• SECOND-DERIVATIVE TEST FOR RELATIVE EXTREMA

If $f(x)$ is a function and x_0 is a number such that $f'(x_0) = 0$, then

1. If $f''(x_0) < 0$, $f(x)$ has a relative maximum at $x = x_0$.
2. If $f''(x_0) > 0$, $f(x)$ has a relative minimum at $x = x_0$.
3. If $f''(x_0) = 0$, the test fails. In other words, the test gives no information regarding a relative maximum or relative minimum at $x = x_0$.

Notes:

1. This test applies only to critical values for which $f'(x) = 0$. It does not apply to critical values for which $f'(x)$ is undefined.
2. This test can fail. In other words, it can give no information regarding the nature of the relative extrema at x_0.
3. If either of the above occurs, use the first-derivative test.

• SECOND-DERIVATIVE TEST FOR ABSOLUTE EXTREMA

When a function is continuous over some interval and *only one critical value* **exists in the interval** Given that a function $f(x)$ is continuous over some interval, and x_0 is the only critical value interior to the interval, and $f'(x_0) = 0$, then

1. If $f''(x_0) < 0$, $f(x_0)$ is the **absolute maximum** value of $f(x)$ over the interval.
2. If $f''(x_0) > 0$, $f(x_0)$ is the **absolute minimum** value of $f(x)$ over the interval.
3. If $f''(x_0) = 0$, the test fails.

• TO FIND ABSOLUTE EXTREMA

For Continuous Functions Defined on Closed Intervals To find the absolute extrema of a continuous function $f(x)$ on the closed interval $[a, b]$:

1. Find all critical values of $f(x)$ in $[a, b]$.
2. Evaluate $f(x)$ at the endpoints a and b and at the critical values found in step 1.
3. Write the largest value found in step 2. This is the *absolute maximum* value of $f(x)$ on the interval $[a, b]$.
4. Write the smallest value found in step 2. This is the *absolute minimum* value of $f(x)$ on the interval $[a, b]$.

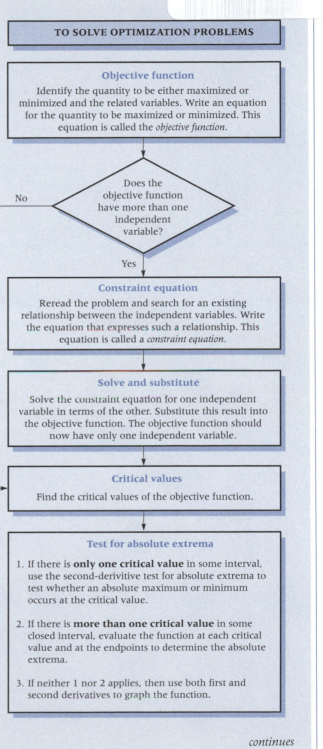

TO SOLVE OPTIMIZATION PROBLEMS

Objective function
Identify the quantity to be either maximized or minimized and the related variables. Write an equation for the quantity to be maximized or minimized. This equation is called the *objective function*.

Does the objective function have more than one independent variable?

No

Yes

Constraint equation
Reread the problem and search for an existing relationship between the independent variables. Write the equation that expresses such a relationship. This equation is called a *constraint equation*.

Solve and substitute
Solve the constraint equation for one independent variable in terms of the other. Substitute this result into the objective function. The objective function should now have only one independent variable.

Critical values
Find the critical values of the objective function.

Test for absolute extrema
1. If there is **only one critical value** in some interval, use the second-derivative test for absolute extrema to test whether an absolute maximum or minimum occurs at the critical value.

2. If there is **more than one critical value** in some closed interval, evaluate the function at each critical value and at the endpoints to determine the absolute extrema.

3. If neither 1 nor 2 applies, then use both first and second derivatives to graph the function.

continues

Continued

• TO SOLVE RELATED-RATE PROBLEMS

1. Identify and list the variables involved. Draw a sketch, if possible.
2. Find an equation that relates the variables.
3. Identify and list the rates of change that are given and those that must be determined.
4. Differentiate the equation of step 2 implicitly with respect to time, t. Solve for the derivative that gives the desired rate of change.
5. Substitute in all given values.

• DERIVATIVE RULE FOR EXPONENTIAL FUNCTIONS

If $y = e^u$, where u is a differentiable function of x, then

$$\frac{dy}{dx} = e^u \frac{du}{dx}$$

• DERIVATIVE RULE FOR LOGARITHMIC FUNCTIONS

If $y = \ln u$, where u is differentiable function of x, then

$$\frac{dy}{dx} = \frac{1}{u} \cdot \frac{du}{dx}$$

• INDEFINITE INTEGRAL FORMULAS

If k and c are constants:

1. $\int x^n \, dx = \frac{x^{n+1}}{n+1} + c \quad (n \neq -1)$
2. $\int k f(x) \, dx = k \int f(x) \, dx$
3. $\int k \, dx = kx + c$
4. $\int [f(x) \pm g(x)] \, dx = \int f(x) \, dx \pm \int g(x) \, dx$
5. $\int e^x \, dx = e^x + c$
6. $\int e^{kx} \, dx = \frac{1}{k} e^{kx} + c$
7. $\int x^{-1} \, dx = \int \frac{1}{x} \, dx = \ln |x| + c$

• AREA UNDER A CURVE

If $f(x) \geq 0$ over the interval $a \leq x \leq b$, the area bounded by the graph of $f(x)$ and the x-axis over the interval $a \leq x \leq b$, as illustrated in the figure below, is given by

$$\int_a^b f(x) \, dx = F(b) - F(a)$$

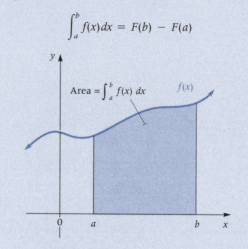

• INTEGRATION BY SUBSTITUTION

$$\int u^n \, du = \frac{1}{n+1} u^{n+1} + c \quad (n \neq -1)$$

If $u = f(x)$ and $du = f'(x) \, dx$, then

$$\int e^u \, du = e^u + c$$

If $u = f(x)$ and $du = f'(x) \, dx$, then

$$\int \frac{du}{u} = \ln |u| + c$$

• INTEGRATION BY PARTS

If u and v are differentiable functions of x, then

$$\int u \, dv = uv - \int v \, du$$

• PARTIAL DERIVATIVES

If $z = f(x, y)$, then

1. The partial derivative of z with respect to x is

$$f_x = \frac{\partial z}{\partial x} = \begin{array}{l} \text{instantaneous rate of change} \\ \text{of } z \text{ with respect to } x \end{array}$$

continues

APPLIED CALCULUS
FOR BUSINESS AND THE
SOCIAL AND NATURAL SCIENCES

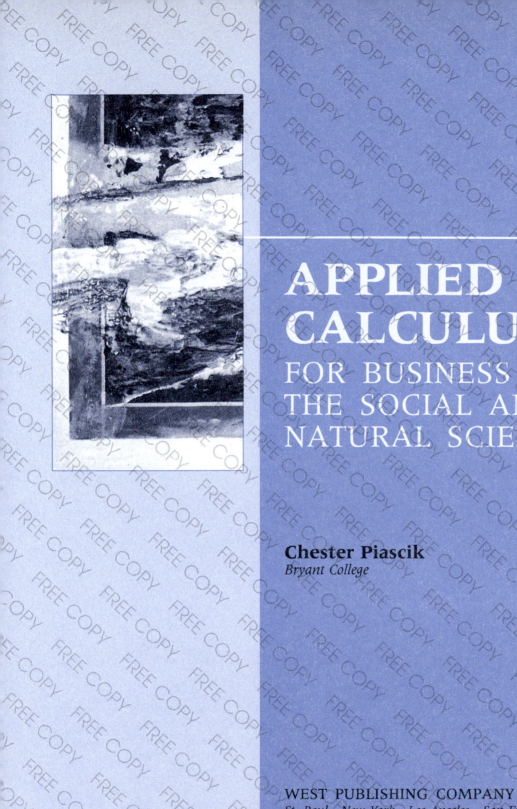

APPLIED CALCULUS

FOR BUSINESS AND THE SOCIAL AND NATURAL SCIENCES

Chester Piascik
Bryant College

WEST PUBLISHING COMPANY
St. Paul   New York   Los Angeles   San Francisco

Copyedit:	*Sherry Goldbecker*
Art:	*Christine Ventley and Edward Rose, Visual Graphic Systems*
Composition:	*The Clarinda Company*
Index:	*E. Virginia Hobbs*
Text design:	*Geri Davis, Quadrata, Inc.*
Answers:	*Gloria Langer*
Cover image:	*"Boarderline" by David Graves, copyright © 1991*
Cover design:	*Geri Davis and Dick Hannus, Quadrata, Inc.*

COPYRIGHT © 1992   By WEST PUBLISHING COMPANY
50 W. Kellogg Boulevard
P.O. Box 64526
St. Paul, MN 55164-0526

Library of Congress Cataloging-in-Publication Data

Piascik, Chester.
    Applied calculus for business and the social and natural sciences
/ Chester Piascik.
        p.   cm.
    Includes index.
    ISBN 0-314-91851-5
    1. Calculus.   I. Title.
QA303. P5365   1992
515--dc20

91-25351
CIP

To my wife, Francine

Contents

Preface

This text is designed to provide the calculus concepts needed by students in business, economics, and the social and natural sciences. From past experience, I have found the algebra backgrounds of these students to be varied. Thus, one of my goals has been to make this text as readable as possible without sacrificing its mathematical content. Clear, direct, and concise explanations enhance this text's readability and provide the student with insightful and meaningful interpretations of an abundant supply of examples and applications. Also, an algebra review is included in Chapter R at the end of the text. This chapter can be covered at the beginning of the course, skipped, or used as a reference throughout the text. In addition to preliminary material, this chapter contains a thorough introduction to the distributive law, multiplying binomials, and factoring. These sections have been written so that they can be assigned to students for self-study or review. Also, algebra refreshers are included prior to Chapters 2 and 3.

• *Graphics*

Another goal of this text is to train the student to think graphically. Wherever appropriate, graphics and graphical analyses are used to illustrate and reinforce the presentation of mathematical concepts. An abundance of graphs in two-color format complement the text's presentation. For example, graphics are used to develop an intuitive understanding of limits, continuity, and differentiability in Chapter 2. Also, Chapter 3 on curve sketching and optimization presents a thorough exposition of graphing functions, using both first and second derivatives. This occurs prior to the section on optimization where optimal solutions are determined without necessarily graphing functions. However, the solid graphical background of the previous sections provides a foundation for the optimization problem-solving procedure of Section 3-4. Additionally, graphs of exponential and logarithmic functions are discussed at the beginning of Chapter 5 prior to introducing their derivatives.

• *Flexibility*

Topics are organized to allow the instructor maximum flexibility. For example, Chapter 1 can be covered with varying degrees of intensity or omitted, depending on students' backgrounds. The first three sections of Chapter 5 on exponential and logarithmic functions can be covered at the end of Chapter 1. Section 5-3 can be omitted without loss of continuity. Many of the sections in Chapter 4 on applications of the derivative, Chapter 7 on further topics of integration, and the latter part of Chapter 8 can be omitted. Chapter 9 on trigonometric functions can be either omitted or covered as desired.

• *Critical Thinking/Problem Solving*

Throughout this text, there is continuing emphasis on student interpretation of results—on understanding what the answer means. This feature is one of many that distinguish this text from its competitors. Wherever appropriate, the text includes explanations that interpret the meanings of results. This develops students' critical thinking and problem-solving skills. Also, procedures used to solve problems are codified and used. For example, Section 3-4 provides an optimization problem-solving procedure that is applied throughout the section. Color screens and annotations are used to show the development of equations and the progress through solution procedures.

• *Careful Attention to Pedagogy*

Excellent coherent explanations throughout this text enhance its readability. Concepts are developed from specific examples to general theory to provide insight into the method of mathematical discovery.

An introductory application opens each chapter to pique student interest and enhance motivation. The application is solved later in the chapter.

In-section and in-chapter summaries, problem-solving procedures, and highlighted formulas appear throughout the text. These are used to summarize ideas and procedures and synthesize related ideas into conceptual entities.

Chapter highlights, being for the most part verbal in nature, appear at the end of each chapter to consolidate the information in the chapter and let the student know what is really happening. These are referenced by section and, therefore, their study takes a student through the main concepts of each section within a chapter.

End-of-section exercises follow each section and end-of-chapter exercises follow each chapter to provide a plentiful supply of problem-solving opportunities for students.

• *Applications*

Relevant and timely applications permeate this text. These range from Uniform CPA Examination problems to examples illustrating market dynamics, economics, managerial concepts, finance and investment, quality and productivity problems in industry, and social and natural science problems.

• *Examples*

This text contains an abundance of examples to reinforce explanations and discussions. Wherever appropriate, color screens and annotations are used to provide step-by-step details of problem-solving procedures.

• *Extra Dividends*

Many chapters are followed by sections dealing with topics and applications that are extensions of chapter concepts. Such sections are entitled "Extra Dividends." Specifically, Chapter 1 contains material on goodness of fit. In addition to setting the stage for the method of least squares, these sections show students how linear and quadratic models are fit to real-world data. These sections and Section 5-3 form a thread through the text that culminates in a discussion of the method of least squares in Section 8-4.

The exponential and logarithmic functions chapter is followed by a discussion of stock market forecasting that utilizes properties of logarithms. Other chapters are followed by discussions of such topics as response surfaces and using Newton's method to determine rates of return on investments.

• *Calculator Exercises*

Although calculators are appropriate for many exercises, some exercises are specifically designated for solution with a calculator. These calculator exercises are marked with the symbol ▥.

• *Computer Exercises*

Where appropriate, some exercises are intended for solution by computer. Such exercises are labeled "Computer Exercises." Also, some exercises not labeled as computer exercises lend themselves to computer solution. This is true for exercises on limits, difference quotients, the trapezoidal rule, Simpson's rule, and Newton's method.

• *Answers*

Answers to all odd-numbered end-of-section exercises, all odd-numbered end-of-chapter exercises, and all chapter highlight questions appear at the end of the text.

• *Supplements*

An **Instructor's Manual** containing step-by-step solutions to all exercises is available.

A **Student's Solutions Manual** containing step-by-step solutions to all odd-numbered exercises is available.

A **computer software package** entitled WESTWARE created by Mark Harris is available to adopters. The package has a spreadsheet format for data entry, generation and manipulation, and viewing tabular results. Among the topics included are graphing (including multiple graphs on the same screen and the option to print the graph), exponential and logarithmic functions, least-squares lines, polynomials, and multiple linear regression. Also included is a means for iterating formulas so that data can be generated for graphs, limits, Newton's method, numerical integration, etc. This software package comes complete with documentation.

A set of **overhead transparencies** containing summaries, procedures, and figures useful for class lectures is available to adopters.

A **computerized test bank** is available to adopters.

• *Acknowledgements*

I wish to thank the many reviewers of this manuscript for their valuable suggestions. These include

Rohan Attele
University of North Carolina — Charlotte

Ronald Barnes
University of Houston, Downtown

Christie Bishop
Rochester Institute of Technology

Patricia Blitch
Lander College

Michael Bradley
Merrimack College

Gail A. Broome
Providence College

Richard Byrne
Portland State University

Eleanor Canter
Wentworth Institute of Technology

Raymond Coughlin
Temple University

James Crenshaw
Southern Illinois University at Carbondale

Duane Deal
Ball State University

Joseph Evans
Middle Tennessee State University

Sally Fischbeck
Rochester Institute of Technology

Nancy Fisher
University of Alabama

Patricia Hirschy
Delaware Technical and Community College

John S. Jeffries
New Mexico Highlands University

Joyce Longman
Villanova University

Laurence Maher
University of North Texas

Richard Marshall
East Michigan University

Donald Mason
Elmhurst College

James McKinney
California State Polytechnic University, Pamona

Robert A. Moreland
Texas Tech University

William Perry
Texas A & M University

Wes Sanders
Sam Houston State University

Neil Schwertman
California State University—Chico

Thomas Shilgalis
Illinois State University

William Soule
University of Maine

John Spellman
Southwest Texas State University

Jon D. Weerts
Triton College

David Weinstein
California State University—Northridge

Carroll G. Wells
Western Kentucky University

Wiley Williams
University of Louisville

I thank my colleagues at Bryant College for their comments and suggestions regarding this manuscript. In particular, I thank Helen Baron, Kristen Kennedy, Robert Muksian, Patricia Odell, Frederick Reinhardt, Martin Rosenzweig, Phyllis Schumacher, Richard Smith, and Robert Wall. A very special thanks goes to Alan Olinsky for suggestions and ideas regarding computer applications and pedagogy.

I thank Robert Girasole of Salve Regina College for theory and data on stock market activity. A special thanks goes to Gloria Langer for an excellent job in preparing the *Instructor's Manual*, the *Student's Solutions Manual*, and answers to homework exercises. Another special thanks goes to Michael Bradley of Merrimack College for an excellent job in preparing the test bank. Also, I thank Mark Harris for a dedicated and conscientious effort in developing the computer software package for this text.

I thank Robyn Langlais for her patient and persistent effort in typing many portions of this manuscript.

I thank the staff of West Educational Publishing for their dedicated efforts in the production of this text. In particular, I wish to extend my thanks and gratitude to Christine Hurney, my production editor. Her excellent organizational skills, and careful attention to all the many details of the project kept it moving along throughout the production phase. I thank Kathryn Grimes for her initiative and resourcefulness in developing materials for the marketing of this text. Special thanks go to my editors Ron Pullins and Denise Bayko. I thank Ron for providing this author with excellent editorial support and inspiration to strive for excellence. I thank Denise for excellent editorial support and conscientious persistent effort towards the goal of producing an excellent text. Last, but not least, a special thank you to Greg Pond, who first brought my project to the attention of the appropriate people at West.

1

FUNCTIONS, MODELS, AND GRAPHING

Introductory Application

Revenue and Cost Functions and Break-Even Points

Revenue Function

In this Chapter, we will learn that if the unit selling price of a particular product is constant, the resulting revenue function is linear. However, for some businesses, the unit selling prices of their products depend on the demand levels of the products. Such a relationship between unit selling price and demand is given by a demand equation

$$p = f(x)$$

where p denotes the unit price and x denotes the number of units demanded of the product. The sales revenue function is defined as follows:

$$\text{sales revenue} = (\text{number of units sold})(\text{unit price})$$
$$R(x) = xp$$
$$= xf(x)$$

If the demand equation is linear, the sales revenue function usually resembles the curve of Figure 1-A. Studying the graph of the revenue function of Figure 1-A, notice that sales revenue increases up to a certain point and then decreases as the number of units sold increases. In Section 1-3, we will explain in greater detail why this occurs.

Break-Even Analysis

If a business' cost function is linear, then a graph of both the cost and sales revenue functions is typified by that of Figure 1-B. Note, in Figure 1-B, that the intersection points of the graphs of the cost and revenue functions are the points where sales revenue = cost. These points are called break-even points. We will discuss such cases more fully in Section 1-7.

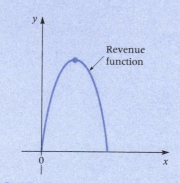

FIGURE 1-A

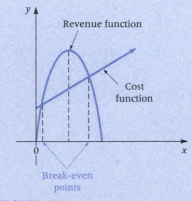

FIGURE 1-B

1-1

• FUNCTIONS

A **function** is a rule that associates a unique **output value** with each element in a set of possible **input values.** Consider, for example, the conversion of temperature from degees Fahrenheit to degrees Celsius. Given a temperature in degrees Fahrenheit (input value), we can find the corresponding value in degrees Celsius (output value) by the following rule:

$$\underbrace{\text{Celsius temperature}}_{\substack{\text{output} \\ \text{value}}} = \frac{5}{9} \underbrace{(\text{Fahrenheit temperature}}_{\substack{\text{input} \\ \text{value}}} - 32)$$

If C is temperature in degrees Celsius and F is temperature in degrees Fahrenheit, then this rule may be expressed by the equation

$$C = \frac{5}{9}(F - 32)$$

To determine the Celsius temperature (output value) associated with 50 degrees Fahrenheit, we substitute $F = 50$ (input value) into the equation and obtain

$$C = \frac{5}{9}(50 - 32)$$

$$= \frac{5}{9}(18)$$

$$= 10 \text{ degrees Celsius}$$

Thus, 10 degrees Celsius is associated with 50 degrees Fahrenheit. Since only one value of C is associated with a value of F, then this equation defines C as a function of F.

Observing the equation

$$C = \frac{5}{9}(F - 32)$$
$$\underset{\substack{\text{output} \\ \text{value}}}{\uparrow} \quad \underset{\substack{\text{input} \\ \text{value}}}{\uparrow}$$

note that the output value, C, is dependent on the input value, F. Thus, C is called the **dependent variable,** and F is called the **independent variable.** This relationship is usually indicated by saying that C is a *function* of F.

Functional Notation

Often a letter is used to represent a function. Specifically, if the letter f is used to name the function defined by the equation

$$y = 5x^2 + 2x + 7$$

then the dependent variable, y, is represented by the symbol $f(x)$, read "f of x." Thus, the preceding equation is written

$$f(x) = 5x^2 + 2x + 7$$

To find the output value associated with $x = 3$, we replace x with 3 to obtain

$$f(3) = 5(3)^2 + 2(3) + 7$$
$$= 45 + 6 + 7$$
$$= 58$$

Rectangular Coordinate System

It is often useful to graph functions on a plane called the **rectangular coordinate system.** Such a system consists of two perpendicular real number lines in the plane, as shown in Figure 1-1. The horizontal number line is called the **x-axis,** and the vertical number line is called the **y-axis.** The point where the lines intersect is the zero point of both lines and is called the **origin.**

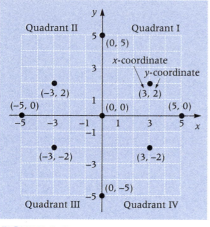

FIGURE 1-1

The plane consists of infinitely many **points.** Each point is assigned an **ordered pair** of numbers which locates its position relative to both axes. For example, looking at Figure 1-1, the ordered pair $(3, 2)$ is associated with the point that may be plotted by starting at the origin and moving 3 units to the right horizontally and then 2 units upward vertically. The numbers 3 and 2 of the ordered pair $(3, 2)$ are called the **x-coordinate** and **y-coordinate,** respectively.

Similarly, the ordered pair $(-3, 2)$ in Figure 1-1 is associated with the point that may be plotted by starting at the origin and moving 3 units to the left horizontally and then 2 units upward vertically. The ordered pair $(-3, -2)$ is associated with the point that may be plotted by starting at the origin and moving 3 units to the left horizontally and then 2 units downward and vertically. The ordered pair $(3, -2)$ is associated with the point that may be plotted by starting at the origin and moving 3 units to the right horizontally and then 2 units downward vertically. The ordered pair $(0, 0)$ is associated with the origin.

Further studying Figure 1-1, we note the following:

1. The x- and y-axes partition the plane into four quadrants, as numbered in the figure.
2. For any point in Quadrant I, the x- and y-coordinates are both positive, i.e., $(+, +)$.
3. For any point in Quadrant II, the x-coordinate is negative and the y-coordinate is positive, i.e., $(-, +)$.
4. For any point in Quadrant III, the x- and y-coordinates are both negative, i.e., $(-, -)$.
5. For any point in Quadrant IV, the x-coordinate is positive and the y-coordinate is negative, i.e., $(+, -)$.
6. Points on the axes belong to no quadrant. Points on the x-axis have y-coordinates of 0, and points on the y-axis have x-coordinates of 0.

Functions As Sets of Ordered Pairs

A function can be expressed as a set of ordered pairs (x, y) such that each value of y is the number associated with its corresponding value of x in ac-

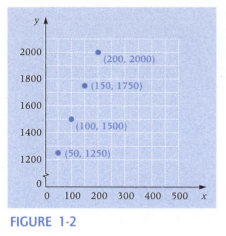

FIGURE 1-2

cordance with the rule defined by the equation. For example, consider the situation of a young entrepreneur manufacturing sneakers. She initially invests $1000 to pay for overhead items such as heat, electricity, etc. Additionally, each pair of sneakers costs $5 to manufacture. Thus, the total cost of producing x pairs of sneakers is given by the equation.

$$y = C(x) = 5x + 1000$$

During the first week of operation, the entrepreneur plans to manufacture either 50, 100, 150, or 200 pairs of sneakers. Table 1-1 shows the output value associated with each input value. The set of input values is called the **domain** of the function, and the set of output values is called the **range** of the function. Observing Table 1-1, note that the domain consists of the set of x-values (in the left column) and that the range consists of the set of y- or $C(x)$-values (in the right column). The function C consists of the set of ordered pairs (x, y) graphed in Figure 1-2.

TABLE 1-1

x	y	$y = C(x) = 5x + 1000$
50	1250	$C(50) = 5(50) + 1000 = 1250$
100	1500	$C(100) = 5(100) + 1000 = 1500$
150	1750	$C(150) = 5(150) + 1000 = 1750$
200	2000	$C(200) = 5(200) + 1000 = 2000$

We are now ready for a more formal definition of a function.

Function

A **function** is a set of ordered pairs (x, y) such that no two ordered pairs have the same first element, x, and different second elements, y. The set of first elements, x, is the **domain** of the function, and the set of second elements, y, is the **range** of the function.

Consider the equation

$$y^2 = x$$

The ordered pairs defined by this equation include $(4, 2)$, $(4, -2)$, $(9, 3)$, and $(9, -3)$. Note that the two numbers $+2$ and -2 are associated with $x = 4$. Since this equation associates more than one y-value for at least one x-value, it is not a function.

To graph the equation $y^2 = x$, we plot the points corresponding to its ordered pairs, some of which are $(4, 2)$, $(4, -2)$, $(9, 3)$, and $(9, -3)$. Figure 1-3 illustrates the graph of this equation. Referring to this illustration, note that since two y-values, $+2$ and -2, are associated with $x = 4$, a vertical line intersects the graph at two points. Generalizing, we have the following **vertical line test** for a function.

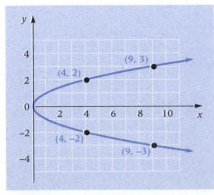

FIGURE 1-3

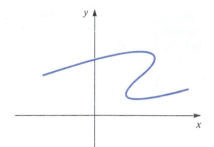

FIGURE 1-4

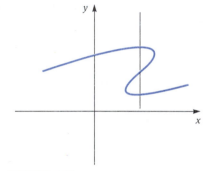

FIGURE 1-5

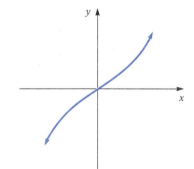

FIGURE 1-6

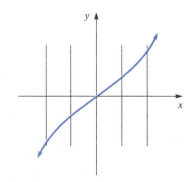

FIGURE 1-7

Vertical Line Test

If a vertical line intersects a graph at more than one point, then that graph does not represent a function.

• **EXAMPLE 1-1**

Use the vertical line test to determine if the graph of Figure 1-4 represents a function.

Solution

Since a vertical line can be drawn that intersects the graph at more than one point (see Figure 1-5), the graph does not represent a function.

• **EXAMPLE 1-2**

Use the vertical line test to determine if the graph of Figure 1-6 represents a function.

Solution

Since it is not possible to draw a vertical line that intersects the graph at more than one point (see Figure 1-7), the graph does represent a function.

•

Often the domain of a function is not specified. If this is the case, it is assumed that the domain is the set of all real numbers for which the function is defined. Consider the function defined by the equation

$$g(x) = \frac{1}{x - 2}$$

Since the domain of g is not specified, it is the set of all real numbers x for which $g(x)$ is defined. Note that $g(x)$ is defined for all real numbers x except $x = 2$, since

$$g(2) = \frac{1}{2 - 2} = \frac{1}{0} \quad \text{which is undefined.}$$

Thus, the domain of g is all real numbers x such that $x \neq 2$.

• **EXAMPLE 1-3**

Specify the domain of h where

$$h(x) = \frac{1}{(x - 3)(x + 5)}$$

Solution

Since the domain of h is not specified, it is the set of all real numbers x for which $h(x)$ is defined. Note that $h(x)$ is defined for all real numbers x except $x = 3$ and $x = -5$, since

$$h(3) = \frac{1}{(3 - 3)(3 + 5)} = \frac{1}{0} \quad \text{which is undefined,}$$

$$h(-5) = \frac{1}{(-5 - 3)(-5 + 5)} = \frac{1}{0} \quad \text{which is undefined.}$$

Thus, the domain of h is all real numbers x such that $x \neq 3$ and $x \neq -5$.

•

• **EXAMPLE 1-4** _____

If $f(x) = \sqrt{x - 7}$, specify the domain of f.

Solution

Since $\sqrt{x - 7}$ is defined as long as $x - 7 \geq 0$ or, equivalently, $x \geq 7$, then the domain of f is all real numbers x such that $x \geq 7$.

We now give an example showing further calculations with functional notation.

• **EXAMPLE 1-5** _____

Given that $f(x) = 3x^2 - 2x + 5$, calculate each of the following:

a) $f(4)$

b) $f(x + h)$

c) $f(x + h) - f(x)$

d) $\dfrac{f(x + h) - f(x)}{h}$

Solutions

a) Since $f(x) = 3x^2 - 2x + 5$, then $f(4)$ is calculated by replacing x with 4. This gives us

$$f(4) = 3(4)^2 - 2(4) + 5$$
$$= 45$$

b) Since $f(x) = 3x^2 - 2x + 5$, then $f(x + h)$ is calculated by replacing x with $x + h$. Therefore, we have

$$f(x + h) = 3(x + h)^2 - 2(x + h) + 5$$
$$= 3(x^2 + 2hx + h^2) - 2x - 2h + 5$$
$$= 3x^2 + 6hx + 3h^2 - 2x - 2h + 5$$

c) Subtracting $f(x) = 3x^2 - 2x + 5$ from the result of part b yields

$$f(x + h) - f(x) = 3x^2 + 6hx + 3h^2 - 2x - 2h + 5 - (3x^2 - 2x + 5)$$
$$= 6hx + 3h^2 - 2h$$

d) Dividing the result of part c by h, we obtain

$$\frac{f(x + h) - f(x)}{h} = \frac{6hx + 3h^2 - 2h}{h}$$
$$= 6x + 3h - 2$$

This result is called a **difference quotient** and will be discussed further in Chapter 2.

We now illustrate more functions and their graphs.

• **EXAMPLE 1-6**   **Parcel Cost.** _____

A private parcel service charges the following rates for delivering small packages:

- $1.00 for a package weighing less than 4 ounces
- $1.50 for a package weighing at least 4 ounces but less than 20 ounces
- $2.00 for a package weighing at least 20 ounces but less than 32 ounces

The service does not deliver packages weighing 32 ounces or more. Express delivery cost as a function of weight and graph the function.

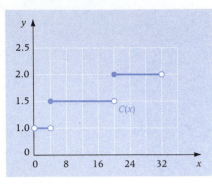

FIGURE 1-8

Solution

If x is the weight of a package, its delivery cost, $C(x)$, is given by

$$C(x) = \begin{cases} 1.00 & \text{if } 0 < x < 4 \\ 1.50 & \text{if } 4 \leq x < 20 \\ 2.00 & \text{if } 20 \leq x < 32 \end{cases}$$

Note that the domain of $C(x)$ is the interval $0 < x < 32$. The graph of $C(x)$ appears in Figure 1-8.

• **EXAMPLE 1-7** **Call Options.**

A stock investor, believing that the price of a share of stock of Amtech, Inc., will rise to approximately \$80 per share during the next 6 months, buys a contract entitling her to buy a specified number of shares of Amtech for \$50 per share during the next 6-month time interval. The investor paid \$10 per share for this contract. Determine the investor's profit function per share of stock.

Solution

This type of contract, which entitles an investor to buy a specified number of shares of a given stock at a given price (called the **striking price**) during a given time interval, is termed a **call option.** The investor's profit is dependent on the stock's market price per share. Thus, we let $P(x)$ denote the investor's profit per share at the stock's market price of x dollars per share. If the stock's market price per share is less than or equal to the striking price (\$50), then the option is worthless to the investor, and, thus, the investor suffers a loss (i.e., a negative profit) of \$10 per share, the price paid for the option. This is written as

$$P(x) = -10 \quad \text{if} \quad 0 \leq x \leq 50$$

If the stock's market price per share exceeds the striking price of \$50 during the given 6-month time interval, then the investor could exercise the option and buy the stock for \$50 per share and obtain a profit per share of

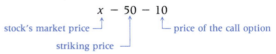

This assumes that the investor sells the stock for x dollars per share and is written as

$$P(x) = x - 50 - 10 \quad \text{if } x > 50$$

Thus, the profit function is defined as

$$P(x) = \begin{cases} -10 & \text{if } 0 \leq x \leq 50 \\ x - 60 & \text{if } x > 50 \end{cases}$$

and its graph appears in Figure 1-9.

If a stock's market price rises rapidly during a given time interval, a call option allows an investor to enjoy a substantial percentage gain with a small investment. For example, if Amtech's market price per share were to reach \$80 within the given 6-month time interval, the investor would earn a profit of $80 - 50 - 10 = \$20$ per share on an investment of \$10 per share, the price paid for the call option. This constitutes a 200% (i.e., $\frac{20}{10} \times 100$) rate of return during the 6-month time interval. One can understand why investors buy call options.

FIGURE 1-9

Note that each function in Examples 1-6 and 1-7 is defined by more than one formula. Functions that are defined by more than one formula are said to be **piecewise defined.** We now discuss another piecewise-defined function.

Absolute Value Function

In Section R-1 of Chapter R, we define the absolute value of a number x. We now define the **absolute value function,** $a(x)$, as

$$a(x) = |x| = \begin{cases} x & \text{if } x \text{ is positive or zero} \\ -x & \text{if } x \text{ is negative} \end{cases}$$

Note that this function associates a non-negative number with itself. Associated with each negative number is its additive inverse. Thus, $(-3, 3)$, $(-1, 1)$, $(-1/2, 1/2)$, $(0, 0)$, $(1, 1)$, $(2, 2)$, and $(5/2, 5/2)$ are some of the ordered pairs belonging to the absolute value function. The graph of $a(x)$ appears in Figure 1-10.

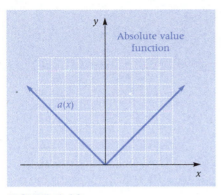

FIGURE 1-10

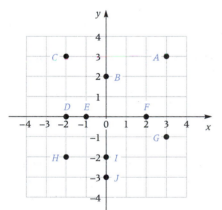

FIGURE 1-11

TABLE 1-2

x	$f(x)$
0	
1	
2	
3	

Exercises 1-1

1. A function is defined by the equation

$$y = 3x - 2$$

   a) Which number does this equation associate with $x = 0$?
   b) Which number does this equation associate with $x = 4$?

2. A function is defined by the equation

$$y = 3x^2 - 4x + 5$$

   a) Which number does this equation associate with $x = 0$?
   b) Which number does this equation associate with $x = 2$?

3. If $f(x) = -2x + 7$, calculate each of the following:
   a) $f(0)$ b) $f(1)$
   c) $f(5)$ d) $f(-3)$

4. If $w(r) = r^3 - 7r^2 + 8r - 5$, calculate each of the following:
   a) $w(0)$ b) $w(2)$
   c) $w(-2)$ d) $w(4)$

5. If $z(t) = \dfrac{5}{t + 7}$, calculate each of the following:
   a) $z(0)$ b) $z(1)$
   c) $z(-6)$ d) $z(8)$

6. For each of the points A through J of Figure 1-11, find the associated ordered pair.

7. Plot each of the following points on the rectangular coordinate system: $(0, 0)$, $(2, 0)$, $(-5, 0)$, $(0, 2)$, $(0, 5)$, $(3, 1)$, $(5, 2)$, $(-7, 3)$, $(-8, -2)$, $(9, -3)$.

8. Plot the following points on the rectangular coordinate system, and state the quadrant in which each is located: $(4, 2)$, $(5, 8)$, $(-9, 3)$, $(-2, 1)$, $(-3, -5)$, $(-2, -7)$, $(8, -3)$, $(9, 2)$.

9. Graph the function defined by

$$f(x) = 3x + 2$$

   with domain equal to the set of x-values in Table 1-2.

TABLE 1-3

x	$S(x)$
1/4	
1/2	
1	
2	

10. Graph the function defined by

$$S(x) = \frac{1}{x}$$

with domain equal to the set of x-values in Table 1-3.

11. If $f(x) = \dfrac{5}{(x-2)(x+7)}$, specify the domain of f.

12. If $g(x) = \dfrac{8}{(x-5)}$, specify the domain of g.

13. If $f(x) = \sqrt{x-2}$, specify the domain of f.

14. If $g(x) = \sqrt{2x+5}$, specify the domain of g.

15. If $h(x) = \dfrac{8}{(x-3)^2}$, specify the domain of h.

16. If $f(x) = \dfrac{6}{x^2 + x}$, specify the domain of f.

17. Which of the graphs in Figure 1-12 are graphs of functions?

18. Which of the graphs in Figure 1-13 are graphs of functions?

19. Does the equation $y^2 = x + 5$ define a function? Why or why not?

20. Does the equation $y^2 = 4x + 1$ define a function? Why or why not?

21. Given that $f(x) = x^2 - 4x + 5$, calculate each of the following:

   a) $f(x + h)$

   b) $f(x + h) - f(x)$

   c) $\dfrac{f(x + h) - f(x)}{h}$

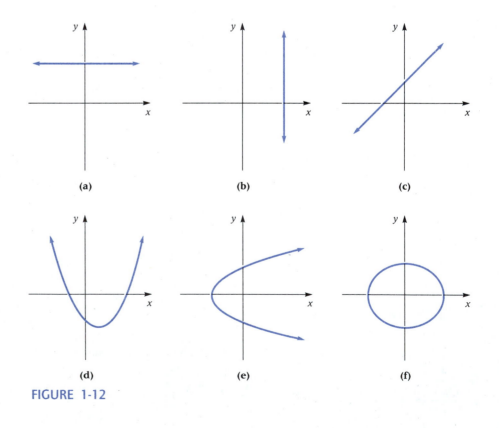

FIGURE 1-12

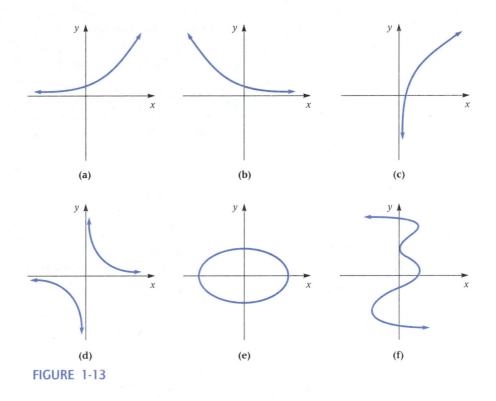

FIGURE 1-13

22. Given that $f(x) = -3x^2 + 5x - 2$, calculate each of the following:
   a) $f(x + h)$
   b) $f(x + h) - f(x)$
   c) $\dfrac{f(x + h) - f(x)}{h}$

23. Given that $f(x) = 5x^2 - 2x + 4$, calculate the difference quotient

$$\frac{f(x + h) - f(x)}{h}$$

24. Given that $f(x) = -2x^2 + 3x - 9$, calculate the difference quotient

$$\frac{f(x + h) - f(x)}{h}$$

25. Given that $g(x) = x^3 - 4x^2 + 5x - 9$, calculate the difference quotient

$$\frac{g(x + h) - g(x)}{h}$$

26. Given that $g(x) = 2x^3 - 3x + 5$, calculate the difference quotient

$$\frac{g(x + h) - g(x)}{h}$$

27. Graph the function defined by

$$h(x) = \begin{cases} 2 & \text{if } x < 1 \\ 4 & \text{if } 1 \leq x < 6 \\ x & \text{if } x \geq 6 \end{cases}$$

28. Graph the function defined by

$$k(x) = \begin{cases} 3 & \text{if } x \le 4 \\ x & \text{if } 4 < x \le 9 \\ 9 & \text{if } x > 9 \end{cases}$$

29. A parcel service charges the following rates for delivering small packages:
    - $1.25 for a package weighing less than 8 ounces
    - $2.00 for a package weighing at least 8 ounces and at most 16 ounces
    - $5.00 for a package weighing more than 16 ounces and at most 40 ounces

    The service delivers no packages weighing more than 40 ounces.
    a) Express delivery cost as a function of weight.
    b) Graph the function of part a.

30. *Call options.* An investor bought a call option entitling him to buy a specified number of shares of Biotech, Inc., for $30 per share during the next 3-month time interval. The investor paid $5 per share for the call option. Determine the investor's profit function per share of stock. Also, graph the profit function.

31. *Put options.* An investor, believing that the price of a share of stock of Amex, Inc., will drop to approximately $10 per share during the next 6 months, buys a contract entitling him to sell a specified number of shares of Amex for $35 per share during the next 6-month time interval. The investor is actually selling shares of stock that he does not own. However, the investor will replace these sold shares by buying the same number of shares at a lower market price. The investor paid $7 per share for this contract. This type of contract, which entitles an investor to sell a specified number of shares of a given stock at a given price (called the **striking price**) during a given time interval, is called a *put option.* Determine the investor's profit function per share of stock for this put option. Also, graph the profit function. Remember that the investor's profit is dependent on the stock's market price per share.

32. *Wind power.* In designing a windmill, an engineer must use the fact that power y available in wind varies with the cube of wind speed. Thus, if x represents wind speed (in miles per hour), we have

$$y = kx^3$$

where k is a constant real number.
a) If a 25-mile-an-hour wind produces 5000 watts, find k.
b) How many watts of power will a 35-mile-per-hour wind produce?

1-2 • SLOPE AND EQUATIONS OF STRAIGHT LINES

Consider the straight line drawn through the two points $(2, 8)$ and $(4, 11)$ in Figure 1-14. Suppose we place the point of a pencil at $(2, 8)$ and move along the line toward $(4, 11)$. As the pencil moves along the line, its x- and y-coordinates change. When the pencil reaches $(4, 11)$, its total vertical change (i.e., change in y) is $11 - 8 = 3$ units, and its total horizontal change (i.e., change in x) is $4 - 2 = 2$ (see Figure 1-15). The ratio 3/2 rep-

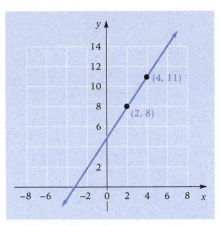

FIGURE 1-14

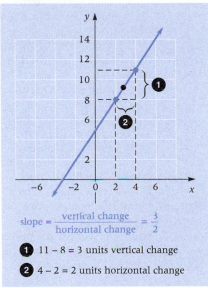

$$\text{slope} = \frac{\text{vertical change}}{\text{horizontal change}} = \frac{3}{2}$$

① $11 - 8 = 3$ units vertical change

② $4 - 2 = 2$ units horizontal change

FIGURE 1-15

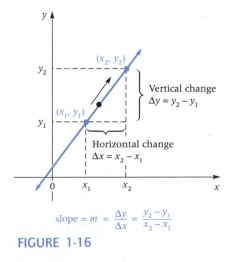

$$\text{slope} = m = \frac{\Delta y}{\Delta x} = \frac{y_2 - y_1}{x_2 - x_1}$$

FIGURE 1-16

resents the rate of change of vertical position (y) with respect to horizontal position (x) and is called the **slope** of the straight line. The slope 3/2 implies that as the pencil moves along the straight line, for every 2 units of horizontal change to the right the pencil experiences 3 units of vertical change upward.

In general, if (x_1, y_1) and (x_2, y_2) represent two points through which a straight line passes (see Figure 1-16) and we move along the straight line from (x_1, y_1) to (x_2, y_2) then the vertical change is denoted by Δy (read "delta y"), and our horizontal change is denoted by Δx (read "delta x"). Furthermore, $\Delta y = y_2 - y_1$ and $\Delta x = x_2 - x_1$ and the slope m of the straight line is determined by the following formula.

$$\text{Slope} = m = \frac{\Delta y}{\Delta x} = \frac{y_2 - y_1}{x_2 - x_1}$$

A property of a straight line is that its slope is the same no matter where it is measured. In other words, we can find the slope of a line by calculating the ratio $\Delta y / \Delta x$ from any two points on the line.

• EXAMPLE 1-8

A particle moves along the straight line from $(3, 11)$ to $(5, 7)$.

a) Find its vertical change, Δy.
b) Find its horizontal change, Δx.
c) Find the slope of the straight line.
d) Interpret the result of part c.

Solutions

a) We let $(x_1, y_1) = (3, 11)$, the point at which the particle starts, and $(x_2, y_2) = (5, 7)$. Then the vertical change is $\Delta y = y_2 - y_1 = 7 - 11 = -4$ (see Figure 1-17 on page 14).

b) The horizontal change is $\Delta x = x_2 - x_1 = 5 - 3 = 2$ (see Figure 1-17).

c) The slope is given by

$$m = \frac{\Delta y}{\Delta x} = \frac{-4}{2} = -2$$

d) Referring to Figure 1-17, as the particle moves along the straight line from $(3, 11)$ to $(5, 7)$, the fact that the slope $\Delta y / \Delta x = -4/2 = -2/1$ means that for each unit of horizontal change to the right, the particle experiences 2 units of vertical change downward. If the particle were moving along the straight line from $(5, 7)$ to $(3, 11)$, as shown in Figure 1-18, then $\Delta y = 11 - 7 = 4$ and $\Delta x = 3 - 5 = -2$ so that $\Delta y / \Delta x = 4/(-2) = 2/(-1)$. Here, as the particle moves from $(5, 7)$ to $(3, 11)$, for each unit of horizontal change to the left, it experiences 2 units of vertical change upward.

Compare the straight line of Figure 1-15 with those of Figures 1-17 and 1-18. Note that a straight line with *positive slope* slants *upward to the right* whereas a straight line with *negative slope* slants *downward to the right*. This is illustrated in the following box.

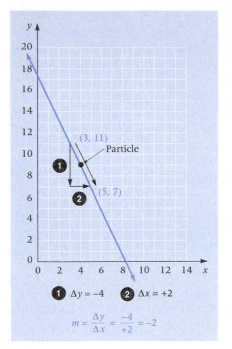

FIGURE 1-17

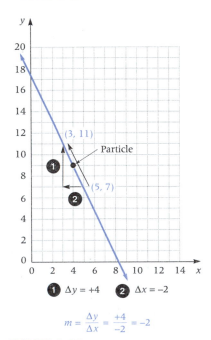

FIGURE 1-18

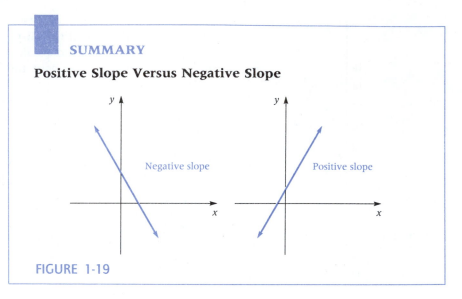

FIGURE 1-19

Constant Rate of Change

Figure 1-20 again illustrates the straight line in Figure 1-14. Referring to Figure 1-20, suppose we move up along the line away from $(4, 11)$ so that we experience 2 units of horizontal change to the right. Since the slope of the straight line is 3/2, then for each 2 units of horizontal change to the right, we experience 3 units of vertical change upward. Hence, we will be located at point $(4 + 2, 11 + 3) = (6, 14)$.

Again referring to Figure 1-20, suppose we begin at point $(2, 8)$ and move down along the straight line until we experience 2 units of horizontal change to the left. Since the slope of the straight line is 3/2 or $-3/(-2)$, then for each 2 units of horizontal change to the left, we experience 3 units of vertical change downward. Hence, we will now be located at point $(2 - 2, 8 - 3) = (0, 5)$. Note that movement along this straight line results in the constant rate of change 3/2 of vertical position with respect to horizontal position.

Again refer to Figure 1-20. Note that the straight line crosses the y-axis at $(0, 5)$. This point is called the **y-intercept** of the straight line. The point where the straight line crosses the x-axis is called the **x-intercept** of the straight line. We will learn a more formal method for determining the x- and y-intercepts of a straight line in Section 1-3.

Slope and Equations of Straight Lines

Study the straight line of Figure 1-20. Recall that this straight line was illustrated at the beginning of this section with the two points $(2, 8)$ and $(4, 11)$. After determining the slope to be 3/2, the rate of change concept was used to find other points on the line, specifically $(6, 14)$ and $(0, 5)$. The concept of slope can be used to determine other points on the line.

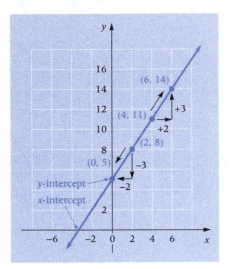

FIGURE 1-20

However, there is a better way. We must realize that the x- and y-coordinates of any point (x, y) on a straight line are related by an equation. Such an equation is called an **equation of the straight line.** An equation of a straight line exhibits the relationship between the x- and y-coordinates of any point (x, y) on the line.

SUMMARY

Slope and Rate of Change

In general, movement along a straight line of slope m results in m vertical units gained for each horizontal unit gained. Thus, the slope, m, is the rate of change of vertical position (y) with respect to horizontal position (x), as is illustrated below.

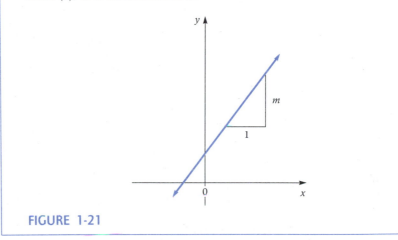

FIGURE 1-21

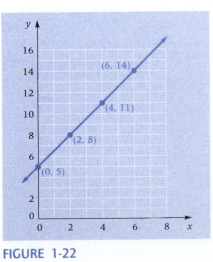

FIGURE 1-22

We will now determine the equation of the straight line of Figure 1-22. Choose one of the known points on the line, say, $(2, 8)$. Let (x, y) represent any point on the line. Since the slope of the straight line is 3/2, the slope between (x, y) and $(2, 8)$ must equal 3/2. Hence,

$$\frac{y - 8}{x - 2} = \frac{3}{2}$$

Multiplying both sides by $x - 2$, we obtain

$$y - 8 = \frac{3}{2}(x - 2)$$

This equation is called the **point-slope form** of the equation of the straight line. Observe that the coordinates of the point, $(2, 8)$, and the slope, 3/2, appear conspicuously in the equation—hence, the term *point-slope form.*

Solving the point-slope form for y, we obtain

$$y = \frac{3}{2}(x - 2) + 8$$

or

$$y = \frac{3}{2}x + 5$$

This equation is called the **slope-intercept form** of the equation of the straight line. Note that the slope, 3/2, and the y-intercept, 5, appear conspicuously in the equation—hence, the term *slope-intercept form*.

Thus, the equation

$$y = \frac{3}{2}x + 5$$

exhibits the relationship between the x and y coordinates of any point (x, y) on the straight line. Observe that the points of the straight line satisfy its equation.

$$(0, 5) \qquad 5 = \frac{3}{2}(0) + 5$$

$$(2, 8) \qquad 8 = \frac{3}{2}(2) + 5$$

$$(4, 11) \qquad 11 = \frac{3}{2}(4) + 5$$

$$(6, 14) \qquad 14 = \frac{3}{2}(6) + 5$$

As previously mentioned, an equation of a straight line may be used to find other points on the line. Specifically, if $x = -4$, then

$$y = \frac{3}{2}(-4) + 5 = -1$$

Thus, $(-4, -1)$ is a point on this straight line. And if $x = 8$, then

$$y = \frac{3}{2}(8) + 5 = 17$$

Therefore, $(8, 17)$ is also a point on the line.

We now state the following generalizations

Equation

An equation of a straight line reveals the relationship between the x- and y-coordinates of any point (x, y) on the line.

Point-Slope Form

Given a point (x_1, y_1) on a straight line of slope m (see Figure 1-23), the **point-slope form** of the equation of that straight line is

$$y - y_1 = m(x - x_1)$$

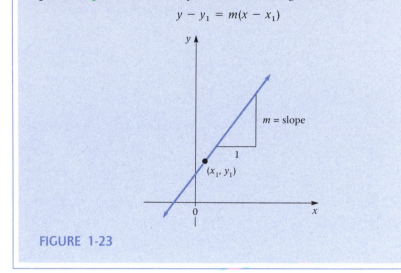

FIGURE 1-23

Slope-Intercept Form

If the point-slope form is solved for y (see Figure 1-24), the resulting equation is the **slope-intercept form**

$$y = mx + b$$

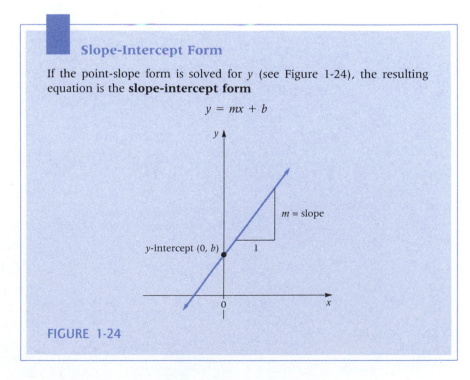

FIGURE 1-24

• **EXAMPLE 1-9**

A straight line passes through (4, 7) and (9, 17).

a) Find its equation in point-slope form.
b) Convert the point-slope form into the slope-intercept form.
c) Find the point on this straight line corresponding to $x = 5$.
d) Sketch this straight line.

Solutions

a) If $(x_1, y_1) = (4, 7)$ and $(x_2, y_2) = (9, 17)$,* then

$$m = \frac{y_2 - y_1}{x_2 - x_1} = \frac{17 - 7}{9 - 4} = \frac{10}{5} = 2$$

Substituting $(x_1, y_1) = (4, 7)$ and $m = 2$ into the point-slope form

$$y - y_1 = m(x - x_1)$$

we obtain

$$y - 7 = 2(x - 4)$$

b) Solving for y gives us

$$y = 2(x - 4) + 7$$

or

$$y = 2x - 1$$

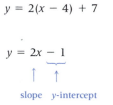

slope   y-intercept

c) If $x = 5$, then $y = 2(5) - 1 = 9$. Thus, (5, 9) is a point on this line.
d) Observing the slope-intercept form, note that $(0, -1)$ is the y-intercept of this straight line. Using a straightedge, we connect the y-intercept with another point on the straight line, say, (5, 9). The resulting graph is illustrated in Figure 1-25. Note that the points (4, 7) and (9, 17) also appear on the line.

• **EXAMPLE 1-10**

A straight line has a slope of 6 and a y-intercept of -3. Find the equation of this line.

Solution

Substituting $m = 6$ and $b = -3$ into the slope-intercept form

$$y = mx + b$$

yields

$$y = 6x - 3$$

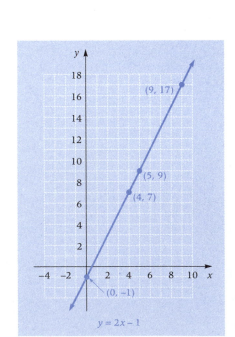

FIGURE 1-25

*Either point may be chosen as (x_1, y_1) or (x_2, y_2).

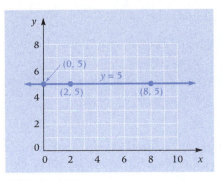

FIGURE 1-26

Horizontal Lines

Consider the straight line passing through the points $(2, 5)$ and $(8, 5)$. Since the y-coordinates are equal, the line passing through these points is horizontal (see Figure 1-26), and its slope is 0, as is determined below.

$$m = \frac{\Delta y}{\Delta x} = \frac{5 - 5}{8 - 2} = \frac{0}{6} = 0$$

Observing Figure 1-26, note that the y-intercept is 5. Substituting $m = 0$ and $b = 5$ into the slope-intercept form

$$y = mx + b$$

we obtain

$$y = 0x + 5$$

or

$$y = 5$$

The equation $y = 5$ expresses the fact that the y-coordinate of any point on this horizontal straight line is 5.

Horizontal Line

In general, the equation

$$y = b$$

represents a horizontal straight line with a y-intercept of b. Every horizontal line has a slope of 0.

Vertical Lines

Consider the straight line passing through the points $(3, 2)$ and $(3, 7)$. Since the x-coordinates are equal, the straight line is vertical (see Figure 1-27). Its x-intercept is 3. Because any point on this vertical line has an x-coordinate of 3, the equation of the line is appropriately $x = 3$.

The slope of this vertical line is

$$m = \frac{\Delta y}{\Delta x} = \frac{7 - 2}{3 - 3} = \frac{5}{0} \qquad \text{which is undefined.}$$

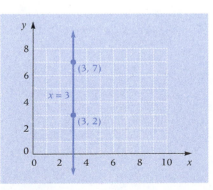

FIGURE 1-27

Vertical Line

In general, the equation

$$x = k$$

represents a vertical straight line with an x-intercept of k. Every vertical line has an undefined slope.

Linear Equations

Up to this point, we have encountered equations of straight lines in either the *point-slope form*

$$y - y_1 = m(x - x_1)$$

or the *slope-intercept form*

$$y = mx + b$$

These equations, which represent straight lines, are called **linear equations.** Linear equations occur in forms other than the preceding. For example,

$$3x + 5y = 16$$

is a linear equation. This is verified by converting it into slope-intercept form. Solving for y yields

$$5y = -3x + 16$$

$$y = -\frac{3}{5}x + \frac{16}{5}$$

General Form

In general, equations of the form

$$ax + by = c$$

where a, b, and c are constant real numbers, with a and b not both 0, are linear equations. This form is called the **general form** of a linear equation.

• **EXAMPLE 1-11**

Convert $4x - 7y = 18$ into slope-intercept form.

Solution

Solving for y yields

$$-7y = -4x + 18$$

$$y = \frac{-4}{-7}x + \frac{18}{-7}$$

or

$$y = \underset{\underset{\text{slope}}{\uparrow}}{\frac{4}{7}x} - \underset{\underset{y\text{-intercept}}{\uparrow}}{\frac{18}{7}}$$

Parallel Lines

Slope, the ratio of vertical change to horizontal change resulting from movement along a straight line, is an indication of the steepness of a straight line. Straight lines that are equally steep are said to be parallel, and therefore, have the same slope.

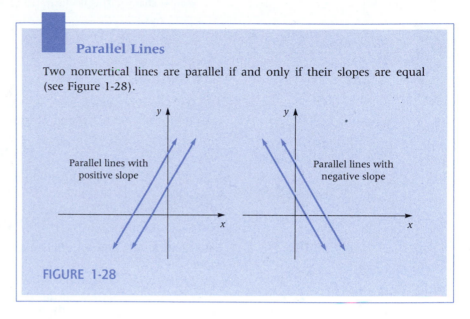

Parallel Lines

Two nonvertical lines are parallel if and only if their slopes are equal (see Figure 1-28).

Parallel lines with positive slope

Parallel lines with negative slope

FIGURE 1-28

• **EXAMPLE 1-12** ───────────────────────

A straight line is parallel to the line $2x + 3y = 12$ and passes through the point $(3, 9)$.

a) Find its equation   **b)** Graph both lines

Solutions

a) We first find the slope of the line $2x + 3y = 12$ by converting it into slope intercept form $y = mx + b$. Hence,

$$2x + 3y = 12 \qquad \text{Given line}$$
$$3y = -2x + 12$$
$$y = -\frac{2}{3}x + 4 \qquad \text{Slope-intercept form}$$
$$\underbrace{\qquad}_{\text{slope}}$$

From the slope-intercept form, the slope of the given line is $-2/3$, and, of course, the slope of the parallel line is also $-2/3$. Using the point-slope form, we find the equation of the parallel line.

$$y - y_1 = m(x - x_1) \qquad \text{Point-slope form}$$

Letting $(x_1, y_1) = (3, 9)$ and $m = -2/3$ gives

$$y - 9 = -\frac{2}{3}(x - 3)$$
$$y - 9 = -\frac{2}{3}x + 2$$
$$y = -\frac{2}{3}x + 11 \qquad \text{Equation of parallel line}$$

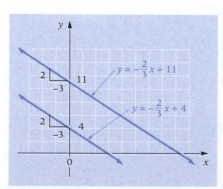

FIGURE 1-29

b)   Each line is graphed by placing our straightedge at its y-intercept and setting its pitch so that there are 2 units of vertical change for every -3 units of horizontal change. This is illustrated in Figure 1-29 on page 21.

•

Applications

Tax Function

The tax rate schedule Table 1-4 gives the amount of 1989 federal income tax due for people filing singly with taxable income of at most $93,130.

PROBLEM

Write the equations for the amount of federal income tax due at the various income levels, and graph the result.

SOLUTION

Let x denote the amount of taxable income and $T(x)$ the respective federal income tax.

From the *first line* of the schedule, if $0 < x \le 18{,}550$, $T(x) = 0.15x$.

From the *second line* of the schedule, if $18{,}550 < x \le 44{,}900$, $T(x) = 2782.50 + 0.28(x - 18{,}550)$.

From the *third line of the schedule,* if $44{,}900 < x \le 93{,}130$, $T(x) = 10{,}160.50 + 0.33(x - 44{,}900)$.

This is written as

$$T(x) = \begin{cases} 0.15x & \text{if} \quad 0 < x \le 18{,}550 \\ 2782.50 + 0.28(x - 18{,}550) & \text{if } 18{,}550 < x \le 44{,}900 \\ 10{,}160.50 + 0.33(x - 44{,}900) & \text{if } 44{,}900 < x \le 93{,}130 \end{cases}$$

The graph of $T(x)$ is given in Figure 1-30. Notice that the different slopes indicate the tax rates.

Specifically, for a person filing singly with taxable income of $60,000, the first $18,550 of taxable income is taxed at a rate of 15%; taxable income over $18,550, but not over $44,900, is taxed at a rate of 28%; taxable income over $44,900, but not over $93,130, is taxed at a rate of 33%. Thus, the federal income tax due on taxable income of $60,000 is given by

$$T(60{,}000) = 10{,}160.50 + 0.33(60{,}000 - 44{,}900)$$

$$= \$15{,}143.50 \quad \text{Federal income tax due on taxable income of \$60,000}$$

TABLE 1-4 **Tax rate schedule**

Taxable income		Federal income tax	
over	but not over		of the amount over
$ 0	$18,550	15%	$ 0
$18,550	44,900	$2782.50 + 28%	18,550
$44,900	93,130	$10,160.50 + 33%	44,900

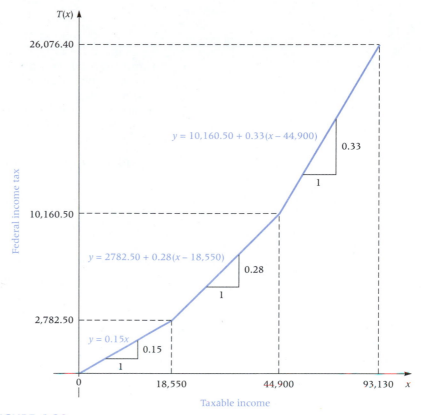

FIGURE 1-30

We close this section by providing a summary of the most common forms of linear equations.

SUMMARY

Linear Equations

1. Point-Slope Form

$$y - y_1 = m(x - x_1)$$ Slope m, line passes through (x_1, y_1)

2. Slope-Intercept Form

$$y = mx + b$$ Slope m, y-intercept $= b$

3. General Form

$$ax + by = c$$ a, b, and c are constant real numbers, with a and b not both 0

4. Horizontal Line

$$y = b$$ y-intercept $= b$, slope $= 0$, no x-intercept

5. Vertical Line

$$x = k$$ x-intercept $= k$, no y-intercept, slope undefined

Note that a linear equation does not contain a variable with a nonzero exponent other than 1.

Exercises 1-2

1. A particle traveled along the straight line from $(2, 5)$ to $(6, 8)$.
   a) Find Δy, the change in y. b) Find Δx, the change in x.
   c) Find the slope. d) Interpret the slope.
2. A particle traveled along the straight line from $(4, 12)$ to $(7, 16)$.
   a) Find Δy, the change in y. b) Find Δx, the change in x.
   c) Find the slope. d) Interpret the slope.

Find the slope of the straight line passing through each of the following pairs of points.

3. $(4, 5), (7, 16)$ 4. $(1, 4), (6, 13)$
5. $(-1, 3), (7, 5)$ 6. $(0, 6), (9, 4)$
7. $(-4, 3), (-5, -7)$ 8. $(5, 9), (8, 7)$
9. $(-8, -2), (-3, -9)$ 10. $(2, 11), (5, -3)$

11. Graphically interpret each of the slopes found in Exercises 3, 8, and 10.

For each of the following, graph the straight line, given slope m through the indicated point:

12. $m = 1/3, (0, 0)$ 13. $m = -1/3, (0, 0)$
14. $m = 5, (1, 8)$ 15. $m = -2, (2, 1)$
16. $m = 6/5, (0, 1)$ 17. $m = -3/4, (4, -5)$
18. $m = 6/5, (10, 13)$ 19. $m = -5/3, (0, 2)$

Find the slope of the straight line passing through each of the following pairs of points, and graph the line.

20. $(4, 6), (-7, 6)$ 21. $(-9, -3), (-8, -3)$
22. $(8, 1), (11, 1)$ 23. $(4, -2), (-6, -2)$
24. $(5, 3), (5, -1)$ 25. $(6, 4), (6, -4)$
26. $(-2, 16), (-2, 4)$ 27. $(4, -6), (4, 9)$

For each of the following, find the equation, in point-slope form, of the straight line passing through the given pair of points. Then convert the equation into slope-intercept form, and sketch the straight line.

28. $(1, 4), (3, 8)$ 29. $(4, -1), (9, -8)$
30. $(5, -10), (7, -14)$ 31. $(3, 2), (7, 10)$
32. $(-2, -3), (-5, 9)$ 33. $(5, 5), (7, 7)$
34. $(4, 12), (6, 18)$ 35. $(5, -3), (4, 2)$

For each of the following, find the equation, in point-slope form, of the straight line passing through the given point and having slope m. Then convert the equation into slope-intercept form, and sketch the straight line.

36. $(4, 3), m = 2$ 37. $(5, -1), m = -3$
38. $(0, -2), m = -4$ 39. $(-4, -9), m = 6$
40. $(-7, 2), m = -1/2$ 41. $(0, 6), m = 5$
42. $(3, 1), m = -1/4$ 43. $(-4, 7), m = 1$

For each of the following linear equations, determine which of the given points lie on its corresponding straight line:

44. $3x - 5y = 30; (0, -6), (5, 2), (10, 0), (15, 3)$
45. $2x + 7y = 21; (7, 1), (3, 0), (4, -3), (14, -1)$
46. $8x + 6y = 0; (0, 0), (1, 5), (-2, 8/3), (7, 13/7)$
47. $y = 6x + 3; (0, 6), (1, 9), (-1/2, 0), (-1, -3)$

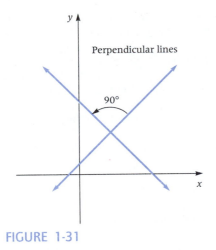

Perpendicular lines

90°

FIGURE 1-31

48. $f(x) = 2x + 4$; $(0, 4)$, $(1, 5)$, $(-1, 2)$, $(-2, 0)$
49. $g(x) = -3x$; $(0, 0)$, $(1, -3)$, $(2, -6)$, $(5, 14)$

For each of the following, find the equation of the straight line passing through the given pair of points. Also, sketch the straight line.

50. $(4, 2)$, $(4, 7)$　　　　　　**51.** $(-3, 1)$, $(-3, 9)$
52. $(5, -9)$, $(8, -9)$　　　　　**53.** $(4, 1)$, $(6, 1)$

For each of the following, find the equation of the straight line passing through the given point and having slope m. Also, sketch the straight line.

54. $(4, 3)$, $m = 0$　　　　　　　**55.** $(-8, 1)$, $m = 0$
56. $(9, -1)$, m is undefined　　　**57.** $(7, 2)$, m is undefined

58. Find the equation of the straight line passing through $(9, -5)$ and parallel to $6x + 2y = 18$. Sketch both lines.

59. Straight lines intersecting each other at right angles (90°) are said to be perpendicular. Figure 1-31 illustrates two perpendicular straight lines. Slopes of perpendicular straight lines are negative reciprocals of each other. In other words, if a straight line has slope m, then a straight line perpendicular to it has slope $-1/m$. This relationship between slopes of perpendicular lines does not hold for vertical or horizontal lines

Find the equation of the straight line passing through $(5, 6)$ and perpendicular to $y = 3x - 2$. Sketch both lines.

60. Find the equation of the straight line passing through $(8, -2)$ and perpendicular to $4x - 3y = 24$. Sketch both lines.

Which of the following pairs of straight lines are parallel?

61. $y = 6x - 14$, $y = 6x + 13$　　**62.** $3x - 2y = 15$, $6x - 4y = 60$
63. $y = -4x + 8$, $y = 4x + 16$　　**64.** $5x - 8y = 11$, $6x + y = 13$

Which of the following pairs of straight lines are perpendicular?

65. $y = 3x + 5$, $y = -(1/3)x + 16$　**66.** $y = 6x + 5$, $y = -6x + 5$
67. $y = 2x - 3$, $2y + x = 10$　　　**68.** $3x + 6y = 11$, $5x + 2y = 13$

Convert each of the following linear equations into slope-intercept form.

69. $3x - 5y = 11$　　　　　　　**70.** $x = -2y + 15$
71. $3x - 2y = 0$　　　　　　　　**72.** $2x + 5y + 16 = 0$

Which of the following equations are linear?

73. $y = 6x - 54$　　　　　　　　**74.** $y = x^2 - 4x$
75. $y = 3x^2 - 4$　　　　　　　**76.** $y^2 = 5x + 7$
77. $3x - 4y = 5$　　　　　　　　**78.** $y = xy + 7$
79. $y = x^3 - 5$　　　　　　　　**80.** $y^3 = x + 4$

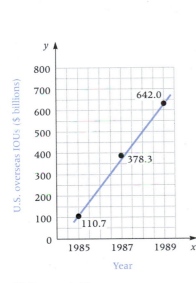

U.S. overseas IOUs ($ billions)

642.0

378.3

110.7

1985　1987　1989

Year

U.S. Department of Commerce

FIGURE 1-32

Applications

81. *U.S. overseas IOUs.* U.S. net foreign debt (overseas IOUs) for each of the three years is given in Figure 1-32.
　a) Find the slope of the straight line of the figure.
　b) Interpret the slope.
　c) Find the equation of the straight line. Express the final result in slope-intercept form.
　d) If U.S. net foreign debt follows the trend of this straight line, predict U.S. net foreign debt for the year 1992.

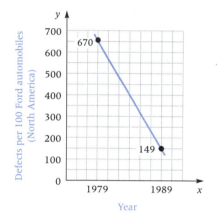

Fortune, April 9, 1990

FIGURE 1-33

82. *Market share: U.S. automobiles.* General Motors' share of the U.S. automobile market slipped from 46.3% to 34.7% during the years from 1979 to 1989 as indicated in Figure 1-33.
a) Find the slope of the straight line of the figure.
b) Interpret the slope.
c) Find the equation of the straight line. Express the final result in slope-intercept form.
d) If General Motors' market share continues to decline at the same rate, predict its market share for the year 1993.

83. *Defects: U.S. automobiles.* The number of defects per 100 vehicles for Ford's North American operations declined from 670 to 149 during the years from 1979 to 1989, as indicated in Figure 1-34
a) Find the slope of the straight line of the figure.
b) Interpret the slope.
c) Find the equation of the straight line. Express the final answer in slope-intercept form.
d) If Ford's defects continue to decline at the same rate, predict its defects per 100 vehicles (North America) for the year 1991.

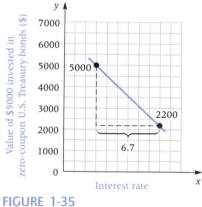

Fortune, April 9, 1990

FIGURE 1-34

84. *Investment.* A money manager noted that $5000 invested in zero-coupon U.S. Treasury bonds would have declined in value to $2200 over a 4-year time interval beginning January 1, 1977, during which time interest rates rose 6.7 percentage points. This is illustrated in Figure 1-35.
a) Find the slope of the straight line of the figure.
b) Interpret the slope.

85. *Investment.* A $5000 investment in gold would have increased in value to $22,000 over a 4-year time interval beginning January 1, 1977, during which time inflation rose from 6.5% to 13.3%. This is illustrated in Figure 1-36.
a) Find the slope of the straight line of the figure.
b) Interpret the slope.

86. *Tax function.* The tax rate schedule in Table 1-5 gives the amount of 1989 federal income tax due for married people filing jointly with taxable income of at most $155,320.
a) Write the equations for the amount of federal income tax due at the various income levels.
b) Graph the result of part a.

87. *Tax function.* The tax rate schedule in Table 1-6 gives the amount of 1989 federal income tax due for married people filing separately with taxable income of at most $117,895.
a) Write the equations for the amount of federal income tax due at the various income levels.
b) Graph the result of part a.

FIGURE 1-35

TABLE 1-5 Tax rate schedule

Taxable income		Federal income tax	
over	but not over		of the amount over
$ 0	$ 30,950	15%	$ 0
30,950	74,850	$4642.50 + 28%	30,950
74,850	155,320	$16,934.50 + 33%	74,850

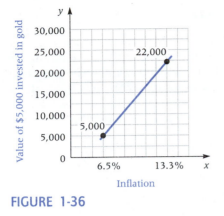

FIGURE 1-36

TABLE 1-6 Tax rate schedule

Taxable income		Federal income tax	
over	but not over		of the amount over
$ 0	$ 15,475	15%	$ 0
15,475	37,425	$2321.25 + 28%	15,475
37,425	117,895	$8467.25 + 33%	37,425

1-3 • GRAPHING LINEAR EQUATIONS

Since all straight lines, except vertical straight lines, are graphs of functions, their equations define **linear functions.** In this section, we will discuss the graphing of linear functions given their equations. In Section 1-2, we graphed a linear function by determining two points on the straight line and connecting them with a straightedge. In this section, instead of determining any two points on the straight line, we will determine the x-intercept and the y-intercept. Recall from Section 1-2 that the y-intercept is the point at which the straight line crosses the y-axis. Thus, the x-intercept is the point at which the straight line crosses the x-axis.

We now graph the linear function defined by

$$2x - 3y = 12$$

by finding its x-intercept and y-intercept.

x-Intercept

As previously mentioned, the x-intercept of a straight line is the point where the straight line crosses the x-axis. Thus, the x-intercept is located on the x-axis, and, therefore, its y-coordinate is 0. Since the x-intercept is also located on the straight line, its coordinates must satisfy the equation of the straight line. Thus, to determine the x-intercept of a straight line, we set $y = 0$ in its equation and solve for x. Using the straight line

$$2x - 3y = 12$$

as an example, we set $y = 0$ and solve for x to determine its x-intercept. Hence,

$$2x - 3(0) = 12$$
$$2x = 12$$
$$x = 6$$

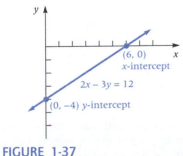

FIGURE 1-37

The x-intercept (6, 0) is illustrated in Figure 1-37.

y-Intercept

As mentioned earlier, the *y*-intercept of a straight line is the point where the straight line crosses the *y*-axis. Thus, the *y*-intercept is located on the *y*-axis, and, therefore, its *x*-coordinate is 0. Since the *y*-intercept is also located on the straight line, its coordinates must satisfy the equation of the straight line. Thus, to determine the *y*-intercept of a straight line, we set $x = 0$ in its equation and solve for *y*. Hence, for the straight line

$$2x - 3y = 12$$

we obtain

$$2(0) - 3y = 12$$
$$-3y = 12$$
$$y = -4$$

The *y*-intercept $(0, -4)$ is illustrated in Figure 1-37.

The straight line defined by $2x - 3y = 12$ is graphed in Figure 1-37.

• EXAMPLE 1-13

Graph $-7x + 2y = 28$.

Solution

First, we find the *x*-intercept. We set $y = 0$ and solve for *x*. Hence,

$$-7x + 2(0) = 28$$
$$-7x = 28$$
$$x = -4$$

Thus, the *x*-intercept is $(-4, 0)$. Next, we determine the *y*-intercept. We set $x = 0$ and solve for *y*. Hence,

$$-7(0) + 2y = 28$$
$$2y = 28$$
$$y = 14$$

Therefore, the *y*-intercept is $(0, 14)$. The straight line is graphed in Figure 1-38.

• EXAMPLE 1-14

Sketch the graph of $y = f(x) = -3x - 2$.

Solution

First, find the *x*-intercept. Set $y = 0$ and solve for *x*. Therefore,

$$0 = -3x - 2$$
$$3x = -2$$
$$x = -\frac{2}{3}$$

Thus, the *x*-intercept is $(-2/3, 0)$. Then find the *y*-intercept. Since the equation $y = -3x - 2$ is in the slope-intercept form, by inspection we determine the *y*-intercept to be $(0, -2)$. The straight line is graphed in Figure 1-39.

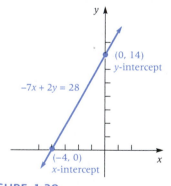

FIGURE 1-38

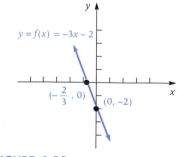

FIGURE 1-39

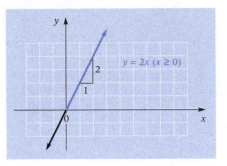

FIGURE 1-40

• **EXAMPLE 1-15**

Graph $y = 2x$, $x \geq 0$.

Solution

The equation $y = 2x$ is in the slope-intercept form $y = mx + b$, with $m = 2$ and $b = 0$. Thus, the y-intercept is the origin, $(0, 0)$. Since the origin is also the x-intercept, we do not have two distinct intercepts to connect with a straightedge. However, if we place our straightedge at the origin and set it so that the slope is 2, we have the straight line of Figure 1-40. The restriction $x \geq 0$ implies that we are to consider only that portion of the line above the interval $x \geq 0$. Accordingly, we have sketched this portion of the line in color.

Before proceeding to the next example, we should study the graphing summary following Example 1-16.

• **EXAMPLE 1-16**

Graph $2x + 5y = 0$.

Solution

Setting $x = 0$ to find the y-intercept yields $y = 0$, and setting $y = 0$ to find the x-intercept yields $x = 0$. Thus, both intercepts are at the origin, $(0, 0)$. This is so because the equation $2x + 5y = 0$, when solved for y, becomes $y = (-2/5)x$. Since $y = (-2/5)x$ is of the form $y = mx$, with $m \neq 0$, then, as is discussed in the graphing summary following this example, its graph goes through the origin and has a negative slope. The graph appears in Figure 1-41.

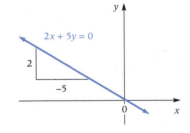

FIGURE 1-41

To Graph a Linear Equation

To graph a linear equation of the form $ax + by = c$,

1. Find the y-intercept. Set $x = 0$ and solve for y. Mark the y-intercept on the y-axis.
2. Find the x-intercept. Set $y = 0$ and solve for x. Mark the x-intercept on the x-axis.
3. Connect the intercepts with a straightedge.

To graph a linear equation in slope-intercept form, $y = mx + b$,

1. Find the y-intercept. The y-intercept is given by b. Mark the y-intercept on the y-axis.
2. Find the x-intercept. Set $y = 0$ and solve for x. Mark the x-intercept on the x-axis.
3. Connect the intercepts with a straightedge.

To graph a linear equation of the form $y = mx$, with $m \neq 0$, note the following:

1. Such an equation is in slope-intercept form, with $b = 0$. Thus, its y-intercept is the origin, $(0, 0)$.
2. Since the origin is also the x-intercept of the straight line, we do not have two distinct intercepts to connect with a straightedge.

continues

To Graph a Linear Equation—_Continued_

3. To graph such a linear equation, we place our straightedge at the origin and set it so that the slope is m. The resulting straight line will resemble one of those shown in Figure 1-42.

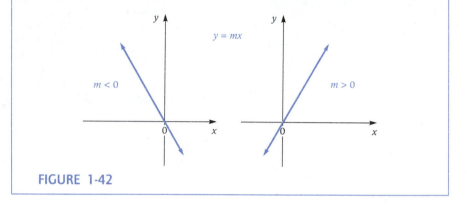

FIGURE 1-42

Exercises 1-3

Graph each of the following linear equations by finding the x and y intercepts:

1. $4x - 6y = 24$
2. $5x + 3y = 45$
3. $-3x + 2y = 8$
4. $5x - 6y = 10$
5. $2x + 7y = 11$
6. $-3x - 5y = 9$
7. $y = -4x + 13$
8. $f(x) = -2x + 15$
9. $f(x) = 6x + 4$
10. $g(x) = (5/2)x + 13$

Graph each of the following linear equations:

11. $y = 2x$
12. $f(x) = -3x$
13. $3x + 2y = 0$
14. $2x - 5y = 0$
15. $g(x) = 7x$
16. $f(x) = (-1/2)x$
17. $f(x) = x$
18. $y = -x$

Graph each of the following:

19. $f(x) = 3x + 5, x \geq 0$
20. $g(x) = 4x, x \geq 0$
21. $f(x) = 2x + 3, x \geq 1$
22. $h(x) = 3x - 15, x \geq 5$

1-4   • LINEAR MODELS

In this section, we present some applications of linear functions. The functions presented will serve as models for later applications in this text.

Cost, Revenue, and Profit Functions

Cost Function.   A manufacturer of chairs can produce 10 chairs at a total cost of \$1100, while 50 such chairs cost \$3500. The **total cost** in each case consists of two components:

1. **Fixed costs,** which include costs that must be paid no matter how few or how many units of product are produced (fixed costs usually include rent, insurance, taxes, etc.).
2. **Variable costs,** which include costs that vary in direct proportion to the number of units of product produced (variable costs usually include material costs, labor costs, and other costs directly attributed to the cost of the product).

Thus,

$$\text{total cost} = \text{variable cost} + \text{fixed cost}$$

If x = number of chairs produced and y = total cost, then we will determine

a)   The variable cost per chair.
b)   The equation relating x and y.

a)   Since 10 chairs cost \$1100 and 50 chairs cost \$3500, we let (x_1, y_1) = $(10, 1100)$ and $(x_2, y_2) = (50, 3500)$. The variable cost per chair is given by the slope of the straight line passing through the two points. Hence,

$$m = \frac{\Delta y}{\Delta x} = \frac{y_2 - y_1}{x_2 - x_1} = \frac{3500 - 1100}{50 - 10} = \frac{2400}{40} = 60$$

Note that the production of 40 additional chairs costs an additional \$2400. Thus, the variable cost per chair is the slope, i.e., \$60 (see Figure 1-43.)

b)   We assume that x and y are linearly related and, therefore, use the point-slope form to find the equation of the straight line passing through the two points, $(10, 1100)$ and $(50, 3500)$. Substituting $(x_1, y_1) = (10, 1100)$ and $m = 60$ into the point-slope form

$$y - y_1 = m(x - x_1)$$

we obtain

$$y - 1100 = 60(x - 10)$$

Solving for y, we have

$$y = 60(x - 10) + 1100$$

or

$$y = 60x + 500$$

variable cost   fixed cost

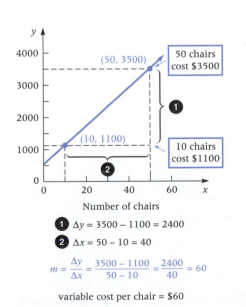

1 $\Delta y = 3500 - 1100 = 2400$

2 $\Delta x = 50 - 10 = 40$

$$m = \frac{\Delta y}{\Delta x} = \frac{3500 - 1100}{50 - 10} = \frac{2400}{40} = 60$$

variable cost per chair = \$60

FIGURE 1-43

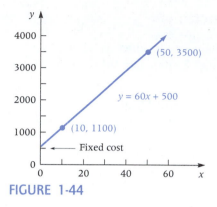

FIGURE 1-44

Since the equation $y = 60x + 500$ relates total cost to number of units produced, it is called a **cost equation.** The function that it defines is called a **cost function** (see Figure 1-44). Note that only the first quadrant portion of the graph of the cost function is shown since the function has meaning only for non-negative values of x.

Since fixed cost is not directly attributed to the cost of the product, it can be defined as the cost of producing 0 units. It is determined by substituting $x = 0$ into the cost equation and solving for y to obtain $y = 60(0) + 500 = 500$. Note that the fixed cost equals the y-intercept (see Figure 1-44).

The variable cost is the product of the variable cost per unit (i.e., the slope, $m = 60$) and the number of units produced (x).

SUMMARY

Linear Cost Function

In general, if total cost (C) and number of units produced (x) are linearly related, then the cost function is defined by

$$C(x) = vx + F \qquad (x \geq 0)$$

where $C(x)$ = cost of producing x units, v = variable cost per unit, and F = fixed cost. The graph of such a cost function appears in Figure 1-45.

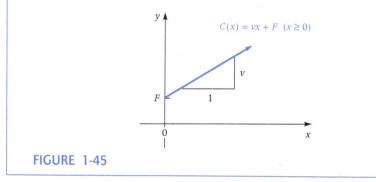

FIGURE 1-45

Revenue Function. Suppose the chair manufacturer of the above illustrative example sells the chairs that he produces for $110. If $R(x)$ = total sales revenue gained from selling x chairs, then

$$\text{sales revenue} = (\text{unit selling price})(\text{number of units sold})$$

or

$$R(x) = 110x$$

The function, R, which relates total sales revenue to number of units sold, is called a **sales revenue function.** Its graph appears in Figure 1-46. Note

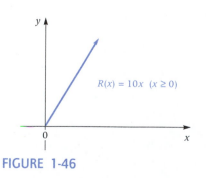

FIGURE 1-46

that only the first quadrant portion of the graph of the revenue function is shown since the function has meaning only for non-negative values of x.

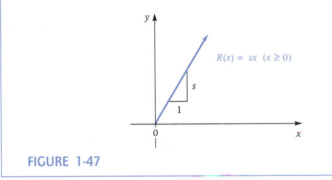

SUMMARY

Sales Revenue Function

In general, if total sales revenue (R) and number of units sold (x) are linearly related, then the sales revenue function is given by

$$R(x) = sx \qquad (x \geq 0)$$

where $R(x)$ = total sales revenue gained from selling x units and s = unit selling price. Its graph is given in Figure 1-47.

FIGURE 1-47

Profit Function. Suppose the chair manufacturer of the above illustrative examples wishes to determine the equation that relates total profit (P) to number of units sold (x). The function that defines this relationship is called a **profit function** and is found by the formula

$$\text{profit} = \text{revenue} - \text{cost}$$

Thus, if $P(x)$ = profit gained from selling x chairs, then

$$P(x) = R(x) - C(x)$$

Since, as determined in the previous illustrative examples, $R(x) = 110x$ and $C(x) = 60x + 500$, then substituting these results into the above equation gives

$$
\begin{aligned}
P(x) &= 110x - (60x + 500) \\
&= 110x - 60x - 500 \\
&= 50x - 500
\end{aligned}
$$

This result is graphed in Figure 1-48. Note that only the first and fourth quadrant portion of the graph of the profit function is shown since the function has meaning only for non-negative values of x.

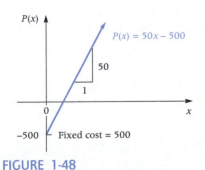

FIGURE 1-48

SUMMARY

Profit Function

In general, given a linear cost function $C(x) = vx + F$ and a sales revenue function $R(x) = sx$ where $x =$ number of units produced and sold, $v =$ variable cost per unit, $F =$ fixed cost, and $s =$ unit selling price, the profit function is determined as follows:

$$P(x) = R(x) - C(x)$$
$$= sx - (vx + F)$$
$$P(x) = (s - v)x - F \qquad (x \geq 0)$$

The slope, $s - v$, of the profit function is called the *unit contribution margin*.

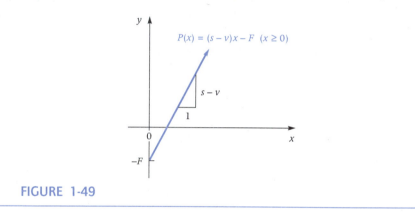

FIGURE 1-49

Demand and Supply Functions

Demand Function. Demand (q) for a product is sometimes linearly related to the product's unit price (p). The equation describing such a relationship between demand and unit price is called a **demand equation,** and its associated function is called a **demand function.**

Consider a case where 20 units of some commodity are demanded by the marketplace when the unit price of that commodity is \$45, whereas 40 units are demanded at a unit price of \$30. We must determine the linear equation relating demand (q) to unit price (p).

Typically, demand (q) is a function of unit price (p), or, in other words, $q = f(p)$. However, since most economists graph the relationship between demand (q) and unit price (p) by writing (p) on the vertical axis and (q) on the horizontal axis, we will also follow this convention. Thus, we summarize the information of the previous paragraph in Table 1-7 by listing first q and then p.

To determine the linear equation relating q and p, we first find the slope

$$m = \frac{\Delta p}{\Delta q} = \frac{30 - 45}{40 - 20} = \frac{-15}{20} = -\frac{3}{4}$$

Rewriting the point-slope form

$$y - y_1 = m(x - x_1)$$

TABLE 1-7

q	p	Ordered pairs (q, p)
20	\$45	(20, 45)
40	\$30	(40, 30)

with p replacing y and q replacing x, we have

$$p - p_1 = m(q - q_1)$$

Arbitrarily selecting $(q_1, p_1) = (40, 30)$, we substitute this result into the above equation along with $m = -3/4$ to obtain

$$p - 30 = -\frac{3}{4}(q - 40)$$

Solving for p, we first multiply $q - 40$ by $-3/4$ (using the distributive law) to obtain

$$p - 30 = -\frac{3}{4}q - \left(-\frac{3}{4}\right)(40)$$

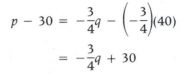

$$= -\frac{3}{4}q + 30$$

and then we add 30 to both sides to obtain the demand equation

$$p = -\frac{3}{4}q + 60$$

which is graphed in Figure 1-50. Observing the graph of the demand function in Figure 1-50, note that its slope is negative. This is typically the case for demand functions since an increase in unit price usually results in a decrease in demand. Note that only the first quadrant portion of the graph of the demand function is shown since the function has meaning only for non-negative values of q and p.

We also note that a demand equation can be written in the form $q = f(p)$. Specifically, if we were to solve the above demand equation for q, we would obtain

$$q = -\frac{4}{3}p + 80$$

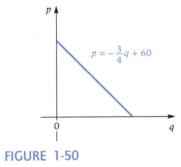

FIGURE 1-50

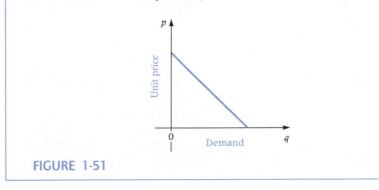

SUMMARY

Linear Demand Functions

A demand function expresses a relationship between demand (q) for some product and the product's unit price (p). The graph of a linear demand function has a *negative slope* and resembles that of Figure 1-51.

FIGURE 1-51

Supply Function. If a given commodity is selling at a unit price of $18, suppliers are willing to produce 30 units of this commodity. However, if the commodity is selling at a unit price of $28, then suppliers are willing to produce 60 units of this commodity. Note that suppliers are willing to produce more of this commodity if it is selling at a higher price than if it is selling at a lower price. This is typical of what usually occurs in the marketplace for most commodities.

An equation that expresses the relationship between the supply for some product and the product's unit price is called a **supply equation,** and its associated function is called a **supply function.** Assuming that supply and demand are linearly related, we now determine the supply equation for the above commodity.

We let p denote unit price and q denote the number of units supplied. As with demand functions, we will consider p the dependent variable and q the independent variable. Thus, we summarize the information of the first paragraph in Table 1-8.

Finding the slope, we obtain

$$m = \frac{\Delta p}{\Delta q} = \frac{28 - 18}{60 - 30} = \frac{10}{30} = \frac{1}{3}$$

As with our previous demand problem, we rewrite the point-slope form

$$y - y_1 = m(x - x_1)$$

by replacing y with p and x with q to obtain

$$p - p_1 = m(q - q_1)$$

Arbitrarily selecting $(q_1, p_1) = (30, 18)$, we substitute this result into the above equation along with $m = 1/3$ to obtain

$$p - 18 = \frac{1}{3}(q - 30)$$

Solving for p, we first multiply $q - 30$ by 1/3 to obtain

$$p - 18 = \frac{1}{3}q - 10$$

and then we add 18 to both sides to obtain the supply equation

$$p = \frac{1}{3}q + 8$$

which is graphed in Figure 1-52. Observing the graph of the supply function in Figure 1-52, note that its slope is positive. This is typically the case for supply functions since an increase in unit price usually results is an increase in supply. Note that only the first quadrant portion of the graph of the supply function is shown since the function has meaning only for non-negative values of q and p.

TABLE 1-8

q	p	Ordered pairs (q, p)
30	$18	(30, 18)
60	$28	(60, 28)

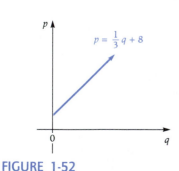

FIGURE 1-52

We also note that a supply equation can be written in the form $q = f(p)$. Specifically, if we were to solve the above supply equation for q, we would obtain

$$q = 3p - 24$$

SUMMARY

Linear Supply Functions

A supply function expresses a relationship between supply (q) for some product and the product's unit price (p). The graph of a linear supply function has a *positive slope* and resembles that of Figure 1-53.

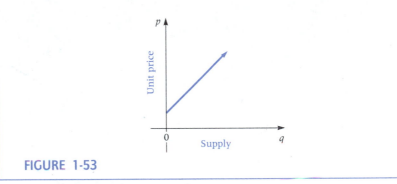

FIGURE 1-53

Consumption Function

TABLE 1-9

x	y
56	50
76	67.2

Table 1-9 exhibits a relationship between a nation's disposable income, x (in billions of dollars), and personal consumption expenditures, y (in billions of dollars). The equation that expresses the relationship between these two quantities defines a **consumption function.** If x and y are linearly related, the slope between the two points in Table 1-9 is

$$m = \frac{\Delta y}{\Delta x} = \frac{y_2 - y_1}{x_2 - x_1} = \frac{67.2 - 50}{76 - 56} = \frac{17.2}{20} = 0.86$$

Economists call this result the **marginal propensity to consume,** abbreviated **MPC.** Since MPC = 0.86, then for each dollar increase in disposable income, consumption increases by $0.86. In other words, 86% of each additional dollar earned is spent, and 14% is saved.

The linear equation relating x and y is determined below. We arbitrarily choose $(x_1, y_1) = (56, 50)$ and substitute this result along with $m = 0.86$ into the point-slope form

$$y - y_1 = m(x - x_1)$$

to obtain

$$y - 50 = 0.86(x - 56)$$

Solving for y, we obtain

$$y = 0.86x + 1.84$$

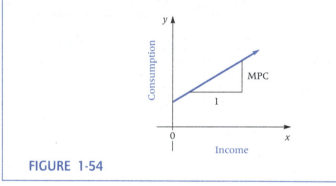
Linear Depreciation

Most assets decrease in value over a period of time. This decrease in value is called **depreciation.** Suppose a company spends $11,000 (total cost) for a truck expected to last 5 years **(economic life),** at which time it will probably be worth $1000 **(salvage value).** For tax purposes, such an asset may be considered to depreciate each year by a fixed amount determined as follows:

$$\frac{\text{depreciable amount}}{\text{economic life}} = \frac{\text{total cost} - \text{salvage value}}{\text{economic life}} = \frac{11{,}000 - 1000}{5}$$

$$= \$2000$$

$$\uparrow$$
$$\text{annual depreciation}$$

Therefore, after 1 year, the value of the truck, y, is

$$y = 11{,}000 - 2000 = \$9000$$

After 2 years, the value of the truck, y, is

$$y = 11{,}000 - 2000(2) = \$7000$$

After 3 years, the value of the truck, y, is

$$y = 11{,}000 - 2000(3) = \$5000$$

After x years, the value of the truck, y, is

$$y = 11{,}000 - 2000x$$

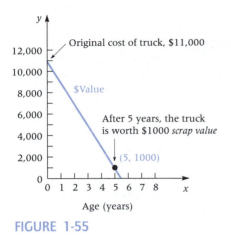

y-axis values: 12,000; 10,000; 8,000; 6,000; 4,000; 2,000; 0

Original cost of truck, $11,000

$Value

After 5 years, the truck is worth $1000 *scrap value*

(5, 1000)

x-axis: 0 1 2 3 4 5 6 7 8

Age (years)

FIGURE 1-55

Thus, the linear equation $y = 11{,}000 - 2000x$ relates the value of the truck, y, to its age, x, in years. This method of depreciation is called the **straight-line method.** The equation is graphed in Figure 1-55.

We will now determine formulas for the y-intercept and slope of the linear equation relating the value of an asset with its age in years. Referring to the linear equation

$$y = 11{,}000 - 2000x$$

y-intercept (total cost)   slope (annual depreciation)

note that the y-intercept, 11,000, is the total cost of the asset and that the slope, -2000, indicates that the value of the truck decreases by $2000 per year.

We generalize as follows.

SUMMARY

Linear Depreciation

If

C = total cost of an asset

n = number of years of economic life of the asset

S = salvage value of the asset

then the linear equation relating the value, y, of the asset with its age, x, in years is given by

$$y = C - \left(\frac{C - S}{n}\right)x$$

Note that the y-intercept is C and the *slope* is

$$-\left(\frac{C - S}{n}\right)$$

• EXAMPLE 1-17

The Beefup Company buys a refrigerator for $20,000. The refrigerator has an economic life of 10 years, after which time it will probably have a salvage value of $2000. Find the linear equation relating the value, y, of the refrigerator to its age, x. Use the straight-line method of depreciation.

Solution

We know that $C = \$20{,}000$, $n = 10$, and $S = \$2000$. Substituting these values into the linear equation

$$y = C - \left(\frac{C - S}{n}\right)x$$

gives us

$$y = 20,000 - \left(\frac{20,000 - 2000}{10}\right)x$$

$$= 20,000 - 1800x$$

•

Exercises 1-4

Cost Functions

1. If 60 units of some product cost $1400 and 40 units cost $1200 to manufacture, then
   a) Determine the variable cost per unit.
   b) Determine the linear cost equation.
   c) Determine the fixed cost.
   d) Graph the cost function.

2. If 20 units of some product cost $2500 and 50 units cost $3400 to produce, then
   a) Determine the variable cost per unit.
   b) Determine the linear cost equation.
   c) Determine the fixed cost.
   d) Graph the cost function.

3. If 30 units of some commodity cost $2200 and 70 units cost $4200 to produce, then
   a) Determine the variable cost per unit.
   b) Determine the linear cost equation.
   c) Determine the fixed cost.
   d) Determine the total cost of producing 50 units.

4. If 30 units of some commodity cost $3100 and 50 units cost $3500 to manufacture, then
   a) Determine the variable cost per unit.
   b) Determine the linear cost equation.
   c) Determine the fixed cost.
   d) Determine the total cost of producing 70 units.

For each of the following, determine the equation of the linear cost function and also the total cost of producing 100 units.

5. Variable cost per unit = $20 and fixed cost = $1000
6. Variable cost per unit = $70 and fixed cost = $900
7. $F = \$8700$ and $v = \$15$
8. $F = \$5000$ and $v = \$90$

Cost, Sales Revenue, and Profit Functions

For each of the following, determine the linear cost, sales revenue, and profit equations. Graph each equation.

9. Variable cost per unit = $40, fixed cost = $900, and unit selling price = $70
10. Variable cost per unit = $90, fixed cost = $2000, and unit selling price = $100
11. $F = \$8000$, $v = \$100$, and $s = \$140$

12. $F = \$9000$, $v = \$50$, and $s = \$80$
13. $F = \$7500$, $v = \$25$, and $s = \$40$
14. $F = \$6000$, $v = \$90$, and $s = \$110$

Demand Functions

For each of the following, determine the equation defining the linear demand function. Graph the result.

15. If clocks are priced at $5 each, there will be a demand for 75 clocks; if clocks are priced at $10 each, the demand will decrease to 50 clocks.
16. At a unit price of $10, 500 units of some product will be demanded; at a unit price of $30, only 300 units will be demanded.

17.

q	p
50	$120
80	$60

18.

q	p
90	$40
30	$80

19.

q	p
300	$200
100	$600

Solve each of the following demand equations for q.

20. $4p + 3q = 12$
21. $6p + 5q = 30$
22. $p + 2q = 8$
23. $2p + q = 6$

Solve each of the following demand equations for p.

24. $6p + 4q = 24$
25. $p + 3q = 6$
26. $p + 5q = 20$
27. $8p + 5q = 40$

Supply Functions

For each of the following, determine the supply equation and graph the result.

28. If gadgets are priced at $9 each, suppliers are willing to produce 86 gadgets. If a gadget's price drops to $5, suppliers are willing to produce only 46 gadgets.
29. At a unit price of $20, suppliers are willing to produce 10 units of some product; at a unit price of $120, suppliers are willing to produce 30 units.

30.

q	p
50	$65
80	$80

31.

q	p
30	$100
90	$120

32.

q	p
20	$ 50
50	$110

Solve each of the following supply equations for q.

33. $4p - 3q = 12$
34. $5p - 4q = 20$

Solve each of the following supply equations for p.

35. $3p - 5q = 30$
36. $4p - 5q = 40$

Consumption Functions

For Exercises 37–39, if x denotes income and y denotes consumption, then
a) Calculate and interpret the MPC.

b) Determine the equation defining the linear consumption function.
c) Graph the result of part b.

37.

x	y
80	58
90	65

38.

x	y
50	44
80	68

39.

x	y
100	97
200	187

TABLE 1-10

x	y
48	44
68	60

40. Table 1-10 presents the relationship between a nation's disposable income, x (in billions of dollars), and personal consumption expenditures, y (in billions of dollars).
  a) Calculate the MPC.
  b) According to the MPC of part a, for each dollar increase in disposable income, consumption increases by how much?
  c) Another rate of change is the *marginal propensity to save,* abbreviated MPS. It is defined as

$$MPS = 1 - MPC$$

  Calculate the MPS for the nation of this example.
  d) According to the MPS calculated in part c, for each dollar increase in disposable income, how many additional dollars are saved?
  e) Determine the equation defining the linear consumption function.
  f) Graph the result of part e.

TABLE 1-11

x	y
60	55
90	79

41. Table 1-11 presents the relationship between a nation's disposable income, x (in billions of dollars), and personal consumption expenditures, y (in billions of dollars).
  a) Calculate and interpret the MPC.
  b) Calculate and interpret the MPS.
  c) Determine the equation defining the linear consumption function.
  d) Calculate the personal consumption expenditures corresponding to disposable income to $85 billion.

Linear Depreciation

In each of the following cases, determine the equation relating the value, y, of an asset to its age, x (in years).

42. $C = \$500{,}000, n = 5, s = \$50{,}000$
43. $C = \$90{,}000, n = 4, s = \$10{,}000$
44. $C = \$60{,}000, n = 6, s = 0$
45. $C = \$45{,}000, n = 3, s = 0$

46. A corporation buys an automobile for $10,500. The automobile's useful life is 5 years, after which time it will have a scrap value of $500.
  a) Find the linear equation relating the value of the automobile, y, to its age, x. Use the linear depreciation method.
  b) Sketch this linear equation.
  c) What is the value of the automobile after 3 years?
47. Made-Fresh Bakery buys an oven for $30,000. The useful life of the oven is 10 years, after which time it will have a scrap value of $1000.
  a) Find the linear equation relating the value of the oven, y, to its age, x.
  b) Graph the linear function defined by the equation of part a.
  c) What is the value of the oven after 6 years?

1-5 • GRAPHING CONCEPTS

In this section, we discuss graphing concepts that enable us to quickly sketch the graphs of functions whose equations are derived from equations of functions with known graphs. Also, we will use these graphing concepts to explain the graphs of functions, where appropriate, in this chapter.

Vertical Shifts

We begin with the graph of the absolute value function

$$f(x) = |x|$$

that was discussed earlier. Recall that to each non-negative number, the absolute value function associates the non-negative number; to each negative number, the absolute value function associates the negative number's additive inverse.

We now consider the graph of the function

$$y = |x| + 4$$

The y-values of this new function are 4 greater than those of the absolute value function. Thus, the graph of $y = |x| + 4$ is obtained from the graph of $y = |x|$ by *lifting the graph* of $y = |x|$ *vertically by 4 units*. This is called a **vertical shift** and is illustrated in Figure 1-56.

Also, the graph of

$$y = |x| - 4$$

is obtained from the graph of $y = |x|$ by *lowering the graph* of $y = |x|$ *vertically by 4 units* as the y-values of $y = |x| - 4$ are 4 less than those of $y = |x|$. This *vertical shift* is also illustrated in Figure 1-56.

We generalize as follows.

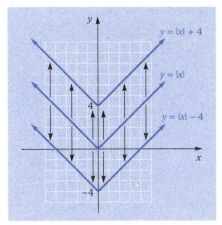

FIGURE 1-56

SUMMARY

Vertical Shifts

Assume the graph of $y = f(x)$ is known.

1. The graph of $y = f(x) + c$, where $c > 0$, is obtained by *lifting the graph* of $y = f(x)$ *vertically by c units*, as illustrated in Figure 1-57.
2. The graph of $y = f(x) - c$, where $c > 0$, is obtained by *lowering the graph* of $y = f(x)$ *vertically by c units*, as illustrated in Figure 1-57.

continues

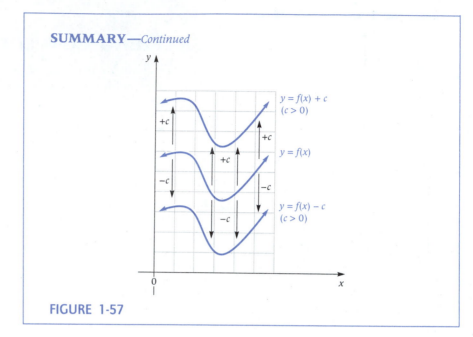

FIGURE 1-57

Horizontal Shifts

Consider the graph of

$$y = |x - 5|$$

as illustrated in Figure 1-58. Note that for any given value of y, the x-coordinates of points on $y = |x - 5|$ are 5 greater than those of $y = |x|$. Thus, the graph of $y = |x - 5|$ is obtained by *shifting the graph* of $y = |x|$ *horizontally to the right by 5 units*, as illustrated in Figure 1-58. This is an example of a **horizontal shift.**

Observe also in Figure 1-58 that the graph of the function

$$y = |x + 5|$$

is obtained by *shifting the graph* of $y = |x|$ *horizontally to the left by 5 units*. This is because for any given value of y, the x-coordinates of points on $y = |x + 5|$ are 5 less than those of $y = |x|$.

We generalize as follows.

SUMMARY

Horizontal Shifts

Assume that the graph of $y = f(x)$ is known.
1. The graph of $y = f(x - c)$, where $c > 0$, is obtained by *shifting the graph* of $y = f(x)$ *horizontally to the right by* c *units,* as illustrated in Figure 1-59.
2. The graph of $y = f(x + c)$, where $c > 0$, is obtained by *shifting the graph* of $y = f(x)$ *horizontally to the left by* c *units,* as illustrated in Figure 1-59.

continues

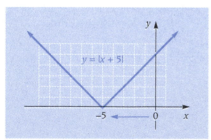

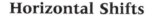

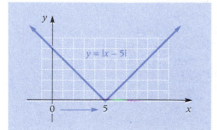

FIGURE 1-58

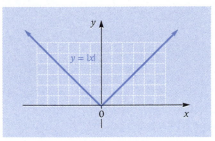

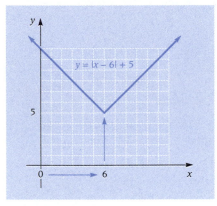

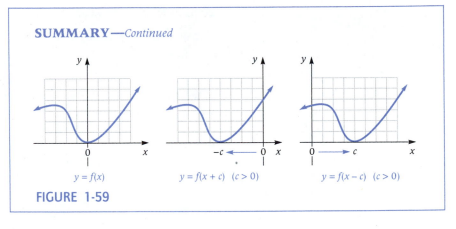

FIGURE 1-59

$y = f(x)$ $y = f(x + c)$ $(c > 0)$ $y = f(x - c)$ $(c > 0)$

• **EXAMPLE 1-18** _____

Graph $y = |x - 6| + 5$.

Solution

This graph involves a horizontal shift followed by a vertical shift. First, the graph of $y = |x - 6|$ is obtained by shifting the graph of $y = |x|$ horizontally to the right by 6 units. Then the graph of $y = |x - 6| + 5$ is obtained by lifting the graph of $y = |x - 6|$ vertically by 5 units. This is illustrated in Figure 1-60.

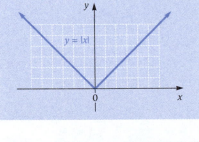

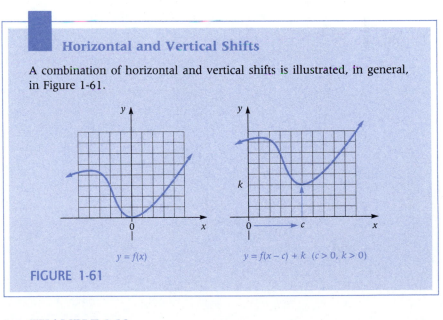

Horizontal and Vertical Shifts

A combination of horizontal and vertical shifts is illustrated, in general, in Figure 1-61.

$y = f(x)$ $y = f(x - c) + k$ $(c > 0, k > 0)$

FIGURE 1-61

$y = |x - 6| + 5$

FIGURE 1-60

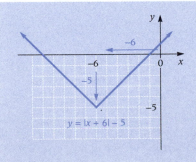

$y = |x + 6| - 5$

FIGURE 1-62

• **EXAMPLE 1-19** _____

Graph $y = |x + 6| - 5$.

Solution

The graph of $y = |x + 6|$ is obtained by shifting the graph of $y = |x|$ horizontally to the left by 6 units. Then the graph of $y = |x + 6| - 5$ is obtained by lowering the graph of $y = |x + 6|$ vertically by 5 units. This is illustrated in Figure 1-62.

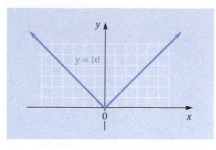

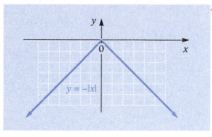

FIGURE 1-63

Reflections in the *x*-Axis

Consider the function

$$y = -|x|$$

Since the *y*-values of the function $y = -|x|$ are the negatives of those of $y = |x|$, then the graph of $y = -|x|$ is obtained by *drawing the graph* of $y = |x|$ *upside down.* This is called a **reflection in the *x*-axis** and is illustrated in Figure 1-63.

We generalize as follows.

SUMMARY

Reflections in the *x*-Axis

Assume the graph of $y = f(x)$ is known. The graph of $y = -f(x)$ is obtained by *drawing the graph* of $y = f(x)$ *upside down,* as illustrated in Figure 1-64.

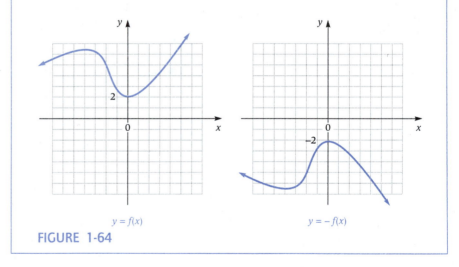

FIGURE 1-64

• **EXAMPLE 1-20** _____

Graph $y = -|x - 3| + 5$.

Solution

We begin with the graph of $y = |x|$ and shift it horizontally to the right 3 units to obtain the graph of $y = |x - 3|$. Then we draw the graph of $y = |x - 3|$ upside down (reflection in the *x*-axis) to obtain the graph of $y = -|x - 3|$. Finally, we lift the graph of $y = -|x - 3|$ vertically 5 units (vertical shift) to obtain the graph of $y = -|x - 3| + 5$. This is illustrated in Figure 1-65.

Horizontal shift

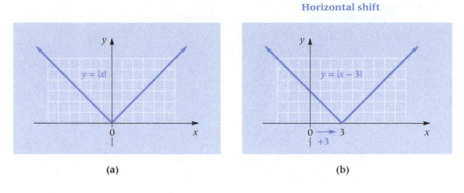

(a)   (b)

Reflection in the *x*-axis   Vertical shift

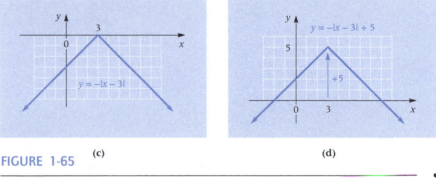

FIGURE 1-65   (c)   (d)

**Symmetry with respect to the
vertical axis (even functions)**

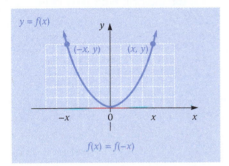

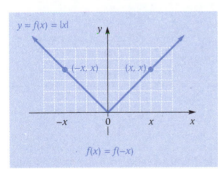

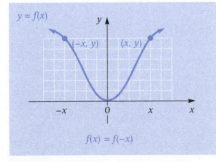

FIGURE 1-66

Symmetry

Observe the graphs of Figure 1-66. Note that for any of these graphs, if (x, y) is on the graph, then $(-x, y)$ is also on the graph. In other words, $f(-x) = f(x)$ for such functions. If a function f satisfies the above condition, it is called an **even function,** and its graph is **symmetrical with respect to the vertical axis.**

Observe the graphs of Figure 1-67 on page 48. Note that for any of these graphs, if (x, y) is on the graph, then $(-x, -y)$ is on the graph. In other words, $f(-x) = -f(x)$ for such functions. If a function satisfies this condition, it is called an **odd function,** and its graph is **symmetrical with respect to the origin.**

We generalize as follows.

SUMMARY

Symmetry

1. **Symmetry with respect to the vertical axis.** If $f(-x) = f(x)$, then f is an **even function,** and its graph is symmetrical with respect to the vertical axis, as illustrated in Figure 1-68.

continues

**Symmetry with respect to the orgin
(odd functions)**

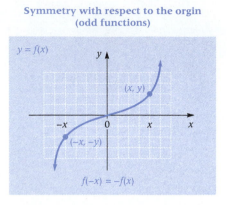

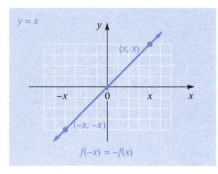

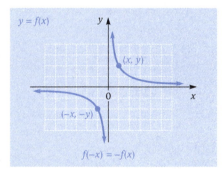

FIGURE 1-67

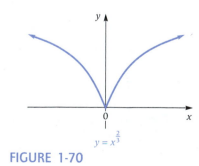

FIGURE 1-70

SUMMARY—*Continued*

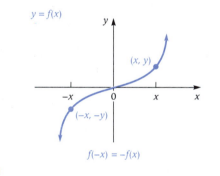

FIGURE 1-68

2. **Symmetry with respect to the origin.** If $f(-x) = -f(x)$, then f is an **odd function,** and its graph is symmetrical with respect to the origin, as illustrated in Figure 1-69.

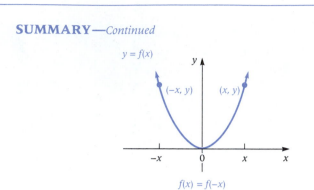

FIGURE 1-69

• **EXAMPLE 1-21** _____

Note that

$$f(x) = x^{2/3}$$

is an even function, as indicated by its table of x- and y-values below. Specifically, $f(-x) = f(x)$, and the graph of f is symmetrical with respect to the y-axis, as illustrated in Figure 1-70.

x	-3	-2	-1	0	1	2	3
$f(x)$	2.08	1.59	1	0	1	1.59	2.08

• **EXAMPLE 1-22** _____

Note that

$$f(x) = x^{1/3}$$

is an odd function, as indicated by its table of x- and y-values below. Specifically, $f(-x) = -f(x)$, and the graph of f is symmetrical with respect to the origin, as illustrated in Figure 1-71.

x	-3	-2	-1	0	1	2	3
$f(x)$	-1.44	-1.26	-1	0	1	1.26	1.44

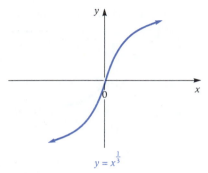

$y = x^{\frac{1}{3}}$

FIGURE 1-71

Exercises 1-5

Graph each of the following.

1. $y = -|x - 2|$ **2.** $y = -|x + 6|$ **3.** $y = |x - 8| + 2$
4. $y = -|x - 6| + 4$ **5.** $y = -|x + 3| - 8$ **6.** $y = -|x + 7| - 9$

Observe the graph of $f(x) = x^{2/3}$ of Figure 1-70, Example 1-21. Then graph each of the following.

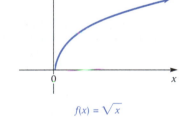

$f(x) = \sqrt{x}$

FIGURE 1-72

7. $f(x) = (x - 3)^{2/3}$ **8.** $f(x) = (x + 4)^{2/3}$
9. $f(x) = (x + 7)^{2/3} + 5$ **10.** $f(x) = (x - 6)^{2/3} - 2$
11. $f(x) = -(x - 5)^{2/3}$ **12.** $f(x) = -(x + 2)^{2/3}$
13. $f(x) = -(x - 3)^{2/3} - 1$ **14.** $f(x) = -(x + 2)^{2/3} + 4$

Observe the graph of $f(x) = x^{1/3}$ of Figure 1-71, Example 1-22. Then graph each of the following.

15. $f(x) = (x + 2)^{1/3}$ **16.** $f(x) = (x - 5)^{1/3}$
17. $f(x) = (x - 2)^{1/3} + 9$ **18.** $f(x) = (x + 1)^{1/3} - 2$
19. $f(x) = -(x - 1)^{1/3}$ **20.** $f(x) = -(x + 2)^{1/3}$
21. $f(x) = -(x - 5)^{1/3} + 2$ **22.** $f(x) = -(x - 4)^{1/3} + 7$

The graph of $f(x) = \sqrt{x}$ is given in Figure 1-72. Graph each of the following.

23. $f(x) = \sqrt{x - 5}$ **24.** $f(x) = \sqrt{x + 2}$
25. $f(x) = \sqrt{x + 9} + 2$ **26.** $f(x) = \sqrt{x - 4} - 6$
27. $f(x) = -\sqrt{x}$ **28.** $f(x) = -\sqrt{x} + 1$
29. $f(x) = -\sqrt{x - 3}$ **30.** $f(x) = -\sqrt{x + 1} - 2$

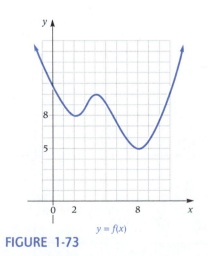

$y = f(x)$

FIGURE 1-73

The graph of some function f is given in Figure 1-73. Graph each of the following.

31. $y = f(x - 2)$ **32.** $y = f(x + 4)$ **33.** $y = -f(x)$
34. $y = -f(x - 6)$ **35.** $y = f(x - 1) + 4$ **36.** $y = -f(x) + 5$
37. $y = -f(x - 2) + 1$ **38.** $y = -f(x + 1) - 2$ **39.** $y = -f(x) - 6$

For each of the graphs below, state whether the function is odd, even, or neither.

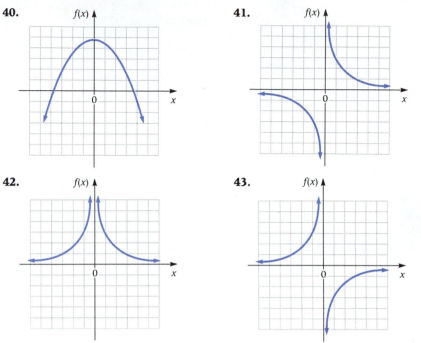

40.

41.

42.

43.

For each of the following:

a) Determine whether the function is odd, even, or neither by filling in the ind - cated table of x- and $f(x)$-values. Use a calculator if necessary.

b) Sketch a graph by plotting the points from part a.

44. $f(x) = x^2$

x	-3	-2	-1	0	1	2	3
$f(x)$							

45. $f(x) = x^3$

x	-3	-2	-1	0	1	2	3
$f(x)$							

46. $f(x) = 1/(1 + x^2)$

x	-3	-2	-1	$-1/2$	0	1/2	1	2	3
$f(x)$									

47. $f(x) = 1/x$

x	-3	-2	-1	$-1/2$	0	1/2	1	2	3
$f(x)$									

48. $f(x) = (x - 2)^2$

x	−3	−2	−1	0	1	2	3
$f(x)$							

Applications

Cost, Revenue, and Profit Functions

The graphs of cost, revenue, and profit functions for some product are given in Figure 1-74.

49. Indicate the effect on the graph of the cost function of a $100 increase in the fixed cost.

50. Indicate the effect on the graph of the profit function of a $100 increase in the fixed cost.

Market Dynamics: Supply, Demand, Equilibrium

In Section 1-4, we learned that a demand function relates the unit price of some product to the demand for that product. Also, a supply function relates the unit price of some product to the number of units supplied of the product. In Section 1-4, we worked with linear supply and demand functions. Thus, their corresponding graphs were straight lines. If the graph of a demand function is nonlinear, its graph is usually referred to as a **demand curve.** Analogously, if the graph of a supply function is nonlinear, its graph is called a **supply curve.**

51. The graphs of the supply and demand functions for some product are given in Figure 1-75. If the demand for this product increases by 5 units, then the graph of the demand function will shift horizontally to the right by 5 units, as illustrated. State the new equilibrium price.

52. Consider the supply and demand curves of Figure 1-76. If the supply of this product increases by 4 units, then the graph of the supply function will shift horizontally to the right by 4 units. State the new equilibrium price.

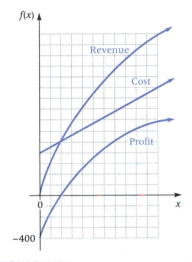

FIGURE 1-74

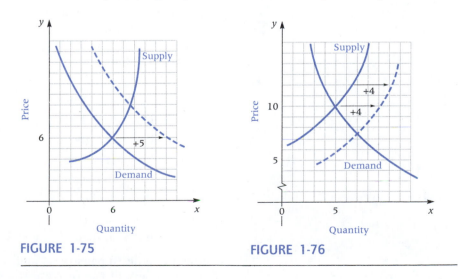

FIGURE 1-75

FIGURE 1-76

1-6 • QUADRATIC FUNCTIONS AND THEIR GRAPHS

In this and the next section, we will learn to graph equations like

$$y = 3x^2 - 4x + 7$$

Such an equation defines a **quadratic function.** Note that the highest-powered term of a quadratic equation is of the **second degree.**

$$y = f(x) = 3x^2 - 4x + 7$$

second-degree   first-degree   constant
term   term   term

In general, any equation of the form

$$y = ax^2 + bx + c$$

where a, b, and c are constant real numbers and $a \neq 0$, is called a **quadratic equation.** Without the restriction $a \neq 0$, the equation becomes the linear equation $y = bx + c$.

If the quadratic equation

$$y = 3x^2 - 4x + 7$$

is compared with the general form

$$y = ax^2 + bx + c$$

then $a = 3$, $b = -4$, and $c = 7$.

As a start in learning to graph quadratic functions, we consider the simplest of all quadratic equations, which is

$$y = x^2$$

Comparing this equation with the general quadratic form, $y = ax^2 + bx + c$, we have $a = 1$, $b = 0$, and $c = 0$.

A sketch of $y = x^2$ may be obtained by finding some ordered pairs (x, y) satisfying the equation and plotting their corresponding points on the rectangular coordinate system. Arbitrarily choosing values of x and finding their corresponding y-values, we have the following:

x-Value	Equation $(y = x^2)$	Ordered Pair (x, y)
If $x = -3$, then	$y = (-3)^2 = 9$	$(-3, 9)$
If $x = -2$, then	$y = (-2)^2 = 4$	$(-2, 4)$
If $x = -1$, then	$y = (-1)^2 = 1$	$(-1, 1)$
If $x = 0$, then	$y = 0^2 = 0$	$(0, 0)$
If $x = 1$, then	$y = 1^2 = 1$	$(1, 1)$
If $x = 2$, then	$y = 2^2 = 4$	$(2, 4)$
If $x = 3$, then	$y = 3^2 = 9$	$(3, 9)$

Plotting the ordered pairs (x, y) and sketching the curve through them, we obtain the graph of Figure 1-77. This graph form is called a **parabola.** In

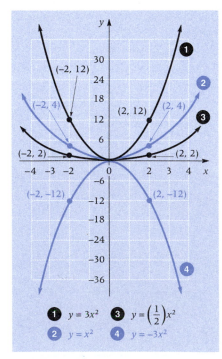

FIGURE 1-77

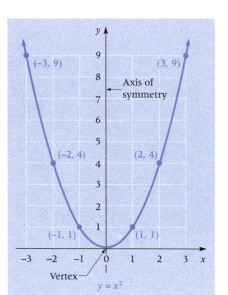

FIGURE 1-78

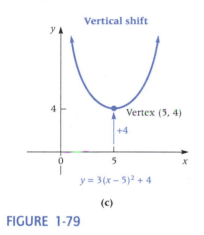

$y = 3x^2$

(a)

Horizontal shift

$y = 3(x - 5)^2$

(b)

Vertical shift

Vertex (5, 4)

+4

$y = 3(x - 5)^2 + 4$

(c)

FIGURE 1-79

fact, the graph of any quadratic function is a parabola. Note that the origin, $(0, 0)$, is the lowest point on the parabola $y = x^2$ of Figure 1-77. The lowest point on the parabola is called the **vertex.** Thus, $(0, 0)$ is the vertex of $y = x^2$.

Still referring to the parabola $y = x^2$ of Figure 1-77 note that the y-axis separates the parabola into two symmetrical parts, each the mirror image of the other. Such a vertical line passing through the vertex is called the **axis of symmetry.**

We now consider quadratic equations of the form

$$y = ax^2$$

with $a \neq 1$. If $a > 0$, then the parabola has the same general shape as $y = x^2$ of Figure 1-77, but it is narrowed if $a > 1$ and widened if $a < 1$. If $a < 0$, then the y-coordinates are negative, and the parabola appears below the x-axis. To illustrate these comments, see the graphs of $y = x^2$ $y = 3x^2$, $y = (1/2)x^2$, and $y = -3x^2$ in Figure 1-78.

The graphs of quadratic functions with $a > 0$ are said to *open up,* whereas those with $a < 0$ are said to *open down.* Thus, the graphs of $y = x^2$, $y = 3x^2$, and $y = (1/2)x^2$ of Figure 1-78 are described as opening up, while the graph of $y = -3x^2$ is said to open down. Note that for a parabola that *opens down,* its **vertex** is the *highest point* on the parabola.

We now consider the graph of the quadratic function defined by

$$y = 3(x - 5)^2 + 4$$

The graph of this function can be sketched by drawing the graph of $y = 3x^2$, shifting it horizontally to the right by 5 units, and then shifting the result vertically by 4 units. This is illustrated in Figure 1-79.

> In general, the graph of the quadratic function defined by
> $$y = a(x - h)^2 + k$$
> 1. Opens up if $a > 0$ and opens down if $a < 0$.
> 2. Has its vertex at (h, k).
> 3. Has the line $x = h$ as its axis of symmetry.

We now consider quadratic equations of the form

$$y = f(x) = ax^2 + bx + c$$

We will derive a formula for the $x =$ coordinate of the vertex, (h, k), in terms of a, b, and c by expressing the equation $y = a(x - h)^2 + k$ in the form $y = ax^2 + bx + c$. We begin with $y = a(x - h)^2 + k$ and replace $(x - h)^2$ with its equivalent expression, $x^2 - 2hx + h^2$, to obtain

$$y = a(x^2 - 2hx + h^2) + k$$

Simplifying this expression, we get

$$y = ax^2 - 2ahx + ah^2 + k$$

Comparing this result with the general quadratic form, $y = ax^2 + bx + c$, we have

$$b = -2ah \quad \text{and} \quad c = ah^2 + k$$

Solving the equation $b = -2ah$ for h, we obtain

$$h = \frac{-b}{2a} \qquad \textit{x-coordinate of vertex}$$

Of course, the corresponding y-coordinate of the vertex is obtained by substituting the above result into the quadratic equation. Thus, the y-coordinate of the vertex is given by

$$f(-b/2a) \qquad \textit{y-coordinate of vertex}$$

We now consider the following example.

• **EXAMPLE 1-23** _____

Graph $y = f(x) = 3x^2 + 5x + 2$.

Solution

Comparing this equation with the form $y = f(x) = ax^2 + bx + c$, we have $a = 3$, $b = 5$, and $c = 2$. Since a is positive, the parabola opens up. The $x =$ coordinate of the vertex, (h, k), is

$$h = -\frac{b}{2a} = -\frac{5}{2(3)} = -\frac{5}{6} \qquad \textit{x-coordinate of vertex}$$

The y-coordinate of the vertex is

$$f\left(-\frac{b}{2a}\right) = f\left(-\frac{5}{6}\right) = 3\left(-\frac{5}{6}\right)^2 + 5\left(-\frac{5}{6}\right) + 2 = -\frac{1}{12} \qquad \textit{y-coordinate of vertex}$$

Thus, the vertex is $(-5/6, -1/12)$.

The y-intercept is

$$y = f(0) = 3(0^2) + 5(0) + 2 = 2$$

The x-intercepts are found by setting $y = 0$ and solving for x. Hence,

$$0 = 3x^2 + 5x + 2$$
$$0 = (3x + 2)(x + 1)$$
$$3x + 2 = 0 \qquad\qquad x + 1 = 0$$
$$x = -\frac{2}{3} \qquad\qquad x = -1$$

Therefore, the x-intercepts are $(-2/3, 0)$ and $(-1, 0)$. The graph appears in Figure 1-80.

_____ •

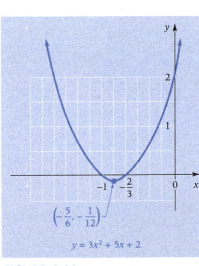

$$\left(-\frac{5}{6}, -\frac{1}{12}\right)$$

$$y = 3x^2 + 5x + 2$$

FIGURE 1-80

Quadratic Formula

When finding the x-intercepts of a parabola, we must often solve a quadratic equation of the form

$$ax^2 + bx + c = 0$$

where a, b, and c are constant real numbers and $a \neq 0$. Sometimes such an equation may be solved by factoring, as was the case in Example 1-23. A more general method is given by the **quadratic formula.***

> **Quadratic Formula**
>
> $$x = \frac{-b \pm \sqrt{b^2 - 4ac}}{2a}$$

We will review the use of the quadratic formula by calculating the x-intercepts of the parabola of Example 1-23. Substituting $a = 3$, $b = 5$, and $c = 2$ into the quadratic formula

$$x = \frac{-b \pm \sqrt{b^2 - 4ac}}{2a}$$

gives us

$$x = \frac{-5 \pm \sqrt{5^2 - 4(3)(2)}}{2(3)}$$

$$= \frac{-5 \pm \sqrt{25 - 24}}{6} = \frac{-5 \pm \sqrt{1}}{6}$$

$$= \frac{-5 \pm 1}{6} = \begin{cases} \dfrac{-5 + 1}{6} = -\dfrac{2}{3} \\[2mm] \dfrac{-5 - 1}{6} = -1 \end{cases}$$

Thus, the x-intercepts are $(-2/3, 0)$ and $(-1, 0)$.

Two x-intercepts: $b^2 - 4ac > 0$

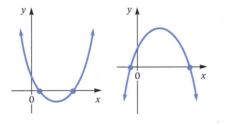

One x-intercept: $b^2 - 4ac = 0$

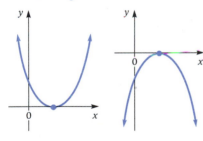

No x-intercepts: $b^2 - 4ac < 0$

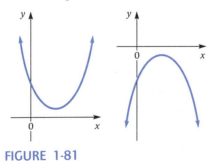

FIGURE 1-81

> The expression $b^2 - 4ac$, which appears under the square root sign in the quadratic formula, determines the character of the solutions. Hence, it is called the **discriminant.** Specifically,
>
> **1.** If $b^2 - 4ac > 0$, there are two real solutions (two x-intercepts).
> **2.** If $b^2 - 4ac = 0$, there is one real solution (one x-intercept).
> **3.** If $b^2 - 4ac < 0$, there are no real solutions (no x-intercepts).

Each of the above situations is illustrated in Figure 1-81.
We now give a procedure for graphing a quadratic function.

*A derivation of the quadratic formula is given in Appendix B.

To Graph a Quadratic Function

To graph a quadratic function whose equation is in the form

$$y = f(x) = ax^2 + bx + c$$

1. Determine whether the parabola *opens up* or *down*.
   Rule: If $a > 0$, parabola opens up.
   If $a < 0$, parabola opens down.
2. Find the *y-intercept*.

$$y = f(0) = a(0)^2 + b(0) + c = c$$

   Hence, the *y*-intercept is always $(0, c)$.

3. Find the coordinates of the *vertex* (____, ____).
$$\underset{-b/2a}{\uparrow} \qquad \underset{f(-b/2a)}{\uparrow}$$

4. Find any *x-intercepts*. Set $y = 0$ and solve the resulting equation for *x*.
   Note:
   • You might have to factor.
   • You might have to use the quadratic formula.
   • There will be two, one, or no *x*-intercept.

• **EXAMPLE 1-24** _____

Graph $f(x) = x^2 - 2x - 8$.

Solution

Note that $a = 1$, $b = -2$, and $c = -8$.

1. The parabola opens up since $a > 0$ ($a = 1$).
2. The *y*-intercept is $(0, c) = (0, -8)$.
3. Vertex (____, ____)

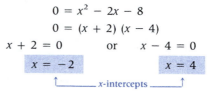

$$\frac{-b}{2a} = \frac{-(-2)}{2(1)}$$
$$= 1$$

x-coordinate

y-coordinate

$$f(1) = 1^2 - 2(1) - 8 = -9$$

4. *x*-intercepts

$$0 = x^2 - 2x - 8$$
$$0 = (x + 2)(x - 4)$$
$$x + 2 = 0 \qquad \text{or} \qquad x - 4 = 0$$
$$\boxed{x = -2} \qquad\qquad \boxed{x = 4}$$

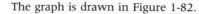

x-intercepts

The graph is drawn in Figure 1-82.

• **EXAMPLE 1-25** _____

Graph $f(x) = -x^2 + 6x$.

Solution

Note that $a = -1$, $b = 6$, and $c = 0$.

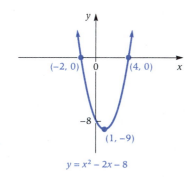

$(-2, 0)$ 0 $(4, 0)$

-8

$(1, -9)$

$y = x^2 - 2x - 8$

FIGURE 1-82

1. The parabola opens down since $a < 0$ ($a = -1$).
2. The y-intercept is $(0, c) = (0, 0)$.

3. Vertex (——, ——)

$$x\text{-coordinate:} \quad -b/2a = -6/2(-1) = 3$$
$$y\text{-coordinate:} \quad f(3) = -(3)^2 + 6(3) = 9$$

4. x-intercepts

$$0 = -x^2 + 6x$$
$$0 = x(-x + 6)$$
$$x = 0 \quad \text{or} \quad -x + 6 = 0$$
$$\boxed{x = 0} \qquad\qquad \boxed{x = 6}$$
$$\underbrace{}_{\text{x-intercepts}}$$

The parabola is drawn in Figure 1-83.

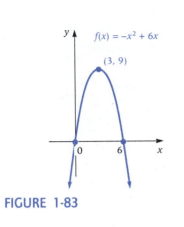

$f(x) = -x^2 + 6x$

$(3, 9)$

FIGURE 1-83

• **EXAMPLE 1-26** _____

Graph $f(x) = x^2 - 6x + 9$.

Solution

Note that $a = 1$, $b = -6$, and $c = 9$.

1. The parabola opens up since $a > 0$ ($a = 1$).
2. The y-intercept is $(0, c) = (0, 9)$.

3. Vertex (——, ——)

$$x\text{-coordinate:} \quad -b/2a = -(-6)/2(1) = 3$$
$$y\text{-coordinate:} \quad f(3) = 3^2 - 6(3) + 9 = 0$$

4. x-intercepts

$$0 = x^2 - 6x + 9$$
$$0 = (x - 3)^2 \qquad \text{Perfect square}$$
$$0 = x - 3$$
$$x = 3 \qquad \text{Only one } x\text{-intercept}$$

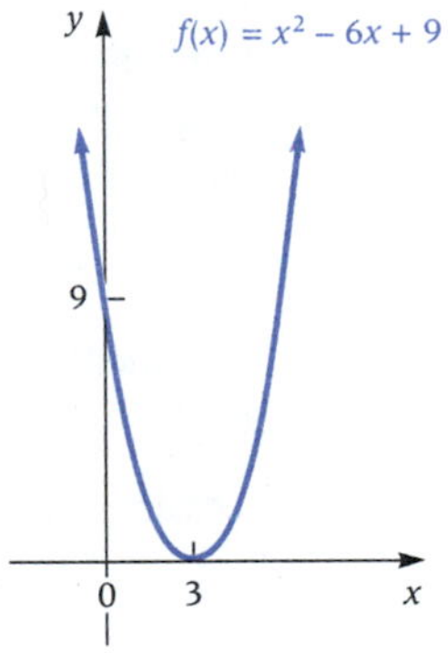

The parabola is drawn in Figure 1-84.

$f(x) = x^2 - 6x + 9$

FIGURE 1-84

Exercises 1-6

1. Graph each of the following:
   a) $y = 5x^2$ b) $y = -5x^2$
   c) $y = (1/2)x^2$ d) $y = -(1/2)x^2$

2. Graph the following on the same set of axes: $y = x^2$, $y = 6x^2$, $y = (1/4)x^2$.
3. Graph the following on the same set of axes: $y = -x^2$, $y = -4x^2$, $y = -(1/3)x^2$.
4. Graph the following on the same set of axes: $f(x) = x^2$, $f(x) = 3x^2$, $f(x) = 7x^2$.

Graph each of the following by using a vertical shift.

5. $y = x^2 + 7$ **6.** $f(x) = 3x^2 + 5$
7. $y = x^2 - 9$ **8.** $y = -x^2 + 9$
9. $f(x) = 2x^2 - 8$ **10.** $y = -4x^2 + 36$

Graph each of the following by using a horizontal shift.

11. $y = (x - 3)^2$

12. $y = (x + 3)^2$

13. $y = 4(x - 1)^2$

14. $y = 4(x + 1)^2$

15. $f(x) = -2(x + 5)^2$

16. $f(x) = -2(x - 3)^2$

Graph each of the following by shifting.

17. $y = 2(x - 1)^2 + 3$

18. $y = -(x - 4)^2 - 1$

19. $f(x) = 3(x - 2)^2 - 1$

20. $f(x) = -3(x - 2)^2 + 4$

21. $y = -3(x + 2)^2 - 5$

22. $y = 4(x + 3)^2 - 2$

23. $f(x) = (x + 3)^2 - 1$

24. $f(x) = (x - 2)^2 + 4$

25. $f(x) = -(x + 2)^2 + 1$

26. $f(x) = -(x - 3)^2 + 2$

Graph each of the following.

27. $y = 2x^2 + 8x$

28. $f(x) = -3x^2 + 7x$

29. $f(x) = x^2 - 5x$

30. $y = -x^2 + 8x$

31. $y = -2x^2 + 6x$

32. $y = 3x^2 - 2x$

33. $y = x^2 - 6x + 5$

34. $y = x^2 - 2x - 3$

35. $f(x) = x^2 - 6x - 16$

36. $f(x) = x^2 - 8x + 7$

37. $y = x^2 - 2x - 15$

38. $y = x^2 - 8x + 15$

39. $y = x^2 - 4x - 5$

40. $y = x^2 + 7x + 6$

41. $f(x) = -5x^2 + 6x + 4$

42. $y = x^2 - 8x + 16$

43. $y = -x^2 + 8x - 16$

44. $f(x) = x^2 + x + 1$

45. $f(x) = x^2 - 10x + 26$

46. $y = 2x^2 - 3x + 6$

47. $f(x) = 2x^2 + 4x + 1$

48. $f(x) = x^2 - 6x + 7$

49. $f(x) = x^2 - 10x + 25$

50. $f(x) = x^2 + 10x + 25$

51. $y = x^2 - 6x + 9$

52. $f(x) = x^2 + 6x + 9$

Equations in Factored Form

If the equation of a quadratic function is given in factored form, such as

$$f(x) = a(x - x_1)(x - x_2)$$

where a, x_1, and x_2 are constants, then the x-intercepts are easily determined as shown below.

$$0 = a(x - x_1)(x - x_2)$$

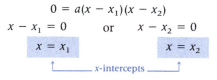

Then, since the x-coordinate of the vertex lies midway between the x-intercepts (due to symmetry), it is determined as shown below.

$$x\text{-coordinate of vertex} = \frac{x_1 + x_2}{2}$$

The y-coordinate of the vertex is determined as indicated below.

$$y\text{-coordinate of vertex} = f\left(\frac{x_1 + x_2}{2}\right)$$

The sign of coefficient a indicates whether the parabola opens up or down. Specifically, if a is positive, the parabola opens up, and if a is negative, the parabola opens down. The y-intercept is determined by setting $x = 0$ and solving for y.

Using the above comments, graph each of the following.

53. $y = (x - 2)(x + 3)$

54. $f(x) = (x + 1)(x - 5)$

55. $y = 4(x - 2)(x + 3)$

56. $y = -2(x + 1)(x - 5)$

57. $f(x) = (x - 6)^2$ **58.** $y = -(x - 6)^2$
59. $y = -5(x + 1)^2$ **60.** $f(x) = (x + 6)(x - 6)$
61. $y = (x - 2)(x + 2)$ **62.** $f(x) = (x + 6)(x + 6)$
63. $y = -3(x - 2)(x + 2)$ **64.** $f(x) = 4(x + 1)(x - 1)$

1-7 • APPLICATIONS OF QUADRATIC FUNCTIONS

Revenue, Cost, and Profit Functions

Revenue Function. We begin this section by discussing, in greater detail, the introductory application to this chapter. Recall that sometimes the unit selling price of a firm's product depends on the demand level of the product. Such a relationship is given by a demand equation

$$p = f(x)$$

where p denotes the unit price and x denotes the number of units demanded of the product. The sales revenue function is determined as follows.

sales revenue = (number of units sold)(unit price)

$$R(x) = xp$$

$$= xf(x)$$

As an example, suppose we are given the demand equation

$$p = -20x + 14,100$$

and asked to find the sales revenue function $R(x)$. We proceed as follows.

$$R(x) = xp$$

$$= x(-20x + 14,100)$$
$$= -20x^2 + 14,100x$$

This revenue function is graphed in Figure 1-85(a). Observe that the vertex point gives the maximum sales revenue. Thus, the maximum sales revenue of $2,485,125 is realized when 352.5 units of the product are sold. Later in this text, we will use calculus concepts to maximize or minimize quantities.

Studying the graph of the revenue function of Figure 1-85(a), observe that after the vertex point, sales revenue decreases as the number of units sold increases. This is because of the nature of the relationship between unit price and demand as given by the demand equation. Note that as demand increases, unit price decreases. Thus, as more and more units of this product are sold, they are sold at lower and lower unit prices. This ultimately results in decreases in sales revenue as the number of units sold increases.

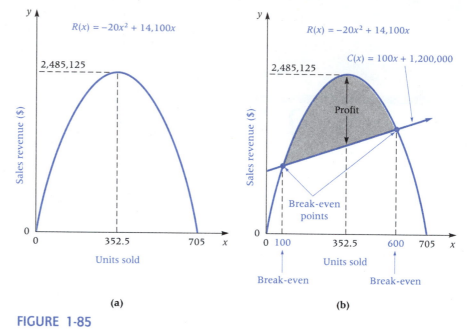

(a)

(b)

FIGURE 1-85

Cost Function. If this product has a fixed cost of $1,200,000 and a unit variable cost of $100, then the cost function is given by

$$C(x) = 100x + 1,200,000$$

Figure 1-85(b) gives a graph of both the cost and sales revenue functions on the same set of axes.

Break-Even Analysis. Note that the intersection points of the graphs of the cost and revenue functions of Figure 1-85(b) are the points where sales revenue = cost. These points are called the **break-even points.** Also note that a positive profit results if the number of units sold lies between the x-coordinates of the break-even points. We will use the profit function to determine the break-even points.

Profit Function: Break-Even Analysis. Using the revenue and cost functions discussed above, we find the equation of the profit function as follows.

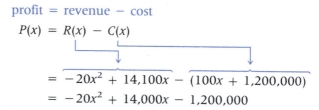

$$\text{profit} = \text{revenue} - \text{cost}$$
$$P(x) = R(x) - C(x)$$
$$= -20x^2 + 14,100x - (100x + 1,200,000)$$
$$= -20x^2 + 14,000x - 1,200,000$$

The graph of the profit function is given in Figure 1-86.

Since the break-even points are the points where sales revenue = cost, or, in other words, profit = 0, we find the break-even points by finding the

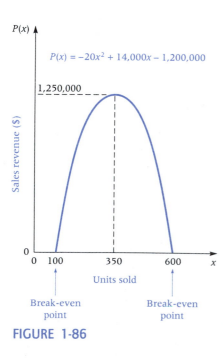

FIGURE 1-86

x-intercepts of the profit function. Thus, we set $P(x) = 0$ and solve for x to obtain

$$0 = -20x^2 + 14{,}000x - 1{,}200{,}000$$
$$0 = -20(x^2 - 700x + 60{,}000)$$
$$0 = -20(x - 100)(x - 600)$$
$$x - 100 = 0 \quad \text{or} \quad x - 600 = 0$$
$$\boxed{x = 100} \qquad\qquad \boxed{x = 600} \qquad \text{x-intercepts}$$

break-even points

Thus, a positive profit is realized as long as the number of units sold, x, lies within the interval $100 < x < 600$.

Studying the graph of the profit function of Figure 1-86 note also that the vertex point gives the maximum profit. Thus, the maximum profit of \$1,250,000 occurs when 350 units of this product are sold. We will, in later chapters, use calculus concepts to find maximum or minimum quantities.

Optimal Unit Price. If $x = 350$ units of this product are sold, then profit is maximized at \$1,250,000. Substituting $x = 350$ into the demand equation

$$p = -20x + 14{,}100$$

gives the unit price that yields the maximum profit for this product. Hence,

$$p = -20(350) + 14{,}100$$
$$= \$7100 \qquad \text{optimal unit price}$$

Supply, Demand, and Market Equilibrium

In Section 1-4, we learned that a demand function relates the unit price of some product to the corresponding demand; a supply function relates the unit price to the corresponding supply. Given the *supply function*

$$p = x^2 + 1 \qquad (x > 0)$$

and the *demand function*

$$p = (x - 5)^2 \qquad (0 < x \le 5)$$

where p denotes the unit price in dollars and x denotes the number of units of the product supplied or demanded in millions of units, find the equilibrium point.

The equilibrium point is the intersection of the graphs of the supply and demand functions. In other words, the equilibrium point is the point at which supply equals demand. Thus, to find the equilibrium point, we set the supply equation equal to the demand equation. Hence,

$$\text{supply} = \text{demand}$$
$$(x - 5)^2 = x^2 + 1$$
$$x^2 - 10x + 25 = x^2 + 1$$
$$-10x = -24$$
$$x = 2.4 \qquad \text{equilibrium quantity}$$

We find the equilibrium price by substituting $x = 2.4$ into either the supply or the demand equation.

Supply Function
$$p = (2.4 - 5)^2 = \$6.76 \leftarrow$$

Demand Function ——— equilibrium price
$$p = (2.4)^2 + 1 = \$6.76 \leftarrow$$

Equilibrium Point. Thus, when supply = demand = 2.4 million units, the equilibrium price is $6.76 per unit. The graphs of the supply and demand functions are given in Figure 1-87.

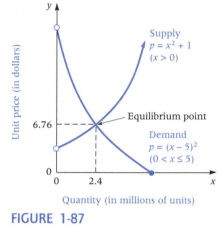

Supply
$p = x^2 + 1$
$(x > 0)$

Equilibrium point

Demand
$p = (x - 5)^2$
$(0 < x \le 5)$

6.76

2.4

Quantity (in millions of units)

Unit price (in dollars)

FIGURE 1-87

• **EXAMPLE 1-27** **Quality Control and Profits.** ——————

This problem is adapted from one that appeared on a past Uniform CPA Examination. MacKenzie Park sells its trivets for $0.25 per unit. The variable cost is $0.10 per trivet. Production capacity is limited to 15,000 trivets per day.

The company does not maintain an inspection system, but has an agreement to reimburse the wholesaler $0.50 for each defective unit the wholesaler finds. The wholesaler uses a method of inspection that detects all defective units. The number of defective units in each lot of 300 units is equal to the daily unit production rate divided by 200. Let x = daily production in units.

a) Determine the algebraic expression that represents the number of defective units per day.
b) Determine the function that expresses the total daily contribution to profit, including the reimbursement to the wholesaler for defective units.
c) What is the maximum daily profit? How many units are produced daily in order to yield the maximum daily profit?

Solutions

a) If x = daily production in units and a lot contains 300 units, then $x/300$ lots are produced in a day. Each of the $x/300$ lots contains $x/200$ defective units. Thus, the number of defective units per day is

$$\frac{x}{200} \cdot \frac{x}{300} = \frac{x^2}{60,000}$$

b) First, we have

$$\text{profit} = \text{sales revenue} - \text{cost} - \text{reimbursement}$$
$$P(x) = 0.25x - 0.10x - 0.50\left(\frac{x^2}{60,000}\right)$$
$$= 0.15x - \frac{x^2}{120,000}$$

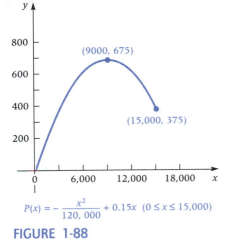

$$P(x) = -\frac{x^2}{120,000} + 0.15x \quad (0 \leq x \leq 15,000)$$

FIGURE 1-88

Thus, the profit function is defined by

$$P(x) = -\frac{x^2}{120,000} + 0.15x \quad (0 \leq x \leq 15,000)$$

Its graph appears in Figure 1-88. Since $0 \leq x \leq 15,000$, the parabola is drawn as a solid line over this interval.

c) As seen in Figure 1-88, the vertex, (9000, 675), is the maximum point on the parabola. Thus, when 9000 units are produced daily, the daily profit will be maximized at $675.

• **EXAMPLE 1-28**   **Time Series.** ───────────────

A company's annual profits, P (in millions of dollars), are related to the time, t (in years), since its incorporation by the function

$$P(t) = 0.4t^2 + 30 \quad (t > 0)$$

Graph the function P and find the company's annual profit for the third year.

Solution

The graph of P is drawn by beginning with the graph of $0.4t^2$ and shifting it vertically by 30 units, as is illustrated in Figure 1-89.

The company's annual profit for the third year is given by

$$P(3) = 0.4(3)^2 + 30$$
$$= \$33.6 \text{ million}$$

This corresponding point is illustrated in Figure 1-89.   •

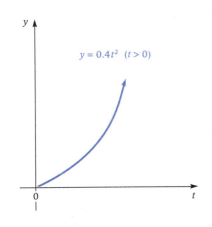

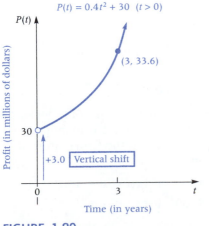

FIGURE 1-89

Light: Parabolic Reflectors

Parabolas possess the following properties when used as reflectors of light.

> **SUMMARY**
>
> **Properties of Parabolic Reflectors**
>
> **Property 1**   If light rays (from some light source such as the sun or some other object) parallel to the axis of symmetry are directed toward a parabola, then such light rays will focus at a single point called the **focus,** as illustrated in Figure 1-90. The vertical distance along the axis of symmetry from the vertex of the parabola to the focus is given by
>
> $$p = \frac{1}{4a}$$
>
> where a is the coefficient of the x^2-term in the equation of the parabola.
> *continues*

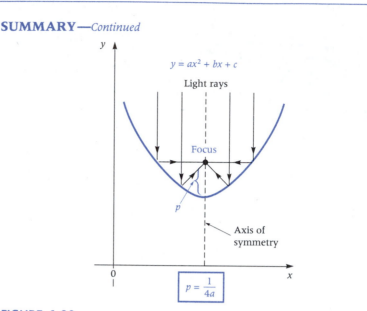

$$y = ax^2 + bx + c$$

Light rays

Focus

Axis of
symmetry

$$p = \frac{1}{4a}$$

FIGURE 1-90

Property 2 If the source of light is located at the focus of a parabola, then light rays will reflect parallel to the axis of symmetry. This is graphically illustrated by reversing the direction of the arrows in Figure 1-90.

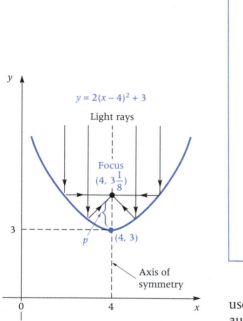

$$y = 2(x - 4)^2 + 3$$

Light rays

Focus
$(4, 3\frac{1}{8})$

p

$(4, 3)$

Axis of
symmetry

FIGURE 1-91

Because they possess the above properties, parabolic reflectors are used for TV dishes, solar collectors, satellite communications, flashlights, automobile headlights, and more.

As an example, if the light rays are directed toward the parabola

$$y = 2(x - 4)^2 + 3$$

as illustrated in Figure 1-91, then the distance, p, from the vertex to the focus is

$$p = \frac{1}{4a} = \frac{1}{4(2)} = \frac{1}{8}$$

Thus, the focus is given by the point $(4, 3\frac{1}{8})$, as illustrated in Figure 1-91.

Productivity: Chemical Process Yield

The productivity of a chemical process is measured in terms of its yield. After running a chemical process many times, a chemical company discovered that the yield, y, of the process is dependent on the temperature, x (in degrees Celsius), as given by the function

$$y = f(x) = \begin{cases} -(x - 130)^2 + 800 & \text{if } 110 < x \leq 130 \\ -(x - 150)^2 + 1300 & \text{if } 130 < x \leq 150 \end{cases}$$

Since this function is defined by more than one formula, then, as was discussed in Section 1-1, it is said to be **piecewise defined.** The parabola

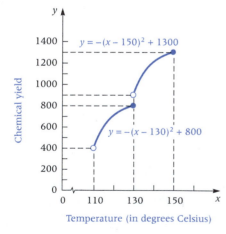

$$y = -(x - 150)^2 + 1300$$

Chemical yield

$$y = -(x - 130)^2 + 800$$

Temperature (in degrees Celsius)

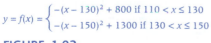

$$y = f(x) = \begin{cases} -(x - 130)^2 + 800 \text{ if } 110 < x \leq 130 \\ -(x - 150)^2 + 1300 \text{ if } 130 < x \leq 150 \end{cases}$$

FIGURE 1-92

$y = -(x - 130)^2 + 800$ over the interval $110 < x \le 130$ constitutes the first piece; the parabola $y = -(x - 150)^2 + 1300$ over the interval $130 < x \le 150$ constitutes the second piece. The graph of f is given in Figure 1-92.

Exercises 1-7

Revenue Functions

For each of the following demand dequations, p denotes the unit price in dollars, and x denotes the number of units demanded of some product.
a) Determine the equation of the revenue function, $R(x)$.
b) Graph the revenue function.
c) State the maximum sales revenue.
d) How many units must be sold in order to achieve the maximum sales revenue?
e) Substitute the result of part d into the demand equation to determine the unit price that maximizes sales revenue.

1. Demand function: $p = -2x + 100$
2. Demand function: $p = -3x + 180$
3. Demand function: $p = -4x + 320$
4. Demand function: $p = -5x + 1000$
5. Demand function: $p = -6x + 1800$
6. Demand function: $p = -3x + 240$

Revenue, Cost, and Profit Functions; Break-Even Analysis

For each of the following, p denotes the unit price in dollars, and x denotes the number of units produced and sold of some product.
a) Determine the equation of the revenue function, $R(x)$.
b) Graph both the revenue and cost functions on the same set of axes.
c) How many units of the product should be produced and sold in order to break even?
d) State the interval over which profit is positive.
e) Determine the equation of the profit function.
f) Graph the profit function.
g) Using the profit function, determine the break-even points. Verify that they agree with the answer to part c.
h) Using the profit function, state the interval over which profit is positive. Verify that this answer agrees with that of part d.
i) State the maximum profit.
j) How many units of the product should be produced and sold in order to maximize profit?
k) Find the unit price that yields the maximum profit.

7. Demand function: $p = -x + 1200$
    Cost function: $C(x) = 200x + 160,000$
8. Demand function: $p = -2x + 2400$
    Cost function: $C(x) = 400x + 180,000$
9. Demand function: $p = -2x + 2700$
    Cost function: $C(x) = 300x + 540,000$
10. Demand function: $p = -x + 2200$
    Cost function: $C(x) = 800x + 240,000$

Supply, Demand, and Market Equilibrium

For each of the following supply and demand functions, p denotes the unit price in dollars, and x denotes the number of units supplied or demanded of some product in millions of units.

a) Determine the equilibrium quantity.
b) Determine the equilibrium price.
c) Graph both the supply and demand functions on the same set of axes.

11. Supply function: $p = x^2 + 12$ $\quad(x > 0)$
  Demand function: $p = (x - 6)^2$ $\quad(0 < x \le 6)$

12. Supply function: $p = x^2 + 3$ $\quad(x > 0)$
  Demand function: $p = (x - 3)^2$ $\quad(0 < x \le 3)$

13. Supply function: $p = x^2 + 16$ $\quad(x > 0)$
  Demand function: $p = (x - 8)^2$ $\quad(0 < x \le 8)$

14. Supply function: $p = x^2 + 20$ $\quad(x > 0)$
  Demand function: $p = (x - 10)^2$ $\quad(0 < x \le 10)$

15. *Quality control and profits.* The Container Corporation manufactures wooden barrels. Each barrel costs $200 to produce and sells for $270. The barrels are manufactured in production lots. Each production lot contains 500 barrels. Quality control procedures have revealed that there are $x/20$ defective barrels per lot where $x =$ the number of barrels produced per month. Each defective barrel costs the company an additional $50 to repair.
  a) Find the equation that relates profit, P, with monthly production volume.
  b) Graph the equation of part a.
  c) Determine the maximum profit.
  d) Determine the monthly production volume, x, that maximizes profit.

Time Series

16. A company's annual profits, P (in millions of dollars), are related to the time, t (in years), since its incorporation by the function

$$P(t) = 0.6t^2 + 20 \qquad (t > 0)$$

  a) Graph the function P.
  b) Find the company's annual profit for the second year.
  c) Find the company's annual profit for the fourth year.
  d) Find the company's annual profit for the fifth year.

17. A company's annual profits, P (in millions of dollars), are related to the time, t (in years), since its incorporation by the function

$$P(t) = 0.8(t - 2)^2 + 40 \qquad (t > 0)$$

  a) Graph the function P.
  b) Find the company's annual profit for the second year.
  c) Find the company's annual profit for the fourth year.
  d) Find the company's annual profit for the fifth year.

18. *Earnings per share.* The annual earnings per share (abbreviated EPS and expressed in dollars) of a corporation is calculated by dividing the corporation's annual earnings by the number of shares of its stock outstanding. That is,

$$EPS = \frac{\text{annual earnings}}{\text{number of shares of stock outstanding}}$$

The EPS is helpful in evaluating the performance of a corporation.

Assume that the EPS, denoted by y, for a corporation is related to the time, t (in years), since its incorporation by the function

$$y = 0.9(t - 3)^2 + 35 \qquad (t > 0)$$

a) Graph the function defined by the above equation.
b) Find the EPS for the second year.
c) Find the EPS for the third year.
d) Find the EPS for the fifth year.
e) Find the EPS for the sixth year.

19. *Production possibility curve.* A textile company produces amounts x and y of two different jeans using the same production process. The amounts x and y are related by the equation

$$y = -0.10x^2 + 30 \qquad (0 \le x \le 17)$$

Since the amounts x and y give the production possibilities for the two different jeans, the graph of the above equation is called a **production possibility curve.**

a) Graph the production possibility curve defined by the above equation.
b) Determine the production possibility for $x = 5$.
c) Determine the production possibility for $x = 10$.
d) If the company wants to produce an amount x such that it is twice as much as amount y (i.e., $x = 2y$), what amounts x and y should be produced?

20. *Cost.* The Haskins Company produces ornamental bells. The equation

$$C(x) = x^2 - 100x + 2900 \qquad (x \ge 0)$$

relates total daily production cost, C, to daily production, x, of bells.

a) Graph the cost function C.
b) Find the total daily production cost for a daily production level of $x = 650$ bells.
c) How many bells should the company produce daily in order to minimize daily production cost?
d) State the minimum daily production cost.

21. *Projectile.* A ball is projected vertically into the air. The function defined by

$$s(t) = -16t^2 + 192t \qquad (0 \le t \le 12)$$

gives the height of the ball (in feet) above the ground t seconds after it is projected into the air.

a) Graph the function s
b) When does the ball reach maximum height? What maximum height does it reach?
c) When is the ball at zero height?

Parabolic Reflectors

Assume that for each of the following parabolas, rays of light parallel to the axis of symmetry are directed toward the parabola, as illustrated in Figure 1-93. Find the coordinates of the focus for each parabola.

22. $y = x^2$
23. $y = 0.5(x - 7)^2$
24. $y = (x - 2)^2 + 6$
25. $y = 2(x - 1)^2 + 3$
26. $y = 0.5(x - 3)^2 + 1$
27. $y = 0.1(x - 4)^2 + 5$

28. *Satellite dish.* Satellite dishes are used to transmit and receive radio signals. The cross-sectional center of a parabolic satellite dish is given by the equation

$$y = 0.5x^2$$

Give the x- and y-coordinates of the location of the transmitter and receiver.

29. *Solar collector.* A parabolic solar collector focuses sunlight into a container

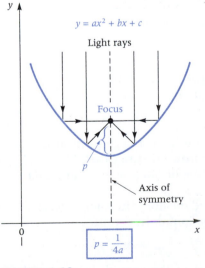

$y = ax^2 + bx + c$

Light rays

Focus

p

Axis of symmetry

$p = \dfrac{1}{4a}$

FIGURE 1-93

called a furnace. If the cross-sectional center of the solar collector is given by the equation

$$y = 0.25x^2$$

find the x- and y-coordinates of the location of the furnace.

30. *Flashlight.* The cross-sectional center of a parabolic reflector used in a flashlight is given by the equation

$$y = 0.125x^2$$

Determine the x- and y-coordinates of the location of the bulb.

31. *Productivity: Chemical process yield.* A chemical company has discovered that the yield, y, of a chemical process depends on its reaction time, t (in hours), as given by the function

$$y = f(t) = \begin{cases} (t - 5)^2 + 40 & \text{if } 1 < t \le 5 \\ (t - 10)^2 + 12 & \text{if } 5 < t \le 10 \end{cases}$$

a) Graph $f(t)$.
Compute the process yield for
b) $t = 3$ c) $t = 4$ d) $t = 6$ e) $t = 8$

32. *Delivery time.* The delivery time, y (in hours), for a manufacturer's product depends on the distance to be shipped, x (in thousands of miles), and the mode of transportation as given by the function

$$y = f(x) = \begin{cases} -(x - 2)^2 + 50 & \text{if } 0 < x \le 2 \text{ (by truck)} \\ -(x - 4)^2 + 60 & \text{if } 2 < x \le 4 \text{ (by rail)} \end{cases}$$

a) Graph $f(x)$.
According to the above function
b) For what shipping distances does the manufacturer ship by rail?
c) For what shipping distances does the manufacturer ship by truck?
Determine the delivery time for each of the following shipping distances
d) $x = 0.5$ e) $x = 1$ f) $x = 2.5$ g) $x = 3$

1-8 • SOME SPECIAL POLYNOMIAL AND RATIONAL FUNCTIONS

Polynomial Functions

In Sections 1-2, 1-3, and 1-4, we discussed linear functions. Recall that a linear function is defined by an equation of the form

$$f(x) = mx + b$$

Since the highest-powered term, mx, is of the first degree, linear functions are sometimes called **first-degree polynomial functions.** The graphs of first-degree polynomial functions are straight lines, as we learned in Section 1-4.

In Sections 1-6 and 1-7, we discussed quadratic functions. Recall that a quadratic function is defined by an equation of the form

$$f(x) = ax^2 + bx + c \qquad (a \ne 0)$$

Since the highest-powered term, ax^2, is of the second degree, quadratic functions are sometimes called **second-degree polynomial functions.**

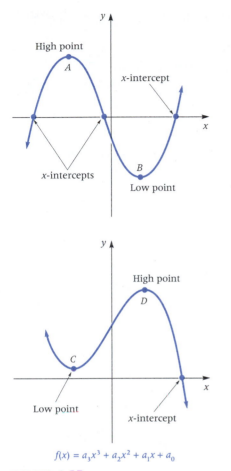

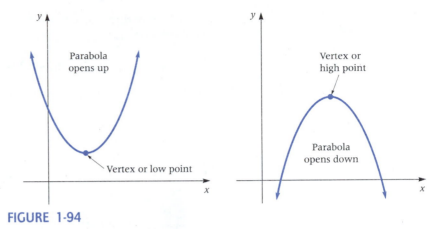

FIGURE 1-94

$$f(x) = a_3 x^3 + a_2 x^2 + a_1 x + a_0$$

FIGURE 1-95

The graphs of second-degree polynomial functions are parabolas (see Figure 1-94), as we learned in Sections 1-6 and 1-7. Note that a second-degree quadratic function (a parabola) has one point, the vertex, where its graph changes direction (see Figure 1-94). Also, a second-degree polynomial function has at most two x-intercepts.

An equation such as

$$f(x) = x^3 - 5x^2 + 3x + 9$$

defines a **third-degree polynomial function** since the highest-powered term, x^3, is of the third degree. The general form of the equation of a third-degree polynomial function is

$$f(x) = a_3 x^3 + a_2 x^2 + a_1 x + a_0$$

where a_3, a_2, a_1, and a_0 are constant real numbers and $a_3 \neq 0$. Figure 1-95 illustrates possible shapes of graphs of third-degree polynomial functions. The points labeled A, B, C, and D, called high/low points, in Figure 1-95 are places where the graph of $f(x)$ changes direction. A third-degree polynomial function has at most two high/low points and at most three x-intercepts.

In general, an equation of the form

$$f(x) = a_n x^n + a_{n-1} x^{n-1} + \ldots + a_2 x^2 + a_1 x + a_0$$

where n is a positive integer, and a_n, a_{n-1}, . . ., a_2, a_1, and a_0 are constant real numbers, and $a_n \neq 0$, defines the **nth-degree polynomial function.** *An nth-degree polynomial function has at most* n $-$ 1 *high/low points and at most* n x-*intercepts.*

• **EXAMPLE 1-29**

The graph of a polynomial function appears in Figure 1-96. Its degree must be at least what number?

Solution

The graph has 4 high/low points. Since the graph of a polynomial function of degree n has at most $n - 1$ such points, then the degree of the polynomial function in Figure 1-94 is at least 5. Also, the graph has 5 x-intercepts, which implies that the degree of the polynomial function is at least 5.

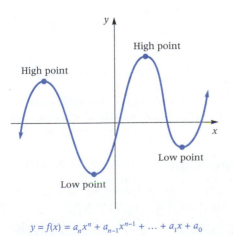

$$y = f(x) = a_n x^n + a_{n-1} x^{n-1} + \ldots + a_1 x + a_0$$

FIGURE 1-96

We now turn our attention to the graphs of some special case polynomial functions.

Special Case Polynomial Functions

We first consider the graphs of polynomial functions defined by equations of the form

$$f(x) = ax^n$$

where a is a constant coefficient and n is a positive integer. We consider the following two cases and their graphs in the following summary box.

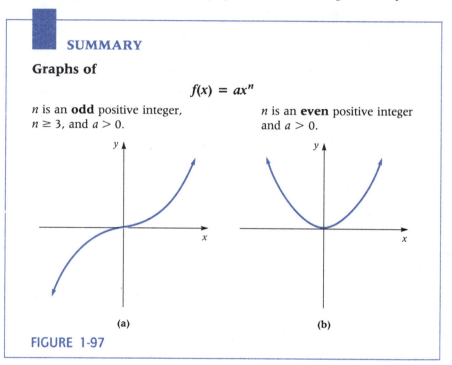

SUMMARY

Graphs of

$$f(x) = ax^n$$

n is an **odd** positive integer, $n \geq 3$, and $a > 0$.

n is an **even** positive integer and $a > 0$.

(a)   (b)

FIGURE 1-97

FIGURE 1-98

Thus, the graphs of $y = 2x^3$, $y = 3x^7$, and $y = 10x^9$ resemble those of Figure 1-97(a), whereas the graphs of $y = 3x^2$, $y = 7x^4$, and $y = 8x^{10}$ resemble those of Figure 1-97(b).

Also, the graphs of $y = -3x^5$, $y = -2x^7$, and $y = -8x^9$ are reflections in the x-axis of those resembling Figure 1-97(a). These resemble the graph of Figure 1-98.

The graphs of $y = -3x^4$, $y = -5x^8$, and $y = -6x^{10}$ are reflections in the x-axis of those resembling Figure 1-97(b). These resemble the graph of Figure 1-99.

Graphs of Some Rational Functions

If a function $f(x)$ is defined as the quotient of two polynomials, it is called a **rational function.** Thus, a rational function $f(x)$ is defined by

$$f(x) = \frac{g(x)}{h(x)}$$

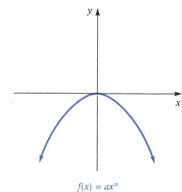

$f(x) = ax^n$
($a < 0$, n is an even positive integer)

FIGURE 1-99

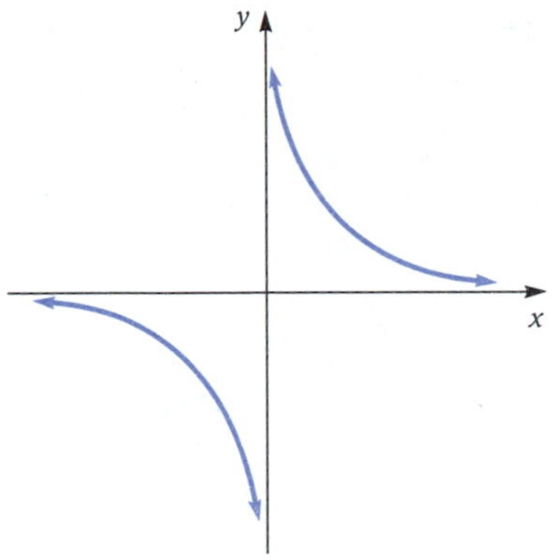

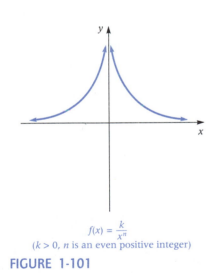

$$f(x) = \frac{k}{x^n}$$
$(k > 0,\ n \text{ is an odd positive integer})$

FIGURE 1-100

where $g(x)$ and $h(x)$ are polynomials and $h(x) \neq 0$. In this section, we will discuss the graphs of a special category of rational functions defined by equations of the form

$$y = f(x) = \frac{k}{x^n}$$

where k is a constant real number, n is a positive integer, and $x \neq 0$. We begin with rational functions defined by equations of the form

$$y = f(x) = \frac{k}{x^n}$$

where $k > 0$ and n is an *odd positive integer*. The graphs of such functions are typified by the graph in Figure 1-100. Observing Figure 1-100, note that as x takes on values closer and closer to 0, the graph of $f(x)$ gets closer and closer to the vertical line $x = 0$ (i.e., the y-axis). Such a vertical line is called a **vertical asymptote.** *Vertical asymptotes occur at values of* x *for which the denominator of a rational function $= 0$ and the numerator $\neq 0$.* Note that the graph of $f(x)$ approaches different ends of the vertical asymptote from different sides. Further study of the graph in Figure 1-100 reveals that as x takes on values of larger and larger magnitude, the graph of $f(x)$ gets closer and closer to the horizontal line $y = 0$ (i.e., the x-axis). Such a horizontal line is called a **horizontal asymptote.**

For example, the graphs of $y = 2/x^5$, $y = 3/x^7$, and $y = 6/x^3$ resemble that in Figure 1-100.

Now we consider rational functions defined by equations of the form

$$y = f(x) = \frac{k}{x^n}$$

$$f(x) = \frac{k}{x^n}$$
$(k > 0,\ n \text{ is an even positive integer})$

FIGURE 1-101

where $k > 0$ and n is an *even positive integer*. The graphs of such functions are typified by the graph in Figure 1-101. Studying this graph, note that the y-axis is a vertical asymptote and that the graph of $f(x)$ approaches the same end of this vertical asymptote from different sides. Also, the x-axis is a horizontal asymptote. For example, the graphs of $y = 5/x^4$, $y = 8/x^6$, and $y = 3x^8$ resemble that in Figure 1-101.

We summarize as follows.

SUMMARY

Graphs of

$$f(x) = \frac{k}{x^n} \qquad (k > 0)$$

n is an **odd** positive integer. $\qquad$ n is an **even** positive integer.

continues

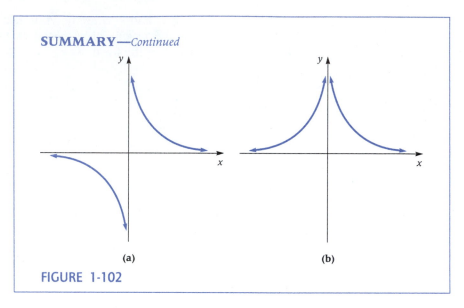

SUMMARY—*Continued*

(a)   (b)

FIGURE 1-102

Of course, if $k < 0$, then the resulting graphs are reflections about the x-axis of those in Figure 1-102.

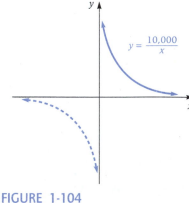

Applications

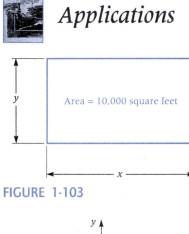

Area = 10,000 square feet

FIGURE 1-103

$y = \dfrac{10{,}000}{x}$

FIGURE 1-104

• **EXAMPLE 1-30**   **Area.**

A rectangular pasture must be enclosed so that the enclosed area equals 10,000 square feet, as illustrated in Figure 1-103. Draw a graph showing the possible x and y dimensions.

Solution

Since the enclosed area must be 10,000 square feet, then

$$xy = 10{,}000$$

Solving for y gives

$$y = \frac{10{,}000}{x}$$

Note that this equation is of the form $f(x) = k/x^n$, where n is an odd positive integer and $k > 0$. Thus, its graph resembles that of Figure 1-102(a). The graph of y versus x is drawn in Figure 1-104. Since x and y must be positive, we have drawn the portion of the graph in the first quadrant as a solid curve.

• **EXAMPLE 1-31**   **Production Possibility Curve.** _____

A firm produces x units of Product A and y units of Product B. The equation

$$y = \frac{2{,}000{,}000}{x^2} \qquad (00 \le x \le 500)$$

relates x and y and thus gives the production possibilities between these two products. The graph of y versus x is therefore called a **production possibility curve.**

a)   Graph the production possibility curve.
b)   State the production possibility for $x = 200$.

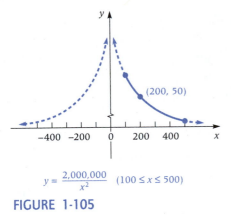

$$y = \frac{2,000,000}{x^2} \quad (100 \le x \le 500)$$

FIGURE 1-105

Solutions

a) The equation

$$y = \frac{2,000,000}{x^2}$$

is of the form $y = k/x^n$, where n is even and $k > 0$. Its graph is drawn in Figure 1-105.

b) When $x = 200$,

$$y = \frac{2,000,000}{(200)^2} = 50$$

Thus, when $x = 200$ units of Product A are produced, $y = 50$ units of Product B are produced. This is illustrated in Figure 1-105.

                                                                              •

Average Cost Per Unit. If $C(x)$ denotes the total cost of producing x units of some product, then the *average cost per unit* is given by

$$\overline{C}(x) = \frac{\text{total production cost}}{\text{number of units produced}}$$

01.106/3

or, in other words,

$$\overline{C}(x) = \frac{C(x)}{x} \quad (x > 0)$$

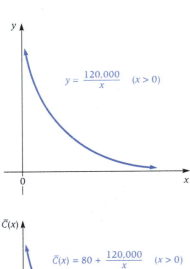

$$y = \frac{120,000}{x} \quad (x > 0)$$

The function $\overline{C}$ is called an **average cost function.**

As an example, if

$$C(x) = 80x + 120,000$$

then the *average cost per unit* is given by

$$\overline{C}(x) = \frac{80x + 120,000}{x} \quad (x > 0)$$

Dividing each term of the numerator by x, we obtain the equivalent expression for $\overline{C}(x)$ given below.

$$\overline{C}(x) = 80 + \frac{120,000}{x} \quad (x > 0)$$

We graph the function $\overline{C}$ by noting that the term $120,000/x$ is of the form $f(x) = k/x^n$, where n is an odd positive integer and $k > 0$. Thus, we draw the graph of $\overline{C}$ by beginning with the graph of $y = 120,000/x$ and shifting it vertically by 80 units, as illustrated in Figure 1-106. Since $x > 0$, only that corresponding portion of the graph is drawn as a solid curve.

Studying the graph of Figure 1-106, note that the average cost per unit approaches the variable cost per unit, 80 (the horizontal asymptote), as the number of units, x, gets larger and larger. This is because the fixed cost is averaged out over the x units and becomes rather insignificant when x is

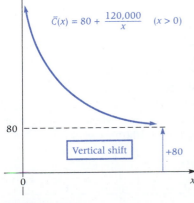

$$\overline{C}(x) = 80 + \frac{120,000}{x} \quad (x > 0)$$

Vertical shift   +80

FIGURE 1-106

very large. We illustrate this numerically by computing the average cost per unit for each of the following production levels. Hence,

$$\overline{C}(10,000) = 80 + \frac{120,000}{10,000}$$

$$= 80 + 12 = \$92 \text{ per unit}$$

$$\overline{C}(100,000) = 80 + \frac{120,000}{100,000}$$

$$= 80 + 1.2 = \$81.20 \text{ per unit}$$

Exercises 1-8

State the degree of each polynomial function.

1. $y = -6x + 7$

2. $f(x) = 6x^4 - 8x + 9$

3. $f(x) = 9x^8 + 4x^6 - 8x^3 + 6$

4. $y = -x^2 + 3x + 4$

5. $y = 4x^3 - 8x^2 + 7x + 3$

6. $f(x) = x^5 - 8x^4 + x^3$

7. The graph of a polynomial function appears in Figure 1-107. Its degree must be at least what number?

8. The graph of a polynomial function appears in Figure 1-108. Its degree must be at least what number?

9. Show why graphs of equations of the form $f(x) = ax^n$, where $n \geq 3$ is an odd positive integer and $a > 0$, resemble that of Figure 1-97(a). Use $f(x) = x^3$ as an example and fill in the following table:

x	-4	-3	-2	-1	0	1	2	3	4
$f(x)$									

10. Show why graphs of equations of the form $f(x) = ax^n$, where n is an even positive integer and $a > 0$, resemble that of Figure 1-97(b). Use $f(x) = x^4$ as an example and fill in the following table:

x	-4	-3	-2	-1	0	1	2	3	4
$f(x)$									

Graph each of the following.

11. $f(x) = x^2$

12. $f(x) = 5x^2$

13. $f(x) = x^4$

14. $y = x^6$

15. $y = -4x^2$

16. $y = -x^6$

17. $y = x^3$

18. $f(x) = -2x^3$

19. $f(x) = x^5$

20. $f(x) = 4x^7$

21. $f(x) = -2x^5$

22. $y = -4x^7$

23. Show why graphs of equations of the form $f(x) = k/x^n$, where n is an odd positive integer and $k > 0$, resemble that of Figure 1-102(a). Use $f(x) = 1/x^3$ as an example and fill in the following table:

x	-4	-3	-2	-1	0	1	2	3	4
$f(x)$									

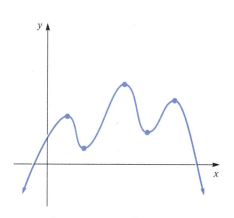

$y = f(x) = a_n x^n + a_{n-1} x^{n-1} + \ldots + a_1 x + a_0$

FIGURE 1-107

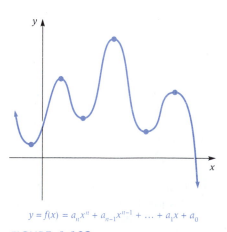

$y = f(x) = a_n x^n + a_{n-1} x^{n-1} + \ldots + a_1 x + a_0$

FIGURE 1-108

24. Show why graphs of equations of the form $f(x) = k/x^n$, where n is an even positive integer and $k > 0$, resemble that of Figure 1-102(b). Use $f(x) = 1/x^4$ as an example and fill in the following table:

x	-4	-3	-2	-1	0	1	2	3	4
$f(x)$									

Graph each of the following:

25. $y = 3/x^2$

26. $f(x) = 4/x^3$

27. $f(x) = 5/x^7$

28. $y = 6/x^4$

29. $f(x) = 2/x^5$

30. $y = 7/x^2$

31. $y = 5/x^3$

32. $f(x) = 8/x^7$

33. $y = 6/x^8$

34. $y = 10/x^{12}$

35. $f(x) = 4/x^5$

36. $f(x) = 3/x$

37. $y = -6/x^8$

38. $y = -3/x^4$

39. $y = -5/x^3$

40. $y = -3/x$

41. $y = -7/x^6$

42. $y = -4/x^5$

Use horizontal and vertical shifts to graph the following.

43. $y = 2(x - 5)^4$

44. $y = 2(x - 4)^5$

45. $y = 5(x + 2)^3$

46. $y = 3(x - 1)^6$

47. $y = (x - 2)^4 + 5$

48. $y = (x - 3)^6 + 7$

49. $y = (x + 5)^3 - 2$

50. $y = (x + 7)^5 - 1$

51. $y = 3/(x - 5)$

52. $y = 4/(x - 2)^2$

53. $y = 2/(x + 5)^6$

54. $y = 1/(x + 7)^3$

55. $y = \dfrac{7}{(x - 2)^4} + 3$

56. $y = \dfrac{3}{(x - 5)^2} - 4$

57. $y = \dfrac{2}{(x - 3)^5} - 1$

58. $y = \dfrac{1}{(x + 1)^5} + 2$

Applications

59. *Area.* A rectangular pasture of dimensions x feet by y feet must be enclosed so that the enclosed area equals 30,000 square feet. Draw a graph of y versus x.

60. *Production possibility curve.* A company produces x units of Product A and y units of Product B. The equation

$$y = \frac{4,000,000}{x^2} \qquad (100 \le x \le 400)$$

relates x and y and thus gives the production possibilities for these two products.
a) Graph the production possibility curve.
b) State the production possibility for $x = 100$.
c) State the production possibility for $x = 200$.
d) State the production possibility for $x = 400$.

61. *Production possibility curve.* A company produces x units of Product A and y units of Product B. The equation

$$y = \frac{200,000}{x} \qquad (1000 \le x \le 5000)$$

relates x and y and thus gives the production possibilities for these two products.
a) Graph the production possibility curve.
b) State the production possibility for $x = 1000$.

c) State the production possibility for $x = 2000$.
d) State the production possibility for $x = 4000$.
e) State the production possibility for $x = 5000$.

62. *Demand curve.* The equation

$$p = \frac{10,000}{x - 3} \qquad (3 < x \leq 4003)$$

gives the relationship between the unit price, p, and the number of units demanded, x, for some product.
a) Graph the demand curve.
b) Find the unit price when the demand is 1003 units.
c) Find the unit price when the demand is 2003 units.
d) Find the unit price when the demand is 4003 units.

63. *Demand curve.* The equation

$$p = \frac{20,000}{x - 10} \qquad (10 < x \leq 5010)$$

gives the relationship between the unit price, p, and the number of units demanded, x, for some product.
a) Graph the demand curve.
b) Find the unit price when the demand is 1010 units.
c) Find the unit price when the demand is 2010 units.
d) Find the unit price when the demand is 4010 units.
e) Find the unit price when the demand is 5010 units.

Average Cost Functions

For each of the following, $C(x)$ denotes the total cost (in dollars) of producing x units of some product.
a) Determine the equation of the average cost function.
b) Graph the result of part a.
c) Evaluate $\overline{C}(1000)$, $\overline{C}(10,000)$, and $\overline{C}(100,000)$, and interpret the results.
d) As the production level increases, the average cost per unit is approaching what value?

64. $\overline{C}(x) = 40x + 80,000$

65. $\overline{C}(x) = 50x + 40,000$

66. $\overline{C}(x) = 100x + 90,000$

67. $\overline{C}(x) = 20x + 60,000$

68. *Quality/productivity: Loss functions.* The graphs of Figures 1-109 and 1-110 give the loss in dollars to a producer of some product. The notations LSL and USL denote lower specification limit and upper specification limit, respectively. As an example, if a product, say, a disk, must be made to diameter specification limits of

3.50 inches ± 0.10 inches

then the LSL = 3.50 − 0.10 = 3.40 inches, and the USL = 3.50 + 0.10 = 3.60 inches. Thus, such a disk is considered to be within specification if

3.40 inches < disk diameter < 3.60 inches

a) According to the loss function of Figure 1-109, does the company incur a loss if its product remains within the specification limits?
b) According to the loss function of Figure 1-109, if the product deviates from the average, but remains within the specification limits, does the company incur a loss?
Note: Experts in the field of quality/productivity refer to this type of loss function as "the old thinking."

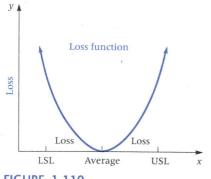

FIGURE 1-109

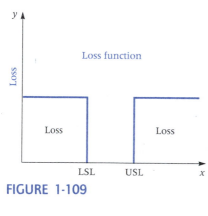

FIGURE 1-110

c) According to the loss function of Figure 1-110, does the company incur a loss as soon as its product deviates from the average?

d) According to the loss function of Figure 1-110, if the product deviates from the average, but remains within the specification limits, does the company incur a loss?

Note: Experts in the field of quality/productivity refer to this type of loss function as "the new thinking."

EXTRA DIVIDENDS

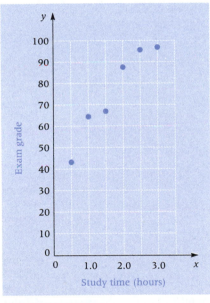

FIGURE 1-111

• *Model Fitting: Goodness of Fit (Linear Models)*

Table 1-12 gives a set of data that relates grades obtained on a mathematics exam by a very small class to the number of hours studied for the exam. Specifically, for each student, x denotes the number of hours that the student studied for the mathematics exam and y denotes the exam grade for that student.

Figure 1-111 gives a plot of the data points (x, y). Figure 1-112 on page 78 gives a plot of the data and the graph of the straight line

$$y = 20x + 40$$

TABLE 1-12

	Study time						
x	(in hours)	0.5	1.0	1.5	2.0	2.5	3.0
y	Exam grade	43	64	68	88	97	99

that appears to capture the relationship between x and y. Observe, in Figure 1-112, that the fitted values are determined by substituting the x-values into the equation of the fitted linear model. Hence, the fitted values are simply the y-coordinates of points on the fitted line.

We will not be concerned with how the equation (or, in other words, the linear model) $y = 20x + 40$ was obtained. Such discussion is the topic of Section 8-4. In this section, we address the issue of assessing the goodness of fit of a straight line fit to a set of data points.

• *Goodness of Fit*

To assess the goodness of fit of a model fit to a set of data, we determine, for each data point, the vertical distance between the given data point and the fitted line, as illustrated in Figure 1-113. Such vertical distances are called **residuals** and indicate the extent to which the fitted model does not fit the data points. An overall measure of the extent to which the fitted model (in this case, the straight line) does not fit the data is given by the sum of the squares of the residuals. This result is called the sum of squares error and is denoted by S, as is shown on the next page.

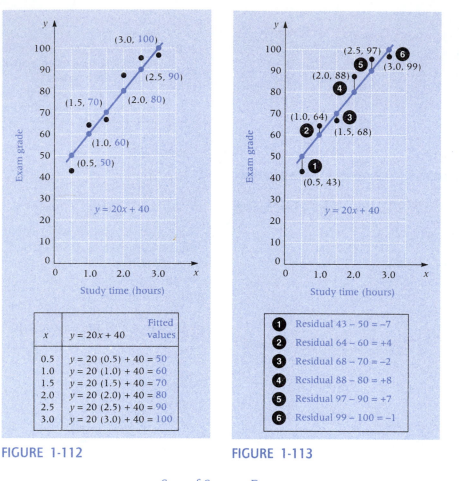

FIGURE 1-112

FIGURE 1-113

x	y = 20x + 40	Fitted values
0.5	y = 20 (0.5) + 40 =	50
1.0	y = 20 (1.0) + 40 =	60
1.5	y = 20 (1.5) + 40 =	70
2.0	y = 20 (2.0) + 40 =	80
2.5	y = 20 (2.5) + 40 =	90
3.0	y = 20 (3.0) + 40 =	100

1. Residual 43 − 50 = −7
2. Residual 64 − 60 = +4
3. Residual 68 − 70 = −2
4. Residual 88 − 80 = +8
5. Residual 97 − 90 = +7
6. Residual 99 − 100 = −1

Sum of Squares Error

$$S = (43 - 50)^2 + (64 - 60)^2 + (68 - 70)^2 + (88 - 80)^2 + (97 - 90)^2 \\ + (99 - 100)^2$$

$$= (-7)^2 + (4)^2 + (-2)^2 + (8)^2 + (7)^2 + (-1)^2$$

$$= 183 \quad \text{Sum of squares error}$$

If another straight line, say

$$y = 10x + 60$$

is fitted to the set of data points, it can be determined whether or not this line is a better fit to the data by computing the sum of squares error for this line and comparing the result with that of the previous line, $y = 20x + 40$. The better-fitting line is the one that has a smaller sum of squares error. The residuals for the new line, $y = 10x + 60$, are illustrated in Figure 1-114, and the sum of squares error is computed below.

Sum of Squares Error

$$S = (43 - 65)^2 + (64 - 70)^2 + (68 - 75)^2 + (88 - 80)^2 + (97 - 85)^2 \\ + (99 - 90)^2$$

$$= (-22)^2 + (-6)^2 + (-7)^2 + (8)^2 + (12)^2 + (9)^2$$

$$= 858 \quad \text{Sum of squares error}$$

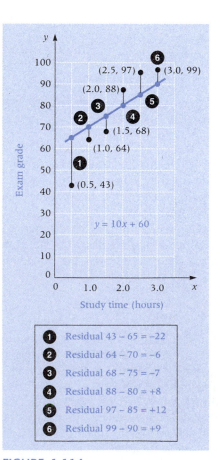

1. Residual 43 − 65 = −22
2. Residual 64 − 70 = −6
3. Residual 68 − 75 = −7
4. Residual 88 − 80 = +8
5. Residual 97 − 85 = +12
6. Residual 99 − 90 = +9

FIGURE 1-114

Since the sum of squares error for the first line is less than that for the second line, the first line, $y = 20x + 40$, better-fits this set of data than does the second line, $y = 10x + 60$.

We summarize as follows.

To Determine Goodness of Fit

The **goodness of fit** of a model fitted to a given set of data points is determined as follows:

1. Compute the **fitted values** by substituting the x-values of the data points into the equation of the fitted model.
2. Compute the **residual** for each data point in accordance with the formula.

$$\text{residual} = \text{data value} - \text{fitted value}$$

3. Compute the **sum of squares error, S,** as given below.

$$S = \text{sum of the squares of the residuals}$$

Note: The sum of squares error is an overall measure of the extent to which the fitted model does not fit the data.

Note: If more than one model is fit to the same set of data points, then the model resulting in the **smallest** sum of squares error is the better-fitting model for the set of data point.

If different types of models are fit to a given set of data points, the sum of squares error can be used to determine which type of model better fits the data according to this criterion. The model resulting in the smaller sum of squares error is the better-fitting model.

Lastly, we mention that in Section 8-4, we will learn how to find the equation of a straight line that best fits a set of data points. This entails the use of calculus, which we will study in subsequent chapters of this text.

Exercises

For each of the following sets of data, the equations of two fitted linear models are given.

a) Determine the sum of squares error for each fitted linear model.

b) Write the equation of the better-fitting linear model.

1. | x | 2 | 4 | 6 | 8 | 9 |
   |-----|---|---|----|----|----|
   | y | 7 | 9 | 13 | 16 | 25 |

   $y = 2x + 1$
   $y = 3x - 2$

2. | x | 1 | 3 | 4 | 7 | 9 |
   |-----|---|----|----|----|----|
   | y | 9 | 13 | 16 | 24 | 35 |

   $y = 3x + 5$
   $y = 4x + 1$

3. | x | 2 | 3 | 7 | 8 | 9 |
   |-----|---|---|----|----|----|
   | y | 6 | 9 | 19 | 28 | 35 |

   $y = 4x - 3$
   $y = 3x + 2$

4. | x | 2 | 4 | 5 | 8 | 9 |
   |-----|---|----|----|----|----|
   | y | 9 | 19 | 27 | 38 | 47 |

   $y = 5x - 1$
   $y = 4x + 5$

Applications

Time Series

A set of data that relates some quantity to time is called a **time series.** The data in Exercises 5, 6, and 7 constitute time series. For these exercises, the variable, x, denotes successive time periods, such as weeks, months, quarters, or years, and the variable, y, denotes the quantity related to time.

5. *Stock prices: S&P 500.* The following data give quarterly values of Standard & Poors 500 Composite Index (denoted S&P 500), which measures stock market movement. The S&P 500 values given here begin with the second quarter of 1985 and end with the third quarter of 1988. The successive quarters are denoted by $x = 1, x = 2, \ldots, x = 14$.

x	1	2	3	4	5	6	7
y S&P 500	153.18	166.10	167.24	180.66	191.85	182.08	211.28
x	8	9	10	11	12	13	14
y S&P 500	238.90	250.84	231.32	242.17	291.70	304.00	337.00

The following two linear models are fit to this set of data:

$$y = 13x + 130 \qquad y = 20x + 70$$

a) Determine the sum of squares error for each fitted linear model.
b) Write the equation of the better-fitting linear model.

6. *Stock prices: S&P 500.* The following data give quarterly values of Standard & Poors 500 Composite Index (denoted S&P 500), which measures stock market movement. The S&P 500 values given here begin with the fourth quarter of 1972 and end with the third quarter of 1974. The successive quarters are denoted by $x = 1, x = 2, \ldots, x = 8$.

x	1	2	3	4	5	6	7	8
y S&P 500	118.05	111.52	104.26	108.43	97.55	93.98	86.00	63.54

The following two linear models are fit to this set of data:

$$y = -7x + 130 \qquad y = -10x + 140$$

a) Determine the sum of squares error for each fitted linear model.
b) Write the equation of the better-fitting linear model.

7. *Systolic Blood Pressure (SBP).* A person's systolic blood pressure (SBP) is recorded weekly with the following results:

x Week	1	2	3	4	5	6	7	8	9
y SBP	125	128	130	129	135	138	140	146	145

The following two linear models are fit to this set of data:

$$y = 3x + 120 \qquad y = 4x + 115$$

a) Determine the sum of squares error for each fitted linear model.
b) Write the equation of the better-fitting linear model.

8. *Education.* The data below relate undergraduate grade point average (GPA) to starting salary (in thousands of dollars) for a sample of recent graduates at a small liberal arts college.

x GPA	2.5	3.0	2.4	3.5	2.1	2.6
y Starting salary	15.5	19.7	15.2	22.8	14.6	15.8

The following two linear models are fit to this set of data:

$$y = 6x + 1 \qquad y = 7x - 1$$

a) Determine the sum of squares error for each fitted linear model.
b) Write the equation of the better-fitting linear model.

9. *Medical science.* The data below relate serum cholesterol level (in milligrams/100 milliters) with age for a sample of adult males.

x Age	20	35	27	40	49	55
y Cholesterol	210	279	230	190	252	287

The following two linear models are fit to the set of data:

$$y = 2x + 170 \qquad y = 3x + 100$$

a) Determine the sum of squares error for each fitted linear model.
b) Write the equation of the better-fitting linear model.

EXTRA DIVIDENDS

• *Model Fitting: Goodness of Fit (Quadratic Models)*

In the previous Extra Dividends entitled "Model Fitting: Goodness of fit," we discussed how to determine the goodness of fit of linear models fit to given sets of data. This Extra Dividends applies the same concepts to nonlinear models. Specifically, if we are given a nonlinear model fit to a set of data, its goodness of fit is determined as it was in the previously mentioned section—by computing the sum of squares error. Although these concepts were summarized in the previous Extra Dividends, we repeat the summary here for completeness. We also note again that we are not concerned with how the fitted model is obtained. Such discussion is the topic of Section 8-4.

To Determine Goodness of Fit

The **goodness of fit** of a model fitted to a given set of data points is determined as follows:

1. Compute the **fitted values** by substituting the x-values of the data points into the equation of the fitted model. These are simply the y-coordinates of points on the graph of the fitted model.

2. Compute the **residual** for each data point in accordance with the formula

$$\text{residual} = \text{data value} - \text{fitted value}$$

3. Compute the **sum of squares error, S,** as given below.

$$S = \text{sum of the squares of the residuals}$$

Note: The sum of squares error is an overall measure of the extent to which the fitted model does not fit the data.
Note: If more than one model is fit to the same set of data points, then the model resulting in the **smallest** sum of squares error is the better-fitting model for the set of data points.

We now consider Table 1-13, a set of data relating annual sales revenues (in thousands of dollars) with time (in years). We learned in the previous Extra Dividends that a set of data that relates some quantity to time is called a **time series.** For time series data, the successive time periods are denoted by $x = 1$, $x = 2$, . . . , etc. Although we use the variable x to denote the successive time periods, the letter t is also often used.

TABLE 1-13

Years	1985	1986	1987	1988	1989	1990	1991
x	1	2	3	4	5	6	7
y revenues	90	120	190	220	340	420	580

The data of Table 1-13 are plotted in Figure 1-115. Observe that the data appear to exhibit a nonlinear trend. This is made more explicit in Figure 1-116, where it is observed that a nonlinear model might be a better fit to the data than a linear model.

Figure 1-117 gives a plot of the data and the fitted quadratic model (i.e., a parabola)

$$y = 10x^2 + 70$$

that appears to capture the relationship between x and y. Observe, in Figure 1-117, that the fitted values are determined by substituting the x-values into the equation of the fitted model. As mentioned earlier, we will not be concerned with how the quadratic model, $y = 10x^2 + 70$, was obtained as this will be discussed in Section 8-4. Here we address the issue of assessing the goodness of fit of a nonlinear model fit to a set of data points.

• *Goodness of Fit*

As discussed in the previous Extra Dividends, to assess the goodness of fit of a model fit to a set of data points, we determine, for each data point, the vertical distance between the given data point and the graph of the fitted model, as illustrated in Figure 1-118. Recall that these vertical distances are called **residuals** and indicate the extent to which the fitted model does not fit the data points. Also, as discussed earlier, an overall measure of the extent to which the fitted model (in this case, the parabola $y = 10x^2 + 70$) does not fit the data is given by the sum of squares error and is denoted by S, as is shown below

Sum of Squares Error

$$S = (90 - 80)^2 + (120 - 110)^2 + (190 - 160)^2 + (220 - 230)^2$$
$$+ (340 - 320)^2 + (420 - 430)^2 + (580 - 560)^2$$
$$= (10)^2 + (10)^2 + (30)^2 + (-10)^2 + (20)^2 + (-10)^2 + (20)^2$$
$$= 2100 \quad \text{Sum of squares error}$$

Figure 1-119 illustrates the goodness of fit of the linear model.

$$y = 80x - 40$$

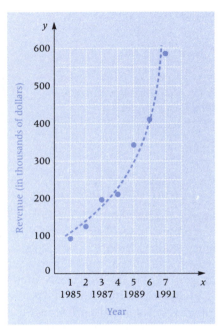

FIGURE 1-115

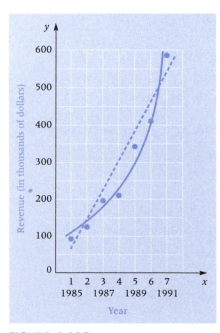

FIGURE 1-116

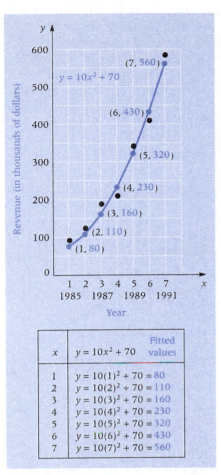

FIGURE 1-117

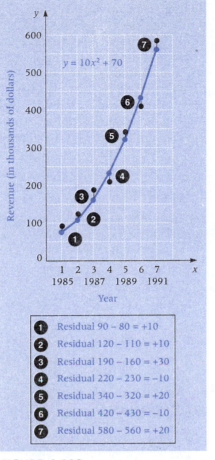

FIGURE 1-118

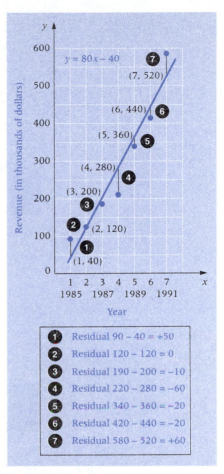

FIGURE 1-119

to the set of data points in Table 1-13. The sum of squares error is computed below.

Sum of Squares Error

$$S = (90 - 40)^2 + (120 - 120)^2 + (190 - 200)^2 + (220 - 280)^2$$
$$+ (340 - 360)^2 + (420 - 440)^2 + (580 - 520)^2$$
$$= (50)^2 + (0)^2 + (-10)^2 + (-60)^2 + (-20)^2 + (-20)^2 + (60)^2$$
$$= 10{,}600 \quad \text{Sum of squares error}$$

Comparing the sum of squares error of the linear model, 10,600, with that of the quadratic model, 2100, it is apparent that the quadratic model, having a smaller sum of squares error, is the better-fitting model for this set of data.

• Best-Fitting Models

We have stated that in Section 8-4 of this text, we will learn how to fit models to data. Actually, we will learn more than that. We will learn how to determine the best-fitting linear model for a set of data, how to determine the best-fitting quadratic model for a set of data, etc. We caution that the linear model fit to the data of Table 1-13 is not necessarily the best-fitting linear model for the data. The quadratic model $y = 10x^2 + 70$ is not necessarily the best-fitting quadratic model for this set of data. Thus, when our comparison of the goodness of fit of both models indicated the quadratic model to be the better-fitting model, that does not necessarily imply that the best-fitting quadratic model fits this set of data better than the best-fitting linear model does. This determination can be made by comparing the sum of squares error for both best-fitting models.

Exercises

For each of the following sets of data, the equations of two fitted models are given.
a) Determine the sum of squares error for each fitted model.
b) Select the better-fitting model.

1.

x	1	2	3	4	5
y	40	80	200	300	530

$y = 20x^2 + 10$
$y = 100x - 90$

2.

x	2	3	5	7	10
y	35	60	150	240	530

$y = 5x^2 + 20$
$y = 45x - 40$

Application

3. *Time series: GNP.* Figure 1-120 gives a MINITAB plot of quarterly U.S. gross national product (GNP) from 1970 through 1980. Also given are the equa-

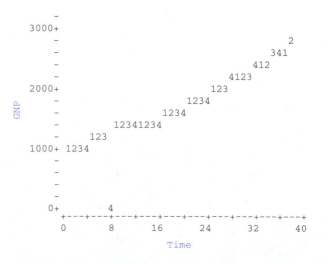

Each digit 1, 2, 3, and 4 indicates which quarter of a particular year's GNP is plotted at that location.

* This graph was drawn using the MINITAB statisitical software package. The annotations have been added.

FIGURE 1-120

tions of two fitted models and their associated sum of squares errors. Select the better-fitting model.

Fitted Model	*Sum of Squares Error*
$y = 48.4x + 768$	1,568,435
$y = 1.2x^2 + 1111$	1,596,801

CHAPTER 1 HIGHLIGHTS

• *Concepts*

Your ability to answer the following questions is one indicator of the depth of your mastery of this chapter's important concepts. Note that the questions are grouped under various topic headings. For any question that you cannot answer, refer to the section of the chapter indicated by the topic heading. Pay particular attention to the summary boxes within a section.

1-1 FUNCTIONS

1. Explain the following terms: function, domain, range, dependent variable, independent variable, ordered pair, x-coordinate, y-coordinate, x-axis, y-axis, origin, quadrant.
2. A function is usually defined by a (an) _____ that expresses a (an) _____ between two quantities.
3. How can we determine whether or not a given graph represents a function?
4. Draw a graph of the absolute value function.
5. If a function is defined by more than one formula, the function is said to be _____ defined.

1-2 SLOPE AND EQUATIONS OF STRAIGHT LINES

6. Which of the following do not represent slope?
   a) Steepness of a straight line.
   b) Rate of change of the dependent variable with respect to the independent variable.
   c) Vertical change/horizontal change.
   d) Horizontal change/vertical change.
7. A straight line, $y = mx + b$, has slope = $-5/3$. State the effect on y if x increases by 3 units.
8. Draw a graph that typifies a straight line with
   a) Positive slope.   b) Negative slope.
   c) Zero slope.   d) Undefined slope.
9. A straight line with an equation of the form $y = mx$ passes through the _____.
10. A horizontal straight line has an equation of the form _____.
11. A vertical straight line has an equation of the form _____.
12. A linear equation in slope-intercept form is easily graphed by first plotting the _____ and then drawing the straight line upward to the right if its slope is _____ or upward to the left if its slope is _____.
13. A tax function is an example of a piecewise-defined function. The different slopes of a tax function represent _____ _____.

1-3 GRAPHING LINEAR EQUATIONS

14. Explain the following terms: x-intercept, y-intercept.
15. An x-intercept has a y-coordinate that equals _____.

16. A y-intercept has an x-coordinate that equals _____.

17. State the procedure for graphing a linear equation of the form $ax + by = c$.

18. State the procedure for graphing a linear equation of the form $y = mx$.

1-4 LINEAR MODELS

Cost, Revenue, and Profit Functions

19. A cost function expresses a relationship between what two quantities?

20. A sales revenue function expresses a relationship between what two quantities?

21. A profit function expresses a relationship between what two quantities?

22. Give an interpretation of the slope of a linear cost function.

23. The y-intercept of a cost function is the _____ _____ ; explain this term.

Demand and Supply Functions

24. A demand equation relates the quantities _____ and _____.

25. A supply equation relates the quantities _____ and _____.

Consumption Function and MPC

26. A consumption function relates the quantities _____ and _____.

27. Give an interpretation of the MPC.

Linear Depreciation

28. Give the linear equation that relates the value of an asset to its age. Interpret its y-intercept and slope.

1-5 GRAPHING CONCEPTS

Explain each of the following terms, and indicate how it is related to the equation of a graph.

29. Vertical shift

30. Horizontal shift

31. Reflection in the x-axis

32. Symmetry with respect to the vertical axis

33. Symmetry with respect to the origin

1-6 QUADRATIC FUNCTIONS AND THEIR GRAPHS

34. Write the general form of a quadratic equation; write the formula for the x-coordinate of the vertex; the y-intercept is given by $(0, \underline{\quad})$.

35. Give the rule for determining whether a parabola opens up or down.

36. Give the procedure for finding the x-intercept(s) of a parabola.

37. A parabola may have as many as ____ x-intercepts.

38. If a parabola has exactly one x-intercept, then the x-intercept is also the _____.

1-7   APPLICATIONS OF QUADRATIC FUNCTIONS

39. Sales revenue is determined by beginning with the formula

$$\text{sales revenue} = (\underline{\hspace{3cm}})(\underline{\hspace{3cm}})$$

40. A profit equation is determined by beginning with the formula

$$\text{profit} = (\underline{\hspace{3cm}}) - (\underline{\hspace{3cm}})$$

41. Given a profit equation, state the procedure for determining the break-even points.

42. Given the supply and demand equations, state the procedure for determining the equilibrium point.

43. If an equation relates some quantity to time, its graph is called a(an) _____.

1-8   SOME SPECIAL POLYNOMIAL AND RATIONAL FUNCTIONS

44. Write the general form for the equation of an nth-degree polynomial function.

45. An nth-degree polynomial function has at most ____ high/low points and at most ____ x-intercepts.

46. Draw the graph that typifies equations of the form $f(x) = ax^n$, where n is an odd positive integer, $n \geq 3$, and $a > 0$.

47. Draw the graph that typifies equations of the form $f(x) = ax^n$, where n is an even positive integer and $a > 0$.

48. Draw the graph that typifies equations of the form $f(x) = k/x^n$, where n is an odd positive integer and $k > 0$.

49. Draw the graph that typifies equations of the form $f(x) = k/x^n$, where n is an even positive integer and $k > 0$.

50. Give the procedure for determining vertical asymptotes of rational functions.

51. If $C(x)$ denotes the total cost of producing x units of some product, write the equation that gives the average cost per unit.

REVIEW EXERCISES

• *Functions and Functional Notation*

For each of the following, calculate $f(0)$, $f(1)$, and $f(3)$.

1. $f(x = 4x - 2$ **2.** $f(x) = 5x + 3$

3. $f(x) = x^2 + 2x - 1$ **4.** $f(x) = \dfrac{3x + 5}{x + 1}$

For each of the following, calculate the difference quotient

$$\frac{f(x + h) - f(x)}{h}$$

5. $f(x) = 4x + 8$ **6.** $f(x) = x^2 + 6x - 5$
7. $f(x) = x^2 - 4x + 3$ **8.** $f(x) = x^3 - x^2 + 7$

Specify the domain of each of the following functions.

9. $f(x) = \sqrt{x - 4}$ **10.** $f(x) = \sqrt{x + 8}$

11. $f(x) = \dfrac{x + 6}{(x - 7)(x + 5)}$ **12.** $f(x) = \dfrac{4x + 10}{x - 2}$

• Functions and Graphs

State whether each of the following is the graph of a function.

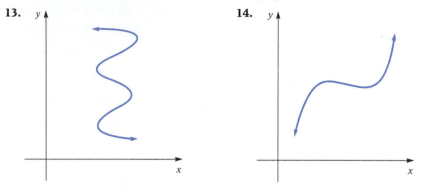

13.

14.

Graph each of the following.

15. $f(x) = \begin{cases} 2 & \text{if } x \le 3 \\ 5 & \text{if } 3 < x \le 8 \\ x & \text{if } x > 8 \end{cases}$

16. $g(x) = \begin{cases} -1 & \text{if } x \le 2 \\ x & \text{if } 2 < x \le 5 \\ 7 & \text{if } x > 5 \end{cases}$

17. *Call options.* An investor bought a call option entitling her to buy a specified number of shares of a stock for $20 per share during the next 3 months. The investor paid $4 per share for the call option. Determine the investor's profit function per share of stock. Graph the profit function.

• Slope and Equations of Straight Lines

Find the slope of the straight line passing through each of the following pairs of points.

18. $(3, -7)$ and $(-8, 26)$

19. $(6, 5)$ and $(4, -3)$

Find the equation of the straight line passing through each of the following pairs of points. Express the answer in slope-intercept form.

20. $(-1, 6)$ and $(4, 16)$

21. $(3, -2)$ and $(5, 8)$

For each of the following, determine which of the given points lie on the straight line.

22. $2x + 5y = 20$: $(0, 4)$, $(10, 0)$, $(2, 4)$, $(5, 2)$, $(3, 4)$

23. $4x - 2y = 10$: $(1, -3)$, $(2, 5)$, $(0, -5)$, $(3, 0)$, $(-1, -2)$

Draw the graph of a straight line that passes through the origin and has

24. Positive slope.

25. Negative slope.

Draw the graph of a straight line that passes through $(3, 4)$ and

26. Has slope $= 0$.

27. Has an undefined slope.

Write the equation of the straight line of

28. Exercise 26.

29. Exercise 27.

Which of the following pairs of straight lines are parallel?

30. $y = 5x + 7$, $y = 4x - 9$

31. $2x + 6y = 30$, $-4x - 12y = 24$

32. *Defects: U.S. automobiles.* The number of defects per 100 vehicles for Chrysler's North American operations declined from 810 to 175 during the years from 1979 to 1989.
    a) Find the slope of the straight line that indicates this trend.
    b) Interpret the slope.
    c) Find the equation of the straight line. Express the final answer in slope-intercept form.
    d) If Chrysler's defects continue to decline at the same rate, predict its defects per 100 vehicles (North America) for the year 1991.

• *Graphing Linear Equations*

Graph each of the following by finding the x- and y-intercepts.

33. $5x - 2y = 20$
34. $y = 7x - 14$
35. $f(x) = 6x$
36. $3x - 6y = 0$

• *Cost, Revenue, and Profit Functions*

For Exercises 37 and 38, determine the linear cost, sales revenue, and profit equations. Graph each on the same set of axes. Determine the break-even point.

37. Variable cost per unit = $30, fixed cost = $1200, and unit selling price = $50
38. Variable cost per unit = $80, fixed cost = $1600, and unit selling price = $120

• *Supply, Demand, and Equilibrium Point*

Determine the supply and demand equations and the equilibrium point.

39. *Demand:* If a given product is priced at $7 per unit, there is a demand for 4 units; if the product is priced at $6 per unit, there is a demand for 8 units.
    Supply: If the product is priced at $9 per unit, suppliers are willing to produce 4 units; if the product is priced at $23 per unit, suppliers are willing to produce 12 units.

• *Consumption Function, MPC, and MPS*

For Exercises 40 and 41, if x denotes income and y denotes consumption, then
    a) Calculate and interpret the MPC.
    b) Calculate and interpret the MPS.
    c) Determine the equation defining the linear consumption function.

40.

x	y
50	85
60	94

41.

x	y
40	62
70	86

• *Linear Depreciation*

42. A construction company buys a truck for $80,000. The useful life of the truck is 5 years, after which time it will have a scrap value of $5000.
    a) Find the linear equation relating the value of the truck, y, to its age, x.

b) Graph the result of part a.

c) What is the value of the truck after 3 years?

• *Graphing Concepts*

Graph each of the following.

43. $y = |x - 7|$ **44.** $y = |x + 5| - 3$ **45.** $y = -|x + 2| + 1$

For Exercises 46–48, determine whether the function is odd, even, or neither by filling in the indicated table of x- and $f(x)$-values.

46. $f(x) = x^4$

x	−3	−2	−1	0	1	2	3
$f(x)$							

47. $f(x) = 1/x^3$

x	−3	−2	−1	0	1	2	3
$f(x)$							

48. $f(x) = 3x - 4$

x	−3	−2	−1	0	1	2	3
$f(x)$							

• *Quadratic Functions*

Graph Exercises 49–60.

49. $f(x) = x^2 - 25$ **50.** $f(x) = -x^2 + 36$
51. $f(x) = -3(x + 2)^2 + 4$ **52.** $f(x) = (x - 5)^2 - 3$
53. $y = -4x^2 + 24x$ **54.** $y = 5x^2 - 30x$
55. $f(x) = x^2 + 2x - 15$ **56.** $f(x) = x^2 - 9x + 8$
57. $f(x) = x^2 - 8x + 16$ **58.** $f(x) = x^2 + 10x + 25$
59. $y = (x + 4)(x - 6)$ **60.** $y = (x - 7)(x - 9)$

61. *Revenue function.* Given the demand equation $p = -2x + 140$, where p denotes the unit price in dollars and x denotes the number of units demanded of some product,

a) Determine the equation of the revenue function, $R(x)$.

b) Graph the revenue function.

c) State the maximum sales revenue.

d) How many units must be sold in order to achieve the maximum sales revenue?

e) Substitute the result of part d into the demand equation to determine the unit price that maximizes sales revenue.

62. *Revenue, cost, and profit functions; Break-even analysis.* Given the following:

$$\text{Demand function: } p = -2x + 2700$$

$$\text{Cost function: } C(x) = 300x + 400{,}000$$

where p denotes the unit price in dollars and x denotes the number of units produced and sold of some product,

a) Determine the equation of the revenue function, $R(x)$.
b) Graph both the revenue and cost functions on the same set of axes.
c) How many units of the product should be produced and sold in order to break even?
d) State the interval over which profit is positive.
e) Determine the equation of the profit function.
f) Graph the profit function.
g) Using the profit function, determine the break-even points. Verify that they agree with the answer to part c.
h) Using the profit function, state the interval over which profit is positive. Verify that this answer agrees with that of part d.
i) State the maximum profit.
j) How many units of the product should be produced and sold in order to maximize profit?

63. *Supply, demand, and market equilibrium.* For the following supply and demand functions, p denotes the unit price in dollars and x denotes the number of units supplied or demanded of some product in millions of units.

$$\text{Supply function: } p = x^2 + 8 \qquad (x > 0)$$
$$\text{Demand function: } p = (x - 4)^2 \qquad (0 < x \le 4)$$

a) Determine the equilibrium quantity.
b) Determine the equilibrium price.
c) Graph both the supply and demand functions on the same set of axes.

64. *Time series.* A company's annual profits, P (in millions of dollars), are related to the time, t (in years), since its incorporation by the function

$$P(t) = 0.8t^2 + 40 \qquad (t > 0)$$

a) Graph the function $P(t)$.
b) Find the company's annual profit for the third year.
c) Find the company's annual profit for the sixth year.

• Some Special Polynomial and Rational Functions

Graph Exercises 65–74.

65. $y = x^6$ **66.** $y = x^5$ **67.** $y = 5x^8$ **68.** $y = -7x^4$
69. $y = 3/x^4$ **70.** $y = 6/x^7$ **71.** $y = -8/x^3$ **72.** $y = -2/x^2$
73. $y = -4(x - 2)^4 + 3$ **74.** $y = 2/(x - 5)^5$

75. *Production possibility curve.* A company produces x units of Product A and y units of Product B. The equation

$$y = 8{,}000{,}000/x^2 \qquad (200 \le x \le 800)$$

relates x and y and thus gives the production possibilities for the two products.
a) Graph the production possibility curve.
b) State the production possibility for $x = 200$.
c) State the production possibility for $x = 600$.
d) State the production possibility for $x = 800$.

76. *Demand curve.* The equation

$$p = 40{,}000/(x - 20) \qquad (20 < x < 8020)$$

gives the relationship between the unit price, p, and the number of units demanded, x, of some product.
a) Graph the demand curve.
b) Find the unit price when the demand is 1020 units.
c) Find the unit price when the demand is 6020 units.

77. *Average cost function.* The total cost in dollars of producing x units of some product is given by

$$C(x) = 800x + 480{,}000 \qquad (x > 0)$$

a) Determine the equation of the average cost function.
b) Graph the result of part a.
c) Evaluate $\overline{C}(2000)$, $\overline{C}(10{,}000)$, and $\overline{C}(100{,}000)$, and interpret the results.
d) As the production level increases, the average cost per unit is approaching what value?

Algebra Refresher

EXPONENTS

Rational Exponents

$$x^{1/n} = \sqrt[n]{x}$$

Examples: $\quad x^{1/2} = \sqrt{x} \qquad x^{1/3} = \sqrt[3]{x} \qquad x^{1/4} = \sqrt[4]{x}$

Worksheet

Fill in the blanks.

$x^{1/5} = \sqrt[\ ]{x}$ Answer: $\sqrt[5]{x}$ $\sqrt[7]{x} = x^{-/-}$ Answer: $x^{1/7}$

$x^{1/9} = \sqrt[\ ]{x}$ Answer: $\sqrt[9]{x}$ $\sqrt[8]{x} = x^{-/-}$ Answer: $x^{1/8}$

$$x^{m/n} = \sqrt[n]{x^m}$$

Examples: $\quad x^{5/2} = \sqrt{x^5} \qquad x^{5/3} = \sqrt[3]{x^5} \qquad x^{7/4} = \sqrt[4]{x^7}$

Worksheet

Fill in the blanks.

$x^{2/3} = \sqrt[3]{x^{-}}$ Answer: $\sqrt[3]{x^2}$ $x^{9/4} = \sqrt[\ ]{x^{-}}$ Answer: $\sqrt[4]{x^9}$

$\sqrt[5]{x^8} = x^{-/-}$ Answer: $x^{8/5}$ $\sqrt[7]{x^6} = x^{-/-}$ Answer: $x^{6/7}$

Negative Exponents

$$x^{-n} = \frac{1}{x^n}$$

Examples: $\quad x^{-2} = \frac{1}{x^2} \qquad x^{-1/3} = \frac{1}{\sqrt[3]{x}} \qquad x^{-5/4} = \frac{1}{\sqrt[4]{x^5}}$

Worksheet

Fill in the blanks.

$x^{-3} = \underline{\qquad}$ Answer: $\dfrac{1}{x^3}$ $x^{-1/4} = \underline{\qquad}$ Answer: $\dfrac{1}{\sqrt[4]{x}}$

$x^{-1/5} = \underline{\qquad}$ Answer: $\dfrac{1}{\sqrt[5]{x}}$ $x^{-5/3} = \underline{\qquad}$ Answer: $\dfrac{1}{\sqrt[3]{x^5}}$

$x^{-4/3} = \underline{\qquad}$ Answer: $\dfrac{1}{\sqrt[3]{x^4}}$ $\dfrac{1}{\sqrt[5]{x^6}} = \underline{\qquad}$ Answer: $x^{-6/5}$

$\dfrac{1}{\sqrt{x^7}} = \underline{\qquad}$ Answer: $x^{-7/2}$ $\dfrac{1}{\sqrt[4]{x^7}} = \underline{\qquad}$ Answer: $x^{-7/4}$

The contents of this page and other exponent laws are discussed in Section R-3.

DIFFERENTIATION

Introductory Application

Marginal Revenue

Given the demand equation

$$p = -x + 10 \qquad (0 \leq x \leq 10)$$

where p denotes the unit selling price and x denotes the number of units demanded of some product,

a) Determine the equation for total sales revenue, $R(x)$.

b) Determine the equation for marginal revenue.

c) Determine the marginal revenue at sales level $x = 3$ units. Interpret the result.

In Chapter 1, we learned to determine the equation of a sales revenue function, given a demand equation. In this chapter, we will learn that marginal revenue represents the additional revenue gained from the sale of one more unit of product.

The above problem is solved in Example 2-28.

Calculus is the branch of mathematics that concerns itself with the *rate of change* of one quantity with respect to another quantity. Calculus is considered to have been invented by Isaac Newton and Gottfried Wilhelm von Leibnitz working independently at the close of the seventeenth century. Calculus is separated into two parts: **differential calculus** and **integral calculus.** Differential calculus is involved with a certain quantity called a **derivative.** In this chapter, we will learn what a derivative is, how to calculate a derivative, and how a derivative is used. Integral calculus will be considered in Chapters 6 and 7.

2-1   • LIMITS

The concept of limit is very important for the formal development of calculus. In this section, we will give a brief introduction to limits.

When we apply the concept of limit, we examine what happens to the *y*-values of a function $f(x)$ as x gets closer and closer to (but does not reach) some particular number, called *a*. If the *y*-values also get closer and closer to a single number, L, then the number L is said to be the *limit of the function as x approaches a*. Thus, we say that **L is the limit of $f(x)$ as x approaches a.** This is written in mathematical shorthand as

$$\lim_{x \to a} f(x) = L$$

where the symbol $\to$ stands for the word *approaches*. If the *y*-values of the function do not get closer and closer to a single number as x gets closer and closer to a, then the function has no limit as x approaches a. Figure 2-1 gives the graph of the function

$$f(x) = 2x + 1$$

along with a table of x and $f(x)$ values.

We wish to determine the limit of f(x) = 2x + 1 *as* x *approaches 3.*

To determine $\lim_{x \to 3} f(x)$, we let x take on values that approach 3 from the left and record the corresponding $f(x)$ values, as illustrated in the table of Figure 2-1. Note that as x approaches 3 from the left (i.e., $x < 3$), $f(x)$ approaches 7. This is a **left-hand limit** and is written as

$$\lim_{x \to 3^-} f(x) = 7$$

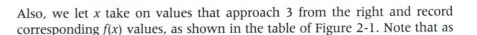

Also, we let x take on values that approach 3 from the right and record corresponding $f(x)$ values, as shown in the table of Figure 2-1. Note that as

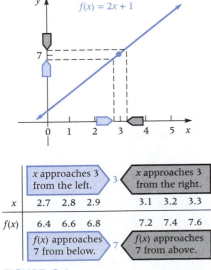

$f(x) = 2x + 1$

	x approaches 3 from the left.		3	x approaches 3 from the right.		
x	2.7	2.8	2.9	3.1	3.2	3.3
$f(x)$	6.4	6.6	6.8	7.2	7.4	7.6
	f(x) approaches 7 from below.		7	f(x) approaches 7 from above.		

FIGURE 2-1

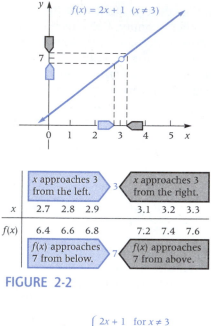

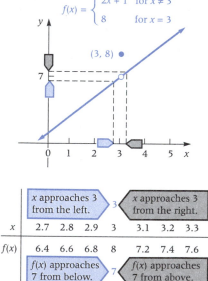

FIGURE 2-2

FIGURE 2-3

x approaches 3 from the right (i.e., $x > 3$) $f(x)$ approaches 7. This is a **right-hand limit** and is written as

$$\lim_{x \to 3^+} f(x) = 7$$

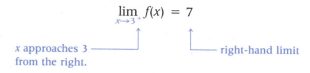

Since the left-hand limit, 7, equals the right-hand limit, 7, then we say that 7 is the limit of $f(x)$ as x approaches 3. In other words, the $f(x)$ values approach the same number—in this case, 7—as x approaches 3 from both sides. Thus, we write

$$\lim_{x \to 3} f(x) = 7$$

We note that if the point $(3, 7)$ is omitted from the function $f(x)$, then the $\lim_{x \to 3} f(x)$ is unaffected and is still 7, as is shown in Figure 2-2.

Also, if the function $f(x)$ is assigned a value different from 7 when $x = 3$, as illustrated in Figure 2-3, then the $\lim_{x \to 3} f(x)$ is unaffected and is still 7, as we show in Figure 2-3.

Nonexistence of Limits

We now give an example where a *limit does not exist* at a particular point. We consider an income tax function, $T(x)$, which gives the amount of federal income tax for taxable income x. This tax function was under consideration during a past tax reform movement. We note that present-day tax functions possess a somewhat similar structure. Thus, $T(x)$ is defined below, and its graph is given in Figure 2-4.

Tax Function

$$T(x) = \begin{cases} 0.15x & \text{for } 0 \le x \le 29{,}300 \\ 0.27x - 3561 & \text{for } x > 29{,}300 \end{cases}$$

Studying the tax function $T(x)$, note that for taxable income up to and including \$29,300, the federal income tax is 15% of such income. However, for taxable income in excess of \$29,300, the federal income tax is 27% of such income, minus \$3561.

We want to determine the limit, if it exists, of T(x) *as* x *approaches 29,300.*

Thus, we let x take on values that approach 29,300 from the left and record the corresponding $T(x)$ values, as illustrated in the table of Figure 2-4. Note that as x approaches 29,300 from the left, $T(x)$ approaches 4395. Thus,

$$\lim_{x \to 29{,}300^-} T(x) = 4395$$

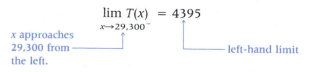

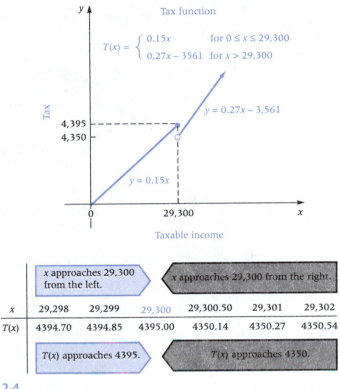

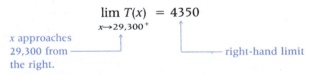

FIGURE 2-4

Also, we let x take on values that approach 29,300 from the right and record the corresponding $T(x)$ values, as illustrated in Figure 2-4. Observe that as x approaches 29,300 from the right, $T(x)$ approaches 4350. Thus,

$$\lim_{x \to 29,300^+} T(x) = 4350$$

x approaches 29,300 from the right. ⎯⎯ right-hand limit

Since the left-hand limit, 4395, does not equal the right-hand limit, 4350, then

$$\lim_{x \to 29,300} T(x) \quad does\ not\ exist.$$

• **EXAMPLE 2-1** ⎯⎯⎯⎯⎯⎯⎯⎯⎯⎯⎯⎯⎯⎯⎯⎯⎯⎯⎯

Find the limit of the function $f(x) = x^2$ as x approaches 3.

Solution

Table 2-1 on page 100 contains a listing of x and y values of $f(x) = x^2$ as x takes on values near 3. Observe that as x gets closer and closer to 3 from each side, $f(x)$ gets closer to 9 from each side. Thus, we say that 9 is the limit of $f(x)$ as x approaches 3. This is written in mathematical shorthand as

$$\lim_{x \to 3} f(x) = 9$$

Since $f(x) = x^2$, this expression may also be written as

$$\lim_{x \to 3} x^2 = 9$$

TABLE 2-1 $y = f(x) = x^2$

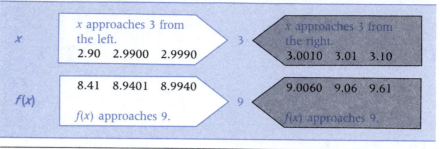

We now give the following definition of limit.

Limit

1.   Let a and L be numbers and $f(x)$ a function. If, as x approaches the number a from each side, the values of $f(x)$ approach the single value L, then L is said to be the **limit of $f(x)$ as x approaches a**. We write this in mathematical shorthand as

$$\lim_{x \to a} f(x) = L$$

2.   This means that the left-hand limit equals the right-hand limit or, in other words,

$$\lim_{x \to a^-} f(x) = L = \lim_{x \to a^+} f(x)$$

3.   The $\lim_{x \to a} f(x)$ does not depend on the value of $f(x)$ at $x = a$. Whether or not the function, $f(x)$ is defined at $x = a$ does not affect the limit or its existence or nonexistence at $x = a$.

4.   In other words,

$$\lim_{x \to a} f(x) = L$$

means that the values of $f(x)$ approach, without necessarily being equal to, L as x approaches, without necessarily being equal to, a.

• **EXAMPLE 2-2**

If $f(x) = x$, find $\lim_{x \to 4} f(x)$ or, in other words, $\lim_{x \to 4} x$.

Solution

We make a table of x and y values as x approaches 4 (see Table 2-2). Note that as x approaches 4 from each side, the values of $f(x)$ approach 4. Thus, $4 = \lim_{x \to 4} f(x)$ or, equivalently, $4 = \lim_{x \to 4} x$.

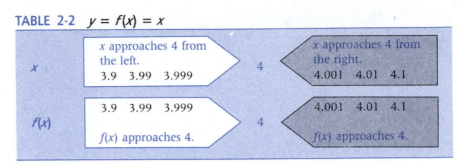

TABLE 2-2 $y = f(x) = x$

x	x approaches 4 from the left.	4	x approaches 4 from the right.
	3.9 3.99 3.999	4	4.001 4.01 4.1
$f(x)$	3.9 3.99 3.999	4	4.001 4.01 4.1
	$f(x)$ approaches 4.		$f(x)$ approaches 4.

We now look at situations where the function is not given as a formula. Instead, we have only the graph. We can still find the limit, if it exists.

• **EXAMPLE 2-3**

For each of the graphs of Figure 2-5, determine if $\lim_{x \to 7} h(x)$ exists. If the limit exists, state its numerical value.

Solutions

a) As x gets closer and closer to 7 from each side, the values of $h(x)$ get closer and closer to the single value 6. Thus, $\lim_{x \to 7} h(x) = 6$. Note that this function has a limit at all other values of x shown on this graph.

b) As x gets closer and closer to 7 from the left, the values of $h(x)$ get closer and closer to 5. As x gets closer and closer to 7 from the right, the values of $h(x)$ get closer and closer to 8. Since the values of $h(x)$ do not approach the same value from each side, the function has no limit as $x \to 7$. Note that this function has a limit at all other values of x shown on this graph.

c) As x gets closer and closer to 7, the values of $h(x)$ get larger and larger and do not approach a single number. Thus, $\lim_{x \to 7} h(x)$ does not exist. Note that this function has a limit at all other values of x shown on this graph.

•

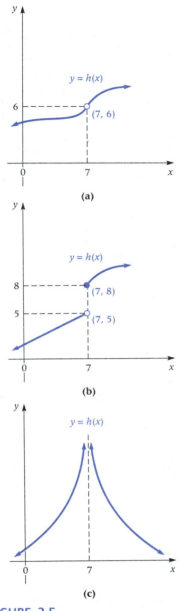

FIGURE 2-5

Limit Properties

In the previous examples of this section, we determined the limits of functions by applying the definition of limit. Many times, limits of functions are determined in a much simpler manner by using **limit properties.** The following limit properties are stated without verification.

Limit Properties   For each of the following, assume that $\lim_{x \to a} f(x)$ and $\lim_{x \to a} g(x)$ both exist. Also, let a, c, k, and r be constant real numbers, with $r > 0$.

Property 1   *Limit of a Constant.*

$$\lim_{x \to a} c = c$$

This property states that the limit of a constant function is the constant value. Thus, for example, we write

$$\lim_{x \to 2} 5 = 5 \qquad \lim_{x \to -1} 8 = 8 \qquad \lim_{x \to a} -4 = -4 \qquad \lim_{x \to 6} 9 = 9$$

Property 2   *Limit of a Sum or Difference.*

$$\lim_{x \to a} [f(x) \pm g(x)] = \lim_{x \to a} f(x) \pm \lim_{x \to a} g(x)$$

This property states that the limit of a sum or difference is the sum or difference of the individual limits, provided that these limits exist. Thus, if $f(x) = x$ and $g(x) = 5$, then

$$\begin{aligned}
\lim_{x \to 4} [f(x) + g(x)] &= \lim_{x \to 4} (x + 5) \\
&= \lim_{x \to 4} x + \lim_{x \to 4} 5 \\
&= 4 + 5 \\
&= 9 \\
\lim_{x \to 4} [f(x) - g(x)] &= \lim_{x \to 4} (x - 5) \\
&= \lim_{x \to 4} x - \lim_{x \to 4} 5 \\
&= 4 - 5 \\
&= -1
\end{aligned}$$

Property 3   *Limit of a Constant Times a Function.*

$$\lim_{x \to a} kf(x) = k \lim_{x \to a} f(x)$$

This property states that the limit of a constant times a function is the constant times the limit of the function, provided, of course, that the limit exists. Thus, if $f(x) = x$ and $k = 3$, then

$$\begin{aligned}
\lim_{x \to 4} kf(x) &= \lim_{x \to 4} 3x \\
&= 3 \lim_{x \to 4} x \\
&= 3(4) \\
&= 12
\end{aligned}$$

Property 4   *Limit of a Function to a Power.*

$$\lim_{x \to a} [f(x)]^r = \left[\lim_{x \to a} f(x) \right]^r$$

This property states that the limit of a function raised to a power is the power of the limit, provided, of course, that the limit exists. Thus, if $f(x) = x$ and $r = 3$, then

$$\begin{aligned}
\lim_{x \to 4} [f(x)]^r &= \lim_{x \to 4} x^3 \\
&= \left[\lim_{x \to 4} x \right]^3 \\
&= 4^3 \\
&= 64
\end{aligned}$$

Property 5   *Limit of a Product.*

$$\lim_{x \to a} [f(x)g(x)] = \left[\lim_{x \to a} f(x) \right]\left[\lim_{x \to a} g(x) \right]$$

This property states that the limit of a product is the product of the limits, provided that these limits exist. Thus, if $f(x) = x^3$ and $g(x) = x + 5$, then

$$\lim_{x \to 4} [f(x)g(x)] = \lim_{x \to 4} x^3(x + 5)$$
$$= \left[\lim_{x \to 4} x^3\right]\left[\lim_{x \to 4} (x + 5)\right]$$
$$= 4^3(4 + 5)$$
$$= 64(9)$$
$$= 576$$

Note that we have previously determined that $\lim_{x \to 4} x^3 = 4^3 = 64$ and that $\lim_{x \to 4}(x + 5) = 4 + 5 = 9$.

Property 6   *Limit of a Quotient.*
If $\lim_{x \to a} g(x) \neq 0$, then

$$\lim_{x \to a} \frac{f(x)}{g(x)} = \frac{\lim_{x \to a} f(x)}{\lim_{x \to a} g(x)}$$

This property states that the limit of a quotient is the quotient of the limits, provided that the limits exist and that the limit of the denominator is not zero. Thus, if $f(x) = x^3$ and $g(x) = x + 5$, then

$$\lim_{x \to 4} \frac{f(x)}{g(x)} = \lim_{x \to 4} \frac{x^3}{x + 5}$$
$$= \frac{\lim_{x \to 4} x^3}{\lim_{x \to 4} (x + 5)}$$
$$= \frac{4^3}{(4 + 5)}$$
$$= \frac{64}{9}$$

Again, recall that we have previously determined that $\lim_{x \to 4} x^3 = 4^3 = 64$ and that $\lim_{x \to 4}(x + 5) = 9$.

• **EXAMPLE 2-4** _____

Compute the following limits:

a) $\lim_{x \to 5} x$ **b)** $\lim_{x \to 5} x^4$

c) $\lim_{x \to 5} 3x^4$ **d)** $\lim_{x \to 5}(3x^4 - 275)$

e) $\lim_{x \to 5} \sqrt{3x^4 - 275}$ **f)** $\lim_{x \to 5} \frac{\sqrt{3x^4 - 275}}{x^3}$

Solutions

a) In Example 2-2, we showed that $\lim_{x \to 4} x = 4$. In a similar manner, we could show that $\lim_{x \to 5} x = 5$.

b) $\lim_{x \to 5} x^4 = \left(\lim_{x \to 5} x\right)^4$ By Property 4
$= 5^4$ By Part a
$= 625$

c) $\lim_{x\to 5} 3x^4 = 3 \lim_{x\to 5} x^4$ By Property 3

$= 3(625)$ By Part b

$= 1875$

d) $\lim_{x\to 5} (3x^4 - 275) = \lim_{x\to 5} 3x^4 - \lim_{x\to 5} 275$ By Property 2

Since $\lim_{x\to 5} 3x^4 = 1875$ by part c and $\lim_{x\to 5} 275 = 275$ by property 1, the result is

$$\lim_{x\to 5}(3x^4 - 275) = 1875 - 275$$
$$= 1600$$

e) $\lim_{x\to 5} \sqrt{3x^4 - 275} = \lim_{x\to 5}(3x^4 - 275)^{1/2}$

$= \left[\lim_{x\to 5}(3x^4 - 275)\right]^{1/2}$ By Property 4

Since $\lim_{x\to 5}(3x^4 - 275) = 1600$ from part d, then we have

$$\left[\lim_{x\to 5}(3x^4 - 275)\right]^{1/2} = 1600^{1/2}$$
$$= 40$$

f) $\lim_{x\to 5} \dfrac{\sqrt{3x^4 - 275}}{x^3} = \dfrac{\lim_{x\to 5} \sqrt{3x^4 - 275}}{\lim_{x\to 5} x^3}$ By Property 6

In part e, we determined that $\lim_{x\to 5} \sqrt{3x^4 - 275} = 40$. By Property 4 and part a, we determine that $\lim_{x\to 5} x^3 = (\lim_{x\to 5} x)^3 = 5^3 = 125$. Hence, we obtain

$$\frac{\lim_{x\to 5} \sqrt{3x^4 - 275}}{\lim_{x\to 5} x^3} = \frac{40}{125} = \frac{8}{25}$$

• EXAMPLE 2-5

If

$$f(x) = \frac{x^2 - 36}{x - 6}$$

compute $\lim_{x\to 6} f(x)$.

Solution

Note that $f(x)$ is not defined at $x = 6$ since $f(6) = (6^2 - 36)/(6 - 6) = 0/0$, which is undefined. However, we can consider $\lim_{x\to 6} f(x)$ since the limit as x approaches 6 depends only on values of x *near* 6 without consideration of the value at $x = 6$. To evaluate $\lim_{x\to 6} f(x)$, note that if $x \neq 6$,

$$\frac{x^2 - 36}{x - 6} = \frac{(x - 6)(x + 6)}{x - 6}$$
$$= x + 6$$

Hence,

$$\lim_{x\to 6} \frac{x^2 - 36}{x - 6} = \lim_{x\to 6} (x + 6)$$
$$= 12$$

A graph of $f(x)$ appears in Figure 2-6. Observing this figure, note that the graph of $f(x)$ is the graph of the straight line $y = x + 6$ with the point (6, 12) excluded. The open circle at (6, 12) indicates that this point is excluded from the graph.

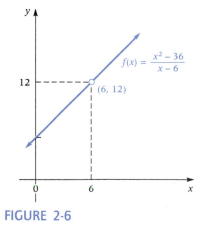

FIGURE 2-6

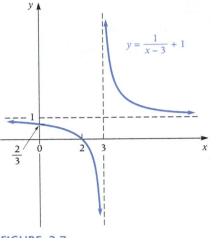

FIGURE 2-7

Infinity and Limits

Consider the function

$$f(x) = \frac{1}{x - 3} + 1$$

The graph of this function appears in Figure 2-7. Observing this figure, note that as x takes on larger and larger positive numbers (i.e., as x increases without bound), the value of $f(x)$ approaches 1. (Recall that the horizontal line $y = 1$ is a *horizontal asymptote* in this case.) For such a situation, we say that 1 is the limit of $f(x)$ as x approaches infinity. The statement "x increases without bound" is equivalently expressed in mathematical terms as "x approaches infinity." Infinity is denoted by the symbol ∞. Thus, $x \to \infty$ means that x is increasing without bound (i.e., x exceeds any positive number). Similarly, $x \to -\infty$ means that x is decreasing without bound (i.e., x is getting more and more negative). Therefore, the fact that the values of $f(x)$ of Figure 2-7 approach 1 as x approaches ∞ is written as

$$\lim_{x \to \infty} f(x) = 1$$

Observe also that as x becomes more and more negative (i.e., as x decreases without bound), the value of $f(x)$ approaches 1. Thus, we say that the limit of $f(x)$ as x approaches negative infinity is 1 and write

$$\lim_{x \to -\infty} f(x) = 1$$

• **EXAMPLE 2-6** _____

Observe the graph of $f(x) = 1/x^2$ in Figure 2-8. Determine

$$\lim_{x \to -\infty} \frac{1}{x^2}$$

Solution

Since $1/x^2$ approaches 0 as x decreases without bound, we obtain

$$\lim_{x \to -\infty} \frac{1}{x^2} = 0$$

_____ •

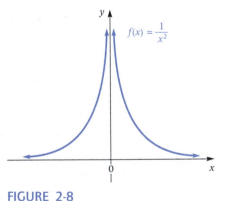

FIGURE 2-8

Observing Figure 2-8, note that $1/x^2$ approaches 0 as x increases without bound. Thus, we can say

$$\lim_{x \to \infty} \frac{1}{x^2} = 0$$

Similar results would be obtained for the functions $1/x$, $1/x^3$, . . . , $1/x^n$, where n is any positive real number. Thus, we state the following in the box on the following page.

For any positive real number n

$$\lim_{x \to -\infty} \frac{1}{x^n} = 0 \text{ and } \lim_{x \to \infty} \frac{1}{x^n} = 0$$

Also, by limit property 5,

$$\lim_{x \to -\infty} \frac{k}{x^n} = 0 \text{ and } \lim_{x \to \infty} \frac{k}{x^n} = 0$$

for any constant k.

• **EXAMPLE 2-7** _____

Determine

$$\lim_{x \to \infty} \frac{3}{x^2 + 5}$$

Solution

As x increases without bound, so does $x^2 + 5$. Thus, the fraction $3/(x^2 + 5)$ approaches 0 as x approaches ∞. Hence, we have

$$\lim_{x \to \infty} \frac{3}{x^2 + 5} = 0$$

• **EXAMPLE 2-8** _____

Determine

$$\lim_{x \to \infty} \frac{x^2 + 3x}{4x^2 + 9}$$

Solution

Note that as x increases without bound, so do both the numerator and the denominator. To determine the limit of their quotient, we factor out the highest power of x in the numerator and also the highest power of x in the denominator to obtain

$$\frac{x^2 + 3x}{4x^2 + 9} = \frac{x^2\left(1 + \dfrac{3}{x}\right)}{x^2\left(4 + \dfrac{9}{x^2}\right)}$$

$$= \frac{1 + \dfrac{3}{x}}{4 + \dfrac{9}{x^2}}$$

Now, as x increases without bound, $3/x$ and $9/x^2$ both approach 0, so the numerator, $1 + 3/x$, approaches 1, and the denominator, $4 + 9/x^2$, approaches 4. Thus, using property 6, we calculate

$$\lim_{x \to \infty} \frac{x^2 + 3x}{4x^2 + 9} = \frac{1}{4}$$

Exercises 2-1

For each of the following functions $f(x)$, determine whether or not $\lim_{x \to 5} f(x)$ exists. If $\lim_{x \to 5} f(x)$ does exist, state its value.

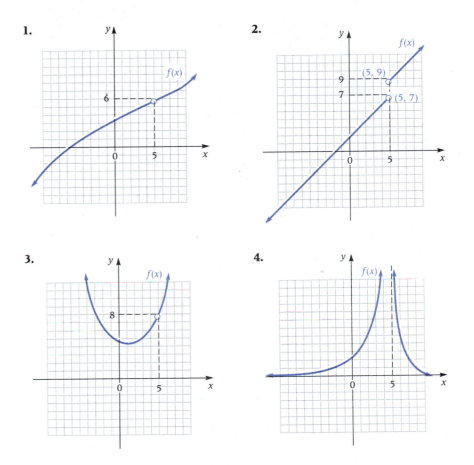

For each of the following functions $h(x)$, determine whether or not $\lim_{x \to 7} h(x)$ exists. If $\lim_{x \to 7} h(x)$ does exist, state its value.

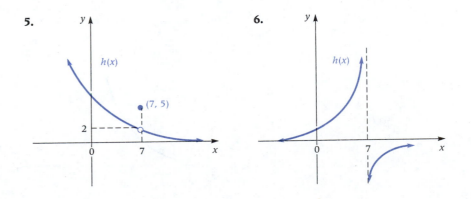

7.

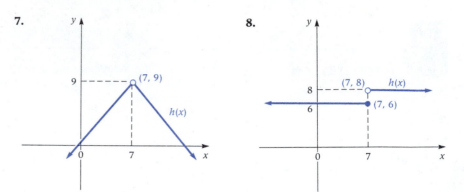

8.

For each of the following functions $f(x)$, determine whether or not $\lim_{x \to \infty} f(x)$ exists. If $\lim_{x \to \infty} f(x)$ does exist, state its value.

9.

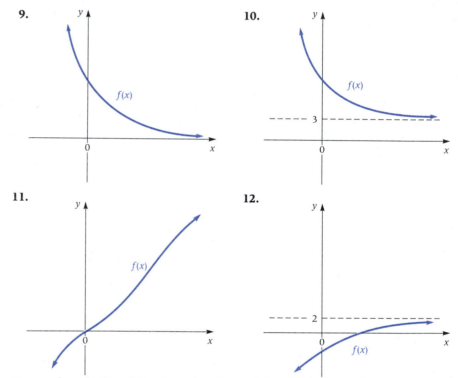

10.

11.

12.

For each of the following functions $g(x)$, determine whether or not $\lim_{x \to -\infty} g(x)$ exists. If $\lim_{x \to -\infty} g(x)$ does exist, state its value.

13.

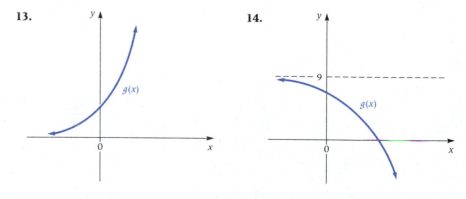

14.

15.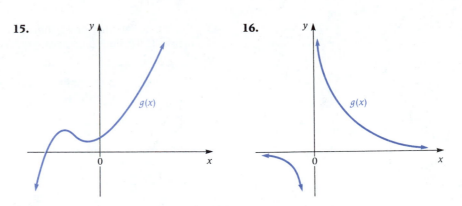

16.

Determine the value of each of the following limits. If the limit does not exist, then state this.

17. $\lim\limits_{x \to 2}(4x + 7)$

18. $\lim\limits_{x \to 1} \dfrac{2x^2 - 2x}{x - 1}$

19. $\lim\limits_{x \to 5} \dfrac{x}{x - 5}$

20. $\lim\limits_{x \to 2} \sqrt{3x^2 + 4}$

21. $\lim\limits_{x \to 0} \dfrac{x^2 - 5x}{x}$

22. $\lim\limits_{x \to 5} \dfrac{x^2 - 25}{x - 5}$

23. $\lim\limits_{x \to 3} \dfrac{x^2 - x - 6}{x - 3}$

24. $\lim\limits_{x \to 8} \dfrac{1}{(x - 8)^2}$

25. $\lim\limits_{x \to \infty} \dfrac{9}{x^3}$

26. $\lim\limits_{x \to \infty} \dfrac{5x^3 - 4x}{2x^3 - 3}$

27. $\lim\limits_{x \to \infty} \dfrac{4}{3x - 7}$

28. $\lim\limits_{x \to \infty} \dfrac{6x^4 - 8x^2}{3x^3 + 2x}$

29. $\lim\limits_{x \to 1}(8x - 5)$

30. $\lim\limits_{x \to 3} \sqrt{5x^2 + 4}$

31. $\lim\limits_{x \to -3} \dfrac{x}{x + 3}$

32. $\lim\limits_{x \to 8} \dfrac{x^2 - 64}{x - 8}$

33. $\lim\limits_{x \to 2} \dfrac{x^2 + 3x - 10}{x - 2}$

34. $\lim\limits_{x \to 5} \dfrac{1}{x^2 - 25}$

35. $\lim\limits_{x \to 0} \dfrac{x^3 - 4x^2 + 5x}{x}$

36. $\lim\limits_{x \to \infty} \dfrac{2x + 3}{x + 7}$

37. $\lim\limits_{x \to -\infty} \dfrac{1}{x^2}$

38. $\lim\limits_{x \to -\infty} \dfrac{5}{x^3}$

39. $\lim\limits_{x \to \infty} \dfrac{3x^2 - 2x}{5x^3 + x}$

40. $\lim\limits_{x \to \infty} \dfrac{5x^3 - 7x}{2x^2 + 3}$

41. Determine whether or not $\lim\limits_{x \to 0} |x|/x$ exists by filling in the table below. If the limit does exist, give its value.

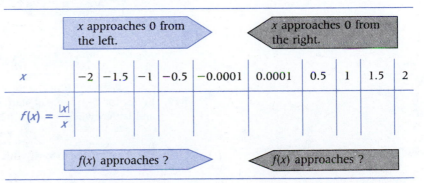

		x approaches 0 from the left.					x approaches 0 from the right.			
x		-2	-1.5	-1	-0.5	-0.0001	0.0001	0.5	1	1.5	2
$f(x) = \dfrac{|x|}{x}$											
		$f(x)$ approaches ?					$f(x)$ approaches ?			

42. Determine whether or not $\lim_{x \to 1} |x - 1|/(x - 1)$ exists by filling in the table below. If the limit does exist, give its value.

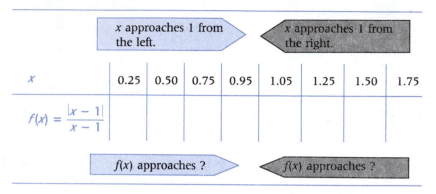

x approaches 1 from the left.				x approaches 1 from the right.			
x 0.25	0.50	0.75	0.95	1.05	1.25	1.50	1.75
$f(x) = \dfrac{|x-1|}{x-1}$							

$f(x)$ approaches ? $f(x)$ approaches ?

43. Using a calculator, determine whether or not $\lim_{x \to 4} (\sqrt{x} - 2)/(x - 4)$ exists by filling in the table below. If the limit does exist, give its value.

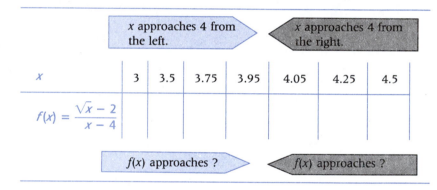

x approaches 4 from the left.				x approaches 4 from the right.		
x 3	3.5	3.75	3.95	4.05	4.25	4.5
$f(x) = \dfrac{\sqrt{x}-2}{x-4}$						

$f(x)$ approaches ? $f(x)$ approaches ?

44. Using a calculator, determine whether or not $\lim_{x \to 9} (\sqrt{x} - 3)/(x - 9)$ exists. If the limit does exist, give its value.

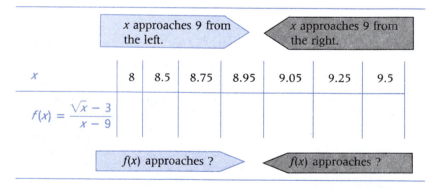

x approaches 9 from the left.				x approaches 9 from the right.		
x 8	8.5	8.75	8.95	9.05	9.25	9.5
$f(x) = \dfrac{\sqrt{x}-3}{x-9}$						

$f(x)$ approaches ? $f(x)$ approaches ?

45. In Section 5-1, we will learn that the expression $(1 + 1/x)^x \to e$ as x gets larger and larger, where e = 2.718281828 to nine decimal places. Thus, we can say

$$\lim_{x \to \infty} (1 + 1/x)^x = e$$

Use a calculator to verify this limit by filling in the following table.

		x approaches ∞			
x	1,000	10,000	100,000	1,000,000	10,000,000
$f(x) = (1 + 1/x)^x$					

f(x) approaches ?

46. Verify that $\lim_{x \to \infty} 1/x = 0$ by filling in the table below. Illustrate graphically.

		x approaches ∞			
x	100	1,000	10,000	100,000	1,000,000
$f(x) = 1/x$					

f(x) approaches ?

47. Verify that $\lim_{x \to \infty} 1/x^2 = 0$ by filling in the table below. Illustrate graphically.

		x approaches ∞			
x	100	1,000	10,000	100,000	1,000,000
$f(x) = 1/x^2$					

f(x) approaches ?

48. *Tax function.* For taxable income, x, where $0 \leq x \leq 155{,}320$, the amount of federal income tax due for a tax year is given by

$$T(x) = \begin{cases} 0.15x & \text{for } 0 \leq x \leq 30{,}950 \\ 0.28x - 4023.5 & \text{for } 30{,}950 < x \leq 74{,}850 \\ 0.33x - 7766 & \text{for } 74{,}850 < x \leq 155{,}320 \end{cases}$$

a) Graph the function $T(x)$.
b) Determine $\lim_{x \to 30{,}950} T(x)$.
c) Determine $\lim_{x \to 74{,}850} T(x)$.

49. *Tax function.* For taxable income x, the amount of tax due is given by

$$T(x) = \begin{cases} 0.20x & \text{for } 0 \leq x \leq 40{,}000 \\ 0.30x - 3800 & \text{for } x > 40{,}000 \end{cases}$$

a) Graph the function $T(x)$.
b) Determine $\lim_{x \to 40{,}000} T(x)$.

Computer Exercises

Use a computer to generate a table of x and $f(x)$ values to determine each of the following.

50. $\lim\limits_{x \to 2} \dfrac{x - 2}{x^2 - 4}$

51. $\lim\limits_{x \to 6} \dfrac{x^2 - 36}{x - 6}$

52. $\lim\limits_{x \to \infty} x^{1/x}$

53. $\lim\limits_{x \to 0^+} x^x$

54. $\lim\limits_{x \to 1} \dfrac{x^3 + x^2 - 2x}{x^3 - x}$

55. $\lim\limits_{x \to 3} \dfrac{x^3 + 2x^2 - 15x}{x^3 - x^2 - 6x}$

2-2 • CONTINUITY

Look at the graphs in Figure 2-9. Notice that the graph of $y = x^2$ has no breaks, whereas the graph of $y = 1/(x - 3)^2$ has a break at $x = 3$. Since the graph of the function defined by $y = x^2$ has no breaks, it is said to be continuous at all values of x. In other words, we can trace this graph without lifting our pencil from the paper. Since the graph of the function defined by $y = 1/(x - 3)^2$ has a break at $x = 3$, it is said to be discontinuous at $x = 3$.

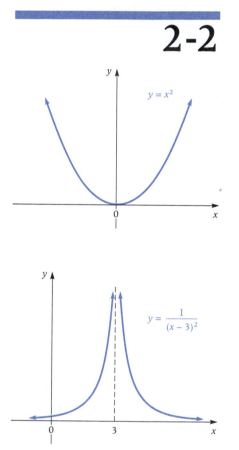

> In general, a function $f(x)$ is **continuous** at $x = a$ if its graph has no break at $x = a$.

This definition is a graphical approach to the concept of continuity. Continuity can be defined in terms of limits. Specifically, a function $f(x)$ is continuous at $x = a$ if

$$\lim_{x \to a} f(x) = f(a)$$

The above statement implies that a function is continuous at $x = a$ if the limit of the function as x approaches a equals the value of the function at $x = a$. This also implies that the function must be defined at $x = a$ and that the limit of the function as x approaches a must exist. We summarize below.

FIGURE 2-9

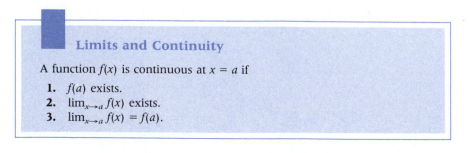

Limits and Continuity

A function $f(x)$ is continuous at $x = a$ if

1. $f(a)$ exists.
2. $\lim_{x \to a} f(x)$ exists.
3. $\lim_{x \to a} f(x) = f(a)$.

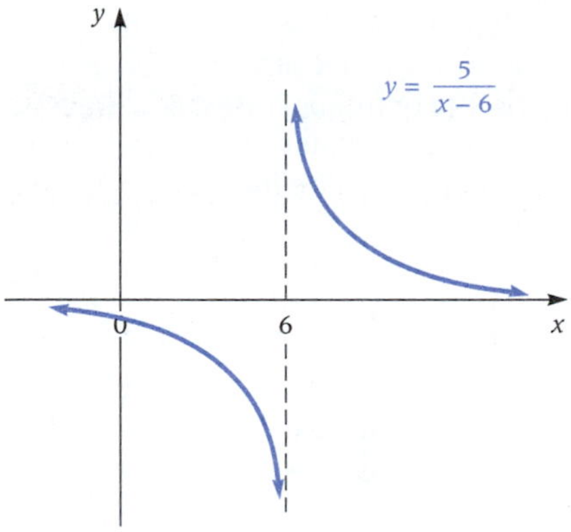

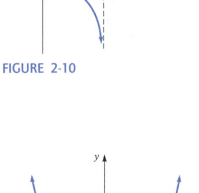

FIGURE 2-10

• **EXAMPLE 2-9** _____

Look at the graph of $f(x) = 5/(x - 6)$ in Figure 2-10.

a) Is $f(x)$ continuous at $x = 8$?
b) Is $f(x)$ continuous at $x = 6$?

Solutions

a) The function is continuous at $x = 8$ since its graph has no break at $x = 8$.
b) The function is not continuous at $x = 6$ since its graph has a break at $x = 6$. In terms of limits, the function is not continuous at $x = 6$ because $f(6)$ is undefined (does not exist). This violates condition 1 of our definition on page 112.

Continuity Over an Interval

Observing the graph of Figure 2-10, note that the function is continuous at all values of x to the right of $x = 6$. Another way of stating this is to say that $f(x)$ *is continuous over the interval* x > 6. Also, note in Figure 2-10, that the function $f(x)$ is continuous at all values of x to the left of $x = 6$. Thus, we say that $f(x)$ *is continuous over the interval* x < 6. Thus, we state the following.

> A function is **continuous over an interval** if it is continuous at each point in the interval.

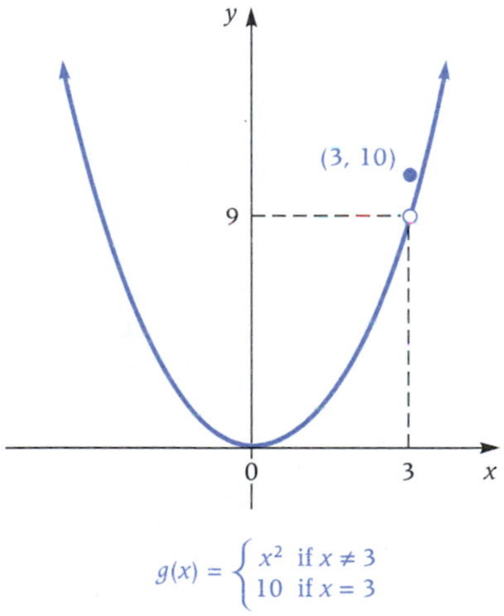

$g(x) = \begin{cases} x^2 & \text{if } x \neq 3 \\ 10 & \text{if } x = 3 \end{cases}$

FIGURE 2-11

• **EXAMPLE 2-10** _____

A function is defined as follows:

$$g(x) = \begin{cases} x^2 & \text{if } x \neq 3 \\ 10 & \text{if } x = 3 \end{cases}$$

The graph of $g(x)$ appears in Figure 2-11.

a) Is $g(x)$ continuous at $x = 2$?
b) Where is $g(x)$ discontinuous? Where is $g(x)$ continuous?

Solutions

a) This function is continuous at $x = 2$ since its graph has no break at $x = 2$.
b) This function is discontinuous at $x = 3$ since its graph has a break at $x = 3$. In terms of limits, $g(x)$ is discontinuous at $x = 3$ because condition 3 of our definition of continuity on page 112 is violated. In other words, $\lim_{x \to 3} g(x) \neq g(3)$ since $\lim_{x \to 3} g(x) = 9$, but $g(3) = 10$. We note that $g(x)$ is continuous over the intervals $x < 3$ and $x > 3$.

• **EXAMPLE 2-11** _____

Where is $f(x) = (x^2 - 4)/(x - 2)$ discontinuous? Since

$$\frac{x^2 - 4}{x - 2} = \frac{(x - 2)(x + 2)}{(x - 2)} = x + 2$$

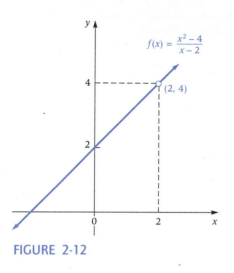

$f(x) = \dfrac{x^2 - 4}{x - 2}$

(2, 4)

FIGURE 2-12

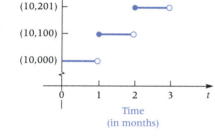

(10,303.01)

(10,201)

(10,100)

(10,000)

Time
(in months)

FIGURE 2-13

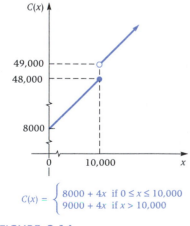

$C(x)$

49,000

48,000

8000

10,000

$C(x) = \begin{cases} 8000 + 4x & \text{if } 0 \le x \le 10{,}000 \\ 9000 + 4x & \text{if } x > 10{,}000 \end{cases}$

FIGURE 2-14

$f(x) = x + 2$ if $x \ne 2$. The graph of $f(x)$ is the straight line $y = x + 2$ minus the point (2, 4) (see Figure 2-12). Since the graph of $f(x)$ has a break at $x = 2$, $f(x)$ is discontinuous at $x = 2$. In terms of limits, $f(x)$ is discontinuous at $x = 2$ because $f(2)$ is undefined (does not exist). Therefore, condition 1 of our definition of continuity on page 112 is violated. Thus, $g(x)$ is continuous over the intervals $x < 2$ and $x > 2$.

• **EXAMPLE 2-12   Compound Interest.** _____

Ten thousand dollars is deposited into a savings account for 3 months at an interest rate of 12% compounded monthly. The interest rate per compounding period is 12%/12, or 1% per month. A full month must pass before interest is added.

At the end of the first month, the account's balance is

$$10{,}000 + 10{,}000(.01) = \$10{,}100$$

At the end of the second month, the account's balance is

$$10{,}100 + 10{,}100(.01) = \$10{,}201$$

At the end of the third month, the account's balance is

$$10{,}201 + 10{,}201(.01) = \$10{,}303.01$$

A graph of the *account's balance* versus *time, t (in months)*, appears in Figure 2-13. Where is the graph discontinuous?

Solution

Since the graph has breaks at $t = 1$, $t = 2$, and $t = 3$, it is discontinuous at $t = 1$, $t = 2$, and $t = 3$. These discontinuities occur at the end of each month when interest is computed and added to the account's balance.

• **EXAMPLE 2-13   Cost Analysis.** _____

Technic, Inc., manufactures electronic circuitry for computers. For a particular unit, the TE104, there is a variable cost of $4 per unit and a fixed cost of $8000 for the first 10,000 units produced. If the number of units manufactured exceeds 10,000, the fixed cost increases by $1000.

a)   Define the cost function.
b)   Graph the cost function.
c)   Where is the cost function discontinuous?

Solutions

a)   If $C(x)$ is the cost of manufacturing x units of TE104,

$$C(x) = \begin{cases} 8000 + 4x & \text{if } 0 \le x \le 10{,}000 \\ 9000 + 4x & \text{if } x > 10{,}000 \end{cases}$$

b)   The graph of $C(x)$ appears in Figure 2-14.
c)   Since the graph of $C(x)$ has a break at $x = 10{,}000$, then $C(x)$ is discontinuous at $x = 10{,}000$.

In the previous section, we stated limit properties, which we used to determine limits of some functions. Similar properties hold for continuity. We state these in the box below.

> **SUMMARY**
>
> **Continuity Properties**
>
> 1. *Constant function.* If $f(x) = k$ where k is a constant, then $f(x)$ is continuous for all x. In other words, a constant function is continuous for all values of x.
> 2. *Power functions.* Functions of the form $f(x) = x^n$ and $g(x) = \sqrt[n]{x}$, where n is a positive integer, are continuous for all values x of their respective domains.
> 3. *Sum, difference, and product.* If $f(x)$ and $g(x)$ are continuous at a point, then $f(x) + g(x)$, $f(x) - g(x)$, and $f(x) \cdot g(x)$ are continuous at that point.
> 4. *Quotient.* If $f(x)$ and $g(x)$ are continuous at a point, then $f(x)/g(x)$ is continuous at that point provided that $g(x) \neq 0$ at the point.

We also include the following statement about continuity regarding polynomial and rational functions. This statement follows directly from the continuity properties.

> **Continuity for Polynomial and Rational Functions**
>
> Any polynomial function is continuous at all values of x. Any rational function is continuous at all values of x, where its denominator does not equal 0.

Exercises 2-2

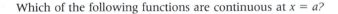

Which of the following functions are continuous at $x = a$?

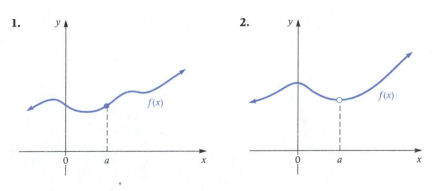

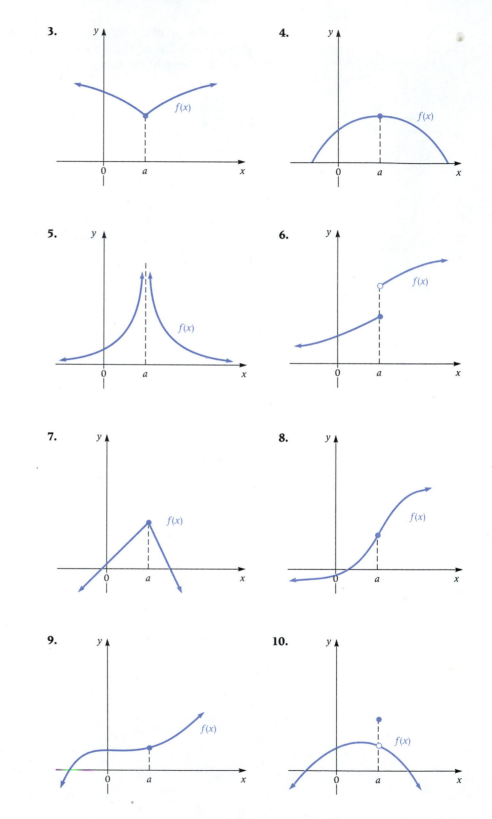

3.

4.

5.

6.

7.

8.

9.

10.

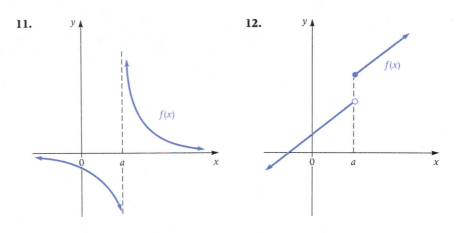

13. Graph $f(x) = 5/x^3$. Where is this function discontinuous?

14. Graph $f(x) = 4/x^2$. Where is this function discontinuous?

15. Graph the following function:

$$f(x) = \begin{cases} x^3 & \text{if } x \neq 2 \\ 10 & \text{if } x = 2 \end{cases}$$

Where is this function discontinuous?

16. Graph the following function:

$$g(x) = \begin{cases} x^4 & \text{if } x \neq 1 \\ 2 & \text{if } x = 1 \end{cases}$$

Where is this function discontinuous?

17. Graph $f(x) = (x^2 - 25)/(x - 5)$. Where is this function discontinuous?

18. Graph $g(x) = (x^2 - 81)/(x + 9)$. Where is this function discontinuous?

19. *Compound interest.* One-hundred thousand dollars is deposited into a savings account for 1 year at 12% compounded quarterly. If interest is added at the end of each quarter,
   a) Find the account's balance for each quarter.
   b) Draw a graph of the account's balance versus time, t (in quarters).
   c) Where is the graph in part b discontinuous?

20. *Cost analysis.* Gameron, Inc., manufactures games for computers. For a particular game, there is a variable cost of $10 per unit and a fixed cost of $20,000 for the first 100,000 units produced. If the number of units produced exceeds 100,000, the fixed cost increases by $5000.
   a) Define the cost function.
   b) Graph the cost function.
   c) Where is the cost function discontinuous?

21. *Cost analysis.* A company makes office supplies. For one of its products, there is a variable cost of $30 per unit and a fixed cost of $40,000 for the first 50,000 units produced. If the number of units produced exceeds 50,000, the fixed cost increases by $10,000.
   a) Define the cost function.
   b) Graph the cost function.
   c) Where is the cost function discontinuous?

22. The **greatest integer function** is defined as:

$$f(x) = [x] = \begin{cases} \text{the greatest integar that} \\ \text{is less than or equal to } x \end{cases}$$

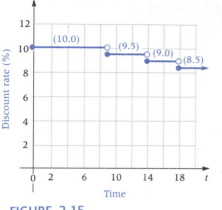

FIGURE 2-15

Specifically, $f(4.73) = [4.73] = 4, f(8.641) = [8.641] = 8$, and $f(-2.315) = [-2.315] = -3$, etc. For a positive number, x, this function cuts off the decimal portion of x. For a negative non-integer, x, this function associates the next lower integer.

    a) Graph $f(x)$ for $-2 \le x \le 4$.

    b) Where is this function discontinuous?

23. *Tax function.* Consider the tax function of Figure 2-4.

    a) Where is this function discontinuous?

    b) Where is this function continuous?

24. *Discount rate.* The interest rate charged by Federal Reserve banks for direct loans to member banks is called the *discount rate*. Figure 2-15 gives a graph of the discount rate for some time period. Where is the function discontinuous?

25. *Chemical production.* A chemical company discovers that the yield, y, of a given chemical process is dependent on its temperature, x (in degrees Celsius), as by the function

$$f(x) = \begin{cases} -(x - 120)^2 + 600 & \text{for} \quad 100 \le x \le 120 \\ -(x - 140)^2 + 1050 & \text{for} \quad 120 < x \le 140 \end{cases}$$

    a) Graph $f(x)$.

    b) For which value(s) of x is $f(x)$ discontinuous?

2-3 • AVERAGE RATE OF CHANGE

At the same instant that a test driver begins his journey around a track, a stopwatch is started. The function defined by

$$y = f(x) = 10x^2 \qquad (x \ge 0)$$

expresses the total distance, y (in miles), traveled by the driver during the first x hours. Thus, during the first 3 hours, the driver has traveled a total distance of

$$y = f(3) = 10(3)^2 = 90 \text{ miles}$$

During the first 5 hours, the driver has traveled a total distance of

$$y = f(5) = 10(5)^2 = 250 \text{ miles}$$

We now pose the following question:

What is the driver's average speed during the time interval between the end of the third hour and the end of the fifth hour?

Figure 2-16 gives a graph of $y = f(x) = 10x^2$, where $x \ge 0$. Since the driver has traveled 90 miles during the first 3 hours and 250 miles during the first 5 hours, he has traveled

$$\Delta y = 250 - 90 = 160 \text{ miles}$$

during the time interval $\Delta x = 5 - 3 = 2$ from $x = 3$ to $x = 5$ (see Figure 2-16). Dividing by the length of the time interval, we have

$$\frac{\Delta y}{\Delta x} = \frac{250 - 90}{5 - 3} = \frac{160}{2} = 80 \text{ miles per hour}$$

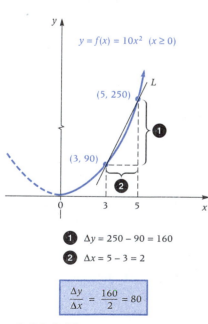

① $\Delta y = 250 - 90 = 160$

② $\Delta x = 5 - 3 = 2$

$$\frac{\Delta y}{\Delta x} = \frac{160}{2} = 80$$

FIGURE 2-16

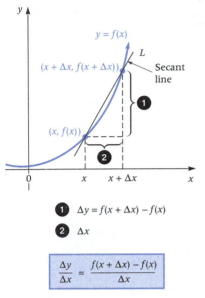

➊ $\Delta y = f(x + \Delta x) - f(x)$

➋ Δx

$$\frac{\Delta y}{\Delta x} = \frac{f(x + \Delta x) - f(x)}{\Delta x}$$

FIGURE 2-17

as the **average speed,** or **average rate of change** of distance with respect to time. Note that the average speed (or average rate of change of distance with respect to time) is the slope of the straight line, L, passing through the points $(3, 90)$ and $(5, 250)$ of the graph of $y = f(x) = 10x^2$ in Figure 2-16. Such a straight line intersecting the graph in at least two points is called a **secant line** (Figure 2-17).

In general, the slope of a secant line passing through two points of the graph of a function is the average rate of change of that function over the respective interval. Observing Figure 2-17, note that the secant line passes through the points $(x, f(x))$ and $(x + \Delta x, f(x + \Delta x))$. Thus, the average rate of change of the function $y = f(x)$ over the interval from x to $x + \Delta x$ is given by the expression

$$\frac{f(x + \Delta x) - f(x)}{\Delta x}$$

Note that Δx is the horizontal distance between the two points $(x, f(x))$ and $(x + \Delta x, f(x + \Delta x))$. We summarize below.

Average Rate of Change

The average rate of change of a function $f(x)$ is given by the formula

$$\frac{f(x + \Delta x) - f(x)}{\Delta x} \qquad (\Delta x \neq 0)$$

The above expression, called the **difference quotient,** gives the slope of the secant line passing through $(x, f(x))$ and $(x + \Delta x, f(x + \Delta x))$, as illustrated in Figure 2-17.

We now give a procedure for determining a general formula for the difference quotient for any given function $f(x)$.

To Determine a Formula for the Difference Quotient

Step 1   Given a formula for $f(x)$, replace x with $x + \Delta x$ to obtain

$$f(x + \Delta x)$$

Step 2   Subtract $f(x)$ from the result of step 1 (and simplify) to obtain

$$\Delta y = f(x + \Delta x) - f(x)$$

Step 3   Divide the result of step 2 by Δx (and simplify) to obtain a formula for the difference quotient

$$\frac{\Delta y}{\Delta x} = \frac{f(x + \Delta x) - f(x)}{\Delta x}$$

This result gives a formula for the *average rate of change* for the given function $f(x)$ as we move from x to $x + \Delta x$.

As an example, we compute a formula for the difference quotient (i.e., the average rate of change) of the function defined by

$$y = f(x) = 10x^2$$

Step 1   We replace x with $x + \Delta x$ to obtain

$$
\begin{aligned}
f(x + \Delta x) &= 10(x + \Delta x)^2 \\
&= 10[x^2 + 2x(\Delta x) + (\Delta x)^2] \\
&= 10x^2 + 20x(\Delta x) + 10(\Delta x)^2
\end{aligned}
$$

Step 2   We subtract $f(x)$ from the result of step 1 to obtain

$$y = f(x + \Delta x) - f(x)$$

$$= \overbrace{10x^2 + 20x(\Delta x) + 10(\Delta x)^2}^{f(x+\Delta x)} - \overbrace{10x^2}^{f(x)}$$

$$= 20x(\Delta x) + 10(\Delta x)^2$$

Step 3   We divide the result of step 2 by Δx to obtain

$$
\begin{aligned}
\frac{\Delta y}{\Delta x} &= \frac{f(x + \Delta x) - f(x)}{\Delta x} \\
&= \frac{20x(\Delta x) + 10(\Delta x)^2}{\Delta x} \\
&= 20x + 10(\Delta x) \qquad \text{\color{blue}{Formula for Difference Quotient}}
\end{aligned}
$$

This result gives a formula for the *average rate of change* between any two points of the function $f(x)$.

Thus, if we want to determine the average rate of change (that is, the slope of the secant line) between the points $(3, 90)$ and $(5, 250)$ of $f(x) = 10x^2$, we let $x = 3$ and $\Delta x = 5 - 3 = 2$. Then

$$
\begin{aligned}
\frac{\Delta y}{\Delta x} &= 20x + 10(\Delta x) \\
&= 20(3) + 10(2) \\
&= 80
\end{aligned}
$$

is the average rate of change from $x = 3$ to $x + \Delta x = 3 + 2 = 5$. Note that this equals the result previously determined in Figure 2-16.

If $x = 3$ and $\Delta x = 1$, then

$$
\begin{aligned}
\frac{\Delta y}{\Delta x} &= 20x + 10(\Delta x) \\
&= 20(3) + 10(1) \\
&= 70
\end{aligned}
$$

is the average rate of change from $x = 3$ to $x + \Delta x = 3 + 1 = 4$. In other words, during the interval from $x = 3$ to $x = 4$, the average speed was 70 miles per hour. Observe, in Figure 2-18, that this is the slope of the secant line passing through the points $(3, 90)$ and $(4, 160)$.

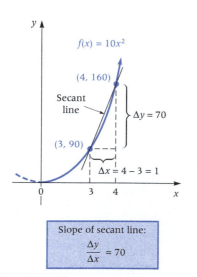

FIGURE 2-18

• EXAMPLE 2-14   **Revenue Function.** _____

The total sales revenue R, gained from selling x units of a product is given by

$$R(x) = -0.2x^2 + 8000x \qquad (0 \le x \le 20{,}000)$$

a) Determine the formula for the average rate of change of sales revenue with respect to x.

b) Use the result of part a to determine the average rate of change of sales revenue with respect to x as x changes from $x = 10{,}000$ to $x = 14{,}000$.

c) Interpret the result of part b.

Solutions

a) The formula for average rate of change (i.e., the difference quotient) is determined by finding

$$\frac{\Delta R}{\Delta x} = \frac{R(x + \Delta x) - R(x)}{\Delta x}$$

This quantity is determined as follows.

Step 1 Replace x in $R(x)$ with $x + \Delta x$ to obtain

$$\begin{aligned}
R(x + \Delta x) &= -0.2(x + \Delta x)^2 + 8000(x + \Delta x) \\
&= -0.2[x^2 + 2x(\Delta x) + (\Delta x)^2] + 8000x + 8000(\Delta x) \\
&= -0.2x^2 - 0.4x(\Delta x) - 0.2(\Delta x)^2 + 8000x + 8000(\Delta x)
\end{aligned}$$

Step 2 Subtract $R(x)$ from the result of step 1 to obtain

$$\Delta R = R(x + \Delta x) - R(x)$$

$$\overbrace{= -0.2x^2 - 0.4x(\Delta x) - 0.2(\Delta x)^2 + 8000x + 8000(\Delta x)}^{R(x + \Delta x)}$$

$$- \underbrace{(-0.2x^2 + 8000x)}_{R(x)}$$

$$= -0.4x(\Delta x) - 0.2(\Delta x)^2 + 8000(\Delta x)$$

Step 3 Divide the result of step 2 by Δx to obtain

$$\begin{aligned}
\frac{\Delta R}{\Delta x} &= \frac{R(x + \Delta x) - R(x)}{\Delta x} \\
&= \frac{-0.4x(\Delta x) - 0.2(\Delta x)^2 + 8000(\Delta x)}{\Delta x} \\
&= -0.4x - 0.2(\Delta x) + 8000 \qquad \text{\color{blue}Formula for Difference Quotient}
\end{aligned}$$

This result gives the formula for the average rate of change of sales revenue with respect to x.

b) Since x changes from $x = 10{,}000$ to $x = 14{,}000$, then $\Delta x = 14{,}000 - 10{,}000 = 4000$. Substituting $x = 10{,}000$ and $\Delta x = 4000$ into the result of part a gives

$$\begin{aligned}
\frac{\Delta R}{\Delta x} &= -0.4x - 0.2(\Delta x) + 8000 \\
&= -0.4(10{,}000) - 0.2(4000) + 8000 \\
&= 3200
\end{aligned}$$

as the average rate of change of sales revenue with respect to x as x changes from $x = 10{,}000$ to $x = 14{,}000$. This result is illustrated graphically in Figure 2-19. Observe that the average rate of change, 3200, is the slope of the secant line in Figure 2-19.

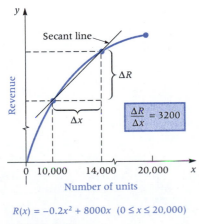

$R(x) = -0.2x^2 + 8000x \quad (0 \le x \le 20{,}000)$

FIGURE 2-19

c) The result of part b is interpreted as follows: As x changes from $x = 10{,}000$ to $x = 14{,}000$, an additional unit sold yields $3200 of sales revenue, on the average.

•

Direct Computation of Average Rate of Change

The average rate of change between two specific points of a function can be computed directly without having to determine the general formula for the difference quotient.

As an example, we return to the function defined by

$$y = f(x) = 10x^2$$

and compute the *average rate of change* from $x = 3$ to $x = 4$. Using the formula

$$\frac{\Delta y}{\Delta x} = \frac{f(x + \Delta x) - f(x)}{\Delta x}$$

we substitute $x = 3$ and $\Delta x = 4 - 3 = 1$ into the above formula to obtain

$$\frac{\Delta y}{\Delta x} = \frac{f(3 + 1) - f(3)}{1}$$

$$= \frac{f(4) - f(3)}{1}$$

Since $f(4) = 10(4^2) = 160$ and $f(3) = 10(3^2) = 90$, the above formula becomes

$$\frac{\Delta y}{\Delta x} = \frac{160 - 90}{1}$$

$$= \frac{70}{1} = 70 \qquad \text{Average Rate of Change}$$

Note that this result agrees with that previously obtained in Figure 2-18.

• **EXAMPLE 2-15** _____

Look at the graph of

$$f(x) = x^3$$

given in Figure 2-20. Use a calculator to compute the slopes of the secant lines corresponding to the respective values of Δx, and write the results in the Table 2-3.

Solutions

For $x = 1$ and $\Delta x = 0.75$,

$$\frac{\Delta y}{\Delta x} = \frac{f(x + \Delta x) - f(x)}{\Delta x}$$

$$= \frac{f(1 + 0.75) - f(1)}{0.75}$$

$$= \frac{f(1.75) - f(1)}{0.75}$$

$$= \frac{5.3594 - 1}{0.75} \approx 5.8125 \qquad \text{Answer}$$

Calculator
$f(1.75) = (1.75)^3 \approx 5.3594$
$f(1) = (1)^3 = 1$

TABLE 2-3

x	Δx	$\dfrac{f(x + \Delta x) - f(x)}{\Delta x}$
1	0.75	
1	0.50	
1	0.25	

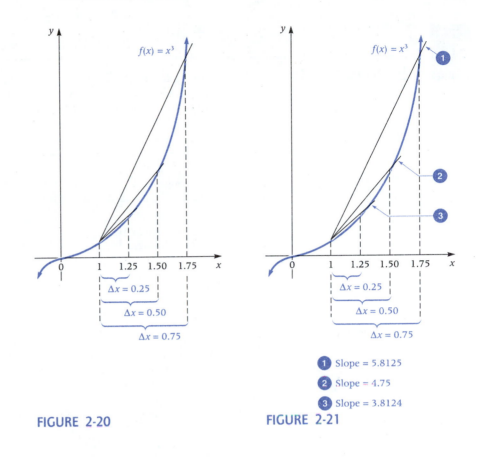

FIGURE 2-20

FIGURE 2-21

① Slope = 5.8125

② Slope = 4.75

③ Slope = 3.8124

For $x = 1$ and $\Delta x = 0.50$,

$$\frac{\Delta y}{\Delta x} = \frac{f(x + \Delta x) - f(x)}{\Delta x}$$

$$= \frac{\overbrace{f(1 + 0.50)}^{1.5} - f(1)}{0.50}$$

Calculator
$f(1.5) = (1.5)^3$
$= 3.375$

$$= \frac{3.375 - 1}{0.50} = 4.75 \qquad \text{Answer}$$

For $x = 1$ and $\Delta x = 0.25$,

$$\frac{\Delta y}{\Delta x} = \frac{f(x + \Delta x) - f(x)}{\Delta x}$$

$$= \frac{\overbrace{f(1 + 0.25)}^{1.25} - f(1)}{0.25}$$

Calculator
$f(1.25) = (1.25)^3$
≈ 1.9531

$$\approx \frac{1.9531 - 1}{0.25} = 3.8124 \qquad \text{Answer}$$

The above results are entered in Table 2-4 and also in Figure 2-21.

TABLE 2-4

x	Δx	$\dfrac{f(x + \Delta x) - f(x)}{\Delta x}$
1	0.75	5.8125
1	0.50	4.75
1	0.25	3.8124

Exercises 2-3

1. *Prime rate.* The *prime interest rate,* often called the *prime rate,* is the interest rate that banks charge their most credit-worthy borrowers. Table 2-5 gives the prime rate for a succession of weeks during a past time period.

TABLE 2-5

t time (weeks)	1	2	3	4	5	6	7	8	9	10
y prime rate (%)	15¼	16½	16¾	17¼	17¾	18½	19	19½	20	19½

Determine the average rate of change of the prime rate over the time interval from
a) $t = 2$ to $t = 6$.
b) $t = 1$ to $t = 9$.

2. *Medical research.* In a study attempting to measure bodily response to stress, a person's *systolic blood pressure* (SBP) is recorded at 1-minute intervals following a stress-inducing stimulus. The results are given in Table 2-6.

TABLE 2-6

x minutes	1	2	3	4	5	6	7	8	9	10
y SBP	160	200	190	185	180	172	156	150	148	148

Determine the average rate of change in SBP over the interval from
a) $x = 1$ to $x = 2$.
b) $x = 3$ to $x = 8$.

3. *Dow Jones average.* The graph of Figure 2-22 illustrates the Dow Jones industrial average (DJIA) during a past time period. Find the average rate of change of the DJIA over the indicated time interval.

4. *Dow Jones average.* The graph of Figure 2-23 illustrates the Dow Jones industrial average (DJIA) during a past time period. Find the average rate of change of the DJIA over the indicated time interval.

5. *Yield curve.* The graph of Figure 2-24 gives the yields on U.S. Treasury securities of various maturities on a given day. Determine the average rate of change of yield with respect of maturity from
a) $x = 2$ to $x = 10$.
b) $x = ¼$ to $x = 30$.

6. *Yield curve.* The graph of Figure 2-25 gives the yields on U.S. Treasury securities of various maturities on a given day. Determine the average rate of change of yield with respect to maturity from
a) $x = 2$ to $x = 10$.
b) $x = 2$ to $x = 30$.

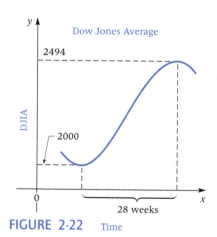

FIGURE 2-22   Time

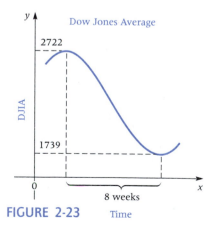

FIGURE 2-23   Time

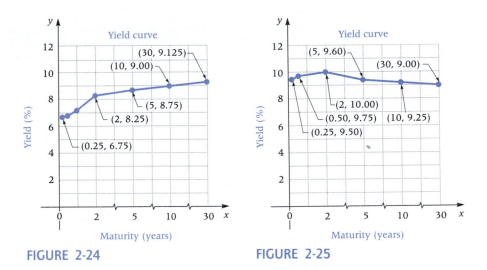

FIGURE 2-24   FIGURE 2-25

7. *Inflation rate.* A graph of the annual inflation rate for China is given in Figure 2-26. Determine the average rate of change of the inflation rate from
   a) $x = 3$ to $x = 8$.
   b) $x = 6$ to $x = 8$.
   c) $x = 3$ to $x = 5$.

8. *Learning curve.* The number of nondefectives produced by a newly hired apprentice at Hi-Tech Industries is given in Figure 2-27. Determine the average rate of change of nondefectives from
   a) $x = 2$ to $x = 5$.
   b) $x = 5$ to $x = 10$.

9. *Population growth.* The graph of Figure 2-28 gives the population of a city during a given time period. Determine the average rate of change of the population during the time interval from
   a) $x = 2$ to $x = 6$.
   b) $x = 3$ to $x = 7$.
   c) $x = 5$ to $x = 10$.

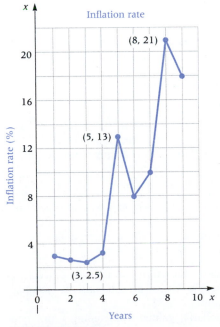

FIGURE 2-26

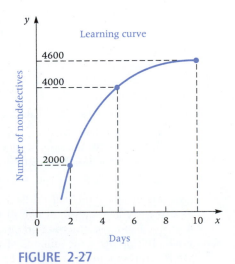

FIGURE 2-27

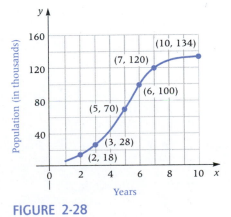

FIGURE 2-28

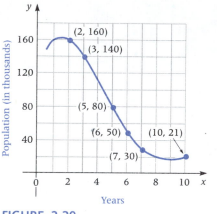

FIGURE 2-29

10. *Population decline.* The graph of Figure 2-29 gives the population of a city during a given time period. Determine the average rate of change of the population during the time interval from
   a) $x = 2$ to $x = 5$.
   b) $x = 3$ to $x = 7$.
   c) $x = 6$ to $x = 10$.

For each of the following, determine the formula for the difference quotient.

11. $f(x) = 3x$ 12. $f(x) = -6x$
13. $f(x) = -2x + 5$ 14. $f(x) = 4x - 7$
15. $f(x) = 4x^2$ 16. $f(x) = -6x^2$
17. $f(x) = x^2 - 5x + 8$ 18. $f(x) = -2x^2 + 3x$
19. $f(x) = -5x^2 + 9$ 20. $f(x) = 3x^2 - 4$
21. $f(x) = x^2 - 2x + 1$ 22. $f(x) = x^2 + 5x - 3$
23. $f(x) = 2x^2 - x + 4$ 24. $f(x) = -3x^2 + 2x + 1$
25. $f(x) = x^3$ 26. $f(x) = x^3 - 6x$
27. $f(x) = x^4$ 28. $f(x) = x^4 - 3x^2 + 1$
29. $f(x) = x^4 + x^2 + 4x$ 30. $f(x) = x^4 - 2x^2 + 3x$

For each of the following, first determine the formula for the average rate of change of y with respect to x over the interval from x to $x + \Delta x$. Then use this result to calculate the average rate of change over the given interval, and interpret this result graphically.

31. $f(x) = x^2 - 4x + 5$ from $x = 2$ to $x = 6$
32. $f(x) = x^2 - 3x$ from $x = 1$ to $x = 3$
33. $f(x) = 4x + 7$ from $x = 2$ to $x = 3$
34. $f(x) = -2x^2 + 8$ from $x = 1$ to $x = 4$
35. $f(x) = -3x^2 - 2x + 1$ from $x = 2$ to $x = 5$
36. $f(x) = x^3 - 16x$ from $x = 0$ to $x = 2$

37. *Sales revenue.* The Great Glove Company manufactures gloves. Its total sales revenue, R, is given by

$$R = f(x) = x^2 - 6x + 9 \qquad (x \geq 3)$$

where x is the number of pairs of gloves sold. Find the average rate of change of sales revenue with respect to number of pairs of gloves sold over the interval $4 \leq x \leq 6$. Show the graphical interpretation.

38. *Cost.* The total cost of producing x units of some product is given by

$$C(x) = 3x^2 + 80,000 \qquad (0 \leq x \leq 100)$$

Find the average rate of change of cost with respect to the number of units produced as x changes from $x = 50$ to $x = 55$. Interpret graphically.

39. *Cost.* The total cost, C (in millions of dollars), of producing x (in hundreds) units of a product is given by

$$C(x) = 0.5x^2 + 10,000 \qquad (0 \leq x \leq 1000)$$

Find the average rate of change of cost with respect to x as x changes from $x = 200$ to $x = 220$. Interpret graphically.

40. *Projectile.* A ball is projected vertically into the air. The function defined by

$$S(t) = -16t^2 + 192t \qquad (0 \leq t \leq 12)$$

gives the height of the ball (in feet) above the ground at time, t (in seconds). Find the average rate of change of height with respect to time as t changes from $t = 1$ to $t = 4$. Interpret graphically.

41. *Profit.* The profit, P (in millions of dollars), gained from selling x (in thousands) units of a product is given by

$$P(x) = -0.1x^2 + 4x - 30 \qquad (10 \leq x \leq 30)$$

TABLE 2-7

x	Δx	$\dfrac{f(x + \Delta x) - f(x)}{\Delta x}$
2	0.80	
2	0.40	
2	0.20	

TABLE 2-8

x	Δx	$\dfrac{f(x + \Delta x) - f(x)}{\Delta x}$
4	0.75	
4	0.50	
4	0.25	

TABLE 2-9

x	Δx	$\dfrac{f(x + \Delta x) - f(x)}{\Delta x}$
2	0.80	
2	0.40	
2	0.20	

TABLE 2-10

x	Δx	$\dfrac{f(x + \Delta x) - f(x)}{\Delta x}$
1	0.60	
1	0.40	
1	0.20	

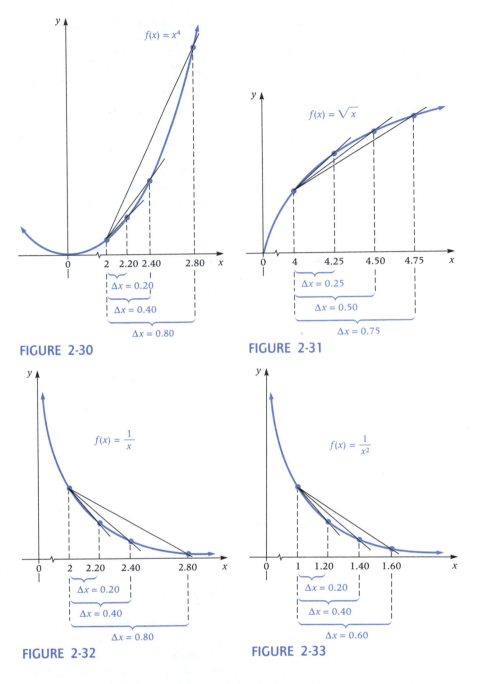

FIGURE 2-30

FIGURE 2-31

FIGURE 2-32

FIGURE 2-33

Find the average rate of change of profit with respect to x as x changes from $x = 12$ to $x = 15$. Interpret graphically.

42. Look at the graph of $f(x) = x^4$, given in Figure 2-30. Use a calculator to compute the slopes of the secant lines corresponding to the respective values of Δx, and write the results in Table 2-7.

43. Look at the graph of $f(x) = \sqrt{x}$, given in Figure 2-31. Use a calculator to compute the slopes of the secant lines corresponding to the respective values of Δx, and write the results in Table 2-8.

44. Look at the graph of $f(x) = 1/x$, given in Figure 2-32. Use a calculator to compute the slopes of the secant lines corresponding to the respective values of Δx, and write the results in Table 2-9 on page 127.

45. Look at the graph of $f(x) = 1/x^2$, given in Figure 2-33 on page 127. Use a calculator to compute the slopes of the secant lines corresponding to the respective values of Δx, and write the results in Table 2-10 on page 127.

2-4 • THE DERIVATIVE

In the previous section, we discussed the relationship between the distance, y (in miles), traveled by a driver and the time elapsed, x (in hours). These two quantities are related by the equation

$$y = f(x) = 10x^2 \qquad (x \geq 0)$$

Instantaneous Rate of Change

The formula for the average rate of change of y with respect to x over the interval from x to $x + \Delta x$ is given by

$$\frac{f(x + \Delta x) - f(x)}{\Delta x} = 20x + 10(\Delta x)$$

The average rate of change of y with respect to x when x changes from $x = 3$ to $x = 5$ is determined by substituting $x = 3$ and $\Delta x = 5 - 3 = 2$ into the formula for average rate of change, $20x + 10(\Delta x)$, to give

$$20(3) + 10(2) = 80$$

Thus, the driver's average speed during the time interval from $x = 3$ to $x = 5$ is 80 miles per hour. Graphically, this is the slope of the secant line, passing through $(3, 90)$ and $(5, 250)$ of Figure 2-34.

The driver's average speed (i.e., average rate of change of y with respect to x) during the time interval from $x = 3$ to $x = 4$ is determined by substituting $x = 3$ and $\Delta x = 4 - 3 = 1$ into the formula for average rate of change, $20x + 10(\Delta x)$, to give

$$20(3) + 10(1) = 70$$

Thus, the driver's average speed during the time interval from $x = 3$ to $x = 4$ is 70 miles per hour. Graphically, this is the slope of the secant line M, passing through $(3, 90)$ and $(4, 160)$ in Figure 2-34.

Now what is the driver's speed at $x = 3$? This result is called the **instantaneous speed** or **instantaneous rate of change** of y with respect to x at $x = 3$. It is determined by first calculating a formula for the instantaneous rate of change of y with respect to x at point $(x, f(x))$. This formula is determined by calculating the average rate of change

$$\frac{f(x + \Delta x) - f(x)}{\Delta x} = 20x + 10(\Delta x)$$

letting Δx get very small (i.e., we let $\Delta x \to 0$) to obtain

$$20x + 10(0) = 20x$$

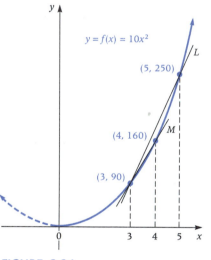

$y = f(x) = 10x^2$

$(5, 250)$

$(4, 160)$

$(3, 90)$

FIGURE 2-34

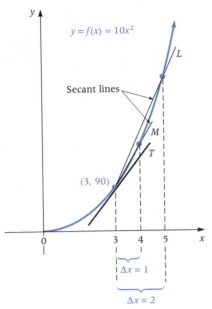

$y = f(x) = 10x^2$

L

Secant lines

M

T

(3, 90)

0   3   4   5   x

$\Delta x = 1$

$\Delta x = 2$

Observe:
As $\Delta x \to 0$, secant lines approach the tangent line T.

$f'(3) = 60$ is the slope of tangent line T.

FIGURE 2-35

This result, $20x$, is called the **derivative** of the function $f(x) = 10x^2$ and is denoted by **$f'(x)$**. Thus, the derivative

$$f'(x) = 20x$$

gives the formula for the instantaneous rate of change of y with respect to x at any point $(x, f(x))$ of the function defined by $y = f(x) = 10x^2$.

To determine the instantaneous rate of change at $x = 3$, we evaluate the derivative at $x = 3$ to obtain

$$f'(3) = 20(3) = 60$$

Thus, the driver's speed at $x = 3$ is 60 miles per hour. That is, at $x = 3$, the car's speedometer reading indicated a speed of 60 miles per hour. Graphically, this is the limit of the slopes of the secant lines L and M in Figure 2-35 as Δx approaches zero. As Δx approaches zero, the slopes of the secant lines L and M approach the slope of tangent line T. Thus, the slope of tangent line T is $f'(3)$, which equals 60. Tangent line T touches the curve $y = 10x^2$ at the point $(3, 90)$.

The instantaneous rate of change of y with respect to x at any point $(x, f(x))$ on the graph of a function $f(x)$ is given by the derivative of $f(x)$. The derivative is denoted by $f'(x)$ and is determined by calculating

$$\frac{f(x + \Delta x) - f(x)}{\Delta x}$$

and letting Δx approach zero (i.e., $\Delta x \to 0$). In other words, the derivative or the instantaneous rate of change of y with respect to x is the limit of the average rate of change as $\Delta x \to 0$ (provided this limit exists). This written as

$$f'(x) = \lim_{\Delta x \to 0} \frac{f(x + \Delta x) - f(x)}{\Delta x}$$

In summary, we state the following.

SUMMARY

Instantaneous Rate of Change

The **instantaneous rate of change of y with respect to x** at any point $(x, f(x))$ on the graph of a function $y = f(x)$ is given by the **derivative $f'(x)$** which is defined by

$$f'(x) = \lim_{\Delta x \to 0} \frac{f(x + \Delta x) - f(x)}{\Delta x}$$

provided this limit exists. Graphically, the *derivative is the slope of the straight line tangent to the graph of the function at $(x, f(x))$*, as shown in Figure 2-36. The derivative, $f'(x)$, is determined by the following procedure:

Step 1 Calculate the difference quotient

$$\frac{f(x + \Delta x) - f(x)}{\Delta x}$$

continues

SUMMARY—*Continued*

Step 2 Let $\Delta x \to 0$ and calculate the resulting limit.

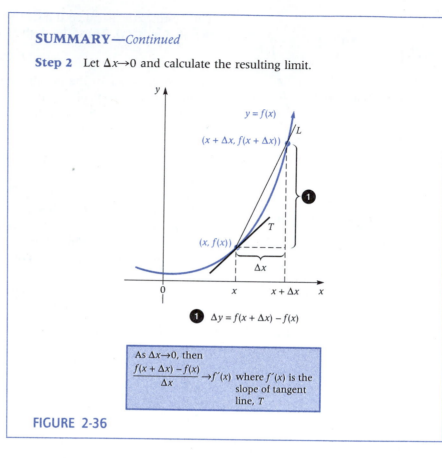

1 $\Delta y = f(x + \Delta x) - f(x)$

As $\Delta x \to 0$, then

$$\frac{f(x + \Delta x) - f(x)}{\Delta x} \to f'(x)$$ where $f'(x)$ is the slope of tangent line, T

FIGURE 2-36

• **EXAMPLE 2-16** _____

For the function defined by

$$y = f(x) = x^3$$

a) Calculate $f'(x)$.
b) Determine the instantaneous rate of change of y with respect to x at $x = 2$.
c) Find the equation of the tangent line to the graph of $f(x)$ at $x = 2$.

Solutions

a) **Step 1** Since

$$f(x + \Delta x) = (x + \Delta x)^3$$
$$= x^3 + 3x^2(\Delta x) + 3x(\Delta x)^2 + (\Delta x)^3$$

then

$$\frac{f(x + \Delta x) - f(x)}{\Delta x} = \frac{\overbrace{x^3 + 3x^2(\Delta x) + 3x(\Delta x)^2 + (\Delta x)^3}^{f(x + \Delta x)} - \overbrace{x^3}^{f(x)}}{\Delta x}$$
$$= 3x^2 + 3x(\Delta x) + (\Delta x)^2$$

Step 2 Letting $\Delta x \to 0$, we have

$$f'(x) = 3x^2$$

which we call the derivative of $f(x) = x^3$.

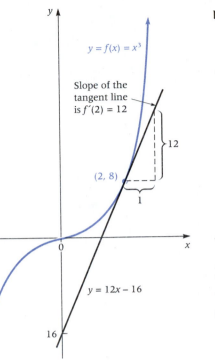

FIGURE 2-37

b) Evaluating $f'(x)$ at $x = 2$ gives

$$f'(2) = 3(2)^2$$
$$= 12$$

c) The slope of the tangent line at $x = 2$ is given by $f'(2) = 12$, as shown in Figure 2-37. Since $f(2) = 2^3 = 8$, then the point of tangency is $(2, f(2)) = (2, 8)$. Thus, the tangent line passes through $(2, 8)$ and has a slope of 12. Using the slope-intercept form, $y = mx + b$, of the equation of a straight line, we have

$$y = 12x + b$$

We determine b by substituting the coordinates of $(2, 8)$ into this equation and solving for b to obtain

$$8 = 12(2) + b$$
$$b = -16$$

Thus, the equation of the tangent line is $y = 12x - 16$.

Numerical Computation

The derivative of a function at a point can be approximated by numerical computation. As an example, we consider approximating the derivative of

$$f(x) = x^3$$

at $x = 2$ by using a calculator to compute the value of the difference quotient

$$\frac{f(x + \Delta x) - f(x)}{\Delta x}$$

at $x = 2$ and smaller and smaller values of Δx, as illustrated in Table 2-11(a) and (b) and Figure 2-38(a) and (b) on page 132.

Observe that Table 2-11(a) has positive Δx-values, and, therefore, the secant lines are drawn to the right of $x = 2$, as illustrated in Figure 2-38(a). On the other hand, Table 2-11(b) has negative Δx-values, and, therefore, the secant lines are drawn to the left of $x = 2$, as illustrated in Figure 2-38(b). Note that as $\Delta x \to 0$, the difference quotient, $[f(x + \Delta x) - f(x)]/\Delta x$, approaches 12 for both positive and negative Δx-values. Graphically, the slopes of the secant lines to both the *right* and the *left* of $x = 2$ are approaching 12. Recall that this agrees with our previous computation of $f'(2)$ in Example 2-16.

Round-Off Error

Computers are also used to numerically approximate derivatives. We hasten to mention that numerical approximation of derivatives via the difference quotient—whether by calculator or by computer—entails consideration of round-off error. Round-off error is the result of the fact that a computer or calculator stores, processes, and displays numbers to a limited number of significant digits. Although further discussion of this issue is beyond the scope of this text, it should be noted that computer or calculator results of the numerical approximation of derivatives should always be checked for reasonableness.

TABLE 2-11(a)

x	Δx	$\dfrac{f(x + \Delta x) - f(x)}{\Delta x}$
2	0.1	12.610000
2	0.01	12.060100
2	0.001	12.006001
2	0.0001	12.000600
2	0.00001	12.000014

approaching 12

TABLE 2-11(b)

x	Δx	$\dfrac{f(x + \Delta x) - f(x)}{\Delta x}$
2	-0.1	11.410000
2	-0.01	11.940100
2	-0.001	11.994001
2	-0.0001	11.999397
2	-0.00001	11.999954

approaching 12

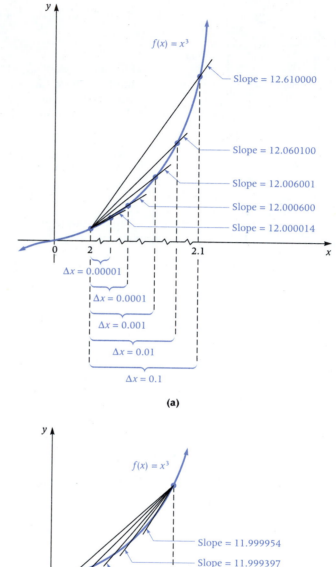

(a)

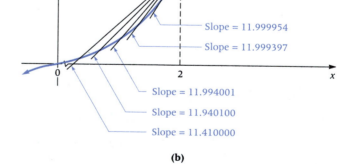

(b)

FIGURE 2-38

Exercises 2-4

For each of the following functions, find the formula for $f'(x)$.

1. $f(x) = x^2$
2. $f(x) = 4x^2$
3. $f(x) = 6x^3$
4. $f(x) = x^3$
5. $f(x) = x^4$
6. $f(x) = -3x^4$
7. $f(x) = 3x$
8. $f(x) = 5x$
9. $f(x) = x^2 - 5x + 7$
10. $f(x) = x^2 + 3x + 1$
11. $f(x) = -3x^2 + 4x$
12. $f(x) = -2x^2 + 6x$
13. $f(x) = 5x^2 + 6$
14. $f(x) = 3x^2 + 11$
15. $f(x) = x^3 - x^2 + 5x$
16. $f(x) = x^3 + 2x^2 + 9x$

For each of the following functions, find $f'(1), f'(2)$, and $f'(-2)$.

17. $f(x) = x^2 - 4x + 1$
18. $f(x) = x^2 + 3x + 2$
19. $f(x) = x^2 + 6x$
20. $f(x) = x^2 - 4x$
21. $f(x) = -3x^2 + 5$
22. $f(x) = -2x^2 + 9$
23. $f(x) = x^2 - 5x + 4$
24. $f(x) = x^2 - 5x + 2$
25. $f(x) = x^3 - 5x^2 + 7$
26. $f(x) = x^3 - 2x^2 + 5$
27. $f(x) = 2x^3 - 3x^2 + 9$
28. $f(x) = 4x^3 - 3x^2 + 1$

For each of the following functions, find the instantaneous rate of change of y with respect to x at each of the given points. Illustrate graphically.

29. $y = f(x) = x^2 - 10x$ at $x = 2$ and $x = 3$
30. $y = f(x) = x^3 + 2$ at $x = 3$ and $x = 4$
31. $y = f(x) = 5x + 7$ at $x = 4$ and $x = 5$
32. $y = f(x) = -x^2 + 8$ at $x = 1$ and $x = 3$

Find the derivative of each of the following.

33. $y = f(x) = 3x^2 - 5$
34. $y = f(x) = 2x^3 + 8$
35. $y = f(x) = 5x^2 - 3x + 1$
36. $y = f(x) = 4x - 6$
37. $y = f(x) = x^2 - 3x + 5$
38. $y = f(x) = x^4 - 5$

For each of the following functions, find the instantaneous rate of change of y with respect to x at the given point. Also, find the equation of the tangent line. Then graph the function and its tangent line on the same axis system.

39. $y = f(x) = x^2 - 4x + 5$ at $x = 2$
40. $y = f(x) = x^2 - 3x$ at $x = 1$
41. $y = f(x) = 4x + 7$ at $x = 2$
42. $y = f(x) = -2x^2 + 8$ at $(1, 6)$
43. $y = f(x) = x^2 - 16x$ at $x = 1$
44. $y = f(x) = x^4 - 36x^2$ at $x = 3$

45. *Sales revenue.* The Quality Hat Company manufactures hats. Its total sales revenue, y, is given by
$$y = f(x) = -3x^2 + 60x \qquad (0 \le x \le 20)$$
where x is the number of hats sold.
   a) Calculate $f'(x)$
   b) Calculate the instantaneous rate of change of sales revenue with respect to the number of hats sold at $x = 3$.
   c) Find the equation of the tangent line to the graph of $y = f(x) = -3x^2 + 60x$ at $x = 3$.

Numerical Computation

46. Look at the graph of $f(x) = x^4$ in Figure 2-39 on page 135. Use a calculator to approximate $f'(2)$ by filling in the difference quotient columns of Table 2-12(a) and (b). Draw the graph for Table 2-12(b). As $\Delta x \to 0$, the values of the difference quotient appear to be approaching what number?

TABLE 2-12(a)

x	Δx	$\dfrac{f(x + \Delta x) - f(x)}{\Delta x}$
2	0.1	
2	0.01	
2	0.001	
2	0.0001	
2	0.00001	

TABLE 2-12(b)

x	Δx	$\dfrac{f(x + \Delta x) - f(x)}{\Delta x}$
2	−0.1	
2	−0.01	
2	−0.001	
2	−0.0001	
2	−0.00001	

approaching ?

47. Look at the graph of $f(x) = \sqrt{x}$ in Figure 2-40 on page 135. Use a calculator to approximate $f'(4)$ by filling in the difference quotient columns of Tables 2-13(a) and (b). Draw the graph for Table 2-13(b). As $\Delta x \to 0$, the values of the difference quotient appear to be approaching what number?

TABLE 2-13(a)

x	Δx	$\dfrac{f(x + \Delta x) - f(x)}{\Delta x}$
4	0.1	
4	0.01	
4	0.001	
4	0.0001	
4	0.00001	

TABLE 2-13(b)

x	Δx	$\dfrac{f(x + \Delta x) - f(x)}{\Delta x}$
4	−0.1	
4	−0.01	
4	−0.001	
4	−0.0001	
4	−0.00001	

approaching ?

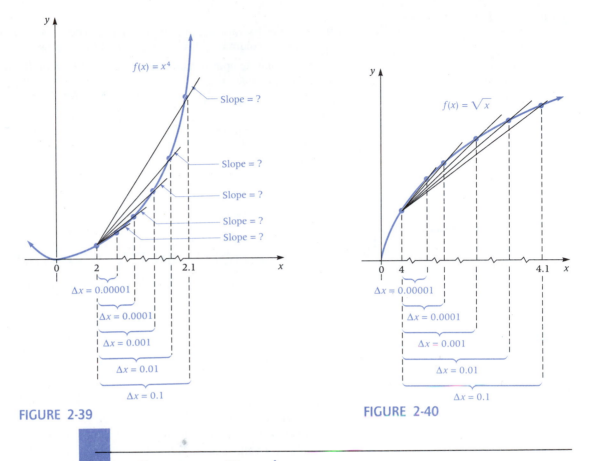

FIGURE 2-39

FIGURE 2-40

Computer Exercises

48. If $f(x) = 1/x$, use a computer to approximate $f'(2)$ by filling in the difference quotient columns of Table 2-14(a) and (b).

TABLE 2-14(a)

x	Δx	$\dfrac{f(x + \Delta x) - f(x)}{\Delta x}$
2	0.1	
2	0.01	
2	0.001	
2	0.0001	
2	0.00001	

TABLE 2-14(b)

x	Δx	$\dfrac{f(x + \Delta x) - f(x)}{\Delta x}$
2	−0.1	
2	−0.01	
2	−0.001	
2	−0.0001	
2	−0.00001	

TABLE 2-15(a)

x	Δx	$\dfrac{f(x + \Delta x) - f(x)}{\Delta x}$
1	0.1	
1	0.01	
1	0.001	
1	0.0001	
1	0.00001	

TABLE 2-15(b)

x	Δx	$\dfrac{f(x + \Delta x) - f(x)}{\Delta x}$
1	−0.1	
1	−0.01	
1	−0.001	
1	−0.0001	
1	−0.00001	

49. If $f(x) = 1/x^2$, use a computer to approximate $f'(1)$ by filling in the difference quotient columns of Table 2-15 (a) and (b) on page 135.

Use a computer to approximate the derivative of each of the following functions at the indicated value of x.

50. $f(x) = 3x + 4$, $x = 5$

51. $f(x) = 7x - 2$, $x = -1$

52. $f(x) = 5x^2 + 3x - 2$, $x = 2$

53. $f(x) = 3x^2 - 2x + 5$, $x = 1$

54. $f(x) = (3x + 4)/(x - 5)$, $x = 1$

55. $f(x) = (4x - 7)/(x + 3)$, $x = 2$

56. $f(x) = \sqrt{5x + 4}$, $x = 1$

57. $f(x) = \sqrt{2x + 10}$, $x = 3$

58. $f(x) = 3/(\sqrt{x} + 5)$, $x = 4$

59. $f(x) = 5/(\sqrt{x} + 8)$, $x = 9$

2-5 • DIFFERENTIABILITY AND CONTINUITY

Up to this point, we have defined the derivative of a function $f(x)$ to be

$$f'(x) = \lim_{\Delta x \to 0} \frac{f(x + \Delta x) - f(x)}{\Delta x}$$

Differentiability

If this limit does not exist at certain values of x, the function $f(x)$ does not have a derivative at those values of x. In general, if a function $f(x)$ has a derivative at $x = a$, then $f(x)$ is said to be **differentiable** at $x = a$.

In this section, we will show situations where a function is not differentiable at a value of x—say, $x = a$. Recall that the derivative of a function $f(x)$ evaluated at $x = a$ is the slope of the tangent line to the graph of the function at $(a, f(a))$. Thus, if the graph of the function has a vertical tangent line at $x = a$, the function is not differentiable at $x = a$ since the slope of a vertical line is undefined.

We summarize as follows.

> ### Differentiability
>
> A function is said to be differentiable at a point if its derivative exists at that point.
>
> **Graphical Interpretation.** A function is said to be differentiable at a point if its graph has a unique nonvertical tangent line at that point.

As an example, consider the function

$$f(x) = x^{2/3}$$

Its graph appears in Figure 2-41. Observe that the graph of $f(x)$ has unique nonvertical tangent lines at all values of x except $x = 0$. At $x = 0$, notice how the graph of $f(x)$ comes to a sharp point, and, therefore, we can draw many tangent lines, one of which is the (vertical) y-axis. Let us see what

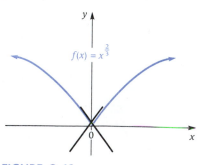

$f(x) = x^{\frac{2}{3}}$

FIGURE 2-41

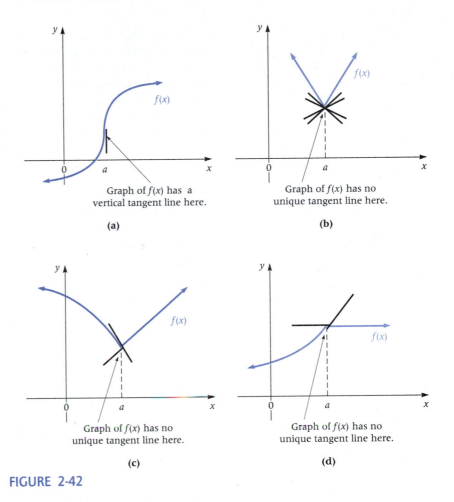

FIGURE 2-42

happens to the derivative at $x = 0$. Since $f(x) = x^{2/3}$, then, as will be shown in Example 2-20, we determine that

$$f'(x) = \frac{2}{3}x^{-1/3}$$

$$= \frac{2}{3\sqrt[3]{x}}$$

Hence, we have

$$f'(0) = \frac{2}{3\sqrt[3]{0}} \qquad \text{which is undefined}$$

Thus, the function $f(x)$ has no derivative at $x = 0$. Observe that $f(x)$ has a derivative at all other values of x since the ratio $2/3\sqrt[3]{x}$ is defined for all values of x except $x = 0$. Figure 2-42(a) contains the graph of another function that has a vertical tangent line at $x = a$ and, thus, is not differentiable at $x = a$.

If the graph of a function has no tangent line at $x = a$, the function is not differentiable at $x = a$. Figures 2-42(b), (c), and (d) contains graphs of functions that do not have tangent lines at $x = a$ and, hence, are not differentiable at $x = a$.

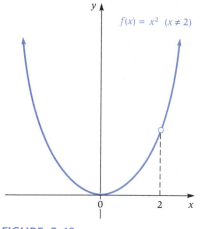

FIGURE 2-43

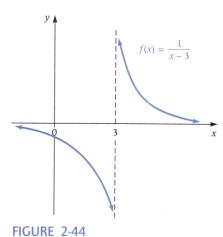

FIGURE 2-44

If a function is not defined at a value of x, then it is not differentiable there. Specifically, let us consider the function defined by $f(x) = x^2$ for all values of x except $x = 2$. The graph of this function is the parabola $y = x^2$ excluding the point $(2, 4)$ (see Figure 2-43). Since the point $(2, 4)$ does not belong to the function $f(x)$ as defined, the graph of $f(x)$ has a break at $(2, 4)$. Thus, we cannot evaluate $f(2)$ to use in the definition of the derivative $f'(x) = \lim_{\Delta x \to 0} [f(x + \Delta x) - f(x)]/\Delta x$. Hence, there is no tangent line to the graph of $f(x)$ at $(2, 4)$, and $f(x)$ is not differentiable there.

Continuity

The graph of Figure 2-43 again brings up the topic of **continuity.** Recall that a function $f(x)$ is continuous at all values of x if its graph has no breaks. Thus, the function in Figure 2-43 is not continuous at $x = 2$, but is continuous at all other values of x.

Continuity and Differentiability

Observe that the rational function

$$f(x) = \frac{1}{x - 3}$$

whose graph appears in Figure 2-44, is continuous at all values of x except $x = 3$. Note that its derivative (which will be determined in Example 2-34), is

$$f'(x) = \frac{-1}{(x - 3)^2}$$

and is undefined at $x = 3$.

The functions in Figures 2-43 and 2-44 illustrate the fact that if a function $f(x)$ is not continuous at a value of x, then it is not differentiable there. Do not misinterpret this statement by concluding that if a function $f(x)$ is continuous at a value of x, then it is differentiable there. This is not necessarily true. If we observe the graph in Figure 2-41, we see a function, $f(x) = x^{2/3}$, which is continuous at $x = 0$, but not differentiable there. An inspection of the graphs in Figure 2-42 reveals functions continuous at $x = a$, but not differentiable there.

We now state, without proof, the following facts, which are usually proven in more formal calculus texts.

> 1. If a function is differentiable at a point, then it is continuous at that point.
> 2. If a function is not continuous at a point, then it is not differentiable at that point.

We now summarize on pages 139-140 situations where a function is not differentiable.

• EXAMPLE 2-17

For each of the following functions, study its derivative and state where the derivative does not exist. The solutions are given at the bottom of page 140.

Function	*Derivative*

a) $f(x) = (x - 7)^{5/2}$ $\qquad f'(x) = \dfrac{5}{2}(\sqrt{x - 7})^3$

b) $f(x) = (8 - x)^{1/5}$ $\qquad f'(x) = \dfrac{-1}{5(\sqrt[5]{8 - x})^4}$

The solutions are given at the bottom of page 140.

SUMMARY

Situations Where a Function Is Not Differentiable

A function is not differentiable

1. Where the graph of the function has a *sharp point* (see Figure 2-45).

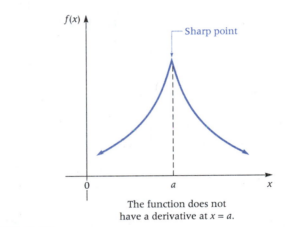

The function does not
have a derivative at $x = a$.

FIGURE 2-45

2. Where the graph of the function has a *vertical tangent line* (see Figure 2-46).

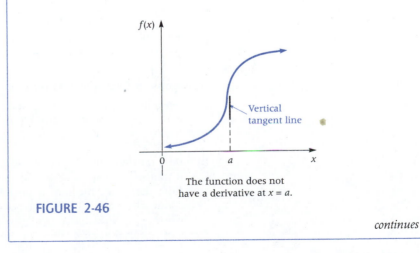

The function does not
have a derivative at $x = a$.

FIGURE 2-46

continues

SUMMARY—*Continued*

3. Where the function is *not continuous* (see Figure 2-47).

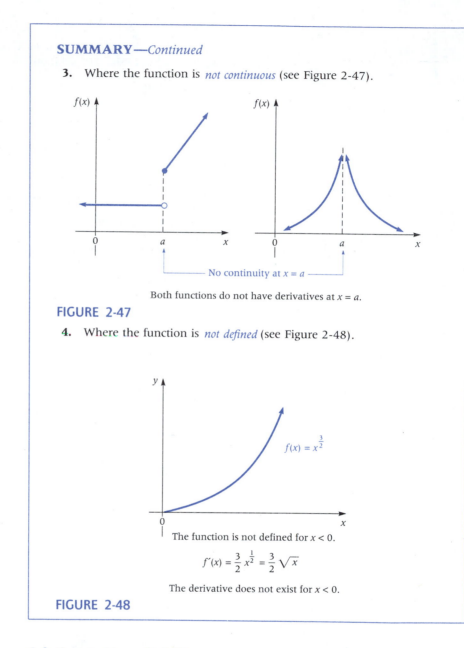

— No continuity at $x = a$ —

Both functions do not have derivatives at $x = a$.

FIGURE 2-47

4. Where the function is *not defined* (see Figure 2-48).

$f(x) = x^{\frac{3}{2}}$

The function is not defined for $x < 0$.

$$f'(x) = \frac{3}{2} x^{\frac{1}{2}} = \frac{3}{2} \sqrt{x}$$

The derivative does not exist for $x < 0$.

FIGURE 2-48

Solutions to Example 2-17 on page 139

a) Since the square root (or, for that matter, any even root) of a negative number is undefined, the derivative $f'(x) = \frac{5}{2}(\sqrt{x - 7})^3$ does not exist at values of x where $x - 7 < 0$. Since $x - 7 < 0$ for $x < 7$, then $f'(x)$ does not exist for $x < 7$.

b) Here the derivative does not exist at values of x where the denominator equals 0. Since this occurs at $x = 8$, then the derivative does not exist at $x = 8$. Note that since the root is an odd root, we do not have to be concerned about where $8 - x$ is negative because an odd root of a negative number does exist.

Exercises 2-5

1. Which of the functions in Figure 2-49 are differentiable at $x = a$?
2. Which of the functions in Figure 2-50 on page 142 are continuous at $x = a$, but not differentiable at $x = a$?
3. Given the function defined by

$$f(x) = \frac{1}{(x - 5)^2}$$

with

$$f'(x) = \frac{-2}{(x - 5)^3}$$

a) Graph $f(x)$.
b) For which value(s) of x is $f(x)$ not continuous?
c) For which value(s) of x is $f(x)$ not differentiable?

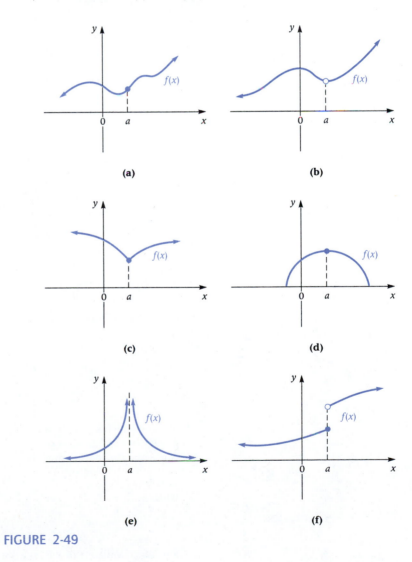

(a)

(b)

(c)

(d)

(e)

(f)

FIGURE 2-49

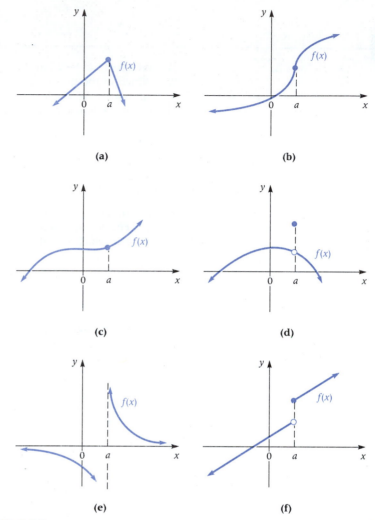

(a) **(b)**

(c) **(d)**

(e) **(f)**

FIGURE 2-50

4. Given the function defined by

$$f(x) = \frac{1}{(x - 3)^2(x + 5)}$$

with

$$f'(x) = \frac{-(3x + 7)}{(x - 3)^3(x + 5)^2}$$

a) For which value(s) of x is $f(x)$ not continuous?
b) For which value(s) of x is $f(x)$ not differentiable?

5. Given the function defined by

$$f(x) = x^{1/3}$$

with

$$f'(x) = \frac{1}{3\sqrt[3]{x^2}}$$

For which value(s) of x is $f(x)$ not differentiable?

6. Given that

$$f(x) = \begin{cases} x^2 & \text{if } x \neq 3 \\ 10 & \text{if } x = 3 \end{cases}$$

   a) Graph $f(x)$.
   b) Where is this function discontinuous?
   c) Where is this function not differentiable?

7. Given that

$$f(x) = \begin{cases} x^2 + 5 & \text{if } x \neq 4 \\ 20 & \text{if } x = 4 \end{cases}$$

   a) Graph $f(x)$.
   b) Where is this function discontinuous?
   c) Where is this function not differentiable?

8. Given that $f(x) = (x^2 - 25)/(x - 5)$
   a) Graph $f(x)$.
   b) Where is this function discontinuous?
   c) Where is this function not differentiable?

9. Given that $f(x) = (x^2 - 81)/(x + 9)$
   a) Graph $f(x)$.
   b) Where is this function discontinuous?
   c) Where is this function not differentiable?

10. For what values of x is the absolute value function, $f(x) = |x|$, not differentiable?

For each of the following functions, study its derivative and state where the derivative does not exist.

Function	Derivative
11. $f(x) = \sqrt{x - 5}$	$f'(x) = \dfrac{1}{2\sqrt{x - 5}}$
12. $f(x) = \sqrt{x + 3}$	$f'(x) = \dfrac{1}{2\sqrt{x + 3}}$
13. $f(x) = \dfrac{1}{x - 2}$	$f'(x) = \dfrac{-1}{(x - 2)^2}$
14. $f(x) = \dfrac{1}{x - 9}$	$f'(x) = \dfrac{-1}{(x - 9)^2}$
15. $f(x) = \dfrac{x + 5}{x - 1}$	$f'(x) = \dfrac{-6}{(x - 1)^2}$
16. $f(x) = \dfrac{x - 2}{x + 1}$	$f'(x) = \dfrac{3}{(x + 1)^2}$
17. $f(x) = \dfrac{1}{\sqrt{x - 3}}$	$f'(x) = \dfrac{-1}{2\sqrt{(x - 3)^3}}$
18. $f(x) = (2x - 1)^{1/3}$	$f'(x) = \dfrac{2}{3\sqrt[3]{(2x - 1)^2}}$
19. $f(x) = (7 - x)^{4/5}$	$f'(x) = \dfrac{-4}{5\sqrt[5]{7 - x}}$
20. $f(x) = (9 - x)^{1/5}$	$f'(x) = \dfrac{-1}{5\sqrt[5]{(9 - x)^4}}$
21. $f(x) = (4x - 1)^{3/5}$	$f'(x) = \dfrac{12}{5\sqrt[5]{(4x - 1)^2}}$
22. $f(x) = (x + 4)^{3/2}$	$f'(x) = \dfrac{3}{2}\sqrt{x + 4}$
23. $f(x) = (x - 6)^{5/2}$	$f'(x) = \dfrac{5}{2}(\sqrt{x - 6})^3$

2-6 • RULES FOR FINDING DERIVATIVES

Alternative Notations for the Derivative

The derivative of a function $y = f(x)$ is a function that is denoted by the symbol $f'(x)$. Alternative notations are

$$\frac{dy}{dx} \qquad y' \qquad \frac{d}{dx}[f(x)] \qquad D_x y \qquad D_x[f(x)]$$

Thus, the derivative $f'(x) = 20x$ of the function $y = f(x) = 10x^2$ may also be expressed with any of the following notations:

$$\frac{dy}{dx} = 20x \qquad y' = 20x \qquad \frac{d}{dx}(10x^2) = 20x \qquad D_x y = 20x \qquad D_x(10x^2) = 20x$$

Up to this point, we have been calculating derivatives of functions $y = f(x)$ by using the definition of the derivative $f'(x) = \lim_{\Delta x \to 0} [f(x + \Delta x) - f(x)]/\Delta x$. Since this is a tedious process, we will introduce some rules to expedite the calculation of derivatives.

The first rule pertains to calculating the derivative of a function defined by an equation of the form

$$f(x) = k$$

where k is a constant. Such a function is called a **constant function.** Since

$$\frac{f(x + \Delta x) - f(x)}{\Delta x} = \frac{k - k}{\Delta x} = \frac{0}{\Delta x} = 0$$

and $\lim_{\Delta x \to 0}(0) = 0$, then $f'(x) = 0$. Thus, we state the **constant function rule.**

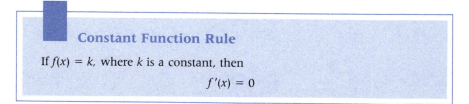

Constant Function Rule

If $f(x) = k$, where k is a constant, then

$$f'(x) = 0$$

The constant function rule states that the derivative of a constant function is 0. Thus, if $f(x) = 5$, then $f'(x) = 0$. If $y = -7$, then $dy/dx = 0$.

Another useful rule pertains to derivatives of functions defined by equations of the form

$$f(x) = x^n$$

where n is a real number. It is called the **power rule** and is stated in the following box. The proof of the case where n is a positive integer appears in Appendix A.

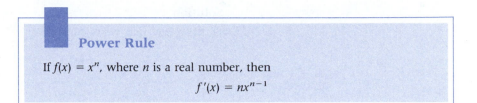

Power Rule

If $f(x) = x^n$, where n is a real number, then

$$f'(x) = nx^{n-1}$$

Note that the derivative of x^n is found by writing the exponent, n, as the coefficient of x with an exponent that is 1 less than n, as illustrated below.

$$f(x) = x^n$$

$$f'(x) = nx^{n-1} \quad \longleftarrow \quad \text{This exponent is 1 less than that of } x^n.$$

The following are illustrations of the use of the power rule:

- If $f(x) = x^3$, then $f'(x) = 3x^{3-1} = 3x^2$.
- If $f(x) = x^6$, then $f'(x) = 6x^{6-1} = 6x^5$.
- If $f(x) = x^{-8}$, then $f'(x) = -8x^{-8-1} = -8x^{-9}$ or $-8/x^9$.
- If $f(x) = x$, then $f'(x) = 1x^{1-1} = 1x^0 = 1$.

• **EXAMPLE 2-18**

If $y = f(x) = \sqrt{x}$, find the following.

a) dy/dx
b) $f'(16)$

Solutions

a) Since $y = f(x) = \sqrt{x} = x^{1/2}$, then, using the power rule, we have

$$\frac{dy}{dx} = \frac{1}{2}x^{1/2-1} = \frac{1}{2}x^{-1/2} = \frac{1}{2\sqrt{x}}$$

b) Since $dy/dx = f'(x)$, then

$$f'(16) = \frac{1}{2\sqrt{16}} = \frac{1}{(2)(4)} = \frac{1}{8}$$

• **EXAMPLE 2-19**

If $y = 1/x^2$, find dy/dx.

Solution

Since $y = 1/x^2 = x^{-2}$, using the power rule, we have

$$\frac{dy}{dx} = -2x^{-2-1} = -2x^{-3} = \frac{-2}{x^3}$$

• **EXAMPLE 2-20**

If $f(x) = x^{2/3}$, find $f'(x)$.

Solution

By the power rule, we calculate

$$f'(x) = \frac{2}{3}x^{2/3 - 1} = \frac{2}{3}x^{-1/3} = \frac{2}{3\sqrt[3]{x}}$$

Using the power rule, we may easily calculate the derivative of a function of the form $y = x^n$, where n is a real number. However, additional rules are needed if we wish to determine the derivatives of such functions as

$$y = 3x^7$$
$$y = 6x^3 - 4x^2 + 8x - 5$$
$$y = (x^3 + 7)(x^2 - 3x + 5)$$

One such rule, the **constant multiplier rule,** is stated here.

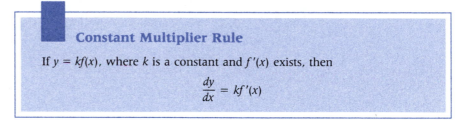

> **Constant Multiplier Rule**
>
> If $y = kf(x)$, where k is a constant and $f'(x)$ exists, then
>
> $$\frac{dy}{dx} = kf'(x)$$

The constant multiplier rule states that the derivative of a constant times a function is the constant times the derivative of the function.

To prove the constant multiplier rule, we let $y(x) = kf(x)$ and note that

$$\frac{dy}{dx} = \lim_{\Delta x \to 0} \frac{y(x + \Delta x) - y(x)}{\Delta x}$$

$$= \lim_{\Delta x \to 0} \frac{kf(x + \Delta x) - kf(x)}{\Delta x}$$

$$= \lim_{\Delta x \to 0} k\frac{f(x + \Delta x) - f(x)}{\Delta x}$$

By limit property 3, this result becomes

$$\frac{dy}{dx} = k \lim_{\Delta x \to 0} \frac{f(x + \Delta x) - f(x)}{\Delta x}$$

$$= kf'(x)$$

As previously stated, the constant multiplier rule states that if a function, $f(x)$, is multiplied by a constant, k, then the derivative of the new function, $kf(x)$, is k times the derivative of the original function.

Thus, if $y = 3x^7$, we have

$$\frac{dy}{dx} = 3(7x^6) = 21x^6$$

• **EXAMPLE 2-21**

If $f(x) = 6/x^3$, find $f'(x)$.

Solution

Since $f(x) = 6x^{-3}$, then by the constant multiplier rule and the power rule,

$$f'(x) = 6(-3x^{-3-1}) = -18x^{-4} = \frac{-18}{x^4}$$

Another useful rule for finding derivatives, the **sum or difference rule,** is stated here.

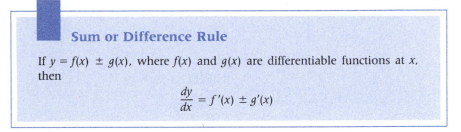

Sum or Difference Rule

If $y = f(x) \pm g(x)$, where $f(x)$ and $g(x)$ are differentiable functions at x, then

$$\frac{dy}{dx} = f'(x) \pm g'(x)$$

The sum or difference rule states that the derivative of a sum or a difference of two functions is the sum or difference of their derivatives. It may be generalized to more than two functions.

Thus, the function

$$y = 6x^4 + 8x^2$$

is of the form

$$y = f(x) + g(x)$$

with $f(x) = 6x^4$ and $g(x) = 8x^2$. Since $f'(x) = 24x^3$ and $g'(x) = 16x$, then according to the sum rule,

$$\frac{dy}{dx} = f'(x) + g'(x)$$

$$= 24x^3 + 16x$$

To prove the sum or difference rule, we let $y(x) = f(x) \pm g(x)$ and note that

$$\frac{dy}{dx} = \lim_{\Delta x \to 0} \frac{y(x + \Delta x) - y(x)}{\Delta x}.$$

$$= \lim_{\Delta x \to 0} \frac{[f(x + \Delta x) \pm g(x + \Delta x)] - [f(x) \pm g(x)]}{\Delta x}$$

$$= \lim_{\Delta x \to 0} \frac{[f(x + \Delta x) - f(x)] \pm [g(x + \Delta x) - g(x)]}{\Delta x}$$

$$= \lim_{\Delta x \to 0} \left[\frac{f(x + \Delta x) - f(x)}{\Delta x} \pm \frac{g(x + \Delta x) - g(x)}{\Delta x} \right]$$

By limit property 2, this result becomes

$$\frac{dy}{dx} = \lim_{\Delta x \to 0} \frac{f(x + \Delta x) - f(x)}{\Delta x} \pm \lim_{\Delta x \to 0} \frac{g(x + \Delta x) - g(x)}{\Delta x}$$

$$= f'(x) \pm g'(x)$$

• **EXAMPLE 2-22** _____

If $y = x^3 - 4x^2 + 15x - 10$, find dy/dx.

Solution

$$\frac{dy}{dx} = \frac{d}{dx}(x^3) + \frac{d}{dx}(-4x^2) + \frac{d}{dx}(15x) + \frac{d}{dx}(-10)$$
$$= 3x^2 - 8x + 15 + 0$$
$$= 3x^2 - 8x + 15$$

• **EXAMPLE 2-23** _____

If

$$y = x^5 - 8x^2 + \frac{6}{x^2} + 50$$

find dy/dx.

Solution

First rewrite the equation as

$$y = x^5 - 8x^2 + 6x^{-2} + 50$$

Then

$$\frac{dy}{dx} = \frac{d}{dx}(x^5) + \frac{d}{dx}(-8x^2) + \frac{d}{dx}(6x^{-2}) + \frac{d}{dx}(50)$$
$$= 5x^4 - 16x - 12x^{-3} + 0$$
$$= 5x^4 - 16x - \frac{12}{x^3}$$

• **EXAMPLE 2-24** _____

Find the equation of the tangent line to $f(x) = 3x^2 - 12x + 13$ at $x = 3$.

Solution

The slope of the tangent line for $x = 3$ is given by $f'(3)$. Calculating $f'(x)$, we have

$$f'(x) = 6x - 12 \qquad \text{Derivative of function}$$

Hence,

$$f'(3) = 6(3) - 12$$
$$= 6 \qquad \text{Slope of tangent line}$$

The point of tangency is $(3, f(3))$. Since

$$f(3) = 3(3)^2 - 12(3) + 13$$
$$= 4 \qquad \text{y-Coordinate of point of tangency}$$

the point of tangency is $(3, 4)$. Using the slope-intercept form, $y = mx + b$, of the equation of a straight line, we have

$$y = 6x + b$$

We determine b by substituting the coordinates of $(3, 4)$ into this equation and solving for b to obtain

$$4 = 6(3) + b$$
$$b = -14$$

Thus, the equation of the tangent line is $y = 6x - 14$ (see Figure 2-51). We could have found the equation of the tangent line by using the point-slope form. This method is used in Example 2-26.

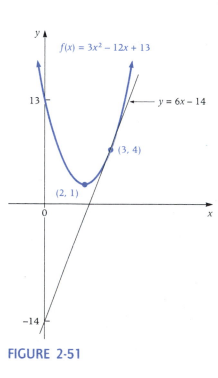

FIGURE 2-51

Notation

Given that $y = f(x) = 3x^2 - 4x + 5$, the instantaneous rate of change of y with respect to x is given by $f'(x)$ or

$$\frac{dy}{dx} = 6x - 4$$

If we wish to evaluate dy/dx [or $f'(x)$] at $x = 3$, this is indicated by $f'(3)$ or, alternatively, by

$$\left.\frac{dy}{dx}\right|_{x - 3} = 6(3) - 4 = 14$$

Thus, given a function $y = f(x)$, its derivative evaluated at $x = a$ is given by either

$$f'(a) \qquad \text{or} \qquad \left.\frac{dy}{dx}\right|_{x = a}$$

sometimes letters other than x and y appear in equations. If $q = z^3 + 8z^2 + 10z + 9$, then the *instantaneous rate of change of q with respect to z* is given by dq/dz where

$$\frac{dq}{dz} = \frac{d}{dz}(z^3) + \frac{d}{dz}(8z^2) + \frac{d}{dz}(10z) + \frac{d}{dz}(9)$$

$$= 3z^2 + 16z + 10 + 0$$

$$= 3z^2 + 16z + 10$$

• **EXAMPLE 2-25** _____

A ball moves in the path of a straight line. The distance, s (in feet), of the ball from its starting point after t seconds have elapsed is given by

$$s = -3t^2 + 48t \quad (0 \le t \le 16)$$

a) Find the formula giving the ball's instantaneous speed.
b) Find the ball's instantaneous speed at $t = 2$.

Solutions

a) The ball's instantaneous speed is given by the rate of change of distance with respect to time or ds/dt.

$$\frac{ds}{dt} = \frac{d}{dt}(-3t^2) + \frac{d}{dt}(48t)$$

$$= -6t + 48$$

b) $\left.\dfrac{ds}{dt}\right|_{t = 2} = -6(2) + 48 = 36$

Thus, at $t = 2$, the ball's instantaneous speed is 36 feet per second.

• **EXAMPLE 2-26**   **Investment Portfolio.** _____

The value, y (in millions of dollars), of an investment portfolio is related to time, x (in years), since inception by the equation

$$y = f(x) = 5x^2 \quad (x \ge 0)$$

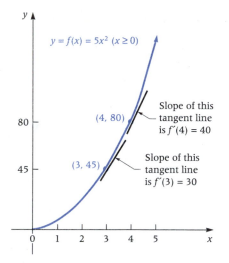

FIGURE 2-52

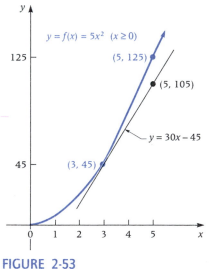

FIGURE 2-53

a) Calculate $f'(x)$.

b) Determine the instantaneous rate of change of value with respect to time at $x = 3$ and at $x = 4$. Illustrate these results graphically. Is the instantaneous rate of change the same for each year?

c) If the instantaneous rate of change of value with respect to time were to remain constant for $x \geq 3$, determine the portfolio's value at $x = 5$. (This is, of course, a different portfolio for $x > 3$ than the original.)

Solutions

a) $f'(x) = 10x$

b) Since $f'(3) = 10(3) = 30$, the portfolio's value is increasing at the rate of $30 million per year at $x = 3$.

Since $f'(4) = 10(4) = 40$, the portfolio's value is increasing at the rate of $40 million per year at $x = 4$.

The rate of change is not the same for each year. These results are graphically illustrated in Figure 2-52.

c) If the rate of change of value with respect to time were to remain constant for $x \geq 3$, then the new portfolio's value will be given by the equation of the tangent line in Figure 2-53 for $x \geq 3$. The slope of the tangent line at $x = 3$ is given by $f'(3) = 30$. Since $f(3) = 5(3^2) = 45$, then the point of tangency is $(3, f(3)) = (3, 45)$. Thus, the tangent line passes through $(3, 45)$ and has a slope of 30.

Using the point-slope form of the equation of a straight line

$$y - y_1 = m(x - x_1)$$

where

$$m = 30 \text{ and } (x_1, y_1) = (3, 45)$$

we have

$$y - 45 = 30(x - 3) \qquad \text{Point-slope form}$$

Solving for y gives the slope-intercept form. Hence,

$$y - 45 = 30x - 90$$
$$y = 30x - 45 \qquad \text{Equation of tangent line}$$

Thus, the equation of the tangent line is $y = 30x - 45$.

The new portfolio's value at $x = 5$ is determined by substituting 5 into the equation of the tangent line to yield

$$y = 30(5) - 45$$
$$= 105$$

Thus, if the instantaneous rate of change of value with respect to time remains constant for $x \geq 3$, the new portfolio's value at $x = 5$ is $105 million. If the instantaneous rate of change does not remain constant, but varies according to the derivative, then the original portfolio's value at $x = 5$ is $125 million (i.e., $f(5) = 5(5^2) = 125$), as shown in Figure 2-53.

Marginal Cost and Marginal Revenue

Suppose the total cost of producing x units of some commodity is given by the cost function

$$C(x) = -0.01x^2 + x + 175 \qquad (0 \leq x \leq 50)$$

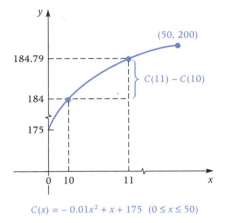

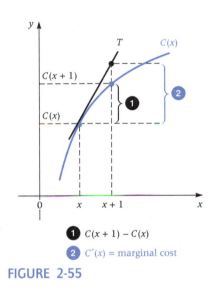

$C(x) = -0.01x^2 + x + 175 \quad (0 \le x \le 50)$

FIGURE 2-54

① $C(x + 1) - C(x)$

② $C'(x) = $ marginal cost

FIGURE 2-55

Then the total cost of producing 10 units is

$$C(10) = -0.01(10)^2 + 10 + 175$$
$$= \$184$$

Thus, at production level $x = 10$, the total cost is \$184.

If we want to determine the additional cost of producing 1 more unit at production level $x = 10$, we must calculate the total cost of producing $10 + 1 = 11$ units and subtract from this result the total cost of producing 10 units. Hence, we find

$$C(11) = -0.01(11)^2 + 11 + 175$$
$$= \$184.79$$

And the additional cost of producing 1 more unit is

$$C(11) - C(10) = 184.79 - 184$$
$$= \$0.79$$

Observing Figure 2-54, note that $C(11) - C(10)$ is the *vertical distance* between the points $(10, 184)$ and $(11, 184.79)$ of the cost function.

In general, for a cost function, $C(x)$, the additional cost of producing *1 more unit* at production level x is

$$C(x + 1) - C(x)$$

In practice, this quantity is usually approximated by the derivative $C'(x)$, which is called the **marginal cost.** Observing Figure 2-55, note that the marginal cost, $C'(x)$, is the slope of the tangent line, T. However, since the horizontal distance between x and $x + 1$ is 1, then $C'(x)$ is the vertical distance indicated. Note that $C'(x)$ is an approximation of $C(x + 1) - C(x)$. Thus, returning to the cost function

$$C(x) = -0.01x^2 + x + 175$$

the marginal cost at production level $x = 10$ is $C'(10)$ and is determined by

$$C'(x) = -0.02x + 1$$
$$C'(10) = -0.02(10) + 1$$
$$= \$0.80$$

Thus, at production level $x = 10$, 1 more unit costs approximately \$0.80.

Similarly, given a revenue function, $R(x)$, its derivative, $R'(x)$, is called the **marginal revenue.** It approximates the quantity $R(x + 1) - R(x)$, which is the additional revenue derived from producing and selling 1 more unit.

We summarize in the following boxes.

SUMMARY

Marginal Cost

If

$C(x) =$ the *total cost* of producing x units of some product

then its derivative,

$C'(x) =$ the *marginal cost*

which is the approximate cost of producing 1 more unit when the production level is x units. The graphical interpretation appears in Figure 2-56.

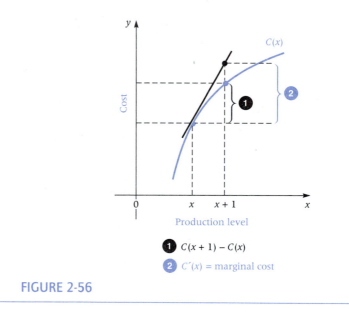

1 $C(x + 1) - C(x)$

2 $C'(x) =$ marginal cost

FIGURE 2-56

SUMMARY

Marginal Revenue

If

$R(x) =$ the *total revenue* gained from selling x units of some product

then its derivative,

$R'(x) =$ the *marginal revenue*

which is the approximate revenue gained from selling 1 more unit when the sales level is x units. The graphical interpretation appears in Figure 2-57.

continues

SUMMARY—*Continued*

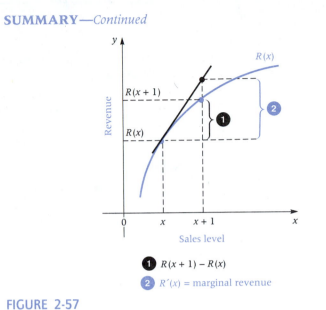

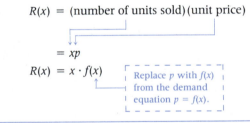

FIGURE 2-57

Comment.   Given a demand equation

$$p = f(x)$$

where p denotes the unit price of some product and x denotes the number of units demanded, the equation for total sales revenue is given by

$$R(x) = (\text{number of units sold})(\text{unit price})$$

$$= xp$$

$$R(x) = x \cdot f(x) \qquad \boxed{\text{Replace } p \text{ with } f(x) \text{ from the demand equation } p = f(x).}$$

• **EXAMPLE 2-27**

The total cost of producing x units of some product is given by

$$C(x) = -0.02x^2 + 4x + 8000 \qquad (0 \le x \le 100)$$

a)   Find the equation for marginal cost.
b)   Find the marginal cost at a production level of $x = 60$ units. Interpret the result.

Solutions

a)   The equation for marginal cost is given by

$$C'(x) = -0.04x + 4$$

b)   The marginal cost at $x = 60$ is

$$C'(60) = -0.04(60) + 4$$
$$= \$1.60$$

Thus, at production level $x = 60$, 1 more unit costs approximately $1.60.

• **EXAMPLE 2-28** _____

Given the demand equation

$$p = -x + 10 \qquad (0 \le x \le 10)$$

where p denotes the unit selling price and x denotes the number of units demanded of some product,

a)   Determine the equation for total sales revenue, $R(x)$.
b)   Determine the equation for marginal revenue.
c)   Determine the marginal revenue at sales level $x = 3$ units. Interpret the result.

Solutions

a)   The *total sales revenue* is given by

$$R(x) = (\text{number of units sold})(\text{unit price})$$

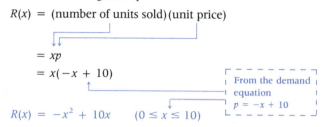

$$= xp$$
$$= x(-x + 10)$$

From the demand equation $p = -x + 10$

$$R(x) = -x^2 + 10x \qquad (0 \le x \le 10)$$

b)   The equation for *marginal revenue* is given by

$$R'(x) = -2x + 10$$

c)   The *marginal revenue at $x = 3$* is given by

$$R'(3) = -2(3) + 10$$
$$= \$4$$

Thus, at sales level $x = 3$ units, approximately \$4 of revenue is gained from selling 1 more unit.

_____   •

Exercises 2-6

For each of the following, find dy/dx.

1. $y = x^3$ **2.** $y = x^{10}$ **3.** $y = x^{20}$
4. $y = x^{1/5}$ **5.** $y = 4x$ **6.** $y = x^{-3}$
7. $y = 1/x^6$ **8.** $y = 1/x$ **9.** $y = x^5$
10. $y = x^9$ **11.** $y = 1/x^3$ **12.** $y = 1/\sqrt{x^5}$
13. $y = x^{-1/4}$ **14.** $y = -40$ **15.** $y = 6$

For each of the following, find $f'(x)$.

16. $f(x) = x^5$ **17.** $f(x) = -x^8$
18. $f(x) = 4x^2$ **19.** $f(x) = -3/x^2$
20. $f(x) = 4/x$ **21.** $f(x) = 5/\sqrt{x^3}$
22. $f(x) = -2/(\sqrt[3]{x})^4$ **23.** $f(x) = 1/6$

For each of the following, find $f'(4)$.

24. $f(x) = 3\sqrt{x}$ **25.** $f(x) = 5/\sqrt{x}$
26. $f(x) = -2/\sqrt{x^3}$ **27.** $f(x) = 8\sqrt{x^3}$
28. $f(x) = 5/x^2$ **29.** $f(x) = -2/x^3$

For each of the following, find dy/dx.

30. $y = 3x^2 - 2x + 5$

31. $y = x^2 - 8x$

32. $y = -4x^2 + 6$

33. $y = 8x^2 + 10$

34. $y = x^3 + 4x^2 + 1$

35. $y = x^3 + 2x^2 + 9$

Find the derivative of each of the following.

36. $f(x) = 5x^7 - 8x^3 + 6x - 8$

37. $y = x^6 - x^5 + 4/x^2 + 9$

38. $f(x) = -8x^3 + 6x^2 - 6x + 9$

39. $y = -5x^3 - 6x^2 + 8x - 4$

40. $y = x(x^3 - 4x^2 + 3x - 8)$

41. $y = x^3(x^2 - 6x + 8)$

Find each of the following.

42. $\dfrac{d}{dx}(4x^2 - 5)$

43. $\dfrac{d}{dx}(3x^2 + 7)$

44. $\dfrac{d}{dx}(5x^2 + 2)$

45. $\dfrac{d}{dx}(-2x^2 + 1)$

46. $\dfrac{d}{dx}(8x^2 - 3)$

47. $\dfrac{d}{dx}(-3x^3 + 4)$

48. $\dfrac{d}{dx}(x^2 - 2x)$

49. $\dfrac{d}{dx}(x^3 - 4x^2 + 5)$

50. $\dfrac{d}{dx}(\sqrt{x} + 1/x)$

51. $\dfrac{d}{dx}(1/\sqrt{x} + 4\sqrt{x})$

Determine each of the following.

52. $\dfrac{d}{dt}(t^3 - t^2 + 8)$

53. $\dfrac{d}{dt}(-3t^2 + 8t + 7)$

54. $\dfrac{d}{dz}(z^4 - 8z^2 + 1)$

55. $\dfrac{d}{dw}(w^3 - 5w + 8)$

For each of the following, find $\dfrac{dy}{dx}\bigg|_{x=1}$.

56. $y = x^2 - 3x + 5$

57. $y = -2x^3 + 4x$

58. $y = 3\sqrt{x} + 4$

59. $y = -6/\sqrt{x} + 7$

For each of the following, find $\dfrac{dy}{dx}\bigg|_{x=4}$.

60. $y = 4x^2 - 8x + 5$

61. $y = -3x^3 + 7x$

62. $y = 6x^2 - \sqrt{x}$

63. $y = \sqrt{x} - 4/\sqrt{x}$

Determine y' for each of the following.

64. $y = 8x^2 - 3x + 5$

65. $y = -3x^2 + 2x + 1$

66. $y = -x^3 - 2x^2 + 5x + 1$

67. $y = x^3 + 6x^2 + 8x + 7$

68. $y = x^4 - 5x^2 - 7x + 8$

69. $y = x^5 - 6x^3 + 6x + 5$

Determine each of the following.

70. $D_x(30x^3)$

71. $D_x(5x^{10})$

72. $D_x(9/x^4)$

73. $D_x(-3/x^2)$

74. $D_x(8x^2 - 4x + 6)$

75. $D_x(4x^3 - 6x^2 + 4x + 8)$

76. Find the equation of the tangent line to $f(x) = x^2 - 10x + 28$ at $x = 7$. Illustrate graphically.

77. Find the equation of the tangent line to $f(x) = 2x^3 + 5$ at $x = 1$. Illustrate graphically.

78. Find the equation of the tangent line to $f(x) = -3x^2 + 18x$ at $x = 4$. Illustrate graphically.

Applications

79. *Annual profits.* A company's annual profit, P, is related to time, x, by the equation

$$P(x) = 0.03x^2 + 5 \qquad (x \geq 0)$$

where $P(x)$ is the profit (in millions of dollars) for the xth year the company has been operating.
a) Find the rate of change of profit at the second year. Interpret the result.
b) Find the rate of change of profit at $x = 3$. Interpret the result.
c) If the rate of change of profit remains constant at and beyond the third year, find the equation relating P and x for $x \geq 3$. Calculate the profit for the seventh year.

80. *Investment portfolio.* The value, y (in millions of dollars), of an investment portfolio is related to time, x (in years), since inception by the equation

$$y = f(x) = 4x^2 \qquad (x \geq 0)$$

a) Calculate $f'(x)$.
b) Determine the instantaneous rate of change of value with respect to time at $x = 2$ and at $x = 3$. Illustrate these results graphically. Is the instantaneous rate of change the same for each year?
c) If the instantaneous rate of change of value with respect to time were to remain constant for $x \geq 2$, determine the portfolio's value at $x = 4$. (We are assuming a different portfolio for $x > 2$ than the original.)

81. *Investment portfolio.* The value, y (in millions of dollars), of an investment portfolio is related to time, x (in years), since inception by the equation

$$y = f(x) = 6x^2 \qquad (x \geq 0)$$

a) Calculate $f'(x)$.
b) Determine the instantaneous rate of change of value with respect to time at $x = 2$ and at $x = 3$. Illustrate these results graphically. Is the rate of change the same for each year?
c) If the rate of change of value with respect to time remains constant for $x \geq 3$, determine the portfolio's value at $x = 5$. (We are assuming a different portfolio for $x > 3$ than the original.)

82. *Production cost.* The cost of producing x units of some commodity is given by the cost function defined by

$$C(x) = 5x^2 + 100 \qquad (x \geq 0)$$

a) Find the equation for marginal cost.
b) Find the marginal cost at $x = 3$. Interpret the result.
c) Illustrate the graphical interpretation of the answer to part b.

83. *Sales revenue.* The revenue derived from selling x units of some item is given by the revenue function defined by

$$R(x) = -2x^2 + 60x \qquad (0 \leq x \leq 30)$$

a) Find the equation for marginal revenue.
b) Find the marginal revenue at $x = 10$. Interpret the result.
c) Illustrate the graphical interpretation of the answer to part b.

84. *Sales revenue.* The demand for tricycles, x, is related to the price per tricycle, p, by the equation

$$p = -2x + 40 \qquad (0 \leq x \leq 20)$$

   a) Find the revenue function, $R(x)$.
   b) Find the equation for marginal revenue.
   c) Find the marginal revenue at $x = 5$. Interpret the result.
   d) Find the marginal revenue at $x = 7$. Interpret the result.
   e) Illustrate the graphical interpretation of the answers to parts c and d.

85. *Projectile.* At the same instant a ball is projected into the air, a stopwatch is started. The function defined by

$$S(x) = -16x^2 + 64x \qquad (0 \leq x \leq 4)$$

expresses the height (in feet) above the ground of the ball after x seconds have elapsed.

   a) At what speed (in feet per second) is the ball traveling after 1 second has elapsed (i.e., at $x = 1$)?
   b) At what speed is the ball traveling at $x = 2$?
   c) At what speed is the ball traveling at $x = 3$?
   d) Sketch $S(x)$ and illustrate the graphical interpretations of parts a through c.

86. *Production cost.* The Ding Dong Company manufactures ornamental bells. The function

$$C(x) = x^2 - 100x + 2900 \qquad (x \geq 0)$$

relates total daily production cost, C, with daily production, x, of bells.

   a) Find the equation for marginal cost.
   b) Find the marginal cost at $x = 40$. Interpret the result.
   c) Find the marginal cost at $x = 50$. Interpret the result.
   d) Find the marginal cost at $x = 70$. Interpret the result.

87. *Profit.* Consider the profit function defined by

$$P(x) = 4x - \frac{x^3}{1,000,000} \qquad (0 \leq x \leq 2000)$$

Marginal profit is defined in the same manner as marginal revenue and marginal cost.

   a) Find the equation for marginal profit.
   b) Find the marginal profit at $x = 100$. Interpret the result.
   c) Find the marginal profit at $x = 1900$. Interpret the result.

88. *Sales revenue.* Consider the revenue function defined by

$$R(x) = -\frac{1}{100}x^3 + 16x \qquad (0 \leq x \leq 40)$$

   a) Find the equation for marginal revenue.
   b) Find the marginal revenue at $x = 10$. Interpret the result.
   c) Find the marginal revenue at $x = 30$. Interpret the result.

89. *Learning curve.* The number of units produced, y, by a trainee after x hours of instruction is given by

$$y = 90 \sqrt{x} \qquad (x \geq 0)$$

   a) Determine the equation for the trainee's production rate.
   b) Determine the trainee's production rate after 4 hours of instruction.
   c) Determine the trainee's production rate after 9 hours of instruction.

90. *Air pollution.* In a given geographical region, the concentration of pollution (in parts per million) in the air is given by

$$y = \frac{0.3}{x^2} \qquad (x > 0)$$

where x denotes the distance (in miles) from a large industrial area. Determine the instantaneous rate of change of concentration at

a) $x = 1$ mile.   b) $x = 3$ miles.

91. *Population growth.* The population, P, of a certain city is related to time, t (in years), by the function

$$P(t) = 4000t^2 + 200,000$$

where $t = 0$ denotes the year 19X0, $t = 1$ denotes the year 19X1, etc.

a) Determine the formula for the instantaneous rate of change of the population with respect to time.
b) Determine the instantaneous rate of change of the population at $t = 3$.
c) Determine the instantaneous rate of change of the population at $t = 6$.

2-7 • THE PRODUCT AND QUOTIENT RULES

Often we must find the derivative of a product of functions such as

$$y = (x^3 - 8x)(x^4 - 15)$$

The derivative, dy/dx, may be determined by the **product rule,** which is stated as follows. Its proof appears in Appendix A.

> **Product Rule**
>
> If $y = f(x)s(x)$, where $f(x)$ and $s(x)$ are differentiable functions at x, then
>
> $$\frac{dy}{dx} = f(x)s'(x) + s(x)f'(x)$$

The product rule states that the derivative of the product $f(x)s(x)$ is $f(x)$ times the derivative of $s(x)$ plus $s(x)$ times the derivative of $f(x)$. In other words, the derivative dy/dx of the product of two functions is given by

$$\frac{dy}{dx} = (\text{first})\left(\begin{matrix}\text{derivative} \\ \text{of second}\end{matrix}\right) + (\text{second})\left(\begin{matrix}\text{derivative} \\ \text{of first}\end{matrix}\right)$$

Thus, for the function

$$y = (x^3 - 8x)(x^4 - 15)$$

we note that $f(x) = x^3 - 8x$ is the first function and $s(x) = x^4 - 15$ is the second function. Hence,

$$\frac{dy}{dx} = (\text{first})\left(\begin{matrix}\text{derivative} \\ \text{of second}\end{matrix}\right) + (\text{second})\left(\begin{matrix}\text{derivative} \\ \text{of first}\end{matrix}\right)$$

$$= (x^3 - 8x)(4x^3) + (x^4 - 15)(3x^2 - 8)$$

$$= 7x^6 - 40x^4 - 45x^2 + 120$$

• **EXAMPLE 2-29**

If $y = (x^5 - 6x^3 + 5)(x^{10} - 8x^2)$, find dy/dx.

Solution

The first function of our product is $f(x) = x^5 - 6x^3 + 5$, and the second function is $s(x) = x^{10} - 8x^2$. By the product rule, we have

$$\frac{dy}{dx} = (\text{first})\binom{\text{derivative}}{\text{of second}} + (\text{second})\binom{\text{derivative}}{\text{of first}}$$
$$= (x^5 - 6x^3 + 5)(10x^9 - 16x) + (x^{10} - 8x^2)(5x^4 - 18x^2)$$
$$= 15x^{14} - 78x^{12} + 50x^9 - 120x^6 + 240x^4 - 80x$$

• **EXAMPLE 2-30**

If $g(x) = (5x + 3)(2x - 1)$, find $g'(x)$

a) By using the product rule.
b) Without using the product rule.

Solutions

a) Using the product rule, we have

$$g'(x) = (5x + 3)(2) + (2x - 1)(5)$$
$$= (10x + 6) + (10x - 5)$$
$$= 20x + 1$$

b) Without using the product rule, we must multiply the binomial factors $5x + 3$ and $2x - 1$ of $g(x)$ to obtain

$$g(x) = 10x^2 + x - 3$$

Since the result is a polynomial, its derivative is

$$g'(x) = 20x + 1$$

Observe that this result agrees with the final answer for part a.

Application

• **EXAMPLE 2-31**   **Agriculture: Peach Growing.**

If a peach grower harvests her peach crop now, she will pick on the average 200 pounds per tree, and she will get $0.72 per pound for her peaches. From past experience, the grower has learned that for each additional week that she waits, the yield per tree will increase by 20 pounds, while the price will decrease by $0.04 per pound.

a) Write the equation that gives the total sales revenue per tree, R, as a function of the number of weeks, x, that the peach grower should wait before harvesting.
b) Determine the formula for dR/dx.
c) Evaluate dR/dx at $x = 2$ and interpret the result.

Solutions

a) We must determine an equation for the total sales revenue per tree, R. Hence,

$$R = (\text{price per pound})(\text{number of pounds})$$

TABLE 2-16

Decision	Price per pound
Harvest now	$0.72
Wait 1 week	$0.72 − 0.04
Wait 2 weeks	$0.72 − 0.04(2)
Wait 3 weeks	$0.72 − 0.04(3)
.	.
.	.
.	.
Wait x weeks	$0.72 − 0.04$x$

TABLE 2-17

Decision	Number of pounds
Harvest now	200
Wait 1 week	200 + 20
Wait 2 weeks	200 + 20(2)
Wait 3 weeks	200 + 20(3)
.	.
.	.
.	.
Wait x weeks	200 + 20x

Let's focus on the *price per pound*. If the peach grower harvests now, the price per pound is $0.72. For each additional week that she waits, the price per pound decreases by $0.04. This is illustrated in Table 2-16.

Thus, the sales revenue equation is

$$R = \text{(price per pound)(number of pounds)}$$
$$= (0.72 − 0.04x)\text{(number of pounds)}$$

Now we focus on the *number of pounds*. If the peach grower harvests now, she will harvest 200 pounds per tree. For each week that she waits, the number of pounds harvested per tree increases by 20 pounds. This is illustrated in Table 2-17.

Thus, the sales revenue equation is

$$R = \text{(price per pound)(number of pounds)}$$

$$R = (0.72 − 0.04x)(200 + 20x)$$

b) Using the product rule, we find

$$\frac{dR}{dx} = (0.72 − 0.04x)(20) + (200 + 20x)(−0.04)$$

$$= −1.6x + 6.4$$

c)

$$\frac{dR}{dx}\bigg|_{x = 2} = −1.6(2) + 6.4 = 3.2$$

Thus, after 2 weeks have elapsed, the sales revenue per tree is increasing at the rate of $3.20 per tree.

Quotient Rule

To find the derivative of the quotient of functions such as

$$y = \frac{x^5 − 9x}{3x^2 − 8}$$

we must use the **quotient rule,** which is stated as follows. Its proof appears in Appendix A.

> **Quotient Rule**
>
> If $y = n(x)/d(x)$, where $n(x)$ and $d(x)$ are differentiable functions at x and $d(x) \neq 0$, then
>
> $$\frac{dy}{dx} = \frac{d(x)n'(x) − n(x)d'(x)}{[d(x)]^2}$$

The quotient rule states that the derivative dy/dx of a quotient of two functions is given by

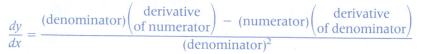

Thus, for the function

$$y = \frac{x^5 - 9x}{3x^2 - 8}$$

the numerator is $n(x) = x^5 - 9x$, and the denominator is $d(x) = 3x^2 - 8$. By the quotient rule, we have

$$\frac{dy}{dx} = \frac{(\text{denominator})\binom{\text{derivative}}{\text{of numerator}} - (\text{numerator})\binom{\text{derivative}}{\text{of denominator}}}{(\text{denominator})^2}$$

$$= \frac{(3x^2 - 8)(5x^4 - 9) - (x^5 - 9x)(6x)}{(3x^2 - 8)^2}$$

$$= \frac{9x^6 - 40x^4 + 27x^2 + 72}{(3x^2 - 8)^2}$$

• **EXAMPLE 2-32**

If

$$y = \frac{x^8 - 3x}{2x^5 - 9}$$

find dy/dx.

Solution

The numerator is $n(x) = x^8 - 3x$, and the denominator is $d(x) = 2x^5 - 9$. By the quotient rule,

$$\frac{dy}{dx} = \frac{(\text{denominator})\binom{\text{derivative}}{\text{of numerator}} - (\text{numerator})\binom{\text{derivative}}{\text{of denominator}}}{(\text{denominator})^2}$$

$$= \frac{(2x^5 - 9)(8x^7 - 3) - (x^8 - 3x)(10x^4)}{(2x^5 - 9)^2}$$

$$= \frac{6x^{12} - 72x^7 + 24x^5 + 27}{(2x^5 - 9)^2}$$

• **EXAMPLE 2-33**

If

$$f(x) = \frac{6x^4 - 8x^2}{x}$$

find $f'(x)$

a) By using the quotient rule.
b) Without using the quotient rule.

Solutions

a) Using the quotient rule, we have

$$f'(x) = \frac{(x)(24x^3 - 16x) - (6x^4 - 8x^2)(1)}{x^2}$$

$$= \frac{24x^4 - 16x^2 - 6x^4 + 8x^2}{x^2}$$

$$= \frac{18x^4 - 8x^2}{x^2}$$

$$= 18x^2 - 8$$

b) Without using the quotient rule, we must divide $6x^4 - 8x^2$ by x to obtain

$$f(x) = 6x^3 - 8x$$

Hence, the derivative of the resulting polynomial is

$$f'(x) = 18x^2 - 8$$

Observe that this result agrees with the final answer for part a.

• **EXAMPLE 2-34** _____

Find the equation of the straight line tangent to $f(x) = 1/(x - 3)$ at $x = 4$.

Solution

The slope of the tangent line is given by $f'(4)$. Using the quotient rule, we calculate

$$f'(x) = \frac{(x - 3)(0) - (1)(1)}{(x - 3)^2}$$

$$= \frac{-1}{(x - 3)^2} \qquad \text{Derivative of Function}$$

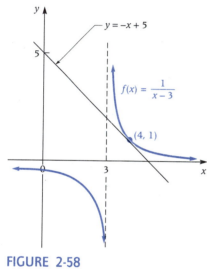

$f(x) = \dfrac{1}{x - 3}$

$y = -x + 5$

$(4, 1)$

FIGURE 2-58

Hence,

$$f'(4) = \frac{-1}{(4 - 3)^2} = -1 \qquad \text{Slope of Tangent Line}$$

The point of tangency is $(4, f(4))$. Since

$$f(4) = \frac{1}{4 - 3} = 1 \qquad y - \text{Coordinate of Point of Tangency}$$

the point of tangency is $(4, 1)$. Using the slope-intercept form, $y = mx + b$, of the equation of a straight line, we have

$$y = -1x + b$$

We determine b by substituting the coordinates of $(4, 1)$ into the equation and solving for b to obtain

$$1 = -1(4) + b$$
$$b = 5$$

Thus, the equation of the tangent line is $y = -x + 5$ (see Figure 2-58).

Application

• **EXAMPLE 2-35** **Average Cost.**

If $C(x)$ = total cost of producing x units of some product, then the **average cost per unit** is given by

$$\overline{C}(x) = \frac{C(x)}{x} \qquad (x > 0)$$

Given the cost function defined by

$$C(x) = 8x + 100$$

a) Determine the equation for average cost, $\overline{C}(x)$.
b) Determine the formula for $\overline{C}'(x)$.
c) Compute $\overline{C}'(5)$ and interpret the result.

Solutions

a) $\overline{C}(x) = \dfrac{C(x)}{x}$

$\qquad = \dfrac{8x + 100}{x} \qquad (x > 0)$

b) Using the quotient rule, we find

$$\overline{C}'(x) = \dfrac{x(8) - (8x + 100)(1)}{x^2}$$

$$= \dfrac{-100}{x^2}$$

c) $\overline{C}'(5) = \dfrac{-100}{5^2} = -4$

Thus, at a production level of 5 units, the average cost per unit is decreasing by \$4 per unit.

Sometimes we must use the product and quotient rules together within a single problem. Example 2-36 illustrates such a situation.

• **EXAMPLE 2-36** ───────────────────────

If

$$y = \dfrac{(x^2 - 3x + 5)(4x - 1)}{x + 3}$$

find dy/dx.

Solution

Note that the formula for y is a quotient, the numerator of which is a product. Thus, we begin by using the quotient rule.

$$\dfrac{dy}{dx} = \dfrac{(\text{denominator})\binom{\text{derivative}}{\text{of numerator}} - (\text{numerator})\binom{\text{derivative}}{\text{of denominator}}}{(\text{denominator})^2}$$

$$= \dfrac{(x + 3)\dfrac{d}{dx}[(x^2 - 3x + 5)(4x - 1)] - (x^2 - 3x + 5)(4x - 1)\dfrac{d}{dx}(x + 3)}{(x + 3)^2}$$

Note that we must use the product rule in the numerator of the above to find d/dx $[(x^2 - 3x + 5)(4x - 1)]$. Thus, the above expression becomes

$$\dfrac{dy}{dx} = \dfrac{(x + 3)\,[(x^2 - 3x + 5)(4) + (4x - 1)(2x - 3)] - (x^2 - 3x + 5)(4x - 1)(1)}{(x + 3)^2}$$

$$= \dfrac{(x + 3)(4x^2 - 12x + 20 + 8x^2 - 2x - 12x + 3) - (4x^3 - 13x^2 + 23x - 5)}{(x + 3)^2}$$

$$= \dfrac{(x + 3)(12x^2 - 26x + 23) - 4x^3 + 13x^2 - 23x + 5}{(x - 3)^2}$$

$$= \dfrac{12x^3 + 10x^2 - 55x + 69 - 4x^3 + 13x^2 - 23x + 5}{(x - 3)^2}$$

$$= \dfrac{8x^3 + 23x^2 - 78x + 74}{(x - 3)^2}$$

In Example 2-36, we began with the quotient rule since the function was written as a quotient of two expressions. Since one of these expressions was a product, we had to use the product rule within the quotient rule. Sometimes we encounter examples where the function is a product of expressions, one or more of which are quotients. For such cases, we would have to begin with the product rule and then use the quotient rule within the product rule. We will encounter such problems in the exercises.

Exercises 2-7

Find the derivative of each of the following.

1. $y = (x^2 + 4x + 5)(x^3 - 2x^2 + 7)$

2. $y = (4x^5 - 9x^3 + 7x)(x^7 - 8x^6 + 4)$

3. $f(x) = (x^3 - 2x + 6)(x^2 - 3x + 2)$

4. $g(x) = (5x^3 + 6)(x^2 - 8x + 4)$

5. $y = (x^3 - x^2 - 2)(x^2 - x - 1)$

For each of the following, find dy/dx.

6. $y = (x^3 - 8x + 4)(3x^2 - 6x + 1)$

7. $y = (x^7 - 6x^2)(4x^2 - 3x + 4)$

8. $y = (8x + 4)(6x^3 + 4x)$

9. $y = (5x^2 - 3x + 1)(3x^4 - 7)$

10. $y = (3\sqrt{x} + 4x^2)(4/\sqrt{x} + x)$

Find the derivative of each of the following.

11. $y = \dfrac{x^2 - 4x + 5}{x^3 - 3x + 9}$

12. $y = \dfrac{x^3 - x^2 + 5x}{x^2 - 2x + 1}$

13. $f(x) = \dfrac{x^3}{x + 5}$

14. $y = \dfrac{x + 6}{x^4}$

15. $g(x) = \dfrac{x^3 + 7}{x^4}$

16. $y = \dfrac{x^3}{x^2 - 3}$

17. $y = 8 - \dfrac{6}{x - 2} + \dfrac{3x}{5x + 1}$

18. $y = 4 + \dfrac{2}{x + 5} - \dfrac{5x}{6x - 7}$

19. $y = \dfrac{x^3 + 9}{x^2 - 9}$

20. $y = \dfrac{x^4 - 6}{x^3 + 1}$

For each of the following, find dy/dx.

21. $y = \dfrac{1}{x^2 - 3x}$

22. $y = \dfrac{1}{x^4 - 5x}$

23. $y = \dfrac{4x + 1}{3x^2 - 2x}$

24. $y = \dfrac{3x + 2}{5x^2 - 3x}$

25. $y = \dfrac{5x^3 - 2x + 1}{\sqrt[5]{x}}$

26. $y = \dfrac{4x^2 - x + 7}{\sqrt[3]{x}}$

27. $y = \dfrac{x^4 - 8x^3 + 5x + 1}{5x^3 - 7x^2 + 3}$

28. $y = \dfrac{x^3 - 8x^2 + 3x + 1}{x^2 - 6x + 1}$

29. $y = \dfrac{\sqrt{x} + x}{x - 1/\sqrt{x}}$

30. $y = \dfrac{x + 1/\sqrt{x}}{\sqrt{x} - 1}$

For each of the following, find $\left. \dfrac{dy}{dx} \right|_{x = 1}$.

31. $y = \dfrac{x^2 - 3x + 1}{x^3 - 2x}$

32. $y = \dfrac{x^3 - 4x^2 + 2}{x^2 + 6x + 1}$

33. $y = \dfrac{\sqrt{x} + 6x}{x - 2/\sqrt{x}}$

34. $y = \dfrac{5x - 2}{2x^3 + 3}$

Find the derivatives of each of the following.

35. $y = (x^3 - 4x^2 + 5)(x^2 - 8x + 7)$

36. $y = \dfrac{x^2 - 3x}{x^3 + 16}$

37. $y = \dfrac{(x^3 - 4x + 7)(x^2 - 2x)}{x^3 - 6x + 1}$

38. $f(x) = \dfrac{x^4 - 8x^2 + 6}{(x^3 + 5)(x^2 - 3x)}$

39. $y = \dfrac{(x^3 - 6x^2 + 5)(x^2 - 4x)}{(x^5 - 8x^2)(x^3 + 1)}$

40. $f(x) = (x^3 + 4)\left(\dfrac{x^4 - 2}{x^5 + 1}\right)$

41. $g(t) = (t^5 - 4)\left(\dfrac{t^3 + 6}{t^4 + 7}\right)$

42. $f(x) = \dfrac{\dfrac{5}{4x} - 3}{\dfrac{6}{x^5} + 9}$

43. $y = (x^2 - 4x + 1)\left(\dfrac{x^3 - 5x}{x^2 + 6}\right)$

44. If $f(x) = -4/x^3$, find $f'(x)$ by using
   a) The power rule.
   b) The quotient rule.

45. If $y = x^3(x^6 - 8x^2)$, find dy/dx
   a) Without using the product rule.
   b) By using the product rule.

46. If $f(x) = (x - 1)/(x + 3)$, find $f'(2)$.

47. If $f(x) = (x^2 + 2)(x^3 - 2x + 5)$, calculate $f'(1)$.

48. If $f(x) = (x + 1)(x + 2)(x - 5)$, find $f'(3)$.

49. Find the equation of the straight line tangent to $f(x) = (x^2 - 9)(x + 5)$ at $x = 1$.

50. Find the equation of the straight line tangent to $f(x) = 1/x$ at $x = 3$. Illustrate graphically.

51. Find the equation of the straight line tangent to $f(x) = 1/x^2$ at $x = 7$. Illustrate graphically.

52. Find the equation of the straight line tangent to

$$f(x) = \frac{x^2}{x - 3}$$

at $x = 4$.

53. Find the equation of the straight line tangent to

$$f(x) = \frac{(x^2 - 36)(x + 4)}{x^2 - 81}$$

at $x = 1$.

Applications

54. *Apple growing.* If an apple grower harvests his crop now, he will pick on the average 300 pounds per tree, and he will get $0.50 per pound for his apples. For each week that the grower waits before harvesting, the yield per tree will increase by 20 pounds, while the price will decrease by $0.02 per pound.
   a) Write the equation that gives total sales revenue, R, per tree as a function of x, the number of weeks that the grower waits before harvesting.
   b) Determine the formula for dR/dx.
   c) Evaluate dR/dx at $x = 3$ and interpret the result.

55. *Sales revenue.* The unit price, p (in dollars), of some product is changing with time, t (in months), in accordance with the equation

$$p = 10 + 2t$$

The demand, x, for the product is changing with time, t, in accordance with the equation

$$x = 20 + 0.2t^2$$

a) Write the equation for sales revenue, R, as a function of t.
b) Determine the formula for dR/dt.
c) Evaluate dR/dt at $t = 2$ and interpret the result.

Average cost. For each of the following cost functions,
a) Determine the formula for average cost per unit, $\overline{C}(X)$.
b) Determine the formula for $\overline{C}'(x)$.
c) Find $\overline{C}'(4)$, $\overline{C}'(5)$, and $\overline{C}'(6)$, and interpret the results.

56. $C(x) = 5x + 100$ **57.** $C(x) = 10x + 500$
58. $C(x) = -x^2 + 20x$ **59.** $C(x) = -x^2 + 30x$

60. *Production possibility curve.* The equation

$$y = \frac{500(x - 300)}{x - 320} \qquad (0 \le x \le 300)$$

relates the number of units of products A and B that can be produced during a week. Here x and y denote the number of units produced of Products A and B, respectively.
a) Determine the formula for dy/dx.
b) Evaluate dy/dx at $x = 20$, $x = 30$, and $x = 50$, and interpret the results.

61. *Cost-benefit analysis.* The equation

$$y = \frac{30}{110 - x} \qquad (0 \le x \le 100)$$

expresses the relationship between the cost, y (in millions of dollars), of removing $x\%$ of a pollutant from the atmosphere.
a) Determine the formula for dy/dx.
b) Evaluate dy/dx at $x = 60$, $x = 80$, and $x = 90$, and interpret the results.

62. *Bacteria population.* The equation

$$B(t) = 800\left(1 + \frac{6t}{90 + t^2}\right)$$

gives the number of bacteria, $B(t)$ (in millions), present in a culture at a given time, t (in weeks).
a) Determine the formula for $B'(t)$.
b) Compute $B'(2)$ and $B'(3)$, and interpret the results.

2-8 • THE CHAIN RULE

Different Variables

As we have seen, if $y = f(x)$, then its derivative is denoted by dy/dx. If letters other than y and x are dependent and independent variables, respectively, then the symbol dy/dx must be changed accordingly. Consider the function

$$z = t^3 - 8t^2 + 15t - 7$$

Since the dependent and independent variables are z and t, respectively, the derivative is denoted by dz/dt. Thus,

$$\frac{dz}{dt} = 3t^2 - 16t + 15$$

• **EXAMPLE 2-37** _____

Find the derivative of the function $w = r^4 - 8r^2 + 5$.

Solution

$dw/dr = 4r^3 - 16r$

• **EXAMPLE 2-38** _____

If $y = u^3$, then find its derivative

Solution

$dy/du = 3u^2$

We are now ready to discuss another useful rule for finding derivatives. It is called the **chain rule** and is stated here without proof.

> **Chain Rule**
>
> If $y = f(u)$ is a differentiable function of u and $u = g(x)$ is a differentiable function of x, then
>
> $$\frac{dy}{dx} = \frac{dy}{du}\frac{du}{dx}$$

The chain rule states that if y is a function of u and u is a function of x, then the derivative of y with respect to x (i.e., dy/dx) equals the derivative of y with respect to u (i.e., dy/du)times the derivative of u with respect to x (i.e., du/dx).

As an example, consider the function

$$y = (\underbrace{6x^2 - 5}_{u})^{10}$$

If we let $u = 6x^2 - 5$, then the function may be expressed as

$$y = f(u) = u^{10}$$
$$\text{where } u = 6x^2 - 5$$

Thus, the derivative, dy/dx, is calculated by using the chain rule. Hence, we write

$$\frac{dy}{dx} = \frac{dy}{du}\frac{du}{dx}$$

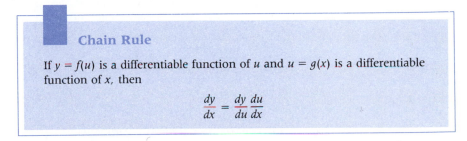

Replacing u by its equivalent expression, $6x^2 - 5$, we have

$$\frac{dy}{dx} = 10(6x^2 - 5)^9(12x)$$

$$= 120x(6x^2 - 5)^9$$

Applications

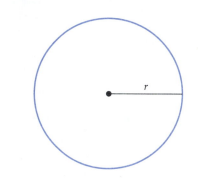

• **EXAMPLE 2-39** **Oil Spill.**

An oil tanker hits a reef and begins spilling oil over the ocean surface. The oil spill takes the form of a circle with the radius, r (in feet), increasing as a function of time in accordance with the equation

$$r = 3t^2$$

where t is the time elapsed (in days) since the tanker began leaking oil. Given that the circumference of a circle is

$$C = 2\pi r$$

where r is its radius and $\pi \approx 3.1416$.

a) Find the formula for the instantaneous rate of change of the circumference with respect to time, dC/dt.

b) Compute dC/dt after 5 days (i.e., $t = 5$).

Solutions

a) Since C is a function of r and r is a function of t, then, by the chain rule,

$$\frac{dC}{dt} = \frac{dC}{dr}\frac{dr}{dt}$$

$$= (2\pi)(6t)$$

$$= 12\pi t$$

b)

$$\left.\frac{dC}{dt}\right|_{t=5} = 12\pi(5)$$

$$= 60\pi$$

$$\approx 188.5 \text{ feet/day}$$

Thus, 5 days after the tanker began leaking oil, the circumference of the oil slick is increasing at the rate of 188.5 feet/day.

• **EXAMPLE 2-40** **Medical Science.** _____

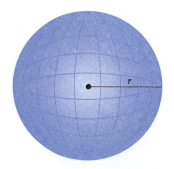

The volume, V, of a sphere is given by

$$V = \frac{4}{3}\pi r^3$$

where r is the radius of the sphere. A tumor, having the shape of a sphere, is increasing in a manner such that its radius, r (in centimeters), is enlarging in accordance with the function

$$r = 0.008t^3$$

where t denotes elapsed time in months.

a) Determine the formula for the instantaneous rate of change of volume, V, with respect to time, t.

b) Determine the instantaneous rate of change of volume with respect to time at $t = 4$ months.

Solutions

a) We want to determine dV/dt. Since V is a function of r such that $V = (4/3)\pi r^3$, we find

$$\frac{dV}{dr} = \frac{4}{3}\pi(3r^2)$$

$$= 4\pi r^2$$

Since r is a function of t such that $r = 0.008t^3$, we find

$$\frac{dr}{dt} = 0.024t^2$$

Using the chain rule, we write

$$\frac{dV}{dt} = \frac{dV}{dr}\frac{dr}{dt}$$

$$= (4\pi r^2)(0.024t^2)$$

$$= 0.096\pi r^2 t^2$$

Since $r = 0.008t^3$, we substitute $0.008t^3$ for r in the above expression for dV/dt to obtain an expression for dV/dt in terms of t. Hence,

$$\frac{dV}{dt} = 0.096\pi r^2 t^2$$

$$= 0.096\pi(0.008t^3)^2 t^2$$

$$= 0.000006144\pi t^8 = (6.144 \times 10^{-6})\pi t^8$$

b)

$$\frac{dV}{dt}\bigg|_{t=4} = (6.144 \times 10^{-6})\pi(4)^8$$

$$\approx 0.4027\pi \approx 1.27 \text{ cm}^3/\text{month}$$

Thus, at $t = 4$ months, the volume of the tumor is increasing at the rate of 1.27 cubic centimeters per month.

• EXAMPLE 2-41   Cost.

The total cost, C (in thousands of dollars), of producing x (in hundreds) units of some commodity is given by

$$C = 0.1x^3 + 9 \qquad (x \geq 0)$$

where x is related to time, t (in months), by the equation

$$x = 2t + 5 \qquad (t \geq 0)$$

Find the rate of change of cost with respect to time at $t = 4$.

Solution

We seek

$$\frac{dC}{dt}\bigg|_{t=4}$$

Since C is a function of x and x is a function of t, by the chain rule,

$$\frac{dC}{dt} = \frac{dC}{dx}\frac{dx}{dt}$$

Since $dC/dx = 0.3x^2$ and $dx/dt = 2$,

$$\frac{dC}{dt} = 0.3x^2(2)$$

$$= 0.6x^2$$

Substituting $x = 2t + 5$ into this result gives dc/dt in terms of t. Hence,

$$\frac{dC}{dt} = 0.6(2t + 5)^2$$

Evaluating this result at $t = 4$ gives

$$\frac{dC}{dt}\bigg|_{t=4} = 0.6[2(4) + 5]^2$$

$$= 0.6(13)^2 = 101.4$$

Thus, at $t = 4$, production cost is increasing at the rate of 101.4 thousand dollars per month.

General Power Rule

For functions of the form

$$y = u^n$$

where $u = f(x)$

the chain rule becomes

$$\frac{dy}{dx} = \frac{dy}{du}\frac{du}{dx}$$

$$= nu^{n-1}\frac{du}{dx}$$

This result is called the **general power rule,** which is formally stated in the following box.

> ### General Power Rule
>
> If $y = u^n$, where u is a differentiable function of x, then
>
> $$\frac{dy}{dx} = nu^{n-1}\frac{du}{dx}$$

Specifically, if

$$y = (x^6 - 8x)^{20}$$

where $u = x^6 - 8x$ and $n = 20$, we find

$$\frac{dy}{dx} = nu^{n-1}\frac{du}{dx}$$

$$= 20(x^6 - 8x)^{19}(6x^5 - 8)$$

• EXAMPLE 2-42

If $y = (x^5 - 9x^2)^{11}$, find dy/dx.

Solution

We write the above as

$$y = (x^5 - 9x^2)^{11}$$

or

$$y = u^{11}$$

where $u = x^5 - 9x^2$

Using the general power rule,

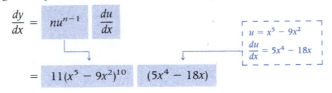

$$\frac{dy}{dx} = nu^{n-1} \quad \frac{du}{dx}$$

$u = x^5 - 9x^2$

$\dfrac{du}{dx} = 5x^4 - 18x$

$$= 11(x^5 - 9x^2)^{10} \quad (5x^4 - 18x)$$

• EXAMPLE 2-43

If $y = \sqrt{x^5 - 8}$, find dy/dx.

Solution

We rewrite the above as

$$y = (x^5 - 8)^{1/2}$$

or

$$y = u^{1/2}$$

where $u = x^5 - 8$

Using the general power rule,

$$\frac{dy}{dx} = nu^{n-1} \quad \frac{du}{dx}$$

$u = x^5 - 8$

$\dfrac{du}{dx} = 5x^4$

$$= \frac{1}{2}(x^5 - 8)^{1/2-1} \quad (5x^4)$$

$$= \frac{5}{2}x^4(x^5 - 8)^{-1/2}$$

$$= \frac{5x^4}{2\sqrt{x^5 - 8}}$$

Sometimes we must use the chain rule together with the product or quotient rules. The following two examples illustrate such situations.

• EXAMPLE 2-44

If $y = (x^3 - 6)^5(2x + 9)^8$, find dy/dx.

Solution

Since we have a product of two functions, we must first use the product rule. Hence, we calculate

$$\frac{dy}{dx} = (\text{first})\left(\begin{array}{c}\text{derivative}\\\text{of second}\end{array}\right) + (\text{second})\left(\begin{array}{c}\text{derivative}\\\text{of first}\end{array}\right)$$

$$= (x^3 - 6)^5 \cdot 8(2x + 9)^7(2) + (2x + 9)^8 \cdot 5(x^3 - 6)^4(3x^2)$$

Note that the chain rule was used to find the "derivative of second" and the "derivative of first." When simplified, the preceding result becomes

$$\frac{dy}{dx} = 16(x^3 - 6)^5(2x + 9)^7 + 15x^2(2x + 9)^8(x^3 - 6)^4$$

$$= (x^3 - 6)^4(2x + 9)^7(46x^3 + 135x^2 - 96)$$

• **EXAMPLE 2-45** _____

If

$$y = \left(\frac{x^2 + 3}{x^5 + 4}\right)^{20}$$

find dy/dx.

Solution

Since $u = (x^2 + 3)/(x^5 + 4)$ and $n = 20$, then we have

$$\frac{dy}{dx} = nu^{n-1}\frac{du}{dx}$$

$$= 20\left(\frac{x^2 + 3}{x^5 + 4}\right)^{19}\left[\frac{(x^5 + 4)(2x) - (x^2 + 3)(5x^4)}{(x^5 + 4)^2}\right]$$

Note that du/dx is computed by the quotient rule. When simplified, this result becomes

$$\frac{dy}{dx} = 20\left(\frac{x^2 + 3}{x^5 + 4}\right)^{19}\left[\frac{(-3x^6 - 15x^4 + 8x)}{(x^5 + 4)^2}\right]$$

$$= \frac{20(x^2 + 3)^{19}(-3x^6 - 15x^4 + 8x)}{(x^5 + 4)^{21}}$$

Application

• **EXAMPLE 2-46   Compound Interest.**

Five thousand dollars is deposited in an account earning interest at the rate of $r\%$ compounded monthly. At the end of 6 years, the balance in the account is given by

$$S = 5000\left(1 + \frac{r}{1200}\right)^{72}$$

Find the instantaneous rate of change of S with respect to r for these rates: $r = 6\%$, 8%, and 10%.

Solutions

We seek dS/dr evaluated at the above rates, r. Using the general power rule, we let $u = 1 + (r/1200)$ and find

$$\frac{dS}{dr} = 5000 \cdot \overset{nu^{n-1}}{72\left(1 + \frac{r}{1200}\right)^{71}} \overset{\frac{du}{dr}}{\left(\frac{1}{1200}\right)}$$

$$= 300\left(1 + \frac{r}{1200}\right)^{71}$$

For $r = 6$,

$$\frac{dS}{dr} = 300\left(1 + \frac{6}{1200}\right)^{71} \approx \$427.48$$

Thus, at a rate of 6% compounded monthly, the instantaneous rate of change of the account's balance is $427.48 per percentage point.

For $r = 8$,

$$\frac{dS}{dr} = 300\left(1 + \frac{8}{1200}\right)^{71} \approx \$480.85$$

Thus, at a rate of 8% compounded monthly, the instantaneous rate of change of the account's balance is $480.85 per percentage point.

For $r = 10$,

$$\frac{dS}{dr} = 300\left(1 + \frac{10}{1200}\right)^{71} \approx \$540.77$$

Thus, at a rate of 10% compounded monthly, the instantaneous rate of change of the account's balance is $540.77 per percentage point.

Exercises 2-8

1. If $z = t^5 - 4t^3 + 7t - 8$, find dz/dt.
2. If $h = w^3 - 4w^2 + 8w - 9$, find dh/dw.
3. If $y = u^5$, find dy/du.
4. If $u = x^2$, find du/dx.
5. If $y = 3u^6 - 8u^5 + 4u - 8$, find dy/du.
6. If $u = 8x^2 - 3x + 5$, find du/dx.
7. If $f(u) = -7u^3 - 8u^2 + 6$, find $f'(u)$.
8. If $g(t) = 8t^2 - 4t + 5$, find $g'(t)$.

Find the derivative of each of the following.

9. $y = (x^3 + 5)^{11}$ 10. $y = (x^6 - 4x + 9)^{1/2}$
11. $y = (x^3 - 6x)^{-4}$ 12. $f(x) = (x^3 + x^2 + 9x)^{-5}$
13. $f(x) = (x^4 - 9)^{15}$ 14. $y = 1/\sqrt{x^3 - 8x}$
15. $y = 1/\sqrt[3]{(x^6 - 8x)^2}$ 16. $f(x) = (x^6 - 9x^2)^{-2/5}$
17. $y = (x^3 - 4x^2 + 5)^{20}$ 18. $y = 1/(x^4 - 8x^3 + 5)^{10}$

Find the derivative of each of the following.

19. $y = (x^3 - 4x)^{10}(x^2 + 5)$ 20. $y = x(x^2 - 4x + 5)^4$
21. $y = \left(\dfrac{5x - 3}{8 - x^4}\right)^7$ 22. $y = \left(\dfrac{2x + 1}{x^2 - 5x}\right)^9$
23. $y = \dfrac{(5x - 3)^7}{(8 - x^4)^7}$ 24. $y = \dfrac{(2x + 1)^9}{(x^2 - 5x)^9}$
25. $y = [(5x - 3)(x^2 - 1)]^{10}$ 26. $y = [(6x - 7)(x^3 - 2)]^8$
27. $y = (5x - 3)^{10}(x^2 - 1)^{10}$ 28. $y = (6x - 7)^8(x^3 - 2)^8$
29. $y = (x^3 - 4x^2)^5(x^2 - 1)^3$ 30. $y = (x^2 - 4x)^6(x^2 - 5)^4$
31. $y = (x^3 + 1)^5 + (x^2 - 2)^7$ 32. $y = (x^4 + 8)^9 + (x^2 - 6)^3$
33. $y = (\sqrt{x} + 9)^5$ 34. $y = (\sqrt{x} - 3)^8$

For each of the following, find dy/dx.

35. $y = x\sqrt{x^3 + 1}$ 36. $y = x^4\sqrt{x^2 + 8x}$
37. $y = x^3/\sqrt{x + 1}$ 38. $y = x^5/\sqrt{x^2 + 5}$

For each of the following, find $\dfrac{dy}{dx}\Big|_{x = 1}$.

39. $y = 1/(x^3 + 4)$ 40. $y = x^2\sqrt{x^3 + 1}$
41. $y = x/\sqrt{x^3 + 9}$ 42. $y = \left(\dfrac{3x}{x - 6}\right)^3$

43. Find the equation of the straight line tangent to $f(x) = (x - 7)^5$ at $x = 3$.
44. Find the equation of the straight line tangent to $f(x) = 1/(x - 1)^2$ at $x = 3$.

Applications

45. *Cost.* The total cost, C, of the producing x units of some commodity is given by

$$C = x^3 + 9 \qquad (x \geq 0)$$

The number of units produced, x, is a function of the number of days, t, subsequent to the start of a production run. The variable x is related to t by the equation

$$x = 5t + 4 \qquad (t \geq 0)$$

a) Find the formula for the rate of change of cost with respect to time.
b) Evaluate the result of part a at $t = 6$ and interpret the result.

46. *Cost.* The total cost, C (in millions of dollars), of producing x (in thousands) units of some commodity is given by

$$C = 0.2x^3 + 10 \qquad (x \geq 0)$$

where x is related to time, t (in months), by the equation

$$x = 4t + 3 \qquad (t \geq 0)$$

Find the rate of change of production cost with respect to time at $t = 5$.

47. *Cost.* The total cost, C (in millions of dollars), of producing x units of some commodity is given by

$$C = 0.01x^3 + 8 \qquad (x \geq 0)$$

If production is increasing in accordance with the equation

$$x = 50t + 90$$

where t is the number of months since production of this commodity began, find the rate of change of cost with respect to time, t (in months), at a production level of 200 units.

48. *Revenue.* The revenue, R (in thousands of dollars), gained from selling x units of some product is given by

$$R = -4x^2 + 80x \qquad (0 \leq x \leq 20)$$

If sales are increasing in accordance with the equation

$$x = 30t + 20$$

where t is the number of months this product has been marketed, find the rate of change of revenue with respect to time, t (in months), at a sales level of 4 units.

49. *Compound interest.* Ten thousand dollars is deposited in an account earning interest at the rate of r% compounded quarterly. At the end of 7 years, the balance in the account is given by

$$S = 10,000 \left(1 + \frac{r}{400} \right)^{28}$$

a) Find the formula for the instantaneous rate of change of S with respect to r.

b) Find $\left. \dfrac{dS}{dr} \right|_{r = 8}$ and interpret the result.

c) Find $\left. \dfrac{dS}{dr} \right|_{r = 10}$ and interpret the result.

50. *Compound interest.* Fifteen thousand dollars is deposited into an account earning interest at the rate of $r\%$ compounded annually. At the end of 5 years, the balance in the account is given by

$$S = 15{,}000 \left(1 + \frac{r}{100}\right)^5$$

   a) Find the formula for the instantaneous rate of change of S with respect to r.

   b) Find $\left.\dfrac{dS}{dr}\right|_{r=6}$ and interpret the result.

   c) Find $\left.\dfrac{dS}{dr}\right|_{r=10}$ and interpret the result.

51. *Annuity.* At the end of each year, $6000 is deposited into an account earning interest at the rate of $r\%$ compounded annually. At the end of 8 years, the balance in the account is given by

$$S = \left(\frac{600{,}000}{r}\right)\left[\left(1 + \frac{r}{100}\right)^8 - 1\right]$$

   a) Find the formula for the instantaneous rate of change of S with respect to r.

   b) Find $\left.\dfrac{dS}{dr}\right|_{r=8}$ and interpret the result.

   c) Find $\left.\dfrac{dS}{dr}\right|_{r=10}$ and interpret the result.

52. *Annuity.* At the end of each quarter, $2000 is deposited into an account earning interest at the rate of $r\%$ compounded quarterly. At the end of 6 years, the balance in the account is given by

$$S = \left(\frac{800{,}000}{r}\right)\left[\left(1 + \frac{r}{400}\right)^{24} - 1\right]$$

   a) Find the formula for the instantaneous rate of change of S with respect r.

   b) Find $\left.\dfrac{dS}{dr}\right|_{r=8}$ and interpret the result.

   c) Find $\left.\dfrac{dS}{dr}\right|_{r=10}$ and interpret the result.

CHAPTER 2 HIGHLIGHTS

• *Concepts*

Your ability to answer the following questions is one indicator of the depth of your mastery of this chapter's important concepts. Note that the questions are grouped under various topic headings. For any question that you cannot answer, refer to the appropriate section of the chapter indicated by the topic heading. Pay particular attention to the summary boxes within a section.

2-1   LIMITS

1. Explain the term *limit*.
2. If a given function has a limit at a value of x, then this implies that the left-hand limit equals the _____-_____ _____ at that value of x.

3. Is it possible for a function to have a limit at a value of x even though the function is not defined at that value of x?

4. State six limit properties and explain each.

5. As x approaches positive or negative infinity, expressions of the form k/x^n, where n is a positive real number and k is a constant, approach _____.

6. If a function, $f(x)$, approaches L as x approaches positive (or negative) infinity, then graphically the line $y = L$ is a(n) _____ _____.

2-2 CONTINUITY

7. Explain continuity from a graphical perspective.

8. Explain continuity in terms of limits.

9. Explain what it means for a function to be continuous over an interval.

10. State and explain four continuity properties.

11. For which values of x are polynomial functions continuous?

12. For which values of x are rational functions continuous?

2-3 AVERAGE RATE OF CHANGE

13. Write the expression for the average rate of change of a function, $f(x)$, over the interval from x to $x + \Delta x$. This expression is called the _____ _____.

14. Graphically, the average rate of change between two points of a function is the slope of the _____ _____ passing through the points.

2-4 THE DERIVATIVE

15. Use limits to write an expression for the derivative.

16. Graphically, a derivative is the _____ of the _____ line to the graph of a function at a point.

2-5 DIFFERENTIABILITY AND CONTINUITY

17. A function is differentiable at a point if its _____ exists at that _____.

18. Graphically, what does it mean for a function to be differentiable at a point?

19. If a function is continuous at a point, does this imply that the function is differentiable at the point?

20. If a function is differentiable at a point, does this imply that the function is continuous at the point?

21. If a function is not continuous at a point, does this imply that it is not differentiable at the point?

2-6 RULES FOR FINDING DERIVATIVES

State and explain each of the following derivative rules.

22. Constant function rule

23. Power rule

24. Constant multiplier rule

25. Sum or difference rule

26. Explain the terms *marginal cost* and *marginal revenue*.

2-7 THE PRODUCT AND QUOTIENT RULES

State and explain each of the following derivative rules.

27. Product rule

28. Quotient rule

2-8   THE CHAIN RULE

State and explain each of the following derivative rules.

29.   Chain rule   **30.**   General power rule

REVIEW EXERCISES

• *Limits and Continuity*

For Exercises 1–6, determine whether or not $\lim_{x \to 2} f(x)$ exists.

1. $f(x) = \dfrac{1}{x-2}$

2. $f(x) = \dfrac{x^2-4}{x-2}$

3. $f(x) = 4x + 8$

4. $f(x) = \begin{cases} 2x-1 & \text{for } x \le 2 \\ x^2 & \text{for } x > 2 \end{cases}$

5. $f(x) = \dfrac{\sqrt{x} - \sqrt{2}}{x-2}$

6. $f(x) = \begin{cases} x^2 + 5 & \text{for } x \ne 2 \\ 12 & \text{for } x = 2 \end{cases}$

7–12.   For Exercises 1–6, state where the function is discontinuous.

13.   *Compound interest.* One thousand dollars is deposited into a savings account for 2 years at 8% compounded semiannually. If interest is added at the end of each half-year,
a)   Find the account's balance for each half-year.
b)   Draw a graph of the account's balance versus time, t (in half-years).
c)   Where is the graph of part b discontinuous?

14.   *Cost analysis.* A company makes machine parts. For one of its products, the variable cost is $40 per unit, and the fixed cost is $50,000 for the first 10,000 units produced. When the production level exceeds 10,000 units, the fixed cost increases by $8000.
a)   Define the cost function.
b)   Graph the cost function.
c)   Where is the cost function discontinuous?

• *Average Rate of Change*

For Exercises 15 and 16, determine the formula for the difference quotient.

15. $f(x) = x^2 - 3x + 5$

16. $f(x) = x^3 + 5x^2 - 2x + 6$

17–18.   For Exercises 15 and 16, use the formula for the difference quotient to determine the average rate of change of y with respect to x over the interval from $x = 1$ to $x = 3$.

19.   *Sales revenue.* The total sales revenue gained from producing x units of some product is given by

$$R(x) = -x^2 + 8000x \qquad (0 \le x \le 8000)$$

Determine the average rate of change of sales revenue with respect to x over the interval
a) $1000 \le x \le 3000$.   b) $1000 \le x \le 2000$.
c)   Interpret the result of part a.   d)   Interpret the result of part b.
e)   Give a graphical interpretation of the result of part a.
f)   Give a graphical interpretation of the result of part b.

• *Derivatives and Derivative Rules*

For Exercises 20–23, find

a) $f'(x)$ b) $f'(1)$ c) $f'(-2)$

20. $f(x) = x^2 - 6x - 5$ **21.** $f(x) = -5x^2 + 2x + 7$
22. $f(x) = x^3 - 3x^2 + 6x$ **23.** $f(x) = x^8 - 8x$

24. *Sales revenue.* Return to Exercise 19 and determine
    a) $R'(x)$ b) $R'(1000)$
    c) Interpret the result of part b.
    d) Give a graphical interpretation of the result of part b.
25. *Population growth.* The population, P, of a given city is related to time, t (in years), by the function

$$P(t) = 5000t^2 + 300{,}000$$

where $t = 0$ denotes the year 19X0, $t = 1$ denotes the year 19X1, etc.
    a) Determine the formula for the instantaneous rate of change of population with respect to time.
    Determine the instantaneous rate of change of the population at each of the following values of t and interpret the results.
    b) $t = 4$ c) $t = 6$ d) $t = 9$
26. Find the equation of the tangent line to $y = -x^2 + 9x$ at each of the following values of x and illustrate the results graphically.
    a) $x = 2$ b) $x = 3$ c) $x = 6$

For Exercises 27–41, find dy/dx.

27. $y = (x^2 + 4x + 7)(x^3 + 3x^2 + 8)$
28. $y = (x^3 - 4x^2 + 3)(x^5 + 6x^4 + 2)$
29. $y = (x^4 - 6x + 1)^6$ **30.** $y = x^5 + 6x^3 - 8x$
31. $y = 1/(x^2 + 8x + 2)^9$ **32.** $y = (x^3 + 5x + 8)^7$
33. $y = (x^3 + x^2 + 4)^5(x^2 + 4x + 5)$
34. $y = \dfrac{x^3 + 2x^2 - 5x}{x^2 - 4x + 8}$ **35.** $y = \dfrac{x^4 + 5x^2 + 7}{x^3 - 6x + 8}$
36. $y = \dfrac{(x^2 - 5)^8}{x^2 + 36}$ **37.** $y = \dfrac{(x^4 + 4x + 7)^9}{x^3 - 4x + 2}$
38. $y = (x^5 - 7x)\left(\dfrac{x^4 + 8x}{x^2 + 6}\right)$ **39.** $y = (x^8 + 9)\left(\dfrac{x^2 - 9}{x^4 + 7}\right)^6$
40. $y = (x + 1/\sqrt{x})(x + 3)$ **41.** $y = [(x + 6)/(x - 5)]^8$

42. *Sales revenue.* The unit price, p (in dollars), of some product is changing with demand, x, in accordance with the equation

$$p = 300 + 50x$$

The demand, x, is changing with time, t (in days), in accordance with the equation

$$x = 400 + 0.5t^3$$

    a) Determine the formula for dR/dt.
    b) Evaluate dR/dt at $t = 6$ and interpret the result.
43. *Average cost.* The cost of producing x units of some product is given by

$$C(x) = 8x + 240$$

    a) Determine the formula for the average cost per unit $\bar{C}(x)$.
    b) Determine the formula for $\bar{C}'(x)$.
    c) Find $\bar{C}'(5)$, $\bar{C}'(20)$, and $\bar{C}'(50)$, and interpret the results.

44. *Compound interest.* Twenty thousand dollars is deposited into an account earning interest at the rate of r% compounded annually. At the end of 8 years, the balance in the account is given by

$$S = 20{,}000[1 + (r/100)]^8$$

a) Find the formula for the instantaneous rate of change of S with respect to r.

b) Evaluate the result of part a at $r = 7$ and interpret the result.

c) Evaluate the result of part a at $r = 9$ and interpret the result.

45. *Annuity.* At the end of each year, $9000 is deposited into an account earning interest at the rate of r% compounded annually. At the end of 6 years, the balance in the account is given by

$$S = (900{,}000/r)([(1 + (r/100)]^6 - 1)$$

a) Find the formula for the instantaneous rate of change of S with respect to r.

b) Evaluate the result of part a at $r = 8$ and interpret the result.

c) Evaluate the result of part a at $r = 10$ and interpret the result.

• *Differentiability and Continuity*

For Exercises 46 and 47:

a) For which value(s) of x is $f(x)$ not continuous?

b) For which value(s) of x is $f(x)$ not differentiable?

46. $f(x) = 1/(x - 7)^3$　　　　　　　**47.** $f(x) = \sqrt{x - 5}$

For Exercises 48–50, for which value(s) of x is $f(x)$ not differentiable?

48. $f(x) = |x|$　　　　**49.** $f(x) = x^{1/5}$　　　　**50.** $f(x) = x^{4/5}$

Algebra Refresher

FACTORING

Difference of Two Squares

$$a^2 - b^2 = (a - b)(a + b)$$

Examples $x^2 - 36 = (x - 6)(x + 6)$ $x^2 - 7 = (x - \sqrt{7})(x + \sqrt{7})$

Worksheet

Fill in the blanks.

$x^2 - 25 = ($_____$)($_____$)$ Answer: $(x - 5)(x + 5)$

$x^2 - 81 = ($_____$)($_____$)$ Answer: $(x - 9)(x + 9)$

$x^2 - 19 = ($_____$)($_____$)$ Answer: $(x - \sqrt{19})(x + \sqrt{19})$

Trinomials

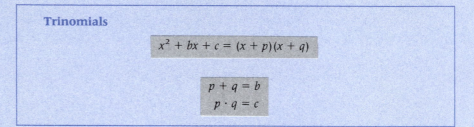

$$x^2 + bx + c = (x + p)(x + q)$$

$$p + q = b$$
$$p \cdot q = c$$

Examples $x^2 + 5x + 6 = (x + 3)(x + 2)$ $x^2 - 2x - 15 = (x - 5)(x + 3)$

Worksheet

Fill in the blanks.

$x^2 + 5x - 6 = ($_____$)($_____$)$ Answer: $(x + 6)(x - 1)$

$x^2 - 5x + 6 = ($_____$)($_____$)$ Answer: $(x - 2)(x - 3)$

$x^2 - 4x - 21 = ($_____$)($_____$)$ Answer: $(x - 7)(x + 3)$

$x^2 - 8x + 16 = ($_____$)($_____$)$ Answer: $(x - 4)(x - 4)$

$x^2 + 6x + 9 = ($_____$)($_____$)$ Answer: $(x + 3)(x + 3)$

3

CURVE SKETCHING AND OPTIMIZATION

Introductory Application

Optimization: Quality Control and Profits

Sharp Industries produces table knives. Each knife costs $6 to produce and sells for $9. The quality control manager has determined from past data that out of x knives that are produced during any given day, the fraction defective for the day is given by $x^2/20{,}000{,}000$, where $100 \leq x \leq 1500$. Each defective knife costs the company an additional $20.

a) Determine the equation that gives daily profit, P, as a function of daily production volume, x.

b) Determine the maximum daily profit and the daily production volume that yields the maximum daily profit.

In this chapter, we discuss optimization procedures that enable us to solve problems such as the one above. The above problem is solved in Example 3-20.

3-1

• HIGHER-ORDER DERIVATIVES

The Second Derivative

The derivative of a function, $y = f(x)$, commonly denoted by $f'(x)$, dy/dx, y', or $D_x y$ is called a **first derivative.** The derivative of a first derivative is called the **second derivative** and is denoted by any of the following symbols:

$$f''(x) \qquad f^{(2)}(x) \qquad \frac{d^2 y}{dx^2} \qquad y'' \qquad y^{(2)}(x) \qquad D_x^2 y \qquad D_x^2[f(x)]$$

Thus, if

$$f(x) = x^4 - 8x^3 + 7x^2 - 15$$

the first derivative is

$$f'(x) = 4x^3 - 24x^2 + 14x$$

and the second derivative is

$$f''(x) = 12x^2 - 48x + 14$$

• EXAMPLE 3-1

If $f(x) = x^5 - 8x^4 + 7x^3 - 5$, find $f'(x), f''(x)$, and $f''(1)$.

Solution

$$f'(x) = 5x^4 - 32x^3 + 21x^2$$

The derivative of $f'(x)$ is

$$f''(x) = 20x^3 - 96x^2 + 42x$$

Evaluating $f''(x)$ at $x = 1$ gives

$$f''(1) = 20(1)^3 - 96(1)^2 + 42(1) = -34$$

The derivative of the second derivative is called the **third derivative** and is denoted by any of the following symbols:

$$f'''(x) \qquad f^{(3)}(x) \qquad \frac{d^3 y}{dx^3} \qquad y''' \qquad y^{(3)}(x) \qquad D_x^3 y \qquad D_x^3[f(x)]$$

Analogously, the derivative of the third derivative is called the fourth derivative, the derivative of the fourth derivative is called the fifth derivative, etc. In general, the **nth derivative** of a function $y = f(x)$ is denoted by any of the following symbols:

$$f^{(n)}(x) \qquad \frac{d^n y}{dx^n} \qquad y^{(n)} \qquad y^{(n)}(x) \qquad D_x^n y \qquad D_x^n[f(x)]$$

• EXAMPLE 3-2

If $y = x^4 - 2x^3 + 5x^2 - 3x + 4$, find dy/dx, d^2y/dx^2, d^3y/dx^3, and $\left.\dfrac{d^3 y}{dx^3}\right|_{x=2}$.

Solution

$$\frac{dy}{dx} = 4x^3 - 6x^2 + 10x - 3$$

The derivative of dy/dx is

$$\frac{d^2y}{dx^2} = 12x^2 - 12x + 10$$

The derivative of d^2y/dx^2 is

$$\frac{d^3y}{dx^3} = 24x - 12$$

Evaluating d^3y/dx^3 at $x = 2$ gives

$$\frac{d^3y}{dx^3}\bigg|_{x=2} = 24(2) - 12 = 36$$

• **EXAMPLE 3-3** _____

If $f(x) = x^5 - 6x^4 + 3x^2 + 5$, find $f'(x), f''(x), f'''(x), f^{(4)}(x)$, and $f^{(4)}(3)$.

Solution

$$f'(x) = 5x^4 - 24x^3 + 6x$$

The derivative of $f'(x)$ is

$$f''(x) = 20x^3 - 72x^2 + 6$$

The derivative of $f''(x)$ is

$$f'''(x) = 60x^2 - 144x$$

The derivative of $f'''(x)$ is

$$f^{(4)}(x) = 120x - 144$$

Evaluating $f^{(4)}(x)$ at $x = 3$ gives

$$f^{(4)}(3) = 120(3) - 144 = 216$$

_____ •

Acceleration

A second derivative d^2y/dx^2 of a function $y = f(x)$ gives the instantaneous rate of change of the first derivative with respect to x. If $S = f(t)$, then d^2S/dt^2 gives the instantaneous rate of change of the first derivative with respect to t. Thus, if a ball moves in the path of a straight line and its distance, S (in feet), from its starting point after t seconds have elapsed is given by

$$S = -4t^2 + 36t \qquad (0 \le t \le 9)$$

then the formula for the ball's instantaneous speed (or velocity) is given by

$$\frac{dS}{dt} = -8t + 36$$

The ball's instantaneous speed (or velocity) at $t = 2$ is given by

$$\frac{dS}{dt}\bigg|_{t=2} = -8(2) + 36 = 20$$

Thus, at $t = 2$, the ball's instantaneous speed is 20 ft/sec.

The ball's instantaneous speed at $t = 3$ is given by

$$\frac{dS}{dt}\bigg|_{t=3} = -8(3) + 36 = 12$$

Thus, at $t = 3$, the ball's speed is 12 ft/sec.

Note that the ball's instantaneous speed changes as t changes. The instantaneous rate of change of speed with respect to time is called **instantaneous acceleration** and is given in this case by

$$\frac{d^2S}{dt^2} = -8$$

Thus, the ball's instantaneous acceleration is -8 ft/sec^2 (i.e., -8 feet per second per second).

The concept of acceleration is most clearly explained by considering a person driving an automobile. If the speedometer reads 50 on the mph scale, then the car is moving at a speed of 50 mph. As long as the speedometer remains at 50 mph, the car is moving at a constant speed, and the acceleration (the rate of change of speed with respect to time) is 0. If the driver further depresses the gas pedal, the speedometer's reading increases beyond 50 mph, and the acceleration is greater than 0. If the driver releases pressure on the gas pedal, the acceleration is less than 0, and the speed decreases. Negative acceleration is called **deceleration.** Specifically, the *negative* acceleration, $d^2S/dt^2 = -8$, of the ball of the above illustrative example indicates that the ball's speed is *decreasing* at a rate of 8 feet per second per second.

Exercises 3-1

For each of the following, find $f'(x)$ and $f''(x)$.

1. $f(x) = x^3 - 4x^2 + 7x - 9$
2. $f(x) = x^4 - 7x^3 + 8x - 3$
3. $f(x) = x^5 - 8x^3 + 2x^2 + 4x + 1$
4. $f(x) = (x - 1)/(x + 6)$
5. $f(x) = (x^3 + 1)(x^2 - x + 4)$
6. $f(x) = (x^2 + 5)(x^3 - x + 1)$
7. $f(x) = (x + 1)^4(x - 2) + 6$

For each of the following, find dy/dx and d^2y/dx^2.

8. $y = x^4 - 8x^3 + 6x - 9$
9. $y = x^3 - 2x^2 + 8x - 3$
10. $y = x^8 - 10x^2 + 4x + 1$
11. $y = (x^4 + 6)/(x^3 - 7)$
12. $y = (x^2 + 5)(x^3 - x + 6)$
13. $y = (x - 4)^3(x - 7) + 8$
14. If $f(x) = x^3 - 4x^2 + 7x + 9$, find $f'(x), f''(x), f'(2)$, and $f''(4)$.
15. If $g(x) = (x^2 - 1)/(x - 5)$, find $g'(x), g''(x)$, and $g''(2)$.
16. If $y(x) = (x + 1)(x + 3)^2$, find $y'(x), y''(x)$, and $y''(2)$.
17. If $y = x^4 - 5x^3 + 6x^2 + 3x + 1$, find $\dfrac{dy}{dx}, \dfrac{dy}{dx}\bigg|_{x=1}, \dfrac{d^2y}{dx^2}$, and $\dfrac{d^2y}{dx^2}\bigg|_{x=1}$.
18. If $y = x^5 - 8x^4 + 6x^3 - 9x^2 + 4$, find $\dfrac{dy}{dx}, \dfrac{dy}{dx}\bigg|_{x=2}, \dfrac{d^2y}{dx^2}$, and $\dfrac{d^2y}{dx^2}\bigg|_{x=2}$.
19. If $f(x) = x^4 - 6x^3 + 8x^2 - 4x - 5$, find $f'(x), f''(x), f'(1)$, and $f''(3)$.
20. If $f(x) = (x^3 - 1)(x^2 + x - 4)$, find $f'(x), f'(2), f''(x)$, and $f''(2)$.

21. If $f(x) = x^6 - 8x^5 + 6x^4 - 2x^3 + x + 5$, find $f'(x)$, $f''(x)$, $f'''(x)$, $f^{(4)}(x)$, and $f^{(4)}(3)$.

22. If $f(x) = x^7 - 4x^6 + 3x^4 + 6x - 9$, find $f'(x)$, $f''(x)$, $f'''(x)$, $f^{(4)}(x)$, $f^{(5)}(x)$, and $f^{(5)}(1)$.

23. If $f(x) = x^4 - 6x^3 + 4x^2 - 8x + 1$, find $f'(x)$, $f''(x)$, $f'''(x)$, $f^{(4)}(x)$, $f^{(5)}(x)$, and $f^{(6)}(x)$.

24. *Projectile.* A ball moves in the path of a straight line. Its distance, S (in feet), from its starting point after t seconds have elapsed is given by

$$S = -4t^2 + 32t \qquad (0 \le t \le 8)$$

a) Find the ball's instantaneous speed at $t = 1$ and $t = 2$.
b) Find the ball's instantaneous acceleration at $t = 1$ and $t = 2$.

25. *Projectile.* A ball is projected vertically into the air. The function defined by

$$S = -16t^2 + 192t \qquad (0 \le t \le 12)$$

gives the height of the ball (in feet) above the ground at time t (in seconds).

a) Find the ball's instantaneous speed at $t = 2$, at $t = 3$, and at $t = 8$.
b) Find the ball's instantaneous acceleration at $t = 2$, at $t = 3$, and at $t = 8$.

3-2 • CRITICAL VALUES AND THE FIRST DERIVATIVE

Consider the graph in Figure 3-1. In this chapter, we will be concerned with identifying the x- and y-coordinates of points such as A and B. We first begin by identifying points of relative maxima and relative minima. Point A $(x_1, f(x_1))$ is an example of a **relative maximum** point because it is *higher* than any of its neighboring points on the graph of $f(x)$. Mathematically, this is expressed by saying that $f(x_1) > f(x)$ for all values of x near x_1. Point B $(x_2, f(x_2))$ in Figure 3-1 is an example of a **relative minimum** point because it is *lower* than any of its neighboring points on the graph of $f(x)$. Mathematically, this is expressed by saying that $f(x_2) < f(x)$ for all values of x near x_2. More precisely, a point $(x_1, f(x_1))$ is called a relative maximum point of the function $f(x)$ if $f(x_1) > f(x)$ for all x-values in some open interval containing x_1 and in the domain of f (see Figure 3-2).* A point $(x_2, f(x_2))$ is called a relative minimum point of the function $f(x)$ if $f(x_2) < f(x)$ for all x-values in some open interval containing x_2 and in the domain of f (see Figure 3-2).

Points of relative maxima and relative minima should be distinguished from points of absolute maxima and absolute minima. Referring to Figure 3-2, point A $(x_1, f(x_1))$ is a relative maximum point because it is higher than any of its neighboring points on the graph of $f(x)$. However, it is not the highest point on the graph of $f(x)$. Observe that point C $(b, f(b))$ is higher than point A. If we choose the domain of $f(x)$ to be the closed interval $a \le x \le b$, then point C is the highest point on the graph of $f(x)$.† Hence, its y-coordinate is called the **absolute maximum** value of $f(x)$. Similarly, observe that point B $(x_2, f(x_2))$ is a relative minimum point because it is lower than any of its neighboring points on the graph of $f(x)$. However, it is not the lowest point on the graph of the function. That dis-

FIGURE 3-1

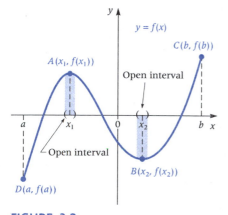

FIGURE 3-2

---

*An open interval does not contain its endpoints.
†A closed interval does contain its endpoints.

tinction is attributed to the point $D\,(a, f(a))$. Thus, the y-coordinate of point $D\,(a, f(a))$ is called the **absolute minimum** value of $f(x)$. Note that if the domain of $f(x)$ is the set of all real numbers, then there is neither an absolute maximum nor an absolute minimum since the function $f(x)$ extends downward indefinitely to the left and upward indefinitely to the right. Thus, we state the following.

SUMMARY

Relative Extrema

Relative Maximum

1. A point $(x_0, f(x_0))$ is a **relative maximum point** of a function $f(x)$ if $f(x_0) > f(x)$ for all x-values in some open interval containing x_0.
2. $f(x_0)$ is a **relative maximum value** (or, simply, *relative maximum*) of the function $f(x)$.
3. A relative maximum point is higher than any of its neighboring points on the graph of $f(x)$.

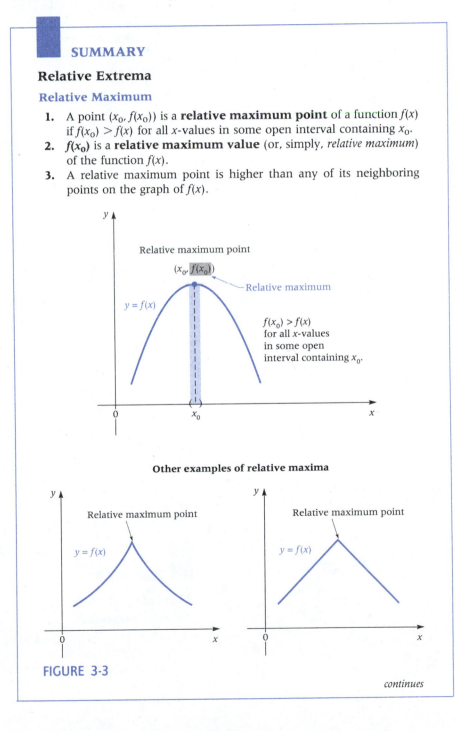

FIGURE 3-3

continues

SUMMARY—*Continued*

Relative Minimum

1. A point $(x_0, f(x_0))$ is a **relative minimum point** of a function $f(x)$ if $f(x_0) < f(x)$ for all x-values in some open interval containing x_0.
2. $f(x_0)$ is a **relative minimum value** (or, simply, *relative minimum*) of the function $f(x)$.
3. A relative minimum point is lower than any of its neighboring points on the graph of $f(x)$.

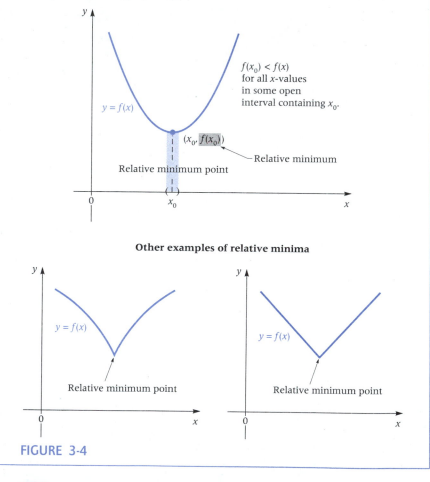

FIGURE 3-4

SUMMARY

Absolute Extrema

Absolute Maximum

1. A point $(x_0, f(x_0))$ is an **absolute maximum point** of a function $f(x)$ if $f(x_0) \geq f(x)$ for all x-values over which $f(x)$ is defined. $f(x_0)$ is the **absolute maximum value** (or, simply, *absolute maximum*) of

continues

SUMMARY—*Continued*

the function $f(x)$. The absolute maximum, $f(x_0)$, is the largest value of the function, $f(x)$ for all x-values over which $f(x)$ is defined.

2. A function can have more than one absolute maximum point, but only one absolute maximum. If a function has more than one absolute maximum point, then all such points have the same value of $f(x)$ (i.e., the same y-value). Thus, there is no point on the graph of $f(x)$ that is higher than an absolute maximum point. Study Figure 3-5.

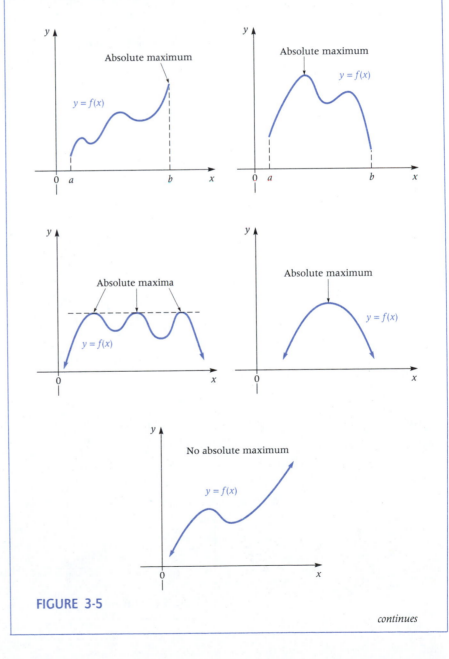

FIGURE 3-5

continues

SUMMARY—*Continued*

Absolute Minimum

1. A point $(x_0, f(x_0))$ is an **absolute minimum point** of a function $f(x)$ if $f(x_0) \leq f(x)$ for all x-values over which $f(x)$ is defined. $\boldsymbol{f(x_0)}$ is the **absolute maximum value** (or, simply, *absolute minimum*) of the function $f(x)$. The absolute minimum, $f(x_0)$, is the smallest value of the function $f(x)$ for all x-values over which $f(x)$ is defined.

2. A function can have more than one absolute minimum point, but only one absolute minimum. If a function has more than one absolute minimum point, then all such points have the same value of $f(x)$ (i.e., the same y-value). Thus, there is no point on the graph of $f(x)$ that is lower than an absolute minimum point. Study Figure 3-6.

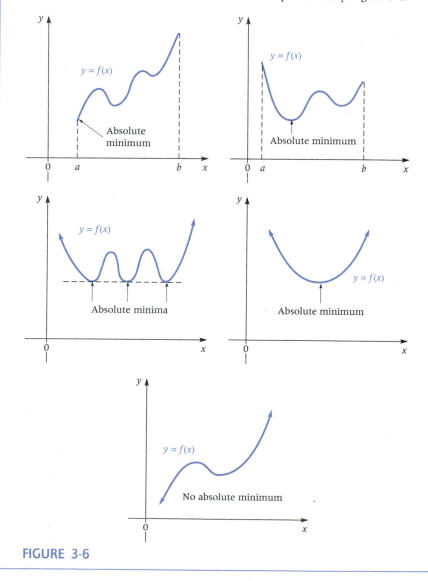

FIGURE 3-6

We also state the following.

> ### Extreme Value Theorem
>
> A continuous function defined on a closed interval will have both an absolute maximum and an absolute minimum at points in the interval.

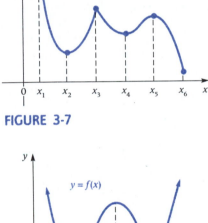

FIGURE 3-7

• **EXAMPLE 3-4**

Consider the graph in Figure 3-7.

a) Identify all relative maximum and minimum points and their respective relative maximum and minimum values.

b) Identify the absolute maximum and minimum points and their respective absolute maximum and minimum values.

Solutions

a) The relative maximum points are $(x_3, f(x_3))$ and $(x_5, f(x_5))$. Thus, $f(x_3)$ and $f(x_5)$ are relative maximum values of $f(x)$ or, simply, relative maxima. The relative minimum points are $(x_2, f(x_2))$ and $(x_4, f(x_4))$. Thus, $f(x_2)$ and $f(x_4)$ are relative minimum values of $f(x)$ or, simply, relative minima.

b) Here there is only one absolute maximum point, $(x_1, f(x_1))$. Thus, $f(x_1)$ is the absolute maximum value or, simply, absolute maximum of $f(x)$. Also, there is only one absolute minimum point, $(x_6, f(x_6))$. Thus, $f(x_6)$ is the absolute minimum value or, simply, absolute minimum of $f(x)$.

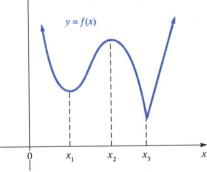

FIGURE 3-8

• **EXAMPLE 3-5**

Consider the graph in Figure 3-8.

a) Identify all relative extrema.

b) Identify all absolute extrema.

Solutions

a) $f(x_2)$ is a relative maximum; $f(x_1)$ and $f(x_3)$ are relative minima.

b) $f(x_3)$ is an absolute minimum. There is no absolute maximum as the graph of $f(x)$ continues upward indefinitely.

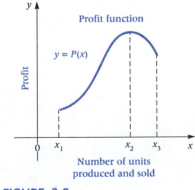

FIGURE 3-9

• **EXAMPLE 3-6**

Consider the graph of the profit function in Figure 3-9.

a) How many units should be produced and sold in order to maximize profit?

b) What is the maximum profit? Is this a relative maximum? Is this an absolute maximum?

Solutions

a) x_2 units should be produced and sold in order to maximize profit.

b) The maximum profit is given by $P(x_2)$. $P(x_2)$ is both a relative maximum and an absolute maximum.

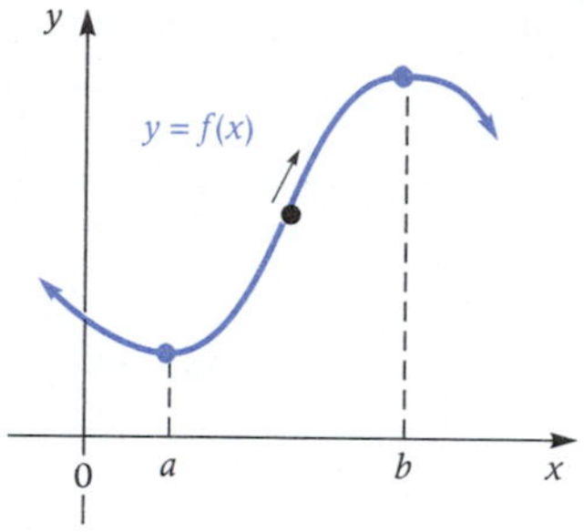

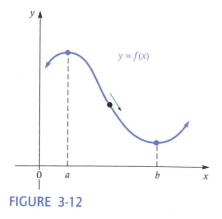

FIGURE 3-10

Increasing and Decreasing Functions

An important concept in graphing is identifying values of x for which a function $f(x)$ is increasing or decreasing. Consider the graph in Figure 3-10. If we place the point of a pencil on the graph of $f(x)$ at $x = a$ and move along the graph of $f(x)$ from $x = a$ to $x = b$, as indicated by the arrow above the black point in Figure 3-10, then our pencil will be moving uphill on the graph of $f(x)$. Thus, we say that $f(x)$ is increasing over the interval $a < x < b$. A more formal definition of an increasing function is given in the following box.

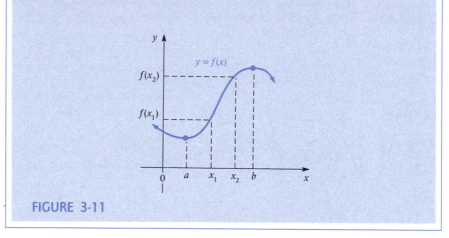

Increasing Function

Let x_1 and x_2 be any x-values in the interval $a < x < b$ such that $x_2 > x_1$ (see Figure 3-11). The function $f(x)$ is **increasing** over the interval $a < x < b$ if $f(x_2) > f(x_1)$.

FIGURE 3-11

Consider the graph in Figure 3-12. If we move our pencil along the graph of $f(x)$ from $x = a$ to $x = b$, then our pencil will be moving downhill on the graph of $f(x)$. Thus, we say that $f(x)$ is decreasing over the interval $a < x < b$. A more formal definition of a decreasing function is given in the following box.

FIGURE 3-12

Decreasing Function

Let x_1 and x_2 be any x-values in the interval $a < x < b$ such that $x_2 > x_1$ (see Figure 3-13). The function $f(x)$ is **decreasing** over the interval $a < x < b$ if $f(x_2) < f(x_1)$.

continues

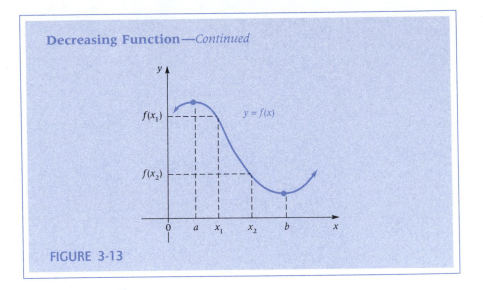

Decreasing Function—*Continued*

FIGURE 3-13

• **EXAMPLE 3-7** _____

Consider the graph in Figure 3-14.

a)   State the interval(s) over which the function $f(x)$ is increasing.
b)   State the interval(s) over which the function $f(x)$ is decreasing.
c)   Identify all relative maxima and relative minima.
d)   Identify the absolute maximum and absolute minimum values of $f(x)$.

Solutions

a)   The function $f(x)$ is increasing over the intervals $a < x < b$ and $c < x < d$.
b)   The function $f(x)$ is decreasing over the intervals $b < x < c$ and $d < x < e$.
c) $f(b)$ and $f(d)$ are relative maxima; $f(c)$ is a relative minimum.
d)   The absolute maximum is $f(d)$; the absolute minimum is $f(c)$.

                                                                              •

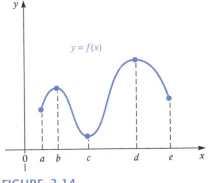

FIGURE 3-14

We will now be concerned mainly with graphing functions and with determining their relative maxima and relative minima. In this regard, we consider the graph of the function illustrated in Figure 3-15 on page 194. Observe that certain segments of the function are identified as either increasing or decreasing. Specifically, the function $f(x)$ is *increasing* as we move along its path from point D to point A and from point B to point C. Thus, the function is said to be increasing on each of the intervals $a < x < x_1$ and $x_2 < x < b$. Note that, within these intervals, any tangent line to the function has a *positive slope*. Since the slope of a tangent line is the derivative of the function at the point of tangency, we state the following.

> *Given that* f(x) *is differentiable on the interval* a < x < b, *then* f(x) *is increasing on this interval if* f'(x) > 0 *for all values of* x *within* a <).

Again referring to Figure 3-15 on page 194, observe that the function is *decreasing* as we move along its path from point A to point B. The function is said to be decreasing on the interval $x_1 < x < x_2$. Any tangent line to the function within this interval has a *negative slope*. Thus, we state the following.

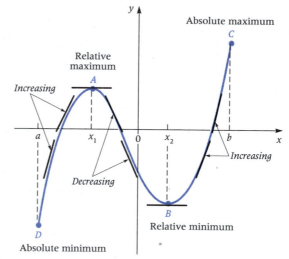

FIGURE 3-15

Given that f(x) *is differentiable on the interval* a < x < b, *then* f(x) *is decreasing on this interval if* f'(x) < 0 *for all values of* x *within* a < x < b.

Thus, for a given function, we can use the first derivative to determine where the function is increasing or decreasing, as summarized in the following box.

SUMMARY

First Derivative and Increasing and Decreasing Functions

Given a function $f(x)$ that is differentiable on some open interval, then

- If $f'(x) > 0$ for all values of x in the open interval, then $f(x)$ is **increasing** on the interval (see Figure 3-16).

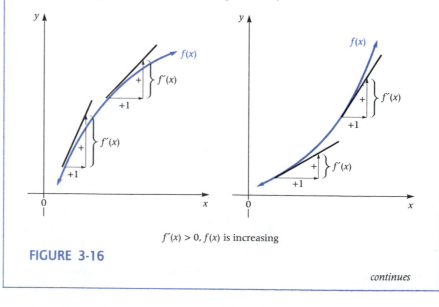

$f'(x) > 0, f(x)$ is increasing

FIGURE 3-16

continues

SUMMARY—*Continued*

- If $f'(x) < 0$ for all values of x in some open interval, then $f(x)$ is **decreasing** on the interval (see Figure 3-17).

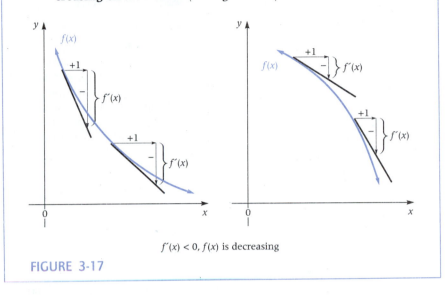

$f'(x) < 0$, $f(x)$ is decreasing

FIGURE 3-17

Once again observing Figure 3-15, note that at a point of relative maximum or relative minimum, the tangent line is *horizontal*. Hence, its *slope is 0*. Since the slope of a tangent line is the derivative of the function, then $f'(x) = 0$ for values of x where $f(x)$ has either relative maxima or minima. We now state the following.

If a function $f(x)$ *has either a relative minimum or a relative maximum at* $x = x_0$ *and is differentiable at* $x = x_0$, *then*

$$f'(x_0) = 0$$

Thus, we can usually identify relative maxima and relative minima by finding the values of x for which $f'(x) = 0$. This assumes that $f(x)$ is differentiable at the points of relative maxima and minima. However, this is not always the case. An example of a function that is not differentiable at a relative minimum is $f(x) = x^{2/3}$. Observing its graph in Figure 3-18, note that the point $(0, 0)$ is a relative minimum point since it is lower than any of its neighboring points. However, since the graph of $f(x)$ comes to a sharp point at $x = 0$, then $f(x)$ is not differentiable there. Hence, $f'(0)$ does not exist. Therefore, in order to identify points of relative maxima and relative minima of a continuous function $f(x)$, we should follow the subsequent procedure.

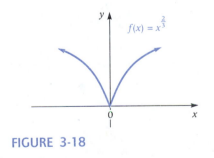

FIGURE 3-18

To Identify Candidates for Relative Extrema

Find $f'(x)$ and determine those values of x for which $f'(x) = 0$. Additionally, look for values of x at which $f'(x)$ does not exist.

Values of x at which either $f'(x) = 0$ or $f'(x)$ does not exist are called **critical values.** We summarize as follows.

SUMMARY

Critical Values and Relative Extrema

1. **Critical values** of x are those values of x at which either $f'(x) = 0$ or $f'(x)$ is undefined, and $f(x)$ is defined.
2. **Existence of Relative Extrema.** Given that $f(x)$ is continuous over some open interval, then relative maxima or minima, if they exist, occur at critical values of x.
   Note: This does not mean that all critical values yield relative extrema. We should understand that a critical value may or may not yield relative extrema. In other words, critical values yield candidates for relative extrema.

• EXAMPLE 3-8

Find the critical values of $f(x) = 2x^3 - 3x^2 - 36x + 7$.

Solution

Here we calculate

$$f'(x) = 6x^2 - 6x - 36$$

Since we seek values of x for which $f'(x) = 0$, we set $f'(x) = 0$ and solve for x to obtain

$$6x^2 - 6x - 36 = 0$$
$$6(x^2 - x - 6) = 0$$
$$6(x - 3)(x + 2) = 0$$

Thus, $x = 3$ and $x = -2$ are critical values. Since there are no values of x at which $f'(x)$ does not exist, these are the only critical values. Computing the corresponding y-coordinates, we have

$$f(3) = 2(3)^3 - 3(3)^2 - 36(3) + 7 = -74$$
$$f(-2) = 2(-2)^3 - 3(-2)^2 - 36(-2) + 7 = 51$$

Hence, the points $(3, -74)$ and $(-2, 51)$ are candidates for relative maximum and minimum points.

• EXAMPLE 3-9

Find the critical values of $f(x) = x^{2/3}$.

Solution

Here we calculate

$$f'(x) = \frac{2}{3}x^{-1/3}$$

$$= \frac{2}{3} \cdot \frac{1}{x^{1/3}} = \frac{2}{3} \cdot \frac{1}{\sqrt[3]{x}}$$

A sign chart for $f'(x)$ is given in Table 3-1.

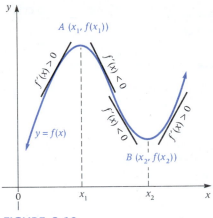

FIGURE 3-19

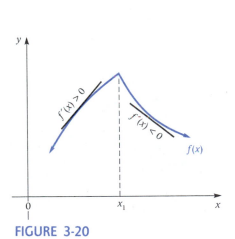

FIGURE 3-20

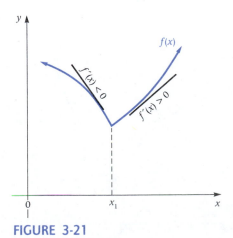

FIGURE 3-21

TABLE 3-1

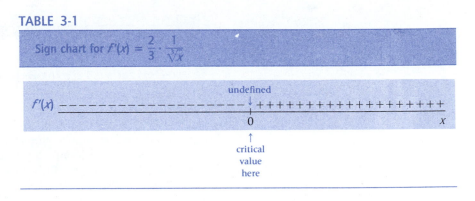

Sign chart for $f'(x) = \dfrac{2}{3} \cdot \dfrac{1}{\sqrt[3]{x}}$

Note that there are no values of x for which $f'(x) = 0$. However, $f'(x)$ does not exist at $x = 0$. Thus, $x = 0$ is the only critical value. Computing the corresponding y-coordinate, we have

$$f(0) = 0^{2/3} = 0$$

Therefore, $(0, 0)$ is a candidate for a relative maximum or minimum point.

Recall, from Section 2-5, that the graph of $f(x) = x^{2/3}$ is as given in Figure 3-18.

First-Derivative Test

A critical value may or may not lead to a relative maximum or minimum point. In other words, not every critical value yields a relative maximum or minimum point. Thus, we need a test to determine whether a critical value yields either a relative maximum or a relative minimum, or neither. One such test is called the **first-derivative test** since it is based on the first derivative, $f'(x)$, of a function $f(x)$.

We will explain the first-derivative test by referring to the function in Figure 3-19. Observing the relative maximum point A $(x_1, f(x_1))$, note that the tangent line to the left of x_1 has a positive slope, whereas the tangent line to the right of x_1 has a negative slope. Thus, if x_1 is a critical value of $f(x)$, then x_1 yields a relative maximum if $f'(x) > 0$ for all nearby values of x to the left of x_1 and $f'(x) < 0$ for all nearby values of x to the right of x_1. This is true even if $f'(x_1)$ does not exist (see Figure 3-20). For a relative minimum, the reverse holds. Observing the relative minimum point B $(x_2, f(x_2))$ in Figure 3-19, note that the tangent line to the left of x_2 has a negative slope, whereas the tangent line to the right of x_2 has a positive slope. Thus, if x_2 is a critical value of $f(x)$, then x_2 yields a relative minimum if $f'(x) < 0$ for all nearby values of x to the left of x_2 and $f'(x) > 0$ for all nearby values of x to the right of x_2. This also is true even if $f'(x_2)$ does not exist, as illustrated in Figure 3-21. Thus, we now state the first-derivative test.

SUMMARY

First-Derivative Test for Relative Extrema

If x_0 is a critical value of $f(x)$ (in other words, $f'(x_0) = 0$ or $f'(x_0)$ is undefined) where $f(x_0)$ is defined, then

1. $f(x_0)$ is a **relative maximum** of $f(x)$ if $f'(x)$ is positive for all nearby values of x to the left of x_0 and $f'(x)$ is negative for all nearby values of x to the right of x_0 (see Figure 3-22).

2. $f(x_0)$ is a **relative minimum** of $f(x)$ if $f'(x)$ is negative for all nearby values of x to the left of x_0 and $f'(x)$ is positive for all nearby values of x to the right of x_0 (see Figure 3-23).

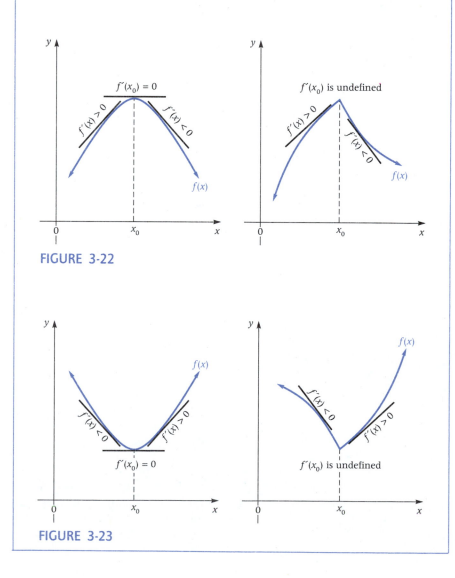

FIGURE 3-22

FIGURE 3-23

• EXAMPLE 3-10

Find the relative maxima and minima of the function $f(x) = x^3 + 3x^2 - 72x + 9$.

Solution

First, we find

$$f'(x) = 3x^2 + 6x - 72$$

Setting $f'(x) = 0$ and solving for x yields

$$3x^2 + 6x - 72 = 0$$
$$3(x^2 + 2x - 24) = 0$$
$$3(x + 6)(x - 4) = 0$$

Thus, $x = -6$ and $x = 4$ are critical values. Since there are no values of x at which $f'(x)$ does not exist, these are the only critical values. We now apply the first-derivative test by analyzing the sign of $f'(x)$, as illustrated in Table 3-2.

Studying Table 3-2 on page 200, note that the sign of $3(x + 6)$ is the same as the sign of $(x + 6)$ since the *positive* constant multiplier, 3, does not change the sign of $(x + 6)$. Since $f'(x) > 0$ for all nearby values of x to the left of $x = -6$ and $f'(x) < 0$ for all nearby values of x to the right of $x = -6$, then, by the first-derivative test, a relative maximum exists at $x = -6$. Also, since $f'(x) < 0$ for all nearby values of x to the left of $x = 4$ and $f'(x) > 0$ for all nearby values of x to the right of $x = 4$, then, by the first derivative test, a relative minimum exists at $x = 4$.

Computing the y-coordinates corresponding to the relative maximum and minimum, we have

$$f(-6) = (-6)^3 + 3(-6)^2 - 72(-6) + 9 = 333 \qquad \text{Relative maximum}$$
$$f(4) = 4^3 + 3(4)^2 - 72(4) + 9 = -167 \qquad \text{Relative minimum}$$

Plotting the relative maximum and minimum points and the y-intercept on the rectangular coordinate system gives us the graph in Figure 3-24. Observe that it is not difficult to determine the general nature of the graph of $f(x)$, which appears in Figure 3-25, since $f(x)$ is increasing for those values of x at which $f'(x) > 0$ and decreasing for those values of x at which $f'(x) < 0$.

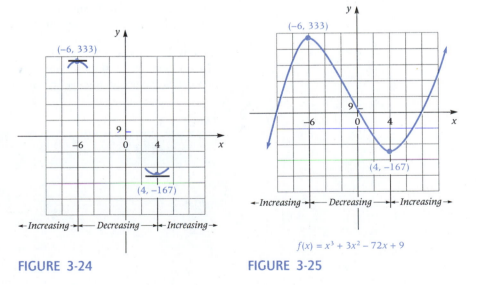

FIGURE 3-24

FIGURE 3-25

TABLE 3-2

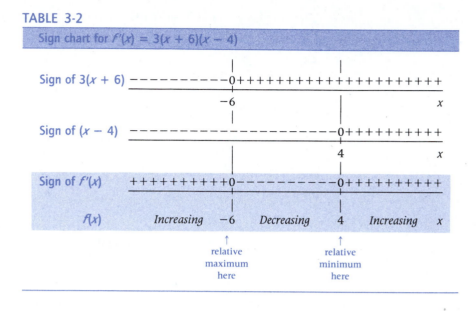

Remember that a sign change in $f'(x)$ indicates the occurrence of a relative extremum. The nature of the sign change indicates whether the relative extremum is either a maximum or a minimum.

• EXAMPLE 3-11

Find any relative maxima and minima of the function $f(x) = x^{2/3}$.

Solution

In Example 3-9, we calculated

$$f'(x) = \frac{2}{3} \cdot \frac{1}{x^{1/3}}$$

which yielded a critical value of $x = 0$. Applying the first-derivative test, we analyze the sign of $f'(x)$. Note that, as illustrated in Table 3-3, the sign of $f'(x)$ is the same as the sign of $x^{1/3} = \sqrt[3]{x}$. If $x > 0$, then $\sqrt[3]{x} > 0$, and, hence, $f'(x) > 0$. If $x < 0$, then $\sqrt[3]{x} < 0$, and, hence, $f'(x) < 0$. Since $f'(x) < 0$ for all nearby values of x to the left of $x = 0$ and $f'(x) > 0$ for all nearby values of x to the right of $x = 0$, then, by the first-derivative test, a relative minimum exists at $x = 0$. Note that $f(0) = 0^{2/3} = 0$.

TABLE 3-3

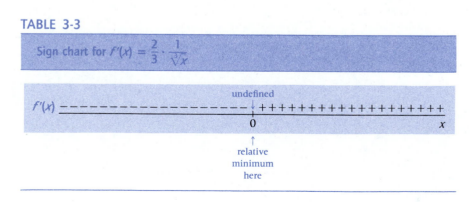

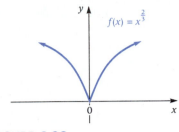

$f(x) = x^{\frac{2}{3}}$

FIGURE 3-26

Although the preceding information does not enable us to sketch a graph of $f(x)$, its graph is included in Figure 3-26.

• **EXAMPLE 3-12   Sales Revenue.** _____

The sales revenue, R (in millions of dollars), gained from selling x (in thousands) units of a particular product is given by

$$R(x) = -x^3 - 6x^2 + 180x \qquad (0 \le x \le 10)$$

a) Graph the function $R(x)$ and determine the relative and absolute extrema.
b) How many units of this product should be produced and sold in order to maximize the sales revenue? What is the maximum sales revenue?

Solutions

a) We find

$$R'(x) = -3x^2 - 12x + 180$$

Setting $R'(x) = 0$ and solving for x yields

$$0 = -3x^2 - 12x + 180$$
$$0 = -3(x^2 + 4x - 60)$$
$$0 = -3(x - 6)(x + 10)$$

Thus, $x = 6$ and $x = -10$ are critical values. We rule out $x = -10$ since the function $R(x)$ is defined over the interval $0 \le x \le 10$. Since there are no values of x at which $R(x)$ does not exist, then $x = 6$ is the only relevant critical value. We now apply the first-derivative test by analyzing the sign of $R'(x)$ in Table 3-4. Although we include the sign chart for all values of x, we are concerned only with that portion over the interval $0 \le x \le 10$. Accordingly, we have shaded the corresponding portion in Table 3-4.

Note that the sign chart of Table 3-4 indicates the occurrence of a relative maximum at the critical value $x = 6$. Then we find the y-coordinate

TABLE 3-4

Sign chart for $R'(x) = -3(x - 6)(x + 10)$

Sign of $-3(x - 6)$ + 0 – – – – – – – – – –

6   10 x

Sign of $(x + 10)$ – – – – – – – – – – 0 +

–10   10 x

Sign of $R'(x)$ – – – – – – – – – 0 + + + + + + + + + + 0 – – – – – – – – –

–10   6   10 x

$R(x)$

relative minimum here   relative maximum here

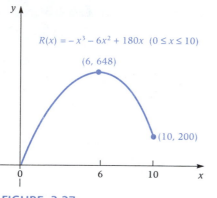

$R(x) = -x^3 - 6x^2 + 180x \quad (0 \le x \le 10)$

(6, 648)

(10, 200)

FIGURE 3-27

corresponding to $x = 6$ along with the y-coordinates of the endpoints of the interval $0 \le x \le 10$. Hence,

$$R(6) = -(6)^3 - 6(6)^2 + 180(6) = 648$$
$$R(0) = -(0)^3 - 6(0)^2 + 180(0) = 0$$
$$R(10) = -(10)^3 - 6(10)^2 + 180(10) = 200$$

The graph of $R(x)$ is sketched in Figure 3-27. Note that both a relative maximum and an absolute maximum occur at $x = 6$. An absolute minimum occurs at $x = 0$.

b) Thus, $x = 6$ thousand (remember that x is in thousands) units must be produced and sold in order to maximize sales revenue. The maximum sales revenue is given by the absolute maximum, $R(6) = 648$ million (remember that $R(x)$ is in millions) dollars.

Exercises 3-2

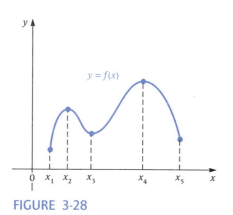

$y = f(x)$

FIGURE 3-28

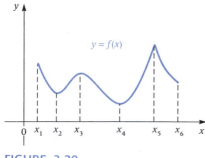

$y = f(x)$

FIGURE 3-29

1. Consider the graph of Figure 3-28.
   a) State the interval(s) over which the function $f(x)$ is increasing.
   b) State the interval(s) over which the function $f(x)$ is decreasing.
   c) Identify all relative maxima and minima.
   d) Identify the absolute maximum and minimum values of $f(x)$.
2. Consider the graph of Figure 3-29.
   a) State the interval(s) over which $f(x)$ is increasing.
   b) State the interval(s) over which $f(x)$ is decreasing.
   c) Identify all relative maxima and minima.
   d) Identify the absolute maximum and minimum values of $f(x)$.

For each of the following sign charts, assume that the function $f(x)$ is continuous over the interval $(-\infty, \infty)$.
a) State the interval(s) over which the function $f(x)$ is increasing.
b) State the interval(s) over which the function $f(x)$ is decreasing.
c) State where relative maxima or minima occur.

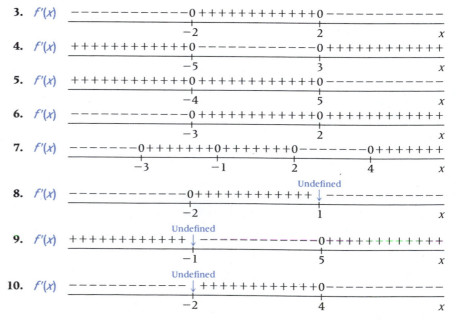

3. $f'(x)$ $----------0+++++++++++0----------$
   $-2 \qquad 2 \qquad x$

4. $f'(x)$ $+++++++++++0-----------0+++++++++++$
   $-5 \qquad 3 \qquad x$

5. $f'(x)$ $+++++++++++0+++++++++++0-----------$
   $-4 \qquad 5 \qquad x$

6. $f'(x)$ $----------0+++++++++++0+++++++++++$
   $-3 \qquad 2 \qquad x$

7. $f'(x)$ $------0+++++++0+++++++0------0+++++++$
   $-3 \qquad -1 \qquad 2 \qquad 4 \qquad x$

8. $f'(x)$ $----------0+++++++++++ \quad \text{Undefined} \downarrow ----------$
   $-2 \qquad 1 \qquad x$

9. $f'(x)$ $+++++++++++ \quad \text{Undefined} \downarrow -----------0+++++++++++$
   $-1 \qquad 5 \qquad x$

10. $f'(x)$ $---------- \quad \text{Undefined} \downarrow +++++++++++0----------$
    $-2 \qquad 4 \qquad x$

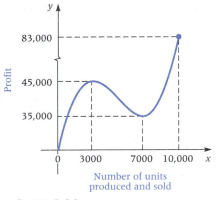

FIGURE 3-30

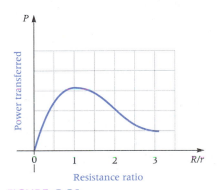

FIGURE 3-31

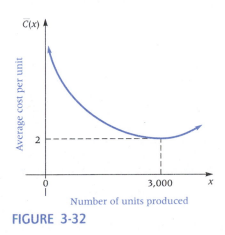

FIGURE 3-32

11. *Profit function.* Consider the graph of the profit function in Figure 3-30.
    a) State the interval(s) over which profit is increasing.
    b) State the interval(s) over which profit is decreasing.
    c) Identify all relative extrema.
    d) How many units should be produced and sold in order to maximize profit?
    e) What is the maximum profit? Is this a relative maximum? Is this an absolute maximum?

12. *Physics: Power transfer.* When energy, such as electrical energy, is transferred from a source to a system (such as from a battery to an electrical system), the power, P, transferred to the system is a function of the ratio of the external resistance, R (the resistance of the system), to the internal resistance, r (the resistance of the source). Figure 3-31 gives a graph of this relationship.
    a) What resistance ratio, R/r, yields the maximal power transfer? Is this a relative maximum? Is this an absolute maximum?
    b) What relationship must exist between R and r in order for the maximal power transfer to occur?

13. *Average cost per unit.* Figure 3-32 gives a graph of the average cost per unit, $\overline{C}$, versus the number of units produced, x.
    a) How many units should be produced in order to minimize the average cost per unit?
    b) What is the minimum average cost per unit? Is this a relative minimum? Is this an absolute minimum?

For each of the following, use the first derivative to
a) Determine the interval(s) over which the function is increasing.
b) Determine the interval(s) over which the function is decreasing.
c) Determine any relative maxima and minima.

14. $y = x^2 + 2x - 15$
15. $y = 3x + 5$
16. $y = -2x + 8$
17. $y = -x^2 + 8x$
18. $y = 2x^3 + 15x^2 - 36x + 1$
19. $f(x) = 3x^4 - 4x^3 + 10$
20. $f(x) = 4x^3 - 72x^2 + 24x - 5$
21. $y = \sqrt{x^2 + 4}$
22. $y = \sqrt{x^2 + 9}$
23. $y = (x - 5)^3$
24. $y = \dfrac{x + 5}{x - 4}$
25. $y = \dfrac{x + 3}{x + 1}$

For each of the following, use the first derivative to
a) Determine the interval(s) over which the function is increasing.
b) Determine the interval(s) over which the function is decreasing.
c) Determine any relative maxima and minima.
d) Graph the function.

26. $y = x^2 + 8x + 5$
27. $y = -x^2 + 8x + 9$
28. $f(x) = -4x^2 + 32x + 19$
29. $y = x^3 - 6x^2$
30. $f(x) = 2x^3 + 3x^2 - 36x + 8$
31. $y = x^4 - 8x^2$
32. $f(x) = 3x^4 - 8x^3 + 20$
33. $y = x^4 + 5$

34. Find any relative maxima and minima of the function defined by $f(x) = x^{4/3}$. Use the first-derivative test.

35. Consider the function defined by

$$f(x) = x^3 + 6x^2 - 15x + 1 \qquad (-10 \le x \le 11)$$

Use the first-derivative test to find all relative maximum and relative minimum points. Also, determine the absolute maximum and minimum values of $f(x)$. Graph $f(x)$.

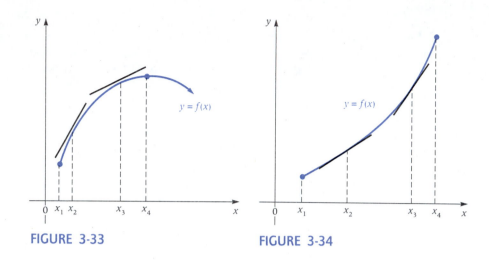

FIGURE 3-33 **FIGURE 3-34**

36. Consider the function defined by

$$f(x) = -x^3 - 9x^2 + 21x + 4 \qquad (-8 \le x \le 10)$$

Use the first-derivative test to find all relative maximum and relative minimum points. Also, determine the absolute maximum and minimum values of $f(x)$. Graph $f(x)$.

37. Use the first derivative to show that the x-coordinate of the vertex of a quadratic equation of the form $f(x) = ax^2 + bx + c$ is $-b/2a$.

38. Consider the graph in Figure 3-33.
   a) State the interval over which $f(x)$ is increasing.
   b) Observe the slopes of the tangent lines at $x = x_2$ and $x = x_3$. Is $f'(x_3) < f'(x_2)$? As one moves along the graph of $f(x)$ from $x = x_1$ to $x = x_4$, are the values of $f(x)$ increasing at an increasing rate, or are they increasing at a decreasing rate?

39. Consider the graph in Figure 3-34.
   a) State the interval over which $f(x)$ is increasing.
   b) Observe the slopes of the tangent lines at $x = x_2$ and $x = x_3$. Is $f'(x_3) > f'(x_2)$? As one moves along the graph of $f(x)$ from $x = x_1$ to $x = x_4$, are the values of $f(x)$ increasing at an increasing rate, or are they increasing at a decreasing rate?

Applications

40. *Projectile.* At the same instant a ball is projected into the air, a stopwatch is activated. The function

$$S(x) = -16x^2 + 96x \qquad (0 \le x \le 6)$$

gives the height (in feet) above the ground of the ball after x seconds have elapsed.
   a) State the interval(s) over which the height of the ball is increasing.
   b) State the interval(s) over which the height of the ball is decreasing.
   c) Identify all relative extrema.
   d) Graph the function, $S(x)$.
   e) When does the ball reach its maximum height? Is this a relative maximum? Is this an absolute maximum?
   f) What is the maximum height?

41. *Revenue function.* The sales revenue gained from selling x units of some product is given by
$$R(x) = -x^2 + 40x \qquad (0 \leq x \leq 40)$$
    a) State the interval(s) over which sales revenue is increasing.
    b) State the interval(s) over which sales revenue is decreasing.
    c) Identify all relative extrema.
    d) Graph the function, $R(x)$.
    e) What sales volume maximizes sales revenue? Is this a relative maximum? Is this an absolute maximum?
    f) What is the maximum sales revenue?

42. *Profit function.* The profit gained from producing and selling x units of some product is given by
$$P(x) = 3x - \frac{x^3}{1{,}000{,}000} \qquad (0 \leq x \leq 1500)$$
    a) State the interval(s) over which profit is increasing.
    b) State the interval(s) over which profit is decreasing.
    c) Identify any relative extrema.
    d) Graph the profit function.
    e) How many units should be produced and sold in order to maximize profit? Is this a relative maximum? Is this an absolute maximum?
    f) What is the maximum profit?

43. *Social science: Survey costs.* The total cost of surveying x respondents for a behavioral research study is given by
$$C(x) = 20(x - 100)^2 + 1000 \qquad (x \geq 90)$$
    a) State the interval(s) over which the function $C(x)$ is increasing.
    b) State the interval(s) over which the function $C(x)$ is decreasing.
    c) Graph the function, $C(x)$.
    d) How many respondents should be surveyed in order to minimize the total survey cost? Is this a relative minimum? Is this an absolute minimum?
    e) Find the minimum total survey cost.

44. *Learning.* An educational institution that specializes in teaching foreign languages to executives has determined that the length of time (in minutes) per word it takes a typical executive to learn x new words is given by
$$L(x) = 0.1(x - 10)^2 + 0.5 \qquad (0 \leq x \leq 20)$$
    a) State the interval(s) over which the function $L(x)$ is increasing.
    b) State the interval(s) over which the function $L(x)$ is decreasing.
    c) Graph the function, $L(x)$.
    d) How many words should be given to an executive to learn so that the learning time per word is minimized? Is this a relative minimum? Is this an absolute minimum?
    e) Find the minimum learning time per word.

3-3

• CONCAVITY AND THE SECOND DERIVATIVE

In Section 3-2, we discussed the first-derivative test for determining whether a critical value yields a relative maximum, a relative minimum, or

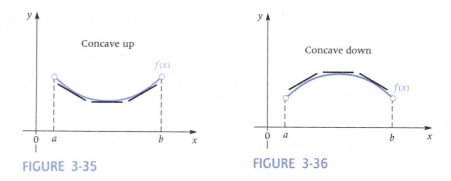

FIGURE 3-35   FIGURE 3-36

neither. Another test exists for making this determination, called the **second-derivative test.** In order to apply it, we must first consider the second derivative.

Graphical Interpretation of the Second Derivative

In order to discuss the graphical interpretation of the second derivative, we must define the terms *concave up* and *concave down* as they relate to functions. A function $f(x)$ is said to be **concave up** on an interval $a < x < b$ if each tangent line to the graph of $f(x)$ lies below the graph of $f(x)$ (see Figure 3-35). A function $f(x)$ is said to be **concave down** on an interval $a < x < b$ if each tangent line to the graph of $f(x)$ lies above its graph (see Figure 3-36). In Chapter 1, we classified the graphs of quadratic functions (parabolas) as either opening up or opening down. In terms of concavity, a parabola that opens up is said to be concave up, and a parabola that opens down is said to be concave down (see Figure 3-37).

We now consider the graph in Figure 3-38. Observe that $f(x)$ is concave up the interval $a < x < x_0$ and concave down on the interval $x_0 < x < b$. At $x = x_0$, the graph of $f(x)$ changes in concavity. Such a point, where a curve changes in concavity, is called an **inflection point.** Note that as we move along the concave-up portion of the curve from $(a, f(a))$ toward $(x_0, f(x_0))$, the slopes of the tangent lines are increasing. Thus, $f'(x)$ is increasing on the interval $a < x < x_0$. Since $f'(x)$ is increasing on the interval $a < x < x_0$, then its derivative $f''(x) > 0$. Analogously, as we move along the concave-down portion of the curve from $(x_0, f(x_0))$ to $(b, f(b))$, the slopes of the tangent lines are decreasing. Thus, $f'(x)$ is decreasing on the interval $x_0 < x < b$. Since $f'(x)$ is decreasing on the interval $x_0 < x < b$, then its derivative $f''(x) < 0$. At the inflection point, x_0, the second derivative $f''(x_0) = 0$. Therefore, as we move along a concave-up portion of the graph of a function, the first derivative is increasing, and, thus, the second derivative is positive. As we move along a concave-down portion, the first derivative is decreasing, and, thus, the second derivative is negative. At an inflection point, the first derivative is neither increasing nor decreasing, and, thus, the second derivative is often 0. However, this is not always the case (see Exercise 45 at the end of this section). A true test of the existence of an inflection point at $x = x_0$ is a change in sign of the second derivative at $x = x_0$. We summarize as follows.

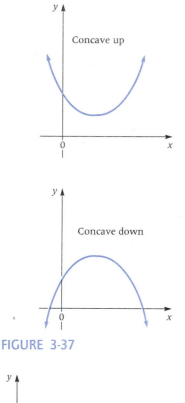

FIGURE 3-37

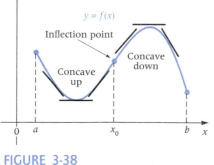

FIGURE 3-38

SUMMARY

Second Derivative and Concavity

1. A function $f(x)$ is concave up at all values of x for which $f''(x) > 0$, as illustrated in Figure 3-39.
2. A function $f(x)$ is concave down at all values of x for which $f''(x) < 0$, as illustrated in Figure 3-40.
3. If $f''(x)$ changes sign at $x = x_0$, than an inflection point occurs at $x = x_0$ (see Figure 3-41).

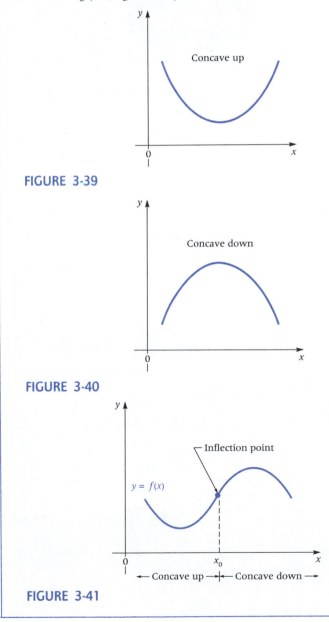

FIGURE 3-39

FIGURE 3-40

FIGURE 3-41

TABLE 3-5 First and second derivatives and shape of graph

Sign of $f'(x)$	Positive	Negative	Negative	Positive
Sign of $f''(x)$	Negative	Negative	Positive	Positive
Is $f(x)$ increasing or decreasing?	Increasing	Decreasing	Decreasing	Increasing
Concavity of $f(x)$	Concave down	Concave down	Concave up	Concave up
Shape of graph of $f(x)$				

Table 3-5 summarizes the results of both first and second derivatives and the shape of the graph of the function.

• **EXAMPLE 3-13** _____

Use both first and second derivatives to graph

$$f(x) = x^4 - 6x^2 + 10$$

Identify all relative and absolute extrema and inflection points.

Solution

First-Derivative Analysis

First, we find

$$f'(x) = 4x^3 - 12x$$
$$= 4x(x^2 - 3) \quad\quad\boxed{\text{Use difference of two squares.}}$$
$$= 4x(x - \sqrt{3})(x + \sqrt{3})$$

TABLE 3-6

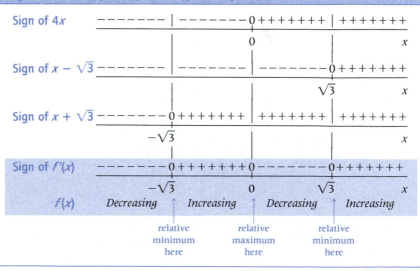

Setting $f'(x) = 0$ and solving for x gives critical values of

$$x = 0, x = \sqrt{3}, \text{ and } x = -\sqrt{3}$$

Since there are no values of x at which $f'(x)$ does not exist, these are the only critical values.

We now analyze the sign of $f'(x)$ to determine where $f(x)$ is increasing or decreasing and to determine points of relative extrema. A sign chart of $f'(x)$ is given in Table 3-6 on page 208. Note that relative minima occur at critical values $x = \pm\sqrt{3}$ and a relative maximum occurs at the critical value $x = 0$. We find the y-coordinates corresponding to the critical values. Hence,

$$f(0) = (0)^4 - 6(0)^2 + 10 = 10$$
$$f(-\sqrt{3}) = (-\sqrt{3})^4 - 6(-\sqrt{3})^2 + 10 = 1$$
$$f(\sqrt{3}) = (\sqrt{3})^4 - 6(\sqrt{3})^2 + 10 = 1$$

We begin to graph $f(x)$ in Figure 3-42 and include the above results.

Second-Derivative Analysis

We find

$$f''(x) = 12x^2 - 12$$
$$= 12(x^2 - 1)$$
$$= 12(x - 1)(x + 1)$$

and construct its sign chart in Table 3-7.

From Table 3-7, we learn that inflection points occur at $x = \pm 1$. Computing their y-coordinates, we obtain

$$f(-1) = (-1)^4 - 6(-1)^2 + 10 = 5$$
$$f(1) = (1)^4 - 6(1)^2 + 10 = 5$$

The results of the second-derivative analysis are summarized in Figure 3-43 on page 210, and the graph of $f(x)$ is sketched.

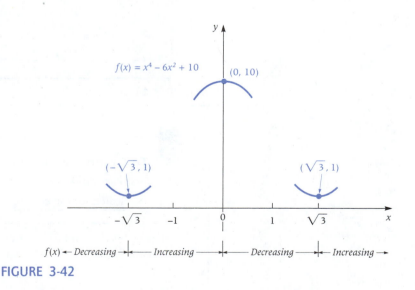

FIGURE 3-42

TABLE 3-7

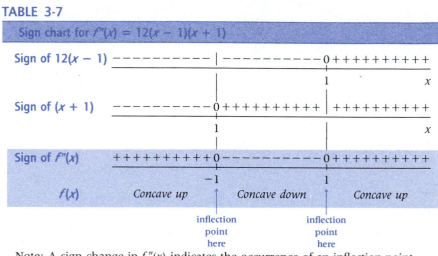

Sign chart for $f''(x) = 12(x - 1)(x + 1)$		

Sign of $12(x - 1)$ $- - - - - - - - - - | - - - - - - - - - - 0 + + + + + + + + +$

Sign of $(x + 1)$ $- - - - - - - - - - 0 + + + + + + + + + + | + + + + + + + + + +$

Sign of $f''(x)$ $+ + + + + + + + + + 0 - - - - - - - - - - 0 + + + + + + + + +$

$f(x)$ Concave up   Concave down   Concave up

inflection point here   inflection point here

Note: A sign change in $f''(x)$ indicates the occurrence of an inflection point.

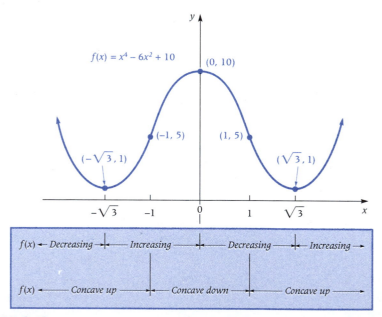

$f(x) = x^4 - 6x^2 + 10$

FIGURE 3-43

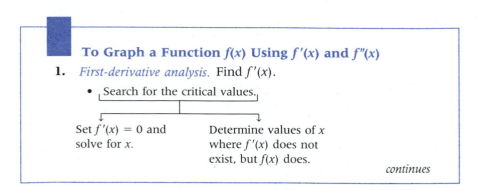

To Graph a Function $f(x)$ Using $f'(x)$ and $f''(x)$

1. *First-derivative analysis.* Find $f'(x)$.

   • Search for the critical values.

   Set $f'(x) = 0$ and solve for x.

   Determine values of x where $f'(x)$ does not exist, but $f(x)$ does.

   continues

> **To Graph a Function $f(x)$ Using $f'(x)$ and $f''(x)$—***Continued***
>
> - Draw a sign chart for $f'(x)$ This will indicate where $f(x)$ is increasing or decreasing and any relative extrema.
> - Find the y-coordinates of any relative extrema.
>
> **2.** *Second-derivative analysis.* Find $f''(x)$.
>
> - Draw a sign chart for $f''(x)$. This will indicate where $f(x)$ is concave up or down and any inflection points.
> - Find the y-coordinates of any inflection points.
>
> **3.** *Graph of $f(x)$.*
>
> - Summarize the results of steps 1 and 2 on a graph.
> - Plot the relative extrema and inflection points.
> - Plot the points of any x- and y-intercepts that are easily determined.
> - Sketch the graph of $f(x)$.

• **EXAMPLE 3-14   Cost Function.** ──────────────────

The ABC Container Company manufactures plastic bottles. Its cost function is defined by

$$C(x) = (x - 5)^3 + 1025$$

where x is the number (in millions) of bottles produced and $C(x)$ is the total cost (in thousands of dollars). Find all relative maxima and minima and inflection points of $C(x)$, and sketch its graph.

Solution

First-Derivative Analysis

$$C'(x) = 3(x - 5)^2$$

> Critical value:
> $x = 5$

Sign chart for $C'(x) = 3(x - 5)^2$

Sign of $C'(x)$	$++++++++++++++++++0+++++++++++++++++++$	
$C(x)$	Increasing 5 Increasing	x

Note that $C'(x)$ does not change sign at the critical value $x = 5$. This means that no relative extremum occurs at $x = 5$. However, since $C'(x) = 0$ at $x = 5$, the tangent line is horizontal there. This means that the graph of $C(x)$ is flat at $x = 5$.

Second-Derivative Analysis

$$C''(x) = 6(x - 5)$$

Sign chart for $C''(x) = 6(x - 5)$

Sign of $C''(x)$	$------------------0++++++++++++++++++$	
$C(x)$	Concave down 5 Concave up	x

An inflection point occurs at $x = 5$. Hence, its y-coordinate is

$$C(5) = (5 - 5)^3 + 1025 = 1025$$

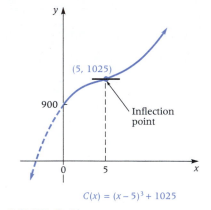

$$C(x) = (x - 5)^3 + 1025$$

FIGURE 3-44

Graph of $C(x)$

The above results are summarized in Figure 3-44, and the graph of $C(x)$ is sketched. Assuming $x \geq 0$, our curve is drawn as a solid line in the first quadrant.

The shape of $C(x)$ is typical of nonlinear cost functions of some large companies. The marginal cost, $C'(x)$, is decreasing at values of x to the left of the inflection point since the company is making efficient use of its fixed costs. However, at values of x to the right of the inflection point, the marginal cost, $C'(x)$, is increasing since the company has reached a point—the inflection point—at which the variable cost begins to escalate.

Rational Functions

The next few examples involve rational functions. Recall that a function $f(x)$ is a rational function if it can be written as

$$f(x) = \frac{N(x)}{D(x)} \quad \begin{array}{l} \leftarrow \text{numerator function} \\ \leftarrow \text{denominator function} \end{array}$$

where $N(x)$ and $D(x)$ are polynomial functions. When graphing rational functions, we should be watchful for both vertical and horizontal asymptotes. Remember that vertical asymptotes occur at values of x where the denominator, $D(x)$, equals zero and the numerator does not. Thus, if a function has a vertical asymptote at a value of x, then the function is undefined at that x-value. Horizontal asymptotes, if they exist, are determined by evaluating $\lim_{x \to -\infty} f(x)$ and $\lim_{x \to \infty} f(x)$. We elaborate on the above in the succeeding boxes.

SUMMARY

Vertical Asymptotes

1. A rational function

$$f(x) = \frac{N(x)}{D(x)}$$

where $N(x)$ and $D(x)$ are polynomials, has a **vertical asymptote** at $x = a$ if and only if

$$\lim_{x \to a} f(x) = \infty \ (\text{or} \ -\infty)$$

This means that the values of $f(x)$ increase or decrease without bound as $x \to a$. Thus, the graph of $f(x)$ rises or falls without bound and gets closer and closer to the line $x = a$, the **vertical asymptote**, as illustrated in Figure 3-45.

continues

SUMMARY—*Continued*

Vertical asymptotes at *x = a*

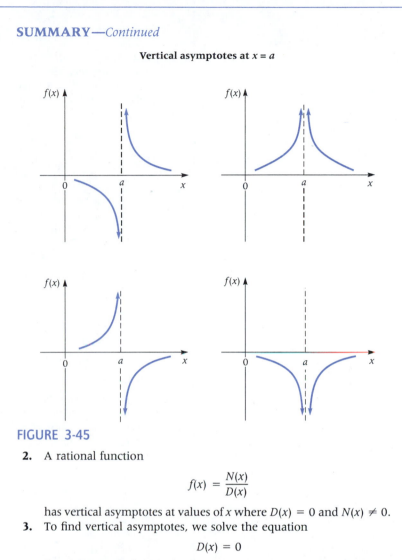

FIGURE 3-45

2. A rational function

$$f(x) = \frac{N(x)}{D(x)}$$

has vertical asymptotes at values of *x* where $D(x) = 0$ and $N(x) \neq 0$.

3. To find vertical asymptotes, we solve the equation

$$D(x) = 0$$

for *x*. This assumes that $N(x)$ and $D(x)$ have no common factors. In other words, if $D(a) = 0$, then $N(a) \neq 0$.

SUMMARY

Limits at Infinity and Horizontal Asymptotes

- A function $f(x)$ has a horizontal asymptote if and only if either

$$\lim_{x \to \infty} f(x) = L \qquad \text{or} \qquad \lim_{x \to -\infty} f(x) = M$$

where L and M are constants. Also, it might be the case that $L = M$.

- If $\lim_{x \to \infty} f(x) = L$, then the values of $f(x)$ approach the single num-

continues

SUMMARY—*Continued*

ber L as x gets larger and larger without bound. Thus, the graph of $f(x)$ approaches the horizontal line $y = L$ as $x \to \infty$. For such a case, the line $y = L$ is a **horizontal asymptote** of the function $f(x)$, as illustrated in Figure 3-46.

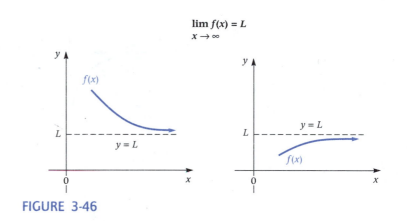

FIGURE 3-46

• If $\lim_{x \to -\infty} f(x) = M$, then the values of $f(x)$ approach the single number M as x gets more and more negative. Thus, the graph of $f(x)$ approaches the horizontal line $y = M$ as $x \to -\infty$. For such a case, the line $y = M$ is a **horizontal asymptote** of the function $f(x)$, as illustrated in Figure 3-47.

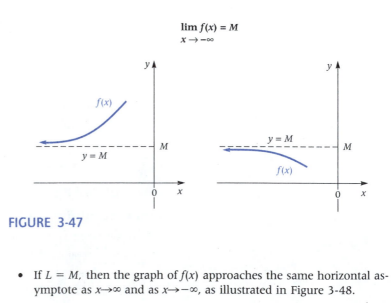

FIGURE 3-47

• If $L = M$, then the graph of $f(x)$ approaches the same horizontal asymptote as $x \to \infty$ and as $x \to -\infty$, as illustrated in Figure 3-48.

continues

SUMMARY—*Continued*

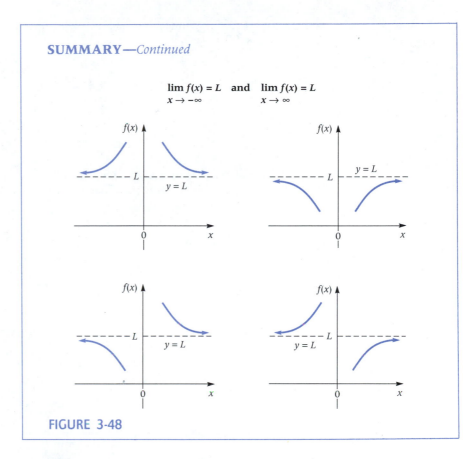

$$\lim_{x \to -\infty} f(x) = L \quad \text{and} \quad \lim_{x \to \infty} f(x) = L$$

FIGURE 3-48

When evaluating limits, we note that if $n > 0$,

1. $\displaystyle\lim_{x \to \infty} \frac{1}{x^n} = 0$.

2. $\displaystyle\lim_{x \to -\infty} \frac{1}{x^n} = 0$ as long as x^n is defined for negative x-values.

• **EXAMPLE 3-15**

Sketch the graph of $f(x) = 2x + (32/x)$.

Solution

First-Derivative Analysis

$$f'(x) = 2 - 32x^{-2}$$

$$= 2 - \frac{32}{x^2}$$

Search for Critical Values

Note that $f'(x)$ is undefined at $x = 0$. Ordinarily, this would mean that $x = 0$ is a critical value. However, this is not the case here since $f(x)$ is undefined at $x = 0$. As a matter of fact, $f(x)$ has a vertical asymptote at $x = 0$.

Setting $f'(x) = 0$ and solving for x yields

$$0 = 2 - \frac{32}{x^2}$$

$$\frac{32}{x^2} = 2$$

$$2x^2 = 32$$

$$x^2 = 16$$

$$x = \pm 4 \qquad \text{Critical Values}$$

Draw a Sign Chart for $f'(x)$

We rewrite the equation for $f'(x)$ as follows:

$$f'(x) = 2\left(\frac{x^2}{x^2}\right) - \frac{32}{x^2}$$

$$= \frac{2x^2}{x^2} - \frac{32}{x^2}$$

$$= \frac{2x^2 - 32}{x^2} = \frac{2(x-4)(x+4)}{x^2}$$

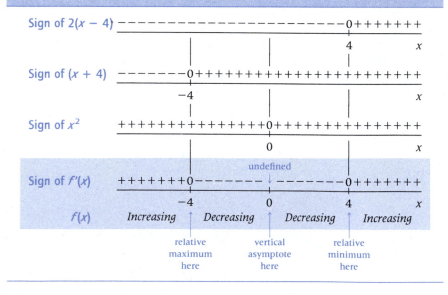

Find the y-coordinates of any relative extrema

$$f(-4) = 2(-4) + \frac{32}{-4} = -16$$

$$f(4) = 2(4) + \frac{32}{4} = 16$$

Second-Derivative Analysis

$$f''(x) = 64x^{-3} = \frac{64}{x^3}$$

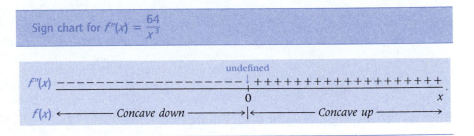

Sign chart for $f''(x) = \dfrac{64}{x^3}$

$$f''(x) \quad \underset{0}{\underbrace{- - - - - - - - - - - - - - - - - - - -}} \overset{\text{undefined}}{\underset{}{\Big\downarrow}} {+ + + + + + + + + + + + + + + + + + + +}$$

$f(x)$ ⟵ ——— Concave down ———⟶ | ⟵——— Concave up ———⟶

Vertical Asymptotes

Rewrite the equation for $f(x)$ as

$$f(x) = 2x\left(\frac{x}{x}\right) + \frac{32}{x} = \frac{2x^2 + 32}{x}$$

and note that at $x = 0$, the denominator is 0. Hence, as stated earlier, $f(x)$ has a vertical asymptote at $x = 0$.

Horizontal Asymptotes

$$\lim_{x \to \infty}\left(2x + \frac{32}{x}\right) = \lim_{x \to \infty}(2x) + \lim_{x \to \infty}\left(\frac{32}{x}\right)$$

$$= \infty + 0 = \infty$$

$$\lim_{x \to -\infty}\left(2x + \frac{32}{x}\right) = \lim_{x \to -\infty}(2x) + \lim_{x \to -\infty}\left(\frac{32}{x}\right)$$

$$= -\infty + 0 = -\infty$$

There are no horizontal asymptotes.

Graph of $f(x)$

The graph of $f(x)$ is sketched in Figure 3-49.

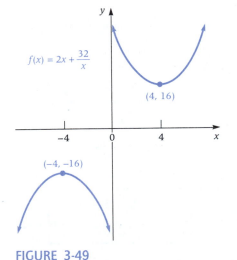

$f(x) = 2x + \dfrac{32}{x}$

(4, 16)

(−4, −16)

FIGURE 3-49

• EXAMPLE 3-16

Sketch the graph of

$$y = f(x) = \frac{x}{x^2 + 4}$$

Solution

First-Derivative Analysis

Using the quotient rule, we find

$$f'(x) = \frac{(x^2 + 4)(1) - x(2x)}{(x^2 + 4)^2}$$

$$= \frac{4 - x^2}{(x^2 + 4)^2}$$

$$= \frac{(2 - x)(2 + x)}{(x^2 + 4)^2}$$

Search for Critical Values

Setting $f'(x) = 0$ and solving for x gives critical values of $x = -2$ and $x = 2$. Since there are no values of x at which $f'(x)$ does not exist, these are the only critical values.

Draw a Sign Chart for $f'(x)$

We now analyze the sign of $f'(x)$ to determine where $f(x)$ is increasing or decreasing and to determine relative maximum and minimum points. These results are illustrated in Figure 3-50. Studying Figure 3-50, note that the sign of $f'(x)$ reveals the values of x for which $f(x)$ is increasing and decreasing. Also, by the first-derivative test, we determine the relative maximum and minimum points. Specifically, since $f'(x) < 0$ for nearby values of x to the left of $x = -2$ and $f'(x) > 0$ for nearby values of x to the right of $x = -2$, then, by the first-derivative test, a relative minimum point occurs at $x = -2$. Computing its y-coordinate, we obtain

$$f(-2) = \frac{-2}{(-2)^2 + 4} = -\frac{1}{4} \qquad \textcolor{blue}{\text{Relative Minimum}}$$

and $(-2, -1/4)$ is a relative minimum point.

Also, since $f'(x) > 0$ for nearby values of x to the left of $x = 2$ and $f'(x) < 0$ for

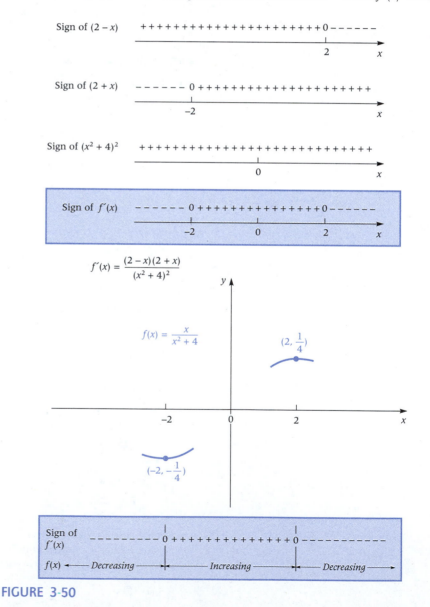

FIGURE 3-50

nearby values of x to the right of $x = 2$, then, by the first-derivative test, a relative maximum occurs at $x = 2$. Computing its y-coordinate, we obtain

$$f(2) = \frac{2}{(2)^2 + 4} = \frac{1}{4} \qquad \text{Relative Maximum}$$

and $(2, 1/4)$ is a relative maximum point.

Second-Derivative Analysis

We now analyze the second derivative to determine the concavity of $f(x)$. Computing the derivative of $f'(x)$, we obtain

$$f''(x) = \frac{(x^2 + 4)^2(-2x) - (-x^2 + 4)(2)(x^2 + 4)(2x)}{(x^2 + 4)^4}$$

$$= \frac{(x^2 + 4)(-2x)[(x^2 + 4) + (-2x^2 + 8)]}{(x^2 + 4)^{43}}$$

$$= \frac{2x(x^2 - 12)}{(x^2 + 4)^3}$$

$$= \frac{2x(x - \sqrt{12})(x + \sqrt{12})}{(x^2 + 4)^3}$$

> Use difference of two squares:
> $x^2 - 12 = (x - \sqrt{12})(x + \sqrt{12})$.

The sign of $f''(x)$ appears in Figure 3-51 on page 220. Since $f''(x) < 0$ for $x < -\sqrt{12}$ and for $0 < x < \sqrt{12}$, the graph of $f(x)$ is concave down over these intervals. Since $f''(x) > 0$ for $-\sqrt{12} < x < 0$ and for $x > \sqrt{12}$, the graph of $f(x)$ is concave up over these intervals. Since $f''(x)$ changes sign at $x = -\sqrt{12}$, $x = 0$, and $x = \sqrt{12}$, inflection points occur at these values of x. The y-coordinates of the inflection points are computed as follows:

$$f(-\sqrt{12}) = \frac{-\sqrt{12}}{(-\sqrt{12})^2 + 4} = \frac{-2\sqrt{3}}{16} = -\frac{\sqrt{3}}{8} \approx -0.22$$

$$f(\sqrt{12}) = \frac{\sqrt{12}}{(\sqrt{12})^2 + 4} = \frac{2\sqrt{3}}{16} = \frac{\sqrt{3}}{8} \approx 0.22$$

$$f(0) = 0$$

Thus, $(-\sqrt{12}, -0.22)$, $(\sqrt{12}, 0.22)$, and $(0, 0)$ are inflection points. Note that $(0, 0)$ is both the x-intercept and the y-intercept.

Vertical Asymptotes

Note that there are no vertical asymptotes since the denominator, $x^2 + 4$, does not equal 0 for any x-values.

Horizontal Asymptotes

Since $f(x)$ is a rational function, we examine its behavior as $x \to \infty$ and $x \to -\infty$ to find any horizontal asymptotes. Factoring out the highest-powered terms of both the numerator and the denominator of $f(x) = x/(x^2 + 4)$ gives

$$\frac{x}{x^2 + 4} = \frac{x(1)}{x^2\left(1 + \dfrac{4}{x^2}\right)}$$

$$= \frac{1}{x} \cdot \frac{1}{1 + \dfrac{4}{x^2}}$$

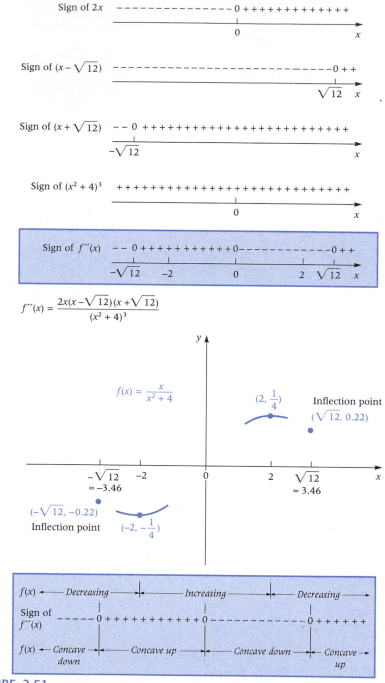

$$f''(x) = \frac{2x(x - \sqrt{12})(x + \sqrt{12})}{(x^2 + 4)^3}$$

FIGURE 3-51

As $x \to \infty$, $4/x^2 \to 0$ and $1/x \to 0$ so that

$$\frac{1}{x} \cdot \frac{1}{1 + \dfrac{4}{x^2}} \to 0 \cdot 1 = 0$$

Hence, $\lim_{x \to \infty} f(x) = 0$, making $y = 0$ a horizontal asymptote. A similar manner of reasoning gives $\lim_{x \to -\infty} f(x) = 0$.

Graph of $f(x)$

The graph of $f(x)$ appears in Figure 3-52.

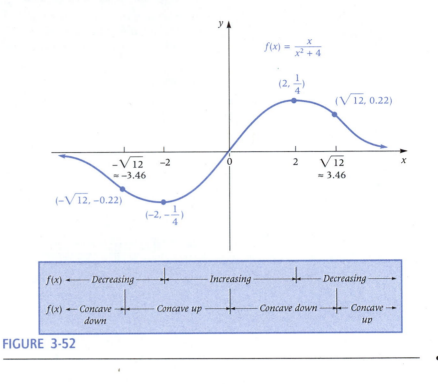

FIGURE 3-52

Exercises 3-3

1. Consider the graph of Figure 3-53.
    a) State the interval(s) over which the function $f(x)$ is concave up.
    b) State the interval(s) over which the function $f(x)$ is concave down.
    c) Identify any inflection points.
    d) Identify any relative extrema.
2. Consider the graph of Figure 3-54.
    a) State the interval(s) over which the function $f(x)$ is concave up.
    b) State the interval(s) over which the function $f(x)$ is concave down.
    c) Identify any inflection points.
    d) Identify any relative extrema.

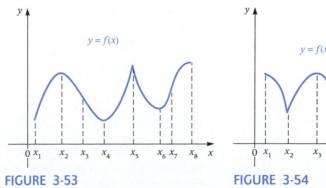

FIGURE 3-53

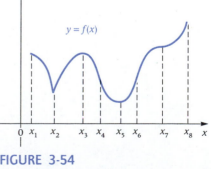

FIGURE 3-54

For each of the following sign charts, assume that the function $f(x)$ is continuous over the interval $(-\infty, \infty)$.

a) State the interval(s) over which the function $f(x)$ is concave up.
b) State the interval(s) over which the function $f(x)$ is concave down.
c) Identify any inflection points.

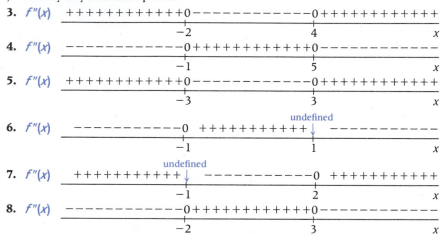

For each of the following, use both first and second derivatives to graph the function. Identify all relative and absolute extrema and inflection points.

9. $y = x^2 - 2x + 4$
10. $f(x) = x^3 + 6x^2 - 36x + 8$
11. $y = x^3 - 12x^2 - 27x - 1$
12. $f(x) = (1/3)x^3 - 4x + 8$
13. $f(x) = 5x^4 - 20x^3 + 7$
14. $f(x) = 5x^6 - 54x^5 + 60x^4 + 10$
15. $y = x^3 - 3x + 2$
16. $y = x^3 - 27x + 2$

17. $f(x) = (x - 5)^3$ 18. $f(x) = (x - 6)^8$
19. $y = (x + 3)^{10} + 2$ 20. $y = (x - 8)^5 + 2$
21. $y = (x + 2)(x - 5)^4 + 6$ 22. $y = (x - 1)^3(x + 6) + 1$
23. $f(x) = (x - 4)^3(x + 2)^2$ 24. $f(x) = x^3(x - 1)(x + 6)^4$
25. $y = x^3$ 26. $f(x) = x^6$
27. $f(x) = x^{4/3}$ 28. $f(x) = (x + 1)/x$

29. $y = \dfrac{-6}{x^2 + 2}$ 30. $y = \dfrac{8}{x^2 + 1}$

31. $f(x) = \dfrac{x}{x^2 + 1}$ 32. $y = \dfrac{x - 1}{x^2}$

33. $f(x) = \dfrac{800}{x} + 2x$ 34. $y = \dfrac{x + 1}{x^2}$

35. $f(x) = \dfrac{(x - 3)^2}{x + 1}$ 36. $f(x) = \dfrac{1}{x} - 3$

37. $f(x) = \dfrac{x^2(x - 2)}{(x - 1)^3}$ 38. $y = \dfrac{1}{(x - 3)^2}$

39. $f(x) = \dfrac{20}{x} + x + 9$ 40. $y = \dfrac{6}{x} + x + 5$

41. $f(x) = x^3 - 16x^2$ $(-5 \le x \le 6)$

42. $f(x) = -\dfrac{1}{100}x^3 + 16x$ $(-10 \le x \le 40)$

43. $f(x) = x^3 - 5x^2 + 7x - 3$ $(0 \le x \le 4)$
44. $f(x) = x^3 - 12x^2 + 45x - 50$ $(1 \le x \le 10)$

45. Given the function defined by $f(x) = x^{1/3}$:
    a) For which values of x is the graph of $f(x)$ concave up?
    b) For which values of x is the graph of $f(x)$ concave down?
    c) At which values of x does the graph of $f(x)$ change in concavity? Is $f''(x)$ defined there?
    d) Graph $f(x)$.

Applications

46. *Profit function*. The profit from producing x units of some commodity is given by the function

    $$P(x) = -0.01x^3 + 1.20x^2 - 21x + 50{,}000 \qquad (10 \leq x \leq 80)$$

    a) Find any relative maxima, minima, and inflection points of $P(x)$, and sketch its graph.
    b) How many units must be sold in order to yield the maximum profit?
    c) What is the maximum profit? Is this an absolute maximum?

47. *Water pollution*. The amount of oxygen (measured in milligrams of oxygen per liter of water) in a pond x weeks after the dumping of organic waste is given by

    $$f(x) = \frac{x^2 - x + 4}{x^2 + 4} \qquad (x \geq 0)$$

    a) Use both first- and second-derivative analyses to sketch the graph of $f(x)$.
    b) Determine the initial level of oxygen in the pond.
    c) For how many weeks after dumping organic waste is the oxygen level decreasing?
    d) How many weeks after dumping organic waste does the oxygen level begin to increase?
    e) What is the minimum oxygen level? When does it occur?
    f) What is the maximum oxygen level? When does it occur?
    g) After organic waste is dumped into the pond, does the amount of oxygen reach its initial level?

48. *Average cost per unit*. Given the cost function

    $$C(x) = 5x + 1000 \qquad (x > 0)$$

    where x is the number of units produced, the average cost per unit is given by

    $$\overline{C}(x) = \frac{C(x)}{x}$$
    $$= \frac{5x + 1000}{x} \qquad (x > 0)$$

    a) Use both first and second derivatives to graph the function, $\overline{C}(x)$.
    b) Identify any relative and absolute extrema.

49. *Average cost per unit*. Given the cost function

    $$C(x) = x^2 - 4x + 64 \qquad (x > 0)$$

    where x is the number of units produced, the average cost per unit is given by

    $$\overline{C}(x) = \frac{C(x)}{x}$$
    $$= \frac{x^2 - 4x + 64}{x} \qquad (x > 0)$$

    a) Use both first and second derivatives to graph the function, $\overline{C}(x)$.
    b) Identify any relative and absolute extrema.
    c) What production level minimizes the average cost per unit?
    d) What is the minimum average cost per unit?

50. *Learning.* A center for educational research has determined that the length of time (in minutes) it takes an average individual to learn x new words in a particular foreign language at a single study session is given by

$$L(x) = 0.1(x - 2)^3 + 8 \qquad (0 \le x \le 10)$$

a) Use both first and second derivatives to graph the function, $L(x)$.
b) Identify any relative and absolute extrema.
c) Identify any inflection points.
d) Graph the first derivative, $L'(x)$.
e) Identify any relative and absolute extrema of $L'(x)$.
f) How many new words should an average individual learn at a single study session in order to minimize $L'(x)$? Is this an absolute minimum value of $L'(x)$?

51. *Advertising and sales.* The sales revenue, R (in thousands of dollars), for a product is related to its advertising expenses, x (in thousands of dollars), by the equation

$$R(x) = -0.01x^3 + 6x^2 \qquad (0 \le x \le 500)$$

a) Use both first and second derivatives to graph the function, $R(x)$.
b) Identify any relative and absolute extrema.
c) Identify any inflection points.
d) Graph the first derivative, $R'(x)$.
e) Identify any relative and absolute extrema of $R'(x)$.
f) What level of advertising expenses maximizes $R'(x)$?

3-4 • OPTIMIZATION

In the previous two sections, we used the first and second derivatives to sketch graphs of functions. This enabled us to determine relative and absolute maximum and minimum values of functions.

In this section, we will be concerned with determining maximum or minimum values of functions without having to graph the functions. In other words, our goal will be to determine the maximum or minimum value of some quantity, Q, where $Q = f(x)$, and the value of x at which Q is either maximized or minimized. Our goal will not be to sketch the graph of $Q = f(x)$, although we will at times use graphical concepts to support conclusions regarding the optimality of our answers.

To find maximum and minimum values of functions without graphing the functions, we will first find critical values and then use a test to determine whether maxima, minima, or neither occurs at individual critical values. Up to this point in this text, the first-derivative test has been used to determine whether relative maxima, minima, or neither occurs at individual critical values.

Now we present another test, the second-derivative test, to determine the nature of relative extrema in certain situations. The advantage of the second-derivative test is that it is easier and faster to apply than the first-derivative test. However, the second-derivative test has limitations, and, therefore, the first-derivative test should be used if the second-derivative test fails or cannot be used.

■ **SUMMARY**

Second-Derivative Test for Relative Extrema

If $f(x)$ is a function and x_0 is a number such that $f'(x_0) = 0$, then

1. If $f''(x_0) < 0$, $f(x)$ has a relative maximum at $x = x_0$.
2. If $f''(x_0) > 0$, $f(x)$ has a relative minimum at $x = x_0$.
3. If $f''(x_0) = 0$, the test fails. In other words, the test gives no information regarding a relative maximum or relative minimum at $x = x_0$.

Notes:

1. This test applies only to critical values for which $f'(x) = 0$. It does not apply to critical values for which $f'(x)$ is undefined.
2. This test can fail. In other words, it can give no information regarding the nature of the relative extrema at x_0.
3. If either of the above occurs, use the first-derivative test.

We now give an example illustrating the use of the second-derivative test.

• EXAMPLE 3-17

Find the relative maximum and minimum values for

$$f(x) = x + \frac{9}{x}$$

Solution

First Derivative

$$f'(x) = 1 - \frac{9}{x^2}$$

$$0 = 1 - \frac{9}{x^2}$$

$$\frac{9}{x^2} = 1$$

$$x^2 = 9$$

$$x = \pm 3 \qquad \text{Critical Values}$$

Note that $x = 0$ is not a critical value despite the fact that $f'(0)$ is undefined. This is because $f(0)$ is undefined.

Second-Derivative Test

$$f''(x) = \frac{18}{x^3}$$

$$f''(-3) = \frac{18}{(-3)^3} < 0$$

critical value ⌐

By the second-derivative test, a relative maximum occurs at $x = -3$.

$$f''(3) = \frac{18}{(3)^3} > 0$$

critical value ⌐

By the second-derivative test, a relative minimum occurs at $x = 3$.

Find the relative extrema.

$$f(-3) = -3 + \frac{9}{-3} = -6 \qquad \text{Relative Maximum}$$

$$f(3) = 3 + \frac{9}{3} = 6 \qquad \text{Relative Minimum}$$

We now give an applied example illustrating the use of the second-derivative test.

• **EXAMPLE 3-18   Minimizing Average Cost Per Unit.** ____

The total cost of producing x units of some product is given by

$$C(x) = x^2 - 60x + 1600 \qquad (x > 0)$$

and the average cost per unit, when producing x units, is given by

$$\overline{C}(x) = \frac{C(x)}{x} \qquad (x > 0)$$

$$= \frac{x^2 - 60x + 1600}{x} \qquad (x > 0)$$

How many units should be produced in order to minimize the average cost per unit, $\overline{C}(x)$?

Solution

First Derivative

Using the quotient rule, we determine that

$$\overline{C}'(x) = \frac{x(2x - 60) - (x^2 - 60x + 1600)(1)}{x^2}$$

$$= \frac{x^2 - 1600}{x^2}$$

$$= \frac{(x - 40)(x + 40)}{x^2}$$

Critical Values

$x = 0$	$x = -40$	$x = 40$
↑	↑	↑
$\overline{C}'(0)$ is undefined. Rule out $x = 0$ because $\overline{C}(0)$ is undefined. Also, the restriction, $x > 0$, rules out $x = 0$.	$\overline{C}'(-40) = 0.$ Rule out $x = -40$ because of the restriction, $x > 0$.	$\overline{C}'(40) = 0.$ This is the only relevant critical value.

Second Derivative

We write the first derivative as

$$\overline{C}'(x) = \frac{x^2 - 1600}{x^2}$$

Using the quotient rule, we find

$$\overline{C}''(x) = \frac{x^2(2x) - (x^2 - 1600)(2x)}{(x^2)^2}$$

$$= \frac{3200x}{x^4} = \frac{3200}{x^3} \qquad \text{Second Derivative}$$

Second-Derivative Test

We evaluate the second-derivative at the critical value $x = 40$ to obtain

$$\overline{C}''(40) = \frac{3200}{(40)^3} = \frac{1}{20}$$

which is positive. Therefore, by the second-derivative test, a relative minimum exists at $x = 40$. The relative minimum is

$$\overline{C}(40) = \frac{(40)^2 - 60(40) + 1600}{40} = \$20 \text{ per unit}$$

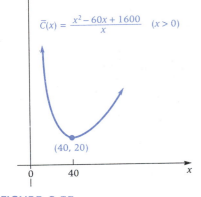

$$\overline{C}(x) = \frac{x^2 - 60x + 1600}{x} \quad (x > 0)$$

(40, 20)

FIGURE 3-55

Absolute Extrema

We have determined, in Example 3-18, that a relative minimum exists at $x = 40$. A much stronger result would be to determine that an absolute minimum occurs at $x = 40$. We do this by noting that $\overline{C}(x)$ is defined only for positive values of x (i.e., the restriction, $x > 0$). Next note that the second derivative

$$\overline{C}''(x) = \frac{3200}{x^3}$$

is positive for $x > 0$, and, therefore, the graph of $\overline{C}(x)$ is concave up over the interval $x > 0$. This implies that the graph of $\overline{C}(x)$ has the appearance of that of Figure 3-55 and then the relative minimum at the critical value $x = 40$ is an absolute minimum. Thus, the minimum average cost is $20 per unit, and it occurs at a production level of $x = 40$ units.

Example 3-18 illustrates a special situation where a continuous function has only one critical value in some interval (the interval can be closed, open, half-closed, etc.). This case occurs so often in applications that we present a special second-derivative test for determining whether an absolute maximum, an absolute minimum, or neither occurs at the critical value.

SUMMARY

Second-Derivative Test for Absolute Extrema

When a function is continuous over some interval and *only one critical value* exists in the interval: Given that a function $f(x)$ is continuous over some interval, and x_0 is the only critical value interior to the interval, and $f'(x_0) = 0$, then

1. If $f''(x_0) < 0$, $f(x_0)$ is the **absolute maximum** value of $f(x)$ over the interval (see Figure 3-56).

continues

SUMMARY—*Continued*

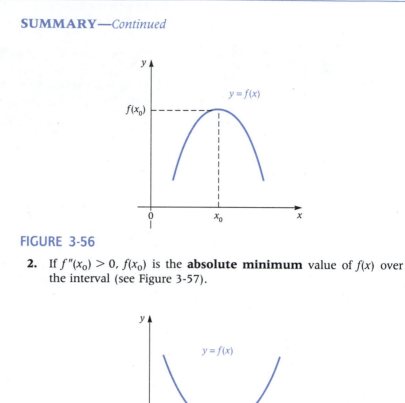

FIGURE 3-56

2. If $f''(x_0) > 0$, $f(x_0)$ is the **absolute minimum** value of $f(x)$ over the interval (see Figure 3-57).

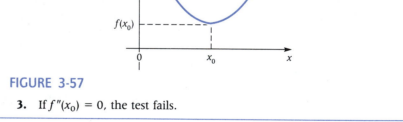

FIGURE 3-57

3. If $f''(x_0) = 0$, the test fails.

Since many optimization problems and applications involve the determination of absolute maximum and minimum values of functions defined over closed intervals, we now give a procedure for such situations.

To Find Absolute Extrema

For Continuous Functions Defined on Closed Intervals. To find the absolute extrema of a continuous function $f(x)$ on the closed interval $[a, b]$:

1. Find all critical values of $f(x)$ in $[a, b]$.
2. Evaluate $f(x)$ at the endpoints a and b and at the critical values found in step 1.

continues

To Find Absolute Extrema—*Continued*

3. Write the largest value found in step 2. This is the *absolute maximum* value of $f(x)$ on the interval $[a, b]$.
4. Write the smallest value found in step 2. This is the *absolute minimum* value of $f(x)$ on the interval $[a, b]$.

• **EXAMPLE 3-19** _____

Determine the absolute extrema for

$$f(x) = x^3 - 6x^2 - 36x + 10 \qquad (-3 \leq x \leq 9)$$

Solution

Critical Values

$$\begin{aligned}
f'(x) &= 3x^2 - 12x - 36 \\
&= 3(x^2 - 4x - 12) \\
&= 3(x - 6)(x + 2)
\end{aligned}$$

Setting $f'(x) = 0$ and solving for x gives

$$\begin{aligned}
x - 6 &= 0 & x + 2 &= 0 \\
x &= 6 & x &= -2
\end{aligned}$$

$\llcorner$ critical values $\lrcorner$

These are the only critical values since there are no values of x at which $f'(x)$ is undefined.

Evaluate f(x) *at Critical Values and at Endpoints*

$$f(6) = (6)^3 - 6(6)^2 - 36(6) + 10 = -206 \qquad \leftarrow \text{absolute}$$
critical value $\longrightarrow$ $\qquad\qquad\qquad\qquad\qquad\qquad\qquad\qquad\qquad$ minimum

$$f(-2) = (-2)^3 - 6(-2)^2 - 36(-2) + 10 = 50 \qquad \leftarrow \text{absolute}$$
critical value $\longrightarrow$ $\qquad\qquad\qquad\qquad\qquad\qquad\qquad\qquad\qquad$ maximum

$$f(-3) = (-3)^3 - 6(-3)^2 - 36(-3) + 10 = 37$$
endpoint $\longrightarrow$

$$f(9) = (9)^3 - 6(9)^2 - 36(9) + 10 = -71$$
endpoint $\longrightarrow$

Thus, the absolute maximum value of $f(x)$ is 50, and it occurs at $x = -2$; the absolute minimum value of $f(x)$ is -206, and it occurs at $x = 6$.

$\bullet$

Since the remainder of this section entails solving applied optimization problems, we now present a procedure for solving such problems in Figure 3-58.

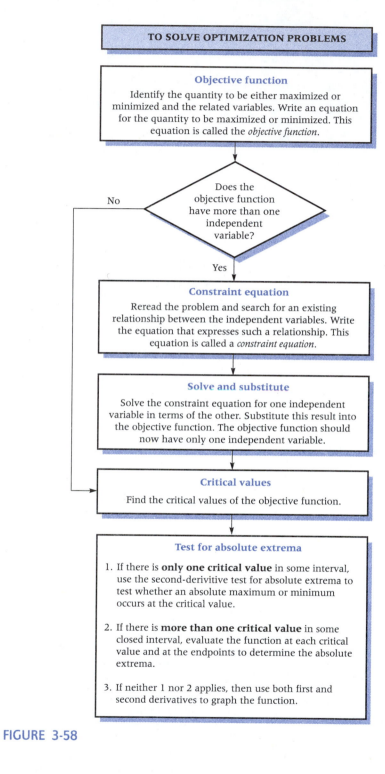

FIGURE 3-58

• **EXAMPLE 3-20   Quality Control and Profits.** _____

Sharp Industries produces table knives. Each knife costs $6 to produce and sells for $9. The quality control manager has determined from past data that out of x knives that are produced during any given day, the fraction defective for the day is given by $x^2/20{,}000{,}000$, where $100 \leq x \leq 1500$. Each defective knife costs the company an additional $20.

a)   Determine the equation that gives daily profit, P, as a function of daily production volume, x.

b)   Determine the maximum daily profit and the daily production volume that yields the maximum daily profit.

Solutions

Objective Function

a)   A unit profit of $9 − $6 = $3 is made on each knife. The daily profit is given by

$$P = 3x - (\text{additional cost of the defective knives})$$

The number of defective knives produced in a day is determined by multiplying the fraction defective and the daily production volume. Hence,

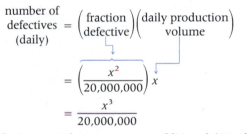

$$\begin{aligned}\text{number of defectives (daily)} &= \left(\text{fraction defective}\right)\left(\text{daily production volume}\right)\\ &= \left(\frac{x^2}{20{,}000{,}000}\right)x\\ &= \frac{x^3}{20{,}000{,}000}\end{aligned}$$

Since each defective costs the company an additional $20, then

$$\text{additional cost of the defective knives} = 20 \cdot \frac{x^3}{20{,}000{,}000} = \frac{x^3}{1{,}000{,}000}$$

Thus, the daily profit is given by

Objective function

$$P(x) = 3x - \frac{x^3}{1{,}000{,}000} \qquad (100 \leq x \leq 1500)$$

Critical Values

$$P'(x) = 3 - \frac{3x^2}{1{,}000{,}000}$$

$$0 = 3 - \frac{3x^2}{1{,}000{,}000}$$

$$\frac{3x^2}{1{,}000{,}000} = 3$$

$$x^2 = \frac{3{,}000{,}000}{3} = 1{,}000{,}000$$

$$x = \pm 1000$$

We rule out $x = -1000$ because $100 \leq x \leq 1500$. Thus,

$x = 1000$ is the only critical value

Test for Absolute Extrema

Second-Derivative Test

$$P''(x) = \frac{-6x}{1,000,000}$$

$$P''(1000) = \frac{-6(1000)}{1,000,000} < 0$$

By the second-derivative test for absolute extrema, the function $P(x)$ has an absolute maximum at $x = 1000$. Hence,

$$P(1000) = 3(1000) - \frac{(1000)^3}{1,000,000}$$

$$= 2000 \qquad \text{Absolute maximum}$$

Note: We could also have used the procedure for finding absolute extrema of continuous functions defined on closed intervals instead of the second-derivative test for absolute extrema.

• **EXAMPLE 3-21**   **Apple Growing: Maximizing Revenue.**

From past experience, an apple grower knows that if the apples are harvested now, each tree will yield on the average 130 pounds, and the grower will sell the apples for $0.64 per pound. However, for each additional week that the grower waits before harvesting, the yield per tree will increase by 5 pounds, while the price per pound will decrease by $0.02. How many weeks should the grower wait before harvesting the apples in order to maximize the sales revenue per tree? What is the maximum sales revenue per tree?

Solution

Objective Function

Let x = number of weeks the grower waits. The sales revenue per tree is given by

$$R = \left(\begin{array}{c}\text{number of pounds} \\ \text{per tree}\end{array}\right)\left(\begin{array}{c}\text{price per} \\ \text{pound}\end{array}\right)$$

$$R(x) = (130 + 5x)(0.64 - 0.02x)$$

Critical Values

Using the product rule, we find

$$R'(x) = (130 + 5x)(-0.02) + (0.64 - 0.02x)(5)$$

$$R'(x) = 0.60 - 0.20x$$

$$0 = 0.60 - 0.20x$$

$$x = 3 \qquad \text{Only critical value}$$

Test for Absolute Extrema

Second-Derivative Test

$$R''(x) = -0.20$$

$$R''(3) = -0.20 < 0$$

Therefore, by the second-derivative test for absolute extrema, the function $R(x)$ has an absolute maximum at $x = 3$.

$$R(3) = (130 + 5 \cdot 3)(0.64 - 0.02 \cdot 3)$$
$$= (145)(0.58)$$
$$= \$84.10 \qquad \text{Absolute maximum}$$

Thus, the grower should wait 3 weeks before harvesting in order to attain the maximum sales revenue per tree of $84.10.

• EXAMPLE 3-22

The manager of an ocean resort wants to enclose a rectangular area of beach along the ocean. There must be at least 500 feet of frontage along the ocean, as illustrated in Figure 3-59. Find the dimensions that maximize the enclosed area if 2000 feet of fencing are available. Find the maximum area.

Solution

Objective Function

We wish to maximize the enclosed area, which is given by

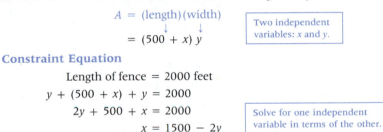

$$A = (\text{length})(\text{width})$$
$$= (500 + x) y$$

Two independent variables: x and y.

Constraint Equation

$$\text{Length of fence} = 2000 \text{ feet}$$
$$y + (500 + x) + y = 2000$$
$$2y + 500 + x = 2000$$
$$x = 1500 - 2y$$

Solve for one independent variable in terms of the other.

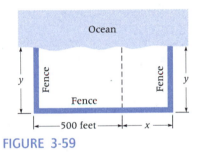

Ocean

Fence

y Fence   Fence y

Fence

|←——500 feet——→|←— x —→|

FIGURE 3-59

Note: We could have solved for y in terms of x. However, we chose to solve for x in terms of y in order to avoid fractions. Substitute $1500 - 2y$ for x into the objective function.

Objective Function

$$A(y) = (500 + 1500 - 2y)y$$
$$= (2000 - 2y)y$$
$$= 2000y - 2y^2 \qquad (y > 0)$$

Note that y is the independent variable

Critical Values

$$A'(y) = 2000 - 4y$$
$$0 = 2000 - 4y$$
$$y = 500 \qquad \text{Only critical value}$$

Test for Absolute Extrema

Second-Derivative Test

$$A''(y) = -4$$
$$A''(500) = -4 < 0$$

Thus, by the second-derivative test for absolute extrema, the function $A(x)$ has an absolute maximum when $y = 500$ feet.

We determine x by substituting $y = 500$ into the constraint equation solved for x. Hence,

$$x = 1500 - 2y$$
$$= 1500 - 2(500) = 500 \text{ feet}$$

Thus, the dimensions of the enclosed area are

$$500 + x \text{ by } y$$
$$500 + 500 \text{ by } 500$$
1000 feet by 500 feet

The maximum area is given by

$$A = (\text{length})(\text{width})$$
$$= (1000)(500)$$
$$= 500{,}000 \text{ square feet}$$

Note: We could have determined the maximum area by evaluating $A(500)$.

• **EXAMPLE 3-23**   **Minimizing Surface Area Cost.** _____

A company makes prefabricated steel buildings. One of its models is illustrated in Figure 3-60. The building must be 8 feet high and have a volume of 20,000 cubic feet. If the material for the sides costs $20 per square foot and the material for the roof costs $30 per square foot, determine the dimensions of the building that will minimize its cost. Also, determine the minimum cost. Do not consider the cost of the floor.

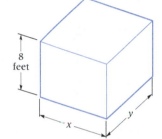

FIGURE 3-60

Solution

Objective Function

We want to minimize cost, which is given by

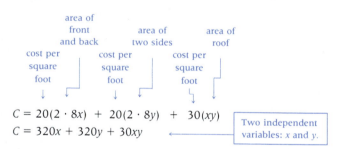

$$C = 20(2 \cdot 8x) + 20(2 \cdot 8y) + 30(xy)$$
$$C = 320x + 320y + 30xy$$

Two independent variables: x and y.

Constraint Equation

$$\text{Volume} = 20{,}000 \text{ cubic feet}$$
$$8xy = 20{,}000$$
$$y = \frac{2500}{x}$$

Solve for one independent variable in terms of the other.

Substitute $2500/x$ for y into the objective function.

Objective Function

$$C = 320x + 320\left(\frac{2500}{x}\right) + 30x\left(\frac{2500}{x}\right)$$
$$C(x) = 320x + \frac{800{,}000}{x} + 75{,}000 \qquad (x > 0)$$

Critical Values

$$C'(x) = 3200 - \frac{8,000,000}{x^2}$$

$$0 = 3200 - \frac{8,000,000}{x^2}$$

$$\frac{8,000,000}{x^2} = 3200$$

$$x^2 = \frac{8,000,000}{3200} = 2500$$

$$x = \pm 50 \quad\longleftarrow\quad \boxed{\text{We disregard } x = -50 \text{ because}}$$
$$x = 50 \quad \text{Only critical value} \qquad \text{of the restriction, } x > 0.$$

We note that $C'(x)$ is undefined at $x = 0$. However, $x = 0$ is not a critical value since $C(0)$ is undefined.

Test for Absolute Extrema

Second-Derivative Test

$$C''(x) = \frac{16,000,000}{x^2}$$

$$C''(50) = \frac{16,000,000}{(50)^2} > 0$$

Thus, by the second-derivative test for absolute extrema, the function $C(x)$ has an absolute minimum when $x = 50$.

We determine y by substituting $x = 50$ into the secondary equation solved for y. Hence,

$$y = \frac{2500}{x}$$

$$= \frac{2500}{50} = 50 \text{ feet}$$

Thus, the base of the building should be 50 feet by 50 feet. The total cost is given by substituting $x = 50$ into the objective function to obtain

$$C(50) = 320(50) + \frac{800,000}{50} + 75,000$$

$$= \$107,000 \qquad \text{Absolute minimum cost}$$

• EXAMPLE 3-24   Maximizing Profit. _____

A company manufactures a product used in the computer industry. The unit price, p (in thousands of dollars), and demand, x (in hundreds of units), are related by the equation

$$x = \frac{8100}{p^2} \qquad (p > 0)$$

The cost, C (in thousands of dollars), of producing the items is given by

$$C(x) = 5x + 120 \qquad (x > 0)$$

The company wishes to determine

a)   The demand level, x, for which profit is maximized.
b)   The unit price, p, for which profit is maximized.
c)   The maximum profit.

Solutions

Objective Function

a) Since we seek a value of x that maximizes profit, P, we must write profit in terms of x. If $P(x)$ = profit gained from selling x units and $R(x)$ = sales revenue gained from selling x units, then

$$P(x) = R(x) - C(x)$$

We must determine an equation for $R(x)$. Hence,

$$\text{sales revenue} = (\text{number of units sold})(\text{unit price})$$

or

$$R(x) = xp \qquad \qquad \overset{\text{Constraint}}{\underset{\text{equation}}{\rule{0pt}{0pt}}}$$

where x and p are related by the equation $x = 8100/p^2$. Solving for p gives $p = 90/\sqrt{x}$. Substituting this result for p into the formula for $R(x)$ gives

$$R(x) = x\left(\frac{90}{\sqrt{x}}\right)$$
$$= 90x^{1/2}$$

Hence,

$$P(x) = R(x) - C(x)$$
$$= 90x^{1/2} - (5x + 120)$$
$$= 90x^{1/2} - 5x - 120 \qquad \text{Objective function}$$

where P is in thousands of dollars and $x > 0$.

Critical Values

We now seek critical values of $P(x)$ by finding

$$P'(x) = 45x^{-1/2} - 5$$

Setting $P'(x) = 0$ and solving for x gives, successively,

$$0 = 45x^{-1/2} - 5$$
$$5 = \frac{45}{\sqrt{x}}$$
$$\sqrt{x} = 9$$
$$x = 81 \qquad \text{Only critical value}$$

Thus, $x = 81$ is a critical value. Since there are no positive values of x at which $P'(x)$ does not exist, this is the only critical value.

Test for Absolute Extrema

We now apply the second-derivative test to determine the nature of the critical value, $x = 81$. Hence, we differentiate $P'(x)$ to obtain

$$P''(x) = -22.5x^{-3/2}$$
$$= \frac{-22.5}{\sqrt{x^3}}$$

Since $P''(x) < 0$ at $x = 81$, then, by the second-derivative test for absolute extrema, an absolute maximum occurs at $x = 81$.

Thus, in order to maximize profit, the company should produce and sell 8100 units (remember that since x was defined in terms of hundreds of units, $x = 81$ means 81 hundred units).

b) The variables x and p are related by $x = 8100/p^2$, which, when solved for p, gives

$$p = \frac{90}{\sqrt{x}}$$

Substituting $x = 81$ into this equation gives

$$p = \frac{90}{\sqrt{81}} = 10$$

as the unit price at which profit is maximized. Since p is defined in terms of thousands of dollars, the company must charge $10,000 (i.e., $p = 10$ means $10,000) per 100 units for this product in order to maximize profit.

c) The maximum profit is $P(81)$. Since

$$P(x) = 90\sqrt{x} - 5x - 120$$

then

$$P(81) = 90\sqrt{81} - 5(81) - 120$$
$$= 285$$

Since P is given in terms of thousands of dollars, the *maximum profit* is $285,000.

In Example 3-24 we determined $P'(x)$ and set it equal to zero in order to maximize the profit, $P(x)$. Since

$$P(x) = R(x) - C(x)$$

where $R(x)$ and $C(x)$ denote sales revenue and cost, respectively, then differentiating both sides with respect to x gives

$$P'(x) = R'(x) - C'(x)$$

Setting $P'(x) = 0$ gives the equation

$$0 = R'(x) - C'(x)$$

or

$$R'(x) = C'(x)$$

Since $R'(x)$ gives marginal revenue and $C'(x)$ gives marginal cost, this equation implies that *profit is maximized when marginal revenue equals marginal cost*. Graphically, profit is maximized when the slope of the revenue graph equals the slope of the cost graph, as illustrated in Figure 3-61.

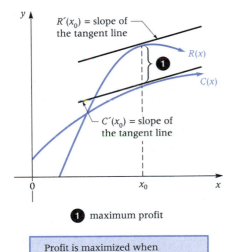

1 maximum profit

Profit is maximized when marginal revenue = marginal cost.

FIGURE 3-61

Exercises 3-4

Use the second-derivative test to find relative maxima and minima for each of the following.

1. $y = x^2 - 8x + 9$

2. $y = x^2 - 10x + 50$

3. $y = x^3 - 6x^2 + 7$

4. $y = x^3 - 12x^2 + 15$

5. $f(x) = x^3 - 3x + 5$

6. $f(x) = x^3 - 12x + 10$

7. $f(x) = 2x^3 + 3x^2 - 12x + 1$

8. $f(x) = x^3 - 3x^2 - 9x + 5$

9. $f(x) = x^3 - 3x^2 - 45x + 9$
10. $f(x) = 2x^3 - 9x^2 - 24x + 6$
11. $f(x) = x^4 - 8x^2 + 6$
12. $f(x) = x^4 - 18x^2 - 11$
13. $y = x + \dfrac{25}{x}$
14. $y = x + \dfrac{81}{x}$
15. $f(x) = x + \dfrac{27}{x^3}$
16. $f(x) = x + \dfrac{4}{x^2}$

Determine the absolute extrema for each of the following.

17. $f(x) = x^2 - 16x + 9$
18. $f(x) = x^2 - 10x + 4$
19. $f(x) = -x^2 + 8x + 3$
20. $f(x) = -x^2 + 10x + 6$
21. $f(x) = 4\sqrt{x} - x$
22. $f(x) = 8\sqrt{x} - x$
23. $f(x) = x^3 - 27x + 4 \quad (-4 \le x \le 4)$
24. $f(x) = x^3 - 48x + 9 \quad (-5 \le x \le 5)$
25. $f(x) = 9 + 5x + 125/x \quad (x > 0)$
26. $f(x) = 3 + 4x + 64/x \quad (x > 0)$
27. $f(x) = 2x + 54/x^3 \quad (x > 0)$
28. $f(x) = 6 + 3x + 12/x^2 \quad (x > 0)$
29. $f(x) = 5(x - 2)^3 \quad (0 \le x \le 4)$
30. $f(x) = 5(x + 1)^3 \quad (-3 \le x \le 0)$
31. $f(x) = (x - 1)(x - 4)^2 \quad (0 \le x \le 6)$
32. $f(x) = (x - 1)(x - 5)^3 \quad (0 \le x \le 7)$

General Word Problems

33. Find two numbers whose sum is 24 and whose product is as large as possible.
34. Find two numbers whose difference is 30 and whose product is as small as possible.
35. Find two numbers whose sum is 600 and whose sum of squares is as small as possible.
36. Find two numbers whose sum is 800 and whose sum of squares is as small as possible.

Applications

37. *Average cost.* The total cost of producing x units of some product is given by
$$C(x) = x^2 - 80x + 3600 \quad (x > 0)$$
How many units should be produced in order to minimize the average cost per unit?

38. *Energy costs.* The heating and cooling costs for a building with no insulation are $853,333 per year. If x inches ($0 \le x \le 9$) of insulation are added, the combined heating and cooling costs will be $2,560,000/(x + 3)$ dollars per year. If it costs $200,000 for each inch (thickness) of insulation added, then the total energy cost (insulation cost + combined heating and cooling cost) for 5 years is given by

Insulation cost   Combined heating and cooling cost
$$C(x) = 200{,}000x + 5\left(\frac{2{,}560{,}000}{x + 3}\right) \quad (0 \le x \le 9)$$

   a) How many inches of insulation should be added in order to minimize the total energy costs over a 5-year period?
   b) Using the result of part a, what are the savings over a 5-year period?
39. *Energy costs.* The heating and cooling costs for a building with no insulation are $590,625 per year. If x inches ($0 \le x \le 10$) of insulation are added, the

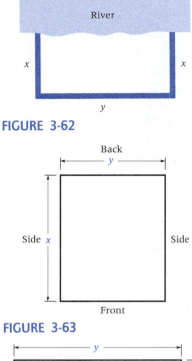

FIGURE 3-62

FIGURE 3-63

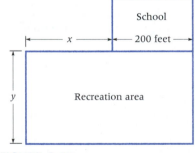

FIGURE 3-64

FIGURE 3-65

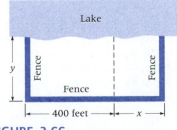

FIGURE 3-66

heating and cooling costs will be $2,362,500/(x + 4)$ dollars per year. If it costs \$175,000 for each inch of insulation added,

a) How many inches of insulation should be added in order to minimize the total energy costs over a 6-year period?

b) Using the result of part (a), what are the savings over a 6-year period?

40. *Projectile.* A ball is projected vertically into the air. The function $S(t) = -16t^2 + 192t$ gives the height, S (in feet), above the ground of the ball at time, t (in seconds). When does the ball reach maximum height, and what is the maximum height?

41. *Area.* A park manager has 400 feet of fence to enclose a rectangular area alongside a river. No fence is needed along the river (see Figure 3-62). Use calculus to determine the dimensions x and y that maximize the enclosed area.

42. *Enclosure cost.* A city recreation department is planning to enclose a rectangular area of 125,000 square feet for a playground (see Figure 3-63). If the fence along the sides costs \$10 per foot and the fence along the front and back costs \$20 per foot, find the dimensions of the playground that minimize the fence cost.

43. *Enclosure.* A zoo manager wishes to enclose an area of 20,000 square feet into 3 cages of equal size, as illustrated in Figure 3-64. Find the dimensions x and y that minimize the length of fence used.

44. *Enclosure.* A park manager has 2000 feet of fence with which to enclose a rectangular area. Determine the dimensions of the rectangle that yield the maximum area.

45. *Enclosure.* Show that the maximum area enclosed by a rectangle with a fixed perimeter will always result in a square.

46. *Recreation area.* A school department wishes to enclose a recreation area adjacent to its high school, as illustrated in Figure 3-65. Find the dimensions that maximize the enclosed area if

a) 3200 feet of fencing is available.

b) 4800 feet of fencing is available.

47. *Enclosure.* A recreation manager wants to enclose a rectangular area of beach along a lake. There must be at least 400 feet of frontage along the lake, as illustrated in Figure 3-66. Find the dimensions that maximize the enclosed area if 1800 feet of fencing is available.

Profit. For each of the following, determine

a) The equation for profit, $P(x)$.

b) The number of units, x, for which profit is maximized.

c) The maximum profit.

48. $R(x) = -2x^2 + 400x$; $C(x) = 40x + 5000$
49. $R(x) = -4x^2 + 3200x$; $C(x) = 200x + 10,000$
50. $R(x) = 10x$, $C(x) = 0.01x^2 + 0.4x + 20$
51. $R(x) = 20x$, $C(x) = 0.01x^2 + 0.2x + 40$

Profit. For each of the following, assume that p denotes the unit price (in dollars) of some product and x denotes the demand for the product. Determine

a) The equation for revenue, $R(x)$.

b) The equation for profit, $P(x)$.

c) The demand level, x, for which profit is maximized.

d) The unit price, p, for which profit is maximized.

e) The maximum profit.

52. $p = -4x + 1600$, $C(x) = 40x + 3000$
53. $p = -5x + 3000$, $C(x) = 50x + 6000$
54. $p = -8x + 6400$, $C(x) = 60x + 8000$
55. $p = -2x + 2000$, $C(x) = 30x + 4000$

56. *Tax.* For Exercise 52, suppose a tax of $8 per unit produced is imposed on the producer. This modifies the cost equation so that

$$C(x) = \text{original cost} + \text{tax}$$
$$= 40x + 3000 + 8x$$
$$= 48x + 3000 \qquad \text{Modified cost equation}$$

a) Find the demand level, x, for which profit is maximized.
b) Find the unit price, p, for which profit is maximized.
c) How has the tax changed the price the producer charges for the product? (*Hint:* Compare the result of part b with that of Exercise 52(d).)
d) What portion of the tax is passed on to the consumer? (*Hint:* Use the result of part c.)

57. *Tax.* For Exercise 53, suppose a tax of $20 per unit produced is imposed on the producer. This modifies the cost equation so that

$$C(x) = \text{original cost} + \text{tax}$$
$$= 50x + 6000 + 20x$$
$$= 70x + 6000 \qquad \text{Modified cost equation}$$

a) Find the demand level, x, for which profit is maximized.
b) Find the unit price, p, for which profit is maximized.
c) How has the tax changed the price the producer charges for the product? (*Hint:* Compare the result of part b with that of Exercise 53(d).)
d) What portion of the tax is passed on to the consumer? (*Hint:* Use the result of part c.)

58. *Tax.* For Exercise 54, suppose a tax of $16 per unit produced is imposed on the producer.

a) Find the modified cost equation.
b) Find the demand level, x, for which profit is maximized.
c) Find the unit price, p, for which profit is maximized.
d) How has the tax changed the price the producer charges for the product? (*Hint:* Compare the result of part c with that of Exercise 54(d).
e) What portion of the tax is passed on to the consumer? (*Hint:* Use the result of part d.)

59. *Profit.* A company manufactures a product used in the computer industry. The unit price, p (in thousands of dollars), and the demand, x (in hundreds of units), are related by the equation

$$x = \frac{6400}{p^2} \qquad (p > 0)$$

The cost, C (in thousands of dollars), of producing the items is given by

$$C(x) = 8x + 50 \qquad (x > 0)$$

The company wishes to determine
a) The demand level, x, for which profit is maximized.
b) The unit price, p, for which profit is maximized.
c) The maximum profit.

60. *Quality control and profits.* Time Industries produces watches. Each watch costs $30 to produce and sells for $38. From past experience, it has been determined that out of x watches that are produced during any given day, the fraction defective for the day is given by $x^2/10{,}000{,}000$, where $0 \le x \le 2500$. Each defective watch costs the company an additional $15.

a) Determine the equation that gives daily profit, P, as a function of daily production volume, x.

b) Determine the maximum daily profit and the daily production volume that yields the maximum daily profit.

61. *Apple growing: Revenue per tree.* If an apple grower harvests her crop now, she will pick on the average 120 pounds per tree. She will get $0.48 per pound for the apples. From past experience, the grower knows that for each additional week she waits, the yield per tree will increase by about 10 pounds, while the price will decrease by about $0.03 per pound. Determine how many weeks the grower should wait in order to maximize sales revenue. What is the maximum sales revenue?

62. *Rental income.* An apartment building contains 100 apartments. If the rent is $300 per month, all apartments will be rented. However, for each additional $50 increase in the monthly rent, 5 additional apartments will become vacant.
   a) Find the equation that gives the total monthly rental income, R, in terms of x, the number of $50 increases in monthly rent.
   b) How many $50 increases in monthly rent will maximize the total monthly rental income?
   c) Determine the maximum total monthly rental income.

63. *Continuing education income.* If an educational institution charges $1000 for a full-day workshop in time management, 40 managers usually enroll for the workshop. For each $50 decrease in the fee, 5 additional managers enroll for the workshop.
   a) Determine the equation that gives workshop income as a function of the number of $50 decreases in the fee.
   b) How many $50 decreases in the workshop fee will maximize the workshop income?
   c) Determine the maximum workshop income.

64. *Volume.* A company manufactures open boxes from square pieces of tin that are 60 inches on each side. The process involves cutting equal squares from the corners of each piece of tin and folding up the flaps to form sides, as illustrated in Figure 3-67.
   a) What size square should be cut from each corner in order to maximize the volume of the box?
   b) Determine the maximum volume.
   c) Is the answer to part b an absolute maximum?

65. *Volume.* A company manufactures open boxes from square pieces of tin that are 18 inches on each side. The process involves cutting equal squares from the corners of each piece of tin and folding up the flaps to form sides. What size square should be cut from each corner in order to maximize the volume of the box?

66. *Surface area.* A company manufactures the open trash bin illustrated in Figure 3-68. Each bin must be 6 feet high and have a volume of 294 cubic feet. Find the dimensions x and y of the base that minimize the total surface area of a bin. (*Note:* The total surface area is the sum of the areas of the sides and bottom).

67. *Material cost.* A company manufactures the open trash bin illustrated in Figure 10-69. Each bin must be 6 feet high and have a volume of 192 cubic feet. If the material for the front and back costs $5 per square foot, the material for the sides costs $10 per square foot, and the material for the bottom costs $20 per square foot, find the dimensions x and y of the base that minimize the total cost.

Maximum sustainable harvest. If a population (of living things such as whales, salmon, mink, etc.) of size P grows to $f(P)$ at the end of some unit of time, then, if $f(P) > P$, the amount

$$f(P) - P$$

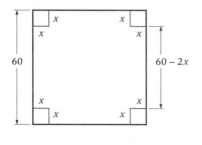

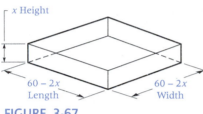

FIGURE 3-67

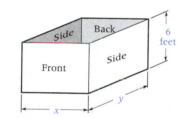

FIGURE 3-68

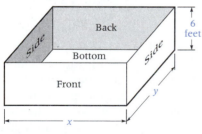

FIGURE 3-69

could be *removed* or *harvested* from the population, and the population size would not fall below the initial population size, P. The function $f(P)$ reveals the growth pattern of the population and is thus called a **reproduction curve.** The quantity, $f(P) - P$, represents the amount harvested. We let H denote this quantity. Thus, H is a function of P and

$$H(P) = f(P) - P \qquad \text{Amount harvested}$$

We wish to determine the initial population size, P, which maximizes the amount harvested, $H(P)$. In other words, we want to determine the value of P that maximizes H. The maximum value of H is called the *maximum sustainable harvest.*

Determine the maximum sustainable harvest for each of the following reproduction curves, $f(P)$.

68. $f(P) = -0.05P^2 + 10P$
69. $f(P) = -0.01P^2 + 4P$
70. $f(P) = -0.02P^2 + 10P$, where P is measured in thousands
71. $f(P) = 60\sqrt{P}$, where P is measured in thousands
72. $f(P) = 20\sqrt{P}$, where P is measured in thousands
73. $f(P) = 1.10P$
74. $f(P) = 1.06P$

75. *Construction costs.* A construction company must lay a water line from point A on shore (see Figure 3-70) to point D on an island. The island is 9 miles offshore, as shown in Figure 3-70. It costs $600 per mile to run the water line along the shoreline and $800 per mile to run the water line underwater. At what point along the shoreline should the water line proceed under water in order to minimize the total construction cost?

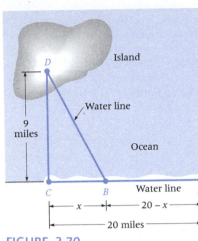

FIGURE 3-70

3-5 • MINIMIZING INVENTORY COST

A very important cost for many companies is that of financing and maintaining inventories. In this section, we develop a model for determining and minimizing total annual inventory cost. We begin with a discussion of the following typical situation.

A distributor of tires usually sells 100,000 tires per year. For each order for tires placed, it costs the distributor $20. Additionally, the cost of carrying 1 tire in inventory for a year is $4. The graph in Figure 3-71 illustrates the depletion of the distributor's inventory of tires over time, t. We assume that the annual demand is proportionally distributed throughout the year. In other words, if a work year consists of 50 weeks, then the weekly demand is $100,000/50 = 2000$ tires. Observing the graph of inventory level versus time in Figure 3-71, note that at $t = 0$, the initial inventory is Q tires. At $t = 1$ and $t = 2$, the inventory has reached a level of 0 tires. Thus, at $t = 1$ and $t = 2$, an order is placed for Q tires, and the inventory is immediately replenished.

The distributor must find an answer to the following question:

Each time an order is placed for tires, how many tires (Q) should be ordered so that the total annual inventory cost is minimized?

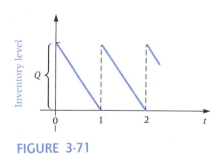

FIGURE 3-71

Objective Function

The total annual inventory cost, C, is calculated by the following formula:

$$C = \text{ordering cost} + \text{carrying cost}$$

The **ordering cost** is calculated by multiplying the cost of placing an order by the number of orders placed in a year. Since 100,000 tires are usually ordered annually in quantities of Q tires per order, the number of orders per year is 100,000/Q. Thus, since the cost of placing each order is $20, we have

$$\text{ordering cost} = 20\left(\frac{100,000}{Q}\right)$$

The **carrying cost** is calculated by multiplying the cost of carrying 1 unit in inventory for a year by the average number of units in inventory. The average inventory is $(0 + Q)/2 = Q/2$, since the inventory level varies from 0 to Q. Thus, since the cost of carrying 1 tire in inventory for a year is $4, we obtain

$$\text{carrying cost} = 4\left(\frac{Q}{2}\right)$$

Therefore, the *total annual inventory cost* is calculated as

$$C(Q) = 20\left(\frac{100,000}{Q}\right) + 4\left(\frac{Q}{2}\right) \qquad \text{Objective function}$$

Simplifying, we obtain

$$C(Q) = \frac{2,000,000}{Q} + 2Q \qquad (Q > 0)$$

Critical Values

Since we must find the value of Q that minimizes $C(Q)$, we calculate $C'(Q)$, as follows:

$$C'(Q) = \frac{-2,000,000}{Q^2} + 2$$

A critical value is $Q = 0$. However, we exclude $Q = 0$ since it is not in the domain $Q > 0$. We set $C'(Q) = 0$ to obtain

$$0 = \frac{-2,000,000}{Q^2} + 2$$

Solving for Q^2 yields

$$Q^2 = 1,000,000$$
$$Q = \pm 1000$$

We disregard the critical value $Q = -1000$ since it is outside the domain $Q > 0$. Thus, there is only one relevant critical value:

$$Q = 1000 \qquad \text{Only critical value}$$

Test for Absolute Extrema

Applying the second-derivative test to $Q = 1000$, we have

$$C''(Q) = \frac{4,000,000}{Q^3}$$

$$C''(1000) = \frac{4,000,000}{1000^3} = \frac{4}{1000} \quad \text{which is positive}$$

Therefore, by the second-derivative test for absolute extrema, an absolute minimum exists at $Q = 1000$.

Thus, in order to minimize the total annual inventory cost, the distributor should order tires in lots of 1000 tires. The minimum annual inventory cost is

$$C(1000) = \frac{2,000,000}{1000} + 2(1000)$$

$$= \$4000 \qquad \text{Absolute minimum}$$

Graph of $C(Q)$

Since $C''(Q) > 0$ for all values of Q in the interval $Q > 0$, the cost function, $C(Q)$, is concave up over the interval $Q > 0$. This and the fact that $C'(1000) = 0$ imply that the graph of $C(Q)$ has the appearance of that shown in Figure 3-72.

We generalize as follows.

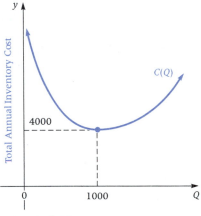

FIGURE 3-72

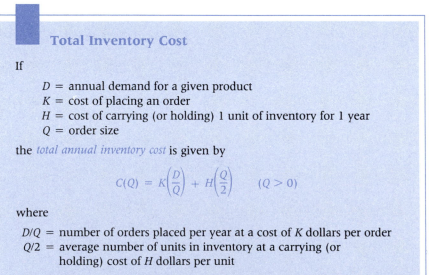

Total Inventory Cost

If

     D = annual demand for a given product
     K = cost of placing an order
     H = cost of carrying (or holding) 1 unit of inventory for 1 year
     Q = order size

the *total annual inventory cost* is given by

$$C(Q) = K\left(\frac{D}{Q}\right) + H\left(\frac{Q}{2}\right) \qquad (Q > 0)$$

where

     D/Q = number of orders placed per year at a cost of K dollars per order
     $Q/2$ = average number of units in inventory at a carrying (or holding) cost of H dollars per unit

The graph of $C(Q)$ has the appearance of that of Figure 3-73.

continues

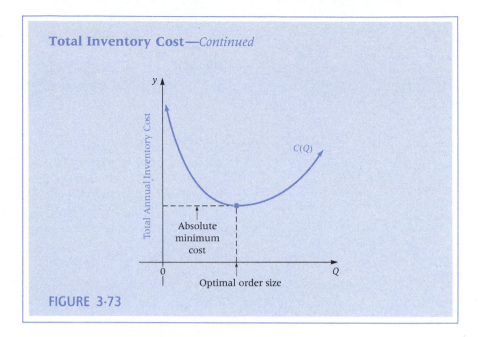

Total Inventory Cost—*Continued*

FIGURE 3-73

Unit Holding Cost

The holding cost, H, per unit of inventory includes financing costs (i.e., cost of capital) and other costs associated with holding inventory, such as insurance costs, taxes, breakage costs, etc. Often H is given as a percentage of the cost of 1 unit of inventory. For example, let's assume that each tire purchased by the distributor of the preceding discussion costs $20. If the distributor borrows money to buy tires at an annual rate of 19%, then the finance cost of each tire is $(0.19)(20) = \$3.80$ per year. If the annual insurance cost is $20,000, then the insurance cost per tire is $20,000/100,000 = \$0.20$ per tire. Thus, the breakdown of H, the annual holding cost per tire (assuming there are no other holding costs), is:

Finance cost	$3.80
Insurance cost	0.20
	$4.00

If we wish to express $H = \$4$ as a percentage of the cost per tire, then H is 20% (i.e., $4/20 = 0.20$) of the cost of each tire.

• EXAMPLE 3-25

One of many products sold by a discount store is a special model video-cassette recorder (VCR). Each such VCR costs the store $200. The annual demand is 200,000 units. Ordering costs are $40 per order, and the annual holding cost per unit is 8% of the cost of a VCR.

a) Determine the equation for the total annual inventory cost.
b) Determine the order size that minimizes the total annual inventory cost.

c) Determine the minimum total annual inventory cost.

d) Determine the number of orders placed in a year for this particular VCR.

Solutions

a) The total annual inventory cost is given by

$$C(Q) = K\frac{D}{Q} + H\frac{Q}{2}$$

where

Q = order size

K = $40 (cost of placing 1 order)

D = 200,000 (annual demand)

H = (0.08)($200) = $16 (unit annual holding cost)

Thus

$$C(Q) = 40\left(\frac{200,000}{Q}\right) + 16\left(\frac{Q}{2}\right)$$

$$= \frac{8,000,000}{Q} + 8Q \quad (Q > 0)$$

b) Calculating $C'(Q)$ gives

$$C'(Q) = \frac{-8,000,000}{Q^2} + 8$$

A critical value is $Q = 0$, which we exclude because it is not in the domain $Q > 0$. Setting $C'(Q) = 0$ yields

$$0 = \frac{-8,000,000}{Q^2} + 8$$

Solving for Q^2 gives

$$Q^2 = 1,000,000$$

$$Q = \pm 1000$$

We disregard the critical value $Q = -1000$ since it is outside the domain $Q > 0$. Thus, there is only one relevant critical value:

$$Q = 1000 \qquad \text{Only critical value}$$

Applying the second-derivative test to $Q = 1000$, we have

$$C''(Q) = \frac{16,000,000}{Q^3}$$

$$C''(1000) = \frac{16,000,000}{1000^3}$$

$$= 0.016 \qquad \text{which is positive}$$

Therefore, by the second-derivative test for absolute extrema, an *absolute minimum* exists at $Q = 1000$.

Thus, in order to minimize the total annual inventory cost, the store should order this particular model of VCR in lots of 1000.

c) The *minimum annual inventory cost* is

$$C(1000) = \frac{8,000,000}{1000} + 8(1000)$$

$$= \$16,000$$

d) The *number of orders placed in a year* for this VCR is given by

$$\frac{D}{Q} = \frac{200{,}000}{1000}$$

$$= 200 \text{ orders}$$

Exercises 3-5

1. It costs a moped distributor $100 to place an order for Q mopeds. Also, it costs $20 per year to keep 1 moped in inventory. The distributor usually sells 25,000 mopeds annually.
   a) Find the formula for total inventory cost as a function of Q.
   b) What order size, Q, minimizes the total inventory cost?
2. A bicycle manufacturer finds that it costs $1500 to order Q bicycles. Also, it costs $3 per year to keep a bicycle in inventory. The manufacturer expects to sell 4,900,000 bicycles this year.
   a) Find the formula for total inventory cost as a function of Q.
   b) What production lot size, Q, minimizes the total inventory cost?
   c) What is the minimum total inventory cost?
3. A store sells 300,000 units of a particular model of color television. Each TV costs the store $500. Ordering costs are $60 per order, and the carrying cost per unit per year is 5% of the cost of the TV.
   a) Determine the equation for the total annual inventory cost.
   b) Determine the order size that minimizes the total annual inventory cost.
   c) Determine the minimum total annual inventory cost.
   d) Determine the number of orders placed in a year for this TV.
4. A computer store sells 400,000 units of a particular model home computer. Each computer costs the store $1000. Ordering costs are $80 per order, and annual holding costs per unit are 10% of the cost of a computer.
   a) Determine the equation for the total annual inventory cost.
   b) Determine the order size that minimizes the total annual inventory cost.
   c) Determine the minimum total annual inventory cost.
   d) Determine the total number of orders placed in a year for this computer.
5. A distributor of heating and cooling equipment sells 500,000 units of a particular model of air conditioner. Ordering costs are $100 per order. The annual finance charge for 500,000 units of this air conditioner is $7,000,000, and the annual insurance costs are $1,000,000. There are no other holding costs.
   a) Calculate the annual holding cost per air conditioner.
   b) Determine the equation for the total annual inventory cost.
   c) Determine the order size that minimizes the total annual inventory cost.
   d) Determine the minimum total annual inventory cost.
   e) Determine the number of orders placed in a year for this air conditioner.
6. Determine an equation for the value of Q that minimizes the total annual inventory cost

$$C(Q) = K\frac{D}{Q} + H\frac{Q}{2} \quad (Q > 0)$$

by following the steps.

Step 1 Find $C'(Q)$ by differentiating $C(Q)$ with respect to Q. Treat K, D, and H as positive constants.

Step 2 Set $C'(Q) = 0$, and solve for Q^2 and then Q. Call this minimizing value Q^*.

7. Verify that the equation for Q^* determined in Exercise 6 yields an absolute minimum for $C(Q)$ by following the steps:

   Step 1   Find $C''(Q)$ by differentiating $C'(Q)$ with respect to Q. Treat K, D, and H as positive constants.

   Step 2   Analyze the sign of $C''(Q)$.

EXTRA DIVIDENDS

• *The Production Lot Size Model—Medisoap, Inc.*

The inventory model in Section 3-5 assumed that items of inventory arrive in lots of size Q. However, there are real-life situations where items of inventory are supplied at a constant rate during a given time interval. This is characteristic of a production situation where a production run to manufacture a total of Q units is set up and the items are supplied to the inventory stockpile at a constant rate per time unit until the production run has been completed. The graph of inventory level versus time for such a situation appears in Figure 3-74.

We let

$$P = \text{annual production rate}$$
$$D = \text{annual demand rate}$$

where $P > D$, and note that these may be expressed in time units other than 1 year. If, for example, we wish to express P and D as daily rates, then we simply divide these annual rates by the number of work days in a year. The result is a daily production rate and a daily demand rate. Observing the graph in Figure 3-74, note that inventory is being produced (and supplied) at a rate, P (adjusted by a divisor for a daily, weekly, or monthly rate), and, simultaneously, is being sold at a rate, D (adjusted by a divisor for a daily, weekly, or monthly rate), during the production phase of the inventory cycle. This situation is illustrated in Figure 3-75. If $P = $ production rate or rate of inflow of inventory into the stockpile and $D = $ rate of outflow, then $P - D$ is the net rate of inflow of inventory into

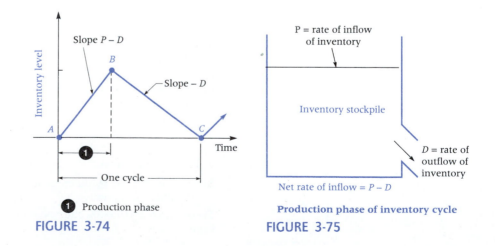

FIGURE 3-74

FIGURE 3-75

Production phase of inventory cycle

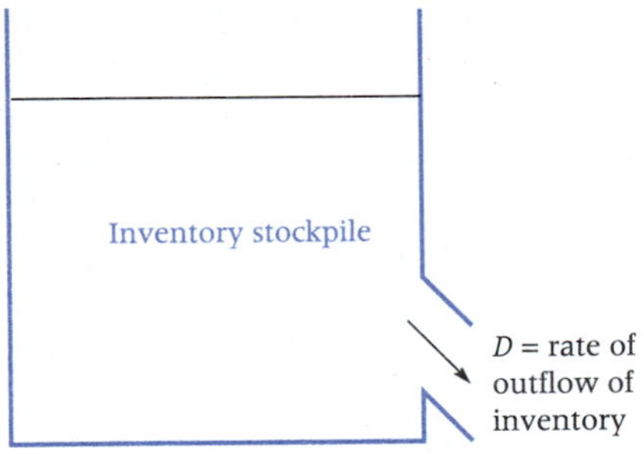

Inventory stockpile

D = rate of outflow of inventory

Post-production phase of inventory cycle

FIGURE 3-76

the stockpile during the production phase of the inventory cycle. As shown in Figure 3-74, $P - D$ is the slope of the line segment AB.

During the latter phase of the inventory cycle, no production is taking place; therefore, only the outflow of inventory at demand rate, D, is occurring. The slope, $-D$, of the line segment BC indicates that inventory is decreasing at an annual rate of D units. This is illustrated in Figure 3-76.

The **total annual inventory cost** associated with this production lot size inventory model is given by

$$C(Q) = K\frac{D}{Q} + H\left(\frac{P - D}{P}\right)\frac{Q}{2} \quad (Q > 0)$$

where

Q = number of units of inventory manufactured during a production run

D = annual demand rate

P = annual production rate

K = cost of setting up a production run

H = annual holding cost per unit of inventory

For this equation, the first component, $K(D/Q)$, gives the annual set-up cost for the production runs; the second component, $H[(P - D)/P](Q/2)$, gives the annual holding cost. Since K, D, H, and P are constants, *we seek a value of Q that minimizes the total annual inventory cost, $C(Q)$.*

We now consider the following specific example. Medisoap, Inc., manufactures a special type of medicated soap. Medisoap can produce this soap at an annual rate of 480,000 cases. The annual demand is estimated to be 320,000 cases. It costs Medisoap $400 to set up a production run. The annual holding cost per case of soap is $12.

Exercises

1. Determine the equation defining the total annual inventory cost for Medisoap.
2. Determine the value of Q that minimizes the total annual inventory cost.
3. Determine the minimum total annual inventory cost.
4. Determine the annual set-up cost.
5. Determine the annual holding cost.
6. Determine an equation for the value of Q that minimizes the total annual inventory cost

$$C(Q) = K\frac{D}{Q} + H\left(\frac{P - D}{P}\right)\frac{Q}{2} \quad (Q > 0)$$

by following these steps.

Step 1 Find $C'(Q)$ by differentiating $C(Q)$ with respect to Q. Treat K, D, P, and H as positive constants.

Step 2 Set $C'(Q) = 0$, and solve for Q^2 and then Q. Call this minimizing value Q^*.

7. Verify that the equation for Q^* determined in Exercise 6 yields an absolute minimum for $C(Q)$ by following these steps.

Step 1 Find $C''(Q)$ by differentiating $C'(Q)$ with respect to Q. Treat K, D, P, and H as positive constants.

Step 2 Analyze the sign of $C''(Q)$.

CHAPTER 3 HIGHLIGHTS

• *Concepts*

Your ability to answer the following questions is one indicator of the depth of your mastery of this chapter's important concepts. Note that the questions are grouped under various topic headings. For any question that you cannot answer, refer to the appropriate section of the chapter indicated by the topic heading. Pay particular attention to the summary boxes within a section.

3-1 HIGHER-ORDER DERIVATIVES

1. How does one find a second derivative of a function?
2. How does one find a third derivative of a function?
3. If the distance, S, gained by a moving particle is given by a function, $S = f(t)$, where t denotes time, then
   a) Explain the term *velocity* and indicate how it is determined.
   b) Explain the term *acceleration* and indicate how it is found.

3-2 CRITICAL VALUES AND THE FIRST DERIVATIVE

4. Draw each of the following:
   a) A relative maximum point where the first derivative is 0
   b) A relative minimum point where the first derivative is 0
   c) A relative maximum point where the first derivative is undefined
   d) A relative minimum point where the first derivative is undefined
5. Draw two types of curve segments that are
   a) Increasing.   b) Decreasing.
6. a) If the first derivative of some function is positive over some interval, what does this indicate about the function over that interval?
   b) If the first derivative of some function is negative over some interval, what does this indicate about the function over that interval?
7. a) Define *critical values*.
   b) Do critical values always yield relative extrema?
   c) How do we determine whether or not a critical value yields a relative extremum?
   d) Can a relative extremum occur at a value of x that is not a critical value?
8. According to the first-derivative test for relative extrema,
   a) How do we determine whether or not a relative maximum occurs at a critical value?
   b) How do we determine whether or not a relative minimum occurs at a critical value?
9. a) State the difference between relative extrema and absolute extrema.
   b) Is it possible for a relative extremum to also be an absolute extremum? Draw graphs to support your answer.
   c) Is an absolute extremum always a relative extremum? Draw graphs to support your answer.

3-3   CONCAVITY AND THE SECOND DERIVATIVE

10. Draw a curve segment that is increasing and
   a) Concave down.   b) Concave up.
11. Draw a curve segment that is decreasing and
   a) Concave down.   b) Concave up.
12. a) If the second derivative of some function is positive over some interval, what does this indicate about the function over the interval?
   b) If the second derivative of some function is negative over some interval, what does this indicate about the function over the interval?
13. a) What is an inflection point?
   b) How do we determine the existence of an inflection point?
14. How do we determine the existence of vertical asymptotes?
15. Is a function defined at any of its vertical asymptotes?
16. How do we determine the existence of horizontal asymptotes?

3-4   OPTIMIZATION

17. Does the second-derivative test for relative extrema apply to
   a) All critical values?
   b) Critical values for which $f'(x) = 0$?
   c) Critical values for which $f'(x)$ is undefined?
18. If $f(x)$ is a function and x_0 is a number such that $f'(x_0) = 0$, then, according to the second-derivative test for relative extrema,
   a) If $f''(x_0) > 0$, what does this indicate?
   b) If $f''(x_0) < 0$, what does this indicate?
   c) If $f''(x_0) = 0$, what does this indicate?
19. If the second-derivative test for relative extrema fails, or if a critical value is such that $f'(x)$ is undefined, what test should be used to determine the existence or nonexistence of relative extrema?
20. Is the second-derivative test for relative extrema used to graph a function?
21. Is the second-derivative test for relative extrema used mainly to determine relative extrema without having to graph functions?
22. Can the second-derivative test for absolute extrema be used if two or more critical values exist in some interval of interest?
23. State the second-derivative test for absolute extrema.
24. State the procedure for finding absolute extrema of continuous functions defined on closed intervals.

3-5   MINIMIZING INVENTORY COST

25. State the two components that constitute total annual inventory cost. Give the formula for and explain each component.

REVIEW EXERCISES

• *Higher-Order Derivatives*

For Exercises 1-4, find
a) $f'(x)$ b) $f''(x)$ c) $f'(1)$ d) $f''(1)$

1. $f(x) = x^2 - 6x + 8$ **2.** $f(x) = x^4 - 2x^3 + 6x^2 + 9$
3. $f(x) = x^6 - 8x^4 + 7$ **4.** $f(x) = (x - 4)^2(x^2 + 6)$

5. *Projectile.* A ball moves in the path of a straight line. Its distance, S (in feet), from its starting point after t seconds have elapsed is given by
$$S(t) = -2t^2 + 80t \qquad (0 \le t \le 40)$$

    a) Find the ball's instantaneous speed at $t = 5$ and $t = 10$.
    b) Find the ball's instantaneous acceleration at $t = 5$ and $t = 10$.

• *Critical Values and the First Derivative*

For Exercises 6-9, use the first derivative to
a) Determine any critical values.
b) Determine the interval(s) over which the function is increasing.
c) Determine the interval(s) over which the function is decreasing.
d) Determine any relative maxima and minima.
e) Graph the function.

  6. $f(x) = 2x^3 - 18x^2 + 30x + 5$ **7.** $f(x) = 2x^3 + 3x^2 - 60x + 8$
  8. $f(x) = x^4 - 32x^2 + 10$ **9.** $f(x) = x^3 - 24x^2 + 6$

10. *Revenue function.* The sales revenue gained from selling x units of some product is given by

$$R(x) = -6x^2 + 600x \qquad (0 \le x \le 50)$$

a) State the interval(s) over which sales revenue is increasing.
b) State the interval(s) over which sales revenue is decreasing.
c) Identify all relative extrema.
d) Graph $R(x)$.
e) What sales volume maximizes sales revenue? Is this a relative maximum? Is this an absolute maximum?
f) What is the maximum sales revenue?

• *Concavity and the Second Derivative*

For Exercises 11-16, use both first and second derivatives to graph the function. Identify all relative and absolute extrema and inflection points.

  11. $f(x) = 3x^4 - 8x^3 + 6x^2 + 2$ **12.** $f(x) = 3x^4 - 16x^3 + 24x^2 + 4$
  13. $f(x) = x^{6/5}$ **14.** $f(x) = 1800/x + 2x$
  15. $f(x) = 10/(x^2 + 4)$ **16.** $f(x) = (x + 8)/x$

17. *Average cost per unit.* Given the cost function

$$C(x) = x^2 - 8x + 100 \qquad (x > 0)$$

where x is the number of units produced,
a) Determine the formula for the average cost per unit.
b) Use both first and second derivatives to graph the average cost function.
c) Identify any relative and absolute extrema.
d) What production level minimizes the average cost per unit?
e) What is the minimum average cost per unit?

• *Optimization*

Use the second-derivative test to find relative extrema for Exercises 18-21.

  18. $f(x) = x^2 - 10x + 8$ **19.** $f(x) = x^3 - 15x^2 + 48x + 4$
  20. $f(x) = x^3 - 9x^2 - 48x + 12$ **21.** $f(x) = x + 100/x$

Determine the absolute extrema for Exercises 22-27.

  22. $f(x) = x^2 - 20x + 5$
  23. $f(x) = 3\sqrt{x} - x$
  24. $f(x) = x^3 - 75x + 10$ $(-10 \le x \le 10)$
  25. $f(x) = 7 + 3x + 48/x$ $(x > 0)$

26. $f(x) = 6(x - 4)^3$ $\quad (0 \leq x \leq 7)$

27. $f(x) = 8 + 2x + 128/x^3$ $\quad (x > 0)$

Solve Exercises 28-34. Try to verify the existence of absolute extrema.

28. Find two numbers whose difference is 20 and whose product is as small as possible.

29. *Enclosure.* A person has 800 feet of fence to enclose a rectangular area. Use calculus to determine the dimensions that maximize the enclosed area.

30. *Enclosure.* A farmer must enclose a rectangular area of 40,000 square feet. Use calculus to determine the dimensions that minimize the length of fence used.

31. *Revenue.* A cable television company currently charges $20 per month for its service and has 5000 subscribers. Market surveys indicate that the number of subscribers will increase by 400 for each $1 decrease in the monthly rate.
   a) Determine the monthly rate that maximizes revenue.
   b) What is the maximum revenue?
   c) How many subscribers will produce the maximum revenue?

32. *Building cost.* A home improvement center is designing a greenhouse that is to have the shape of a box with a square base. The material for the floor costs $5 per square foot; the material for the roof and three sides is glass and costs $20 per square foot; the material for the fourth side is wood and costs $4 per square foot. If the greenhouse is to have a volume of 400 cubic feet, find the dimensions that minimize its cost.

33. *Enclosure.* A rectangular storage area containing 800 square feet is to be enclosed outside a shopping mall. Three sides are to consist of cedar fencing at a cost of $10 per foot; the fourth side is to consist of chain link fencing at a cost of $20 per foot. Find the dimensions that minimize the cost.

• *Minimizing Inventory Cost*

34. A distributor of cameras sells 600,000 cameras per year. The cost of placing an order for cameras is $5. The cost of holding 1 camera in inventory for 1 year is $6.
   a) Determine the equation for the total annual inventory cost, $C(Q)$.
   b) Each time the distributor places an order for cameras, how many should be ordered so that the total annual inventory cost is minimized?
   c) Determine the minimum total annual inventory cost.
   d) How many orders will be placed per year?

4

APPLICATIONS
OF THE
DERIVATIVE

Introductory Application

Newton's Method: Break-Even Point

The profit, P (in millions of dollars), gained from selling x (in thousands) units of some product is given by

$$P(x) = 2x^3 - 9x^2 + 6x - 3 \qquad (x \geq 0)$$

Approximate a break-even point that occurs in the vicinity of $x = 3.5$.

The break-even points are given by the x-intercepts of the profit function. These are easily determined if the right-hand side of the profit equation can be factored. If this is not the case, then Newton's method provides a procedure for approximating x-intercepts. This is discussed in Section 4-5, and the above problem is solved in Example 4-19.

4-1 • IMPLICIT DIFFERENTIATION

Up to this point, we have found derivatives of functions that were defined *explicitly in terms of x*. For example, the equation

$$y = f(x) = x^3 - 4x^2 + 5$$

defines y (or $f(x)$) explicitly in terms of x because y is written completely in terms of x and constants. If this equation were written as

$$y - x^3 + 4x^2 - 5 = 0$$

or

$$f(x) - x^3 + 4x^2 - 5 = 0$$

then y (or $f(x)$) is said to be defined implicitly in terms of x. Thus, if y is not written completely in terms of x and constants, then y is said to be defined **implicitly in terms of x.**

There are cases where y (or $f(x)$) cannot be defined explicitly in terms of x and also where it is difficult to do so. Consider the equation

$$xy^2 + x^2 + y = 2$$

It is difficult to solve this equation for y so that y is expressed explicitly in terms of x. Thus, we suppose that y (or $f(x)$) is defined implicitly in terms of x by the given equation and proceed as follows.

If we assume that y is a differentiable function of x—say, $y = f(x)$—then dy/dx is found by a method called **implicit differentiation.** To differentiate an expression such as

$$xy^2 + x^2 + y = 2$$

implicitly, we differentiate each side of the equation with respect to x, *term by term*, to obtain

$$\frac{d}{dx}(xy^2) + \frac{d}{dx}(x^2) + \frac{d}{dx}(y) = \frac{d}{dx}(2) \tag{1}$$

Since y is a differentiable function of x and xy^2 is a product, we must use the product rule to find $(d/dx)(xy^2)$. Hence

$$\frac{d}{dx}(xy^2) = x\frac{d}{dx}(y^2) + y^2\frac{d}{dx}(x)$$

$$= x \cdot 2y\frac{dy}{dx} + y^2(1)$$

Note that we used the general power rule to find

$$\frac{d}{dx}(y^2) = 2y\frac{dy}{dx}$$

Thus,

$$\frac{d}{dx}(xy^2) = 2xy\frac{dy}{dx} + y^2$$

and equation (1) becomes

$$2xy\frac{dy}{dx} + y^2 + 2x + \frac{dy}{dx} = 0$$

Combining terms with dy/dx gives

$$2xy\frac{dy}{dx} + \frac{dy}{dx} = -2x - y^2$$

Factoring out dy/dx, we have

$$(2xy + 1)\frac{dy}{dx} = -2x - y^2$$

Solving for dy/dx gives

$$\frac{dy}{dx} = \frac{-2x - y^2}{2xy + 1}$$

Note that dy/dx is expressed in terms of x and y.

• **EXAMPLE 4-1**

For the equation $x^2 + y^2 = 16$:

a) Find the dy/dx by implicit differentiation.
b) Find the slope of the tangent line at $(3, \sqrt{7})$.

Solutions

a) Differentiating both sides with respect to x, term by term, gives

$$\frac{d}{dx}(x^2) + \frac{d}{dx}(y^2) = \frac{d}{dx}(16) \qquad (2)$$

Treating y as a function of x and using the general power rule,

$$\frac{d}{dx}(y^2) = 2y\frac{dy}{dx}$$

Thus, equation (2) becomes

$$2x + 2y\frac{dy}{dx} = 0$$

Solving for dy/dx yields

$$\frac{dy}{dx} = \frac{-2x}{2y} = \frac{-x}{y}$$

b) The circle* defined by $x^2 + y^2 = 16$ is graphed in Figure 4-1. Note that $(3, \sqrt{7})$ is a point on the circle since its coordinates satisfy the equation $x^2 + y^2 = 16$. To find the slope of the tangent line at $(3, \sqrt{7})$, we must evaluate dy/dx at $(3, \sqrt{7})$. Hence,

$$\frac{dy}{dx} = \frac{-x}{y}$$

$$\left.\frac{dy}{dx}\right|_{(3, \sqrt{7})} = \frac{-3}{\sqrt{7}} \approx -1.13$$

Thus, the slope of the tangent line at $(3, \sqrt{7})$ is $-3/\sqrt{7}$, or approximately -1.13.

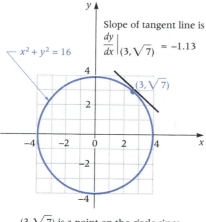

Slope of tangent line is $\left.\dfrac{dy}{dx}\right|_{(3, \sqrt{7})} \approx -1.13$

$x^2 + y^2 = 16$

$(3, \sqrt{7})$ is a point on the circle since

$$x^2 + y^2 = 16$$
$$(3)^2 + (\sqrt{7})^2 = 16$$

FIGURE 4-1

*Equations of circles are discussed in Appendix B.

• **EXAMPLE 4-2** _____

For the equation $xy - 2y = 5$:

a) Find dy/dx by implicit differentiation.
b) Express y explicitly in terms of x, and find dy/dx.
c) Compare the results of parts a and b.

Solutions

a) Beginning with $xy - 2y = 5$, we differentiate both sides with respect to x, term by term, to obtain

$$\frac{d}{dx}(xy) - \frac{d}{dx}(2y) = \frac{d}{dx}(5)$$

Treating y as a function of x and using the appropriate differentiation rule, we obtain

$$x\frac{dy}{dx} + y - 2\frac{dy}{dx} = 0$$

Combining terms containing dy/dx gives

$$(x - 2)\frac{dy}{dx} = -y$$

Solving for dy/dx gives

$$\frac{dy}{dx} = \frac{-y}{x - 2}$$

b) $xy - 2y = 5$ can be written as $(x - 2)y = 5$. Solving for y explicitly yields

$$y = \frac{5}{x - 2}$$

Hence,

$$\frac{dy}{dx} = \frac{-5}{(x - 2)^2}$$

c) From part a, $dy/dx = -y/(x - 2)$. We solved the equation $xy - 2y = 5$ for y to obtain $y = 5/(x - 2)$. Substituting this result for y into the equation for dy/dx gives

$$\frac{dy}{dx} = \frac{-5/(x - 2)}{(x - 2)} = \frac{-5}{(x - 2)^2}$$

This answer is identical to that of part b.

_____ •

dy/dx and dx/dy

If an equation defines y as a function of x, such as

$$y = 4x - 3$$

then the expression for the rate of change of y with respect to x is

$$\frac{dy}{dx} = 4$$

Suppose we wish to find an expression for the *instantaneous rate of change of x with respect to y*, dx/dy. We can solve the equation $y = 4x - 3$ for x to obtain

$$x = \frac{1}{4}y + 3$$

and differentiate with respect to y to obtain

$$\frac{dx}{dy} = \frac{1}{4}$$

Note that $dx/dy = 1/(dy/dx)$. Is this true in general? In other words, can we find dx/dy as the reciprocal of dy/dx without having to solve the equation for x and then differentiate with respect to y? The answer to both questions is yes, provided certain conditions hold. We will use implicit differentiation and the chain rule to show why.

Let $y = f(x)$ be an equation defining y as a function of x and $x = g(y)$ be its equivalent equation obtained by solving for x in terms of y. We begin with

$$y = f(x)$$

and differentiate both sides with respect to y to obtain

$$\frac{d}{dy}(y) = \frac{d}{dy}(f(x))$$

Since x is also a function of y, we apply the chain rule to obtain

$$\frac{d}{dy}(y) = \frac{d}{dx}(f(x))\frac{dx}{dy}$$

Since $(d/dy)(y) = 1$ and $(d/dx)(f(x)) = f'(x)$, the equation becomes

$$1 = f'(x)\frac{dx}{dy}$$

Solving for dx/dy yields

$$\frac{dx}{dy} = \frac{1}{f'(x)}$$

Since $f'(x) = dy/dx$, the equation becomes as follows.

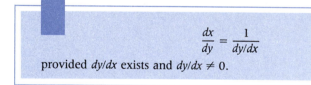

$$\frac{dx}{dy} = \frac{1}{dy/dx}$$

provided dy/dx exists and $dy/dx \neq 0$.

• **EXAMPLE 4-3**

If $y = x^2 - 8x + 10$, then find dx/dy.

Solution

Since y is expressed in terms of x, we find dy/dx.

$$\frac{dy}{dx} = 2x - 8$$

Now

$$\frac{dx}{dy} = \frac{1}{dy/dx}$$

$$= \frac{1}{2x - 8} \qquad \text{provided that } x \neq 4$$

Exercises 4-1

Use implicit differentiation to find dy/dx for each of the following.

1. $xy^3 + x^4 + y = 8$ **2.** $x^2 + y^2 = 60$

3. $xy^5 + x^3 + y^4 = 10$ **4.** $x^3 + y^2 = 80$

5. $x^3 + y^6 = 8xy$ **6.** $\sqrt{x} + \sqrt{y} = 10$

7. $(x - y)(x^2 + y^2) = 9$ **8.** $x^2/4 + y^2/25 = 1$

9. $(x + y)^4 = x^2 + y^2$ **10.** $(x + y)(x + 3y) = 10$

For each of the following, find the slope of the tangent line to the curve at the indicated point.

11. $x^3 + xy^2 + y^4 = 21$, $(1, 2)$ **12.** $y^3 - x^2 + xy = 29$, $(2, 3)$

13. $x^2 - 3xy + 5y^2 = 15$, $(-2, 1)$ **14.** $3x + 4y^2 - y = 57$, $(-1, 4)$

15. $4x - 2y^2 + 5y = -7$, $(-1, 3)$ **16.** $x^3 - 2xy + y^2 = 4$, $(1, 3)$

17. For the equation $x^2 + y^2 = 64$:
   a) Find dy/dx by implicit differentiation.
   b) Find the slope of the tangent line at $(4, 4\sqrt{3})$.
   c) Find the equation of the tangent line of part b.
   d) Include a graphical interpretation of parts a through c.

18. For the equation $(x - 3)^2 + (y - 6)^2 = 25$:
   a) Find dy/dx by implicit differentiation.
   b) Find the slope of the tangent line at $(7, 9)$.
   c) Find the equation of the tangent line of part b.
   d) Include a graphical interpretation of parts a through c.

19. If $y = 6x + 10$, find dx/dy.

20. If $y = 3x^2 - 8x$, find dx/dy.

21. If $y = 4x^2 - 3x + 7$, find dx/dy.

22. If $y = 6x^2 - 2x + 1$, find dx/dy.

23. Given that $y = x^2 - 4x$,
   a) Find dx/dy.
   b) Evaluate dx/dy at $x = 3$.
   c) Interpret the result of part b as a rate of change.

24. Given that $y = -4x^2 + 36x$,
   a) Find dx/dy.
   b) Evaluate dx/dy at $x = 2$.
   c) Interpret the result of part b as a rate of change.

25. *Demand.* For some commodity, demand, q, and unit price, p, are related by

$$q = p^2 - 20p + 101 \quad (0 < p \leq 10)$$

   a) Find dp/dq.
   b) Evaluate dp/dq at $p = 7$.
   c) Interpret the result of part b as a rate of change.

26. *Demand.* For some commodity, demand, q, and unit price, p, are related by

$$q = p^2 - 40p + 405 \quad (0 < p \leq 20)$$

   a) Find dp/dq.
   b) Evaluate dp/dq at $p = 10$.
   c) Interpret the result of part b as a rate of change.

Physics: Velocity. A particle starts at point 0 and moves along a horizontal line, as illustrated to the left. The distance between the particle and its starting point, 0, after t seconds have elapsed is given by S. If S and t are related as follows, then, for each of the following, find a formula for the velocity, dS/dt.

Particle

27. $S^3 - 2St + 4t^3 - 2t = 0$ **28.** $S^2 - St + t^2 = 5$
29. $S^4 - 3St^2 + t^3 = 6$ **30.** $S^3 + 4St - t^2 = 9$

4-2 • RELATED RATES

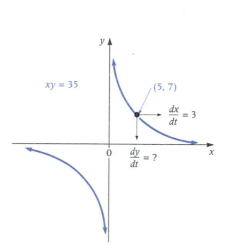

FIGURE 4-2

In this section, we will encounter word problems—the solutions to which involve equations with variables that are implicit functions of time. Typically we will have to determine rates of change of such variables with respect to time. Since such variables will not usually be defined explicitly in terms of time, we will have to differentiate implicitly with respect to time to determine the rates of change.

For example, suppose a point moves along the graph of

$$xy = 35$$

in such a manner that its x-coordinate is increasing at the rate of 3 units per second when the point is at $(5, 7)$ (see Figure 4-2). Find the rate of change of the y-coordinate at that moment.

Here x and y are functions of time, t. We want to determine a formula for dy/dt. Since x and y are not defined explicitly in terms of t, we must implicitly differentiate each side of the equation $xy = 35$ with respect to t. This gives

$$\frac{d}{dt}(xy) = \frac{d}{dt}(35)$$

Since x and y are functions of t, we must use the product rule to differentiate the left-hand side. The derivative of 35, a constant, is 0. Hence, we have

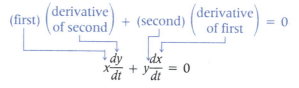

$$x\frac{dy}{dt} + y\frac{dx}{dt} = 0$$

Note that the derivatives dx/dt and dy/dt are related by the above equation. Hence, they are called **related rates.** Solving for dy/dt gives

$$x\frac{dy}{dt} = -y\frac{dx}{dt}$$

$$\frac{dy}{dt} = -\frac{y}{x} \cdot \frac{dx}{dt} \qquad \text{Formula for } dy/dt$$

Substituting 5 for x, 7 for y, and 3 for dx/dt gives

$$\frac{dy}{dt} = -\frac{7}{5}(3) = -4.2 \text{ units per second}$$

Thus, the y-coordinate is decreasing at a rate of 4.2 units per second.

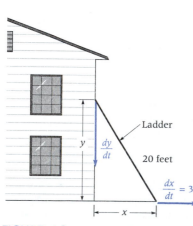

FIGURE 4-3

• **EXAMPLE 4-4**

A 20-foot ladder is resting against a building, as illustrated in Figure 4-3. The bottom of the ladder is sliding away from the building at a rate of 3 feet per second.

a) Use implicit differentiation to find a formula for dy/dt, the rate at which the top of the ladder is sliding downward.

b) How fast is the top of the ladder sliding downward when the bottom of the ladder is 12 feet away from the building?

Solutions

a) Observing Figure 4-3 and using the Pythagorean theorem, we obtain the equation

$$x^2 + y^2 = 20^2$$

Since x and y are changing as time elapses, then x and y are functions of time, t (in seconds). Since we want to determine a formula for dy/dt, we differentiate both sides of the above equation, term by term, with respect to t. This gives

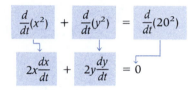

$$2x\frac{dx}{dt} + 2y\frac{dy}{dt} = 0$$

Solving for dy/dt, we obtain

$$2y\frac{dy}{dt} = -2x\frac{dx}{dt}$$

$$\frac{dy}{dt} = \frac{-2x}{2y} \cdot \frac{dx}{dt}$$

$$= -\frac{x}{y} \cdot \frac{dx}{dt} \qquad \text{This expression gives } dy/dt \text{ in terms of } x, y, \text{ and } dx/dt.$$

Since the ladder is sliding away from the wall (i.e., horizontally) at 3 feet per second, then

$$\frac{dx}{dt} = 3$$

Substituting this into the above formula for dy/dt gives

$$\frac{dy}{dt} = -\frac{x}{y}(3)$$

$$= -\frac{3x}{y} \qquad \text{This expression gives } dy/dt \text{ in terms of } x \text{ and } y \text{ when } dx/dt = 3.$$

b) When the ladder is 12 feet away from the building, then $x = 12$. Substituting into the equation

$$x^2 + y^2 = 20^2$$

gives

$$12^2 + y^2 = 20^2$$

or

$$144 + y^2 = 400$$
$$y^2 = 256$$
$$y = 16$$

Thus, when $x = 12$, $y = 16$. Substituting these results into the formula for dy/dt gives

$$\frac{dy}{dt} = -\frac{3x}{y}$$

$$= -\frac{3(12)}{16} = -2.25 \text{ feet per second}$$

Hence, the top of the ladder is sliding downward at a rate of 2.25 feet per second. The minus sign indicates that the top of the ladder is sliding *downward*.

• **EXAMPLE 4-5** _____

The unit price, p, of some product is related to the number of units sold, x, by the demand equation

$$p = 400 - \frac{x}{1000} \qquad \text{Demand equation}$$

The cost of producing x units of this product is given by

$$C(x) = 50x + 16{,}000 \qquad \text{Cost equation}$$

The number of units produced and sold, x, is increasing at a rate of 200 units per week. When the number of units produced and sold is 10,000, determine the instantaneous rate of change with respect to time, t (in weeks), of

a) Sales revenue. **b)** Cost. **c)** Profit.

Solutions

a) We determine the equation for sales revenue, R.

$$R = (\text{unit price})\binom{\text{number of}}{\text{units sold}}$$

$$= px$$

$$= \left(400 - \frac{x}{1000}\right)x$$

$$R = 400x - \frac{x^2}{1000} \qquad \text{Revenue equation}$$

Since x is changing as time, t, elapses, then R is changing as time elapses. We want to find dR/dt. Differentiating both sides of the revenue equation with respect to t gives

$$\frac{d}{dt}(R) = \frac{d}{dt}(400x) - \frac{d}{dt}\left(\frac{x^2}{1000}\right)$$

$$\frac{dR}{dt} = 400\frac{dx}{dt} - \frac{x}{500} \cdot \frac{dx}{dt}$$

$$= \left(400 - \frac{x}{500}\right)\frac{dx}{dt}$$

Since x is increasing at a rate of 200 units per week, $dx/dt = 200$. Substituting 200 for dx/dt and 10,000 for x, we obtain

$$\frac{dR}{dt} = \left(400 - \frac{10{,}000}{500}\right)(200) = \$76{,}000 \text{ per week}$$

Thus, sales revenue is increasing at a rate of $76,000 per week.

b) We want to find dC/dt where

$$C = 50x + 16{,}000$$

Since x changes with time, C also changes with time. Thus, to find dC/dt, we differentiate both sides of the cost equation with respect to t to obtain

$$\frac{d}{dt}(C) = \frac{d}{dt}(50x) + \frac{d}{dt}(16,000)$$

$$\frac{dC}{dt} = 50\frac{dx}{dt} + 0$$

$$= 50\frac{dx}{dt}$$

Substituting 200 for dx/dt gives

$$\frac{dC}{dt} = 50(200) = \$10,000 \text{ per week}$$

Thus, the cost is increasing at a rate of $10,000 per week

c) We want to find dP/dt where

$$P = R - C \qquad \text{Profit equation}$$

Since R and C change with time, then P changes with time. To find dP/dt, we differentiate both sides of the above profit equation with respect to time to obtain

$$\frac{dP}{dt} = \frac{dR}{dt} - \frac{dC}{dt}$$

from part a

from part b

$$\frac{dP}{dt} = \$76,000 - \$10,000 = \$66,000 \text{ per week}$$

Thus, profit is increasing at a rate of $66,000 per week.

We now state a procedure for solving related-rate problems.

To Solve Related-Rate Problems

1. Identify and list the variables involved. Draw a sketch, if possible.
2. Find an equation that relates the variables.
3. Identify and list the rates of change that are given and those that must be determined.
4. Differentiate the equation of step 2 implicitly with respect to time, t. Solve for the derivative that gives the desired rate of change.
5. Substitute in all given values.

• EXAMPLE 4-6

A metal cylinder, when heated, expands in such a manner that its radius, r, increases at a rate of 0.20 centimeter per minute and its height, h, increases at a rate of 0.15 centimeter per minute (see Figure 4-4). Determine the rate of change of the volume of the cylinder when its radius is 10 centimeters and its height is 25 centimeters.

Solution

Step 1 *Identify and list the variables.* r = radius, h = height, V = volume, and t = time in minutes.

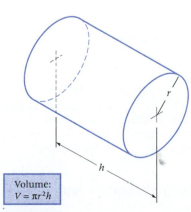

Volume:
$V = \pi r^2 h$

FIGURE 4-4

Step 2 *Write the equation.* The volume of a cylinder is given by

$$V = \pi r^2 h$$

where $\pi \approx 3.1416$.

Step 3 *Identify and list the rates of change.*

$$\frac{dr}{dt} = 0.20 \quad \leftarrow \text{The radius is increasing at 0.20 centimeter per minute.}$$

$$\frac{dh}{dt} = 0.15 \quad \leftarrow \text{The height is increasing at 0.15 centimeter per minute.}$$

$$\frac{dV}{dt} = ? \quad \leftarrow \text{This must be determined.}$$

Step 4 *Differentiate implicitly.* As determined in step 2, the volume of a cylinder is given by

$$V = \pi r^2 h$$

Since r and h are changing with time, then V is also changing with time. We must find dV/dt.

Differentiating each side of the above equation with respect to t gives

$$\frac{d}{dt}(V) = \frac{d}{dt}(\pi r^2 h)$$

We must use the product rule to find the derivative of the right-hand side since r and h are functions of t. Hence,

$$\frac{dV}{dt} = (\text{first})\binom{\text{derivative}}{\text{of second}} + (\text{second})\binom{\text{derivative}}{\text{of first}}$$

$$\frac{dV}{dt} = \pi r^2 \frac{dh}{dt} + h \cdot 2\pi r \frac{dr}{dt}$$

$$= \pi r^2 \frac{dh}{dt} + 2\pi r h \frac{dr}{dt}$$

Step 5 *Substitute in the given values.* Since $dr/dt = 0.20$ and $dh/dt = 0.15$, we substitute these along with $r = 10$ and $h = 25$ into the above equation for dV/dt to obtain

$$\frac{dV}{dt} = \pi(10)^2(0.15) + 2\pi(10)(25)(0.20)$$

$$= 15\pi + 100\pi$$

$$= 115\pi$$

$$\approx 361.28 \text{ cubic centimeters per minute}$$

Thus, the volume of the cyclinder is increasing at approximately 361.28 cubic centimeters per minute.

• EXAMPLE 4-7 _____

The cylinder in Example 4-6 is expanding in such a manner that its radius is increasing at 0.30 centimeter per minute and its height is increasing at a rate of 0.25 centimeter per minute. Determine the rate of change of the surface area of the cylinder when its radius is 10 centimeters and its height is 25 centimeters.

Solution

Step 1 *Identify and list the variables.* r = radius, h = height, S = surface area, and t = time.

Step 2 *Write the equation.* The surface area of a cylinder is given by

$$\underset{\underset{\displaystyle 2\pi r^2}{\uparrow}}{\overset{\text{area of top}}{\underset{\text{and bottom}}{}}} \quad \underset{\underset{\displaystyle 2\pi rh}{\uparrow}}{\overset{\text{area of}}{\underset{\text{side}}{}}}$$

$$S = \quad 2\pi r^2 \quad + \quad 2\pi rh$$

Step 3 *Identify and list the rates of change.*

$$\frac{dr}{dt} = 0.30 \;\leftarrow \text{The radius is increasing at 0.30 centimeter per minute.}$$

$$\frac{dh}{dt} = 0.25 \;\leftarrow \text{The height is increasing at 0.25 centimeter per minute.}$$

$$\frac{dS}{dt} = ? \quad\;\leftarrow \text{This must be determined.}$$

Step 4 *Differentiate implicitly.* As determined in step 2, the surface area is given by

$$S = 2\pi r^2 + 2\pi rh$$

where *r* and *h* are changing with time. We must find *dS/dt*. Differentiating each side of the equation for *S* with respect to *t* gives

$$\frac{d}{dt}(S) = \boxed{\frac{d}{dt}(2\pi r^2)} + \boxed{\frac{d}{dt}(2\pi rh)}$$

Use the product rule.

$$\frac{dS}{dt} = \left(2\pi \cdot 2r\frac{dr}{dt}\right) + \overbrace{2\pi r\frac{dh}{dt} + \left(h \cdot 2\pi \frac{dr}{dt}\right)}$$

$$= (4\pi r + 2\pi h)\frac{dr}{dt} + 2\pi r\frac{dh}{dt}$$

$$= 2\pi(2r + h)\frac{dr}{dt} + 2\pi r\frac{dh}{dt}$$

Step 5 *Substitute in the given values.* Since *dr/dt* = 0.30 and *dh/dt* = 0.25, we substitute these along with *r* = 10 and *h* = 25 into the above equation for *dS/dt* to obtain

$$\frac{dS}{dt} = 2\pi(2 \cdot 10 + 25)(0.30) + 2\pi(10)(0.25)$$

$$= 27\pi + 5\pi$$

$$= 32\pi \approx 100.53 \text{ square centimeters per minute}$$

Thus, the surface area is increasing at the rate of approximately 100.53 square centimeters per minute.

• EXAMPLE 4-8

Rubbish is dumped into the container of Figure 4-5 at the rate of 20 cubic feet per day. Assuming that the rubbish is evenly distributed within the container, how fast is the depth of the rubbish increasing?

Solution

Step 1 *Identify and list the variables.* *h* = depth of rubbish and *t* = time in days.

Step 2 *Write the equation.* The volume of the rubbish is given by

$$V = (\text{length})(\text{width})(\text{height})$$

$$= (10)(8)h$$

$$= 80h$$

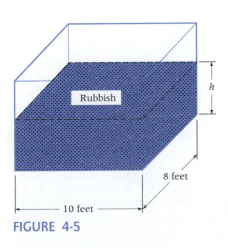

FIGURE 4-5

Step 3 *Identify and list the rates of change.*

$$\frac{dV}{dt} = 20 \leftarrow \text{Rubbish is dumped into the container at a rate}$$
of 20 cubic feet per day.

$$\frac{dh}{dt} = ? \leftarrow \text{This must be determined.}$$

Step 4 *Differentiate implicitly.* We differentiate with respect to t the formula for the volume of the rubbish, as shown below.

$$\frac{d}{dt}(V) = \frac{d}{dt}(80h)$$

$$\frac{dV}{dt} = 80\frac{dh}{dt}$$

Now we solve the above result for dh/dt to obtain

$$\frac{dh}{dt} = \frac{1}{80} \cdot \frac{dV}{dt}$$

Step 5 *Substitute in the given values.* We substitute 20 in place of dV/dt in the above equation to obtain

$$\frac{dh}{dt} = \frac{1}{80}(20) = 0.25 \text{ feet per day.}$$

Thus, the depth of the rubbish is increasing at a rate of 0.25 feet per day.

Exercises 4-2

For Exercises 1-12, assume x and y are functions of t. Determine the indicated rate, given the other information.

1. $y = 3x^2 + 4x$; $dx/dt = -1$, $x = 2$, $dy/dt = ?$
2. $y = 5x^2 - 7$; $dx/dt = 2$, $x = 3$, $dy/dt = ?$
3. $y = 4x^2 + 9$; $dy/dt = 4$, $x = 2$, $dx/dt = ?$
4. $y = 6x^3 - 1$; $dy/dt = 6$, $x = 1$, $dx/dt = ?$
5. $2y^2 + 3x = 8$; $dx/dt = 3$, $x = 2$, $y = 1$, $dy/dt = ?$
6. $x^2 + y^2 = 16$; $dy/dt = -3$, $x = 2$, $y = 2$, $dx/dt = ?$
7. $3x^2 + 2y^2 = 30$; $dx/dt = -2$, $x = 2$, $y = 3$, $dy/dt = ?$
8. $2y^3 + x^2 = 7$; $dy/dt = -1$, $x = 3$, $y = -1$, $dx/dt = ?$
9. $y^2 + xy = 6$; $dx/dt = 1$, $x = 5$, $y = 1$, $dy/dt = ?$
10. $x^2 - xy + 6 = 0$; $dy/dt = -4$, $x = 3$, $y = 5$, $dx/dt = ?$
11. $x^3 - xy + 4 = 0$; $dx/dt = -1$, $x = 2$, $y = 6$, $dy/dt = ?$
12. $y^3 + xy = 48$; $dy/dt = 2$, $x = 7$, $y = 3$, $dx/dt = ?$

13. A point moves on the graph of $xy = 8$ in such a manner that its y-coordinate is increasing at a rate of 2 units per second when the point is at $(2, 4)$. Find the rate of change of the x-coordinate at that moment.

14. A point moves on the graph of $4x^2 + 2y^2 = 18$ in such a manner that its x-coordinate is decreasing at a rate of 3 units per second when the point is at $(2, 1)$. Find the rate of change of the y-coordinate at that moment.

Applications

15. *Ladder.* A 25-foot ladder is resting against a building, as shown in Figure 4-6. The bottom of the ladder is sliding away from the building at a rate of 4 feet per second. Determine the rate at which the top of the ladder is sliding downward when the ladder is 20 feet from the building.

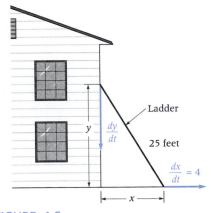

FIGURE 4-6

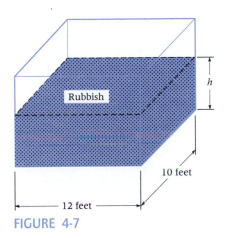

FIGURE 4-7

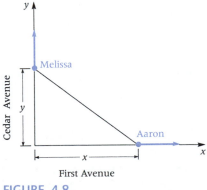

FIGURE 4-8

16. *Revenue, cost, profit.* The unit price, p, of some product is related to the number of units sold, x, by the demand equation

$$p = 200 - \frac{x}{1000}$$

The cost of producing x units of this product is given by

$$C = 40x + 12{,}000$$

The number of units produced and sold, x, is increasing at a rate of 300 units per week. When the number of units produced and sold is 20,000, determine the instantaneous rate of change with respect to time, t (in weeks), of
a) Sales revenue.   b) Cost.   c) Profit.

17. *Revenue, cost, profit.* Given are the following revenue, cost, and profit equations

$$R = 800x - \frac{x^2}{10}$$
$$C = 40x + 5000$$
$$P = R - C$$

where x denotes the number of units produced and sold. When production is at 2000 units and increasing at a rate of 100 units per month, determine the instantaneous rate of change with respect to time, t (in months), of
a) Sales revenue.   b) Cost.   c) Profit.

18. *Cylinder: Volume.* A metal cylinder is heated and expands so that its radius increases at a rate of 0.40 centimeter per minute and its height increases at a rate of 0.30 centimeter per minute. Determine the rate of change of the volume of the cylinder when its radius is 20 centimeters and its height is 40 centimeters.

19. *Cylinder: Surface area.* Determine the rate of change of the surface area of the cylinder in Exercise 18.

20. *Cylinder: Surface area.* The cylinder of Exercise 18 is heated and expands so that its radius is increasing at 0.35 centimeter per minute and its height is increasing at 0.25 centimeter per minute. Determine the rate of change of the surface area of the cylinder when its radius is 30 centimeters and its height is 50 centimeters.

21. *Rubbish disposal.* Rubbish is dumped into the container of Figure 4-7 at the rate of 30 cubic feet per day. If the rubbish is evenly distributed within the container, how fast is the depth of the rubbish increasing?

22. *Jogging.* Two people, Melissa and Aaron, begin jogging at the intersection of First and Cedar Avenues (see Figure 4-8). Melissa jogs along Cedar Avenue at the rate of 350 yards per minute, while Aaron jogs along First Avenue at the rate of 300 yards per minute. How fast is the distance between them increasing
a) After 1 minute?   b) After 2 minutes?

23. *Radar speed check.* A state trooper, parked 40 feet away from Interstate 95 (see Figure 4-9 on page 270), uses radar to determine that the straight-line distance between himself and an oncoming vehicle is decreasing at the rate of 80 feet per second at the instant when the straight-line distance between both is 200 feet.
a) Determine the speed (in feet per second) of the oncoming car.
b) Using the facts that 5280 feet = 1 mile and 3600 seconds = 1 hour, convert the answer for part a to miles per hour.

24. *Baseball.* A batter hits a ball along the third-base line at a speed of 50 feet per second, as illustrated in Figure 4-10 on page 270. How fast is the distance between the ball and first base changing 1 second after the ball is hit?

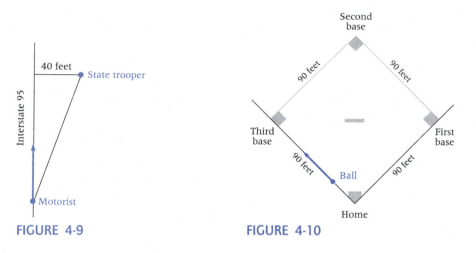

FIGURE 4-9   **FIGURE 4-10**

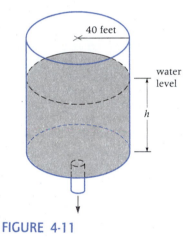

FIGURE 4-11

Resistors in series

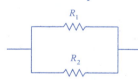

FIGURE 4-12

Resistors in parallel

R_1

R_2

FIGURE 4-13

25. *Sphere: Volume.* A spherical balloon is inflated so that its radius is increasing at the rate of 2 centimeters per minute. Determine the rate of change of volume when the radius is 20 centimeters. Use the fact that the volume of a sphere is given by

$$V = \frac{4}{3}\pi r^3$$

where r is the radius and $\pi \approx 3.1416$.

26. *Sphere: Surface area.* Use the fact that the surface area of a sphere is given by

$$S = 4\pi r^2$$

where r is the radius and $\pi \approx 3.1416$, to determine the rate of change of the surface area of the balloon of Exercise 25.

27. *Water usage.* A town stores its water in the cylindrical tank of Figure 4-11. During peak usage time, water flows out of the tank at a rate of 4000 cubic feet per hour. How fast is the depth of the water in the tank decreasing during peak usage time?

28. *Physics: Boyle's law.* According to Boyle's law, the volume, V, of an enclosed gas and the pressure, P, exerted on it are related by the equation

$$PV = k$$

where k is a constant. The above formula holds if the temperature of the gas remains constant. If the volume of the gas increases at a rate of 6 cubic inches per minute, determine the rate of change of pressure (in pounds per square inch per minute) when the volume is 500 cubic inches and the pressure is 25 pounds per square inch.

29. *Physics: Electricity.* If two resistances, R_1 and R_2 (measured in ohms), are connected in series, as illustrated in Figure 4-12, the combined resistance, R, is given by

$$R = R_1 + R_2$$

If R_1 and R_2 are increasing at 0.4 and 0.6 ohms per second, respectively, find the rate of change of the combined resistance, R.

30. *Physics: Electricity.* If two resistances, R_1 and R_2 (measured in ohms), are connected in parallel, as illustrated in Figure 4-13, the combined resistance, R, is given by

$$\frac{1}{R} = \frac{1}{R_1} + \frac{1}{R_2}$$

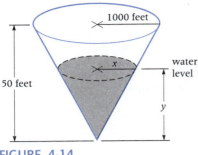

FIGURE 4-14

If R_1 and R_2 are increasing at 0.2 and 0.4 ohms per second, respectively, find the rate of change of the combined resistance when $R_1 = 150$ ohms and $R_2 = 200$ ohms.

31. *Reservoir.* A town's reservoir has the shape of the cone of Figure 4-14. If water is flowing into the reservoir at the rate of 200 cubic feet per minute, how fast is the depth of the water, y, changing when $y = 30$ feet? Use the fact that the volume of the portion of the cone that is filled with water is given by

$$V = \frac{1}{3}\pi x^2 y$$

where $\pi \approx 3.1416$. Also, you will need the relationship

$$\frac{x}{y} = \frac{1000}{50}$$

which is determined from similar triangles.

32. *Reservoir.* For the reservoir of Example 31, if, instead of water flowing into the reservoir, water is flowing out of the reservoir at the rate of 300 cubic feet per minute, how fast is the depth of the water, y, changing when $y = 40$ feet?

4-3 • ELASTICITY OF DEMAND

Frequently economists and managers wish to measure the responsiveness of consumers to changes in the price of a given commodity. This is accomplished by calculating a ratio, called the elasticity of demand, for the commodity. Elasticity of demand measures the sensitivity of demand to changes in price. Specifically, **elasticity of demand** is a ratio that compares the proportionate change in the quantity of a product demanded to the proportionate change in price. That is,

$$\text{elasticity of demand} = \frac{\%\text{ change in quantity demanded}}{\%\text{ change in price}}$$

To calculate elasticity of demand, we must be given an equation (defining a demand function) that relates the commodity's demand, q, with its unit price, p. Let $q = f(p)$* be a differentiable demand function, as illustrated in Figure 4-15. Observing the graph of Figure 4-15, if the unit price changes from p to $p + \Delta p$, then the demand changes from q to $q + \Delta q$. Thus, the percent change in quantity demanded is $(\Delta q/q)100$, the percent change in price is $(\Delta p/p)100$, and the elasticity of demand, E, is

$$E = \frac{\dfrac{\Delta q}{q}100}{\dfrac{\Delta p}{p}100}$$

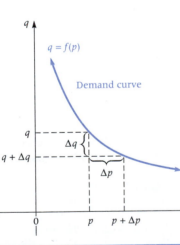

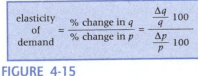

$$\begin{array}{l}\text{elasticity}\\ \text{of}\\ \text{demand}\end{array} = \frac{\%\text{ change in }q}{\%\text{ change in }p} = \frac{\dfrac{\Delta q}{q}\,100}{\dfrac{\Delta p}{p}\,100}$$

FIGURE 4-15

---

*When constructing supply and demand functions, economists consider quantity, q, to be dependent on price, p. However, when considering market mechanisms, p is defined as a function of q. In this section, we assume $q = f(p)$ unless otherwise specified.

The right-hand side of this equation can be rearranged as

$$E = \frac{p}{q} \cdot \frac{\Delta q}{\Delta p}$$

This formula is a measure of *arc elasticity of demand*. If the change in p is small (i.e., Δp is close to 0), then $\Delta q / \Delta p$ is approximated by dq/dp, and the limit of the arc elasticity as $\Delta p \to 0$ is

$$E = \frac{p}{q} \cdot \frac{dq}{dp}$$

This formula gives the *point elasticity of demand* at point (p, q).

In this text, we assume what is typical of most demand functions— that is, as the price of a commodity increases, its quantity demanded decreases. Thus, dq/dp is negative. This, plus the assumptions that $p > 0$ and $q > 0$, implies that elasticity of demand, as defined by $E = (p/q)(dq/dp)$, is negative.

SUMMARY

Point Elasticity of Demand
Given a demand function defined by an equation of the form $q = f(p)$, where q denotes demand and p denotes unit price, then the **point elasticity of demand** is given by

$$E = \frac{p}{q} \cdot \frac{dq}{dp}$$

This is interpreted as

$$E = \frac{\% \text{ change in quantity demanded}}{\% \text{ change in price}}$$

We note that elasticity, as given by the above formula, is negative. We identify three cases:

1. If $|E| = 1$, then the percent change in demand equals the percent change in price. In this case, demand is said to have **unit elasticity.**
2. If $|E| > 1$, then the percent change in demand is greater than the percent change in price. In this case, demand is said to be **elastic.**
3. If $|E| < 1$, then the percent change in demand is less than the percent change in unit price. In this case, demand is said to be **inelastic.**

• **EXAMPLE 4-9** _____

The demand for a given commodity is given by

$$q = \frac{p}{p - 5} \quad (p > 5)$$

where p is the unit price.

a) Find the formula for point elasticity of demand.
b) Evaluate the formula in part a at $p = 7$.
c) Interpret the result of part b.

Solutions

a) First, we find dq/dp.

$$\frac{dq}{dp} = \frac{(p-5)(1) - (p)(1)}{(p-5)^2} = \frac{-5}{(p-5)^2}$$

Substituting this result for dq/dp and $p(p-5)$ for q into the formula

$$E = \frac{p}{q} \cdot \frac{dq}{dp}$$

yields

$$E = \left(\frac{p}{p/(p-5)}\right)\left(\frac{-5}{(p-5)^2}\right)$$

$$= \left(\frac{p(p-5)}{p}\right)\left(\frac{-5}{(p-5)^2}\right)$$

$$= \frac{-5}{p-5}$$

This result gives the formula for point elasticity of demand.

b) Substituting $p = 7$ into the formula

$$E = \frac{-5}{p-5}$$

gives

$$E = \frac{-5}{7-5}$$

$$= \frac{-5}{2} = -2.5 \qquad \text{Demand is elastic.}$$

c) Since

$$E = \frac{\% \text{ change in quantity demanded}}{\% \text{ change in price}}$$

the result, $E = -2.5$, means that if the price increases by 1% when $p = 7$, the quantity demanded will decrease by approximately 2.5%. Also, if the price decreases by 1% when $p = 7$, the quantity demanded will increase by approximately 2.5%.

• **EXAMPLE 4-10** _____

The demand (in pounds) for E-Z Chew peanuts is given by

$$q = -60p + 480 \qquad (0 < p < 7)$$

where p is the price (in dollars) of peanuts per pound.

a) Find the formula for point elasticity of demand.
b) Evaluate the formula of part a at $p = 3$.
c) Interpret the result of part b.
d) Determine the values of p for which demand is elastic.

Solutions

a) First, we find $dq/dp = -60$. Substituting this result for dq/dp and $-60p + 480$ for q into the formula

$$E = \frac{p}{q} \cdot \frac{dq}{dp}$$

yields

$$E = \left(\frac{p}{-60p + 480}\right)(-60)$$

$$= \frac{-60p}{-60(p - 8)}$$

$$= \frac{p}{p - 8}$$

This result gives the formula for point elasticity of demand.

b) Substituting $p = 3$ into the formula

$$E = \frac{p}{p - 8}$$

gives

$$E = \frac{3}{3 - 8}$$

$$= \frac{3}{-5} = -0.6$$

c) Since

$$E = \frac{\% \text{ change in quantity demanded}}{\% \text{ change in price}}$$

the result, $E = -0.6$, means that if the price increases by 1% when $p = 3$, the quantity demanded will decrease by approximately 0.6%. Also, if the price decreases by 1% when $p = 3$, the quantity demanded will increase by approximately 0.6%. Since $|E| < 1$, demand for E-Z Chew peanuts is inelastic.

d) Demand is elastic if $|E| > 1$. This plus the fact that $E < 0$ implies that $E < -1$. Hence,

$$\frac{p}{p - 8} < -1$$

To solve for p, we multiply both sides by $p - 8$. Note that $p - 8$ is negative since $0 < p < 7$. Thus, we must reverse the inequality when we multiply by $p - 8$. This gives

$$p > -1(p - 8)$$
$$p > -p + 8$$
$$2p > 8$$
$$p > 4$$

Thus, demand is elastic for values of p such that $p > 4$. However, since values of p were originally restricted to the interval $0 < p < 7$, then demand is elastic for values of p within the interval $4 < p < 7$.

•

Elasticity and Marginal Revenue

A relationship between marginal revenue and point elasticity of demand is determined as follows. If q units are demanded at price p so that $p = f(q)$ where f is differentiable, then the total sales revenue is given by

$$R(q) = (\text{quantity demanded})(\text{unit price})$$

$$= q \cdot p$$

Since $p = f(q)$, the above becomes

$$R(q) = q \cdot f(q)$$

The equation for marginal revenue is obtained by differentiating this formula with respect to q. Using the product rule, we obtain

$$R'(q) = q \cdot f'(q) + f(q) \cdot 1$$

Substituting dp/dq for $f'(q)$ and p for $f(q)$ into this equation results in

$$R'(q) = q\frac{dp}{dq} + p$$

Factoring out p, we have

$$R'(q) = p\left(\frac{q}{p} \cdot \frac{dp}{dq} + 1\right)$$

Since $dp/dq = 1/(dq/dp)$, provided $dq/dp \neq 0$, the equation becomes

$$R'(q) = p\left(\frac{1}{\frac{p}{q} \cdot \frac{dq}{dp}} + 1\right)$$

Since $E = (p/q)(dq/dp)$, then this equation becomes

$$R'(q) = p\left(\frac{1}{E} + 1\right) \qquad \text{Marginal Revenue}$$

We assume what is typical of most demand functions—that $p > 0$ and $E < 0$. Thus,

1. If demand is elastic (in other words, $|E| > 1$), then $E < -1$, $(1/E + 1) > 0$, and marginal revenue is positive.
2. If demand is inelastic (in other words, $|E| < 1$), then $-1 < E < 0$, $(1/E + 1) < 0$, and marginal revenue is negative.

We summarize as follows.

SUMMARY

Elasticity and Marginal Revenue

Demand	*Marginal Revenue*
Elastic	Positive
Inelastic	Negative

Exercises 4-3

For each of the demand functions below, find the formula for point elasticity of demand.

1. $q = -3p + 90$ 2. $q = -2p + 60$
3. $q = -p + 40$ 4. $q = -p + 30$
5. $q = 3(p - 4)^2$ 6. $q = 2(p - 5)^2$

7. $q = 40 - 10\sqrt{p}$

8. $q = 30 - 5\sqrt{p}$

9. $q = \sqrt{200 - p}$

10. $q = \sqrt{400 - p}$

11. $q = p/(p - 10)$

12. $q = p/(p - 20)$

13. Elasticity of demand for some commodity is given to be -1.5 at $p = 10$.
   a) Interpret this result.
   b) Is demand elastic or inelastic at $p = 10$?

14. Elasticity of demand for some product is given to be -0.70 at $p = 6$.
   a) Interpret this result.
   b) Is demand elastic or inelastic at $p = 6$?

15. Elasticity of demand for some commodity is given to be -0.80 at $p = 20$.
   a) Interpret this result.
   b) Is demand elastic or inelastic at $p = 20$?

16. Elasticity of demand for some commodity is given to be -1.3 at $p = 30$.
   a) Interpret this result.
   b) Is demand elastic or inelastic at $p = 30$?

17. The demand for bracelets is given by

$$q = -2p + 130 \qquad (0 < p < 65)$$

where p is the price per bracelet.
   a) Find the formula for point elasticity of demand.
   b) Evaluate the formula in part a at $p = 50$.
   c) Interpret the result of part b.

18. The demand for some commodity is given by

$$q = -3p + 15 \qquad (0 < p < 5)$$

where p is the unit price.
   a) Find the formula for point elasticity of demand.
   b) Evaluate the formula in part a at $p = 2$.
   c) Interpret the result of part b.

19. The demand for a given commodity is given by

$$q = \frac{p}{p - 8} \qquad (p > 8)$$

where p is the unit price.
   a) Find the formula for point elasticity of demand.
   b) Find the elasticity of demand at $p = 10$.
   c) Interpret the result of part b.

20. The demand for a product is given by

$$q = \sqrt{80 - p} \qquad (0 < p < 80)$$

where p is the unit price.
   a) Find the formula for point elasticity of demand.
   b) Find the elasticity of demand at $p = 16$.
   c) Interpret the result of part b.

21. The demand for a product is given by

$$q = 3(p - 10)^2 \qquad (0 < p < 10)$$

where p is the unit price.
   a) Find the formula for point elasticity of demand.
   b) Find the elasticity of demand at $p = 4$.
   c) Interpret the result of part b.

22. The demand for a given commodity is given by

$$q = 300 - 20\sqrt{p} \qquad (0 < p < 225)$$

where p is the unit price.

a) Find the formula for point elasticity of demand.
b) Find the elasticity of demand at $p = 100$.
c) Interpret the result of part b.
d) Find the elasticity of demand at $p = 49$.
e) Interpret the result of part d.
f) Find the elasticity of demand at $p = 121$.
g) Interpret the result of part f.

23. The demand for a given product is given by

$$q = \frac{10,000}{p} \qquad (p > 0)$$

where p is the unit price.
a) Find the formula for point elasticity of demand.
b) Interpret the result of part a.
c) For which values of p is demand elastic?
d) For which values of p is demand inelastic?

24. The demand for a given product is given by

$$q = \frac{c}{p} \qquad (p > 0)$$

where p is the unit price and c is a constant such that $c > 0$. Show that this demand equation has unit elasticity.

25. The demand for a product is given by

$$q = \sqrt{100 - p} \qquad (0 < p < 100)$$

where p is the unit price.
a) Find the formula for point elasticity of demand.
b) For which values of p is demand elastic?
c) For which values of p is demand inelastic?
d) For which value of p does demand have unit elasticity?

26. The demand for a product is given by

$$q = -4p + 100 \qquad (0 < p < 25)$$

where p is the unit price.
a) Find the formula for point elasticity of demand.
b) For which values of p is demand elastic?
c) For which values of p is demand inelastic?
d) For which values of p does demand have unit elasticity?

4-4 • DIFFERENTIALS

Up to this point, we have been using the symbol dy/dx to denote the derivative of y with respect to x. We now give meaning to the symbols dy and dx.

Consider a differentiable function $y = f(x)$ and its tangent line T at the point $P(x, f(x))$, as shown in Figure 4-16 on page 278. The vertical distance between the points $P(x, f(x))$ and $Q(x + \Delta x, f(x + \Delta x))$ is Δy. Since the slope of the tangent line T is $f'(x)$, then

$$\frac{dy}{\Delta x} = f'(x)$$

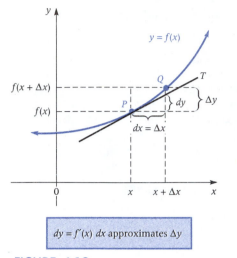

$dy = f'(x)\,dx$ approximates Δy

FIGURE 4-16

If we let $dx = \Delta x$, then

$$dy = f'(x)\,dx$$

Notice that dy is that portion of Δy shown in the figure. If dx is small (i.e., close to 0), then dy closely approximates the vertical distance Δy. For that reason, dy is called the *differential approximation to* Δy or, equivalently, the **differential of y.** Thus,

$$\Delta y \approx dy$$
$$f(x + \Delta x) - f(x) \approx dy$$

and

$$f(x + \Delta x) \approx f(x) + dy$$

The last equation above provides a useful approximation to $f(x + \Delta x)$ because it is usually easier to calculate the quantity $f(x) + dy$ than it is to calculate $f(x + \Delta x)$ for most nonlinear functions.

> **Differentials**
>
> If $y = f(x)$ defines a differentiable function of x, then
>
> 1. The differential of x, written dx, is an arbitrary real number (usually small).
> 2. The differential of y, written dy, is the product of $f'(x)$ and dx. In other words,
>
> $$dy = f'(x)\,dx$$
>
> dy approximates Δy, as illustrated in Figure 4-16.

The following two examples illustrate the computation of differentials.

• **EXAMPLE 4-11** _____

If $y = f(x) = x^3 - 5x^2 + 6x + 7$, find dy.

Solution

First, find $f'(x)$. Hence, $f'(x) = 3x^2 - 10x + 6$. Then

$$dy = f'(x)\,dx$$
$$= (3x^2 - 10x + 6)\,dx$$

• **EXAMPLE 4-12** _____

If $y = f(x) = x^2 + 5x - 6$,

a) Find dy.
b) Evaluate dy at $x = 3$ and $dx = 0.1$.

Solutions

a) We first find $f'(x) = 2x + 5$. Then

$$dy = f'(x)\,dx$$
$$= (2x + 5)\,dx$$

b) When $x = 3$ and $dx = 0.1$, then

$$dy = (2x + 5)dx$$
$$= [2(3) + 5](0.1)$$
$$= (11)(0.1) = 1.1$$

We now give examples using differentials as approximations.

• **EXAMPLE 4-13**

Approximate $\sqrt{36.12}$ by using differentials.

Solution

Let $f(x) = \sqrt{x}$. Then

$$f'(x) = \frac{1}{2}x^{-1/2} = \frac{1}{2\sqrt{x}}$$

and

$$dy = f'(x)dx$$
$$= \frac{1}{2\sqrt{x}}dx$$

Observing Figure 4-17, we evaluate dy at $x = 36$ and $dx = \Delta x = 0.12$ to obtain

$$dy = \frac{1}{2\sqrt{36}}(0.12)$$

$$= \frac{1}{(2)(6)}(0.12) = 0.01$$

Since

$$f(x + \Delta x) \approx f(x) + dy$$

then

$$f(36.12) \approx f(36) + dy$$
$$= 6 + 0.01 = 6.01 \qquad \text{Approximation}$$

The actual value of $\sqrt{36.12}$ to 5 decimal places is 6.00999.

• **EXAMPLE 4-14** **Profit.**

The profit, $P(x)$ (in millions of dollars), gained from producing x (in thousands) units of some product is given by

$$P(x) = -x^2 + 9x - 14 \qquad (2 \leq x \leq 7)$$

If the production level, x, changes from 3.5 to 3.75, use differentials to approximate the change in profit.

Solution

Since x changes from 3.5 to 3.75, then $dx = \Delta x = 3.75 - 3.5 = 0.25$. Thus, we seek to evaluate the differential dP when $x = 3.5$ and $dx = 0.25$. Hence, $P'(x) = -2x + 9$ and

$$dP = P'(x)dx$$
$$= (-2x + 9)dx$$

Evaluating dP at $x = 3.5$ and $dx = 0.25$ yields

$$dP = [-2(3.5) + 9](0.25)$$
$$= (2)(0.25) = 0.50$$

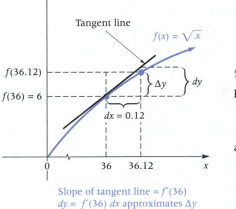

Tangent line

$f(x) = \sqrt{x}$

$f(36.12)$

$f(36) = 6$

Δy } dy

$dx = 0.12$

0 36 36.12 x

Slope of tangent line $= f'(36)$
$dy = f'(36)\ dx$ approximates Δy

FIGURE 4-17

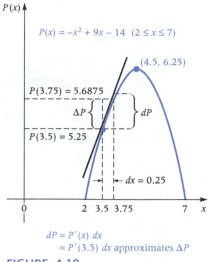

$P(x) = -x^2 + 9x - 14 \quad (2 \le x \le 7)$

$(4.5, 6.25)$

$P(3.75) = 5.6875$

ΔP { } dP

$P(3.5) = 5.25$

$dx = 0.25$

$2 \quad 3.5 \quad 3.75 \qquad 7 \quad x$

$dP = P'(x)\,dx$
$= P'(3.5)\,dx$ approximates ΔP

FIGURE 4-18

Thus, the approximate change in profit is 0.50 million dollars. Note that the actual change in profit is given by $P(3.75) - P(3.5) = 5.6875 - 5.25 = 0.4375$. A graphical interpretation appears in Figure 4-18.

• **EXAMPLE 4-15** **Wind Power.**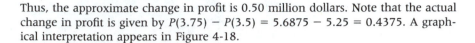

According to Betz's Law, the available power in wind, P (in kilowatts), for a windmill with a rotor diameter of 20 feet is given by

$$P(x) = 0.000948x^3 \qquad (x \ge 0)$$

where x is the wind speed in miles per hour (mph). If the wind speed changes from 10 mph to 12 mph, approximate the change in power.

Solution

Since x changes from 10 mph to 12 mph, then $dx = \Delta x = 12 - 10 = 2$. Thus, we seek to evaluate the differential, dP, when $x = 10$ and $dx = 2$. Hence, $P'(x) = 0.002844x^2$ and

$$dP = P'(x)\,dx$$
$$= (0.002844x^2)\,dx$$

Evaluating dP at $x = 10$ and $dx = 2$ yields

$$dP = [0.002844(10^2)](2)$$
$$= (0.2844)(2) = 0.5688$$

Thus, the approximate change in power is 0.5688 kilowatts.

• **EXAMPLE 4-16** **Cost.**

The cost, C (in millions of dollars), of producing x (in thousands) units of a product is given by

$$C(x) = 0.1x^2 + 10{,}000 \qquad (0 \le x \le 1000)$$

If the production level, x, changes from 500 to 501, find the approximate change in cost.

Solution

Since x changes from 500 to 501, then $dx = \Delta x = 501 - 500 = 1$. Thus, we seek to evaluate the differential, dC, when $x = 500$ and $dx = 1$. Hence, $C'(x) = 0.2x$ and

$$dC = C'(x)\,dx$$
$$= (0.2x)\,dx$$

evaluating dC at $x = 500$ and $dx = 1$ yields

$$dC = [0.2(500)](1)$$
$$= (100)(1) = 100$$

Thus, the approximate change in cost is 100 million dollars.

Consider the differentiable function $y = f(x)$ in Figure 4-19. When x changes by an amount Δx, the *percent change in y* is given by

$$\frac{\Delta y}{y}100$$

Using differentials, the *percent change in y* is approximated by

$$\frac{dy}{y}100$$

The following example illustrates the use of this concept.

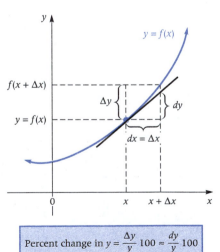

$y = f(x)$

$f(x + \Delta x)$

Δy { } dy

$y = f(x)$

$dx = \Delta x$

$0 \qquad x \quad x + \Delta x \qquad x$

Percent change in $y = \dfrac{\Delta y}{y}100 \approx \dfrac{dy}{y}100$

FIGURE 4-19

• EXAMPLE 4-17   Construction Cost. ─────────────

A 1-story building costs $1000 per square foot to construct. Thus, the cost of constructing a square 1-story building x feet on each side is given by

$$C(x) = 1000x^2 \qquad (x \geq 0)$$

a) Use differentials to approximate the percent change in cost if each side changes from 30 feet to 33 feet.

b) Use differentials to approximate the percent change in cost if each side increases by 5% from 30 feet.

Solutions

a) Since x changes from 30 to 33, then $dx = \Delta x = 33 - 30 = 3$. We first seek to evaluate dC/C when $x = 30$ and $dx = 3$. Since $dC = C'(x)dx$, we determine that $C'(x) = 2000x$ so that $dC = (2000x)dx$. Hence,

$$\frac{dC}{C} = \frac{2000x\,dx}{1000x^2}$$

$$= \frac{2dx}{x}$$

Evaluating dC/C at $x = 30$ and $dx = 3$ gives

$$\frac{dC}{C} = \frac{2(3)}{30} = 0.20$$

Thus, the approximate percent change in cost when $x = 30$ and $dx = 3$ is

$$\frac{dC}{C} \cdot 100 = (0.20)(100)$$

$$= 20\%$$

b) If x increases by 5% from 30 feet, then $dx = \Delta x = 0.05(30) = 1.5$. We seek to evaluate dC/C when $x = 30$ and $dx = 1.5$. From part a, we obtain

$$\frac{dC}{C} = \frac{2dx}{x}$$

Evaluating dC/C at $x = 30$ and $dx = 1.5$ gives

$$\frac{dC}{C} = \frac{2(1.5)}{30} = 0.10$$

Thus, the approximate percent change in cost when $x = 30$ and $dx = 1.5$ is

$$\frac{dC}{C} \cdot 100 = (0.10)(100)$$

$$= 10\%$$

Exercises 4-4

Find dy for each of the following:

1. $y = x^3$

2. $y = x^2 - 8x + 9$

3. $y = f(x) = 8x^4 + 1$

4. $y = 1/x^3$

5. $y = 3x\sqrt{x}$

6. $y = f(x) = x^3(2x + 5)$

7. $y = 8(1 + 4/x)$

8. $y = \sqrt{x^4 + 9}$

9. $y = \sqrt[3]{x}$

10. $y = \sqrt[5]{x}$

11. If $y = x^2 - 6x + 5$, find dy and evaluate it at $x = 9$ and $dx = 0.5$.

12. If $y = f(x) = 0.4(x - 5)^3$, find dy and evaluate it at $x = 8$ and $dx = 0.7$.

13. If $y = f(x) = 1/(x - 9)^2$, find dy and evaluate it at $x = 3$ and $dx = 0.1$.

14. If $y = f(x) = \sqrt{x}$, find dy and evaluate it at $x = 25$ and $dx = 0.14$.

15. If $y = x^3 - 8x + 5$, find dy and evaluate it at $x = 4$ and $dx = 0.4$.

16. If $y = \sqrt{x^2 - 3x + 7}$, find dy and evaluate it at $x = 6$ and $dx = 0.8$.

Use differentials to approximate each of the following:

17. $\sqrt{81.68}$ **18.** $\sqrt[3]{27.94}$ **19.** $\sqrt{65}$

20. $\sqrt[4]{17}$ **21.** $\sqrt[4]{15.8}$ **22.** $\sqrt[5]{33}$

23. *Revenue.* The sales revenue, R (in millions of dollars), gained from selling x (in thousands) units of some product is given by

$$R(x) = -x^2 + 10x \qquad (0 \le x \le 5)$$

If x changes from 3.6 to 3.75, use differentials to approximate the change in sales revenue. Find the actual change in sales revenue.

24. *Revenue.* If the price of a widget is p dollars, the total sales revenue (in millions of dollars) gained from selling widgets is given by

$$R(p) = -200p^2 + 100p \qquad (0 \le p \le 0.50)$$

If the unit price, p, changes from \$0.15 to \$0.19, use differentials to approximate the change in sales revenue. Find the actual change in sales revenue.

25. *Demand.* The relation between unit price, p (in dollars), and demand, q (in millions of units), for gadgets is given by

$$p = 6/\sqrt{q} \qquad (q > 0)$$

If the demand, q, changes from 25 to 26, use differentials to approximate the change in unit price.

26. *Wind power.* The available power in wind, P (in kilowatts), for a windmill with a rotor diameter of 10 feet is given by

$$P(x) = 0.000237x^3 \qquad (x \ge 0)$$

where x is the wind speed in miles per hour (mph). If the wind speed changes from 12 mph to 13 mph, use differentials to approximate the change in power.

27. *Cost.* The cost, C (in millions of dollars), of producing x (in thousands) units of a product is given by

$$C(x) = 0.15x^2 + 7000 \qquad (0 \le x \le 500)$$

If the production level, x, changes from 200 to 201, find the approximate change in cost. Find the actual change in cost. Include a graphical interpretation.

28. *Average cost.* A company produces tires for trucks. The total cost, $C(x)$, of producing x tires is given by $C(x) = 50x + 30,000$. If

$$\overline{C} = \frac{\text{total cost}}{\text{number of tires produced}}$$

then $\overline{C}$ is the *average cost per tire*. The equation

$$\overline{C}(x) = \frac{C(x)}{x} \qquad (x > 0)$$

relates the average cost per tire, $\overline{C}$, with x, the number of tires produced. If the production level changes from 100 to 101, use differentials to approximate the change in average cost.

29. *Average cost.* The total cost of producing x units of some commodity is given by $C(x) = 100x + 50,000$.

a) Find the equation for the average cost per unit, $\overline{C}(x)$.

b) If the production level changes from 200 to 201, use differentials to approximate the change in average cost.

30. If $y = 0.6x^2 + 8$, use differentials to approximate the percent change in y as x changes from 6 to 6.2. Find the actual percent change in y. Include a graphical interpretation.

31. *Cost.* The cost, C(in dollars), of producing x units of some product is given by

$$C(x) = 0.25x^2 + 8000 \qquad (0 \le x \le 6000)$$

If the production level, x, changes from 40 to 41, use differentials to approximate the percent change in cost.

32. If $y = 0.8x^2 + 10$, use differentials to approximate the percent change in y when x increases by 8% from a value of 5.

33. *Construction cost.* A 1-story building costs $500 per square foot to construct. If x denotes the length of each side in feet, then
    a) Use differentials to approximate the percent change in cost when each side changes from 20 feet to 22 feet.
    b) Use differentials to approximate the percent change in cost when each side increases by 5% from 20 feet.

4-5 • NEWTON'S METHOD

Newton's Method for Approximating the x-Intercepts of a Function

To find the x-intercepts of the graph of a function $y = f(x)$, we set $y = 0$ and solve the resulting equation for x. This process is quite simple for linear and quadratic equations. If the function is linear (i.e., of the form $y = mx + b$), we obtain $0 = mx + b$ with $x = -b/m$. If the function is quadratic (i.e., of the form $y = ax^2 + bx + c$), we can either try to factor $ax^2 + bx + c$ or use the quadratic formula

$$x = \frac{-b \pm \sqrt{b^2 - 4ac}}{2a}$$

If the function is of degree higher than 2, we attempt factorization. However, some polynomial functions are not factorable, and some are not easily factored. Thus, we need a method for *approximating* the x-intercepts of a function. Such a method exists and is called **Newton's method.**

To understand Newton's method, consider the function $y = f(x)$ in Figure 4-20. Assume that we do not know the value of the x-intercept, r. We choose x_0 as an initial approximation of r. Then we find the equation of the tangent line to the function at x_0. Since the slope of the tangent line is $f'(x_0)$ and the point of tangency is $(x_0, f(x_0))$, then using the point-slope form

$$y - y_1 = m(x - x_1)$$

the equation of the tangent line is shown to be

$$y - f(x_0) = f'(x_0)(x - x_0)$$

Observing Figure 4-20, note that the x-intercept of the tangent line is a bet-

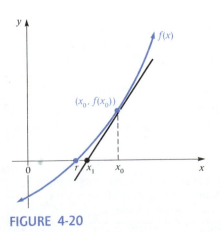

FIGURE 4-20

ter approximation of r. To find the x-intercept of the tangent line, we set $y = 0$ and solve for x. Hence, we write

$$0 - f(x_0) = f'(x_0)(x - x_0)$$

and obtain

$$x = x_0 - \frac{f(x_0)}{f'(x_0)}$$

If we denote the x-intercept of the tangent line by x_1, this equation becomes

$$x_1 = x_0 - \frac{f(x_0)}{f'(x_0)}$$

We now repeat the process, replacing x_0 with x_1, to obtain a better approximation

$$x_2 = x_1 - \frac{f(x_1)}{f'(x_1)}$$

Continuing this iterative process, if we have obtained x_n as an approximation of r, then a better approximation is as follows.

$$x_{n+1} = x_n - \frac{f(x_n)}{f'(x_n)}$$

It is essential that at each iteration $f'(x_n) \neq 0$. We terminate the process when $|x_{n+1} - x_n|$ is less than our desired level of accuracy.

SUMMARY

Newton's Method

Approximating x-intercepts of a Function. Let $f(x)$ be a differentiable function of x over the interval $a < x < b$. Let r denote an x-intercept of $f(x)$ in the interval $a < x < b$. In other words, $f(r) = 0$ and r is called a zero of $f(x)$.

To approximate r by Newton's Method, follow these steps.

Step 1 Choose x_0 as an initial approximation of r.

Step 2 Compute a better approximate using the formula

$$x_{n+1} = x_n - \frac{f(x_n)}{f'(x_n)}$$

Step 3 If $|x_{n+1} - x_n|$ is less than the desired level of accuracy, terminate the process. That is, let x_{n+1} be a final approximation of r. Otherwise, return to step 2 and compute the next approximation.

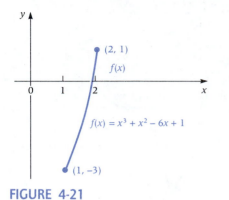

FIGURE 4-21

• **EXAMPLE 4-18**

Use Newton's method to approximate a positive x-intercept of the function

$$f(x) = x^3 + x^2 - 6x + 1$$

Solution

We first test various x-values to determine a sign change in $f(x)$. Since $f(1) = -3$ and $f(2) = +1$, then $f(x)$ crosses the x-axis at some value between $x = 1$ and $x = 2$ (see Figure 4-21). We may choose either $x_0 = 1$ or $x_0 = 2$ as our initial approximation. Choosing $x_0 = 2$, we must compute $f'(2)$. Hence, we calculate

$$f'(x) = 3x^2 + 2x - 6$$
$$f'(2) = 3(2)^2 + 2(2) - 6$$
$$= 10$$

The next approximation, x_1, is calculated to be

$$x_1 = x_0 - \frac{f(x_0)}{f'(x_0)}$$
$$= 2 - \frac{1}{10}$$
$$= 1.9000$$

where calculations are carried out to 4 decimal places.
   We then calculate $f(x_1)$ and $f'(x_1)$. Thus, we obtain

$$f(x_1) = f(1.9) = (1.9)^3 + (1.9)^2 - 6(1.9) + 1 = 0.0690$$
$$f'(x_1) = f'(1.9) = 3(1.9)^2 + 2(1.9) - 6 = 8.6300$$

The next approximation, x_2, is calculated to be

$$x_2 = x_1 - \frac{f(x_1)}{f'(x_1)}$$
$$= 1.9000 - \frac{0.0690}{8.6300}$$
$$\approx 1.8920$$

We then calculate $f(x_2)$ and $f'(x_2)$. Thus, we obtain

$$f(x_2) = f(1.8920)$$
$$= (1.8920)^3 + (1.8920)^2 - 6(1.8920) + 1$$
$$\approx 0.0004$$
$$f'(x_2) = f'(1.8920)$$
$$= 3(1.8920)^2 + 2(1.8920) - 6$$
$$\approx 8.5230$$

The next approximation, x_3, is

$$x_3 = x_2 - \frac{f(x_2)}{f'(x_2)}$$
$$= 1.8920 - \frac{0.0004}{8.5230}$$

Since $0.0004/8.5230$ is 0.0000 (to 4 decimal places), then

$$x_3 \approx 1.8920$$

A graphical interpretation of this appears in Figure 4-22.

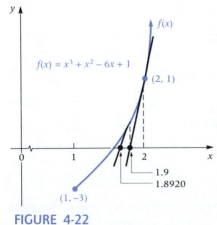

FIGURE 4-22

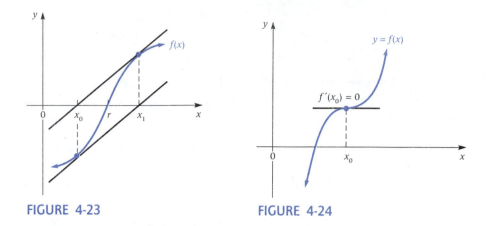

FIGURE 4-23   **FIGURE 4-24**

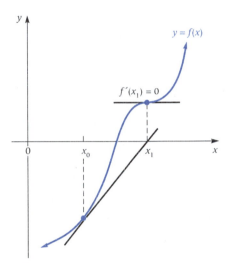

FIGURE 4-25

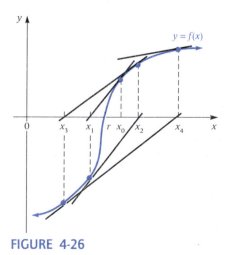

FIGURE 4-26

With Newton's method, the x_n's usually get closer and closer to the x-intercept very rapidly. However, in some instances, this may not be the case. As as example, consider the graph of Figure 4-23. Note that if x_0 is the initial approximation of r, then the x_n's will go back and forth between x_0 and x_1. No matter how many iterations we perform using the formula

$$x_{n+1} = x_n - \frac{f(x_n)}{f'(x_n)}$$

we will obtain either x_0 or x_1 without getting any closer to r.

Another instance where Newton's method fails is presented in Figure 4-24. Observe that for the initial choice x_0, $f'(x_0) = 0$. This situation can be remedied by choosing a different value for x_0. The graph of Figure 4-25 presents a situation where Newton's method fails because $f'(x_n) = 0$ for some n (in this case, $n = 1$). Here, too, the situation can be remedied by choosing a different value for x_0.

The graph of Figure 4-26 illustrates an instance where the values of x_n do not get closer and closer to the x-intercept, r. In fact, successive values of x_n are getting farther and farther away from r. Such a situation is often not dependent on the choice of x_0. Thus, Newton's method fails for such a situation, and we should look for some other root-finding method.

The next example illustrates the application of Newton's method to approximate a break-even point for a profit function. We used a Lotus® 1-2-3® worksheet to do our computations. The computer output is given in the solution.

• **EXAMPLE 4-19**   **Break-Even Point.** ⎯⎯⎯⎯⎯⎯⎯

The profit, P (in millions of dollars), gained from selling x (in thousands) units of some product is given by

$$P(x) = 2x^3 - 9x^2 + 6x - 3 \qquad (x \geq 0)$$

Use Newton's method with $x_0 = 3.5$ to approximate a break-even point that occurs in that vicinity.

Solution

Using $x_0 = 3.5$ as an initial approximation gives the following computer output.

Computer Output

x	P(x)	P'(x)
3.5	-6.5	16.5
3.893939	1.984528	26.88567
3.820125	0.077455	24.79790
3.817002	0.000135	24.71099
3.816996	0.000000	24.71084
3.816996	-8.9E-16	24.71084

Studying the computer output, note that the last two approximations are the same to 6 decimal places. Hence,

final approximation = 3.816996

However, observe that the following computer output gives the above results after the Lotus 1-2-3 worksheet is adjusted to a wider column width to allow for a greater number of decimal places.

Computer Output
(Wider Column Width)

x	P(x)	P'(x)
3.5	-6.5	16.5
3.8939393939	1.9845284804	26.885674931
3.820125793	0.0774551822	24.797902172
3.817002336	0.0001357497	24.710998949
3.8169968425	0.0000000004	24.710846208
3.8169968424	-8.8817841970E-16	24.710846207
3.8169968424	-8.8817841970E-16	24.710846207
3.8169968424	-8.8817841970E-16	24.710846207

Note the greater accuracy. We have included more iterations than necessary in order to demonstrate the level of accuracy attained. Studying the computer output, a more accurate approximation is

final approximation = 3.8169968424

Thus, when approximately 3.8169968424 thousand units (or, 3817 units, rounded to the nearest whole number) of this product are produced and sold, the company breaks even.

Exercises 4-5

For each function of Exercises 1–4, verify that the function has an x-intercept in the given interval. Use Newton's method with the given value of x_0 to approximate the x-intercept.

1. $f(x) = x^3 - 5x^2 - x + 6$; $1 < x < 2$; $x_0 = 1$
2. $f(x) = x^3 - 7x^2 + 7x + 17$; $3 < x < 4$; $x_0 = 3$
3. $f(x) = x^3 - 2x^2 - x - 1$; $2 < x < 3$; $x_0 = 2$
4. $f(x) = x^3 - 4x^2 - x + 5$; $-2 < x < -1$; $x_0 = -1$
5. Use Newton's method to approximate $\sqrt{5}$ by approximating the positive x-intercept of $f(x) = x^2 - 5$. Use $x_0 = 2$.
6. Use Newton's method to approximate $\sqrt[3]{2}$ by approximating the x-intercept of $f(x) = x^3 - 2$. Use $x_0 = 1$.

7. *Break-even point.* The profit, P (in millions of dollars), gained from selling x (in thousands) units of some product is given by

$$P(x) = x^3 - 70x^2 + 1400x - 8001 \qquad (0 \leq x \leq 18)$$

   Use Newton's method to find the break-even point, which occurs in the interval $10 < x < 11$. Use $x_0 = 10$.

8. *Break-even point.* The profit, P (in thousands of dollars), gained from selling x (in hundreds) units of some commodity is given by

$$P(x) = x^3 - 35x^2 + 350x - 1001 \qquad (0 \leq x \leq 9)$$

   Use Newton's method to find the break-even point, which occurs in the interval $5 < x < 6$. Use $x_0 = 5$.

9. Verify that the function defined by $f(x) = x^3 - 7x - 5$ has an x-intercept in the interval $2 < x < 3$.
   a) Use Newton's method with $x_0 = 2$ to approximate the x-intercept.
   b) Use Newton's method with $x_0 = 3$ to approximate the x-intercept.
   c) Compare the results of parts a and b.

10. Verify that the function defined by $f(x) = x^3 - 5x^2 - x + 6$ has an x-intercept in the interval $4 < x < 5$.
    a) Use Newton's method with $x_0 = 4$ to approximate the x-intercept.
    b) Use Newton's method with $x_0 = 5$ to approximate the x-intercept.
    c) Compare the results of parts a and b.

EXTRA DIVIDENDS

• *Using Newton's Method to Find Rates of Return*

For any financial transaction, the value of an amount of money changes with time as a result of the application of interest. To *accumulate* or *bring forward* a single payment, R, for n periods at an interest rate, i, per period, we multiply R by $(1 + i)^n$, as illustrated in Figure 4-27. To *bring back* or *discount* a single payment, R, for n periods at an interest rate of i per period, we multiply R by $(1 + i)^{-n}$, as shown in Figure 4-28. We will use these concepts to solve the following problem.

Bringing forward a single payment R

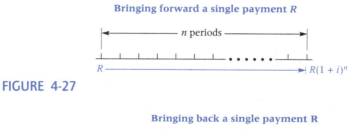

FIGURE 4-27

Bringing back a single payment R

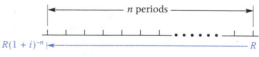

FIGURE 4-28

A 2-year U.S. Treasury note is selling at $98.84 per $100 of face value. The note earns interest at 9%, payable in 4 semiannual installments of $4.50 [i.e., $(0.09/2)(100)$] each. Find the yield to maturity.

The time diagram in Figure 4-29 illustrates the cash flows involved. Since the note is to be redeemed at face value at the end of 2 years, the last cash flow, $104.50, includes the redemption value of $100 plus the interest payment of $4.50. Since the holder of this note has paid $98.84 for an investment with the cash inflows shown in Figure 4-29, we discount or bring back the cash inflows to the beginning of the time line. If j = the unknown interest rate (i.e., the yield to maturity), then the interest rate per 6-month conversion period is $i = j/2$. Figure 4-30 illustrates the discounting of the cash inflows.

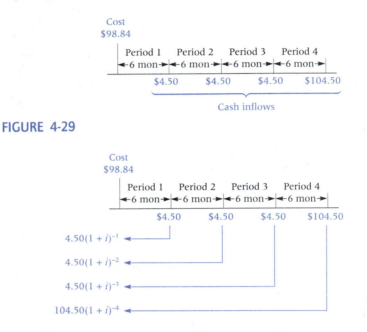

FIGURE 4-29

FIGURE 4-30

In order to attain the yield to maturity, j, the discounted cash inflows must equal the cost of the note. Hence,

$$98.84 = 4.50(1 + i)^{-1} + 4.50(1 + i)^{-2} + 4.50(1 + i)^{-3} + 104.50(1 + i)^{-4}$$

If we let $x = (1 + i)^{-1}$, then the equation becomes

$$98.84 = 4.50x + 4.50x^2 + 4.50x^3 + 104.50x^4$$

or

$$0 = 104.50x^4 + 4.50x^3 + 4.50x^2 + 4.50x - 98.84$$

Thus, we must solve this equation for x. This is equivalent to finding the roots of

$$f(x) = 104.50x^4 + 4.50x^3 + 4.50x^2 + 4.50x - 98.84$$

Since $f(0) < 0$ (i.e., $f(0) = -98.84$) and $f(1) > 0$ (i.e., $f(1) = 19.16$), we conclude that a root occurs within the interval $0 \leq x \leq 1$. If we choose an initial estimate of $x_0 = 1$, then the following computer output is obtained.

Computer Output

x	$f(x)$	$f'(x)$
1	19.16	445
0.956943	1.162358	391.7738
0.953976	0.005196	388.2741
0.953963	0.000000	388.2584
0.953963	−5.6E-16	388.2584

Thus,

$$x = 0.953963 \qquad \text{Final approximation}$$

Since $x = (1 + i)^{-1} = 0.953963$ and $1 + i = 1/0.953963 = 1.048259$, then $i = 1.048259 - 1 = 0.048259$. Since $i = j/2$, where j is the yield to maturity, then $j = 2i$, or $j = 2(0.048259) = 0.096518$. Thus, the yield to maturity is approximately

$$9.65\% \text{ compounded semiannually} \qquad \text{Yield to maturity}$$

Computer Exercises

1. If the U.S. Treasury note discussed in this case sold for $96 per $100 of face value, find the yield to maturity.
2. If the U.S. Treasury note discussed in this case sold for $99.50 per $100 of face value, find the yield to maturity.
3. A 2-year U.S. Treasury note is selling at $95 per $100 of face value. The note earns interest at 10% payable in four semiannual installments of $5 (i.e., (0.10/2)(100)) each. Find the yield to maturity.
4. A 2-year U.S. Treasury note is selling at $97.50 per $100 of face value. The note earns interest at 8% payable in 4 semiannual installments. Find the yield to maturity.

Amortization

Recall that if a loan of A dollars is repaid (or amortized) with n payments of R dollars each, then the formula relating these two quantities is given by

$$A = (R/i)[1 - (1 + i)^{-n}]$$

where i is the interest rate per period. We note that each payment is made at the end of the payment period and that the payment periods coincide with the interest periods.

5. A 30-year home mortgage for $100,000 is to be amortized with monthly payments of $900. Find the interest rate.
6. A 20-year mortgage for $60,000 is to be amortized with monthly payments of $500. Find the interest rate.
7. A 30-year mortgage for $200,000 is to be amortized with monthly payments of $1700 each. Find the interest rate.
8. A 15-year mortgage for $150,000 is to be amortized with monthly payments of $1200. Find the interest rate.

Add-on Interest

If a loan is amortized by the add-on interest method, the simple interest is computed on the principal for the full term of the loan and then added to the principal. This sum is divided by the number of payments to give the periodic payment. The true interest rate can be determined by applying Newton's method to the amortization formula preceding Exercise 5.

For each of the following loans,
a)   Determine the periodic payment by the add-on interest method.
b)   Use Newton's method to find the true interest rate.

9. $40,000 loan, quarterly payments for 10 years, interest rate is 9%.
10. $30,000 loan, annual payments for 20 years, interest rate is 8%.

Sinking Fund

Recall that if a person wishes to accumulate a future amount of S dollars by making periodic deposits of R dollars into a fund, then the formula relating these two quantities is given by

$$S = (R/i)[1 + i)^n - 1]$$

where i is the interest rate per period. We assume that each payment is made at the end of the payment period and that payment periods coincide with interest periods.

11. A person wants to accumulate a savings account valued at $180,000 upon retirement in 20 years. The person wants to save $200 per month toward this goal. Determine the interest rate that must be earned in order to achieve this goal.
12. A city must set up a fund to retire a debt of $2,000,000 five years from now. If the city wants to make monthly deposits of $26,000 toward this goal, find the interest rate that must be earned by the fund.
13. A financial planner is setting up a retirement fund for a client. The fund must have a value of $300,000 20 years from now. If the client can afford to make monthly payments of $400, find the interest rate that must be earned by the fund.
14. A sinking fund must have a value of $140,000 at the end of 10 years. This is to be accomplished by making quarterly payments of $2200. Find the interest rate that must be earned by the fund.

CHAPTER 4 HIGHLIGHTS

• Concepts

Your ability to answer the following questions is one indicator of the depth of your mastery of this chapter's important concepts. Note that the questions are grouped under various topic headings. For any question that you cannot answer, refer to the appropriate section of the chapter indicated by the topic heading. Pay particular attention to the summary boxes within a section.

4-1   IMPLICIT DIFFERENTIATION

1. What does it mean for a function to be defined implicitly in terms of x?

4-2 RELATED RATES

2. In a related-rate problem, each variable is assumed to be a function of _____.

3. State the procedure for solving related-rate problems.

4-3 ELASTICITY OF DEMAND

4. Elasticity of demand = (_____)/(_____).

5. Use the derivative to give the formula for elasticity of demand. Elasticity, as given by this formula, is always _____.

6. State and explain the three cases for elasticity of demand.

7. If demand is elastic, then marginal revenue is _____.

8. If demand is inelastic, then marginal revenue is _____.

4-4 DIFFERENTIALS

9. Give the formula for the differential of y, dy.

10. Give a graphical interpretation for the differential of y, dy.

11. Using differentials, give the formula for the percent change in y.

4-5 NEWTON'S METHOD

12. Newton's method is used to approximate the _____ of a function.

13. Give the formula for Newton's method.

14. When using Newton's method, how do we know when to stop?

15. Is it possible that Newton's method might fail in some instances? Review any such instances in the text.

REVIEW EXERCISES

• Implicit Differentiation

Use implicit differentiation to find dy/dx for Exercises 1–4.

1. $xy^4 + x^3 + y = 3$ **2.** $x^2 + y^2 = 40$
3. $(x - y)(x + y^3) = 7$ **4.** $x + y = 30$

For Exercises 5 and 6, find the slope of the tangent line to the curve at the indicated point.

5. $x^2 + y^2 = 20$ (4, 2)   **6.** $x^4 + xy^3 + y^2 = 19$ (2, 1)
7. If $y = 8x^2 + 6x + 4$, find dx/dy.

• Related Rates

8. A point moves on the graph of $xy = 20$ in such a manner that its x-coordinate is increasing at a rate of 3 units per second when the point is at (4, 5). Find the rate of change of the y-coordinate at that moment.

9. A point moves on the graph of $5x^2 + 3y^2 = 47$ in such a manner that its y-coordinate is increasing at a rate of 2 units per second when the point is at (2, 3). Find the rate of change of the x-coordinate at that moment.

10. *Ladder.* A 30-foot ladder is resting against a building. The bottom of the ladder is sliding away from the building at a rate of 5 feet per second. Determine the rate at which the top of the ladder is sliding downward.

11. *Sphere: Volume.* A spherical balloon is inflated so that its radius is increasing at the rate of 1.5 centimeters per minute. Determine the rate of change of volume when the radius is 18 centimeters. Use the fact that the volume of a sphere is given by

$$V = \frac{4}{3}\pi r^3$$

where r is the radius and $\pi \approx 3.1416$.

• *Elasticity of Demand*

Exercises 12–15 each give a demand function. Find the formula for point elasticity of demand.

12. $q = -4p + 80$ **13.** $q = 4(p - 7)^2$

14. $q = 80 - 20p$ **15.** $q = p/(p - 30)$

16. The demand for a product is given by

$$q = -8p + 160 \qquad (0 < p < 20)$$

    a) Find the formula for point elasticity of demand.
    b) Evaluate the result of part a at $p = 10$.
    c) Interpret the result of part b.

17. Elasticity of demand for some product is given to be -1.4 at $p = 20$.
    a) Interpret this result.
    b) Is demand elastic or inelastic at $p = 20$?

18. Elasticity of demand for some product is given to be -0.90 at $p = 50$.
    a) Interpret this result.
    b) Is demand elastic or inelastic at $p = 50$?

• *Differentials*

Find dy for Exercises 19–22.

19. $y = x^3 - 4x^2 + 5$ **20.** $y = x^2 + 4x - 8$

21. $y = 4x^2\sqrt{x}$ **22.** $y = \sqrt{x^2 + 20}$

23. If $y = x^2 + 2x + 3$, find dy and evaluate it at $x = 4$ and $dx = 0.05$.

24. *Cost.* The total cost, C (in dollars), of producing x units of some product is given by

$$C(x) = 0.40x^2 + 6000 \qquad (0 \le x \le 5000)$$

If the production level, x, changes from 100 to 101, use differentials to approximate the
    a) Change in total cost.   b) Percent change in total cost.

25. *Revenue.* The sales revenue, R (in millions of dollars), gained from selling x (in thousands) units of some product is given by

$$R(x) = -x^2 + 40x \qquad (0 \le x \le 20)$$

If x changes from 10 to 10.5, use differentials to approximate the
    a) Change in revenue.   b) Percent change in revenue.

• *Newton's Method*

For each function of Exercises 26 and 27, verify that the function has an x-intercept in the given interval. Use Newton's Method with the given value of x_0 to approximate the x-intercept.

26. $f(x) = x^3 - 4x + 2$; $1 < x < 2$; $x_0 = 2$

27. $f(x) = x^3 - 6x^2 + 9x - 1$; $2 < x < 3$; $x_0 = 2$

28. *Break-even point.* The profit, P (in millions), gained from selling x (in thousands) units of some product is given by

$$P(x) = -x^3 + 2x + 10 \qquad (0 < x < 3)$$

Use Newton's method to approximate the break-even point which occurs in the interval $2 < x < 3$. Use $x_0 = 2$.

5

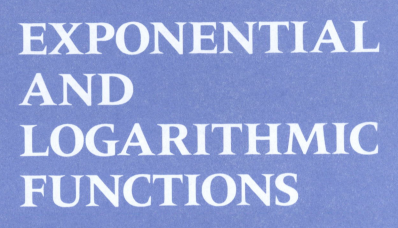

EXPONENTIAL AND LOGARITHMIC FUNCTIONS

Introductory Application

Market Penetration: Long-Range Forecasting

The exponential function defined by

$$y = A - Be^{-mx}$$

where A, B, and m are positive constants, is used to model market penetration of a product that exhibits rapid sales growth upon introduction into the marketplace. The above function is called the **modified exponential model.** Its graph appears in Figure 5-A. Note that x denotes time (in years), y denotes the percentage of the market penetrated by the product, and the constant, A, denotes the market saturation level—not to exceed 100% ($A = 100$). Observe that the graph of Figure 5-A indicates rapid sales growth upon introduction of the product (at $x = 0$). This sales growth continues for some time until it eventually slows as the market reaches saturation level.

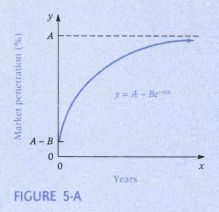

FIGURE 5-A

• EXAMPLE

The market penetration for television sets has followed the modified exponential model.

•

In this chapter, we discuss exponential and logarithmic functions, including the modified exponential model and the logistic growth model, along with other applications.

In this chapter, we will discuss functions used to describe growth and decay of various quantities. Such functions are called **exponential functions.** We will also consider **logarithms** and **logarithmic functions.** The derivatives of exponential and logarithmic functions will be discussed along with various applications.

5-1   • EXPONENTIAL FUNCTIONS AND THEIR GRAPHS

Consider two quantities, y and x, related by the equation

$$y = 2^x$$

Since the variable x is an exponent, such an equation defines an exponential function. The constant 2, is called the **base.** A graph and a table of x- and y-values are illustrated in Figure 5-1 and Table 5-1, respectively. Observing the graph of Figure 5-1, note that $(0, 1)$ is the y-intercept. Since 2^x approaches 0 as x takes on negative values of larger and larger magnitude, the graph of $y = 2^x$ approaches the x-axis as x takes on negative values far away from the origin. Thus, the x-axis is a horizontal asymptote.

Note that Table 5-1 shows values of 2^x for rational values of x. It is possible to evaluate 2^x for irrational values of x by approximating each irrational value of x by rational values. For example, $2^{\sqrt{3}}$ may be approximated to varying degrees of accuracy by considering the sequence of rational powers

$$2^1, 2^{1.7}, 2^{1.73}, 2^{1.732}, \ldots$$

Recall that $\sqrt{3} \approx 1.732$. Thus, as the exponents get closer and closer to $\sqrt{3}$, the corresponding powers of 2 get closer and closer to $2^{\sqrt{3}}$. Therefore, the exponential function defined by $y = 2^x$ has all of the real numbers as its domain, and its graph is the continuous curve illustrated in Figure 5-1.

We now consider the function defined by the equation

$$y = 2^{-x}$$

Again, since the variable x appears as an exponent, this equation defines an exponential function. Note that the exponent, $-x$, has a negative sign. The graph of $y = 2^{-x}$ and a table of $x-$ and $y-$ values are given on page 298 in Figure 5-2 and Table 5-2, respectively.

Studying the graph of Figure 5-2, we see that $(0, 1)$ is the y-intercept. Note that 2^{-x} approaches 0 as x takes on larger and larger positive values. Thus, the x-axis is a horizontal asymptote. The graphs of $y = 2^x$ and $y = 2^{-x}$ are reflections of one another through the y-axis.

We now consider the function defined by

$$y = 5 \cdot 2^x$$

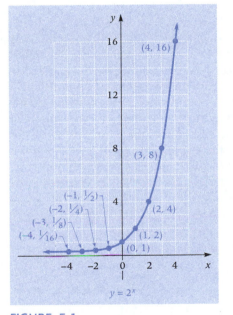

FIGURE 5-1

TABLE 5-1

x	$y = 2^x$
-4	$y = 2^{-4} = (1/2)^4 = 1/16$
-3	$y = 2^{-3} = (1/2)^3 = 1/8$
-2	$y = 2^{-2} = (1/2)^2 = 1/4$
-1	$y = 2^{-1} = (1/2)^1 = 1/2$
0	$y = 2^0 = 1$
1	$y = 2^1 = 2$
2	$y = 2^2 = 4$
3	$y = 2^3 = 8$
4	$y = 2^4 = 16$

FIGURE 5-2

TABLE 5-2

x	$y = 2^{-x}$
-4	$y = 2^{-(-4)} = 2^4 = 16$
-3	$y = 2^{-(-3)} = 2^3 = 8$
-2	$y = 2^{-(-2)} = 2^2 = 4$
-1	$y = 2^{-(-1)} = 2^1 = 2$
0	$y = 2^{-(0)} = 2^0 = 1$
1	$y = 2^{-1} = \dfrac{1}{2}$
2	$y = 2^{-2} = \dfrac{1}{2^2} = \dfrac{1}{4}$
3	$y = 2^{-3} = \dfrac{1}{2^3} = \dfrac{1}{8}$
4	$y = 2^{-4} = \dfrac{1}{2^4} = \dfrac{1}{16}$

Since the variable x appears as an exponent, this equation also defines an exponential function. Its graph and a table of x- and y-values are illustrated in Figure 5-3 and Table 5-3, respectively. Looking at Figure 5-3, note that $(0, 5)$ is the y-intercept and that the x-axis is a horizontal asymptote.

If we compare the graphs of $y = 2^x$ and $y = 5 \cdot 2^x$ by sketching both functions on the same axis system, we obtain Figure 5-4. Note that the x-axis is the horizontal asymptote for both functions. Also, $(0, 1)$ is the y-intercept of $y = 2^x$, whereas $(0, 5)$ is the y-intercept of $y = 5 \cdot 2^x$. Observe that the graph of $y = 5 \cdot 2^x$ is similar to the graph of $y = 2^x$. The only effects of the constant multiplier, 5, on the graph of $y = 2^x$ are changes in its y-intercept and curvature. This is because the y-values of $y = 5 \cdot 2^x$ are 5 times those of $y = 2^x$.

TABLE 5-3

x	$y = 5 \cdot 2^x$
-3	$y = 5 \cdot 2^{-3} = 5 \cdot (1/2)^3 = 5/8$
-2	$y = 5 \cdot 2^{-2} = 5 \cdot (1/2)^2 = 5/4$
-1	$y = 5 \cdot 2^{-1} = 5 \cdot (1/2)^1 = 5/2$
0	$y = 5 \cdot 2^0 = 5 \cdot 1 = 5$
1	$y = 5 \cdot 2^1 = 5 \cdot 2 = 10$
2	$y = 5 \cdot 2^2 = 5 \cdot 4 = 20$
3	$y = 5 \cdot 2^3 = 5 \cdot 8 = 40$
4	$y = 5 \cdot 2^4 = 5 \cdot 16 = 80$

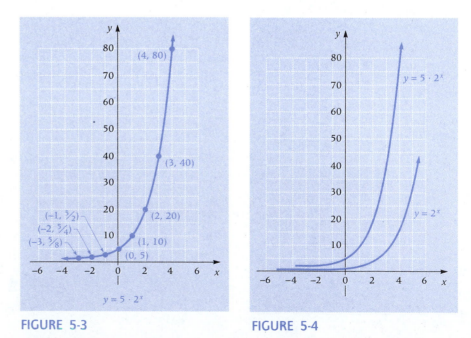

FIGURE 5-3

FIGURE 5-4

Step 1
Begin with the graph $y = 5 \cdot 2^x$.

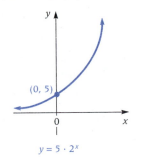

$y = 5 \cdot 2^x$

Step 2
Draw the graph of $y = 5 \cdot 2^x$ upside down to obtain the graph of $y = -5 \cdot 2^x$.

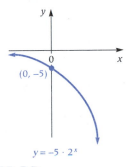

$y = -5 \cdot 2^x$

FIGURE 5-5

We note that if the constant multiplier is negative—say, -5,—then the y-values of the function $y = -5 \cdot 2^x$ are the negatives of those of $y = 5 \cdot 2^x$, and, therefore, the graph of $y = -5 \cdot 2^x$ is a reflection on the x-axis of the graph of $y = 5 \cdot 2^x$, as illustrated in Figure 5-5. In other words, the graph of $y = -5 \cdot 2^x$ can be obtained by drawing the graph of $y = 5 \cdot 2^x$ upside down.

Base e

The following discussion will involve values of the expression

$$\left(1 + \frac{1}{x}\right)^x$$

as x gets larger and larger. This expression occurs so often in mathematics that we use a calculator to evaluate it for larger and larger values of x as illustrated below.

$$\left(1 + \frac{1}{1000}\right)^{1000} = 2.716923924. \ldots$$

$$\left(1 + \frac{1}{10,000}\right)^{10,000} = 2.718145918. \ldots$$

$$\left(1 + \frac{1}{100,000}\right)^{100,000} = 2.718268237. \ldots$$

$$\left(1 + \frac{1}{1,000,000}\right)^{1,000,000} = 2.718281828. \ldots$$

$$\left(1 + \frac{1}{10,000,000}\right)^{10,000,000} = 2.718281828. \ldots$$

Note how $(1 + 1/x)^x$ is approaching a single value close to 2.718281828 to nine decimal places. Mathematicians have assigned the letter e to the limiting value of the expression $(1 + 1/x)$ as x gets larger and larger. In other words,

as x gets larger and larger, and e denotes the irrational number whose decimal expansion to nine decimal places is given as follows.

$$e = 2.718281828$$

We note that powers of e (i.e., e^2, e^3, $e^{1.5}$, $e^{-1.67}$, etc.) can be computed by using a calculator. Also, Appendix C gives values of e^x and e^{-x} for various values of x.

Up to this point, we have graphed exponential functions with base 2. However, we often encounter exponential functions with base e. Some examples include $y = e^x$, $y = e^{-x}$, $y = 5e^x$, and $y = -5e^x$. Since we have already graphed $y = 2^x$, $y = 2^{-x}$, $y = 5 \cdot 2^x$, and $y = -5 \cdot 2^x$, we note that the graphs of these equations resemble those of $y = e^x$, $y = e^{-x}$, $y = 5e^x$, and $y = -5e^x$, respectively.

We now summarize the concepts discussed up to this point in this section.

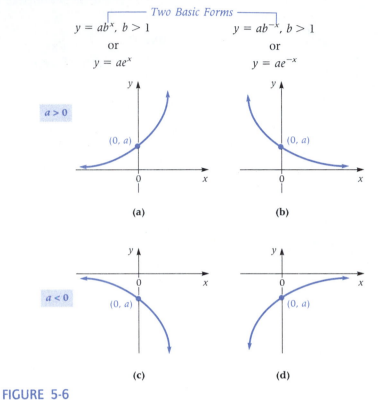

■ **SUMMARY**

Graphs of Exponential Functions

Two Basic Forms

$y = ab^x,\ b > 1$ $y = ab^{-x},\ b > 1$

or   or

$y = ae^x$ $y = ae^{-x}$

$a > 0$

(a)   (b)

$a < 0$

(c)   (d)

FIGURE 5-6

Note: The graphs for $a < 0$ are reflections (in other words, drawn upside down) of those for $a > 0$.

• **EXAMPLE 5-1**

a) The graphs of $y = 5 \cdot 3^x$, $y = e^x$, and $y = 4e^x$ resemble that of Figure 5-6(a).

b) The graphs of $y = 5 \cdot 3^{-x}$, $y = e^{-x}$, and $y = 7e^{-x}$ resemble that of Figure 5-6(b).

c) The graphs of $y = -4 \cdot 2^x$, $y = -e^x$, and $y = -8e^x$ resemble that of Figure 5-6(c).

d) The graphs of $y = -5 \cdot 3^{-x}$. $y = -e^{-x}$, and $y = -6e^{-x}$ resemble that of Figure 5-6(d).

•

$y = ab^x + c$ and $y = ab^{-x} + c$ Where $b > 1$

Sometimes we encounter an exponential function defined by an equation such as

$$y = 3e^x + 2$$

Step 1
Begin with the graph of $y = 3e^x$.

Step 2 *Vertical shift*
Lift the graph of $y = 3e^x$ vertically by 2 units to obtain the graph of $y = 3e^x + 2$.

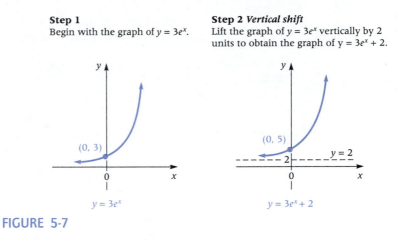

FIGURE 5-7

Since the constant 2 is added to $y = 3e^x$, the y-values of $y = 3e^x + 2$ are 2 *greater than* those of $y = 3e^x$. Hence, $y = 3e^x + 2$ may be sketched by beginning with the graph of $y = 3e^x$ and *lifting it vertically by 2 units* (see Figure 5-7). As discussed in Chapter 2, this is called a **vertical shift.** Note that the horizontal line $y = 2$ is the horizontal asymptote for $y = 3e^x + 2$.

Step 1
Begin with the graph of $y = -2e^x$.

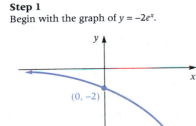

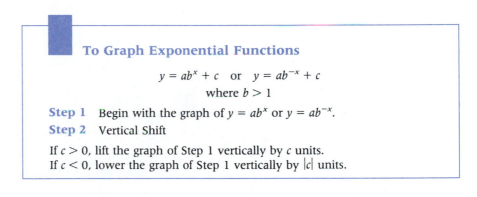

To Graph Exponential Functions

$$y = ab^x + c \quad \text{or} \quad y = ab^{-x} + c$$
$$\text{where } b > 1$$

Step 1   Begin with the graph of $y = ab^x$ or $y = ab^{-x}$.

Step 2   Vertical Shift

If $c > 0$, lift the graph of Step 1 vertically by c units.
If $c < 0$, lower the graph of Step 1 vertically by $|c|$ units.

Step 2 *Vertical shift*
Lower the graph of $y = -2e^x$ vertically by 1 unit to obtain the graph of $y = -2e^x - 1$.

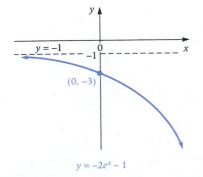

FIGURE 5-8

• **EXAMPLE 5-2**

Sketch $f(x) = -2e^x - 1$.

Solution

Compare this equation with the general form $y = ab^x + c$, where $a = -2$ (a negative number), $b = e$, and $c = -1$. The graph is sketched in Figure 5-8.

• **EXAMPLE 5-3**

Sketch $y = -4e^{-x} + 6$.

Solution

This function is of the form $y = ab^{-x} + c$, where $a = -4$ (a negative number), $b = e$, and $c = 6$. Its graph is sketched in Figure 5-9 on page 302.

Step 1
Begin with the graph of $y = -4e^{-x}$.

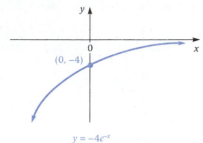

Step 2 *Vertical shift*
Lift the graph of $y = -4e^{-x}$ vertically by 6 units to obtain the graph of $y = -4e^{-x} + 6$.

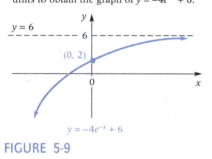

FIGURE 5-9

All of the equations defining exponential functions in this section have appeared in either of the following two forms:

$$y = ab^x + c \qquad (b > 1)$$

or

$$y = ab^{-x} + c \qquad (b > 1)$$

Note that for each form, $b > 1$. We now consider the cases for which $b \le 1$. If $b = 1$, then $b^x = 1^x = 1$ for all finite x-values. Thus, the equation $y = ab^x + c$ becomes the horizontal line $y = a + c$. The same happens to the form $y = ab^{-x} + c$. We have little interest in such exponential functions.

We now show that the case in which $0 < b < 1$ is not really a new case at all. If $0 < b < 1$, then b^x may be written as b_1^{-x}, with $b_1 = 1/b$ and $b_1 > 1$. For example, $(1/2)^x = 2^{-x}$, $(1/3)^x = 3^{-x}$, $(2/5)^x = (5/2)^{-x}$, etc. Also, b^{-x} becomes b_1^x, with $b_1 = 1/b$ and $b_1 > 1$. For example, $(1/2)^{-x} = 2^x$, $(1/3)^{-x} = 3^x$, $(2/5)^{-x} = (5/2)^x$, etc. Thus, the equation $y = ab^x + c$, with $0 < b < 1$, may be written as $y = ab_1^{-x} + c$, with $b_1 > 1$, since $b_1 = 1/b$. Also, the equation $y = ab^{-x} + c$, with $0 < b < 1$, may be rewritten as $y = ab_1^x + c$, with $b_1 > 1$, since $b_1 = 1/b$.

If $b \le 0$, we have little interest in equations of the form $y = ab^x + c$ or $y = ab^{-x} + c$ since the function is not defined at many x-values. Specifically, if $b = 0$ and $x = -1$, then $y = ab^x + c$ is undefined; if $b = -4$ and $x = 1/2$, then $y = ab^x + c$ is undefined.

We state the following property.

If $b > 0$, there is a value k such that

$$b = e^k$$

In other words, any positive number b can be expressed as e^k.*

Exponential Functions with Terms e^{kx} and e^{-kx}

Since

$$b^x = (e^k)^x = e^{kx}$$

equations of the forms

$$y = ab^x + c \qquad (b > 1)$$

and

$$y = ab^{-x} + c \qquad (b > 1)$$

*We will learn how to find k in Section 5-2.

Step 1
Begin with the graph of $y = -3e^{-0.05x}$.

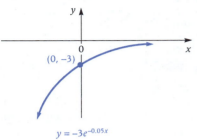

$(0, -3)$

$y = -3e^{-0.05x}$

Step 2 *Vertical shift*
Lift the graph of $y = -3e^{-0.05x}$ vertically by 7 units to obtain the graph of $y = -3e^{-0.05x} + 7$.

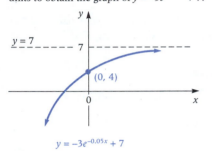

$y = 7$

$(0, 4)$

$y = -3e^{-0.05x} + 7$

FIGURE 5-10

may be restated as

$$y = ae^{kx} + c \qquad (k > 0)$$

and

$$y = ae^{-kx} + c \qquad (k > 0)$$

respectively. Therefore, the procedures of this section also apply to sketching exponential functions expressed in the latter forms that contain the terms e^{kx} and e^{-kx}.

• EXAMPLE 5-4

Sketch $y = -3e^{-0.05x} + 7$.

Solution

The graph is sketched in Figure 5-10.

Before ending this section, we state the following property.

If $b > 0$ and $b \neq 1$, then $b^x = b^y$ if and only if $x = y$.

For example, if $3^{18} = 3^{2x}$, then $2x = 18$ and $x = 9$. If $5^{40} = 5^{4x}$, then $4x = 40$ and $x = 10$.

Applications

Radioactive Decay

A radioactive substance loses its mass (or, if you prefer, weight) as time passes. Specifically, its mass, y, is related to the time elapsed, t, by an equation of the form

$$y = ae^{-kt} \qquad (k > 0)$$

Note that at $t = 0$, the initial mass is

$$y = ae^{-k(0)}$$
$$= a \cdot 1$$
$$= a$$

The letter k represents a constant associated with the specific radioactive substance being considered. If, for a particular radioactive substance, the initial mass is $a = 1000$ grams and $k = 0.70$, then the equation

$$y = 1000e^{-0.70t}$$

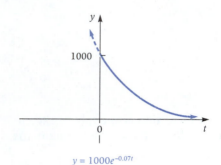

1000

0   t

$y = 1000e^{-0.07t}$

FIGURE 5-11

relates its mass, y (in grams), with the time elapsed, t (in minutes). Thus, at $t = 1$ (after 1 minute has elapsed), the mass is

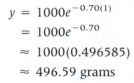

$$y = 1000e^{-0.70(1)}$$
$$= 1000e^{-0.70}$$
$$\approx 1000(0.496585)$$
$$\approx 496.59 \text{ grams}$$

The graph of $y = 1000e^{-0.70t}$ is illustrated in Figure 5-11. Observe that the radioactive mass is decreasing as time is increasing.

Newton's Law of Cooling

Newton's law of cooling expresses the relationship between the temperature of a cooling object and the time elapsed since cooling first began. According to Newton's law of cooling, if

y = temperature of a cooling object after t units of time

c = temperature of the medium surrounding the cooling object

then the exponential function

$$y = ae^{-kt} + c$$

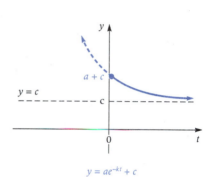

$a + c$

$y = c$

c

0   t

$y = ae^{-kt} + c$

FIGURE 5-12

relates temperature, y, with time, t. The letters a and k represent constants associated with the cooling object. A sketch of the general function $y = ae^{-kt} + c$ appears in Figure 5-12. The constants a and k are non-negative. Studying Figure 5-12, we note that the temperature y of the cooling object approaches the temperature c of the surrounding medium as t gets larger and larger. Thus, the temperature of a cooling object will not fall below the temperature of the surrounding medium.

As a specific example, consider a cup of tea heated to 210°F. The room temperature is 70°F. Here, the exponential function

$$y = 140e^{-0.01t} + 70 \qquad (t \geq 0)$$

relates the temperature, y, of the tea with the time elapsed, t (in minutes). Hence, after 10 minutes have elapsed ($t = 10$), we find that

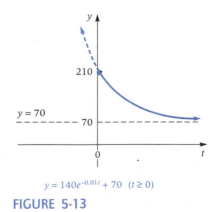

210

$y = 70$ 70

0   t

$y = 140e^{-0.01t} + 70 \quad (t \geq 0)$

FIGURE 5-13

$$y = 140e^{-0.01(10)} + 70$$
$$= 140e^{-0.1} + 70$$
$$\approx 140(0.904837) + 70$$
$$\approx 126.67718 + 70$$
$$\approx 196.7$$

Thus, the object at this point in time has cooled to a temperature of approximately 197°F. The graph of $y = 140e^{-0.01t} + 70$ is sketched in Figure 5-13.

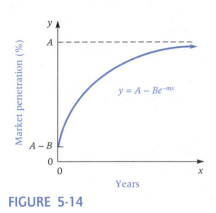

FIGURE 5-14

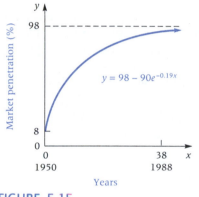

FIGURE 5-15

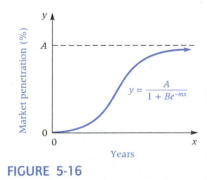

FIGURE 5-16

Market Penetration: Long-Range Forecasting

We discuss two exponential functions used to model and, thus, forecast the market penetration of products introduced into the marketplace. The first is called the modified exponential model, and the second is called the logistic growth model.

Modified Exponential Model. As discussed in the introductory application to this chapter, the exponential function defined by

$$y = A - Be^{-mx}$$

where A, B, and m are positive constants, is used to model market penetration of a product that exhibits rapid sales growth upon introduction into the marketplace. The above function is called the **modified exponential model.** Its graph appears in Figure 5-14. Note that x denotes time (in years), y denotes the percentage of the market penetrated by the product, and the constant, A, denotes the market saturation level—not to exceed 100% ($A = 100$). Observe that the graph of Figure 5-14 indicates rapid sales growth upon introduction of the product (at $x = 0$). This sales growth continues for some time until it eventually slows as the market reaches saturation level.

The market penetration for television sets has followed the modified exponential model, as illustrated in Figure 5-15. The equation

$$y = 98 - 90e^{-0.19x}$$

approximates the relationship between market penetration and time exhibited by the curve of Figure 5-15. Here $x = 0$ corresponds to the year 1950, and $x = 38$ corresponds to the year 1988.

USING THE MODEL TO FORECAST We forecast the percentage of the market penetrated by television sets for the year 1995 by substituting $x = 45$ into the equation of the model to obtain

$$y = 98 - 90e^{-0.19(45)} \quad \text{Use a calculator}$$
$$\approx 97.98 \quad \text{Forecast}$$

Thus, approximately 97.98% of all households are projected to have television sets in 1995.

Logistic Growth Model. The exponential function defined by

$$y = \frac{A}{1 + Be^{-mx}}$$

where A, B, and m are positive constants, is used to model market penetration of a product that exhibits slow sales growth when first introduced into the marketplace, then a period of rapid growth followed by a gradual decline in growth, and, finally, no growth as the market reaches saturation level. This is illustrated in Figure 5-16, which gives the graph of the above function. This function is called the **logistic growth model;** the variable,

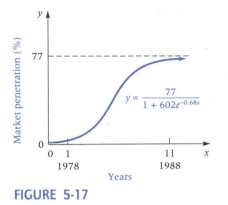

FIGURE 5-17

x, denotes time (in years), y denotes the percentage of the market penetrated by the product, and the constant, A, denotes the market saturation level—not to exceed 100% ($A = 100$).

The market penetration for videocassette recorders (VCRs) has followed the logistic growth model, as illustrated in Figure 5-17. The equation

$$y = \frac{77}{1 + 602e^{-0.68x}}$$

approximates the relationship between market penetration and time exhibited by the curve of Figure 5-17. Here $x = 1$ corresponds to the year 1978, and $x = 11$ corresponds to the year 1988.

USING THE MODEL TO FORECAST We forecast the percentage of the market penetrated by videocassette recorders for the year 1995 by substituting $x = 18$ into the equation of the model to obtain

$$y = \frac{77}{1 + 602e^{-0.68(18)}} \qquad \text{Use a calculator}$$

$$\approx 76.77 \qquad \text{Forecast}$$

Thus, approximately 76.77% of all households are projected to have videocassette recorders in 1995.

Exercises 5-1

Sketch the following. Identify the y-intercept and the horizontal asymptote in each case.

1. $f(x) = 5^x$ **2.** $y = 3^x$ **3.** $y = 4^x$
4. $f(x) = 4 \cdot 5^x$ **5.** $y = 2 \cdot 3^x$ **6.** $y = 3 \cdot 4^x$
7. $f(x) = -4 \cdot 5^x$ **8.** $f(x) = -2 \cdot 3^x$ **9.** $y = -3 \cdot 4^x$
10. $y = 3e^x$ **11.** $f(x) = 7e^x$ **12.** $y = 10e^x$
13. $y = -3e^x$ **14.** $y = -7e^x$ **15.** $y = -10e^x$
16. $y = 2 \cdot 3^x + 5$ **17.** $f(x) = -3 \cdot 4^x + 8$
18. $f(x) = 4e^x + 1$ **19.** $y = 4e^x - 1$
20. $y = -2e^x + 8$ **21.** $f(x) = -2e^x - 5$
22. $y = 5^{-x}$ **23.** $f(x) = 3^{-x}$
24. $y = 4^{-x}$ **25.** $y = 4 \cdot 5^{-x}$
26. $f(x) = 2 \cdot 3^{-x}$ **27.** $y = 3 \cdot 4^{-x}$
28. $y = -4 \cdot 5^{-x}$ **29.** $f(x) = -2 \cdot 3^{-x}$
30. $y = -3 \cdot 4^{-x}$ **31.** $y = 3e^{-x}$
32. $y = 7e^{-x}$ **33.** $y = 10e^{-x}$
34. $y = -3e^{-x}$ **35.** $f(x) = -7e^{-x}$
36. $y = -10e^{-x}$ **37.** $y = 2 \cdot 3^{-x} + 5$
38. $f(x) = -3 \cdot 4^{-x} + 8$ **39.** $f(x) = 4e^{-x} + 1$
40. $y = 4e^{-x} - 1$ **41.** $y = -2e^{-x} + 30$
42. $f(x) = -2e^{-x} - 5$ **43.** $y = 30e^{-x} + 30$
44. $f(x) = 50 - 50e^{-x}$ **45.** $y = 10(1 - e^{-x})$
46. $f(x) = -5(1 - e^{-x})$ **47.** $y = (1/2)^x$
48. $y = (2/3)^x$ **49.** $y = (1/2)^{-x}$

50. $f(x) = (2/3)^{-x}$

51. $y = 5 \cdot (1/5)^x + 1$

52. $f(x) = -4 \cdot (1/6)^{-x} + 2$

53. $y = 3e^{2x} + 1$

54. $f(x) = 4e^{-3x} + 1$

55. $f(x) = -2e^{0.05x} + 1$

56. $y = 3e^{-0.02x} - 5$

57. $y = 10e^{0.07x}$

58. $y = -5e^{0.03x}$

59. $f(x) = 7e^{-0.10x}$

60. $y = -3e^{-0.06x}$

61. $y = 10(1 - e^{-0.20x})$

62. $y = -2e^{-0.3x} - 6$

63. $y = -8e^{-0.40x}$

64. $y = 70e^{-0.50x} + 10$

Applications

65. *Bacteria growth.* A certain type of bacteria triples its numbers each day. Initially, there were 500,000 such bacteria present. Let y represent the number of bacteria present and t represent the number of days elapsed.
  a) Find the equation that relates y and t.
  b) Sketch the graph of the equation of part a.
  c) How many bacteria are present after 4 days?
  d) How many bacteria are present after 6 days?

66. *Depreciation.* A certain car depreciates in such a way that it loses two-thirds of its value each year. The car initially cost $4000. Let y represent the car's value (in dollars) at the end of the xth year.
  a) Find the equation that relates y and x.
  b) Sketch the graph of the equation of part a.
  c) Find the car's value at the end of the fourth year.
  d) Find the car's value at the end of the fifth year.

67. *Time series.* The annual sales, y (in millions of dollars), of a particular company are related to time, t, by the equation

$$y = 3 \cdot 2^t$$

with $t = 0$ corresponding to the year 19x0, $t = 1$ corresponding to the year 19x1, etc.
  a) Sketch $y = 3 \cdot 2^t$.
  b) Find the annual sales for years 19x0, 19x1, and 19x2.

68. *Time series.* The annual earnings per share of AKD Corporation are related to time by the equation

$$y(t) = e^{0.1t}$$

where $y(t)$ represents the earnings per share for year t. Note that $t = 0$ corresponds to the year 19x0, $t = 1$ corresponds to the year 19x1, etc.
  a) Sketch $y(t) = e^{0.1t}$.
  b) Find the earnings per share for years 19x0, 19x1, 19x2, and 19x3.

69. *Maintenance cost.* The annual maintenance cost, y, of a machine is related to the number of years it is run, t, by the equation

$$y = 1000e^{0.05t} \qquad (t \geq 0)$$

  a) Sketch $y = 1000e^{0.05t}$, $t \geq 0$.
  b) Find the annual maintenance cost after the machine has run for 2 years.

70. *Population decline.* The population, $P(t)$, of a certain city is related to time, t (in years), by the exponential function

$$P(t) = 10,000e^{-0.03t}$$

Note that $t = 0$ corresponds to the year 19x0, $t = 1$ corresponds to the year 19x1, etc.

a) Sketch $P(t) = 10,000e^{-0.03t}$.

b) Find this city's population for 19x0, 19x1, 19x2, and 19x3.

71. *Radioactive decay.* A certain radioactive substance decays in accordance with the equation

$$y(t) = 2000e^{-0.60t} \qquad (t \geq 0)$$

where $y(t)$ represents the mass (in grams) related to time, t (in hours).

a) Sketch $y(t) = 2000e^{-0.60t}$.

b) Calculate the initial mass of the substance.

c) Calculate the mass of the substance after 1/2 hour has elapsed.

d) Calculate the mass of the substance after 3 hours have elapsed.

Learning Curve

Psychologists have found that when a person learns a new task, learning is rapid at first. Then, as time passes, learning tends to taper off. Once the task is mastered, the person's level of performance approaches an upper limit. The function that relates a learner's performance with the time elapsed is called a **learning curve.** Learning curves are often expressed by exponential functions.

72. *Learning curve.* Consider the learning curve expressed by the exponential function

$$y = 40 - 40e^{-0.2x} \qquad (x \geq 0)$$

Here, the performance, y, is the number of items produced by the worker during the xth day following the training period.

a) Sketch $y = 40 - 40e^{-0.2x}$.

b) How many items are produced during the third day following the training period?

c) This worker's daily production will never exceed how many units?

73. *Learning curve.* The graph of the exponential function defined by

$$N(x) = 50 - 50e^{-0.3x} \qquad (x \geq 0)$$

is a learning curve, where $N(x)$ represents the number of items produced by an assembly line worker during the xth day after the training period.

a) Sketch $N(x) = 50 - 50e^{-0.3x}$.

b) How many items are produced during the fifth day following the training period?

c) This worker's daily production will never exceed how many units?

74. *Newton's law of cooling.* The temperature, y, of a heated cup of coffee is related to the time elapsed, t (in minutes), by the equation

$$y = 150e^{-0.02t} + 65 \qquad (t \geq 0)$$

a) Sketch $y = 150e^{-0.02t} + 65$.

b) Calculate the temperature of the coffee before cooling began.

c) Calculate the temperature of the coffee after 5 minutes have elapsed.

d) What is the room temperature?

e) The temperature of the coffee will not decline below what value?

75. *Newton's law of cooling.* A coroner determines that the temperature, T, of a murder victim's body is related to the time elapsed, t (in hours), since death by the equation

$$T = 38.6e^{-0.05t} + 60 \qquad (t \geq 0)$$

a) Sketch $T = 38.6e^{-0.05t} + 60$.
b) What is the room temperature?
c) Calculate the dead body's temperature after 2 hours have elapsed.

76. *Sales.* The function defined by

$$y = 3.6e^{0.02x} \qquad (x \geq 0)$$

approximates the relationship between sales, y (in billions of dollars), and advertising expenditure, x (in millions of dollars).
a) Sketch $y = 3.6e^{0.02x}$.
b) Calculate the expected sales for an advertising expenditure of $5 million.

77. *Market penetration: Long-range forecasting.* The percentage of market penetration for a product x years after it has been introduced is given by

$$y = 80 - 60e^{-0.70x}$$

a) Graph $y = 80 - 60e^{-0.70x}$ for $x \geq 0$.
b) Determine the percentage of market penetration for the second year.
c) Determine the percentage of market penetration for the tenth year.
d) Determine the saturation level.

78. *Market penetration: Long-range forecasting.* The percentage of market penetration for a product x years after it has been introduced is given by

$$y = \frac{80}{1 + 200e^{-0.90x}}$$

a) Determine the percentage of market penetration for the second, sixth, and twelfth years.
b) Determine the saturation level.

5-2 • LOGARITHMIC FUNCTIONS

Logarithm

If three numbers, L, b, and N (and $b > 0$, $b \neq 1$, and $N > 0$), are related in such a way that

$$N = b^L$$

then the exponent, L, is defined as "the logarithm of N to the base b." This definition is written in shorthand notation as

$$L = \log_b N$$

Thus, the statement $N = b^L$ has the same meaning as the statement $L = \log_b N$. The statement $N = b^L$ is written in **exponential form.** The statement $L = \log_b N$ is written in **logarithmic form.** Specifically, the statement $9 = 3^2$ may be expressed in logarithmic form as $2 = \log_3 9$, read "2 equals the log of 9 to the base 3."

• **EXAMPLE 5-5** _____

Rewrite the statement $5^3 = 125$ in logarithmic form.

Solution

$3 = \log_5 125$, read "3 equals the log of 125 to the base 5."

• **EXAMPLE 5-6** _____

Rewrite the statement $10^4 = 10,000$ in logarithmic form.

Solution

$4 = \log_{10} 10,000$, read "4 equals the log of 10,000 to the base 10."

Studying the preceding examples, we note that a **logarithm** is an *exponent* of a number called the **base.** Thus, the statement

$$2 = \log_{10} 100$$

has the same meaning as the statement

$$10^2 = 100$$

Note that 2, the logarithm, is the exponent of 10, the base.

• **EXAMPLE 5-7** _____

Find y if $y = \log_2 8$.

Solution

Since $y = \log_2 8$ means $2^y = 8$, then $y = 3$. Thus, 3 is the log of 8 to the base 2.

• **EXAMPLE 5-8** _____

Find $\log_{10} 100$.

Solution

Let $y = \log_{10} 100$. Translated into exponential form, the statement becomes $10^y = 100$. Hence, $y = 2$. Thus, 2 is the log of 100 to the base 10.

Different Bases

We again emphasize that a logarithm is an exponent of a number called the base (study Examples 5-5 through 5-8). Two bases are most commonly used: **base 10** and **base e.** Base-10 logarithms are called **common logarithms.** Base-e logarithms are called **natural logarithms,** or **Napierian logarithms.** The following notation is used to distinguish between common logarithms and natural logarithms. Specifically, the common logarithm of x, $\log_{10} x$, is abbreviated $\log x$; the natural logarithm of x, $\log_e x$, is abbreviated $\ln x$. Thus, the statement $y = \log x$ means $10^y = x$; the statement $y = \ln x$ means $e^y = x$.

• **EXAMPLE 5-9** _____

Find log 10.

Solution

Let $L = \log 10$. Rewriting the statement in exponential form, we have

$$10^L = 10$$

Hence, $L = 1$. Thus, the common logarithm of 10 is 1.

• **EXAMPLE 5-10** _____

Find $\ln e$.

Solution

Let $L = \ln e$. Rewriting this statement in exponential form gives us

$$e^L = e$$

Hence, $L = 1$. Thus, the natural logarithm of e is 1.

• **EXAMPLE 5-11** _____

In Section 5-1, we stated that for any positive number, b, there is a value k such that $b = e^k$. Find k.

Solution

Rewriting the statement $b = e^k$ in logarithmic form, we have

$$k = \ln b$$

Thus, $b = e^k = e^{\ln b}$

Calculators and Logarithms

Appendix C contains common logarithm tables to find common logarithms of numbers and natural logarithm tables to find natural logarithms of numbers. However, if a student has a calculator with "log" and "ln" buttons, then the common log of a number may be easily found by using the "log" button, and the natural log of a number may be determined by using the "ln" button.

• **EXAMPLE 5-12** _____

Use a calculator to determine each of the following:

a) $\ln 5396$ b) $\ln 8.43$
c) $\ln 0.765$ d) $\log 0.492$

Solutions

	Enter	Key	Result
a)	5396	ln	8.593413
b)	8.43	ln	2.131796
c)	0.765	ln	−0.267879
d)	0.492	log	−0.308035

We note that the answers are truncated to six decimal places.

TABLE 5-4

$y = \log x$, or $x = 10^y$	Ordered pairs (x, y)
If $y = -3$, then $x = 10^{-3} = 1/1000$	$(1/1000, -3)$
If $y = -2$, then $x = 10^{-2} = 1/100$	$(1/100, -2)$
If $y = -1$, then $x = 10^{-1} = 1/10$	$(1/10, -1)$
If $y = 0$, then $x = 10^0 = 1$	$(1, 0)$
If $y = 1$, then $x = 10^1 = 10$	$(10, 1)$
If $y = 2$, then $x = 10^2 = 100$	$(100, 2)$
If $y = 3$, then $x = 10^3 = 1000$	$(1000, 3)$

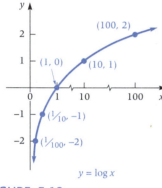

FIGURE 5-18

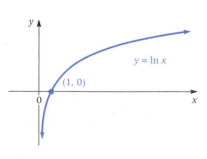

x-intercept
$y = \ln x$ means $x = e^y$.
If $y = 0$, then $x = e^0 = 1$.
Hence, $(1, 0)$ is the x-intercept.

FIGURE 5-19

• **EXAMPLE 5-13** _____

Find x for each of the following:

a) $\ln x = 0.783$ **b)** $\log x = 2.863$

Solutions

a) $\ln x = 0.783$

Rewriting this statement in exponential form, we have

$$x = e^{0.783}$$
$$\approx 2.188 \quad \text{Use the } \boxed{e^x} \text{ button on a calculator.}$$

b) $\log x = 2.863$

Rewriting this statement in exponential form gives

$$x = 10^{2.863}$$
$$\approx 729.458 \quad \text{Use the } \boxed{y^x} \text{ or } \boxed{x^y} \text{ button on a calculator.}$$

Logarithmic Functions

Consider two variables, x and y, related by the equation

$$y = \log x \qquad (x > 0)$$

Since this is an equation with two variables, it may be graphed by computing a table of x- and y-values. Such a table is easily obtained by rewriting the equation $y = \log x$ in exponential form as $10^y = x$ and then choosing arbitrary y-values (see Table 5-4). The graph is sketched in Figure 5-18.

The equation $y = \log x$ defines a logarithmic function. The graph of $y = \log x$, illustrated in Figure 5-18, is typical of the graph of a logarithmic function with a *base greater than 1*. Studying Figure 5-18, we see that $(1, 0)$ is the x-intercept and that the y-axis is a vertical asymptote. Also, note that $y = \log x$ is undefined for $x \leq 0$. A few trial values of x will indicate why. If $x = 0$, then $y = \log 0$ means $10^y = 0$. But no value of y exists such that $10^y = 0$. Thus, $\log 0$ is undefined. However, as y takes on negative values of larger magnitude, 10^y approaches 0, and the y-axis is a vertical asymptote. If x is a negative number, such as $x = -3$, then $y = \log - 3$ means $10^y = -3$. Again, no value of y exists such that $10^y = -3$.

• **EXAMPLE 5-14** _____

Sketch the graph of $y = \ln x$.

Solution

Since this logarithmic function has base e (a number greater than 1), its graph will resemble that of $y = \log x$. See Figure 5-19.

Properties of Logarithms

Logarithms obey certain rules called **properties of logarithms.** These properties simplify much of our work with logarithms. They also enable us to perform certain arithmetic operations using logarithms. We now state the five properties of logarithms.

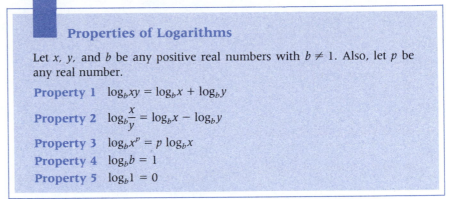

Properties of Logarithms

Let x, y, and b be any positive real numbers with $b \neq 1$. Also, let p be any real number.

Property 1 $\log_b xy = \log_b x + \log_b y$

Property 2 $\log_b \dfrac{x}{y} = \log_b x - \log_b y$

Property 3 $\log_b x^p = p \log_b x$

Property 4 $\log_b b = 1$

Property 5 $\log_b 1 = 0$

Since it is important to understand the meaning of these properties of logarithms, we will consider each in turn.

Property 1 $\log_b xy = \log_b x + \log_b y$

This property states that *the logarithm of a product of two numbers is equal to the sum of their logarithms.* The following are a few numerical illustrations of this property:

$$\log_2 (8 \cdot 32) = \log_2 8 + \log_2 32$$

$$\log (5.23 \times 100) = \log 5.23 + \log 100$$

$$\ln (3 \cdot 7) = \ln 3 + \ln 7$$

Property 2 $\log_b \dfrac{x}{y} = \log_b x - \log_b y$

This property states that *the logarithm of a quotient of two numbers is equal to the difference of their logarithms.* The following are a few numerical illustrations of this property:

$$\log_2 \frac{64}{16} = \log_2 64 - \log_2 16$$

$$\log \frac{5.63}{100} = \log 5.63 - \log 100$$

$$\ln \frac{40}{3} = \ln 40 - \ln 3$$

Property 3 $\log_b x^p = p \log_b x$

This property states that *the logarithm of the pth power of a number is equal to p times the logarithm of the number.* The following are a few numerical illustrations of this property:

$$\log_2 4^3 = 3 \log_2 4$$

$$\ln 8^2 = 2 \ln 8$$

$$\log 3^{1/2} = \frac{1}{2}(\log 3)$$

Property 4 $\log_b b = 1$

This property states that *the logarithm of its base is 1*. Thus,

$$\log_5 5 = 1 \quad \log_3 3 = 1 \quad \log 10 = 1 \quad \ln e = 1$$

Property 5 $\log_b 1 = 0$

This property states that *the logarithm of 1 is 0*. Thus,

$$\log_5 1 = 0 \quad \log_3 1 = 0 \quad \log 1 = 0 \quad \ln 1 = 0$$

We now give the proofs of the properties of logarithms.

Proofs of Properties of Logarithms

Note that the properties of logarithms are simply translations of laws of exponents.

Property 1   Let $L_1 = \log_b x$ and $L_2 = \log_b y$. Rewriting these statements in exponential form, we have

$$x = b^{L_1} \qquad y = b^{L_2}$$

Thus,

$$\begin{aligned} xy &= b^{L_1} \cdot b^{L_2} \\ &= b^{L_1 + L_2} \end{aligned}$$

Rewriting the statement $xy = b^{L_1 + L_2}$ in logarithmic form, we obtain

$$\log_b xy = L_1 + L_2$$

Since $L_1 = \log_b x$ and $L_2 = \log_b y$, the preceding statement may be rewritten as

$$\log_b xy = \log_b x + \log_b y$$

Property 2   Let $L_1 = \log_b x$ and $L_2 = \log_b y$. Rewriting these statements in exponential form results in

$$x = b^{L_1} \qquad y = b^{L_2}$$

Thus,

$$\begin{aligned} \frac{x}{y} &= \frac{b^{L_1}}{b^{L_2}} \\ &= b^{L_1 - L_2} \end{aligned}$$

Rewriting the statement $x/y = b^{L_1 - L_2}$ in logarithmic form, we have

$$\log_b \frac{x}{y} = L_1 - L_2$$

Since $L_1 = \log_b x$ and $L_2 = \log_b y$, the preceding statement may be rewritten as

$$\log_b \frac{x}{y} = \log_b x - \log_b y$$

Property 3 Let $L = \log_b x$. Rewriting this statement in exponential form, we have

$$x = b^L$$

Raising both sides to the pth power, we obtain

$$x^p = (b^L)^p$$
$$= b^{Lp}$$
$$= b^{pL}$$

Rewriting the statement $x^p = b^{pL}$ in logarithmic form gives us

$$\log_b x^p = pL$$

Since $L = \log_b x$, this statement may be rewritten as

$$\log_b x^p = p \log_b x$$

Property 4 Let $L = \log_b b$. This statement is rewritten in exponential form as

$$b^L = b$$

Hence, $L = 1$ and

$$\log_b b = 1$$

Property 5 Let $L = \log_b 1$. This statement is rewritten as

$$b^L = 1$$

Hence, $L = 0$ and

$$\log_b 1 = 0$$

• EXAMPLE 5-15

Given that $\log 3 = 0.4771$ and $\log 5 = 0.6990$, find each of the following using the properties of logarithms:

a) $\log 15$ **b)** $\log 625$
c) $\log \sqrt{5}$ **d)** $\log 0.6$

Solutions

a) $\log 15 = \log (5 \cdot 3)$

$\qquad = \log 5 + \log 3$ Property 1

$\qquad = 0.6990 + 0.4771$

$\qquad = 1.1761$

b) $\log 625 = \log 5^4$

$\qquad = 4 \log 5$ Property 3

$\qquad = 4(0.6990)$

$\qquad = 2.7960$

c) $\log \sqrt{5} = \log 5^{1/2}$

$\qquad = \dfrac{1}{2}(\log 5)$ Property 3

$\qquad = \dfrac{1}{2}(0.6990)$

$\qquad = 0.3495$

d) $\log 0.6 = \log \dfrac{3}{5}$

$\qquad\qquad = \log 3 - \log 5 \qquad$ Property 2

$\qquad\qquad = 0.4771 - 0.6990$

$\qquad\qquad = -0.2219$

• **EXAMPLE 5-16**

Express each of the following in simpler form:

a) $\log\left(\dfrac{A}{BC}\right)$

b) $\log\left(\dfrac{A}{B}\right)^{.706}$

Solutions

a) $\log\left(\dfrac{A}{BC}\right) = \log A - \log (BC) \qquad$ Property 2

$\qquad\qquad = \log A - [\log B + \log C] \qquad$ Property 1

$\qquad\qquad = \log A - \log B - \log C$

b) $\log\left(\dfrac{A}{B}\right)^{.706} = .706 \log \dfrac{A}{B} \qquad$ Property 3

$\qquad\qquad = .706 \, [\log A - \log B] \qquad$ Property 2

$\qquad\qquad = .706 \log A - .706 \log B$

We now state two more properties of logarithms that are useful in many applications. These properties are indicated by the graphs of logarithmic functions (Figures 5-18 and 5-19).

> **Property 6**
>
> $\log_b x = \log_b y$ if and only if $x = y$
>
> where x, y, and b are positive real numbers with $b \neq 1$.

> **Property 7**
>
> $\log_b x > \log_b y$ if and only if $x > y$
>
> where x, y, and b are positive real numbers with $b \neq 1$.

We now give an example where logarithms are used to solve for one quantity in terms of another.

• **EXAMPLE 5-17**

The demand, x (in millions), for a product is related to its unit price, p (in dollars), by the equation

$$p = e^{5 - 0.2x}$$

a) Express the demand, x, in terms of unit price, p.
b) Calculate the demand associated with a unit price of $6.

Solution

a) Taking the natural logarithm of each side, we have

$$\ln p = 5 - 0.2x$$

Solving for x yields

$$x = \frac{\ln p - 5}{-0.2}$$

b) Since $p = \$6$, then

$$x = \frac{\ln p - 5}{-0.2}$$
$$= \frac{\ln 6 - 5}{-0.2}$$
$$\approx \frac{1.791759 - 5}{-0.2}$$
$$\approx 16.04 \text{ million units}$$

Doubling Time: Exponential Growth

If a quantity, y, is related to time, t, by the exponential model

$$y = y^0 e^{kt}$$

where y_0 and k are positive constants, then the *initial value of y* (i.e., the value of y at $t = 0$) is

$$y = y_0 e^{k(0)}$$
$$= y_0 e^0$$
$$= y_0(1)$$
$$= y_0$$

The time it takes for the quantity y_0 to double itself is determined by setting $y = 2y_0$ and solving the resulting equation for t. Hence,

$$y = y_0 e^{kt}$$
$$2y_0 = y_0 e^{kt} \qquad \text{Set } y = 2y_0.$$
$$2 = e^{kt} \qquad \text{Multiply both sides by } 1/y_0.$$
$$kt = \ln 2 \qquad \text{Rewrite in logarithmic form.}$$
$$t = \frac{\ln 2}{k} \qquad \text{Doubling time}$$

For example, if

$$y = 1000e^{0.10t}$$

where t denotes time (in years), the initial value of y is 1000, and the doubling time is given by

$$t = \frac{\ln 2}{0.10}$$

$$= \frac{0.6931}{0.10}$$

$$= 6.931 \text{ years} \qquad \text{Doubling time}$$

Exercises 5-2

Rewrite each of the following statements in logarithmic notation:

1. $5^2 = 25$ **2.** $4^2 = 16$ **3.** $2^6 = 64$

4. $10^5 = 100,000$ **5.** $10^{-2} = 0.01$ **6.** $10^1 = 10$

7. $t^w = S$ **8.** $4^3 = 64$ **9.** $b^{x+y} = N$

Find y for each of the following:

10. $y = \log_3 9$ **11.** $y = \log_9 81$

12. $y = \log_2 8$ **13.** $y = \log_3 1$

14. $y = \log_2 16$ **15.** $y = \log_7 7$

16. $y = \log_{10} 1$ **17.** $y = \log_{10} 10$

18. $y = \log_{10} 100$ **19.** $y = \log_{10} 1000$

20. $y = \log_{10} 10,000$ **21.** $y = \log_{10} 100,000$

22. $y = \ln 1$ **23.** $y = \ln e^2$

Find each of the following logarithms:

24. $\log_3 81$ **25.** $\log_2 32$ **26.** $\log_4 16$

27. $\log_3 1$ **28.** $\log_5 1$ **29.** $\log_8 1$

30. $\log 1$ **31.** $\log 10$ **32.** $\log 100$

33. $\log 1000$ **34.** $\log 10,000$ **35.** $\log 100,000$

36. Sketch the graph of $y = \log_2 x$. What is the x-intercept?

37. Sketch the graph of $y = \log_3 x$. What is the x-intercept?

Given that $\log 2 = 0.3010$ and $\log 7 = 0.8451$, find each of the following using the properties of logarithms:

38. $\log 14$ **39.** $\log 3.5$ **40.** $\log \frac{2}{7}$

41. $\log 49$ **42.** $\log 98$ **43.** $\log 56$

44. $\log \sqrt{2}$ **45.** $\log \sqrt[3]{2}$ **46.** $\log \sqrt{7}$

47. $\log \sqrt{14}$ **48.** $\log \sqrt[5]{7}$ **49.** $\log \sqrt{98}$

Given that $\log 3.71 = 0.5694$, find each of the following using the properties of logarithms. (Remember that $\log 10 = 1$.)

50. $\log 37.1$ **51.** $\log 371$ **52.** $\log 3710$

53. $\log 37,100$ **54.** $\log 371,000$ **55.** $\log 0.371$

56. $\log 0.0371$ **57.** $\log 0.00371$ **58.** $\log 0.000371$

Given that $\ln 3 = 1.098612$ and $\ln 2 = 0.693147$, find each of the following using the properties of logarithms:

59. $\ln 6$ **60.** $\ln 1.5$ **61.** $\ln \frac{2}{3}$

62. $\ln 81$ **63.** $\ln 8$ **64.** $\ln 12$

65. $\ln \sqrt{3}$ **66.** $\ln \sqrt[3]{2}$ **67.** $\ln 0.75$

Using a calculator with a "log" button, find each of the following:

68. log 4.76

69. log 8.73

70. log 92.1

71. log 4760

72. log 0.0673

73. log 0.80

Using a calculator with an "ln" button, find each of the following.

74. ln 2.8

75. ln 10

76. ln 25

77. ln 0.15

78. ln 0.60

79. ln 80

Find x for each of the following:

80. $\log x = 0.7738$

81. $\log x = 0.9047$

82. $\log x = 2.7738$

83. $\log x = 3.9047$

84. $\log x = 1.4698$

85. $\log x = 5.4099$

86. $\ln x = 0.6419$

87. $\log x = 1.3610$

88. $\ln x = 3.6889$

89. $\ln x = 1.7047$

Express each of the following numbers as e^k:

90. 7

91. 3.4

92. 14

93. 5.5

94. 750

Use properties of logarithms to express each of the following in simpler form.

95. $\log \left(\dfrac{xy}{z} \right)$

96. $\log \left(\dfrac{x}{y} \right)^{5.83}$

97. $\log (x^2 y)$

98. $\log (xy)^7$

99. $\log \sqrt{xy}$

100. $\log \sqrt{\dfrac{xy}{z}}$

Applications

101. *Sales.* A company's sales, $S(x)$ (in thousands of dollars), are related to advertising expenditure, x (in thousands of dollars), by the equation

$$S(x) = 100,000 + 8000 \ln (x + 2)$$

a) Calculate the sales associated with each of the following advertising expenditures: $1000, $3000, $10,000, and $20,000.

b) Calculate $S(21) - S(20)$ and interpret the answer.

c) If the company increases its advertising expenditures from $30,000 to $31,000, find the corresponding increase in sales.

102. *Sales.* A company's sales, $S(x)$ (in thousands), are related to advertising expenditures, x, (in thousands of dollars), by the equation

$$S(x) = 200,000 + 10,000 \ln x$$

a) Calculate the sales associated with each of the following advertising expenditures: $2000, $5000, $10,000, and $30,000.

b) Calculate $S(13) = S(12)$ and interpret the answer.

c) If the company increases its advertising expenditure from $19,000 to $20,000, find the corresponding increase in sales.

103. *Revenue.* A company's sales revenue, $R(x)$ (in thousands of dollars), is related to the number of units sold, x, by the equation

$$R(x) = 10 \log(20x + 1)$$

a) Calculate and interpret each of the following: $R(1)$, $R(2)$, $R(5)$, and $R(10)$.

b) Calculate $R(11) - R(10)$ and interpret the answer.

c)   If the company increases its sales from 20 units to 21 units, calculate the increase in sales revenue.

104. *Cost.* A company's total production cost, $C(x)$ (in dollars), is related to the number of units produced, x, by the equation.

$$C(x) = 9000 + 10 \ln(x + 1)$$

a)   Calculate and interpret each of the following: $C(0)$, $C(1)$, $C(5)$, and $C(10)$.
b)   Calculate $C(19) - C(18)$ and interpret the answer.
c)   If the company increases its production from 12 units to 13 units, calculate the increase in total production cost.

105. *Tripling time: Exponential growth.* If a quantity, y, is related to time, t, by the exponential model

$$y = y_0 e^{kt}$$

where y_0 and k are positive constants, verify that the tripling time is given by

$$t = \frac{\ln 3}{k}$$

If

$$y = 2000 e^{0.20t}$$

where t denotes time in days,
a)   Determine the initial value of y.
b)   Determine the tripling time.
c)   Determine the quadrupling time.

106. *Doubling time.* If a quantity, y, is related to time, t, by the exponential model

$$y = y_0 b^{kt}$$

where y_0, k, and b are positive constants such that $b > 1$ and $b \neq e$, verify that the doubling time is given by

$$t = \frac{\ln 2}{k \ln b}$$

107. *Population growth.* The population, P, of a certain town is related to time, t (in years), by the exponential function

$$P = 1000 e^{0.05t}$$

a)   How long will it take for the population to double itself?
b)   How long will it take for the population to triple itself?

108. *Demand.* The demand, x (in billions), for a product is related to its unit price, p (in dollars), by the equation

$$p = e^{8 - 0.3x}$$

a)   Express demand, x, in terms of unit price, p.
b)   Find the demand associated with a unit price of $9.

109. *Supply.* The supply, y (in millions), for a product is related to its unit price, p (in dollars), by the supply equation

$$p = e^{1 + 0.3y}$$

a) Express supply, y, in terms of unit price, p.

b) Find the supply associated with a unit price of $10.

5-3 • FITTING EXPONENTIAL MODELS (OPTIONAL)

In this section, we discuss fitting an exponential model of the form

$$y = ab^x$$

to a set of data points. First, we restate the above equation in logarithmic form by taking the natural logarithm of each side to obtain

$$
\begin{aligned}
\ln y &= \ln ab^x && \text{Logarithm property 6} \\
&= \ln a + \ln b^x && \text{Logarithm property 2} \\
&= \ln a + x \ln b && \text{Logarithm property 3} \\
&= \ln a + (\ln b)x
\end{aligned}
$$

Thus, the exponential equation $y = ab^x$ is restated in logarithmic form as $\ln y = \ln a + (\ln b)x$. Observe that the logarithmic form expresses a linear relationship between the variables $\ln y$ and x. This means that for points (x, y) on the graph of the exponential function $y = ab^x$, the graph of the corresponding points $(x, \ln y)$ is a straight line. In other words, if a plot of y-values versus x-values has the graph of an exponential function $y = ab^x$, then a plot of $\ln y$-values versus x-values has the graph of a straight line. Thus, given points (x, y) of an exponential model $y = ab^x$, the coefficients a and b are determined by fitting the linear model $\ln y = \ln a + (\ln b)x$ (straight line) to the points $(x, \ln y)$ and then by determining a and b, given their logarithms. We note that common logarithms can be used in place of natural logarithms.

To Fit an Exponential Model

The **exponential model**

$$y = ab^x$$

is restated in **logarithmic form** as

$$\ln y = \ln a + (\ln b)x \qquad \text{Linear form}$$

             ⌐ slope

       ⌐ $\ln y$-intercept

This has the following implications:

1. If a plot of y-values versus x-values has the graph of an exponential function $y = ab^x$, then a plot of $\ln y$-values versus x-values has the graph of a straight line, as is illustrated in Figure 5-20.

continues

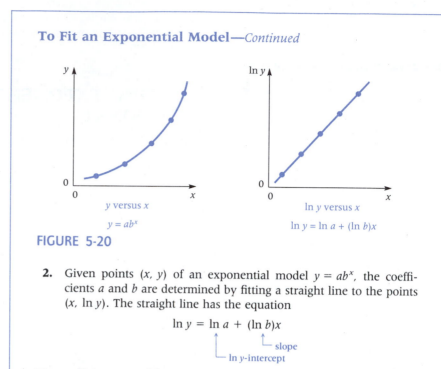

To Fit an Exponential Model—*Continued*

y versus x

$y = ab^x$

ln y versus x

$\ln y = \ln a + (\ln b)x$

FIGURE 5-20

2. Given points (x, y) of an exponential model $y = ab^x$, the coefficients a and b are determined by fitting a straight line to the points $(x, \ln y)$. The straight line has the equation

$$\ln y = \ln a + (\ln b)x$$

ln y-intercept ⟍ ⟋ slope

The coefficients a and b are determined from their logarithms.
Note: Common logarithms can be used in place of natural logarithms.

As an example, we will determine the coefficients a and b of the exponential model $y = ab^x$ whose graph contains the points $(1, 3)$ and $(5, 30)$. Use the following procedure.

Step 1 *Replace the y-value of each given data point with its logarithm.* Use either common or natural logarithms. We will use natural logarithms.

Using a calculator, we find that $\ln 3 \approx 1.10$ and $\ln 30 \approx 3.40$. This gives the corresponding points $(1, 1.10)$ and $(5, 3.40)$, which are plotted in Figure 5-21.

Step 2 *Find the equation of the straight line passing through the new points* $(x, \ln y)$. Begin by finding the slope.

$$\text{slope} = \frac{3.40 - 1.10}{5 - 1}$$

$$= \frac{2.30}{4} \approx 0.58$$

Using the point-slope form

$$y - y_1 = m(x - x_1)$$

with y replaced by $\ln y$, we choose the point $(1, 1.10)$ to obtain

$$\ln y - 1.10 = 0.58(x - 1)$$

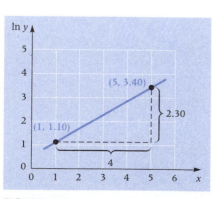

FIGURE 5-21

Simplifying, we get

$$\ln y - 1.10 = 0.58x - 0.58$$
$$= 0.58x - 0.58$$
$$\ln y = 0.58x - 0.58 + 1.10$$
$$\ln y = 0.58x + 0.52 \qquad \text{Logarithmic form}$$

This last equation is our answer in logarithmic form. However, it must be written in the exponential form $y = ab^x$.

Step 3 *Use the definition of a logarithm to determine the coefficients* a *and* b *of the exponential equation* y = ab^x. The above equation, when written as

$$\ln y = 0.52 + 0.58x$$

is of the form

$$\ln y = \ln a + (\ln b)x$$

where

$$\ln a = 0.52 \qquad \text{and} \qquad \ln b = 0.58$$

Rewriting the above in exponential form allows us to solve for a and b (with a calculator) as indicated below.

$$a = e^{0.52} \qquad\qquad b = e^{0.58}$$
$$\approx 1.68 \qquad\qquad \approx 1.79$$

Thus, the exponential model

$$y = ab^x$$

containing the points (1, 3) and (5, 30) is given by

$$y = 1.68(1.79^x)$$

Application

Earnings Per Share

Annual earnings per share (EPS) in dollars of a corporation are determined by dividing the corporation's annual earnings by the number of shares of its stock outstanding. That is,

$$\text{EPS} = \frac{\text{annual earnings}}{\text{number of shares of stock outstanding}}$$

The EPS is used to evaluate the performance of a corporation.

The EPS for Lotus Development Corporation is given for the indicated years in Table 5-5 on page 324. Note that the years are coded, with $x = 1$ corresponding to 1986, $x = 2$ to 1987, . . ., $x = 5$ to 1990. Graphs of y- versus x-values and $\ln y$- versus x-values are given in Figure 5-22 on page 324. Observe that the graph of $\ln y$- versus x-values appears to have a linear trend. Thus, we fit the linear form

$$\ln y = \ln a + (\ln b)x$$

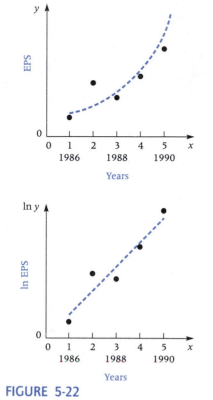

FIGURE 5-22

TABLE 5-5   **Lotus Development Corporation: Earnings per share**

Years	1986	1987	1988	1989	1990
x = coded years	1	2	3	4	5
y = EPS	1.03	1.58	1.29	1.61	2.30
ln y	0.0296	0.4574	0.2546	0.4762	0.8329

Step 1   We use the first and last data points with ln y-values, $(1, 0.0296)$ and $(5, 0.8329)$.

Step 2   The slope is given by

$$m = \frac{0.8329 - 0.0296}{5 - 1}$$

$$= \frac{0.8033}{4}$$

$$= 0.20 \qquad \text{Slope}$$

Using the point-slope form

$$y - y_1 = m(x - x_1)$$

with y replaced by ln y, we choose the point $(5, 0.8329)$ to obtain

$$\ln y - 0.8329 = 0.20(x - 5)$$

$$= 0.20x - 1$$

Solving for ln y gives

$$\ln y = 0.20x - 0.17 \qquad \text{Logarithmic form}$$

Step 3   The above result, when rewritten as

$$\ln y = -0.17 + 0.20x$$

is of the form

$$\ln y = \ln a + (\ln b)x$$

where

$$\ln a = -0.17 \qquad \text{and} \qquad \ln b = 0.20$$

Hence,

$$a = e^{-0.17} \qquad\qquad b = e^{0.20}$$

$$\approx 0.84 \qquad\qquad\qquad \approx 1.22 \qquad \text{Use a calculator}$$

Thus, the fitted exponential model, $y = ab^x$, is given by

$$y = 0.84(1.22^x)$$

Using the Model to Forecast.   If the EPS for Lotus Development Corporation continue to grow in accordance with the above model, then the 1991 EPS are forecast by substituting $x = 6$ into the equation as given below.

$$y = 0.84(1.22^6)$$

$$\approx 0.84(3.2973)$$

$$\approx 2.77 \qquad \text{1991 EPS}$$

Caution: Although we used the first and last data points to fit the linear model ln y = ln a + (ln b)x, this does not necessarily give the best-fitting linear model. For this example, it does provide a reasonably good fit to the set of data points. Recall the goodness of fit of a model was discussed in the "Extra Dividends" following Chapter 1. Those concepts also apply to exponential models. Although we do not pursue the goodness of fit of exponential models here, we will learn how to determine the equation of a best-fitting model to a set of data points in Section 8-4.

Exercises 5-3

Determine the coefficients a and b of the exponential model $y = ab^x$ whose graph passes through the following given points.

1. (2, 6) and (8, 40)
2. (1, 8) and (5, 50)
3. (3, 20) and (6, 70)
4. (4, 10) and (7, 80)
5. (1, 15) and (5, 85)
6. (3, 27) and (8, 92)

Applications

Earnings Per Share

In exercises 7-9 the EPS of a company is given for a period. For each exercise
a) Fit the exponential model $y = ab^x$ by using the points appearing in color screen.
b) Assuming that the EPS continue to grow in accordance with the model determined in part a, forecast the next year's EPS.

7. **Kellogg Company**

Year	1980	1981	1982	1983	1984	1985	1986	1987	1988	1989
x	1	1	3	4	5	6	7	8	9	10
EPS	1.21	1.35	1.49	1.59	1.68	2.28	2.58	3.20	3.90	3.46

8. **Bristol-Myers Squibb Company**

Year	1980	1981	1982	1983	1984	1985	1986	1987	1988	1989
x	1	2	3	4	5	6	7	8	9	10
EPS	1.02	1.15	1.30	1.50	1.73	1.93	2.07	2.47	2.88	1.43

9. **Ford Motor Company**

Year	1983	1984	1985	1986	1987	1988	1989
x	1	2	3	4	5	6	7
EPS	3.43	5.27	4.55	6.16	9.05	10.96	8.22

10. *Population growth.* The population of a particular town has grown exponentially from 20,000 in 1985 to 50,000 in 1990.
    a) Determine the equation of the exponential model $y = ab^x$ whose curve passes through the two data points.
    b) If the town's population continues to grow in accordance with the model derived in part a, forecast the town's population for 1991.

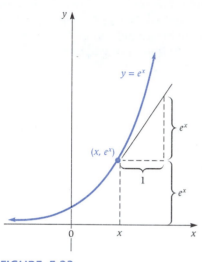

FIGURE 5-23

5-4

• DERIVATIVES OF EXPONENTIAL FUNCTIONS

In this section, we discuss rules for finding derivatives of exponential functions. Our first rule involves the exponential function $y = e^x$.

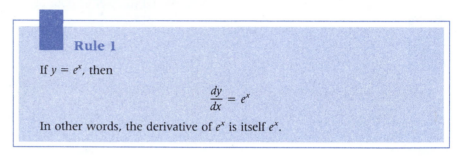

Rule 1

If $y = e^x$, then

$$\frac{dy}{dx} = e^x$$

In other words, the derivative of e^x is itself e^x.

The graphical implication, of course, is that the slope of the graph of $y = e^x$ at the point (x, e^x) is the height e^x, as shown in Figure 5-23.

An informal proof of rule 1 is as follows. If $y = f(x) = e^x$, then

$$\frac{dy}{dx} = f'(x)$$

$$= \lim_{\Delta x \to 0} \frac{f(x + \Delta x) - f(x)}{\Delta x}$$

$$= \lim_{\Delta x \to 0} \frac{e^{x + \Delta x} - e^x}{\Delta x}$$

$$= \lim_{\Delta x \to 0} \frac{e^x e^{\Delta x} - e^x}{\Delta x}$$

$$= \lim_{\Delta x \to 0} e^x \frac{e^{\Delta x} - 1}{\Delta x}$$

$$= e^x \lim_{\Delta x \to 0} \frac{e^{\Delta x} - 1}{\Delta x} \qquad \text{Limit property 3}$$

It is shown below that

$$\lim_{\Delta x \to 0} \frac{e^{\Delta x} - 1}{\Delta x} = 1$$

Thus, the resulting expression for dy/dx becomes

$$\frac{dy}{dx} = e^x \cdot 1 = e^x$$

To show that $\lim_{\Delta x \to 0} \dfrac{e^{\Delta x} - 1}{\Delta x} = 1$, we note that, by definition,

$$e = \lim_{x \to \infty} \left(1 + \frac{1}{x}\right)^x$$

This can be restated as

$$e = \lim_{x \to 0} (1 + x)^{1/x}$$

In terms of Δx,

$$e = \lim_{\Delta x \to 0} (1 + \Delta x)^{1/\Delta x}$$

so that for small values of Δx,

$$e \approx (1 + \Delta x)^{1/\Delta x}$$

and, therefore,

$$e^{\Delta x} \approx 1 + \Delta x$$

since

$$[(1 + \Delta x)^{1/\Delta x}]^{\Delta x} = (1 + \Delta x)^{\Delta x/\Delta x} = 1 + \Delta x$$

Substituting this result into the expression

$$\frac{e^{\Delta x} - 1}{\Delta x}$$

gives

$$\lim_{\Delta x \to 0} \frac{e^{\Delta x} - 1}{\Delta x} = 1$$

• **EXAMPLE 5-18**

If $y = 8e^x$, find dy/dx.

Solution

Using rule 1 and the constant multiplier rule, we have

$$\frac{dy}{dx} = 8\frac{d}{dx}(e^x) = 8e^x$$

• **EXAMPLE 5-19**

If $y = e^u$, find dy/du.

Solution

Using rule 1, we write

$$\frac{dy}{du} = e^u$$

We now consider exponential functions such as

$$y = e^{x^2 - 3x}$$

This function is of the form

$$y = e^u$$

where u is a function of x. The derivative of such a function is found by applying the chain rule to exponential functions. Recall that, according to the chain rule, if y is a function of u and u is a function of x, then

$$\frac{dy}{dx} = \frac{dy}{du} \cdot \frac{du}{dx}$$

Since $y = e^u$, then $dy/du = e^u$. Hence, we have

$$\frac{dy}{dx} = e^u \frac{du}{dx}$$

Thus, we have the following rule.

Rule 2

If $y = e^u$, where u is a differentiable function of x, then

$$\frac{dy}{dx} = e^u \frac{du}{dx}$$

Returning to the function

$$y = e^{x^2 - 3x}$$

with $u = x^2 - 3x$, its derivative is

$$\frac{dy}{dx} = e^u \frac{du}{dx}$$

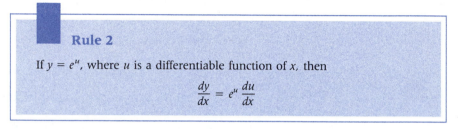

$$= e^{x^2 - 3x}(2x - 3) \qquad \boxed{\begin{array}{l} u = x^2 - 3x \\ \dfrac{du}{dx} = 2x - 3 \end{array}}$$

• EXAMPLE 5-20

If $y = e^{x^5 - 8x}$, find dy/dx.

Solution

Since $u = x^5 - 8x$, then $du/dx = 5x^4 - 8$. Hence, we obtain

$$\frac{dy}{dx} = e^u \frac{du}{dx}$$

$$= e^{x^5 - 8x}(5x^4 - 8)$$

• EXAMPLE 5-21

If $y = 7e^{5x}$, find dy/dx.

Solution

Since $u = 5x$, then $du/dx = 5$. Using rule 2 and the constant multiplier rule, we have

$$\frac{dy}{dx} = 7e^{5x}(5)$$

$$= 35e^{5x}$$

• **EXAMPLE 5-22** _____

If $f(t) = 800e^{-0.5t}$, find

a) $f'(t)$
b) $f'(6)$

Solutions

a) $f'(t) = 800e^{-0.5t}(-0.5)$
      $= -400e^{-0.5t}$
b) $f'(6) = -400e^{-0.5(6)}$
        $= -400e^{-3}$
        $\approx -400(0.049787)$
        ≈ -19.91

Applications

• **EXAMPLE 5-23**

If $1000 is invested for x years at 8% compounded continuously, then the total amount is given by $S(x) = 1000e^{0.08x}$.

a) Find $S'(x)$.
b) Find $S'(2)$ and interpret.
c) Find $S'(5)$ and interpret.
d) If, for each year beyond the fifth, interest is computed as simple interest instead of interest compounded continuously, find the total amount at the end of the tenth year. Compare this result with what the total amount should be under normal conditions.

Solutions

a) $S'(x) = 1000e^{0.08x}(0.08)$
         $= 80e^{0.08x}$
b) $S'(2) = 80e^{0.08(2)}$
          $= 80e^{0.16}$
          $\approx 80(1.173511)$
          $\approx \$93.88$

Thus, at the end of the second year, the total amount is instantaneously increasing by $93.88 per year.

c) $S'(5) = 80e^{0.08(5)}$
          $= 80e^{0.40}$
          $\approx 80(1.491825)$
          $\approx \$119.35$

Thus, at the end of the fifth year, the total amount is instantaneously increasing by $119.35 per year.

d) If, for each year beyond the fifth, interest is computed as simple interest instead of interest compounded continuously, the total amount increases by the same constant amount for each year beyond the fifth. Then its graph is represented by the tangent line to $S(x)$ at $x = 5$ (see Figure 5-24 on page 330). Since the slope of the tangent line is $S'(5) = 119.35$ and its point of tangency is $(5, S(5))$, or $(5, 1491.83)$, then according to the point-slope form

$$y - y_1 = m(x - x_1)$$

its equation is

$$y - 1491.83 = 119.35(x - 5)$$
$$y = 119.35x + 895.08$$

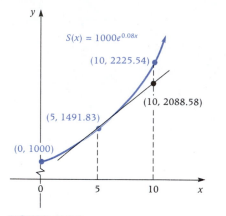

$S(x) = 1000e^{0.08x}$

(10, 2225.54)

(10, 2088.58)

(5, 1491.83)

(0, 1000)

FIGURE 5-24

Thus, at the end of the tenth year ($x = 10$), the total amount is

$$y = 119.35(10) + 895.08$$
$$= \$2088.58$$

Note that under normal conditions of 8% compounded continuously, the total amount at the end of the tenth year is

$$S(10) = 1000e^{0.08(10)}$$
$$= 1000e^{0.80}$$
$$\approx 1000(2.225541)$$
$$\approx \$2225.54$$

These amounts are graphically illustrated in Figure 5-24.

• **EXAMPLE 5-24**   **Population Growth.** _____

The population, $P(t)$, of a city is related to time, t (in years), by the equation

$$P(t) = 60,000e^{0.08t}$$

where $t = 1$ denotes the end of year 19X1, $t = 2$ denotes the end of year 19X2, . . . , etc. Find the rate of change of the population

a)   At $t = 5$. **b)**   At $t = 9$.

Solutions

First, we determine

$$P'(t) = 60,000e^{0.08t}(0.08)$$
$$= 4800e^{0.08t}$$

a) $P'(5) = 4800e^{0.08(5)}$
$$= 4800e^{0.40}$$
$$\approx 4800(1.491825)$$
$$\approx 7161$$

Thus, at $t = 5$ (the end of year 19X5), the city's population is growing at the rate of approximately 7161 people per year.

b) $P'(9) = 4800e^{0.08(9)}$
$$= 4800e^{0.72}$$
$$\approx 4800(2.054433)$$
$$\approx 9861$$

Thus, at $t = 9$ (the end of year 19X9), the city's population is growing at the rate of approximately 9861 people per year.

• **EXAMPLE 5-25**   **Market Penetration: Modified Exponential Model.** _____

In Section 5-1, we learned that the model

$$y = 98 - 90e^{-0.19x}$$

expresses the relationship between y, the percentage of the market penetrated by television sets, and x, the time in years, where $x = 0$ corresponds to the year 1950, . . . , and $x = 38$ corresponds to the year 1988.

a)   Find dy/dx.
b)   Evaluate dy/dx at $x = 1$ and interpret the result.
c)   Evaluate dy/dx at $x = 5$ and interpret the result.
d)   Evaluate dy/dx at $x = 20$ and interpret the result.

Solutions

a) $\dfrac{dy}{dx} = (-90)e^{-0.19x}(-0.19) = 17.1e^{-0.19x}$

b) At $x = 1$,

$$\frac{dy}{dx} = 17.1e^{-0.19(1)} \approx 17.1(0.8270) \approx 14.14$$

Thus, at $x = 1$ (the year 1951), the percentage of the market penetrated by television sets was increasing at a rate of 14.14 percentage points per year.

c) At $x = 5$,

$$\frac{dy}{dx} = 17.1e^{-0.19(5)} = 17.1e^{-0.95} \approx 17.1(0.3867) \approx 6.61$$

Thus, at $x = 5$ (the year 1955), the percentage of the market penetrated by television sets was increasing at a rate of 6.61 percentage points per year.

d) At $x = 20$,

$$\frac{dy}{dx} = 17.1e^{-0.19(20)} = 17.1e^{-3.8} \approx 17.1(0.0223) \approx 0.38$$

Thus, at $x = 20$ (the year 1970), the percentage of the market penetrated by television sets was increasing at a rate of 0.38 percentage points per year.

Comparing the results of parts b, c, and d, note how the increase in market penetration declines with increasing time. This is illustrated graphically in Figure 5-25 by the slopes of the tangent lines at $x = 1$, 5, and 20.

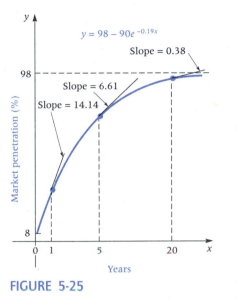

$y = 98 - 90e^{-0.19x}$

Slope = 0.38

Slope = 6.61

Slope = 14.14

Market penetration (%)

Years

FIGURE 5-25

Up to this point, we have calculated the derivatives of exponential functions having base e. The next rule tells us how to calculate derivatives of exponential functions with other bases. We consider functions with equations of the form $y = b^u$, where u is a function of x, $b > 0$, and $b \neq e$.

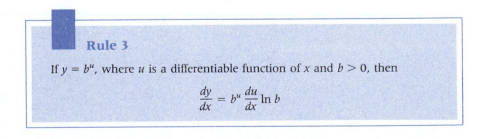

Rule 3

If $y = b^u$, where u is a differentiable function of x and $b > 0$, then

$$\frac{dy}{dx} = b^u \frac{du}{dx} \ln b$$

Note that if $b = e$, then rule 3 becomes rule 2. The proof of rule 3 appears as follows.

PROOF OF RULE 3

We make use of the fact stated in Section 5-2 that any positive number b can be expressed as $e^{\ln b}$. Hence,

$$y = b^u$$
$$= (e^{\ln b})^u$$
$$= e^{u \ln b}$$

Using rule 2 of this section, we find

$$\frac{dy}{dx} = e^{u \ln b} \frac{d}{dx}(u \ln b)$$

$$= e^{u \ln b} \frac{du}{dx} \ln b \qquad \text{Constant multiplier rule}$$

Replacing $e^{u \ln b}$ with b^u, this equation becomes

$$\frac{dy}{dx} = b^u \frac{du}{dx} \ln b$$

• **EXAMPLE 5-26** ─────────────────────────

If $y = 5^{x^7 - 4x}$, find dy/dx.

Solution

Note that $b = 5$, $u = x^7 - 4x$, and $du/dx = 7x^6 - 4$. Hence, we get

$$\frac{dy}{dx} = b^u \frac{du}{dx} \ln b$$
$$= 5^{x^7 - 4x}(7x^6 - 4) \ln 5$$
$$\approx 5^{x^7 - 4x}(7x^6 - 4)(1.609438)$$

─── •

We now do a few examples involving the product and quotient rules.

• **EXAMPLE 5-27** ─────────────────────────

If $y = x^4 e^{3x}$, find dy/dx.

Solution

Using the product rule, we have

$$\frac{dy}{dx} = (\text{first})(\text{derivative of second}) + (\text{second})(\text{derivative of first})$$

$$\frac{dy}{dx} = x^4 e^{3x}(3) + e^{3x}(4x^3)$$

$$= 3x^4 e^{3x} + 4x^3 e^{3x} \qquad \text{Simplifying}$$
$$= x^3 e^{3x}(3x + 4) \qquad \text{Factoring using the distributive law}$$

• **EXAMPLE 5-28** ─────────────────────────

If $y = \dfrac{e^{8x}}{x^5}$, find dy/dx.

Solution

Using the quotient rule, we have

$$\frac{dy}{dx} = \frac{(\text{denominator})\begin{pmatrix}\text{derivative}\\\text{of numerator}\end{pmatrix} - (\text{numerator})\begin{pmatrix}\text{derivative}\\\text{of denominator}\end{pmatrix}}{(\text{denominator})^2}$$

$$\frac{dy}{dx} = \frac{x^5 e^{8x}(8) - e^{8x}(5x^4)}{(x^5)^2}$$

$$= \frac{8x^5 e^{8x} - 5x^4 e^{8x}}{x^{10}} \qquad \text{Simplifying}$$

$$= \frac{x^4 e^{8x}(8x - 5)}{x^{10}} \qquad \text{Factoring using the distributive law}$$

$$= \frac{e^{8x}(8x - 5)}{x^6}$$

Exercises 5-4

Find the derivative of each of the following:

1. $y = e^{4x}$
2. $y = e^{-x}$
3. $y = 4e^{-2x}$
4. $y = -e^{-x}$
5. $f(x) = -2e^{-0.1x}$
6. $f(x) = e^x$
7. $y = e^{x^5 - 7x}$
8. $f(x) = 6e^{x^3 - 2x}$
9. $y = e^{2x-5}$
10. $f(x) - 4e^{3x^2 + 4x}$
11. $y = 4^{x^2 - 3x}$
12. $f(x) = 2^{3x^2 - 5x}$
13. $y = 4^{-0.02x}$
14. $f(x) = -2(3^{-x})$
15. $y = (x^5 - 4x^2)e^{x^4 - 7x}$
16. $y = (x^3 - 2)e^{-x^2}$
17. $f(x) = (x^4 + 8x)e^{x^3 + 5x}$
18. $y = x^2 e^{x^5 + 6}$
19. $y = \dfrac{e^x + e^{-x}}{x}$
20. $y = \dfrac{3e^x - e^{-x}}{x}$
21. $y = \dfrac{e^x - e^{-x}}{x}$
22. $y = e^{\sqrt{4 - x^2}}$
23. $f(x) = \dfrac{e^{x^3 - 4x}}{x^2 - 3x}$
24. $f(x) = \dfrac{e^{x+6}}{x + 6}$
25. $y = e^{\sqrt{25 - x^2}}$
26. $y = e^{-x^2}$
27. $y = e^{\sqrt{x}}$
28. $y = x^2 e^{-4x}$
29. $y = \dfrac{800}{1 + 40e^{-3x}}$
30. $y = \dfrac{60}{1 - 20e^{5x}}$
31. $y = \dfrac{1000}{5 - 80e^{-2x}}$
32. $y = \dfrac{70}{1 + 60e^{-2x}}$
33. $y = (4x + e^{-x})^2$
34. $y = (2x - e^x)^2$
35. $f(x) = \sqrt{x + e^{-x}}$
36. $f(x) = \sqrt{x - e^x}$
37. $y = \sqrt{x^2 + e^{-x^2}}$
38. $y = \sqrt{x^3 - e^{-x^2}}$

39. Find the equation of the straight line tangent to $f(x) = e^x$ at $x = 0$. Graph $f(x)$ and its tangent line.
40. Find the equation of the straight line tangent to $f(x) = e^{-x}$ at $x = 1$. Graph $f(x)$ and its tangent line.

Applications

41. *Continuous compounding.* If $10,000 is invested for x years at 10% compounded continuously, then the total amount is given by

$$S(x) = 10{,}000e^{0.10x}$$

a) Find $S'(x)$.
b) Find $S'(3)$ and interpret.
c) Find $S'(4)$ and interpret.
d) Find the rate of change of the total amount at $x = 5$.
e) If the total amount increases by the same amount for each year beyond the fifth, find the total amount at the end of the ninth year. Compare this with what the total amount should be under normal conditions.
f) Graphically illustrate part e.

42. *Continuous compounding.* If $50,000 is invested for x years at 9% compounded continuously, then the total amount is given by

$$S(x) = 50{,}000e^{0.09x}$$

a) Find $S'(x)$.
b) Find $S'(2)$ and interpret.
c) Find $S'(3)$ and interpret.
d) Find the rate of change of the total amount at $x = 4$.
e) If the total amount increases by the same amount for each year beyond the fourth, find the total amount at the end of the seventh year. Compare this with what the total amount should be under normal conditions.
f) Graphically illustrate part e.

43. *Employee growth.* The number of employees, $P(x)$, of a certain company is related to time, x (in years), by the exponential function defined by

$$P(x) = 1000e^{0.06x} \qquad (x \geq 0)$$

a) Find the rate of change of the number of employees at $x = 5$. Is the number of employees increasing or decreasing at this point?
b) Find the rate of change of the number of employees at $x = 10$. Is the number of employees increasing or decreasing at this point?
c) If the number of employees increases by a constant amount for each year beyond the tenth, find the number of employees at $x = 13$.
d) Graphically illustrate part c.

44. *Sales decay.* If a product is not advertised, then its monthly sales decay is in accordance with the equation

$$y(t) = 2000e^{-0.60t} \qquad (t \geq 0)$$

where $y(t)$ represents monthly sales at time t (in months).
a) Find $y'(t)$.
b) Find the rate of change of sales at $t = 1/2$.
c) How fast are sales decaying at $t = 2$?

45. *Learning curve.* The function defined by

$$N(x) = 50 - 50e^{-0.3x} \qquad (x \geq 0)$$

is a learning curve, where $N(x)$ represents the number of items produced by an assembly-line worker during the xth day after the training period. Is daily production increasing or decreasing at $x = 5$, and at what rate?

46. *Temperature.* The temperature of a heated cup of coffee, y, is related to the time elapsed, t (in minutes), by

$$y = 150e^{-0.02t} + 65 \qquad (t \geq 0)$$

Is the temperature increasing or decreasing at $t = 5$, and at what rate?

47. *Market penetration: Modified exponential model.* The percentage of market penetration for a product x years after it has been introduced is given by

$$y = 90 - 82e^{-0.30x}$$

   a) Find dy/dx.
   b) Evaluate dy/dx at $x = 1$ and interpret the result.
   c) Evaluate dy/dx at $x = 6$ and interpret the result.
   d) Evaluate dy/dx at $x = 25$ and interpret the result.
   e) Interpret the results of parts b, c, and d graphically.

48. *Radioactive decay.* A certain radioactive substance decays in accordance with the equation

$$f(t) = 4000e^{-0.60t} \qquad (t > 0)$$

where $f(t)$ denotes the mass (in grams) at time t (in hours). Determine the rate of change of the substance's mass

   a) At $t = 5$. b) At $t = 10$.

49. *Population growth.* In a scientific experiment, a population of fruit flies grows in accordance with the equation

$$N(t) = 10,000e^{0.05t}$$

where $N(t)$ denotes the number of fruit flies present t days after the beginning of the experiment. Determine the rate of growth of the fruit flies

   a) At $t = 10$. b) At $t = 20$.

5-5 • DERIVATIVES OF LOGARITHMIC FUNCTIONS

We first consider the derivative of the logarithmic function

$$y = \ln x$$

When written in exponential form, the statement $y = \ln x$ is equivalent to

$$e^y = x$$

Taking the derivative of each side with respect to x and using the chain rule, we have

$$e^y \frac{dy}{dx} = 1$$

Solving for dy/dx, we obtain

$$\frac{dy}{dx} = \frac{1}{e^y}$$

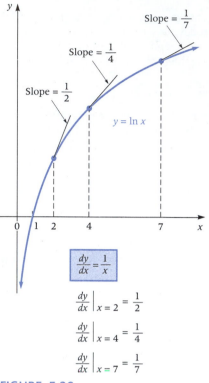

Slope = $\frac{1}{7}$

Slope = $\frac{1}{4}$

Slope = $\frac{1}{2}$

$y = \ln x$

$$\frac{dy}{dx} = \frac{1}{x}$$

$$\frac{dy}{dx}\bigg|_{x=2} = \frac{1}{2}$$

$$\frac{dy}{dx}\bigg|_{x=4} = \frac{1}{4}$$

$$\frac{dy}{dx}\bigg|_{x=7} = \frac{1}{7}$$

FIGURE 5-26

Since $e^y = x$, this expression becomes

$$\frac{dy}{dx} = \frac{1}{x}$$

We have just proven the following rule.

Rule 4

If $y = \ln x$, then

$$\frac{dy}{dx} = \frac{1}{x}$$

Using rule 4, we determine the slopes of tangent lines to the function $y = \ln x$, as illustrated in Figure 5-26.

• **EXAMPLE 5-29** _____

If $y = 5 \ln x$, find dy/dx.

Solution

Using rule 1 and the constant multiplier rule, we have

$$\frac{dy}{dx} = 5\frac{d}{dx}(\ln x)$$

$$= 5 \cdot \frac{1}{x} = \frac{5}{x}$$

• **EXAMPLE 5-30** _____

If $y = \ln u$, find dy/du.

Solution

Using rule 4, we have

$$\frac{dy}{du} = \frac{1}{u}$$

By applying the chain rule, we can find the derivatives of functions of the form

$$y = \ln u$$

where u is a function of x. According to the chain rule, if y is a function of u and u is a function of x, then

$$\frac{dy}{dx} = \frac{dy}{du} \cdot \frac{du}{dx}$$

If $y = \ln u$, then $dy/du = 1/u$. Hence,

$$\frac{dy}{dx} = \frac{1}{u} \cdot \frac{du}{dx}$$

We now have the following rule.

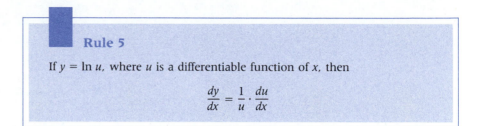

Rule 5

If $y = \ln u$, where u is a differentiable function of x, then

$$\frac{dy}{dx} = \frac{1}{u} \cdot \frac{du}{dx}$$

• **EXAMPLE 5-31** _____

If $y = \ln (x^3 - 5x^2 + 6)$, find dy/dx.

Solution

Let $u = x^3 - 5x^2 + 6$. Then $du/dx = 3x^2 - 10x$. Using rule 5, we have

$$\frac{dy}{dx} = \frac{1}{u} \cdot \frac{du}{dx}$$

$$= \frac{1}{x^3 - 5x^2 + 6}(3x^2 - 10x)$$

$$= \frac{3x^2 - 10x}{x^3 - 5x^2 + 6}$$

• **EXAMPLE 5-32** _____

If $f(x) = e^{x^5-7} \ln (x^8 - 3x)$, find $f'(x)$.

Solution

We begin by using the product rule.

$$f'(x) = (\text{first})\left(\begin{array}{c}\text{derivative}\\\text{of second}\end{array}\right) + (\text{second})\left(\begin{array}{c}\text{derivative}\\\text{of first}\end{array}\right)$$

$$f'(x) = \boxed{e^{x^5-7}} \cdot \boxed{\frac{8x^7 - 3}{x^8 - 3x}} + \boxed{\ln (x^8 - 3x)} \cdot \boxed{e^{x^5-7} \cdot (5x^4)}$$

$$= \left[\frac{8x^7 - 3}{x^8 - 3x} + 5x^4 \ln (x^8 - 3x)\right] e^{x^5-7}$$

• **EXAMPLE 5-33** _____

If $y = \sqrt{\ln (x^3 + 8)}$, find dy/dx.

Solution

Rewrite $y = \sqrt{\ln (x^3 + 8)}$ as

$$y = [\ln(x^3 + 8)]^{1/2}$$

and apply the general power rule to obtain

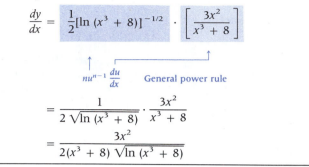

$$\frac{dy}{dx} = \frac{1}{2}[\ln{(x^3 + 8)}]^{-1/2} \cdot \left[\frac{3x^2}{x^3 + 8}\right]$$

$$nu^{n-1}\frac{du}{dx} \qquad \text{General power rule}$$

$$= \frac{1}{2\sqrt{\ln{(x^3 + 8)}}} \cdot \frac{3x^2}{x^3 + 8}$$

$$= \frac{3x^2}{2(x^3 + 8)\sqrt{\ln{(x^3 + 8)}}}$$

Rules 4 and 5 for finding the derivatives of logarithmic functions have applied only to those functions involving natural logarithms. The following rule applies to logarithmic functions with arbitrary bases—that is, to logarithmic functions with equations of the form $y = \log_b u$, where u is a function of x, $b > 0$, and $b \neq 1$.

Rule 6

If $y = \log_b u$, where u is a differentiable function of x, $b > 0$, and $b \neq 1$, then

$$\frac{dy}{dx} = \frac{1}{u\ln{b}} \cdot \frac{du}{dx}$$

The proof of this rule is given below. Note that if $b = e$, then rule 6 becomes rule 5.

PROOF OF RULE 6

When written in exponential form, the statement $y = \log_b u$ becomes

$$b^y = u$$

Taking the derivative of both sides with respect to x, we obtain

$$b^y\frac{dy}{dx}\ln{b} = \frac{du}{dx}$$

Solving for dy/dx yields

$$\frac{dy}{dx} = \frac{1}{b^y\ln{b}} \cdot \frac{du}{dx}$$

Since $b^y = u$, this equation becomes

$$\frac{dy}{dx} = \frac{1}{u\ln{b}} \cdot \frac{du}{dx}$$

• EXAMPLE 5-34 _____

If $y = \log_{10}(x^6 - 9x^3)$, find dy/dx.

Solution

Since $b = 10$ and $u = x^6 - 9x^3$, then, using rule 6, we have

$$\frac{dy}{du} = \frac{1}{u \ln b} \cdot \frac{du}{dx}$$

$$= \frac{1}{(x^6 - 9x^3)\ln 10}(6x^5 - 27x^2) \qquad \underset{\text{\small$\frac{du}{dx}$}}{\underbrace{\qquad}}$$

$$\approx \frac{6x^5 - 27x^2}{2.302585(x^6 - 9x^3)}$$

• EXAMPLE 5-35 _____

If $y = x^2 \ln x$, find dy/dx.

Solution

Using the product rule, we have

$$\frac{dy}{dx} = x^2(1/x) + (\ln x)(2x)$$

$$= x + 2x \ln x \qquad \text{\color{blue}Simplifying}$$

$$= x(1 + 2 \ln x) \qquad \text{\color{blue}Factoring using the distributive law}$$

• EXAMPLE 5-36 _____

If $y = \sqrt[3]{\ln(4 + x^2)}$, find dy/dx.

Solution

First, rewrite the above as

$$y = [\ln(4 + x^2)]^{1/3}$$

and then use the general power rule (Section 2-8) with rule 5 to obtain

$$\frac{dy}{dx} = nu^{n-1}\frac{du}{dx}$$

$$\frac{dy}{dx} = \frac{1}{3}[\ln(4 + x^2)]^{-2/3}\left(\frac{2x}{4 + x^2}\right) \qquad \boxed{\color{blue}[\ln(4 + x^2)]^{-2/3} =}$$

$$= \frac{2x}{3(4 + x^2)\sqrt[3]{[\ln(4 + x^2)]^2}} \qquad \boxed{\color{blue}\dfrac{1}{\sqrt[3]{[\ln(4 + x^2)]^2}}}$$

Sometimes properties of logarithms are used to simplify differentiation. The next example illustrates such a situation.

• EXAMPLE 5-37 _____

Use properties of logarithms to find dy/dx for

$$y = \ln \frac{(x^2 - 1)^3}{\sqrt{3 - 5x}}$$

Solution

Rewriting the above as

$$y = \ln \frac{(x^2 - 1)^3}{(3 - 5x)^{1/2}}$$

and using properties of logarithms on the right-hand side gives

$$y = \ln[(x^2 - 1)^3] - \ln[(3 - 5x)^{1/2}] \qquad \text{Logarithm of a quotient}$$
$$= 3 \ln(x^2 - 1) - (1/2)\ln(3 - 5x) \qquad \text{Logarithm of a power}$$

Now we find the derivative

$$\frac{dy}{dx} = 3\left(\frac{2x}{x^2 - 1}\right) - \frac{1}{2}\left(\frac{-5}{3 - 5x}\right)$$
$$= \frac{6x}{x^2 - 1} + \frac{5}{2}\left(\frac{1}{3 - 5x}\right)$$

Application

• **EXAMPLE 5-38** **Advertising Expenditures and Sales.**

A company's sales, $S(x)$ (in dollars), are related to advertising expenditures, x (in thousands of dollars), by the model.

$$S(x) = 200,000 + 800,000 \ln x$$

a) Determine the formula for the rate of change of S with respect to x.
b) Find $S'(5)$ and interpret.
c) Find $S'(20)$ and interpret.

Solutions

a) $S'(x) = 800,000\left(\dfrac{1}{x}\right) = \dfrac{800,000}{x}$

b) $S'(5) = 800,000/5 = 160,000$. This means that when advertising expenditures are 5 thousand dollars, an additional 1 thousand dollars spent on advertising results in $160,000 of additional sales.

c) $S'(20) = 800,000/20 = 40,000$. This means that when advertising expenditures are 20 thousand dollars, an additional 1 thousand dollars spent on advertising results in $40,000 of additional sales.

Comparing parts b and c, note that at higher levels of advertising expenditures, additional money spent on advertising results in less additional sales.

•

Exercises 5-5

Find the derivative of each of the following.

1. $y = 6 \ln x$ **2.** $y = -8 \ln x$
3. $y = \ln 3x$ **4.** $y = \ln 5x$
5. $f(x) = \ln(x^2 - 4x)$ **6.** $f(x) = -2 \ln(x^2 + 1)$
7. $f(x) = \ln(x^2 - 4x + 1)$ **8.** $f(x) = \ln(-x^6 + 3x)$
9. $y = x^4 + 3 \ln x$ **10.** $y = x^2 - 4 \ln x$

11. $f(x) = \dfrac{1}{x^3} - 7 \ln x$ **12.** $f(x) = \dfrac{1}{x^5} + 9 \ln x$

13. $y = 5\sqrt{x} - 3 \ln x$ **14.** $y = -8\sqrt{x} + 2 \ln x$

15. $y = x^3 \ln(x^2 + 5)$

16. $y = x^5 \ln(x^3 - 6)$

17. $y = \dfrac{\ln x^7}{x^9}$

18. $y = \dfrac{\ln x^8}{x^4}$

19. $y = (x^2 + 1) \ln(x^2 + 5)$

20. $y = (x^3 + 4) \ln(x^2 + 36)$

21. $y = \dfrac{x^2 + 6}{\ln(x^2 + 1)}$

22. $y = \dfrac{x^3 + 4}{\ln(x^2 + 25)}$

23. $y = [\ln(x^6 - 8x^3)]^{10}$

24. $y = [\ln(x^4 - 6x)]^8$

25. $y = \sqrt{\ln(x^3 + 7)}$

26. $y = \sqrt{\ln(x^6 + 5)}$

27. $y = \ln(\sqrt{x^3 + 7})$

28. $y = \ln(\sqrt{x^6 + 5})$

29. $y = \dfrac{e^x}{\ln x}$

30. $y = e^x \ln x$

31. $y = \dfrac{x^3 e^x}{\ln x}$

32. $y = \dfrac{x^2 e^{-x}}{\ln x}$

33. $f(x) = [\ln(x^3 - 2x)]e^{x^4 - 8}$

34. $f(x) = [\ln(x^5 - 7x)]e^{x^6 - 2}$

35. $y = \dfrac{\ln x^3}{\ln x^2}$

36. $y = \dfrac{\ln x^2}{\ln x^4}$

37. $y = \log_{10} 5x$

38. $y = \log_{10}(3x - 4)$

39. $y = \log_6(x^3 + 8x)$

40. $y = \log_3(2x^8 - 1)$

41. $y = \log_2(x^3 - 4x)$

42. $\log_4(x^5 - 2x^3)$

For Exercises 43–48, use properties of logarithms to find dy/dx.

43. $y = \ln \dfrac{x^5}{\sqrt{x^3 + 7}}$

44. $y = \ln \dfrac{x^2}{\sqrt[3]{x^4 - 9}}$

45. $y = \ln \dfrac{(x^3 + 7)^5}{\sqrt{4 - 5x}}$

46. $y = \ln \dfrac{(x^2 + 2)^3}{\sqrt{5 - 6x}}$

47. $y = \ln[(x^2 + 7)^4(x^6 - 5)^3]$

48. $y = \ln[(x^2 - 7)^5(x^3 + 8)^2]$

Applications

49. *Learning curve.* The function defined by

$$N(x) = 1000 \ln(0.5x)$$

is a learning curve, where $N(x)$ denotes the number of items produced by a new worker during the xth day following a training period.

a) Find the formula for the rate of change of N with respect to x.

b) Find $N'(4)$ and interpret.

c) Find $N'(8)$ and interpret.

50. *Advertising expenses.* A company's sales, $S(x)$ (in dollars), are related to advertising expenditures, x (in thousands of dollars), by the equation

$$S(x) = 300,000 + 500,000 \ln x$$

a) Determine the formula for the rate of change of S with respect to x.

b) Find $S'(10)$ and interpret.

c) Find $S'(15)$ and interpret.

51. *Cost.* The total cost of producing x units of some product is given by

$$C(x) = 9000 + 10 \ln(x + 1)$$

a) Find $C'(x)$.

b) Find $C'(10)$ and interpret.

c) Find $C'(20)$ and interpet.

52. *Continuous compounding.* The equation

$$t = \dfrac{\ln 2}{r}$$

gives the time, t (in years), it takes money to double at an interest rate of $r \cdot 100\%$ compounded continuously.

a) Find dt/dr.

b) Evaluate dt/dr at $r = 0.08$ and interpret the result.

c) Evaluate dt/dr at $r = 0.10$ and interpret the result.

d) Evaluate dt/dr at $r = 0.20$ and interpret the result.

53. *Continuous compounding.* The equation

$$t = \frac{\ln 3}{r}$$

gives the time, t (in years), it takes money to triple at an interest rate of $r \cdot 100\%$ compounded continuously.

a) Find dt/dr.

b) Evaluate dt/dr at $r = 0.08$ and interpret the result.

c) Evaluate dt/dr at $r = 0.10$ and interpret the result.

d) Evaluate dt/dr at $r = 0.20$ and interpret the result.

e) Evaluate dt/dr at $r = 0.30$ and interpret the result.

EXTRA DIVIDENDS

• *Stock Market Forecasting*

The *Value Line Investment Survey*, a reputable investment advisory newsletter, gave the following equation for predicting the Dow Jones Industrial Average (DJIA) for a given future year.

DJIA Forecast for t^{th} Year*

$$P_t = 1.021 P_{t-1} \cdot E^{0.236} \cdot D^{0.301} \cdot A^{-0.391}$$

Here, P_{t-1} = DJIA for the previous $(t - 1)$ year

$$E = \frac{\text{earnings } t}{\text{earnings } (t - 1)} = \text{ratio of } t^{\text{th}} \text{ to } (t - 1) \text{ year earnings of the Dow Jones Industrial stocks}$$

$$D = \frac{\text{dividends } t}{\text{dividends } (t - 1)} = \text{ratio of } t^{\text{th}} \text{ year to } (t - 1) \text{ year dividends of the Dow Jones Industrial stocks}$$

$$A = \frac{\text{Aaa BOND YLD } t}{\text{Aaa BOND YLD } (t - 1)} = \text{ratio of } t^{\text{th}} \text{ year to } (t - 1) \text{ year yields of Aaa corporate bonds}$$

For example, if earnings are expected to increase by 8% next year, then

$$E = \frac{\text{earnings } t}{\text{earnings } (t - 1)} = 1.08$$

*Copyright © 1989 by Value Line, Inc.; used by permission.

If dividends are expected to increase by 5% next year, then

$$D = \frac{\text{dividends } t}{\text{dividends } (t - 1)} = 1.05$$

If aaa corporate bond yields are expected to decrease by 3% next year, then

$$A = \frac{\text{Aaa BOND YLD } t}{\text{Aaa BOND YLD } (t - 1)} = 1 - 0.03 = 0.97$$

PROBLEM

We will use the properties of logarithms to determine the effect on the DJIA forecast of

1. An increase in earnings
2. A decrease in earnings
3. An increase in dividends
4. A decrease in dividends
5. An increase in Aaa Bond Yields
6. A decrease in Aaa Bond Yields

SOLUTION

First, we must rewrite the equation in a form that is easier to analyze. We take the natural logarithm (or, if one prefers, the common logarithm) of each side to obtain

$$\ln P_t = \ln 1.021 + \ln P_{t-1} + \ln E^{0.236} + \ln D^{0.301} + \ln A^{-0.391}$$

property 1

$$\ln P_t = \ln 1.021 + \ln P_{t-1} + 0.236 \ln E + 0.301 \ln D + (-0.391) \ln A$$

property 3

At this point, we restate the following logarithmic property, which is determined by studying the graph of the logarithmic function illustrated in Figure 5-27.

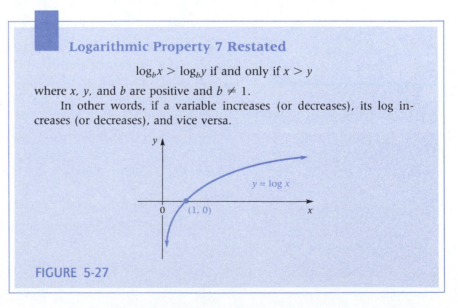

Logarithmic Property 7 Restated

$$\log_b x > \log_b y \text{ if and only if } x > y$$

where x, y, and b are positive and $b \neq 1$.

In other words, if a variable increases (or decreases), its log increases (or decreases), and vice versa.

$y = \log x$

$(1, 0)$

FIGURE 5-27

We now address our previously stated concerns.

1. If earnings are projected to increase for the next year, then the earnings ratio will be greater than 1, and, therefore, its natural logarithm (look at the graph of the logarithm function of Figure 5-27) will be positive. This result, when multiplied by 0.236, gives an increase in $\ln P_t$, which, by logarithmic property 7, implies an increase in P_t (the DJIA for the future year). This assumes that dividends and bond yields remain constant.

2. If earnings are projected to decrease for the next year, then the earnings ratio will be greater than 0, but smaller than 1, and, therefore, its natural logarithm (look at the graph of the logarithm function of Figure 5-27) will be negative. This result, when multiplied by 0.236, gives a decrease in $\ln P_t$, which, by logarithmic property 7, implies a decrease in P_t (the DJIA for the future year). This assumes that dividends and bond yields remain constant.

3. P_t will increase. The reasoning is the same as that for part 1.

4. P_t will decrease. The reasoning is the same as that for part 2.

5. If Aaa bond yields are projected to increase for the next year. Then the Aaa ratio will be greater than 1, and, therefore, its natural logarithm (look at the graph of the logarithm function of Figure 5-27) will be positive. This result, when multiplied by -0.391, gives a decrease in $\ln P_t$ which, by logarithmic property 7, implies a decrease in P_t (the DJIA for the future year). This assumes that earnings and dividends remain constant.

6. If Aaa bond yields are projected to decrease for the next year, then the Aaa ratio will be greater than 0, but smaller than 1, and, therefore, its natural logarithm (look at the graph of the logarithm function of Figure 5-27) will be negative. This result, when multiplied by -0.391, gives an increase in $\ln P_t$ which, by logarithmic property 7, implies an increase in P_t (the DJIA for the future year). This assumes that earnings and dividends remain constant.

FORECAST

We now forecast next year's DJIA under the following assumptions:

1. Previous year DJIA closing price: 2166
2. 7.5% increase in earnings
3. 10.2% increase in dividends
4. 1.5% increase in Aaa bond yields

Thus,

$$\ln P_t = \ln 1.021 + \ln 2166 + 0.236 \ln 1.075 \\ + 0.301 \ln 1.102 - 0.391 \ln 1.015$$

$$\ln P_t = 0.0208 + 7.6806 + 0.236(0.0723) \\ + 0.301(0.0971) - 0.391(0.0149)$$

$$\ln P_t = 7.7419$$

Rewriting this result in exponential form gives

$$P_t = e^{7.7419}$$

$$= 2302.84 \qquad \text{Use } e^x \text{ key on calculator.}$$

Thus, the DJIA forecast for the next year is 2302.84.

We note that, using statistical analysis techniques beyond the scope of this text, this forecast can be expanded into an interval within which the DJIA can be expected to fall with a predictable probability.

CHAPTER 5 HIGHLIGHTS

• *Concepts*

Your ability to answer the following questions is one indicator of the depth of your mastery of this chapter's important concepts. Note that the questions are grouped under various topic headings. For any question that you cannot answer, refer to the appropriate section of the chapter indicated by the topic heading. Pay particular attention to the summary boxes within a section.

5-1 EXPONENTIAL FUNCTIONS AND THEIR GRAPHS

For Exercises 1-4, draw the graph that typifies each function.

1. $y = ae^x$, $a > 0$
2. $y = ae^{-x}$, $a > 0$
3. $y = ae^x$, $a < 0$
4. $y = ae^{-x}$, $a < 0$
5. Give the procedure for graphing exponential functions of the form $y = ab^x + c$ or $y = ab^{-x} + c$, where $b > 1$.
6. Write the equation for Newton's law of cooling. Explain the dependent and independent variables.
7. Write the equations for the two market penetration models. Explain the dependent and independent variables.

5-2 LOGARITHMIC FUNCTIONS

8. A logarithm is a(an) _____ of a number that is called a base.
9. Base e logarithms are called _____ logarithms.
10. Base 10 logarithms are called _____ logarithms.
11. For any positive number b, there is a value k such that $b = e^k$, where $k =$ _____ .
12. Draw the graph of the logarithmic function $y = \ln x$. The x-intercept is (____, 0). Is there a y-intercept? Is the function defined for $x < 0$?
13. State the seven properties of logarithms. Explain each property using examples.

5-3 FITTING EXPONENTIAL MODELS (OPTIONAL)

14. Write the linear form that corresponds to the exponential model $y = ab^x$.
15. For points (x, y) of the exponential function $y = ab^x$, the graph of the corresponding points $(x, \ln y)$ is a(an) _____ .

5-4 DERIVATIVES OF EXPONENTIAL FUNCTIONS

16. State the rule for finding the derivative of $y = e^x$.
17. State the rule for finding the derivative of $y = e^u$, where u is a differentiable function of x.
18. State the rule for finding the derivative of $y = b^u$, where u is a differentiable function of x and $b > 0$.

5-5 DERIVATIVES OF LOGARITHMIC FUNCTIONS

19. State the rule for finding the derivative of $y = \ln x$.
20. State the rule for finding the derivative of $y = \ln u$, where u is a differentiable function of x.
21. State the rule for finding the derivative of $y = \log_b u$, where u is a differentiable function of x, $b > 0$, and $b \neq 1$.

REVIEW EXERCISES

• *Exponential Functions*

Graph the following.

1. $y = 7^x$ **2.** $y = 7^{-x}$ **3.** $y = e^x$ **4.** $y = e^{-x}$

5. $y = 8e^x$ **6.** $y = -3e^x$ **7.** $y = -5e^{-x}$ **8.** $y = -e^x$

9. $f(x) = 4 + 2e^x$ **10.** $f(x) = -2 + 5e^{-x}$

11. $f(x) = 9 - 2e^{-x}$ **12.** $f(x) = 6 - 4e^x$

13. $f(x) = -1 + 5e^{-x}$ **14.** $f(x) = 2 + e^{3x}$

15. $f(x) = 5 + e^{-2x}$ **16.** $f(x) = 3 - e^{-x}$

17. *Time series.* The annual income, y (in millions of dollars), of a firm is related to time, t (in years), by the equation

$$y = 5e^t$$

where $t = 0$ denotes the year 19x0, $t = 1$ denotes the year 19x1, and so on.
a) Graph $y = 5e^t$ for $t \geq 0$.
b) Determine the annual earnings for the years 19x2, 19x3, and 19x5.

18. *Time series: Sales decay.* The annual sales, y (in millions of dollars), of a company are given by

$$y = 10e^{-t}$$

where $t = 0$ denotes the year 19x0, $t = 1$ denotes the year 19x1, and so on.
a) Graph $y = 10e^{-t}$ for $t \geq 0$.
b) Determine the annual sales for the years 19x0, 19x2, and 19x5.

19. *Market penetration: Long-range forecasting.* The percentage of market penetration for a product x years after it has been introduced is given by

$$y = 80 - 74e^{-0.27x}$$

a) Graph $y = 80 - 74e^{-0.27x}$ for $x \geq 0$.
b) Determine the percentage of market penetration for the third year.
c) Determine the percentage of market penetration for the tenth year.
d) Determine the saturation level.

20. *Market penetration: Long-range forecasting.* The percentage of market penetration for a product x years after it has been introduced is given by

$$y = \frac{90}{1 + 400e^{-0.80x}}$$

a) Determine the percentage of market penetration for the second, seventh, and twelfth years.
b) Determine the saturation level.

• *Logarithmic Functions*

Rewrite the following in logarithmic notation.

21. $10^4 = 10,000$ **22.** $5^3 = 125$

23. $y = e^x$

Find the logarithm for each of the following.

24. $\log_2 8$ **25.** $\log_3 9$ **26.** $\ln e^2$

27. $\log 1$ **28.** $\ln 1$ **29.** $\log 10$

Using a calculator with an "ln" button, find each the following.

30. $\ln 23$ **31.** $\ln 0.987$ **32.** $\ln 356$

Find x for the following.

33. $\log x = 0.8875$ **34.** $\ln x = 2.1576$

35. $\log x = 4.56$

Express each of the following as e^k.

36. 5   **37.** 4.6   **38.** 0.45

Use properties of logarithms to express the following in simpler form:

39. $\log (st/r)$ **40.** $\log (x^3y)$ **41.** $\log (uv)^5$

42. $\log (x/y)^4$ **43.** $\log uv$ **44.** $\log uv/w$

45. Graph $y = \ln x$

46. *Demand.* The demand, x (in millions), for a product is related to its unit price, p (in dollars), by the equation

$$p = e^{4-0.2x}$$

a) Express demand, x, in terms of unit price, p.
b) Find the demand associated with a unit price of $4.

• *Fitting Exponential Models*

47. Determine the coefficients a and b of the exponential model $y = ab^x$, whose graph passes through the points $(2, 8)$ and $(5, 60)$.

48. *Health care's share of GNP.* The U.S. health care industry's share of the gross national product (% of GNP) for the years 1965 to 2010 is given below: (Estimates are given for years beyond 1990.)

x = Coded Years	1	2	3	4	5	6	7
y = % of GNP	6	8	11	12	15.5	20	28

a) Fit the exponential model $y = ab^x$ by using the points appearing in color screens.
b) Assuming that each x-value denotes a time interval of approximately 7½ years, forecast health care's share of GNP for the next 7½ year time interval beyond the year 2010.

• *Derivatives of Exponential Functions*

For Exercises 49–62, find the derivative.

49. $y = e^{5x}$ **50.** $y = e^{-7x}$

51. $y = e^{8x+5}$ **52.** $y = 2^{3x+2}$

53. $y = (x^2 + 8x)e^{5x+9}$ **54.** $y = (x^4 - 7)e^{-x}$

55. $y = (4e^x - e^{-x})/x$ **56.** $y = [e^{x+8}]/(x - 4)$

57. $y = x^3 e^{6x}$ **58.** $y = e^{4\sqrt{x}}$

59. $y = 600/(1 + 20e^{5x})$ **60.** $y = 400/(1 + 10e^{-2x})$

61. $y = (8x + e^x)^2$ **62.** $y = (6x - e^{-4x})^{1/2}$

63. *Continuous compounding.* If $40,000 is invested for x years at 8% compounded continuously, the total amount is given by

$$S(x) = 40,000e^{0.08x}$$

a) Find $S'(x)$.
b) Find $S'(3)$ and interpret.
c) Find $S'(6)$ and interpret.

64. *Continuous compounding.* If in Exercise 63, the total amount increases by the same amount for each year beyond the sixth, find the total amount at the end of the tenth year. Compare this with what the total amount should be under normal conditions, and illustrate graphically.

Market penetration. The percentage of market penetration for a product x years after it has been introduced is given by each of the functions of Exercises 65 and 66.

a) Find $f'(x)$.
b) Find $f'(3)$ and interpret.
c) Find $f'(8)$ and interpret.

65. $f(x) = 90 - 50e^{-0.60x}$

66. $f(x) = \dfrac{70}{1 + 300e^{-0.80x}}$

• *Derivatives of Logarithmic Functions*

For Exercises 67–78, find the derivative.

67. $y = -7 \ln x$ **68.** $y = \ln 9x$

69. $y = \ln(x^3 - 6x^2)$ **70.** $y = \ln(x^6 + 5x)$

71. $y = x^2 \ln(x^3 + 7x)$ **72.** $y = x^7 - 6 \ln x$

73. $y = [\ln(x^5 + 6x^2)]^8$ **74.** $y = \ln(x^7 - 6x^2)$

75. $y = e^{3x+5} \ln x$ **76.** $y = \log_5(x^2 + 6x)$

77. $y = [\ln(x^5 - 6x^2)]e^{8x}$ **78.** $y = [\ln x^7]e^{6x+5}$

79. *Cost.* The total cost of producing x units of some product is given by

$$C(x) = 20{,}000 + 40 \ln(x + 3)$$

a) Find $C'(x)$.
b) Find $C'(17)$ and interpret.
c) Find $C'(22)$ and interpret.

6

INTEGRATION

Introductory Application

Marginal Cost/Cost

Sometimes we are given a marginal cost equation, $C'(x)$, and must determine the cost equation, $C(x)$. Consider, for example, a firm that produces picture frames. At a production level of x frames, the marginal cost is

$$C'(x) = 4x + 5$$

Find the cost equation, $C(x)$, if the fixed cost is $500.

In this chapter, we will discuss situations where we are given a derivative, $f(x)$, and must determine the equation of a function $F(x)$ such that $F'(x) = f(x)$. In other words, we must determine the equation of a function, given its derivative.

The above problem is solved in Example 6-10.

6-1 • ANTIDIFFERENTIATION

In Chapters 2 and 5, we discussed the calculations of derivatives $f'(x)$ of functions $f(x)$. The operation of calculating a derivative of a function is called **differentiation.** The result, $f'(x)$, is of course itself a function; it is called the derivative of the function $f(x)$. In this chapter, we will perform an operation that is the *reverse* of differentiation. It is called **antidifferentiation.** We will encounter problems in which we are given a function, $f(x)$, and must determine a function, $F(x)$, such that $F'(x) = f(x)$. Such a function $F(x)$ is called an antiderivative of $f(x)$.

> **Antiderivative**
>
> Given a function $f(x)$, $F(x)$ is an antiderivative of $f(x)$ if
> $$F'(x) = f(x)$$

• EXAMPLE 6-1

Find an antiderivative of $f(x) = x^2$.

Solution

We seek a function $F(x)$ whose derivative is x^2. One such function is

$$F(x) = \frac{1}{3}x^3$$

since $F'(x) = x^2$. Another such function is

$$F(x) = \frac{1}{3}x^3 + 5$$

since $F'(x) = x^2$ because the derivative of a constant (in this case, 5) is 0. In fact, all antiderivatives of $f(x)$ are functions of the form

$$F(x) = \frac{1}{3}x^3 + c$$

where c is an arbitrary constant. The graph of all antiderivatives $F(x)$ is a family of curves, as illustrated in Figure 6-1.

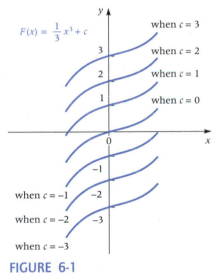

$F(x) = \frac{1}{3}x^3 + c$

when $c = 3$
when $c = 2$
when $c = 1$
when $c = 0$
when $c = -1$
when $c = -2$
when $c = -3$

FIGURE 6-1

• EXAMPLE 6-2

Find antiderivatives of $f(x) = e^x$.

Solution

We seek a function $f(x)$ whose derivative is e^x. Since e^x is its own derivative, then $F(x) = e^x$.

Also, if

$$F(x) = e^x + c$$

where c is an arbitrary constant, then

$$F'(x) = e^x$$

since the derivative of a constant is 0.

We now state the following.

> If $F(x)$ and $G(x)$ are antiderivatives of a function $f(x)$, then
> $$F(x) = G(x) + c$$
> where c is a constant.
>
> In other words, if a function $f(x)$ has two antiderivatives, $F(x)$ and $G(x)$, they differ by only a constant.

• EXAMPLE 6-3

Find antiderivatives of $f(x) = x^3$.

Solution

We seek all functions $F(x)$ such that $F'(x) = x^3$. One such function is

$$F(x) = \frac{1}{4}x^4$$

since $F'(x) = x^3$. In fact, all functions of the form

$$F(x) = \frac{1}{4}x^4 + c$$

where c is an arbitrary constant, represent the family of antiderivatives of $f(x) = x^3$ since $F'(x) = x^3$.

Note that in Examples 6-1 and 6-3, we have determined antiderivatives of functions of the form

$$f(x) = x^n \qquad (n \neq -1)$$

We now state a general rule for finding the antiderivatives of such functions.

> **Rule 6-1**
>
> If $n \neq -1$, the family of antiderivatives of functions of the form $f(x) = x^n$ is given by the set of all functions of the form
> $$F(x) = \frac{x^{n+1}}{n+1} + c$$
> where c is an arbitrary constant.

Note that if $F(x) = [1/(n+1)]x^{n+1} + c$, then $F'(x) = x^n$.

Indefinite Integrals

The family of antiderivatives of a function $f(x)$ is denoted by

$$\int f(x)\, dx$$

The symbol $\int$ is called an integral sign. The entire expression $\int f(x)\ dx$ is called the **indefinite integral** of $f(x)$. The process for finding $\int f(x)\ dx$ is called **indefinite integration.** The symbol dx indicates that we are integrating with respect to the variable x. Thus, rule 6-1 is restated as follows.

Rule 6-1 (Restated)   Power Rule

$$\int x^n\ dx = \frac{1}{n+1}x^{n+1} + c \qquad (n \neq -1)$$

• **EXAMPLE 6-4** _____

If $f(x) = \sqrt{x}$, find $\int f(x)\ dx$.

Solution

Since $f(x) = \sqrt{x} = x^{1/2}$, then, using rule 6-1 with $n = 1/2$, we have

$$\int x^{1/2}\ dx = \frac{1}{\frac{1}{2}+1}x^{1/2+1} + c$$

$$= \frac{2}{3}x^{3/2} + c$$

Note that the derivative of $\frac{2}{3}x^{3/2} + c$ is $x^{1/2}$.

_____ •

Note: Remember that we can always check an indefinite integral by taking its derivative.

• **EXAMPLE 6-5** _____

Determine $\int (1/x^2)\ dx$.

Solution

Since $1/x^2 = x^{-2}$, then, using rule 6-1 with $n = -2$, we have

$$\int x^{-2}\ dx = \frac{1}{-2+1}x^{-2+1} + c$$

$$= -x^{-1} + c$$

$$= -\frac{1}{x} + c$$

Observe that the derivative of $-x^{-1} + c$ is x^{-2}.

_____ •

Up to this point, we have used rule 6-1 to determine the antiderivatives, or indefinite integrals, of functions of the form $f(x) = x^n$, where $n \neq -1$. We now consider functions of the form

$$f(x) = kx^n \qquad (n \neq -1)$$

where k is a constant. Rule 6-2 provides a useful property of integrals that enables us to find the indefinite integrals of such functions.

Rule 6-2   Constant Multiplier Rule

$$\int kf(x)\, dx = k \int f(x)\, dx$$

Rule 6-2 states that the indefinite integral of a constant, k, times a function, $f(x)$, is equal to the constant, k, times the indefinite integral of the function, $f(x)$. This is the result of reversing the constant multiplier rule for derivatives. Specifically, we have

$$\int 5x^3\, dx = 5 \int x^3\, dx$$

$$= 5\left(\frac{1}{4}x^4 + c_1\right)$$

where c_1 is an arbitrary constant. Multiplying the expression inside the parentheses by 5, the result becomes $(5/4)x^4 + 5c_1$. Since c_1 is an arbitrary constant, then $5c_1$ is an arbitrary constant and may be written as c. Hence, we have

$$\int 5x^3\, dx = \frac{5}{4}x^4 + c$$

• **EXAMPLE 6-6** _____

Find $\int 8x\, dx$.

Solution

Using rules 6-2 and 6-1, we have

$$\int 8x\, dx = 8 \int x\, dx$$

$$= 8\left(\frac{1}{2}x^2 + c_1\right)$$

$$= \frac{8}{2}x^2 + 8c_1$$

$$= 4x^2 + 8c_1$$

Rewriting the arbitrary constant, $8c_1$, as c, we obtain

$$\int 8x\, dx = 4x^2 + c$$

• **EXAMPLE 6-7** _____

Find $\int 9\, dx$.

Solution

Since $9 = 9x^0$, we have

$$\int 9\, x^0\, dx = 9 \int x^0\, dx$$

$$= 9\,(x + c_1)$$

$$= 9x + 9c_1$$

Rewriting the arbitrary constant, $9c_1$, as c, we obtain

$$\int 9\, dx = 9x + c$$

In general, since the derivative of $kx + c$ is k, where k is a nonzero constant and c is a constant, then we state the following special case of the constant multiplier rule.

> **Rule 6-3**
>
> In general, if k is a constant, then
>
> $$\int k\, dx = kx + c$$
>
> where c is an arbitrary constant.

Indefinite Integral of a Sum or Difference

Sometimes, we must determine the indefinite integral of a sum or difference, $f(x) \pm g(x)$, of two functions, $f(x)$ and $g(x)$. If we reverse the sum or difference rule for derivatives, we obtain Rule 6-4, which enables us to integrate a sum or difference of two functions.

> **Rule 6-4   Sum or Difference Rule**
>
> $$\int (f(x) \pm g(x))\, dx = \int f(x)\, dx \pm \int g(x)\, dx$$

Rule 6-4 states that the indefinite integral of a sum or difference of two functions is the sum or difference of their individual integrals. For example,

$$\int (5x^7 + 7x)\, dx = \int 5x^7\, dx + \int 7x\, dx$$

$$= \left(\frac{5}{8}x^8 + c_1\right) + \left(\frac{7}{2}x^2 + c_2\right)$$

$$= \frac{5}{8}x^8 + \frac{7}{2}x^2 + c$$

For simplicity, the sum of the arbitrary constants, c_1 and c_2, is replaced by a single arbitrary constant, c.

Rule 6-4 may be extended to sums or differences that involve a finite number of three or more functions. Hence,

$$\int \left(9x^6 - \frac{1}{2}x^2 + 4 \right) dx = \boxed{\int 9x^6 \, dx} - \boxed{\int \frac{1}{2}x^2 \, dx} + \boxed{\int 4 \, dx}$$

$$= \frac{9}{7}x^7 - \frac{1}{6}x^3 + 4x + c$$

Note that it is not necessary to write the arbitrary constants associated with the individual indefinite integrals. Their sum is denoted by a single arbitrary constant, c.

• **EXAMPLE 6-8**

Determine $\int (3x^2 - x^{-5} - 7) \, dx$.

Solution

$$\int (3x^2 - x^{-5} - 7) \, dx = \int 3x^2 \, dx - \int x^{-5} \, dx - \int 7 \, dx$$

$$= \frac{3}{3}x^3 - \frac{1}{-4}x^{-4} - 7x + c$$

$$= x^3 + \frac{1}{4}x^{-4} - 7x + c$$

$$= x^3 + \frac{1}{4x^4} - 7x + c$$

Sometimes the independent variable is denoted by a letter other than x. Such a case is illustrated in Example 6-9.

• **EXAMPLE 6-9**

Find $\int (u^5 - 8u + 3) \, du$.

Solution

$$\int (u^5 - 8u + 3) \, du = \int u^5 \, du - \int 8u \, du + \int 3 \, du$$

$$= \frac{1}{6}u^6 - \frac{8}{2}u^2 + 3u + c$$

$$= \frac{1}{6}u^6 - 4u^2 + 3u + c$$

The next example illustrates a situation where we are given a marginal cost equation, $C'(x)$, and must integrate to determine the cost equation, $C(x)$.

Applications

• **EXAMPLE 6-10   Cost.**

A firm produces picture frames. At a production level of x frames, the marginal cost is

$$C'(x) = 4x + 5$$

Find the cost equation, $C(x)$, if the fixed cost is $500.

Solution

Here we calculate

$$C(x) = \int C'(x)\, dx$$

$$= \int (4x + 5)\, dx$$

$$= 2x^2 + 5x + c$$

Since the fixed cost is $500, then $C(0) = 500$. Hence,

$$500 = 2(0^2) + 5(0) + c$$

$$= c$$

Thus, we obtain

$$C(x) = 2x^2 + 5x + 500$$

• **EXAMPLE 6-11   Capital Formation.**

The value, V, of an investment fund changes over time, t (in years), at the rate

$$V'(t) = 18{,}000t^2$$

The amount in the fund at the end of the fourth year ($t = 4$) is $1,134,000.

a) Find the equation defining V as a function of t.
b) Find the value of the fund at the end of the sixth year ($t = 6$).

Solutions

a) Here

$$V(t) = \int 18{,}000t^2\, dt$$

$$= 6000t^3 + c$$

The condition that $V(4) = 1{,}134{,}000$ allows us to solve for the arbitrary constant, c. Hence,

$$1{,}134{,}000 = 6000(4)^3 + c$$

$$= 384{,}000 + c$$

$$c = 750{,}000$$

Thus,

$$V(t) = 6000t^3 + 750{,}000$$

b) The value of the fund at the end of the sixth year is given by

$$V(6) = 6000(6)^3 + 750{,}000$$

$$= \$2{,}046{,}000$$

Indefinite Integrals of Exponential Functions

We have already stated that since e^x is its own derivative, then its family of antiderivatives is given by $e^x + c$, where c is an arbitrary constant. This means that

$$\int e^x \, dx = e^x + c$$

We also note that since the derivative of $(1/k)e^{kx}$, where k is a nonzero constant, is $(1/k)ke^{kx}$, which simplifies to e^{kx}, then

$$\int e^{kx} \, dx = \frac{1}{k}e^{kx} + c$$

Thus, we state the following.

> ### Rule 6-5
>
> If k is a constant,
>
> **a)** $\displaystyle\int e^x \, dx = e^x + c$
>
> **b)** $\displaystyle\int e^{kx} \, dx = \frac{1}{k}e^{kx} + c \qquad (k \neq 0)$
>
> where c is the arbitrary constant of integration.

We now give some examples of the above rule.

• EXAMPLE 6-12

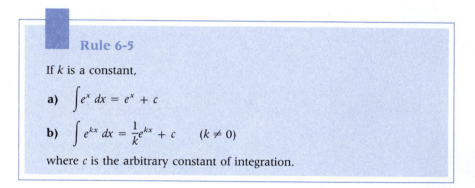

a) $\displaystyle\int 7e^x \, dx = 7\int e^x \, dx = 7e^x + c$

              constant   rule
              multiplier   6-5(a)
              rule

b) $\displaystyle\int e^{3x} \, dx = \frac{1}{3}e^{3x} + c$

         rule 6-5(b)

c) $\displaystyle\int e^{-5t} \, dt = \frac{1}{-5}e^{-5t} + c = -\frac{1}{5}e^{-5t} + c$

         rule 6-5(b)

d) $\displaystyle\int 4e^{(6/5)x} \, dx = 4\left(\frac{1}{6/5}e^{(6/5)x}\right) + c$

$$= 4\left(\frac{5}{6}\right)e^{(6/5)x} + c$$

$$= \frac{10}{3}e^{(6/5)x} + c$$

Indefinite Integrals Involving Logarithmic Functions

In Section 6-2, we learned that the derivative of $\ln x$ is $1/x$. We now show that the derivative of $\ln |x|$ is $1/x$ for $x \neq 0$ by considering two cases:

1. If $x > 0$, then $|x| = x$, so that

$$\frac{d}{dx}\left(\ln |x|\right) = \frac{d}{dx}\left(\ln x\right) = \frac{1}{x}$$

2. If $x < 0$, then $|x| = -x$, so that

$$\frac{d}{dx}\left(\ln |x|\right) = \frac{d}{dx}\left[\ln (-x)\right] = \frac{1}{-x}(-1) = \frac{1}{x}$$

Thus, Rule 6-6 holds.

Rule 6-6

$$\int x^{-1}\, dx = \int \frac{1}{x}\, dx = \ln |x| + c \qquad (x \neq 0)$$

We now provide some examples of the above rule.

• **EXAMPLE 6-13** _____

a) $\displaystyle \int \frac{5}{x}\, dx = 5 \int \frac{1}{x}\, dx = 5 \ln |x| + c$

              constant   rule 6-6
              multiplier
              rule

b) $\displaystyle \int \left(\frac{8}{x} + e^{-3x}\right) dx = \int \frac{8}{x}\, dx + \int e^{-3x}\, dx$

              sum or difference
              rule

$$= 8 \ln |x| + \frac{1}{-3}e^{-3x} + c$$

$$= 8 \ln |x| - \frac{1}{3}e^{-3x} + c$$

c) $\displaystyle \int \left(\frac{7}{x} - \frac{6}{\sqrt{x}}\right) dx = \int \frac{7}{x}\, dx - \int 6x^{-1/2}\, dx$

              sum or difference $\dfrac{6}{\sqrt{x}} = \dfrac{6}{x^{1/2}} = 6x^{-1/2}$
              rule

$$= 7 \ln |x| - 6\,\frac{x^{(-1/2)+1}}{-\frac{1}{2}+1} + c$$

$$= 7 \ln |x| - 6\left(\frac{2}{1}\right)x^{1/2} + c$$

$$= 7 \ln |x| - 12\sqrt{x} + c$$

d) For this part, we use algebra to simplify the expression before integrating.

$$\int \frac{e^x - 2x^2 - xe^x}{x^2 e^x}\, dx = \int \left(\frac{e^x}{x^2 e^x} - \frac{2x^2}{x^2 e^x} - \frac{xe^x}{x^{2\cdot 1} e^x} \right) dx$$

$$= \int \left(\frac{1}{x^2} - \frac{2}{e^x} - \frac{1}{x} \right) dx$$

$$= \int \left(x^{-2} - 2e^{-x} - \frac{1}{x} \right) dx$$

$$= \frac{x^{-1}}{-1} - 2\left(\frac{1}{-1} \right) e^{-x} - \ln |x| + c$$

$$= -\frac{1}{x} + 2e^{-x} - \ln |x| + c$$

We now summarize the indefinite integral formulas of this section.

SUMMARY

Indefinite Integral Formulas

If k and c are constants:

1. $\displaystyle \int x^n\, dx = \frac{x^{n+1}}{n+1} + c \qquad (n \neq -1)$

2. $\displaystyle \int k f(x)\, dx = k \int f(x)\, dx$

3. $\displaystyle \int k\, dx = kx + c$

4. $\displaystyle \int [f(x) \pm g(x)]\, dx = \int f(x)\, dx \pm \int g(x)\, dx$

5. $\displaystyle \int e^x\, dx = e^x + c$

6. $\displaystyle \int e^{kx}\, dx = \frac{1}{k} e^{kx} + c$

7. $\displaystyle \int x^{-1}\, dx = \int \frac{1}{x}\, dx = \ln |x| + c$

Marginal Tax Rates

The **marginal tax rate** gives the amount of federal income tax due on each additional dollar of taxable income. Table 6-1 gives the marginal tax rates for married people filing jointly and qualifying widow(er)s with taxable annual incomes not exceeding $155,320 for the 1989 tax year. We exclude the case where the annual taxable income exceeds $155,320 as this entails complications that we choose to avoid here.

TABLE 6-1

| Taxable income | | Marginal tax rate |
over	but not over	
$0	$30,950	15%
$30,950	$74,850	28%
$74,850	$155,320	33%

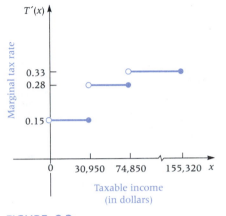

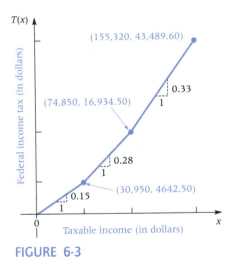

FIGURE 6-2

FIGURE 6-3

We let

$$x = \text{taxable annual income in dollars}$$

$$T(x) = \text{amount of federal income tax (in dollars)}$$
$$\text{due for taxable income } x$$

$$T'(x) = \text{marginal tax rate for taxable income } x$$

Thus, the *marginal tax rate*, $T'(x)$, can be written as

$$T'(x) = \begin{cases} 0.15 & \text{if} \quad\quad 0 < x \le 30{,}950 \\ 0.28 & \text{if } 30{,}950 < x \le 74{,}850 \\ 0.33 & \text{if } 74{,}850 < x \le 155{,}320 \end{cases}$$

The graph of $T'(x)$ is given in Figure 6-2. Note the existence of three tax brackets, depending on the amount of taxable income.

The *amount of federal income tax due* is given by the *tax function*

$$T(x) = \begin{cases} 0.15x & \text{if} \quad\quad 0 < x \le 30{,}950 \\ 4642.50 + 0.28(x - 30{,}950) & \text{if } 30{,}950 < x \le 74{,}850 \\ 16{,}934.50 + 0.33(x - 74{,}850) & \text{if } 74{,}850 < x \le 155{,}320 \end{cases}$$

The graph of $T(x)$ is given in Figure 6-3. Again, note the existence of three tax brackets, depending on the amount of taxable income. The first $30,950 of annual income is taxed at 15%. Thus, for annual taxable income over $30,950, but not exceeding $74,850 (or, in other words, the second tax bracket), the tax on the first $30,950 is 0.15(30,950) = $4642.50; the amount over $30,950 is taxed at 28%. For annual taxable income over $74,850, but not exceeding $155,320 (or, in other words, the third tax bracket), the tax on the first $30,950 is $4642.50, the tax on the next $43,900 (i.e., $74,850 − $30,950) is 0.28(43,900) = $12,292. This amount, added to $4642.50, gives a sum of $16,934.50, which is the tax on the first $74,850 of annual taxable income. The amount of income over $74,850 is taxed at 33%.

Thus, for an annual taxable income of $40,000, the amount of federal income tax due is given by

$$T(40{,}000) = 4642.50 + 0.28(40{,}000 - 30{,}950)$$

This is the tax on the first $30,950 of taxable income at 15%.   This amount is taxed at 28%.

$$= 4642.50 + 0.28(9050)$$

$$= \$7176.50 \quad \text{Federal Income Tax}$$

For an annual taxable income of $100,000, the amount of federal income tax due is given by

$$T(100,000) = 16,934.50 + 0.33(\underbrace{100,000 - 74,850})$$

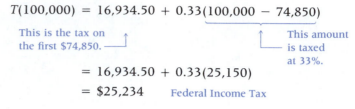

This is the tax on the first $74,850.

This amount is taxed at 33%.

$$= 16,934.50 + 0.33(25,150)$$

$$= \$25,234 \qquad \text{Federal Income Tax}$$

Exercises 6-1

For each of the following, verify that $F(x)$ is an antiderivative of $f(x)$.

1. $f(x) = 7x^6$, $F(x) = x^7$

2. $f(x) = 7x^6$, $F(x) = x^7 - 5$

3. $f(x) = x^2 - 8x + 5$, $F(x) = \frac{1}{3}x^3 - 4x^2 + 5x + 1$

4. $f(x) = \frac{1}{\sqrt[5]{x}}$, $F(x) = \frac{5}{4}\sqrt[5]{x^4} + 9$

5. $f(x) = e^{2x}$, $F(x) = \frac{1}{2}e^{2x}$

6. $f(x) = e^{-7x}$, $F(x) = -\frac{1}{7}e^{-7x}$

7. $f(x) = \frac{1}{x}$, $F(x) = \ln x$

8. $f(x) = \frac{3}{x}$, $F(x) = 3 \ln x$

Find each of the indefinite integrals.

9. $\displaystyle\int x^{12}\, dx$

10. $\displaystyle\int 5\, dx$

11. $\displaystyle\int \frac{10}{\sqrt{x}}\, dx$

12. $\displaystyle\int \frac{dx}{x^3}$

13. $\displaystyle\int \sqrt[4]{x}\, dx$

14. $\displaystyle\int 20\sqrt{x}\, dx$

15. $\displaystyle\int \frac{1}{x^9}\, dx$

16. $\displaystyle\int x^{-1/6}\, dx$

17. $\displaystyle\int \sqrt[3]{x^2}\, dx$

18. $\displaystyle\int \frac{1}{\sqrt[7]{x}}\, dx$

19. $\displaystyle\int \frac{-4}{\sqrt[7]{x^2}}\, dx$

20. $\displaystyle\int \frac{1}{\sqrt[3]{x^5}}\, dx$

21. $\displaystyle\int \frac{-3}{\sqrt{x}}\, dx$

22. $\displaystyle\int \frac{8}{x^{1/3}}\, dx$

23. $\displaystyle\int \frac{1}{\sqrt[5]{x^2}}\, dx$

24. $\displaystyle\int e^x\, dx$

25. $\displaystyle\int e^{5x}\, dx$

26. $\displaystyle\int e^{-x}\, dx$

27. $\displaystyle\int e^{-4x}\, dx$

28. $\displaystyle\int 6e^{-2x}\, dx$

29. $\displaystyle\int 8e^{2x}\, dx$

30. $\displaystyle\int \frac{9}{x}\, dx$

31. $\displaystyle\int \frac{-4}{x}\, dx$

32. $\displaystyle\int \frac{600}{x}\, dx$

33. $\displaystyle\int \frac{300}{x}\, dx$

34. $\int \dfrac{1}{2x}\, dx$

35. $\int \dfrac{1}{5x}\, dx$

36. $\int \dfrac{1}{x^5}\, dx$

37. $\int \dfrac{1}{x^6}\, dx$

38. $\int \dfrac{6}{x^4}\, dx$

39. $\int \dfrac{8}{x^7}\, dx$

40. $\int (3x^2 - 8x + 5)\, dx$

41. $\int (4x^3 - 16)\, dx$

42. $\int (2x^7 - 6x^4 - 1)\, dx$

43. $\int (x^5 - 7x)\, dx$

44. $\int \left(5x^4 - \sqrt{x} + \dfrac{7}{\sqrt{x}}\right) dx$

45. $\int \left(x^3 - \dfrac{4}{x^2} + 6\right) dx$

46. $\int (u^4 - 6u^2 + 5)\, du$

47. $\int (t^3 - 2t^2)\, dt$

48. $\int (v^2 - 1)\, dv$

49. $\int (y^6 - 5y^4 + 1)\, dy$

50. $\int \left(t^6 - \dfrac{2}{t^2} + \dfrac{6}{\sqrt{t}}\right) dt$

51. $\int \left(4u^3 - \dfrac{8}{\sqrt{u}} + \dfrac{5}{u^2}\right) du$

52. $\int (5x^{-1} + e^{3x})\, dx$

53. $\int (7x^{-1} + e^{4x})\, dx$

54. $\int \left(\dfrac{3}{x} + e^{-2x}\right) dx$

55. $\int \left(\dfrac{9}{x} + e^{-x}\right) dx$

56. $\int \left(\dfrac{2}{x} - e^{6x}\right) dx$

57. $\int \left(\dfrac{4}{x} - e^{-5x}\right) dx$

58. $\int \left(\dfrac{3}{x^2} + \dfrac{1}{x}\right) dx$

59. $\int \left(\dfrac{4}{x^3} + \dfrac{2}{x}\right) dx$

60. $\int \left(\dfrac{5}{x^3} + e^{-2x}\right) dx$

61. $\int \left(\dfrac{6}{x^4} - e^{4x}\right) dx$

62. $\int (x^{-4} - e^{-x})\, dx$

63. $\int (x^{-2} + e^{-x})\, dx$

64. $\int (x^{-1} + x^{-3} + e^{-2x})\, dx$

65. $\int (x^{-1} - x^{-2} - e^x)\, dx$

Use algebra to rewrite each of the following so that the indefinite integral rules of this section can be applied, and then complete the integration.

66. $\int \dfrac{1 - x^5}{x^2}\, dx$

67. $\int \dfrac{x^6 - 4x}{x^3}\, dx$

68. $\int (3x + 2)^2\, dx$

69. $\int (x - 1)^2\, dx$

70. $\int \dfrac{4x - e^x}{xe^x}\, dx$

71. $\int \dfrac{e^x - x}{xe^x}\, dx$

72. $\int (x + 1)(x - 1)\, dx$

73. $\int (x + 2)(x - 2)\, dx$

74. $\int (x + 1)(x - 4)\, dx$

75. $\int (x - 3)(x + 2)\, dx$

76. $\int \dfrac{x^2 - 1}{x - 1}\, dx$

77. $\int \dfrac{x^2 - 4}{x + 2}\, dx$

Applications

78. *Cost.* The Safe Ride Company produces tires. At a production level of x tires, the marginal cost is

$$C'(x) = 8x + 2$$

Find the cost function, $C(x)$, if the fixed cost is $1000.

79. *Cost.* Given the marginal cost function

$$C'(x) = 6x^2 + 4x - 5$$

find the cost function, $C(x)$, if the fixed cost is $800.

80. *Cost.* Given the marginal cost function

$$C'(x) = 6x + 1$$

find the cost function, $C(x)$, if the total cost of producing 2 units is $900.

81. *Capital formation.* The value, V, of a mutual fund changes over time, t (in years), at the rate

$$V'(t) = 24{,}000t^2$$

The initial amount (i.e., at $t = 0$) in the fund is $1,000,000.
a) Find the equation defining V as a function of t.
b) Find the value of the mutual fund at the end of the fifth year (i.e., at $t = 5$).

82. *Marginal propensity to save.* The marginal propensity to save, $S'(x)$, is a function of a nation's income, x (in billions of dollars), as defined by the equation

$$S'(x) = 0.5 - 0.12x^{-1/2} \qquad (x > 0)$$

If $S = 0$ when $x = 81$, then
a) Find the equation defining total savings, $S(x)$.
b) Find the total savings at a national income of $144 billion.

Velocity/Distance. For each of the following, the velocity (or speed) of a moving particle after t seconds have elapsed is given by the formula for $v(t)$. Determine the formula for distance traveled, $S(t)$, after t seconds have elapsed if $S(0)$ is as given. Use the fact that $v(t) = S'(t)$.

83. $v(t) = 6t^2$, $S(0) = 2$
84. $v(t) = 3t$, $S(0) = 4$
85. $v(t) = 3t^2$, $S(0) = 6$

Acceleration/Velocity. For each of the following, the acceleration (or rate of change of velocity with respect to time) is given by the formula for $a(t)$. Determine the formula for velocity, $v(t)$, if $v(0)$ is as given. Use the fact that $a(t) = v'(t)$.

86. $a(t) = 2t$, $v(0) = 10$
87. $a(t) = 4t$, $v(0) = 30$
88. $a(t) = t^2 + 4$, $v(0) = 2$

89. *Biomedical: Wound healing.* The area, A (in square centimeters), of a wound that is healing is changing at a rate given by

$$\frac{dA}{dt} = -40t^{-3} \qquad (1 \leq t \leq 6)$$

where t is the time (in days) elapsed since the wound was inflicted.
a) Determine the formula for area, $A(t)$, if $A(1) = 19.5$.
b) Determine the area of the wound after 5 days.

90. *Population growth.* The growth rate of a city is given by

$$\frac{dP}{dt} = 10{,}000e^{0.10t} \qquad (0 \leq t \leq 10)$$

where $P(t)$ is the population t years after the city was chartered.
a) Determine the formula for $P(t)$ if $P(0) = 100,000$.
b) Determine the population 6 years after the city was chartered.

6-2 • THE DEFINITE INTEGRAL AND AREA UNDER A CURVE

In Section 6-1, we discussed indefinite integrals of functions $f(x)$. We will now consider the concept and the mechanics of computing a *definite integral*. A definite integral results in a numerical value. A definite integral of a function $f(x)$ is evaluated over an interval of x-values. The endpoints of this interval are called *limits of integration*. We now illustrate the concept of a definite integral by the following example.

Definite Integrals

Consider a firm producing some commodity. At a production level of x units, the marginal cost is

$$C'(x) = 6x + 8$$

The antiderivative of the marginal cost is

$$C(x) = \int (6x + 8)\, dx$$
$$= 3x^2 + 8x + c$$

If we are told that the fixed cost is $600, then we determine the arbitrary constant to be $c = 600$. Hence, the cost function is

$$C(x) = 3x^2 + 8x + 600$$

Suppose we wish to determine the *total net change* in cost if production rises from $x = 10$ to $x = 15$. This total net change in cost is determined by evaluating

$$C(15) - C(10)$$

Since

$$C(15) = 3(15^2) + 8(15) + 600 = \$1395$$

and

$$C(10) = 3(10^2) + 8(10) + 600 = \$980$$

the total net change in cost is

$$C(15) - C(10) = \$1395 - \$980$$
$$= \$415$$

Thus, as production changes from $x = 10$ to $x = 15$, the total cost increases by $415.

In general, if a and b are numbers and $F(x)$ is a function, then the quantity

$$F(b) - F(a)$$

is the **total net change** of $F(x)$ over the interval from $x = a$ to $x = b$. The quantity $F(b) - F(a)$ is often abbreviated by the symbol

$$F(x) \Big|_a^b$$

We now define a **definite integral.**

Definite Integral

Let a and b be numbers and $f(x)$ a continuous function with an antiderivative, $F(x)$. Then the **definite integral** of $f(x)$ from $x = a$ to $x = b$ is denoted and defined by

$$\int_a^b f(x) \, dx = F(x) \Big|_a^b = F(b) - F(a)$$

The numbers a and b are called **limits of integration.**

The definite integral $\int_a^b f(x) \, dx$ is the total change of the antiderivative, $F(x)$, over the interval from $x = a$ to $x = b$. It is assumed that $f(x)$ is continuous over the interval $a \leq x \leq b$.

● **EXAMPLE 6-14** _____

Find $\int_1^2 x^2 \, dx$.

Solution

Here we write

$$\int_1^2 x^2 \, dx = F(x) \Big|_1^2 = F(2) - F(1)$$

where

$$F(x) = \frac{1}{3}x^3 + c$$

Hence, we have

$$F(2) - F(1) = \left[\frac{1}{3}(2^3) + c \right] - \left[\frac{1}{3}(1^3) + c \right]$$

$$= \left(\frac{8}{3} + c \right) - \left(\frac{1}{3} + c \right)$$

$$= \frac{7}{3}$$

Notice that the definite integral does not depend on the choice of the arbitrary constant, c. Thus, we will choose $c = 0$ when computing definite integrals.

● **EXAMPLE 6-15** _____

Find $\int_{-1}^3 (8x^3 - 4x + 5) \, dx$.

Solution

$$\int_{-1}^{3} (8x^3 - 4x + 5)\, dx = \underbrace{2x^4 - 2x^2 + 5x}_{F(x)}\Big|_{-1}^{3}$$

$$= F(3) - F(-1)$$
$$= [2(3^4) - 2(3^2) + 5(3)] - [2(-1)^4 - 2(-1)^2 + 5(-1)]$$
$$= (162 - 18 + 15) - (2 - 2 - 5)$$
$$= 164$$

• **EXAMPLE 6-16** _____

Find $\int_0^5 e^x\, dx$.

Solution

$$\int_0^5 e^x\, dx = \underbrace{e^x}_{F(x)}\Big|_0^5 = F(5) - F(0)$$

$$= e^5 - e^0$$
$$\approx 148.41 - 1 = 147.41$$

• **EXAMPLE 6-17** _____

Find $\int_2^9 x^{-1}\, dx$.

Solution

$$\int_2^9 x^{-1}\, dx = \underbrace{\ln|x|}_{F(x)}\Big|_2^9 = F(9) - F(2)$$

$$= \ln|9| - \ln|2|$$
$$\approx 2.1972 - 0.6931 = 1.5041$$

Definite integrals are used to find *areas under curves*. Since this is an important use of definite integrals, we now develop this topic.

Area Under a Curve

Suppose we had to compute the area bounded by the curve $f(x) = x^2$, the x-axis, and the vertical lines $x = 0$ and $x = 1$ (see Figure 6-4). We could obtain an approximation by arbitrarily dividing the interval $0 \le x \le 1$ into, say, four subintervals and then covering the shaded area with the four rectangles, as shown in Figure 6-5.

Observe that each rectangle has a width of 1/4 unit. Also, note that the height of each rectangle is given by the y-coordinate of the upper right-hand corner point (of the rectangle) on the graph of the function,

$$f(x) = x^2$$

Thus, the height of the first rectangle is

$$f\left(\frac{1}{4}\right) = \left(\frac{1}{4}\right)^2 = \frac{1}{16}$$

the height of the second rectangle is

$$f\left(\frac{1}{2}\right) = \left(\frac{1}{2}\right)^2 = \frac{1}{4}$$

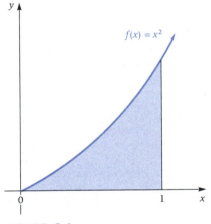

FIGURE 6-4

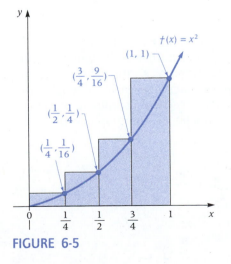

FIGURE 6-5

the height of the third rectangle is

$$f\left(\frac{3}{4}\right) = \left(\frac{3}{4}\right)^2 = \frac{9}{16}$$

and the height of the fourth rectangle is

$$f(1) = (1)^2 = 1$$

Since the area of each rectangle is the width times the height, the sum of the areas of the rectangles is

$$A_1 = \left[\frac{1}{4} \cdot f\left(\frac{1}{4}\right)\right] + \left[\frac{1}{4} \cdot f\left(\frac{1}{2}\right)\right] + \left[\frac{1}{4} \cdot f\left(\frac{3}{4}\right)\right] + \left[\frac{1}{4} \cdot f(1)\right]$$

$$= \left(\frac{1}{4} \cdot \frac{1}{16}\right) + \left(\frac{1}{4} \cdot \frac{1}{4}\right) + \left(\frac{1}{4} \cdot \frac{9}{16}\right) + \left(\frac{1}{4} \cdot 1\right)$$

$$= \frac{15}{32} \text{ square unit}$$

Of course, this approximation is greater than the actual area and is therefore called an *upper approximation*. Figure 6-6 illustrates the use of rectangles to obtain an approximation less than the actual area. Observing Figure 6-6, note that the sum of the areas of the rectangles is

$$A_2 = \left[\frac{1}{4} \cdot f\left(\frac{1}{4}\right)\right] + \left[\frac{1}{4} \cdot f\left(\frac{1}{2}\right)\right] + \left[\frac{1}{4} \cdot f\left(\frac{3}{4}\right)\right]$$

$$= \left(\frac{1}{4} \cdot \frac{1}{16}\right) + \left(\frac{1}{4} \cdot \frac{1}{4}\right) + \left(\frac{1}{4} \cdot \frac{9}{16}\right)$$

$$= \frac{7}{32} \text{ square unit}$$

Since A_2 is less than the actual area, it is called a *lower approximation*. The actual area, A, lies somewhere between A_1 and A_2. Hence,

$$\frac{7}{32} < A < \frac{15}{32}$$

Riemann Sum

A more accurate approximation of this area, A, in Figure 6-4 is obtained by dividing the interval $0 \le x \le 1$ into a greater number of subintervals and summing the areas of the respective rectangles. In Figure 6-7, we divide the interval $0 \le x \le 1$ into n subintervals, each of length $1/n$. Again, the height of each rectangle is given by the y-coordinate of the upper right-hand corner point (of the rectangle) on the graph of the function.

$$f(x) = x^2$$

Thus, the height of the first rectangle is

$$f\left(\frac{1}{n}\right) = \left(\frac{1}{n}\right)^2 = \frac{1^2}{n^2}$$

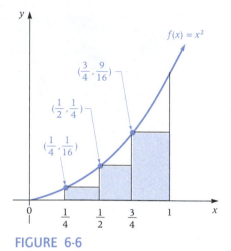

FIGURE 6-6

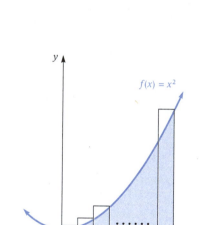

FIGURE 6-7

the height of the second rectangle is

$$f\left(\frac{2}{n}\right) = \left(\frac{2}{n}\right)^2 = \frac{2^2}{n^2}$$

and the height of the nth rectangle is

$$f\left(\frac{n}{n}\right) = \left(\frac{n}{n}\right)^2 = \frac{n^2}{n^2}$$

Since the area of each rectangle is the width times the height, the sum of the areas of the respective rectangles is

$$S = \left[\frac{1}{n} \cdot f\left(\frac{1}{n}\right)\right] + \left[\frac{1}{n} \cdot f\left(\frac{2}{n}\right)\right] + \ldots + \left[\frac{1}{n} \cdot f\left(\frac{n}{n}\right)\right]$$

$$= \left(\frac{1}{n} \cdot \frac{1^2}{n^2}\right) + \left(\frac{1}{n} \cdot \frac{2^2}{n^2}\right) + \ldots + \left(\frac{1}{n} \cdot \frac{n^2}{n^2}\right)$$

$$= \frac{1}{n^3}(1^2 + 2^2 + \ldots + n^2)$$

It can be verified that

$$1^2 + 2^2 + \ldots + n^2 = \frac{n(n + 1)(2n + 1)}{6}$$

Substituting this result into the preceding equation for S yields

$$S = \frac{1}{n^3}\left[\frac{n(n + 1)(2n + 1)}{6}\right]$$

$$= \frac{(n + 1)(2n + 1)}{6n^2}$$

$$= \frac{2n^2 + 3n + 1}{6n^2}$$

$$= \frac{2n^2}{6n^2} + \frac{3n}{6n^2} + \frac{1}{6n^2}$$

$$= \frac{1}{3} + \frac{1}{2n} + \frac{1}{6n^2}$$

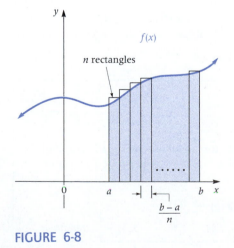

FIGURE 6-8

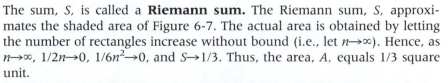

The sum, S, is called a **Riemann sum.** The Riemann sum, S, approximates the shaded area of Figure 6-7. The actual area is obtained by letting the number of rectangles increase without bound (i.e., let $n \to \infty$). Hence, as $n \to \infty$, $1/2n \to 0$, $1/6n^2 \to 0$, and $S \to 1/3$. Thus, the area, A, equals 1/3 square unit.

In summary, if $f(x)$ is a non-negative continuous function over the interval $a \le x \le b$, then the area, A, between $f(x)$ and the x-axis from $x = a$ to $x = b$ may be approximated by the sum of areas of rectangles, as illustrated in Figure 6-8.

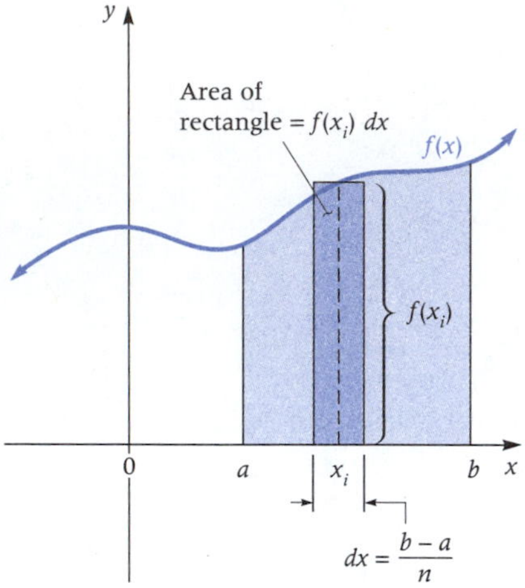

$$y$$

Area of
rectangle $= f(x_i)\, dx$

$f(x)$

$f(x_i)$

0   a x_i b x

$$dx = \frac{b - a}{n}$$

FIGURE 6-9

Each rectangle is constructed as follows:

1. The interval $a \leq x \leq b$ is divided into n subintervals, each of width $dx = (b - a)/n$.
2. The height of the ith rectangle is $f(x_i)$, where x_i may be any point in the ith subinterval (see Figure 6-9).

Thus, the area between $f(x)$ and the x-axis from $x = a$ to $x = b$ is approximated by the Riemann sum,

$$S = f(x_1)\, dx + f(x_2)\, dx + \ldots + f(x_n)\, dx$$

As $n \to \infty$, the Riemann sum approaches the area, A.

Fundamental Theorem of Calculus

We now state a result that relates area under a curve to the antiderivative. This result is called the **fundamental theorem of calculus.** An informal argument for the theorem appears later in this section.

> **SUMMARY**
>
> **Fundamental Theorem of Calculus**
>
> Let $f(x)$ be defined and continuous over the interval $a \leq x \leq b$. Let $F(x)$ be an antiderivative of $f(x)$. Then the limit of every possible Riemann sum equals
>
> $$\int_a^b f(x)\, dx = F(b) - F(a)$$

The fundamental theorem of calculus allows us to compute the area under the graph of a continuous non-negative function $f(x)$ over the interval $a \leq x \leq b$ by $\int_a^b f(x)\, dx = F(b) - F(a)$, where $F(x)$ is an antiderivative of $f(x)$ (see Figure 6-10). We note that the restriction that $f(x)$ be non-negative is needed only when the fundamental theorem is used to find area. However, later in this section, we will learn how to apply the fundamental theorem to find area when $f(x)$ is negative over some interval. We summarize as follows.

> **SUMMARY**
>
> **Area Under a Curve**
>
> If $f(x) \geq 0$ over the interval $a \leq x \leq b$, the area bounded by the graph of $f(x)$ and the x-axis over the interval $a \leq x \leq b$, as illustrated in Figure 6-10, is given by
>
> $$\int_a^b f(x)\, dx = F(b) - F(a)$$
>
> *continues*

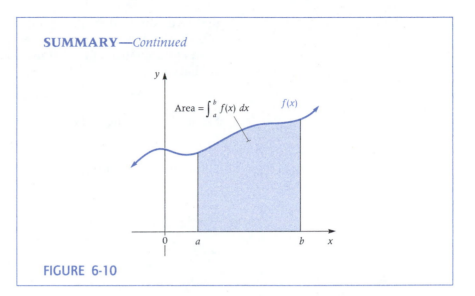

SUMMARY—*Continued*

Area $= \int_a^b f(x)\, dx$

$f(x)$

FIGURE 6-10

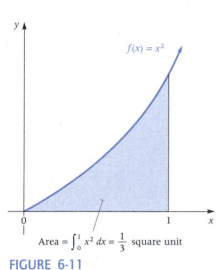

$f(x) = x^2$

Area $= \int_0^1 x^2\, dx = \dfrac{1}{3}$ square unit

FIGURE 6-11

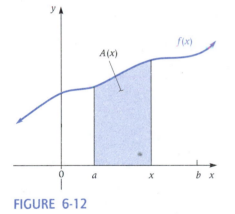

$A(x)$

$f(x)$

FIGURE 6-12

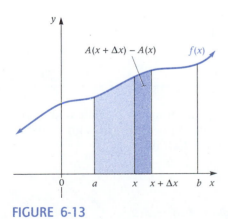

$A(x + \Delta x) - A(x)$

$f(x)$

FIGURE 6-13

Thus, for our illustrative example, the actual area between $f(x) = x^2$ and the x-axis from $x = 0$ to $x = 1$ is given by

$$\int_0^1 x^2\, dx = \underbrace{\frac{1}{3}x^3}_{F(x)} \Big|_0^1$$

$$= F(1) - F(0)$$

$$= \frac{1}{3} - 0$$

$$= \frac{1}{3} \text{ square unit}$$

This result is illustrated in Figure 6-11.

Before proceeding with more examples, we now present an informal argument for the fundamental theorem of calculus.

Let $A(x)$ be a function that represents the area between $f(x)$ and the x-axis (see Figure 6-12) from a to x, where x is any number within the interval $a \leq x \leq b$. Note that $A(a) = 0$ and $A(b)$ represents the area over the entire interval $a \leq x \leq b$. If Δx is a small positive number, then $A(x + \Delta x) - A(x)$ is the area of the darker shaded region of Figure 6-13. This darker shaded region is approximately a rectangle with height $f(x)$, width Δx, and area $\Delta x \cdot f(x)$. Hence, we may write

$$A(x + \Delta x) - A(x) \approx \Delta x \cdot f(x)$$

where the approximation gets better as Δx approaches 0. Dividing this expression by Δx, we obtain

$$\frac{A(x + \Delta x) - A(x)}{\Delta x} \approx f(x)$$

Since the approximation becomes better as Δx approaches 0, the quotient, $[A(x + \Delta x) - A(x)]/\Delta x$, approaches $f(x)$. From the definition of a derivative, we know that the quotient, $[A(x + \Delta x) - A(x)]/\Delta x$, approaches $A'(x) = f(x)$. Since x is any number within the interval $a \leq x \leq b$, then $A(x)$ is an antiderivative of $f(x)$. Thus, if $F(x)$ is any other antiderivative of $f(x)$, we have

$$A(x) = F(x) + c$$

Since $A(a) = 0$, then $A(a) = F(a) + c = 0$ and

$$c = -F(a)$$

Substituting this into $A(x) = F(x) + c$ gives us

$$A(x) = F(x) - F(a)$$

Hence,

$$A(b) = F(b) - F(a)$$
$$= \int_a^b f(x) \, dx$$

Note that the fundamental theorem requires that the function $f(x)$ be non-negative over the interval $a \leq x \leq b$. If $f(x)$ is *negative* over the interval $a \leq x \leq b$, the definite integral, $\int_a^b f(x) \, dx$, results in a value that is the negative of the area between $f(x)$ and the x-axis from $x = a$ to $x = b$. In such a case, the area between the x-axis and the curve is the absolute value of the definite integral, $\int_a^b f(x) \, dx$. This is illustrated in Example 6-19.

We now state the following properties of definite integrals.

SUMMARY

Properties of Definite Integrals

1. $\displaystyle\int_a^a f(x) \, dx = 0$

2. $\displaystyle\int_a^b f(x) \, dx = - \int_b^a f(x) \, dx$

3. $\displaystyle\int_a^b k \cdot f(x) \, dx = k \int_a^b f(x) \, dx$ (k is a constant)

4. $\displaystyle\int_a^b [f(x) \pm g(x)] \, dx = \int_a^b f(x) \, dx \pm \int_a^b g(x) \, dx$

5. $\displaystyle\int_a^b f(x) \, dx = \int_a^c f(x) \, dx + \int_c^b f(x) \, dx$

We verify properties 1 and 2 and explain property 5, while noting that properties 3 and 4 parallel the constant multiplier and the sum or difference rules for indefinite integrals. If $F'(x) = f(x)$, then

1. $\displaystyle\int_a^a f(x) \, dx = F(a) - F(a) = 0$

2. $\displaystyle\int_a^b f(x) \, dx = F(b) - F(a), \int_b^a f(x) \, dx = F(a) - F(b)$

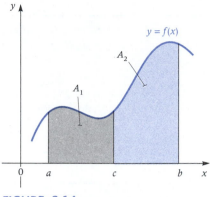

FIGURE 6-14

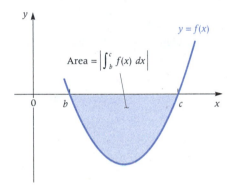

FIGURE 6-15

Since $F(b) - F(a) = -[F(a) - F(b)]$, then

$$\int_a^b f(x)\, dx = -\int_b^a f(x)\, dx$$

3. For $f(x) > 0$ and $a < c < b$, this property indicates that the area from $x = a$ to $x = b$ equals the sum of the component areas, A_1 and A_2 (see Figure 6-14). This allows us to split the interval over which a definite integral is evaluated. Although this property makes most sense when c lies within the interval $a < x < b$, it holds for any value of c for which both $f(x)$ and $F(x)$ are defined.

Areas Below the x-Axis

If $f(x) < 0$ over some interval $b < x < c$, the corresponding area between the graph of $f(x)$ and the x-axis lies below the x-axis (see Figure 6-15). The definite integral $\int_b^c f(x)\, dx$ results in a value that is the negative of the area, so the absolute value of such a definite integral gives the area, as indicated in Figure 6-15.

The following box provides a procedure for determining areas that lie above and below the x-axis.

■ SUMMARY

Areas Above and Below the x-Axis

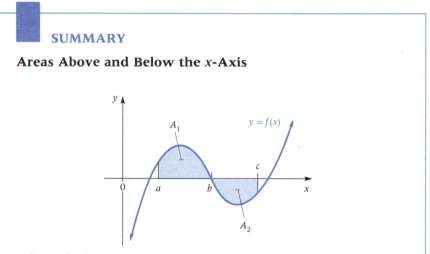

FIGURE 6-16

For a situation where the indicated area lies above and below the x-axis, as illustrated in Figure 6-16, the total area, A, is determined by finding the separate areas, A_1 and A_2, and summing the results. Hence,

$$A = A_1 + A_2$$

where

$$A_1 = \int_a^b f(x)\, dx \qquad \text{and} \qquad A_2 = \left| \int_b^c f(x)\, dx \right|$$

In the following box, we state a procedure that should be followed when finding areas.

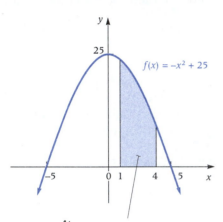

$$Area = \int_1^4 (-x^2 + 25)\, dx = 54 \text{ square units}$$

FIGURE 6-17

> **To Find Areas**
>
> 1. Graph the function.
> 2. Find any x-intercepts.
> 3. Shade the area to be found.
> 4. Note whether the shaded area contains any regions that lie below the x-axis as well as above the x-axis.
> 5. Evaluate the appropriate definite integrals.

• EXAMPLE 6-18

Find the area between the x-axis and the curve $f(x) = -x^2 + 25$ from $x = 1$ to $x = 4$.

Solution

A sketch of $f(x)$ and the indicated area appears in Figure 6-17. The shaded area is computed by the definite integral

$$\int_1^4 (-x^2 + 25)\, dx = \underbrace{-\frac{1}{3}x^3 + 25x}_{F(x)} \Big|_1^4$$

$$= F(4) - F(1)$$

$$= \left[-\frac{1}{3}(4^3) + 25(4) \right] - \left[-\frac{1}{3}(1^3) + 25(1) \right]$$

$$= \frac{236}{3} - \frac{74}{3}$$

$$= \frac{162}{3}$$

$$= 54 \text{ square units}$$

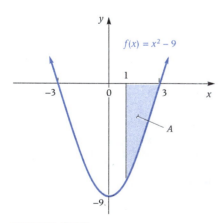

FIGURE 6-18

• EXAMPLE 6-19

Find the area between the x-axis and the curve $f(x) = x^2 - 9$ from $x = 1$ to $x = 3$.

Solution

A sketch of $f(x)$ and the indicated area appears in Figure 6-18. Observe that $f(x) \le 0$ over the interval $1 \le x \le 3$, and, thus, the shaded area appears below the x-axis. To determine the area, A, we begin by computing the definite integral as follows:

$$\int_1^3 (x^2 - 9)\, dx = \underbrace{\frac{1}{3}x^3 - 9x}_{F(x)} \Big|_1^3$$

$$= F(3) - F(1)$$

$$= \left[\frac{1}{3}(3^3) - 9(3) \right] - \left[\frac{1}{3}(1^3) - 9(1) \right]$$

$$= -18 - \left(-8\frac{2}{3} \right)$$

$$= -9\frac{1}{3}$$

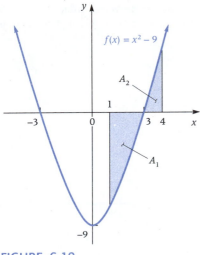

$f(x) = x^2 - 9$

A_2

A_1

FIGURE 6-19

The definite integral results in a negative number because the area is located below the x-axis. Thus,

$$A = \left| -9\frac{1}{3} \right| = 9\frac{1}{3} \text{ square units}$$

•

Example 6-20 illustrates a situation where some of the desired area is above the x-axis and some is below the x-axis.

• **EXAMPLE 6-20**

Find the area between the x-axis and the curve $f(x) = x^2 - 9$ from $x = 1$ to $x = 4$.

Solution

A sketch of $f(x)$ and the indicated area appears in Figure 6-19. Observe that $f(x) \leq 0$ over the interval $1 \leq x \leq 3$ and $f(x) \geq 0$ over the interval $3 \leq x \leq 4$. Thus, part of the area appears below the x-axis, and part appears above the x-axis. Each part must be determined separately. Since A_1, the area below, was determined in Example 6-19, we now compute A_2 as follows:

$$A_2 = \int_3^4 (x^2 - 9)\, dx = \underbrace{\frac{1}{3}x^3 - 9x}_{F(x)} \Big|_3^4$$

$$= F(4) - F(3)$$

$$= \left[\frac{1}{3}(4^3) - 9(4) \right] - \left[\frac{1}{3}(3^3) - 9(3) \right]$$

$$= \left(\frac{64}{3} - 36 \right) - (-18)$$

$$= 3\frac{1}{3} \text{ square units}$$

Thus, the total area is

$$A = A_1 + A_2$$

$$= 9\frac{1}{3} + 3\frac{1}{3}$$

$$= 12\frac{2}{3} \text{ square units}$$

Application

• **EXAMPLE 6-21**   **Velocity/Distance.**

The velocity (or speed), v (in feet per second), of a moving particle after t seconds have elapsed is given by

$$v(t) = 3t^2 + 2t \qquad (t \geq 0)$$

Determine the distance traveled by the particle from the end of the third second to the end of the sixth second or, in other words, over the interval $3 \leq t \leq 6$.

Solution

We first sketch a graph of the function in Figure 6-20 and shade the area over the indicated interval.

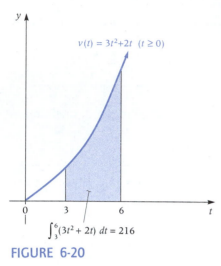

$$\int_3^6 (3t^2 + 2t)\, dt = 216$$

FIGURE 6-20

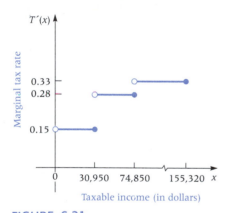

FIGURE 6-21

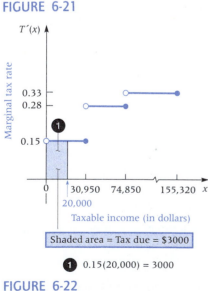

Shaded area = Tax due = $3000

① 0.15(20,000) = 3000

FIGURE 6-22

Since $v(t) = S'(t)$, where $S(t)$ denotes the distance traveled after t seconds have elapsed, then the distance traveled during the time interval $3 \leq t \leq 6$ is given by

$$\int_3^6 S'(t)\, dt = \int_3^6 v(t)\, dt$$

$$= \int_3^6 (3t^2 + 2t)\, dt$$

$$= (t^3 + t^2) \Big|_3^6$$

$$= (6^3 + 6^2) - (3^3 + 3^2)$$

$$= 216 \text{ feet}$$

Marginal Tax Rates

As we learned in the preceding section, the marginal tax rate gives the amount of federal income tax due on each additional dollar of taxable income. For married people filing jointly and qualifying widow(er)s with taxable incomes not exceeding $155,320 during the 1989 tax year, the marginal tax rate, $T'(x)$, is given by the function

$$T'(x) = \begin{cases} 0.15 & \text{if} \quad\quad 0 < x \leq 30{,}950 \\ 0.28 & \text{if } 30{,}950 < x \leq 74{,}850 \\ 0.33 & \text{if } 74{,}850 < x \leq 155{,}320 \end{cases}$$

where x denotes annual taxable income in dollars.

The graph of $T'(x)$ is given in Figure 6-21. Note that

the area under the graph of T'(x) *gives the amount of federal income tax due.*

Thus, for taxable income of $20,000, the amount of federal income tax due is given by the area over the interval $0 < x \leq 20{,}000$ (see Figure 6-22), which can be determined by the definite integral

$$\int_0^{20{,}000} T'(x)\, dx = \int_0^{20{,}000} 0.15\, dx$$

$$= 0.15x \Big|_0^{20{,}000}$$

$$= 0.15(20{,}000) - 0.15(0)$$

$$= \$3000$$

This is illustrated in Figure 6-22, where the area is determined by multiplying the length and width of the rectangle. Note that the definite integral agrees with the result of Figure 6-22.

For taxable income of $40,000, the amount of federal income tax due

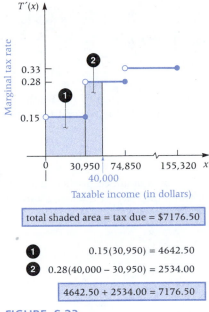

Marginal tax rate

0.33

0.28

0.15

0   30,950   74,850   155,320 x
            40,000

Taxable income (in dollars)

total shaded area = tax due = $7176.50

1   0.15(30,950) = 4642.50

2   0.28(40,000 – 30,950) = 2534.00

4642.50 + 2534.00 = 7176.50

FIGURE 6-23

is given by the area over the interval $0 < x \leq 40,000$ (see Figure 6-23). This area can be determined by the definite integral

$$\int_0^{40,000} T'(x)\ dx$$

Since $T'(x)$ is piecewise defined by different formulas on either side of the discontinuity at $x = 30,950$, the above definite integral is evaluated as the sum of the definite integrals given below.

$$\int_0^{30,950} 0.15\ dx + \int_{30,950}^{40,000} 0.28\ dx$$

Note that we have split the interval $0 < x \leq 40,000$ at the point of discontinuity, $x = 30,950$. In general, this is permissible for a function $f(x)$ defined over some interval if $|f(x)| < M$ (where M is a constant) for all values of x in the interval, and if $f(x)$ has at most a finite number of discontinuities over the interval.

Evaluating each definite integral gives the following results:

$$\int_0^{30,950} 0.15\ dx = 0.15x \Big|_0^{30,950}$$

$$= 0.15(30,950) - 0.15(0)$$

$$= 4642.50$$

$$\int_{30,950}^{40,000} 0.28\ dx = 0.28x \Big|_{30,950}^{40,000}$$

$$= 0.28(40,000) - 0.28(30,950)$$

$$= 0.28(40,000 - 30,950)$$

$$= 2534$$

Thus,

$$\int_0^{40,000} T'(x)\ dx = 4642.50 + 2534 = \$7176.50 \qquad \text{Tax Due}$$

This is illustrated in Figure 6-23, where the area of each rectangle is determined by multiplying its length and width. Note that the definite integral agrees with the result of Figure 6-23.

Exercises 6-2

Evaluate each of the following.

1. $\displaystyle\int_1^3 4x^3\ dx$

2. $\displaystyle\int_2^5 \frac{-6}{x^2}\ dx$

3. $\displaystyle\int_0^1 (4x + 1)\ dx$

4. $\displaystyle\int_{-2}^4 (8x^3 - 6x^2 + 2)\ dx$

5. $\displaystyle\int_1^4 \frac{4}{x^3}\ dx$

6. $\displaystyle\int_1^{27} 5\sqrt[3]{x}\ dx$

7. $\displaystyle\int_1^5 \frac{10}{x}\ dx$

8. $\displaystyle\int_2^4 \frac{8}{x}\ dx$

9. $\int_0^3 e^x \, dx$

10. $\int_1^{10} e^{-x} \, dx$

11. $\int_0^2 e^{-2x} \, dx$

12. $\int_0^1 e^{-4x} \, dx$

Area Approximation

Find both lower and upper approximations of the area bounded by the x-axis and the curve $f(x) = -x^2 + 4$ from $x = 0$ to $x = 1$ by dividing the interval $0 \le x \le 1$ into the following.

13. 4 subintervals
14. 10 subintervals

Find both lower and upper approximations of the area bounded by the x-axis and the curve $f(x) = 2x^2$ from $x = 1$ to $x = 2$ by dividing the interval $1 \le x \le 2$ into the following.

15. 5 subintervals
16. 10 subintervals

Riemann Sum

17. Using the formula

$$1 + 2 + \ldots + n = \frac{n(n + 1)}{2}$$

in conjunction with a Riemann sum as developed in this section, find the area bounded by the x-axis and the graph of $f(x) = x$ from $x = 0$ to $x = 1$. Check your answer by using $F(1) - F(0)$.

18. Using the formula

$$1^3 + 2^3 + \ldots + n^3 = \left[\frac{n(n + 1)}{2} \right]^2$$

in conjunction with a Riemann sum as developed in this section, find the area bounded by the x-axis and the graph of $f(x) = x^3$ over the interval $0 \le x \le 1$. Check your answer by using $F(1) - F(0)$.

19. Find the area between the curve $f(x) = 3x^2$ and the x-axis from $x = 0$ to $x = 1$ by using
    a) The Riemann sum as developed in this section.
    b) The definite integral.

Definite Integral Versus Area Approximation

20. Use the definite integral to determine the area bounded by the x-axis and the curve $f(x) = -x^2 + 4$ from $x = 0$ to $x = 1$. Compare your answer with those in Exercises 13 and 14.

21. Use the definite integral to determine the area bounded by the x-axis and the curve $f(x) = 2x^2$ from $x = 1$ to $x = 2$. Compare your answer with those in Exercises 15 and 16.

Definite Integrals and Areas

22. Find the area between the x-axis and the curve $f(x) = 3x^2 + 5$ from $x = 2$ to $x = 5$. Graph the curve and shade the desired area.

23. Find the area between the x-axis and the curve $y = x^3$ from $x = 0$ to $x = 4$. Graph the curve and shade the desired area.

24. Find the area between the x-axis and the curve $f(x) = -3x^2 + 24x$ from $x = 0$ to $x = 8$. Graph the curve and shade the desired area.
25. Find the area between the x-axis and the curve $f(x) = 1/x^2$ from $x = 1$ to $x = 3$. Graph the curve and shade the desired area.
26. Find the area between the x-axis and the curve $y = 2x + 6$ from $x = 0$ to $x = 2$. Graph the curve and shade the desired area.
27. Find the area between the x-axis and the curve $y = -2x + 8$ from $x = 0$ to $x = 3$. Graph the curve and shade the desired area.
28. Find the area between the x-axis and the curve $y = -x$ from $x = -2$ to $x = 0$. Graph the curve and shade the desired area.
29. Find the area between the x-axis and the curve $y = -2x$ from $x = -3$ to $x = -1$. Graph the curve and shade the desired area.
30. Find the area between the x-axis and the curve $y = -x^2 + 16$ from $x = 0$ to $x = 4$. Graph the curve and shade the desired area.
31. Find the area between the x-axis and the curve $y = -x^2 + 25$ from $x = 0$ to $x = 5$. Graph the curve and shade the desired area.
32. Find the area between the x-axis and the curve $y = -4x^2 + 32x$ from $x = 0$ to $x = 8$. Graph the curve and shade the desired area.
33. Find the area between the x-axis and the curve $y = -5x^2 + 20x$ from $x = 0$ to $x = 4$. Graph the curve and shade the desired area.
34. Find the area between the x-axis and the curve $y = x^2 - 4x + 5$ from $x = 0$ to $x = 2$. Graph the curve and shade the desired area.
35. Find the area between the x-axis and the curve $y = x^2 - 6x + 12$ from $x = 0$ to $x = 4$. Graph the curve and shade the desired area.
36. Find the area between the x-axis and the curve $y = x^2 - 10x + 30$ from $x = 1$ to $x = 2$. Graph the curve and shade the desired area.
37. Find the area between the x-axis and the curve $y = x^2 - 2x + 8$ from $x = -3$ to $x = 3$. Graph the curve and shade the desired area.
38. Find the area between the x-axis and the curve $y = e^x$ from $x = 0$ to $x = 2$. Graph the curve and shade the desired area.
39. Find the area between the x-axis and the curve $y = e^{-x}$ from $x = 0$ to $x = -3$. Graph the curve and shade the desired area.
40. Find the area between the x-axis and the curve $y = e^{-x}$ from $x = 0$ to $x = 3$. Graph the curve and shade the desired area.
41. Find the area between the x-axis and the curve $y = e^x$ from $x = -1$ to $x = 1$. Graph the curve and shade the desired area.
42. Find the area between the x-axis and the curve $y = 1/x$ from $x = 1$ to $x = 4$. Graph the curve and shade the desired area.
43. Find the area between the x-axis and the curve $y = 1/x$ from $x = 1$ to $x = 5$. Graph the curve and shade the desired area.
44. Find the area between the x-axis and the curve $y = 1/x^2$ from $x = 1$ to $x = 2$. Graph the curve and shade the desired area.
45. Find the area between the x-axis and the curve $y = 1/x^4$ from $x = 2$ to $x = 4$. Graph the curve and shade the desired area.
46. Find the area between the x-axis and the curve $y = x^4$ from $x = -2$ to $x = 2$. Graph the curve and shade the desired area.
47. Find the area between the x-axis and the curve $y = x^5$ from $x = 0$ to $x = 1$. Graph the curve and shade the desired area.

Areas Above and Below the x-Axis

For each of the following, find the area bounded by the x-axis and the function over the indicated interval. Graph the function and shade the desired area.

48. $y = x^2 - 9, 0 \le x \le 6$

49. $y = x^2 - 4, 0 \le x \le 3$

50. $y = x, -2 \le x \le 2$

51. $y = -x, -4 \le x \le 4$

52. $y = -x^2 + 1, 0 \le x \le 3$

53. $y = -x^2 + 4, 0 \le x \le 3$

54. $y = 4x - 12, 0 \le x \le 4$

55. $y = -2x + 6, 0 \le x \le 6$

56. $y = x^3, -1 \le x \le 1$

57. $y = -x^3, -2 \le x \le 4$

58. $y = x^2 - 4x - 5, 3 \le x \le 6$

59. $y = x^2 - x - 2, 0 \le x \le 3$

60. $y = -1 + 1/x, 0.5 \le x \le 4$

61. $y = -1 + 4/x, 1 \le x \le 6$

62. $y = -1 + 4/x^2, 1 \le x \le 4$

63. $y = -1 + 9/x^2, 1 \le x \le 6$

64. $y = 3x^2 - 27, 0 \le x \le 4$

65. $y = -3x^2 + 12, 0 \le x \le 6$

Applications

Marginal cost/Cost. For each marginal cost function, $C'(x)$, where x denotes the number of units produced, determine the total change in cost over the interval $a \le x \le b$ by using the definite integral

$$\int_a^b C'(x) \, dx = C(b) - C(a)$$

66. $C'(x) = 10x + 50, 5 \le x \le 10$

67. $C'(x) = 20x + 100, 10 \le x \le 20$

68. $C'(x) = 30x + 600, 20 \le x \le 30$

Marginal revenue/Revenue. For each marginal revenue function, $R'(x)$, where x denotes the number of units sold, determine the total change in revenue over the interval $a \le x \le b$ by using the formula

$$\int_a^b R'(x) \, dx = R(b) - R(a)$$

69. $R'(x) = -2x + 100, 10 \le x \le 30$

70. $R'(x) = -4x + 800, 20 \le x \le 50$

71. $R'(x) = -8x + 400, 5 \le x \le 40$

Velocity/Distance. Each of the following functions gives the velocity (or speed), v (in feet per second), of a moving particle after t seconds have elapsed. Find the distance traveled by the particle over the indicated interval.

72. $v(t) = 3t^2 + 4t, 0 \le t \le 3$

73. $v(t) = 6t^2 + 5t, 0 \le t \le 6$

74. $v(t) = 4t^3, 1 \le t \le 2$

75. $v(t) = 6t^5, 0 \le t \le 1$

76. *Oil leak.* Oil is leaking from a tanker at the rate of

$$L'(t) = 50t + 20$$

gallons per hour, where t denotes elapsed time (in hours) since the leak began.

a) Find the total number of gallons that have leaked during the first hour (or, in other words, during the time interval $0 \le t \le 1$).

b) Find the total number of gallons that have leaked during the first 2 hours.

c) Find the total number of gallons that have leaked during the third hour (or, in other words, during the time interval $2 \le t \le 3$).

77. *Natural gas leak.* A truck carrying natural gas gets stuck at a low underpass and leaks natural gas at the rate of

$$L'(t) = 10t + 20$$

cubic feet per minute, where t denotes time (in minutes) elapsed since the gas first began leaking.

a) Find the total amount of natural gas that has leaked during the first 5 minutes.

b) Find the total amount of gas that has leaked during the first 10 minutes.

c) Find the total amount of gas that has leaked during the fifth minute (i.e., $4 \leq t \leq 5$).

d) Find the total amount of gas that has leaked during the sixth minute.

78. *Timber depletion.* In a given geographic area, timber is being depleted at the rate of

$$D'(t) = 2000e^t$$

trees per year, where t denotes time in years, with $t = 0$ denoting the present year.

a) How many trees will be cut down during the first year?

b) How many trees will be cut down during the second year?

c) How many trees will be cut down during the third year?

79. *Marketing.* The weekly rate of increase in sales of a new product is given by

$$S'(t) = 100 - 100e^{-0.20t}$$

where t denotes the number of weeks since the beginning of an advertising campaign for the product. Determine the total sales during

a) The first 5 weeks.   b) The first 10 weeks.

80. *Population growth.* The population, P, of a state is growing at an annual rate given by

$$P'(t) = 4000e^{0.10t}$$

where t denotes the time elapsed (in years) since the end of last year. Find the total increase in population during the next

a) 2 years.   b) 4 years.   c) 6 years.   d) 10 years.

81. *Job growth.* For a given state, the annual rate of increase of jobs is given by

$$J'(t) = 100e^{-0.05t}$$

where t denotes the time elapsed (in years) since the end of last year. Find the total increase in jobs during the next

a) 2 years.   b) 3 years.   c) 5 years.   d) 10 years.

Marginal tax rates. For single tax filers with annual taxable incomes not exceeding $93,130 during the 1989 tax year, the federal marginal tax rate, $T'(x)$, is given by the function

$$T'(x) = \begin{cases} 0.15 & \text{if} \quad\quad 0 < x \leq 18{,}550 \\ 0.28 & \text{if } 18{,}550 < x \leq 44{,}900 \\ 0.33 & \text{if } 44{,}900 < x \leq 93{,}130 \end{cases}$$

Find the appropriate area under the graph of $T'(x)$ by integration in order to determine the amount of federal income tax due on the following taxable incomes.

82. $14,000	**83.** $18,400	**84.** $19,000
85. $30,000	**86.** $43,000	**87.** $50,000
88. $60,000	**89.** $80,000	**90.** $90,000

6-3 • AREA BETWEEN TWO CURVES

Sometimes we must determine the area between the graphs of two continuous functions, $f(x)$ and $g(x)$, over an interval, $a \leq x \leq b$, as

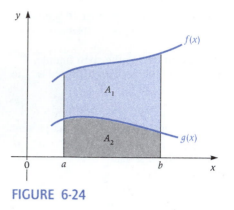

FIGURE 6-24

illustrated by the shaded area A_1 of Figure 6-24. The shaded area A_1 is determined by noting the following:

1. The area A_2 is the area between the graph of $g(x)$ and the x-axis over the interval $a \leq x \leq b$. Therefore, it is determined by the definite integral given below.

$$A_2 = \int_a^b g(x) \, dx$$

2. The area $A_1 + A_2$ is the area between the x-axis and the graph of $f(x)$ over the interval $a \leq x \leq b$. Therefore, it is determined by the definite integral given below.

$$A_1 + A_2 = \int_a^b f(x) \, dx$$

3. This implies that

$$A_1 = \int_a^b f(x) \, dx - \int_a^b g(x) \, dx$$

$$= \int_a^b [f(x) - g(x)] \, dx$$

where $f(x) \geq g(x)$ over the interval $a \leq x \leq b$. This formula holds even if $f(x)$ or $g(x)$ is negative for values of x in the interval $a \leq x \leq b$.

We summarize as follows.

SUMMARY

Area Between Two Curves

The area between the graphs of two continuous functions, f and g, over an interval, $a \leq x \leq b$, where $f(x) \geq g(x)$ (as illustrated in Figure 6-25), is given by the definite integral

$$\int_a^b [f(x) - g(x)] \, dx$$

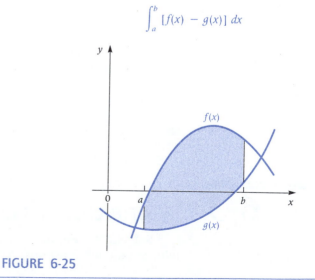

FIGURE 6-25

• **EXAMPLE 6-22**

Find the area between $f(x) = x + 6$ and $g(x) = x^2$ from $x = 1$ to $x = 2$.

Solution

A sketch of both functions appears in Figure 6-26. We must determine the x-coordinates of both intersection points of the functions. Setting

$$f(x) = g(x)$$

we have

$$x + 6 = x^2$$

Solving for x yields

$$0 = x^2 - x - 6$$
$$0 = (x - 3)(x + 2)$$
$$x - 3 = 0 \qquad x + 2 = 0$$
$$x = 3 \qquad\quad x = -2$$

The area included between the two curves from $x = 1$ to $x = 2$ is shaded in Figure 6-27. This area is determined by the definite integral

$$\int_1^2 [f(x) - g(x)]\, dx$$

where

$$f(x) - g(x) = x + 6 - x^2$$
$$= -x^2 + x + 6$$

Thus, we have

$$\int_1^2 [f(x) - g(x)]\, dx = \int_1^2 (-x^2 + x + 6)\, dx$$

$$= \underbrace{-\frac{1}{3}x^3 + \frac{1}{2}x^2 + 6x \Big|_1^2}_{F(x)}$$

$$= F(2) - F(1)$$

$$= \frac{34}{3} - \frac{37}{6}$$

$$= \frac{31}{6} \text{ square units}$$

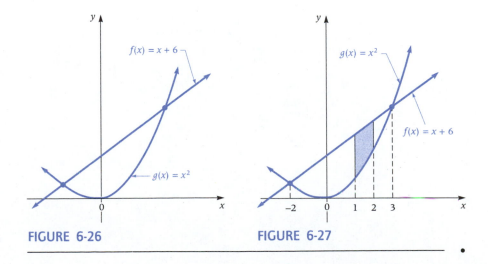

FIGURE 6-26   **FIGURE 6-27**

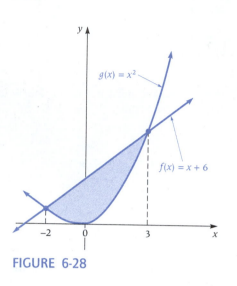

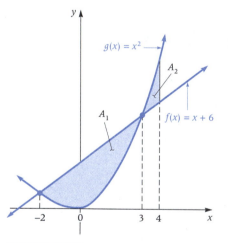

FIGURE 6-28

FIGURE 6-29

• **EXAMPLE 6-23**

Find the total area bounded by the graphs of $f(x) = x + 6$ and $g(x) = x^2$ in Example 6-22.

Solution

We seek the shaded area in Figure 6-28. This area is determined by the definite integral

$$\int_{-2}^{3} [f(x) - g(x)] \, dx = \int_{-2}^{3} (-x^2 + x + 6) \, dx$$

$$= \underbrace{-\frac{1}{3}x^3 + \frac{1}{2}x^2 + 6x}_{F(x)} \Big|_{-2}^{3}$$

$$= F(3) - F(-2)$$

$$= \frac{27}{2} - \left(-\frac{22}{3}\right)$$

$$= \frac{125}{6} \text{ square units}$$

• **EXAMPLE 6-24**

Find the area included between the graphs of the functions $f(x) = x + 6$ and $g(x) = x^2$ in Examples 6-22 and 6-23 from $x = -2$ to $x = 4$.

Solution

We seek the shaded area in Figure 6-29. Observing Figure 6-29, note that for the area between $x = 3$ and $x = 4$, $g(x) \geq f(x)$. Thus, we must determine area A_2 separately by the definite integral

$$\int_{3}^{4} [g(x) - f(x)] \, dx$$

Since

$$g(x) - f(x) = x^2 - (x + 6)$$
$$= x^2 - x - 6$$

then we have

$$\int_{3}^{4} [g(x) - f(x)] \, dx = \int_{3}^{4} (x^2 - x - 6) \, dx$$

$$= \underbrace{\frac{1}{3}x^3 - \frac{1}{2}x^2 - 6x}_{F(x)} \Big|_{3}^{4}$$

$$= F(4) - F(3)$$

$$= -\frac{32}{3} - \left(-\frac{27}{2}\right)$$

$$= -\frac{64}{6} + \frac{81}{6}$$

$$= \frac{17}{6} \text{ square units}$$

Since area A_1 was determined in Example 6-23, the total area, A, is

$$A = A_1 + A_2$$
$$= \frac{125}{6} + \frac{17}{6}$$
$$= \frac{71}{3} \text{ square units}$$

• EXAMPLE 6-25

Find the area between the graphs of $f(x) = 2x + 8$ and $g(x) = -3x^2$ from $x = -1$ to $x = 2$.

Solution

A sketch of both functions is given in Figure 6-30. Since the graphs of Figure 6-30 indicate that the curves do not intersect, we do not have to determine intersection points. The area to be determined is shaded in Figure 6-30 and is given by the definite integral

$$\int_{-1}^{2} [f(x) - g(x)] \, dx$$

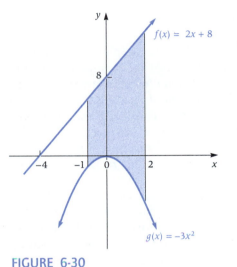

FIGURE 6-30

where

$$f(x) - g(x) = 2x + 8 - (-3x^2)$$
$$= 3x^2 + 2x + 8$$

Thus,

$$\int_{-1}^{2} [f(x) - g(x)] \, dx = \int_{-1}^{2} [3x^2 + 2x + 8] \, dx$$
$$= x^3 + x^2 + 8x \Big|_{-1}^{2}$$
$$= F(2) - F(-1)$$
$$= [2^3 + 2^2 + 8(2)] - [(-1)^3 + (-1)^2 + 8(-1)]$$
$$= [28] - [-8] = 36 \text{ square units}$$

Application

Consumers' and Producers' Surpluses

Suppose a product has the supply function $p = S(q)$ and the demand function $p = D(q)$, as illustrated in Figure 6-31 on page 386. Assume that p denotes the unit price (in dollars) of this product and q denotes the number of units supplied or demanded. Thus, the supply function, $p = S(q)$, gives the unit price at which suppliers are willing to produce q units of this product; the demand function, $p = D(q)$, gives the unit price at which consumers are willing to buy q units of this product. Note that, at the equilibrium point, supply = demand = q_E units and the unit price stabilizes at p_E dollars.

However, when the market is at equilibrium, there are still some consumers who would have paid a unit price higher than the equilibrium price, p_E. Since these consumers would have paid a unit price p, where $p > p_E$, then the area under the demand curve, but above the horizontal line, $p = p_E$, represents the increase in unit price times demand, or the ad-

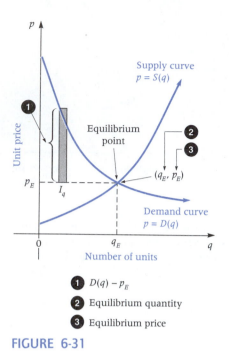

1 $D(q) - p_E$

2 Equilibrium quantity

3 Equilibrium price

FIGURE 6-31

ditional revenue that would have been paid by these consumers (see Figure 6-31). Since the market is at equilibrium, this additional revenue is not paid by consumers; thus, it is the total amount of money saved by consumers as a result of the market being at equilibrium and is called the **consumers' surplus.** Since the consumers' surplus (denoted CS) is represented by the area under the demand curve, but above the horizontal line, $p = p_E$, over the interval $0 \leq q \leq q_E$, as illustrated in Figure 6-32, it is determined by the definite integral

$$\text{CS} = \int_0^{q_E} [D(q) - p_E] \, dq$$

Also, there are producers who are willing to supply this product at prices lower than its equilibrium price, p_E. Since these producers would have received a unit price p, where $p < p_E$, then the area between the supply curve and the horizontal axis [the gray area of Figure 6-33] represents the amount of revenue that would have been received by these producers. However, since the market is at equilibrium, then producers will sell q_E units at a unit price of p_E dollars to receive total revenue of $p_E q_E$ dollars. This total revenue is represented by the area of the rectangle (colored area + gray area) of Figure 6-33(a). Thus, the area between the horizontal line, $p = p_E$, and the supply curve [the colored area of Figure 6-33(a)] represents the additional revenue gained by producers as a result of the market being at equilibrium. This additional revenue is called the **producers' surplus** and is denoted PS. The producers' surplus is determined by the definite integral

$$\text{PS} = \int_0^{q_E} [p_E - S(q)] \, dq$$

as is illustrated in Figure 6-33(b).

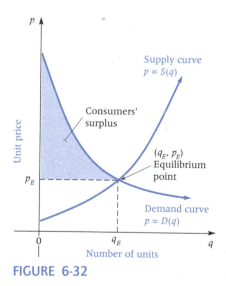

FIGURE 6-32

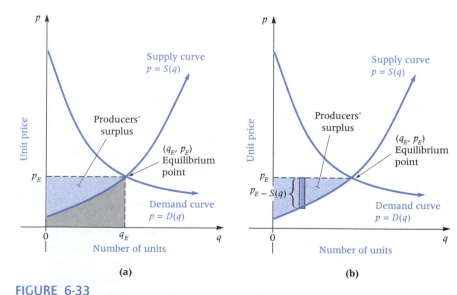

(a)

(b)

FIGURE 6-33

We summarize as follows.

SUMMARY

Consumers' and Producers' Surpluses

Given a demand function, $p = D(q)$, and a supply function, $p = S(q)$, where p denotes the unit price and q denotes the number of units supplied or demanded of some product (see Figure 6-34), then

1. The consumers' surplus is given by

$$CS = \int_0^{q_E} [D(q) - p_E] \, dq$$

2. The producers' surplus is given by

$$PS = \int_0^{q_E} [P_E - S(q)] \, dq$$

3. The corresponding areas are given in Figure 6-34.

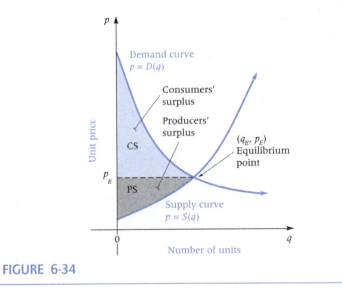

FIGURE 6-34

• EXAMPLE 6-26

Given the demand function

$$p = (q - 10)^2 \qquad (0 \leq q \leq 10)$$

and the supply function

$$p = q^2 \qquad (0 \leq q \leq 10)$$

where p denotes the unit price in dollars and q denotes the number of units of some product, find the consumers' and producers' surpluses.

Solution

We first graph both functions and indicate the areas to be found as CS and PS in Figure 6-35.

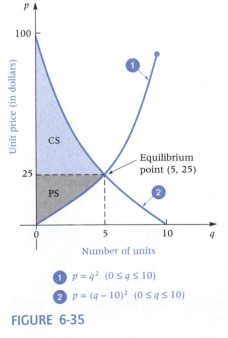

1 $p = q^2 \quad (0 \leq q \leq 10)$

2 $p = (q - 10)^2 \quad (0 \leq q \leq 10)$

FIGURE 6-35

Next we find the equilibrium point by equating the values of p given by the supply and demand functions. Hence,

$$(q - 10)^2 = q^2$$
$$q^2 - 20q + 100 = q^2$$
$$-20q = -100$$
$$q = 5 \qquad \text{Equilibrium quantity}$$

We find the equilibrium price by evaluating either

$$p = S(5) = 5^2 = 25$$

$$\text{or} \qquad \text{Equilibrium price}$$

$$p = D(5) = (5 - 10)^2 = 25$$

The coordinates of the equilibrium point are indicated in Figure 6-35.

The consumers' surplus is determined as follows:

$$\text{CS} = \int_0^5 [D(q) - p_E]\, dq$$

$$= \int_0^5 [(q - 10)^2 - 25]\, dq$$

$$= \int_0^5 [(q^2 - 20q + 100) - 25]\, dq$$

$$= \int_0^5 (q^2 - 20q + 75)\, dq$$

$$= \left. \left(\frac{1}{3} q^3 - 10q^2 + 75q \right) \right|_0^5$$

$$= \left[\frac{1}{3}(5^3) - 10(5^2) + 75(5) \right] - 0$$

$$= \frac{500}{3} = 166.67$$

Thus, the consumers' surplus is $166.67

The producers' surplus is determined below.

$$\text{PS} = \int_0^5 [p_E - S(q)]\, dq$$

$$= \int_0^5 (25 - q^2)\, dq$$

$$= \left. \left(25q - \frac{1}{3} q^3 \right) \right|_0^5$$

$$= \left[25(5) - \frac{1}{3}(5^3) \right] - 0$$

$$= \frac{250}{3} = 83.33$$

Thus, the producers' surplus is $83.33.

Exercises 6-3

For each of the following, graph the functions and find the area between the graphs of the functions over the indicated interval.

1. $f(x) = 2x + 20$, $g(x) = x^2 + 5$; $1 \le x \le 3$
2. $f(x) = x$, $g(x) = x^3$; $0 \le x \le 1$
3. $f(x) = x^2$, $g(x) = x^3$; $0 \le x \le 1$
4. $f(x) = 2x^2 + 4$, $g(x) = x^2 + 3$; $0 \le x \le 3$
5. $y = 3x^2 + 5$, $y = x^2 + 5$; $0 \le x \le 2$
6. $y = x$, $y = x^4$; $0 \le x \le 1$
7. $f(x) = x$, $g(x) = x^5$; $0 \le x \le 1$
8. $f(x) = \sqrt{x}$, $g(x) = x$; $0 \le x \le 4$
9. $f(x) = 2x + 5$, $g(x) = 1$; $0 \le x \le 3$
10. $f(x) = 2x + 8$, $g(x) = 3$; $0 \le x \le 4$
11. $y = -x + 4$, $y = 3/x$; $1 \le x \le 3$
12. $y = -x + 6$, $y = 8/x$; $2 \le x \le 4$
13. $f(x) = -x + 5$, $g(x) = 6/x$; $2 \le x \le 3$
14. $f(x) = -x + 10$, $g(x) = 24/x$; $4 \le x \le 6$
15. $f(x) = e^x$, $g(x) = 1$; $0 \le x \le 2$
16. $f(x) = e^{-x}$, $g(x) = 1$; $0 \le x \le 4$
17. $y = -x$, $y = x$; $0 \le x \le 2$
18. $y = -x$, $y = x$; $-2 \le x \le 0$
19. $y = x^4$, $y = x^3$; $0 \le x \le 1$
20. $y = x$, $y = 1/x$; $-2 \le x \le -1$
21. $y = e^x$, $y = e^{-x}$; $0 \le x \le 1$
22. $f(x) = -x^2 + 8$, $g(x) = 2x$; $0 \le x \le 2$
23. $f(x) = -x^2 + 6$, $g(x) = x$; $-3 \le x \le 2$
24. $f(x) = -x^2 + 10$, $g(x) = 3x$; $-5 \le x \le 2$
25. $y = x + 1$, $y = 2$; $0 \le x \le 4$
26. $y = x + 3$, $y = 5$; $0 \le x \le 6$
27. $f(x) = x$, $g(x) = x^2$; $0 \le x \le 3$
28. $f(x) = x^3$, $g(x) = x^2$; $0 \le x \le 6$
29. $f(x) = x$, $g(x) = x^3$; $-1 \le x \le 4$
30. $y = \sqrt{x}$, $y = x$; $0 \le x \le 4$
31. $y = -x^2 + 5$, $y = 1$; $-2 \le x \le 6$
32. $y = -x^2 + 12$, $y = 3$; $-3 \le x \le 6$
33. $f(x) = e^x$, $g(x) = e^{-x}$; $-2 \le x \le 3$
34. $f(x) = -x + 4$, $g(x) = 3/x$; $1 \le x \le 4$
35. $f(x) = -x + 6$, $g(x) = 8/x$; $2 \le x \le 6$

Consumers' and producers' surpluses. Find the consumers' and producers' surpluses for each of the following.

36. $p = D(q) = -0.5q + 8$, $p = S(q) = 2q + 0.5$
37. $p = D(q) = -0.5q + 20$, $p = S(q) = q + 8$
38. $p = D(q) = (q - 20)^2$, $p = S(q) = q^2 + 40$
39. $p = D(q) = (q - 30)^2$, $p = S(q) = q^2 + 300$
40. $p = D(q) = -2q + 80$, $p = S(q) = 3q + 5$
41. $p = D(q) = (q - 40)^2$, $p = S(q) = q^2 + 640$

Marginal analysis. For a given product, a company's sales revenue changes with time at a rate of $R'(t)$ dollars per month and its cost changes with time at the rate of $C'(t)$ dollars per month. Then the total profit (for the product) accumulated during the time interval $a \le t \le b$, as illustrated in Figure 6-36, is given by

$$\int_a^b [R'(t) - C'(t)]\, dt$$

where t is given in months. For each of the following, determine the total profit accumulated during the indicated time interval.

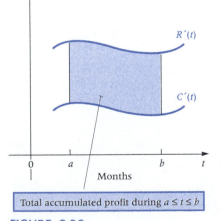

Total accumulated profit during $a \le t \le b$

FIGURE 6-36

42. $R'(t) = 50t^2 + 10$, $C'(t) = t + 5$; $0 \le t \le 10$
43. $R'(t) = 20t + 5$, $C'(t) = 4t + 2$; $2 \le t \le 6$
44. $R'(t) = -t^2 + 1600$, $C'(t) = 10$; $0 \le t \le 20$
45. $R'(t) = 1000e^t + 1000$, $C'(t) = 2t + 4$; $0 \le t \le 8$

6-4 • INTEGRATION BY SUBSTITUTION

Up to this point, we have been finding indefinite integrals of functions consisting of sums of terms of the form

$$kx^n, \; e^{kx}, \text{ and } \frac{1}{x}$$

where k and n are constants and $n \ne -1$. In this section, we will learn a technique that will enable us to find indefinite integrals of a greater variety of functions. The technique will involve the **substitution** principle. Since the substitution principle involves writing expressions for differentials, we briefly review this procedure.

Differentials

If $u = f(x)$ defines a differentiable function of x and dx is any real number, then, as discussed in Section 4-4, the quantity

$$du = f'(x) \, dx$$

is called the **differential of u.** Thus, if

$$u = f(x) = x^3$$

then

$$du = f'(x) \, dx$$
$$= 3x^2 \, dx$$

Differentials have a special meaning, as was discussed in Section 4-4. However, here we will need to determine only the formula for du, given some equation $u = f(x)$.

• **EXAMPLE 6-27** _____

If $u = x^6$, find the differential du.

Solution

Since $u = f(x) = x^6$, then $f'(x) = 6x^5$. Hence,

$$du = f'(x) \, dx$$
$$= 6x^5 \, dx$$

• **EXAMPLE 6-28** _____

If $u = x^4 - 8x^2 + 16$, find du.

Solution

Since $u = f(x) = x^4 - 8x^2 + 16$, then $f'(x) = 4x^3 - 16x$. Hence,

$$du = f'(x)\, dx$$
$$= (4x^3 - 16x)\, dx$$

In rule 6-1 of Section 6-1, we saw that

$$\int x^n\, dx = \frac{1}{n+1}x^{n+1} + c \qquad (n \neq -1)$$

This rule may be restated in terms of the variable u. If x is replaced by u and dx by du, then we have rule 6-7.

Rule 6-7

$$\int u^n\, du = \frac{1}{n+1}u^{n+1} + c \qquad (n \neq -1)$$

Rule 6-7 will be used in conjunction with the substitution principle to integrate the functions in this section.

We now consider the problem of finding

$$\int (x^3 - 4)^7\, 3x^2\, dx$$

In order to determine this indefinite integral, we will restate the problem in an equivalent, but simpler, form by substituting the variable u in place of $x^3 - 4$ and then making appropriate symbolic changes. Hence, we let

$$u = x^3 - 4$$

Then we have

$$du = 3x^2\, dx$$

Substitution

Thus, the indefinite integral

$$\int \underbrace{(x^3 - 4)}_{u}^{7}\ \underbrace{3x^2\, dx}_{du}$$

becomes simply

$$\int u^7\, du$$

This result is integrated by using rule 6-7. Hence, we obtain

$$\int u^7\, du = \frac{1}{8}u^8 + c$$

Since the solution

$$\frac{1}{8}u^8 + c$$

is written in terms of u, we must rewrite it in terms of x. Since

$$u = x^3 - 4$$

replacing u with $x^3 - 4$ in the solution yields

$$\frac{1}{8}(x^3 - 4)^8 + c$$

Hence, we have

$$\int (x^3 - 4)^7 \, 3x^2 \, dx = \frac{1}{8}(x^3 - 4)^8 + c$$

the validity of which can be verified by differentiation as given below.
   Check:

$$\frac{d}{dx}\left[\frac{1}{8}(x^3 - 4)^8 + c\right] = \frac{1}{8} \cdot 8(x^3 - 4)^7(3x^2) + 0$$
$$= (x^3 - 4)^7(3x^2)$$

• **EXAMPLE 6-29**

   Find $\int (x^5 - 6)^9 \, 5x^4 \, dx$.

Solution

Let $u = x^5 - 6$. Then

$$du = 5x^4 \, dx \quad \Big\} \text{ Substitution}$$

Hence,

$$\int (\underbrace{x^5 - 6}_{u})^9 \, \underbrace{5x^4 \, dx}_{du} = \int u^9 \, du$$
$$= \frac{1}{10}u^{10} + c$$

Replacing u with $x^5 - 6$ gives

$$\int (x^5 - 6)^9 \, 5x^4 \, dx = \frac{1}{10}(x^5 - 6)^{10} + c$$

We now consider a problem in which du does not appear explicitly in the function to be integrated. Consider the indefinite integral

$$\int (x^3 - 7)^5 \, x^2 \, dx$$

If $u = x^3 - 7$, then

$$du = 3x^2 \, dx \quad \Big\} \text{ Substitution}$$

In order to rewrite the integral in terms of u, the $x^2\ dx$ term must equal du.

$$\int (x^3 - 7)^5\ x^2\ dx = \int u^5 \ \underline{\ ?\ }$$

Since $du = 3x^2\ dx$, we must multiply $x^2\ dx$ by 3 and compensate by multiplying the integral by 1/3 to obtain

$$\frac{1}{3} \int \underbrace{(x^3 - 7)^5}_{u}\ \underbrace{3x^2\ dx}_{du}$$

Our multiplying $x^2\ dx$ by 3 and the integral by 1/3 is allowed by rule 6-2 of Section 6-1, which states that the integral of a constant times a function is equal to the constant times the integral of the function. It must be noted that this works only for a *constant multiplier*. It does not apply to variables. Also, if the x^2 term was not present in the original problem, we could not have used the substitution technique. Example 6-32 illustrates such a situation in greater detail. Thus, in our example,

$$\frac{1}{3} \int \underbrace{(x^3 - 7)^5}_{u}\ \underbrace{3x^2\ dx}_{du} = \frac{1}{3} \int u^5\ du$$

$$= \frac{1}{3} \cdot \frac{1}{6} u^6 + c$$

$$= \frac{1}{18}(x^3 - 7)^6 + c$$

• **EXAMPLE 6-30**

Find

$$\int \frac{x^4\ dx}{\sqrt{x^5 - 9}}$$

Solution

We write

$$\int \frac{x^4\ dx}{\sqrt{x^5 - 9}} = \int (x^5 - 9)^{-1/2}\ x^4\ dx$$

Letting $u = x^5 - 9$ gives us

$$du = 5x^4\ dx$$

Hence, we obtain

$$\int (x^5 - 9)^{-1/2}\ x^4\ dx = \frac{1}{5} \int \underbrace{(x^5 - 9)^{-1/2}}_{u}\ \underbrace{5x^4\ dx}_{du}$$

$$= \frac{1}{5} \int u^{-1/2}\ du$$

$$= \frac{1}{5} \cdot \frac{1}{1/2} u^{1/2} + c$$

$$= \frac{2}{5}(x^5 - 9)^{1/2} + c$$

• **EXAMPLE 6-31** _____

Find $\int (2x^3 - 5)^{11} \, 5x^2 \, dx$.

Solution

Letting $u = 2x^3 - 5$ gives us

$$du = 6x^2 \, dx$$

Hence, we obtain

$$\int (2x^3 - 5)^{11} \, 5x^2 \, dx = \frac{5}{6} \int \underbrace{(2x^3 - 5)^{11}}_{u} \cdot \underbrace{\frac{6}{5} \cdot 5x^2 \, dx}_{du}$$

Multiply $5x^2 \, dx$ by 6/5 to obtain du.

$$= \frac{5}{6} \int u^{11} \, du$$

Multiply the integral by 5/6, the reciprocal of 6/5.

$$= \frac{5}{6} \cdot \frac{1}{12} u^{12} + c$$

$$= \frac{5}{72}(2x^3 - 5)^{12} + c$$

We now give an example where du cannot be formed.

• **EXAMPLE 6-32** _____

Find

$$\int \frac{x^3 \, dx}{(x^5 + 6)^4}$$

Solution

We rewrite the above integral as

$$\int (x^5 + 6)^{-4} x^3 \, dx$$

and let $u = x^5 + 6$. This gives

$$du = 5x^4 \, dx$$

Hence, we have

$$\int \underbrace{(x^5 + 6)^{-4}}_{u} \underbrace{x^3 \, dx}_{?} = \int u^{-4} \underline{\quad ? \quad}$$

$$\underset{\longmapsto\text{—————}}{} du = 5x^4 \, dx$$

Although we would like to multiply $x^3 \, dx$ by $5x$ to give $5x^4 \, dx$, as shown below,

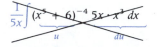

we cannot do this because $5x$ is not a constant. Thus, this integral cannot be evaluated by the substitution rules presented in this text. As of now, we have no way to evaluate this integral.

Definite Integrals: Substitution Method

When evaluating a definite integral using the substitution method, either of two computational procedures can be used. One procedure involves writing the antiderivative in terms of x and evaluating the definite integral using the original limits of integration. A second procedure is to write the antiderivative in terms of the substitution variable u, change the original limits (given in terms of x) to corresponding values of u, and then evaluate the definite integral (written in terms of u) using the new limits (written as values of u). Accordingly, this procedure is called **change of limits.** The next two examples illustrate both procedures to evaluate the same definite integral.

• **EXAMPLE 6-33**

Evaluate

$$\int_1^3 (9 - x^2)^4 x \, dx$$

using the original limits of integration.

Solution

Letting $u = 9 - x^2$ gives

$$du = -2x \, dx \quad \Big\} \text{ Substitution}$$

so that

$$\int_1^3 (9 - x^2)^4 x \, dx = \frac{1}{-2} \int_1^3 \underbrace{(9 - x^2)^4}_{u} \underbrace{(-2)x \, dx}_{du}$$

$$= \frac{1}{-2} \cdot \frac{1}{5}(9 - x^2)^5 \Big|_1^3 \quad \begin{array}{l}\text{Write antiderivative in terms of } x.\\ \text{Use original limits of integration.}\end{array}$$

$$= -\frac{1}{10}[(9 - 3^2)^5 - (9 - 1^2)^5]$$

$$= -\frac{1}{10}[(0)^5 - (8)^5] = 3276.8$$

• **EXAMPLE 6-34**

Evaluate

$$\int_1^3 (9 - x^2)^4 x \, dx$$

by using the change of limits procedure.

Solution

Letting $u = 9 - x^2$ gives

$$du = -2x \, dx \quad \Big\} \text{ Substitution}$$

Change Limits

Lower limit: When $x = 1$, $u = 9 - x^2 = 9 - 1^2 = 8$.

Upper limit: When $x = 3$, $u = 9 - x^2 = 9 - 3^2 = 0$.

Note that the upper limit is smaller than the lower limit. This sometimes happens with the change of limits procedure. Do not change the order of the limits and proceed with the integration in the usual manner.

Make the substitution, write the antiderivative in terms of u, and use the new limits. Hence,

$$\int_1^3 (9 - x^2)^4 x \, dx = -\frac{1}{2} \int_1^3 \underbrace{(9 - x^2)^4}_{u} \underbrace{(-2)x \, dx}_{du}$$

$$= -\frac{1}{2} \int_8^0 u^4 \, du \qquad \text{Use the new limits.}$$

$$= -\frac{1}{2} \cdot \frac{1}{5} u^5 \Big|_8^0 \qquad \begin{array}{l}\text{Write the antiderivative}\\\text{in terms of } u.\end{array}$$

$$= -\frac{1}{10}[0^5 - 8^5] = 3276.8 \qquad \text{Use the new limits.}$$

Note that this answer agrees with that of the previous example.

Exercises 6-4

Determine each of the following.

1. $\displaystyle\int (x^3 - 7)^{10} 3x^2 \, dx$

2. $\displaystyle\int (x^2 - 3)^4 2x \, dx$

3. $\displaystyle\int (x^3 - 4x)^5 (3x^2 - 4) \, dx$

4. $\displaystyle\int (5x + 6)^{12} 5 \, dx$

5. $\displaystyle\int (x^4 - 8)^9 x^3 \, dx$

6. $\displaystyle\int (2x^5 - 7)^6 x^4 \, dx$

7. $\displaystyle\int (x - 3)^9 \, dx$

8. $\displaystyle\int (x^3 - 4)^{1/2} x^2 \, dx$

9. $\displaystyle\int (x^4 + 6)^5 5x^3 \, dx$

10. $\displaystyle\int (x^4 - 8x + 5)^7 (2x^3 - 4) \, dx$

11. $\displaystyle\int (x^6 + 9)^{10} 2x^5 \, dx$

12. $\displaystyle\int (4x^3 - 1)^{11} 5x^2 \, dx$

13. $\displaystyle\int \frac{x^2}{(x^3 - 5)^{10}} dx$

14. $\displaystyle\int \sqrt{(4x^2 + 5)} \, x \, dx$

15. $\displaystyle\int \frac{x^3}{\sqrt{x^4 - 6}} dx$

16. $\displaystyle\int \sqrt[3]{(x^3 - 9)^4} \, x^2 \, dx$

17. $\displaystyle\int \frac{dx}{(3x - 5)^4}$

18. $\displaystyle\int \frac{5x^2 \, dx}{\sqrt[5]{(x^3 - 9)^2}}$

Evaluate each of the following:

19. $\displaystyle\int_2^4 (\sqrt{x^2 + 9}) x \, dx$

20. $\displaystyle\int_1^2 (x^4 - 3)^3 x^3 \, dx$

21. $\displaystyle\int_3^5 \frac{x \, dx}{(x^2 - 5)^2}$

22. $\displaystyle\int_0^1 (x^2 + 2x)^3 (x + 1) \, dx$

23. Find the area between the x-axis and the curve $f(x) = (x - 5)^3$ from $x = 5$ to $x = 7$. Sketch $f(x)$ and shade the desired area.

24. Find the area between the x-axis and the curve $f(x) = (x + 4)^3$ from $x = -4$ to $x = 0$. Sketch $f(x)$ and shade the desired area.

25. Find the area between the x-axis and the curve $y = 1/(x - 6)^2$ from $x = 0$ to $x = 5$. Sketch the function and shade the desired area.

26. Find the area between the x-axis and the function $f(x) = 1/(x - 5)^3$ from $x = 6$ to $x = 8$. Sketch $f(x)$ and shade the desired area.

27. Consider the indefinite integral

$$\int (x^3 - 5)^{10} x \, dx$$

Why can't this indefinite integral be determined by the techniques of this section? [Of course, this indefinite integral can be determined by using the time-consuming process of expanding $(x^3 - 5)^{10}$.]

Applications

28. *Revenue flow.* If the rate of flow of revenue into a mutual fund is given by

$$R'(t) = 50t + 20t\sqrt{1 + t^2}$$

where t is given in months, find the total revenue obtained during the first 2 years.

29. *Oil leak.* An oil tanker is leaking crude oil at the rate of $B'(t)$ barrels per hour, where t is the number of hours since the leak began. If

$$B'(t) = 200t + 50$$

how many barrels of oil will have leaked into the water during the first 2 days?

30. *Population growth.* Executive Realty Corporation has recently completed a new development called Hidden Valley Estates. The population of Hidden Valley Estates has been growing at the rate of $P'(t)$ individuals per month, where t is the number of months elapsed since December 31 of the past year. If

$$P'(t) = 100 + 18t$$

find the total increase in population during the first three-quarters of the present year.

31. *Profit.* The rate of change of the annual profit of a firm is given by

$$P'(x) = 500,000x + 100,000$$

where x denotes the number of years after December 31 of a particular year. Find the equation for $P(x)$, given the initial condition that $P(2) = 1,000,000$.

32. *Cash reserves.* The rate of change of the cash reserves of a scholarship fund is given by

$$C'(x) = \frac{x}{(x^2 + 4)^2}$$

where x denotes time (in years) since the inception of the fund and $C'(x)$ is given in millions of dollars. Find the equation for $C(x)$ if the fund had 8.2 million dollars one year after its inception.

• INTEGRALS INVOLVING EXPONENTIAL AND LOGARITHMIC FUNCTIONS

In Chapter 5, we used the chain rule to derive the following rule for differentiating exponential functions: If $y = e^u$, where u is a function of x, then

$$\frac{dy}{dx} = e^u \frac{du}{dx}$$

We use this rule to find the derivative of the exponential function

$$y = e^{x^3 + 7}$$

Hence,

$$\frac{dy}{dx} = e^{x^3 + 7}(3x^2)$$

Since integration is the reverse process of differentiation, the integral of a derivative results in the original function. Thus, for the above example,

$$\int e^{x^3 + 7}(3x^2)\, dx = e^{x^3 + 7} + c$$

where c is an arbitrary constant. Note the form of the above integral. Specifically, if we let

$$u = x^3 + 7$$

then Substitution

$$du = 3x^2\, dx$$

and the integrand (the expression following the integral sign) is of the form

$$e^u\, du$$

as is illustrated below.

$$\int \overbrace{e^{x^3 + 7}}^{u}\ \overbrace{3x^2\, dx}^{du} = \overbrace{e^{x^3 + 7}}^{u} + c$$

The above discussion suggests the following rule.

Rule 6-8

If $u = f(x)$ and $du = f'(x)\, dx$, then

$$\int e^u\, du = e^u + c$$

Note that this rule is a restatement of the formula (from Section 6-1)

$$\int e^x \, dx = e^x + c$$

with $u = f(x)$ replacing x and $du = f'(x) \, dx$ replacing dx.

Rule 6-8 may be used in conjunction with the substitution principle to integrate exponential functions with base e. Consider

$$\int e^{x^8 - 5} x^7 \, dx$$

If we let $u = x^8 - 5$, then

$$du = 8x^7 \, dx \left.\right\} \text{Substitution}$$

Thus, we obtain

$$\int e^{x^8 - 5} x^7 \, dx = \frac{1}{8} \int e^{\overbrace{x^8 - 5}^{u}} \underbrace{8x^7 \, dx}_{du}$$

$$= \frac{1}{8} \int e^u \, du$$

$$= \frac{1}{8} e^u + c$$

$$= \frac{1}{8} e^{x^8 - 5} + c$$

Check by finding the derivative:

$$\frac{d}{dx}\left(\frac{1}{8} e^{x^8 - 5} + c\right) = \frac{1}{8} e^{x^8 - 5} (8x^7) + c = e^{x^8 - 5}(x^7)$$

• **EXAMPLE 6-35**

Find $\int e^{x^3 - 6} 2x^2 \, dx$.

Solution

Let $u = x^3 - 6$. Then

$$du = 3x^2 \, dx \left.\right\} \text{Substitution}$$

Thus, we have

$$\int e^{x^3 - 6} 2x^2 \, dx = \frac{2}{3} \int e^{\overbrace{x^3 - 6}^{u}} \underbrace{\frac{3}{2} 2x^2 \, dx}_{du}$$ Multiply the integrand by 3/2 to form du.

$$= \frac{2}{3} \int e^u \, du$$ Multiply the integral by the reciprocal of 3/2, 2/3.

$$= \frac{2}{3} e^u + c$$

$$= \frac{2}{3} e^{x^3 - 6} + c$$

In Section 6-1, we stated the formula

$$\int \frac{dx}{x} = \ln|x| + c$$

Using reasoning similar to that employed to develop rule 6-8 for exponential functions, we state the following rule.

> **Rule 6-9**
>
> If $u = f(x)$ and $du = f'(x)\,dx$, then
>
> $$\int \frac{du}{u} = \ln|u| + c$$

Rule 6-9 may be used in conjunction with the substitution principle to integrate functions that may be expressed in the form du/u. Consider, for instance,

$$\int \frac{x\,dx}{x^2 - 1}$$

If we let $u = x^2 - 1$, then

$$du = 2x\,dx \quad \Big\} \text{ Substitution}$$

Hence, we have

$$\int \frac{x\,dx}{x^2 - 1} = \frac{1}{2} \int \frac{\overset{du}{\overbrace{2x\,dx}}}{\underset{u}{\underbrace{x^2 - 1}}}$$

$$= \frac{1}{2} \int \frac{du}{u}$$

$$= \frac{1}{2} \ln|u| + c$$

$$= \frac{1}{2} \ln|x^2 - 1| + c$$

• **EXAMPLE 6-36**

Find

$$\int \frac{x^6\,dx}{x^7 + 15}$$

Solution

Let $u = x^7 + 15$. Then

$$du = 7x^6\,dx \quad \Big\} \text{ Substitution}$$

Hence, we find

$$\int \frac{x^6\ dx}{x^7 + 15} = \frac{1}{7} \int \frac{\overbrace{7x^6\ dx}^{du}}{\underbrace{x^7 + 15}_{u}}$$

$$= \frac{1}{7} \int \frac{du}{u}$$

$$= \frac{1}{7} \ln |u| + c$$

$$= \frac{1}{7} \ln |x^7 + 15| + c$$

• **EXAMPLE 6-37**   **Revenue Flow.** _____

The rate of flow of revenue (in dollars) into a firm is given by

$$R'(t) = \frac{10{,}000{,}000}{5 + t} \qquad (t \geq 0)$$

where t is time (in years). Determine the total revenue flowing in during the time interval $4 \leq t \leq 20$.

Solution

We first graph $R'(t)$ in Figure 6-37. The shaded area denotes the total revenue flow that must be determined. We seek

$$\int_4^{20} R'(t)\ dt = R(20) - R(4)$$

Hence,

$$\int_4^{20} R'(t)\ dt = \int_4^{20} \frac{10{,}000{,}000}{5 + t}\ dt \qquad \text{Substitution}$$
$$\qquad\qquad u = 5 + t$$
$$= \underbrace{10{,}000{,}000 \ln |5 + t|}_{R(t)} \Big|_4^{20} \qquad du = dt$$

$$= R(20) - R(4)$$

$$= 10{,}000{,}000 \ln |5 + 20| - 10{,}000{,}000 \ln |5 + 4|$$

$$= 10{,}000{,}000(\ln 25 - \ln 9)$$

$$= 10{,}000{,}000(\ln 25/9) \qquad \text{Property of logarithms}$$

$$\approx 10{,}000{,}000(1.0216512) = \$10{,}216{,}512 \qquad \text{Total revenue flow}$$

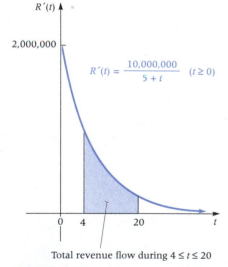

$R'(t) = \dfrac{10{,}000{,}000}{5 + t} \quad (t \geq 0)$

Total revenue flow during $4 \leq t \leq 20$

FIGURE 6-37

Exercises 6-5

Determine each of the following:

1. $\displaystyle\int e^x\ dx$

2. $\displaystyle\int e^{-x}\ dx$

3. $\displaystyle\int e^{4x}\ dx$

4. $\displaystyle\int_0^1 e^{-3x}\ dx$

5. $\displaystyle\int e^{x/2}\,dx$

6. $\displaystyle\int 6e^{-0.3x}\,dx$

7. $\displaystyle\int e^{x^3-5}x^2\,dx$

8. $\displaystyle\int \frac{x\,dx}{e^{x^2}}$

9. $\displaystyle\int x^3 e^{x^4+6}\,dx$

10. $\displaystyle\int x e^{x^2+1}\,dx$

11. $\displaystyle\int (x+1)e^{x^2+2x}\,dx$

12. $\displaystyle\int e^{5x-2}\,dx$

13. $\displaystyle\int \frac{5\,dx}{x}$

14. $\displaystyle\int \frac{dx}{x+1}$

15. $\displaystyle\int \frac{x}{x^2+1}\,dx$

16. $\displaystyle\int \frac{x^3\,dx}{x^4-1}$

17. $\displaystyle\int \frac{6x^2\,dx}{x^3+4}$

18. $\displaystyle\int \frac{5x\,dx}{x^2-4}$

19. $\displaystyle\int \frac{-x\,dx}{5x^2-6}$

20. $\displaystyle\int \frac{-4x^2}{x^3+5}\,dx$

Evaluate each of the following.

21. $\displaystyle\int_0^4 e^x\,dx$

22. $\displaystyle\int_0^2 x e^{x^2/2}\,dx$

23. $\displaystyle\int_0^1 x e^{-x^2}\,dx$

24. $\displaystyle\int_0^1 (t+1)\,e^{t^2+2}\,dt$

25. $\displaystyle\int_1^4 (1/x)\,dx$

26. $\displaystyle\int_2^6 (8/x)\,dx$

27. $\displaystyle\int_1^6 (-6/x)\,dx$

28. $\displaystyle\int_1^5 (-4/t)\,dt$

Determine each of the following.

29. $\displaystyle\int \frac{(\ln x)^2}{x}\,dx$

30. $\displaystyle\int \frac{\ln 4x}{x}\,dx$

31. $\displaystyle\int \frac{(\ln 3x)^4}{x}\,dx$

32. $\displaystyle\int \frac{e^x\,dx}{5+e^x}$

33. $\displaystyle\int \frac{x-2}{x^2-4x+1}\,dx$

34. $\displaystyle\int \frac{x-4}{x^2-8x+5}\,dx$

35. $\displaystyle\int \frac{1}{x\ln x}\,dx$

36. $\displaystyle\int \frac{1}{x(\ln x)^3}\,dx$

37. $\displaystyle\int \frac{1}{x\ln x^2}\,dx$

38. $\displaystyle\int \frac{4}{x\ln x^2}\,dx$

39. Find the area bounded by the x-axis and $f(x) = e^{-2x}$ from $x = 0$ to $x = 1$. Sketch $f(x)$ and shade the desired area.

40. Find the area bounded by the x-axis and the curve $f(x) = 1/(x-2)$ from $x = 3$ to $x = 6$. Sketch $f(x)$ and shade the desired area.

41. Find the area bounded by the x-axis and $f(x) = 1/(x-9)$ from $x = 1$ to $x = 4$. Sketch $f(x)$ and shade the desired area.

Applications

42. *Revenue flow.* If the rate of flow of revenue into a firm is given by

$$R'(t) = \frac{10{,}000{,}000}{t+5}$$

where t is measured in years, find the total revenue obtained during the interval $0 \leq t \leq 4$.

43. *Revenue flow.* If the rate of flow of revenue into a firm is given by

$$R'(t) = 100t + 10e^{-t}$$

where t is measured in years, find the total revenue obtained during the interval $1 \leq t \leq 10$.

44. *Drug reaction.* After a certain cancer-inducing drug is injected into a mouse, cancer cells increase at the rate of $D'(t)$ cells per day, where t is the number of days following the drug injection. If

$$D'(t) = 100e^{5t}$$

find the total increase in cancer cells during the first 2 days following the drug injection.

45. *Bacteria growth.* The rate of growth of a population of bacteria is given by

$$B'(x) = \frac{10{,}000}{5x + 1}$$

where x denotes time in days. Find the equation for $B(x)$, given that $B(2) = 9000$.

46. *Cash reserves.* The rate of change of the cash reserves of an emergency fund is given by

$$C'(x) = xe^{x^2}$$

where x denotes time in years since the fund's inception and $C'(x)$ is given in thousands of dollars. Find the equation for $C(x)$ if the fund's value was 30 thousand dollars 2 years after its inception.

6-6 • INTEGRATION BY PARTS

Try to determine the indefinite integral

$$\int xe^x \, dx$$

If we attempt to use the substitution principle, we let $u = x$; then $du = dx$, and we realize that $\int xe^x \, dx$ cannot be expressed in the form $\int e^u \, du$ since $x \, dx$ does not equal and cannot be modified (by multiplication by a constant) to equal du. This problem cannot be integrated by any of the substitution techniques discussed up to this point.

A useful technique to solve the above problem is integration by parts. The integration by parts technique involves application of the formula below.

SUMMARY

Integration by Parts

If u and v are differentiable functions of x, then

$$\int u \, dv = uv - \int v \, du$$

The above formula is derived from the product rule for differentiation as follows: Let u and v be differentiable functions of x. Then, by the product rule,

$$\frac{d}{dx}(uv) = u\frac{dv}{dx} + v\frac{du}{dx}$$

Integrating both sides with respect to x gives

$$\int \frac{d}{dx}(uv)\,dx = \int u\frac{dv}{dx}\,dx + \int v\frac{du}{dx}\,dx$$

Since the integral of the derivative of uv is uv, the left-hand side of the above formula becomes uv, so that the formula is rewritten as

$$uv = \int u\,dv + \int v\,du$$

Solving the above equation for $\int u\,dv$ gives

$$\int u\,dv = uv - \int v\,du$$

The arbitrary constant is included when $\int v\,du$ is determined.

To apply integration by parts to evaluate the indefinite integral

$$\int xe^x\,dx$$

we must express the integral in the form

$$\int u\,dv$$

Also, we must determine u and dv so that $\int v\,du$ can be easily determined by one of our known integration techniques. Note that if

$$u = x \qquad \text{and} \qquad dv = e^x\,dx$$

then

$$du = dx \qquad \text{and} \qquad v = \int e^x\,dx$$
$$= e^x$$

> Omit the constant of integration here.
> Include it when $\int v\,du$ is determined.

Thus, applying the integration by parts formula, we have

$$\int u\,dv = uv - \int v\,du$$

or

$$\int x\,e^x\,dx = xe^x - \int e^x\,dx$$

Note that $\int e^x\,dx$ is easily determined to be $e^x + c$. Thus, our final answer is

$$\int xe^x\,dx = xe^x - e^x + c$$

The integration by parts technique depends on the proper choice of u and dv. To illustrate this point, we attempt the above problem with a different choice of u and dv.

Wrong Choice of u and dv. Let

$$u = e^x \qquad \text{and} \qquad dv = x\,dx$$

then

$$du = e^x\,dx \qquad \text{and} \qquad v = \int x\,dx$$

$$= \frac{1}{2}x^2$$

so that

$$\int u\,dv = uv - \int v\,du$$

becomes

$$\int e^x x\,dx = e^x\,[(1/2)x^2] - \int (1/2)x^2 e^x\,dx$$

Note that the integral $\int (1/2)x^2 e^x\,dx$ is more complex than the original integral $\int xe^x\,dx$ and, thus, cannot be determined by any of the substitution techniques discussed up to this point. This indicates a wrong choice of u and dv.

Arbitrary Constant of Integration

When using the integration by parts formula,

$$\int u\,dv = uv - \int v\,du$$

v is determined by integrating dv. At this point, we omit the arbitrary constant of integration and include it at the end of the procedure when we evaluate $\int v\,du$. This simplifies the integration by parts process. Its legitimacy is shown by replacing v with $v + c$ (where c is an arbitrary constant) in the integration by parts formula to obtain the result

$$\int u\,dv = u(v + c) - \int (v + c)\,du$$

$$= uv + uc - \int v\,du - \int c\,du$$

$$= uv + uc - \int v\,du - cu$$

Since $uc = cu$, the above equation reduces to the integration by parts formula

$$\int u\, dv = uv - \int v\, du$$

We now provide another example of the application of integration by parts.

• **EXAMPLE 6-38** _____

Evaluate $\int x\sqrt{x - 2}\, dx$.

Solution

Let

$$u = x \quad \text{and} \quad dv = \sqrt{x - 2}\, dx.$$

Then

$$du = dx \quad \text{and} \quad v = \int (x - 2)^{1/2}\, dx$$

$$= \frac{2}{3}(x - 2)^{3/2}$$

Applying the integration by parts formula, we have

$$\int u\, dv = uv - \int v\, du$$

or

$$\int \underbrace{x}_{u}\ \underbrace{\sqrt{x - 2}\, dx}_{dv} = x\frac{2}{3}(x - 2)^{3/2} - \int \frac{2}{3}(x - 2)^{3/2}\, dx$$

$$= \frac{2}{3}x(x - 2)^{3/2} - \frac{4}{15}(x - 2)^{5/2} + c$$

SUMMARY

Guidelines for Choosing u and dv

1. Make certain that dv can be integrated.
2. Make certain that the integral $\int v\, du$ either can be integrated or is of a simpler form than the original integral, $\int u\, dv$.

• **EXAMPLE 6-39** _____

Evaluate $\int x \ln x\, dx$.

Solution

Let

$$u = \ln x \quad \text{and} \quad dv = x\, dx$$

Then

$$du = \frac{1}{x} dx \qquad \text{and} \qquad v = \int x \, dx$$

$$= \frac{1}{2} x^2$$

Applying the integration by parts formula, we have

$$\int u \, dv = uv - \int v \, du$$

or

$$\int \underbrace{(\ln x)}_{u} \underbrace{x \, dx}_{dv} = \underbrace{(\ln x)}_{u} \underbrace{\frac{1}{2} x^2}_{v} - \int \underbrace{\frac{1}{2} x^2}_{v} \underbrace{\frac{1}{x} dx}_{du}$$

$$= \frac{1}{2} x^2 \ln x - \int \frac{1}{2} x \, dx$$

$$= \frac{1}{2} x^2 \ln x - \frac{1}{4} x^2 + c$$

• EXAMPLE 6-40

Evaluate

$$\int \frac{xe^x}{(x + 1)^2} dx$$

Solution

Remember that we must choose u and dv so that $\int v \, du$ is evaluated by one of our known integration techniques. Let

$$u = xe^x \qquad \text{and} \qquad dv = \frac{1}{(x + 1)^2} dx$$

Then

$$du = (xe^x + e^x) \, dx \qquad \text{and} \qquad v = \int \frac{1}{(x + 1)^2} dx$$

$$= (x + 1)e^x \, dx \qquad\qquad = -\frac{1}{x + 1}$$

Using the integration by parts formula, we have

$$\int u \, dv = uv - \int v \, du$$

or

$$\int \frac{xe^x}{(x + 1)^2} dx = \underbrace{xe^x}_{u} \underbrace{\left(-\frac{1}{x + 1} \right)}_{v} - \int \underbrace{-\frac{1}{x + 1}}_{v} \underbrace{(x + 1)e^x \, dx}_{du}$$

$$= -\frac{xe^x}{x + 1} + \int e^x \, dx$$

Since $\int e^x \, dx = e^x + c$, the above becomes

$$\int \frac{xe^x}{(x + 1)^2} dx = -\frac{xe^x}{x + 1} + e^x + c$$

Sometimes we must use the integration by parts formula repeatedly in a given problem. The next example illustrates such a case.

• **EXAMPLE 6-41** _____

Evaluate $\int x^2 e^x\, dx$.

Solution

Let

$$u = x^2 \quad \text{and} \quad dv = e^x\, dx$$

Then

$$du = 2x\, dx \quad \text{and} \quad v = \int e^x\, dx$$
$$= e^x$$

Using the integration by parts formula, we have

$$\int u\, dv = uv - \int v\, du$$

or

$$\int \underbrace{x^2}_{u} \underbrace{e^x\, dx}_{dv} = \underbrace{x^2}_{u}\underbrace{e^x}_{v} - \int \underbrace{2x}\,\underbrace{e^x}_{v}\, dx \qquad (1)$$

Note that $\int 2xe^x\, dx$ is of a form simpler than the original integral. Thus, we apply the integration by parts formula again to evaluate $\int 2xe^x\, dx$. Letting

$$u = 2x \quad \text{and} \quad dv = e^x\, dx$$

then

$$du = 2\, dx \quad \text{and} \quad v = \int e^x\, dx$$
$$= e^x$$

Again, using the integration by parts formula, we have

$$\int u\, dv = uv - \int v\, du$$

or

$$\int 2xe^x\, dx = \underbrace{2x}\,\underbrace{e^x}_{v} - \int \underbrace{e^x}_{v}\,\underbrace{2\, dx}_{du}$$
$$= 2xe^x - \int 2e^x\, dx$$

Substituting this result into equation (1), we have

$$\int x^2 e^x\, dx = x^2 e^x - \left(2xe^x - \int 2e^x\, dx\right)$$
$$= x^2 e^x - 2xe^x + \int 2e^x\, dx$$
$$= x^2 e^x - 2xe^x + 2e^x + c$$
$$= (x^2 - 2x + 2)e^x + c$$

Application

• **EXAMPLE 6-42**   **Marginal Cost/Cost.**

The marginal cost (in dollars per unit) for some product is given by

$$C'(x) = \ln x \qquad (x > 1)$$

where x denotes the number of units produced. Find the increase in total cost as the number of units produced changes from $x = 5$ to $x = 10$.

Solution

As discussed in Section 6-2, we seek the value of the definite integral,

$$\int_5^{10} C'(x)\, dx = \int_5^{10} \ln x\, dx$$

We first evaluate the corresponding indefinite integral by letting

$$u = \ln x \qquad \text{and} \qquad dv = dx$$

Then

$$du = \frac{1}{x}\, dx \qquad \text{and} \qquad v = \int dx$$
$$= x$$

Using the integration by parts formula, we have

$$\int u\, dv = uv - \int v\, du$$

$$C(x) = x \ln x - \int x \cdot \frac{1}{x}\, dx = x \ln x - \int dx$$
$$= x \ln x - x + c$$

Hence,

$$\int_5^{10} \ln x\, dx = (x \ln x - x)\, \Big|_5^{10}$$

$$= C(10) - C(5)$$
$$= (10 \ln 10 - 10) - (5 \ln 5 - 5)$$
$$= 10 \ln 10 - 5 \ln 5 - 5$$
$$\approx 10(2.3026) - 5(1.6094) - 5$$
$$\approx \$9.98 \qquad \text{Increase in total cost}$$

We now summarize correct choices of u and dv for some of the most common integral forms evaluated by integration by parts.

SUMMARY

Common Integral Forms and Correct Choices of u and dv

Assume that n, k, a, and b are constants.

1. For integrals of the form $\int x^n e^{kx}\, dx$, let $u = x^n$ and $dv = e^{kx}\, dx$. (See Example 6-41 and the illustrative example on page 403.

continues

> **SUMMARY**—*Continued*
>
> **2.** For integrals of the form $\int x^n (\ln x)^k \, dx$, let $u = (\ln x)^k$ and $dv = x^n \, dx$. (See Example 6-39.)
>
> **3.** For integrals of the form $\int x(ax + b)^n \, dx$, let $u = x$ and $dv = (ax + b)^n \, dx$. (See Example 6-38.)

Exercises 6-6

Use integration by parts to find each of the following integrals.

1. $\displaystyle\int xe^{3x} \, dx$

2. $\displaystyle\int x\sqrt{x + 5} \, dx$

3. $\displaystyle\int \frac{x}{\sqrt{x - 3}} \, dx$

4. $\displaystyle\int xe^{-5x} \, dx$

5. $\displaystyle\int \frac{x}{e^x} \, dx$

6. $\displaystyle\int \ln x \, dx$

7. $\displaystyle\int \frac{x}{(x - 4)^3} \, dx$

8. $\displaystyle\int x(x + 6)^4 \, dx$

9. $\displaystyle\int \frac{x}{e^{4x}} \, dx$

10. $\displaystyle\int x^2 \ln x \, dx$

11. $\displaystyle\int x^3 \ln x \, dx$

12. $\displaystyle\int \frac{xe^{3x}}{(3x + 1)^2} \, dx$

13. $\displaystyle\int x(x - 9)^5 \, dx$

14. $\displaystyle\int x\sqrt{x - 6} \, dx$

15. $\displaystyle\int \frac{x}{(6 + 5x)^2} \, dx$

16. $\displaystyle\int \frac{x + 2}{e^x} \, dx$

17. $\displaystyle\int \frac{x}{\sqrt{5 + 3x}} \, dx$

18. $\displaystyle\int \frac{\ln x}{x^4} \, dx$

19. $\displaystyle\int 3x\sqrt{3x + 7} \, dx$

20. $\displaystyle\int x(e^x - 1) \, dx$

21. $\displaystyle\int x \ln 9x \, dx$

22. $\displaystyle\int 5x(5x - 1)^3 \, dx$

23. $\displaystyle\int x^3 e^x \, dx$

24. $\displaystyle\int x^4 e^x \, dx$

25. Referring to Exercises 23 and 24 above, verify the formula

$$\int x^n e^x \, dx = x^n e^x - n \int x^{n-1} e^x \, dx$$

where n is a positive integer.

26. Use the integration by parts formula twice to evaluate $\int x^2(x + 7)^{10} \, dx$.

Use integration by parts for Exercises 27–29.

27. $\displaystyle\int (\ln x)^2 \, dx$

28. $\displaystyle\int (\ln x)^3 \, dx$

29. Verify the formula

$$\int (\ln x)^n \, dx = x(\ln x)^n - n \int (\ln x)^{n-1} \, dx$$

where n is a positive integer.

30. Determine the area bounded by the x-axis and the curve $f(x) = \ln x$ from $x = 1$ to $x = 3$.

31. Determine the area bounded by the x-axis and the curve $f(x) = xe^x$ from $x = 0$ to $x = 2$.

32. Determine the area bounded by the x-axis and the curve $f(x) = x \ln x$ from $x = 1$ to $x = 3$.

33. Determine the area bounded by the x-axis and the curve $f(x) = x^3 e^{x^2}$ from $x = 0$ to $x = 1$.

For Exercises 34–39, some require integration by parts, while others require techniques discussed in this chapter. Find each of the following.

34. $\int 2x^3 e^{x^3} \, dx$ **35.** $\int x^2 e^x \, dx$ **36.** $\int 2xe^x \, dx$

37. $\int \dfrac{1}{x + 6} \, dx$ **38.** $\int \dfrac{x}{x + 6} \, dx$ **39.** $\int \dfrac{x}{2x + 9} \, dx$

Applications

40. *Revenue.* For a given product, a company's sales revenue changes with time at a rate of $R'(t)$ dollars per month, where t is given in months. Find the total sales revenue accumulated during the time interval $0 \le t \le 1$ if

$$R'(t) = 10{,}000te^t$$

41. *Profit.* For a given product, a company's profit changes at a rate given by

$$P'(t) = 2000te^{0.2t}$$

where t is given in months. Find the total profit accumulated during the first 6 months.

42. *Population growth.* The population of a town grows at a rate given by

$$P'(t) = 200te^{2t}$$

where t is in years. Find the total accumulated population growth during the first 4 years.

43. *Medical research.* After a certain experimental drug is injected into a mouse infected with cancer, cancer cells decrease at the rate of $D'(t)$ cells per day, where t is the number of days following the drug injection. If

$$D'(t) = 10{,}000te^{-t}$$

find the total accumulated decrease in cancer cells during the first 2 days following the drug injection.

44. *Marginal cost/Cost.* Find the total cost equation, $C(x)$, if the marginal cost function is given by

$$C'(x) = 10 \ln x \qquad (x > 1)$$

where x denotes the number of units produced and $C(1) = 20$.

45. *Marginal revenue/Revenue.* Find the sales revenue equation, $R(x)$, if the marginal revenue function is given by

$$R'(x) = x^3(\ln x) \qquad (x > 1)$$

where x denotes the number of units sold and $R(1) = 80$.

6-7 • USING TABLES OF INTEGRALS

In Sections 6-4 and 6-5, we integrated functions by using the substitution principle in conjunction with the formulas

$$\int u^n \, du = \frac{1}{n+1} u^{n+1} + c \qquad (n \neq -1)$$

$$\int e^u \, du = e^u + c$$

$$\int \frac{du}{u} = \ln |u| + c$$

These formulas allow us to integrate a variety of functions. However, the functions are limited to those that can be expressed in one of these forms. There are many functions that must be integrated by other methods.

Table 9 of Appendix C lists additional integral forms. Such a table is called a **table of integrals.** A more complete table of integrals appears in *CRC Standard Mathematical Tables.** Table 6-2 is an abridged version of a table of integrals. We now illustrate how a table of integrals is used.

TABLE 6-2 Table of integrals (Abridged)

1. $\displaystyle\int \frac{du}{\sqrt{a^2 + u^2}} = \ln |u + \sqrt{a^2 + u^2}| + c$

2. $\displaystyle\int \frac{du}{a^2 - u^2} = \frac{1}{2a} \ln \left|\frac{a + u}{a - u}\right| + c$

3. $\displaystyle\int u^n e^u \, du = u^n e^u - n \int u^{n-1} e^u \, du$

4. $\displaystyle\int \frac{du}{u^2(a + bu)} = -\frac{1}{au} + \frac{b}{a^2} \ln \left|\frac{a + bu}{u}\right| + c$

• **EXAMPLE 6-43**

Find

$$\int \frac{dx}{\sqrt{36 + x^2}}$$

Solution

Scanning the integral forms in Table 6-2, note that this integral is of the form

$$\int \frac{du}{\sqrt{a^2 + u^2}} = \ln |u + \sqrt{a^2 + u^2}| + c$$

with $a^2 = 36$, $u = x$, and $du = dx$. Substituting 36 for a^2, x for u, and dx for du into this form, we have

$$\int \frac{dx}{\sqrt{36 + x^2}} = \ln |x + \sqrt{36 + x^2}| + c$$

*CRC Standard Mathematical Tables. 27th ed. Boca Raton, Fl.: CRC Press, 1984.

• **EXAMPLE 6-44** _____

Find

$$\int \frac{dx}{x^2(3 - 5x)}$$

Solution

Scanning the integral forms of Table 6-2, we see that this integral is of the form

$$\int \frac{du}{u^2(a + bu)} = -\frac{1}{au} + \frac{b}{a^2} \ln \left| \frac{a + bu}{u} \right| + c$$

with $a = 3$, $b = -5$, $u = x$, and $du = dx$. Substituting 3 for a, -5 for b, x for u, and dx for du into this form, we obtain

$$\int \frac{dx}{x^2(\underset{\uparrow}{3} - \underset{\uparrow}{5}x)} = -\frac{1}{3x} + \frac{-5}{3^2} \ln \left| \frac{3 - 5x}{x} \right| + c$$
$$\qquad\qquad a \quad b$$

$$= -\frac{1}{3x} - \frac{5}{9} \ln \left| \frac{3 - 5x}{x} \right| + c$$

• **EXAMPLE 6-45** _____

Find $\int x^2 e^x \, dx$.

Solution

Scanning the integral forms in Table 6-2, we determine this integral to be of the form

$$\int u^n e^u \, du = u^n e^u - n \int u^{n-1} e^u \, du$$

with $n = 2$, $u = x$, and $du = dx$. Substituting 2 for n, x for u, and dx for du into this form yields

$$\int x^2 e^x \, dx = x^2 e^x - 2 \int x e^x \, dx$$

In this case, we see that the initial solution actually contains an indefinite integral that must be evaluated. Examining its nature, we see that we can use the same form to evaluate $\int x e^x \, dx$. This time $n = 1$. Hence,

$$\int x e^x \, dx = x e^x - \int e^x \, dx$$
$$= x e^x - e^x + c_1$$

Combining the two results, we see that

$$\int x^2 e^x \, dx = x^2 e^x - 2 \int x e^x \, dx$$
$$= x^2 e^x - 2(x e^x - e^x + c_1)$$
$$= x^2 e^x - 2x e^x + 2e^x - 2c_1$$
$$= x^2 e^x - 2x e^x + 2e^x + c$$

where $-2c_1 = c$ is an arbitrary constant.

_____ •

Application

• **EXAMPLE 6-46** **Velocity/Distance.**

The velocity, v (in feet per second), of a moving particle is given by

$$v(t) = \frac{1}{t(5 - t)} \qquad (1 \le t \le 4)$$

where t denotes the time (in seconds) elapsed. Find the distance traveled by the particle during the time interval $1 \le t \le 4$.

Solution

Since $v(t) = S'(t)$, where $S(t)$ denotes distance (in feet), we seek the value of the definite integral

$$\int_1^4 v(t)\ dt = \int_1^4 \frac{1}{t(5 - t)}\ dt$$

Scanning the integral forms of Table 9 in Appendix c, we see that this integral is of the form

$$\int \frac{du}{u(a + bu)} = -\frac{1}{a} \ln \left| \frac{a + bu}{u} \right| + c$$

with $u = t$, $du = dt$, $a = 5$, and $b = -1$. Using the above form,

$$\int_1^4 \frac{1}{t(5 - t)}\ dt = -\frac{1}{5} \ln \left| \frac{5 - t}{t} \right| \Big|_1^4$$

$$= (-1/5)\ [\ln | (5 - 4)/4 | - \ln | (5 - 1)/1 |]$$

$$= (-1/5)\ (\ln | 1/4 | - \ln | 4 |)$$

$$= (-1/5)(\ln 1 - \ln 4 - \ln 4) \qquad \text{Property of logs}$$

$$= (-1/5)(0 - 2 \ln 4) \qquad \text{ln 1 = 0}$$

$$= (-1/5)(-\ln 4^2) \qquad \text{Property of logs}$$

$$\approx (-1/5)(-2.7726)$$

$$\approx 0.55 \text{ feet} \qquad \text{Distance traveled}$$

Exercises 6-7

Using Table 6-2 find each of the following:

1. $\displaystyle\int \frac{dx}{\sqrt{81 + x^2}}$

2. $\displaystyle\int \frac{dx}{\sqrt{x^2 + 64}}$

3. $\displaystyle\int_0^8 \frac{dx}{\sqrt{x^2 + 36}}$

4. $\displaystyle\int \frac{dx}{4 - x^2}$

5. $\displaystyle\int \frac{-7\ dx}{81 - x^2}$

6. $\displaystyle\int \frac{dx}{x^2(5 + 3x)}$

7. $\displaystyle\int \frac{3\ dx}{x^2(4 - 7x)}$

8. $\displaystyle\int x^2 e^{5x}\ dx$

9. $\displaystyle\int_0^1 x^3 e^x\ dx$

10. $\displaystyle\int_0^2 \frac{dx}{\sqrt{x^2 + 25}}$

Using Table 9 of Appendix C, find each of the following:

11. $\int \ln 5x \, dx$

12. $\int \ln(3x - 1) \, dx$

13. $\int \dfrac{dx}{x\sqrt{5 - 2x}}$

14. $\int \dfrac{dx}{x\sqrt{2 + 6x}}$

15. $\int \dfrac{dx}{\sqrt{x^2 - 100}}$

16. $\int \dfrac{dx}{x^2 - 64}$

17. $\int \dfrac{dx}{x\sqrt{25 - x^2}}$

18. $\int \dfrac{dx}{x\sqrt{x^2 + 4}}$

19. $\int (36 - x^2)^{-3/2} \, dx$

20. $\int_0^7 \dfrac{dx}{(x^2 + 49)^{3/2}}$

21. $\int (\ln x)^2 \, dx$

22. $\int (\ln x)^3 \, dx$

23. $\int x^2 \ln x \, dx$

24. $\int x^3 \ln x \, dx$

25. $\int (x^2 + 25)^{-3/2} \, dx$

26. $\int (16 - x^2)^{-3/2} \, dx$

27. $\int (x + 1) \ln(x + 1) \, dx$

28. $\int (x + 1)^2 \ln(x + 1) \, dx$

29. $\int \dfrac{4}{x(3 + 7x)} \, dx$

30. $\int \dfrac{6}{x\sqrt{4 - x^2}} \, dx$

Applications

31. *Velocity/Distance.* The velocity, v (in feet per minute), of a moving particle is given by

$$v(t) = \frac{1}{64 - t^2} \qquad (0 \le t \le 6)$$

where t denotes time (in minutes) elapsed. Find the total distance traveled by the particle over the time interval $0 \le t \le 6$.

32. *Marginal profit/Profit.* The marginal profit (in dollars per unit) for some product is given by

$$P'(x) = \frac{1}{x^2 - 100} \qquad (x > 10)$$

where x denotes the number of units produced and sold. Find the increase in profit as the number of units produced and sold changes from $x = 11$ to $x = 15$.

Water pollution. Raw sewage discharged into a bay is accumulating at the rate of $R'(t)$ gallons per hour, where t denotes the time (in hours) elapsed. For Exercises 33 and 34, find the total amount of sewage accumulated during the time interval $0 \le t \le 10$.

33. $R'(t) = \dfrac{200}{\sqrt{t^2 + 1}} \qquad (t \ge 0)$

34. $R'(t) = 500 \left(1 - \dfrac{1}{\sqrt{t^2 + 1}} \right) \qquad (t \ge 0)$

CHAPTER 6 HIGHLIGHTS

• *Concepts*

Your ability to answer the following questions is one indicator of the depth of your mastery of this chapter's important concepts. Note that the questions are grouped under various topic headings. For any question that you cannot answer, refer to the appropriate section of the chapter indicated by the topic heading. Pay particular attention to the boxes within a section.

6-1   ANTIDIFFERENTIATION

1. If $F(x)$ is an antiderivative of $f(x)$, then $F'(x) = $ _____.
2. If a function has two antiderivatives, they differ by only a(n) _____.
3. State and explain each of the following rules:
   a) Power rule   b) Constant multiplier rule
   c) Sum or difference rule

4. $\int k\, dx = $ _____   5. $\int e^x\, dx = $ _____

6. $\int e^{kx}\, dx = $ _____   7. $\int x^{-1}\, dx = $ _____

8. Explain the term *marginal tax rate*.

6-2   THE DEFINITE INTEGRAL AND AREA UNDER A CURVE

9. Explain each of the following terms: definite integral, limits of integration, Riemann sum.
10. Explain the fundamental theorem of calculus.
11. Give the procedure for finding areas.
12. Explain how to find an area where a portion of the area lies above the x-axis and a portion lies below the x-axis.

6-3   AREA BETWEEN TWO CURVES

13. Explain, using graphs, how to find the area between two curves.
14. Explain the term *consumers' surplus,* and indicate how it is determined.
15. Explain the term *producers' surplus,* and indicate how it is determined.

6-4   INTEGRATION BY SUBSTITUTION

16. State the rule for determining $\int u^n\, du$. Explain the quantity du.

6-5   INTEGRALS INVOLVING EXPONENTIAL AND LOGARITHMIC FUNCTIONS

17. State the rule for determining $\int e^u\, du$. Explain the quantity du.
18. State the rule for determining $\int du/u$. Explain the quantity du.

6-6   INTEGRATION BY PARTS

19. State the formula for integration by parts.

6-7   USING TABLES OF INTEGRALS

20. Explain the term *tables of integrals*.

REVIEW EXERCISES

• *Antidifferentiation*

Find the indefinite integral for Exercises 1–16.

1. $\int x^4 \, dx$ **2.** $\int dx/x^2$ **3.** $\int (20/x) \, dx$ **4.** $\int e^x \, dx$

5. $\int e^{-x} \, dx$ **6.** $\int (7/x) \, dx$ **7.** $\int 7 \, dx$ **8.** $\int x \, dx$

9. $\int (5x^4 + 6x^2 - 8x + 4) \, dx$ **10.** $\int (x^3 - 2x + 7) \, dx$

11. $\int (4x^{-1} + e^{6x}) \, dx$ **12.** $\int (x^{-1} - x^{-4} - e^{-x}) \, dx$

13. $\int [(4 - x^6)/x^2] \, dx$ **14.** $\int [(8x - e^x)/xe^x] \, dx$

15. $\int (x - 5)(x + 5) \, dx$ **16.** $\int [(x^2 - 9)/(x + 3)] \, dx$

17. *Marginal cost.* The marginal cost for some product is given by

$$C'(x) = 9x^2 + 4x - 1$$

where x is the production level. Find the cost function, $C(x)$, if the fixed cost is $5000.

18. *Velocity/Distance.* The velocity, v, of a moving particle after t seconds have elapsed is given by

$$v(t) = 9t^2$$

Determine the formula for the distance traveled, $S(t)$, by the particle after t seconds have elapsed if $S(0) = 5$.

• *The Definite Integral and Area*

Evaluate Exercises 19–24.

19. $\int_1^4 (8x + 2) \, dx$ **20.** $\int_1^3 (6x^2 - 2x + 4) dx$

21. $\int_2^5 (20/x) \, dx$ **22.** $\int_0^1 e^x dx$

23. $\int_1^4 (40/\sqrt{x}) \, dx$ **24.** $\int_0^2 e^{-4x} dx$

Area. For Exercises 25–29, find the area between the x-axis and the graph of $f(x)$ over the indicated interval. Include a graph and shade the desired area.

25. $f(x) = -x^2 + 36$ from $x = 0$ to $x = 6$
26. $f(x) = -x^2 + 16$ from $x = -4$ to $x = 4$
27. $f(x) = x^4 + 10$ from $x = 0$ to $x = 2$
28. $f(x) = -2x^2 + 6x$ from $x = 0$ to $x = 8$
29. $f(x) = x^2 - 4$ from $x = 0$ to $x = 4$
30. Find the area between two curves, $f(x) = x^2$ and $g(x) = 4x$, from $x = 1$ to $x = 2$. Graph both functions and shade the desired area.
31. Find the area between two curves, $f(x) = -x^2 + 16$ and $g(x) = x^2 - 16$, from $x = -4$ to $x = 4$. Graph both functions and shade the desired area.

Consumers' and producers' surpluses. Find the consumers' and producers' surpluses for Exercises 32 and 33.

32. $p = D(q) = (q - 10)^2$, $p = S(q) = q^2 + 20$

33. $p = D(q) = -4q + 56$, $p = S(q) = 2q + 8$

• *Integration by Substitution*

Determine Exercises 34–43.

34. $\displaystyle\int (x^2 + 8)^6 x \, dx$

35. $\displaystyle\int (x^4 + 6x)^5 (4x^3 + 6) \, dx$

36. $\displaystyle\int e^{x+4} \, dx$

37. $\displaystyle\int e^{x^2 + 6} x \, dx$

38. $\displaystyle\int x^2 \sqrt{x^3 + 9} \, dx$

39. $\displaystyle\int [x/(x^2 + 4)] \, dx$

40. $\displaystyle\int [x^2/(x^3 + 6)^7] \, dx$

41. $\displaystyle\int [(\ln 5x)^3/x] \, dx$

42. $\displaystyle\int [e^x/(7 + e^x)] \, dx$

43. $\displaystyle\int (x^2 + 10x - 7)^6 (x + 5) \, dx$

• *Integration by Parts*

Use integration by parts to determine Exercises 44–47.

44. $\displaystyle\int x e^{8x} \, dx$

45. $\displaystyle\int x \sqrt{x - 8} \, dx$

46. $\displaystyle\int x \ln 4x \, dx$

47. $\displaystyle\int [x/(8 + 5x)] \, dx$

• *Tables of Integrals*

Use Table 9 of Appendix C to determine Exercises 48–55.

48. $\displaystyle\int \frac{1}{\sqrt{x^2 + 25}} \, dx$

49. $\displaystyle\int \frac{1}{7 - x} \, dx$

50. $\displaystyle\int \ln (4x + 5) \, dx$

51. $\displaystyle\int \frac{1}{x\sqrt{7 - 2x}} \, dx$

52. $\displaystyle\int \frac{1}{\sqrt{x^2 - 36}} \, dx$

53. $\displaystyle\int (x^2 + 16)^{-3/2} \, dx$

54. $\displaystyle\int (x + 3) \ln (x + 3) \, dx$

55. $\displaystyle\int x^2 e^{8x} \, dx$

Applications

56. *Revenue.* The rate of flow of revenue (in dollars) into a firm is given by

$$R'(t) = 200t + 50e^{-t}$$

where t is given in years. Find the total revenue gained during the interval $0 \le t \le 5$.

57. *Population growth.* The population of a given community has been growing at the rate of $P'(t)$ individuals per month, where t is the number of months elapsed since December 31 of the past year. If

$$P'(t) = 0.25t e^t$$

find the total increase in the population during the first 8 months of this year.

7

FURTHER TOPICS OF INTEGRATION

Introductory Application

Probability: Interarrival Time

The interarrival time, x (i.e., the time between two successive arrivals), of customers at a particular bank is exponentially distributed, with $k = 10$. Find the probability that the interarrival time is between 0.1 and 0.5 minute.

In this chapter, we will learn that an exponentially distributed random variable has a density function typified by the graph of Figure 7-A. Furthermore, the above probability is given by the shaded area under the graph of the density function in Figure 7-A. This problem is solved in Example 7-11.

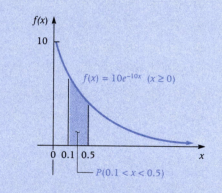

$f(x) = 10e^{-10x}$ $(x \geq 0)$

$P(0.1 < x < 0.5)$

FIGURE 7-A

7-1 • CONTINUOUS MONEY FLOW

In previous sections of this text, we have encountered situations where money flowed into a firm's treasury at a rate of $R'(t)$ dollars, where t denotes time. In this section, we will consider such problems under the added assumption that the money flow, once received, earns interest that is compounded continuously at a nominal rate, r. In order to simplify our notation, we will use $f(x)$, instead of $R'(t)$, to denote the rate of money flow. Also, we assume that x denotes time in years; therefore, $f(x)$ denotes an annual rate of money flow, and r denotes an annual rate at which interest is compounded continuously.

There are many business situations (as when chain stores, large manufacturing operations, or toll roads and bridges receive revenues) where the flow of revenue is most accurately approximated by a continuous flow of money into a fund. An analogy can be drawn between a liquid flowing into a container and money flowing into a fund, as illustrated in Figure 7-1. Again, $f(x)$ denotes the rate of money flow (in dollars per year).

We now review the case where the continuous money flow does not earn interest.

Total Money Flow

If money flows into a fund at a rate, $f(x)$, during a time interval, $0 \le x \le t$, then the total amount of money accumulated is given by

$$\int_0^t f(x)\, dx$$

This is the area under the graph of $f(x)$, as shown in Figure 7-1.

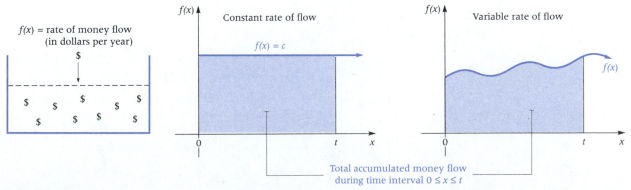

$f(x)$ = rate of money flow
(in dollars per year)

Constant rate of flow

$f(x) = c$

Variable rate of flow

$f(x)$

Total accumulated money flow
during time interval $0 \le x \le t$

FIGURE 7-1

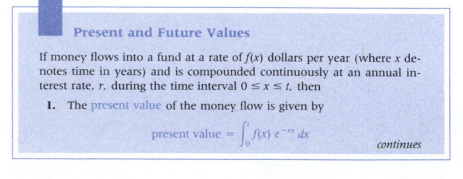

$f(x)$

$f(x)$

0

Δx_i

t

x

Present value
$f(x_i)\,\Delta x_i e^{-rx_i}$

Area of rectangle
$= f(x_i)\,\Delta x_i$
$\approx$ total accumulated
money flow during
the interval
of length Δx_i

FIGURE 7-2

Interest-Earning Money Flows

We now consider the case where the continuous money flow earns interest. We will develop formulas for the present and future values of such money flows. We first begin with present value by considering the graph of Figure 7-2. Note that the area of the rectangle at $x = x_i$, $f(x_i)\,\Delta x_i$, approximates the total (accumulated) money flow during the time interval of length Δx_i. The present value of this incremental accumulated money flow is given by

$$f(x_i)\,\Delta x_i e^{-rx_i}$$

where r is the annual interest rate compounded continuously. The sum of all such incremental present values, where Δx_i gets smaller and smaller (or, equivalently, as the number of such rectangles increases without bound), results in the definite integral given below.

$$\text{Present value} = \int_0^t f(x)\, e^{-rx}\, dx$$

We note that the **present value** is the single-sum equivalent at time $x = 0$ of the total money flow including interest earned at an annual rate, r, compounded continuously during the time interval.

The **future value** of the continuous money flow is the total accumulated money flow plus interest earned during the time interval. The future value is determined by multiplying the present value by e^{rt}. Thus, the future value is given by the definite integral below.

$$\text{Future value} = e^{rt}\int_0^t f(x)\, e^{-rx}\, dx$$

or

$$\text{Future value} = e^{rt}(\text{present value})$$

We summarize these results below.

> ### Present and Future Values
>
> If money flows into a fund at a rate of $f(x)$ dollars per year (where x denotes time in years) and is compounded continuously at an annual interest rate, r, during the time interval $0 \le x \le t$, then
>
> **1.** The present value of the money flow is given by
>
> $$\text{present value} = \int_0^t f(x)\, e^{-rx}\, dx$$
>
> *continues*

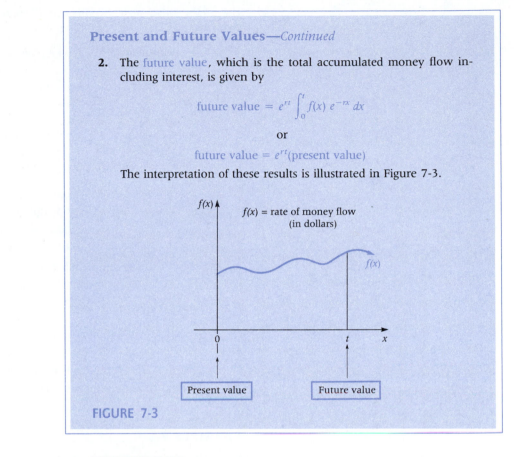

Present and Future Values—*Continued*

2. The future value, which is the total accumulated money flow including interest, is given by

$$\text{future value} = e^{rt} \int_0^t f(x)\, e^{-rx}\, dx$$

or

$$\text{future value} = e^{rt}(\text{present value})$$

The interpretation of these results is illustrated in Figure 7-3.

$f(x)$ = rate of money flow (in dollars)

$f(x)$

Present value

Future value

FIGURE 7-3

• **EXAMPLE 7-1**

Revenues from a manufacturing operation flow continuously into a firm's treasury at the rate of $f(x)$ dollars per year where

$$f(x) = 60{,}000$$

and x denotes time in years.

a) Find the total money flow at the end of 5 years (or, in other words, over the time interval $0 \le x \le 5$).

b) If the money flow, over the time interval $0 \le x \le 5$, is compounded continuously at 6%, find its present value.

c) If the money flow, over the time interval $0 \le x \le 5$, is compounded continuously at 6%, find its future value.

Solutions

a) The *total money flow (without interest)* is given by

$$\int_0^5 f(x)\, dx = \int_0^5 60{,}000\, dx$$

$$= 60{,}000x \Big|_0^5$$

$$= 60{,}000(5) - 60{,}000(0)$$

$$= \$300{,}000 \qquad \text{Total Money Flow}$$

b) The *present value*, at 6% compounded continuously, of the money flow is given by

$$\text{present value} = \int_0^5 f(x)\, e^{-rx}\, dx$$

$$= \int_0^5 60{,}000 e^{-0.06x}\, dx$$

$$= \frac{60{,}000}{-0.06} \int_0^5 \overbrace{e^{-0.06x}}^{u} \underbrace{(-0.06)\, dx}_{du}$$

$$= -1{,}000{,}000 e^{-0.06x} \Big|_0^5$$

$$= -1{,}000{,}000\left(e^{-0.06(5)} - e^{-0.06(0)}\right)$$

$$= -1{,}000{,}000\left(e^{-0.30} - 1\right)$$

$$\approx -1{,}000{,}000(0.740818 - 1)$$

$$= \$259{,}182 \qquad \text{Present Value}$$

c) The *future value*, at 6% compounded continuously, of the money flow is given by

$$\text{future value} = e^{rt} \int_0^t f(x)\, e^{-rx}\, dx$$

$$= e^{rt}(\text{present value})$$

$$= e^{0.06(5)}(259{,}182)$$

$$= e^{0.30}(259{,}182) = \$349{,}859 \qquad \text{Future Value}$$

This is the total amount of money flow including interest into the firm's treasury after 5 years.

• **EXAMPLE 7-2** _____

Revenues flow into a fund at the rate of $f(x)$ dollars per year, where

$$f(x) = 8000x$$

and x denotes time in years.

a) Find the total money flow (no interest) at the end of 4 years.
b) If the money flow, over the time interval $0 \le x \le 4$, is compounded continuously at 10%, find its present value.
c) If the money flow, over the time interval $0 \le x \le 4$, is compounded continuously at 10%, find its future value.

Solutions

a) The *total money flow* is given by

$$\int_0^4 8000x\, dx = 4000x^2 \Big|_0^4$$

$$= 4000(4^2) - 4000(0^2)$$

$$= \$64{,}000$$

b) The *present value* at 10% compounded continuously, is given by

$$\text{present value} = \int_0^4 f(x)\, e^{-rx}\, dx$$

$$= \int_0^4 8000x e^{-0.10x}\, dx$$

This integral may be evaluated either by using formula 7 of our table of integrals (see Table 9 in Appendix C) or by integrating by parts. This form is

$$\int u e^u \, du = e^u (u - 1) + c$$

We must find $\int 8000 x e^{-0.10x} \, dx$ by using this form. Using the substitution principle, we let $u = -0.10x$. Then $du = -0.10 \, dx$, and the integral becomes

$$\frac{8000}{(-0.10)^2} \int \underbrace{(-0.10)x}_{u} \underset{\uparrow}{\overset{\overbrace{}^{u}}{e^{-0.10x}}} \underbrace{(-0.10) \, dx}_{du} = 800{,}000 \int u e^u \, du$$

We must multiply by -0.10 twice, once for du and then for u.

$$= 800{,}000 e^u (u - 1) + c$$

Replacing u with $-0.10x$ gives the result below.

$$= 800{,}000 e^{-0.10x}(-0.10x - 1)$$

Hence,

$$\int_0^4 8000 x e^{-0.10x} \, dx = \underbrace{800{,}000 e^{-0.10x}(-0.10x - 1)}_{F(x)} \Big|_0^4$$

$$= F(4) - F(0)$$
$$= 800{,}000 [e^{-0.40}(-1.40) - e^0(-1)]$$
$$\approx 800{,}000(-0.938448 + 1)$$
$$\approx \$49{,}241.55 \qquad \text{Present Value}$$

c) The *future value*, at 10% compounded continuously, is given by

$$\text{future value} = e^{rt} \int_0^t f(x) \, e^{-rx} \, dx$$

$$= e^{rt}(\text{present value})$$
$$\approx e^{0.10(4)}(49{,}241.55)$$
$$\approx \$73{,}459.76 \qquad \text{Future Value}$$

This is the total money flow including interest over 4 years.

Exercises 7-1

For Exercises 1–16, assume revenues flow into a fund at the rate of $f(x)$ dollars per year, where x denotes time in years.
a) Find the total money flow (no interest) at the end of 5 years.
b) If the money flow, over the time interval $0 \le x \le 5$, is compounded continuously at 9%, find its present value.
c) If the money flow, over the time interval $0 \le x \le 5$, is compounded continuously at 9%, find its future value.

1. $f(x) = 2000$ 2. $f(x) = 3000$
3. $f(x) = 60{,}000$ 4. $f(x) = 40{,}000$
5. $f(x) = 6000x$ 6. $f(x) = 4000x$
7. $f(x) = 0.8x$ 8. $f(x) = 0.6x$

9. $f(x) = 3000e^{0.05x}$ **10.** $f(x) = 20,000e^{-0.10x}$

11. $f(x) = 40,000e^{-0.04x}$ **12.** $f(x) = 8000e^{0.02x}$

13. $f(x) = 0.20x + 1000$ **14.** $f(x) = 0.60x + 1200$

15. $f(x) = 2500 - 250x$ **16.** $f(x) = 10,000 - 100x$

17. *Sales revenue.* Sales revenue flows continuously into the treasury of a super-market at the rate of $f(x)$ dollars per year (x = time in years), where $f(x) = 10,000$ during the time interval $0 \le x \le 7$.
   a) Find the total money flow (no interest) at the end of 7 years.
   b) If the money flow, over the time interval $0 \le x \le 7$, is compounded continuously at 10%, find its present value.
   c) If the money flow, over the time interval $0 \le x \le 7$, is compounded continuously at 10%, find its future value.

18. *Toll road revenue.* Money from toll roads in a given state flows into the state treasury at the rate of $f(x)$ dollars per year (x = time in years), where $f(x) = 9,500,000x$ during the time interval $0 \le x \le 5$.
   a) Find the total money flow (no interest) at the end of 5 years.
   b) If the money flow, over the time interval $0 \le x \le 5$, is compounded continuously at 8%, find its present value.
   c) If the money flow, over the time interval $0 \le x \le 5$, is compounded continuously at 8%, find its future value.

19. *Sales revenue.* Sales revenue flows continuously into the treasury of a retail store outlet at the rate of $f(x)$ dollars per year (x = time in years), where $f(x) = 10,000,000x$ during the time interval $0 \le x \le 4$.
   a) Find the total money flow (no interest) at the end of 4 years.
   b) If the money flow, over the time interval $0 \le x \le 4$, is compounded continuously at 12%, find its present value.
   c) If the money flow, over the time interval $0 \le x \le 4$, is compounded continuously at 12%, find its future value.

20. *Mutual fund revenue.* Revenue flows continuously into a mutual fund at the rate of $f(x)$ dollars per year (x = time in years), where $f(x) = 10,000,000x^2$ during the time interval $0 \le x \le 6$.
   a) Find the total money flow (no interest) at the end of 6 years.
   b) If the money flow, over the time interval $0 \le x \le 6$, is compounded continuously at 10%, find its present value.
   c) If the money flow, over the time interval $0 \le x \le 6$, is compounded continuously at 10%, find its future value.

7-2 • IMPROPER INTEGRALS

Suppose we wish to compute the area between the x-axis and the curve $f(x) = e^x$ *over the interval* $-\infty < x \le 0$ [see Figure 7-4 (a)]. Studying Figure 7-4 (a), note that the shaded region has no bound as $x \to -\infty$. Since the shaded region has no bound as $x \to -\infty$, we begin to compute its area by finding

$$\int_a^0 e^x \, dx$$

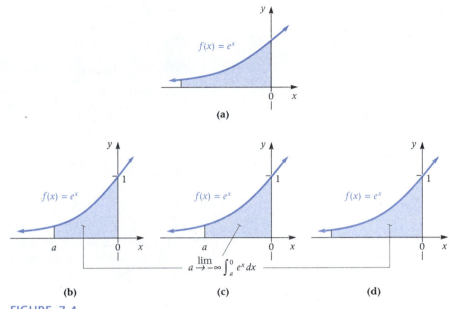

FIGURE 7-4

where a is a real number, as illustrated in Figure 7-4 (b). Hence,

$$\int_a^0 e^x\, dx = e^x\Big|_a^0$$

$$= e^0 - e^a$$

$$= 1 - e^a$$

As $a \to -\infty$, then the definite integral $\int_a^0 e^x\, dx$ becomes

$$\lim_{a \to -\infty}\int_a^0 e^x\, dx = \lim_{a \to -\infty}(1 - e^a)$$

$$= 1 - 0$$

$$= 1$$

as illustrated by the graphs in Figure 7-4(b), (c), and (d). Since $\lim_{a \to -\infty}\int_a^0 e^x\, dx = 1$, then the shaded area in Figure 7-4 (a) is 1. The fact that

$$\int_a^0 e^x\, dx \text{ approaches 1 as } a \to -\infty$$

is written as

$$\int_{-\infty}^0 e^x\, dx = 1$$

An integral such as $\int_{-\infty}^0 e^x\, dx$ where either one or both limits of integration are infinite is called an **improper integral.** Since the definite integral $\int_a^0 e^x\, dx$ approaches a *finite number* as $a \to -\infty$, then the improper integral $\int_{-\infty}^0 e^x\, dx$ is said to be *convergent*. If this were not the case, then the improper integral would be said to be *divergent*.

We define three types of improper integrals.

> ### Improper Integrals
>
> If the function $f(x)$ is continuous over the indicated intervals, and if the indicated limits exist, then
>
> **1.** $\displaystyle \int_a^\infty f(x)\,dx = \lim_{b\to\infty} \int_a^b f(x)\,dx,$
>
> **2.** $\displaystyle \int_{-\infty}^b f(x)\,dx = \lim_{a\to-\infty} \int_a^b f(x)\,dx,$ and
>
> **3.** $\displaystyle \int_{-\infty}^\infty f(x)\,dx = \int_{-\infty}^c f(x)\,dx + \int_c^\infty f(x)\,dx,$
>
> where a, b, and c are real numbers.
>
> *Note:* If the right-hand-side expressions exist, then the improper integrals are said to be **convergent.** If the right-hand-side expressions do not exist, then the improper integrals are said to be **divergent.**

• **EXAMPLE 7-3**

Find the area between the x-axis and the curve $f(x) = 1/x$ over the interval $1 \le x < \infty$, as illustrated in Figure 7-5.

Solution

We seek to evaluate the improper integral

$$\int_1^\infty \frac{1}{x}\,dx$$

by letting $b > 1$ denote a real number and computing the definite integral $\int_1^b (1/x)\,dx$. Hence,

$$\int_1^b \frac{1}{x}\,dx = \ln|x| \Big|_1^b$$
$$= \ln|b| - \ln|1|$$
$$= \ln|b| - 0$$
$$= \ln|b|$$

Now, as $b\to\infty$, $\ln|b|\to\infty$, and the definite integral $\int_1^b (1/x)\,dx$ does not approach a finite number. Thus, the improper integral $\int_1^\infty (1/x)\,dx$ is divergent, and the shaded area in Figure 7-5 is infinite.

• **EXAMPLE 7-4**

Determine whether the improper integral

$$\int_2^\infty \frac{1}{x^2}\,dx$$

is convergent or divergent.

Solution

We let $b > 2$ denote a real number and compute the definite integral

$$\int_2^b \frac{1}{x^2}\,dx$$

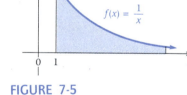

FIGURE 7-5

Hence,

$$\int_2^b \frac{1}{x^2}\,dx = \int_2^b x^{-2}\,dx$$

$$= -\frac{1}{x}\Big|_2^b$$

$$= -\frac{1}{b} - \left(-\frac{1}{2}\right)$$

$$= -\frac{1}{b} + \frac{1}{2}$$

Now, as $b\to\infty$, $-1/b\to 0$, so that

$$\int_2^b \frac{1}{x^2}\,dx \to 0 + \frac{1}{2} = \frac{1}{2}$$

Since the definite integral $\int_2^b (1/x^2)\,dx$ approaches 1/2 as $b\to\infty$, then the improper integral $\int_2^\infty (1/x^2)\,dx = 1/2$ and thus is convergent.

Present Value of a Perpetual Flow

In certain situations (e.g., where interest from a perpetual bond or income from an indestructible asset such as land is earned), a continuous stream of money flows forever (i.e., perpetually). We will now show how to find the present value of such a perpetual flow. If a continuous stream of money flows perpetually into a fund at a rate of $f(x)$ dollars per year (x = time in years) during the time interval $0 \le x < \infty$, and if this money flow is compounded continuously at an annual interest rate of r, then its present value at $x = 0$ is given by the improper integral

$$\int_0^\infty f(x)\,e^{-rx}\,dx$$

• **EXAMPLE 7-5** _____

Income from a piece of land flows continuously into a trust fund at a constant rate of $f(x)$ = \$600,000 per year (x = time in years) and is compounded continuously at 10%. If this flow continues forever (i.e., $0 \le x < \infty$), find its present value.

Solution

The present value at $x = 0$ is given by

$$\int_0^\infty 600{,}000e^{-0.10x}\,dx$$

We must evaluate the definite integral $\int_0^b 600{,}000e^{-0.10x}\,dx$. We let $b > 0$ denote a real number and compute the definite integral $\int_0^b 600{,}000e^{-0.10x}\,dx$. Hence.

$$\int_0^b 600{,}000e^{-0.10x}\,dx = -6{,}000{,}000e^{-0.10x}\Big|_0^b$$

$$= -6{,}000{,}000e^{-0.10b} - (-6{,}000{,}000e^0)$$

$$= -6{,}000{,}000e^{-0.10b} + 6{,}000{,}000$$

Now, as $b\to\infty$, $e^{-0.10b}\to 0$, so that

$$\int_0^b 600{,}000e^{-0.10x}\,dx \to 0 + 6{,}000{,}000 = 6{,}000{,}000$$

Thus, the improper integral

$$\int_0^\infty 600{,}000e^{-0.10x}\,dx = 6{,}000{,}000$$

and the present value is $6,000,000. Thus, $6,000,000 invested now at 10% compounded continuously will provide for payments at the rate of $600,000 per year forever.

• **EXAMPLE 7-6** **Radioactive Waste.** _____

The rate (in tons per year) at which radioactive waste is being released into the atmosphere is given by

$$f(t) = 2000e^{-0.05t} \qquad (t \ge 0)$$

where t denotes time in years. If this flow of radioactive waste continues indefinitely, find the total amount released.

Solution

The *total amount released* is given by the improper integral

$$\int_0^\infty 2000e^{-0.05t}\,dt = \lim_{b\to\infty}\int_0^b 2000e^{-0.05t}\,dt$$

We must evaluate the definite integral

$$\int_0^b 2000e^{-0.05t}\,dt = \frac{2000}{-0.05}e^{-0.05t}\Big|_0^b$$

$$= -40{,}000e^{-0.05b} - (-40{,}000e^{-0.05(0)})$$

$$= -40{,}000e^{-0.05b} + 40{,}000$$

Now, as $b\to\infty$, $e^{-0.05b}\to 0$, so that

$$\int_0^b 2000e^{-0.05t}\,dt \to 0 + 40{,}000 = 40{,}000$$

Thus, the improper integral

$$\int_0^\infty 2000e^{-0.05t}\,dt = 40{,}000 \qquad \text{Total amount (in tons) of radioactive waste released}$$

Exercises 7-2

Evaluate whichever of the following improper integrals converge.

1. $\displaystyle\int_1^\infty \frac{dx}{x^2}$

2. $\displaystyle\int_1^\infty \frac{dx}{x^4}$

3. $\displaystyle\int_6^\infty \frac{dx}{x}$

4. $\displaystyle\int_2^\infty \frac{dx}{x^3}$

5. $\displaystyle\int_3^\infty \frac{dx}{x+1}$

6. $\displaystyle\int_1^\infty \frac{dx}{2x+5}$

7. $\displaystyle\int_0^\infty e^{-2x}dx$

8. $\displaystyle\int_0^\infty e^{-4x}dx$

9. $\displaystyle\int_0^\infty xe^{-x}dx$

10. $\displaystyle\int_0^\infty xe^{-2x}dx$

11. $\displaystyle\int_{-\infty}^0 e^{2x}dx$

12. $\displaystyle\int_{-\infty}^0 e^{x}dx$

13. $\displaystyle\int_4^\infty x^{-1/2}dx$

14. $\displaystyle\int_8^\infty x^{-1/3}dx$

15. $\displaystyle\int_1^\infty \frac{dx}{(x+2)^2}$

16. $\displaystyle\int_0^\infty \frac{dx}{(x+4)^3}$

17. $\displaystyle\int_0^\infty xe^{-x^2}dx$

18. $\displaystyle\int_1^\infty x^2 dx$

19. $\displaystyle\int_{-\infty}^{\infty} xe^{-x^2}dx$ **20.** $\displaystyle\int_{2}^{\infty} \frac{\ln x}{x}\, dx$ **21.** $\displaystyle\int_{1}^{\infty} \frac{dx}{\sqrt{x+6}}$

22. $\displaystyle\int_{8}^{\infty} \frac{dx}{\sqrt{x-7}}$ **23.** $\displaystyle\int_{0}^{\infty} x^3 dx$ **24.** $\displaystyle\int_{1}^{\infty} \frac{(2x+4)}{x^2+4x}\, dx$

Area

25. Find the area between the x-axis and the curve $y = e^{-x}$ over the interval $0 \le x < \infty$. Sketch the function and shade the desired area.

26. Find the area between the x-axis and the curve $f(x) = 1/(x-3)^2$ over the interval $10 \le x < \infty$. Sketch the function and shade the desired area.

27. Find the area between the x-axis and the curve $f(x) = 1/(x-3)^2$ over the interval $4 \le x < \infty$. Sketch the function and shade the desired area.

28. Find the area between the x-axis and the curve $f(x) = 1/(x-1)^3$ over the interval $2 \le x < \infty$. Sketch the function and shade the desired area.

29. Find the area between the x-axis and the curve $f(x) = 1/(x-1)^3$ over the interval $3 \le x < \infty$. Sketch the function and shade the desired area.

30. Find the area between the x-axis and the curve $y = e^x$ over the interval $-\infty < x \le 0$. Sketch the function and shade the desired area.

Applications

31. *Perpetual flow.* A perpetual bond yields a continuous flow of interest at a constant rate of $f(x) = \$40{,}000$ per year (x = time in years). If this perpetual flow is compounded continuously at 9%, find its present value.

32. *Perpetual flow.* A piece of land yields a continuous flow of revenue at a constant rate of $800,000 per year. If this perpetual flow is compounded continuously at 12%, find its present value.

33. *Perpetual flow: Endowment fund.* A college wishes to establish an endowment fund to provide for annual scholarships in the amount of $20,000. If the fund is to be invested at 10% compounded continuously, how much should be solicited from donors for this fund now?

34. *Perpetual flow: Endowment fund.* A donor wishes to establish an endowment fund to provide a hospital with annual $50,000 research grants. If the fund is to be invested at 9% compounded continuously, how much should the donor provide to set up the fund?

35. *Radioactive waste.* The rate at which radioactive waste is being released into the atmosphere is given by

$$f(t) = 8000e^{-0.04t} \qquad (t \ge 0)$$

where t denotes time in years. If this flow of radioactive waste continues indefinitely, find the total amount released.

36. *Radioactive waste.* The rate at which radioactive waste is being released into the atmosphere is given by

$$f(t) = 6000e^{-0.03t} \qquad (t \ge 0)$$

where t denotes time in years. If this flow continues indefinitely, find the total amount released.

37. *Water pollution.* In a given area, toxic chemicals from a nearby dump are seeping into the groundwater at a rate of

$$f(t) = \frac{600}{(1+t)^3} \qquad (t \ge 0)$$

gallons per year, where t denotes time in years. If this seepage continues indefinitely, find the total amount of seepage.

7-3 • PROBABILITY DISTRIBUTIONS

TABLE 7-1 Box full of numbers

1	(20%)
3	(50%)
5	(15%)
8	(10%)
10	(5%)

TABLE 7-2

x	$P(x)$
1	.20
3	.50
5	.15
8	.10
10	.05
	1.00

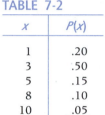

FIGURE 7-6

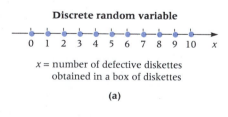

Discrete random variable

x = number of defective diskettes obtained in a box of diskettes

(a)

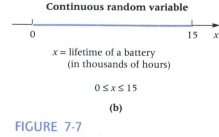

Continuous random variable

x = lifetime of a battery (in thousands of hours)

$0 \leq x \leq 15$

(b)

FIGURE 7-7

Frequently, in business and industry, chance events take the form of numerical outcomes. The numerical outcomes are denoted by a letter—say, x—which is called a **random variable.** We now discuss this concept in detail.

Consider a simple type of gambling machine—a box full of numbers (see Table 7-1). Observing Table 7-1, note that the box contains the numbers 1, 3, 5, 8, and 10. Specifically, in the proportions shown, 20% of all the numbers in the box are 1s, 50% are 3s, 15% are 5s, 10% are 8s, and 5% are 10s.

A chance experiment consists of selecting 1 number from the box. The number selected may be taken to a cashier who will pay the player a dollar amount equal to the number. Observing the percentages in Table 7-1, it is obvious that the player has a 20% probability of winning $1, a 50% probability of winning $3, a 15% probability of winning $5, a 10% probability of winning $8, and a 5% probability of winning $10.

Since the outcomes of this chance experiment are numerical values, they may be listed in tabular form, as shown in Table 7-2. Observing Table 7-2, note that the numerical values 1, 3, 5, 8, and 10 are denoted by a letter—in this case, x. Since the values of x are chance outcomes, x is called a **random variable.** Observe that the probability of occurrence of each x-value is listed in the "$P(x)$" column (i.e., the "probability of x" column). Such a display of values of random variables and their corresponding probabilities is called a **probability distribution.** As shown in Table 7-2, the sum of the probabilities of a probability distribution is 1. Figure 7-6 graphically illustrates this probability distribution. Since the random variable, x, takes on a finite number of values, it is called a **discrete random variable,** and its probability distribution is termed a **discrete probability distribution.** If a random variable can take on all possible values within an interval of numbers, it is termed a **continuous random variable,** and its probability distribution is called a **continuous probability distribution.**

An example of a discrete random variable is given by the number of defective diskettes obtained in a box of 10 diskettes, as is illustrated in Figure 7-7(a). The lifetime (in thousands of hours) of a battery is an example of a continuous random variable, as is illustrated in Figure 7-7(b).

We now give an example illustrating an application of a discrete random variable.

• EXAMPLE 7-7

The manager of Howie's Hamburger Stand has kept a record of daily demand for hamburgers during the past 400 days. For example, on precisely 20 of the 400 days, there was a demand for $x = 100$ hamburgers. The complete results are shown in Table 7-3. Such a display of data is called a **frequency (f) distribution.**

a) Convert this frequency distribution into a probability distribution by expressing the frequency of occurrence as a percentage for each x-value.

TABLE 7-3

x (Demand)	f (# days)
100	20
110	80
120	200
130	80
140	20
	400

TABLE 7-4

x	P(x)	
100	.05	←20/400
110	.20	←80/400
120	.50	←200/400
130	.20	←80/400
140	.05	←20/400
	1.00	

TABLE 7-5

x	P(x)
1	.25
3	.25
5	.25
7	.25
	1.00

b) Find the probability that daily demand is 130 hamburgers.
c) Find the probability that daily demand is at most 130 hamburgers.
d) How many hamburgers should be kept on hand in order to satisfy daily demand 95% of the time?

Solutions

a) Dividing each frequency value by the total frequency, 400, we have the probability distribution in Table 7-4.

b) Observing Table 7-4, we note that the probability that daily demand is 130 hamburgers is .20. This is expressed symbolically as

$$P(x = 130) = P(130) = .20$$

c) The probability that daily demand is at most 130 is

$$P(x \leq 130) = P(130) + P(120) + P(110) + P(100)$$
$$= .20 + .50 + .20 + .05$$
$$= .95$$

d) Since there is a 95% probability (see part c) that daily demand will be at most 130 hamburgers, then 130 hamburgers should be kept on hand in order to satisfy demand 95% of the time.

Uniform Distributions

Consider for a moment a box of numbers whose distribution is given by the discrete probability distribution in Table 7-5. A graph of this probability distribution appears in Figure 7-8. If a chance experiment consists of selecting 1 number from the box, the chance outcomes of 1, 3, 5, and 7 have equal probabilities of occurring. Thus, we say that the random variable, x, is *uniformly distributed*.

Now consider a uniformly distributed random variable, x, having possible values within the interval $1 \leq x \leq 7$. Since x is a continuous random variable, it takes on an infinite number of possible values. Thus, we can no longer list all possible individual values of x and their probabilities as we do with a discrete random variable. Instead, we use a graph to illustrate the distribution of the random variable, x, over the interval $1 \leq x \leq 7$. Since the random variable, x, is uniformly distributed over the interval $1 \leq x \leq 7$, the graph of its probability distribution takes on a *constant value* over the interval $1 \leq x \leq 7$, as illustrated in Figure 7-9.

With a probability distribution of a continuous random variable, the

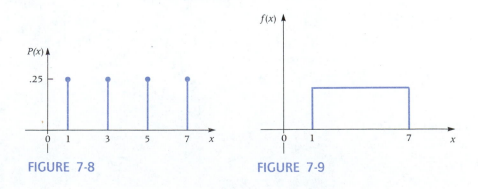

FIGURE 7-8   **FIGURE 7-9**

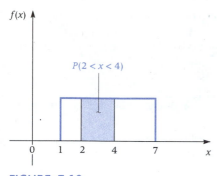

FIGURE 7-10

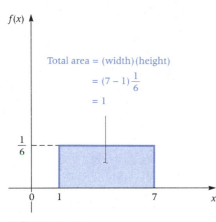

FIGURE 7-11

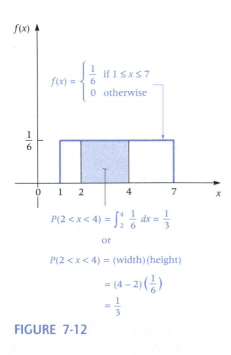

FIGURE 7-12

area between its graph and the *x*-axis measures *probability*. Thus, if a chance experiment consists of selecting a number from the interval $1 \leq x \leq 7$ in Figure 7-9, the probability that the selected number lies between 2 and 4, or, in other words,

$$P(2 < x < 4)$$

is represented by the shaded area in Figure 7-10. Since the random variable, *x*, represents all values within the interval $1 \leq x \leq 7$, then $P(1 \leq x \leq 7) = 1$. Therefore, the total area between the graph of the probability distribution and the *x*-axis over the interval $1 \leq x \leq 7$ equals 1, and the height of the graph is 1/6 (see Figure 7-11) since the enclosed area is a rectangle. Hence,

$$P(2 < x < 4) = (\text{width})(\text{height})$$
$$= (4 - 2)\left(\frac{1}{6}\right)$$
$$= \frac{1}{3}$$

Note that with a continuous random variable, we determine the probability that the random variable has a value within a specified interval. Such a probability is given by the area between the graph of the probability distribution and the *x*-axis *over the specified interval*. We do not attempt to determine the probability that a random variable takes on an individual value since the area above an individual value is zero. Thus, if a continuous random variable, *x*, is defined over some interval that includes the real numbers *a* and *b*, where $a < b$, then $P(x = a) = 0$, $P(x = b) = 0$, and $P(a < x < b) = P(a \leq x \leq b)$. As an example, for the uniformly distributed random variable in Figure 7-10, $P(2 < x < 4) = P(2 \leq x \leq 4) = 1/3$.

A continuous probability distribution is usually described by a function, called its **probability density function.** The probability density function for the preceding uniform distribution is given by

$$f(x) = \begin{cases} \dfrac{1}{6} & \text{if } 1 \leq x \leq 7 \\ 0 & \text{otherwise} \end{cases}$$

Thus, since the probability is represented by the area under the graph (see Figure 7-12), the probability $P(2 < x < 4)$ can also be determined by the definite integral

$$\int_2^4 f(x)\,dx = \int_2^4 \frac{1}{6}\,dx$$
$$= \frac{1}{6}x \Big|_2^4$$
$$= \frac{1}{6}(4) - \frac{1}{6}(2)$$
$$= \frac{1}{3}$$

We summarize as follows.

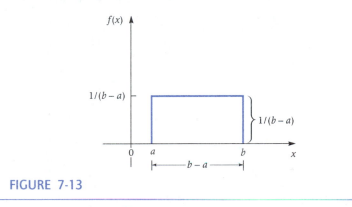

SUMMARY

Uniform Distribution

If a random variable, x, is **uniformly distributed** over the interval $a \leq x \leq b$, its probability density function is given by

$$f(x) = \begin{cases} \dfrac{1}{b - a} & \text{for } a \leq x \leq b \\ 0 & \text{otherwise} \end{cases}$$

The graph of $f(x)$ appears in Figure 7-13. Observe that the base of the rectangle has length $b - a$, while the height is $1/(b - a)$, so that the enclosed area is $(b - a)[1/(b - a)] = 1$.

FIGURE 7-13

• **EXAMPLE 7-8** **Waiting Time.**

The time (in minutes) a customer waits at a department store's counter is a uniformly distributed random variable, x, having possible values within the interval $0 \leq x \leq 5$. Find the probability that an arriving customer will wait at most 4 minutes.

Solution

We seek $P(0 \leq x \leq 4)$. This probability is represented by the shaded area in Figure 7-14. Since the shaded area is rectangular, the probability may be determined by the product $4(1/5)$. Hence,

$$P(0 \leq x \leq 4) = 4\left(\frac{1}{5}\right)$$

$$= .8$$

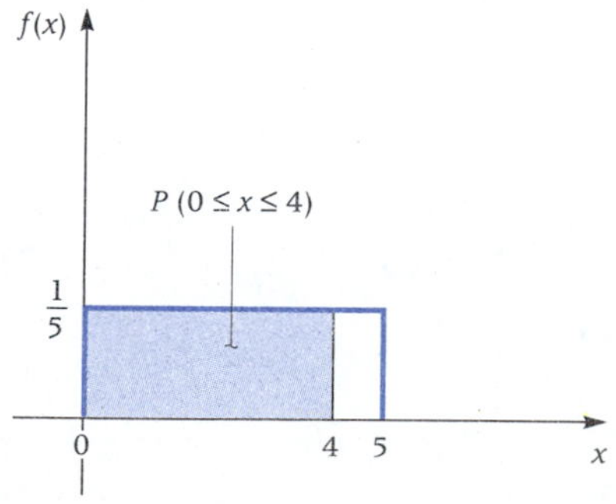

Using the definite integral to find the shaded area yields the same result. Therefore,

$$P(0 \leq x \leq 4) = \int_0^4 \frac{1}{5}\, dx = \frac{1}{5}x \Big|_0^4$$

$$= \frac{1}{5}(4) - \frac{1}{5}(0)$$

$$= .8 \qquad \text{Probability of a customer waiting at most 4 minutes}$$

$f(x)$

$P(0 \leq x \leq 4)$

$\dfrac{1}{5}$

$0 \qquad 4 \quad 5 \qquad x$

FIGURE 7-14

We now summarize the concept of probability density functions.

SUMMARY

Probability Density Function

Let x be a continuous random variable. A function $f(x)$ is a probability density function over some interval $a \leq x \leq b$ if

1. $f(x) \geq 0$ for $a \leq x \leq b$.
2. The area under the graph of the density function over the interval $[a, b]$ equals 1. In other words,

$$\int_a^b f(x)\, dx = 1$$

as illustrated in Figure 7-15.

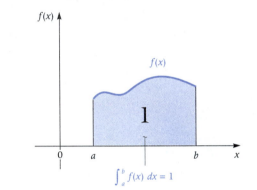

FIGURE 7-15

3. If $[c, d]$ is a subinterval of $[a, b]$, then

$$P(c \leq x \leq d) = \int_c^d f(x)\, dx$$

as illustrated in Figure 7-16.

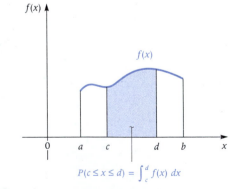

FIGURE 7-16

Note: The above holds if the interval $[a, b]$ is replaced with $(-\infty, b]$, $[a, \infty)$, or $(-\infty, \infty)$.

• **EXAMPLE 7-9**   **Product Lifetime.** _____

The length of life (in years) of a certain brand of battery is a continuous random variable with density function

$$f(x) = \frac{10}{3x^2} \quad (2 \le x \le 5)$$

a) Verify that the area under the graph of $f(x)$ over the interval [2, 5] equals 1.

b) Find the probability that a battery of this brand will last between 3 and 4 years.

c) Find the probability that a battery of this brand will last at most 4 years.

d) Find the probability that a battery of this brand will last at least 4 years.

Solutions

a)
$$\int_2^5 \frac{10}{3x^2}\, dx = \int_2^5 \frac{10}{3}x^{-2}\, dx$$

$$= \frac{10}{3}\frac{x^{-1}}{-1}\Big|_2^5$$

$$= -\frac{10}{3x}\Big|_2^5$$

$$= -\frac{10}{3(5)} - \left[-\frac{10}{3(2)}\right]$$

$$= -\frac{10}{15} + \frac{10}{6}$$

$$= -\frac{20}{30} + \frac{50}{30} = 1$$

b) The probability that a battery of this brand will last anywhere from 3 to 4 years is

$$P(3 \le x \le 4) = \int_3^4 \frac{10}{3x^2}\, dx$$

$$= -\frac{10}{3x}\Big|_3^4$$

$$= -\frac{10}{3(4)} - \left[-\frac{10}{3(3)}\right]$$

$$= \frac{5}{18} \approx .28$$

This is illustrated in Figure 7-17.

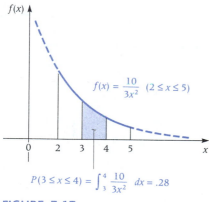

$f(x)$

$$f(x) = \frac{10}{3x^2} \quad (2 \le x \le 5)$$

0   2   3   4   5 x

$$P(3 \le x \le 4) = \int_3^4 \frac{10}{3x^2}\, dx = .28$$

FIGURE 7-17

c) The probability that a battery of this brand will last at most 4 years is

$$P(2 \le x \le 4) = \int_2^4 \frac{10}{3x^2}\, dx$$

$$= -\frac{10}{3x}\Big|_2^4$$

$$= -\frac{10}{3(4)} - \left[-\frac{10}{3(2)}\right]$$

$$= -\frac{10}{12} + \frac{10}{6}$$

$$= \frac{5}{6} \approx .83$$

This is illustrated in Figure 7-18.

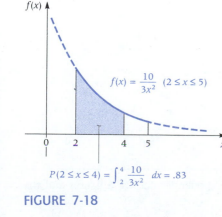

$f(x)$

$$f(x) = \frac{10}{3x^2} \quad (2 \le x \le 5)$$

0   2   4   5 x

$$P(2 \le x \le 4) = \int_2^4 \frac{10}{3x^2}\, dx = .83$$

FIGURE 7-18

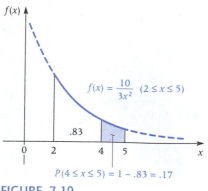

$f(x) = \dfrac{10}{3x^2}$ $(2 \le x \le 5)$

.83

$P(4 \le x \le 5) = 1 - .83 = .17$

FIGURE 7-19

d) The probability that a battery of this brand will last at least 4 years is $P(4 \le x \le 5)$, which is illustrated in Figure 7-19. Since this area is the complement of the area corresponding to $P(2 \le x \le 4)$, which was determined in part c, we easily determine

$$P(4 \le x \le 5) = 1 - P(2 \le x \le 4)$$

$$= 1 - \frac{5}{6}$$

$$= \frac{1}{6} \approx .17$$

We note that this same result could have been determined by the definite integral

$$\int_4^5 \frac{10}{3x^2}\, dx = \frac{1}{6} \approx .17$$

We now discuss another probability distribution called the exponential distribution.

SUMMARY

Exponential Distribution

If a random variable, x, is distributed in accordance with the density function

$$f(x) = \begin{cases} ke^{-kx} & \text{if } x \ge 0 \\ 0 & \text{otherwise} \end{cases}$$

where the constant $k > 0$, then x is said to be **exponentially distributed.** A graph of the exponential density function appears in Figure 7-20.

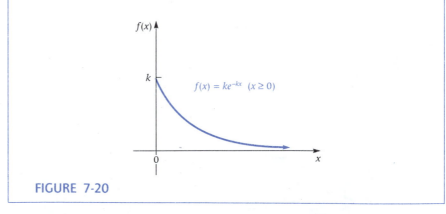

$f(x) = ke^{-kx}$ $(x \ge 0)$

FIGURE 7-20

• EXAMPLE 7-10 _____

Show that the total area between the exponential density function and the x-axis is 1.

Solution

We must show that the improper integral

$$\int_0^\infty ke^{-kx}\, dx$$

with constant $k > 0$, converges to 1. Hence, we let $b > 0$ denote a real number and compute the definite integral

$$\int_0^b ke^{-kx}\, dx = -e^{-kx}\Big|_0^b$$

$$= -e^{-kb} - (-e^{-k(0)})$$

$$= -e^{-kb} - (-1)$$

$$= -e^{-kb} + 1$$

Since $-e^{-kb} \to 0$ as $b \to \infty$, then

$$\int_0^b ke^{-kx}\, dx \to 0 + 1 = 1$$

and thus the total area equals 1.

• **EXAMPLE 7-11**   **Interarrival Time.** _____

The interarrival time, x (i.e., the time between two successive arrivals), of customers at a particular bank is exponentially distributed, with $k = 10$. Find the probability that the interarrival time is between 0.1 and 0.5 minute.

Solution

We seek the shaded area in Figure 7-21. Thus, we have

$$P(0.1 < x < 0.5) = \int_{0.1}^{0.5} 10e^{-10x}\, dx$$

$$= -e^{-10x}\Big|_{0.1}^{0.5}$$

$$= -e^{-10(0.5)} - (-e^{-10(0.1)})$$

$$= -e^{-5} + e^{-1}$$

$$\approx -.006738 + .367879$$

$$\approx .3611 \quad \text{Probability that the interarrival time is between 0.1 and 0.5 minute}$$

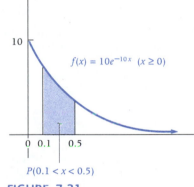

$f(x)$

10

$f(x) = 10e^{-10x}\ (x \geq 0)$

$0\ \ 0.1\ \ \ \ 0.5$ x

$P(0.1 < x < 0.5)$

FIGURE 7-21

Exercises 7-3

1. *Waiting time.* A customer's waiting time, x (in minutes), is a random variable that is uniformly distributed over the interval $0 \leq x \leq 20$. If a customer arrives at this restaurant, find the probability that he or she must wait
   a) At least 12 minutes.
   b) Less than 5 minutes.
   c) Between 5 and 10 minutes.

2. *Product life.* The length of life (in years) of a certain brand of battery is a random variable, x, distributed in accordance with the probability density function

$$f(x) = \begin{cases} -6x^2 + 6x & \text{if } 0 \leq x \leq 1 \\ 0 & \text{otherwise} \end{cases}$$

a) Sketch $f(x)$ and verify that $\int_0^1 f(x)\,dx = 1$.
b) Find the probability that a battery lasts longer than 3/4 year.
c) Find $P(0 \le x \le 0.2)$.
d) If the batteries are unconditionally guaranteed for 2 months, what percentage will be returned?

3. A random variable, x, is uniformly distributed over the interval $2 \le x \le 7$.
   a) Determine its probability density function, $f(x)$.
   b) Find $P(2 \le x \le 3)$.
   c) Find $P(4 \le x \le 6)$.

4. A random variable, x, is distributed in accordance with a probability density function of the form $f(x) = kx$ (where k is a constant) over the interval $0 \le x \le 4$.
   a) Determine k.
   b) Sketch $f(x)$.
   c) Calculate $P(0 \le x \le 2)$.
   d) Calculate $P(3 \le x \le 4)$.
   e) Calculate $P(1 \le x \le 2)$.

5. *Interarrival time.* The interarrival times (in minutes) of incoming calls at a certain switchboard are exponentially distributed, with $k = 5$. Find the probability that the time between two successive arrivals is
   a) Less than 0.1 minute.
   b) Between 0.2 and 0.6 minute.
   c) Longer than 0.4 minute.

6. *Interarrival time.* At a certain self-service gas station, the interarrival times (in minutes) are exponentially distributed, with $k = 0.5$. Find the probability that the interarrival time is
   a) Less than 0.6 minute.
   b) Between 0.2 and 0.8 minute.
   c) Longer than 1 minute.

7. A random variable, x, is exponentially distributed, with $k = 2$. Find each of the following.
   a) $P(0.5 \le x \le 1)$
   b) $P(0 \le x \le 1.5)$
   c) $P(x \ge 3)$

8. *Reliability.* Let the random variable, x, represent the length of life of some mechanical component with probability density function $f(x)$. If t is a given length of time, then

$$P(x > t) = \int_t^\infty f(x)\,dx$$

Since this integral represents the probability that the component's lifetime exceeds t units of time (see Figure 7-22), it is called the **reliability function** and is denoted by $R(t)$. Hence,

$$R(t) = P(x > t) = \int_t^\infty f(x)\,dx$$

a) Find $R(t)$ for an exponential density function, with $k = 0.8$.
b) Find $R(1)$ and interpret.
c) Find $R(5)$ and interpret.

9. *Reliability.* The length of life (in years) of circuitry in a certain brand of calculator is exponentially distributed, with $k = 0.5$.
   a) Find the reliability function, $R(t)$.
   b) Find $R(1)$ and interpret.
   c) Find $R(4)$ and interpret.

$f(x)$

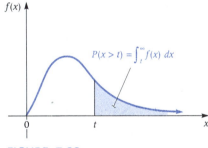

$P(x > t) = \int_t^\infty f(x)\,dx$

0   t x

FIGURE 7-22

7-4

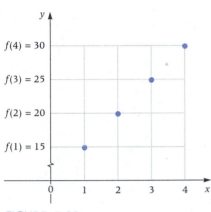

FIGURE 7-23

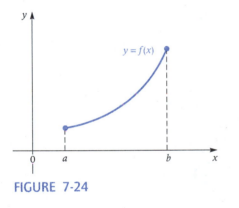

FIGURE 7-24

• APPLICATIONS: AVERAGE VALUE AND VOLUME

Average Value of a Function

Consider a firm that produces either 1, 2, 3, or 4 units of some commodity. If the variable cost per unit is \$5 and the fixed cost is \$10, then the cost function is defined by

$$f(x) = 5x + 10$$

with domain consisting of the x-values given in Table 7-6. A graph of the cost function, $f(x)$, appears in Figure 7-23. The **average value,** Av, of the function is determined by summing the y-coordinates of $f(x)$ and dividing this result by the number of points. Hence,

$$Av = \frac{f(1) + f(2) + f(3) + f(4)}{4}$$

$$= \frac{15 + 20 + 25 + 30}{4}$$

$$= 22.5$$

Thus, the average cost is \$22.50.

In general, given a function $f(x)$ with domain consisting of the x-values $x_1, x_2, \ldots, x_n$, the average value, Av, of $f(x)$ is given by

$$Av = \frac{f(x_1) + f(x_2) + \ldots + f(x_n)}{n}$$

If $f(x)$ is a continuous function defined over the interval $a \leq x \leq b$ (see Figure 7-24), its average value cannot be computed by the above formula since the domain $a \leq x \leq b$ contains infinitely many values. The average value of such a continuous function is determined by the formula

$$\frac{1}{b - a} \int_a^b f(x) \, dx$$

An explanation of this formula for determining the average value of a continuous function, $f(x)$, defined over the interval $a \leq x \leq b$ is presented in the succeeding paragraph.

Divide the interval $a \leq x \leq b$ into n subintervals, each of length $(b - a)/n$, and choose n x-values, $x_1, x_2, \ldots, x_n$, such that x_1 is in the first subinterval, x_2 is in the second subinterval, . . . , and x_n is in the nth sub-

TABLE 7-6

x	y	$y = f(x) = 5x + 10$
1	15	$f(1) = 5(1) + 10 = 15$
2	20	$f(2) = 5(2) + 10 = 20$
3	25	$f(3) = 5(3) + 10 = 25$
4	30	$f(4) = 5(4) + 10 = 30$

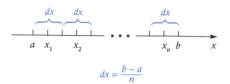

$$dx = \frac{b - a}{n}$$

FIGURE 7-25

interval, as illustrated in Figure 7-25. The average value of $f(x)$ over these n particular x-values is

$$\frac{f(x_1) + f(x_2) + \ldots + f(x_n)}{n}$$

This can be rewritten as

$$\left[f(x_1) \cdot \frac{1}{n} \right] + \left[f(x_2) \cdot \frac{1}{n} \right] + \ldots + \left[f(x_n) \cdot \frac{1}{n} \right]$$

Multiplying the above by $(b - a)/(b - a)$ gives

$$\frac{1}{b - a} \left[f(x_1) \cdot \frac{b - a}{n} + f(x_2) \cdot \frac{b - a}{n} + \ldots + f(x_n) \cdot \frac{b - a}{n} \right]$$

If we let $dx = (b - a)/n$, this becomes

$$\frac{1}{b - a} \left[f(x_1) \, dx + f(x_2) \, dx + \ldots + f(x_n) \, dx \right]$$

As the number of x-values becomes arbitrarily large, or, in other words, as $n \rightarrow \infty$, then

$$f(x_1) \, dx + f(x_2) \, dx + \ldots + f(x_n) \, dx$$

becomes the definite integral

$$\int_a^b f(x) \, dx$$

and the average value of $f(x)$ over the interval $a \leq x \leq b$ becomes

$$\frac{1}{b - a} \int_a^b f(x) \, dx$$

We summarize the following.

Average Value of a Function

The average value of a continuous function, $f(x)$, over the interval $[a, b]$ is given by

$$\frac{1}{b - a} \int_a^b f(x) \, dx$$

• **EXAMPLE 7-12**

Find the average value of $f(x) = 3x^2$ over the interval $1 \leq x \leq 3$.

Solution

A graph of $f(x)$ appears in Figure 7-26. Since

$$\text{average value} = \frac{1}{b - a} \int_a^b f(x) \, dx$$

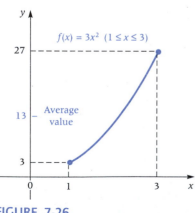

FIGURE 7-26

then for the function in Figure 7-26, $a = 1$, $b = 3$, and $f(x) = 3x^2$. Hence,

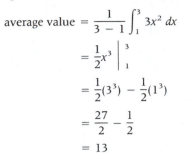

$$\text{average value} = \frac{1}{3 - 1} \int_1^3 3x^2 \, dx$$

$$= \frac{1}{2}x^3 \bigg|_1^3$$

$$= \frac{1}{2}(3^3) - \frac{1}{2}(1^3)$$

$$= \frac{27}{2} - \frac{1}{2}$$

$$= 13$$

• **EXAMPLE 7-13**

The function $R(x) = -3x^2 + 18x$ represents the sales revenue (in millions of dollars) received from selling x (in thousands) units of some item. If $0 \le x \le 3$, then find the average sales revenue.

Solution

A graph of $R(x)$ appears in Figure 7-27. The average sales revenue is the average value of $R(x)$ over the interval $0 \le x \le 3$. Thus,

$$\text{average sales revenue} = \frac{1}{3 - 0} \int_0^3 R(x) \, dx$$

$$= \frac{1}{3} \int_0^3 (-3x^2 + 18x) \, dx$$

$$= \frac{1}{3}(-x^3 + 9x^2) \bigg|_0^3$$

$$= \frac{1}{3}\left[-(3^3) + 9(3^2)\right] - \frac{1}{3}(0)$$

$$= 18 - 0 = 18$$

Thus, the average sales revenue is $18 million when sales are between 0 and 3 thousand units.

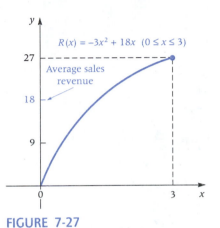

$R(x) = -3x^2 + 18x \quad (0 \le x \le 3)$

Average sales revenue

FIGURE 7-27

Geometric Interpretation

Consider the function $f(x)$ in Figure 7-28 and the shaded area from $x = a$ to $x = b$. Suppose we want to determine the height, H, of the rectangle in Figure 7-29 having the same area as that shaded under $f(x)$ in Figure 7-28. Since

$$\text{area of rectangle} = \text{area under curve}$$

then

$$H(b - a) = \int_a^b f(x) \, dx$$

Solving for H, we have

$$H = \frac{1}{b - a} \int_a^b f(x) \, dx$$

Note that H equals the *average value of the function* $f(x)$ over the interval $a \le x \le b$.

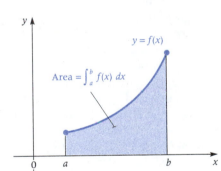

$y = f(x)$

$\text{Area} = \int_a^b f(x) \, dx$

FIGURE 7-28

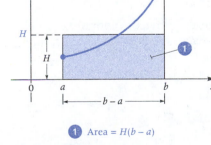

$y = f(x)$

❶ Area = $H(b - a)$

FIGURE 7-29

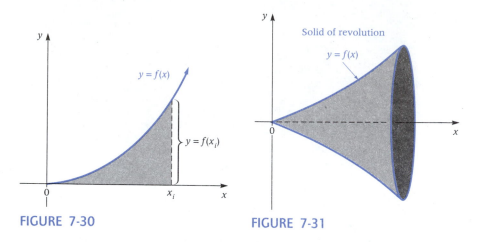

FIGURE 7-30   **FIGURE 7-31**

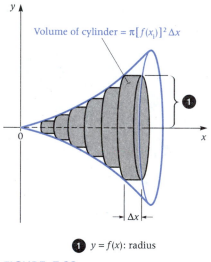

 $y = f(x)$: radius

FIGURE 7-32

Volume of a Solid of Revolution

Consider a function defined by

$$y = f(x)$$

with a graph as illustrated in Figure 7-30. If we rotate the graph of $y = f(x)$ and the shaded area of Figure 7-30 about rhe x-axis, the result is the three-dimensional solid of Figure 7-31. A solid formed by such a rotation of the graph of $y = f(x)$ is called a **solid of revolution.**

We now discuss the determination of the *volume* of a solid of revolution. The volume of a solid of revolution is approximated by the sum of volumes of cylinders, each of height Δx, as illustrated in Figure 7-32. We note that height is measured along the x-axis since the cylinder is on its side.

The volume of each of the approximating cylinders is given by

$$\text{volume} = \pi\,(\text{radius})^2(\text{height})$$
$$= \pi\,[f(x_i)]^2\,\Delta x$$

Volume of a cylinder

Thus, the volume, V, of the solid of revolution is approximated by the sum of all such cylinders as given below.

$$V = \pi[f(x_1)]^2\,\Delta x + \pi[f(x_2)]^2\,\Delta x + \ldots + \pi[(f(x_n)]^2\,\Delta x$$

As the number of approximating cylinders approaches infinity, the height (or thickness) of each such cylinder approaches 0, and the actual volume is given by the definite integral

$$\int_a^b \pi[f(x)]^2\,dx$$

We summarize as follows.

Volume of a Solid of Revolution

The volume, V, of a solid of revolution formed by rotating about the x-axis the region between the graph of $y = f(x)$ and the x-axis from $x = a$ to $x = b$ (see Figure 7-33) is given by

$$V = \int_a^b \pi [f(x)]^2 \, dx$$

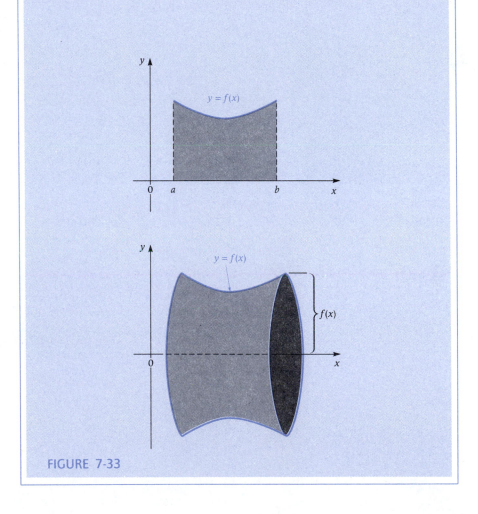

FIGURE 7-33

• EXAMPLE 7-14

Find the volume of the solid of revolution formed by rotating about the x-axis the region between the graph of $y = \sqrt{x}$ and the x-axis from $x = 0$ to $x = 2$.

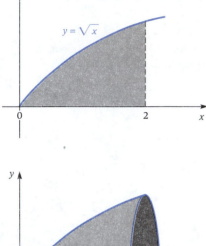

FIGURE 7-34

Solution

We first graph the function $y = \sqrt{x}$, shade the region, and draw the solid of revolution in Figure 7-34. The volume, V, is given by

$$V = \int_0^2 \pi [f(x)]^2 \, dx$$

$$= \int_0^2 \pi (\sqrt{x})^2 \, dx$$

$$= \int_0^2 \pi x \, dx$$

$$= \frac{\pi x^2}{2} \Big|_0^2$$

$$= \frac{\pi (2)^2}{2} - \frac{\pi (0)^2}{2}$$

$$= 2\pi \approx 6.28 \qquad \text{Volume}$$

• **EXAMPLE 7-15**

Find the volume of the solid of revolution formed by rotating about the x-axis the region between the graph of $y = x^2$ and the x-axis from $x = 1$ to $x = 4$.

Solution

We first graph $y = x^2$, shade the region, and draw the solid of revolution in Figure 7-35.

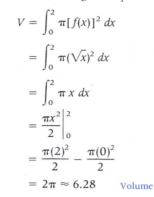

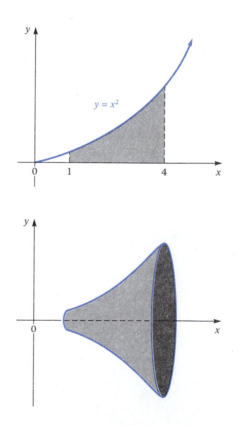

FIGURE 7-35

The volume, V, is given by

$$V = \int_1^4 \pi [f(x)]^2 \, dx$$

$$= \int_1^4 \pi (x^2)^2 \, dx$$

$$= \int_1^4 \pi x^4 \, dx$$

$$= \left. \frac{\pi x^5}{5} \right|_1^4$$

$$= \frac{\pi (4)^5}{5} - \frac{\pi (1)^5}{5}$$

$$= \frac{1023\pi}{5} \approx 642.44 \qquad \text{Volume}$$

Exercises 7-4

Average Value

Find the average value of each function over the indicated interval.

1. $f(x) = -3x + 15$, $0 \le x \le 5$
2. $f(x) = x^2$, $1 \le x \le 4$
3. $f(x) = \sqrt{x}$, $1 \le x \le 4$
4. $f(x) = 1/x$, $1 \le x \le 3$
5. $f(x) = -3x^2 + 6$, $0 \le x \le 1$
6. $f(x) = e^x$, $0 \le x \le 1$
7. Find the average value of the function $f(x) = -2x + 10$ over the interval $0 \le x \le 5$. Graph $f(x)$ and illustrate the geometric interpretation of its average value.
8. Find the average value of the function $f(x) = -3x^2 + 27$ over the interval $0 \le x \le 3$. Graph $f(x)$ and illustrate the geometric interpretation of its average value.

Applications

9. *Revenue.* The sales revenue gained from selling x units of some commodity is given by

$$R(x) = -5x^2 + 40$$

If $0 \le x \le 2$, then find the average sales revenue. Graph $R(x)$ and illustrate the geometric interpretation of its average value.

10. *Population.* The population of a certain town is related to time, t (in years), by the exponential function defined by

$$P(t) = 1000e^{0.05t}$$

Note that $t = 0$ corresponds to the year 19X0, $t = 1$ corresponds to the year 19X1, etc. Find the average population over the interval $0 \le t \le 10$.

11. *Temperature.* The temperature, y, of a heated cup of coffee is related to the time, t (in minutes), elapsed by the exponential function defined by

$$y = 150e^{-0.02t} \qquad (t \ge 0)$$

Find the average temperature during the first 5 minutes (i.e., $0 \le t \le 5$).

12. *Radioactive decay.* A certain radioactive substance decays in accordance with the function defined by

$$y(t) = 2000e^{-0.06t} \qquad (t \ge 0)$$

where $y(t)$ is the mass (in grams) at time t (in hours). Find the average mass of the radioactive substance during the first 3 hours.

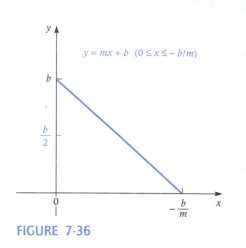

FIGURE 7-36

13. *Compound amount.* A sum of $10,000 is deposited in a bank that pays interest at the rate of 8% compounded continuously. Find the average value of this bank account over the next 5 years.

14. *Average inventory.* An oil company stores its home heating oil in large tanks, each with a capacity of 100,000 gallons. After a tank has been filled, its level of inventory (oil) is related to the time (in days) elapsed since filling by the function defined by

$$I(t) = -5t + 100 \qquad (t \geq 0)$$

where $I(t)$ is the amount of oil (in thousands of gallons) in the tank t days after filling.
   a) Graph $I(t)$.
   b) Find the number of days before the tank is empty.
   c) Find the average level of inventory during the time interval determined by part b.

15. Show that the average value of the linear function $y = mx + b$ in Figure 7-36 over the interval $0 \leq x \leq -b/m$ is $b/2$.

Volume

For each of the following, find the volume of the solid of revolution formed by rotating about the x-axis the region between the graph of the given function and the x-axis over the indicated interval. Illustrate graphically.

16. $y = 2x$ from $x = 0$ to $x = 1$
17. $y = -4x + 8$ from $x = 0$ to $x = 2$
18. $y = 3x^2$ from $x = 1$ to $x = 2$
19. $y = -6x^2 + 6$ from $x = 0$ to $x = 1$
20. $y = e^x$ from $x = 1$ to $x = 3$
21. $y = e^{-x}$ from $x = 0$ to $x = 1$
22. $y = 1/x$ from $x = 1$ to $x = 2$
23. $y = \sqrt{x}$ from $x = 1$ to $x = 4$
24. *Sphere.* $y = \sqrt{1 - x^2}$ from $x = -1$ to $x = 1$
25. *Sphere.* $y = \sqrt{4 - x^2}$ from $x = -2$ to $x = 2$
26. *Sphere.* $y = \sqrt{9 - x^2}$ from $x = -3$ to $x = 3$
27. *Sphere.* $y = \sqrt{16 - x^2}$ from $x = -4$ to $x = 4$

7-5   • THE TRAPEZOIDAL RULE

Sometimes we must evaluate a definite integral $\int_a^b f(x)\, dx$ where $f(x)$ cannot be antidifferentiated (or can be antidifferentiated only with much difficulty) by any of the elementary integration techniques. In such a situation, the definite integral may sometimes be *numerically approximated*. Two such approximation techniques use the so-called **trapezoidal rule** and **Simpson's rule.** In this section, we will discuss the trapezoidal rule. Simpson's rule will be discussed in the next section.

When discussing both approximation techniques, it is helpful to think in terms of area under a curve. Since the trapezoidal rule uses areas of trapezoids to approximate the area between the x-axis and a continuous

Trapezoids

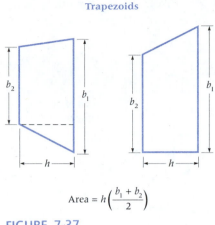

$$\text{Area} = h\left(\frac{b_1 + b_2}{2}\right)$$

FIGURE 7-37

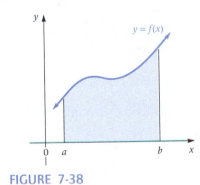

FIGURE 7-38

curve over a defined interval, we will first discuss trapezoids and the formula for the area of a trapezoid.

A trapezoid is a four-sided figure—two sides of which are parallel. Figure 7-37 illustrates two trapezoids. The parallel sides of a trapezoid are called **bases,** and their lengths are denoted by b_1 and b_2. The perpendicular distance between the two parallel sides is called the height of the trapezoid and is denoted by h. The area of a trapezoid is the product of its height and the average length of its two bases. Thus, for a trapezoid

$$\text{area} = h\left(\frac{b_1 + b_2}{2}\right)$$

as indicated in Figure 7-37.

We now develop the trapezoidal rule for approximating the definite integral $\int_a^b f(x)\,dx$, where $f(x)$ is a continuous function over the interval $a \leq x \leq b$ (see Figure 7-38). For convenience, we assume that the continuous function $f(x)$ is non-negative over the interval $a \leq x \leq b$. The area between the x-axis and the curve (see Figure 7-38) from $x = a$ to $x = b$ is given by the definite integral

$$\int_a^b f(x)\,dx$$

The area given by this definite integral is approximated by dividing the interval $a \leq x \leq b$ into n subintervals, each of length $(b - a)/n$, as illustrated in Figure 7-39. Observe that above each subinterval, there exists a trapezoid whose area approximates the area between the curve and the x-axis over that subinterval. Let's look at the trapezoid over the subinterval $x_{i-1} \leq x \leq x_i$. Its bases have lengths $f(x_{i-1})$ and $f(x_i)$; its height h has length $(b - a)/n$. Thus, its area is given by the product of its height, h, and the average of its two bases, or

$$\text{area} = h\left[\frac{f(x_{i-1}) + f(x_i)}{2}\right]$$
$$= \frac{b - a}{n}\left[\frac{f(x_{i-1}) + f(x_i)}{2}\right]$$

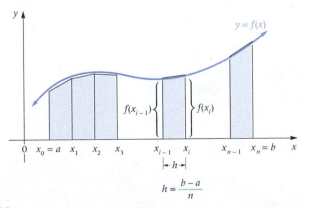

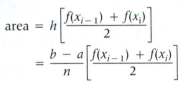

FIGURE 7-39

If we sum the areas of the n trapezoids of Figure 7-39, we obtain

$$
\overbrace{\frac{b-a}{n}\left[\frac{f(x_0)+f(x_1)}{2}\right]}^{\substack{\text{area of first}\\\text{trapezoid}}}+\overbrace{\frac{b-a}{n}\left[\frac{f(x_1)+f(x_2)}{2}\right]}^{\substack{\text{area of second}\\\text{trapezoid}}}+\ldots
$$

$$
+\overbrace{\frac{b-a}{n}\left[\frac{f(x_{i-1})+f(x_i)}{2}\right]}^{\substack{\text{area of }i\text{th}\\\text{trapezoid}}}+\ldots+\overbrace{\frac{b-a}{n}\left[\frac{f(x_{n-1})+f(x_n)}{2}\right]}^{\substack{\text{area of }n\text{th}\\\text{trapezoid}}}
$$

Factoring out $(b-a)/2n$, we obtain

$$
\frac{b-a}{2n}\left[f(x)_0+\underbrace{f(x_1)+f(x_1)}_{2f(x_1)}+\underbrace{f(x_2)+}_{2f(x_2)}\ldots+\underbrace{f(x_i)+}_{2f(x_i)}\ldots+\underbrace{f(x_{n-1})}_{2f(x_{n-1})}+f(x_n)\right]
$$

Studying this expression, note that with exception of $f(x_0)$ and $f(x_n)$, for each x_i, there are two $f(x_i)$s. Thus, the expression may be written as

$$
\frac{b-a}{2n}\left[f(x_0)+2f(x_1)+2f(x_2)+\ldots+2f(x_{n-1})+f(x_n)\right]
$$

This expression approximates $\int_a^b f(x)\,dx$, which gives the area between the curve and the x-axis over the interval $a \le x \le b$. We summarize as follows.

Trapezoidal Rule

If $f(x)$ is a continuous function over the interval $a \le x \le b$, then

$$
\int_a^b f(x)\,dx \approx \frac{b-a}{2n}\left[f(x_0)+2f(x_1)+2f(x_2)+\ldots+2f(x_{n-1})+f(x_n)\right]
$$

• **EXAMPLE 7-16** _____

Use the trapezoidal rule with $n=6$ to approximate $\int_0^3 e^{-x^2}\,dx$.

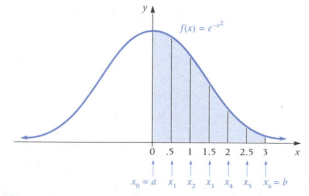

FIGURE 7-40

TABLE 7-7

x	$f(x) = e^{-x^2}$	Coefficient	Product
$x_0 = 0.0$	1.000000	1	1.000000
$x_1 = 0.5$	0.778801	2	1.557602
$x_2 = 1.0$	0.367880	2	0.735760
$x_3 = 1.5$	0.105399	2	0.210798
$x_4 = 2.0$	0.018316	2	0.036632
$x_5 = 2.5$	0.001930	2	0.003860
$x_6 = 3.0$	0.000123	1	0.000123
			Sum = 3.544775

Solution

The graphical representation appears in Figure 7-40. Our computations appear in Table 7-7. Observe that each value of $f(x_i)$ is multiplied by the appropriate coefficient to yield the associated value in the product column. The sum of the values in the product column is then multiplied by $(b - a)/2n$. Thus, according to the trapezoidal rule,

$$\int_a^b f(x)\, dx \approx \frac{b-a}{2n}\Big[f(x_0) + 2f(x_1) + 2f(x_2) + \ldots + 2f(x_{n-1}) + f(x_n) \Big]$$

For this example, $a = 0$, $b = 3$, $n = 6$, and $f(x) = e^{-x^2}$. Thus, the trapezoidal rule becomes

$$\int_0^3 e^{-x^2}\, dx \approx \frac{3-0}{(2)(6)}\Big[e^{-(0.0)^2} + 2e^{-(0.5)^2} + 2e^{-(1.0)^2} + 2e^{-(1.5)^2} + 2e^{-(2.0)^2} + 2e^{-(2.5)^2} + e^{-(3)^2} \Big]$$

$$\approx \frac{1}{4}[3.544775] \approx 0.886194$$

from Table 7-7

Applications

FIGURE 7-41

Standard Normal Curve

If a random variable, x, is distributed in accordance with the density function

$$f(x) = \frac{1}{\sqrt{2\pi}} e^{-x^2/2} \qquad \text{over } (-\infty, \infty)$$

then x is said to have a **standard normal distribution.** The graph of the density function, which is given in Figure 7-41, is called the **standard normal curve.**

We now give trapezoidal approximations to the definite integral

$$\int_0^3 \frac{1}{\sqrt{2\pi}} e^{-x^2/2}\, dx$$

TABLE 7-8

n	Trapezoidal rule approximation
10	0.4985514
20	0.4986252
50	0.4986463
100	0.4986492
200	0.4986502

for various values of n. These results, which are given in Table 7-8, approximate the shaded area of Figure 7-41. We used a computer to obtain these trapezoidal approximations. Of course, the shaded area gives $P(0 \le x \le 3)$.

Error Estimates

Since the trapezoidal rule gives an approximation of the value of a definite integral, it is necessary to be concerned about how close the approximation is to the exact value of the definite integral. From the explanation presented in this section, it is clear that as the number of subintervals, n, increases, the corresponding trapezoidal approximation gets closer to the exact value of the definite integral. The difference between the exact value of a definite integral and an approximation is called **error** and is defined below.

> **Error**
>
> The error, E, in approximating a definite integral is defined to be
> $$E = |\text{exact value} - \text{approximation}|$$

More advanced texts prove the following result:

> **Error in Trapezoidal Rule**
>
> The error in approximating $\int_a^b f(x)\, dx$ by the trapezoidal rule is at most
> $$\frac{K(b - a)^3}{12n^2}$$
> where K is the maximum value of $|f''(x)|$ over the interval $[a, b]$.
> *Note:* The error decreases as n, the number of subintervals, increases.

• **EXAMPLE 7-17** _____

Determine the maximum error in approximating $\int_0^3 e^{-x^2}\, dx$ with $n = 6$.

Solution

The error is at most $K(b - a)^3/12n^2$, where K is the maximum value of $|f''(x)|$ over the interval $0 \le x \le 3$. We begin to determine K by computing $f''(x)$. Hence,

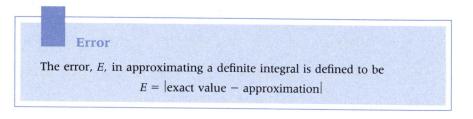

$$f(x) = e^{-x^2}$$
$$f'(x) = e^{-x^2}(-2x) = -2xe^{-x^2}$$
$$f''(x) = -2x(e^{-x^2})(-2x) + e^{-x^2}(-2)$$
$$= 2e^{-x^2}(2x^2 - 1)$$

Using the optimization methods of Chapter 3, it can be determined that the maximum value of $|f''(x)|$ over the interval $[0, 3]$ is $|f''(0)| = 2$. Therefore, the error in approximating $\int_0^3 e^{-x^2} dx$ with $n = 6$ is at most

$$\frac{K(b-a)^3}{12n^2} = \frac{2(3-0)^3}{12(6^2)}$$

$$= 0.125000$$

This means that

$$\text{approximation} - \text{error} \leq \int_0^3 e^{-x^2} dx \leq \text{approximation} + \text{error}$$

$$0.886194 - 0.125000 \leq \int_0^3 e^{-x^2} dx \leq 0.886194 + 0.125000$$

or

$$0.761194 \leq \int_0^3 e^{-x^2} dx \leq 1.011194$$

Determining the Number of Subintervals

The formula for the approximation error of the trapezoidal rule is used to determine n, the number of subintervals needed to get an approximation to a desired degree of accuracy. This is illustrated in Example 7-18.

• **EXAMPLE 7-18**

Assume that the approximation error, 0.125, in Example 7-17 is too large for our purposes. Determine n so that the error is at most 0.01.

Solution

This means that we must determine n so that

$$\frac{K(b-a)^3}{12n^2} \leq 0.01$$

Substituting $K = 2$, $b = 3$, and $a = 0$ into the above inequality yields

$$\frac{9}{2n^2} \leq 0.01$$

Solving for n^2 gives

$$\frac{9}{2}\left(\frac{1}{0.01}\right) \leq n^2$$

$$450 \leq n^2$$

Since $n > 0$,

$$n \geq \sqrt{450} \approx 21.21$$

Thus, we choose $n = 22$ (since $n \geq 21.21$) in order that the error in approximating $\int_0^3 e^{-x^2} dx$ is at most 0.01.

Exercises 7-5

For Exercises 1–10

a) use the trapezoidal rule with the indicated value of n to approximate the value of the definite integral. Round your answers to six decimal places.

b) find the exact value of the definite integral, and compare this result with the answer to part a.

1. $\int_1^2 \frac{1}{x}\, dx,\ n = 4$

2. $\int_1^3 \frac{1}{x^2}\, dx,\ n = 4$

3. $\int_1^3 x^2\, dx,\ n = 4$

4. $\int_0^3 x^3\, dx,\ n = 6$

5. $\int_0^2 \frac{1}{x+1}\, dx,\ n = 8$

6. $\int_1^2 \frac{1}{x+4}\, dx,\ n = 4$

7. $\int_1^2 (3x^2 + 1)\, dx,\ n = 4$

8. $\int_0^4 \sqrt{x}\, dx,\ n = 8$

9. $\int_0^3 \sqrt{x}\, dx,\ n = 6$

10. $\int_0^2 (6x^2 + 4)\, dx,\ n = 8$

For Exercises 11–22, use the trapezoidal rule with the indicated value of n to approximate the value of the definite integral. Round your answers to six decimal places.

11. $\int_0^2 e^{-x^2}\, dx,\ n = 8$

12. $\int_1^2 e^{-x^2}\, dx,\ n = 4$

13. $\int_0^3 e^{-0.5x^2}\, dx,\ n = 6$

14. $\int_0^3 \sqrt{x^2 + 1}\, dx,\ n = 6$

15. $\int_0^1 \frac{1}{\sqrt{x^2 + 1}}\, dx,\ n = 6$

16. $\int_0^1 \frac{1}{x^2 + 1}\, dx,\ n = 6$

17. $\int_0^2 \sqrt{x^2 + 1}\, dx,\ n = 8$

18. $\int_0^2 \sqrt{x^3 + 1}\, dx,\ n = 4$

19. $\int_0^3 \frac{1}{\sqrt{x^3 + 1}}\, dx,\ n = 6$

20. $\int_4^6 x\sqrt{x - 4}\, dx,\ n = 4$

21. $\int_2^4 \ln x\, dx,\ n = 8$

22. $\int_3^5 \ln x\, dx,\ n = 8$

Error

23. Determine the error for Exercise 1.
24. Determine the error for Exercise 2.
25. Determine the error for Exercise 5.
26. Determine the error for Exercise 6.
27. Determine the error for Exercise 21.
28. Determine the error for Exercise 22.

Determining the Number of Subintervals

29. Determine n so that the error in approximating $\int_1^2 x^{-1}dx$ by the trapezoidal rule is at most 0.0001.
30. Determine n so that the error in approximating $\int_2^4 x^{-2}dx$ by the trapezoidal rule is at most 0.0001.
31. Determine n so that the error in approximating $\int_0^2 (x + 1)^{-1}dx$ by the trapezoidal rule is at most 0.0001.
32. Determine n so that the error in approximating $\int_2^4 \ln x\, dx$ by the trapezoidal rule is at most 0.0001.
33. Determine n so that the error in approximating $\int_1^3 \ln x\, dx$ by the trapezoidal rule is at most 0.0001.
34. Determine n so that the error in approximating $\int_0^1 \ln (x^2 + 1)\, dx$ by the trapezpidal rule is at most 0.0001.

Applications

35. *Semicircle.* Use the trapezoidal rule with $n = 8$ to approximate the area between the semicircle $y = \sqrt{1 - x^2}$ and the x-axis, as illustrated in Figure 7-42. Round your answer to six decimal places. Check the accuracy of your answer by using the fact that the area A of a circle of radius r is given by $A = \pi r^2$.

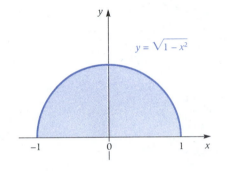

FIGURE 7-42

36. *Bridge suspension.* A bridge of length 100 feet is suspended by a parabolic cable whose equation is equal to $y = x^2/200$, as illustrated in Figure 7-43.

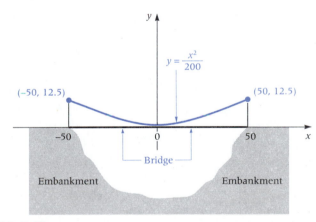

FIGURE 7-43

The length of the cable is given by the definite integral

$$\int_{-50}^{50} \sqrt{1 + (y')^2}\, dx = 2\int_{0}^{50} \sqrt{1 + (x/100)^2}\, dx$$

Use the trapezoidal rule with $n = 10$ to approximate the length of the parabolic cable.

37. *Travel distance.* A driver records speedometer readings every 5 minutes during an automobile trip that lasts 30 minutes. The results are given in the Table 7-9,

TABLE 7-9

Time (minutes)	Speed (mph)
0	0
5	45
10	50
15	42
20	55
25	58
30	48

with an accompanying graphic illustration in Figure 7-44. Observe in Figure 7-44 that time has been converted to *hours* to correspond with speed, which is given in miles per *hour*.

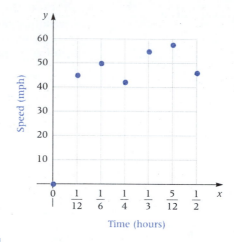

FIGURE 7-44

The total distance traveled is given by the definite integral

$$\int_0^{1/2} v(t)\, dt$$

Use the trapezoidal rule to approximate the total distance traveled.

38. *Rocket launch.* The velocity readings (in miles per hour) of a rocket during takeoff are recorded at 1-second intervals with the following results:

$$0, 10, 30, 60, 90, 120, 150, 180, 210, 240, 270$$

A graphical illustration appears in Figure 7-45. Observe in Figure 7-45 that time is given in *hours* to correspond with velocity, which is given in miles per *hour*.

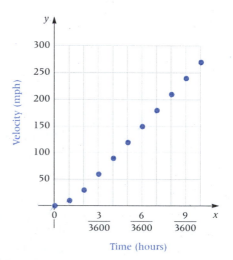

FIGURE 7-45

Use the trapezoidal rule to approximate the total distance traveled by the rocket during the first 10 seconds.

39. *Probability.* Use the trapezoidal rule with $n = 4$ to approximate the normal probability given by the definite integral

$$\int_0^2 \frac{1}{\sqrt{2\pi}} e^{-x/2} \, dx$$

Round your answer to six decimal places.

40. *Land measurement.* A developer wishes to determine the area of the parcel of land illustrated in Figure 7-46.
  a) Use the trapezoidal rule to approximate the area.
  b) If 43,560 square feet equals 1 acre, then how many acres are in the parcel in Figure 7-46?

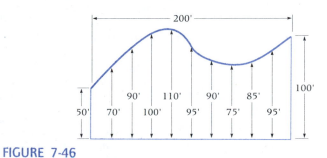

FIGURE 7-46

41. *Land measurement.* Use the trapezoidal rule to approximate the area (in square feet) of the parcel of land illustrated in Figure 7-47.

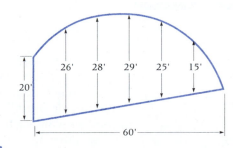

FIGURE 7-47

42. *Water flow.* Engineers must determine the amount of water flowing down a particular river. The first step involves the determination of the area of a vertical cross-section of the river. Depth measurements are made every 10 feet along an imaginary line crossing the river. The results are given in Figure

7-48. Use the trapezoidal rule to approximate the area of the vertical cross-section.

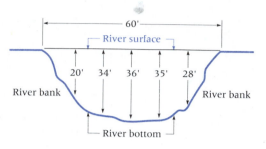

FIGURE 7-48

Computer Exercises

Use the trapezoidal rule with $n = 100$ to approximate each of the following definite integrals.

43. $\displaystyle\int_0^3 (x^2 + 4)\, dx$

44. $\displaystyle\int_0^2 \sqrt{4 - x^2}\, dx$

45. $\displaystyle\int_0^1 \frac{1}{x^2 + 4}\, dx$

46. $\displaystyle\int_2^6 \frac{1}{\sqrt{x - 1}}$

47. $\displaystyle\int_{-3}^3 e^{-x^2}\, dx$

48. $\displaystyle\int_8^{10} \ln(x - 7)\, dx$

49. *Bridge suspension.* Use the trapezoidal rule with $n = 100$ to approximate the definite integral of Exercise 36.

50. *Probability.* Use the trapezoidal rule with $n = 100$ to approximate the normal probability given by the definite integral

$$\int_0^3 \frac{1}{\sqrt{2\pi}}\, e^{-x^2/2}\, dx$$

7-6 • SIMPSON'S RULE

As discussed in Section 7-5, sometimes we must evaluate a definite integral $\int_a^b f(x)\, dx$ where $f(x)$ cannot be integrated (or can be integrated only with much difficulty) by any of the elementary integration techniques. In such a situation, the definite integral may sometimes be *numerically approximated*. One such approximation technique is the trapezoidal rule, which was discussed in Section 7-5. Another such approximation technique is **Simpson's rule,** which we will discuss in this section.

When discussing Simpson's rule as a method of aprproximating a definite integral $\int_a^b f(x)\, dx$, where $f(x)$ is a continuous function over the interval $a \leq x \leq b$, it is helpful to think in terms of the area under a curve. Figure 7-49 illustrates the area, between the x-axis and the graph of $f(x)$ from $x = a$ to $x = b$, that is given by $\int_a^b f(x)\, dx$. For convenience, we assume that $f(x)$ is non-negative over the interval $a \leq x \leq b$.

FIGURE 7-49

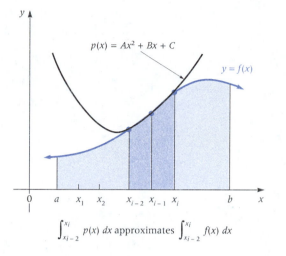

$$\int_{x_{i-2}}^{x_i} p(x)\,dx \text{ approximates } \int_{x_{i-2}}^{x_i} f(x)\,dx$$

FIGURE 7-50

Developing Simpson's rule involves approximating $f(x)$ by parabolas over subintervals within the interval $a \le x \le b$. Specifically, Figure 7-50 illustrates the approximation of $f(x)$ by the parabola $p(x) = Ax^2 + Bx + C$ over the interval $x_{i-2} \le x \le x_i$. Thus, $\int_{x_{i-2}}^{x_i} p(x)\,dx$ approximates $\int_{x_{i-2}}^{x_i} f(x)\,dx$. It can be algebraically proven that

$$\int_{x_{i-2}}^{x_i} p(x)\,dx = \frac{x_i - x_{i-2}}{6}\left[p(x_{i-2}) + 4p\left(\frac{x_{i-2} + x_i}{2}\right) + p(x_i) \right]$$

We require the partition of the interval $a \le x \le b$ into n subintervals, each of length $(b - a)/n$, where n *is even*. We combine pairs of subintervals into the larger subintervals

$$a \le x \le x_2, \; x_2 \le x \le x_4, \; \ldots, \; x_{n-2} \le x \le x_n$$

and approximate $f(x)$ by a parabola $p(x) = Ax^2 + Bx + C$ over each of these larger subintervals, as illustrated in Figure 7-50. Observing Figure 7-50, note that within each such subinterval $x_{i-2} \le x \le x_i$, there are three points $(x_{i-2}, f(x_{i-2}))$, $(x_{i-1}, f(x_{i-1}))$, and $(x_i, f(x_i))$ through which the parabola $p(x)$ passes. For these three points, $p(x_{i-2}) = f(x_{i-2})$, $p(x_{i-1}) = f(x_{i-1})$, and $p(x_i) = f(x_i)$. Thus, the area between the curve $f(x)$ and the x-axis over the interval $x_{i-2} \le x \le x_i$ is approximated by the area between the parabola $p(x)$ and the x-axis over the interval $x_{i-2} \le x \le x_i$. This approximation is given by

$$\int_{x_{i-2}}^{x_i} p(x)\,dx = \frac{x_i - x_{i-2}}{6}\left[p(x_{i-2}) + 4p\left(\frac{x_{i-2} + x_i}{2}\right) + p(x_i) \right]$$

Since $p(x_{i-2}) = f(x_{i-2})$, $p(x_{i-1}) = f(x_{x-1})$, $p(x_i) = f(x_i)$, and $(x_{i-2} + x_i)/2 = x_{i-1}$, this formula becomes

$$\int_{x_{i-2}}^{x_i} p(x)\,dx = \frac{x_i - x_{i-2}}{6}\left[f(x_{i-2}) + 4f(x_{i-1}) + f(x_i) \right]$$

Since the length, $x_i - x_{i-2}$, of the interval $x_{i-2} \leq x \leq x_i$ is twice the length, $(b - a)/n$, of each of the subintervals, $x_{i-1} \leq x \leq x_i$, then

$$x_i - x_{i-2} = 2\left(\frac{b - a}{n}\right)$$

and the expression $(x_i - x_{i-2})/6$ of the formula for $\int_{x_{i-2}}^{x_i} p(x)\, dx$ is replaced by

$$\frac{\left[\dfrac{2(b - a)}{n}\right]}{6} = \frac{b - a}{3n}$$

to yield

$$\int_{x_{i-2}}^{x_i} p(x)\, dx = \frac{b - a}{3n}\left[f(x_{i-2}) + 4f(x_{i-1}) + f(x_i)\right]$$

The area between the curve $f(x)$ and the x-axis over the interval $a \leq x \leq b$ is approximated by the sum of the areas between $n/2$ parabolas and the x-axis over subintervals $x_{i-2} \leq x \leq x_i$. Summing the $n/2$ areas gives the following approximation to $\int_a^b f(x)\, dx$.

$$\int_a^b f(x)\, dx \approx \frac{b - a}{3n}\Big[(f(x_0) + 4f(x_1) + f(x_2)) + (f(x_2) + 4f(x_3) + f(x_4)) +$$

$$(f(x_4) + 4f(x_5) + f(x_6)) + \ldots + (f(x_{n-2}) + 4f(x_{n-1}) + f(x_n)) \Big]$$

$$\approx \frac{b - a}{3n}\Big[f(x_0) + 4f(x_1) + 2f(x_2) + 4f(x_3) + 2f(x_4) + \ldots + 4f(x_{i-1}) + f(x_n) \Big]$$

This expression approximates $\int_a^b f(x)\, dx$, which gives the area between the curve $f(x)$ and the x-axis over the interval $a \leq x \leq b$. Note that terms with odd subscripts have coefficients of 4, while those with even subscripts have coefficients of 2 except $f(x_0)$ and $f(x_n)$, which have coefficients of 1. We summarize as follows.

Simpson's Rule

If $f(x)$ is a continuous function over the interval $a \leq x \leq b$, and **n is even,** then

$$\int_a^b f(x)\, dx \approx \frac{b - a}{3n}\Big[f(x_0) + 4f(x_1) + 2f(x_2) + 4f(x_3) + 2f(x_4) + \ldots$$

$$+ 4f(x_{n-1}) + f(x_n) \Big]$$

• **EXAMPLE 7-19** _____

Use Simpson's rule with $n = 6$ to approximate $\int_0^3 e^{-x^2}\, dx$.

Solution

The graphical representation appears in Figure 7-51. Our computations appear in Table 7-10. Observe that each value of $f(x_i)$ is multiplied by the appropriate coefficient to yield the product column. The sum of these products is an important component of Simpson's rule.

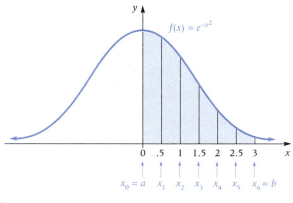

FIGURE 7-51

TABLE 7-10

x	$f(x) = e^{-x^2}$	Coefficient	Product
$x_0 = 0.0$	1.000000	1	1.000000
$x_1 = 0.5$	0.778801	4	3.115204
$x_2 = 1.0$	0.367880	2	0.735760
$x_3 = 1.5$	0.105339	4	0.421596
$x_4 = 2.0$	0.018316	2	0.036632
$x_5 = 2.5$	0.001930	4	0.007720
$x_6 = 3.0$	0.000123	1	0.000123
			Sum = 5.317035

According to Simpson's rule,

$$\int_a^b f(x)\, dx \approx \frac{b-a}{3n}\Big[f(x_0) + 4f(x_1) + 2f(x_2) + 4f(x_3) + 2f(x_4) + 4f(x_5) + f(x_6)\Big]$$

For this example, $a = 0$, $b = 3$, $n = 6$, and $f(x) = e^{-x^2}$. Thus, Simpson's rule becomes

$$\int_0^3 e^{-x^2}\, dx \approx \frac{3-0}{3(6)}\Big[e^{-(0.0)^2} + 4e^{-(0.5)^2} + 2e^{-(1.0)^2} + 4e^{-(1.5)^2} + 2e^{-(2.0)^2} + 4e^{-(2.5)^2} + 2e^{-(3.0)^2}\Big]$$

$$\approx \frac{1}{6}\Big[\underset{\substack{\nearrow \\ \text{from Table 7-10}}}{5.317035}\Big] \approx 0.886173$$

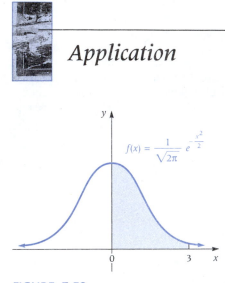

Application

FIGURE 7-52

Standard Normal Curve

As stated in Section 7-5, if a random variable, x, is distributed in accordance with the density function

$$f(x) = \frac{1}{\sqrt{2\pi}} e^{-x^2/2} \qquad \text{over } (-\infty, \infty)$$

then x is said to have a **standard normal distribution.** The graph of the density function, which is given in Figure 7-52, is called the **standard normal curve.**

We now use Simpson's rule to approximate the definite integral

$$\int_0^3 \frac{1}{\sqrt{2\pi}} e^{-x^2/2} \, dx$$

for various values of n. These results, which are given in Table 7-11, approximate the shaded area of Figure 7-52. We used a computer to obtain these Simpson rule approximations. Of course, the shaded area gives $P(0 \leq x \leq 3)$.

Comparing these results with the trapezoidal approximations of Table 7-8 in Section 7-5, note that the trapezoidal rule required $n = 200$ subintervals to obtain the same approximation determined by Simpson's rule with only $n = 30$ subintervals.

TABLE 7-11

n	Simpson rule approximation
10	0.4986498
15	0.4986502
20	0.4986503
30	0.4986502
40	0.4986502

Error Estimates

Since Simpson's rule gives an approximation to the value of a definite integral, it is necessary to be concerned about how close the approximation is to the exact value of the definite integral. From the explanation presented in this section, it is clear that as the number of subintervals, n, increases, the corresponding Simpson rule approximation gets closer to the exact value of the definite integral. The difference between the exact value of a definite integral and an approximation is called **error** and is defined below.

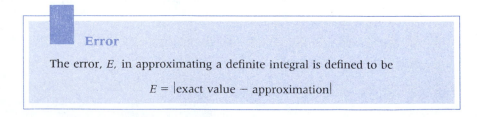

Error

The error, E, in approximating a definite integral is defined to be

$$E = |\text{exact value} - \text{approximation}|$$

More advanced texts prove the following result:

> **Error in Simpson's Rule**
>
> The error in approximating $\int_a^b f(x)\,dx$ by Simpson's rule is at most
>
> $$\frac{K(b-a)^5}{180n^4}$$
>
> where K is the maximum value of $|f^{(4)}(x)|$ over the interval $[a, b]$.
> *Note:* The error decreases as n, the number of subintervals, increases.

• EXAMPLE 7-20

Determine the maximum error in approximating $\int_0^3 e^{-x^2}\,dx$ with $n = 6$.

Solution

The error is at most $K(b-a)^5/180n^4$, where K is the maximum value of $|f^{(4)}(x)|$ over the interval $0 \le x \le 3$. We begin to determine K by computing $f^{(4)}(x)$. Hence,

$$f(x) = e^{-x^2}$$
$$f'(x) = -2xe^{-x^2}$$
$$f''(x) = 2e^{-x^2}(2x^2 - 1)$$
$$f'''(x) = 8xe^{-x^2}(1.5 - x^2)$$
$$f^{(4)}(x) = e^{-x^2}(16x^4 - 48x^2 + 12)$$

Using the optimization methods of Chapter 3, it can be determined that the maximum value of $|f^{(4)}(x)|$ over the interval $[0, 3]$ is $|f^{(4)}(0)| = 12$. Thus, K, the maximum value of $|f^{(4)}(x)|$ over the interval $0 \le x \le 3$, equals 12.

The error in approximating $\int_0^3 e^{-x^2}\,dx$ with $n = 6$ is at most

$$\frac{K(b-a)^5}{180n^4} = \frac{12(3-0)^5}{180(6^4)}$$
$$= 0.0125$$

This means that

$$\text{approximation} - \text{error} \le \int_0^3 e^{-x^2}dx \le \text{approximation} + \text{error}$$

$$0.886173 - 0.012500 \le \int_0^3 e^{-x^2}\,dx \le 0.886173 + 0.012500$$

or

$$0.873673 \le \int_0^3 e^{-x^2}\,dx \le 0.898673$$

Determining the Number of Subintervals

The formula for the maximum approximation error of Simpson's rule is used to determine n, the number of subintervals needed to get an approximation to a desired degree of accuracy. This is illustrated in Example 7-21.

• **EXAMPLE 7-21** _____

Assume that the approximation error, 0.0125, in Example 7-20 is too large for our purposes. Determine n so that the error is at most 0.01.

Solution

This means that we must determine n so that

$$\frac{K(b - a)^5}{180n^4} \le 0.01$$

Substituting $K = 12$, $b = 3$, and $a = 0$ into this inequality yields

$$\frac{81}{5n^4} \le 0.01$$

Solving for n^4 gives

$$\frac{81}{5}\left(\frac{1}{0.01}\right) \le n^4$$

$$1620 \le n^4$$

Since $n > 0$,

$$n \ge \sqrt[4]{1620} \approx 6.34$$

Thus, we choose $n = 8$ (since n must be both even and at least 6.34) in order that the error in approximating $\int_0^3 e^{-x^2}\, dx$ is at most 0.01.

•

Trapezoidal Rule Versus Simpson's Rule

In Sections 7-5 and 7-6, we have approximated $\int_0^3 e^{-x^2}\, dx$ by both the trapezoidal rule and Simpson's rule with $n = 6$ and have computed the error in both cases. The maximum error with the trapezoidal approximation was 0.125, whereas the maximum error with Simpson's rule was 0.0125. Clearly, in this example, Simpson's rule gave the better approximation for $n = 6$. Also, comparing the results of Examples 7-18 and 7-21, we found that in order for the maximum error not to exceed 0.01, the trapezoidal rule required $n = 22$ subintervals, whereas Simpson's rule required only $n = 8$ subintervals. For a given value of n, Simpson's rule usually gives a better approximation than the trapezoidal rule. Hence, it is a built-in feature of some calculators.

At this point, the question arises "Why bother studying the trapezoidal rule if Simpson's rule usually gives a better approximation?" A partial answer is that it is easier to determine n, the number of subintervals required to assure a desired level of accuracy, with the trapezoidal rule than with Simpson's rule. This is because the maximum error estimate of the trapezoidal rule involves the computation of only the second derivative, whereas Simpson's rule requires computation of the fourth derivative. Also, the trapezoidal rule estimate can be adjusted to provide a much better approximation to $\int_a^b f(x)\, dx$ by adding the quantity

$$\left(\frac{f'(a) - f'(b)}{12}\right)\left(\frac{b - a}{n}\right)^2$$

When this quantity is added to the trapezoidal rule formula, the result is the **adjusted trapezoidal rule** for approximating $\int_a^b f(x)\,dx$.

> ### Adjusted Trapezoidal Rule
>
> If $f(x)$ is continuous over the interval $a \le x \le b$, then
>
> $$\int_a^b f(x)\,dx \approx \frac{b-a}{2n}\Big[f(x_0) + 2f(x_1) + 2f(x_2) + \ldots + 2f(x_{n-1}) + f(x_n)\Big]$$
> $$+ \left(\frac{f'(a) - f'(b)}{12}\right)\left(\frac{b-a}{n}\right)^2$$

Error Estimates

The error of approximating $\int_a^b f(x)\,dx$ by the adjusted trapezoidal rule is at most

$$\frac{K(b-a)^5}{720n^4}$$

where K is the maximum value of $|f^{(4)}(x)|$ over the interval $a \le x \le b$.

Exercises 7-6

For Exercises 1–10
a) use Simpson's rule with the indicated value of n to approximate the value of the definite integral. Round your answers to six decimal places.
b) find the exact value of the definite integral, and compare this result with the answer to part (a).

1. $\displaystyle\int_1^2 \frac{1}{x}\,dx,\ n = 4$

2. $\displaystyle\int_1^3 \frac{1}{x^2}\,dx,\ n = 4$

3. $\displaystyle\int_1^3 x^2\,dx,\ n = 4$

4. $\displaystyle\int_0^3 x^3\,dx,\ n = 6$

5. $\displaystyle\int_0^2 \frac{1}{x+1}\,dx,\ n = 8$

6. $\displaystyle\int_1^2 \frac{1}{x+4}\,dx,\ n = 4$

7. $\displaystyle\int_1^2 (3x^2 + 1)\,dx,\ n = 4$

8. $\displaystyle\int_0^4 \sqrt{x}\,dx,\ n = 8$

9. $\displaystyle\int_0^3 \sqrt{x}\,dx,\ n = 6$

10. $\displaystyle\int_0^2 (6x^2 + 4)\,dx,\ n = 8$

For Exercises 11–22, use Simpson's rule with the indicated value of n to approximate the value of the definite integral. Round your answers to six decimal places.

11. $\displaystyle\int_0^2 e^{-x^2}\,dx,\ n = 8$

12. $\displaystyle\int_1^2 e^{-x^2}\,dx,\ n = 4$

13. $\displaystyle\int_0^3 e^{-0.5x^2}\,dx,\ n = 6$

14. $\displaystyle\int_0^3 \sqrt{x^2 + 1}\,dx,\ n = 6$

15. $\displaystyle\int_0^1 \frac{1}{\sqrt{x^2 + 1}}\, dx, \; n = 6$

16. $\displaystyle\int_0^1 \frac{1}{x^2 + 1}\, dx, \; n = 6$

17. $\displaystyle\int_0^2 \sqrt{x^2 + 1}\, dx, \; n = 8$

18. $\displaystyle\int_0^2 \sqrt{x^3 + 1}\, dx, \; n = 4$

19. $\displaystyle\int_0^3 \frac{1}{\sqrt{x^3 + 1}}\, dx, \; n = 6$

20. $\displaystyle\int_4^6 x\sqrt{x - 4}\, dx, \; n = 4$

21. $\displaystyle\int_2^4 \ln x\, dx, \; n = 8$

22. $\displaystyle\int_3^5 \ln x\, dx, \; n = 8$

Error

23. Determine the error for Exercise 1.
24. Determine the error for Exercise 2.
25. Determine the error for Exercise 5.
26. Determine the error for Exercise 6.
27. Determine the error for Exercise 21.
28. Determine the error for Exercise 22.

Determining the Number of Subintervals

29. Determine n so that the error in approximating $\int_1^2 x^{-1}\, dx$ by Simpson's rule is at most 0.0001.

30. Determine n so that the error in approximating $\int_2^4 x^{-2}\, dx$ by Simpson's rule is at most 0.0001.

31. Determine n so that the error in approximating $\int_0^2 (x + 1)^{-1}\, dx$ by Simpson's rule is at most 0.0001.

32. Determine n so that the error in approximating $\int_2^4 \ln x\, dx$ by Simpson's rule is at most 0.0001.

33. Determine n so that the error in approximating $\int_1^3 \ln x\, dx$ by Simpson's rule is at most 0.0001.

34. Determine n so that the error in approximating $\int_0^1 \ln (x^2 + 1)\, dx$ by Simpson's rule is at most 0.0001.

Applications

35. *Semicircle.* Use Simpson's rule with $n = 8$ to approximate the area between the semicircle $y = \sqrt{1 - x^2}$ and the x-axis, as illustrated in Figure 7-53. Round your answer to six decimal places. Check the accuracy of your answer by using the fact that the area A of a circle of radius r is given by $A = \pi r^2$.

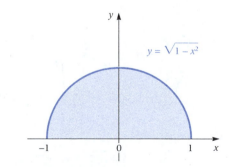

FIGURE 7-53

36. *Bridge suspension.* A bridge of length 100 feet is suspended by a parabolic cable whose equation is equal to $y = x^2/200$, as illustrated in Figure 7-54. The length of the cable is given by the definite integral

$$\int_{-50}^{50} \sqrt{1 + (y')^2} \, dx = 2 \int_{0}^{50} \sqrt{1 + (x/100)^2} \, dx$$

Use Simpson's rule with $n = 10$ to approximate the length of the parabolic cable.

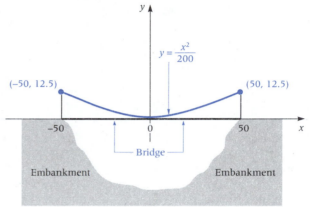

FIGURE 7-54

37. *Travel distance.* A driver records speedometer readings every 5 minutes during an automobile trip that last 30 minutes. The results are given in the Table 7-12 below, with an accompanying graphical illustration in Figure 7-55. Observe in Figure 7-55 that time has been converted to *hours* to correspond with speed, which is given in miles per *hour*. The total distance traveled is given by the definite integral

$$\int_{0}^{1/2} v(t) \, dt$$

Use Simpson's rule to approximate the total distance traveled.

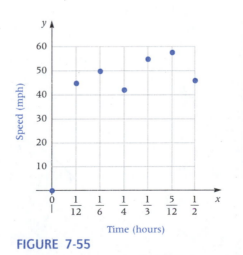

FIGURE 7-55

TABLE 7-12

Time (minutes)	Speed (mph)
0	0
5	45
10	50
15	42
20	55
25	58
30	48

38. *Rocket launch.* The velocity readings (in miles per hour) of a rocket during takeoff are recorded at 1-second intervals with the following results:

$$0, 10, 30, 60, 90, 120, 150, 180, 210, 240, 270$$

A graphical illustration appears in Figure 7-56. Observe in Figure 7-56 that time has been converted to *hours* to correspond with velocity, which is given in miles per *hour*. Use Simpson's rule to approximate the total distance traveled by the rocket during the first 10 seconds.

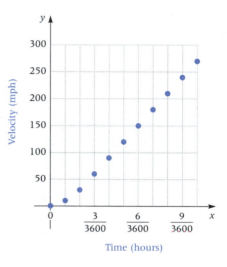

FIGURE 7-56

39. *Probability.* Use Simpson's rule with $n = 4$ to approximate the normal probability given by the definite integral

$$\int_0^2 \frac{1}{\sqrt{2\pi}} e^{-x^2/2} \, dx$$

Round your answer to six decimal places.

40. *Land measurement.* A developer wishes to determine the area of the parcel of land illustrated in Figure 7-57.
a) Use Simpson's rule to approximate the area.
b) If 43,560 square feet equals 1 acre, then how many acres are in the parcel in Figure 7-57.

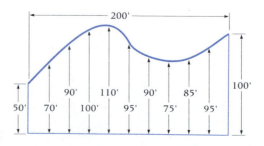

FIGURE 7-57

41. *Land measurement.* Use Simpson's rule to approximate the area (in square feet) of the parcel of land illustrated in Figure 7-58.

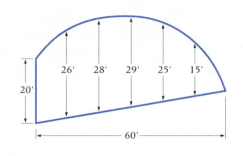

FIGURE 7-58

42. *Water flow.* Engineers must determine the amount of water flowing down a particular river. The first step involves the determination of the area of a vertical cross-section of the river. Depth measurements are made every 10 feet along an imaginary line crossing the river. The results are given in Figure 7-59. Use Simpson's rule to approximate the area of the vertical cross-section.

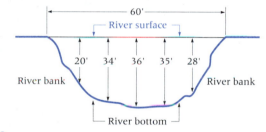

FIGURE 7-59

Computer Exercises

Use Simpson's rule with $n = 100$ to approximate each of the following definite integrals.

43. $\int_0^3 (x^2 + 4)\, dx$

44. $\int_0^2 \sqrt{4 - x^2}\, dx$

45. $\int_0^1 \frac{1}{x^2 + 4}\, dx$

46. $\int_2^6 \frac{1}{\sqrt{x - 1}}$

47. $\int_{-3}^3 e^{-x^2}\, dx$

48. $\int_8^{10} \ln(x - 7)\, dx$

49. *Bridge suspension.* Use Simpson's rule with $n = 100$ to approximate the definite integral of Exercise 36.

50. *Probability.* Use Simpson's rule with $n = 100$ to approximate the normal probability given by the definite integral

$$\int_0^3 \frac{1}{\sqrt{2\pi}}\, e^{-x^2/2}\, dx$$

7-7 • DIFFERENTIAL EQUATIONS

In this section, we will encounter equations involving derivatives. An equation that contains one or more derivatives is called a **differential equation.** A differential equation expresses a relationship between a rate of change and other variables. The equation

$$\frac{dy}{dx} - 2xy^2 = 0$$

is an example of a differential equation. Since this differential equation involves the variables x and y, its **solution** is an equation that (1) *relates the variables* x *and* y; and (2) *satisfies the differential equation.*

Separation of Variables

The solution to the above differential equation is found by the method of **separation of variables.** To solve this differential equation by the separation of variables method, we must rewrite it so that the variable y occurs only on one side of the equation and x only on the other. If we treat dy/dx as a quotient of differentials, the differential equation may be rewritten as

$$\frac{dy}{dx} = 2xy^2 \qquad \text{Adding } 2xy^2 \text{ to both sides}$$

$$\frac{dy}{y^2} = 2x\, dx \qquad \text{Dividing both sides by } y^2 \text{ and multiplying both sides by } dx$$

or

$$y^{-2}dy = 2x\, dx$$

Note that y occurs only on one side of the equation and x only on the other. Hence, the variables are separated.

Integrating both sides of the equation, we have

$$\int y^{-2}dy = \int 2x\, dx$$

$$\frac{y^{-1}}{-1} = x^2 + C$$

$$y = \frac{-1}{x^2 + C}$$

where C is an arbitrary constant. Thus, the proposed solution to the differential equation is the set of functions of the form

$$y = \frac{-1}{x^2 + C} \qquad \text{Solution}$$

Verifying Solutions

To verify that this proposed solution actually does satisfy the differential equation, we compute dy/dx and substitute it and the result for y into the differential equation. Since $y = -1/(x^2 + C)$, then

$$\frac{dy}{dx} = \frac{2x}{(x^2 + C)^2}$$

Substituting $2x/(x^2 + C)^2$ for dy/dx and $-1/(x^2 + C)$ for y into the differential equation

$$\frac{dy}{dx} - 2xy^2 = 0$$

gives

$$\frac{2x}{(x^2 + C)^2} - 2x\left(\frac{-1}{x^2 + C}\right)^2 = 0$$

Simplifying this equation results in

$$\frac{2x}{(x^2 + C)^2} - \frac{2x}{(x^2 + C)^2} = 0$$

Thus, the proposed solution satisfies the differential equation.

General Solution

Since the solution, $y = -1/(x^2 + C)$, contains an arbitrary constant, C, it is called a **general solution** to the differential equation $(dy/dx) - 2xy^2 = 0$. The general solution represents an entire family of solutions to the differential equation. If C takes on a specific value, say $C = 5$, then the solution becomes

$$y = \frac{-1}{x^2 + 5}$$

This result is called a **particular solution** to the differential equation.

Usually, a desired particular solution is determined from further specified information called **initial conditions** (or **boundary conditions**) for the variables. For example, if we are given the initial condition that

$$y = 2 \text{ when } x = 3 \qquad \text{Initial condition}$$

then these values are substituted into the general solution

$$y = \frac{-1}{x^2 + C}$$

to give

$$2 = \frac{-1}{3^2 + C}$$

Solving for C yields

$$-\frac{1}{2} = 3^2 + C$$

$$C = -9\frac{1}{2}$$

Thus, the particular solution, in this instance, is

$$y = \frac{-1}{x^2 - 9.5} \qquad \text{Particular solution}$$

Of course, the initial conditions (or boundary conditions) ensure that the graph of the particular solution passes through $(3, 2)$.

• **EXAMPLE 7-22** _____

Consider the differential equation

$$y^2\frac{dy}{dx} - 4x^2 = 0$$

a) Solve by the method of separation of variables.
b) Verify that the general solution of part a satisfies the differential equation.
c) Find the particular solution for the initial condition that $y = 5$ when $x = 2$.

Solutions

a) Adding $4x^2$ to both sides of the differential equation and multiplying by dx gives

$$y^2 dy = 4x^2\, dx$$

Integrating both sides of this equation yields

$$\int y^2 dy = \int 4x^2\, dx$$

$$\frac{1}{3}y^3 = \frac{4}{3}x^3 + C_1$$

where C_1 is an arbitrary constant.

Attempting to solve for y in terms of x, we multiply both sides of this equation by 3 to obtain

$$y^3 = 4x^3 + 3C_1$$

Since C_1 is an arbitrary constant, $3C_1$ is also an arbitrary constant, which we denote by C. Thus, the equation becomes

$$y^3 = 4x^3 + C$$

Taking the cube root of each side gives

$$y = \sqrt[3]{4x^3 + C} \qquad \text{General solution}$$

b) Rewriting our general solution as

$$y = (4x^3 + C)^{1/3}$$

and computing dy/dx gives

$$\frac{dy}{dx} = \frac{1}{3}(4x^3 + C)^{-2/3}(12x^2)$$

$$= 4x^2(4x^3 + C)^{-2/3}$$

Substituting $4x^2(4x^3 + C)^{-2/3}$ for dy/dx and $(4x^3 + C)^{2/3}$ for y^2 into the differential equation

$$y^2\frac{dy}{dx} - 4x^2 = 0$$

gives

$$(4x^3 + C)^{2/3} \cdot 4x^2(4x^3 + C)^{-2/3} - 4x^2 = 0$$

Simplifying this gives

$$4x^2 - 4x^2 = 0$$

and thus the solution satisfies the differential equation.

c) Substituting the initial condition that $y = 5$ when $x = 2$ into the general solution

$$y = \sqrt[3]{4x^3 + C}$$

we have

$$5 = \sqrt[3]{4(2)^3 + C}$$

Solving for C gives

$$5 = \sqrt[3]{32 + C}$$
$$5^3 = 32 + C$$
$$125 = 32 + C$$
$$C = 93$$

Thus, the particular solution is

$$y = \sqrt[3]{4x^3 + 93}$$

Exponential Growth and Decay

There are many situations where the rate of change of some quantity with respect to time is proportional to the quantity. For example, let P be the population of a city at time t (in years); then dP/dt is the rate of change of the city's population with respect to time. If the population's rate of change is proportional to the population, P, then

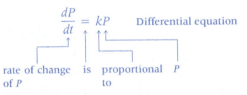

$$\frac{dP}{dt} = kP \qquad \text{Differential equation}$$

rate of change   is   proportional P
of P to

where k is the constant of proportionality. To solve this differential equation, we separate the variables to obtain

$$\frac{dP}{P} = kdt$$

Integrating both sides gives

$$\int \frac{dP}{P} = \int kdt$$
$$\ln |P| = kt + C$$

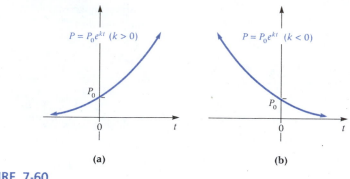

FIGURE 7-60

where C is an arbitrary constant of integration. Rewriting this result in exponential form, we have

$$P = e^{kt+C}$$

Using laws of exponents, we can rewrite this equation as

$$P = e^{kt} \cdot e^C$$

Since C is an arbitrary constant, e^C is also an arbitrary constant, which we denote by P_0. Thus, the solution to our differential equation is written as

$$P = P_0 e^{kt} \qquad \text{Solution}$$

Its possible graphs appear in Figure 7-60. If $k > 0$, then the city's population is exhibiting exponential growth, and k is the growth rate [see Figure 7-60(a)]. If $k < 0$, then the city's population is exhibiting exponential decay, and k is the decay rate [see Figure 7-60(b)]. Note that P_0 is the population at time $t = 0$ since

$$\begin{aligned} P &= P_0 e^{k(0)} \\ &= P_0(1) \\ &= P_0 \end{aligned}$$

• **EXAMPLE 7-23** **Continuous Compounding of Interest.** ⎯

Show that the continuous compounding of interest is an example of exponential growth.

Solution

Let $S = S(t)$ be the value of an investment at time, t (in years). If interest is compounded m times a year at an annual rate, r, each conversion period has a length of $1/m$ years (see Figure 7-61). Thus, the interest earned during a conversion period of length $\Delta t = 1/m$ years is given by $\Delta S = S(t + \Delta t) - S(t)$, as illustrated in Figure 7-61. Since

$$\text{interest} = (\text{principal})(\text{rate})(\text{time})$$

then

$$\Delta S = S(t) \cdot r \cdot \Delta t$$

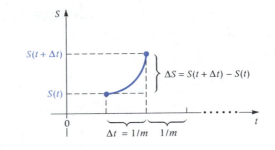

FIGURE 7-61

where $S(t)$ is the value of the investment at the beginning of a conversion period of length Δt years. Dividing both sides of this equation by Δt gives

$$\frac{\Delta S}{\Delta t} = rS(t)$$

If interest is compounded continuously, the number of conversion periods in one year, m, increases without bound (i.e., $m \to \infty$). Since $\Delta t = 1/m$, then $\Delta t \to 0$ as $m \to \infty$ and $\Delta S/\Delta t \to dS/dt$. In other words, $\lim_{\Delta t \to 0} \Delta S/\Delta t = dS/dt$. Thus, the equation becomes the differential equation

$$\frac{dS}{dt} = rS \qquad \text{Differential equation}$$

This differential equation indicates that the rate of change of S with respect to time, t, is proportional to S (where S is the value of the investment at time t) when interest is compounded continuously at an annual rate, r. Note that the annual rate r is the constant of proportionality.

In the discussion preceding this example, we have shown that a general solution to this type of differential equation is given by

$$S = S_0 e^{rt}$$

where S_0 is the value of the investment at time $t = 0$. In other words, $S_0 = P$, the principal or original amount invested. Thus, the above general solution is written as

$$S = Pe^{rt} \qquad \text{Solution}$$

Newton's Law of Cooling

If an object is placed in a surrounding medium of different temperature, then Newton's law of cooling states that the rate of change of temperature of the object is proportional to the difference between its present temperature and the temperature of its surrounding medium. If $y = y(t)$ is the temperature of the object at time t and the constant m is the temperature of the surrounding medium, then Newton's law of cooling results in the differential equation

$$\frac{dy}{dt} = k(y - m) \qquad (y \geq m)$$

where k is the constant of proportionality. The following example illustrates the solution of this differential equation.

• **EXAMPLE 7-24** _____

a) Solve the differential equation

$$\frac{dy}{dt} = k(y - m) \qquad (y \geq m)$$

where k and m are constants.

b) If the constant temperature of the surrounding medium is 60°F, find a particular solution given the following boundary conditions:

1. At time $t = 0$, the temperature of the object is 230°F.
2. At time $t = 10$, the temperature of the object is 190°F.

Solutions

a) Separating the variables, we divide both sides of the differential equation by $y - m$ and multiply both sides by dt to obtain

$$\frac{dy}{y - m} = kdt$$

Integrating both sides, we have

$$\int \frac{dy}{y - m} = \int kdt$$
$$\ln |y - m| = kt + C$$

where C is an arbitrary constant of integration. Rewriting this result in exponential form gives

$$y - m = e^{kt+C}$$

Using laws of exponents, we can rewrite this equation as

$$y - m = e^{kt} \cdot e^{C}$$

Since e^{C} is a constant, we denote it by A. Thus, the equation becomes

$$y - m = Ae^{kt}$$

Adding m to both sides, the general solution becomes

$$y = Ae^{kt} + m$$

b) Since the constant temperature of the _surrounding medium_ is 60°F, then $m = 60$. The above solution becomes

$$y = Ae^{kt} + 60$$

The _first boundary condition_ specifies that at $t = 0$, $y = 230$. Substituting these values for t and y into this equation gives

$$230 = Ae^{k(0)} + 60$$

Solving for A, we have

$$230 = A(1) + 60$$
$$A = 170$$

The solution becomes

$$y = 170e^{kt} + 60$$

The _second boundary condition_ specifies that at $t = 10$, $y = 190$. Substituting these values for t and y into the above equation gives

$$190 = 170e^{k(10)} + 60$$

Solving for k, we obtain

$$130 = 170e^{10k}$$

$$\frac{130}{170} = e^{10k}$$

$$10k = \ln\left(\frac{130}{170}\right)$$

$$k = \frac{1}{10}\ln\left(\frac{130}{170}\right)$$

$$\approx \frac{1}{10}(-0.27) = -0.027$$

Thus, the particular solution is

$$y = 170e^{-0.027t} + 60$$

Exercises 7-7

For each of the following differential equations, solve by the method of separation of variables, and verify that the general solution satisfies the differential equation.

1. $dy/dt = 8y$
2. $dy/dx = xy$
3. $dy/dx = xy^3$
4. $dy/dx = x^3y$
5. $y^3\dfrac{dy}{dx} - 3x^2 = 0$
6. $x^2\dfrac{dy}{dx} - 2x^4y^3 = 0$
7. $dy/dx = x^2e^y$
8. $dy/dx = y/x$
9. $dy/dx = y^3x^2$
10. $dy/dx = \dfrac{y}{x + 3}$
11. $\dfrac{dy}{dx} - x\sqrt{x^2 + 5} = 0$
12. $dydx = \dfrac{1}{xy + y}$

Solve each of the following by the method of separation of variables.

13. $(4 + x)\dfrac{dy}{dx} - 5y = 0$
14. $\dfrac{dy}{dt} - te^{t^2} = 0$
15. $\dfrac{dy}{dx} - y^2e^x = 0$
16. $\dfrac{dy}{dt} = \dfrac{t^3y^2}{t^4 + 10}$
17. $\dfrac{dy}{dx} = e^{x-y}$
18. $\dfrac{dy}{dt} = \dfrac{3t(y - 2)}{t^2 + 5}$

19. Verify that $y = ke^{(1/2)t^2}$, where k is a constant, is a solution of the differential equation

$$\frac{dy}{dt} = ty$$

Do not solve the differential equation.

20. Verify that $y = \dfrac{1}{4}(\ln x + c)^2$ is a solution of the differential equation

$$x\frac{dy}{dx} = \sqrt{y}$$

Do not solve the differential equation.

21. Find a particular solution for

$$y^2\frac{dy}{dx} - 3x^2 = 0$$

given that $x = 2$ when $y = 4$.

22. Find a particular solution for

$$y^4\frac{dy}{dx} - x^3 = 0$$

given that $x = 2$ when $y = 1$.

23. Find a particular solution of

$$x^2\frac{dy}{dx} + y = 0$$

given that $y = e$ when $x = 1$.

Applications

Continuous compounding. Assume interest is compounded continuously at each of the following annual rates. S denotes the value (in dollars) of an investment at time t (in years).
a)   Write the differential equation for the rate of change of S.
b)   Write the solution to the differential equation of part a.
c)   If the initial amount invested is $5000, find its value after 9 years.

24. Annual rate = 6%   **25.** Annual rate = 7%
26. Annual rate = 8%   **27.** Annual rate = 9%
28. Annual rate = 10%   **29.** Annual rate = 11%

30. *Asset growth.* The growth rate of a company's assets is directly proportional to the amount of assets, y.
a)   Find the differential equation expressing this relationship.
b)   Solve the differential equation of part a.
c)   Find a particular solution given the following boundary conditions:
   1. At $t = 0$, $y = \$100,000$.
   2. At $t = 5$, $y = \$900,000$.

31. *Radioactive decay.* The mass (or weight) of a radioactive substance decreases at a rate that is directly proportional to the mass, y.
a)   Find the differential equation expressing this relationship.
b)   Solve the differential equation of part a.
c)   Find a particular solution given the following boundary conditions:
   1. At $t = 0$, the mass is 40,000 grams.
   2. At $t = 4$, the mass is 20,000 grams.

32. *Depreciation.* A certain machine loses value at a rate that is directly proportional to its value, v.
a)   Find the differential equation expressing this relationship.
b)   Solve the differential equation of part a.
c)   Find a particular solution given the following boundary conditions:
   1. The cost (or initial value) of the machine is $60,000.
   2. At $t = e$ the machine is worth $30,000.
d)   Find the machine's value at $t = 5$.

33. *Inverse proportions.* If a quantity, y, is **inversely proportional** to a quantity x, then $y = k/x$ for some constant $k \neq 0$. The Weber-Fechner Law of psychology states that the rate of change of a reaction, R, with respect to a stimulus, S, is inversely proportional to the stimulus. Hence

$$\frac{dR}{dS} = \frac{k}{S}$$

for some constant $k \neq 0$.

a) Solve the differential equation $dR/dS = k/S$.
b) Find a particular solution given the following boundary conditions:
    1. $R = 5$ when $S = 1$.
    2. $R = 6$ when $S = 10$.

34. *Psychology.* The Brentano-Stevens Law of psychology states that the rate of change of a reaction, R, with respect to a stimulus, S, is directly proportional to the ratio R/S. Hence,

$$\frac{dR}{dS} = k \cdot \frac{R}{S}$$

where k is the constant of proportionality.
a) Solve this differential equation.
b) Find a particular solution given the following boundary conditions:
    1. $R = 3$ when $S = 1$.
    2. $R = 5$ when $S = 3$.

35. *Water pollution.* Water containing 50% pollutant is seeping into a pond at the rate of 4 gallons per hour. The resulting mixture of polluted water and pond water runs over a dam at the rate of 4 gallons per hour. The pond contains 10,000 gallons of water. If P is the amount of pollutant (in gallons) in the pond at time t (in hours), then the rate of change of P with respect to t is given by

$$\frac{dP}{dt} = \left(\begin{array}{c} \text{rate at which} \\ \text{pollutant runs} \\ \text{in} \end{array} \right) - \left(\begin{array}{c} \text{rate at which} \\ \text{pollutant runs} \\ \text{out} \end{array} \right)$$

a) Verify that this formula results in the differential equation

$$\frac{dP}{dt} = 2 - \frac{4P}{10,000}$$

b) Solve the differential equation of a.
c) Find a particular solution given the boundary condition that the pond initially contained pollutant-free water.
d) Find the amount of pollutant in the pond at the end of 10,000 hours.

36. *Glucose injection.* Sometimes it is necessary to inject glucose into a person's bloodstream. Suppose glucose is injected into a person's blood at the rate of r grams per minute. At the same time that glucose enters the blood, it is converted and removed at a rate directly proportional to the amount of glucose present. If G is the amount of glucose present in the blood at time t (in minutes), then
a) verify that the rate of change of glucose with respect to time t is given by

$$\frac{dG}{dt} = r - kG$$

where k is the constant of proportionality.
b) solve the differential equation of part a. Remember that r and k are constants.

37. *Newton's law of cooling.* A piece of meat is placed in a freezer where the temperature is maintained at 5°F. Find a particular solution to the differential equation resulting from Newton's law of cooling given the following additional boundary conditions:
1. The initial temperature of the meat was 40°F.
2. After the meat was in the freezer for 2 hours, its temperature was 15°F.

38. *Newton's law or cooling.* A carton of milk is removed from a refrigerator and placed in a room where the temperature is maintained at 65°F. Find a partic-

ular solution to the differential equation resulting from Newton's law of cooling given the following additional boundary conditions:
1. The initial temperature of the milk was 45°F.
2. After the milk was in the room for 1 hour, its temperature was 55°F.

CHAPTER 7 HIGHLIGHTS

● *Concepts*

Your ability to answer the following questions is one indicator of the depth of your mastery of this chapter's concepts. Note that the questions are grouped under various topic headings. For any question that you cannot answer, refer to the appropriate section of the chapter indicated by the topic heading. Pay particular attention to the boxes within a section.

7-1 CONTINUOUS MONEY FLOW

1. State and explain the formula for total money flow.
2. State and explain the formulas for present and future values of continuous money flows.

7-2 IMPROPER INTEGRALS

3. Give the three types of improper integrals. Explain the terms *convergent* and *divergent*.
4. State and explain the formula for the present value of a perpetual flow.

7-3 PROBABILITY DISTRIBUTIONS

5. Explain each of the following terms: discrete random variable, continuous random variable.
6. Give the formula for the density function of the uniform distribution, and draw its graph.
7. State and explain three properties of probability density functions.
8. Give the formula for the density function of the exponential distribution, and draw its graph.

7-4 APPLICATIONS: AVERAGE VALUE AND VOLUME

9. Give the formula for the average value of a function, and explain its geometric interpretation.
10. State and explain the formula for a volume of a solid of revolution.

7-5 THE TRAPEZOIDAL RULE

11. State and explain the formula for the trapezoidal rule.
12. Give the formula for determining the maximum error in approximating a definite integral by the trapezoidal rule.

7-6 SIMPSON'S RULE

13. State and explain the formula for Simpson's rule.
14. Give the formula for determining the maximum error in approximating a definite integral by Simpson's rule.

7-7 DIFFERENTIAL EQUATIONS

15. What is a differential equation?
16. Explain the method of separation of variables.

17. Explain each of the following terms:
General solution, initial conditions, particular solution
18. How do you verify a solution to a differential equation?
19. State and explain the differential equation for the continuous compounding of interest.
20. State and explain the differential equation for Newton's law of cooling.

REVIEW EXERCISES

• *Continuous Money Flow*

For Exercises 1–4, assume revenues flow into a fund at the rate of $f(x)$ dollars per year, where x denotes time in years.
a) Find the total money flow (no interest) at the end of 4 years.
b) If the money flow, over the time interval $0 \le x \le 4$, is compounded continuously at 8%, find its present value.
c) If the money flow, over the time interval $0 \le x \le 4$, is compounded continuously at 8%, find its future value.

1. $f(x) = 5000$ 　　　　　　　　　**2.** $f(x) = 2000x$
3. $f(x) = 2000e^{0.10x}$ 　　　　　　　**4.** $f(x) = 4000 - 40x$

• *Improper Integrals*

Evaluate whichever of the following improper integrals converge.

5. $\displaystyle\int_1^\infty (1/x)\, dx$ 　　　　　　　**6.** $\displaystyle\int_1^\infty (1/x^2)\, dx$

7. $\displaystyle\int_0^\infty e^{-x}\, dx$ 　　　　　　　**8.** $\displaystyle\int_9^\infty x^{-1/2}\, dx$

9. $\displaystyle\int_1^\infty [1/(x + 4)^2]\, dx$ 　　　　**10.** $\displaystyle\int_0^\infty [1/(x + 9)^3]\, dx$

11. *Perpetual flow: Endowment fund.* A college wishes to establish an endowment fund to provide $100,000 annually. If the fund is to be invested at 8% compounded continuously, how much should be provided now to set up the fund?

• *Probability Distributions*

12. *Uniform distribution.* A random variable, x, is uniformly distributed over the interval $4 \le x \le 9$.
a) Graph its density function.
b) Determine $P(4 \le x \le 7)$ and shade the corresponding area on the graph.
13. *Uniform distribution.* At a given bus stop, a bus going to a certain destination appears every 20 minutes. The time (in minutes) a bus rider spends waiting at this bus stop is a random variable uniformly distributed over the interval $0 \le x \le 20$. If a bus rider arrives at this bus stop, find the probability that she (he) must wait
a) At least 15 minutes. 　　　　　　b) At most 12 minutes.
c) Between 5 and 17 minutes. 　　　　d) Between 6 and 15 minutes.
14. *Exponential distribution.* A random variable x is exponentially distributed, with $k = 0.25$. Graph the density function and find
a) $P(0 < x < 2)$ 　　　　　　　　b) $P(1 < x < 3)$
c) $P(x > 2)$ 　　　　　　　　　　d) $P(x > 1)$

15. *Service time: Exponential distribution.* The time (in minutes) it takes to change an automobile's oil at a service center is exponentially distributed, with $k = 0.10$. Find the probability that an oil change takes
    a) At most 5 minutes.
    b) At most 12 minutes.
    c) At least 8 minutes.
    d) At least 10 minutes.

16. Given the probability distribution with density function

$$f(x) = 4 - 8x \qquad (0 \leq x \leq 0.5)$$

    a) Graph $f(x)$.
    b) Verify that the total area is 1.
    c) Find $P(0 < x < 0.3)$.
    d) Find $P(0 < x < 0.4)$.

• *Average Value of a Function*

For Exercises 17 and 18, find the average value of the function over the indicated interval.

17. $f(x) = -5x + 20, \ 0 \leq x \leq 4$

18. $f(x) = -x^2 + 25, \ -5 \leq x \leq 5$

19. *Revenue.* The sales revenue gained from selling x units of some product is given by

$$R(x) = -6x^2 + 240x$$

    If $0 \leq x \leq 20$, find the average sales revenue.

20. *Compound amount.* A sum of \$40,000 is deposited in a bank that pays interest at 9% compounded continuously. Find the average value of this bank account
    a) Over the next 3 years.
    b) Over the next 6 years.

• *Volume*

For Exercises 21–23, find the volume of the solid of revolution formed by rotating about the x-axis the region between the graph of the given function and the x-axis over the indicated interval. Illustrate graphically.

21. $y = 6x^2$ from $x = 0$ to $x = 4$
22. $y = 1/x^2$ from $x = 1$ to $x = 3$
23. $y = -x^2 + 4$ from $x = 0$ to $x = 2$
24. *Sphere.* $y = \sqrt{25 - x^2}$ from $x = -5$ to $x = 5$

• *Trapezoidal Rule*

For each of Exercises 25 and 26, use the trapezoidal rule with the indicated value of n to approximate the value of the definite integral.

25. $\displaystyle \int_1^5 (1/x^3) \, dx, \ n = 8$

26. $\displaystyle \int_0^2 e^{-0.5x} \, dx, \ n = 4$

27. Determine the error for Exercise 25.

28. Determine n so that the error in approximating $\int_0^5 (x + 4)^{-2} \, dx$ is at most 0.0001.

• *Simpson's Rule*

For Exercises 29 and 30, use Simpson's rule with the indicated value of n to approximate the value of the definite integral.

29. $\int_1^4 (x^2 + 5)^{1/2}\, dx,\ n = 6$ **30.** $\int_1^5 \ln x\, dx,\ n = 8$

31. Determine the error for Exercise 30.

32. Determine n so that the error in approximating $\int_1^3 x^{-3}\, dx$ is at most 0.0001.

• *Differential Equations*

For Exercises 33–36, solve the differential equation by the method of separation of variables, and verify that the general solution satisfies the differential equation.

33. $dy/dx = x^2 y^4$ **34.** $y^4 \dfrac{dy}{dx} - 6x^3 = 0$

35. $\dfrac{dy}{dx} - y^3 e^x = 0$ **36.** $\dfrac{dy}{dx} = \dfrac{4}{x + xy}$

Continuous compounding. For Exercises 37 and 38, assume interest is compounded continuously at each of the following rates. S denotes the value (in dollars) of an investment at time t (in years).
a) Write the differential equation for the rate of change of S.
b) Write the solution to the differential equation of part a.
c) If the initial amount invested is $8000, find its value after 6 years.

37. Annual rate $= 12\%$ **38.** Annual rate $= 9.5\%$

39. *Asset growth.* The growth rate of a company's annual profits is directly proportional to the amount of annual profit, P.
   a) Write the differential equation expressing this relationship.
   b) Solve the differential equation of part a.
   c) Find a particular solution given the following initial conditions:
      1. At $t = 0$, $P = \$4{,}000{,}000$.
      2. At $t = 4$, $P = \$28{,}000{,}000$.

40. *Worker productivity.* The rate, dy/dt, at which a worker produces a new product is related to the worker's daily production, y, by the differential equation

$$dy/dt = 0.4(200 - y)$$

where t denotes the number of days the worker has been working on the product.
   a) Solve the above differential equation.
   b) Find a particular solution given the initial condition that the worker produced 50 units during the first day ($t = 0$) working on this product.
   c) Find the number of units produced by this worker during the 21st day ($t = 20$).

8

FUNCTIONS OF SEVERAL VARIABLES

Introductory Application

Cost, Revenue, and Profit Functions: Two Products

A firm manufactures two competing brands of a given product. Let p_1 and p_2 be the case selling prices (in dollars) of brands 1 and 2, respectively. If x_1 cases of brand 1 and x_2 cases of brand 2 are demanded by the market, then the relationships between the unit (case) selling prices and the demands for the competing brands are given by the equations

$$x_1 = 80 - 2p_1 + p_2$$
$$x_2 = 30 + p_1 - p_2$$

If $40 and $30 are the unit case costs of brands 1 and 2, respectively, determine the case selling prices, p_1 and p_2, that maximize total profit, $P(p_1, p_2)$.

This problem is solved in Example 8-24.

8-1 • FUNCTIONS OF SEVERAL VARIABLES

A function such as

$$y = f(x) = x^3 + \frac{4}{x} + 17$$

has dependent variable y and independent variable x. Since there is only one independent variable, $f(x)$ is called a **function of one variable.** If a function has two independent variables—say, x and y—it is called a **function of two variables** and is usually denoted by $f(x, y)$. If a function has three independent variables—say, x, y, and w—it is called a **function of three variables** and may be denoted by $f(x, y, w)$. In general, functions of more than one variable are called **multivariate functions.**

As a specific example, we consider a company producing metal tanks. It has been determined that the daily production cost, z, is dependent on the daily number of tanks produced, x, and the daily number of person-hours used, y. These quantities are related by the multivariate function

$$z = f(x, y) = x^2 - 8x + y^2 - 12y + 1500$$

If, during a given day, the company produced $x = 2$ tanks and used $y = 5$ person-hours of labor, then the daily production cost is

$$z = f(2, 5) = 2^2 - 8(2) + 5^2 - 12(5) + 1500 = \$1453$$

A function of two variables, $z = f(x, y)$, associates a single value of z with each ordered pair of real numbers, (x, y). The set of all such ordered pairs (x, y) is the **domain** of f, and the set of all such possible values of z is called the **range** of f. If the domain of a function of two variables, $z = f(x, y)$, is not specified, then it is the set of all ordered pairs (x, y) for which the function is defined.

• EXAMPLE 8-1

Consider the function defined by

$$z = f(x, y) = \frac{x^2 + y^2 + 8}{(x - 4)(y + 3)}$$

a) Compute $f(2, 5)$.
b) Specify the domain of f.

Solutions

a) $f(2, 5) = \dfrac{(2)^2 + (5)^2 + 8}{(2 - 4)(5 + 3)}$

$= \dfrac{37}{-16} = -\dfrac{37}{16}$

Hence, the function f associates $-37/16$ with the ordered pair $(2, 5)$.

b) Since the domain of f is not specified, it is the set of all ordered pairs (x, y) for which f is defined. The function f is defined for all ordered pairs (x, y) such that $x \neq 4$ and $y \neq -3$.

• **EXAMPLE 8-2   Wind Power.** _____

According to Betz's Law, the available power in wind, P (in kilowatts), for a windmill with a rotor diameter of D feet and wind speed of V miles per hour (mph) is given by

$$P(D, V) = 0.0000023694D^2V^3$$

If the wind speed is 20 mph, find the power produced by a windmill with a rotor diameter of 10 feet.

Solution

Our answer is given by $P(10, 20)$. Hence,

$$P(10, 20) = 0.0000023694(10^2)(20^3)$$
$$= 1.8955 \text{ kilowatts}$$

The concepts of the preceding paragraphs of this section can be generalized to functions of n variables, where n is a whole number. Specifically, if, with each ordered n-tuple of real numbers $(x_1, x_2, \ldots, x_n)$, the equation $z = f(x_1, x_2, \ldots, x_n)$ associates a unique value of z, then f is called a function of $x_1, x_2, \ldots,$ and x_n. The set of all such ordered n-tuples is the *domain* of f, and the set of all such values of z is called the *range* of f. If the domain of a function of n variables is not specified, then it is the set of all ordered n-tuples $(x_1, x_2, \ldots, x_n)$ for which f is defined.

• **EXAMPLE 8-3** _____

Given

$$z = f(x_1, x_2, x_3) = \frac{x_1^2 - 4x_1x_3 + x_2^3 + 8}{(x_1 - 4)(x_3 + 6)}$$

a)   Compute $f(2, 3, 1)$.
b)   Specify the domain of f.

Solutions

a) $f(2, 3, 1) = \dfrac{(2)^2 - 4(2)(1) + (3)^3 + 8}{(2 - 4)(1 + 6)}$

$= \dfrac{31}{-14} = -\dfrac{31}{14}$

The function f associates $-31/14$ with the ordered triple $(2, 3, 1)$.
b)   Since the domain of f is not specified, it is the set of all ordered triples of real numbers (x_1, x_2, x_3) for which f is defined. The function f is defined for all ordered triples (x_1, x_2, x_3) such that $x_1 \neq 4$ and $x_3 \neq -6$.

Revenue Function: Several Products

The sales revenue gained from selling n products is given by

$$R = x_1p_1 + x_2p_2 + \ldots + x_np_n$$

where

$x_i =$ the number of units sold of the ith product
$p_i =$ unit price of the ith product

• EXAMPLE 8-4   Revenue Function: Two Products. _____

Find the equation defining the revenue function, $R(p_1, p_2)$, where the numbers of units sold and the unit prices are related by the equations

$$x_1 = 60 - 2p_1 + p_2$$
$$x_2 = 20 + p_1 - 2p_2$$

Solution

The revenue is given by the equation

$$R = x_1 p_1 + x_2 p_2$$

Substituting the above equations for x_1 and x_2 into the above equation gives

$$R(p_1, p_2) = \overbrace{(60 - 2p_1 + p_2)}^{x_1} p_1 + \overbrace{(20 + p_1 - 2p_2)}^{x_2} p_2$$
$$= -2p_1^2 - 2p_2^2 + 2p_1 p_2 + 60p_1 + 20p_2$$

Note that the revenue function, $R(p_1, p_2)$, gives revenue in terms of the unit prices of the products.

Sales revenue can also be given in terms of x_1 and x_2, as we show in Example 8-5.

• EXAMPLE 8-5   Revenue Function: Two Products. _____

Find the equation defining the revenue function, $R(x_1, x_2)$, where the numbers of units sold and the unit prices are related by the equations

$$p_1 = 59 - 4x_1 - 3x_2$$
$$p_2 = 78 - 3x_1 - 6x_2$$

Note that prices are given in terms of number of units sold.

Solution

The revenue is given by the equation

$$R = x_1 p_1 + x_2 p_2$$

Substituting the equations for p_1 and p_2 into the above equation for revenue gives

$$R(x_1, x_2) = x_1 \overbrace{(59 - 4x_1 - 3x_2)}^{p_1} + x_2 \overbrace{(78 - 3x_1 - 6x_2)}^{p_2}$$
$$= -4x_1^2 - 6x_2^2 - 6x_1 x_2 + 59x_1 + 78x_2$$

Note that the revenue function, $R(x_1, x_2)$, gives revenue in terms of the numbers of units sold of both products.

Cobb-Douglas Production Function

Economists frequently use a model that gives production as a function of labor and capital. One such model is the *Cobb-Douglas production function* which is given by

$$f(x, y) = Cx^a y^{1-a}$$

where C and a are constants with $0 < a < 1$, x = number of units of labor, and y = number of units of capital.

We now consider the following examples.

• **EXAMPLE 8-6** _____

For some company, the number of units produced when using x units of labor and y units of capital is given by the production function

$$f(x, y) = 80x^{1/4}y^{3/4}$$

Find the number of units produced when 625 units of labor and 81 units of capital are used.

Solution

$$f(625, 81) = 80(625)^{1/4}(81)^{3/4}$$
$$= 80(5)(27) = 10,800 \qquad \text{Production}$$

• **EXAMPLE 8-7** _____

Show, in general, for the Cobb-Douglas production function that the doubling of both labor and capital results in the doubling of production.

Solution

We begin with the equation

$$f(x, y) = Cx^ay^{1-a}$$

and replace x with $2x$ and y with $2y$ to obtain

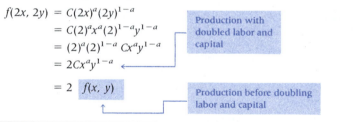

$$f(2x, 2y) = C(2x)^a(2y)^{1-a}$$
$$= C(2)^ax^a(2)^{1-a}y^{1-a} \qquad \text{Production with doubled labor and capital}$$
$$= (2)^a(2)^{1-a}\,Cx^ay^{1-a}$$
$$= 2Cx^ay^{1-a}$$

$$= 2\;\boxed{f(x, y)} \qquad \text{Production before doubling labor and capital}$$

Graphs of Functions of Two Variables

A function of two variables is graphed in a **three-dimensional coordinate system.** Such a system consists of three mutually perpendicular real number lines intersecting at the origin of each line, as illustrated in Figure 8-1. The two horizontal number lines are called the x-axis and the y-axis; the vertical number line is called the z-axis. Each point in a three-dimensional coordinate system is denoted by an ordered triple of real numbers (x, y, z), which locates its position relative to the three axes. The origin is denoted by the ordered triple $(0, 0, 0)$. For example, looking at Figure 8-1, the ordered triple $(2, 1, 5)$ is associated with the point that is plotted as follows:

1. Starting at the origin, move 2 units in the positive direction along the x-axis.

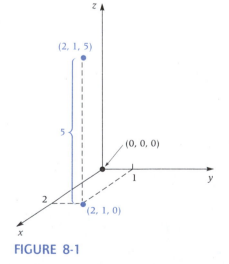

FIGURE 8-1

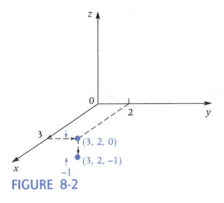

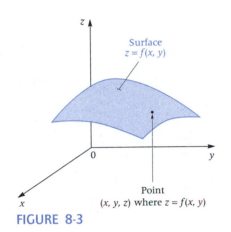

2. Then move 1 unit horizontally in the positive direction parallel to the *y*-axis.

3. Last, move 5 units vertically in the positive direction parallel to the *z*-axis.

• **EXAMPLE 8-8** _____

Plot the point given by $(3, 2, -1)$ in the three-dimensional coordinate system.

Solution

Observing Figure 8-2, we begin at the origin, move 3 units in the positive direction along the *x*-axis, then 2 units horizontally in the positive direction parallel to the *y*-axis, and, finally, 1 unit vertically in the negative direction parallel to the *z*-axis.

_____ •

The graph of a function of two variables

$$z = f(x, y)$$

consists of a set of points (x, y, z) such that the variables are related by the equation $z = f(x, y)$. In general, the set of such points constitutes a surface in three-dimensional space, as is illustrated in Figure 8-3.

Figure 8-4 on page 492 gives the graphs of some specific functions of two variables.

The plane of Figure 8-4(a) consists of all points (x, y, z) such that $x = x_0$, where x_0 is a constant; the plane of Figure 8-4(b) consists of all points (x, y, z) such that $y = y_0$, where y_0 is a constant.

The plane of Figure 8-4(c) consists of all points (x, y, z) such that $2x + 4y + z = 12$. The *x*-intercept is determined by setting both *y* and *z* equal to 0 and solving the resulting equation for *x*; the *y*-intercept is determined by setting both *x* and *z* equal to zero and solving the resulting equation for *y*; the *z*-intercept is determined by setting both *x* and *y* equal to zero and solving the resulting equation for *z*. The *xz*-trace is the intersection of the plane with the *xz*-plane; its equation is determined by setting $y = 0$ in the original equation. Thus, the *xz*-trace is the straight line $2x + z = 12$. The *xy*- and *yz*-traces are defined and obtained in a similar manner.

The plane of Figure 8-4(d) consists of all points (x, y, z) such that $5x + 3y = 30$. The surface of Figure 8-4(e) consists of all points (x, y, z) such that $z = x^2$. Note that the *xz*-trace of this surface is the parabola $z = x^2$.

The surface of Figure 8-4(f) consists of all points (x, y, z) such that $z = x^2 + y^2$. Here the *xz*-trace (set $y = 0$) is the parabola $z = x^2$, and the *yz*-trace (set $x = 0$) is the parabola $z = y^2$.

The surface of Figure 8-4(g) consists of all points (x, y, z) such that $z = y^2 - x^2$. The *yz*-trace (set $x = 0$) is the parabola $z = y^2$, and the *xz*-trace (set $y = 0$) is the parabola $z = -x^2$.

FIGURE 8-2

FIGURE 8-3

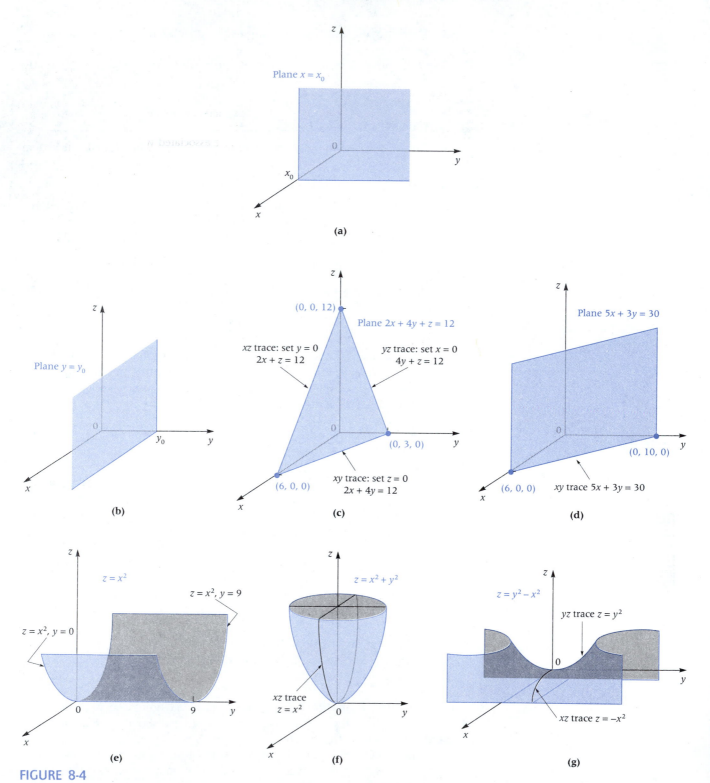

FIGURE 8-4

Exercises 8-1

1. If $f(x, y) = 3x^2 - 4y + 6xy + y^2 + 5$, then compute each of the following:
   a) $f(0, 1)$ b) $f(2, 5)$ c) $f(1, 0)$
2. If $f(x, y) = 3x^4 - 2xy + y^2 - 8x + 1$, then compute each of the following:
   a) $f(1, 3)$ b) $f(-2, 1)$ c) $f(0, -1)$
3. If $z = x^3 - y^4/4$, then find the value of z associated with $x = 2$ and $y = 1$.
4. If $H = P^2 - 5PT^2 - 4/T$, then find the value of H associated with $P = 3$ and $T = 2$.
5. If $z = f(x_1, x_2, x_3) = x_1^2 - 4x_1x_3 + x_3^2 + x_2x_3$, then
   a) z is a function of how many variables?
   b) Compute $f(2, 1, -3)$.
   c) Compute $f(-2, -1, 4)$.
6. If $K = f(H, T, P) = H^2 - 3TP + HP^3 + 5$, then
   a) K is a function of how many variables?
   b) Compute $f(4, -2, 3)$
   c) Compute $f(-3, -1, 5)$.
7. If $g(x_1, x_2, x_3, x_4) = x_1^2 + x_2x_3 + x_3^2x_4^3 + 5$, then
   a) g is a function of how many variables?
   b) Compute $g(1, -1, 2, -3)$.
   c) Compute $g(-1, 0, -3, 4)$.
8. If $f(x, y) = (3x^2 - 2xy + 5y)/(x - 2)(x + 4)$, then specify the domain of f.
9. If $g(x, y) = 4x^2 + 5x^3/y + 8/(x - 2)$, then specify the domain of g.
10. If $f(x_1 x_2, x_3) = (x_1^2 + 5x_2x_3)/(x_2 - 4)$, then specify the domain of f.
11. If $f(x, y) = (x^3 - 4xy + y^2)/\sqrt{x - 3}$, then specify the domain of f.
12. If $f(x, y) = (x^2 + 4xy + 6y)/\sqrt{x^2 - 25}$, then specify the domain of f.
13. If $f(x, y) = \ln(x/y)$, then specify the domain of f.

Plot each of the following points in a three-dimensional coordinate system.

14. $(5, 3, 9)$ 15. $(-1, 5, 2)$ 16. $(2, -3, -5)$
17. $(3, 2, -4)$ 18. $(4, 6, 9)$ 19. $(-2, 1, 8)$

Applications

20. *Revenue function: Two products.*
    a) Find the equation defining the revenue function, $R(p_1, p_2)$, where the numbers of units sold and the unit prices are related by the equations

    $$x_1 = 80 - p_1 - 2p_2$$
    $$x_2 = 25 + 2p_1 - p_2$$

    b) Find the revenue if the unit prices of the first and second products are $5 and $8, respectively.

21. *Revenue function: Two products.*
    a) Find the equation defining the revenue function, $R(x_1, x_2)$, where the numbers of units sold and the unit prices are related by the equations

    $$p_1 = 90 - 4x_1 - 3x_2$$
    $$p_2 = 60 - 2x_1 - 5x_2$$

    b) Find the revenue gained from selling 3 and 5 units of products 1 and 2, respectively.

22. *Cobb-Douglas production function.* For some firm, the number of units produced when using x units of labor and y units of capital is given by the production function

$$f(x, y) = 100x^{1/5}y^{4/5}$$

Find the number of units produced when 243 units of labor and 32 units of capital are used.

23. *Cost function: Two products.* The total cost (in thousands of dollars) of producing x thousand units of product 1 and y thousand units of product 2 is given by

$$C(x, y) = x^2 + 4y^2 - 2xy + 8x + 6y + 3$$

Find the total cost of producing 3 thousand units of product 1 and 5 thousand units of product 2.

24. *Revenue, cost, profit functions: Two products.* Consider the following revenue and cost functions for x and y units of products 1 and 2, respectively.

$$R(x, y) = -20x^2 - 10y^2 + 200x + 100y + 400xy + 800$$
$$C(x, y) = 10x + 5y + 100$$

a) Using the formula

$$\text{profit} = \text{revenue} - \text{cost}$$

find the equation defining the profit function.

b) Find the profit from selling 10 and 20 units of products 1 and 2, respectively.

25. *Optimum level of energy conservation.* The effectiveness of insulation in resisting heat loss is expressed by a number called its **R-value.** Fiberglass batts of insulation that are 3½ inches thick typically have an R-value of 11. Fiberglass batts of insulation that are 6 inches thick have an R-value of 19. A formula for determining the optimum R-value needed for insulating a building is

$$F(e, i, c) = \sqrt{\frac{1 + e}{c(1 + i)}}$$

where e is the fuel price growth rate (compounded annually), i is the current rate at which money earns interest (compounded annually), and c is the cost (in dollars) per square foot of insulation per unit of R.

a) If fuel prices are increasing at 15% per year (i.e., $e = 0.15$) and money currently earns interest at 10% per year (i.e., $i = 0.10$), compute the optimum R-value for insulation that costs \$0.03 per square foot per unit of R.

b) If fuel prices are increasing at 10% per year (i.e., $e = 0.10$) and money currently earns interest at 12% per year (i.e., $i = 0.12$), compute the optimum R-value for insulation that costs \$0.03 per square foot per unit of R.

8-2 • PARTIAL DERIVATIVES

Recall the company producing metal tanks in Section 8-1. It has been determined that the daily production cost, z, is dependent on the daily number of tanks produced, x, and the daily number of person-hours used, y. These quantities are related by the multivariate function

$$z = f(x, y) = x^2 - 8x + y^2 - 12y + 1500$$

We now consider finding the *instantaneous rate of change of z with respect to* x (i.e., the instantaneous rate of change of cost with respect to the number of tanks produced). This is expressed by finding the derivative of z with respect to x. However, since $z = f(x, y)$ has two independent variables, the derivative of z with respect to one of the independent variables is called a **partial derivative,** or simply a **partial.** Specifically, the derivative of z with respect to x is called the **partial derivative of z with respect to** x and is denoted by any of the following:

$$\frac{\partial z}{\partial x} \qquad f_x(x, y) \qquad f_x$$

The partial derivative of z with respect to x is found by treating x as a variable and the remaining independent variables (in this example, y) as constants and applying the differentiation rules of Chapter 2. Thus, if

$$z = f(x, y) = x^2 - 8x + y^2 - 12y + 1500 \qquad \text{Color screen indicates the variable.}$$

then

$$f_x(x, y) = 2x - 8$$

Similarly, the *instantaneous rate of change of z with respect to* y is expressed by the **partial derivative of z with respect to** **y** and is denoted by any of the following:

$$\frac{\partial z}{\partial y} \qquad f_y(x, y) \qquad f_y$$

The partial derivative of z with respect to y is found by treating y as a variable and the remaining independent variables (in this example, x) as constants. Hence, if

$$z = f(x, y) = x^2 - 8x + y^2 - 12y + 1500 \qquad \text{Color screen indicates the variable.}$$

then

$$f_y(x, y) = 2y - 12$$

If we wish to evaluate $\partial z/\partial x$ at $x = 6$ and $y = 10$, this is denoted by any of the following notations.

$$\frac{\partial z}{\partial x}\bigg|_{\substack{x = 6 \\ y = 10}} \qquad \frac{\partial z}{\partial x}\bigg|_{(6, 10)} \qquad f_x(6, 10)$$

Since $\partial z/\partial x$ or $f_x(x, y)$ is given by

$$f_x(x, y) = 2x - 8$$

then

$$\frac{\partial z}{\partial x}\bigg|_{(6, 10)} \qquad \text{or} \qquad f_x(6, 10)$$

is given by

$$f_x(6, 10) = 2(6) - 8$$
$$= 4$$

Thus, when $x = 6$ tanks are being produced daily and $y = 10$ person-hours are being used daily, the *instantaneous rate of change of cost with respect to the number of tanks produced* (i.e., the *marginal cost*) is \$4. In other words, assuming the number of person-hours used daily does not change, an additional tank costs approximately \$4.

Analogously, if we wish to evaluate $\partial z / \partial y$ at $x = 6$ and $y = 10$, this is denoted by any of the following notations:

$$\left.\frac{\partial z}{\partial y}\right| \begin{array}{l} x = 6 \\ y = 10 \end{array} \qquad \left.\frac{\partial z}{\partial y}\right|(6, 10) \qquad f_y(6, 10)$$

Since $\partial z / \partial y$ or $f_y(x, y)$ is given by

$$f_y(x, y) = 2y - 12$$

then

$$\left.\frac{\partial z}{\partial y}\right|(6, 10) \qquad \text{or} \qquad f_y(6, 10)$$

is given by

$$f_y(6, 10) = 2(10) - 12$$
$$= 8$$

Thus, when $x = 6$ tanks are being produced daily and $y = 10$ person-hours are being used daily, an additional person-hour costs approximately \$8. This assumes the number of tanks produced daily remains fixed.

We summarize as follows.

Partial Derivatives

If $z = f(x, y)$, then

1. The **partial derivative of z with respect to x** is

$$f_x = \frac{\partial z}{\partial x} = \text{instantaneous rate of change of } z \text{ with respect to } x$$

   assuming that y is held constant. To find f_x, use the derivative rules (i.e., the power rule, product rule, quotient rule, etc.) of Chapters 2 and 5, while treating y as a constant.

2. The **partial derivative of z with respect to y** is

$$f_y = \frac{\partial z}{\partial y} = \text{instantaneous rate of change of } z \text{ with respect to } y$$

   assuming that x is held constant. To find f_y, use the derivative rules (i.e., the power rule, product rule, quotient rule, etc.) of Chapters 2 and 5, while treating x as a constant.

• EXAMPLE 8-9

If $z = f(x, y) = 3x^2 + 4x^2y^3 - 6x + 8y - 9$, then find each of the following:

a) f_x **b)** $f_x(1, 2)$ **c)** f_y **d)** $f_y(2, -1)$

Solutions

a) We find f_x from

$$f(x, y) = 3\;\boxed{x^2}\; + 4\;\boxed{x^2}\;y^3 - 6\;\boxed{x}\; + 8y - 9 \qquad \text{Color screens indicate the variable.}$$

by using the power rule, treating x as a variable and y as a constant. Hence,

$$f_x(x, y) = 6x + 8xy^3 - 6$$

> Note that for the term $4x^2y^3$, $4y^3$ is treated as the constant coefficient of x^2. Thus, the derivative with respect to x is $4y^3(2x) = 8xy^3$.

b) $f_x(1, 2) = 6(1) + 8(1)(2)^3 - 6$
$$= 64$$

c) We find f_y from

$$f(x, y) = 3x^2 + 4x^2\;\boxed{y^3}\; - 6x + 8\;\boxed{y}\; - 9 \qquad \text{Color screens indicate the variable.}$$

by using the power rule, treating y as a variable and x as a constant. Hence,

$$f_y(x, y) = 12x^2y^2 + 8$$

> Note that for the term $4x^2y^3$, $4x^2$ is treated as the constant coefficient of y^3. Thus, the derivative with respect to y is $4x^2(3y^2) = 12x^2y^2$.

d) $f_y(2, -1) = 12(2)^2(-1)^2 + 8$
$$= 56$$

Graphical Interpretation of Partial Derivatives

Up to this point, we have discussed the computation and application of partial derivatives. We now focus on the graphical interpretation of partial derivatives.

Consider a function of two variables defined by

$$z = f(x, y)$$

and assume its graph is the surface in Figure 8-5. Since $\partial z/\partial x$ or $f_x(x, y)$ is the instantaneous rate of change of z with respect to x, while y is held constant, then $\partial z/\partial x$ or $f_x(x, y)$ is formally defined as

$$f_x(x, y) = \lim_{\Delta x \to 0} \frac{f(x + \Delta x, y) - f(x, y)}{\Delta x} \qquad \text{Formal definition of } f_x$$

If we evaluate $f_x(x, y)$ at $x = x_0$ and $y = y_0$, where x_0 and y_0 are constant real numbers, then $f_x(x_0, y_0)$ gives the slope of the straight line tangent to the curve $z = f(x, y_0)$ on the graph of $f(x)$ at (x_0, y_0, z_0), where $z_0 = f(x_0, y_0)$, as illustrated in Figure 8-5. The curve $z = f(x, y_0)$ is the intersection of the plane $y = y_0$ and the surface $z = f(x, y)$, as shown in Figure 8-5.

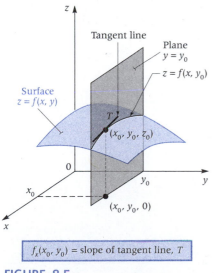

$f_x(x_0, y_0) = $ slope of tangent line, T

FIGURE 8-5

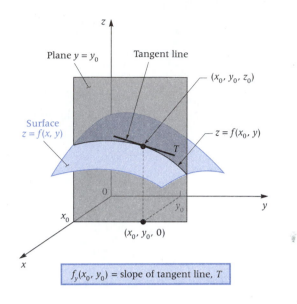

$$f_y(x_0, y_0) = \text{slope of tangent line, } T$$

FIGURE 8-6

Analagously, $\partial z/\partial y$ or $f_y(x, y)$ is defined as

$$f_y(x, y) = \lim_{\Delta y \to 0} \frac{f(x, y + \Delta y) - f(x, y)}{\Delta y} \qquad \text{Formal definition of } f_y$$

If we evaluate $f_y(x, y)$ at $x = x_0$ and $y = y_0$, where x_0 and y_0 are constant real numbers, then $f_y(x_0, y_0)$ gives the slope of the straight line tangent to the curve $z = f(x_0, y)$ on the graph of $f(x, y)$ at (x_0, y_0, z_0), where $z_0 = f(x_0, y_0)$, as illustrated in Figure 8-6. The curve $z = f(x_0, y)$ is the intersection of the plane $x = x_0$ and the surface $z = f(x, y)$, as shown in Figure 8-6.

We now give more examples of partial derivatives.

• **EXAMPLE 8-10** _____

If $f(x, y) = \ln (x^2 + y^2)$, find

a) f_x **b)** f_y

Solutions

Using the rule that the derivative of $\ln u$ is $1/u$ times the derivative of u, we let $u = x^2 + y^2$ and obtain the following:

$$
\begin{array}{cc}
\overset{\frac{1}{u}}{} & \overset{\frac{\partial u}{\partial x}}{}
\end{array}
$$

a) $f_x(x, y) = \dfrac{1}{x^2 + y^2} \ (2x) = \dfrac{2x}{x^2 + y^2}$

$$
\begin{array}{cc}
\overset{\frac{1}{u}}{} & \overset{\frac{\partial u}{\partial y}}{}
\end{array}
$$

b) $f_y(x, y) = \dfrac{1}{x^2 + y^2} \ (2y) = \dfrac{2y}{x^2 + y^2}$

• **EXAMPLE 8-11** _____

If $f(x, y) = e^{x^2 + y^3}$, find each of the following:

a) f_x **b)** f_y

Solutions

Using the rule that the derivative of e^u is e^u times the derivative of u, we let $u = x^2 + y^3$ and obtain the following:

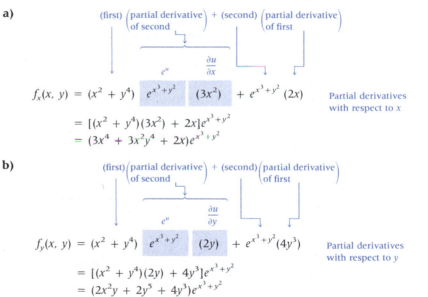

a) $\quad f_x(x, y) = \boxed{e^{x^2+y^3}} \; \boxed{(2x)} = 2xe^{x^2+y^3}$

b) $\quad f_y(x, y) = \boxed{e^{x^2+y^3}} \; \boxed{(3y^2)} = 3y^2e^{x^2+y^3}$

• **EXAMPLE 8-12** _____

If $f(x, y) = (x^2 + y^4)e^{x^3+y^2}$, find each of the following:

a) $\quad f_x$ b) $\quad f_y$

Solutions

Since the function $f(x, y)$ is a product of two functions, we must use the product rule. Also, within the product rule, we must use the rule that the derivative of e^u is e^u times the derivative of u. Of course, all derivatives are partial derivatives.

a)

(first) $\left(\begin{array}{c}\text{partial derivative}\\\text{of second}\end{array}\right)$ + (second) $\left(\begin{array}{c}\text{partial derivative}\\\text{of first}\end{array}\right)$

$$f_x(x, y) = (x^2 + y^4) \; \boxed{e^{x^3+y^2}} \; \boxed{(3x^2)} + e^{x^3+y^2}\,(2x) \qquad \text{Partial derivatives with respect to } x$$

$$= [(x^2 + y^4)(3x^2) + 2x]e^{x^3+y^2}$$

$$= (3x^4 + 3x^2y^4 + 2x)e^{x^3+y^2}$$

b)

(first) $\left(\begin{array}{c}\text{partial derivative}\\\text{of second}\end{array}\right)$ + (second) $\left(\begin{array}{c}\text{partial derivative}\\\text{of first}\end{array}\right)$

$$f_y(x, y) = (x^2 + y^4) \; \boxed{e^{x^3+y^2}} \; \boxed{(2y)} + e^{x^3+y^2}(4y^3) \qquad \text{Partial derivatives with respect to } y$$

$$= [(x^2 + y^4)(2y) + 4y^3]e^{x^3+y^2}$$

$$= (2x^2y + 2y^5 + 4y^3)e^{x^3+y^2}$$

Applications

• **EXAMPLE 8-13**

The revenue, z, derived from selling x calculators and y adding machines is given by the function

$$z = f(x, y) = -x^2 + 8x - 2y^2 + 6y + 2xy + 50$$

a) At a sales level of $x = 4$ calculators and $y = 3$ adding machines, find the marginal revenue resulting from the sale of 1 additional calculator.

b) At a sales level of $x = 4$ calculators and $y = 3$ adding machines, find the marginal revenue resulting from the sale of 1 additional adding machine.

Solutions

a) Since the marginal revenue resulting from the sale of 1 additional calculator is defined as the instantaneous rate of change of z with respect to x, we calculate f_x by treating x as a variable and y as a constant. We thus obtain

$$f_x(x, y) = -2x + 8 + 2y$$
$$f_x(4, 3) = -2(4) + 8 + 2(3) = 6 \qquad \text{Marginal Revenue}$$

Therefore, at $x = 4$ and $y = 3$, sales revenue is increasing at the rate of approximately $6 per calculator sold. Hence, the *marginal revenue* is $6.

b) Since the marginal revenue resulting from the sale of 1 additional adding machine is defined as the instantaneous rate of change of z with respect to y, we calculate f_y by treating y as a variable and x as a constant. Here we get

$$f_y(x, y) = -4y + 6 + 2x$$
$$f_y(4, 3) = -4(3) + 6 + 2(4) = 2 \qquad \text{Marginal Revenue}$$

Thus, at $x = 4$ and $y = 3$, sales revenue is increasing at the rate of approximately $2 per adding machine. Hence, the *marginal revenue* is $2.

Cobb-Douglas Production Function

As stated in Section 8-1 economists frequently use a model that gives production as a function of labor and capital. One such model is the Cobb-Douglas production function, which is given by

$$f(x, y) = Cx^a y^{1-a}$$

where C is a positive constant and $0 < a < 1$. Here $f(x, y)$ denotes the number of units produced using x units of labor and y units of capital. The partial derivatives are interpreted below.

$$f_x = \text{marginal productivity of labor}$$
$$f_y = \text{marginal productivity of capital}$$

We now consider the following example.

• **EXAMPLE 8-14** _____

For some firm, the number of units produced when using x units of labor and y units of capital is given by the production function

$$f(x, y) = 80x^{1/4}y^{3/4}$$

a) Find the equations for both marginal productivities.
b) Evaluate and interpret the results of part a when 625 units of labor and 81 units of capital are used.

Solutions

a) Equations for marginal productivities:

$$f_x(x, y) = 80\left(\frac{1}{4}\right)x^{-3/4}y^{3/4} = 20x^{-3/4}y^{3/4} \qquad \text{Labor}$$

$$f_y(x, y) = 80x^{1/4}\left(\frac{3}{4}\right)y^{-1/4} = 60x^{1/4}y^{-1/4} \qquad \text{Capital}$$

b)
$$f_x(625, 81) = 60(625)^{-3/4}(81)^{3/4}$$

$$= 60\left(\frac{1}{125}\right)(27) = 12.96 \qquad \text{Marginal Productivity of Labor}$$

Thus, when 625 units of labor and 81 units of capital are used, 1 more unit of labor results in approximately 12.96 more units of production.

$$f_y(625, 81) = 60(625)^{1/4}(81)^{-1/4}$$

$$= 60(5)\left(\frac{1}{3}\right) = 100 \qquad \text{Marginal Productivity of Capital}$$

Thus, when 625 units of labor and 81 units of capital are used, 1 more unit of capital results in approximately 100 more units of production.

Second Partial Derivatives

The partial derivative of a partial derivative is called a **second partial derivative,** or simply a **second partial.** Specifically, if $z = f(x, y)$, then there are four second partials:

1. The partial derivative of $\partial z/\partial x$ with respect to x, or

$$\frac{\partial}{\partial x}\left(\frac{\partial z}{\partial x}\right)$$

This is denoted by any of the following:

Take the first partial with respect to x. Then take the partial of that result again with respect to x.

$$\frac{\partial^2 z}{\partial x^2} \qquad f_{xx}(x, y) \qquad f_{xx}$$

2. The partial derivative of $\partial z/\partial y$ with respect to y, or

$$\frac{\partial}{\partial y}\left(\frac{\partial y}{\partial y}\right)$$

This is denoted by any of the following:

Take the first partial with respect to y. Then take the partial of that result again with respect to y.

$$\frac{\partial^2 z}{\partial y^2} \qquad f_{yy}(x, y) \qquad f_{yy}$$

3. The partial derivative of $\partial z/\partial y$ with respect to x, or

$$\frac{\partial}{\partial x}\left(\frac{\partial z}{\partial y}\right)$$

This is denoted by any of the following:

Take the first partial with respect to y. Then take the partial of that result with respect to x.

$$\frac{\partial^2 z}{\partial x \partial y} \qquad f_{yx}(x, y) \qquad f_{yx}$$

4. The partial derivative of $\partial z/\partial x$ with respect to y, or

$$\frac{\partial}{\partial y}\left(\frac{\partial z}{\partial x}\right)$$

This is denoted by any of the following:

Take the first partial with respect to x. Then take the partial of that result with respect to y.

$$\frac{\partial^2 z}{\partial y \partial x} \qquad f_{xy}(x, y) \qquad f_{xy}$$

Therefore, if

$$z = f(x, y) = x^5 - y^4 + 3x^2y^6 + 18$$

then

$$f_x = 5x^4 + 6xy^6$$

The derivative of f_x with respect to x is f_{xx}. Thus, treating x as a variable and y as a constant, we differentiate f_x with respect to x to obtain

$$f_{xx} = 20x^3 + 6y^6$$

The derivative of f_x with respect to y is f_{xy}. Returning to f_x, we treat y as a variable and x as a constant and differentiate f_x with respect to y to obtain

$$f_{xy} = 36xy^5$$

Returning to $z = f(x, y) = x^5 - y^4 + 3x^2y^6 + 18$, we calculate

$$f_y = -4y^3 + 18x^2y^5$$

The derivative of f_y with respect to y is f_{yy}. Treating x as a constant and y as a variable, we differentiate f_y with respect to y to obtain

$$f_{yy} = -12y^2 + 90x^2y^4$$

The derivative of f_y with respect to x is f_{yx}. Returning to f_y, we treat x as a variable and y as a constant and differentiate f_y with respect to x to obtain

$$f_{yx} = 36xy^5$$

Observe that $f_{xy} = f_{yx}$. This is always true if f_x, f_y, f_{xy}, and f_{yx} are all continuous. In this text, $f_{xy} = f_{yx}$ for all functions $z = f(x, y)$.

• **EXAMPLE 8-15** ──────────────────────────────

If $z = f(x, y) = 3x^2 + 4y^5 - 8x^3y^6 + 15$, calculate each of the following:

a) f_x b) f_{xx} c) $f_{xx}(1, 0)$ d) f_{xy}
e) f_y f) f_{yy} g) f_{yx} h) $f_{yx}(-1, 1)$

Solutions

a) $f_x = 6x - 24x^2y^6$
b) $f_{xx} = 6 - 48xy^6$
c) $f_{xx}(1, 0) = 6 - 48(1)(0)^6 = 6$
d) $f_{xy} = -144x^2y^5$
e) $f_y = 20y^4 - 48x^3y^5$
f) $f_{yy} = 80y^3 - 240x^3y^4$
g) $f_{yx} = -144x^2y^5$
h) $f_{yx}(-1, 1) = -144(-1)^2(1)^5 = -144$

Exercises 8-2

1. If $f(x, y) = 3x^2 + 4y^3 + 6xy - x^2y^3 + 5$, find each of the following:
  a) f_x b) f_y c) $f_x(1, -1)$ d) $f_y(2, 1)$

2. If $f(x, y) = 4x^2 - 2y^4 + 6x^2y^2 - xy + 3$, find each of the following:
  a) f_x b) f_y c) $f_x(-1, 2)$ d) $f_y(0, 2)$

3. If $z = x^3 + y^5 - 8xy + 2x^3y^2 + 11$, find each of the following:
  a) $\dfrac{\partial z}{\partial x}$ b) $\dfrac{\partial z}{\partial y}$

4. $f_x(x, y) = 5x^2 + 8y^4 - 2x^3y^6 + 7xy + 9$, find each of the following:
  a) $f_x(x, y)$ b) $f_y(x, y)$
  c) $f_x(1, 2)$ d) $f_y(0, 3)$

5. If $f(x, y) = 8x^3 - 2y^2 - 7x^5y^8 + 8xy^2 + y + 6$, find each of the following:
  a) $f_x(x, y)$ b) $f_y(x, y)$
  c) $f_x(1, 2)$ d) $f_y(1, 2)$

6. If $s = x^3 + 4y^2 + y^4 - xy + x^3y^2 + 18$, find each of the following:
  a) $\dfrac{\partial s}{\partial x}$ b) $\dfrac{\partial s}{\partial y}$

7. If $z = 4x^6 - 8x^3 - 7x + 6xy + 8y + x^3y^5$, find each of the following:
  a) $\dfrac{\partial z}{\partial x}$ b) $\dfrac{\partial z}{\partial y}$ c) $\dfrac{\partial^2 z}{\partial x^2}$
  d) $\dfrac{\partial^2 z}{\partial y^2}$ e) $\dfrac{\partial^2 z}{\partial x \partial y}$ f) $\dfrac{\partial^2 z}{\partial y \partial x}$

8. If $f(x, y) = 4x^2 - 8y^3 + 6x^5y^2 + 4x + 6y + 9$, find each of the following:
  a) $f_x(x, y)$ b) $f_y(x, y)$
  c) $f_x(2, 1)$ d) $f_y(0, 2)$
  e) $f_{xx}(x, y)$ f) $f_{yy}(x, y)$
  g) $f_{xx}(2, 1)$ h) $f_{yy}(1, 0)$
  i) $f_{xy}(x, y)$ j) $f_{yx}(x, y)$
  k) $f_{xy}(2, 3)$ l) $f_{yx}(2, 3)$

9. If $f(x, y) = 1000 - x^3 - y^2 + 4x^3y^6 + 8y$, find each of the following:
  a) f_x b) f_y c) f_{xx} d) f_{yy}
  e) f_{xy} f) f_{yx} g) $f_x(2, -1)$ h) $f_{yy}(1, 3)$

10. If $f(x, y) = \ln (x^3 + y^2)$, find each of the following:
  a) f_x b) f_y c) f_{xx} d) f_{yy}

11. If $z = x^3 e^{x^2 + y^2}$, find each of the following:
  a) $\dfrac{\partial z}{\partial x}$ b) $\dfrac{\partial z}{\partial y}$

12. If $z = \dfrac{x^3 + 4xy^2}{2x - 3y}$, find each of the following:
  a) $\dfrac{\partial z}{\partial x}$ b) $\dfrac{\partial z}{\partial y}$

13. If $f(x, y) = (x^3 + y^2)e^{2x + 3y + 5}$, find each of the following:
  a) $f_x(x, y)$ b) $f_y(x, y)$ c) $f_x(0, 1)$

14. If $f(x, y) = (x^2 + 2y^5) \cdot \ln (x^2 + 2y + y^3)$, find each of the following:
  a) f_x b) f_y c) $f_x(1, 0)$ d) $f_y(1, 0)$

Applications

15. *Cost.* The cost of producing x washers and y dryers is given by

$$C(x, y) = 40x + 200y + 10xy + 300$$

Presently, 50 washers and 90 dryers are being produced. Find the marginal cost of producing
a) 1 more washer.   b) 1 more dryer.

16. *Revenue.* The revenue derived from selling x toasters and y broilers is given by

$$R(x, y) = 2x^2 + y^2 + 4x + 5y + 1000$$

At present, the retailer is selling 30 toasters and 50 broilers. Which of these two product lines should be expanded in order to yield the greater increase in revenue?

17. *Profit.* The annual profit of a certain hotel is given by

$$P(x, y) = 100x^2 + 4y^2 + 2x + 5y + 100{,}000$$

where x is the number of rooms available for rent and y is the monthly advertising expenditures. Presently, the hotel has 90 rooms available and is spending $1000 per month on advertising.
a) If an additional room is constructed in an unfinished area, how will this affect annual profits?
b) If an additional dollar is spent on monthly advertising expenditures, how will this affect annual profit?

18. *Competitive pricing.* Two brands of ice cream, Farmer's Delight and Mellow Creme, are competing for the same market. The demands (in cases) for Farmer's Delight and Mellow Creme are represented by D_f and D_m, respectively. If x is the price of one case of Farmer's Delight and y is the price of one case of Mellow Creme, then

$$D_f = 5000 - 50x + 25y - 2xy$$
$$D_m = 6000 + 30x - 20y - xy$$

In economics, these two products are said to be competitive at those values of x and y for which

$$\frac{\partial D_f}{\partial y} > 0 \quad \text{and} \quad \frac{\partial D_m}{\partial x} > 0$$

Find those prices at which these two products are competitive.

8-3 • RELATIVE MAXIMA AND MINIMA (FUNCTIONS OF TWO VARIABLES)

Relative maxima and minima of multivariate functions are defined in a manner similar to that used for single variable functions. The graphs in Figure 8-7 illustrate relative maximum and minimum points of multivariate functions. Notice that the point labeled "Relative minimum" is lower than any of its neighboring points and that the point labeled "Relative maximum" is higher than any of its neighboring points.

Specifically, a function $z = f(x, y)$ is said to have a *relative maximum* at the point (x_0, y_0) if $f(x_0, y_0) \geq f(x, y)$ for all points (x, y) neighboring (x_0, y_0). A function $z = f(x, y)$ is said to have a *relative minimum* at the point (x_0, y_0) if $f(x_0, y_0) \leq f(x, y)$ for all points (x, y) neighboring (x_0, y_0).

To determine relative maxima and relative minima of functions of two variables, we use the first-derivative rule for functions of two variables.

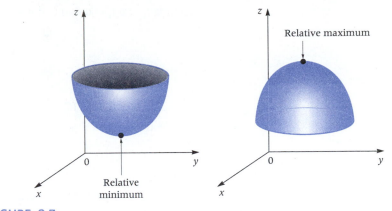

FIGURE 8-7

> ### First-Derivative Rule for Functions of Two Variables
>
> If the function $z = f(x, y)$ has either a relative maximum or a relative minimum at a point (x_0, y_0), and if $f_x(x_0, y_0)$ and $f_y(x_0, y_0)$ exist, then
>
> $$f_x(x_0, y_0) = 0$$
> $$f_y(x_0, y_0) = 0$$

This rule states that if a function $z = f(x, y)$ has either a relative maximum or a relative minimum at a point (x_0, y_0) and if both partial derivatives $\partial z/\partial x$ and $\partial z/\partial y$ exist at (x_0, y_0), then it is necessary that both partial derivatives, when evaluated at $x = x_0$ and $y = y_0$, to be equal to 0. This is because at a relative maximum or minimum located at (x_0, y_0), the slope, $f_x(x_0, y_0)$, of the tangent line parallel to the xz-plane is 0 and the slope, $f_y(x_0, y_0)$, of the tangent line parallel to the yz-plane is 0 as is illustrated in Figure 8-8. Such a point (x_0, y_0), at which both partial derivatives $\partial z/\partial x$ and $\partial z/\partial y$ equal 0, is called a critical point of the function $z = f(x, y)$.

Thus, to determine relative maxima and relative minima of functions of two variables, we first search for critical points. A point (x_0, y_0) is called a critical point of $z = f(x, y)$ if

$$f_x(x_0, y_0) = 0 \quad \text{and} \quad f_y(x_0, y_0) = 0$$

Critical points yield candidates for relative maxima/minima.

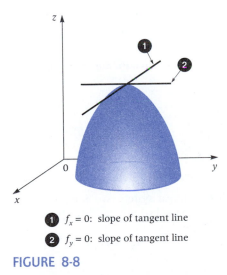

1 $f_x = 0$: slope of tangent line

2 $f_y = 0$: slope of tangent line

FIGURE 8-8

• EXAMPLE 8-16

Find the critical points of the function

$$z = f(x, y) = x^2 - 8x + y^2 - 12y + 1500$$

Solution

We must compute f_x and f_y, set them equal to 0, and solve for x and y. Computing f_x and f_y gives

$$f_x = 2x - 8 \quad \text{and} \quad f_y = 2y - 12$$

Setting f_x and f_y equal to 0 and solving for x and y yields

$$0 = 2x - 8 \qquad 0 = 2y - 12$$
$$x = 4 \qquad y = 6$$

Thus, the point $(x_0, y_0) = (4, 6)$ is the only critical point of the function $z = f(x, y)$.

• **EXAMPLE 8-17** _____

Find the critical points of

$$z = f(x, y) = x^2 + 2xy + 1.5y^2 - 16x + y + 1000$$

Solution

We must compute f_x and f_y, set them equal to 0, and solve for x and y. Computing f_x and f_y gives

$$f_x = 2x + 2y - 16$$
$$f_y = 2x + 3y + 1$$

Setting f_x and f_y equal to 0 gives the linear system

$$0 = 2x + 2y - 16$$
$$0 = 2x + 3y + 1$$

Solving this linear system, we obtain $x = 25$ and $y = -17$. Thus, $(25, -17)$ is the only critical point of the function $z = f(x, y)$.

• **EXAMPLE 8-18** _____

Find the critical points of

$$z = f(x, y) = x^3 + x^2y + 2x - 4y + 8$$

Solution

We must compute f_x and f_y, set them equal to 0, and solve for x and y. Computing f_x and f_y gives

$$f_x = 3x^2 + 2xy + 2$$
$$f_y = x^2 - 4$$

Setting f_x and f_y equal to 0 gives the equations

$$3x^2 + 2xy + 2 = 0$$
$$x^2 - 4 = 0$$

Since this set of equations does not constitute a linear system, we attempt to solve one of the equations for one of its unknowns and substitute the result(s) into the other equation to solve for the remaining unknown.

Solving the second equation, $x^2 - 4 = 0$, gives $x = \pm 2$. Solving the first equation, $3x^2 + 2xy + 2 = 0$, for y gives

$$y = \frac{-3x^2 - 2}{2x}$$

Substituting $x = 2$ into this equation gives

$$y = \frac{-3(2)^2 - 2}{2(2)}$$
$$= \frac{-14}{4} = -\frac{7}{2}$$

Thus, $(2, -7/2)$ is a critical point. Substituting $x = -2$ into the equation for y gives

$$y = \frac{-3(-2)^2 - 2}{2(-2)}$$

$$= \frac{-14}{-4} = \frac{7}{2}$$

Thus, $(-2, 7/2)$ is another critical point.

As previously stated in this section, we first search for critical points when attempting to determine relative maxima and relative minima of functions of two variables. However, a critical point may or may not yield either a relative maximum or a relative minimum. Recall that this is also the case with functions of one variable. Just as we have a second-derivative test for functions of one variable, we also have a similar test to identify the relative maxima and minima of functions of two variables. This test is stated as follows.

Second-Derivative Test for Functions of Two Variables

Let (x_0, y_0) be a critical point of $z = f(x, y)$ such that f_x, f_y, f_{xx}, f_{yy}, and f_{xy} are continuous at (x_0, y_0). Also, let

$$A = f_{xx}(x_0, y_0)$$
$$B = f_{yy}(x_0, y_0)$$
$$C = f_{xy}(x_0, y_0)$$

Then

1. $f(x_0, y_0)$ is a relative maximum if $AB - C^2 > 0$ and $A < 0$.
2. $f(x_0, y_0)$ is a relative minimum if $AB - C^2 > 0$ and $A > 0$.
3. $f(x_0, y_0)$ is a **saddle point** if $AB - C^2 < 0$. (A saddle point is illustrated in the graph of Figure 8-9.)
4. The test fails and no information is given about the point (x_0, y_0) if $AB - C^2 = 0$.

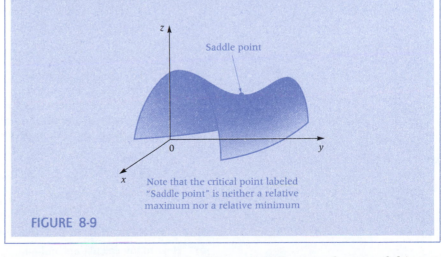

Note that the critical point labeled "Saddle point" is neither a relative maximum nor a relative minimum

FIGURE 8-9

The subsequent examples in this section illustrate the use of this test.

• **EXAMPLE 8-19**

Find any relative maxima and minima of the function

$$z = f(x, y) = x^2 - 8x + y^2 - 12y + 1500$$

Solution

First, we find the critical points. Computing f_x and f_y gives

$$f_x = 2x - 8$$
$$f_y = 2y - 12$$

Setting f_x and f_y equal to 0 and solving for x and y gives $x = 4$ and $y = 6$. Hence, $(4, 6)$ is the only critical point.

We now apply the second-derivative test for functions of two variables. Computing f_{xx}, f_{yy}, and f_{xy} gives

$$f_{xx}(x, y) = 2 \qquad f_{yy}(x, y) = 2 \qquad f_{xy}(x, y) = 0$$

Evaluating each of these at the critical point $(4, 6)$ gives

$$A = f_{xx}(4, 6) = 2$$
$$B = f_{yy}(4, 6) = 2$$
$$C = f_{xy}(4, 6) = 0$$
$$AB - C^2 = 2(2) - 0^2 = 4$$

Since $AB - C^2 > 0$ and $A > 0$, then, according to the second-derivative test, a relative minimum occurs at $(4, 6)$. Thus, the relative minimum value of z is

$$z = f(4, 6) = (4)^2 - 8(4) + 6^2 - 12(6) + 1500 = 1448 \qquad \text{Relative Minimum}$$

At this point, we state a procedure for finding relative maximum and minimum values for functions of two variables.

> **To Find Relative Extrema for Functions of Two Variables**
>
> **1.** Search for critical points.
>   - Find the first-order partials f_x and f_y.
>   - Set the first-order partials equal to zero, and solve for x and y.
>   - Determine all possible ordered pairs (x, y) that satisfy both equations
>
> $$f_x(x, y) = 0 \qquad \text{and} \qquad f_y(x, y) = 0$$
>
>   These are the critical points.
> **2.** Apply the second-derivative test for functions of two variables.
>   - Compute the second-order partials f_{xx}, f_{yy}, and f_{xy}.
>   - Evaluate the second-order partials at each critical point.
>   - Apply the second-derivative test to each critical point.

• **EXAMPLE 8-20**

Consider the function

$$z = f(x, y) = -x^2 + 8x - 2y^2 + 6y + 2xy + 50$$

where z is the sales revenue derived from selling x calculators and y adding machines.

a) How many calculators and adding machines should be sold in order to maximize sales revenue?

b) What is the maximum sales revenue?

Solutions

Critical Points

a) We first calculate f_x and f_y, as follows:

$$f_x = -2x + 8 + 2y$$
$$f_y = -4y + 6 + 2x$$

Setting f_x and f_y equal to 0, we have

$$0 = -2x + 8 + 2y$$
$$0 = -4y + 6 + 2x$$

Solving this linear system for x and y, we obtain $x = 11$ and $y = 7$. Thus, the only critical point is $(11, 7)$.

Second-Derivative Test

We calculate

$$f_{xx} = -2 \qquad f_{yy} = -4 \qquad f_{xy} = 2$$

Since the critical point is $(11, 7)$, then

$$A = f_{xx}(11, 7) = -2$$
$$B = f_{yy}(11, 7) = -4$$
$$C = f_{xy}(11, 7) = 2$$
$$AB - C^2 = -2(-4) - 2^2 = 4$$

Since $AB - C^2 > 0$ and $A < 0$, then, according to the second-derivative test, a relative maximum occurs at $(11, 7)$. Thus, in order to maximize revenue, $x = 11$ calculators and $y = 7$ adding machines must be sold.

b) The maximum sales revenue is

$$z = f(11, 7) = -(11)^2 + 8(11) - 2(7)^2 + 6(7) + 2(11)(7) + 50$$
$$= \$115 \qquad \text{Relative maximum}$$

• EXAMPLE 8-21 ———————————————————

Find any relative maxima and minima of the function

$$f(x, y) = 3x^2 - x^3 + 12y^2 - 8y^3 + 60$$

Solution

Critical Points

$$f_x = 6x - 3x^2 = 0 \qquad f_y = 24y - 24y^2 = 0$$
$$= 3x(2 - x) = 0 \qquad = 24y(1 - y) = 0$$
$$x = 0 \quad x = 2 \qquad y = 0 \quad y = 1$$

Possible ordered pairs (or critical points)

			Verify that $f_x = 0$ and $f_y = 0$	
$x = 0$	$y = 0$	$(0, 0)$	$f_x(0, 0) = 0$	$f_y(0, 0) = 0$
	$y = 1$	$(0, 1)$	$f_x(0, 1) = 0$	$f_y(0, 1) = 0$
$x = 2$	$y = 0$	$(2, 0)$	$f_x(2, 0) = 0$	$f_y(2, 0) = 0$
	$y = 1$	$(2, 1)$	$f_x(2, 1) = 0$	$f_y(2, 1) = 0$

↑
critical points

Since all of the above ordered pairs satisfy both equations, $f_x = 0$ and $f_y = 0$, then they are critical points, as indicated above.

Second-Derivative Test

Second-order partials:

$$f_{xx}(x, y) = 6 - 6x \qquad f_{yy}(x, y) = 24 - 48y \qquad f_{xy}(x, y) = 0$$

Apply the second-derivative test to each critical point.

Critical Point (0, 0)

$$A = f_{xx}(0, 0) = 6 \qquad B = f_{yy}(0, 0) = 24 \qquad C = f_{xy}(0, 0) = 0$$
$$AB - C^2 = (6)(24) - 0^2 = 144$$

Since $A > 0$ and $AB - C^2 > 0$, then, by the second-derivative test for functions of two variables, a relative minimum occurs at $(0, 0)$. Hence,

$$f(0, 0) = 3(0)^2 - (0)^3 + 12(0)^2 - 8(0)^3 + 60 = 60 \qquad \text{Relative minimum}$$

Critical Point (0, 1)

$$A = f_{xx}(0, 1) = 6 \qquad B = f_{yy}(0, 1) = -24 \qquad C = f_{xy}(0, 1) = 0$$
$$AB - C^2 = (6)(-24) - 0^2 = -144$$

Since $AB - C^2 < 0$, a saddle point occurs at $(0, 1)$.

Critical Point (2, 0)

$$A = f_{xx}(2, 0) = -6 \qquad B = f_{yy}(2, 0) = 24 \qquad C = f_{xy}(2, 0) = 0$$
$$AB - C^2 = (-6)(24) - 0^2 = -144$$

Since $AB - C^2 < 0$, a saddle point occurs at $(2, 0)$.

Critical Point (2, 1)

$$A = f_{xx}(2, 1) = -6 \qquad B = f_{yy}(2, 1) = -24 \qquad C = f_{xy}(2, 1) = 0$$
$$AB - C^2 = (-6)(-24) - 0^2 = 144$$

Since $A < 0$ and $AB - C^2 > 0$, a relative maximum occurs at $(2, 1)$. Hence,

$$f(2, 1) = 3(2)^2 - (2)^3 + 12(1)^2 - 8(1)^3 + 60 = 68 \qquad \text{Relative maximum}$$

• EXAMPLE 8-22

Find any relative maxima and minima of the function

$$z = f(x, y) = -x^3 - y^2 + 4xy + 6$$

Solution

Critical Points

First, we find the critical points. Computing f_x and f_y gives

$$f_x = -3x^2 + 4y$$
$$f_y = -2y + 4x$$

Setting f_x and f_y equal to 0, we have

$$-3x^2 + 4y = 0$$
$$-2y + 4x = 0$$

Since this set of equations does not constitute a linear system, we attempt to solve one of the equations for one of its unknowns and substitute the result into the other equation to solve for the remaining unknown.

Solving the second equation, $-2y + 4x = 0$, for y, we obtain

$$y = 2x$$

Substituting this result into the first equation, $-3x^2 + 4y = 0$, gives

$$-3x^2 + 4(2x) = 0$$

or

$$-3x^2 + 8x = 0$$

Solving this equation for x gives

$$x = 0 \quad \text{or} \quad x = \frac{8}{3}$$

Substituting these results into the second equation, $y = 2x$, gives the following results:

- If $x = 0$, then $y = 2(0) = 0$ and $(0, 0)$ is a critical point.
- If $x = 8/3$, then $y = 2(8/3) = 16/3$ and $(8/3, 16/3)$ is a critical point.

Thus, $(0, 0)$ and $(8/3, 16/3)$ are the critical points.

Second-Derivative Test

We now apply the second-derivative test for functions of two variables. Computing f_{xx}, f_{yy}, and f_{xy} gives

$$f_{xx}(x, y) = -6x$$
$$f_{yy}(x, y) = -2$$
$$f_{xy}(x, y) = 4$$

Evaluating each of these at the critical point $(0, 0)$ gives

$$A = f_{xx}(0, 0) = 0$$
$$B = f_{yy}(0, 0) = -2$$
$$C = f_{xy}(0, 0) = 4$$
$$AB - C^2 = 0(-2) - 4^2 = -16$$

Since $AB - C^2 < 0$, then, according to the second-derivative test of this section, a saddle point occurs at $(0, 0)$.

Applying the second-derivative test to the critical point $(8/3, 16/3)$ gives

$$A = f_{xx}(8/3, 16/3) = -6(8/3) = -16$$
$$B = f_{yy}(8/3, 16/3) = -2$$
$$C = f_{xy}(8/3, 16/3) = 4$$
$$AB - C^2 = (-16)(-2) - 4^2 = 16$$

Since $AB - C^2 > 0$ and $A < 0$, then, by the second-derivative test, a relative maximum occurs at $(8/3, 16/3)$. The relative maximum value of z is

$$z = f\left(\frac{8}{3}, \frac{16}{3}\right) = -\left(\frac{8}{3}\right)^3 - \left(\frac{16}{3}\right)^2 + 4\left(\frac{8}{3}\right)\left(\frac{16}{3}\right) + 6$$

$$= \frac{418}{27} \approx 15.48 \qquad \text{Relative maximum}$$

Applications

• **EXAMPLE 8-23**   **Cost, Revenue, Profit.**

Meditech, Inc., produces two products used in the dental industry. Each thousand units of product 1 sells for $100, and each thousand units of product 2 sells for $80. Meditech's analysts have determined that if x thousand units of product 1 and y thousand units of product 2 are produced, the total production cost is given by

$$C(x, y) = 10x^2 + 5y^2 - 10xy - 20x + 5y + 12$$

a) Determine the equation for total sales revenue, $R(x, y)$.
b) Determine the equation for total profit, $P(x, y)$.
c) Determine the number of units of each product that should be produced in order to maximize total profit.

Solutions

a) The total sales revenue is given by

$$R(x, y) = 100x + 80y$$

b) The total profit is given by

$$\begin{aligned} P(x, y) &= R(x, y) - C(x, y) \\ &= 100x + 80y - (10x^2 + 5y^2 - 10xy - 20x + 5y + 12) \\ &= -10x^2 - 5y^2 + 10xy + 120x + 75y - 12 \end{aligned}$$

c) Computing P_x and P_y, we have

$$\begin{aligned} P_x &= -20x + 10y + 120 \\ P_y &= -10y + 10x + 75 \end{aligned}$$

Setting P_x and P_y equal to 0 and solving for x and y yields the critical point, $(19.5, 27)$. Computing P_{xx}, P_{yy}, and P_{xy} and applying the second-derivative test for functions of two variables gives

$$\begin{aligned} P_{xx}(x, y) &= -20 \\ P_{yy}(x, y) &= -10 \\ P_{xy}(x, y) &= 10 \end{aligned}$$

Hence,

$$\begin{aligned} A &= P_{xx}(19.5, 27) = -20 \\ B &= P_{yy}(19.5, 27) = -10 \\ C &= P_{xy}(19.5, 27) = 10 \\ AB - C^2 &= (-20)(-10) - (-10)^2 = 100 \end{aligned}$$

Since $AB - C^2 > 0$ and $A < 0$, then, by the second-derivative test, a relative maximum occurs at $(19.5, 27)$. Thus, 19.5 thousand units of product 1 and 27 thousand units of product 2 should be produced in order to maximize total profit. The maximum profit is

$$P(19.5, 27) = -10(19.5)^2 - 5(27)^2 + 10(19.5)(27) + 120(19.5) + 75(27) - 12$$
$$= \$2170.50 \qquad \text{Relative maximum}$$

• **EXAMPLE 8-24 Cost, Revenue, Profit.** _____

A firm manufactures two competing brands of a given product. Let p_1 and p_2 be the case selling prices (in dollars) of brands 1 and 2, respectively. If x_1 cases of brand 1 and x_2 cases of brand 2 are demanded by the market, then the relationship between the unit (case) prices and the demands for the competing brands are given by the equations

$$\begin{aligned} x_1 &= 80 - 2p_1 + p_2 \\ x_2 &= 30 + p_1 - p_2 \end{aligned}$$

a) Determine the equation for total sales revenue, $R(p_1, p_2)$.
b) If \$40 and \$30 are the unit case costs of brands 1 and 2, respectively, determine the total cost, $C(p_1, p_2)$.
c) Determine the equation for total profit, $P(p_1, p_2)$.
d) Determine the case selling prices, p_1 and p_2, that maximize total profit, $P(p_1, p_2)$.

Solutions

a) Since sales revenue for each brand is *price* × *quantity*, then the total sales revenue is

$$R = p_1 x_1 + p_2 x_2$$

Since we want $R(p_1, p_2)$, we substitute $80 - 2p_1 + p_2$ for x_1 and $30 + p_1 - p_2$ for x_2 to obtain

$$
\begin{aligned}
R(p_1, p_2) &= p_1(80 - 2p_1 + p_2) + p_2(30 + p_1 - p_2) \\
&= -2p_1^2 - p_2^2 + 2p_1 p_2 + 80p_1 + 30p_2
\end{aligned}
$$

b) Multiplying each case cost by the respective demand gives the total cost

$$C = 40x_1 + 30x_2$$

Since we want $C(p_1, p_2)$, we substitute $80 - 2p_1 + p_2$ for x_1 and $30 + p_1 - p_2$ for x_2 to obtain

$$
\begin{aligned}
C(p_1, p_2) &= 40(80 - 2p_1 + p_2) + 30(30 + p_1 - p_2) \\
&= -50p_1 + 10p_2 + 4100
\end{aligned}
$$

c) The total profit is given by

$$
\begin{aligned}
P(p_1, p_2) &= R(p_1, p_2) - C(p_1, p_2) \\
&= (-2p_1^2 - p_2^2 + 2p_1 p_2 + 80p_1 + 30p_2) - (-50p_1 + 10p_2 + 4100) \\
&= -2p_1^2 - p_2^2 + 2p_1 p_2 + 130p_1 + 20p_2 - 4100
\end{aligned}
$$

d) Computing the partial derivatives P_{p1} and P_{p2} gives

$$
\begin{aligned}
P_{p1} &= -4p_1 + 2p_2 + 130 \\
P_{p2} &= -2p_2 + 2p_1 + 20
\end{aligned}
$$

Setting the above partial derivatives equal to 0 and solving for p_1 and p_2 yields the approximate critical point, $(75, 85)$. Computing the second partials and applying the second-derivative test for functions of two variables gives

$$
\begin{aligned}
P_{p1p1}(p_1, p_2) &= -16 \\
P_{p2p2}(p_1, p_2) &= -2 \\
P_{p1p2}(p_1, p_2) &= 2
\end{aligned}
$$

Hence,

$$
\begin{aligned}
A &= P_{p1p1}(75, 85) = -16 \\
B &= P_{p2p2}(75, 85) = -2 \\
C &= P_{p1p2}(75, 85) = 2 \\
AB - C^2 &= (-16)(-2) - 2^2 = 28
\end{aligned}
$$

Since $AB - C^2 > 0$ and $A < 0$, then, by the second-derivative test, a relative maximum occurs at $(75, 85)$. Thus, brand 1 should be priced at $75 per case, and brand 2 should be priced at $85 per case in order to maximize total profit. The maximum profit is

$$
\begin{aligned}
P(75, 85) &= -2(75)^2 - (85)^2 + 2(75)(85) \\
&\quad + 130(75) + 20(85) - 4100 \\
&= \$1625 \qquad \text{Relative maximum}
\end{aligned}
$$

Exercises 8-3

Find any critical points for each of the following:

1. $z = x^2 + 3y^2 - 10x + 48y + 86$

2. $f(x, y) = -2x^2 - 3y^2 + 20x - 30y + 90$

3. $f(x, y) = -x^2 - y^2 + 4x + 8y + xy + 56$
4. $f(x, y) = x^2 + 2y^2 - 10x - 12y + 2xy + 7$
5. $z = 3x^2 + 2y^2 + 24x - 36y + 50$
6. $f(x, y) = -x^2 - 3y^2 + 10x + 54y + 80$
7. $f(x, y) = -x^2 - 5y^2 + 30x + 20y + 3xy + 8$
8. $f(x, y) = 5x^2 + 4y^2 + 6xy + 10x - 64y - 67$
9. $f(x, y) = 2x^3 + x^2y + 5x - 36y + 90$
10. $z = -2x^3 - y^2 + 10xy + 60$
11. $z = -x^2 + y^3 - 12y + 8x + 80$
12. $f(x, y) = x^2 - 2x^3 + 5y^2 - 10y^3 + 65$

Find any relative maxima or relative minima of each of the following:

13. $z = x^2 + 2y^2 - 8x - 20y + 18$
14. $f(x, y) = 2x^2 + y^2 - 28x - 20y + 80$
15. $f(x, y) = 9x - 50y + x^2 + 5y^2 + 100$
16. $z = 40x + 160y - 2x^2 - 4y^2 + 1000$
17. $f(x, y) = 1000 + 80x + 100y - 2x^2 - y^2$
18. $f(x, y) = 4x^2 + 2y^2 + 3xy - 70x - 55y + 1000$
19. $z = 3x^2 + 4y^2 + 2xy - 30x - 32y + 50$
20. $f(x, y) = 4x^2 + 5y^2 + 5xy - 73x - 80y + 6$
21. $z = 200 - 2x^2 - 6y^2 + 2xy + 32x + 28y$
22. $f(x, y) = 80 + 3xy + 42x - 16y - 3x^2 - 2y^2$
23. $z = f(x, y) = 2x^3 + x^2y + 8x - 25y + 800$
24. $f(x, y) = -x^3 - 2y^2 + 30xy + 50$
25. $z = f(x, y) = -x^2 + y^3 - 24y + 10x + 95$
26. $f(x, y) = 2x^2 - x^3 + 4y^2 - 12y^3 + 850$

27. Show that the function defined by

$$f(x, y) = 500 + x^2 - 2y^2 - 18x + 16y$$

has neither a relative maximum nor a relative minimum. Additionally, show that $f(x, y)$ has a saddle point, and find it.

28. Show that the function defined by

$$z = x^2 + 2y^2 + 3xy - 40x - 55y + 100$$

has a saddle point, and find it. Does the function have any relative maxima or minima?

Applications

29. *Profit.* The profit of a company is given by
$$P(x, y) = 1,000,000 + 1600x + 2000y - 4x^2 - 2y^2$$
where x is the unit labor cost and y is the unit raw material cost.
a) Find the unit labor cost and unit raw material cost that maximizes profit.
b) Find the maximum profit.

30. *Cost.* The manager of Freddy's Frogurt Stand has determined that the cost of producing x gallons of strawberry frogurt and y gallons of blueberry frogurt is given by
$$C(x, y) = 2x^2 + 3y^2 + 2xy - 800x - 1400y + 185,000$$
a) How many gallons of each flavor should be produced in order to minimize cost?
b) Find the minimum cost.

31. *Production output.* The weekly output of a firm is given by
$$z(x, y) = 1000x + 1600y + 2xy - 5x^2 - 2y^2$$
where x is the number of hours of labor and y is the number of units of raw material used weekly.

a) How many hours of labor and how many units of raw material should be used weekly in order to maximize output?

b) Find the maximum output.

32. *Cost, revenue, profit.* A firm produces two products, which are used in the automobile industry. Each thousand units of product 1 sells for $200, and each thousand units of product 2 sells for $295. If x thousand units of product 1 are produced and y thousand units of product 2 are produced, the total production cost is given by

$$C(x, y) = 5x^2 + 10y^2 + 5xy - 10x + 15y + 10$$

a) Determine the equation for total sales revenue, $R(x, y)$.

b) Determine the equation for total profit, $P(x, y)$.

c) Determine the number of units of each product that should be produced in order to maximize total profit.

33. *Revenue.* A large bottling company produces two competing brands of soda, Crystal Club and Mineral Club. The demands (in cases) for Crystal Club and Mineral Club are given by x_1 and x_2, respectively. If p_1 is the price for 1 case of Crystal Club and p_2 is the price for 1 case of Mineral Club, then

$$x_1 = 200 - 20p_1 + p_2$$
$$x_2 = 300 - 15p_2 + 2p_1$$

a) Determine the equation for total sales revenue, $R(p_1, p_2)$.

b) How should each brand be priced in order to maximize sales revenue, $R(p_1, p_2)$?

c) Determine the maximum sales revenue.

d) Find the demand for each brand at the optimal prices.

34. *Cost, revenue, profit.* A company manufactures two competing brands of a given product. Let p_1 and p_2 be the case prices (in dollars) of brands 1 and 2, respectively. If x_1 cases of brand 1 and x_2 cases of brand 2 are demanded by the marketplace, then the relationships between unit prices and demands for both competing brands are given by the equations

$$x_1 = 100 - 5p_1 + p_2$$
$$x_2 = 50 + p_1 - p_2$$

a) Determine the equation for total sales revenue, $R(p_1, p_2)$.

b) If $20 and $30 are the unit case costs of brands 1 and 2, respectively, determine the total cost, $C(p_1, p_2)$.

c) Determine the equation for total profit, $P(p_1, p_2)$.

d) Determine the case prices, p_1 and p_2, that maximize total profit, $P(p_1, p_2)$.

35. *Surface area.* A company manufactures boxes such as the one shown in Figure 8-10. If each such box must have a volume of 200 cubic inches, determine the dimensions of the box that minimize its surface area (i.e., surface area = area of four sides + area of top + area of bottom).

36. *Production cost.* A company manufactures boxes such as the one shown in Figure 8-10. Each side costs $5 per square inch to manufacture, and the top and bottom cost $8 per square inch to manufacture. If each box is to have a volume of 200 cubic inches, determine the dimensions that minimize its production cost.

37. *Heating and cooling costs.* A building is to be built in the shape of a rectangular box such as that shown in Figure 8-10. The building is to have a volume of 10,000 cubic feet. The combined annual heating and cooling costs are $10 per square foot for the top of the building (i.e., the roof) and $4 per square foot for the sides. Determine the dimensions of the building that will minimize the combined annual heating and cooling costs.

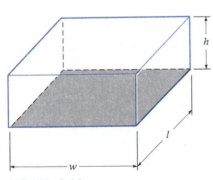

FIGURE 8-10

8-4

• APPLICATION: THE METHOD OF LEASTSQUARES

TABLE 8-1

x Annual advertising expense ($ millions)	y Annual sales ($ millions)
1	14
2	19
4	30
5	33

Table 8-1 gives annual advertising expenses and corresponding annual sales from a sample of 4 years' data for a corporation. The firm's management wishes to determine a mathematical relationship between annual advertising expense, x, and annual sales, y. The given data points (x, y) are plotted in Figure 8-11. Studying this figure, notice that the data points approximately follow the path of a straight line. Although the points do not necessarily lie on the straight line in Figure 8-11, their trend appears to be linear. Thus, the firm's analyst decides to *fit a straight line* to the set of data points. In other words, the analyst wishes to determine the equation $y = mx + b$ of the straight line that *best fits* the set of data points. The equation

$$y = mx + b$$

provides a mathematical model that describes the relationship between annual advertising expense, x, and annual sales, y. Thus, the analyst's problem reduces to finding the slope m and y-intercept b of the straight line $y = mx + b$ that *best fits* the set of data points.

We must understand what the phrase "best fits" might mean as we try to fit a straight line to a set of data points. Although we have discussed this term in previous Extra Dividends at the end of Chapter 1, we again explain it by focusing on the given data point (4, 30) and the point directly below on the straight line, $y = mx + b$, in Figure 8-12. Note that the point on the straight line, $y = mx + b$, directly below (4, 30) has x-coordinate 4 and y-coordinate $m(4) + b$ or $4m + b$. Hence, its ordered pair is $(4, 4m + b)$. The extent to which the straight line, $y = mx + b$, does not fit the data

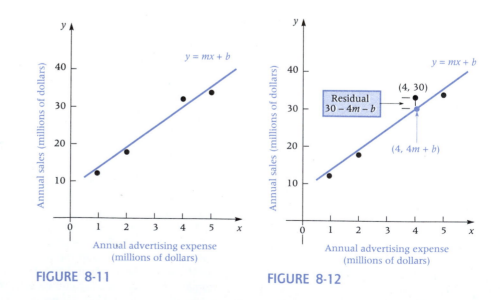

FIGURE 8-11   **FIGURE 8-12**

point (4, 30) could be expressed by the vertical distance between (4, 30) and (4, 4m + b). This vertical distance is called a **residual** and is given by the expression

$$30 - (4m + b)$$

or

$$30 - 4m - b$$

Since this quantity will be negative for points below the line, we determine and use its square

$$(30 - 4m - b)^2$$

Figure 8-13 shows the expressions of such vertical distances, or residuals, and their squares for all of the observed data points. The *best-fitting* straight line is defined as the one that *minimizes the sum of the squares* of the residuals. Since the sum of the squares is a measure of the extent to which the straight line does not pass through the given data points, it is called **sum of squares error** and is denoted by S. Hence,

$$S = (14 - m - b)^2 + (19 - 2m - b)^2 + (30 - 4m - b)^2 + (33 - 5m - b)^2$$

We must determine the slope m and y-intercept b (of the straight line, $y = mx + b$) that *minimize the sum of squares error*. The procedure is called

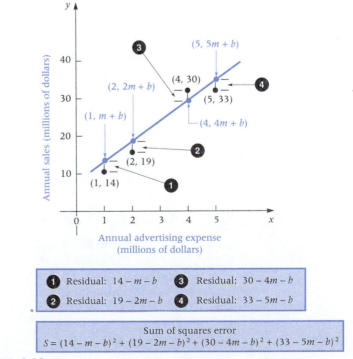

FIGURE 8-13

the **method of least squares.** Note that S is a function of two variables, m and b. To find the values of m and b that minimize S, we determine the partial derivatives with respect to m and b, set them equal to 0, and solve for m and b. Computing $\partial S/\partial m$ and $\partial S/\partial b$ gives

$$\frac{\partial S}{\partial m} = 2(14 - m - b)(-1) + 2(19 - 2m - b)(-2)$$
$$+ 2(30 - 4m - b)(-4) + 2(33 - 5m - b)(-5)$$

$$\frac{\partial S}{\partial b} = 2(14 - m - b)(-1) + 2(19 - 2m - b)(-1)$$
$$+ 2(30 - 4m - b)(-1) + 2(33 - 5m - b)(-1)$$

Setting $\partial S/\partial m$ and $\partial S/\partial b$ equal to 0 and simplifying yields the linear system

$$92m + 24b = 674$$
$$24m + 8b = 192$$

Solving for m and b gives the critical point $(m, b) = (4.9, 9.3)$.

Computing the second partials and applying the second-derivative test for functions of two variables gives

$$S_{mm}(m, b) = 92 \qquad S_{bb}(m, b) = 8 \qquad S_{mb}(m, b) = 24$$

Hence,

$$A = S_{mm}(4.9, 9.3) = 92$$
$$B = S_{bb}(4.9, 9.3) = 8$$
$$C = S_{mb}(4.9, 9.3) = 24$$
$$AB - C^2 = (92)(8) - 24^2 = 160$$

Since $AB - C^2 > 0$ and $A > 0$, then, by the second-derivative test, a relative minimum value of S occurs at $(4.9, 9.3)$.

Thus, the equation of the best-fitting straight line (i.e., the straight line that minimizes the sum of squares error) is

$$y = 4.9x + 9.3 \qquad \text{Regression line}$$

This best-fitting line to a set of data points is called the **least-squares line** or the **regression line,** as indicated above.

Using the Regression Line As a Predictor

The regression line is used to predict y-values corresponding to given x-values. For example, we can predict the annual sales corresponding to the annual advertising expenditure of 3 million dollars by substituting $x = 3$ into the equation of the regression line. Hence,

$$y = 4.9(3) + 9.3$$
$$= 24 \qquad \text{24 million dollars of annual sales}$$
$$\text{correspond to annual advertising}$$
$$\text{expenditures of 3 million dollars.}$$

General Case

It can be shown, in general, that the slope m and the y-intercept b of the least squares or regression line for a set of n data points, (x_1, y_1), (x_2, y_2), . . . , (x_n, y_n), satisfy the linear system

$$nb + \left(\sum_{i=1}^{n} x_i\right) m = \sum_{i=1}^{n} y_i$$

$$\left(\sum_{i=1}^{n} x_i\right) b + \left(\sum_{i=1}^{n} x_i^2\right) m = \sum_{i=1}^{n} x_i y_i$$

where

$$\sum_{i=1}^{n} x_i = x_1 + x_2 + \ldots + x_n$$

$$\sum_{i=1}^{n} y_i = y_1 + y_2 + \ldots + y_n$$

$$\sum_{i=1}^{n} x_i^2 = x_1^2 + x_2^2 + \ldots + x_n^2$$

$$\sum_{i=1}^{n} x_i y_i = x_1 y_1 + x_2 y_2 + \ldots + x_n y_n$$

Note that if we divide the first equation by n, we obtain

$$b + \underbrace{\frac{\sum_{i=1}^{n} x_i}{n}}_{\bar{x}} m = \underbrace{\frac{\sum_{i=1}^{n} y_i}{n}}_{\bar{y}}$$

Since

$$\bar{x} = \frac{\sum_{i=1}^{n} x_i}{n} \qquad \text{Average of the } x\text{-values}$$

$$\bar{y} = \frac{\sum_{i=1}^{n} y_i}{n} \qquad \text{Average of the } y\text{-values}$$

then the above equation can be rewritten as

$$b + \bar{x} m = \bar{y}$$

or

$$\bar{y} = m\bar{x} + b$$

The last equation implies that the regression line always passes through the point $(\bar{x}, \bar{y})$.

Alternate Formulas for m and b

The equations in the color screen on page 519 can be rewritten to give the following formulas for the slope m and the y-intercept b.

$$m = \frac{\sum\limits_{i=1}^{n} x_i y_i - n\bar{x}\bar{y}}{\sum\limits_{i=1}^{n} x_i^2 - n\bar{x}^2} \qquad \text{Slope}$$

$$b = \bar{y} - m\bar{x} \qquad \text{y-Intercept}$$

These enable us to obtain m and b expeditiously without having to solve a linear system. We summarize as follows.

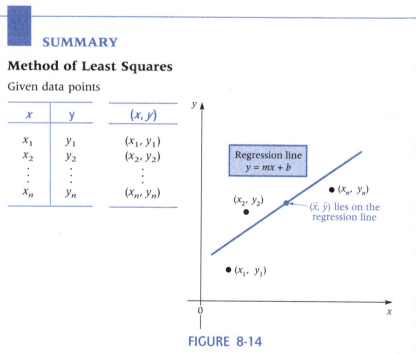

■ SUMMARY

Method of Least Squares

Given data points

x	y	(x, y)
x_1	y_1	(x_1, y_1)
x_2	y_2	(x_2, y_2)
$\vdots$	$\vdots$	$\vdots$
x_n	y_n	(x_n, y_n)

Regression line
$y = mx + b$

$(\bar{x}, \bar{y})$ lies on the regression line

FIGURE 8-14

the **slope m** and the **y-intercept b** of the regression line are given by the formulas

$$m = \frac{\sum\limits_{i=1}^{n} x_i y_i - n\bar{x}\bar{y}}{\sum\limits_{i=1}^{n} x_i^2 - n\bar{x}^2}$$

$$b = \bar{y} - m\bar{x}$$

continues

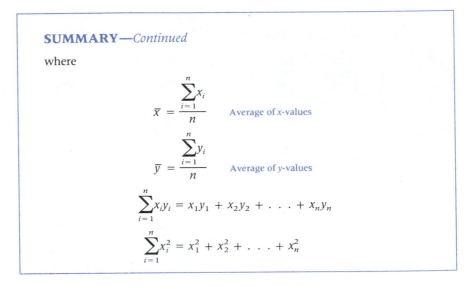

SUMMARY—*Continued*

where

$$\bar{x} = \frac{\sum\limits_{i=1}^{n} x_i}{n} \qquad \text{Average of } x\text{-values}$$

$$\bar{y} = \frac{\sum\limits_{i=1}^{n} y_i}{n} \qquad \text{Average of } y\text{-values}$$

$$\sum_{i=1}^{n} x_i y_i = x_1 y_1 + x_2 y_2 + \ldots + x_n y_n$$

$$\sum_{i=1}^{n} x_i^2 = x_1^2 + x_2^2 + \ldots + x_n^2$$

Applications

Investment Risk Measurement

Table 8-2 gives annual percent changes of net asset values of Fidelity Magellan Fund versus those of the overall stock market as measured by the Standard & Poors 500 Composite Index (S&P 500).

PROBLEM

We want to determine the linear relationship between the performance of Fidelity Magellan Fund and that of the overall market. This relationship is given by the regression line

$$y = mx + b$$

SOLUTION

Using the least squares method as outlined in the box on page 520, our computations appear in Table 8-3. Note that we multiply each x-value by

TABLE 8-2 Annual Percent Changes

		1984	1985	1986	1987	1988
x	S&P 500	6.2	31.3	18.1	4.7	16.2
y	Fidelity Magellan	2.0	43.2	23.7	1.0	22.8

TABLE 8-3

x_i	y_i	x_iy_i	x_i^2
6.2	2.0	12.40	38.44
31.3	43.2	1352.16	979.69
18.1	23.7	428.97	327.61
4.7	1.0	4.70	22.09
16.2	22.8	369.36	262.44
76.5	92.7	2167.59	1630.27

its corresponding y-value to obtain the entries of the x_iy_i column. Also, we square each x-value to obtain the entries of the x_i^2 column.

$$\bar{x} = \frac{\sum\limits_{i=1}^{n} x_i}{n} = \frac{76.5}{5} = 15.3 \qquad \text{Average of } x\text{-values}$$

$$\bar{y} = \frac{\sum\limits_{i=1}^{n} y_i}{n} = \frac{92.7}{5} = 18.54 \qquad \text{Average of } y\text{-values}$$

$$m = \frac{\sum\limits_{i=1}^{n} x_iy_i - n\bar{x}\bar{y}}{\sum\limits_{i=1}^{n} x_i^2 - n\bar{x}^2} = \frac{2167.59 - 5(15.3)(18.54)}{1630.27 - 5(15.3)^2} \approx \frac{749.28}{459.82} \approx 1.63$$

$$b = \bar{y} - m\bar{x} = 18.54 - 1.63(15.3) = -6.40$$

Thus, the regression equation is

$$y = 1.63x - 6.40$$

Slope and Risk

When the performance of a mutual fund or stock (as measured in percent changes) is related to the overall market, as in this example, the slope of the regression line is, in most financial publications, denoted by β (read "beta") and is interpreted in the following box.

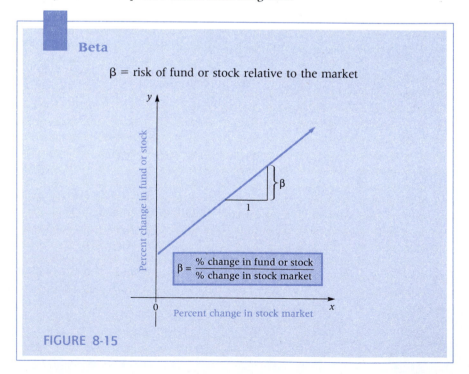

Beta

β = risk of fund or stock relative to the market

$$\beta = \frac{\% \text{ change in fund or stock}}{\% \text{ change in stock market}}$$

FIGURE 8-15

Thus Fidelity Magellan Fund's beta, $\beta = 1.63$, means that if the overall stock market, as measured by the S&P 500, goes up 1 percentage point, then Fidelity Magellan Fund can be expected to go up by 1.63 percentage points. Also, if the overall market goes down 1 percentage point, then Fidelity Magellan Fund can be expected to go down by 1.63 percentage points.

Time Series

Farm Population

Table 8-4 gives U.S. farm population as a percentage of total U.S. population for the years 1958 through 1984. A set of data, such as that of Table 8-4, that relates some quantity versus time is called a **time series.**

TABLE 8-4 **U.S. farm population as a percentage of total U.S. population**

Year	x	y	Year	x	y	Year	x	y	Year	x	y
1958	1	9.8	1965	8	6.4	1972	15	4.6	1979	22	2.8
1959	2	9.3	1966	9	5.9	1973	16	4.5	1980	23	2.7
1960	3	8.7	1967	10	5.5	1974	17	4.3	1981	24	2.5
1961	4	8.1	1968	11	5.2	1975	18	4.1	1982	25	2.4
1962	5	7.7	1969	12	5.1	1976	19	3.8	1983	26	2.5
1963	6	7.1	1970	13	4.7	1977	20	2.8	1984	27	2.4
1964	7	6.7	1971	14	4.5	1978	21	2.9			

x = coded years
y = U.S. farm population as a percentage of total U.S. population

We use the MINITAB statistical software package to plot the y-values versus the x-values. The results appear in Figure 8-16. A graph, such as that of Figure 8-16, that relates some quantity versus time is called a **time series plot.**

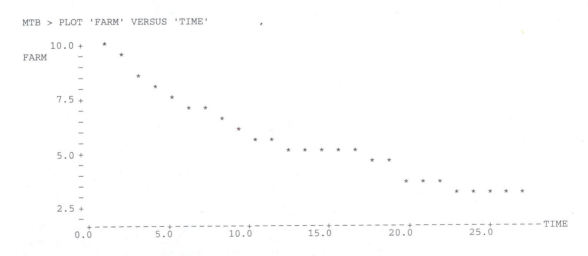

```
MTB > PLOT 'FARM' VERSUS 'TIME'

      10.0 +    *
FARM       -      *
           -
           -       *
           -        *
       7.5 +         *
           -          *   *
           -            *
           -             *
           -              *  *
       5.0 +                 *  *  *  *  *
           -                          *  *
           -                              *  *  *
           -                                     *  *  *  *
       2.5 +
           -
           +---------+---------+---------+---------+---------+------TIME
         0.0       5.0      10.0      15.0      20.0      25.0
```

This graph was drawn using the MINITAB statistical software package.

FIGURE 8-16

PROBLEM

We want to fit a straight line to the set of data points of Figure 8-16. In other words, we want to determine the equation of the regression line

$$y = mx + b$$

for this set of data.

COMPUTER SOLUTION

We use a computer software package to find the equation of the regression line. The results are given below. Also, a graph of the regression line fit to the data is given in Figure 8-17.

Regression Line

$$y = -0.275x + 8.93$$

Sum of Squares Error

7.17

Studying the computer solution, note that the slope of the regression line indicates that during the indicated time period, the U.S. farm population as a percentage of the total U.S. population is decreasing at the rate of 0.275 percentage points per year. Also, note that we have given the sum of squares error (i.e., the sum of the squares of the residuals) below the regression line. The reason for this will be apparent when we study the next example.

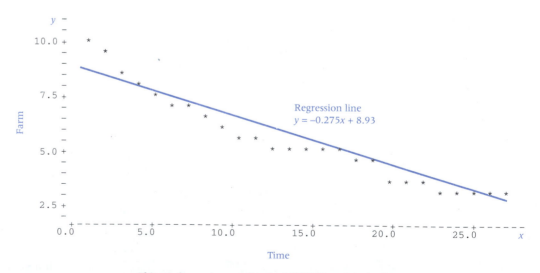

This graph was drawn using the MINITAB statistical software package. The regression line and annotations have been added.

FIGURE 8-17

Nonlinear Regression

Farm Population

Here we continue our analysis of the farm population data given in Table 8-4 and Figure 8-16. Studying the time series plot of Figure 8-16, note that the way that the data trail off at around the coded year $x = 13$ suggests a nonlinear pattern, perhaps an exponential pattern, to the data. This suggests that we try an *exponential model*

PROBLEM

Fit the exponential model

$$y = ab^x$$

to the farm population data of Table 8-4.

COMPUTER SOLUTION

The exponential model

$$y = ab^x \qquad \text{Exponential form}$$

can be written in logarithmic form by taking the natural logarithm (or, for that matter, the common logarithm) of each side to obtain

$$
\begin{aligned}
\ln y &= \ln ab^x \\
&= \ln a + \ln b^x \\
&= \ln a + x \ln b \\
&= \ln a + (\ln b)x \qquad \text{Logarithmic form}
\end{aligned}
$$

Thus, the exponential form, $y = ab^x$, is restated in the equivalent logarithmic form, $\ln y = \ln a + (\ln b)x$. Note that the logarithmic equation

$$\ln y = \ln a + (\ln b)x \qquad \text{ln } y \text{ and } x \text{ are linearly related.}$$

expresses a linear relationship between $\ln y$ and x, where $\ln b$ is the slope and $\ln a$ is the y-intercept. This means that we can fit an exponential model to a set of data points by finding the equation of the regression line relating $\ln y$-values and x-values. Thus, we use a calculator or computer to find the natural logarithms (or, if we prefer, common logarithms) of the y-values of our data. Then we use a computer software package to find the regression line relating the $\ln y$-values and x-values. The results are given in Table 8-5, along with the data and $\ln y$-values.

Studying the results of Table 8-5, note that the sum of squares error (i.e., the sum of the squares of the residuals) is 1.4451 as compared to 7.17 for the linear model of the previous example. The smaller sum of squares error for the exponential model suggests that the exponential model fits the data better than the linear model does.

TABLE 8-5

x	y	$\ln y$
1	9.8	2.28238
2	9.3	2.23001
3	8.7	2.16332
4	8.1	2.09186
5	7.7	2.04122
6	7.1	1.96009
7	6.7	1.90211
8	6.4	1.85630
9	5.9	1.77495
10	5.5	1.70475
11	5.2	1.64866
12	5.1	1.62924
13	4.7	1.54756
14	4.5	1.50408
15	4.6	1.52606
16	4.5	1.50408
17	4.3	1.45862
18	4.1	1.41099
19	3.8	1.33500
20	2.8	1.02962
21	2.9	1.06471
22	2.8	1.02962
23	2.7	0.99325
24	2.5	0.91629
25	2.4	0.87547
26	2.5	0.91629
27	2.4	0.87547

Regression Line

$\ln y = 2.31 - 0.0561x$

$\ln y = \ln a + (\ln b)x$

Sum of Squares Error

1.4451

WRITING THE MODEL IN EXPONENTIAL FORM

Studying the regression line of Table 8-5, note that

$$\ln a = 2.31 \qquad \text{and} \qquad \ln b = -0.0561$$

Rewriting the above in exponential form gives

$$a = e^{2.31} \qquad\qquad b = e^{-0.0561}$$
$$= 10.07$$

Thus, the equivalent exponential form

$$y = ab^x$$

is given by

$$y = 10.07e^{-0.0561x}$$

Its graph is given in Figure 8-18.

Using the concepts of continuous compounding and exponential functions, the exponent, -0.0561, indicates that the U.S. farm population as a percentage of total U.S. population is decreasing at an annual rate of approximately 5.61% compounded continuously. This translates into the effective annual rate given below.

Effective Annual Rate

$$e^{-0.0561} - 1 = -0.0546$$
$$= 5.46\% \text{ decrease per year}$$

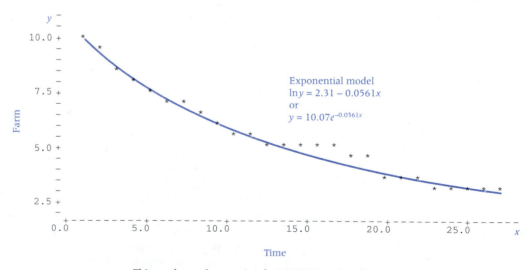

This graph was drawn using the MINITAB statistical software package. The regression line and annotations have been added.

FIGURE 8-18

Quadratic Models

Up to this point in this section, we have presented numerous applications of the least squares method of fitting regression lines to sets of data. We have indicated how to fit linear models and exponential models to data.

We wish to note that the least squares method is used to fit *quadratic models* of the form

$$y = ax^2 + bx + c$$

to sets of data. Graphically, these result in the fitting of a parabola to a set of data points. Here the least squares method is used to find the coefficients a, b, and c of the best-fitting parabola to a set of data points. Specifically, the sum of squares error, S, is a function of a, b, and c. Thus, the coefficients a, b, and c are determined by taking the partial derivatives of S with respect to a, b, and c, respectively; setting them equal to zero; and solving for a, b, and c. In other words, the coefficients a, b, and c are solutions to the linear system

$$S_a(a, b, c) = 0 \qquad S_b(a, b, c) = 0 \qquad S_c(a, b, c) = 0$$

Since such computations are usually long and tedious, we will use a computer software package to fit parabolas to sets of data in the homework exercises.

Multiple Linear Regression Models

Also, the least squares method is used to relate y-values to more than one independent variable. Specifically, if a set of data relates y-values to x_1-values and x_2-values, then a linear relationship between y and a joint combination of x_1 and x_2 is given by the equation

$$y = a + b_1 x_1 + b_2 x_2$$

Such a model is called a *multiple linear regression model*

Exercises 8-4

For each of the following:
a) Find the equation of the linear regression line.
b) Graph the data and the regression line on the same set of axes.
c) Compute the residuals.
d) Compute the sum of squares error.

1.

x	y
2	8
3	10
2	7
5	15

2.

x	y
3	7
2	5
4	10
3	6

3.

x	y
4	8
2	5
8	14
6	9

4.

x	y
5	7
3	4
9	15
7	10

5.

x	y
1	4
2	6
3	7
4	10
5	13

6.

x	y
−2	3
−1	7
0	11
1	15
2	19

7.

x	y
−2	2
−1	4
0	7
1	10
2	12

8.

x	y
−3	5
−1	9
1	12
3	14

A computer was used to fit a linear regression line to each set of data below. Computer results, including residuals, are given next to each set of data. For each of the following:

a) Use the equation of the regression line to estimate y at $x = 3.5$.

b) Compute the sum of squares error.

9.

x	y	Residuals
2	7	1.6890
4	9	−0.8841
6	13	−1.4573
8	16	−3.0305
9	25	3.6829

The regression equation is
$y = 0.74 + 2.29x$.

10.

x	y	Residuals
1	9	1.6520
3	13	−0.6912
4	16	−0.8627
7	24	−2.3775
9	35	2.2794

The regression equation is
$y = 4.18 + 3.17x$.

11.

x	y	Residuals
2	6	1.1340
3	9	0.3093
7	19	−4.9897
8	28	0.1856
9	35	3.3608

The regression equation is
$y = −2.78 + 3.82x$.

12.

x	y	Residuals
2	9	0.3494
4	19	−0.7108
5	27	2.1084
8	38	−2.4337
9	47	1.3855

The regression equation is
$y = −1.01 + 5.18x$.

Goodness-of-Fit. A computer was used to fit both an exponential and a quadratic model to each set of data below. The results, including the sum of squares error for each model, are given for each set of data. Therefore, for each of the following:

a)   State which model best fits the set of data.
b)   Write the exponential model in the form $y = ab^x$.
c)   Use the exponential model to estimate y at $x = 4.5$.
d)   Use the quadratic model to estimate y at $x = 4.5$.

13.

x	y
1	10
3	50
4	90
6	185
2	20

Exponential Model
$\ln y = 1.89 + 0.593x$

Sum of Squares Error
2684.9

Quadratic Model
$y = 4.71x^2 + 2.76x + 0.05$

Sum of Squares Error
40

14.

x	y
1	3
2	5
3	10
4	18
5	30

Exponential Model
$\ln y = 0.495 + 0.589x$

Sum of Squares Error
2.0482

Quadratic Model
$y = 1.64x^2 - 3.16x + 4.60$

Sum of Squares Error
0.11

Applications

Accounting: Cost Segregation

In an Extra Dividends section following Chapter 1, we used a method called the high-low point method to fit a straight line to a set of cost data. The equation of the resulting straight line was used to segregate the fixed and variable portions of cost as follows:

1. The y-intercept of the straight line estimates the fixed cost.
2. The slope of the straight line estimates the variable cost per unit.

For each of the exercises below, we will use the linear regression line to segregate the fixed and variable portions of cost. Specifically, for Exercises 15 and 16, we have used a computer to fit a linear regression line to the data.

15.   *Electric power costs.* The data below give electric power costs associated with various hours of operation for some firm.

x Hours	y Cost ($)
5800	7000
5000	6500
5600	6700
5900	7400

Regression Line
$y = 0.841x + 2211$

a)   State the fixed cost.
b)   State the variable cost per hour.

16. *The following cost data appeared on a past Uniform CPA Examination.* Labor hours and production costs for 4 representative months of a given year are as follows:

Month	Labor hours	Total production costs ($)
September	2500	20,000
October	3500	25,000
November	4500	30,000
December	3500	25,000

Regression Line
$y = 5x + 7500$

a) State the fixed monthly production cost.
b) State the variable production cost per hour.

Investment Risk Measurement

The data below give annual percent changes of the net asset values of various mutual funds versus those of the overall market as measured by the Standard & Poors 500 Composite Index (S&P 500).

Annual percent changes

		1984	1985	1986	1987	1988
x	S&P 500	6.2	31.3	18.1	4.7	16.2
y	Mutual Shares	14.5	26.6	17.0	6.4	30.8
y	20th Century Vista	−16.3	29.5	26.3	6.0	2.4
y	Neuberger Manhattan	6.9	37.2	17.0	0.4	18.3
y	Nicholas Fund	10.0	29.6	11.7	−0.8	18.0

We used a computer to find the equation of the linear regression line relating each fund's performance versus that of the overall stock market as measured by the S&P 500. The results are given below. For each of the following, state the fund's beta and give its interpretation.

17. Mutual Shares
    Regression line: $y = 0.655x + 9.04$
18. 20th Century Vista
    Regression line: $y = 1.38x - 11.5$
19. Neuberger Manhattan
    Regression line: $y = 1.29x - 3.75$
20. Nicholas Fund
    Regression line: $y = 0.957x - 0.94$

Time Series

21. *Gross National Product (GNP).* The data below give the GNP (in billions of dollars) for the United States for the years indicated.

Year	1955	1956	1957	1958	1959	1960	1961
GNP	405.9	428.2	451.0	456.8	495.8	515.3	533.8
Year	1962	1963	1964	1965	1966	1967	1968
GNP	574.6	606.9	649.8	705.1	772.0	816.4	892.7
Year	1969	1970	1971	1972	1973	1974	1975
GNP	963.9	1015.5	1102.7	1212.8	1359.3	1472.8	1598.4
Year	1976	1977	1978	1979	1980	1981	1982
GNP	1782.8	1990.5	2249.7	2508.3	2732.0	3052.6	3166.0
Year	1983	1984	1985	1986			
GNP	3405.7	3765.0	3998.1	4208.5			

A computer was used to fit the exponential moded to the GNP data with coded x-values such that $x = 1$ corresponds to 1955, $x = 2$ to 1956, etc., and y denotes GNP. The result is given below.

Regression line: $\ln y = 5.77 + 0.0785x$

a) Write the equation of the regression line in the form $y = ab^x$.
b) At what annual rate (i.e., compounded annually) has GNP been increasing during this time interval?
c) Using this model, forecast GNP for the years 1987, 1988, and 1989.

22. *Imports.* The data below give U.S. imports (in billions of dollars) for the indicated years.

Year	1967	1968	1969	1970	1971	1972
Imports	42.1	49.3	54.7	60.5	66.1	78.2
Year	1973	1974	1975	1976	1977	1978
Imports	97.3	135.2	130.3	158.9	189.7	223.4
Year	1979	1980	1981	1982	1983	1984
Imports	272.5	318.9	348.9	335.6	358.7	441.4
Year	1985	1986				
Imports	448.6	478.7				

A computer was used to fit the exponential model to the data with coded x-values such that $x = 1$ corresponds to the year 1967, $x = 2$ to 1968, etc., and y denotes imports. The result is given below.

Regression line: $\ln y = 3.64 + 0.138x$

a) Write the equation of the regression line in the form $y = ab^x$.
b) At what annual rate (i.e., compounded annually) have imports been increasing during this time interval?
c) Using this model, forecast U.S. imports for the years 1987, 1988, and 1989.

23. *Exports.* The data below give U.S. exports (in billions of dollars) for the indicated years.

Year	1976	1977	1978	1979	1980	1981
Exports	177.7	191.6	227.5	291.2	351.0	382.8
Year	1982	1983	1984	1985	1986	
Exports	361.9	352.5	382.7	369.8	373.0	

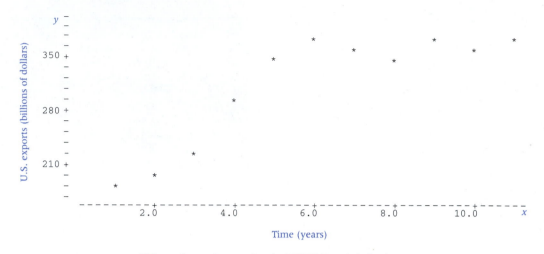

This graph was drawn using the MINITAB statistical software package. The regression line and annotations have been added.

FIGURE 8-19

A computer was used to fit both linear and quadratic models to the data with coded x-values such that $x = 1$ corresponds to the year 1976, $x = 2$ to 1977, etc., and y denotes exports. A time series plot of the data prepared using the Minitab statistical software package is given in Figure 8-19. Also, the computer results are given below.

Linear Model	*Quadratic Model*
$y = 20.8x + 190$	$y = -3.60x^2 + 64x + 96.3$
Sum of Squares Error	*Sum of Squares Error*
15,143	4031

a) State which model better fits the data.
b) Use the linear model to forecast U.S. exports for the years 1987, 1988, and 1989.
c) Figure 8-20 on page 533 gives a Minitab plot of the fitted quadratic model. According to this graph, are U.S. exports increasing, decreasing, or leveling off?
d) Use the quadratic model to forecast U.S. exports for the years 1987, 1988, and 1989.

24. *Systolic blood pressure.* A person's systolic blood pressure (SBP) is recorded weekly, with the following results:

Week	1	2	3	4	5	6	7	8	9
SBP	125	128	130	129	135	138	140	146	145

a) Find the equation of the linear regression line for this time series data.
b) How is this person's blood pressure changing with time?
c) Using the linear model of part a, forecast blood pressure for the tenth week.

25. *Education.* The data below relate undergraduate grade point average (GPA) with starting salary (in thousands of dollars) for a sample of recent graduates of a small liberal arts college.

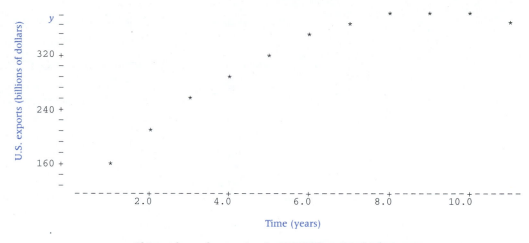

This graph was drawn using the MINITAB statistical software package. The regression line and annotations have been added.

FIGURE 8-20

x GPA	2.5	3.0	2.4	3.5	2.1	2.6
y Starting salary	15.5	19.7	15.2	22.8	14.6	15.8

a) Find the equation of the linear regression line.
b) According to the linear model of part a, state the effect of GPA on starting salary.
c) Estimate the starting salary for a GPA of 2.9.

26. *Medical science.* The data below relate serum cholesterol level (in milligrams/100 milliters) with age for a sample of adult males.

x Age	20	35	27	40	49	55
y Cholesterol	210	279	230	190	252	287

a) Find the equation of the regression line.
b) According to these data, state the effect of age on cholesterol level.
c) Estimate the cholesterol level of a 30-year-old male.

Multiple Linear Regression

27. *Agriculture.* The multiple linear regression model

$$y = 630.4 - 7.8x_1 + 4.3x_2$$

gives the relationship among y, x_1, and x_2, where

y = yield of some crop (in millions of bushels)

x_1 = average temperature (in degrees Fahrenheit) during the growing season

x_2 = average percentage of sunshine during the growing season

a) If x_2 is held constant and x_1 increases by 1 degree Fahrenheit, what effect will this have on crop yield?
b) If x_1 is held constant and x_2 increases by 1 percentage point, what effect will this have on crop yield?

28. *Education.* The multiple linear regression model

$$y = -0.86 + 0.00025x_1 + 0.00513x_2$$

gives the relationship among y, x_1, and x_2, where

$$y = \text{first-year GPA}$$
$$x_1 = \text{SAT mathematics score}$$
$$x_2 = \text{SAT verbal score}$$

for a sample of freshmen students at a college. According to the multiple linear regression model:

a) State the effect on GPA of a 100-point increase in the SAT mathematics score, assuming the SAT verbal score remains constant.

b) State the effect on GPA of a 100-point increase in the SAT verbal score, assuming the SAT mathematics score remains constant.

8-5 • LAGRANGE MULTIPLIERS

Sometimes we must optimize a function $z = f(x, y)$, where x and y are constrained. As an example, consider a factory that burns two types of fuel: BF108 and BF109. The number of tons of pollutant exhausted by the factory in a year is given by

$$z = f(x, y) = x^2 + 2y^2 - xy - 279{,}990$$

where x is the amount (in thousands of gallons) of BF108 fuel used annually and y is the amount (in thousands of gallons) of BF109 fuel used annually. The factory uses a combined amount of 800 thousand gallons of fuel annually. We seek to determine how many thousands of gallons of each type fuel should be burned annually in order to minimize the amount of pollutant exhausted.

Since the factory uses a combined amount of 800 thousand gallons of fuel annually, then

$$x + y = 800$$

Mathematically, our problem is to

$$\text{Minimize } f(x, y) = x^2 + 2y^2 - xy - 279{,}990$$
$$\text{subject to the constraint } g(x, y) = x + y = 800$$

Such a problem may be solved by the method of *Lagrange multipliers.*, A graphical interpretation of this constrained optimization problem is given in Figure 8-21.

In general, the method of Lagrange multipliers is used to solve the following type of problem.

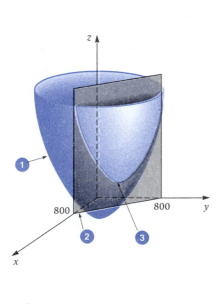

1 Surface: $z = x^2 + 2y^2 - xy - 279{,}900$

2 Constraint: $x + y = 800$

3 Constrained minimum

FIGURE 8-21

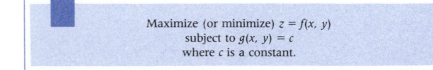

Maximize (or minimize) $z = f(x, y)$
subject to $g(x, y) = c$
where c is a constant.

To use the method of LaGrange multipliers, we define a new function

$$F(x, y, \lambda) = f(x, y) + \lambda(c - g(x, y))$$

where λ is called the **Lagrange multiplier** and the function F is called the **lagrangian function.** Studying the lagrangian function, F, note that since $g(x, y) = c$, then $c - g(x, y) = 0$, and the value of F will equal that of the original function, f. The following is proven in more advanced texts.

> The relative maxima (or minima) of the function $z = f(x, y)$ subject to the constraint $g(x, y) = c$ will be among those points (x_0, y_0) such that (x_0, y_0, λ_0) is a critical point of the lagrangian function, F.

Thus, by finding the values of x, y, and λ that maximize (or minimize) F, we also find the values of x and y that maximize (or minimize) $f(x, y)$ subject to the constraint equation $g(x, y) = c$.

Returning to our problem, we find

$$F(x, y, \lambda) = f(x, y) + \lambda(c - g(x, y))$$
$$= x^2 + 2y^2 - xy - 279{,}900 + \lambda(800 - x - y)$$

We now find the critical values of F.

Calculating F_x, F_y, F_λ, we have

$$F_x = 2x - y - \lambda$$
$$F_y = 4y - x - \lambda$$
$$F_\lambda = 800 - x - y$$

Setting these equal to 0 yields

$$2x - y - \lambda = 0$$
$$4y - x - \lambda = 0$$
$$800 - x - y = 0$$

Solving the first two equations for λ, we have

$$\lambda = 2x - y$$
$$\lambda = 4y - x$$

Equating these two expressions for λ yields

$$2x - y = 4y - x$$
$$-5y = -3x$$
$$y = \frac{3}{5}x$$

Substituting $(3/5)x$ for y into the third equation

$$800 - x - y = 0$$

yields

$$800 - x - \frac{3}{5}x = 0$$

Solving for x, we obtain

$$x = 500$$

Substituting $x = 500$ into

$$y = \frac{3}{5}x$$

we have

$$y = \frac{3}{5}(500)$$

$$= 300$$

We now substitute $x = 500$ and $y = 300$ into either of the equations for λ. Arbitrarily choosing the equation

$$\lambda = 2x - y$$

we obtain

$$\lambda = 2(500) - 300$$

$$= 700$$

Thus, the function F has a *critical point* at

$$x = 500 \qquad y = 300 \qquad \lambda = 700$$

Second Order Conditions

We must now determine whether either a relative maximum of F or a relative minimum of F exists at the critical point in question. To determine the behavior of F (and also f subject to the constraint) at a critical point, we define the matrix

$$H = \begin{bmatrix} 0 & g_x & g_y \\ g_x & f_{xx} & f_{xy} \\ g_y & f_{yx} & f_{yy} \end{bmatrix}$$

The matrix H is called a **bordered Hessian matrix** and must be evaluated at the critical point. The determinant* of H (denoted $|H|$) indicates whether either a relative maximum or a relative minimum exists at the critical point in accordance with the rule stated here.

---

*The evaluation of determinants is presented in Appendix B.

Returning to our example, we compute the elements of H and evaluate them at the critical values of F.

$$g(x, y) = x + y, \; g_x = 1, g_x(500, 300) = 1$$
$$g_y = 1, g_y(500, 300) = 1$$

$$f(x, y) = x^2 + 2y^2 - xy - 279{,}990$$
$$f_x = 2x - y, f_x(500, 300) = 2(500) - 300 = 700$$
$$f_y = 4y - x, f_y(500, 300) = 4(300) - 500 = 700$$

$$f_{xx} = 2, \quad f_{xx}(500, 300) = 2, \quad f_{yy} = 4, \quad f_{yy}(500, 300) = 4$$
$$f_{xy} = -1, f_{xy}(500, 300) = -1, f_{yx} = -1, f_{yx}(500, 300) = -1$$

Thus, H evaluated at the critical values is

$$H = \begin{bmatrix} 0 & 1 & 1 \\ 1 & 2 & -1 \\ 1 & -1 & 4 \end{bmatrix}$$

and $|H| = -8$. Since $|H| < 0$, a relative minimum exists at the critical values $x = 500$, $y = 300$, and $\lambda = 700$. Also, the minimal value of f (i.e., the minimal number of tons of exhausted pollutant) subject to the constraint is given by

$$f(500, 300) = (500)^2 + 2(300)^2 - 500(300) - 279{,}990$$
$$= 10$$

In other words, λ_0 is the rate of change of z with respect to c and thus measures the sensitivity of the optimal value of f to a change in c.

Returning to our original example, recall that $\lambda_0 = 700$. Since $dz/dc = \lambda_0 = 700$, then each unit increase in c (i.e., each additional thousand gallons of fuel used) increases the optimal amount of pollutant exhausted by approximately 700 tons.

We now summarize the method of Lagrange multipliers.

SUMMARY

Method of Lagrange Multipliers

To solve the problem

$$\text{Maximize (or minimize) } z = f(x, y)$$
$$\text{subject to } g(x, y) = c$$
$$\text{where } c \text{ is a constant}$$

1. Determine the lagrangian function

$$F(x, y, \lambda) = f(x, y) + \lambda(c - g(x, y))$$

where λ is the lagrangian multiplier.

2. Search for the critical points.
   - Find the first-order partials F_x, F_y, and F_λ.
   - Set the first-order partials equal to zero and solve for x, y, and λ.
   - Determine all possible ordered triples (x, y, λ) that satisfy all three equations:

$$F_x(x, y, \lambda) = 0 \qquad F_y(x, y, \lambda) = 0 \qquad F_\lambda(x, y, \lambda) = 0$$

These are the critical points of F.

3. Apply the second-order conditions.
   - Compute g_x, g_y, f_{xx}, f_{yy}, f_{xy}, and f_{yx}.
   - Evaluate the above at each critical point, and form the bordered Hessian matrix, H, for each critical point.
   - Evaluate the determinant of each bordered Hessian matrix, H (there will be a bordered Hessian matrix, H, for each critical point), and apply the second-order conditions to each such H as follows.

Second-Order Conditions

If $|H| > 0$, a relative maximum exists
If $|H| < 0$, a relative minimum exists

• EXAMPLE 8-25 _____

Maximize (or minimize) $f(x, y) = -x^2 + 4xy - y^2 + 10$ subject to $x + 2y = 9$.

Solution

Determine the Lagrangian Function

$$F(x, y, \lambda) = f(x, y) + \lambda(c - g(x, y))$$
$$= -x^2 + 4xy - y^2 + 10 + \lambda(9 - x - 2y)$$

Search for the Critical Points

We find the first-order partials and set them equal to 0. Hence,

$$F_x = -2x + 4y - \lambda = 0$$
$$F_y = 4x - 2y - 2\lambda = 0$$
$$F_\lambda = 9 - x - 2y = 0$$

Solving the first two equations for λ, we have

$$\lambda = -2x + 4y$$
$$\lambda = 2x - y$$

Equating these two, we have

$$-2x + 4y = 2x - y$$
$$y = \frac{4}{5}x$$

Substituting $(4/5)x$ for y in the third equation, $9 - x - 2y = 0$, yields

$$9 - x - \frac{8}{5}x = 0$$

Solving for x, we obtain

$$x = \frac{45}{13}$$

Since $y = (4/5)x$, then $y = (4/5)(45/13) = 36/13$. We now substitute $x = 45/13$ and $y = 36/13$ into either equation containing λ. Arbitrarily choosing

$$\lambda = 2x - y$$

we obtain

$$\lambda = 2\left(\frac{45}{13}\right) - \frac{36}{13}$$
$$= \frac{54}{13}$$

Thus, the function F has a critical point at

$$x = \frac{45}{13} \qquad y = \frac{36}{13} \qquad \lambda = \frac{54}{13}$$

Apply the Second-Order Conditions

We must determine whether either a relative maximum or a relative minimum exists at the critical point by determining the bordered Hessian matrix

$$H = \begin{bmatrix} 0 & g_x & g_y \\ g_x & f_{xx} & f_{xy} \\ g_y & f_{yx} & f_{yy} \end{bmatrix}$$

We first compute the elements of H and evaluate them at the critical values of F. Hence,

$$g(x, y) = x + 2y, g_x = 1, g_x(45/13, 36/13) = 1$$
$$g_y = 2, g_y(45/13, 36/13) = 2$$

$$f(x, y) = -x^2 + 4xy - y^2 + 10$$
$$f_x = -2x + 4y, f_x(45/13, 36/13) = -2(45/13) + 4(36/13) = 54/13$$
$$f_y = 4x - 2y, f_y(45/13, 36/13) = 4(45/13) - 2(36/13) = 108/13$$
$$f_{xx} = -2, f_{xx}(45/13, 36/13) = -2, f_{yy} = -2, f_{yy}(45/13, 36/13) = -2$$
$$f_{xy} = 4, f_{xy}(45/13, 36/13) = 4, f_{yx} = 4, f_{yx}(45/13, 36/13) = 4$$

Thus, H evaluated at the critical values is

$$H = \begin{bmatrix} 0 & 1 & 2 \\ 1 & -2 & 4 \\ 2 & 4 & -2 \end{bmatrix}$$

and $|H| = 26$. Since $|H| > 0$, a *relative maximum* exists at the critical values $x = 45/13$, $y = 36/13$, and $\lambda = 54/13$. Also, the maximum value of f subject to the constraint is given by

$$f(45/13, 36/13) = -(45/13)^2 + 4(45/13)(36/13) - (35/13)^2 + 10$$
$$= 373/13 \approx 28.69$$

• EXAMPLE 8-26 _____

Interpret the lagrangian multiplier, λ, for Example 8-25.

Solution

Since $dz/dc = \lambda_0 = 54/13$, then each unit increase in c (where $c = 9$) increases the optimal value of f by approximately $54/13$ units.

Applications

• EXAMPLE 8-27   **Sawmill: Maximizing Cross-Sectional Area of a Beam.**

A sawmill receives logs with a cross-sectional diameter of $\sqrt{2}$ (approximately 1.414) feet. A rectangular beam is cut from each such log, as illustrated in Figure 8-22. Determine the cross-sectional dimensions that result in a beam with maximal cross-sectional area.

Solution

In terms of Figure 8-22, the cross-sectional rectangular dimensions are $2x$ by $2y$. Thus, the cross-sectional area, which we seek to maximize, is $(2x)(2y) = 4xy$. Therefore, our problem is stated mathematically below.

$$\text{Maximize } z = f(x, y) = 4xy$$
$$\text{subject to} \quad \underbrace{x^2 + y^2}_{g(x,\ y)} = 1/2$$

Determine the Lagrangian Function

$$F(x, y, \lambda) = f(x, y) + \lambda(c - g(x, y))$$
$$= 4xy + \lambda(1/2 - x^2 - y^2)$$

Search for Critical Points

We find the first-order partials and set them equal to 0. Hence,

$$F_x = 4y - 2\lambda x = 0$$
$$F_y = 4y - 2\lambda y = 0$$
$$F_\lambda = \frac{1}{2} - x^2 - y^2 = 0$$

Solving the first equation for λ gives $\lambda = 2y/x$. Solving the second equation for λ gives $\lambda = 2x/y$. Setting both expressions for λ equal to each other gives

$$\frac{2y}{x} = \frac{2x}{y} \quad \text{or} \quad y^2 = x^2$$
$$y = \pm x$$

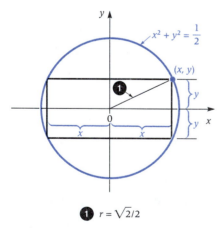

FIGURE 8-22

Substituting $y = \pm x$ into the third equation

$$\frac{1}{2} - x^2 - y^2 = 0$$

gives

$$\frac{1}{2} - x^2 - (\pm x)^2 = 0$$

$$-2x^2 = -\frac{1}{2}$$

$$x^2 = \frac{1}{4}$$

$$x = \pm\frac{1}{2}$$

Due to the symmetry of the problem, as seen in Figure 8-22, we need to consider only positive x- and y-values. In other words, the Lagrange multiplier method has given us all four corner points of the cross-sectional area of the beam, as shown in Figure 8-22. We only need one corner point in order to determine the cross-sectional dimensions. Thus, we substitute $x = 1/2$ and $y = 1/2$ into either equation for λ. Arbitrarily choosing the equation

$$\lambda = \frac{2y}{x}$$

we get

$$\lambda = \frac{2(1/2)}{(1/2)} = 2$$

Thus, the function F has a *critical point* at

$$x = 1/2 \qquad y = 1/2 \qquad \lambda = 2$$

Apply the Second-Order Conditions
We determine the following and evaluate at the critical values of F.

$$g_x(x, y) = 2x \qquad g_x(1/2, 1/2) = 2(1/2) = 1$$
$$g_y(x, y) = 2y \qquad g_y(1/2, 1/2) = 2(1/2) = 1$$
$$f_x = 4y \qquad f_{xx}(x, y) = 0 \qquad f_{xx}(1/2, 1/2) = 0$$
$$f_y = 4x \qquad f_{yy}(x, y) = 0 \qquad f_{yy}(1/2, 1/2) = 0$$
$$f_{xy}(x, y) = 4 \qquad f_{xy}(1/2, 1/2) = 4$$
$$f_{yx}(x, y) = 4 \qquad f_{yx}(1/2, 1/2) = 4$$

The bordered Hessian matrix, H, for our critical point is

$$H = \begin{bmatrix} 0 & 1 & 1 \\ 1 & 0 & 4 \\ 1 & 4 & 0 \end{bmatrix}$$

and its determinant is $|H| = 8$, which is positive. Therefore, by the second-order conditions, a *relative maximum* occurs at the critical values $x = 1/2$, $y = 1/2$, and $\lambda = 2$. Thus, the *maximal cross-sectional area* of the beam is given by

$$f(1/2, 1/2) = 4(1/2)(1/2) = 1 \text{ square foot}$$

• **EXAMPLE 8-28**

Interpret the Lagrange multiplier for Example 8-27.

Solution

$$\lambda_0 = \frac{dz}{dc} = \frac{2 \leftarrow \text{change in cross-sectional area}}{1 \leftarrow \text{change in radius squared}}$$

Thus, for each 1-foot increase in the square of the radius of a log, the maximal cross-sectional area, 1, increases by approximately 2 square feet.

Exercises 8-5

1. Maximize (or minimize)

$$f(x, y) = x^2 - 4xy + y^2 + 200$$

subject to the constraint

$$2x + y = 26$$

2. Maximize (or minimize)

$$f(x, y) = x^2 + 6xy + y^2$$

subject to the constraint

$$x + y = 10$$

3. Maximize (or minimize)

$$f(x, y) = x^2 + 6xy + 2y^2$$

subject to $4x + y = 18$.

4. Maximize (or minimize)

$$f(x, y) = x^2 + 4xy + y$$

subject to $x + y = 12$.

5. Maximize (or minimize)

$$f(x, y) = x^2 + 2xy + y^2 - 3x - 5y$$

subject to $x + y = 18$.

6. Maximize (or minimize)

$$f(x, y) = -y^2 + xy + x$$

subject to $2x + y = 19$.

7. Maximize (or minimize)

$$f(x, y) = x^2 - 5xy + 2y^2$$

subject to $3x + y = 20$.

Lagrange multiplier. Interpret the Lagrange multiplier λ for each of the indicated exercises.

8. Exercise 1   9. Exercise 2   10. Exercise 3
11. Exercise 4   12. Exercise 6   13. Exercise 7

Applications

14. *Profit.* A farmer's profit per square foot of cropland is given by

$$P(x, y) = -x^2 - 5y^2 + 10xy + 4x + 2y - 1100$$

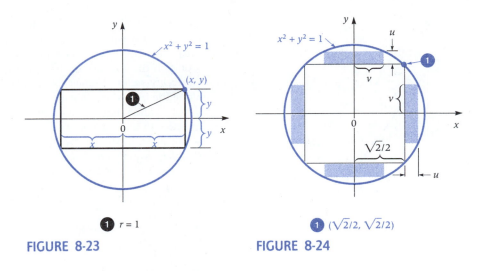

1 $r = 1$

FIGURE 8-23

1 $(\sqrt{2}/2, \sqrt{2}/2)$

FIGURE 8-24

where x is the amount spent on labor per square foot and y is the amount spent on fertilizer per square foot of cropland. If the farmer spends a total of $31.90 per square foot of cropland for labor and fertilizer, then how many dollars per square foot should be allocated to labor and fertilizer in order to maximize the profit per square foot?

15. *Cost.* The total cost of producing x units of product A and y units of product B is given by

$$C(x, y) = x^2 + 4y^2 - 5xy + 2000$$

If a combined total of 40 units is produced daily, then how many units of each product should be produced daily in order to minimize the total cost?

16. *Sawmill: Maximizing cross-sectional area of a beam.* A sawmill receives logs with a cross-sectional diameter of 2 feet. A rectangular beam is cut from each such log, as illustrated in Figure 8-23. Determine the cross-sectional dimensions that result in a beam with maximal cross-sectional area.

17. *Sawmill: Maximizing the use of scrap lumber.* After the beam of Exercise 16 is cut from the log, the remaining scrap lumber is to be used to cut smaller beams, as illustrated in Figure 8-24. Determine the dimensions of the smaller beams that maximize the combined cross-sectional area of the 4 smaller beams.

18. *Cobb-Douglas production function.* For some firm, the number of units produced when using x units of labor and y units of capital is given by the production function

$$z = f(x, y) = 100x^{3/5}y^{2/5}$$

Each unit of labor costs $600, and each unit of capital costs $200. The firm has $700,000 budgeted for combined labor and capital costs.
   a) Write the constraint for the combined labor and capital costs.
   b) Determine the number of units of labor and capital required to maximize production subject to the constraint of part a.
   c) Determine the maximum number of units produced.

19. *Volume.* A box with a square base (see Figure 8-25) is constructed such that the material for the sides costs $1 per square foot and the material for the base costs $3 per square foot. There is no top as the box is open. If each such box is to cost $60, then find its dimensions so that the volume is maximized.

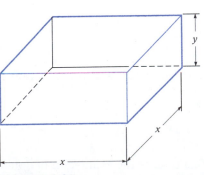

FIGURE 8-25

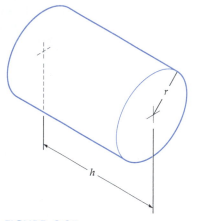

FIGURE 8-26

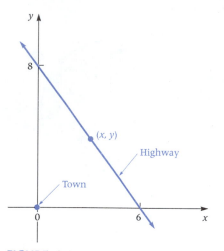

FIGURE 8-27

20. *Cost.* A rubbish container is in the form of a box (as illustrated in Figure 8-25 on page 543) with a square base. It is to cost $14,400. If the material for the sides costs $100 per square foot and the base and top cost $150 per square foot, find the dimensions that maximize its volume.

21. *Emergency facility location.* An emergency facility is to be built somewhere along the highway in Figure 8-26. Since the facility is to service both highway travelers and town residents, at what point on the highway should it be built in order to minimize its distance from the town located at $(0, 0)$? Assume x and y are in miles.

22. *Cylinder.* A cylindrical container (see Figure 8-27) must have a surface area 54π square feet. What dimensions r and h maximize its volume? What is the maximum volume? Use the facts that the volume of a cylinder is given by $\pi r^2 h$ and that the surface area is given by $2\pi rh + 2\pi r^2$.

23. *Cost.* A 1-product company has 2 plants. The cost of producing x units at plant A is given by the cost function

$$C(x) = 80 + x^2/8$$

The cost of producing y units at plant B is given by the cost function

$$C(y) = 100 + y^2/4$$

The total cost of producing x units at plant A and y units at plant B is given by the cost function

$$C(x, y) = C(x) + C(y)$$

If a total of $x + y = 9000$ units is to be made, then how many units should be produced at each plant in order to minimize the total production cost?

Lagrange multiplier. Interpret the Lagrange multiplier λ for each of the indicated exercises.

24. Exercise 14	**25.** Exercise 15	**26.** Exercise 16
27. Exercise 17	**28.** Exercise 18	**29.** Exercise 19
30. Exercise 20	**31.** Exercise 21	**32.** Exercise 22
33. Exercise 23		

8-6 • DOUBLE INTEGRALS

An expression such as

$$\int_4^6 \int_1^2 18x^2y \, dx \, dy$$

which contains two integral signs is an example of a **double integral.** Note that the above expression is of the form

$$\int_c^d \int_a^b f(x, y) \, dx \, dy$$

where a, b, c, and d are constants. We first discuss the evaluation of double integrals and then their graphical interpretation.

To evaluate a double integral, we first evaluate the **inner integral** as indicated below.

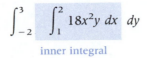

inner integral

Note that the inner integral contains both x and y terms. Since the inner integral contains dx, we treat x as a variable and the remaining variable, y, as a constant. Hence,

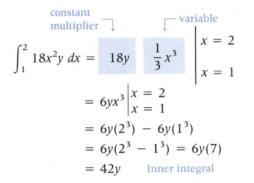

$$= 6yx^3 \Big|_{x=1}^{x=2}$$
$$= 6y(2^3) - 6y(1^3)$$
$$= 6y(2^3 - 1^3) = 6y(7)$$
$$= 42y \qquad \text{Inner integral}$$

Now, we evaluate the **outer integral.**

outer integral

$$\int_{-2}^{3} 42y \; dy$$

evaluated inner integral

Note that this is the integral of the result of the inner integral evaluation. Since the outer integral contains dy, we treat y as a variable. Hence,

$$\int_{-2}^{3} 42y \; dy = 42 \quad \frac{1}{2} y^2 \Big|_{y=-2}^{y=3}$$

$$= 21y^2 \Big|_{y=-2}^{y=3}$$
$$= 21(3^2) - 21 \, (-2)^2$$
$$= 21(9 - 4) = 105 \qquad \text{Final result: double integral}$$

Since the evaluation of double integrals requires that we integrate twice—first, with respect to one variable and, second, with respect to the other variable—they are also called double interated integrals, where the word *iterate* means "to repeat."

• **EXAMPLE 8-29** _____

Evaluate $\int_{-1}^{3} \int_{2}^{4} 6xy^2 \; dy \; dx$.

Solution

First, we evaluate the inner integral as indicated below.

$$\int_{-1}^{3} \boxed{\int_{2}^{4} 6xy^2 \, dy} \, dx$$

inner integral

Since the inner integral contains dy, we treat y as a variable and the remaining variable, x, as a constant. Hence,

$$\int_{2}^{4} 6xy^2 \, dy = 6x \boxed{\frac{1}{3} y^3} \Big|_{\substack{y = 4 \\ y = 2}}$$

$$= 2xy^3 \Big|_{\substack{y = 4 \\ y = 2}}$$

$$= 2x(4^3) - 2x(2^3)$$

$$2x(64 - 8) = 112x \qquad \text{Inner integral}$$

Secondly, we evaluate the outer integral, treating x as a variable as indicated below. Remember, this is the integral of the result of the evaluated inner integral. Hence,

$$\int_{-1}^{3} 112x \, dx = 112 \cdot \frac{1}{2} \cdot x^2 \Big|_{\substack{x = 3 \\ x = -1}}$$

$$= 56x^2 \Big|_{\substack{x = 3 \\ x = -1}}$$

$$= 56(3^2) - 56(-1)^2$$

$$= 56[3^2 - (-1)^2]$$

$$= 56(8) = 448 \qquad \text{Double integral}$$

Variable Limits of Integration

Sometimes, there are variable limits of integration. When this occurs, the variable limits are always located on the inner integral. The outer integral always has constant limits of integration. The next example illustrates a case with variable limits.

• **EXAMPLE 8-30** _____

Evaluate $\displaystyle\int_{0}^{2} \int_{y}^{y^2} 2xy \, dx \, dy$.

Solution

First, we evaluate the inner integral as indicated below.

$$\int_{0}^{2} \boxed{\int_{y}^{y^2} 2xy \, dx} \, dy$$

inner integral

Since the inner integral contains *dx*, we treat *x* as a variable and *y* as a constant. In other words, we integrate with respect to *x*. Hence,

$$\int_{y}^{y^2} 2xy\ dx = 2y\ \left.\frac{1}{2}x^2\right|_{x=y}^{x=y^2}$$

$$= yx^2\Big|_{x=y}^{x=y^2}$$

$$= y(y^2)^2 - y(y^2)$$

$$= y^5 - y^3 \quad \text{Inner integral}$$

Secondly, we evaluate the outer integral, treating *y* as a variable as indicated below. Remember, this is the integral of the result of the evaluated inner integral. Hence,

$$\int_{0}^{2} (y^5 - y^3)\ dy = \frac{1}{6}y^6 - \frac{1}{4}y^4\Big|_{0}^{2}$$

$$= [(1/6)(2^6) - (1/4)(2^4)] - [(1/6)(0^6) - (1/4)(0^4)]$$

$$= \frac{64}{6} - 4 - [0]$$

$$= \frac{40}{6} = \frac{20}{3} \quad \text{Double integral}$$

Graphical Interpretation of Double Integrals

We now consider the graphical interpregation of double integrals of the form

$$\int_{y_1}^{y_2} \int_{x_1}^{x_2} f(x, y)\ dx\ dy$$

where $f(x, y) \geq 0$. Observe, in Figure 8-28, that the limits of integration $x = x_1$, $x = x_2$, $y = y_1$, and $y = y_2$ are boundaries of a rectangular region in the *xy*-plane, and $z = f(x, y)$ represents a surface over the region.

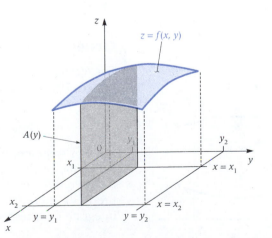

FIGURE 8-28

The inner integral, denoted by $A(y)$, where

$$A(y) = \int_{x_1}^{x_2} f(x, y)\, dx$$

represents the area of the grey plane [denoted by $A(y)$] in Figure 8-28. As this plane moves from $y = y_1$ to $y = y_2$, it forms the **volume** bounded by the surface and the xy-plane over the rectangular region. This *volume* is determined by evaluating the outer integral

$$\int_{y_1}^{y_2} A(y)\, dy$$

We summarize as follows.

Volume

For a function $z = f(x, y)$ that is non-negative over some region (in the xy-plane) bounded by the straight lines $x = x_1$, $x = x_2$, $y = y_1$, and $y = y_2$, the double integral

$$\int_{y_1}^{y_2} \int_{x_1}^{x_2} f(x, y)\, dx\, dy$$

gives the volume of the solid between the surface $z = f(x, y)$ and the xy-plane over the region.

Variable Limits: Graphical Interpretation

If there are variable limits of integration as in the double integral

$$\int_{y_1}^{y_2} \int_{x_1=g(y)}^{x_2=h(y)} f(x, y)\, dx\, dy$$

then the region in the xy-plane is no longer rectangular, but is bounded by the curves $x_1 = g(y)$ and $x_2 = h(y)$ and by the straight lines $y = y_1$ and $y = y_2$, as is illustrated in Figure 8-29.

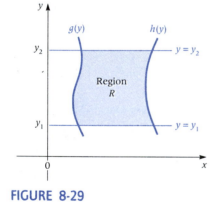

FIGURE 8-29

Order of Integration

For rectangular regions in the xy-plane, the order of integration may be reversed. This means that for constants x_1, x_2, y_1, and y_2, the following holds:

$$\int_{y_1}^{y_2} \left[\int_{x_1}^{x_2} f(x, y)\, dx \right] dy = \int_{x_1}^{x_2} \left[\int_{y_1}^{y_2} f(x, y)\, dy \right] dx$$

For some nonrectangular regions, the order of integration depends on the shape of the region. Specifically, if the region in the xy-plane is such that two sides are straight lines parallel to the y-axis, as is illustrated in Figure 8-30, then, since variable limits are always on the inner integral, we integrate with respect to y first, as indicated by the double integral

$$\int_{x_1}^{x_2} \int_{f(x)}^{g(x)} f(x, y)\, dy\, dx$$

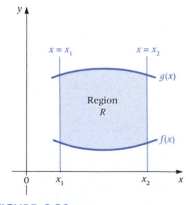

FIGURE 8-30

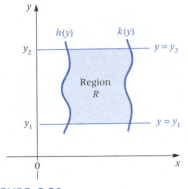

FIGURE 8-31

On the other hand, if the region in the xy-plane is such that two sides are straight lines parallel to the x-axis, as is illustrated in Figure 8-31, then, since variable limits are always on the inner integral, we integrate with respect to x first, as indicated by the double integral

$$\int_{y_1}^{y_2} \int_{h(y)}^{k(y)} f(x, y) \, dx \, dy$$

For other types of nonrectangular regions, double integrals can be integrated in either order. However, determining the variable limits is complicated for more complex regions. Such situations are discussed in more advanced texts.

Application

Probability

A computer module that governs the idle of an automobile engine contains two vital components—components A and B—each of which is replaceable at nominal cost, but at great time expense to the comsumer. For this reason, the lifetime (in years) of each component is of concern to the manufacturer of the module. Both components' lifetimes are considered to be random variables that are jointly distributed in accordance with the probability density function

$$f(x, y) = \begin{cases} e^{-(x + y)} & \text{for } x \geq 0 \text{ and } y \geq 0 \\ 0 & \text{elsewhere} \end{cases}$$

where x denotes the lifetime (in years) of component A and y denotes the lifetime (in years) of component B. This means that the ordered pair (x, y) represents points in the xy-plane where the x-coordinate of a given point denotes a lifetime assumable by component A and the corresponding y-coordinate denotes a lifetime assumable by component B. Furthermore, the probability that x assumes values between a and b and that y assumes val-

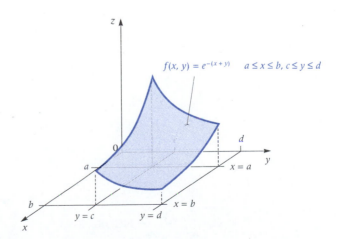

FIGURE 8-32

ues between c and d is given by the volume of the solid between the graph (surface) of the density function and the region in the xy-plane, as indicated in Figure 8-32.

We pause to formally define a joint density function.

Joint Density Function

Continuous Random Variables. A function $z = f(x, y)$ is a joint density function if

1. $f(x, y) \geq 0$ for all (x, y) in some specified region R.

2. $\int_R \int f(x, y) \, dy \, dx = 1$, where the double integral is evaluated over the region R.

PROBLEM

The manufacturer wants to determine the probability that component A has a lifetime of at most 3 years and component B has a lifetime of at most 2 years.

SOLUTION

In terms of probability notation, this probability is written as

$$P(0 \leq x \leq 3 \text{ and } 0 \leq y \leq 2)$$

and is given by the volume under the density function $f(x, y) = e^{-(x + y)}$ over the rectangular region bounded by the straight lines $x = 0$, $x = 3$, $y = 0$, and $y = 2$, as is illustrated in Figure 8-33. Note that this region gives all possible values of both lifetimes of concern to the manufacturer.

This probability (or volume) is given by the double integral

$$\int_0^3 \int_0^2 e^{-(x + y)} \, dy \, dx$$

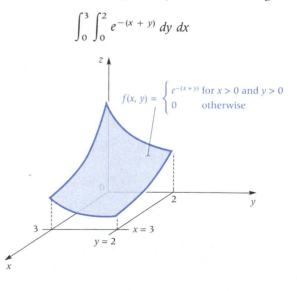

$$f(x, y) = \begin{cases} e^{-(x+y)} & \text{for } x > 0 \text{ and } y > 0 \\ 0 & \text{otherwise} \end{cases}$$

FIGURE 8-33

which we now evaluate. First, we evaluate the inner integral with respect to y. In other words, we treat y as a variable and x as a constant. Hence,

$$\int_0^2 e^{-(x + y)}\, dy = -e^{-(x + y)}\Big|_0^2$$

$$= [-e^{-(x + 2)}] - [-e^{-(x + 0)}]$$

$$= -e^{-(x + 2)} + e^{-x} \qquad \text{Inner integral}$$

Now we evaluate the integral of the above result with respect to x. In other words, we treat x as a variable. Hence,

$$\int_0^3 [-e^{-(x + 2)} + e^{-x}]\, dx = e^{-(x + 2)} - e^{-x}\Big|_0^3$$

$$= [e^{-(3 + 2)} - e^{-3}] - [e^{-(0 + 2)} - e^{-0}]$$

$$= e^{-5} - e^{-3} - e^{-2} + 1$$

$$\approx 0.0067 - 0.0498 - 0.1353 + 1$$

$$\approx 0.8216 \qquad \text{Probability}$$

Thus, there is approximately an 82.16% probability that component A has a lifetime of at most 3 years and component B has a lifetime of at most 2 years.

Exercises 8-6

Evaluate each of the following double integrals.

1. $\int_0^3 \int_1^2 4xy^3\, dy\, dx$

2. $\int_1^4 \int_0^2 (x + y)\, dx\, dy$

3. $\int_1^2 \int_3^6 (2x + 4y)\, dx\, dy$

4. $\int_0^3 \int_{-1}^1 (x - y)\, dy\, dx$

5. $\int_0^1 \int_{x^2}^x (x^2 + y)\, dy\, dx$

6. $\int_{-1}^2 \int_x^{\sqrt{x}} (x^3 + y)\, dy\, dx$

7. $\int_1^4 \int_{y^2}^y (x + 2y)\, dx\, dy$

8. $\int_{-2}^4 \int_1^x (x + 3y^2)\, dy\, dx$

9. $\int_1^2 \int_{-1}^x (x + 4y^3)\, dy\, dx$

10. $\int_1^3 \int_0^x (x^2 + y^2)\, dy\, dx$

11. $\int_1^2 \int_0^4 e^{x+y}\, dx\, dy$

12. $\int_0^4 \int_0^3 e^{2x+y}\, dx\, dy$

13. $\int_0^1 \int_1^2 (4x + 2y + 6)\, dy\, dx$

14. $\int_1^3 \int_0^1 (6 - 2x - 4y)\, dx\, dy$

15. $\int_2^3 \int_1^2 (1/x)\, dx\, dy$

16. $\int_0^1 \int_1^2 \sqrt{x + y}\, dy\, dx$

17. $\int_1^4 \int_1^2 [1/(x + y)]\, dy\, dx$

18. $\int_1^2 \int_1^3 [1/(xy)]\, dx\, dy$

19. $\int_1^4 \int_1^2 (y/x)\, dx\, dy$

20. $\int_1^4 \int_2^6 (x/y)\, dx\, dy$

Reversing the Order of Integration

For each of Exercises 21–24, evaluate the double integral in the order indicated. Then, reverse the order of integration.

21. $\int_1^2 \int_0^4 (4x + 8y) \, dx \, dy$

22. $\int_0^4 \int_2^6 (y - x + 2) \, dy \, dx$

23. $\int_0^3 \int_1^2 (3x^2 + 6y^2) \, dy \, dx$

24. $\int_0^2 \int_1^3 e^{x-y} \, dx \, dy$

Evaluate each of the following double integrals over the indicated region.

25. $\iint e^{2x+4y} \, dy \, dx; \ 0 \leq x \leq 2, 1 \leq y \leq 3$

26. $\iint (x + y) \, dx \, dy; \ 1 \leq x \leq 4, 2 \leq y \leq 5$

27. $\iint (x/y) \, dx \, dy; \ 1 \leq x \leq 3, 2 \leq y \leq 6$

28. $\iint (3x^2 + 4y^3) \, dy \, dx; \ 0 \leq x \leq 2, 1 \leq y \leq 3$

Applications

Probability

29. *Process control.* A company makes washers (see Figure 8-34) with inner and outer diameters denoted by the random variables x and y, respectively, where $0.495 \leq x \leq 0.505$ and $0.995 \leq y \leq 1.005$. The random variables x and y are jointly uniformly distributed in accordance with the density function

$$f(x, y) = \begin{cases} 10{,}000 & \text{if } 0.495 \leq x \leq 0.505, 0.995 \leq y \leq 1.005 \\ 0 & \text{elsewhere} \end{cases}$$

a) Verify that $\int_{0.995}^{1.005} \int_{0.495}^{0.505} 10{,}000 \, dx \, dy = 1$.

b) Find the probability that a washer has an inner diameter within the interval $0.497 \leq x \leq 0.499$ and an outer diameter within the interval $0.998 \leq y \leq 1.001$.

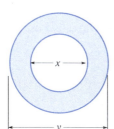

FIGURE 8-34

30. *Military intelligence system: Survival times.* A military spy plane has two computer systems—A and B—on board. The times to failure (in years) of systems A and B are denoted by the random variables x and y, respectively, and are jointly distributed in accordance with the density function

$$f(x, y) = \begin{cases} 2e^{-(2x+y)} & \text{if } x \geq 0, y \geq 0 \\ 0 & \text{otherwise} \end{cases}$$

Find the probability that the survival times for both systems are at most 1 year (in other words, $0 \leq x \leq 1$ and $0 \leq y \leq 1$).

31. *Survey research.* A marketing research firm has prepared two presentations for a particular type of telephone survey. The random variables x and y denote the proportions of subjects that respond to presentations 1 and 2, respectively, and are jointly distributed in accordance with the density function

$$f(x, y) = \begin{cases} (2/3)(2x + y) & \text{if } 0 \leq x \leq 1, 0 \leq y \leq 1 \\ 0 & \text{otherwise} \end{cases}$$

a) Verify that $\displaystyle\int_0^1 \int_0^1 (2/3)(2x + y)\, dx\, dy = 1$

b) Find the probability that at least 50% of the subjects respond to presentation 1 and at least 60% of the subjects respond to presentation 2.

32. For the joint density function of the illustrative probability application in the text, verify that

$$\int_0^\infty \int_0^\infty e^{-(x+y)}\, dx\, dy = 1$$

33. For the joint density function of Exercise 30, verify that

$$\int_0^\infty \int_0^\infty 2e^{-(2x+y)}\, dy\, dx = 1$$

EXTRA DIVIDENDS

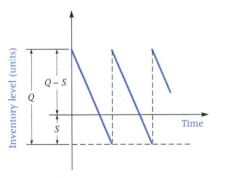

FIGURE 8-35

• *Back-Order Inventory Model—BFI, Inc.*

The distributor of plumbing supplies, BFI, Inc., allows back orders to be taken when demand exceeds the available supply of inventory. This results in the imposition of a stockout cost (or penalty cost) on the average number of back orders. If

D = annual demand (in units) for a given inventory product

K = cost of placing an order

H = annual carrying cost per unit

B = annual stockout cost (or back-order cost) per unit

Q = number of units ordered per order

S = maximum number of back orders allowed

then the total annual inventory cost in such situations is given by

$$C(Q, S) = K\frac{D}{Q} + H\frac{(Q - S)^2}{2Q} + B\frac{S^2}{2Q}$$

Figure 8-35 illustrates a graph of inventory level versus time for such an inventory model.

Using the optimization methods of Section 8-3, it can be determined that the values of Q and S that minimize the total annual inventory cost, C, are given by

$$Q^* = \sqrt{\frac{2DK}{H}\left(\frac{H + B}{B}\right)}$$

$$S^* = Q^*\left(\frac{H}{H + B}\right)$$

One of BFI's products, the BFI307, has an annual demand of 1200, an ordering cost of $5.00 per order, an annual carrying cost of $1.15 per unit, and an annual stockout cost of $2.40 per unit.

Exercises

1. Determine the equation defining the total annual inventory cost.
2. Determine the values of Q and S that minimize the total annual inventory cost.
3. What is the minimum total annual inventory cost?
4. How many back orders are allowed?
5. Every time an order is placed for the BFI307, how many are ordered? After back orders have been set aside, how many are available for sale?

EXTRA DIVIDENDS

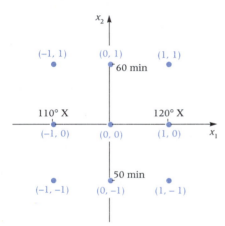

FIGURE 8-36

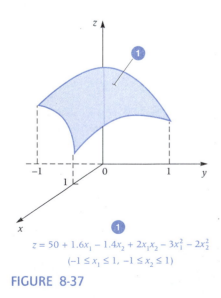

$z = 50 + 1.6x_1 - 1.4x_2 + 2x_1x_2 - 3x_1^2 - 2x_2^2$
$(-1 \le x_1 \le 1, -1 \le x_2 \le 1)$

FIGURE 8-37

• *Using a Response Surface to Increase Industrial Productivity*

Pfichem, Inc., produces a chemical (PFI 707) that is used to clean circuits of computers. The yield (z) in kilograms of the chemical process used to produce PFI 707 is dependent on the *temperature* in degrees Celsius at which the process is run and the *process time* in minutes that the chemical process is allowed to react. The plant manager wants to determine the optimum combination of temperature and process time in order to maximize the yield (z). After running the process at various combinations of temperature and process time, and after analyzing the results, the manager has determined that the process yield (z) is near optimum when the temperature is kept within the interval 100°C to 120°C and the process time is kept within the interval 50 min to 60 min.

To facilitate computational efficiency, these temperature levels are expressed in terms of the coded variable x_1, where $x_1 = -1$ denotes 100°C and $x_1 = 1$ denotes 120°C. Specifically, if C denotes the temperature in degrees Celsius, the equation relating the coded variable x_1 and C is given by

$$x_1 = \frac{C - 110}{10} \qquad (100 \le C \le 120)$$

Similarly, the process time is expressed in terms of the coded variable x_2 such that $x_2 = -1$ denotes 50 minute and $x_2 = 1$ denotes 60 minutes. Specifically, if T denotes the process time in minutes, the equation relating x_2 and T is given by

$$x_2 = \frac{T - 55}{5} \qquad (50 \le T \le 60)$$

The graph of the region denoting feasible near-optimum combinations of temperature and process time appears in Figure 8-36.

The plant manager runs the process repeatedly at each combination of temperature and process time indicated by the colored points of Figure 8-36 and records the corresponding yields, z. Since the values of z indicate how the process yield responds to different combinations of temperature and process time, z is called a **response variable.** The method of least squares is used to fit a model that expresses the relationship between the process yield, z, and the coded variables, x_1 and x_2. This model is given by the equation

$$z = 50 + 1.6x_1 - 1.4x_2 + 2x_1x_2 - 3x_1^2 - 2x_2^2$$

where $-1 \leq x_1 \leq 1$ and $-1 \leq x_2 \leq 1$. The graph of this equation over the region $-1 \leq x_1 \leq 1$ and $-1 \leq x_2 \leq 1$ is the surface sketched in Figure 8-37. Since a point on this surface is denoted by an ordered triple (x_1, x_2, z), where z is the response variable, the surface of Figure 8-37 is called a **response surface.**

Exercises

1. Determine the values of x_1 and x_2 that maximize the process yield, z.
2. Determine the maximum process yield.
3. Determine the optimum combination of temperature in degrees Celsius and process time in minutes in order to maximize the yield, z.

CHAPTER 8 HIGHLIGHTS

• *Concepts*

Your ability to answer the following questions is one indicator of the depth of your mastery of this chapter's important concepts. Note that the questions are grouped under various topic headings. For any question that you cannot answer, refer to the appropriate section of the chapter indicated by the topic heading. Pay particular attention to the summary boxes within a section.

8-1 FUNCTIONS OF SEVERAL VARIABLES

1. Explain each of the following terms: function of two variables, function of three variables, multivariate functions.
2. Draw a three-dimensional coordinate system, and explain how an ordered triple (x, y, z) is plotted.

8-2 PARTIAL DERIVATIVES

3. Given a function $z = f(x, y)$, explain each of the following and indicate how it is determined:
   a) Partial derivative of z with respect to x
   b) Partial derivative of z with respect to y
4. What is a second partial derivative?
5. State the four types of second partials.

8-3 RELATIVE MAXIMA AND MINIMA (FUNCTIONS OF TWO VARIABLES)

6. What is a critical point?
7. If a function $z = f(x, y)$ has relative maxima/minima, do they occur at critical points?
8. Does a critical point always result in a relative extremum?

9. According to the second-derivative test for functions of two variables:
   a) State the conditions for a relative maximum.
   b) State the conditions for a relative minimum.
   c) State the conditions for a saddle point and explain this term.
   d) State the condition for the test failing.
10. Give the procedure for finding relative extrema for functions of two variables.

8-4   APPLICATION: THE METHOD OF LEAST SQUARES

11. What does the method of least squares provide?
12. Give the formulas for determining the slope and y-intercept of a regression line. Explain the components.
13. With regard to investment risk measurement, explain the term *beta*.
14. How does one fit an exponential model to a set of data using the method of least squares?
15. State the three coefficients that must be determined when fitting a quadratic model to a set of data.
16. What is a multiple linear regression model?

8-5   LAGRANGE MULTIPLIERS

17. Describe the type of problem solved by the method of Lagrange multipliers.
18. Outline the method of Lagrange multipliers.
19. Interpret the Lagrange multiplier.

8-6   DOUBLE INTEGRALS

20. What is a double integral?
21. Outline the procedure for determining a double integral.

REVIEW EXERCISES   • *Functions of Two Variables*

1. If $f(x, y) = 2x^2 + 7xy^3 - 6y^4 + 9$, compute each of the following:
   a) $f(1, -1)$ b) $f(-1, 0)$ c) $f(2, 1)$ d) $f(0, -2)$
2. If $f(x, y) = (5x^2 + 6y^2 + 9xy)/(x^2 - 4)$, specify the domain of f.
3. If $f(x, y) = (x^3 + 6xy^2 + 7x - 6)/(x - 4)$, specify the domain of f.

For Exercises 4–6, plot the point in a three-dimensional coordinate system.

4. $(2, 4, 7)$ 5. $(3, -1, 5)$ 6. $(-2, 1, 6)$

• *Partial Derivatives*

7. If $f(x, y) = 2x^2 + 6xy - 8y^4 + 5x + 9$, find each of the following:
   a) $f_x(x, y)$ b) $f_y(x, y)$ c) $f_x(1, 0)$ d) $f_y(-1, 2)$
8. If $g(x, y) = x^4 - 6y^2 - 8x^2y^4 + 9y + 7$, find each of the following:
   a) $g_x(x, y)$ b) $g_y(x, y)$ c) $g_x(-2, 1)$ d) $g_y(1, 2)$
9. If $f(x, y) = x^5 e^{x+y}$, find each of the following:
   a) $f_x(x, y)$ b) $f_y(x, y)$ c) $f_x(1, 0)$ d) $f_y(1, 2)$
10. If $f(x, y) = y^5 \ln (x^3 + 6y^4)$, find each of the following:
    a) $f_x(x, y)$ b) $f_y(x, y)$ c) $f_x(-2, 1)$ d) $f_y(1, -2)$

11. *Cost.* The cost of producing x units of product 1 and y units of product 2 is given by

$$C(x, y) = 80x + 50y + 40xy + 500$$

If 30 units of product 1 and 40 units of product 2 are currently being produced, find the marginal cost of producing an additional unit of
a) Product 1.   b) Product 2.

• ## Second-Order Partial Derivatives

For Exercises 12–15, find each of the following:

a) f_x b) f_{xx} c) f_y d) f_{yy} e) f_{xy} f) f_{yx}
g) $f_{xx}(-1, 3)$ h) $f_{yy}(1, -2)$ i) $f_{xy}(1, 0)$

12. $f(x, y) = x^3 + 4y^2 - 6xy^5 + 9$ 13. $f(x, y) = x^4 e^{x+y}$
14. $f(x, y) = x^5 \ln (x^3 + y^4)$ 15. $f(x, y) = (x^3 + y^5)^4$

• ## Relative Extrema

Find any relative extrema for Exercises 16–19.

16. $f(x, y) = x^2 + y^2 + 6xy + 27x + 21y + 90$
17. $f(x, y) = -x^2 - 2y^2 + 8xy + 32x + 12y + 60$
18. $f(x, y) = 4x^2 - 12x^3 + 6y^2 - 8y^3 + 80$
19. $f(x, y) = -2x^3 - 8y^2 + 24xy + 12$

20. Show that the function defined by

$$f(x, y) = x^2 - 4y^2 - 20x + 24y + 800$$

has no relative extrema. Additionally, show that $f(x, y)$ has a saddle point, and find it.

21. *Sales revenue.* The sales revenue gained from selling x and y units of products A and B, respectively, is given by

$$R(x, y) = -10x^2 - 16y^2 + 48x + 36y$$

Determine the number of units of products A and B that should be sold in order to maximize the sales revenue. Find the maximum sales revenue.

22. *Profit.* A profit function is defined by

$$P(x, y) = -4x^2 - 3y^2 + 54x + 96y - 2xy - 10$$

where x and y denote the sales of gadgets and widgets, respectively. Determine the number of gadgets and widgets that must be sold in order to maximize profit. Find the maximum profit.

23. *Revenue.* A company produces two competing products: A and B. The numbers of units demanded of products A and B are denoted by x_1 and x_2, respectively, and are related to the unit prices, p_1 and p_2, of products A and B, respectively, as given by the following equations:

$$x_1 = 400 - 12p_1 + 14p_2$$
$$x_2 = 600 - 15p_2 + 6p_1$$

a) Determine the equation for total sales revenue, $R(p_1, p_2)$.
b) How should each product be priced in order to maximize the total sales revenue, $R(p_1, p_2)$?
c) Determine the maximum sales revenue.
d) Find the demand for each product at the optimal prices.

• *The Method of Least Squares*

For Exercises 24–26:

a) Find the equation of the linear regression line.
b) Graph the data and the regression line on the same set of axes.
c) Compute the residuals.
d) Compute the sum of squares error.
e) Use the regression line to predict y at $x = 5$.

24.

x	y
1	4
3	10
2	7
6	19

25.

x	y
4	9
8	20
3	8
9	23

26.

x	y
2	7
8	30
7	25
3	8

27. *Investment risk.* The relationship between the percent change of XYZ Mutual Fund and that of the S&P 500 is given by the least squares line

$$y = 1.90x - 1.05$$

Interpret the slope.

28. *Exponential model.* Fit the exponential model to the data points $(1, 3)$, $(2, 17)$, and $(3, 68)$. Write the answer in both logarithmic and exponential forms. Use the model to predict y at $x = 2.5$.

29. *Exponential model.* Fit the exponential model to the data points $(1, 130)$, $(2, 30)$ and $(3, 4)$. Write the answer in both logarithmic and exponential forms. Use the model to predict y at $x = 1.5$.

• *Lagrange Multipliers*

For Exercises 30–32, use the method of Lagrange multipliers.

30. Maximize (or minimize) $f(x, y) = x^2 - 10xy + 2y^2 + 200$ subject to $x + y = 52$.

31. Maximize (or minimize) $f(x, y) = x^2 + 8xy + y^2 + 600$ subject to $x + 2y = 66$.

32. Maximize (or minimize) $f(x, y) = x^2 + 6xy + 4y + 900$ subject to $x + y = 24$.

Interpret the Lagrange multiplier, λ, for each of the indicated exercises.

33. Exercise 30   **34.** Exercise 31   **35.** Exercise 32

36. *Cost.* The total cost of producing x units of product A and y units of product B is given by

$$C(x, y) = x^2 + 3y^2 - 4xy + 6000$$

If a combined total of 800 units is to be produced weekly, then how many units of each product should be produced weekly in order to minimize the total cost? Find the minimum cost. Interpret the Lagrange multiplier.

37. *Container cost.* A company produces a container in the shape of a box with a square base. The cost per square foot for the top and bottom is $5. The cost per square foot for the sides is $10. If the container is to cost $480, find the dimensions that maximize its volume. Interpret the Lagrange multiplier.

• *Double Integrals*

Evaluate each of Exercises 38–41.

38. $\displaystyle\int_{1}^{4}\int_{0}^{2} 6x^2y \; dx \; dy$

39. $\displaystyle\int_{0}^{2}\int_{1}^{4} (3x^2 + 4y^3) \; dy \; dx$

40. $\displaystyle\int_{0}^{1}\int_{1}^{3} e^{x+4y} \; dy \; dx$

41. $\displaystyle\int_{0}^{1}\int_{1}^{y} (3x^2 + y) \; dx \; dy$

Evaluate each of the following double integrals over the indicated region.

42. $\displaystyle\int\int (x/y) \; dx \; dy; \; 2 \le x \le 6, \; 1 \le y \le 5$

43. $\displaystyle\int\int (x + y) \; dy \; dx; \; 1 \le x \le 4, \; 2 \le y \le 8$

TRIGONOMETRIC FUNCTIONS

Introductory Application

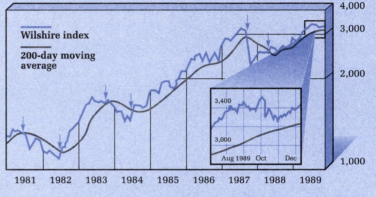

FIGURE 9-A

We begin by observing a graph of the Wilshire 5000, a widely used index of stock market performance. Note the wavelike nature of the index and also its upward trend during the given time period. Stock market analysts are forever trying to decompose such graphs into simpler components in order to forcast future stock market activity. To decompose graphs, such as the one above, into simpler components, it is helpful to understand the following graphical concepts.

Periodicity

Consider the graph of the function illustrated in Figure 9-B. In addition to its wavelike nature, notice how the graph repeats itself at regular intervals. Specifically, as indicated in Figure 9-B, note that for any value of x and a constant p,

$$f(x + p) = f(x)$$

A function that has this property is said to be **periodic.** The smallest value of p for which this property holds is called the **period of the function.**

Periodic functions are used to model economic cycles and time series data that are of a cyclical nature. Although the fitted models often repeat themselves with regularity (in other words, with some period p), actual data values do not usually repeat themselves with the precision of their

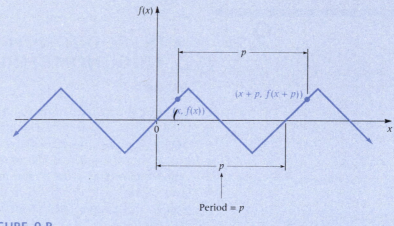

FIGURE 9-B

fitted models. However, studying fitted models exhibiting periodic behavior often gives an analyst intuitive insights that are useful in forecasting future movements of the time series data.

Graphical Concepts

Sometimes time series data contain a combination of periodic behavior and trend. Consider the straight line and periodic function graphs of Figure 9-C(a) and (b). If the y-values of the respective functions are added, the result is the graph of Figure 9-C(c). Observe how the graph of a periodic function and the graph of a linear function combine to form a wavelike graph that moves back and forth about an overall linear trend. The graph of the Wilshire 5000 stock index exhibits such behavior to some extent. Time series data describing monthly sales, annual sales, and annual tax collections, for example, also exhibit similar behavior.

Trigonometric Functions

The preceding paragraphs have involved functions whose graphs exhibit wavelike periodic behavior. In this chapter, we will study such functions. The preceding discussion indicates the need for such a study.

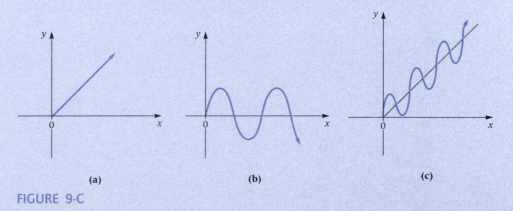

(a)　　　　　　　　(b)　　　　　　　　(c)

FIGURE 9-C

9-1

• INTRODUCTION TO THE TRIGONOMETRIC FUNCTIONS

Angles

Consider the *xy*-axis system and a straight line beginning at the origin, as illustrated in Figure 9-1. The straight line is a ray that rotates in either a clockwise or a counterclockwise manner. At any position, the ray forms an **angle** with the positive half of the *x*-axis. The positive half of the *x*-axis is called the **initial side** of the angle, and the ray is called the **terminal side** of the angle. If the ray rotates *counterclockwise*, the resulting angle is *positive*; if the ray rotates *clockwise*, the resulting angle is *negative*.

Degree Measure

Angles are measured in both degrees and radians. Here, we discuss measuring angles in degrees. If the ray rotates counterclockwise so that it stops along the positive half of the *y*-axis, the resulting angle has a measure of 90°, as shown in Figure 9-2(a). If the ray rotates counterclockwise so that it stops along the negative half of the *x*-axis, the resulting angle has a mea-

Counterclockwise rotation:
Positive angle

Clockwise rotation:
Negative angle

FIGURE 9-1

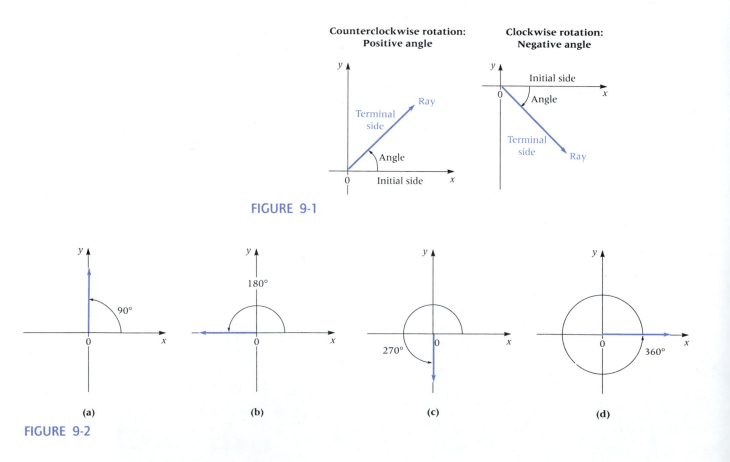

(a) (b) (c) (d)

FIGURE 9-2

sure of 180°, as shown in Figure 9-2(b). If the ray rotates counterclockwise so that it stops along the negative half of the *y*-axis, the resulting angle has a measure of 270°, as shown in Figure 9-2(c). If the ray rotates counter-clockwise so that it makes a complete revolution and stops along the positive half of the *x*-axis, the resulting angle has a measure of 360°, as shown in Figure 9-2(d).

Figure 9-3 illustrates positive angles of 30°, 150°, and 300° and negative angles of −60° and −110°. Observe that the rotating ray is in the same location for angles of −60° and 300°, and for angles of −110° and 250°, as illustrated in Figure 9-3. Also, if the rotating ray makes two complete counterclockwise revolutions, the resulting angle is 2(360°), or 720°, as illustrated in Figure 9-3.

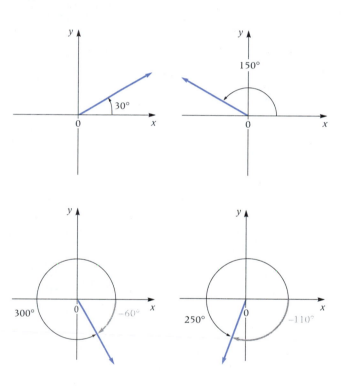

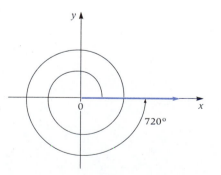

FIGURE 9-3

Radian Measure

Angles are also measured in terms of **radians.** To define a radian, we consider a circle of radius r in Figure 9-4(a) and note the angle formed by the ray. Observe that the counterclockwise-rotating ray has stopped at a position so that the distance along the circumference from the positive half of the x-axis to the ray equals the radius, r. The resulting angle is said to measure 1 radian. An angle that measures 2 radians is illustrated in Figure 9-4(b). Since the circumference of a circle of radius r is $2\pi r$, then the circumference of a circle consists of 2π radii placed end to end, as illustrated in Figure 9-4(c). Thus, a counterclockwise-rotating ray that makes one complete revolution forms an angle of 2π radians. However, since one

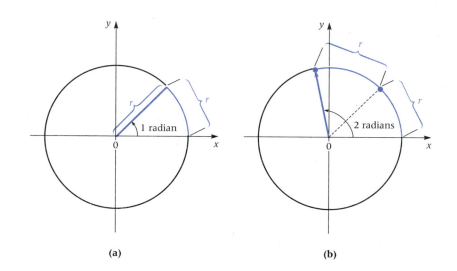

(a) (b)

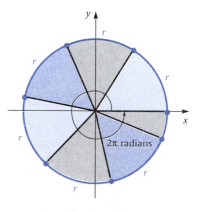

2π radii = circumference
2π radians = 360°

(c)

FIGURE 9-4

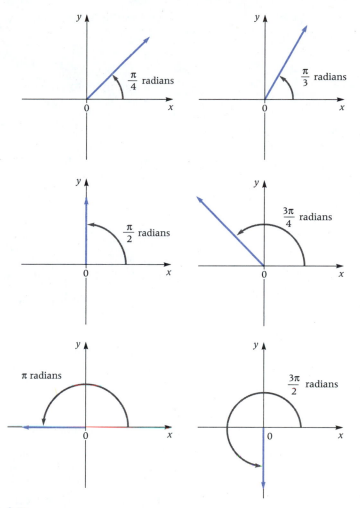

FIGURE 9-5

complete counterclockwise revolution constitutes 360°, then the following relationship holds between degrees and radians:

$$2\pi \text{ radians} = 360°$$

Multiplying both sides of the above by 1/2, 1/4, and 3/4, respectively, gives the following results:

$$\pi \text{ radians} = 180° \qquad \frac{\pi}{2} \text{ radians} = 90° \qquad \frac{3\pi}{2} \text{ radians} = 270°$$

These and other angles are illustrated in Figure 9-5.

Converting from Degrees to Radians

It is sometimes necessary to convert from one angle measure to another. To convert from degrees to radians, we begin with the fact that

$$2\pi \text{ radians} = 360°$$

and multiply both sides by 1/360. This gives the following:

$$1° = \frac{\pi}{180} \text{ radians}$$

Use this result to convert from degrees to radians.

For example, to convert 30° to radians, multiply 30° by $\pi/180$ to obtain

$$30° = 30 \times \frac{\pi}{180} = \frac{\pi}{6} \text{ radians}$$

To convert 80° to radians, multiply 80° by $\pi/180$ to obtain

$$80° = 80 \times \frac{\pi}{180} = \frac{4\pi}{9} \text{ radians}$$

To Convert from Degrees to Radians

Multiply the degree measure by $\pi/180$.

Converting from Radians to Degrees

To convert from radians to degrees, we begin with the relation

$$2\pi \text{ radians} = 360°$$

and multiply both sides by $1/2\pi$ to obtain

$$1 \text{ radian} = \frac{180}{\pi} \text{ degrees}$$

Use this result to convert from radians to degrees.

For example, to convert 3π radians to degrees, multiply 3π radians by $180/\pi$ to obtain

$$3\pi \text{ radians} = 3\pi \times \frac{180}{\pi} = 540°$$

To convert 7 radians to degrees, multiply 7 radians by $180/\pi$ to obtain

$$7 \text{ radians} = 7 \times \frac{180}{\pi} = \frac{1260}{\pi} \text{ degrees}$$

$$\approx \frac{1260}{3.14} = 401.3° \qquad \pi \approx 3.14$$

To Convert from Radians to Degrees

Multiply the radian measure by $180/\pi$.

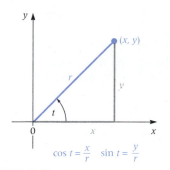

$$\cos t = \frac{x}{r} \quad \sin t = \frac{y}{r}$$

FIGURE 9-6

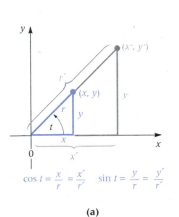

$$\cos t = \frac{x}{r} = \frac{x'}{r'} \quad \sin t = \frac{y}{r} = \frac{y'}{r'}$$

(a)

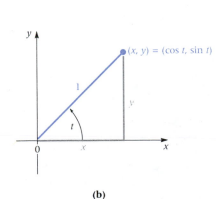

(b)

FIGURE 9-7

Trigonometric Functions

Consider the angle of measure t formed by the ray of length r with endpoint (x, y), as shown in Figure 9-6. By the Pythagorean Theorem,

$$r = \sqrt{x^2 + y^2}$$

The ratio **y/r** is defined as **sin t,** called "sine of t"; the ratio **x/r** is defined as **cos t,** called "cosine of t." Observe that t is an angle and that sin t and cos t are functions of t. Sin t and cos t belong to a class of functions called **trigonometric functions.**

Note that if (x, y) is another point on the ray, the ratios sin t and cos t remain unchanged for a given angle of measure t, as illustrated in Figure 9-7(a). This is due to properties of similar triangles. In subsequent explanations of sin t and cos t, we use a ray (terminal side) of length 1 [see Figure 9-7(b)] to simplify such discussion. Note, in Figure 9-7(b), that since the length of the ray is 1, then

$$\sin t = y/1 = y \quad \text{and} \quad \cos t = x/1 = x$$

and, therefore, the ray of length 1 has the endpoint $(\cos t, \sin t)$.

A complete summary of sin t and cos t is given in the following box. Study this information before proceeding with the remainder of this section.

■ SUMMARY

Sin t and Cos t

Given a ray of length r that forms an angle t with the positive x-axis and has endpoint (x, y), as shown in Figure 9-8, the trigonometric functions sin t and cos t are defined as

$$\sin t = \frac{y}{r} \quad \cos t = \frac{x}{r}$$

where $r = \sqrt{x^2 + y^2}$. Due to properties of similar triangles, the ratios sin t and cos t are constant for a given angle t.

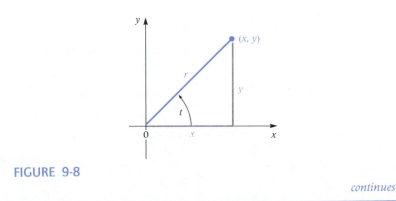

FIGURE 9-8

continues

SUMMARY—*Continued*

For a ray of length 1 that forms an angle t with the positive x-axis and has endpoint (x, y), as shown in Figure 9-9, the trigonometric functions $\sin t$ and $\cos t$ are defined as

$$\sin t = y \qquad \cos t = x$$

and, thus, the endpoint of the ray has coordinates $(\cos t, \sin t)$.

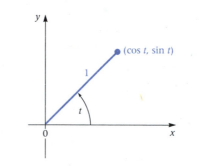

FIGURE 9-9

The trigonometric functions $\sin t$ and $\cos t$ can be interpreted in terms of a right triangle when $0 < t < \pi/2$, as illustrated in Figure 9-10. Note, in Figure 9-10, that

$$\sin t = \frac{\text{opposite side}}{\text{hypotenuse}} \qquad \cos t = \frac{\text{adjacent side}}{\text{hypotenuse}}$$

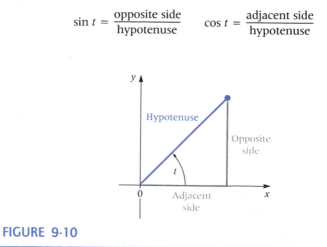

FIGURE 9-10

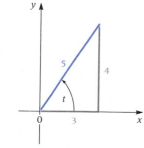

FIGURE 9-11

• **EXAMPLE 9-1**

Find the values of $\sin t$ and $\cos t$ for angle t of Figure 9-11.

Solution

$$\sin t = \frac{\text{opposite side}}{\text{hypotenuse}} \qquad \cos t = \frac{\text{adjacent side}}{\text{hypotenuse}}$$

$$= \frac{y}{r} = \frac{4}{5} \qquad\qquad\qquad = \frac{x}{r} = \frac{3}{5}$$

• EXAMPLE 9-2 _____

Use the triangles of Figure 9-12 to find the values of the following:

a) $\sin 30°$ **b)** $\cos \dfrac{\pi}{6}$ **c)** $\sin 45°$

d) $\cos \dfrac{\pi}{4}$ **e)** $\sin 60°$ **f)** $\cos \dfrac{\pi}{3}$

g) $\sin (-60°)$ **h)** $\cos \left(-\dfrac{\pi}{3} \right)$

Solutions

From Figure 9-12(a), we obtain

a) $\sin 30° = \sin \dfrac{\pi}{6} = \dfrac{1}{2}$ **b)** $\cos \dfrac{\pi}{6} = \cos 30° = \dfrac{\sqrt{3}}{2}$

From Figure 9-12(b), we obtain

c) $\sin 45° = \sin \dfrac{\pi}{4} = \dfrac{1}{\sqrt{2}} = \dfrac{\sqrt{2}}{2}$ **d)** $\cos \dfrac{\pi}{4} = \cos 45° = \dfrac{1}{\sqrt{2}} = \dfrac{\sqrt{2}}{2}$

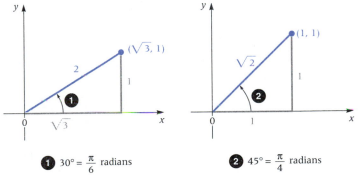

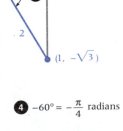
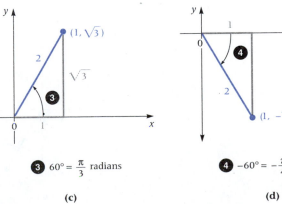

FIGURE 9-12

From Figure 9-12(c), we obtain

e) $\sin 60° = \sin \dfrac{\pi}{3} = \dfrac{\sqrt{3}}{2}$
f) $\cos \dfrac{\pi}{3} = \cos 60° = \dfrac{1}{2}$

From Figure 9-12(d), we obtain

g) $\sin(-60°) = \sin\left(-\dfrac{\pi}{3}\right) = -\dfrac{\sqrt{3}}{2}$
h) $\cos\left(-\dfrac{\pi}{3}\right) = \cos(-60°) = \dfrac{1}{2}$

• **EXAMPLE 9-3** _____

Use the triangles of Figure 9-13 to find the values of the following.

a) $\cos \dfrac{2\pi}{3}$
b) $\sin 120°$
c) $\sin \dfrac{5\pi}{4}$

d) $\cos \dfrac{5\pi}{4}$
e) $\cos 300°$
f) $\sin \dfrac{5\pi}{3}$

g) $\sin\left(-\dfrac{3\pi}{4}\right)$
h) $\cos\left(-\dfrac{3\pi}{4}\right)$

Solutions

From Figure 9-13(a), we determine

a) $\cos \dfrac{2\pi}{3} = \cos 120° = \dfrac{-1}{2}$
b) $\sin 120° = \sin \dfrac{2\pi}{3} = \dfrac{\sqrt{3}}{2}$

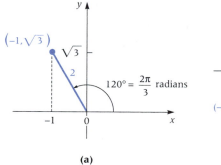

(a)

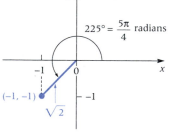

(b)

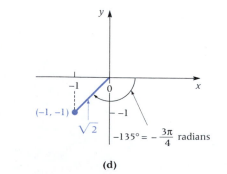

(c)

(d)

FIGURE 9-13

From Figure 9-13(b), we determine

c) $\sin\dfrac{5\pi}{4} = \sin 225° = \dfrac{-1}{\sqrt{2}} = -\dfrac{\sqrt{2}}{2}$ **d)** $\cos\dfrac{5\pi}{4} = \cos 225° = \dfrac{-1}{\sqrt{2}} = -\dfrac{\sqrt{2}}{2}$

From Figure 9-13(c), we determine

e) $\cos 300° = \cos\dfrac{5\pi}{3} = \dfrac{1}{2}$ **f)** $\sin\dfrac{5\pi}{3} = \sin 300° = \dfrac{-\sqrt{3}}{2}$

From Figure 9-13(d), we determine

g) $\sin\left(-\dfrac{3\pi}{4}\right) = \sin(-135°) = \dfrac{-1}{\sqrt{2}} = -\dfrac{\sqrt{2}}{2}$

h) $\cos\left(-\dfrac{3\pi}{4}\right) = \cos(-135°) = \dfrac{-1}{\sqrt{2}} = -\dfrac{\sqrt{2}}{2}$

Periodicity

Observe the angles of the unit circles of Figure 9-14(a) and (b). Note that for Figure 9-14(b), the ray of length 1 has made a complete revolution of 360° or, equivalently, 2π radians from its position in Figure 9-14(a), so that its angle is $t + 2\pi$ radians and its endpoint is at the same location (x, y) as that of Figure 9-14(a). Thus,

$$\sin t = \sin(t + 2\pi) \qquad \text{and} \qquad \cos t = \cos(t + 2\pi)$$

Since the above hold for any value of t, the trigonometric functions $\sin t$ and $\cos t$ are periodic with period 2π. Also, if the ray makes a complete clockwise revolution, then

$$\sin t = \sin(t - 2\pi) \qquad \text{and} \qquad \cos t = \cos(t - 2\pi)$$

Graphs of Sin t and Cos t

Figure 9-15 on page 574 contains a graph of the function $y = \sin t$. Note that values of $\sin t$ fluctuate between -1 and $+1$. Also, note that the graph is wavelike and periodic with period 2π.

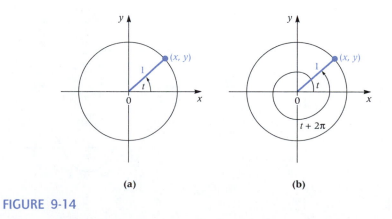

(a)   (b)

FIGURE 9-14

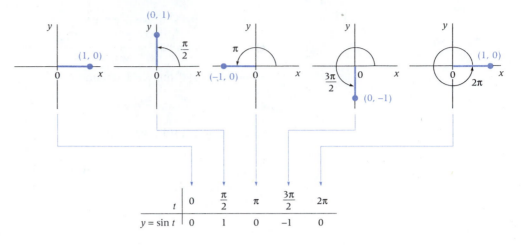

t	0	$\dfrac{\pi}{2}$	π	$\dfrac{3\pi}{2}$	2π
$y = \sin t$	0	1	0	-1	0

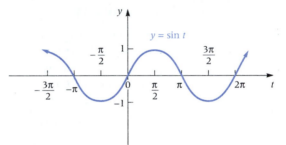

FIGURE 9-15

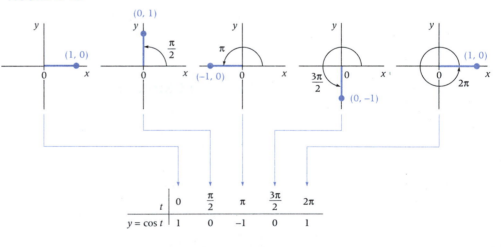

t	0	$\dfrac{\pi}{2}$	π	$\dfrac{3\pi}{2}$	2π
$y = \cos t$	1	0	-1	0	1

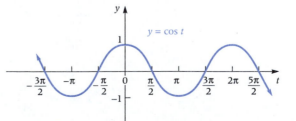

FIGURE 9-16

Figure 9-16 contains a graph of the function $y = \cos t$. As with $\sin t$, note that values of $\cos t$ fluctuate between -1 and $+1$. Again, note that the graph is wavelike and periodic with period 2π.

Comparing the graph of $y = \sin t$ with that of $y = \cos t$, note that $y = \sin t$ is an **odd function** since

$$\sin(-t) = -\sin t$$

and $y = \cos t$ is an **even function** since

$$\cos(-t) = \cos t$$

Other Trigonometric Functions

The functions $\sin t$ and $\cos t$ are the most often used of the six trigonometric functions. The remaining four trigonometric functions are called tangent, cotangent, secant, and cosecant. These are defined as follows.

SUMMARY

Four Other Trigonometric Functions

Given a ray of length r that forms an angle t with the positive x-axis and has endpoint (x, y), as shown in Figure 9-17, four other trigonometric functions are defined as follows:

$$\text{Tangent} \qquad \tan t = \frac{y}{x} = \frac{\sin t}{\cos t}$$

$$\text{Cotangent} \qquad \cot t = \frac{x}{y} = \frac{\cos t}{\sin t}$$

$$\text{Secant} \qquad \sec t = \frac{r}{x} = \frac{1}{\cos t}$$

$$\text{Cosecant} \qquad \csc t = \frac{r}{y} = \frac{1}{\sin t}$$

provided that the denominators do not equal 0.

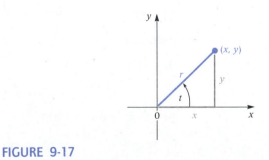

FIGURE 9-17

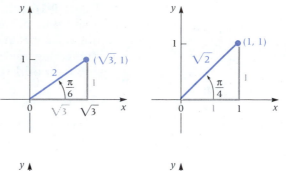

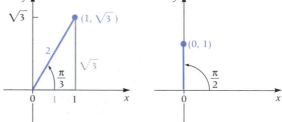

FIGURE 9-18

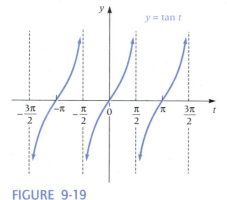

FIGURE 9-19

Tangent. Referring to the angles of Figure 9-18, note that

$$\tan\frac{\pi}{6} = \frac{y}{x} = \frac{1}{\sqrt{3}} = \frac{\sqrt{3}}{3} \qquad \tan\frac{\pi}{4} = \frac{y}{x} = \frac{1}{1} = 1$$

$$\tan\frac{\pi}{3} = \frac{y}{x} = \frac{\sqrt{3}}{1} = \sqrt{3} \qquad \tan\frac{\pi}{2} = \frac{y}{x} = \frac{1}{0} \text{ which is undefined}$$

Since $\tan t = (\sin t)/(\cos t)$, then note than $\tan(\pi/6)$ can also be determined as follows:

$$\tan\frac{\pi}{6} = \frac{\sin(\pi/6)}{\cos(\pi/6)} = \frac{1/2}{\sqrt{3}/2} = \frac{\sqrt{3}}{3}$$

The graph of $y = \tan t$ is given in Figure 9-19. Note that the tangent function is undefined at odd multiples of $\pi/2$ and has a period of π.

• **EXAMPLE 9-4** _____

Refer to the angles of Figure 9-13 on page 572 to determine each of the following:

a) $\tan\dfrac{2\pi}{3}$ **b)** $\tan\dfrac{5\pi}{4}$ **c)** $\tan\dfrac{5\pi}{3}$ **d)** $\tan\left(-\dfrac{3\pi}{4}\right)$

Solutions

a) From Figure 9-13(a),

$$\tan\frac{2\pi}{3} = \frac{y}{x} = \frac{\sqrt{3}}{-1} = -\sqrt{3}$$

b) From Figure 9-13(b),

$$\tan\frac{5\pi}{4} = \frac{y}{x} = \frac{-1}{-1} = 1$$

c) From Figure 9-13(c),

$$\tan \frac{5\pi}{3} = \frac{y}{x} = \frac{-\sqrt{3}}{1} = -\sqrt{3}$$

d) From Figure 9-13(d),

$$\tan \left(-\frac{3\pi}{4} \right) = \frac{y}{x} = \frac{-1}{-1} = 1$$

Note that each of the above could have been determined by using the formula $\tan t = (\sin t)/(\cos t)$.

• **EXAMPLE 9-5**   **Other Trigonometric Functions.** —————

Refer to the angles of Figure 9-13 on page 572 to determine each of the following:

a) $\cot \dfrac{2\pi}{3}$ **b)** $\sec \dfrac{2\pi}{3}$ **c)** $\csc \dfrac{5\pi}{4}$ **d)** $\sec \dfrac{5\pi}{3}$

Solutions

a) From Figure 9-13(a),

$$\cot \frac{2\pi}{3} = \frac{x}{y} = \frac{-1}{\sqrt{3}} = -\frac{\sqrt{3}}{3}$$

b) From Figure 9-13(a),

$$\sec \frac{2\pi}{3} = \frac{r}{x} = \frac{2}{-1} = -2$$

c) From Figure 9-13(b),

$$\csc \frac{5\pi}{4} = \frac{r}{y} = \frac{\sqrt{2}}{-1} = -\sqrt{2}$$

d) From Figure 9-13(c),

$$\sec \frac{5\pi}{3} = \frac{r}{x} = \frac{2}{1} = 2$$

Note that we could have used the formulas

$$\cot t = (\cos t)/(\sin t) \qquad \sec t = 1/(\cos t) \qquad \csc t = 1/(\sin t)$$

to determine the values of the cotangent, secant, and cosecant.

•

Exercises 9-1

Convert each of the following to radian measure.

1. 18°   **2.** 300°   **3.** 240°   **4.** 450°   **5.** −24°   **6.** −120°

Convert each of the following to degree measure.

7. .2π radians   **8.** −.6π radians   **9.** 3 radians
10. 1.4π radians   **11.** 3.2 radians   **12.** −5π radians

Use the triangles of Figure 9-12 on page 571 to find the values of the following.

13. sin 210°   **14.** $\cos \dfrac{5\pi}{6}$ **15.** sin 315°

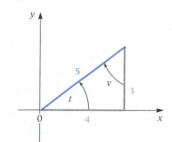

FIGURE 9-20

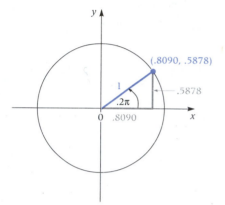

FIGURE 9-21

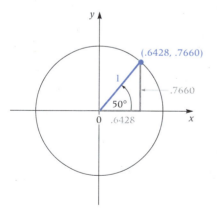

FIGURE 9-22

16. $\cos \dfrac{3\pi}{4}$ **17.** $\sin 120°$ **18.** $\cos \dfrac{2\pi}{3}$

19. $\sin (-120°)$ **20.** $\cos \left(-\dfrac{5\pi}{3}\right)$ **21.** $\sin \left(-\dfrac{3\pi}{4}\right)$

Use the triangle of Figure 9-20 to find the value of each of the following.

22. $\sin t$ **23.** $\cos t$
24. $\sin v$ **25.** $\cos v$

Use the triangle of Figure 9-21 to find the value of each of the following.

26. $\cos 130°$ **27.** $\sin 130°$ **28.** $\cos 230°$
29. $\sin 230°$ **30.** $\sin 310°$ **31.** $\cos 310°$
32. $\sin (-50°)$ **33.** $\cos (-130°)$ **34.** $\sin 410°$
35. $\cos 770°$

Use the triangle of Figure 9-22 to find the value of each of the following.

36. $\sin .2\pi$ **37.** $\cos .2\pi$ **38.** $\cos 1.2\pi$
39. $\sin 1.2\pi$ **40.** $\sin .8\pi$ **41.** $\cos .8\pi$
42. $\sin (-.2\pi)$ **43.** $\cos (-.2\pi)$ **44.** $\sin 2.2\pi$
45. $\cos 4.2\pi$

Use the triangle of Figure 9-23 to find each of the following values.

46. $\sin .4\pi$ **47.** $\cos .4\pi$ **48.** $\cos (-.4\pi)$
49. $\sin (-.4\pi)$ **50.** $\sin 1.4\pi$ **51.** $\cos 1.4\pi$
52. $\sin .6\pi$ **53.** $\cos .6\pi$ **54.** $\cos 2.4\pi$
55. $\sin 2.4\pi$ **56.** $\sin 4.4\pi$ **57.** $\cos 4.4\pi$
58. $\sin (-4.4\pi)$

Use the graph of the sine function to determine the following.

59. $\sin 0$ **60.** $\sin \pi$ **61.** $\sin 2\pi$
62. $\sin 3\pi$ **63.** $\sin 4\pi$ **64.** $\sin (-\pi)$
65. $\sin (-2\pi)$ **66.** $\sin (-3\pi)$ **67.** $\sin (-4\pi)$
68. $\sin (-5\pi)$

Use the graph of the cosine function to determine the following.

69. $\cos 0$ **70.** $\cos \pi$ **71.** $\cos 2\pi$
72. $\cos 3\pi$ **73.** $\cos 4\pi$ **74.** $\cos (-\pi)$
75. $\cos (-2\pi)$ **76.** $\cos (-3\pi)$ **77.** $\cos (-4\pi)$
78. $\cos (-5\pi)$

Given that $\cos .3\pi = .5878$ and $\sin .3\pi = .8090$, use either $\sin(t \pm 2\pi) = \sin t$ or $\cos (t \pm 2\pi) = \cos t$ to determine the following values.

79. $\cos 2.3\pi$ **80.** $\sin 2.3\pi$ **81.** $\cos (-1.7\pi)$ **82.** $\sin 4.3\pi$

In Exercises 83–94, refer to the angles of Figure 9-12 on page 571 to find the following values.

83. $\tan \left(-\dfrac{\pi}{3}\right)$ **84.** $\cot \left(-\dfrac{\pi}{3}\right)$ **85.** $\sec \left(-\dfrac{\pi}{3}\right)$ **86.** $\csc \left(-\dfrac{\pi}{3}\right)$

87. $\cot \dfrac{\pi}{4}$ **88.** $\sec \dfrac{\pi}{4}$ **89.** $\csc \dfrac{\pi}{4}$ **90.** $\sec \dfrac{\pi}{3}$

91. $\csc \dfrac{\pi}{3}$ **92.** $\cot \dfrac{\pi}{3}$ **93.** $\sec \dfrac{\pi}{6}$ **94.** $\csc \dfrac{\pi}{6}$

In Exercises 95–102, use the triangle of Figure 9-21 on this page to find the following values.

95. $\tan 130°$ **96.** $\cot 130°$ **97.** $\sec 130°$ **98.** $\csc 130°$
99. $\tan 230°$ **100.** $\cot 230°$ **101.** $\sec 230°$ **102.** $\csc 230°$

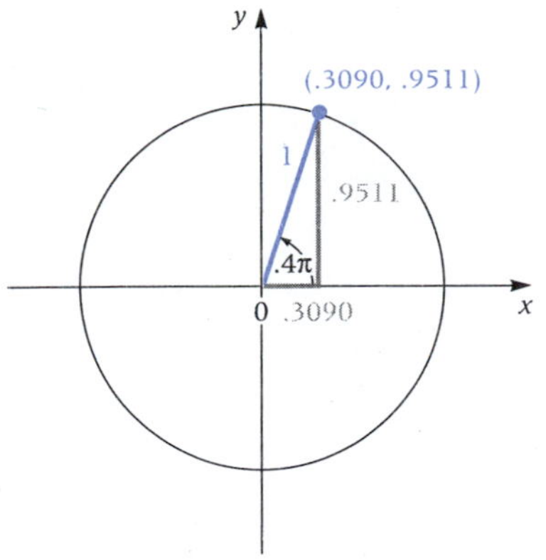

FIGURE 9-23

In Exercises 103–114, use the triangle of Figure 9-22 on page 578 to find the following values.

103. tan $.2\pi$	**104.** cot $.2\pi$	**105.** sec $.2\pi$	**106.** csc $.2\pi$
107. tan $(-.2\pi)$	**108.** cot $(-.2\pi)$	**109.** sec $(-.2\pi)$	**110.** csc $(-.2\pi)$
111. tan 1.2π	**112.** cot 1.2π	**113.** sec 1.2π	**114.** csc 1.2π

In Exercises 115–122, use the graph of the tangent function to determine the following values.

115. tan 0	**116.** tan π	**117.** tan $(-\pi)$	**118.** $\tan \frac{3\pi}{2}$
119. tan 2π	**120.** $\tan\left(-\frac{3\pi}{2}\right)$	**121.** tan (-2π)	**122.** tan (-4π)

Calculator Exercises

Some calculators have keys for trigonometric functions. If your calculator has trigonometric keys, determine whether the angles must be given in degrees or radians. Use a calculator to find the values of the following.

123. sin 26.7°	**124.** cos 146.3°	**125.** cos 2.04°	**126.** sin 192°
127. cos 4.52	**128.** sin (−1.48)	**129.** sin 1.67	**130.** cos 1.4

9-2 • GRAPHING CONCEPTS AND APPLICATIONS

Horizontal and Vertical Shifts

The graphical concepts of horizontal and vertical shifts discussed in Section 1-5 also apply to trigonometric functions. Consider the graphs of $y = \sin t$

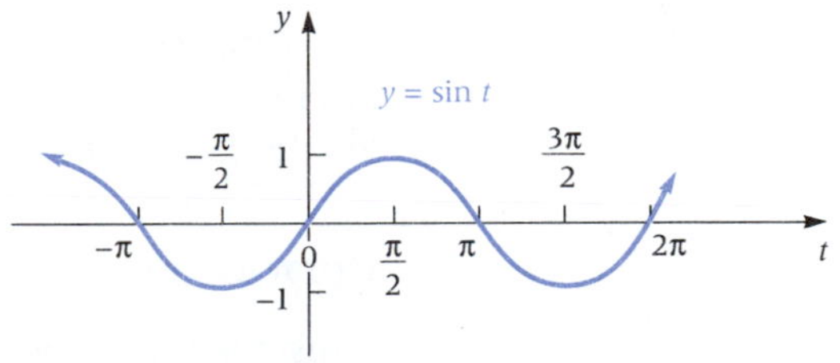

Horizontal shift: Shift the graph of $y = \sin t$ horizontally to the right by $\frac{\pi}{2}$ units to obtain the graph of $y = \sin\left(t - \frac{\pi}{2}\right)$.

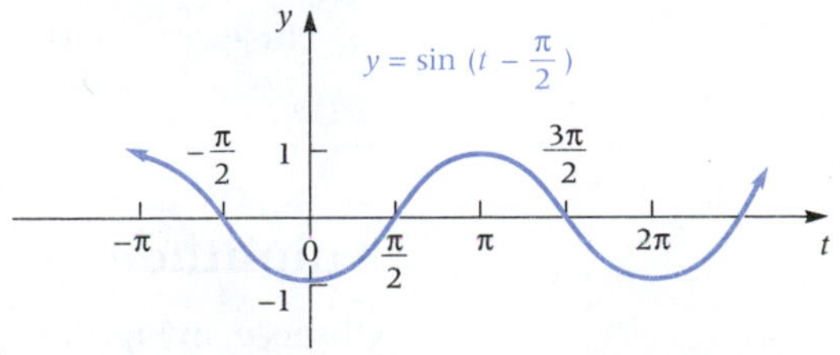

FIGURE 9-24

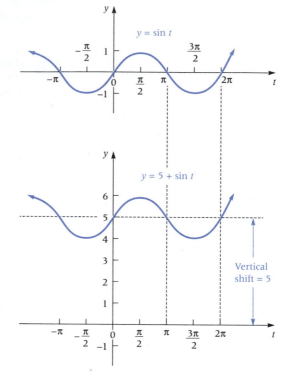

FIGURE 9-25

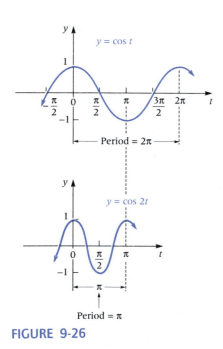

FIGURE 9-26

and $y = \sin\left(t - \dfrac{\pi}{2}\right)$, as illustrated in Figure 9-24. Observe that if we shift the graph of $y = \sin t$ horizontally to the right by $\pi/2$ units, the result is the graph of $y = \sin\left(t - \dfrac{\pi}{2}\right)$. A *horizontal shift* is also called a **phase shift.**

Also, consider the graphs of $y = \sin t$ and $y = 5 + \sin t$, as illustrated in Figure 9-25. Observe that the graph of $y = 5 + \sin t$ is obtained by *shifting* the graph of $y = \sin t$ *vertically* by 5 units.

Periodicity

Consider the graphs of $y = \cos t$ and $y = \cos 2t$, as given in Figure 9-26. Notice that the *period* of $y = \cos 2t$ is *1/2* that $y = \cos t$.

In general, the period of $y = \cos Bt$ is $1/B$ times that of $y = \cos t$; the period of $y = \sin Bt$ is $1/B$ times that of $y = \sin t$.

Amplitude

Observe, in Figure 9-27, the graphs of $y = \cos t$, $y = 3\cos t$, and $y = -3\cos t$. Note that the multiplier 3, of $y = 3\cos t$, *vertically stretches* the graph of

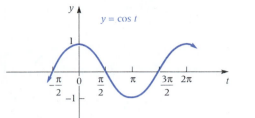

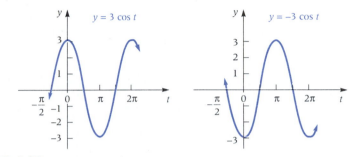

FIGURE 9-27

$y = \cos t$. Additionally, the *negative sign* of the multiplier -3, of $y = -3 \cos t$, turns the graph of $y = 3 \cos t$ *upside down* (reflection in the *x*-axis). The absolute value of such a multiplier, $|3|$ or $|-3|$, is called the **amplitude** of the graph.

SUMMARY

Amplitude and Periodicity

In general, the graphs of $y = A \sin Bt$ and $y = A \cos Bt$, where A and B are constants, have

$$\text{amplitude} = |A| \quad \text{and} \quad \text{period} = \frac{1}{B}(2\pi)$$

as illustrated in Figure 9-28.

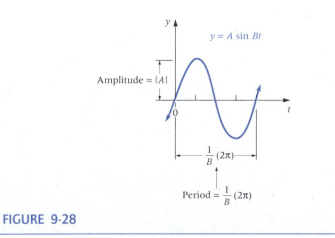

FIGURE 9-28

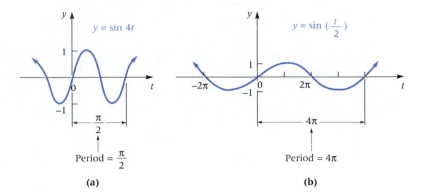

(a)

(b)

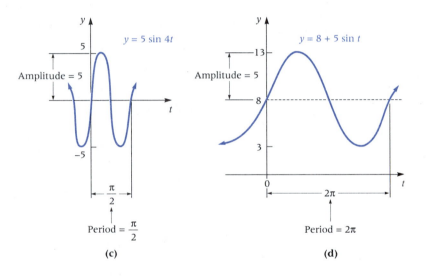

(c)

(d)

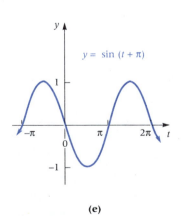

(e)

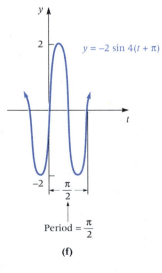

(f)

FIGURE 9-29

• **EXAMPLE 9-6**

Begin with the graph of $y = \sin t$, and graph each of the following:

a) $y = \sin 4t$ **b)** $y = \sin (t/2)$
c) $y = 5 \sin 4t$ **d)** $y = 8 + 5 \sin t$
e) $y = \sin (t + \pi)$ **f)** $y = -2 \sin 4(t + \pi)$

Solutions

The graphs are given in Figure 9-29(a) through (f).

a) The graph of $y = \sin 4t$ has a period that is 1/4 that of $y = \sin t$. Since $y = \sin t$ has a period of 2π, then $y = \sin 4t$ has a period of $\frac{1}{4}(2\pi)$, or $\pi/2$.

b) The graph of $y = \sin (t/2)$ has a period that is $1/(1/2)$, or twice that of $y = \sin t$. Since $y = \sin t$ has a period of 2π, then $y = \sin (t/2)$ has a period of $2(2\pi)$, or 4π.

c) The graph of $y = 5 \sin 4t$ is obtained by stretching the graph of $y = \sin 4t$ so that the amplitude is 5.

d) The graph of $y = 8 + 5 \sin t$ is obtained by shifting the graph of $y = 5 \sin t$ vertically by 8 units.

e) The graph of $y = \sin (t + \pi)$ is obtained by shifting the graph of $y = \sin t$ horizontally to the left by π units.

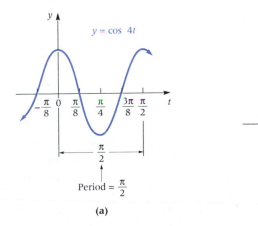

(a)

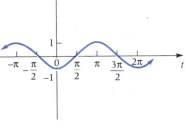

(b)

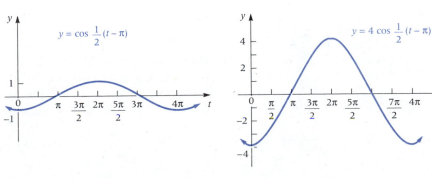

(c)

(d)

FIGURE 9-30

f) The graph of $y = -2 \sin 4(t + \pi)$ is obtained by beginning with the graph of $y = \sin (t + \pi)$, changing its period to $(1/4)(2\pi) = \pi/2$, stretching the resulting graph so that its amplitude is 2, and then turning the result upside down (reflection in the x-axis).

• **EXAMPLE 9-7** _____

Begin with the graph of $y = \cos t$ to graph each of the following:

a) $y = \cos 4t$
b) $y = \cos (t - \pi)$
c) $y = \cos (1/2)(t - \pi)$
d) $y = 4 \cos (1/2)(t - \pi)$

Solutions

The graphs are given in Figure 9-30(a) through (d) on page 583.

a) The graph of $y = \cos 4t$ has a period that is $1/4$ that of $y = \cos t$. Since $y = \cos t$ has a period of 2π, then $y = \cos 4t$ has a period of $(1/4)(2\pi)$, or $\pi/2$.

b) The graph of $y = \cos (t - \pi)$ is obtained by shifting the graph of $y = \cos t$ horizontally to the right by π units.

c) The graph of $y = \cos (1/2)(t - \pi)$ has a period that is $1/(1/2)$, or twice that of $y = \cos (t - \pi)$. Since $y = \cos (t - \pi)$ has a period of 2π, then $y = \cos (1/2)(t - \pi)$ has a period of $2(2\pi)$, or 4π.

d) The graph of $y = 4 \cos (1/2)(t - \pi)$ is obtained by stretching the graph of $y = \cos (1/2)(t - \pi)$ of Figure 9-30(c) so that the amplitude is 4.

_____ •

Applications

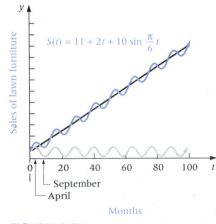

FIGURE 9-31

Seasonal Variation

The grey graph of Figure 9-31 indicates the monthly sales of lawn furniture at a retail outlet in a northeastern region of the united States for a period of 8 years during which there was no annual increase in sales. Note that t denotes time in months, with $t = 0$ corresponding to January 1984. The graph indicates that sales peak near April of any given year and decline to approximately 0 near September. Such a wavelike periodic pattern occurring within a 1-year time period indicates the existence of seasonal variation. In other words, sales of lawn furniture vary according to the season in the northeastern United States. The fact that the wavelike graph moves in a horizontal direction is due to the fact that sales are not increasing from one year to the next.

Trend

If the sales of lawn furniture have an upward trend from one year to the next, their graph could appear as the colored curve of Figure 9-31. The black straight line indicates the upward trend of sales over time. The colored graph is given by the equation

$$S(t) = 11 + 2t + 10 \sin \frac{\pi}{6}t$$

where $S(t)$ denotes sales (in thousands of units) of lawn furniture. The trend and seasonal components of the equation are indicated. Looking at the graph, notice how the seasonal influence (in other words, the seasonal variation) causes the graph to vary about the straight trend line in a wavelike periodic manner.

The sales for January 1991 are given by

$$S(84) = 11 + 2(84) + 10 \sin \left(\frac{\pi}{6} \cdot 84 \right)$$

$$= 11 + 168 + 10 \sin (14\pi)$$

$$= 11 + 168 + 10(0)$$

$$= 179 \text{ thousand units, or } 179,000$$

Modeling Data

The black line of Figure 9-32 is a graph of the annual number of visitors (in thousands) at a particular amusement park over the past 40 years. The annual number of visitors is modeled by the colored curve of

$$N(t) = 10 + e^{0.1t} + 5 \cos \frac{\pi}{4}t$$

where $N(t)$ denotes the annual number of visitors (in thousands) during year t, with $t = 0$ corresponding to the year 1952. Note how the fitted model (colored curve) smooths out the irregularities of the actual data. Observe the upward exponential trend, which is indicated by the $e^{0.1t}$ term in the equation. Note the wavelike periodic pattern about the exponential trend. This indicates that annual attendance is of a cyclical nature with an upward exponential trend.

If annual attendance follows (approximately) the fitted model, then a forecast of the next year's attendance is given by

$$N(41) = 10 + e^{0.1(41)} + 5 \cos \frac{\pi}{4} \cdot 41$$

$$= 10 + e^{4.1} + 5 \cos (10.25\pi)$$

$$\approx 10 + 60.3403 + 5(.7071)$$

$$= 73.8758 \text{ thousand, or } 73,875.8 \qquad \text{Forecast}$$

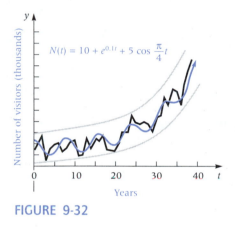

$N(t) = 10 + e^{0.1t} + 5 \cos \frac{\pi}{4}t$

Number of visitors (thousands)

Years

FIGURE 9-32

Cyclicality Versus Seasonal Variation

In the previous application on seasonal variation, we learned that a wavelike periodic pattern occurring within a 1-year time interval indicates the existence of seasonal variation. However, in the amusement park example, the wavelike periodic pattern does not occur within a 1-year time interval, but rather over time intervals of lengths greater than 1 year. Thus, any wavelike periodic pattern that spans more than 1 year indicates the existenhce of a cyclical component to the data. This is the case with the annual attendance data of Figure 9-32.

Variable Amplitude

A chemical company records the viscosity (the internal resistance of a substance to being fluid) of one of its products, chemical B-57, at the end of

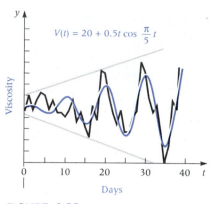

$$V(t) = 20 + 0.5t \cos \frac{\pi}{5}t$$

FIGURE 9-33

each day over a period of 40 days. The graph of the daily viscosity recordings is given by the black line of Figure 9-33. The daily viscosity recordings are modeled by the colored line of

$$V(t) = 20 + 0.5t \cos \frac{\pi}{5}t$$

⌐ variable amplitude

where $V(t)$ denotes the viscosity recording for day t, with $t = 1$ corresponding to the viscosity reading for day 1.

Observing the fitted model (colored curve) of Figure 9-33, notice how the amplitude increases with time, as indicated by the dotted lines. This is due to the variable t, in the term $0.5t$, which gives the amplitude for the model $V(t) = 20 + 0.5t \cos \frac{\pi}{5}t$. This suggests increasing variability in the viscosity recordings of chemical B-57.

Electrical Generators

If a wire loop is rotated so that it cuts the lines of force of a magnetic field, as illustrated in Figure 9-34, an electric current flows through the wire. An electric current can be transmitted by wires to many destinations.

The amount of voltage produced in the wire loop depends on

1. The number of lines of force of the magnetic field that are cut by the wire loop.
2. The speed with which the wire loop cuts the magnetic lines of force (in other words, how fast the wire loop is rotated within the magnetic lines of force).

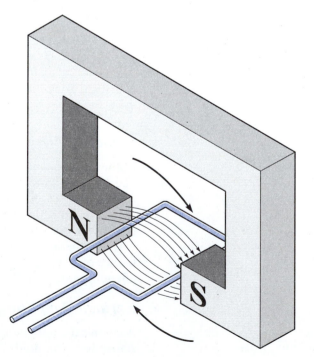

FIGURE 9-34

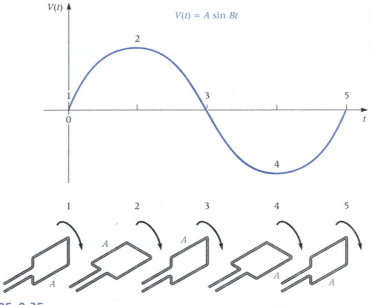

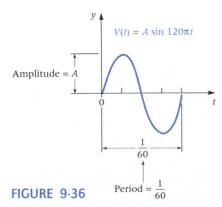

FIGURE 9-35

The amount of voltage produced varies with time according to the function defined by the equation

$$V(t) = A \sin Bt$$

where $V(t)$ is the voltage at time t (in seconds). As illustrated in Figure 9-35, the amount of voltage is 0 when side A of the wire loop is in position 1, 3, or 5 of Figure 9-35. In these positions, side A of the wire loop is not cutting any of the magnetic lines of force, and, therefore, no electric current is generated at these times. The amount of voltage is maximal when the wire loop is rotating so that it is cutting a maximum number of magnetic lines of force. This occurs when side A of the wire loop is at position 2 in Figure 9-35. When side A of the wire loop is in position 4 of Figure 9-35, the amount of voltage is maximal, but the current flows in the opposite direction because side A, the designated cutting side, of the wire loop is cutting the magnetic lines of force in a direction opposite to that at position 2. Thus, the voltage is negative as the wire loop rotates from position 3 to position 5, as indicated by the graph in Figure 9-35.

Electric companies generate electricity so that the period of the graph of the function $V(t) = A \sin Bt$ is 1/60 of a second. Since the period of $V(t) = A \sin Bt$ is $(1/B)(2\pi)$, then $B = 120\pi$ since

$$\frac{1}{B}(2\pi) = \frac{1}{120\pi}(2\pi) = \frac{1}{60}$$

A *period* of 1/60 of a second means it takes 1/60 of a second to generate a full cycle of electrical power, and, therefore, the *frequency* of such cycles is 60 cycles per second. Thus, the amount of voltage produced is given by

$$V(t) = A \sin 120\pi t$$

FIGURE 9-36

with the graph given in Figure 9-36.

Exercises 9-2

Horizontal and Vertical Shifts

Use the concepts of horizontal and/or vertical shifts to graph each of the following.

1. $y = \cos\left(t - \dfrac{\pi}{2}\right)$
2. $y = \cos\left(t + \dfrac{\pi}{2}\right)$

3. $y = \sin\left(t + \dfrac{\pi}{2}\right)$
4. $y = \sin(t - \pi)$

5. $y = \sin(t + \pi)$
6. $y = 6 + \cos t$

7. $y = -2 + \sin t$
8. $y = -1 + \cos t$

9. $y = 4 + \sin(t - \pi)$
10. $y = -2 + \cos(t + \pi)$

Amplitude and Periodicity

Graph each of the following. State the amplitude and period for each graph.

11. $y = 3\cos t$
12. $y = -2\sin 3t$

13. $y = 5\sin(t/3)$
14. $y = 6\cos 5t$

15. $y = -4\cos 2t$
16. $y = \dfrac{\pi}{12}\sin 4t$

17. $y = 5 + 2\sin 4t$
18. $y = -3 + 4\cos 6t$

19. $y = 2 + 3\cos 5\left(t - \dfrac{\pi}{2}\right)$
20. $y = 4 - 2\sin 3\left(t + \dfrac{\pi}{2}\right)$

Applications

21. *Seasonal variation.* Monthly sales of wine (in millions of gallons) for a particular winery are given by

$$y = 20 + 5\sin\frac{\pi}{6}t$$

where t denotes time in months such that $t = 1$ corresponds to January 1987.

a) Graph $y = 20 + 5\sin\dfrac{\pi}{6}t$.

b) State the amplitude and period.

c) Compute wine sales for December 1990.

d) Do wine sales for this winery exhibit either an upward or a downward trend over time? If so, state the direction of trend.

22. *Seasonal variation.* Monthly sales of ice cream (in millions of gallons) at a particular dairy are given by

$$y = 30 + 3t + 10\sin\frac{\pi}{6}t$$

where t denotes time in months such that $t = 1$ corresponds to January 1989.

a) Graph $y = 30 + 3t + 10\sin\dfrac{\pi}{6}t$.

b) State the amplitude and period.

c) Compute ice cream sales for June 1990.

d) Do ice cream sales at this dairy exhibit either an upward or a downward trend over time? If so, state the direction of trend.

e) Indicate the trend component of the above equation.

23. *Seasonal variation.* The quarterly water usage (in thousands of gallons) for a particular community is given by

$$y = 100 + e^{0.2t} + 10 \cos \frac{\pi}{6}t$$

where t denotes time in months such that $t = 0$ corresponds to the first quarter of 1990.

   a) Graph $y = 100 + e^{0.2t} + 10 \cos \frac{\pi}{6}t$.
   b) State the amplitude and period.
   c) Compute the water usage for the third quarter of 1991.
   d) Does water usage exhibit either an upward or a downward trend over time? If so, state the direction of trend.
   e) Indicate the trend component of the above equation.

24. *Cyclicality: Tax collections.* Annual property tax collections (in millions of dollars) for a particular community are given by

$$y = 300 + 50 \sin \frac{\pi}{2}t$$

where t denotes time in years such that $t = 0$ corresponds to 1980.

   a) Graph $y = 300 + 50 \sin \frac{\pi}{2}t$.
   b) State the amplitude and period.
   c) Compute the property tax collected for the year 1990.
   d) Do annual property tax collections exhibit either an upward or a downward trend over time? If so, state the direction of trend.

25. *Cyclicality: Tax collections.* Annual property tax collections (in millions of dollars) for a particular community are given by

$$y = 500 + 10t + 100 \cos \frac{\pi}{2}t$$

where t denotes time in years such that $t = 0$ corresponds to 1980.

   a) Graph $y = 500 + 10t + 100 \cos \frac{\pi}{2}t$.
   b) State the amplitude and period.
   c) Compute the property tax collected for the year 1990.
   d) Do annual property tax collections exhibit either an upward or a downward trend over time? If so, state the direction of trend.
   e) Indicate the trend component of the above equation.

26. *Cyclicality: Stock price.* The price (in dollars) of a share of stock of a given company varies with time in accordance with the model

$$y = 50 + 5 \sin \frac{\pi}{24}t$$

where t denotes time in months, with $t = 0$ corresponding to January 1985.

   a) Graph $y = 50 + 5 \sin \frac{\pi}{24}t$.
   b) State the amplitude and period.
   c) Compute the stock's price for November 1990.
   d) Does the stock's price exhibit either an upward or a downward trend over time? If so, state the direction of trend.

27. *Variable amplitude: Stock price.* The price (in dollars) of a share of stock of a given company varies with time in accordance with the model

$$y = 80 + 0.4t \cos \frac{\pi}{24}t$$

where t denotes time in months, with $t = 0$ corresponding to January 1980.

a) Graph $y = 80 + 0.4t \cos \frac{\pi}{24}t$.

b) State the period.

c) Indicate the variable amplitude component of the above equation. Determine the amplitude at $t = 1$, $t = 5$, $t = 10$, and $t = 20$. Is the amplitude increasing or decreasing over time?

d) Compute the stock's price for January 1991.

e) Does the stock's price exhibit either an upward or a downward trend over time? If so, state the direction of trend.

28. *Variable amplitude: Electric range sales.* Annual electric range sales (in thousands) for a particular brand are given by

$$y = 100 + 3t + 0.5t \sin \frac{\pi}{12}t$$

where t denotes time in years, with $t = 0$ corresponding to 1985.

a) Graph $y = 100 + 3t + 0.5t \sin \frac{\pi}{12}t$.

b) State the period.

c) Indicate the variable amplitude component of the above equation. Determine the amplitude at $t = 1$, $t = 4$, $t = 10$, and $t = 20$. Is the amplitude increasing or decreasing over time?

d) Compute electric range sales for 1991.

e) Do the electric range sales exhibit either an upward or a downward trend over time? If so, indicate the direction of trend.

f) Indicate the trend component of the above equation.

29. *Electrical generators.* The amount of voltage produced by a wind-powered generator varies with time according to the function defined by the equation

$$V(t) = 120 \sin 100\pi t$$

where $V(t)$ is the voltage at time t (in seconds).

a) Graph $V(t) = 120 \sin 100\pi t$.

b) State the amplitude, period, and frequency.

c) State the maximum voltage.

d) Compute the voltage at $t = 5$, $t = 10$, and $t = 20$.

30. *Electrical generators.* The amount of voltage produced by a wind-powered generator varies with time according to the function defined by the equation

$$V(t) = 114 \sin 120\pi t$$

where $V(t)$ is the voltage at time t (in seconds).

a) Graph $V(t) = 114 \sin 120\pi t$.

b) State the amplitude, period, and frequency.

c) State the maximum voltage.

d) Compute the voltage at $t = 5$, $t = 10$, and $t = 20$.

9-3 • DERIVATIVES OF TRIGONOMETRIC FUNCTIONS

In this section we discuss the differentiating of functions involving the sine and cosine functions. We begin by stating the following rules for differentiating $\sin t$ and $\cos t$, with t measured in radians.

$$\frac{d}{dt} \sin t = \cos t \qquad \frac{d}{dt} \cos t = -\sin t$$

The above rules mean that the derivative of the sine function is the cosine function and the derivative of the cosine function is the negative sine function. The justification for these rules is given at the end of this section.

Thus, the formula for the slope of the tangent line to the graph of

$$f(t) = \sin t$$

is given by

$$f'(t) = \cos t$$

At $t = \pi/6$, the above becomes

$$f'(\pi/6) = \cos(\pi/6)$$
$$\approx 0.8660$$

This means that the slope of the tangent line to the graph of $f(t) = \sin t$ at $t = \pi/6$ is 0.8660, as illustrated in Figure 9-37.

The formulas for the derivatives of the sine and cosine functions, when used with the chain rule, become the following.

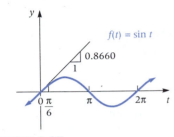

FIGURE 9-37

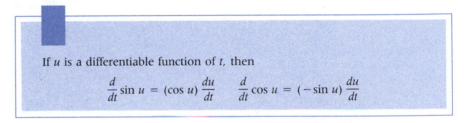

If u is a differentiable function of t, then

$$\frac{d}{dt}\sin u = (\cos u)\frac{du}{dt} \qquad \frac{d}{dt}\cos u = (-\sin u)\frac{du}{dt}$$

• **EXAMPLE 9-8**

Differentiate each of the following with respect to t.

a) $f(t) = \cos(t^2 + 4)$ b) $f(t) = 5\sin 4t$
c) $y = \sin^3 t$ d) $y = (t^3 + 4\cos t)^6$

Solutions

a) If $f(t) = \cos(t^2 + 4)$, then

$$f'(t) = [-\sin(t^2 + 4)](2t) = -2t\sin(t^2 + 4)$$

b) If $f(t) = 5\sin 4t$, then

$$f'(t) = 5(\cos 4t)(4) = 20\cos 4t$$

c) Note that $\sin^3 t = (\sin t)^3$. Thus, $y = \sin^3 t$ means $y = (\sin t)^3$. Using the general power rule and the rule for the derivative of the sine function,

$$\frac{dy}{dt} = 3(\sin t)^2 \frac{d}{dt}\sin t = 3(\sin t)^2\cos t$$

d) If $y = (t^3 + 4 \cos t)^6$, using the general power rule and the rule for the derivative of the cosine function,

$$\frac{dy}{dt} = 6(t^3 + 4 \cos t)^5 \frac{d}{dt}(t^3 + 4 \cos t)$$

$$= 6(t^3 + 4 \cos t)^5(3t^2 - 4 \sin t)$$

• **EXAMPLE 9-9**

Differentiate each of the following with respect to t.

a) $y = t^4 \sin 5t$ **b)** $y = (\cos 3t)/t^2$

Solutions

a) For $y = t^4 \sin 5t$, begin with the product rule to obtain

(first)(derivative of second) + (second)(derivative of first)

$$\frac{dy}{dt} = t^4 \frac{d}{dt} \sin 5t + (\sin 5t) \frac{d}{dt} t^4$$

$$= t^4(\cos 5t)(5) + (\sin 5t)(4t^3)$$

$$= 5t^4 \cos 5t + 4t^3 \sin 5t$$

b) For $y = (\cos 3t)/t^2$, begin with the quotient rule to obtain

(denom.)(deriv. of num.) − (num.)(deriv. of denom.)

$$\frac{dy}{dt} = \frac{(t^2)(-\sin 3t)(3) - (\cos 3t)(2t)}{(t^2)^2} \qquad \text{(denominator)}^2$$

$$= \frac{t(-3t \sin 3t - 2 \cos 3t)}{t^4} = \frac{-3t \sin 3t - 2 \cos 3t}{t^3}$$

Applications

• **EXAMPLE 9-10**   **Profit.**

Monthly profits (in thousands of dollars) of a gift shop are given by

$$P(t) = 20 + 5 \sin \frac{\pi}{6}t$$

where t denotes time in months, with $t = 0$ corresponding to January 1990. Find the rate of change of profits with respect to time at $t = 24$ (January 1992).

Solution

The formula for the rate of change is given by

$$P'(t) = 5\left(\cos \frac{\pi}{6}t\right)\left(\frac{\pi}{6}\right)$$

$$= \frac{5\pi}{6} \cos \frac{\pi}{6}t$$

Evaluating the above result at $t = 24$ gives

$$P'(24) = \frac{5\pi}{6} \cos \frac{\pi}{6}(24)$$

$$= \frac{5\pi}{6} \cos 4\pi$$

$$= \frac{5\pi}{6}(1) \approx \$2.62 \text{ thousand, or } \$2,620$$

Thus, at $t = 24$ (January 1992), monthly profits are changing at the rate of approximately \$2.62 thousand, or \$2620, per month.

• **EXAMPLE 9-11   Optimal Timing: Stock Price Behavior.** —

Monthly closing prices of a particular company's stock have historically exhibited a cyclical pattern and are related to time by the model

$$S(t) = 200 + 10 \cos \frac{\pi}{12}t$$

where t denotes time in months, with $t = 0$ corresponding to January 1987. A stock trader desires to buy this stock at its low price and subsequently sell it at its high price sometime during time interval between September 1991 and March 1993 (equivalently, $56 \le t \le 74$).

a) Determine any relative maxima/minima over the interval $56 \le t \le 74$.
b) Determine the absolute extrema over the interval $56 \le t \le 74$.
c) When should the stock trader plan to buy the stock, and, subsequently, when should the trader plan to sell the stock?

Solution

a) We seek any relative maxima/minima over the interval $56 \le t \le 74$. Hence,

Critical Values

$$S'(t) = 10\left(-\sin \frac{\pi}{12}t\right)\left(\frac{\pi}{12}\right)$$

$$= \frac{-10\pi}{12} \sin \frac{\pi}{12}t$$

$$0 = \frac{-10\pi}{12} \sin \frac{\pi}{12}t \qquad \text{Set } S'(t) = 0 \text{ and solve for } t.$$

$$\frac{\pi}{12}t = 0, \pi, 2\pi, 3\pi, 4\pi, \boxed{5\pi, 6\pi,} 7\pi, \ldots$$

$$t = 0, 12, 24, 36, 48, \boxed{60, 72,} 84, \ldots$$

We have shaded in color the above critical values that lie within the interval $56 \le t \le 74$. Thus, for this problem, the critical values are

$t = 60$, which corresponds to January 1992
$t = 72$, which corresponds to January 1993

Second-Derivative Test

$$S''(t) = \frac{-10\pi}{12}\left(\cos\frac{\pi}{12}t\right)\left(\frac{\pi}{12}\right)$$

$$= \frac{-10\pi^2}{12^2}\cos\frac{\pi}{12}t$$

$$S''(60) = \frac{-10\pi^2}{144}\cos\frac{\pi}{12}(60)$$

$$= \frac{-10\pi^2}{144}\cos 5\pi$$

$$= \frac{-10\pi^2}{144}(-1) > 0 \qquad \text{This implies that a relative minimum occurs at } t = 60.$$

$$S''(72) = \frac{-10\pi^2}{144}\cos\frac{\pi}{12}(72)$$

$$= \frac{-10\pi^2}{144}\cos 6\pi$$

$$= \frac{-10\pi^2}{144}(1) < 0 \qquad \text{This implies that a relative maximum occurs at } t = 72.$$

b) As stated in the box on pages 228-229, to find the absolute extrema for a continuous function defined on a closed interval, we evaluate the function at its critical values and endpoints.

$$S(60) = 200 + 10\cos\left[\frac{\pi}{12}(60)\right] = 190 \longleftarrow \text{absolute minimum}$$

critical value ⤴

$$S(72) = 200 + 10\cos\left[\frac{\pi}{12}(72)\right] = 210 \longleftarrow \text{absolute maximum}$$

critical value ⤴

$$S(56) = 200 + 10\cos\left[\frac{\pi}{12}(56)\right] = 195$$

endpoint ⤴

$$S(74) = 200 + 10\cos\left[\frac{\pi}{12}(74)\right] = 208.66$$

endpoint ⤴

c) The trader should buy the stock at $t = 60$ (January 1992) for $190 per share and sell at $t = 72$ (January 1993) for $210 per share to realize a profit of $210 − $190 = $20 per share. (*Caution:* A stock's price is determined by many factors. A model such as the one in this example is only one of many methods used by stock analysts to time the buying and selling of stocks.)

Justification for Derivative Rules

We now give justification for the derivative rules

$$\frac{d}{dt}\sin t = \cos t \qquad \frac{d}{dt}\cos t = -\sin t$$

To do so, we must first show that the following hold

$$\lim_{t \to 0}\frac{\sin t}{t} = 1 \qquad \lim_{t \to 0}\frac{\cos t - 1}{t} = 0$$

TABLE 9-1

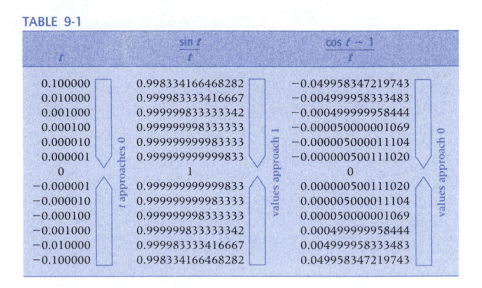

t	$\dfrac{\sin t}{t}$	$\dfrac{\cos t - 1}{t}$
0.100000	0.998334166468282	−0.049958347219743
0.010000	0.999983333416667	−0.004999958333483
0.001000	0.999999833333342	−0.000499999958444
0.000100	0.999999998333333	−0.000050000001069
0.000010	0.999999999983333	−0.000005000011104
0.000001	0.999999999999833	−0.000000500111020
0	1	0
−0.000001	0.999999999999833	0.000000500111020
−0.000010	0.999999999983333	0.000005000011104
−0.000100	0.999999998333333	0.000050000001069
−0.001000	0.999999833333342	0.000499999958444
−0.010000	0.999983333416667	0.004999958333483
−0.100000	0.998334166468282	0.049958347219743

t approaches 0   *values approach 1*   *values approach 0*

by studying Table 9-1, which gives values of $(\sin t)/t$ and $(\cos t - 1)/t$ for small values of t, where t is in radians. Observe that values of $(\sin t)/t$ approach 1 as values of t approach 0. Also, observe that values of $(\cos t - 1)/t$ approach 0 as values of t approach 0.

    To justify the derivative rules, we will also need the following trigonometric identity

$$\sin (t + h) = \sin t \cos h + \cos t \sin h$$

whose justification is usually given in textbooks on trigonometry.

    Now, we justify the derivative rule

$$\frac{d}{dt} \sin t = \cos t$$

Using the definition of a derivative, we have

$$\frac{d}{dt} \sin t = \lim_{h \to 0} \frac{\sin (t + h) - \sin t}{h}$$

We must show that the above limit is $\cos t$. Thus, using the trigonometric identity for $\sin (t + h)$, the difference quotient becomes

$$\frac{\sin t \cos h + \cos t \sin h - \sin t}{h}$$

Rearranging the numerator terms gives

$$\frac{(\sin t \cos h - \sin t) + \cos t \sin h}{h}$$

Factoring out $\sin t$ fom the expression inside the parentheses, we have

$$\frac{\sin t (\cos h - 1) + \cos t \sin h}{h}$$

Using properties of fractions, the above result is rewritten as

$$(\sin t)\,\frac{\cos h - 1}{h} + (\cos t)\,\frac{\sin h}{h}$$

Hence,

$$\frac{d}{dt}\sin t = \lim_{h\to 0}\left[(\sin t)\frac{\cos h - 1}{h} + (\cos t)\,\frac{\sin h}{h}\right]$$

$$= (\sin t)\,\lim_{h\to 0}\frac{\cos h - 1}{h} + (\cos t)\,\lim_{h\to 0}\frac{\sin h}{h} \qquad \text{Limit properties 2 and 3}$$

$$= (\sin t)\cdot 0 + (\cos t)\cdot 1$$

$$= \cos t$$

A procedure similar to the above could be used to justify the derivative rule

$$\frac{d}{dt}\cos t = -\sin t$$

However, we will use an easier method, which depends on the trigonometric identities

$$\cos t = \sin\left(\frac{\pi}{2} - t\right) \qquad \sin t = \cos\left(\frac{\pi}{2} - t\right)$$

whose justifications are given in trigonometry textbooks. Using the first trigonometric identity, we have

$$\frac{d}{dt}\cos t = \frac{d}{dt}\sin\underbrace{\left(\frac{\pi}{2} - t\right)}_{u}$$

$$= \left[\cos\overbrace{\left(\frac{\pi}{2} - t\right)}\right]\overbrace{(-1)}^{du/dt}$$

$$= -\cos\left(\frac{\pi}{2} - t\right)$$

$$= -\sin t$$

Exercises 9-3

Find the derivatives of each of the following with respect to t.

1. $y = \sin 7t$
2. $y = \cos 9t$
3. $y = \cos(t^5 - 3)$
4. $y = \sin(t^3 + 6t)$
5. $y = \sin(5t + 4)$
6. $y = \cos(4t - 9)$
7. $y = 5\sin^4 t$
8. $y = 9t + 3\cos^2 t$
9. $y = t^5\cos 4t$
10. $y = t^6/\sin 5t$
11. $y = (\sin 8t)/t^5$
12. $y = \sin t \cos t$
13. $y = \sin t/\cos t$
14. $y = \sin\sqrt{t^2 + 1}$
15. $y = \cos\sqrt{t^3 - 6}$
16. $y = \sin^3 t \cos t$

17. $y = \cos^4 t \sin t$

18. $y = t^3 - 2 \sin 3t$

19. $y = 3 \cos (t + \pi)$

20. $y = 6 \sin \dfrac{\pi}{3}t$

Find the slope of the tangent line to the graph of each of the following at $t = \pi/3$. Include a graphical interpretation.

21. $y = \cos t$

22. $y = \sin t$

Applications

23. *Sales revenue.* Monthly sales revenues (in thousands of dollars) for a sporting goods outlet are given by

$$R(t) = 200 + 10 \sin \frac{\pi}{6}t$$

where t denotes time in months, with $t = 0$ corresponding to January 1990. Find the rate of change of profits with respect to time at $t = 12$ (January 1991).

24. *Sales.* Monthly sales (in thousands of units) of air conditioners at a wholesale outlet are given by

$$S(t) = 100 + 5 \cos \frac{\pi}{6}t$$

where t denotes time in months, with $t = 0$ corresponding to January 1989. Find the rate of change of monthly sales with respect to time at $t = 18$ (July 1990).

25. *Electricity.* The amount of voltage produced by an electrical generator t seconds after starting is given by

$$V(t) = 120 \sin 120\pi t$$

Find the rate of change of voltage with respect to a time 30 seconds after starting.

26. *Tax revenue.* Sales tax revenues (in millions of dollars) for a given state are related to time by the model

$$R(t) = 50 + 10 \cos \frac{\pi}{6}t$$

where t denotes time in months, with $t = 0$ corresponding to January 1991. During the year 1991 (in other words, $0 \le t \le 11$):
a) Determine the month yielding maximum sales tax revenue and the corresponding maximum sales tax revenue.
b) Determine the month yielding minimum sales tax revenue and the corresponding minimum sales tax revenue.

27. *Profits.* Monthly profits (in thousands of dollars) at a given vacation resort are modeled by

$$P(t) = 150 + 30 \sin \frac{\pi}{6}t$$

where t denotes time in months, with $t = 0$ corresponding to January 1991. During the year 1992 (in other words, $12 \le t \le 23$):
a) Determine the month yielding maximum monthly profit and the corresponding maximum monthly profit.
b) Determine the month yielding minimum monthly profit and the corresponding minimum monthly profit.

28. *Optimal timing: Stock price behavior*. Monthly closing prices of a particular company's stock have historically exhibited a cyclical pattern and are related to time by the model

$$S(t) = 300 + 20 \sin \frac{\pi}{6} t$$

where t denotes time in months, with $t = 0$ corresponding to January 1990. A stock trader desires to buy this stock at its low price and subsequently sell it at its high price sometime during the year 1991 (equivalently, $12 \le t \le 23$). According to the above model, when should the stock trader plan to buy the stock, and, subsequently, when should the trader plan to sell the stock? Determine the optimal profit per share.

29. *Air pollution*. Studies of air quality in a given city have revealed that the amount of air pollution t hours after midnight during a day is given by

$$P(t) = 2 + 0.5 \sin \frac{\pi}{12} (t - 7) \qquad (1 \le t \le 24)$$

a)   During which hour of the day is pollution maximal?
b)   During which hour of the day is pollution minimal?

9-4   • INTEGRATION OF TRIGONOMETRIC FUNCTIONS

Using the definition of the indefinite integral of a function, the differentiation formulas

$$\frac{d}{dt} \sin t = \cos t \qquad \text{and} \qquad \frac{d}{dt} \cos t = -\sin t$$

result in the following integral formulas:

$$\int \cos t \, dt = \sin t + c \qquad \text{and} \qquad \int \sin t \, dt = -\cos t + c$$

• **EXAMPLE 9-12** _____

Find the area between the graph of $y = \cos t$ and the horizontal axis over the interval $0 \le t \le \frac{\pi}{2}$.

Solution

The desired area appears shaded in Figure 9-38 and is given by the definite integral

$$\int_0^{\pi/2} \cos t \, dt = \sin t \Big|_0^{\pi/2} = \sin(\pi/2) - \sin 0$$

$$= 1 - 0 = 1 \qquad \text{Shaded area}$$

•

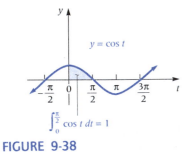

$$\int_0^{\frac{\pi}{2}} \cos t \, dt = 1$$

FIGURE 9-38

The integral formulas preceding Example 9-12 result in the following more general formulas for $u = f(t)$, where u is a differentiable function of t.

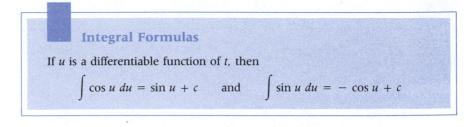

These formulas allow us to use the substitution principle to integrate more complex functions, as is illustrated in the following examples.

• **EXAMPLE 9-13** ────────────────────

Evaluate $\int \sin 5t \, dt$.

Solution

If we let $u = 5t$, then $du = 5 \, dt$, so that

$$\int \sin 5t \, dt = \frac{1}{5} \int \sin 5t \; 5 \, dt = \frac{1}{5}(-\cos u) + c$$

$$= -\frac{1}{5}\cos 5t + c \qquad \text{Answer}$$

Check: Differentiating the answer with respect to t should result in $\sin 5t$. Hence,

$$\frac{d}{dt}\left(-\frac{1}{5}\cos 5t + c\right) = -\frac{1}{5}(-\sin 5t)(5) = \sin 5t$$

• **EXAMPLE 9-14** ────────────────────

Evaluate $\int (\sin t)^3 \cos t \, dt$.

Solution

If we let $u = \sin t$, then $du = \cos t \, dt$, and the above integral is of the form $\int u^n du$. Hence,

$$\int (\sin t)^3 \cos t \, dt = \frac{1}{4}u^4 + c = \frac{1}{4}(\sin t)^4 + c \qquad \text{Answer}$$

• **EXAMPLE 9-15** ────────────────────

Evaluate $\int t^2 \sin t^3 \, dt$.

Solution

If we let $u = t^3$, then $du = 3t^2 \, dt$, so that

$$\int t^2 \sin t^3 \, dt = \frac{1}{3}\int \sin t^3 \; 3t^2 \, dt = \frac{1}{3}(-\cos u) + c$$

$$= -\frac{1}{3}\cos t^3 + c \qquad \text{Answer}$$

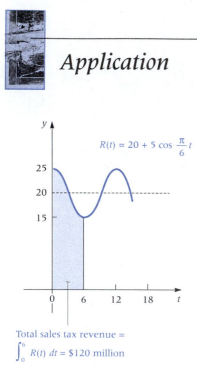

Application

• **EXAMPLE 9-16** **Total Sales Tax Revenue.**

Sales tax revenues (in millions of dollars) flow into a state's treasury at a monthly rate given by

$$R(t) = 20 + 5 \cos \frac{\pi}{6}t$$

where t denotes time in months, with $t = 0$ corresponding to January 1991. Determine the total sales tax revenue flowing into the state's treasury during the following time intervals:

a) From January 1991 to July 1991 ($0 \le t \le 6$)
b) From April 1991 to January 1992 ($3 \le t \le 12$)

Solutions

a) The total tax revenue is given by the area between the graph of $R(t)$ and the horizontal axis over the interval $0 \le t \le 6$, as illustrated by the shaded area in Figure 9-39. This area is given by the following definite integral:

$$\text{Total sales tax revenue} = \int_0^6 R(t) \, dt$$

$$= \int_0^6 \left(20 + 5 \cos \frac{\pi}{6}t \right) dt$$

$$= \left[20t + 5\left(\frac{6}{\pi}\right) \sin \frac{\pi}{6}t \right] \Bigg|_0^6$$

$$= \left(120 + \frac{30}{\pi} \sin \pi \right) - \left(0 + \frac{30}{\pi} \sin 0 \right)$$

$$= (120 + 0) - (0 + 0)$$

$$= \$120 \text{ million} \qquad \text{Total sales tax revenue}$$

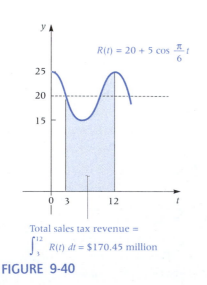

Total sales tax revenue =
$\int_0^6 R(t) \, dt = \$120$ million

FIGURE 9-39

b) We seek the area between the graph of $R(t)$ and the horizontal axis over the interval $3 \le t \le 12$, as illustrated by the shaded area of Figure 9-40. This area is given by the following definite integral:

$$\text{Total sales tax revenue} = \int_3^{12} R(t) \, dt$$

$$= \int_3^{12} \left(20 + 5 \cos \frac{\pi}{6}t \right) dt$$

$$= \left[20t + 5\left(\frac{6}{\pi}\right) \sin \frac{\pi}{6}t \right] \Bigg|_3^{12}$$

$$= \left(240 + \frac{30}{\pi} \sin 2\pi \right) - \left(60 + \frac{30}{\pi} \sin \frac{\pi}{2} \right)$$

$$= (240 + 0) - \left[60 + \frac{30}{\pi}(1) \right]$$

$$\approx 240 - 60 - 9.55$$

$$\approx \$170.45 \text{ million} \qquad \text{Total sales tax revenue}$$

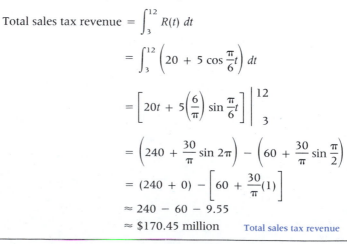

Total sales tax revenue =
$\int_3^{12} R(t) \, dt = \$170.45$ million

FIGURE 9-40

Exercises 9-4

Evaluate each of the following.

1. $\int \cos (2t + 1) \, dt$

2. $\int \sin (6t + 5) \, dt$

3. $\int 5 \sin 4t \, dt$

4. $\int -6 \sin 3t \, dt$

5. $\int (4 + \cos t) \, dt$

6. $\int (8 - 2 \sin t) \, dt$

7. $\int (t^4 - 6 \sin 2t) \, dt$

8. $\int (t^2 + 4 \cos 5t) \, dt$

9. $\int (\sin t)^2 \cos t \, dt$

10. $\int \sin t \cos t \, dt$

11. $\int \sqrt{\sin t} \cos t \, dt$

12. $\int (\sin t / \sqrt{\cos t}) \, dt$

13. $\int \sin t \, (1 - \cos t) \, dt$

14. $\int \cos t \, (1 + \sin t) \, dt$

15. $\int t \sin t^2 \, dt$

16. $\int t^4 \cos t^5 \, dt$

17. $\int (t + 1) \cos (t^2 + 2t) \, dt$

18. $\int (t - 3) \sin (t^2 - 6t) \, dt$

19. $\int (\sin t / \cos t) \, dt$

20. $\int (\cos t / \sin t) \, dt$

For each function, find the area bounded by the graph of the function and the horizontal axis over the interval $0 \le t \le \dfrac{\pi}{4}$. Graph the function, and shade the desired area.

21. $y = \sin 2t$

22. $y = \cos 2t$

23. $y = \cos (t/2)$

24. $y = \sin (t/2)$

Applications

25. *Total revenue.* Sales revenues (in millions of dollars) flow into a firm's treasury at a monthly rate given by

$$R(t) = 40 + 10 \sin \frac{\pi}{6} t$$

where t denotes time in months, with $t = 0$ corresponding to January 1991. Determine the total sales revenues flowing into the firm's treasury during the following time intervals:

a) From April 1991 to October 1991 $(3 \le t \le 9)$
b) From July 1991 to January 1992 $(6 \le t \le 12)$

26. *Total milk production.* Monthly milk production (in thousands of gallons) for a particular region is given by

$$M(t) = 400 + 20 \cos \frac{\pi}{6} t$$

where t denotes time in months, with $t = 0$ corresponding to January 1991. Determine the total milk production during the following time intervals:

a) From January 1991 to July 1991 $(0 \le t \le 6)$
b) From April 1991 to January 1992 $(3 \le t \le 12)$

27. *Total toll revenue.* Monthly toll revenues (in thousands of dollars) for a particular state are given by

$$R(t) = 80 + 10 \cos \frac{\pi}{6}t$$

where t denotes time in months, with $t = 0$ corresponding to January 1991. Determine the total toll revenues during the following time intervals:

a) From January 1991 to October 1991 $(0 \leq t \leq 9)$
b) From April 1991 to April 1992 $(3 \leq t \leq 15)$

CHAPTER 9 HIGHLIGHTS

• *Concepts*

Your ability to answer the following questions is one indicator of the depth of your mastery of this chapter's important concepts. Note that the questions are grouped under various topic headings. For any question that you cannot answer, refer to the appropriate section of the chapter indicated by the topic heading. Pay particular attention to the summary boxes within a section.

9-1 INTRODUCTION TO THE TRIGONOMETRIC FUNCTIONS

1. If the ray that defines the terminal side of an angle rotates clockwise, the resulting angle is _____; if the ray rotates counterclockwise, the resulting angle is _____.
2. State the procedure for converting an angle
    a) From degree measure to radian measure.
    b) From radian measure to degree measure.
3. Give three ways of defining the sine and cosine of an angle.
4. Draw graphs of the sine and cosine functions.
5. Define periodicity, and give the period of the sine and cosine functions.

9-2 GRAPHING CONCEPTS AND APPLICATIONS

6. State the rule for determining the period of $y = \cos Bt$ and $y = \sin Bt$.
7. State the amplitude for $y = A \sin Bt$ and $y = A \cos Bt$.
8. Explain each of the following terms: seasonal variation, trend, cyclicality, variable amplitude.
9. Explain the difference between cyclicality and seasonal variation.
10. *Electrical generators.* Write the equation that gives the amount of voltage produced as a function of time.

9-3 DERIVATIVES OF TRIGONOMETRIC FUNCTIONS

11. The derivative of the sine function is the _____ function; the derivative of the cosine function is the _____ _____.

9-4 INTEGRATION OF TRIGONOMETRIC FUNCTIONS

12. The indefinite integral of the cosine function is _____.
13. The indefinite integral of the sine function is _____.

REVIEW EXERCISES

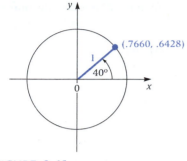

FIGURE 9-41

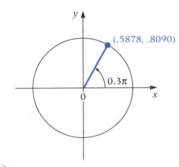

FIGURE 9-42

• *Trigonometric Functions*

Convert each of the following to radian measure.

1. 36°   **2.** −48°   **3.** 156°   **4.** 280°

Convert each of the following to degree measure.

5. 4 radians   **6.** 1.3 radians
7. −2.8π radians   **8.** −8π radians

Use Figure 9-41 to find the value of each of the following.

9. sin 40°   **10.** cos 40°   **11.** cos 140°   **12.** sin 140°
13. cos 220°   **14.** sin 220°   **15.** cos 320°   **16.** sin 320°
17. sin (−40°) **18.** cos (−40°) **19.** cos (−140°) **20.** sin (−140°)

Use Figure 9-42 to find the value of each of the following.

21. sin 0.3π   **22.** cos 0.3π   **23.** cos 0.7π   **24.** sin 0.7π
25. cos 1.3π   **26.** sin 1.3π   **27.** sin 1.7π   **28.** cos 1.7π
29. sin (−0.3π) **30.** cos (−0.3π) **31.** cos 2.7π   **32.** sin 4.7π

Use the graphs of the sine and cosine functions to determine the following.

33. cos 0   **34.** sin π   **35.** cos 2π   **36.** sin (−3π)

• *Graphing Concepts and Applications*

Graph each of the following. State the amplitude and period for each graph.

37. $y = 4 \sin 2t$ **38.** $y = -3 \cos 4t$
39. $y = 3 + 2 \cos t$ **40.** $y = -2 + 5 \sin (t/2)$
41. $y = \sin \left(t - \dfrac{\pi}{4} \right)$ **42.** $y = 5 + 2 \cos \left(t + \dfrac{\pi}{6} \right)$

43. *Seasonal variation.* Monthly sales of wine (in thousands of gallons) at a particular winery are given by

$$y = 80 + 4t + 10 \cos \frac{\pi}{6} t$$

where t denotes time in months such that $t = 0$ corresponds to January 1990.

a) Graph $y = 80 + 4t + 10 \cos \dfrac{\pi}{6} t$.

b) State the amplitude and period.

c) Compute wine sales at this winery for July 1990.

d) Do wine sales at this winery exhibit either an upward or a downward trend over time? If so, state the direction of trend.

e) Indicate the trend component of the above equation.

44. *Variable amplitude: Electric dryer sales.* Annual electric dryer sales (in thousands) for a particular brand are given by

$$y = 200 + e^{0.2t} + 0.4t \cos \frac{\pi}{12} t$$

where t denotes time in years, with $t = 0$ corresponding to the year 1984.

a) Graph $y = 200 + e^{0.2t} + 0.4t \cos \dfrac{\pi}{12} t$.

b) State the period.

c) Indicate the variable amplitude component of the above equation. Determine the amplitude at $t = 2$, $t = 5$, and $t = 10$. Is the amplitude increasing or decreasing over time?

d) Compute electric dryer sales for 1990.

e) Do the electric dryer sales exhibit either an upward or a downward trend over time? If so, indicate the direction of trend.

• *Derivatives of Trigonometric Functions*

Find the derivative of each of the following with respect to t.

45. $y = \cos 7t$

46. $y = \sin (t/6)$

47. $y = \sin (t^3 - 5)$

48. $y = 6 \cos^2 t$

49. $y = 8t - \cos 6t$

50. $y = \sin \sqrt{t^3 + 5}$

51. $y = (\sin 6t)(\cos 5t)$

52. $y = \cos t / \sin t$

53. *Profits.* Monthly profits (in thousands of dollars) at a given health spa are modeled by

$$P(t) = 250 + 20 \cos \frac{\pi}{6}t$$

where t denotes time in months, with $t = 0$ corresponding to January 1990.

a) Find the rate of change of profits with respect to time at $t = 6$ (July 1990).

During the year 1992 (in other words, $24 \le t \le 35$):

b) Determine the month yielding maximum monthly profit and the corresponding maximum monthly profit.

c) Determine the month yielding minimum monthly profit and the corresponding minimum monthly profit.

• *Integration of Trigonometric Functions*

Evaluate each of the following.

54. $\displaystyle\int \sin (4t - 1) \, dt$

55. $\displaystyle\int 6 \cos (2t + 5) \, dt$

56. $\displaystyle\int (5 - 2 \cos t) \, dt$

57. $\displaystyle\int (\cos t)^4 \sin t \, dt$

58. $\displaystyle\int t^2 \sin t^3 \, dt$

59. $\displaystyle\int (t + 2) \cos (t^2 + 4t) \, dt$

60. *Total revenue.* Sales revenues (in millions of dollars) flow into a firm's treasury at a monthly rate given by

$$R(t) = 50 + 10 \cos \frac{\pi}{6}t$$

where t denotes time in months, with $t = 0$ corresponding to January 1990. Determine the total sales revenues flowing into the firm's treasury during the following time intervals:

a) From July 1990 to October 1990 $(6 \le t \le 9)$

b) From March 1991 to January 1992 $(14 \le t \le 24)$

ALGEBRA REVIEW

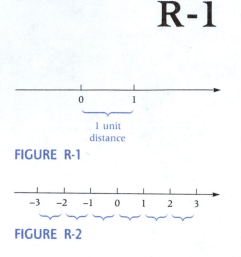

FIGURE R-1

FIGURE R-2

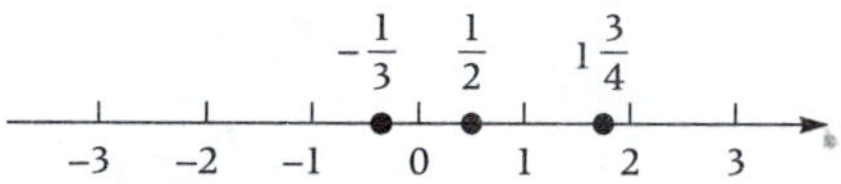

FIGURE R-3

R-1

• THE REAL NUMBERS AND INTERVAL NOTATION

All the numbers we will use in this text can be represented as points on a straight line. Such a representation can be constructed as follows. Begin with a straight line. Choose an arbitrary point, called the **origin,** on the line and label it 0. Then choose another point to the right of 0 and label it 1. Let the distance between 0 and 1 represent 1 unit of measure (see Figure R-1). The point on the straight line 1 unit to the right of 1 is labeled 2, the point 1 unit to the right of 2 is labeled 3, etc. (see Figure R-2). Also, the point on the straight line 1 unit to the left of 0 is labeled −1, the point 1 unit to the left of −1 is labeled −2, the point 1 unit to the left of −2 is labeled −3, etc. (see Figure R-2). The straight line in Figure R-2 is called the **real number line.** There is a one-to-one correspondence between the points on the real number line and the set of real numbers. In other words, each real number is associated with a particular point on this number line. Also, each point on this number line is associated with a particular real number. For example, the fraction 1/2 is associated with the point midway between 0 and 1, the number 1 3/4 is associated with the point three-quarters of the distance between 1 and 2, and the number −1/3 is associated with the point one-third of the distance between 0 and −1 (see Figure R-3).

There are several types of real numbers:

1. *Counting numbers.* These numbers are also called **natural numbers**.

$$1, 2, 3, 4, 5, \ldots *$$

2. *Whole numbers.*

$$0, 1, 2, 3, 4, \ldots$$

3. *Integers.*

$$\ldots, -4, -3, -2, -1, 0, 1, 2, 3, 4, \ldots$$

4. *Rational numbers.* All numbers that can be expressed as a quotient of two integers, where the denominator is not equal to 0. Examples are numbers such as 1/2, 3/4, 4/1, 3, and 1.23. Some rational numbers have decimal expansions that repeat but do not terminate. Some examples are

$$\frac{1}{3} = 0.333. \ldots \text{ which is written as } 0.\overline{3}$$

$$\frac{83}{99} = 0.838383. \ldots \text{ which is written as } 0.\overline{83}$$

5. *Irrational numbers.* These are all real numbers that are not rational. Ir-

---

*Here, the three dots indicate that the numbers continue indefinitely in the same manner.

rational numbers have decimal representations that are nonterminating and nonrepeating. Some examples are

$$\sqrt{2} = 1.4142135. . .*$$
$$\pi = 3.1415926. . .$$
$$e = 2.718281. . .$$
$$-\sqrt{5} = -2.2360679. . .$$

Thus, a real number is either rational or irrational but cannot be both. The rational numbers include the integers, the integers include the whole numbers, and the whole numbers include the counting or natural numbers.

Inequality

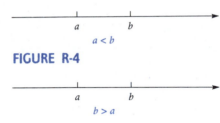

FIGURE R-4

FIGURE R-5

If a number a lies to the left of a number b on the real number line, then "a is less than b." This is written $a < b$ (see Figure R-4). Also, if a number b lies to the right of a number a on the real number line, then "b is greater than a." This is written $b > a$ (see Figure R-5). Thus, the statement "5 is less than 6" is written $5 < 6$, and the statement "8 is greater than 3" is written $8 > 3$.

The complete set of inequality phrases and their respective symbols are summarized as follows.

SUMMARY

Inequality Phrases and Symbols

"Is less than"	$<$
"Is greater than"	$>$
"Is less than or equal to"	$\leq$
"Is greater than or equal to"	$\geq$
"Is not equal to"	$\neq$

Intervals

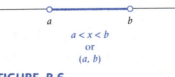

FIGURE R-6

Sometimes it is necessary to refer to all real numbers located between two numbers a and b on the real number line (see Figure R-6). Such a set of numbers is called an **interval** and is expressed as all real numbers x such that

$$a < x < b$$

This interval is also denoted as (a, b). This way of expressing an interval is called **interval notation.** Observe that the endpoints, a and b, are not included in this interval. This situation is graphically expressed by using an open circle at each endpoint (see Figure R-6). An interval that does not

---

*These dots indicate that the decimal representations are nonterminating.

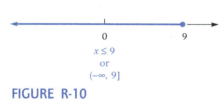

$a \leq x \leq b$
or
$[a, b]$

FIGURE R-7

$5 \leq x \leq 10$
or
$[5, 10]$

FIGURE R-8

FIGURE R-9

$x \leq 9$
or
$(-\infty, 9]$

FIGURE R-10

contain its endpoints is called an *open interval*. If the endpoints are to be included, then the set must be written as

$$a \leq x \leq b$$

or, in terms of interval notation, $[a, b]$. This interval is graphically expressed by using a solid circle at each endpoint (see Figure R-7). An interval that contains its endpoints is called a *closed interval*.

• **EXAMPLE R-1** _____

Graph all real numbers x such that $5 \leq x \leq 10$.

Solution

This interval includes all real numbers between 5 and 10. The endpoints are included. The graph appears in Figure R-8.

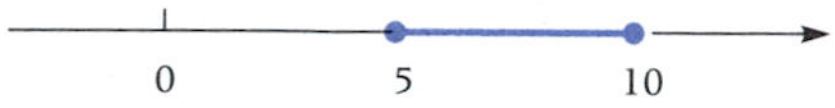

• **EXAMPLE R-2** _____

Express the interval in Figure R-9 by using the variable x and also by using interval notation.

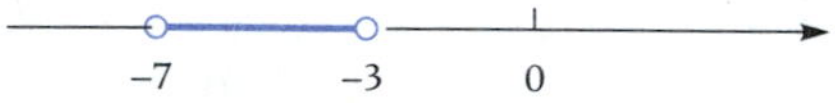

Solution

This interval includes all real numbers between -7 and -3. The endpoints are not included. Hence, the interval is written as all real numbers x such that $-7 < x < -3$. Using interval notation, this interval is also denoted as $(-7, -3)$.

• **EXAMPLE R-3** _____

Graph all real numbers x such that $x \leq 9$.

Solution

This interval includes all real numbers less than or equal to 9. The endpoint, 9, is included. The graph appears in Figure R-10. This interval is also denoted as $(-\infty, 9]$.

•

The symbol $-\infty$ means minus infinity; the symbol ∞ means infinity. We note that ∞ is not a number; it enables us to indicate an interval that is unbounded to the right. $-\infty$ enables us to indicate an interval that is unbounded to the left. Also note that we always use open interval symbols with ∞ or $-\infty$ to indicate that ∞ and $-\infty$ are not actually real numbers that can be achieved by our intervals.

We now give further examples of interval notation.

Interval	Interval notation	Graph
$3 < x \leq 6$	$(3, 6]$	
$-2 \leq x < 4$	$[-2, 4)$	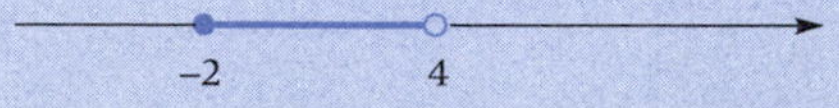
$1 \leq x \leq 7$	$[1, 7]$	

Interval	Interval notation	Graph
$8 \leq x < \infty$	$[8, \infty)$	8
$-\infty < x < 2$	$(-\infty, 2)$	2
$4 < x < 9$	$(4, 9)$	4 9

Absolute Value

The absolute value of a number x, written $|x|$, is defined by

$$|x| = \begin{cases} x & \text{if } x \text{ is positive or zero} \\ -x & \text{if } x \text{ is negative} \end{cases}$$

• EXAMPLE R-4

Evaluate $|-7|$.

Solution

Since -7 is negative, then by the definition of absolute value, $|-7| = -(-7) = 7$.

• EXAMPLE R-5

Evaluate $|8|$.

Solution

Since 8 is positive, then by the definition of absolute value, $|8| = 8$.

• EXAMPLE R-6

Evaluate $|9 - 14|$.

Solution

Since $9 - 14 = -5$, a negative number, then by the definition of absolute value, $|9 - 14| = -(-5) = 5$.

The absolute value of a number is always non-negative. In addition, $|x|$ gives the distance on the real number line between 0 and x, as indicated in Figures R-11 (a) and (b). This is why a number and its negative both have the same absolute value.

The distance between points a and b on the real number line in Figure R-12 is given by either $|a - b|$ or $|b - a|$. Thus, the distance between 7 and 10 on the real number line in Figure R-13 is given by $|7 - 10| = |-3| = 3$. This distance is also given by $|10 - 7| = |3| = 3$.

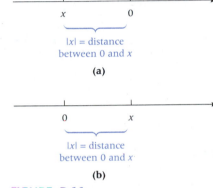

$|x|$ = distance between 0 and x

(a)

$|x|$ = distance between 0 and x

(b)

FIGURE R-11

$|a - b|$ = distance between a and b

FIGURE R-12

$|7 - 10| = 3$
distance between 7 and 10

FIGURE R-13

Exercises R-1

State whether each of the following is true or false.

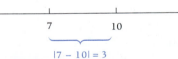

1. $3 < 7$	**2.** $-3 < -7$	**3.** $-2 < -5$
4. $2 < 5$	**5.** $-6 < -2$	**6.** $-3 > -7$
7. $-2 > -5$	**8.** $0 < 5$	**9.** $0 > -3$
10. $9 > 6$	**11.** $8 > 10$	**12.** $-6 < -1$

13. Every counting number is a whole number.
14. Every whole number is an integer.
15. Every counting number is an integer.
16. Every integer is a rational number.
17. Every rational number is a real number.
18. Every integer is a whole number.
19. Every whole number is a counting number.
20. Every irrational number is a real number.
21. 7 is a rational number.
22. 3/5 is a rational number.
23. $-2/3$ is a rational number.
24. $\sqrt{11}$ is a rational number.
25. $\sqrt{11}$ is an irrational number.
26. 3.56345. . . is an irrational number.
27. 4.7065 is an irrational number.
28. 2.767676. . . is a rational number.

Graph each of the following on the real number line.

29. $-5 \leq x \leq -1$ 30. $7 \leq x \leq 11$ 31. $-4 < x < -2$
32. $9 < x < 15$ 33. $-3 < x \leq 2$ 34. $2 \leq x < 9$
35. $5 \leq x$ 36. $x \geq 5$ 37. $x \leq -3$
38. $x < 10$ 39. $x > -2$ 40. $x > 4$
41. $2 < x$ 42. $x \geq -1$ 43. $x \neq 2$
44. $x \neq -3, x \neq 5$

State whether each of the following is an open interval or a closed interval.

45. $3 \leq x \leq 8$ 46. $3 < x < 8$
47. $-4 < x < -1$ 48. $-6 \leq x \leq -2$
49. $8 \leq x \leq 10$ 50. $6 < x \leq 9$

Graph each of the following on the real number line:

51. $[3, 9]$ 52. $(-1, 5)$ 53. $(-\infty, -4]$ 54. $[6, \infty)$
55. $(-\infty, 6)$ 56. $(9, \infty)$ 57. $(4, 9]$ 58. $[2, 9)$

Evaluate each of the following:

59. $|0|$ 60. $|-1|$ 61. $|1|$
62. $|-21|$ 63. $|-2|$ 64. $|15|$
65. $|-15|$ 66. $|-20|$ 67. $|20|$
68. $|5 - 9|$ 69. $|9 - 5|$ 70. $|16 - 7|$
71. $|7 - 16|$ 72. $|14 - 8|$ 73. $|9 - 15|$
74. $|-5 - 3|$ 75. $|-4 - 9|$ 76. $|-6 - 4|$

77. Find the distance between 5 and 11 on the real number line.
78. Find the distance between -3 and 10 on the real number line.
79. Find the distance between -9 and -4 on the real number line.

R-2 • LINEAR EQUATIONS AND INEQUALITIES

Linear Equations in One Variable

A statement such as

$$3x + 5 = 17$$

is a linear equation (equality) in one variable. To find its solution, we first subtract 5 from both sides to obtain

$$3x = 12$$

Then we divide both sides by 3 to obtain the solution

$$x = 4$$

The solution is sketched on the real number line in Figure R-14.

When solving linear equations such as $3x + 5 = 17$, we use the following rules of equalities.

Solution: $x = 4$

FIGURE R-14

■ **SUMMARY**

Rules of Equalities

Rule 1   If the same number is either added to or subtracted from both sides of an equality, the resulting equality remains true.

Rule 2   If both sides of an equality are either multiplied by or divided by the same nonzero number, the resulting equality remains true.

Linear Inequalities

We now consider linear inequalities. In general, if the equal sign (=) of a linear equality such as

$$3x + 5 = 7$$

is replaced by an inequality sign ($<$, $>$, $\leq$, $\geq$), the resulting statement is a linear inequality. Thus, the statements

$$3x + 5 < 7$$
$$3x + 5 > 7$$
$$3x + 5 \leq 7$$
$$3x + 5 \geq 7$$

are examples of linear inequalities. To solve linear inequalities, we may use the following rules of inequalities.

■ **SUMMARY**

Rules of Inequalities

Rule 1   If the same number is either added to or subtracted from both sides of an inequality, the resulting inequality remains true.

Rule 2
a)   If both sides of an inequality are either multiplied by or divided by the same *positive* number, the resulting inequality remains true.
b)   If both sides of an inequality are either multiplied by or divided by the same *negative* number, the original inequality sign must be *reversed* in order for the resulting inequality to remain true.

Note that the rules of equalities also hold for inequalities with the exception involving either multiplication by or division by a negative number. Thus, if

$$2 < 5$$

then

$$-4(2) > -4(5)$$
$$-8 > -20$$

• **EXAMPLE R-7**

Solve the inequality $-5x + 3 \leq 13$ for x, sketch the solution on a real number line, and give the answer in interval notation.

Solution

We first subtract 3 from both sides (rule 1) to obtain

$$-5x \leq 10$$

Then we divide both sides by -5 [rule 2(b)] to get

$$x \geq -2$$

The solution is sketched in Figure R-15.

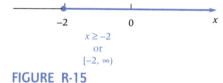

$x \geq -2$
or
$[-2, \infty)$

FIGURE R-15

• **EXAMPLE R-8**

Solve the inequality $3x + 5 < 17$ for x, sketch the solution on a real number line, and give the answer in interval notation.

Solution

Subtracting 5 from both sides (rule 1), we obtain

$$3x < 12$$

Dividing both sides by 3 [rule 2(a)] yields

$$x < 4$$

The solution is sketched in Figure R-16.

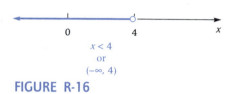

$x < 4$
or
$(-\infty, 4)$

FIGURE R-16

• **EXAMPLE R-9**

Solve the inequality $(-1/2)x + 3 \geq -1$ for x, sketch the solution on a real number line, and give the answer in interval notation.

Solution

Subtracting 3 from both sides (rule 1) gives us

$$-\frac{1}{2}x \geq -4$$

Multiplying both sides by -2 [rule 2(b)] yields

$$x \leq 8$$

The solution is sketched in Figure R-17.

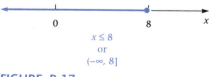

$x \leq 8$
or
$(-\infty, 8]$

FIGURE R-17

Exercises R-2

Solve each of the following.

1. $4x + 8 = 32$
2. $5x + 30 = 80$
3. $-2x + 6 = -12$
4. $-5x + 8 = -52$

5.	$4x - 3 = 21 + 2x$	**6.**	$6x - 7 = 47 - 3x$
7.	$(1/2)x + 6 = 10$	**8.**	$(3/4)x - 2 = 10$
9.	$5y + 2 = 7y - 18$	**10.**	$6z + 4 = 10z - 28$

Solve each of the following inequalities, graph its solution on a real number line, and give the answer in interval notation.

11.	$2x + 4 \le 15$	**12.**	$-3x + 5 \le 32$
13.	$4x - 5 < 25$	**14.**	$5x + 3 > 17$
15.	$-3x + 17 \ge -14$	**16.**	$-6x + 5 > 23$
17.	$-6x - 5 \ge -23$	**18.**	$-3x - 2 \le -14$
19.	$3(x - 5) \ge 18$	**20.**	$-4(x + 7) < 32$

R-3 • EXPONENTS AND RADICALS

Exponents

If x is a number, the product of n $x's$ is denoted by x^n. That is,

$$x^n = \underbrace{x \cdot x \cdot \ldots \cdot x}_{n\ x's}$$

The positive integer n, which indicates the number of times x appears as a factor, is an **exponent.** The number x is called the **base.**

We define a negative exponent as follows:

$$x^{-n} = \frac{1}{x^n} = \frac{1}{\underbrace{x \cdot x \cdot \ldots \cdot x}_{n\ x's}} \qquad (x \ne 0)$$

We define

$$x^0 = 1 \qquad (x \ne 0)$$

Note that 0^0 is undefined.

Laws of Exponents

In this section, we will discuss exponents and the laws governing their algebraic manipulation.

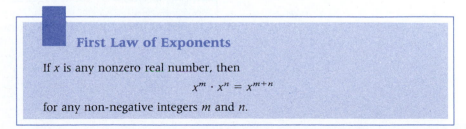

> **First Law of Exponents**
>
> If x is any nonzero real number, then
> $$x^m \cdot x^n = x^{m+n}$$
> for any non-negative integers m and n.

To verify this law, we observe that

$$x^m \cdot x^n = \underbrace{(x \cdot x \cdot \ldots \cdot x)}_{m \ x's}\underbrace{(x \cdot x \cdot \ldots \cdot x)}_{n \ x's}$$

$$= \underbrace{x \cdot x \cdot \ldots \cdot x}_{(m+n) \ x's}$$

$$= x^{m+n}$$

For example,

$$2^3 \cdot 2^4 = 2^{3+4} = 2^7$$
$$5^3 \cdot 5^6 = 5^{3+6} = 5^9$$

> ### Second Law of Exponents
>
> If x is any nonzero real number, then
>
> $$\frac{x^m}{x^n} = x^{m-n}$$
>
> for any non-negative integers m and n.

To verify this law, we note that if $m = 5$ and $n = 2$, then

$$\frac{x^m}{x^n} = \frac{x^5}{x^2} = \frac{\not{x} \cdot \not{x} \cdot x \cdot x \cdot x}{\not{x} \cdot \not{x}}$$

$$= x^{5-2} = x^3$$

And, similarly, we have

$$\frac{5^7}{5^3} = 5^{7-3} = 5^4 = 625$$

$$\frac{4^3}{4^5} = 4^{3-5} = 4^{-2} = \frac{1}{4^2} = \frac{1}{16}$$

It should be noted that the first two laws of exponents also hold true for negative integers m and n.

> ### Third Law of Exponents
>
> If x is any real number, then
>
> $$(x^m)^n = x^{m \cdot n}$$
>
> for all integers m and n.

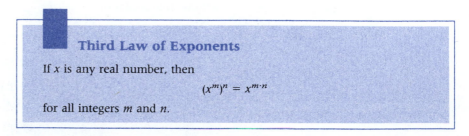

To verify this law, we see that

$$(x^m)^n = \underbrace{x^m \cdot x^m \cdot \ldots \cdot x^m}_{n\ x^m\text{'s}}$$

$$= x^{\overbrace{m+m+\ldots+m}^{n\ m\text{'s}}}$$

$$= x^{m \cdot n}$$

As examples, we have

$$(x^3)^2 = x^{3 \cdot 2} = x^6$$
$$(7^4)^5 = 7^{4 \cdot 5} = 7^{20}$$

Roots and Radicals

We now give meaning to the symbol $\sqrt[n]{x}$, where n is a positive integer. The symbol $\sqrt[n]{x}$ is called a **radical** and is read "the nth root of x." The nth root of x, $\sqrt[n]{x}$, represents a number that when multiplied by itself n times (i.e., raised to the nth power) yields x. Thus, if y is an nth root of x, then

$$y^n = x$$

If $n = 2$, then $\sqrt[2]{x}$ is called the **square root** of x and is usually written $\sqrt{x}$. Thus, $\sqrt{16} = 4$ since $4^2 = 16$. However, the equation $y^2 = 16$ has another solution, -4, since $(-4)^2 = 16$. In such a case, we take the **positive square root,** often called the **principal square root.** Thus, 4 is the principal square root of 16, and we write $\sqrt{16} = 4$. If we want to refer to the **negative square root** of 16, we indicate it by writing $-\sqrt{16} = -4$. Note that $\sqrt{-16}$ is undefined since there is no real number with a square of -16.

If $n = 3$, then $\sqrt[3]{x}$ is called the **cube root** of x. Note that $\sqrt[3]{8} = 2$ since $2^3 = 8$, and that $\sqrt[3]{-8} = -2$ since $(-2)^3 = -8$. Because $n = 3$ and 3 is an odd number, there is no need to define a principal cube root since the cube of a negative number is a negative number and the cube of a positive number is a positive number.

Observe that $\sqrt[4]{16} = 2$ since $2^4 = 16$. However, since $(-2)^4 = 16$, then $-\sqrt[4]{16} = -2$. Again, for even values of n, we call the positive nth root the **principal nth root.**

The preceding comments about $\sqrt[n]{x}$ are summarized as follows:

1. If $x > 0$ and n is even, then there are two solutions to the equation $y^n = x$. One is positive and the other is negative. To avoid ambiguity, we take the positive nth root, often called the principal nth root.
2. If $x < 0$ and n is even, then there are no real nth roots of x.
3. If n is odd, then there is one real nth root of x. Its sign is the same as that of x.
4. If $x = 0$, then the nth root of x is 0.

Rational Exponents

Up to this point, we have discussed only integer exponents. Thus, the first three laws of exponents were restricted to integral exponents. We now take a look at rational exponents. Consider the expression

$$x^{1/n}$$

where n is a nonzero integer. Hence, $1/n$ is a rational exponent. If $x^{1/n}$ is to be well defined, it must obey the laws of exponents. Specifically, the third law of exponents states that

$$(x^m)^n = x^{m \cdot n}$$

If this law is to hold true for $x^{1/n}$, then

$$(x^{1/n})^n = x^{(1/n)n} = x$$

This implies that the product of $x^{1/n}$ multiplied by itself n times equals x. **Hence, $x^{1/n}$ must equal the nth root of x,** or

$$x^{1/n} = \sqrt[n]{x}$$

Thus, $x^{1/n}$ is now defined. Specifically,

$$x^{1/2} = \sqrt{x}$$
$$x^{1/3} = \sqrt[3]{x}$$
$$4^{1/2} = \sqrt{4} = 2$$

Note that $(-4)^{1/2} = \sqrt{-4}$, which is undefined.

Since we have defined the expression $x^{1/n}$ for integral values of n, we now discuss expressions of the form

$$x^{m/n}$$

for integral values of m and n. If the expression $x^{m/n}$ is to be well defined, it must obey the laws of exponents. Specifically, if the third law of exponents is to hold true, then

$$(x^{1/n})^m = x^{(1/n)m} = x^{m/n}$$

Thus, $x^{m/n}$ may be defined as the **mth power of the nth root of x,** or

$$x^{m/n} = (\sqrt[n]{x})^m$$

As examples, we have

$$x^{5/2} = (\sqrt{x})^5$$
$$5^{2/3} = (\sqrt[3]{5})^2$$

Since the third law of exponents also indicates that

$$x^{m/n} = (x^m)^{1/n}$$

then $x^{m/n}$ may also be defined as the **nth root of x^m,** or

$$x^{m/n} = \sqrt[n]{x^m}$$

In summary, if m/n is reduced to lowest terms, we have

$$x^{m/n} = (\sqrt[n]{x})^m = \sqrt[n]{x^m}$$

Thus,

$$x^{5/2} = (\sqrt{x})^5 = \sqrt{x^5}$$
$$5^{2/3} = (\sqrt[3]{5})^2 = \sqrt[3]{5^2}$$

Since we have now defined rational exponents, it is appropriate to state that the first three laws of exponents hold true for all rational exponents m and n for which x^m and x^n are defined.

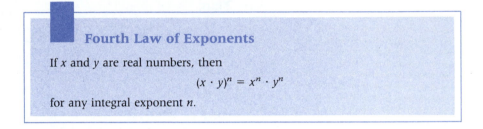

Fourth Law of Exponents

If x and y are real numbers, then

$$(x \cdot y)^n = x^n \cdot y^n$$

for any integral exponent n.

To verify this law, observe that

$$(xy)^n = \underbrace{xy \cdot xy \cdot \ldots \cdot xy}_{n \ xy's}$$

$$= \underbrace{(x \cdot x \cdot \ldots \cdot x)}_{n \ x's}\underbrace{(y \cdot y \cdot \ldots \cdot y)}_{n \ y's}$$

$$= x^n \cdot y^n$$

And, specifically,

$$(4 \cdot 3)^5 = 4^5 \cdot 3^5$$
$$(5x)^3 = 5^3 \cdot x^3 = 125x^3$$
$$(-2xy)^5 = (-2)^5 x^5 y^5 = -32x^5 y^5$$

It should be noted that the fourth law of exponents also holds true for any rational exponent n for which x^n and y^n are defined.

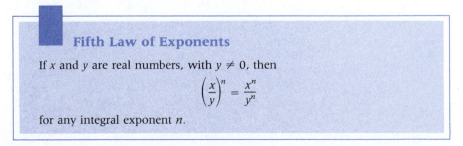

Fifth Law of Exponents

If x and y are real numbers, with $y \neq 0$, then

$$\left(\frac{x}{y}\right)^n = \frac{x^n}{y^n}$$

for any integral exponent n.

To verify this law, note that

$$\left(\frac{x}{y}\right)^n = \underbrace{\frac{x}{y} \cdot \frac{x}{y} \cdot \ \ldots \ \cdot \frac{x}{y}}_{n\frac{x}{y}\text{'s}}$$

$$= \frac{\overbrace{x \cdot x \cdot \ldots \cdot x}^{n\,x\text{'s}}}{\underbrace{y \cdot y \cdot \ldots \cdot y}_{n\,y\text{'s}}}$$

$$= \frac{x^n}{y^n}$$

Thus,

$$\left(\frac{5}{2}\right)^3 = \frac{5^3}{2^3}$$

$$\left(\frac{-3}{y}\right)^4 = \frac{(-3)^4}{y^4} = \frac{81}{y^4}$$

Again, we note that the fifth law of exponents also holds true for any rational exponent n for which x^n and y^n are defined.

Scientific Notation

Any positive number can be expressed in the form

$$c \times 10^n$$

where $1 \le c < 10$ and n is an integral exponent. When a number is expressed in this form, it is said to be in **scientific notation.** Specifically,

$$543 = 5.43 \times 10^2$$
$$84{,}000{,}000 = 8.4 \times 10^7$$
$$0.0003 = 3.0 \times 10^{-4}$$

Exercises R-3

Simplify each of the following. No exponents should appear in the final answer.

1. 3^2

2. $\left(\dfrac{2}{3}\right)^4$

3. $(-5)^2$

4. $(-5)^3$

5. $(4^2)^3$

6. 5^{-3}

7. 2^{-4}

8. $(-3)^{-2}$

9. $\dfrac{2^7}{2}$

10. $\dfrac{(-3)^9}{(-3)^7}$

11. $5^3 \cdot 5^4$

12. $4^2 \cdot 4^3$

13. $\left(\dfrac{3}{5}\right)^2$

14. $\left(\dfrac{4}{3}\right)^0$

15. $(2^{-3})^2$

16. $64^{1/2}$

17. $64^{-1/2}$

18. $216^{1/3}$

19. $16^{1/2}$	**20.** $16^{-1/2}$	**21.** $49^{1/2}$
22. $49^{-1/2}$	**23.** $64^{5/2}$	**24.** $64^{-5/2}$
25. $49^{3/2}$	**26.** $49^{-3/2}$	**27.** $216^{2/3}$
28. $216^{-2/3}$	**29.** 867^0	**30.** $(-3)^0$
31. $49^{5/2}$		

Rewrite each of the following using negative exponents.

32. $\dfrac{1}{3^2}$	**33.** $\dfrac{1}{5^6}$	**34.** $\dfrac{1}{x^7}$
35. $\dfrac{1}{(-5)^3}$	**36.** $\dfrac{1}{x^n}$	**37.** $\dfrac{1}{x^8}$

Rewrite each of the following using rational exponents.

38. $\sqrt[3]{5}$	**39.** $(\sqrt{4})^9$	**40.** $\sqrt[3]{x^5}$
41. $\sqrt[5]{2}$	**42.** $\sqrt{8^7}$	**43.** $\sqrt[3]{9^4}$
44. $\sqrt{5})^3$	**45.** $(\sqrt[3]{5})^7$	**46.** $\sqrt[4]{x}$
47. $\dfrac{1}{\sqrt{5^3}}$	**48.** $\dfrac{1}{(\sqrt[3]{5})^8}$	**49.** $\dfrac{1}{\sqrt{x^5}}$
50. $\dfrac{1}{\sqrt{x^3}}$	**51.** $\dfrac{1}{\sqrt[3]{x^2}}$	**52.** $\dfrac{1}{(\sqrt[3]{x})^7}$

Using the fourth law of exponents, $(x \cdot y)^n = x^n \cdot y^n$, simplify each of the following.

53. $(-3x)^2$	**54.** $(2y)^4$	**55.** $(5xy)^3$
56. $(xyz)^9$	**57.** $(4 \cdot 81)^{1/2}$	**58.** $\sqrt{9 \cdot 64}$

Using the fifth law of exponents, $(x/y)^n = x^n/y^n$, simplify each of the following.

59. $\left(\dfrac{5}{6}\right)^3$	**60.** $\left(\dfrac{x}{y}\right)^4$	**61.** $\left(\dfrac{x}{3}\right)^5$	**62.** $\sqrt[3]{\dfrac{8}{27}}$
63. $\left(\dfrac{x}{5}\right)^2$	**64.** $\left(\dfrac{4}{x}\right)^3$	**65.** $\left(\dfrac{-2}{x}\right)^3$	**66.** $\sqrt{\dfrac{16}{25}}$

Simplify each of the following.

67. $\left(\dfrac{2^{-3} \cdot 2^5}{2^{-2}}\right)^3$	**68.** $3^{1/2} \cdot 3^{5/2}$
69. $\dfrac{3^{-7/2} \cdot 3^{3/2}}{3^{1/2} \cdot 3^{-3/2}}$	**70.** $\left(\dfrac{27^{5/3} \cdot 27^{-1/3}}{27^{1/3}}\right)^2$

Express each of the following in scientific notation.

71. 496	**72.** 5,870,000	**73.** 8,000,000,000
74. 0.00045	**75.** 0.0000008	**76.** 59.5
77. 0.56	**78.** 8730	**79.** 0.00357

R-4

• THE DISTRIBUTIVE LAW AND FACTORING

The Distributive Law

Consider the product of 3 times the sum of $2 + 8$ or

$$3(2 + 8)$$

Such a product can be determined by either of the following two methods:

1. Calculate the sum

$$2 + 8 = 10$$

and multiply the result by 3 to obtain

$$3(2 + 8) = 3(10)$$
$$= 30$$

2. Multiply both 2 and 8 by 3, and add the products to obtain

$$3(2 + 8) = (3 \cdot 2) + (3 \cdot 8)$$
$$= 6 + 24$$
$$= 30$$

Observe that, in the second method, the 3 is *distributed* throughout the sum of 2 + 8. This is a specific illustration of the *distributive law of multiplication over addition.*

> **Distributive Law**
>
> If *a, b,* and *c* are numbers, then
>
> $$a(b + c) = ab + ac$$

• **EXAMPLE R-10** ————————————————————

Using the distributive law, multiply $4(x + 2)$.

Solution

Distributing the 4 throughout the sum of $x + 2$, we have

$$4\ (x + 2) = \boxed{4}\ x + \boxed{4}\ \cdot 2$$
$$= 4x + 8$$

• **EXAMPLE R-11** ————————————————————

Using the distributive law, multiply $3[x + (-5)]$.

Solution

$$3\ (x + (-5)) = \boxed{3}\ x + \boxed{3}\ (-5)$$
$$= 3x - 15$$

Since the sum of $x + (-5)$ is equivalent to the *difference* of $x - 5$, we should realize that the distributive law also holds true for *multiplication over subtraction.* Hence,

$$3\ (x - 5) = \boxed{3}\ x - \boxed{3}\ \cdot 5$$
$$= 3x - 15$$

• **EXAMPLE R-12** ————————————————————

Using the distributive law, multiply $6(2x - 5)$.

Solution

$$\boxed{6}\ (2x - 5) = \boxed{6}\ \cdot 2x - \boxed{6}\ \cdot 5$$
$$= 12x - 30$$

The distributive law may be applied to products involving a sum or difference of more than two numbers, as illustrated in Example R-13.

• **EXAMPLE R-13** _____

Using the distributive law, multiply $-5(x^2 + 3x - 7)$.

Solution

$$-5\,(x^2 + 3x - 7) = \boxed{-5}\;x^2 + \boxed{-5}\cdot 3x - \boxed{(-5)}\,(7)$$
$$= -5x^2 - 15x + 35$$

• **EXAMPLE R-14** _____

Using the distributive law, multiply $-5xy^2(x^3 - 4x^2y)$.

Solution

$$-5xy^2\,(x^3 - 4x^2y) = \boxed{-5xy^2}\cdot x^3 - \boxed{(-5xy^2)}\cdot 4x^2y$$
$$= -5x^4y^2 + 20x^3y^3$$

Factoring

Many times the distributive law is used in *reverse*. This process is called **factoring.** Specifically, if we start with the expression

$$ab + ac$$

and rewrite it as the product

$$a(b + c)$$

then we have factored a from $ab + ac$.

• **EXAMPLE R-15** _____

Factor $3x + 6$.

Solution

$$3x + 6 = \boxed{3}\;x + \boxed{3}\cdot 2$$
$$= \boxed{3}\;(x + 2)$$

• **EXAMPLE R-16** _____

Factor $5x - 10y + 20$.

Solution

$$5x - 10y + 20 = \boxed{5}\;x - \boxed{5}\cdot 2y + \boxed{5}\cdot 4$$
$$= \boxed{5}\;(x - 2y + 4)$$

• **EXAMPLE R-17** _____

Factor $3x^5y^3 - 6x^2y^9$.

Solution

$$3x^5y^3 - 6x^2y^9 = \boxed{3x^2y^3}\cdot x^3 - \boxed{3x^2y^3}\cdot 2y^6$$
$$= \boxed{3x^2y^3}\;(x^3 - 2y^6)$$

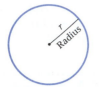

FIGURE R-18

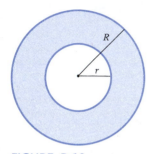

FIGURE R-19

• **EXAMPLE R-18**

Given that the area of a circle of radius r (see Figure R-18) is πr^2 where $\pi \approx$ 3.1415927 to seven decimal places, show that the area of the ring of Figure R-19 is $\pi(R^2 - r^2)$.

Solution

$$\text{area of ring} = \text{area of outer circle} - \text{area of inner circle}$$
$$= \pi R^2 - \pi r^2$$
$$= \pi(R^2 - r^2)$$

• **EXAMPLE R-19**

Using the distributive law, show that $P(1 + i) + P(1 + i)i = P(1 + i)^2$.

Solution

$$P(1 + i) + P(1 + i)i = \boxed{P(1 + i)} \cdot 1 + \boxed{P(1 + i)} \cdot i$$
$$= \boxed{P(1 + i)} (1 + i)$$
$$= P(1 + i)^2$$

• **EXAMPLE R-20**

Factor $7x(x - 5) + 3x(x - 5)$.

Solution

$$7x \boxed{(x - 5)} + 3x \boxed{(x - 5)} = \boxed{(x - 5)} (7x + 3x)$$
$$= (x - 5)10x$$
$$= 10x(x - 5)$$

Exercises R-4

Use the distributive law to multiply each of the following.

1. $3(x + 4)$	**2.** $5(x - 3)$	**3.** $-2(x + 6)$
4. $-5(x - 8)$	**5.** $9(x + 3)$	**6.** $9(2x + 3)$

7. $-4(x^2 - 3x + 7)$ **8.** $6x(x^2 + 2x - 5)$

9. $5x(x^3 - 4x^2 + 4x + 5)$ **10.** $-2x(x^2 + 6x + 7)$

11. $3x^2y^3(x^4 - 5y^2 + 6xy)$ **12.** $-2x^4y^3(x^3 - 6y^2 + 7xy)$

Factor each of the following.

13. $5x + 20$	**14.** $-2x - 8$	**15.** $3x - 27$
16. $8x - 16$	**17.** $6x - 30$	**18.** $4x + 32$
19. $3x^2 - 27x$	**20.** $5x^2 + 60x$	**21.** $-6x^2 + 48x$
22. $-4x^2 - 36x$	**23.** $7x^2 + 28x$	**24.** $9x^2 - 18x$

25. $3x^2y^4 + 6xy^2$ **26.** $4x^3y^5 - 8x^2y^6$

27. $-5x^4y^6 + 20x^3y^7$ **28.** $-2x^5y^3 + 6x^4y^3$

29. $3x^2y^6 + 9x^5y^3 + 6x^3y^4$ **30.** $5x^4y^6 - 10x^3y^7 + 30x^2y^3$

31. $P + Prt$ **32.** $S - Sdt$

33. $P + Pi$ **34.** $ax^2 + bx$

35. $ax^2 - bx$ **36.** $ax^3 + bx^2 + cx$

37. $P(1 + i)^2 + P(1 + i)^2 i$ **38.** $P(1 + i)^3 + P(1 + i)^3 i$

39. $3x(x - 7) + 3x(x + 4)$ **40.** $5x(x + 2) - 2x(x + 2)$

41. $2x(x + 3) - y(x + 3)$ **42.** $3xy(x + 2) - 6x^2(x + 2)$

43. $5xy(x - 2) + 8x^2(x - 2)$ **44.** $4xy^2(x - 1) + 5x^2y(x - 1)$

R-5 • MULTIPLYING BINOMIALS

An algebraic expression containing exactly two terms is called a **binomial.** For example, the expression

$$x + 7$$

is a binomial because it contains two terms, x and 7. The expression

$$4x - 5$$

is a binomial because it contains two terms, $4x$ and -5. The expression

$$x^2 + 6$$

is a binomial because it contains two terms, x^2 and 6. The product of two binomials can be determined by using the distributive law

$$a(b + c) = ab + ac$$

Specifically, the product

$$(x - 3)(x + 5)$$

can be determined by treating the binomial $x - 3$ as a and employing the distributive law as follows:

$$a(b + c) = ab + ac$$

$$(x - 3)(x + 5) = (x - 3)x + (x - 3) \cdot 5$$

$$= x^2 - 3x + 5x - 15$$

$$= x^2 + 2x - 15$$

Observe that the above product can also be determined by the following mechanical procedure, called the **FOIL** method:

Step 1 Multiply the first terms of the binomial factors   F

Step 2 Multiply the outer terms of the binomial factors   O

Step 3 Multiply the inner terms of the binomial factors   I

Step 4 Multiply the last terms of the binomial factors   L

Step 5 Add the above products and simplify if possible.

Using the FOIL method, we again determine the product

$$(x - 3)(x + 5)$$

as follows:

$$(x - 3)(x + 5) = x^2 + 5x - 3x - 15$$
$$= x^2 + 2x - 15$$

• **EXAMPLE R-21** ─────────────────────

Determine the product $(3x - 5)(x + 2)$.

Solution

$$(3x - 5)(x + 2) = 3x^2 + 6x - 5x - 10$$
$$= 3x^2 + x - 10$$

• **EXAMPLE R-22** ─────────────────────

Multiply $(4x + 3)(x - 7)$.

Solution

$$(4x + 3)(x - 7) = 4x^2 - \underline{\quad} + 3x - \underline{\quad}$$
$$= 4x^2 - 25x - 21$$

Answer

$$4x^2 - \underline{28x} + 3x - \underline{21} = 4x^2 - 25x - 21$$

• **EXAMPLE R-23** ─────────────────────

Multiply $(x - 5)(x + 5)$.

Solution

$$(x - 5)(x + 5) = x^2 + 5x - \underline{\quad} - \underline{\quad}$$
$$= x^2 - 25$$

Answer

$$x^2 + 5x - \underline{5x} - \underline{25} = x^2 - 25$$

Notice that the product, $x^2 - 25$, does not contain an x term. That is because the sum of $+5x$ and $-5x$ is 0.

> ### Difference of Two Squares
>
> In general,
>
> $$(x - a)(x + a) = x^2 - a^2$$
>
> where the right-hand expression is called a difference of two squares.

• **EXAMPLE R-24** _____

Determine $(x + 3)^2$.

Solution

$$(x + 3)^2 = (x + 3)(x + 3) = x^2 + \underline{\quad} + 3x + 9$$
$$= x^2 + 6x + 9$$

Answer

$$x^2 + \underline{3x} + 3x + 9 = x^2 + 6x + 9$$

Since the product $x^2 + 6x + 9$ in Example R-24 is equivalent to the square of a binomial, namely $x + 3$, then $x^2 + 6x + 9$ is called a **perfect square.** Notice that when determining the square of a binomial, the products of the inner terms and outer terms are equal. In Example R-24, each is $3x$. Thus, to square a binomial, we can use the following modified procedure.

> ### To Square a Binomial
>
> **Step 1** Square the first term.
> **Step 2** Multiply both terms of the binomial, and double this product.
> **Step 3** Square the last term.
> **Step 4** Add the above products.

For example,

$$(x + 5)^2 = x^2 + 2(5x) + 5^2$$
$$= x^2 + 10x + 25$$
$$(x - 7)^2 = x^2 + 2(-7x) + (-7)^2$$
$$= x^2 - 14x + 49$$
$$(2x - 5)^2 = (2x)^2 + 2[(2x)(-5)] + (-5)^2$$
$$= 4x^2 - 20x + 25$$

Exercises R-5

Determine each of the following products by using the FOIL method.

1. $(x - 2)(x + 3)$	**2.** $(x - 8)(x + 7)$
3. $(x + 1)(x + 5)$	**4.** $(x - 2)(x - 3)$
5. $(x - 8)(x - 7)$	**6.** $(x - 6)(x + 10)$
7. $(3x + 5)(x - 1)$	**8.** $(2x + 1)(3x + 4)$
9. $(4x - 7)(2x + 3)$	**10.** $(5x + 3)(x - 2)$
11. $(7x - 2)(3x + 1)$	**12.** $(9x + 1)(3x - 5)$

Determine each of the following products by using the difference of two squares formula.

13. $(x - 3)(x + 3)$	**14.** $(x - 7)(x + 7)$
15. $(x - 9)(x + 9)$	**16.** $(2x - 1)(2x + 1)$
17. $(3x - 2)(3x + 2)$	**18.** $(4x - 7)(4x + 7)$

Determine each of the following.

19. $(x - 2)^2$	**20.** $(x + 2)^2$
21. $(x + 5)^2$	**22.** $(x - 5)^2$
23. $(2x - 3)^2$	**24.** $(2x + 3)^2$

R-6 • FACTORING

In the previous section, we learned to multiply binomials. For example, we learned that the product $(x - 2)(x + 7)$ can be determined by the FOIL method as follows:

$$(x - 2)(x + 7) = x^2 + 7x - 2x - 14$$
$$= x^2 + 5x - 14$$

If we begin with $x^2 + 5x - 14$ and express it as the product $(x - 2)(x + 7)$, then we have *factored* $x^2 + 5x - 14$. The binomials $x - 2$ and $x + 7$ are called **factors.** Thus, factoring is the reverse of multiplication.

We will demonstrate the factoring process by factoring expressions of the form

$$ax^2 + bx + c$$

where a, b, and c are constants and $a \neq 0$. Also, we will begin with the special case where $a = 1$. Thus, for this special case, the above expression is written as

$$x^2 + bx + c$$

If factored, such an expression is written as the product of two binomials

$$(x + A)(x + B)$$

where A and B are constants. Thus, when we factor the expression $x^2 + bx + c$, we seek two constants, A and B, such that

$$(x + A)(x + B) = x^2 + bx + c \qquad (1)$$

If we apply the FOIL method to the left-hand side of equation (1), we obtain

$$(x + A)(x + B) = x^2 + Bx + Ax + AB$$
$$= x^2 + (B + A)x + AB \qquad (2)$$

Comparing the right-hand sides of equations (1) and (2), note that

$$B + A = b \text{ and } AB = c$$

This result is expressed as follows.

Factoring

When factoring the expression $x^2 + bx + c$ so that

$$(x + A)(x + B) = x^2 + bx + c$$

we seek two constants, A and B, whose sum equals b and whose product equals c.

As an example, let us factor $x^2 + 6x - 27$. This means that we wish to write $x^2 + 6x - 27$ as a product of two factors:

$$(x + A)(x + B)$$

Thus, we seek two numbers, A and B, whose sum is 6 and whose product is -27. The numbers of the pair -3, 9 satisfy the above requirements since $-3 + 9 = 6$ and $-3 \cdot 9 = -27$. Hence,

$$(x - 3)(x + 9) = x^2 + 6x - 27$$

and our two factors are $x - 3$ and $x + 9$.

• **EXAMPLE R-25**

Factor $x^2 + 7x - 30$.

Solution

We wish to determine two factors such that

$$(x + \underline{\quad})(x + \underline{\quad}) = x^2 + 7x - 30$$

Thus, we seek two numbers whose sum is 7 and whose product is -30. The following are possible pairs of numbers whose product is -30:

$$-5, 6 \qquad 5, -6 \qquad -3, 10 \qquad 3, -10$$
$$-30, 1 \qquad 30, -1 \qquad 15, -2 \qquad -15, 2$$

Since the numbers of the pair $-3, 10$ have a sum of 7, then the factors are $x - 3$ and $x + 10$. Hence,

$$(x - 3)(x + 10) = x^2 + 7x - 30$$

Of course, we can always check our factoring by multiplying the factors to determine if their product is the original expression that was factored.

• **EXAMPLE R-26**

Factor $x^2 + 8x + 15$.

Solution

We wish to determine two factors such that

$$(x + \underline{\quad})(x + \underline{\quad}) = x^2 + 8x + 15$$

Thus, we seek two numbers whose sum is 8 and whose product is 15. The following are possible pairs of numbers whose product is 15:

$$3, 5 \qquad -3, -5 \qquad 1, 15 \qquad -1, -15$$

Since the numbers of the pair 3, 5 have a sum of 8, then the factors are $x + 3$ and $x + 5$. Hence,

$$(x + 3)(x + 5) = x^2 + 8x + 15$$

Of course, we can always check our factoring by multiplying the factors to determine if their product is the original expression that was factored.

• **EXAMPLE R-27**

Factor $x^2 - 36$.

Solution

Since $x^2 - 36$ does not contain an x term, we seek two numbers whose sum is 0 and whose product is -36. The numbers are -6 and $+6$. Hence,

$$(x - 6)(x + 6) = x^2 - 36$$

As discussed in the previous section, the expression $x^2 - 36$ in Example R-27 is called a **difference of two squares.** In general, a difference of two squares

$$x^2 - h^2$$

is factored as follows:

$$x^2 - h^2 = (x - h)(x + h)$$

• **EXAMPLE R-28**

Factor $x^2 + 12x + 36$.

Solution

We seek two numbers whose product is 36 and whose sum is 12. The numbers are 6 and 6, and the factors are $x + 6$ and $x + 6$. Hence,

$$(x + 6)(x + 6) = x^2 + 12x + 36$$

or

$$(x + 6)^2 = x^2 + 12x + 36$$

Since the expression $x^2 + 12x + 36$ (in Example R-28), when factored, is written as $(x + 6)^2$, the square of a binomial, then the expression $x^2 + 12x + 36$ is called a **perfect square.** In general, an expression of the form $x^2 + bx + c$ is a perfect square if, when factored, it is written as

$$(x + A)^2 = x^2 + bx + c \qquad (3)$$

where A is a constant.

We now discuss how to recognize a perfect square. Applying the FOIL method to the left-hand side of equation (3), we obtain

$$
\begin{aligned}
(x + A)(x + A) &= x^2 + Ax + Ax + A^2 \\
&= x^2 + 2Ax + A^2 \qquad (4)
\end{aligned}
$$

Comparing the right-hand sides of equations (3) and (4), note that *the coefficient of* x *is twice the square root of the constant* c. Thus, we state the following.

Perfect Square

An expression of the form

$$x^2 + bx + c$$

with $c \geq 0$ is a perfect square if

$$b = \pm 2\sqrt{c}$$

1. If $b = +2\sqrt{c}$, then the expression is written in factored form as

$$(x + \sqrt{c})^2$$

2. If $b = -2\sqrt{c}$, then the expression is written in factored form as

$$(x - \sqrt{c})^2$$

As another example, note that $x^2 - 12x + 36$ is a perfect square since $-12 = -2\sqrt{36}$. Hence,

$$x^2 - 12x + 36 = (x - 6)^2$$

We summarize the following.

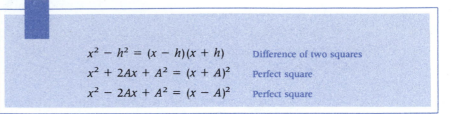

$$x^2 - h^2 = (x - h)(x + h) \qquad \text{Difference of two squares}$$
$$x^2 + 2Ax + A^2 = (x + A)^2 \qquad \text{Perfect square}$$
$$x^2 - 2Ax + A^2 = (x - A)^2 \qquad \text{Perfect square}$$

Exercises R-6

Factor each of the following:

1. $x^2 + 7x - 18$ 2. $x^2 - 7x - 18$
3. $x^2 + 2x - 15$ 4. $x^2 + 10x + 21$
5. $x^2 - 3x + 2$ 6. $x^2 + 13x + 40$
7. $x^2 - 13x + 40$ 8. $x^2 - x + 42$
9. $x^2 - 81$ 10. $x^2 - 64$
11. $x^2 - 49$ 12. $x^2 - 25$
13. $x^2 + 6x + 9$ 14. $x^2 - 6x + 9$
15. $x^2 - 10x + 25$ 16. $x^2 + 10x + 25$
17. $x^2 + 18x + 81$ 18. $x^2 - 18x + 81$
19. $x^2 - 6x - 27$ 20. $x^2 - 100$
21. $x^2 - 4x - 45$ 22. $x^2 - 20x + 100$
23. $x^2 + 7x + 6$ 24. $x^2 + 2x + 1$

R-7 • MORE FACTORING

In the previous section, we demonstrated the factoring process by factoring expressions of the form

$$ax^2 + bx + c$$

where a, b, and c are constants and $a = 1$. In this section, we remove the restriction that $a = 1$. In other words, we will now discuss the factoring of expressions of the form

$$ax^2 + bx + c$$

where a, b, and c are constants, $a \neq 0$, and $a \neq 1$. As an example, we will factor

$$5x^2 + 33x - 14$$

Since the coefficient of x^2 is 5, then by the FOIL method, the product of the x terms of both factors must be $5x^2$. Hence, the x terms of the factors are $5x$ and x, and

$$(5x + \underline{\quad})(x + \underline{\quad}) = 5x^2 + 33x - 14$$

We now seek two numbers whose product is -14. We shall discover that the sum of these two numbers will not be 33, as would be the case if the coefficient of the x^2 term were 1 (i.e., if $a = 1$). The following are pairs of numbers whose product is -14:

$$7, -2 \qquad -7, 2 \qquad -1, 14 \qquad 1, -14$$

Now we must use a trial-and-error approach to determine which pair yields the correct middle term when the factors are multiplied by the FOIL method. We will begin with the pair 7, -2. Hence,

$$
\begin{aligned}
(5x + 7)(x - 2) &\overset{?}{=} 5x^2 + 33x - 14 & (1)\\
&= 5x^2 - 10x + 7x - 14 & (2)\\
&= 5x^2 - 3x - 14 & (3)
\end{aligned}
$$

Note that we have placed a question mark above the equal sign of equation (1). Equations (2) and (3) give the results of multiplying the two factors. Note that since the x term of the product is $-3x$ and not $33x$, then the above factorization is not correct, and we must try another combination of numbers. However, before trying a different pair of numbers, we might interchange the positions of $+7$ and -2. Hence,

$$
\begin{aligned}
(5x - 2)(x + 7) &\overset{?}{=} 5x^2 + 33x - 14 & (4)\\
&= 5x^2 + 35x - 2x - 14 & (5)\\
&= 5x^2 + 33x - 14 & (6)
\end{aligned}
$$

Notice that multiplication by the FOIL method in equations (5) and (6) has resulted in the correct middle term, $33x$. Thus, the above factorization in equation (4) is correct, and

$$5x^2 + 33x - 14 = (5x - 2)(x + 7)$$

• EXAMPLE R-29

Factor $6x^2 - 11x - 35$.

Solution

We wish to determine two factors such that

$$(\underline{}x + \underline{})(\underline{}x + \underline{}) = 6x^2 - 11x - 35$$

Since the coefficient of x^2 is 6, we first seek two numbers whose product is 6. From a number of possibilities, we choose 3 and 2. Hence,

$$(3x + \underline{})(2x + \underline{}) \overset{?}{=} 6x^2 - 11x - 35$$

We hasten to mention that this may not be the correct choice of numbers. This is why we have placed a question mark above the equal sign. However, we have no way of determining this until we choose the numbers for the remaining blanks in our factors and multiply by the FOIL method to determine whether the product equals $6x^2 - 11x - 35$.

Thus, we seek two numbers whose product is -35. From a number of possibilities, we choose 5 and -7. Hence,

$$(3x + 5)(2x - 7) \overset{?}{=} 6x^2 - 11x - 35 \tag{7}$$

$$= 6x^2 - 21x + 10x - 35 \tag{8}$$

$$= 6x^2 - 11x - 35 \tag{9}$$

Note that multiplication by the FOIL method in equations (8) and (9) has resulted in the correct middle term, $-11x$. Thus, the factorization in equation (7) is correct, and

$$6x^2 - 11x - 35 = (3x + 5)(2x - 7)$$

Exercises R-7

Factor each of the following.

1. $2x^2 - x - 28$
2. $6x^2 - 7x - 5$
3. $5x^2 + 18x - 8$
4. $21x^2 - 2x - 8$
5. $6x^2 - 13x - 5$
6. $4x^2 - 13x - 35$
7. $9x^2 - 36$
8. $64x^2 - 49$
9. $4x^2 + 20x + 25$
10. $9x^2 - 12x + 4$
11. $25x^2 - 70x + 49$
12. $81x^2 + 18x + 1$

R-8 • RATIONAL EXPRESSIONS

Expressions involving quotients such as

$$\frac{3x + 15}{2x} \qquad \frac{x^2 - 4x}{x - 7} \qquad \frac{x^2 - 36}{x + 9}$$

are called **rational expressions.** Sometimes we have to simplify or reduce such expressions to their lowest terms. Such simplifications are performed by using the following rules.

Rules Involving Rational Expressions

Assume that N, D, R, and S are expressions such that D and $S \neq 0$.

$$\frac{N \cdot S}{D \cdot S} = \frac{N}{D}$$ Fundamental rule

$$\frac{N}{D} \cdot \frac{R}{S} = \frac{N \cdot R}{D \cdot S}$$ Multiplication rule

$$\frac{N}{D} \div \frac{R}{S} = \frac{N}{D} \cdot \frac{S}{R} \quad (R \neq 0)$$ Division rule

$$\frac{N}{D} + \frac{R}{D} = \frac{N + R}{D}$$ Addition rule

$$\frac{N}{D} - \frac{R}{D} = \frac{N - R}{D}$$ Subtraction rule

The following examples illustrate applications of these rules.

• **EXAMPLE R-30**

Simplify each of the following.

a) $\dfrac{3x + 15}{3} = \dfrac{3(x + 5)}{3} = x + 5$ Factoring, fundamental rule

b) $\dfrac{x^2 + x - 20}{x^2 - 16} = \dfrac{(x - 4)(x + 5)}{(x - 4)(x + 4)} = \dfrac{x + 5}{x + 4}$ Factoring, fundamental rule

• **EXAMPLE R-31**

Perform the indicated operation.

a) $\dfrac{x^2 - 25}{x + 3} \cdot \dfrac{x^2 - 2x - 15}{x^2 - 10x + 25} = \dfrac{(x - 5)(x + 5)}{(x + 3)} \cdot \dfrac{(x - 5)(x + 3)}{(x - 5)(x - 5)}$

$\qquad = x + 5$ Factoring, mulitplication rule, fundamental rule

b) $\dfrac{x^2 + 2x - 8}{x + 6} \div \dfrac{x^2 + 3x - 4}{2x + 12} = \dfrac{x^2 + 2x - 8}{x + 6} \cdot \dfrac{2x + 12}{x^2 + 3x - 8}$ Division rule

$\qquad = \dfrac{(x - 2)(x + 4)}{x + 6} \cdot \dfrac{2(x + 6)}{(x + 4)(x - 1)}$ Factoring; fundamental rule

$\qquad = \dfrac{2(x - 2)}{x - 1}$ or $\dfrac{2x - 4}{x - 1}$ Division rule, factoring, fundamental rule

c) $\dfrac{6}{7x} + \dfrac{8}{7x} = \dfrac{6 + 8}{7x} = \dfrac{14}{7x} = \dfrac{7 \cdot 2}{7x} = \dfrac{2}{x}$ Addition rule, fundamental rule

d) $\dfrac{8}{x} - \dfrac{5}{2x} + \dfrac{4}{3x} = \dfrac{6 \cdot 8}{6 \cdot x} - \dfrac{3 \cdot 5}{3 \cdot 2x} + \dfrac{2 \cdot 4}{2 \cdot 3x} = \dfrac{48}{6x} - \dfrac{15}{6x} + \dfrac{8}{6x}$

$\qquad = \dfrac{48 - 15 + 8}{6x} = \dfrac{41}{6x}$ Addition and subtraction rules; fundamental rule

• **EXAMPLE R-32** _____

Divide by x.

$$\frac{3x + 5}{x} = \frac{3\cancel{x}}{\cancel{x}} + \frac{5}{x} = 3 + \frac{5}{x} \qquad \text{Addition rule; fundamental rule}$$

• **EXAMPLE R-33** _____

Divide.

$$\frac{(1 + i)^{30} - 1}{i} \div (1 + i)^{30} = \frac{(1 + i)^{30} - 1}{i} \div \frac{(1 + i)^{30}}{1}$$

$$= \frac{(1 + i)^{30} - 1}{i} \cdot \frac{1}{(1 + i)^{30}} \qquad \text{Division rule}$$

$$= \frac{(1 + i)^{30} - 1}{(1 + i)^{30} \;\; i} \qquad \text{Multiplication rule}$$

$$= \frac{\dfrac{(1 + i)^{30}}{(1 + i)^{30}} - \dfrac{1}{(1 + i)^{30}}}{i} \qquad \text{Subtraction rule}$$

$$= \frac{1 - (1 + i)^{-30}}{i} \qquad \text{Negative exponent}$$

• **EXAMPLE R-34** _____

Multiply.

$$5x^3 \left(1 + \frac{2}{x} - \frac{3}{x^2} + \frac{6}{x^3}\right) = 1 \cdot 5x^3 + \frac{2 \cdot 5x^3}{x} - \frac{3 \cdot 5x^3}{x^2} + \frac{6 \cdot 5x^3}{x^3}$$

$$= 5x^3 + 10x^2 - 15x + 30$$

• **EXAMPLE R-35** _____

Factor out the highest-powered term: $2x^3 + 4x^2 - 2x + 8$.

Solution

$$\frac{2x^3}{2x^3}(2x^3 + 4x^2 - 2x + 8) = 2x^3 \left(\frac{2x^3 + 4x^2 - 2x + 8}{2x^3}\right)$$

$$= 2x^3 \left(\frac{2x^3}{2x^3} + \frac{4x^2}{2x^3} - \frac{2x}{2x^3} + \frac{8}{2x^3}\right)$$

$$= 2x^3 \left(1 + \frac{2}{x} - \frac{1}{x^2} + \frac{4}{x^3}\right)$$

Exercises R-8

Simplify each of the following.

1. $\dfrac{4x - 28}{2}$

2. $\dfrac{-3x + 18}{3}$

3. $\dfrac{-(2x + 14)}{2}$

4. $\dfrac{5x - 30}{5}$

5. $\dfrac{x^2 - 6x}{x - 6}$

6. $\dfrac{4x^2 - 32x}{x - 8}$

7. $\dfrac{x^2 + 2x - 15}{x^2 - 25}$

8. $\dfrac{x + 8}{x^2 - 64}$

9. $\dfrac{x^2 + 3x - 4}{x^2 - 1}$ **10.** $\dfrac{x^2 + 2x - 8}{x^2 + 5x + 4}$ **11.** $\dfrac{x^2 + 8x + 15}{x^2 + 7x + 10}$

Perform the indicated operations.

12. $\dfrac{x^2 - 49}{x + 2} \cdot \dfrac{x^2 + 3x + 2}{x^2 - 6x - 7}$ **13.** $\dfrac{9}{6x^2} \cdot \dfrac{2x}{3}$

14. $\dfrac{20x^3}{7x} \div \dfrac{10}{21x}$ **15.** $\dfrac{x^2 - 4x - 5}{x^2 + 3x + 2} \cdot \dfrac{x^2 + 5x + 6}{x^2 - 7x + 10}$

16. $\dfrac{x^2 - x - 30}{x^2 - 36} \cdot \dfrac{x^2 + 7x + 6}{x^2 + 7x + 10}$ **17.** $\dfrac{x^2 - 81}{x^2 + 10x + 9} \div \dfrac{x^2 - 7x - 18}{x^2 + 4x + 3}$

18. $\dfrac{x^2 + 2x - 8}{x^2 + x - 2} \div \dfrac{x^2 + x - 12}{x^2 - 1}$

19. $\dfrac{x + 5}{4} + \dfrac{x + 7}{4}$ **20.** $\dfrac{2x + 3}{5} - \dfrac{5x - 7}{10}$ **21.** $\dfrac{5}{x} + \dfrac{8}{2x}$

22. $\dfrac{x}{x - 2} + \dfrac{3}{x + 2}$ **23.** $\dfrac{5}{x + 6} - \dfrac{8}{x}$ **24.** $\dfrac{8}{x - 5} + \dfrac{4}{x + 5}$

25. $\dfrac{5}{x^2 - 36} + \dfrac{9}{x + 6}$ **26.** $\dfrac{4}{x + 8} + \dfrac{3}{x^2 - 64}$ **27.** $\dfrac{7}{x - 9} - \dfrac{5}{x(x - 9)}$

Divide by x.

28. $\dfrac{4x - 9}{x}$ **29.** $\dfrac{2x + 7}{x}$ **30.** $\dfrac{8x - 9}{x}$ **31.** $\dfrac{3x^2 - 36x}{x}$

32. $\dfrac{5x^2 + 30x}{x}$ **33.** $\dfrac{4x^3 - 8x^2 + 6x}{x}$ **34.** $\dfrac{5x^2 - 6x + 8}{x}$

Multiply.

35. $4x^2\left(1 + \dfrac{2}{x} - \dfrac{3}{x^2}\right)$ **36.** $6x^3\left(1 + \dfrac{1}{x} + \dfrac{2}{x^2} - \dfrac{4}{x^3}\right)$

37. $5x^3\left(1 - \dfrac{1}{x} + \dfrac{6}{x^2} - \dfrac{2}{x^3}\right)$ **38.** $x^3\left(2 + \dfrac{3}{x} + \dfrac{8}{x^2} - \dfrac{4}{x^3}\right)$

Factor out the highest-powered term.

39. $x^3 - 4x^2 + 7x + 5$ **40.** $x^4 - 6x^3 + x^2 - x + 9$

41. $x^2 + 7x + 9$ **42.** $x^3 + 6x^2 + 8x + 4$

Divide.

43. $\dfrac{(1 + i)^{20} - 1}{i} \div (1 + i)^{20}$ **44.** $\dfrac{(1 + i)^{36} - 1}{i} \div (1 + i)^{26}$

45. $\dfrac{(1 + i)^{39} - (1 + i)}{i} \div (1 + i)^{38}$ **46.** $\dfrac{(1 + i)^{50} - 1}{i} \div (1 + i)$

EXTRA DIVIDENDS

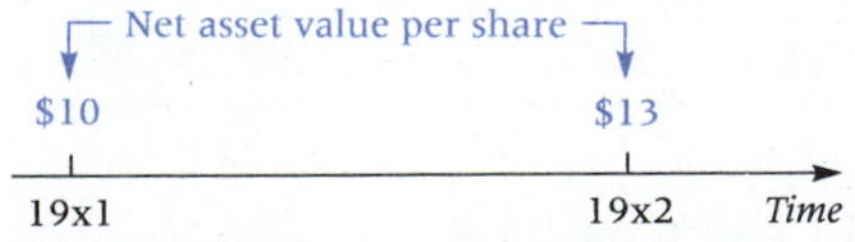

FIGURE R-20

• *Percent Change*

In the business world, assets usually change in value over periods of time. The amount of change is often put into perspective by expressing it as a percentage. For example, if the net asset value per share of mutual fund changes from $10 to $13 during a 1-year time period (see Figure R-20), this constitutes a change (in this case, an increase) of $13 − $10 = $3 per share during the indicated 1-year time period. If we divide the amount of change by the original value (i.e., the net asset value per share at the beginning of the year), the result

$$3/10 = 0.30$$
$$= 30\%$$

gives us the *percent change* (in this case, percent increase) in the net asset value per share of the fund during the indicated time period. We generalize as follows:

● *Percent Change*

If some quantity changes in value during a time interval, as indicated in Figure R-21, then the percent change is given by the following formula:

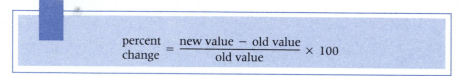

$$\frac{\text{percent}}{\text{change}} = \frac{\text{new value} - \text{old value}}{\text{old value}} \times 100$$

If new value > old value, then the percent change is positive and thus is a percent increase. If new value < old value, then the percent change is negative and thus is a percent decrease.

Thus, if a stock's price changes from \$40 to \$10 during a 3-month time period, the percent change is determined as follows:

$$\text{percent change} = \frac{\text{new value} - \text{old value}}{\text{old value}} \times 100$$

$$= \frac{10 - 40}{40} \times 100$$

$$= \frac{-30}{40} \times 100$$

$$= -0.75 \times 100$$

$$= -75\%$$

Thus, the stock's price has decreased by 75%.

A percent change indicates a relationship between the new value and the old value of an asset. The equation expressing this relationship is determined by beginning with the formula for percent change and solving for the new value. Thus, if p denotes the percent change in decimal form (i.e., before we multiply by 100), OV denotes the old value, and NV denotes the new value, then

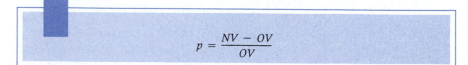

$$p = \frac{NV - OV}{OV}$$

Multiplying both sides of this equation by OV, we have

$$OV \cdot p = NV - OV$$

FIGURE R-21

Solving for NV, we have

$$OV + (OV \cdot p) = NV$$

or

$$NV = OV + (OV \cdot p)$$

Applying the distributive law to the right-hand side, we have

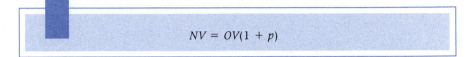

$$NV = OV(1 + p)$$

The boxed equation gives the relationship between the new value and the old value of some asset.

Thus, if an assset's value increases by 40% from $80 during a 6-month time interval, then its new value is given by the formula

$$NV = OV(1 + p)$$

where $p = 0.40$ and $OV = 80$. Hence,

$$
\begin{aligned}
NV &= 80(1 + 0.40) \\
&= 80(1.40) \\
&= 112
\end{aligned}
$$

Thus, the asset's new value at the end of the indicated 6-month time interval is $112.

Also, if an asset's value decreases by 30% from $80 during a specified time interval, then its new value is determined by the formula

$$NV = OV(1 + p)$$

where $p = -0.30$ and $OV = 80$. Hence,

$$
\begin{aligned}
NV &= 80(1 - 0.30) \\
&= 80(0.70) \\
&= 56
\end{aligned}
$$

Thus, the asset's new value at the end of the time period is $56.

Exercises

1. A mutual fund's net asset value per share changes from $40 to $50 during a 1-year time period. Find its percent change.
2. A stock's price changes from $60 to $20 during a 9-month time period. Find its percent change.
3. A stock's price increases by 20% from $60 during a 3-month time period. Find its new price.
4. A stock's price decreases by 30% from $80 during a given month. Find its new price.
5. The price of 1 ounce of gold increased by 40% to $600 during a given month. Find its old price at the beginning of the month.

TABLE R-1

Twentieth Century Growth	43.9%
Fidelity Magellan	48.0
Vanguard Windsor	56.1
Mutual Shares	60.5
Fidelity Puritan	41.9

Investment

Table R-1 gives percent changes of various mutual funds during a selected 3-year time period. If $10,000 were invested at the beginning the selected 3-year period, determine its value at the end of the 3-year period (assuming no withdrawals of either principal or income) for

6. Twentieth Century Growth
7. Fidelity Magellan
8. Vanguard Windsor
9. Mutual Shares
10. Fidelity Puritan

International: Trade

Table R-2 gives total trade (imports and exports in millions of U.S. dollars) in competitive world markets for three countries during various years. Determine the percent change from 1975 to 1980 for

11. United States
12. Soviet Union
13. Japan

Determine the percent change from 1980 to 1985 for

14. United States
15. Soviet Union
16. Japan

TABLE R-2

	1975	1980	1985
United States	$213,992	$477,771	$574,771
Soviet Union	30,791	67,059	65,967
Japan	113,569	271,737	307,652

TABLE R-3

General Electric	451%
Exxon	365
AT&T	348
General Motors	182

Stocks

Table R-3 gives the total return (change in value plus income) for the selected stocks during the decade of the 1980s. If, at the end of the decade, an investor had shares worth $100,000, what was the value of such shares at the beginning of the decade, assuming the shares were purchased at the beginning of the decade and no withdrawals of either principal or income were made? Answer this question if the shares purchased were

17. General Electric
18. Exxon
19. AT&T
20. General Motors

EXTRA DIVIDENDS

TABLE R-4 Price per quart of milk

1990	79¢
1980	56¢

• Using Index Numbers to Measure Change

An **index number** measures the change in some quantity (i.e., price, productivity, inventory, etc.) from one time period to another. The time periods are usually years, although this does not necessarily have to be the case. The time period used as the basis of comparison is called the **base period.** As an example, we consider the price of milk for the years 1990 and 1980, as given in Table R-4.

A simple index number is computed by dividing the 1990 price by the 1980 price. Thus, the ratio

$$\frac{1990 \text{ price}}{1980 \text{ price}} \times 100 = \frac{79\cent}{56\cent} \times 100$$
$$= 1.41 \times 100$$
$$= 141\%$$

gives an index comparing 1990 milk prices to those of 1980.

Since 1980 prices are the basis of the comparison, then 1980 is the *base year* of this index. Note that we multiply by 100 to express the index as a percentage. We will use the symbol

$$I_{80,90}$$

to denote an index number comparing the 1990 price with that of base year 1980. We summarize as follows.

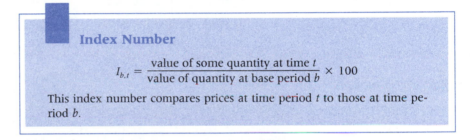

Index Number

$$I_{b,t} = \frac{\text{value of some quantity at time } t}{\text{value of quantity at base period } b} \times 100$$

This index number compares prices at time period t to those at time period b.

Usually, the base period is the earlier time period, although this is not always the case. Thus, for our example comparing milk prices, the index

$$I_{80,90} = 141\%$$

indicates that 1990 milk prices are 141% of those of the base year 1980.

Since the above index compared prices for only one commodity, it is called a **simple index.** Index numbers are usually computed to include prices of a group of commodities. Such index numbers are called **composite index numbers.** The computation of composite index numbers is beyond the scope of this discussion. Here we will stress the use and interpretation of index numbers.

The Bureau of Labor Statistics computes a very important index called the **consumer price index,** abbreviated **CPI.** The CPI is a composite index that measures the change in cost of a fixed market basket of goods and services purchased by a specified group of consumers.

• *Using Index Numbers to Deflate*

Index numbers are often used as price deflators. For example, suppose that in 1988 a construction worker earns $800 per week. A union negotiator wishes to determine the purchasing power of this weekly wage in 1967 dollars. In other words, the union negotiator wants to deflate the 1988 weekly wage to 1967 dollars. To deflate a 1988 price to 1967 dollars, we need an index number (often, the CPI), $I_{67,88}$, that measures the change between 1967 and 1988 prices. Since, from a simplified perspective, the index $I_{67,88}$ is interpreted as a ratio of 1988 prices to 1967 prices, this relationship can be expressed in equation form as

$$I_{67,88} = \frac{1988 \text{ prices}}{1967 \text{ prices}} \times 100$$

Multiplying both sides by the right-hand denominator gives

$$1967 \text{ price} \times I_{67,88} = 1988 \text{ prices} \times 100$$

Solving for 1967 prices, we have

$$1967 \text{ price} = \frac{1988 \text{ price}}{I_{67,88}} \times 100$$

The above boxed formula indicates that a 1988 price is deflated to 1967 dollars by dividing the 1988 price by $I_{67,88}$ and then multiplying by 100. If $I_{67,88} = 250$, then

$$1967 \text{ price} = \frac{1988 \text{ price}}{I_{67,88}} \times 100$$
$$= \frac{800}{250} \times 100$$
$$= 320$$

Thus, the 1988 wage of $800 is the equivalent of $320 in 1967 dollars. Figure R-22 illustrates this relationship from a time diagram point of view.

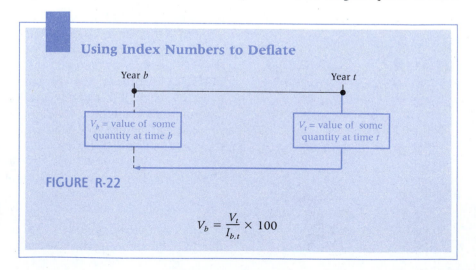

Using Index Numbers to Deflate

Year b Year t

V_b = value of some quantity at time b V_t = value of some quantity at time t

FIGURE R-22

$$V_b = \frac{V_t}{I_{b,t}} \times 100$$

To further illustrate the usefulness of deflating prices, we consider the following example. Suppose the construction worker of the previous example earned $300 per week in 1967. During the time period between 1967 and 1988, his percent increase in weekly wages is given by

$$\frac{800 - 300}{300} \times 100 = \frac{500}{300} \times 100$$
$$= 1.667 \times 100$$
$$= 166.7\%$$

This result is termed a 166.7% increase in nominal wages. However, if we deflate his 1988 wage of $800 to its equivalent in 1967 dollars, $320, then the percent increase in real wages (i.e., wages in 1967 dollars) is given by

$$\frac{320 - 300}{300} \times 100 = \frac{20}{300} \times 100$$
$$= .0667 \times 100$$
$$= 6.67\%$$

Thus, the construction worker's real wages have increased by only 6.67% during the 21-year period. The union negotiator, mentioned earlier, would certainly use this result as an argument for higher future wages.

Exercises

1. In 1970, a commodity sold for $80. Its 1988 price is $140. Compute $I_{70,88}$.
2. In 1980, a 94-pound bag of concrete cost $4.80. Its 1988 price is $6.90. Compute $I_{80,88}$.
3. B-MART's 1988 sales are $23,000,000. If $I_{70,88} = 280$, then deflate the 1988 sales to 1970 dollars.
4. A worker earns $600 per week during 1988. If $I_{79,88} = 240$, then deflate the 1988 wages to 1979 dollars.
5. A wage earner's 1975 income was $15,000, while her 1988 income is $30,000. If $I_{75,88} = 170$, then
   a) Compute the percent increase in nominal income.
   b) Compute the percent increase in real income.
6. A-TECH's 1980 sales were $15,000,000, while its 1988 sales are $40,000,000. If the industry's index is $I_{80,88} = 190$, then
   a) Compute the percent increase in nominal sales.
   b) Compute the percent increase in real sales.

Trade: Value of the Dollar

Figure R-23 gives a graph of index numbers indicating the dollar's value relative to base year 1980 against currencies of its major trading partners.

7. The dollar's value at the end of 1982 was what multiple of its 1980 value?
8. The dollar's value at the end of 1984 was what multiple of its 1980 value?
9. The dollar's value at the end of 1985 was what multiple of its 1980 value?
10. The dollar's value at the end of 1988 was what multiple of its 1980 value?

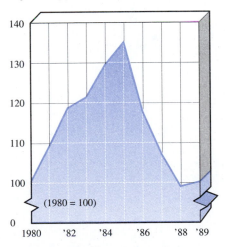

A weaker greenback

The dollar's value against the currencies of its major trading partners

(1980 = 100)

1980 '82 '84 '86 '88 '89

Note: Figure for 1989 reflects the average through November.
USN&WR—Basic data: Atlanta Federal Reserve Board

Copyright ©, Dec. 25, 1989—Jan. 1, 1990,
U.S. News & World Report. Reprinted by permission.

FIGURE R-23

Despite productivity gains...

U.S. manufacturing productivity compared with major industial competitors

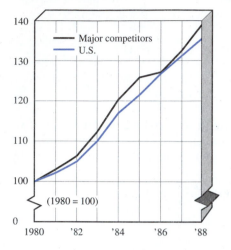

Note: Competitors include 11 industrialized countries. Productivity is worker output per hour.
USN&WR—Basic data: U.S. Dept. of Labor

Copyright ©, Dec. 25, 1989—Jan. 1, 1990, *U.S. News & World Report*. Reprinted by permission.

FIGURE R-24

TABLE R-5   Consumer Price Index (1967 = 100)

	1980	1982	1984
CPI	246.8	289.1	311.1

Productivity

Figure R-24 gives a graph of index numbers indicating productivity relative to base year 1980.

11. U.S. productivity for 1983 was what multiple of its 1980 value?
12. U.S. productivity for 1986 was what multiple of its 1980 value?
13. U.S. productivity for 1987 was what multiple of its 1980 value?
14. U.S. productivity for 1988 was what multiple of its 1980 value?

Consumer Price Index (CPI)

The Table R-5 gives the CPI for various years relative to base year 1967. Give the value in 1967 dollars of goods worth $1000 in

15. 1984 dollars   **16.** 1982 dollars   **17.** 1980 dollars

APPENDIXES

Appendix A
Proofs of Derivative Rules

• POWER RULE

If $f(x) = x^n$, where n is a real number, then

$$f'(x) = nx^{n-1}$$

We will prove the power rule for positive integers n only. Proofs for real numbers n are found in any standard calculus text. To prove the power rule, we must review the binomial theorem for expansion of binomials. The following formulas illustrate equivalent expressions for $(a + b)^n$ for positive integers n:

If $n = 2$, then $(a + b)^2 = a^2 + 2ab + b^2$

If $n = 3$, then $(a + b)^3 = a^3 + 3a^2b + 3ab^2 + b^3$

If $n = 4$, then $(a + b)^4 = a^4 + 4a^3b + 6a^2b^2 + 4ab^3 + b^4$

If $n = 5$, then $(a + b)^5 = a^5 + 5a^4b + 10a^3b^2 + 10a^2b^3 + 5ab^4 + b^5$

The **binomial theorem** provides the following general formula for $(a + b)^n$:

$$(a + b)^n = \binom{n}{0}a^n + \binom{n}{1}a^{n-1}b + \binom{n}{2}a^{n-2}b^2 + \ldots + \binom{n}{n-1}ab^{n-1} + \binom{n}{n}b^n$$

Note that the combinations $\binom{n}{0}, \binom{n}{1}, \binom{n}{2}, \ldots, \binom{n}{n-1}$, and $\binom{n}{n}$ are evaluated as follows:

$$\binom{n}{0} = \frac{n!}{0!n!} = 1$$

$$\binom{n}{1} = \frac{n!}{1!(n-1)!} = n$$

$$\binom{n}{2} = \frac{n!}{2!(n-2)!} = \frac{n(n-1)(n-2)!}{2!(n-2)!} = \frac{n(n-1)}{2}$$

.

.

.

$$\binom{n}{n-1} = \frac{n!}{(n-1)!1!} = \frac{n(n-1)!}{(n-1)!1!} = n$$

$$\binom{n}{n} = \frac{n!}{n!0!} = 1$$

Thus, the binomial theorem may be rewritten as

$$(a + b)^n = a^n + na^{n-1}b + \frac{n(n-1)}{2}a^{n-2}b^2 + \ldots + nab^{n-1} + b^n$$

Returning to the power rule, we now use the binomial theorem to compute

$$f(x + \Delta x) = (x + \Delta x)^n$$

$$= x^n + nx^{n-1}(\Delta x) + \frac{n(n-1)}{2}x^{n-2}(\Delta x)^2 + \ldots + nx(\Delta x)^{n-1} + (\Delta x)^n$$

For our purpose, it is only necessary to notice that

$$f(x + \Delta x) = (x + \Delta x)^n$$

$$= x^n + nx^{n-1}(\Delta x) + (\Delta x)^2 \text{ (a sum of products of powers of } x \text{ and } \Delta x)$$

Thus, the derivative of $f(x) = x^n$ is

$$f'(x) = \lim_{\Delta x \to 0} \frac{f(x + \Delta x) - f(x)}{\Delta x}$$

$$= \lim_{\Delta x \to 0} \frac{x^n + nx^{n-1}\Delta x + \Delta x^2(\text{a sum of products of powers of } x \text{ and } \Delta x) - x^n}{\Delta x}$$

$$= \lim_{\Delta x \to 0} \frac{nx^{n-1}\Delta x + \Delta x^2(\text{a sum of products of powers of } x \text{ and } \Delta x)}{\Delta x}$$

$$= \lim_{\Delta x \to 0} [nx^{n-1} + \Delta x (\text{a sum of products of powers of } x \text{ and } \Delta x)]$$

$$= nx^{n-1}$$

Hence, $f'(x) = nx^{n-1}$.

• PRODUCT RULE

If $y = f(x)s(x)$, where $f(x)$ and $s(x)$ are differentiable functions at x, then

$$\frac{dy}{dx} = f(x)s'(x) + s(x)f'(x)$$

$$\frac{dy}{dx} = \lim_{\Delta x \to 0} \frac{f(x + \Delta x)s(x + \Delta x) - f(x)s(x)}{\Delta x}$$

Adding and subtracting $f(x + \Delta x)s(x)$ to the numerator yields

$$\frac{dy}{dx} = \lim_{\Delta x \to 0} \frac{f(x + \Delta x)s(x + \Delta x) - f(x + \Delta x)s(x) + f(x + \Delta x)s(x) - f(x)s(x)}{\Delta x}$$

$$= \lim_{\Delta x \to 0} \left[f(x + \Delta x) \frac{s(x + \Delta x) - s(x)}{\Delta x} + s(x) \frac{f(x + \Delta x) - f(x)}{\Delta x} \right]$$

By limit property 2 of Section 9-1, this result becomes

$$\frac{dy}{dx} = \lim_{\Delta x \to 0} \left[f(x + \Delta x) \frac{s(x + \Delta x) - s(x)}{\Delta x} \right] + \lim_{\Delta x \to 0} \left[s(x) \frac{f(x + \Delta x) - f(x)}{\Delta x} \right]$$

By limit property 5 of Section 9-1, this becomes

$$\frac{dy}{dx} = \lim_{\Delta x \to 0} f(x + \Delta x) \lim_{\Delta x \to 0} \frac{s(x + \Delta x) - s(x)}{\Delta x} + \lim_{\Delta x \to 0} s(x) \lim_{\Delta x \to 0} \frac{f(x + \Delta x) - f(x)}{\Delta x}$$

Since $f(x)$ is differentiable at x, $f(x)$ is continuous at x, and so $\lim_{\Delta x \to 0} f(x + \Delta x) = f(x)$. Then the preceding expression becomes

$$\frac{dy}{dx} = f(x)s'(x) + s(x)f'(x)$$

• QUOTIENT RULE

If $y = n(x)/d(x)$, where $n(x)$ and $d(x)$ are differentiable functions at x and $d(x) \neq 0$, then

$$\frac{dy}{dx} = \frac{d(x)n'(x) - n(x)d'(x)}{[d(x)]^2}$$

By definition,

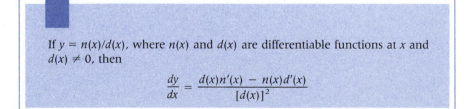

$$\frac{dy}{dx} = \lim_{\Delta x \to 0} \frac{\dfrac{n(x + \Delta x)}{d(x + \Delta x)} - \dfrac{n(x)}{d(x)}}{\Delta x}$$

If we multiply the first term of the numerator by $d(x)/d(x)$ and the second term by $d(x + \Delta x)/d(x + \Delta x)$, we have

$$\frac{dy}{dx} = \lim_{\Delta x \to 0} \frac{\dfrac{n(x + \Delta x)d(x) - d(x + \Delta x)n(x)}{d(x + \Delta x)d(x)}}{\Delta x}$$

$$= \lim_{\Delta x \to 0} \frac{n(x + \Delta x)d(x) - d(x + \Delta x)n(x)}{\Delta x\, d(x + \Delta x)d(x)}$$

Adding and subtracting $n(x)d(x)$ to the numerator yields

$$\frac{dy}{dx} = \lim_{\Delta x \to 0} \frac{n(x + \Delta x)d(x) - n(x)d(x) + n(x)d(x) - d(x + \Delta x)n(x)}{\Delta x\, d(x + \Delta x)d(x)}$$

$$= \lim_{\Delta x \to 0} \frac{d(x)\dfrac{n(x + \Delta x) - n(x)}{\Delta x} - n(x)\dfrac{d(x + \Delta x) - d(x)}{\Delta x}}{d(x + \Delta x)d(x)}$$

By limit properties 2, 5, and 6 of Section 9-1, this expression becomes

$$\frac{dy}{dx} = \frac{\displaystyle\lim_{\Delta x \to 0} d(x) \lim_{\Delta x \to 0} \frac{n(x + \Delta x) - n(x)}{\Delta x} - \lim_{\Delta x \to 0} n(x) \lim_{\Delta x \to 0} \frac{d(x + \Delta x) - d(x)}{\Delta x}}{\displaystyle\lim_{\Delta x \to 0} d(x + \Delta x) \lim_{\Delta x \to 0} d(x)}$$

Since $d(x)$ is differentiable at x, it is continuous at x, and so $\lim_{\Delta x \to 0} d(x + \Delta x) = d(x)$. Hence, the preceding expression becomes

$$\frac{dy}{dx} = \frac{d(x)n'(x) - n(x)d'(x)}{[d(x)]^2}$$

Appendix B
Special Topics

• DERIVATION OF THE QUADRATIC FORMULA

On page 79 of Section 2-2, we stated the quadratic formula for solutions, if any exist, to quadratic equations of the form

$$ax^2 + bx + c = 0 \qquad (a \neq 0)$$

The quadratic formula is derived by beginning with the above equation and dividing both sides by a to obtain

$$x^2 + \frac{b}{a}x + \frac{c}{a} = 0$$

Subtracting c/a from both sides gives

$$x^2 + \frac{b}{a}x = -\frac{c}{a}$$

Adding $(b/2a)^2$ or, equivalently, $b^2/4a^2$ to both sides gives a perfect square for the left-hand side as given below.

$$x^2 + \frac{b}{a}x + \left(\frac{b}{2a}\right)^2 = \frac{b^2}{4a^2} - \frac{c}{a}$$

The left-hand side can be expressed in factored form as indicated below

$$\left(x + \frac{b}{2a}\right)^2 = \frac{b^2}{4a^2} - \frac{c}{a}\left(\frac{4a}{4a}\right)$$

and the (c/a) term is multiplied by $4a/4a$ to give a common denominator. Combining the right-hand-side terms gives

$$\left(x + \frac{b}{2a}\right)^2 = \frac{b^2 - 4ac}{4a^2}$$

Solving the resulting formula for x, we begin by taking the square root of each side to obtain

$$x + \frac{b}{2a} = \pm \sqrt{\frac{b^2 - 4ac}{4a^2}}$$

Using a property of square roots on the right-hand side, the above becomes

$$x + \frac{b}{2a} = \pm \frac{\sqrt{b^2 - 4ac}}{\sqrt{4a^2}}$$

$$= \pm \frac{\sqrt{b^2 - 4ac}}{2a}$$

Adding $-b/2a$ to both sides results in

$$x = -\frac{b}{2a} \pm \frac{\sqrt{b^2 - 4ac}}{2a}$$

$$= \frac{-b \pm \sqrt{b^2 - 4ac}}{2a}$$

Note that

1. There is one real solution if $b^2 - 4ac = 0$. That solution is $-b/2a$.
2. There are no real solutions if $b^2 - 4ac < 0$. This is because the square root of a negative number does not exist.
3. There are two real solutions if $b^2 - 4ac > 0$:

$$x = \frac{-b + \sqrt{b^2 - 4ac}}{2a} \qquad x = \frac{-b - \sqrt{b^2 - 4ac}}{2a}$$

• DISTANCE; THE EQUATION OF A CIRCLE

Sometimes we must find the distance between two points on the rectangular coordinate system. The distance between the two points, (x_1, y_1) and (x_2, y_2), in Figure B-1 is denoted by d. Observe that the vertical dis-

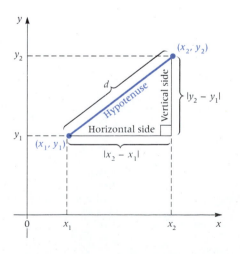

FIGURE B-1

tance between the two points is $|y_2 - y_1|$ and the horizontal distance between the two points is $|x_2 - x_1|$. Also, the vertical distance, $|y_2 - y_1|$, is the length of the vertical side of the right triangle, and the horizontal distance, $|x_2 - x_1|$, the length of the horizontal side of the right triangle. The length of the hypotenuse is the distance, d, between the two points, (x_1, y_1) and (x_2, y_2). According to the Pythagorean theorem,

$$d^2 = \text{(horizontal distance)}^2 + \text{(vertical distance)}^2$$
$$= |x_2 - x_1|^2 + |y_2 - y_1|^2$$
$$= (x_2 - x_1)^2 + (y_2 - y_1)^2$$

Hence,

$$d = \sqrt{(x_2 - x_1)^2 + (y_2 - y_1)^2} \qquad \text{Distance Formula}$$

Since this formula gives the distance between two points, (x_1, y_1) and (x_2, y_2), in the plane, it is called the **distance formula.**

• EXAMPLE B-1

Find the distance between $(1, -2)$ and $(4, 5)$ in Figure B-2.

Solution

Let $(x_1, y_1) = (1, -2)$ and $(x_2, y_2) = (4, 5)$. Then the distance, d, between the points is

$$d = \sqrt{(x_2 - x_1)^2 + (y_2 - y_1)^2}$$
$$= \sqrt{(4 - 1)^2 + [5 - (-2)]^2}$$
$$= \sqrt{3^2 + 7^2}$$
$$= \sqrt{58} \approx 7.62$$

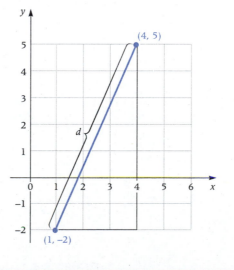

FIGURE B-2

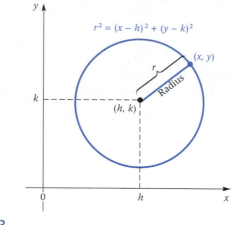

FIGURE B-3

Consider the circle of radius, r, with center at (h, k), as shown in Figure B-3. The circle consists of all points (x, y) that are at distance r from (h, k). Using the distance formula, the distance between a point (x, y) on the circle and the center, (h, k), is given by

$$r = \sqrt{(x - h)^2 + (y - k)^2}$$

Squaring both sides, we have the equation of a circle of radius r and center at (h, k).

$$r^2 = (x - h)^2 + (y - k)^2 \qquad \text{Equation of a circle}$$

Thus, any point (x, y) on the circle satisfies this equation.

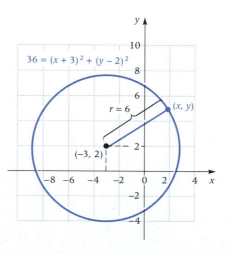

FIGURE B-4

• EXAMPLE B-2

Find the equation of a circle of radius 6 with center at $(-3, 2)$.

Solution

The equation of a circle of radius r and center (h, k) is $r^2 = (x - h)^2 + (y - k)^2$. Since $(h, k) = (-3, 2)$ and $r = 6$, this equation becomes $6^2 = [x - (-3)]^2 + (y - 2)^2$. Thus, the equation of the circle is $36 = (x + 3)^2 + (y - 2)^2$. The circle appears in Figure B-4 on page A-10.

•

Exercises

Find the distance between the following points.

1. $(4, 6)$ and $(7, 10)$
2. $(-1, 2)$ and $(8, 5)$
3. $(3, 0)$ and $(4, 2)$
4. $(-2, 8)$ and $(-1, -3)$
5. $(5, 3)$ and $(5, 7)$
6. $(1, 4)$ and $(8, 4)$
7. $(8, 2)$ and $(6, 9)$
8. $(-6, 2)$ and $(-6, -5)$
9. Find y so that the distance between the origin and the point $(4, y)$ is 6.
10. Find x so that the distance between the origin and the point $(x, 3)$ is 4.
11. Find y so that the distance between $(3, 1)$ and $(7, y)$ is 5.

Find the equation of each of the following circles.

12. Center at $(4, 6)$ and radius is 8
13. Center at $(-2, 5)$ and radius is 3
14. Center at $(4, 0)$ and radius is 6
15. Center at $(0, 3)$ and radius is 5

Graph each of the following:

16. $(x - 2)^2 + (y - 5)^2 = 81$
17. $x^2 + y^2 = 36$
18. $(x + 9)^2 + (y - 1)^2 = 64$
19. $x^2 + (y - 1)^2 = 25$

Answers

1. $d = \sqrt{(7 - 4)^2 + (10 - 6)^2} = \sqrt{3^2 + 4^2} = \sqrt{25} = 5$
2. $d = \sqrt{[8 - (-1)]^2 + (5 - 2)^2} = \sqrt{9^2 + 3^2} = \sqrt{90} \approx 9.49$
3. $d = \sqrt{(4 - 3)^2 + (2 - 0)^2} = \sqrt{1^2 + 2^2} = \sqrt{5} \approx 2.24$
4. $d = \sqrt{[-1 - (-2)]^2 + (-3 - 8)^2} = \sqrt{1^2 + (-11)^2} = \sqrt{122} \approx 11.05$
5. $d = \sqrt{(5 - 5)^2 + (7 - 3)^2} = \sqrt{0^2 + 4^2} = \sqrt{16} = 4$
6. $d = \sqrt{(8 - 1)^2 + (4 - 4)^2} = \sqrt{7^2 + 0^2} = \sqrt{49} = 7$
7. $d = \sqrt{(6 - 8)^2 + (9 - 2)^2} = \sqrt{(-2)^2 + 7^2} = \sqrt{53} \approx 7.28$
8. $d = \sqrt{[-6 - (-6)]^2 + (-5 - 2)^2} = \sqrt{0^2 + (-7)^2} = \sqrt{49} = 7$
9. $6 = \sqrt{(4 - 0)^2 + (y - 0)^2} = \sqrt{4^2 + y^2} = \sqrt{16 + y^2}$, so $36 = 6^2 = (\sqrt{16 + y^2})^2 = 16 + y^2$. Therefore, $y^2 = 36 - 16 = 20$, and so $y = \pm\sqrt{20} \approx \pm 4.47$.
10. $4 = \sqrt{(x - 0)^2 + (3 - 0)^2} = \sqrt{x^2 + 3^2} = \sqrt{x^2 + 9}$, so $16 = 4^2 = (\sqrt{x^2 + 9})^2 = x^2 + 9$. Therefore, $x^2 = 16 - 9 = 7$, and so $x = \pm\sqrt{7} \approx \pm 2.65$.
11. $5 = \sqrt{(7 - 3)^2 + (y - 1)^2} = \sqrt{4^2 + (y - 1)^2} = \sqrt{16 + (y - 1)^2}$, so $25 = 5^2 = [\sqrt{16 + (y - 1)^2}]^2 = 16 + (y - 1)^2$. Therefore, $(y - 1)^2 = 25 - 16 = 9$, and so $y - 1 = \pm 3$. Thus, $y = 3 + 1 = 4$, or $y = -3 + 1 = -2$.
12. $(x - 4)^2 + (y - 6)^2 = 8^2$, or $(x - 4)^2 + (y - 6)^2 = 64$
13. $[x - (-2)]^2 + (y - 5)^2 = 3^2$, or $(x + 2)^2 + (y - 5)^2 = 9$

14. $(x - 4)^2 + (y - 0)^2 = 6^2$, or $(x - 4)^2 + y^2 = 36$
15. $(x - 0)^2 + (y - 3)^2 = 5^2$, or $x^2 + (y - 3)^2 = 25$
16. $(x - 2)^2 + (y - 5)^2 = 81$

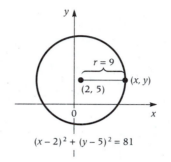

17. $x^2 + y^2 = 36$

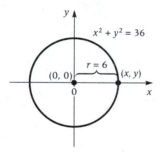

18. $(x + 9)^2 + (y - 1)^2 = 64$

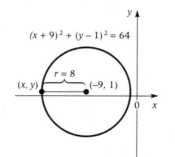

19. $x^2 + (y - 1)^2 = 25$

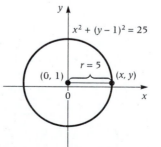

• **DETERMINANTS**

A **determinant** is a number associated with a square matrix. Given a 2×2 matrix

$$A = \begin{bmatrix} a_{11} & a_{12} \\ a_{21} & a_{22} \end{bmatrix}$$

its determinant is denoted by either of the following:

$$|A| \qquad \begin{vmatrix} a_{11} & a_{12} \\ a_{21} & a_{22} \end{vmatrix}$$

The determinant of A is defined as follows:

$$|A| = \begin{vmatrix} a_{11} & a_{12} \\ a_{21} & a_{22} \end{vmatrix} = a_{11}a_{22} - a_{12}a_{21}$$

Thus, if

$$A = \begin{bmatrix} 4 & 3 \\ 8 & 7 \end{bmatrix}$$

its determinant is

$$|A| = \begin{vmatrix} 4 & 3 \\ 8 & 7 \end{vmatrix} = (4)(7) = (3)(8) = 4$$

• EXAMPLE B-3

Find $\begin{vmatrix} -8 & 5 \\ 4 & 6 \end{vmatrix}$.

Solution

$$\begin{vmatrix} -8 & 5 \\ 4 & 6 \end{vmatrix} = (-8)(6) - (5)(4) = -68$$

• EXAMPLE B-4

If

$$A = \begin{bmatrix} -4 & 3 \\ -2 & -1 \end{bmatrix}$$

find the determinant of A.

Solution

$$|A| = (-4)(-1) - (3)(-2) = 10$$

Finding the determinant of a square matrix of a dimension greater than 2×2 is more complicated than in the 2×2 case. In order to find the determinant of a square matrix of dimension greater than 2×2, we must understand the following concept.

> ### Minor of an Element
>
> Each element a_{ij} of a square matrix of dimension $n \times n$ has an associated square matrix of dimension $(n - 1) \times (n - 1)$, which is determined by blocking out the row and column of element a_{ij}. The determinant of the associated $(n - 1) \times (n - 1)$ matrix is called the **minor** of element a_{ij}.

For example, consider the general 3×3 matrix

$$A = \begin{bmatrix} a_{11} & a_{12} & a_{13} \\ a_{21} & a_{22} & a_{23} \\ a_{31} & a_{32} & a_{33} \end{bmatrix}$$

To find the minor of element a_{12}, we block out the row and column of a_{12} as shown here.

$$\begin{bmatrix} a_{11} & a_{12} & a_{13} \\ a_{21} & a_{22} & a_{23} \\ a_{31} & a_{32} & a_{33} \end{bmatrix}$$

The remaining 2×2 matrix is

$$\begin{bmatrix} a_{21} & a_{23} \\ a_{31} & a_{33} \end{bmatrix}$$

Its determinant

$$\begin{vmatrix} a_{21} & a_{23} \\ a_{31} & a_{33} \end{vmatrix} = a_{21}a_{33} - a_{23}a_{31}$$

is the *minor of* a_{12}.

• **EXAMPLE B-5** _____

Find the minor of -2 (located in row 2 and column 2) of matrix B.

$$B = \begin{bmatrix} 1 & 0 & 5 \\ 4 & -2 & -3 \\ 6 & -1 & 8 \end{bmatrix}$$

Solution

We first block out the row and column of -2 as shown below.

$$\begin{bmatrix} 1 & 0 & 5 \\ 4 & -2 & -3 \\ 6 & -1 & 8 \end{bmatrix}$$

The remaining 2×2 matrix is

$$\begin{bmatrix} 1 & 5 \\ 6 & 8 \end{bmatrix}$$

Its determinant,

$$\begin{vmatrix} 1 & 5 \\ 6 & 8 \end{vmatrix} = (1)(8) - (5)(6) = -22$$

is the minor of -2.

Now that we know how to find the minor of an element a_{ij} of a square matrix, we must also understand the following concept.

Cofactor of an Element

Each element a_{ij} of a square matrix has an associated number called the **cofactor** of a_{ij}. The cofactor of an element a_{ij} is determined by the following procedure:

Step 1 Find the *minor* of element a_{ij}.

Step 2 Multiply the minor by $(-1)^{i+j}$, where i is the row number of element a_{ij} and j is the column number of a_{ij}.

We illustrate by finding the cofactor of an element of the matrix

$$M = \begin{bmatrix} 2 & -3 & 3 \\ -6 & 2 & -4 \\ 7 & 2 & -5 \end{bmatrix}$$

Let's find the cofactor of -6, which is located in row 2 and column 1 of matrix M. We first find the *minor of* -6 by blocking out its row and column as shown here

$$\begin{bmatrix} 2 & -3 & 3 \\ -6 & 2 & -4 \\ 7 & 2 & -5 \end{bmatrix}$$

and then finding the determinant of the resulting matrix. Hence,

$$\begin{vmatrix} -3 & 3 \\ 2 & -5 \end{vmatrix} = (-3)(-5) - (3)(2) = 9$$

is the minor of -6. Multiplying 9, the minor of -6, by

$$(-1)^{i+j}$$

where i is the row number of -6 and j is its column number, gives

$$(-1)^{2+1}(9) = -1(9) = -9$$

Thus, -9 is the cofactor of -6.

The minor and cofactor of each element of column 3 of matrix M are given in Table B-1.

TABLE B-1

Element	Minor	Cofactor
Element 3 located in row 1 and column 3 of M	$\begin{vmatrix} -6 & 2 \\ 7 & 2 \end{vmatrix} = -26$	$(-1)^{1+3}(-26) = -26$
Element -4 located in row 2 and column 3 of M	$\begin{vmatrix} 2 & -3 \\ 7 & 2 \end{vmatrix} = 25$	$(-1)^{2+3}(25) = -25$
Element -5 located in row 3 and column 3 of M	$\begin{vmatrix} 2 & -3 \\ -6 & 2 \end{vmatrix} = -14$	$(-1)^{3+3}(-14) = -14$

Now that we know how to determine the cofactor of an element of a square matrix, we are ready to learn how to find the determinant of a square matrix of dimension higher than 2×2. The procedure is as follows.

To Find the Determinant of an $n \times n$ Matrix ($n > 2$)

Step 1 Choose either a row or a column of the original matrix.

Step 2 Multiply each element of this chosen row (or column) by its respective cofactor.

Step 3 Add the products obtained in step 2. The result is the determinant of the matrix.

• **EXAMPLE B-6** _____

Find the determinant of matrix M where

$$M = \begin{bmatrix} 2 & -3 & 3 \\ -6 & 2 & -4 \\ 7 & 2 & -5 \end{bmatrix}$$

Solution

Since the cofactors of the elements in column 3 are given in Table B-1 of this section, we choose column 3 of matrix M. Multiplying each element in column 3 by its respective cofactor and adding the products gives

$$\begin{aligned} |M| &= 3(-26) + (-4)(-25) + (-5)(-14) \\ &= -78 + 100 + 70 \\ &= 92 \end{aligned}$$

• **EXAMPLE B-7** _____

Find the determinant of matrix M of the previous example by choosing row 2.

Solution

The cofactors of -6, 2, and -4 are -9, -31, and -25, respectively. Multiplying each element of row 2 by its respective cofactor and adding the products gives

$$|M| = (-6)(-9) + 2(-31) + (-4)(-25)$$
$$= 54 - 62 + 100$$
$$= 92$$

Note that $|M| = 92$ regardless of the row or column with which we choose to find the determinant of M.

In general, the determinant of a given square matrix is the same number regardless of the row or column chosen.

• **EXAMPLE B-8** ————————————————————————

Find $|A|$ if

$$A = \begin{bmatrix} 1 & 0 & -1 & 4 \\ 0 & 3 & 2 & -4 \\ 2 & 0 & -1 & 0 \\ 5 & 0 & 0 & 0 \end{bmatrix}$$

Solution

Choosing column 2, we determine the cofactor of 3 to be

$$(-1)^{2+2} \begin{vmatrix} 1 & -1 & 4 \\ 2 & -1 & 0 \\ 5 & 0 & 0 \end{vmatrix}$$

We need not determine the cofactors of the 0s since the product of a 0 and its cofactor is 0. We determine that

$$\begin{vmatrix} 1 & -1 & 4 \\ 2 & -1 & 0 \\ 5 & 0 & 0 \end{vmatrix} = 20$$

and, thus, the cofactor of 3 is

$$(-1)^{2+2}(20) = 20$$

Hence,

$$|A| = 3(20) = 60$$

Exercises

1. Find $|D|$ if

$$D = \begin{bmatrix} 2 & -1 & 3 \\ 3 & 2 & -4 \\ 4 & 2 & -5 \end{bmatrix}$$

2. Find $|C|$ if

$$C = \begin{bmatrix} 5 & 3 & 2 \\ 8 & -1 & 4 \\ 1 & 2 & -3 \end{bmatrix}$$

3. Find $|H|$ if

$$H = \begin{bmatrix} 5 & 0 & 4 \\ 3 & 2 & -1 \\ -8 & -5 & 7 \end{bmatrix}$$

4. Find $|K|$ if

$$K = \begin{bmatrix} 0 & -1 & 5 \\ 2 & -3 & -4 \\ 0 & 4 & 7 \end{bmatrix}$$

5. Find $|N|$ if

$$N = \begin{bmatrix} 4 & 0 & 3 & 1 \\ -1 & 0 & 2 & -3 \\ 3 & 5 & 1 & -2 \\ -4 & 0 & -3 & 1 \end{bmatrix}$$

Answers

1. $|D| = -9$
2. $|C| = 93$
3. $|H| = 49$
4. $|K| = 54$
5. $|N| = -110$

Appendix C
Tables

TABLE 1 Common logarithms

x	0	1	2	3	4	5	6	7	8	9
1.0	0.0000	0.0043	0.0086	0.0128	0.0170	0.0212	0.0253	0.0294	0.0334	0.0374
1.1	0.0414	0.0453	0.0492	0.0531	0.0569	0.0607	0.0645	0.0682	0.0719	0.0755
1.2	0.0792	0.0828	0.0864	0.0899	0.0934	0.0969	0.1004	0.1038	0.1072	0.1106
1.3	0.1139	0.1173	0.1206	0.1239	0.1271	0.1303	0.1335	0.1367	0.1399	0.1430
1.4	0.1461	0.1492	0.1523	0.1553	0.1584	0.1614	0.1644	0.1673	0.1703	0.1732
1.5	0.1761	0.1790	0.1818	0.1847	0.1875	0.1903	0.1931	0.1959	0.1987	0.2014
1.6	0.2041	0.2068	0.2095	0.2122	0.2148	0.2175	0.2201	0.2227	0.2253	0.2279
1.7	0.2304	0.2330	0.2355	0.2380	0.2405	0.2430	0.2455	0.2480	0.2504	0.2529
1.8	0.2553	0.2577	0.2601	0.2625	0.2648	0.2672	0.2695	0.2718	0.2742	0.2765
1.9	0.2788	0.2810	0.2833	0.2856	0.2878	0.2900	0.2923	0.2945	0.2967	0.2989
2.0	0.3010	0.3032	0.3054	0.3075	0.3096	0.3118	0.3139	0.3160	0.3181	0.3201
2.1	0.3222	0.3243	0.3263	0.3284	0.3304	0.3324	0.3345	0.3365	0.3385	0.3404
2.2	0.3424	0.3444	0.3464	0.3483	0.3502	0.3522	0.3541	0.3560	0.3579	0.3598
2.3	0.3617	0.3636	0.3655	0.3674	0.3692	0.3711	0.3729	0.3747	0.3766	0.3784
2.4	0.3802	0.3820	0.3838	0.3856	0.3874	0.3892	0.3909	0.3927	0.3945	0.3962
2.5	0.3979	0.3997	0.4014	0.4031	0.4048	0.4065	0.4082	0.4099	0.4116	0.4133
2.6	0.4150	0.4166	0.4183	0.4200	0.4216	0.4232	0.4249	0.4265	0.4281	0.4298
2.7	0.4314	0.4330	0.4346	0.4362	0.4378	0.4393	0.4409	0.4425	0.4440	0.4456
2.8	0.4472	0.4487	0.4502	0.4518	0.4533	0.4548	0.4564	0.4579	0.4594	0.4609
2.9	0.4624	0.4639	0.4654	0.4669	0.4683	0.4698	0.4713	0.4728	0.4742	0.4757
3.0	0.4771	0.4786	0.4800	0.4814	0.4829	0.4843	0.4857	0.4871	0.4886	0.4900
3.1	0.4914	0.4928	0.4942	0.4955	0.4969	0.4983	0.4997	0.5011	0.5024	0.5038
3.2	0.5052	0.5065	0.5079	0.5092	0.5105	0.5119	0.5132	0.5145	0.5159	0.5172
3.3	0.5185	0.5198	0.5211	0.5224	0.5237	0.5250	0.5263	0.5276	0.5289	0.5302
3.4	0.5315	0.5328	0.5340	0.5353	0.5366	0.5378	0.5391	0.5403	0.5416	0.5428
3.5	0.5441	0.5453	0.5465	0.5478	0.5490	0.5502	0.5515	0.5527	0.5539	0.5551
3.6	0.5563	0.5575	0.5587	0.5599	0.5611	0.5623	0.5635	0.5647	0.5658	0.5670
3.7	0.5682	0.5694	0.5705	0.5717	0.5729	0.5740	0.5752	0.5763	0.5775	0.5786
3.8	0.5798	0.5809	0.5821	0.5832	0.5843	0.5855	0.5866	0.5877	0.5888	0.5899
3.9	0.5911	0.5922	0.5933	0.5944	0.5955	0.5966	0.5977	0.5988	0.5999	0.6010
4.0	0.6021	0.6031	0.6042	0.6053	0.6064	0.6075	0.6085	0.6096	0.6107	0.6117
4.1	0.6128	0.6138	0.6149	0.6160	0.6170	0.6180	0.6191	0.6201	0.6212	0.6222
4.2	0.6232	0.6243	0.6253	0.6263	0.6274	0.6284	0.6294	0.6304	0.6314	0.6325

continues

TABLE 1 Common logarithms *(continued)*

x	0	1	2	3	4	5	6	7	8	9
4.3	0.6335	0.6345	0.6355	0.6365	0.6375	0.6385	0.6395	0.6405	0.6415	0.6425
4.4	0.6435	0.6444	0.6454	0.6464	0.6474	0.6484	0.6493	0.6503	0.6513	0.6522
4.5	0.6532	0.6542	0.6551	0.6561	0.6571	0.6580	0.6590	0.6599	0.6609	0.6618
4.6	0.6628	0.6637	0.6646	0.6656	0.6665	0.6675	0.6684	0.6693	0.6702	0.6712
4.7	0.6721	0.6730	0.6739	0.6749	0.6758	0.6767	0.6776	0.6785	0.6794	0.6803
4.8	0.6812	0.6821	0.6830	0.6839	0.6848	0.6857	0.6866	0.6875	0.6884	0.6893
4.9	0.6902	0.6911	0.6920	0.6928	0.6937	0.6946	0.6955	0.6964	0.6972	0.6981
5.0	0.6990	0.6998	0.7007	0.7016	0.7024	0.7033	0.7042	0.7050	0.7059	0.7067
5.1	0.7076	0.7084	0.7093	0.7101	0.7110	0.7118	0.7126	0.7135	0.7143	0.7152
5.2	0.7160	0.7168	0.7177	0.7185	0.7193	7.7202	0.7210	0.7218	0.7226	0.7235
5.3	0.7243	0.7251	0.7259	0.7267	0.7275	0.7284	0.7292	0.7300	0.7308	0.7316
5.4	0.7324	0.7332	0.7340	0.7348	0.7356	0.7364	0.7372	0.7380	0.7388	0.7396
5.5	0.7404	0.7412	0.7419	0.7427	0.7435	0.7443	0.7451	0.7459	0.7466	0.7474
5.6	0.7482	0.7490	0.7497	0.7505	0.7513	0.7520	0.7528	0.7536	0.7543	0.7551
5.7	0.7559	0.7566	0.7574	0.7582	0.7589	0.7597	0.7604	0.7612	0.7619	0.7627
5.8	0.7634	0.7642	0.7649	0.7657	0.7664	0.7672	0.7679	0.7686	0.7694	0.7701
5.9	0.7709	0.7716	0.7723	0.7731	0.7738	0.7745	0.7752	0.7760	0.7767	0.7774
6.0	0.7782	0.7789	0.7796	0.7803	0.7810	0.7818	0.7825	0.7832	0.7839	0.7846
6.1	0.7853	0.7860	0.7868	0.7875	0.7882	0.7889	0.7896	0.7903	0.7910	0.7917
6.2	0.7924	0.7931	0.7938	0.7945	0.7952	0.7959	0.7966	0.7973	0.7980	0.7987
6.3	0.7993	0.8000	0.8007	0.8014	0.8021	0.8028	0.8035	0.8041	0.8048	0.8055
6.4	0.8062	0.8069	0.8075	0.8082	0.8089	0.8096	0.8102	0.8109	0.8116	0.8122
6.5	0.8129	0.8136	0.8142	0.8149	0.8156	0.8162	0.8169	0.8176	0.8182	0.8189
6.6	0.8195	0.8202	0.8209	0.8215	0.8222	0.8228	0.8235	0.8241	0.8248	0.8254
6.7	0.8261	0.8267	0.8274	0.8280	0.8287	0.8293	0.8299	0.8306	0.8312	0.8319
6.8	0.8325	0.8331	0.8338	0.8344	0.8351	0.8357	0.8363	0.8370	0.8376	0.8382
6.9	0.8388	0.8395	0.8401	0.8407	0.8414	0.8420	0.8426	0.8432	0.8439	0.8445
7.0	0.8451	0.8457	0.8463	0.8470	0.8476	0.8482	0.8488	0.8494	0.8500	0.8506
7.1	0.8513	0.8519	0.8525	0.8531	0.8537	0.8543	0.8549	0.8555	0.8561	0.8567
7.2	0.8573	0.8579	0.8585	0.8591	0.8597	0.8603	0.8609	0.8615	0.8621	0.8627
7.3	0.8633	0.8639	0.8645	0.8651	0.8657	0.8663	0.8669	0.8675	0.8681	0.8686
7.4	0.8692	0.8698	0.8704	0.8710	0.8716	0.8722	0.8727	0.8733	0.8739	0.8745
7.5	0.8751	0.8756	0.8762	0.8768	0.8774	0.8779	0.8785	0.8791	0.8797	0.8802
7.6	0.8808	0.8814	0.8820	0.8825	0.8831	0.8837	0.8842	0.8848	0.8854	0.8859
7.7	0.8865	0.8871	0.8876	0.8882	0.8887	0.8893	0.8899	0.8904	0.8910	0.8915
7.8	0.8921	0.8927	0.8932	0.8938	0.8943	0.8949	0.8954	0.8960	0.8965	0.8971
7.9	0.8976	0.8982	0.8987	0.8993	0.8998	0.9004	0.9009	0.9015	0.9020	0.9025
8.0	0.9031	0.9036	0.9042	0.9047	0.9053	0.9058	0.9063	0.9069	0.9074	0.9079
8.1	0.9085	0.9090	0.9096	0.9101	0.9106	0.9112	0.9117	0.9122	0.9128	0.9133
8.2	0.9138	0.9143	0.9149	0.9154	0.9159	0.9165	0.9170	0.9175	0.9180	0.9186
8.3	0.9191	0.9196	0.9201	0.9206	0.9212	0.9217	0.9222	0.9227	0.9232	0.9238
8.4	0.9243	0.9248	0.9253	0.9258	0.9263	0.9269	0.9274	0.9279	0.9284	0.9289
8.5	0.9294	0.9299	0.9304	0.9309	0.9315	0.9320	0.9325	0.9330	0.9335	0.9340
8.6	0.9345	0.9350	0.9355	0.9360	0.9365	0.9370	0.9375	0.9380	0.9385	0.9390
8.7	0.9395	0.9400	0.9405	0.9410	0.9415	0.9420	0.9425	0.9430	0.9435	0.9440
8.8	0.9445	0.9450	0.9455	0.9460	0.9465	0.9469	0.9474	0.9479	0.9484	0.9489
8.9	0.9494	0.9499	0.9504	0.9509	0.9513	0.9518	0.9523	0.9528	0.9533	0.9538
9.0	0.9542	0.9547	0.9552	0.9557	0.9562	0.9566	0.9571	0.9576	0.9581	0.9586
9.1	0.9590	0.9595	0.9600	0.9605	0.9609	0.9614	0.9619	0.9624	0.9628	0.9633

continues

TABLE 1 Common logarithms *(continued)*

x	0	1	2	3	4	5	6	7	8	9
9.2	0.9638	0.9643	0.9647	0.9652	0.9657	0.9661	0.9666	0.9671	0.9675	0.9680
9.3	0.9685	0.9689	0.9694	0.9699	0.9703	0.9708	0.9713	0.9717	0.9722	0.9727
9.4	0.9731	0.9736	0.9741	0.9745	0.9750	0.9754	0.9759	0.9764	0.9768	0.9773
9.5	0.9777	0.9782	0.9786	0.9791	0.9795	0.9800	0.9805	0.9809	0.9814	0.9818
9.6	0.9823	0.9827	0.9832	0.9836	0.9841	0.9845	0.9850	0.9854	0.9859	0.9863
9.7	0.9868	0.9872	0.9877	0.9881	0.9886	0.9890	0.9894	0.9899	0.9903	0.9908
9.8	0.9912	0.9917	0.9921	0.9926	0.9930	0.9934	0.9939	0.9943	0.9948	0.9952
9.9	0.9956	0.9961	0.9965	0.9969	0.9974	0.9978	0.9983	0.9987	0.9991	0.9996

TABLE 2 Natural logarithms

x	ln x	x	ln x	x	ln x
0.1	−2.302585	3.5	1.252763	6.9	1.931521
0.2	−1.609438	3.6	1.280934	7.0	1.945910
0.3	−1.203973	3.7	1.308333	7.1	1.960095
0.4	−0.916291	3.8	1.335001	7.2	1.974081
0.5	−0.693147	3.9	1.360977	7.3	1.987874
0.6	−0.510826	4.0	1.386294	7.4	2.001480
0.7	−0.356675	4.1	1.410987	7.5	2.014903
0.8	−0.223144	4.2	1.435085	7.6	2.028148
0.9	−0.105361	4.3	1.458615	7.7	2.041220
1.0	0.000000	4.4	1.481605	7.8	2.054124
1.1	0.095310	4.5	1.504077	7.9	2.066863
1.2	0.182322	4.6	1.526056	8.0	2.079442
1.3	0.262364	4.7	1.547563	8.1	2.091864
1.4	0.336472	4.8	1.568616	8.2	2.104134
1.5	0.405465	4.9	1.589235	8.3	2.116256
1.6	0.470004	5.0	1.609438	8.4	2.128232
1.7	0.530628	5.1	1.629241	8.5	2.140066
1.8	0.587787	5.2	1.648659	8.6	2.151762
1.9	0.641854	5.3	1.667707	8.7	2.163323
2.0	0.693147	5.4	1.686399	8.8	2.174752
2.1	0.741937	5.5	1.704748	8.9	2.186051
2.2	0.788457	5.6	1.722767	9.0	2.197225
2.3	0.832909	5.7	1.740466	9.1	2.208274
2.4	0.875469	5.8	1.757858	9.2	2.219203
2.5	0.916291	5.9	1.774952	9.3	2.230014
2.6	0.955511	6.0	1.791759	9.4	2.240710
2.7	0.993252	6.1	1.808289	9.5	2.251292
2.8	1.029619	6.2	1.824549	9.6	2.261763
2.9	1.064711	6.3	1.840550	9.7	2.272126
3.0	1.098612	6.4	1.856298	9.8	2.282382
3.1	1.131402	6.5	1.871802	9.9	2.292535
3.2	1.163151	6.6	1.887070	10.0	2.302585
3.3	1.193922	6.7	1.902108	11.0	2.397895
3.4	1.223775	6.8	1.916923	12.0	2.484907

continues

TABLE 2 Natural logarithms *(continued)*

x	ln x	x	ln x	x	ln x
13.0	2.564949	25.0	3.218876	65.0	4.174387
14.0	2.639057	30.0	3.401197	70.0	4.248495
15.0	2.708050	35.0	3.555348	75.0	4.317488
16.0	2.772589	40.0	3.688879	80.0	4.382027
17.0	2.833213	45.0	3.806662	85.0	4.442651
18.0	2.890372	50.0	3.912023	90.0	4.499810
19.0	2.944439	55.0	4.007333	95.0	4.553877
20.0	2.995732	60.0	4.094345	100.0	4.605170

TABLE 3 Exponential functions

x	e^x	e^{-x}	x	e^x	e^{-x}
0.00	1.000000	1.000000	1.40	4.055200	0.246597
0.01	1.010050	0.990050	1.50	4.481689	0.223130
0.02	1.020201	0.980199	1.60	4.953032	0.201897
0.03	1.030455	0.970446	1.70	5.473947	0.182684
0.04	1.040811	0.960789	1.80	6.049647	0.165299
0.05	1.051271	0.951229	1.90	6.685894	0.149569
0.06	1.061837	0.941765	2.00	7.389056	0.135335
0.07	1.072508	0.932394	2.10	8.166170	0.122456
0.08	1.083287	0.923116	2.20	9.025013	0.110803
0.09	1.094174	0.913931	2.30	9.974182	0.100259
0.10	1.105171	0.904837	2.40	11.023176	0.090718
0.11	1.116278	0.895834	2.50	12.182494	0.082085
0.12	1.127497	0.886920	2.60	13.463738	0.074274
0.13	1.138828	0.878095	2.70	14.879732	0.067206
0.14	1.150274	0.869358	2.80	16.444647	0.060810
0.15	1.161834	0.860708	2.90	18.174145	0.055023
0.16	1.173511	0.852144	3.00	20.085537	0.049787
0.17	1.185305	0.843665	3.50	33.115452	0.030197
0.18	1.197217	0.835270	4.00	54.598150	0.018316
0.19	1.209250	0.826959	4.50	90.017131	0.011109
0.20	1.221403	0.818731	5.00	148.413159	0.006738
0.30	1.349859	0.740818	5.50	244.691932	0.004087
0.40	1.491825	0.670320	6.00	403.428793	0.002479
0.50	1.648721	0.606531	6.50	665.141633	0.001503
0.60	1.822119	0.548812	7.00	1096.633158	0.000912
0.70	2.013753	0.496585	7.50	1808.042414	0.000553
0.80	2.225541	0.449329	8.00	2980.957987	0.000335
0.90	2.459603	0.406570	8.50	4914.768840	0.000203
1.00	2.718282	0.367879	9.00	8103.083928	0.000123
1.10	3.004166	0.332871	9.50	13359.726830	0.000075
1.20	3.320117	0.301194	10.00	22026.465795	0.000045
1.30	3.669297	0.272532			

TABLE 4 Compound amount $(1 + i)^n$

n	½%	¾%	1%	1¼%	1½%	1¾%	2%
1	1.005000	1.007500	1.010000	1.012500	1.015000	1.017500	1.020000
2	1.010025	1.015056	1.020100	1.025156	1.030225	1.035306	1.040400
3	1.015075	1.022669	1.030301	1.037971	1.045678	1.053424	1.061208
4	1.020151	1.030339	1.040604	1.050945	1.061364	1.071859	1.082432
5	1.025251	1.038067	1.051010	1.064082	1.077284	1.090617	1.104081
6	1.030378	1.045852	1.061520	1.077383	1.093443	1.109702	1.126162
7	1.035529	1.053696	1.072135	1.090850	1.109845	1.129122	1.148686
8	1.040707	1.061599	1.082857	1.104486	1.126493	1.148882	1.171659
9	1.045911	1.069561	1.093685	1.118292	1.143390	1.168987	1.195093
10	1.051140	1.077583	1.104622	1.132271	1.160541	1.189444	1.218994
11	1.056396	1.085664	1.115668	1.146424	1.177949	1.210260	1.243374
12	1.061678	1.093807	1.126825	1.160755	1.195618	1.231439	1.268242
13	1.066986	1.102010	1.138093	1.175264	1.213552	1.252990	1.293607
14	1.072321	1.110276	1.149474	1.189955	1.231756	1.274917	1.319479
15	1.077683	1.118603	1.160969	1.204829	1.250232	1.297228	1.345868
16	1.083071	1.126992	1.172579	1.219890	1.268986	1.319929	1.372786
17	1.088487	1.135445	1.184304	1.235138	1.288020	1.343028	1.400241
18	1.093929	1.143960	1.196147	1.250577	1.307341	1.366531	1.428246
19	1.099399	1.152540	1.208109	1.266210	1.326951	1.390445	1.456811
20	1.104896	1.161184	1.220190	1.282037	1.346855	1.414778	1.485947
21	1.110420	1.169893	1.232392	1.298063	1.367058	1.439537	1.515666
22	1.115972	1.178667	1.244716	1.314288	1.387564	1.464729	1.545980
23	1.121552	1.187507	1.257163	1.330717	1.408377	1.490361	1.576899
24	1.127160	1.196414	1.269735	1.347351	1.429503	1.516443	1.608437
25	1.132796	1.205387	1.282432	1.364193	1.450945	1.542981	1.640606
26	1.138460	1.214427	1.295256	1.381245	1.472710	1.569983	1.673418
27	1.144152	1.223535	1.308209	1.398511	1.494800	1.597457	1.706886
28	1.149873	1.232712	1.321291	1.415992	1.517222	1.625413	1.741024
29	1.155622	1.241957	1.334504	1.433692	1.539981	1.653858	1.775845
30	1.161400	1.251272	1.347849	1.451613	1.563080	1.682800	1.811362
31	1.167207	1.260656	1.361327	1.469759	1.586526	1.712249	1.847589
32	1.173043	1.270111	1.374941	1.488131	1.610324	1.742213	1.884541
33	1.178908	1.279637	1.388690	1.506732	1.634479	1.772702	1.922231
34	1.184803	1.289234	1.402577	1.525566	1.658996	1.803725	1.960676
35	1.190727	1.298904	1.416603	1.544636	1.683881	1.835290	1.999890
36	1.196681	1.308645	1.430769	1.563944	1.709140	1.867407	2.039887
37	1.202664	1.318460	1.445076	1.583493	1.734777	1.900087	2.080685
38	1.208677	1.328349	1.459527	1.603287	1.760798	1.933338	2.122299
39	1.214721	1.338311	1.474123	1.623328	1.787210	1.967172	2.164745
40	1.220794	1.348349	1.488864	1.643619	1.814018	2.001597	2.208040
41	1.226898	1.358461	1.503752	1.664165	1.841229	2.036625	2.252200
42	1.233033	1.368650	1.518790	1.684967	1.868847	2.072266	2.297244
43	1.239198	1.378915	1.533978	1.706029	1.896880	2.108531	2.343189
44	1.245394	1.389256	1.549318	1.727354	1.925333	2.145430	2.390053
45	1.251621	1.399676	1.564811	1.748946	1.954213	2.182975	2.437854
46	1.257879	1.410173	1.580459	1.770808	1.983526	2.221177	2.486611
47	1.264168	1.420750	1.596263	1.792943	2.013279	2.260048	2.536344
48	1.270489	1.431405	1.612226	1.815355	2.043478	2.299599	2.587070
49	1.276842	1.442141	1.628348	1.838047	2.074130	2.339842	2.638812

continues

TABLE 4 Compound amount $(1 + i)^n$ (continued)

n	½%	¾%	1%	1¼%	1½%	1¾%	2%
50	1.283226	1.452957	1.644632	1.861022	2.105242	2.380789	2.691588
51	1.289642	1.463854	1.661078	1.884285	2.136821	2.422453	2.745420
52	1.296090	1.474833	1.677689	1.907839	2.168873	2.464846	2.800328
53	1.302571	1.485894	1.694466	1.931687	2.201406	2.507980	2.856335
54	1.309083	1.497038	1.711410	1.955833	2.234428	2.551870	2.913461
55	1.315629	1.508266	1.728525	1.980281	2.267944	2.596528	2.971731
56	1.322207	1.519578	1.745810	2.005034	2.301963	2.641967	3.031165
57	1.328818	1.530975	1.763268	2.030097	2.336493	2.688202	3.091789
58	1.335462	1.542457	1.780901	2.055473	2.371540	2.735245	3.153624
59	1.342139	1.554026	1.798710	2.081167	2.407113	2.783112	3.216697
60	1.348850	1.565681	1.816697	2.107181	2.443220	2.831816	3.281031
61	1.355594	1.577424	1.834864	2.133521	2.479868	2.881373	3.346651
62	1.362372	1.589254	1.853212	2.160190	2.517066	2.931797	3.413584
63	1.369184	1.601174	1.871744	2.187193	2.554822	2.983104	3.481856
64	1.376030	1.613183	1.890462	2.214532	2.593144	3.035308	3.551493
65	1.382910	1.625281	1.909366	2.242214	2.632042	3.088426	3.622523
66	1.389825	1.637471	1.928460	2.270242	2.671522	3.142473	3.694974
67	1.396774	1.649752	1.947745	2.298620	2.711595	3.197466	3.768873
68	1.403758	1.662125	1.967222	2.327353	2.752269	3.253422	3.844251
69	1.410777	1.674591	1.986894	2.356444	2.793553	3.310357	3.921136
70	1.417831	1.687151	2.006763	2.385900	2.835456	3.368288	3.999558
71	1.424920	1.699804	2.026831	2.415724	2.877988	3.427233	4.079549
72	1.432044	1.712553	2.047099	2.445920	2.921158	3.487210	4.161140
73	1.439204	1.725397	2.067570	2.476494	2.964975	3.548236	4.244363
74	1.446401	1.738337	2.088246	2.507450	3.009450	3.610330	4.329250
75	1.453633	1.751375	2.109128	2.538794	3.054592	3.673511	4.415835
76	1.460901	1.764510	2.130220	2.570529	3.100411	3.737797	4.504152
77	1.468205	1.777744	2.151522	2.602660	3.146917	3.803209	4.594235
78	1.475546	1.791077	2.173037	2.635193	3.194120	3.869765	4.686120
79	1.482924	1.804510	2.194768	2.668133	3.242032	3.937486	4.779842
80	1.490339	1.818044	2.216715	2.701485	3.290663	4.006392	4.875439
81	1.497790	1.831679	2.238882	2.735254	3.340023	4.076504	4.972948
82	1.505279	1.845417	2.261271	2.769444	3.390123	4.147843	5.072407
83	1.512806	1.859258	2.283884	2.804062	3.440975	4.220430	5.173855
84	1.520370	1.873202	2.306723	2.839113	3.492590	4.294287	5.277332
85	1.527971	1.887251	2.329790	2.874602	3.544978	4.369437	5.382879
86	1.535611	1.901405	2.353088	2.910534	3.598153	4.445903	5.490536
87	1.543289	1.915666	2.376619	2.946916	3.652125	4.523706	5.600347
88	1.551006	1.930033	2.400385	2.983753	3.706907	4.602871	5.712354
89	1.558761	1.944509	2.424389	3.021049	3.762511	4.683421	5.826601
90	1.566555	1.959092	2.448633	3.058813	3.818949	4.765381	5.943133
91	1.574387	1.973786	2.473119	3.097048	3.876233	4.848775	6.061996
92	1.582259	1.988589	2.497850	3.135761	3.934376	4.933629	6.183236
93	1.590171	2.003503	2.522829	3.174958	3.993392	5.019967	6.306900
94	1.598122	2.018530	2.548057	3.214645	4.053293	5.107816	6.433038
95	1.606112	2.033669	2.573538	3.254828	4.114092	5.197203	6.561699
96	1.614143	2.048921	2.599273	3.295513	4.175804	5.288154	6.692933
97	1.622213	2.064288	2.625266	3.336707	4.238441	5.380697	6.826792
98	1.630324	2.079770	2.651518	3.378416	4.302017	5.474859	6.963328
99	1.638476	2.095369	2.678033	3.420646	4.366547	5.570669	7.102594
100	1.646668	2.111084	2.704814	3.463404	4.432046	5.668156	7.244646

TABLE 4 Compound amount $(1 + i)^n$

n	3%	4%	5%	6%	7%	8%	9%
1	1.030000	1.040000	1.050000	1.060000	1.070000	1.080000	1.090000
2	1.060900	1.081600	1.102500	1.123600	1.144900	1.166400	1.188100
3	1.092727	1.124864	1.157625	1.191016	1.225043	1.259712	1.295029
4	1.125509	1.169859	1.215506	1.262477	1.310796	1.360489	1.411582
5	1.159274	1.216653	1.276282	1.338226	1.402552	1.469328	1.538624
6	1.194052	1.265319	1.340096	1.418519	1.500730	1.586874	1.677100
7	1.229874	1.315932	1.407100	1.503630	1.605781	1.713824	1.828039
8	1.266770	1.368569	1.477455	1.593848	1.718186	1.850930	1.992563
9	1.304773	1.423312	1.551328	1.689479	1.838459	1.999005	2.171893
10	1.343916	1.480244	1.628895	1.790848	1.967151	2.158925	2.367364
11	1.384234	1.539454	1.710339	1.898299	2.104852	2.331639	2.580426
12	1.425761	1.601032	1.795856	2.012196	2.252192	2.518170	2.812665
13	1.468534	1.665074	1.885649	2.132928	2.409845	2.719624	3.065805
14	1.512590	1.731676	1.979932	2.260904	2.578534	2.937194	3.341727
15	1.557967	1.800944	2.078928	2.396558	2.759032	3.172169	3.642482
16	1.604706	1.872981	2.182875	2.540352	2.952164	3.425943	3.970306
17	1.652848	1.947900	2.292018	2.692773	3.158815	3.700018	4.327633
18	1.702433	2.025817	2.406619	2.854339	3.379932	3.996019	4.717120
19	1.753506	2.106849	2.526950	3.025600	3.616528	4.315701	5.141661
20	1.806111	2.191123	2.653298	3.207135	3.869684	4.660957	5.604411
21	1.860295	2.278768	2.785963	3.399564	4.140562	5.033834	6.108808
22	1.916103	2.369919	2.925261	3.603537	4.430402	5.436540	6.658600
23	1.973587	2.464716	3.071524	3.819750	4.740530	5.871464	7.257874
24	2.032794	2.563304	3.225100	4.048935	5.072367	6.341181	7.911083
25	2.093778	2.665836	3.386355	4.291871	5.427433	6.848475	8.623081
26	2.156591	2.772470	3.555673	4.549383	5.807353	7.396353	9.399158
27	2.221289	2.883369	3.733456	4.822346	6.213868	7.988061	10.245082
28	2.287928	2.998703	3.920129	5.111687	6.648838	8.627106	11.167140
29	2.356566	3.118651	4.116136	5.418388	7.114257	9.317275	12.172182
30	2.427262	3.243398	4.321942	5.743491	7.612255	10.062657	13.267678
31	2.500080	3.373133	4.538039	6.088101	8.145113	10.867669	14.461770
32	2.575083	3.508059	4.764941	6.453387	8.715271	11.737083	15.763329
33	2.652335	3.648381	5.003189	6.840590	9.325340	12.676050	17.182028
34	2.731905	3.794316	5.253348	7.251025	9.978114	13.690134	18.728411
35	2.813862	3.946089	5.516015	7.686087	10.676581	14.785344	20.413968
36	2.898278	4.103933	5.791816	8.147252	11.423942	15.968172	22.251225
37	2.985227	4.268090	6.081407	8.636087	12.223618	17.245626	24.253835
38	3.074783	4.438813	6.385477	9.154252	13.079271	18.625276	26.436680
39	3.167027	4.616366	6.704751	9.703507	13.994820	20.115298	28.815982
40	3.262038	4.801021	7.039989	10.285718	14.974458	21.724521	31.409420
41	3.359899	4.993061	7.391988	10.902861	16.022670	23.462483	34.236268
42	3.460696	5.192784	7.761588	11.557033	17.144257	25.339482	37.317532
43	3.564517	5.400495	8.149667	12.250455	18.344355	27.366640	40.676110
44	3.671452	5.616515	8.557150	12.985482	19.628460	29.555972	44.336960
45	3.781596	5.841176	8.985008	13.764611	21.002452	31.920449	48.327286
46	3.895044	6.074823	9.434258	14.590487	22.472623	34.474085	52.676742
47	4.011895	6.317816	9.905971	15.465917	24.045707	37.232012	57.417649
48	4.132252	6.570528	10.401270	16.393872	25.728907	40.210573	62.585237
49	4.256219	6.833349	10.921333	17.377504	27.529930	43.427419	68.217908

continues

TABLE 4 Compound amount $(1 + i)^n$ (continued)

n	3%	4%	5%	6%	7%	8%	9%
50	4.383906	7.106683	11.467400	18.420154	29.457025	46.901613	74.357520
51	4.515423	7.390951	12.040770	19.525364	31.519017	50.653742	81.049697
52	4.650886	7.686589	12.642808	20.696885	33.725348	54.706041	88.344170
53	4.790412	7.994052	13.274949	21.938698	36.086122	59.082524	96.295145
54	4.934125	8.313814	13.938696	23.255020	38.612151	63.809126	104.961708
55	5.082149	8.646367	14.635631	24.650322	41.315001	68.913856	114.408262
56	5.234613	8.992222	15.367412	26.129341	44.207052	74.426965	124.705005
57	5.391651	9.351910	16.135783	27.697101	47.301545	80.381122	135.928456
58	5.553401	9.725987	16.942572	29.358927	50.612653	86.811612	148.162017
59	5.720003	10.115026	17.789701	31.120463	54.155539	93.756540	161.496598
60	5.891603	10.519627	18.679186	32.987691	57.946427	101.257064	176.031292
61	6.068351	10.940413	19.613145	34.966952	62.002677	109.357629	191.874108
62	6.250402	11.378029	20.593802	37.064969	66.342864	118.106239	209.142778
63	6.437914	11.833150	21.623493	39.288868	70.986865	127.554738	227.965628
64	6.631051	12.306476	22.704667	41.646200	75.955945	137.759117	248.482535
65	6.829983	12.798735	23.839901	44.144972	81.272861	148.779847	270.845963
66	7.034882	13.310685	25.031896	46.793670	86.961962	160.682234	295.222099
67	7.245929	13.843112	26.283490	49.601290	93.049299	173.536813	321.792088
68	7.463307	14.396836	27.597665	52.577368	99.562750	187.419758	350.753376
69	7.687206	14.972710	28.977548	55.732010	106.532142	202.413339	382.321180
70	7.917822	15.571618	30.426426	59.075930	113.989392	218.606406	416.730086
71	8.155357	16.194483	31.947747	62.620486	121.968650	236.094918	454.235794
72	8.400017	16.842262	33.545134	66.377715	130.506455	254.982512	495.117015
73	8.652018	17.515953	35.222391	70.360378	139.641907	275.381113	539.677547
74	8.911578	18.216591	36.983510	74.582001	149.416840	297.411602	588.248526
75	9.178926	18.945255	38.832686	79.056921	159.876019	321.204530	641.190893
76	9.454293	19.703065	40.774320	83.800336	171.067341	346.900892	698.898074
77	9.737922	20.491187	42.813036	88.828356	183.042055	374.652964	761.798900
78	10.030060	21.310835	44.953688	94.158058	195.854998	404.625201	830.360801
79	10.330962	22.163268	47.201372	99.807541	209.564848	436.995217	905.093274
80	10.640891	23.049799	49.561441	105.795993	224.234388	471.954834	986.551668
81	10.960117	23.971791	52.039513	112.143753	239.930795	509.711221	1075.341318
82	11.288921	24.930663	54.641489	118.872378	256.725950	550.488119	1172.122037
83	11.627588	25.927889	57.373563	126.004721	274.696767	594.527168	1277.613020
84	11.976416	26.965005	60.242241	133.565004	293.925541	642.089342	1392.598192
85	12.335709	28.043605	63.254353	141.578904	314.500328	693.456489	1517.932029
86	12.705780	29.165349	66.417071	150.073639	336.515351	748.933008	1654.545912
87	13.086953	30.331963	69.737925	159.078057	360.071426	808.847649	1803.455044
88	13.479562	31.545242	73.224821	168.622741	385.276426	873.555461	1965.765998
89	13.883949	32.807051	76.886062	178.740105	412.245776	943.439897	2142.684938
90	14.300467	34.119333	80.730365	189.464511	441.102980	1018.915089	2335.526582
91	14.729481	35.484107	84.766883	200.832382	471.980188	1100.428296	2545.723975
92	15.171366	36.903471	89.005227	212.882325	505.018802	1188.462560	2774.839132
93	15.626507	38.379610	93.455489	225.655264	540.370118	1283.539565	3024.574654
94	16.095302	39.914794	98.128263	239.194580	578.196026	1386.222730	3296.786373
95	16.578161	41.511386	103.034676	253.546255	618.669748	1497.120549	3593.497147
96	17.075506	43.171841	108.186410	268.759030	661.976630	1616.890192	3916.911890
97	17.587771	44.898715	113.595731	284.884572	708.314994	1746.241408	4269.433960
98	18.115404	46.694664	119.275517	301.977646	757.897044	1885.940720	4653.683016
99	18.658866	48.562450	125.239293	320.096305	810.949837	2036.815978	5072.514488
100	19.218632	50.504948	131.501258	339.302084	867.716326	2199.761256	5529.040792

TABLE 4 Compound amount $(1 + i)^n$

n	10%	11%	12%	13%	14%	15%	16%
1	1.100000	1.110000	1.120000	1.130000	1.140000	1.150000	1.16000
2	1.210000	1.232100	1.254400	1.276900	1.299600	1.322500	1.34560
3	1.331000	1.367631	1.404928	1.442897	1.481544	1.520875	1.56090
4	1.464100	1.518070	1.573519	1.630474	1.688960	1.749006	1.81064
5	1.610510	1.685058	1.762342	1.842435	1.925415	2.011357	2.10034
6	1.771561	1.870415	1.973823	2.081952	2.194973	2.313061	2.43640
7	1.948717	2.076160	2.210681	2.352605	2.502269	2.660020	2.82622
8	2.143589	2.304538	2.475963	2.658444	2.852586	3.059023	3.27841
9	2.357948	2.558037	2.773079	3.004042	3.251949	3.517876	3.80296
10	2.593742	2.839421	3.105848	3.394567	3.707221	4.045558	4.41144
11	2.853117	3.151757	3.478550	3.835861	4.226232	4.652391	5.11726
12	3.138428	3.498451	3.895976	4.334523	4.817905	5.350250	5.93603
13	3.452271	3.883280	4.363493	4.898011	5.492411	6.152788	6.88579
14	3.797498	4.310441	4.887112	5.534753	6.261349	7.075706	7.98752
15	4.177248	4.784589	5.473566	6.254270	7.137938	8.137062	9.26552
16	4.594973	5.310894	6.130394	7.067326	8.137249	9.357621	10.74800
17	5.054470	5.895093	6.866041	7.986078	9.276464	10.761264	12.46768
18	5.559917	6.543553	7.689966	9.024268	10.575169	12.375454	14.46251
19	6.115909	7.263344	8.612762	10.197423	12.055693	14.231772	16.77652
20	6.727500	8.062312	9.646293	11.523088	13.743490	16.366537	19.46076
21	7.400250	8.949166	10.803848	13.021089	15.667578	18.821518	22.57448
22	8.140275	9.933574	12.100310	14.713831	17.861039	21.644746	26.18640
23	8.954302	11.026267	13.552347	16.626629	20.361585	24.891458	30.37622
24	9.849733	12.239157	15.178629	18.788091	23.212207	28.625176	35.23642
25	10.834706	13.585464	17.000064	21.230542	26.461916	32.918953	40.87424
26	11.918177	15.079865	19.040072	23.990513	30.166584	37.856796	47.41412
27	13.109994	16.738650	21.324881	27.109279	34.389906	43.535315	55.00038
28	14.420994	18.579901	23.883866	30.633486	39.204493	50.065612	63.80044
29	15.863093	20.623691	26.749930	34.615839	44.693122	57.575454	74.00851
30	17.449402	22.892297	29.959922	39.115898	50.950159	66.211772	85.84988
31	19.194342	25.410449	33.555113	44.200965	58.083181	76.143538	99.58586
32	21.113777	28.205599	37.581726	49.947090	66.214826	87.565068	115.51959
33	23.225154	31.308214	42.091533	56.440212	75.484902	100.699829	134.00273
34	25.547670	34.752118	47.142517	63.777439	86.052788	115.804803	155.44317
35	28.102437	38.574851	52.799620	72.068506	98.100178	133.175523	180.31407
36	30.912681	42.818085	59.135574	81.437412	111.834203	153.151852	209.16432
37	34.003949	47.528074	66.231843	92.024276	127.490992	176.124630	242.63062
38	37.404343	52.756162	74.179664	103.987432	145.339731	202.543324	281.45151
39	41.144778	58.559340	83.081224	117.505798	165.687293	232.924823	326.48376
40	45.259256	65.000867	93.050970	132.781552	188.883514	267.863546	378.72116
41	49.785181	72.150963	104.217087	150.043153	215.327206	308.043078	439.31654
42	54.763699	80.087569	116.723137	169.548763	245.473015	354.249540	509.60719
43	60.240069	88.897201	130.729914	191.590103	279.839237	407.386971	591.14434
44	66.264076	98.675893	146.417503	216.496816	319.016730	468.495017	685.72744
45	72.890484	109.530242	163.987604	244.641402	363.679072	538.769269	795.44383
46	80.179532	121.578568	183.666116	276.444784	414.594142	619.584659	922.71484
47	88.197485	134.952211	205.706050	312.382606	472.637322	712.522358	1070.34921
48	97.017234	149.796954	230.390776	352.992345	538.806547	819.400712	1241.60509
49	106.718957	166.274619	258.037669	398.881350	614.239464	942.310819	1440.26190
50	117.390853	184.564827	289.002190	450.735925	700.232988	1083.657442	1670.70380

TABLE 5 Present value $(1 + i)^{-n}$

n	½%	¾%	1%	1¼%	1½%	1¾%	2%
1	0.995025	0.992556	0.990099	0.987654	0.985222	0.982801	0.980392
2	0.990075	0.985167	0.980296	0.975461	0.970662	0.965898	0.961169
3	0.985149	0.977833	0.970590	0.963418	0.956317	0.949285	0.942322
4	0.980248	0.970554	0.960980	0.951524	0.942184	0.932959	0.923845
5	0.975371	0.963329	0.951466	0.939777	0.928260	0.916913	0.905731
6	0.970518	0.956158	0.942045	0.928175	0.914542	0.901143	0.887971
7	0.965690	0.949040	0.932718	0.916716	0.901027	0.885644	0.870560
8	0.960885	0.941975	0.923483	0.905398	0.887711	0.870412	0.853490
9	0.956105	0.934963	0.914340	0.894221	0.874592	0.855441	0.836755
10	0.951348	0.928003	0.905287	0.883181	0.861667	0.840729	0.820348
11	0.946615	0.921095	0.896324	0.872277	0.848933	0.826269	0.804263
12	0.941905	0.914238	0.887449	0.861509	0.836387	0.812058	0.788493
13	0.937219	0.907432	0.878663	0.850873	0.824027	0.798091	0.773033
14	0.932556	0.900677	0.869963	0.840368	0.811849	0.784365	0.757875
15	0.927917	0.893973	0.861349	0.829993	0.799852	0.770875	0.743015
16	0.923300	0.887318	0.852821	0.819746	0.788031	0.757616	0.728446
17	0.918707	0.880712	0.844377	0.809626	0.776385	0.744586	0.714163
18	0.914136	0.874156	0.836017	0.799631	0.764912	0.731780	0.700159
19	0.909588	0.867649	0.827740	0.789759	0.753607	0.719194	0.686431
20	0.905063	0.861190	0.819544	0.780009	0.742470	0.706825	0.672971
21	0.900560	0.854779	0.811430	0.770379	0.731498	0.694668	0.659776
22	0.896080	0.848416	0.803396	0.760868	0.720688	0.682720	0.646839
23	0.891622	0.842100	0.795442	0.751475	0.710037	0.670978	0.634156
24	0.887186	0.835831	0.787566	0.742197	0.699544	0.659438	0.621721
25	0.882772	0.829609	0.779768	0.733034	0.689206	0.648096	0.609531
26	0.878380	0.823434	0.772048	0.723984	0.679021	0.636950	0.597579
27	0.874010	0.817304	0.764404	0.715046	0.668986	0.625995	0.585862
28	0.869662	0.811220	0.756836	0.706219	0.659099	0.615228	0.574375
29	0.865335	0.805181	0.749342	0.697500	0.649359	0.604647	0.563112
30	0.861030	0.799187	0.741923	0.688889	0.639762	0.594248	0.552071
31	0.856746	0.793238	0.734577	0.680384	0.630308	0.584027	0.541246
32	0.852484	0.787333	0.727304	0.671984	0.620993	0.573982	0.530633
33	0.848242	0.781472	0.720103	0.663688	0.611816	0.564111	0.520229
34	0.844022	0.775654	0.712973	0.655494	0.602774	0.554408	0.510028
35	0.839823	0.769880	0.705914	0.647402	0.593866	0.544873	0.500028
36	0.835645	0.764149	0.698925	0.639409	0.585090	0.535502	0.490223
37	0.831487	0.758461	0.692005	0.631515	0.576443	0.526292	0.480611
38	0.827351	0.752814	0.685153	0.623719	0.567924	0.517240	0.471187
39	0.823235	0.747210	0.678370	0.616019	0.559531	0.508344	0.461948
40	0.819139	0.741648	0.671653	0.608413	0.551262	0.499601	0.452890
41	0.815064	0.736127	0.665003	0.600902	0.543116	0.491008	0.444010
42	0.811009	0.730647	0.658419	0.593484	0.535089	0.482563	0.435304
43	0.806974	0.725208	0.651900	0.586157	0.527182	0.474264	0.426769
44	0.802959	0.719810	0.645445	0.578920	0.519391	0.466107	0.418401
45	0.798964	0.714451	0.639055	0.571773	0.511715	0.458090	0.410197
46	0.794989	0.709133	0.632728	0.564714	0.504153	0.450212	0.402154
47	0.791034	0.703854	0.626463	0.557742	0.496702	0.442469	0.394268
48	0.787098	0.698614	0.620260	0.550856	0.489362	0.434858	0.386538
49	0.783128	0.693414	0.614199	0.544056	0.482130	0.427379	0.378958
50	0.779286	0.688252	0.608039	0.537339	0.475005	0.420029	0.371528

continues

TABLE 5 Present value $(1 + i)^{-n}$ *(continued)*

n	½%	¾%	1%	1¼%	1½%	1¾%	2%
51	0.775409	0.683128	0.602019	0.530705	0.467985	0.412805	0.364243
52	0.771551	0.678043	0.596058	0.524153	0.461069	0.405705	0.357101
53	0.767713	0.672995	0.590156	0.517682	0.454255	0.398727	0.350099
54	0.763893	0.667986	0.584313	0.511291	0.447542	0.391869	0.343234
55	0.760093	0.663013	0.578528	0.504979	0.440928	0.385130	0.336504
56	0.756311	0.658077	0.572800	0.498745	0.434412	0.378506	0.329906
57	0.752548	0.653178	0.567129	0.492587	0.427992	0.371996	0.323437
58	0.748804	0.648316	0.561514	0.486506	0.421667	0.365598	0.317095
59	0.745079	0.643490	0.555954	0.480500	0.415435	0.359310	0.310878
60	0.741372	0.638700	0.550450	0.474568	0.409296	0.353130	0.304782
61	0.737684	0.633945	0.545000	0.468709	0.403247	0.347057	0.298806
62	0.734014	0.629226	0.539604	0.462922	0.397288	0.341088	0.292947
63	0.730362	0.624542	0.534261	0.457207	0.391417	0.335221	0.287203
64	0.726728	0.619893	0.528971	0.451563	0.385632	0.329456	0.281572
65	0.723113	0.615278	0.523734	0.445988	0.379933	0.323790	0.276051
66	0.719515	0.610698	0.518548	0.440482	0.374318	0.318221	0.270638
67	0.715935	0.606152	0.513414	0.435044	0.368787	0.312748	0.265331
68	0.712374	0.601639	0.508331	0.429673	0.363337	0.307369	0.260129
69	0.708829	0.597161	0.503298	0.424368	0.357967	0.302082	0.255028
70	0.705303	0.592715	0.498315	0.419129	0.352677	0.296887	0.250028
71	0.701794	0.588303	0.493381	0.413955	0.347465	0.291781	0.245125
72	0.698302	0.583924	0.488496	0.408844	0.342330	0.286762	0.240319
73	0.694828	0.579577	0.483659	0.403797	0.337271	0.281830	0.235607
74	0.691371	0.575262	0.478871	0.398811	0.332287	0.276983	0.230987
75	0.687932	0.570980	0.474129	0.393888	0.327376	0.272219	0.226458
76	0.684509	0.566730	0.469435	0.389025	0.322538	0.267537	0.222017
77	0.681104	0.562511	0.464787	0.384222	0.317771	0.262936	0.217664
78	0.677715	0.558323	0.460185	0.379479	0.313075	0.258414	0.213396
79	0.674343	0.554167	0.455629	0.374794	0.308448	0.253969	0.209212
80	0.670988	0.550042	0.451118	0.370167	0.303890	0.249601	0.205110
81	0.667650	0.545947	0.446651	0.365597	0.299399	0.245308	0.201088
82	0.664329	0.541883	0.442229	0.361083	0.294975	0.241089	0.197145
83	0.661023	0.537849	0.437851	0.356625	0.290615	0.236943	0.193279
84	0.657735	0.533845	0.433515	0.352223	0.286321	0.232868	0.189490
85	0.654462	0.529871	0.429223	0.347874	0.282089	0.228862	0.185774
86	0.651206	0.525927	0.424974	0.343580	0.277920	0.224926	0.182132
87	0.647967	0.522012	0.420766	0.339338	0.273813	0.221058	0.178560
88	0.644743	0.518126	0.416600	0.335148	0.269767	0.217256	0.175059
89	0.641535	0.514269	0.412475	0.331011	0.265780	0.213519	0.171627
90	0.638344	0.510440	0.408391	0.326924	0.261852	0.209847	0.168261
91	0.635168	0.506641	0.404348	0.322888	0.257982	0.206238	0.164962
92	0.632008	0.502869	0.400344	0.318902	0.254170	0.202691	0.161728
93	0.628863	0.499126	0.396380	0.314965	0.250414	0.199204	0.158556
94	0.625735	0.495410	0.392456	0.311076	0.246713	0.195778	0.155448
95	0.622622	0.491722	0.388570	0.307236	0.243067	0.192411	0.152400
96	0.619524	0.488062	0.384723	0.303443	0.239475	0.189102	0.149411
97	0.616442	0.484428	0.380914	0.299697	0.235936	0.185850	0.146482
98	0.613375	0.480822	0.377142	0.295997	0.232449	0.182653	0.143609
99	0.610323	0.477243	0.373408	0.292342	0.229014	0.179512	0.140794
100	0.607287	0.473690	0.369711	0.288733	0.225629	0.176424	0.138033

TABLE 5 Present value $(1 + i)^{-n}$

n	3%	4%	5%	6%	7%	8%	9%
1	0.970874	0.961538	0.952381	0.943396	0.934579	0.925926	0.917431
2	0.942596	0.924556	0.907029	0.889996	0.873439	0.857339	0.841680
3	0.915142	0.888996	0.863838	0.839619	0.816298	0.793832	0.772183
4	0.888487	0.854804	0.822702	0.792094	0.762895	0.735030	0.708425
5	0.862609	0.821927	0.783526	0.747258	0.712986	0.680583	0.649931
6	0.837484	0.790315	0.746215	0.704961	0.666342	0.630170	0.596267
7	0.813092	0.759918	0.710681	0.665057	0.622750	0.583490	0.547034
8	0.789409	0.730690	0.676839	0.627412	0.582009	0.540269	0.501866
9	0.766417	0.702587	0.644609	0.591898	0.543934	0.500249	0.460428
10	0.744094	0.675564	0.613913	0.558395	0.508349	0.463193	0.422411
11	0.722421	0.649581	0.584679	0.526788	0.475093	0.428883	0.387533
12	0.701380	0.624597	0.556837	0.496969	0.444012	0.397114	0.355535
13	0.680951	0.600574	0.530321	0.468839	0.414964	0.367698	0.326179
14	0.661118	0.577475	0.505068	0.442301	0.387817	0.340461	0.299246
15	0.641862	0.555265	0.481017	0.417265	0.362446	0.315242	0.274538
16	0.623167	0.533908	0.458112	0.393646	0.338735	0.291890	0.251870
17	0.605016	0.513373	0.436297	0.371364	0.316574	0.270269	0.231073
18	0.587395	0.493628	0.415521	0.350344	0.295864	0.250249	0.211994
19	0.570286	0.474642	0.395734	0.330513	0.276508	0.231712	0.194490
20	0.553676	0.456387	0.376889	0.311805	0.258419	0.214548	0.178431
21	0.537549	0.438834	0.358942	0.294155	0.241513	0.198656	0.163698
22	0.521893	0.421955	0.341850	0.277505	0.225713	0.183941	0.150182
23	0.506692	0.405726	0.325571	0.261797	0.210947	0.170315	0.137781
24	0.491934	0.390121	0.310068	0.246979	0.197147	0.157699	0.126405
25	0.477606	0.375117	0.295303	0.232999	0.184249	0.146018	0.115968
26	0.463695	0.360689	0.281241	0.219810	0.172195	0.135202	0.106393
27	0.450189	0.346817	0.267848	0.207368	0.160930	0.125187	0.097608
28	0.437077	0.333477	0.255094	0.195630	0.150402	0.115914	0.089548
29	0.424346	0.320651	0.242946	0.184557	0.140563	0.107328	0.082155
30	0.411987	0.308319	0.231377	0.174110	0.131367	0.099377	0.075371
31	0.399987	0.296460	0.220359	0.164255	0.122773	0.092016	0.069148
32	0.388337	0.285058	0.209866	0.154957	0.114741	0.085200	0.063438
33	0.377026	0.274094	0.199873	0.146186	0.107235	0.078889	0.058200
34	0.366045	0.263552	0.190355	0.137912	0.100219	0.073045	0.053395
35	0.355383	0.253415	0.181290	0.130105	0.093663	0.067635	0.048986
36	0.345032	0.243669	0.172657	0.122741	0.087535	0.062625	0.044941
37	0.334983	0.234297	0.164436	0.115793	0.081809	0.057986	0.041231
38	0.325226	0.225285	0.156605	0.109239	0.076457	0.053690	0.037826
39	0.315754	0.216621	0.149148	0.103056	0.071455	0.049713	0.034703
40	0.306557	0.208289	0.142046	0.097222	0.066780	0.046031	0.031838
41	0.297628	0.200278	0.135282	0.091719	0.062412	0.042621	0.029209
42	0.288959	0.192575	0.128840	0.086527	0.058329	0.039464	0.026797
43	0.280543	0.185168	0.122704	0.081630	0.054513	0.036541	0.024584
44	0.272372	0.178046	0.116861	0.077009	0.050946	0.033834	0.022555
45	0.264439	0.171198	0.111297	0.072650	0.047613	0.031328	0.020692
46	0.256737	0.164614	0.105997	0.068538	0.044499	0.029007	0.018984
47	0.249259	0.158283	0.100949	0.064658	0.041587	0.026859	0.017416
48	0.241999	0.152195	0.096142	0.060998	0.038867	0.024869	0.015978
49	0.234950	0.146341	0.091564	0.057546	0.036324	0.023027	0.014659
50	0.228107	0.140713	0.087204	0.054288	0.033948	0.021321	0.013449

continues

TABLE 5 **Present value** $(1 + i)^{-n}$ *(continued)*

n	3%	4%	5%	6%	7%	8%	9%
51	0.221463	0.135301	0.083051	0.051215	0.031727	0.019742	0.012338
52	0.215013	0.130097	0.079096	0.048316	0.029651	0.018280	0.011319
53	0.208750	0.125093	0.075330	0.045582	0.027711	0.016925	0.010385
54	0.202670	0.120282	0.071743	0.043001	0.025899	0.015672	0.009527
55	0.196767	0.115656	0.068326	0.040567	0.024204	0.014511	0.008741
56	0.191036	0.111207	0.065073	0.038271	0.022621	0.013436	0.008019
57	0.185472	0.106930	0.061974	0.036105	0.021141	0.012441	0.007357
58	0.180070	0.102817	0.059023	0.034061	0.019758	0.011519	0.006749
59	0.174825	0.098863	0.056212	0.032133	0.018465	0.010666	0.006192
60	0.169733	0.095060	0.053536	0.030314	0.017257	0.009876	0.005681
61	0.164789	0.091404	0.050986	0.028598	0.016128	0.009144	0.005212
62	0.159990	0.087889	0.048558	0.026980	0.015073	0.008467	0.004781
63	0.155330	0.084508	0.046246	0.025453	0.014087	0.007840	0.004387
64	0.150806	0.081258	0.044044	0.024012	0.013166	0.007259	0.004024
65	0.146413	0.078133	0.041946	0.022653	0.012304	0.006721	0.003692
66	0.142149	0.075128	0.039949	0.021370	0.011499	0.006223	0.003387
67	0.138009	0.072238	0.038047	0.020161	0.010747	0.005762	0.003108
68	0.133989	0.069460	0.036235	0.019020	0.010044	0.005336	0.002851
69	0.130086	0.066788	0.034509	0.017943	0.009387	0.004940	0.002616
70	0.126297	0.064219	0.032866	0.016927	0.008773	0.004574	0.002400
71	0.122619	0.061749	0.031301	0.015969	0.008199	0.004236	0.002201
72	0.119047	0.059374	0.029811	0.015065	0.007662	0.003922	0.002020
73	0.115580	0.057091	0.028391	0.014213	0.007161	0.003631	0.001853
74	0.112214	0.054895	0.027039	0.013408	0.006693	0.003362	0.001700
75	0.108945	0.052784	0.025752	0.012649	0.006255	0.003113	0.001560
76	0.105772	0.050754	0.024525	0.011933	0.005846	0.002883	0.001431
77	0.102691	0.048801	0.023357	0.011258	0.005463	0.002669	0.001313
78	0.099700	0.046924	0.022245	0.010620	0.005106	0.002471	0.001204
79	0.096796	0.045120	0.021186	0.010019	0.004772	0.002288	0.001105
80	0.093977	0.043384	0.020177	0.009452	0.004460	0.002119	0.001014
81	0.091240	0.041716	0.019216	0.008917	0.004168	0.001962	0.000930
82	0.088582	0.040111	0.018301	0.008412	0.003895	0.001817	0.000853
83	0.086002	0.038569	0.017430	0.007936	0.003640	0.001682	0.000783
84	0.083497	0.037085	0.016600	0.007487	0.003402	0.001557	0.000718
85	0.081065	0.035659	0.015809	0.007063	0.003180	0.001442	0.000659
86	0.078704	0.034287	0.015056	0.006663	0.002972	0.001335	0.000604
87	0.076412	0.032969	0.014339	0.006286	0.002777	0.001236	0.000554
88	0.074186	0.031701	0.013657	0.005930	0.002596	0.001145	0.000509
89	0.072026	0.030481	0.013006	0.005595	0.002426	0.001060	0.000467
90	0.069928	0.029309	0.012387	0.005278	0.002267	0.000981	0.000428
91	0.067891	0.028182	0.011797	0.004979	0.002119	0.000909	0.000393
92	0.065914	0.027098	0.011235	0.004697	0.001980	0.000841	0.000360
93	0.063994	0.026056	0.010700	0.004432	0.001851	0.000779	0.000331
94	0.062130	0.025053	0.010191	0.004181	0.001730	0.000721	0.000303
95	0.060320	0.024090	0.009705	0.003944	0.001616	0.000668	0.000278
96	0.058563	0.023163	0.009243	0.003721	0.001511	0.000618	0.000255
97	0.056858	0.022272	0.008803	0.003510	0.001412	0.000573	0.000234
98	0.055202	0.021416	0.008384	0.003312	0.001319	0.000530	0.000215
99	0.053594	0.020592	0.007985	0.003124	0.001233	0.000491	0.000197
100	0.052033	0.019800	0.007604	0.002947	0.001152	0.000455	0.000181

TABLE 5   Present value $(1 + i)^{-n}$

n	10%	11%	12%	13%	14%	15%	16%
1	0.909091	0.900901	0.892857	0.884956	0.877193	0.869565	0.862069
2	0.826446	0.811622	0.797194	0.783147	0.769468	0.756144	0.743163
3	0.751315	0.731191	0.711780	0.693050	0.674972	0.657516	0.640658
4	0.683013	0.658731	0.635518	0.613319	0.592080	0.571753	0.552291
5	0.620921	0.593451	0.567427	0.542760	0.519369	0.497177	0.476113
6	0.564474	0.534641	0.506631	0.480319	0.455587	0.432328	0.410442
7	0.513158	0.481658	0.452349	0.425061	0.399637	0.375937	0.353830
8	0.466507	0.433926	0.403883	0.376160	0.350559	0.326902	0.305025
9	0.424098	0.390925	0.360610	0.332885	0.307508	0.284262	0.262953
10	0.385543	0.352184	0.321973	0.294588	0.269744	0.247185	0.226684
11	0.350494	0.317283	0.287476	0.260698	0.236617	0.214943	0.195417
12	0.318631	0.285841	0.256675	0.230706	0.207559	0.186907	0.168463
13	0.289664	0.257514	0.229174	0.204165	0.182069	0.162528	0.145227
14	0.263331	0.231995	0.204620	0.180677	0.159710	0.141329	0.125195
15	0.239392	0.209004	0.182696	0.159891	0.140096	0.122894	0.107927
16	0.217629	0.188292	0.163122	0.141496	0.122892	0.106865	0.093041
17	0.197845	0.169633	0.145644	0.125218	0.107800	0.092926	0.080207
18	0.179859	0.152822	0.130040	0.110812	0.094561	0.080805	0.069144
19	0.163508	0.137678	0.116107	0.098064	0.082948	0.070265	0.059607
20	0.148644	0.124034	0.103667	0.086782	0.072762	0.061100	0.051385
21	0.135131	0.111742	0.092560	0.076798	0.063826	0.053131	0.044298
22	0.122846	0.100669	0.082643	0.067963	0.055988	0.046201	0.038188
23	0.111678	0.090693	0.073788	0.060144	0.049112	0.040174	0.032920
24	0.101526	0.081705	0.065882	0.053225	0.043081	0.034934	0.028380
25	0.092296	0.073608	0.058823	0.047102	0.037790	0.030378	0.024465
26	0.083905	0.066314	0.052521	0.041683	0.033149	0.26415	0.021091
27	0.076278	0.059742	0.046894	0.036888	0.029078	0.022970	0.018182
28	0.069343	0.053822	0.041869	0.032644	0.025507	0.019974	0.015674
29	0.063039	0.048488	0.037383	0.028889	0.022375	0.017369	0.013512
30	0.057309	0.043683	0.033378	0.025565	0.019627	0.015103	0.011648
31	0.052099	0.039354	0.029802	0.022624	0.017217	0.013133	0.010042
32	0.047362	0.035454	0.026609	0.020021	0.015102	0.011420	0.008657
33	0.043057	0.031940	0.023758	0.017718	0.013248	0.009931	0.007463
34	0.039143	0.028775	0.021212	0.015680	0.011621	0.008635	0.006433
35	0.035584	0.025924	0.018940	0.013876	0.010194	0.007509	0.005546
36	0.032349	0.023355	0.016910	0.012279	0.008942	0.006529	0.004781
37	0.029408	0.021040	0.015098	0.010867	0.007844	0.005678	0.004121
38	0.026735	0.018955	0.013481	0.009617	0.006880	0.004937	0.003553
39	0.024304	0.017077	0.012036	0.008510	0.006035	0.004293	0.003063
40	0.022095	0.015384	0.010747	0.007531	0.005294	0.003733	0.002640
41	0.020086	0.013860	0.009595	0.006665	0.004644	0.003246	0.002276
42	0.018260	0.012486	0.008567	0.005898	0.004074	0.002823	0.001962
43	0.016600	0.011249	0.007649	0.005219	0.003573	0.002455	0.001692
44	0.015091	0.010134	0.006830	0.004619	0.003135	0.002134	0.001458
45	0.013719	0.009130	0.006098	0.004088	0.002750	0.001856	0.001257
46	0.012472	0.008225	0.005445	0.003617	0.002412	0.001614	0.001084
47	0.011338	0.007410	0.004861	0.003201	0.002116	0.001403	0.000934
48	0.010307	0.006676	0.004340	0.002833	0.001856	0.001220	0.000805
49	0.009370	0.006014	0.003875	0.002507	0.001628	0.001061	0.000694
50	0.008519	0.005418	0.003460	0.002219	0.001428	0.000923	0.000599

TABLE 6   Amount of an annuity $s_{\overline{n}|i} = \dfrac{(1 + i)^n - 1}{i}$

n	½%	¾%	1%	1¼%	1½%	1¾%	2%
1	1.000000	1.000000	1.000000	1.000000	1.000000	1.000000	1.000000
2	2.005000	2.007500	2.010000	2.012500	2.015000	2.017500	2.020000
3	3.015025	3.022556	3.030100	3.037656	3.045225	3.052806	0.060400
4	4.030100	4.045225	4.060401	4.075627	4.090903	4.106230	4.121608
5	5.050251	5.075565	5.101005	5.126572	5.152267	5.178089	5.204040
6	6.075502	6.113631	6.152015	6.190654	6.229551	6.268706	6.308121
7	7.105879	7.159484	7.213535	7.268038	7.322994	7.378408	7.434283
8	8.141409	8.213180	8.285671	8.358888	8.432839	8.507530	8.582969
9	9.182116	9.274779	9.368527	9.463374	9.559332	9.656412	9.754628
10	10.228026	10.344339	10.462213	10.581666	10.702722	10.825399	10.949721
11	11.279167	11.421922	11.566835	11.713937	11.863262	12.014844	12.168715
12	12.335562	12.507586	12.682503	12.860361	13.041211	13.225104	13.412090
13	13.397240	13.601393	13.809328	14.021116	14.236830	14.456543	14.680332
14	14.464226	14.703404	14.947421	15.196380	15.450382	15.709533	15.973938
15	15.536548	15.813679	16.096896	16.386335	16.682138	16.984449	17.293417
16	16.614230	16.932282	17.257864	17.591164	17.932370	18.281677	18.639285
17	17.697301	18.059274	18.430443	18.811053	19.201355	19.601607	20.012071
18	18.785788	19.194718	19.614748	20.046192	20.489376	20.944635	21.412312
19	19.879717	20.338679	20.810895	21.296769	21.796716	22.311166	22.840559
20	20.979115	21.491219	22.019004	22.562979	23.123667	23.701611	24.297370
21	22.084011	22.652403	23.239194	23.845016	24.470522	25.116389	25.783317
22	23.194431	23.822296	24.471586	25.143078	25.837580	26.555926	27.298984
23	24.310403	25.000963	25.716302	26.457367	27.225144	28.020655	28.844963
24	25.431955	26.188471	26.973465	27.788084	28.633521	29.511016	30.421862
25	26.559115	27.384884	28.243200	29.135435	30.063024	31.027459	32.030300
26	27.691911	28.590271	29.525631	30.499628	31.513969	32.570440	33.670906
27	28.830370	29.804698	30.820888	31.880873	32.986678	34.140422	35.344324
28	29.974522	31.028233	32.129097	33.279384	34.481479	35.737880	37.051210
29	31.124395	32.260945	33.450388	34.695377	35.998701	37.363293	38.792235
30	32.280017	33.502902	34.784892	36.129069	37.538681	39.017150	40.568079
31	33.441417	34.754174	36.132740	37.580682	39.101762	40.699950	42.379441
32	34.608624	36.014830	37.494068	39.050441	40.688288	42.412200	44.227030
33	35.781667	37.284941	38.869009	40.538571	42.298612	44.154413	46.111570
34	36.960575	38.564578	40.257699	42.045303	43.933092	45.927115	48.033802
35	38.145378	39.853813	41.660276	43.570870	45.592088	47.730840	49.994478
36	39.336105	41.152716	43.076878	45.115505	47.275969	49.566129	51.994367
37	40.532785	42.461361	44.507647	46.679449	48.985109	51.433537	54.034255
38	41.735449	43.779822	45.952724	48.262942	50.719885	53.333624	56.114940
39	42.944127	45.108170	47.412251	49.866229	52.480684	55.266962	58.237238
40	44.158847	46.446482	48.886373	51.489557	54.267894	57.234134	60.401983
41	45.379642	47.794830	50.375237	53.133177	56.081912	59.235731	62.610023
42	46.606540	49.153291	51.878989	54.797341	57.923141	61.272357	64.862223
43	47.839572	50.521941	53.397779	56.482308	59.791988	63.344623	67.159468
44	49.078770	51.900856	54.931757	58.188337	61.688868	65.453154	69.502657
45	50.324164	53.290112	56.481075	59.915691	63.614201	67.598584	71.892710
46	51.575785	54.689788	58.045885	61.664637	65.568414	69.781559	74.330564
47	52.833664	56.099961	59.626344	63.435445	67.551940	72.002736	76.817176

continues

TABLE 6 Amount of an annuity $s_{\overline{n}|i} = \dfrac{(1 + i)^n - 1}{i}$ (continued)

n	½%	¾%	1%	1¼%	1½%	1¾%	2%
48	54.097832	57.520711	61.222608	65.228388	69.565219	74.262784	79.353519
49	55.368321	58.952116	62.834834	67.043743	71.608698	76.562383	81.940490
50	56.645163	60.394257	64.463182	68.881790	73.682828	78.902225	84.579401
51	57.928389	61.847214	66.107814	70.742812	75.788070	81.283014	87.270989
52	59.218031	63.311068	67.768892	72.627097	77.924892	83.705466	90.016409
53	60.514121	64.785901	69.446581	74.534936	80.093765	86.170312	92.816737
54	61.816692	66.271796	71.141047	76.466623	82.295171	88.678292	95.673072
55	63.125775	67.768834	72.852457	78.422456	84.529599	91.230163	98.586534
56	64.441404	69.277100	74.580982	80.402736	86.797543	93.826690	101.558264
57	65.763611	70.796679	76.326792	82.407771	89.099506	96.468658	104.589430
58	67.092429	72.327654	78.090060	84.437868	91.435999	99.156859	107.681218
59	68.427891	73.870111	79.870960	86.493341	93.807539	101.892104	110.834843
60	69.770031	75.424137	81.669670	88.574508	96.214652	104.675216	114.051539
61	71.118881	76.989818	83.486367	90.681689	98.657871	107.507032	117.332570
62	72.474475	78.567242	85.321280	92.815210	101.137740	110.388405	120.679222
63	73.836847	80.156496	87.174443	94.975400	103.654806	113.320202	124.092806
64	75.206032	81.757670	89.046187	97.162593	106.209628	116.303306	127.574662
65	76.582062	83.370852	90.936649	99.377125	108.802772	119.338614	131.126155
66	77.964972	84.996134	92.846015	101.619339	111.434814	122.427039	134.748679
67	79.354797	86.633605	94.774475	103.889581	114.106336	125.659513	138.443652
68	80.751571	88.283357	96.722220	106.188201	116.817931	128.766979	142.212525
69	82.155329	89.945482	98.689442	108.515553	119.570200	132.020401	146.056776
70	83.566105	91.620073	100.676337	110.871998	122.363753	135.330758	149.977911
71	84.983936	93.307223	102.683100	113.257898	125.199209	138.699047	153.977469
72	86.408856	95.007028	104.709931	115.673621	128.077197	142.126280	158.057019
73	87.840900	96.719580	106.757031	118.119542	130.998355	145.613490	162.218159
74	89.280104	98.444977	108.824601	120.596036	133.963331	149.161726	166.462522
75	90.726505	100.183314	110.912847	123.103486	136.972781	152.772056	170.791773
76	92.180138	101.934689	113.021975	125.642280	140.027372	156.445567	175.207608
77	93.641038	103.699199	115.152195	128.212809	143.127783	160.183364	179.711760
78	95.109243	105.476943	117.303717	130.815469	146.274700	163.986573	184.305996
79	95.584790	107.268021	119.476754	133.450662	149.468820	167.856338	188.992115
80	98.067714	109.072531	121.671522	136.118795	152.710852	171.793824	193.771958
81	99.558052	110.890575	123.888237	138.820280	156.001515	175.800216	198.647397
82	101.055842	112.722254	126.127119	141.555534	159.341538	179.876720	203.620345
83	102.561122	114.567671	128.388390	144.324978	162.731661	184.024563	208.692752
84	104.073927	116.426928	130.672274	147.129040	166.172636	188.244992	213.866607
85	105.594297	118.300130	132.978997	149.968153	169.665226	192.539280	219.143939
86	107.122268	120.187381	135.308787	152.842755	173.210204	196.908717	224.526818
87	108.657880	122.088787	137.661875	155.753289	176.808357	201.354620	230.017354
88	110.201169	124.004453	140.038494	158.700206	180.460482	205.878326	235.617701
89	111.752175	125.934486	142.438879	161.683958	184.167390	210.481196	241.330055
90	113.310936	127.878995	144.863267	164.705008	187.929900	215.164617	247.156656
91	114.877490	129.838087	147.311900	167.763820	191.748849	219.929998	253.099789
92	116.451878	131.811873	149.785019	170.860868	195.625082	224.778773	259.161785
93	118.034137	133.800462	152.282869	173.996629	199.559458	229.712401	265.345021
94	119.624308	135.803965	154.805698	177.171587	203.552850	234.732369	271.651921

continues

TABLE 6 Amount of an annuity $s_{\overline{n}|i} = \dfrac{(1 + i)^n - 1}{i}$ *(continued)*

n	½%	¾%	1%	1¼%	1½%	1¾%	2%
95	121.222430	137.822495	157.353755	180.386232	207.606142	239.840185	278.084960
96	122.828542	139.856164	159.927293	183.641059	211.720235	245.037388	284.646659
97	124.442684	141.905085	162.526565	186.936573	215.896038	250.325542	291.339592
98	126.064898	143.969373	165.151831	190.273280	220.134479	255.706239	298.166384
99	127.695222	146.049143	167.803349	193.651696	224.436496	261.181099	305.129712
100	129.333698	148.144512	170.481383	197.072342	228.803043	266.751768	312.232306

TABLE 6 Amount of an annuity $s_{\overline{n}|i} = \dfrac{(1 + i)^n - 1}{i}$

n	3%	4%	5%	6%	7%	8%	9%
1	1.000000	1.000000	1.000000	1.000000	1.000000	1.000000	1.000000
2	2.030000	2.040000	2.050000	2.060000	2.070000	2.080000	2.090000
3	3.090900	3.121600	3.152500	3.183600	3.214900	3.246400	3.278100
4	4.183627	4.246464	4.310125	4.374616	4.439943	4.506112	4.573129
5	5.309136	5.416323	5.525631	5.637093	5.750739	5.866601	5.984711
6	6.468410	6.632975	6.801913	6.975319	7.153291	7.335929	7.523335
7	7.662462	7.898294	8.142008	8.393838	8.654021	8.922803	9.200435
8	8.892336	9.214226	9.549109	9.897468	10.259803	10.636628	11.028474
9	10.159106	10.582795	11.026564	11.491316	11.977989	12.487558	13.021036
10	11.463879	12.006107	12.577893	13.180795	13.816448	14.486562	15.192930
11	12.807796	13.486351	14.206787	14.971643	15.783599	16.645487	17.560293
12	14.192030	15.025805	15.917127	16.869941	17.888451	18.977126	20.140720
13	15.617790	16.626838	17.712983	18.882138	20.140643	21.495297	22.953385
14	17.086324	18.291911	19.598632	21.015066	22.550488	24.214920	26.019189
15	18.598914	20.023588	21.578564	23.275970	25.129022	27.152114	29.360916
16	20.156881	21.824531	23.657492	25.672528	27.888054	30.324483	33.003399
17	21.761588	23.697512	25.840366	28.212880	30.840217	33.750226	36.973705
18	23.414435	25.645413	28.132385	30.905653	33.999033	37.450244	41.301338
19	25.116868	27.671229	30.539004	33.759992	37.378965	41.446263	46.018458
20	26.870374	29.778079	33.065954	36.785591	40.995492	45.761964	51.160120
21	28.676486	31.969202	35.719252	39.992727	44.865177	50.422921	56.764530
22	30.536780	34.247970	38.505214	43.392290	49.005739	55.456755	62.873338
23	32.452884	36.617889	41.430475	46.995828	53.436141	60.893296	69.531939
24	34.426470	39.082604	44.501999	50.815577	58.176671	66.764759	76.789813
25	36.459264	41.645908	47.727099	54.864512	63.249038	73.105940	84.700896
26	38.553042	44.311745	51.113454	59.156383	68.676470	79.954415	93.323977
27	40.709634	47.084214	54.669126	63.705766	74.483823	87.350768	102.723135
28	42.930923	49.967583	58.402583	68.528112	80.697691	95.338830	112.968217
29	45.218850	52.966286	62.322712	73.639798	87.346529	103.965936	124.135356
30	47.575416	56.084938	66.438848	79.058186	94.460786	113.283211	136.307539
31	50.002678	59.328335	70.760790	84.801677	102.073041	123.345868	149.575217
32	52.502759	62.701469	75.298829	80.889778	110.218154	134.213537	164.036987
33	55.077841	66.209527	80.063771	97.343165	118.933425	145.950620	179.800315
34	57.530177	69.857909	85.066959	104.183755	128.258765	158.626670	196.982344
35	60.462082	73.652225	90.320307	111.434780	138.236878	172.316804	215.710755

continues

TABLE 6 Amount of an annuity $s_{\overline{n}|i} = \dfrac{(1 + i)^n - 1}{i}$ *(continued)*

n	3%	4%	5%	6%	7%	8%	9%
36	63.275944	77.598314	95.836323	119.120867	148.913460	187.102148	236.124723
37	66.174223	81.702246	101.628139	127.268119	160.337402	203.070320	258.375948
38	69.159449	85.970336	107.709546	135.904206	172.561020	220.315945	282.629783
39	72.234233	90.409150	114.095023	145.058458	185.640292	238.941221	309.066463
40	75.401260	95.025516	120.799774	154.761966	199.635112	259.056519	337.882445
41	78.663298	99.826536	127.839763	165.047684	214.609570	280.781040	369.291865
42	82.023196	104.819598	135.231751	175.950545	230.632240	304.243523	403.528133
43	85.483892	110.012382	142.993339	187.507577	247.776496	329.583005	440.845665
44	89.048409	115.412877	151.143006	199.758032	266.120851	356.949646	481.521775
45	92.719861	121.029392	159.700156	212.743514	285.749311	386.505617	525.858734
46	96.501457	126.870568	168.685164	226.508125	306.751763	418.426067	574.186021
47	100.396501	132.945390	178.119422	241.098612	329.224386	452.900152	626.862762
48	104.408396	139.263206	188.025393	256.564529	353.270093	490.132164	684.280411
49	108.540648	145.833734	198.426663	272.958401	378.999000	530.342737	746.865648
50	112.796867	152.667084	209.347996	290.335905	406.528929	573.770156	815.083556

TABLE 6 Amount of an annuity $s_{\overline{n}|i} = \dfrac{(1 + i)^n - 1}{i}$

n	10%	11%	12%	13%	14%	15%
1	1.000000	1.000000	1.000000	1.000000	1.000000	1.000000
2	2.100000	2.110000	2.120000	2.130000	2.140000	2.150000
3	3.310000	3.342100	3.374400	3.406900	3.439600	3.472500
4	4.641000	4.709731	4.779328	4.849797	4.921144	4.993375
5	6.105100	6.227801	6.352847	6.480271	6.610104	6.742381
6	7.715610	7.912860	8.115189	8.322706	8.535519	8.753738
7	9.487171	9.732274	10.089012	10.404658	10.730491	11.066799
8	11.435888	11.859434	12.299693	12.757263	13.232760	13.726819
9	13.579477	14.163972	14.775656	15.415707	16.805347	16.785842
10	15.937425	16.722009	17.548735	18.419749	19.337295	20.303718
11	18.531167	19.561430	20.654583	21.814317	23.044516	24.349276
12	21.384284	22.713187	24.133133	25.650178	27.270749	29.001667
13	24.522712	26.211638	28.029109	29.984701	32.088654	34.351917
14	27.974983	30.094918	32.392602	34.882712	37.581065	40.504705
15	31.772482	34.405359	37.279715	40.417464	43.842414	47.580411
16	35.949730	39.189948	42.753280	46.671735	50.980352	55.717472
17	40.544703	44.500843	48.883674	53.739060	59.117601	65.075093
18	45.599173	50.395936	55.749715	61.725138	68.394066	75.836357
19	51.159090	56.939488	63.439681	70.749406	78.969235	88.211811
20	57.274999	64.202832	72.052442	80.946829	91.024928	102.443583
21	64.002499	72.265144	81.698736	92.469917	104.768418	118.810120
22	71.402749	81.214309	92.502584	105.491006	120.435996	137.631638
23	79.543024	91.147884	104.602894	120.204837	138.297035	159.276384
24	88.497327	102.174151	118.155241	136.831465	158.658620	184.167841
25	98.347059	114.413307	133.333870	155.619556	181.870827	212.793017

continues

TABLE 6 Amount of an annuity $s_{\overline{n}|i} = \dfrac{(1 + i)^n - 1}{i}$ *(continued)*

n	10%	11%	12%	13%	14%	15%
26	109.181765	127.998771	150.333934	176.850098	208.332743	245.711970
27	121.099942	143.078636	169.374007	200.840611	238.499327	283.568766
28	134.209936	159.817286	190.698887	227.949890	272.889233	327.104080
29	148.630930	178.397187	214.582754	258.583376	312.093725	377.169693
30	164.494023	199.020878	241.332684	293.199215	356.786847	434.745146
31	181.943425	221.913174	271.292606	332.315113	407.737006	500.956918
32	201.137767	247.323624	304.847719	376.516078	465.820186	577.100456
33	222.251544	275.529222	342.429446	426.463168	532.035012	664.665524
34	245.476699	306.837437	384.520979	482.903380	607.519914	765.365353
35	271.024368	341.589555	431.663496	546.680819	693.572702	881.170156
36	299.126805	380.164406	484.463116	618.749325	791.672881	1014.345680
37	330.039486	422.982490	543.598690	700.186738	903.507084	1167.497532
38	364.043434	470.510564	609.830533	792.211014	1030.998076	1343.622161
39	401.447778	523.266726	684.010197	896.198445	1176.337806	1546.165485
40	442.592556	581.826066	767.091420	1013.704243	1342.025099	1779.090308
41	487.851811	646.826934	860.142391	1146.485795	1530.908613	2046.953854
42	537.636992	718.977896	964.359478	1296.528948	1746.235819	2354.996933
43	592.400692	799.065465	1081.082615	1466.077712	1991.708833	2709.246473
44	652.640761	887.962666	1211.812529	1657.667814	2271.548070	3116.633443
45	718.904837	986.638559	1358.230032	1874.164630	2590.564800	3585.128460
46	791.795321	1096.168801	1522.217636	2118.806032	2954.243872	4123.897729
47	871.974853	1217.747369	1705.883752	2395.250816	3368.838014	4743.482388
48	960.172338	1352.699580	1911.589803	2707.633422	3841.475336	5456.004746
49	1057.189572	1502.496533	2141.980579	3060.625767	4380.281883	6275.405458
50	1163.908529	1668.771152	2400.018249	3459.507117	4994.521346	7217.716277

TABLE 7 Present value of an annuity $a_{\overline{n}|i} = \dfrac{1 - (1 + i)^{-n}}{i}$

n	½%	¾%	1%	1¼%	1½%	1¾%	2%
1	0.995025	0.992556	0.990099	0.987654	0.985222	0.982801	0.980392
2	1.985099	1.977723	1.970395	1.963115	1.955883	1.948699	1.941561
3	2.970248	2.955556	2.940985	2.926534	2.912200	2.897984	2.883883
4	3.950496	3.926110	3.901966	3.878058	3.854385	3.830943	3.807729
5	4.925866	4.889440	4.853431	4.817835	4.782645	4.747855	4.713460
6	5.896384	5.845598	5.795476	5.746010	5.697187	5.688998	5.601431
7	6.862074	6.794638	6.728195	6.662726	6.598214	6.534641	6.471991
8	7.822959	7.736613	7.651678	7.568124	7.485925	7.405053	7.325481
9	8.779064	8.671576	8.566018	8.462345	8.360517	8.260494	8.162237
10	9.730412	9.599580	9.471305	9.345526	9.222185	9.101223	8.982585
11	10.677027	10.520675	10.367628	10.217803	10.071118	9.927492	9.786848
12	11.618932	11.434913	11.255077	11.079312	10.907505	10.739550	10.575341
13	12.556151	12.342345	12.133740	11.930185	11.731532	11.537641	11.348374
14	13.488708	13.243022	13.003703	12.770553	12.543382	12.322006	12.106249
15	14.416625	14.136995	13.865053	13.600546	13.343233	13.092880	12.849264
16	15.339925	15.024313	14.717874	14.420292	14.131264	13.850497	13.577709

continues

TABLE 7 Present value of an annuity $a_{\overline{n}|i} = \dfrac{1 - (1 + i)^{-n}}{i}$ (continued)

n	½%	¾%	1%	1¼%	1½%	1¾%	2%
17	16.258632	15.905025	15.562251	15.229918	14.907649	14.595083	14.291872
18	17.172768	16.779181	16.398269	16.029549	15.672561	15.326863	14.992031
19	18.082356	17.646830	17.226008	16.819308	16.426168	16.046057	15.678462
20	18.987419	18.508020	18.045553	17.599316	17.168639	16.752881	16.351433
21	19.887979	19.362799	18.856983	18.369695	17.900137	17.447549	17.011209
22	20.784059	20.211215	19.660379	19.130563	18.620824	18.130269	17.658048
23	21.675681	21.053315	20.455821	19.882037	19.330861	18.801248	18.292204
24	22.562866	21.889146	21.243387	20.624235	20.030405	19.460686	18.913926
25	23.445638	22.718755	22.023156	21.357269	20.719611	20.108782	19.523456
26	24.324018	23.542189	22.795204	22.081253	21.398632	20.745732	20.121036
27	25.198028	24.359493	23.559608	22.796299	22.067617	21.371726	20.706898
28	26.067689	25.170713	24.316443	23.502518	22.726717	21.986955	21.281272
29	26.933024	25.975893	25.065785	24.200018	23.376076	22.591602	21.844385
30	27.794054	26.775080	25.807708	24.888906	24.015838	23.185849	22.396456
31	28.650800	27.568318	26.542285	25.569290	24.646146	23.769877	22.937702
32	29.503284	28.355650	27.269589	26.241274	25.267139	24.343859	23.468335
33	30.351526	29.137122	27.989693	26.904962	25.878954	24.907970	23.988564
34	31.195548	29.912776	28.702666	27.560456	26.481728	25.462378	24.498592
35	32.035371	30.682656	29.408580	28.207858	27.075595	26.007251	24.998619
36	32.871016	31.446805	30.107505	28.847267	27.660684	26.542753	25.488842
37	33.702504	32.205266	30.799510	29.478783	28.237127	27.069045	25.969453
38	34.529854	32.958080	31.484663	30.102501	28.805052	27.586285	26.440641
39	35.353089	33.705290	32.163033	30.718520	29.364583	28.094629	26.902589
40	36.172228	34.446938	32.834686	31.326933	29.915845	28.594230	27.355479
41	36.987291	35.183065	33.499689	31.927835	30.458961	29.085238	27.799489
42	37.798300	35.913713	34.158108	32.521319	30.994050	29.567801	28.234794
43	38.605274	36.638921	34.810008	33.017475	31.521232	30.042065	28.661562
44	39.408232	37.358730	35.455454	33.686395	32.040622	30.508172	29.079963
45	40.207196	38.073181	36.094508	34.258168	32.552337	30.966263	29.490160
46	41.002185	38.782314	36.727236	34.822882	33.056490	31.416474	29.892314
47	41.793219	39.486168	37.353699	35.380624	33.553192	31.858943	30.286582
48	42.580318	40.184782	37.973959	35.931481	34.042554	32.293801	30.673120
49	43.363500	40.878195	38.588079	36.475537	34.524683	32.721181	31.052078
50	44.142786	41.566447	39.196118	37.012876	34.999688	33.141209	31.423606
51	44.918195	42.249575	39.798136	37.543581	35.467673	33.554014	31.787849
52	45.689747	42.927618	40.394194	38.067734	35.928742	33.959719	32.144950
53	46.457459	43.600614	40.984351	38.585417	36.382997	34.358446	32.495049
54	47.221353	44.268599	41.568664	39.096708	36.830539	34.750316	32.838283
55	47.981445	44.931612	42.147192	39.601687	37.271467	35.135445	33.174788
56	48.737757	45.589689	42.719992	40.100431	37.705879	35.513951	33.504694
57	49.490305	46.242868	43.287121	40.593019	38.133871	35.885947	33.828131
58	50.239109	46.891184	43.848635	41.079524	38.555538	36.251545	34.145226
59	50.984189	47.534674	44.404589	41.560024	38.970973	36.610855	34.456104
60	51.725561	48.173374	44.955038	42.034592	39.380269	36.963986	34.760887
61	52.463245	48.807319	45.500038	42.503301	39.783516	37.311042	35.059693
62	53.197258	49.436545	46.039642	42.966223	40.180804	37.652130	35.352640
63	53.927620	50.061086	46.573903	43.423430	40.572221	37.987351	35.639843
64	54.654348	50.680979	47.102874	43.874992	40.957853	38.316807	35.921415

continues

TABLE 7 Present value of an annuity $a_{\overline{n}|i} = \dfrac{1 - (1 + i)^{-n}}{i}$ *(continued)*

n	½%	¾%	1%	1¼%	1½%	1¾%	2%
65	55.377461	51.296257	47.626608	44.320980	41.337786	38.640597	36.197466
66	56.096976	51.906955	48.145156	44.761462	41.712105	38.958817	36.468103
67	56.812912	52.513107	48.658571	45.196506	42.080891	39.271565	36.733435
68	57.525285	53.114746	49.166901	45.626178	42.444228	39.578934	36.993564
69	58.234115	53.711907	49.670199	46.050547	42.802195	39.881016	37.248592
70	58.939418	54.304622	50.168514	46.469676	43.154872	40.177903	37.498619
71	59.641212	54.892925	50.661895	46.883630	43.502337	40.469683	37.743744
72	60.339514	55.476849	51.150391	47.292474	43.844667	40.756445	37.984063
73	61.034342	56.056426	51.634051	47.696271	44.181938	41.038276	38.219670
74	61.725714	56.631688	52.112922	48.095082	44.514224	41.315259	38.450657
75	62.413645	57.202668	52.587051	48.488970	44.841600	41.587478	38.677114
76	63.098155	57.769397	53.056486	48.877995	45.164138	41.855015	38.899132
77	63.779258	58.331908	53.521274	49.262218	45.481910	42.117951	39.116796
78	64.456973	58.890231	53.981459	49.641696	45.794985	42.376364	39.330192
79	65.131317	59.444398	54.437088	50.016490	46.103433	42.630334	39.539404
80	65.802305	59.994440	54.888206	50.386657	46.407323	42.879935	39.744514
81	66.469956	60.540387	55.334858	50.752254	46.706723	43.125243	39.945602
82	67.134284	61.082270	55.777087	51.113337	47.001697	43.366332	40.142747
83	67.795308	61.620119	56.214937	51.469963	47.292313	43.603275	40.336026
84	68.453042	62.153965	56.648453	51.822185	47.578633	43.836142	40.525516
85	69.107505	62.683836	57.077676	52.170060	47.860722	44.065005	40.711290
86	69.758711	63.209763	57.502650	52.513639	48.138643	44.289931	40.893422
87	70.406678	63.731774	57.923415	52.852977	48.412456	44.510989	41.071982
88	71.051421	64.249900	58.340015	53.188125	48.682222	44.728244	41.247041
89	71.692956	64.764169	58.752490	53.519136	48.948002	44.941764	41.418668
90	72.331300	65.274609	59.160881	53.846060	49.209855	45.151610	41.586929
91	72.966467	65.781250	59.565229	54.168948	49.467837	45.357848	41.751891
92	73.598475	66.284119	59.965573	54.487850	49.722007	45.560539	41.913619
93	74.227338	66.783245	60.361954	54.802815	49.972421	45.759743	42.072175
94	74.853073	67.278655	60.754410	55.113892	50.219134	45.955521	42.227623
95	75.475694	67.770377	61.142980	55.421127	50.462201	46.147933	42.380023
96	76.095218	68.258439	61.527703	55.724570	50.701675	46.337035	42.529434
97	76.711660	68.742867	61.908617	56.024267	50.937611	46.522884	42.675916
98	77.325035	69.223689	62.285759	56.320264	51.170060	46.705537	42.819525
99	77.935358	69.700932	62.659168	56.612606	51.399074	46.885049	42.960319
100	78.542645	70.174623	63.028879	56.901339	51.624704	47.061473	43.098352

TABLE 7 Present value of an annuity $a_{\overline{n}|i} = \dfrac{1 - (1 + i)^{-n}}{i}$

n	3%	4%	5%	6%	7%	8%	9%
1	0.970874	0.961538	0.952381	0.943396	0.934579	0.925926	0.917431
2	1.913470	1.886095	1.859410	1.833393	1.808018	1.783265	1.759111
3	2.828611	2.775091	2.723248	2.673012	2.624316	2.577097	2.531295
4	3.717098	3.629895	3.545951	3.465106	3.387211	3.312127	3.239720

continues

TABLE 7 Present value of an annuity $a_{\overline{n}|i} = \dfrac{1 - (1 + i)^{-n}}{i}$ *(continued)*

n	3%	4%	5%	6%	7%	8%	9%
5	4.579707	4.451822	4.329477	4.212364	4.100197	3.992710	3.889651
6	5.417191	5.242137	5.075692	4.917324	4.766540	4.622880	4.485919
7	6.230283	6.002055	5.786373	5.582381	5.389289	5.206370	5.032953
8	7.019692	6.732745	6.463213	6.209794	5.971299	5.746639	5.534819
9	7.786109	7.435332	7.107822	6.801692	6.515232	6.246888	5.995247
10	8.530203	8.110896	7.721735	7.360087	7.023582	6.710081	6.417658
11	9.252624	8.760477	8.306414	7.886875	7.498674	7.138964	6.805191
12	9.954004	9.385074	8.863252	8.383844	7.942686	7.536078	7.160725
13	10.634955	9.985648	9.393573	8.852683	8.357651	7.903776	7.486904
14	11.296073	10.563123	9.898641	9.294984	8.745468	8.244237	7.786150
15	11.937935	11.118387	10.379658	9.712249	9.107914	8.559479	8.060688
16	12.561102	11.652296	10.837770	10.105895	9.446649	8.851369	8.312558
17	13.166118	12.165669	11.274066	10.477260	9.763223	9.121638	8.543631
18	13.753513	12.659297	11.689587	10.827603	10.059087	9.371887	8.755625
19	14.323799	13.133939	12.085321	11.158116	10.335595	9.603599	8.950115
20	14.877475	13.590326	12.462210	11.469921	10.594014	9.818147	9.128546
21	15.415024	14.029160	12.821153	11.764077	10.835527	10.016803	9.292244
22	15.936917	14.451115	13.163003	12.041582	11.061240	10.200744	9.442425
23	16.443608	14.856842	13.488574	12.303379	11.272187	10.371059	9.580207
24	16.935542	15.246963	13.798642	12.550358	11.469334	10.528758	9.706612
25	17.413148	15.622080	14.093945	12.783356	11.653583	10.674776	9.822580
26	17.876842	15.982769	14.375185	13.003166	11.825779	10.809978	9.928972
27	18.327031	16.329586	14.643034	13.210534	11.986709	10.935165	10.026580
28	18.764108	16.663063	14.898127	13.406164	12.137111	11.051078	10.116128
29	19.188455	16.983715	15.141074	13.590721	12.277674	11.158406	10.198283
30	19.600441	17.292033	15.372451	13.764831	12.409041	11.257783	10.273654
31	20.000428	17.588494	15.592811	13.929086	12.531814	11.349799	10.342802
32	20.388766	17.873551	15.802677	14.084043	12.646555	11.434999	10.406240
33	20.765792	18.147646	16.002549	14.230230	12.753790	11.513888	10.464441
34	21.131837	18.411198	16.192904	14.368141	12.854009	11.586934	10.517835
35	21.487220	18.664613	16.374194	14.498246	12.947672	11.654568	10.566821
36	21.832252	18.908282	16.546852	14.620987	13.035208	11.717193	10.611763
37	22.167235	19.142579	16.711287	14.736780	13.117017	11.775179	10.652993
38	22.492462	19.367864	16.867893	14.846019	13.193473	11.828869	10.690820
39	22.808215	19.584485	17.017041	14.949075	13.264928	11.878582	10.725523
40	23.114772	19.792774	17.159086	15.046297	13.331709	11.924613	10.757360
41	23.412400	19.993052	17.294368	15.138016	13.394120	11.967235	10.786569
42	23.701359	20.185627	17.423208	15.224543	13.452449	12.006699	10.813366
43	23.981902	20.370795	17.545912	15.306173	13.506962	12.043240	10.837950
44	24.254274	20.548841	17.662773	15.383182	13.557908	12.077074	10.860505
45	24.518713	20.720040	17.774070	15.455832	13.605522	12.108402	10.881197
46	24.775449	20.884654	17.880066	15.524370	13.650020	12.137409	10.900181
47	25.024708	21.042936	17.981016	15.589028	13.691608	12.164267	10.917597
48	25.266707	21.195131	18.077158	15.650027	13.730474	12.189136	10.933575
49	25.501657	21.341472	18.168722	15.707572	13.766799	12.212163	10.948234
50	25.729764	21.482185	18.255925	15.761861	13.800746	12.233485	10.961683
51	25.951227	21.617485	18.338977	15.813076	13.832473	12.253227	10.974021

continues

TABLE 7 Present value of an annuity $a_{\overline{n}|i} = \dfrac{1 - (1 + i)^{-n}}{i}$ (continued)

n	3%	4%	5%	6%	7%	8%	9%
52	26.166240	21.747582	18.418073	15.861393	13.862124	12.271506	10.985340
53	26.374990	21.872675	18.493403	15.906974	13.889836	12.288432	10.995725
54	26.577660	21.992957	18.565146	15.949976	13.915735	12.304103	11.005252
55	26.774428	22.108612	18.633472	15.990543	13.939939	12.318614	11.013993
56	26.965464	22.219819	18.698545	16.028814	13.962560	12.332050	11.022012
57	27.150936	22.326749	18.760519	16.064919	13.983701	12.344491	11.029369
58	27.331005	22.429567	18.819542	16.098980	14.003458	12.356010	11.036118
59	27.505831	22.528430	18.875754	16.131113	14.021924	12.366676	11.042310
60	27.675564	22.623490	18.929290	16.161428	14.039181	12.376552	11.047991
61	27.840353	22.714894	18.980276	16.190026	14.055309	12.385696	11.053203
62	28.000343	22.802783	19.028834	16.217006	14.070383	12.394163	11.057984
63	28.155673	22.887291	19.075080	16.242458	14.084470	12.402003	11.062371
64	28.306478	22.968549	19.119124	16.266470	14.097635	12.409262	11.066395
65	28.452892	23.046682	19.161070	16.289123	14.109940	12.415983	11.070087
66	28.595040	23.121810	19.201019	16.310493	14.121439	12.422207	11.073475
67	28.733049	23.194048	19.239066	16.330654	14.132186	12.427969	11.076582
68	28.867038	23.263507	19.275301	16.349673	14.142230	12.433305	11.079433
69	28.997124	23.330296	19.309810	16.367617	14.151617	12.438245	11.082049
70	29.123421	23.394515	19.342677	16.384544	14.160389	12.442820	11.084449
71	29.246040	23.456264	19.373978	16.400513	14.168588	12.447055	11.086650
72	29.365088	23.515639	19.403788	16.415578	14.176251	12.450977	11.088670
73	29.480667	23.572730	19.432179	16.429791	14.183412	12.454608	11.090523
74	29.592881	23.627625	19.459218	16.443199	14.190104	12.457971	11.092223
75	29.701826	23.680408	19.484970	16.455848	14.196359	12.461084	11.093782
76	19.807598	23.731162	19.509495	16.467781	14.202205	12.463967	11.095213
77	29.910290	23.779963	19.532853	16.479039	14.207668	12.466636	11.096526
78	30.009990	23.826888	19.555098	16.489659	14.212774	12.469107	11.097730
79	30.106786	23.872008	19.576284	16.499679	14.217546	12.471396	11.098835
80	30.200763	23.915392	19.596460	16.509131	14.222005	12.473514	11.099849
81	30.292003	23.957108	19.615677	16.518048	14.226173	12.475476	11.100778
82	30.380586	23.997219	19.633978	16.526460	14.230069	12.477293	11.101632
83	30.466588	24.035787	19.651407	16.534396	14.233709	12.478975	11.102414
84	30.550086	24.072872	19.668007	16.541883	14.237111	12.480532	11.103132
85	30.631151	24.108531	19.683816	16.548947	14.240291	12.481974	11.103791
86	30.709855	24.142818	19.698873	16.555610	14.243262	12.483310	11.104396
87	30.786267	24.175787	19.713212	16.561896	14.246040	12.484546	11.104950
88	30.860454	24.207487	19.726869	16.567827	14.248635	12.485691	11.105459
89	30.932479	24.237969	19.739875	16.573421	14.251061	12.486751	11.105926
90	31.002407	24.267278	19.752262	16.578699	14.253328	12.487732	11.106354
91	31.070298	24.295459	19.764059	16.583679	14.255447	12.488641	11.106746
92	31.136212	24.322557	19.775294	16.588376	14.257427	12.489482	11.107107
93	31.200206	24.348612	19.785994	16.592808	14.259277	12.490261	11.107437
94	31.262336	24.373666	19.796185	19.596988	14.261007	12.490983	11.107741
95	31.322656	23.397756	19.805891	16.600932	14.262623	12.491651	11.108019
96	31.381219	24.420919	19.815134	16.604653	14.264134	12.492269	11.108274
97	31.438077	24.443191	19.823937	16.608163	14.265546	12.492842	11.108509
98	31.493279	24.464607	19.832321	16.611475	14.266865	12.493372	11.108724
99	31.546872	24.485199	19.840306	16.614599	14.268098	12.493863	11.108921
100	31.598905	24.504999	19.847910	16.617546	14.269251	12.494318	11.109102

TABLE 7 Present value of an annuity $a_{\overline{n}|i} = \dfrac{1 - (1 + i)^{-n}}{i}$

n	10%	11%	12%	13%	14%	15%	16%
1	0.909091	0.900901	0.892857	0.884956	0.877193	0.869565	0.862069
2	1.735537	1.712523	1.690051	1.668102	1.646661	1.625709	1.605232
3	2.486852	2.443715	2.401831	2.361153	2.321632	2.283225	2.245890
4	3.169865	3.102446	3.037349	2.974471	2.913712	2.854978	2.798181
5	3.790787	3.695897	3.604776	3.517231	3.433081	3.352155	3.274294
6	4.355261	4.230538	4.111407	3.997550	3.888668	3.784483	3.684736
7	4.868419	4.712196	4.563757	4.422610	4.288305	4.160420	4.038565
8	5.334926	5.146123	4.967640	4.798770	4.638864	4.487322	4.343591
9	5.759024	5.537048	5.328250	5.131655	4.946372	4.771584	4.606544
10	6.144567	5.889232	5.650223	5.426243	5.216116	5.018769	4.833227
11	6.495061	6.206515	5.937699	5.686941	5.452733	5.233712	5.028644
12	6.813692	6.492356	6.194374	5.917647	5.660292	5.420619	5.197107
13	7.103356	6.749870	6.423548	6.121812	5.842362	5.583147	5.342334
14	7.366687	6.981865	6.628168	6.302488	6.002072	5.724476	5.467529
15	7.606080	7.190870	6.810864	6.462379	6.142168	5.847370	5.575456
16	7.823709	7.379162	6.973986	6.603875	6.265060	5.954235	5.668497
17	8.021553	7.548794	7.119630	6.729093	6.372859	6.047161	5.748704
18	8.201412	7.701617	7.249670	6.839905	6.467420	6.127966	5.817848
19	8.364920	7.839294	7.365777	6.937969	6.550369	6.198231	5.877455
20	8.513564	7.963328	7.469444	7.024752	6.623131	6.259331	5.928841
21	8.648694	8.075070	7.562003	7.101550	6.686957	6.312462	5.973139
22	8.771540	8.175739	7.644646	7.169513	6.742944	6.358663	6.011326
23	8.883218	8.266432	7.718434	7.229658	6.792056	6.398837	6.044147
24	8.984744	8.348137	7.784316	7.282883	6.835137	6.433771	6.072627
25	9.077040	8.421745	7.843139	7.329985	6.872927	6.464149	6.097092
26	9.160945	8.488058	7.895660	7.371668	6.906077	6.490564	6.118183
27	9.237223	8.547800	7.942554	7.408556	6.935155	6.513534	6.136364
28	9.306567	8.601622	7.984423	7.441200	6.960662	6.533508	6.152038
29	9.369606	8.650110	8.021806	7.470088	6.983037	6.550877	6.165550
30	9.426914	8.693793	8.055184	7.495653	7.002664	6.565980	6.177198
31	9.479013	8.733146	8.084986	7.518277	7.019881	6.579113	6.187240
32	9.526376	8.768600	8.111594	7.538299	7.034983	6.590533	6.195897
33	9.569432	8.800541	8.135352	7.556016	7.048231	6.600463	6.203359
34	9.608575	8.829316	8.156564	7.571696	7.059852	6.609099	6.209792
35	9.644159	8.855240	8.175504	7.585572	7.070045	6.616607	6.215338
36	9.676508	8.878594	8.192414	7.597851	7.078987	6.623137	6.220119
37	9.705917	8.899635	8.207513	7.608718	7.086831	6.628815	6.224241
38	9.732651	8.918590	8.220993	7.618334	7.093711	6.633752	6.227794
39	9.756956	8.935666	8.233030	7.626844	7.099747	6.638045	6.230857
40	9.779051	8.951051	8.243777	7.634376	7.105041	6.641778	6.233497
41	9.799137	8.964911	8.253372	7.641040	7.109685	6.645025	6.235773
42	9.817397	8.977397	8.261939	7.646938	7.113759	6.647848	6.237736
43	9.833998	8.988646	8.269589	7.652158	7.117332	6.650302	6.239427
44	9.849089	8.998780	8.276418	7.656777	7.120467	6.652437	6.240886
45	9.862808	9.007910	8.282516	7.660864	7.123217	6.654293	6.242143
46	9.875280	9.016135	8.287961	7.664482	7.125629	6.655907	6.243227
47	9.886618	9.023545	8.292822	7.667683	7.127744	6.657310	6.244161
48	9.896926	9.030221	8.297163	7.670516	7.129600	6.658531	6.244966
49	9.906296	9.036235	8.301038	7.673023	7.131228	6.659592	6.245661
50	9.914814	9.041653	8.304498	7.675242	7.132656	6.660515	6.246259

TABLE 8 Standard normal curve areas

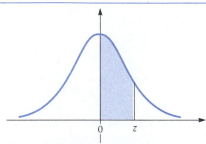

z	.00	.01	.02	.03	.04	.05	.06	.07	.08	.09
0.0	0.0000	0.0040	0.0080	0.0120	0.0160	0.0199	0.0239	0.0279	0.0319	0.0359
0.1	0.0398	0.0438	0.0478	0.0517	0.0557	0.0596	0.0636	0.0675	0.0714	0.0753
0.2	0.0793	0.0832	0.0871	0.0910	0.0948	0.0987	0.1026	0.1064	0.1103	0.1141
0.3	0.1179	0.1217	0.1255	0.1293	0.1331	0.1368	0.1406	0.1443	0.1480	0.1517
0.4	0.1554	0.1591	0.1628	0.1664	0.1700	0.1736	0.1772	0.1808	0.1844	0.1879
0.5	0.1915	0.1950	0.1985	0.2019	0.2054	0.2088	0.2123	0.2157	0.2190	0.2224
0.6	0.2257	0.2291	0.2324	0.2357	0.2389	0.2422	0.2454	0.2486	0.2517	0.2549
0.7	0.2580	0.2611	0.2642	0.2673	0.2704	0.2734	0.2764	0.2794	0.2823	0.2852
0.8	0.2881	0.2910	0.2939	0.2967	0.2995	0.3023	0.3051	0.3078	0.3106	0.3133
0.9	0.3159	0.3186	0.3212	0.3238	0.3264	0.3289	0.3315	0.3340	0.3365	0.3389
1.0	0.3413	0.3438	0.3461	0.3485	0.3508	0.3531	0.3554	0.3577	0.3599	0.3621
1.1	0.3643	0.3665	0.3686	0.3708	0.3729	0.3749	0.3770	0.3790	0.3810	0.3830
1.2	0.3849	0.3869	0.3888	0.3907	0.3925	0.3944	0.3962	0.3980	0.3997	0.4015
1.3	0.4032	0.4049	0.4066	0.4082	0.4099	0.4115	0.4131	0.4147	0.4162	0.4177
1.4	0.4192	0.4207	0.4222	0.4236	0.4251	0.4265	0.4279	0.4292	0.4306	0.4319
1.5	0.4332	0.4345	0.4357	0.4370	0.4382	0.4394	0.4406	0.4418	0.4429	0.4441
1.6	0.4452	0.4463	0.4474	0.4484	0.4495	0.4505	0.4515	0.4525	0.4535	0.4545
1.7	0.4554	0.4564	0.4573	0.4582	0.4591	0.4599	0.4608	0.4616	0.4625	0.4633
1.8	0.4641	0.4649	0.4656	0.4664	0.4671	0.4678	0.4686	0.4693	0.4699	0.4706
1.9	0.4713	0.4719	0.4726	0.4732	0.4738	0.4744	0.4750	0.4756	0.4761	0.4767
2.0	0.4772	0.4778	0.4783	0.4788	0.4793	0.4798	0.4803	0.4808	0.4812	0.4817
2.1	0.4821	0.4826	0.4830	0.4834	0.4838	0.4842	0.4846	0.4850	0.4854	0.4857
2.2	0.4861	0.4864	0.4868	0.4871	0.4875	0.4878	0.4881	0.4884	0.4887	0.4890
2.3	0.4893	0.4896	0.4898	0.4901	0.4904	0.4906	0.4909	0.4911	0.4913	0.4916
2.4	0.4918	0.4920	0.4922	0.4925	0.4927	0.4929	0.4931	0.4932	0.4934	0.4936
2.5	0.4938	0.4940	0.4941	0.4943	0.4945	0.4946	0.4948	0.4949	0.4951	0.4952
2.6	0.4953	0.4955	0.4956	0.4957	0.4959	0.4960	0.4961	0.4962	0.4963	0.4964
2.7	0.4965	0.4966	0.4967	0.4968	0.4969	0.4970	0.4971	0.4972	0.4973	0.4974
2.8	0.4974	0.4975	0.4976	0.4977	0.4977	0.4978	0.4979	0.4979	0.4980	0.4981
2.9	0.4981	0.4982	0.4982	0.4983	0.4984	0.4984	0.4985	0.4985	0.4986	0.4986
3.0	0.4987	0.4987	0.4987	0.4988	0.4988	0.4989	0.4989	0.4989	0.4990	0.4990

TABLE 9 A brief table of integrals

1. $\displaystyle \int u^n \, du = \frac{1}{n+1} u^{n+1} + c \qquad (n \neq -1)$

2. $\displaystyle \int e^u \, du = e^u + c$

continues

TABLE 9   A brief table of integrals *(continued)*

3. $\displaystyle\int \frac{du}{u} = \ln |u| + c$

4. $\displaystyle\int u\,dv = uv - \int v\,du$

5. $\displaystyle\int \frac{du}{\sqrt{a^2 + u^2}} = \ln \left| u + \sqrt{a^2 + u^2}\right| + c$

6. $\displaystyle\int \frac{du}{a^2 - u^2} = \frac{1}{2a} \ln \left|\frac{a + u}{a - u}\right| + c$

7. $\displaystyle\int ue^u\,du = e^u(u - 1) + c$

8. $\displaystyle\int u^n e^u\,du = u^n e^u - n \int u^{n-1} e^u\,du$

9. $\displaystyle\int \frac{du}{u^2(a + bu)} = -\frac{1}{au} + \frac{b}{a^2} \ln \left|\frac{a + bu}{u}\right| + c$

10. $\displaystyle\int \ln u\,du = u \ln |u| - u + c$

11. $\displaystyle\int (\ln u)^n\,du = u(\ln u)^n - n \int (\ln u)^{n-1}\,du \qquad (n \neq -1)$

12. $\displaystyle\int u^n \ln u\,du = u^{n+1} \left[\frac{\ln u}{n + 1} - \frac{1}{(n + 1)^2}\right] + c \qquad (n \neq -1)$

13. $\displaystyle\int \frac{du}{\sqrt{u^2 - a^2}} = \ln \left| u + \sqrt{u^2 - a^2}\right| + c$

14. $\displaystyle\int \frac{du}{u^2 - a^2} = \frac{1}{2a} \ln \left|\frac{u - a}{u + a}\right| + c$

15. $\displaystyle\int \frac{du}{u\sqrt{a^2 - u^2}} = -\frac{1}{a} \ln \left|\frac{a + \sqrt{a^2 + u^2}}{u}\right| + c$

16. $\displaystyle\int \frac{du}{u\sqrt{a^2 + u^2}} = -\frac{1}{a} \ln \left|\frac{a + \sqrt{a^2 + u^2}}{u}\right| + c$

17. $\displaystyle\int \frac{du}{u\sqrt{a + bu}} = \frac{1}{\sqrt{a}} \ln \left|\frac{\sqrt{a + bu} - \sqrt{a}}{\sqrt{a + bu} + \sqrt{a}}\right| + c \qquad (a > 0)$

18. $\displaystyle\int \frac{\sqrt{a^2 - u^2}}{u}\,du = -\sqrt{a^2 - u^2} - a \ln \left|\frac{a + \sqrt{a^2 - u^2}}{u}\right| + c$

19. $\displaystyle\int \frac{du}{u^2\sqrt{a^2 - u^2}} = -\frac{\sqrt{a^2 - u^2}}{a^2 u} + c$

20. $\displaystyle\int \frac{du}{(a^2 - u^2)^{3/2}} = \frac{u}{a^2\sqrt{a^2 - u^2}} + c$

21. $\displaystyle\int \frac{u\,du}{(a + bu)^2} = \frac{1}{b^2} \left[\frac{a}{a + bu} + \ln |a + bu|\right] + c$

22. $\displaystyle\int \sqrt{a^2 + u^2}\,du = \frac{u}{2} \sqrt{a^2 + u^2} + \frac{a^2}{2} \ln \left| u + \sqrt{a^2 + u^2}\right| + c$

23. $\displaystyle\int \frac{du}{(a^2 + u^2)^{3/2}} = \frac{u}{a^2\sqrt{a^2 + u^2}} + c$

24. $\displaystyle\int \frac{du}{u(a + bu)} = -\frac{1}{a} \ln \left|\frac{a + bu}{u}\right| + c$

Answers to Selected Exercises

CHAPTER 1

SECTION 1-1

1. (a) -2 **(b)** 10 **3. (a)** 7 **(b)** 5 **(c)** -3 **(d)** 13

5. (a) $\dfrac{5}{7}$ **(b)** $\dfrac{5}{8}$ **(c)** 5 **(d)** $\dfrac{1}{3}$ **7.**

9.

(graph with points (3, 11), (2, 8), (1, 5), (0, 2))

11. All real x such that $x \neq 2$, $x \neq -7$ **13.** All real x such that $x \geq 2$ **15.** All real x such that $x \neq 3$ **17.** a, c, d
19. *Not* a function: $(4, 3)$ and $(4, -3)$ satisfy equation
21. (a) $f(x + h) = x^2 + 2xh + h^2 - 4x - 4h + 5$
(b) $f(x + h) - f(x) = 2xh + h^2 - 4h$

(c) $\dfrac{f(x + h) - f(x)}{h} = 2x + h - 4$

23. $\dfrac{f(x + h) - f(x)}{h} = 10x + 5h - 2$

25. $\dfrac{g(x + h) - g(x)}{h} = 3x^2 + 3xh + h^2 - 8x - 4h + 5$

27.

29. (a) $C(x) = \begin{cases} 5.00 & \text{if } 16 < x \leq 40 \\ 2.00 & \text{if } 8 \leq x \leq 16 \\ 1.25 & \text{if } 0 < x < 8 \end{cases}$

(b)

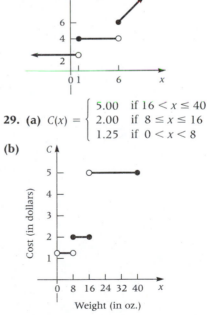

31. $P(x) = \begin{cases} 28 - x & \text{if } 0 \le x \le 35 \\ -7 & \text{if } x > 35 \end{cases}$

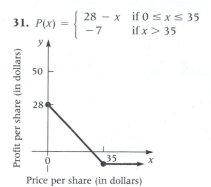

Profit per share (in dollars)

Price per share (in dollars)

SECTION 1-2

1. (a) $\Delta y = 3$ **(b)** $\Delta x = 4$ **(c)** $\dfrac{3}{4}$ **(d)** For every 4 units of horizontal charge to the right there are 3 units of vertical change upward. **3.** $\dfrac{11}{3}$ **5.** $\dfrac{1}{4}$ **7.** 10 **9.** $\dfrac{-7}{5}$

11

① $16 - 5 = 11$ units vertical change

② $7 - 4 = 3$ units horizontal change

Slope $= m = \dfrac{\Delta y}{\Delta x} = \dfrac{11}{3}$

① $7 - 9 = -2$ units vertical change

② $8 - 5 = 3$ units horizontal change

Slope $= m = \dfrac{\Delta y}{\Delta x} = \dfrac{-2}{3}$

continues

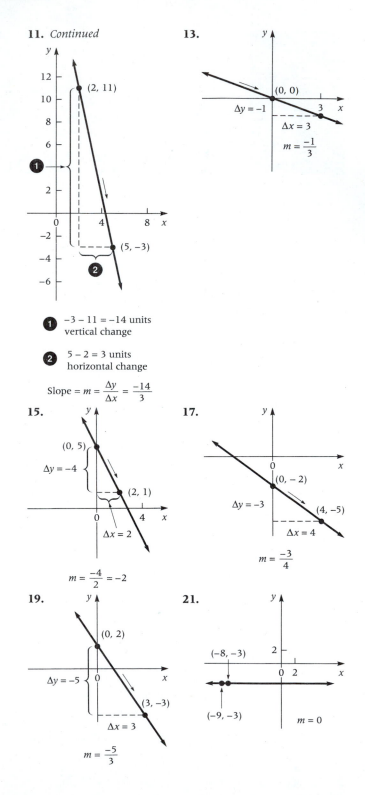

11. *Continued*

① $-3 - 11 = -14$ units vertical change

② $5 - 2 = 3$ units horizontal change

Slope $= m = \dfrac{\Delta y}{\Delta x} = \dfrac{-14}{3}$

13.

$\Delta y = -1$

$\Delta x = 3$

$m = \dfrac{-1}{3}$

15.

$\Delta y = -4$

$\Delta x = 2$

$m = \dfrac{-4}{2} = -2$

17.

$(0, -2)$

$\Delta y = -3$

$\Delta x = 4$

$(4, -5)$

$m = \dfrac{-3}{4}$

19.

$(0, 2)$

$\Delta y = -5$

$(3, -3)$

$\Delta x = 3$

$m = \dfrac{-5}{3}$

21.

$(-8, -3)$

$(-9, -3)$

$m = 0$

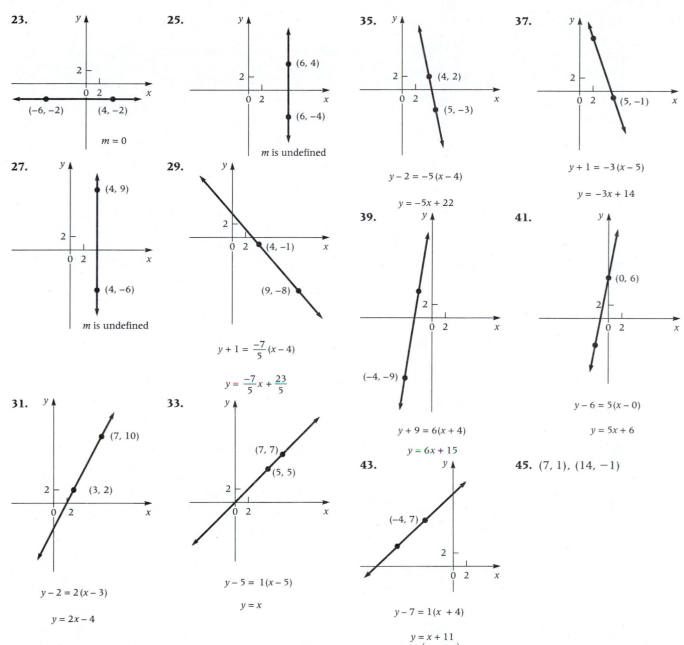

23. $m = 0$ $(-6, -2)$ $(4, -2)$

25. m is undefined $(6, 4)$ $(6, -4)$

27. m is undefined $(4, 9)$ $(4, -6)$

29. $(4, -1)$ $(9, -8)$
$y + 1 = \dfrac{-7}{5}(x - 4)$
$y = \dfrac{-7}{5}x + \dfrac{23}{5}$

31. $(7, 10)$ $(3, 2)$
$y - 2 = 2(x - 3)$
$y = 2x - 4$

33. $(7, 7)$ $(5, 5)$
$y - 5 = 1(x - 5)$
$y = x$

35. $(4, 2)$ $(5, -3)$
$y - 2 = -5(x - 4)$
$y = -5x + 22$

37. $(5, -1)$
$y + 1 = -3(x - 5)$
$y = -3x + 14$

39. $(-4, -9)$
$y + 9 = 6(x + 4)$
$y = 6x + 15$

41. $(0, 6)$
$y - 6 = 5(x - 0)$
$y = 5x + 6$

43. $(-4, 7)$
$y - 7 = 1(x + 4)$
$y = x + 11$

45. $(7, 1), (14, -1)$

47. $(1, 9), \left(\dfrac{-1}{2}, 0\right), (-1, -3)$ **49.** $(0, 0), (1, -3), (2, -6)$

51.

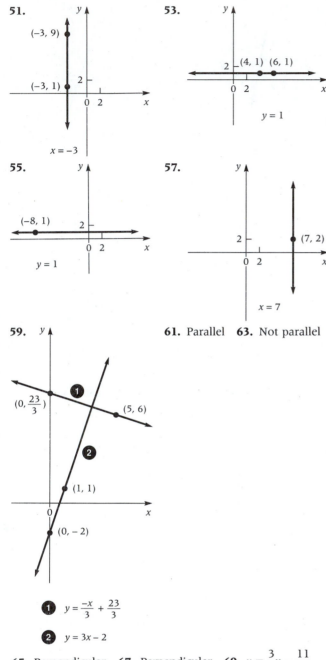

53.

55.

57.

59.

① $y = \dfrac{-x}{3} + \dfrac{23}{3}$

② $y = 3x - 2$

65. Perpendicular **67.** Perpendicular **69.** $y = \dfrac{3}{5}x - \dfrac{11}{5}$

71. $y = \dfrac{3}{2}x$ **73.** Linear **75.** Not linear **77.** Linear

79. Not linear **81. (a)** 132.825 **(b)** U.S. Overseas IOU's are increasing at the rate of 132.825 billion dollars per year during the indicated time interval.
(c) $y - 642 = 132.825(x - 1989)$
or
$y = 132.825x - 263,546.925$

(d) $y = 132.825(1992) - 263,546.925$
$= 1040.475$ billion dollars

83. (a) -52.1 **(b)** Defects per 100 vehicles decreased at the rate of 52.1 per year during the indicated time interval.
(c) $y - 149 = -52.1(x - 1989)$
or
$y = -52.1x + 103,775.9$
(d) $y = -52.1(1991) + 103,775.9$
$= 44.8$

85. (a) 2500 **(b)** The value of the investment increased by $2500 per percentage point increase in inflation.

87. (a)
$$y = \begin{cases} 0.15x & \text{if } 0 < x \le 15,475 \\ 2321.25 + 0.28(x - 15,475) & \\ & \text{if } 15,475 < x \le 37,425 \\ 8467.25 + 0.33(x - 37,425) & \\ & \text{if } 37,425 < x \le 117,895 \end{cases}$$

(b)

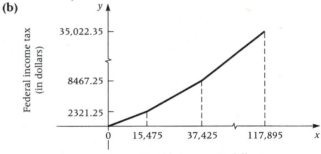

SECTION 1-3

1.

3.

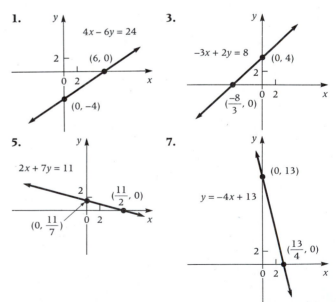

5.

7.

61. Parallel **63.** Not parallel

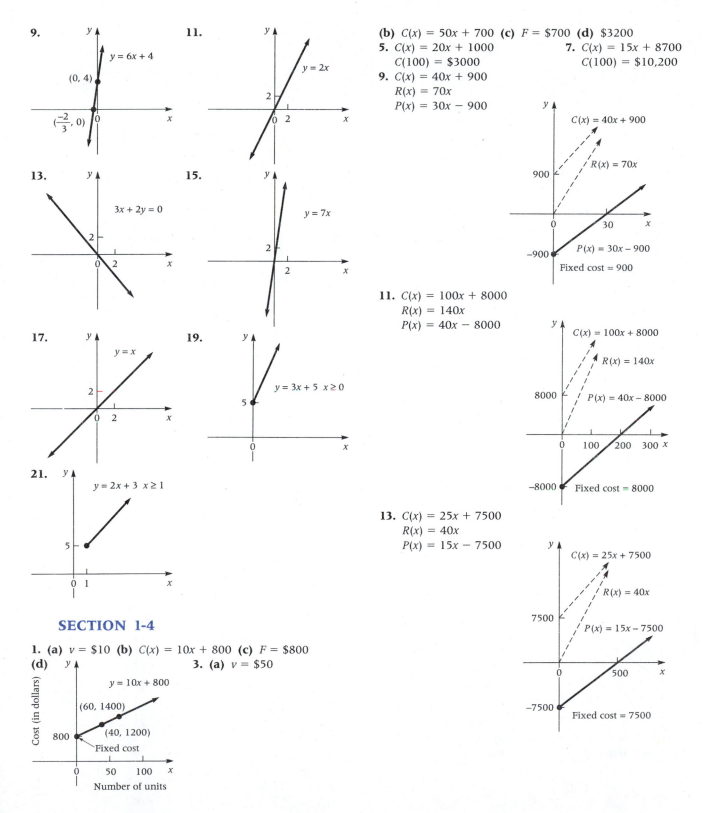

9.

$y = 6x + 4$

$(0, 4)$

$\left(\dfrac{-2}{3}, 0\right)$

11.

$y = 2x$

(b) $C(x) = 50x + 700$ **(c)** $F = \$700$ **(d)** $\$3200$

5. $C(x) = 20x + 1000$
$C(100) = \$3000$

7. $C(x) = 15x + 8700$
$C(100) = \$10{,}200$

9. $C(x) = 40x + 900$
$R(x) = 70x$
$P(x) = 30x - 900$

$C(x) = 40x + 900$
$R(x) = 70x$
900
30
-900
$P(x) = 30x - 900$
Fixed cost $= 900$

13.

$3x + 2y = 0$

15.

$y = 7x$

11. $C(x) = 100x + 8000$
$R(x) = 140x$
$P(x) = 40x - 8000$

$C(x) = 100x + 8000$
$R(x) = 140x$
8000
$P(x) = 40x - 8000$
$100 \quad 200 \quad 300$
-8000 Fixed cost $= 8000$

17.

$y = x$

19.

$y = 3x + 5 \quad x \geq 0$
5

13. $C(x) = 25x + 7500$
$R(x) = 40x$
$P(x) = 15x - 7500$

21.

$y = 2x + 3 \quad x \geq 1$
5
1

$C(x) = 25x + 7500$
$R(x) = 40x$
7500
$P(x) = 15x - 7500$
500
-7500 Fixed cost $= 7500$

SECTION 1-4

1. (a) $v = \$10$ **(b)** $C(x) = 10x + 800$ **(c)** $F = \$800$
(d)

Cost (in dollars)

$y = 10x + 800$

$(60, 1400)$

800

$(40, 1200)$

Fixed cost

$0 \quad 50 \quad 100$

Number of units

3. (a) $v = \$50$

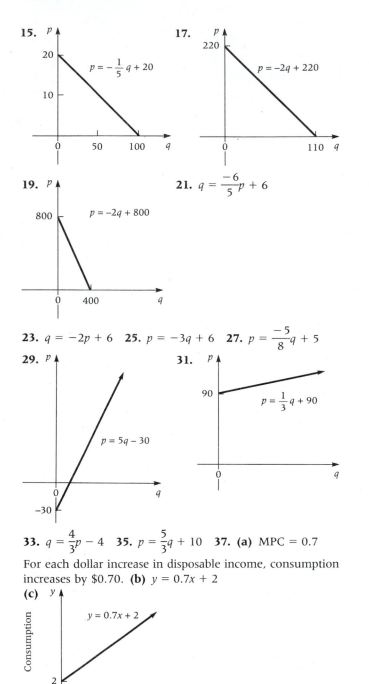

15. $p = -\frac{1}{5}q + 20$

17. $p = -2q + 220$

19. $p = -2q + 800$

21. $q = \frac{-6}{5}p + 6$

23. $q = -2p + 6$ **25.** $p = -3q + 6$ **27.** $p = \frac{-5}{8}q + 5$

29. $p = 5q - 30$

31. $p = \frac{1}{3}q + 90$

33. $q = \frac{4}{3}p - 4$ **35.** $p = \frac{5}{3}q + 10$ **37. (a)** MPC = 0.7

For each dollar increase in disposable income, consumption increases by $0.70. **(b)** $y = 0.7x + 2$

(c) $y = 0.7x + 2$

39. (a) MPC = 0.9 For each dollar increase in disposable income, consumption increases by $0.90. **(b)** $y = 0.9x + 7$

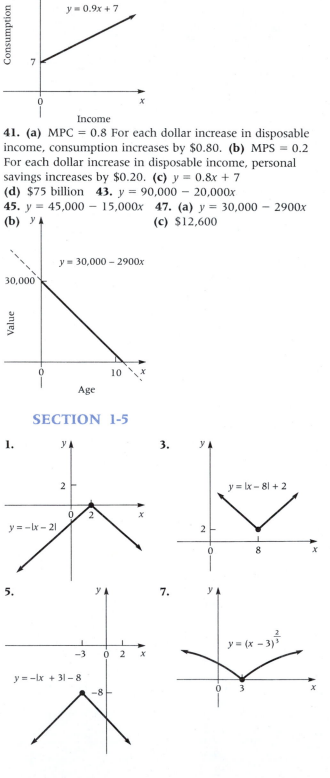

(c) $y = 0.9x + 7$

41. (a) MPC = 0.8 For each dollar increase in disposable income, consumption increases by $0.80. **(b)** MPS = 0.2 For each dollar increase in disposable income, personal savings increases by $0.20. **(c)** $y = 0.8x + 7$
(d) $75 billion **43.** $y = 90,000 - 20,000x$
45. $y = 45,000 - 15,000x$ **47. (a)** $y = 30,000 - 2900x$
(b) **(c)** $12,600

$y = 30,000 - 2900x$

SECTION 1-5

1. $y = -|x - 2|$

3. $y = |x - 8| + 2$

5. $y = -|x + 3| - 8$

7. $y = (x - 3)^{\frac{2}{3}}$

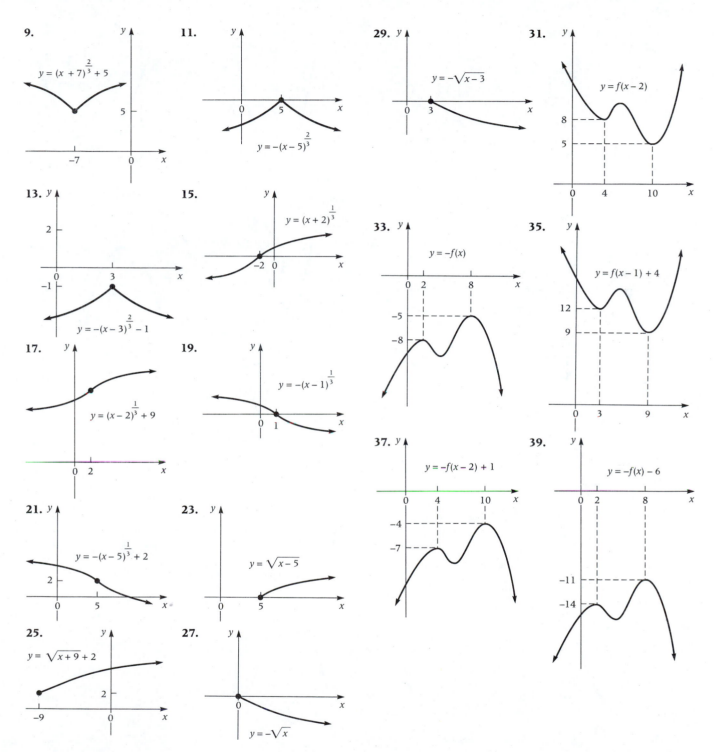

9. $y = (x + 7)^{\frac{2}{3}} + 5$

11. $y = -(x - 5)^{\frac{2}{3}}$

29. $y = -\sqrt{x - 3}$

31. $y = f(x - 2)$

13. $y = -(x - 3)^{\frac{2}{3}} - 1$

15. $y = (x + 2)^{\frac{1}{3}}$

33. $y = -f(x)$

35. $y = f(x - 1) + 4$

17. $y = (x - 2)^{\frac{1}{3}} + 9$

19. $y = -(x - 1)^{\frac{1}{3}}$

37. $y = -f(x - 2) + 1$

39. $y = -f(x) - 6$

21. $y = -(x - 5)^{\frac{1}{3}} + 2$

23. $y = \sqrt{x - 5}$

25. $y = \sqrt{x + 9} + 2$

27. $y = -\sqrt{x}$

41. Odd **43.** Odd **45.** Odd

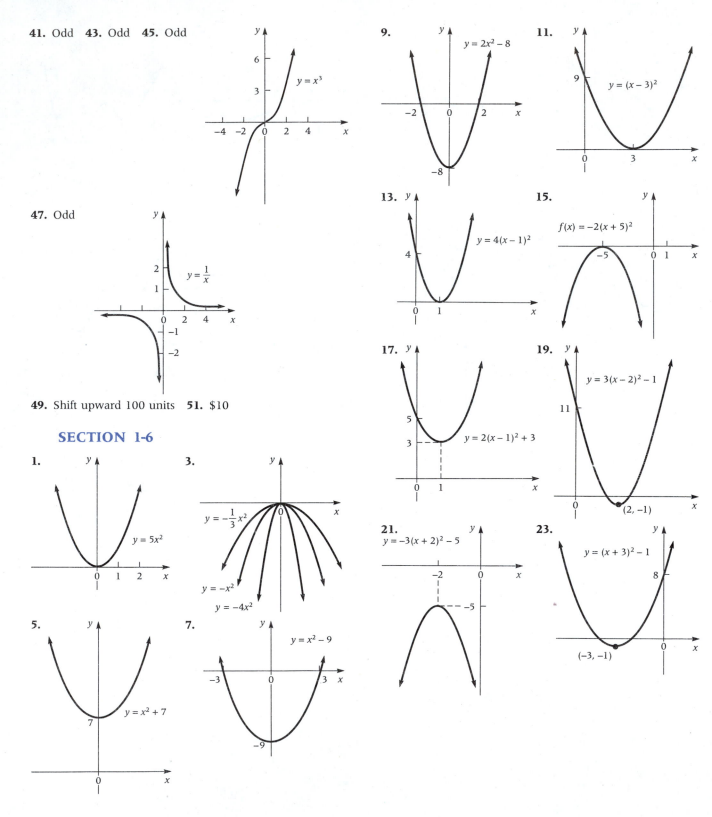

47. Odd

49. Shift upward 100 units **51.** $10

SECTION 1-6

1. $y = 5x^2$

3. $y = -\frac{1}{3}x^2$, $y = -x^2$, $y = -4x^2$

5. $y = x^2 + 7$

7. $y = x^2 - 9$

9. $y = 2x^2 - 8$

11. $y = (x - 3)^2$

13. $y = 4(x - 1)^2$

15. $f(x) = -2(x + 5)^2$

17. $y = 2(x - 1)^2 + 3$

19. $y = 3(x - 2)^2 - 1$, $(2, -1)$

21. $y = -3(x + 2)^2 - 5$

23. $y = (x + 3)^2 - 1$, $(-3, -1)$

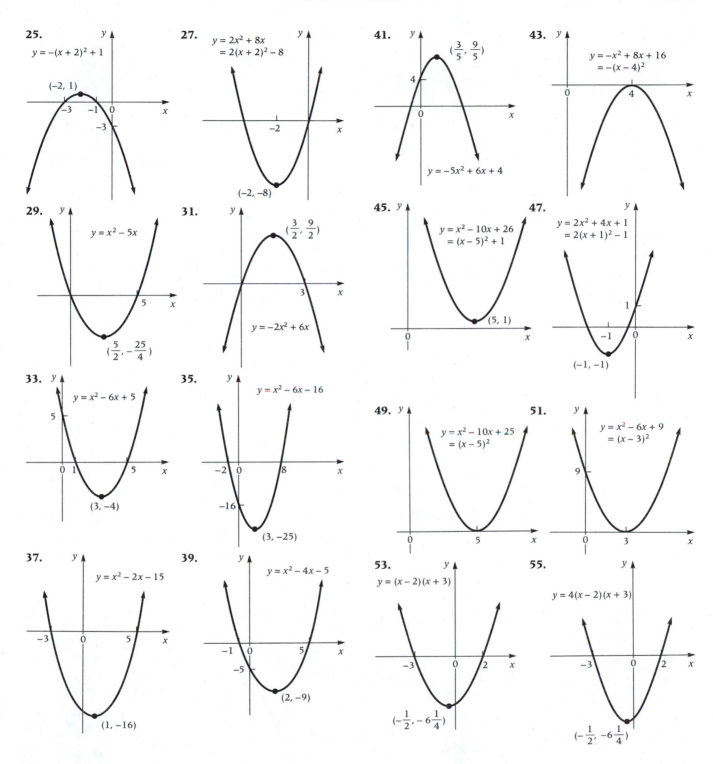

25. $y = -(x + 2)^2 + 1$ $(-2, 1)$

27. $y = 2x^2 + 8x = 2(x + 2)^2 - 8$ $(-2, -8)$

41. $\left(\dfrac{3}{5}, \dfrac{9}{5}\right)$ $y = -5x^2 + 6x + 4$

43. $y = -x^2 + 8x + 16 = -(x - 4)^2$

29. $y = x^2 - 5x$ $\left(\dfrac{5}{2}, -\dfrac{25}{4}\right)$

31. $\left(\dfrac{3}{2}, \dfrac{9}{2}\right)$ $y = -2x^2 + 6x$

45. $y = x^2 - 10x + 26 = (x - 5)^2 + 1$ $(5, 1)$

47. $y = 2x^2 + 4x + 1 = 2(x + 1)^2 - 1$ $(-1, -1)$

33. $y = x^2 - 6x + 5$ $(3, -4)$

35. $y = x^2 - 6x - 16$ $(3, -25)$

49. $y = x^2 - 10x + 25 = (x - 5)^2$

51. $y = x^2 - 6x + 9 = (x - 3)^2$

37. $y = x^2 - 2x - 15$ $(1, -16)$

39. $y = x^2 - 4x - 5$ $(2, -9)$

53. $y = (x - 2)(x + 3)$ $\left(-\dfrac{1}{2}, -6\dfrac{1}{4}\right)$

55. $y = 4(x - 2)(x + 3)$ $\left(-\dfrac{1}{2}, -6\dfrac{1}{4}\right)$

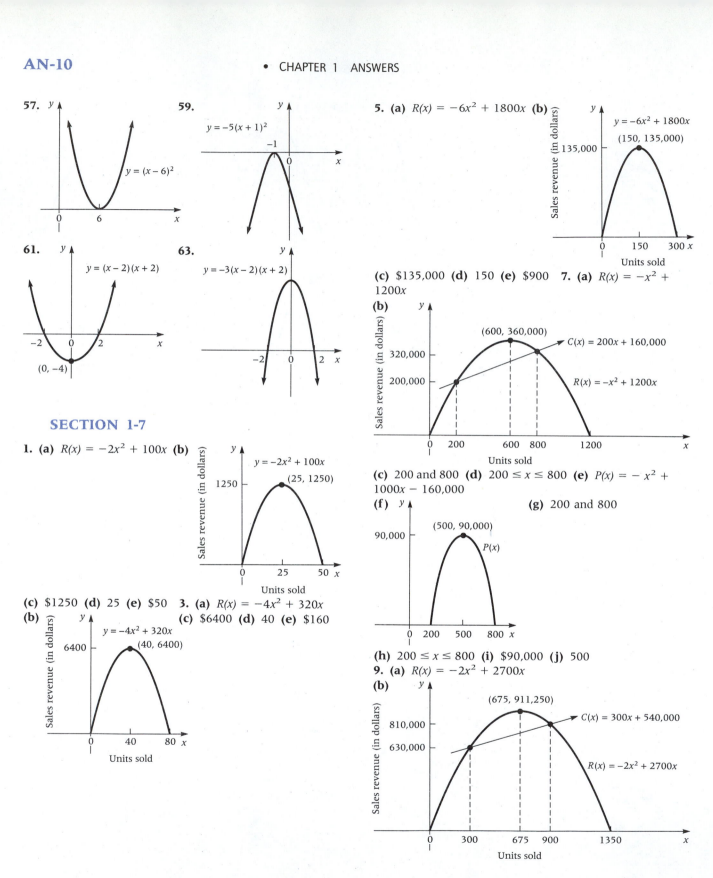

57. $y = (x - 6)^2$

59. $y = -5(x + 1)^2$

61. $y = (x - 2)(x + 2)$, $(0, -4)$

63. $y = -3(x - 2)(x + 2)$

5. (a) $R(x) = -6x^2 + 1800x$ **(b)** $y = -6x^2 + 1800x$, $(150, 135,000)$

(c) $135,000 **(d)** 150 **(e)** $900 **7. (a)** $R(x) = -x^2 + 1200x$

(b) $(600, 360,000)$, $C(x) = 200x + 160,000$, $R(x) = -x^2 + 1200x$

(c) 200 and 800 **(d)** $200 \le x \le 800$ **(e)** $P(x) = -x^2 + 1000x - 160,000$

(f) $(500, 90,000)$, $P(x)$ **(g)** 200 and 800

(h) $200 \le x \le 800$ **(i)** $90,000 **(j)** 500

9. (a) $R(x) = -2x^2 + 2700x$

(b) $(675, 911,250)$, $C(x) = 300x + 540,000$, $R(x) = -2x^2 + 2700x$

SECTION 1-7

1. (a) $R(x) = -2x^2 + 100x$ **(b)** $y = -2x^2 + 100x$, $(25, 1250)$

(c) $1250 **(d)** 25 **(e)** $50 **3. (a)** $R(x) = -4x^2 + 320x$

(b) $y = -4x^2 + 320x$, $(40, 6400)$ **(c)** $6400 **(d)** 40 **(e)** $160

(c) 300 and 900 (d) $300 \le x \le 900$ (e) $P(x) = -2x^2 +$ 2400x − 540,000 (f)

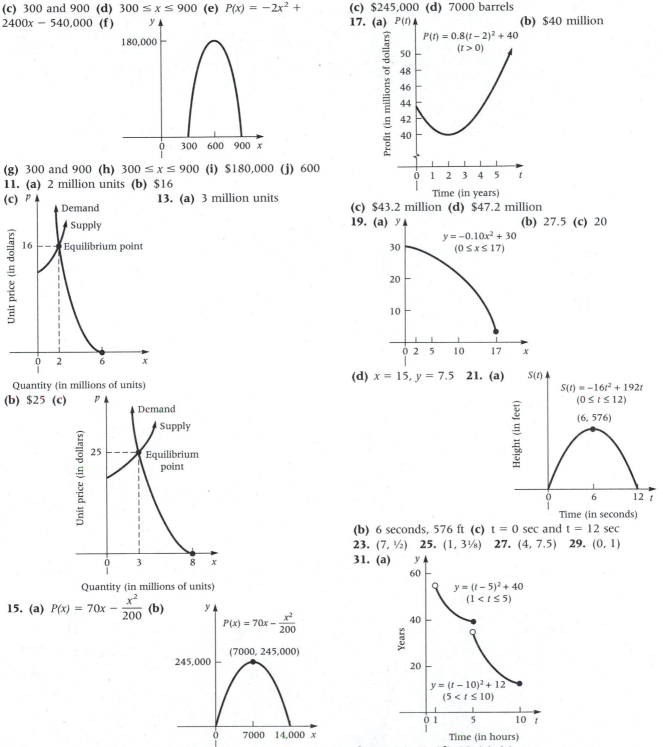

(g) 300 and 900 (h) $300 \le x \le 900$ (i) $180,000 (j) 600
11. (a) 2 million units (b) $16
(c)   13. (a) 3 million units

Quantity (in millions of units)
(b) $25 (c)

Quantity (in millions of units)
15. (a) $P(x) = 70x - \dfrac{x^2}{200}$ (b)

$P(x) = 70x - \dfrac{x^2}{200}$

(7000, 245,000)

245,000

(c) $245,000 (d) 7000 barrels
17. (a) $P(t)$ (b) $40 million

$P(t) = 0.8(t - 2)^2 + 40$
$(t > 0)$

Time (in years)
(c) $43.2 million (d) $47.2 million
19. (a) y (b) 27.5 (c) 20

$y = -0.10x^2 + 30$
$(0 \le x \le 17)$

(d) $x = 15, y = 7.5$ 21. (a) $S(t)$

$S(t) = -16t^2 + 192t$
$(0 \le t \le 12)$

(6, 576)

Time (in seconds)
(b) 6 seconds, 576 ft (c) t = 0 sec and t = 12 sec
23. $(7, \frac{1}{2})$ 25. $(1, 3\frac{1}{8})$ 27. $(4, 7.5)$ 29. $(0, 1)$
31. (a)

$y = (t - 5)^2 + 40$
$(1 < t \le 5)$

$y = (t - 10)^2 + 12$
$(5 < t \le 10)$

Time (in hours)
(b) 44 (c) 41 (d) 28 (e) 16

SECTION 1-8

1. 1 **3.** 8 **5.** 3 **7.** 6

9. $f(x) = x^3$

x	-4	-3	-2	-1	0	1	2	3	4
$f(x)$	-64	-27	-8	-1	0	1	8	27	64

$f(-x) = -f(x)$

etc.

$f(x) = ax^n$
$f(-x) = a(-x)^n$ $n \geq 3$ and odd, $a > 0$
$\qquad = -ax^n = -f(x)$

The graphs of an odd function $f(x) = ax^n$ resemble Figure 2-42.

23. $f(x) = \dfrac{1}{x^3}$

x	-4	-3	-2	-1	0	1	2	3	4
$f(x)$	$-\dfrac{1}{64}$	$-\dfrac{1}{27}$	$-\dfrac{1}{8}$	-1	—	1	$\dfrac{1}{8}$	$\dfrac{1}{27}$	$\dfrac{1}{64}$

$f(-x) = -f(x)$

etc.

$f(x) = \dfrac{k}{x^n}$ n, odd positive; $k > 0$

$f(-x) = \dfrac{k}{(-x)^n}$

$\qquad = -\dfrac{k}{x^n} = -f(x)$

The graphs of $f(x) = \dfrac{k}{x^n}$ (n, odd and positive) resemble Figure 2-47.

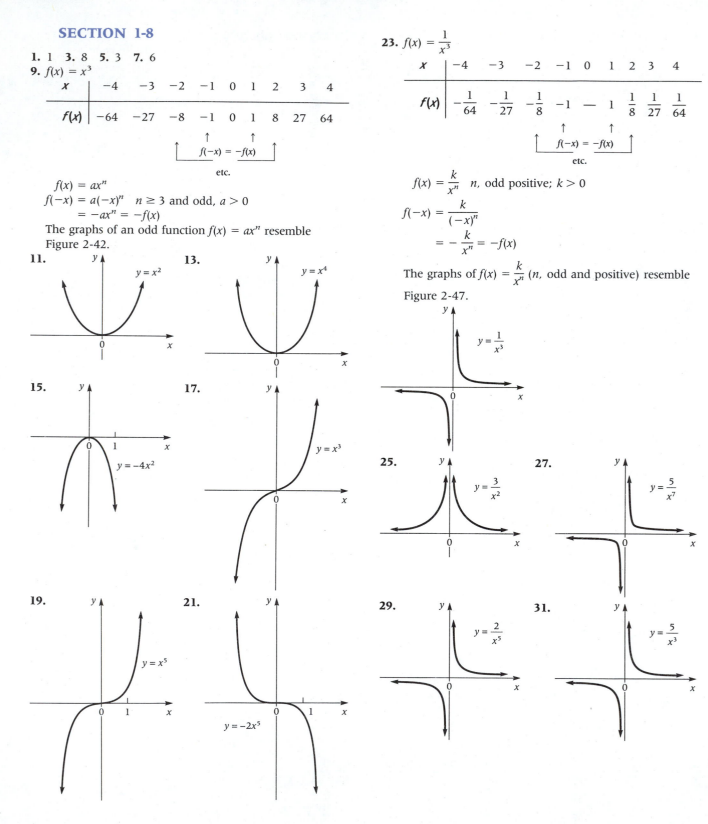

33.

$y = \dfrac{6}{x^8}$

35.

$y = \dfrac{4}{x^5}$

49.

$y = (x + 5)^3 - 2$

$(-5, -2)$

51.

$y = \dfrac{3}{x - 5}$

37.

$y = -\dfrac{6}{x^8}$

39.

$y = -\dfrac{5}{x^3}$

53.

$y = \dfrac{2}{(x + 5)^6}$

55.

$y = \dfrac{7}{(x - 2)^4} + 3$

41.

$y = -\dfrac{7}{x^6}$

43.

$y = 2(x - 5)^4$

1250

57.

$y = \dfrac{2}{(x - 3)^5} - 1$

59.

$y = \dfrac{30,000}{x} \quad (x > 0)$

45.

$y = 5(x + 2)^3$

47.

$y = (x - 2)^4 + 5$

61. (a)

$y = \dfrac{200,000}{x}$

$(1000 \le x \le 5000)$

(b) 200 **(c)** 100 **(d)** 50

(e) 40 **63. (a)**

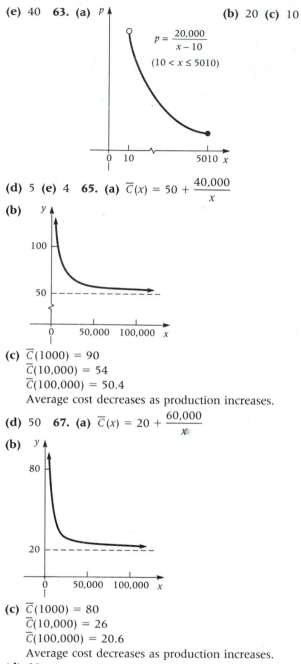

$$p = \frac{20,000}{x-10}$$

$(10 < x \le 5010)$

(b) 20 **(c)** 10

(d) 5 **(e)** 4 **65. (a)** $\overline{C}(x) = 50 + \dfrac{40,000}{x}$

(b)

(c) $\overline{C}(1000) = 90$
$\overline{C}(10,000) = 54$
$\overline{C}(100,000) = 50.4$
Average cost decreases as production increases.

(d) 50 **67. (a)** $\overline{C}(x) = 20 + \dfrac{60,000}{x}$

(b)

(c) $\overline{C}(1000) = 80$
$\overline{C}(10,000) = 26$
$\overline{C}(100,000) = 20.6$
Average cost decreases as production increases.

(d) 20

• EXTRA DIVIDENDS

Model Fitting (Linear Models)

1. (a) For $y = 2x + 1$, $S = 41$
For $y = 3x - 2$, $S = 55$ **(b)** $y = 2x + 1$ is the better fit.

3. (a) For $y = 4x - 3$, $S = 42$
For $y = 3x + 2$, $S = 64$ **(b)** $y = 4x - 3$ is the better fit.
5. (a) For $y = 13x + 130$, $S = 3481.0598$
For $y = 20x + 70$, $S = 15,051.2198$ **(b)** $y = 13x + 130$ is
the better fit. **7. (a)** For $y = 3x + 120$, $S = 27$
For $y = 4x + 115$, $S = 121$ **(b)** $y = 3x + 120$ is the better
fit. **9. (a)** For $y = 2x + 170$, $S = 5462$
For $y = 3x + 100$, $S = 11,786$ **(b)** $y = 2x + 170$ is the
better fit.

• EXTRA DIVIDENDS

Model Fitting (Quadratic Models)

1. For $y = 20x^2 + 10$, $S = 1600$
For $y = 100x - 90$, $S = 16,400$
$y = 20x^2 + 10$ is the better fit
3. $y = 48.4\,x + 768$

• CHAPTER HIGHLIGHTS

1. *Function, domain, range.* A **function** is a rule that
associates a unique output value with each element in a set
of possible input values. The set of input values is called
the **domain** of the function. The set of output values is
called the **range** of the function.
Dependent variable, independent variable. If a function is
defined by an equation such as $y = 5x^2 - 6$, then the value
of y depends upon the value of x. Therefore, y is called the
dependent variable and x is called the **independent**
variable.
Ordered pair, x-coordinate, y-coordinate. Each point in the
rectangular coordinate system is denoted by an **ordered
pair** (x, y) where x is called the **x-coordinate** and y is
called the **y-coordinate**. The x- and y-coordinates indicate
the location of the point relative to the axes.
x-axis, y-axis, origin, quadrant. The **x-axis** is the horizontal
axis of a rectangular coordinate system, and the **y-axis** is
the vertical axis. The point where the axes intersect is
called the **origin**. The x- and y-axes partition the plane into
four regions called **quadrants**. **2.** Equation, relationship
3. *Vertical line test.* If a vertical line intersects a graph at
more than one point, then that graph does not represent a
function. **4.** **5.** Piecewise **6.** d.

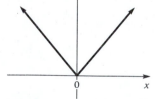

7. y decreases by 5 units. **8. (a)**

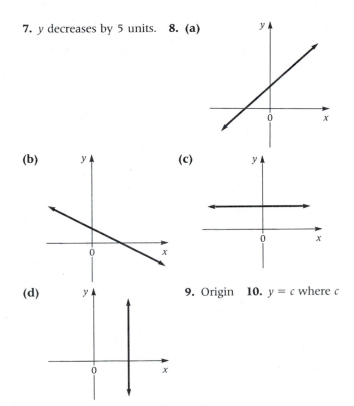

(b) **(c)**

(d) **9.** Origin **10.** $y = c$ where c

is a constant **11.** $x = c$ where c is a constant
12. y-intercept, positive, negative **13.** Tax rates
14. *x-intercept, y-intercept.* The point where a straight line crosses the x-axis is called the **x-intercept**; the point where a straight line crosses the y-axis is called the **y-intercept.** **15.** 0 **16.** 0 **17.** *Step 1:* Find the y-intercept by setting $x = 0$ and solving the resulting equation for y.
Step 2: Find the x-intercept by setting $y = 0$ and solving the resulting equation for x.
Step 3: Connect the intercepts with a straightedge.
18. Place a straightedge at the origin and set it so that the slope is m. **19.** Cost; number of units produced.
20. Sales revenue; number of units produced. **21.** Profit; number of units produced. **22.** Variable cost per unit
23. *Fixed cost:* The cost of producing 0 units. These are costs that must be paid regardless of how few or how many units are produced. **24.** Unit price, demand **25.** Unit price, supply **26.** Consumption, income **27.** The MPC is the slope of a consumption function. The MPC indicates the portion spent of an additional dollar earned.

28. $y = C - \left(\dfrac{C - S}{n}\right)x$ where $C =$ total cost of an asset
$\qquad\qquad\qquad\qquad\qquad\quad S =$ salvage value of the asset
$\qquad\qquad\qquad\qquad\qquad\quad n =$ number of years of asset life

The y-intercept, C, denotes the total cost of the asset. The slope, $(C - S)/n$, is the annual depreciation. **29.** *Vertical shift.* Assume the graph of $y = f(x)$ is known. The graph of $y = f(x) + c$ is obtained by lifting the graph of $y = f(x)$ vertically by c units if $c > 0$ and lowering it by $|c|$ units if $c < 0$. **30.** *Horizontal shift.* Assume that the graph of $y = f(x)$ is known. The graph of $y = f(x - c)$ is obtained by shifting the graph of $y = f(x)$ horizontally to the right by c units if $c > 0$ and horizontally to the left by $|c|$ units if $c < 0$. **31.** *Reflection in the x-axis.* Assume the graph of $y = f(x)$ is known. The graph of $y = -f(x)$ is obtained by drawing the graph of $y = f(x)$ upside down. **32.** The graph of a function $f(x)$ is symmetric with respect to the vertical axis if $f(-x) = f(x)$. This means that if (x, y) is on the graph of $f(x)$, then $(-x, y)$ is also on the graph. Such a function is called an **even function.** **33.** If $f(-x) = -f(x)$, then $f(x)$ is an **odd function** and its graph is symmetric with respect to the origin. **34.** $y = ax^2 + bx + c$ with $a \neq 0$; x-coordinate of the vertex is $-b/2a$; y-intercept $= (0, c)$. **35.** If $a > 0$, the parabola opens up; if $a < 0$, the parabola opens down. **36.** Set $y = 0$ and solve for x or use the quadratic formula $x = (-b \pm \sqrt{b^2 - 4ac})/2a$.
37. 2 **38.** Vertex **39.** Sales revenue = (number of units sold)(unit price) **40.** Profit = sales revenue − cost
41. Set $P(x) = 0$ and solve for x. **42.** Set the supply equation equal to the demand equation and solve for x.
43. Time series **44.** $f(x) = a_n x^n + a_{n-1}x^{n-1} + \ldots + a_1 x + a_0$ **45.** $n - 1, n$ **46.**

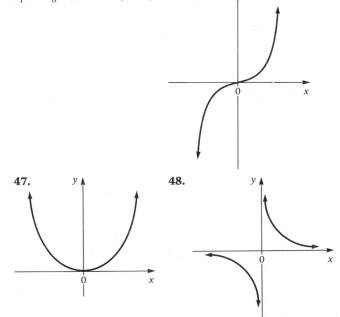

47. **48.**

49.

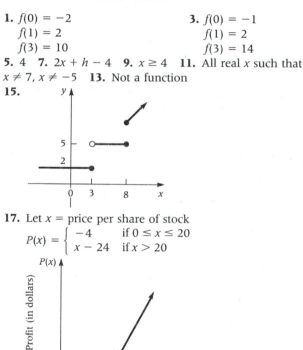

and solve for x. Verify that the numerator does not equal 0 at the solution values of x. If the numerator equals 0 at a solution value of x, then the graph of the rational function does not have a vertical asymptote at that solution value of x. **51.** $\overline{C}(x) = C(x)/x$.

• REVIEW EXERCISES

1. $f(0) = -2$
$f(1) = 2$
$f(3) = 10$

3. $f(0) = -1$
$f(1) = 2$
$f(3) = 14$

5. 4 **7.** $2x + h - 4$ **9.** $x \geq 4$ **11.** All real x such that $x \neq 7, x \neq -5$ **13.** Not a function

15.

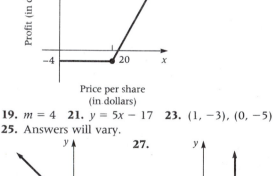

17. Let x = price per share of stock
$$P(x) = \begin{cases} -4 & \text{if } 0 \leq x \leq 20 \\ x - 24 & \text{if } x > 20 \end{cases}$$

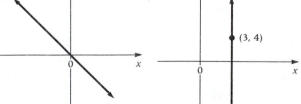

19. $m = 4$ **21.** $y = 5x - 17$ **23.** $(1, -3), (0, -5)$
25. Answers will vary.

27.

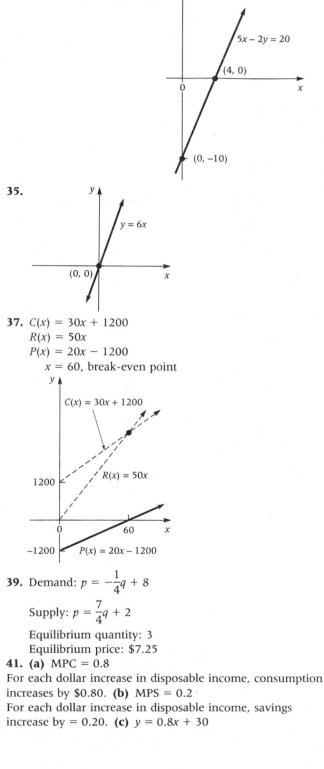

29. $x = 3$ **31.** Parallel **33.**

35.

37. $C(x) = 30x + 1200$
$R(x) = 50x$
$P(x) = 20x - 1200$
$x = 60$, break-even point

39. Demand: $p = -\dfrac{1}{4}q + 8$

Supply: $p = \dfrac{7}{4}q + 2$

Equilibrium quantity: 3
Equilibrium price: $7.25
41. (a) MPC = 0.8
For each dollar increase in disposable income, consumption increases by $0.80. **(b)** MPS = 0.2
For each dollar increase in disposable income, savings increase by = 0.20. **(c)** $y = 0.8x + 30$

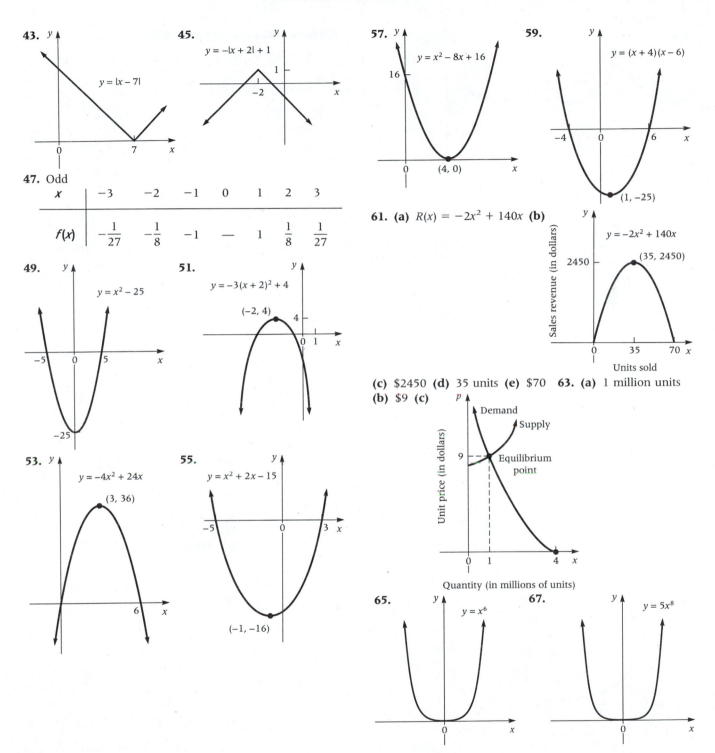

43. $y = |x - 7|$

45. $y = -|x + 2| + 1$

47. Odd

x	-3	-2	-1	0	1	2	3
$f(x)$	$-\dfrac{1}{27}$	$-\dfrac{1}{8}$	-1	—	1	$\dfrac{1}{8}$	$\dfrac{1}{27}$

49. $y = x^2 - 25$

51. $y = -3(x + 2)^2 + 4$ (−2, 4)

53. $y = -4x^2 + 24x$ (3, 36)

55. $y = x^2 + 2x - 15$ (−1, −16)

57. $y = x^2 - 8x + 16$ (4, 0)

59. $y = (x + 4)(x - 6)$ (1, −25)

61. (a) $R(x) = -2x^2 + 140x$ **(b)** $y = -2x^2 + 140x$ (35, 2450)

Sales revenue (in dollars) — Units sold

(c) \$2450 **(d)** 35 units **(e)** \$70 **63. (a)** 1 million units
(b) \$9 **(c)**

Demand / Supply / Equilibrium point

Unit price (in dollars) — Quantity (in millions of units)

65. $y = x^6$

67. $y = 5x^8$

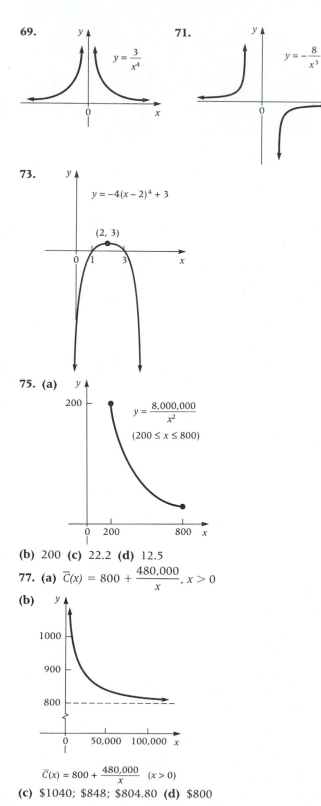

69.

$y = \dfrac{3}{x^4}$

71.

$y = -\dfrac{8}{x^3}$

73.

$y = -4(x-2)^4 + 3$

$(2, 3)$

75. (a)

$y = \dfrac{8{,}000{,}000}{x^2}$

$(200 \leq x \leq 800)$

(b) 200 **(c)** 22.2 **(d)** 12.5

77. (a) $\overline{C}(x) = 800 + \dfrac{480{,}000}{x}, \; x > 0$

(b)

$\overline{C}(x) = 800 + \dfrac{480{,}000}{x} \quad (x > 0)$

(c) $1040; \; 848; \; 804.80$ **(d)** $800

• **CHAPTER 2**

SECTION 2-1

1. 6 **3.** 8 **5.** 2 **7.** 9 **9.** 0 **11.** Does not exist **13.** 0
15. Does not exist **17.** 15 **19.** Does not exist **21.** −5
23. 5 **25.** 0 **27.** 0 **29.** 3 **31.** Does not exist **33.** 7
35. 5 **37.** 0 **39.** 0
41.

x	-2	-1.5	-1	-0.5	-0.0001	0.0001	0.5	1	1.5	2
$f(x) = \dfrac{\lvert x \rvert}{x}$	-1	-1	-1	-1	-1	1	1	1	1	1

$\lim\limits_{x \to 0} f(x)$ does not exist

43.

x	3	3.5	3.75	3.95	4.05	4.25	4.5
$f(x) = \dfrac{\sqrt{x} - 2}{x - 4}$	0.268	0.258	0.254	0.250	0.249	0.246	0.243

$\lim\limits_{x \to 4} f(x) = 0.250$

Note: The limit can also be found algebraically:

$$\lim_{x \to 4} \frac{\sqrt{x} - 2}{x - 4} = \lim_{x \to 4} \frac{1}{\sqrt{x} + 2} = \frac{1}{4}$$

45.

x	$1{,}000$	$10{,}000$	$100{,}000$	$1{,}000{,}000$	$10{,}000{,}000$
$f(x) = \left(1 + \dfrac{1}{x}\right)^x$	2.717	2.7181	2.7183	2.71828	2.718281828

$\lim\limits_{x \to \infty} f(x) = e$

47.

x	100	$1{,}000$	$10{,}000$	$100{,}000$	$1{,}000{,}000$
$f(x) = \dfrac{1}{x^2}$	10^{-4}	10^{-6}	10^{-8}	10^{-10}	10^{-12}

$\lim\limits_{x \to \infty} f(x) = 0$

49. (a)

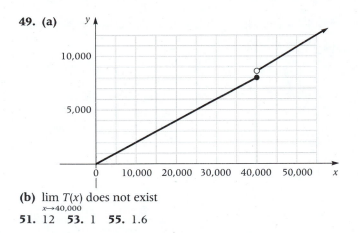

(b) $\lim_{x \to 40,000} T(x)$ does not exist

51. 12   **53.** 1   **55.** 1.6

SECTION 2-2

1. Continuous   **3.** Continuous   **5.** Not continuous
7. Continuous   **9.** Continuous   **11.** Not continuous
13. The function is discontinuous at $x = 0$.

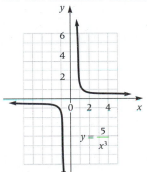

$$y = \frac{5}{x^3}$$

15. The function is discontinuous at $x = 2$.

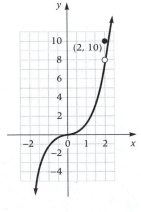

(2, 10)

17. The function is discontinuous at $x = 5$.

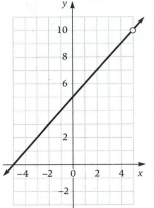

19. (a) $P_0 = \$100,000$; $P_1 = \$103,000$; $P_2 = \$106,090$;
$P_3 = \$109,272.70$; $P_4 = \$112,550.88$
(b)

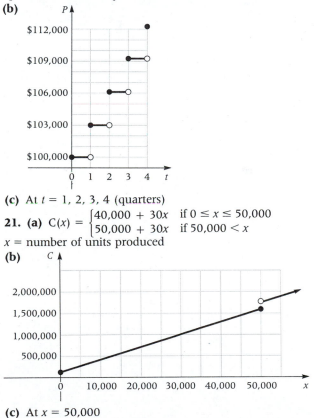

(c) At $t = 1, 2, 3, 4$ (quarters)

21. (a) $C(x) = \begin{cases} 40,000 + 30x & \text{if } 0 \le x \le 50,000 \\ 50,000 + 30x & \text{if } 50,000 < x \end{cases}$
x = number of units produced
(b)

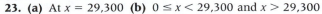

(c) At $x = 50,000$
23. (a) At $x = 29,300$ **(b)** $0 \le x < 29,300$ and $x > 29,300$

25. (a)

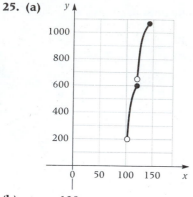

(b) at $x = 120$

SECTION 2-3

1. (a) 0.5 **(b)** 0.59375 **3.** 17.64 points / week
5. (a) 0.09375% / year to maturity **(b)** 0.07983% / year
to maturity **7. (a)** 3.7% / year **(b)** 6.5% / year
(c) 5.25% / year **9. (a)** 20.5 thousands / year
(b) 23 thousands / year **(c)** 12.8 thousands / year
11. 3 **13.** −2 **15.** $8x + 4\Delta x$ **17.** $2x − 5 + \Delta x$
19. $−10x − 5\Delta x$ **21.** $2x − 2 + \Delta x$ **23.** $4x − 1 + 2\Delta x$
25. $3x^2 + 3x\Delta x + (\Delta x)^2$
27. $4x^3 + 6x^2\Delta x + 4x(\Delta x)^2 + (\Delta x)^3$
29. $4x^3 + 2x + 4 + (6x^2 + 1)\Delta x + 4x(\Delta x)^2 + (\Delta x)^3$

31. $\dfrac{\Delta y}{\Delta x} = 2x − 4 + \Delta x$; 4 graphically, $\dfrac{\Delta y}{\Delta x}$ is the slope of
secant line from (2, 1) to (6, 17).

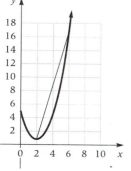

33. 4;4 graphically, $\dfrac{\Delta y}{\Delta x}$ is the slope of the secant line from
(2, 15) to (3, 19)

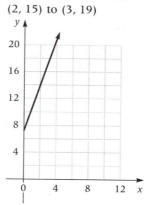

35. $−6x − 2 − 3\Delta x$; −23 graphically, $\dfrac{\Delta y}{\Delta x}$ is the slope of the
secant line from (2, −15) to (5, −84).

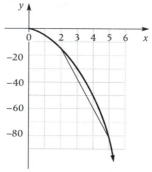

37. 4; graphically, $\dfrac{\Delta R}{\Delta x}$ is the slope of the secant line from
(4, 1) to (6, 9)

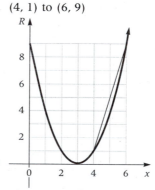

39. 210; The slope of the secant line from 200 to 220 is 210.

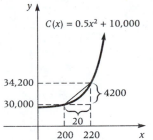

41. 1.3 million dollars/1000 units, this is the slope of the secant line from 12 to 15.

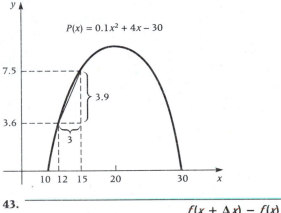

43.

x	Δx	$\dfrac{f(x + \Delta x) - f(x)}{\Delta x}$
4	0.75	.239266
4	0.50	.242641
4	0.25	.246211

45.

x	Δx	$\dfrac{f(x + \Delta x) - f(x)}{\Delta x}$
1	0.60	−1.015625
1	0.40	−1.224490
1	0.20	−1.527777

SECTION 2-4

1. $2x$ **3.** $18x^2$ **5.** $4x^3$ **7.** 3   **9.** $2x - 5$ **11.** $-6x + 4$
13. $10x$ **15.** $3x^2 - 2x + 5$ **17.** -2; 0; -8 **19.** 8; 10; 2
21. -6; -12; 12   **23.** -3; -1; -9 **25.** -7; -8; 32
27. 0; 12; 36

29. $y' = 2x - 10$; $y'(2) = -6$; $y'(3) = -4$

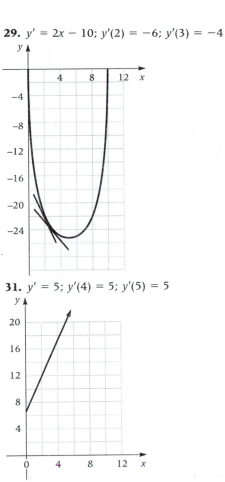

31. $y' = 5$; $y'(4) = 5$; $y'(5) = 5$

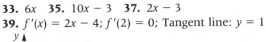

33. $6x$ **35.** $10x - 3$ **37.** $2x - 3$
39. $f'(x) = 2x - 4$; $f'(2) = 0$; Tangent line: $y = 1$

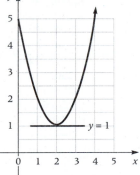

41. $f'(x) = 4$; $f'(2) = 4$; Tangent line: $y = 4x + 7$

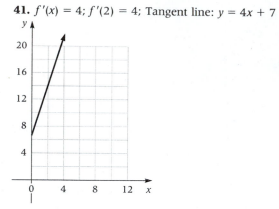

43. $f'(x) = 2x - 16$; $f'(1) = -14$; Tangent line:
$y = -14x - 1$

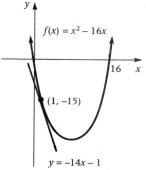

45. (a) $f'(x) = -6x + 60$ **(b)** $f'(3) = 42$ **(c)** $y = 42x + 27$

47.

x	Δx	$\dfrac{f(x + \Delta x) - f(x)}{\Delta x}$
4	0.1	0.2484567
4	0.01	0.2498439
4	0.001	0.2499843
4	0.0001	0.2499980
4	0.00001	0.2500000
4	−0.1	0.2515823
4	−0.01	0.2501564
4	−0.001	0.2500156
4	−0.0001	0.2500012
4	−0.00001	0.2500000

The difference quotient appears to be approaching 0.25.

49.

x	Δx	$\dfrac{f(x + \Delta x) - f(x)}{\Delta x}$
1	0.1	−1.7355372
1	0.01	−1.9703951
1	0.001	−1.9970040
1	0.0001	−1.9997001
1	0.00001	−1.9999710
1	−0.1	−2.3456790
1	−0.01	−2.0304051
1	−0.001	−2.0030040
1	−0.0001	−2.0003000
1	−0.00001	−2.0000300

The difference quotient appears to be approaching −2.
51. 7.0 **53.** 4.0 **55.** 0.76 **57.** 0.25 **59.** −0.006887

SECTION 2-5

1. a and d
3. (a) **(b)** $x = 5$ **(c)** $x = 5$

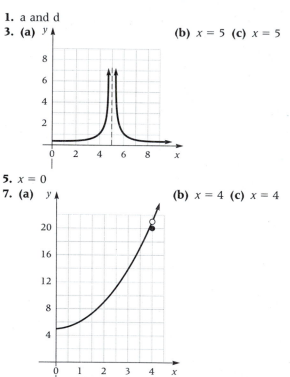

5. $x = 0$
7. (a) **(b)** $x = 4$ **(c)** $x = 4$

9. (a)

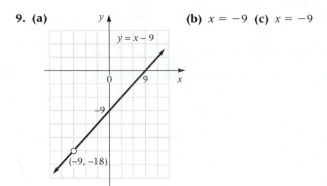

(b) $x = -9$ **(c)** $x = -9$

11. $x \leq 5$ **13.** $x = 2$ **15.** $x = 1$ **17.** $x \leq 3$ **19.** $x = 7$

21. $x = \dfrac{1}{4}$ **23.** $x < 6$

SECTION 2-6

1. $3x^2$ **3.** $20x^{19}$ **5.** 4 **7.** $\dfrac{-6}{x^7}$ **9.** $5x^4$ **11.** $\dfrac{-3}{x^4}$

13. $\dfrac{-1}{4}x^{-5/4}$ **15.** 0 **17.** $-8x^7$ **19.** $6x^{-3}$ **21.** $\dfrac{-15}{2x^{5/2}}$

23. 0 **25.** $\dfrac{-5}{16}$ **27.** 24 **29.** $\dfrac{3}{128}$ **31.** $2x - 8$ **33.** $16x$

35. $3x^2 + 4x$ **37.** $6x^5 - 5x^4 - \dfrac{8}{x^3}$ **39.** $-15x^2 - 12x + 8$

41. $5x^4 - 24x^3 + 24x^2$ **43.** $6x$ **45.** $-4x$ **47.** $-9x^2$

49. $3x^2 - 8x$ **51.** $\dfrac{-1}{2x^{3/2}} + \dfrac{2}{\sqrt{x}}$ **53.** $-6t + 8$ **55.** $3w^2 - 5$

57. -2 **59.** 3 **61.** -137 **63.** $\dfrac{1}{2}$ **65.** $-6x + 2$

67. $3x^2 + 12x + 8$ **69.** $5x^4 - 18x^2 + 6$ **71.** $50x^9$

73. $\dfrac{6}{x^3}$ **75.** $12x^2 - 12x + 4$

77.

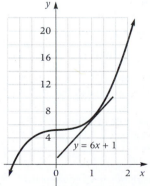

79. (a) 0.12 million dollars/year
(b) 0.18 million dollars/year
(c) $P(x) = 0.18x + 4.73$
  $P(7) = 5.99$ million dollars

81. (a) $12x$ **(b)** $f'(2) = 24$; $f'(3) = 36$; The rate of change is not constant. **(c)** 126 million dollars

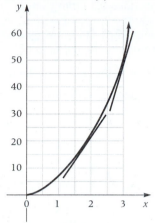

83. (a) $R'(x) = -4x + 60$
(b) $R'(10) = 20$; This is approximately the additional revenue obtained by selling one more unit beyond 10 units. It is the slope of the line tangent to the graph of $R(x)$ at $x = 10$.
(c)

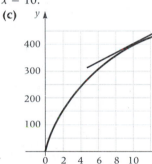

85. (a) 32 ft/sec **(b)** 0 ft/sec **(c)** -32 ft/sec
(d)

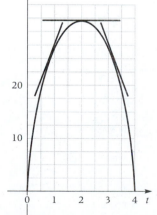

87. (a) Marginal profit $= P'(x) = 4 - \dfrac{3x^2}{1,000,000}$

(b) 3.97; This is the approximate additional profit gained from selling one more unit when at the level of $x = 100$.
(c) -6.83; The approximate change in profit in moving from a sales level of 1900 units to one additional unit is negative.   **89. (a)** $y' = \dfrac{45}{\sqrt{x}}$ units/ hour **(b)** 22.5 units/hour

(c) 15 units/hour   **91. (a)** $P'(t) = 8000t$ people/year
(b) 24,000 people/year **(c)** 48,000 people/year

SECTION 2-7

1. $5x^4 + 8x^3 - 9x^2 - 6x + 28$

3. $(x^3 - 2x + 6)(2x - 3) + (x^2 - 3x + 2)(3x^2 - 2)$
$= 5x^4 - 12x^3 - 6x^2 + 24x - 22$

5. $(x^3 - x^2 - 2)(2x - 1) + (x^2 - x - 1)(3x^2 - 2x)$
$= 5x^4 - 8x^3 - 2x + 2$

7. $(x^7 - 6x^2)(8x - 3) + (4x^2 - 3x + 4)(7x^6 - 12x)$
$= 36x^8 - 21x^7 + 28x^6 - 96x^3 + 54x^2 - 48x$

9. $(5x^2 - 3x + 1)(12x^2) + (3x^4 - 7)(10x - 3)$
$= 30x^5 + 51x^4 - 36x^3 + 12x^2 - 70x + 21$

11. $\dfrac{(x^3 - 3x + 9)(2x - 4) - (x^2 - 4x + 5)(3x^2 - 3)}{(x^3 - 3x + 9)^2}$
$= \dfrac{-x^4 + 8x^3 - 18x^2 + 18x - 21}{(x^3 - 3x + 9)^2}$

13. $\dfrac{2x^3 + 15x^2}{(x + 5)^2}$ **15.** $\dfrac{-x^3 - 28}{x^5}$ **17.** $\dfrac{6}{(x - 2)^2} + \dfrac{3}{(5x + 1)^2}$

19. $\dfrac{x^4 - 27x^2 - 18x}{(x^2 - 9)^2}$ **21.** $\dfrac{-2x + 3}{(x^2 - 3x)^2}$

23. $\dfrac{-2(6x^2 + 3x - 1)}{(3x^2 - 2x)^2}$ **25.** $\dfrac{14x^3 - \frac{8}{5}x - \frac{1}{5}}{x^{6/5}}$

27. $(5x^3 - 7x^2 + 3)(4x^3 - 24x^2 + 5) -$
$\dfrac{(x^4 - 8x^3 + 5x + 1)(15x^2 - 14x)}{(5x^3 - 7x^2 + 3)^2}$
$= \dfrac{5x^6 - 14x^5 + 56x^4 - 38x^3 - 22x^2 + 14x + 15}{(5x^3 - 7x^2 + 3)^2}$

29. $\dfrac{\left(x - \frac{1}{\sqrt{x}}\right)\left(\frac{1}{2\sqrt{x}} + 1\right) - (\sqrt{x} + x)\left(1 + \frac{1}{2x^{3/2}}\right)}{\left(x + \frac{1}{\sqrt{x}}\right)^2}$
$= \dfrac{-\frac{1}{2}\sqrt{x} - \frac{1}{x} - \frac{3}{2\sqrt{x}}}{\left(x + \frac{1}{\sqrt{x}}\right)^2} = \dfrac{-(x\sqrt{x} + 2 - 3\sqrt{x})}{2x\left(x + \frac{1}{\sqrt{x}}\right)^2}$

31. 2 **33.** -21

35. $(x^3 - 4x^2 + 5)(2x - 8) + (x^2 - 8x + 7)(3x^2 - 8x)$
$= 5x^4 - 48x^3 + 117x^2 - 46x - 40$

37. $\dfrac{[x^3 - 6x + 1][(x^3 - 4x + 7)(2x - 2) + (x^2 - 2x)(3x^2 - 4)] - (x^3 - 4x + 7)(x^2 - 2x)(3x^2 - 6)}{(x^3 - 6x + 1)^2}$

39. $\dfrac{(x^5 - 8x^2)(x^3 + 1)[(x^3 - 6x^2 + 5)(2x - 4) + (x^2 - 4x)(3x^2 - 12x)] - (x^3 - 6x^2 + 5)(x^2 - 4x)[(x^5 - 8x^2)(3x^2) + (5x^4 - 16x)(x^3 + 1)]}{[(x^5 - 8x^2)(x^3 + 1)]^2}$

41. $(t^5 - 4)\left[\dfrac{(t^4 + 7)(3t^2) - (t^3 + 6)(4t^3)}{(t^4 + 7)^2}\right] + \left(\dfrac{t^3 + 6}{t^4 + 7}\right)(5t^4)$
$= \dfrac{-t^6 - 24t^3 + 21t^2}{}$ ... $x^4 + 23x^2 - 30$

43. $(x^2 - 4x + 1)\left[\dfrac{(x^2 + 6)(3x^2 - 5) - (x^3 - 5x)(2x)}{(x^2 + 6)^2}\right] + \left(\dfrac{x^3 - 5x}{x^2 + 6}\right)(2x - 4)$

45. (a) $9x^8 - 40x^4 = x^4(9x^4 - 40)$ **(b)** $9x^8 - 40x^4$
47. 11   **49.** $y = 4x - 52$

51. $y = \dfrac{-2}{343}x + \dfrac{3}{49}$

53. $y = \dfrac{47}{128}x + \dfrac{233}{128}$, or $128y - 47x = 233$

55. (a) $R(t) = (10 + 2t)(20 + 0.2t^2)$
$= 200 + 40t + 2t^2 + 0.4t^3$
(b) $(10 + 2t)(0.4t) + (20 + 0.2t^2)2 = 40 + 4t + 1.2t^2$
(c) \$52.80/unit   **57. (a)** $\overline{C}(x) = 10 + \dfrac{500}{x}$ **(b)** $\dfrac{-500}{x^2}$

(c) $\overline{C}'(4) = -31.25$ ⎫ In each case $\overline{C}'(x_0)$ represents the
$\overline{C}'(5) = -20$ ⎬ rate of change of the average cost at
$\overline{C}'(6) = -13.89$ ⎭ $x = x_0$.
At $x = 5$, the average cost per unit in going to $x = 6$ decreases by approximately \$20.
59. (a) $\overline{C}(x) = -x + 30$ **(b)** -1
(c) $\overline{C}'(4) = \overline{C}'(5) = \overline{C}'(6) = -1$
The average cost per unit decreases by \$1 when the production is increased by one unit.

61. (a) $\dfrac{30}{(110 - x)^2}$ **(b)** $\dfrac{dy}{dx}\bigg|_{x = 60} = 0.012;$

$\dfrac{dy}{dx}\bigg|_{x = 80} = 0.0333;$ $\dfrac{dy}{dx}\bigg|_{x = 90} = 0.075;$

In each case $\dfrac{dy}{dx}\Big|x = x_0$ represents the rate of change in the cost y as x is increased. The cost rises more rapidly as x_0 approaches 110.

SECTION 2-8

1. $5t^4 - 12t^2 + 7$ **3.** $5u^4$ **5.** $18u^5 - 40u^4 + 4$
7. $-21u^2 - 16u$ **9.** $33x^2(x^3 + 5)^{10}$
11. $\dfrac{-4(3x^2 - 6)}{(x^3 - 6x)^5} = \dfrac{-12(x^2 - 2)}{(x^3 - 6x)^5}$ **13.** $60x^3(x^4 - 9)^{14}$
15. $\dfrac{-2(6x^5 - 8)}{3(x^6 - 8x)^{5/3}}$ **17.** $20(3x^2 - 8x)(x^3 - 4x^2 + 5)^{19}$
19. $10(x^3 - 4x)^9(3x^2 - 4)(x^2 + 5) + (x^3 - 4x)^{10}(2x)$
21. $7\left(\dfrac{5x - 3}{8 - x^4}\right)^6\left(\dfrac{15x^4 - 12x^3 + 40}{(8 - x^4)^2}\right)$
23. $7\left(\dfrac{5x - 3}{8 - x^4}\right)^6\left(\dfrac{15x^4 - 12x^3 + 40}{(8 - x^4)^2}\right)$
25. $10[(5x - 3)(x^2 - 1)]^9[15x^2 - 6x - 5]$
27. $10[(5x - 3)(x^2 - 1)]^9[15x^2 - 6x - 5]$
29. $6x(x^3 - 4x^2)^5(x^2 - 1)^2 +$
$5(x^3 - 4x^2)^4(3x^2 - 8x)(x^2 - 1)^3$
31. $15x^2(x^3 + 1)^4 + 14x(x^2 - 2)^6$ **33.** $\dfrac{5}{2\sqrt{x}}(\sqrt{x} + 9)^4$
35. $\dfrac{5x^3 + 2}{2\sqrt{x^3 + 1}}$ **37.** $\dfrac{5x^3 + 6x^2}{2(x + 1)^{3/2}}$ **39.** $-\dfrac{3}{25}$ **41.** $\dfrac{17}{20\sqrt{10}}$ or
$\dfrac{17\sqrt{10}}{200}$ **43.** $y = 1280x - 4864$ **45. (a)** $\dfrac{dC}{dt} = 15(5t + 4)^2$
(b) 17,340; The instantaneous rate of change with respect to t at $t = 6$. **47.** 60,000 millions of dollars/month = 60 billion dollars/month **49. (a)** $\dfrac{dS}{dr} = 700\left(1 + \dfrac{r}{400}\right)^{27}$
(b) 1194.82 **(c)** 1363.46; $\dfrac{dS}{dr}$ represents the instantaneous rate of change of S with respect to r. At $r = 10$, for example, the rate of change is \$1363.46/unit change in r.
51. (a) $\dfrac{dS}{dr} = \left(\dfrac{48,000}{r}\right)\left(1 + \dfrac{r}{100}\right)^7 -$
$\left(\dfrac{600,000}{r^2}\right)\left[\left(1 + \dfrac{r}{100}\right)^8 - 1\right]$
(b) 2305.48; An increase of 1% in the interest rate will increase the value of S by approximately \$2305.48
(c) 2492.31; An increase of 1% in the interest rate will increase the value of S by approximately \$2492.31.

• CHAPTER HIGHLIGHTS

1. If the y-values of a function get closer and closer to a single number L as the x-values get closer and closer to a number a, then L is the limit of the function as x approaches a. **2.** Right-hand limit. **3.** Yes.
4. *Property 1:* $\lim\limits_{x \to a} c = c$. This property states that the limit of a constant function is the constant value.

Property 2: $\lim\limits_{x \to a} [f(x) \pm g(x)] = \lim\limits_{x \to a} f(x) \pm \lim\limits_{x \to a} g(x)$. This property states that the limit of a sum (or difference) is the sum (or difference) of the individual limits provided that these limits exist.
Property 3: $\lim\limits_{x \to a} kf(x) = k \lim\limits_{x \to a} f(x)$. This property states that the limit of a constant times a function is the constant times the limit of the function provided that the limit exists.
Property 4: $\lim\limits_{x \to a} [f(x)]^r = [\lim\limits_{x \to a} f(x]^r$. This property states that the limit of a function raised to a power is the power of the limit provided that the limit exists.
Property 5: $\lim\limits_{x \to a} [f(x)g(x)] = [\lim\limits_{x \to a} f(x)][\lim\limits_{x \to a} g(x)]$. This property states that the limit of a product is the product of the limits provided that the limits exist.
Property 6: $\lim\limits_{x \to a} [f(x)/g(x)] = [\lim\limits_{x \to a} f(x)]/[\lim\limits_{x \to a} g(x)]$ provided that $\lim\limits_{x \to a} g(x) \neq 0$. This property states that the limit of a quotient is the quotient of the limits provided that the limits exist and the limit of the denominator is not 0. **5.** 0
6. Horizontal asymptote. **7.** A function is continuous at a point if its graph has no break at that point. **8.** A function f is continuous at $x = a$ if $f(a)$ exists, $\lim\limits_{x \to a} f(x)$ exists, and $\lim\limits_{x \to a} f(x) = f(a)$. **9.** A function is continuous over an interval if it is continuous at each point in the interval.
10. *Property 1: Constant function.* If $f(x) = k$ where k is a constant, then $f(x)$ is continuous for all x. This means that a constant function is continuous for all values of x.
Property 2: Power functions. Functions of the form $f(x) = x^n$ and $g(x) = \sqrt[n]{x}$, where n is a positive integer, are continuous for all values of x in their respective domains.
Property 3: Sum, difference, and product. If $f(x)$ and $g(x)$ are continuous at a point, then $f(x) + g(x)$, $f(x) - g(x)$, and $f(x) \cdot g(x)$ are continuous at that point.
Property 4: Quotient. If $f(x)$ and $g(x)$ are continuous at a point, then $f(x)/g(x)$ is continuous at that point provided that $g(x) \neq 0$ at the point. **11.** Polynomial functions are continuous at all values of x. **12.** A rational function is continuous at all values of x where its denominator does not equal 0. **13.** $[f(x + \Delta x) - f(x)]/\Delta x$; difference quotient
14. Secant line **15.** $\lim\limits_{\Delta x \to 0} [(f(x + \Delta x) - f(x))/\Delta x]$
16. Slope; tangent **17.** Derivative; point
18. The function has a unique nonvertical tangent line at that point. **19.** No **20.** Yes **21.** Yes **22.** If $f(x) = k$ where k is a constant, then $f'(x) = 0$. In other words, the derivative of a constant is 0. **23.** If $f(x) = x^n$ where n is a real number, then $f'(x) = nx^{n-1}$. **24.** If $y = kf(x)$ where k is a constant and $f'(x)$ exists, then $dy/dx = kf'(x)$. In other words, the derivative of a constant times a function is the constant times the derivative of the function.
25. If $y = f(x) \pm g(x)$ where $f(x)$ and $g(x)$ are differentiable functions of x, then $dy/dx = f'(x) \pm g'(x)$. In other words, the derivative of a sum or difference of two functions is the sum or difference of the derivatives. **26.** Marginal cost is

the cost of producing one more unit. Marginal revenue is the revenue gained from selling one more unit.
27. If $y = f(x)s(x)$ where $f(x)$ and $s(x)$ are differentiable functions at x, then $dy/dx = f \cdot s' + s \cdot f'$. In other words, the derivative of a product of two functions is the first times the derivative of the second plus the second times the derivative of the first.   **28.** If $y = n(x)/d(x)$ where $n(x)$ and $d(x)$ are differentiable functions at x and $d(x) \neq 0$, then $dy/dx = [d \cdot n' - n \cdot d']/d^2$. In other words, the derivative of a quotient of two functions is the denominator times the derivative of the numerator minus the numerator times the derivative of the denominator all divided by the square of the denominator.   **29.** If $y = f(u)$ is a differentiable function of u and $u = g(x)$ is a differentiable function of x, then $dy/dx = [dy/du][du/dx]$.   **30.** If $y = u^n$ where u is a differentiable function of x, then $dy/dx = [nu^{n-1}][du/dx]$.

• **REVIEW EXERCISES**

1. Does not exist   **3.** Exists; 16   **5.** Exists; $\dfrac{1}{2\sqrt{2}}$

7. Discontinuous at $x = 2$ **9.** Continuous everywhere
11. Discontinuous at $x = 2$
13. **(a)** $P_0 = \$1000$
$P_1 = \$1040$
$P_2 = \$1081.60$
$P_3 = \$1124.86$
$P_4 = \$1169.86$
(b)

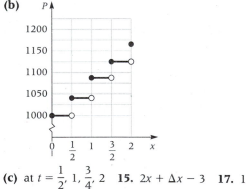

(c) at $t = \dfrac{1}{2}, 1, \dfrac{3}{4}, 2$ **15.** $2x + \Delta x - 3$ **17.** 1

19. **(a)** 4000 **(b)** 5000 **(c)** The value calculated is the slope of the secant line from (1000, 7,000,000) to (3000, 15,000,000). **(d)** The value calculated is the slope

of the secant line from (1000, 7,000,000) to (3000, 12,000,000). **(e)** & **(f)**

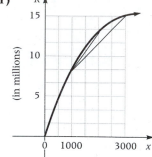

21. **(a)** $-10x + 2$ **(b)** -8 **(c)** 22   **23.** **(a)** $8x^7 - 8$ **(b)** 0
(c) -1032 **25.** **(a)** $10,000t$ people/year **(b)** 40,000
(c) 60,000 **(d)** 90,000
27. $(x^2 + 4x + 7)(3x^2 + 6x) + (x^3 + 3x^2 + 8)(2x + 4)$
$= 5x^4 + 28x^3 + 57x^2 + 58x + 32$

29. $6(x^4 - 6x + 1)^5(4x^3 - 6)$ **31.** $\dfrac{-18(x + 4)}{(x^2 + 8x + 2)^{10}}$

33. $2(x^3 + x^2 + 4)^5(x + 2) +$
$5(x^3 + x^2 + 4)^4(3x^2 + 2x)(x^2 + 4x + 5)$

35. $\dfrac{(x^3 - 6x + 8)(4x^3 + 10x) - (x^4 + 5x^2 + 7)(3x^2 - 6)}{(x^3 - 6x + 8)^2}$

$= \dfrac{-8x^6 - 23x^4 + 32x^3 - 51x^2 + 80x + 42}{(x^3 - 6x + 8)^2}$

37. $9(x^3 - 4x + 2)(x^4 + 4x + 7)^8(4x^3 + 4) -$
$$\dfrac{(x^4 + 4x + 7)^9(3x^2 - 4)}{(x^3 - 4x + 2)^2}$$

39. $6(x^8 + 9)\left(\dfrac{x^2 - 9}{x^4 + 7}\right)^5\left[\dfrac{(x^4 + 7)(2x) - (x^2 - 9)(4x^3)}{(x^4 + 7)^2}\right] +$
$8x^7\left(\dfrac{x^2 - 9}{x^4 + 7}\right)^6$

41. $\dfrac{-88\,(x + 6)^7}{(x - 5)^9}$ **43.** **(a)** $\overline{C}(x) = 8 + \dfrac{240}{x}$ **(b)** $\dfrac{-240}{x^2}$

(c) $\overline{C}'(5) = -9.6$
$\overline{C}'(20) = -0.6$
$\overline{C}'(50) = -0.096$
A value of $\overline{C}'(x_0)$ represents the instantaneous rate of change of the average cost per unit at a production level of x_0.

45. **(a)** $\dfrac{dS}{dr} = -\dfrac{900,000}{r^2}\left[\left(1 + \dfrac{r}{100}\right)^6 - 1\right] +$
$\dfrac{6(900,000)}{r}\left(1 + \dfrac{r}{100}\right)^5\left(\dfrac{1}{100}\right)$

(b) 1665.04; At $r = 8$, a change of 1 unit in r will result in a change of approximately \$1665.04 in S **(c)** 1752.71; At $r = 10$, a change of 1 unit in r will result in an approximate change of \$1752.71 in S.   **47.** **(a)** $x < 5$ because $f(x)$ does not exist for $x < 5$. **(b)** $x \leq 5$ **49.** $x = 0$

• CHAPTER 3

SECTION 3-1

1. $f'(x) = 3x^2 - 8x + 7$
$f''(x) = 6x - 8$
3. $f'(x) = 5x^4 - 24x^2 + 4x + 4$
$f''(x) = 20x^3 - 48x + 4$
5. $f'(x) = 5x^4 - 4x^3 + 12x^2 + 2x - 1$
$f''(x) = 20x^3 - 12x^2 + 24x + 2$
7. $f'(x) = (x + 1)^4 + 4(x + 1)^3(x - 2) = (x + 1)^3(5x - 7)$
$f''(x) = 8(x+1)^3 + 12(x + 1)^2(x - 2) = 4(x + 1)^2(5x - 4)$
9. $\dfrac{dy}{dx} = 3x^2 - 4x + 8$

$\dfrac{d^2y}{dx^2} = 6x - 4$

11. $\dfrac{dy}{dx} = \dfrac{x^6 - 28x^3 - 18x^2}{(x^3 - 7)^2}$

$\dfrac{d^2y}{dx^2} = \dfrac{(x^3 - 7)(6x^5 - 84x^2 - 36x) - 6x^2(x^6 - 28x^3 - 18x^2)}{(x^3 - 7)}$

13. $\dfrac{dy}{dx} = (x - 4)^3 + 3(x - 4)^2(x - 7) = (x - 4)^2(4x - 25)$

$\dfrac{d^2y}{dx} = 6(x - 4)(2x - 11)$

15. $g'(x) = \dfrac{x^2 - 10x + 1}{(x - 5)^2}$

$g''(x) = \dfrac{2(x - 5)^2 - 2(x^2 - 10x + 1)}{(x - 5)^3} = \dfrac{48}{(x - 5)^3}$

$g''(2) = -\dfrac{16}{9} \approx -1.778$

17. $\dfrac{dy}{dx} = 4x^3 - 15x^2 + 12x + 3$

$\left.\dfrac{dy}{dx}\right|_{x = 1} = 4$

$\dfrac{d^2y}{dx^2} = 12x^2 - 30x + 12$

$\left.\dfrac{d^2y}{dx^2}\right|_{x = 1} = -6$

19. $f'(x) = 4x^3 - 18x^2 + 16x - 4$
$f'(1) = -2$
$f''(x) = 12x^2 - 36x + 16$
$f''(3) = 16$
21. $f'(x) = 6x^5 - 40x^4 + 24x^3 - 6x^2 + 1$
$f''(x) = 30x^4 - 160x^3 + 72x^2 - 12x$
$f'''(x) = 120x^3 - 480x^2 + 144x - 12$
$f^{(4)}(x) = 360x^2 - 960x + 144$
$f^{(4)}(3) = 504$
23. $f'(x) = 4x^3 - 18x^2 + 8x - 8$
$f''(x) = 12x^2 - 36x + 8$
$f'''(x) = 24x - 36$

$f^{(4)}(x) = 24$
$f^{(5)}(x) = 0$
$f^{(6)}(x) = 0$

25. (a) $\left.\dfrac{dS}{dt}\right|_{t = 2} = 128$ ft/sec; $\left.\dfrac{dS}{dt}\right|_{t = 3} = 96$ ft/sec;

$\left.\dfrac{dS}{dt}\right|_{t = 8} = -64$ ft/sec (downward) **(b)** $\dfrac{d^2S}{dt^2} = -32$ ft/sec²

at $t = 2, 3,$ and 8

SECTION 3-2

1. (a) $x_1 < x < x_2$ and $x_3 < x < x_4$ **(b)** $x_2 < x < x_3$ and
$x_4 < x < x_5$ **(c)** relative maxima: $f(x_2)$ and $f(x_4)$;
relative minimum: $f(x_3)$ **(d)** absolute maximum: $f(x_4)$;
absolute minimum: $f(x_1)$ **3. (a)** $-2 < x < 2$
(b) $-\infty < x < -2$ and $2 < x < \infty$. **(c)** relative minimum at
$x = -2$; relative maximum at $x = 2$ **5. (a)** $-\infty < x < -4$
and $-4 < x < 5$ **(b)** $5 < x < \infty$ **(c)** relative maximum at
$x = 5$; no relative minima **7. (a)** $-3 < x < -1,$
$-1 < x < 2,$ and $4 < x < \infty$ **(b)** $-\infty < x < -3$ and
$2 < x < 4$ **(c)** relative minima at $x = -3$ and $x = 4$;
relative maxima at $x = 2$ **9. (a)** $-\infty < x < -1$ and
$5 < x < \infty$ **(b)** $-1 < x < 5$ **(c)** relative minimum at $x = 5$;
relative maximum at $x = -1$ **11. (a)** $0 < x < 3000$ and
$7000 < x < 10{,}000$ **(b)** $3000 < x < 7000$ **(c)** 45,000 is a
relative maximum; 35,000 is a relative minimum
(d) 10,000 units **(e)** \$83,000; not a relative maximum;
It is an absolute maximum. **13. (a)** 3000 units
(b) \$2; This is both a relative and an absolute minimum.
15. (a) $-\infty < x < \infty$ **(b)** nowhere **(c)** no relative maxima
or minima **17. (a)** $-\infty < x < 4$ **(b)** $4 < x < \infty$
(c) $f(4) = 16$ is a relative maximum **19. (a)** $1 < x < \infty$
(b) $-\infty < x < 0$ and $0 < x < 1$ **(c)** $f(1) = 9$ is a relative
minimum **21. (a)** $0 < x < \infty$ **(b)** $-\infty < x < 0$
(c) $f(0) = 2$ is a relative minimum **23. (a)** $-\infty < x < 5$
and $5 < x < \infty$ **(b)** Nowhere **(c)** No relative maxima or
minima **25. (a)** Nowhere **(b)** $-\infty < x < -1$ and
$-1 < x < \infty$ **(c)** No relative maxima or minima
27. (a) $-\infty < x < 4$ **(b)** $4 < x < \infty$ **(c)** relative maximum
at $f(4) = 25$ **(d)**

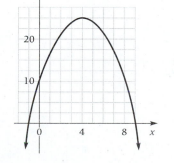

29. (a) $-\infty < x < 0$ and $4 < x < \infty$ **(b)** $0 < x < 4$
(c) relative maximum at $f(0) = 0$; relative minimum at
$f(4) = -32$ **(d)**

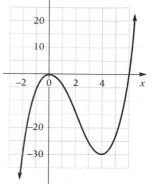

31. (a) $-2 < x < 0$ and $2 < x < \infty$ **(b)** $-\infty < x < -2$ and
$0 < x < 2$ **(c)** relative minima at $f(-2) = -16$ and
$f(2) = -16$; relative maximum at $f(0) = 0$
(d)

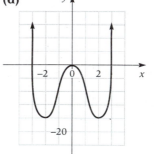

33. (a) $0 < x < \infty$

(b) $-\infty < x < 0$ **(c)** relative minimum at $f(0) = 5$
(d)

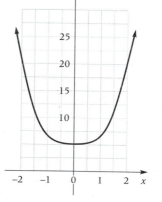

35. relative maximum at

$f(-5) = 101$; relative minimum at $f(1) = -7$; absolute
minimum at $f(-10) = -249$; absolute maximum at
$f(11) = 1893$

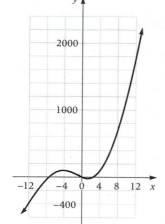

37. $f(x) = ax^2 + bx + c$

$f'(x) = 2ax + b; f'(x) = 0 \Rightarrow x = -\dfrac{b}{2a}$

For $x < -\dfrac{b}{2a}, f'(x) < 0$; for $x > -\dfrac{b}{2a}, f'(x) > 0$.

$\therefore f\left(-\dfrac{b}{2a}\right)$ is a relative minimum of f

39. (a) $x_1 < x < x_4$ **(b)** Increasing at an increasing rate
41. (a) $0 < x < 20$ **(b)** $20 < x < 40$ **(c)** relative
maximum at $R(20) = 400$ **(d)**

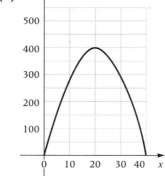

(e) $x = 20$; $R(20)$ is both a relative and an absolute
maximum. **(f)** 144 **43. (a)** $100 < x < \infty$

(b) $90 \le x < 100$ **(c)**

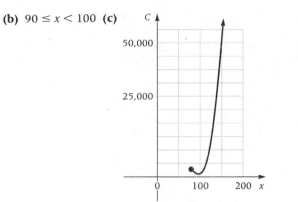

(d) 100; $C(100) = 1000$ is both a relative and an absolute minimum. **(e)** $C(100) = 1000$

SECTION 3-3

1. (a) $x_3 < x < x_5$ and $x_5 < x < x_7$ **(b)** $x_1 < x < x_3$ and $x_7 < x < x_8$ **(c)** $x = x_3$ and $x = x_7$ **(d)** relative maxima occur at $x = x_2$ and $x = x_5$; relative minima occur at $x = x_4$ and $x = x_6$ **3. (a)** $-\infty < x < -2$ and $4 < x < \infty$
(b) $-2 < x < 4$ **(c)** $x = -2$ and $x = 4$
5. (a) $-\infty < x < -3$ and $3 < x < \infty$ **(b)** $-3 < x < 3$
(c) $x = -3$ and $x = 3$ **7. (a)** $-\infty < x < -1$ and $2 < x < \infty$ **(b)** $-1 < x < 2$ **(c)** $x = -1$ and $x = 2$
9.

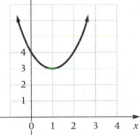

relative minimum: $f(1) = 3$; concave up everywhere; no asymptotes. y-intercept: $(0, 4)$
11. relative maximum: $f(-1) = 13$;
relative minimum: $f(9) = -487$; inflection point at $x = 4$; no asymptotes. y-intercept: $(0, -1)$

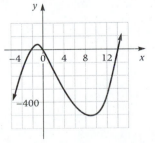

13. relative minimum: $f(3) = -128$; inflection points at $x = 0$ and $x = 2$; no asymptotes. y-intercept: $(0, 7)$

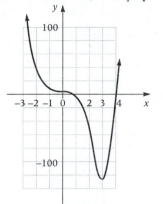

15. relative maximum: $f(-1) = 4$; relative minimum: $f(1) = 0$; inflection point at $x = 0$; no asymptotes. y-intercept: $(0, 2)$

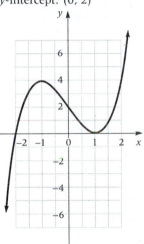

17. no relative extrema. inflection point at $x = 5$; no asymptotes. y-intercept: $(0, -125)$

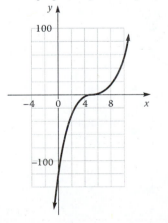

19. relative minimum: $f(-3) = 2$; no inflection points; no asymptotes. y-intercept: $(0, 59{,}051)$

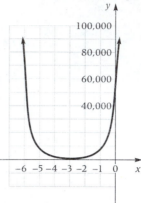

21. relative maximum: $f\left(-\dfrac{3}{5}\right) = 1382.8$;

relative minimum: $f(5) = 6$; inflection point at $x = \dfrac{4}{5}$; no asymptotes. y-intercept: $(0, 1256)$

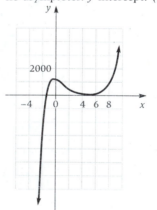

23. relative maximum: $f(-2) = 0$;

relative minimum: $f\left(\dfrac{2}{5}\right) \approx -268.74$;

inflection points at $x = \dfrac{2 - 3\sqrt{6}}{5}$, $x = \dfrac{2 + 3\sqrt{6}}{5}$, and $x = 4$;

no asymptotes. y-intercept: $(0, -256)$

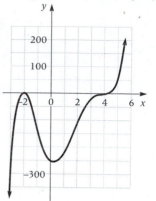

25. no relative extrema; inflection point at $x = 0$; no asymptotes. y-intercept: $(0, 0)$

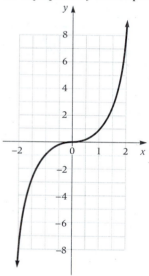

27. relative minimum: $f(0) = 0$; no inflection points; no asymptotes. y-intercept: $(0, 0)$

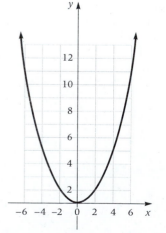

29. relative minimum: $f(0) = -3$;
inflection points at $x = -\sqrt{\dfrac{2}{3}}$ and $x = \sqrt{\dfrac{2}{3}}$;
horizontal asymptote: $y = 0$; y-intercept: $(0, -3)$

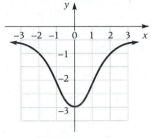

31. relative minimum: $f(-1) = \dfrac{-1}{2}$;

relative maximum: $f(1) = \dfrac{1}{2}$;
inflection points at $x = -\sqrt{3}$, $x = 0$, and $x = \sqrt{3}$;
horizontal asymptote: $y = 0$; y-intercept: $(0, 0)$

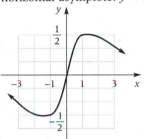

33. relative maximum: $f(-20) = -80$; relative minimum: $f(20) = 80$; no inflection points; vertical asymptote: $x = 0$

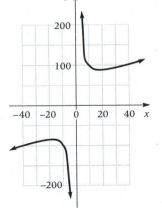

35. relative maximum: $f(-5) = -16$;
relative minimum: $f(3) = 0$; no inflection points;
vertical asymptote: $x = -1$

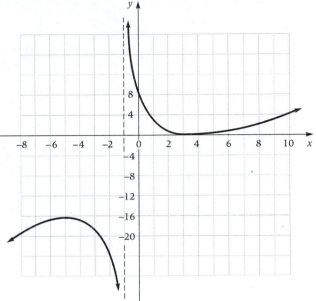

37. relative minimum: $f(0) = 0$;
relative maximum: $f(4) \approx 1.185$;
inflection points at $x = \dfrac{5 - \sqrt{33}}{2} \approx -0.37$ and
$x = \dfrac{5 + \sqrt{33}}{2} \approx 5.37$; vertical asymptote: $x = 1$;
horizontal asymptote: $y = 1$

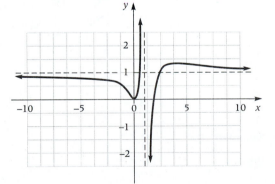

39. relative maximum: $f(-2\sqrt{5}) = 9 - 4\sqrt{5} \approx 0.06$; relative minimum: $f(2\sqrt{5}) = 9 + 4\sqrt{5} \approx 17.9$; no inflection points; vertical asymptote: $x = 0$; oblique asymptote: $y = x + 9$

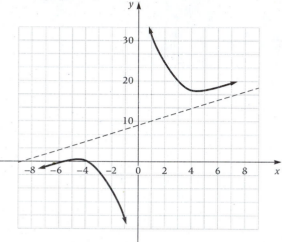

41. relative maximum: $f(0) = 0$; inflection point at $x = \frac{16}{3}$; no asymptotes. y-intecept: $(0, 0)$

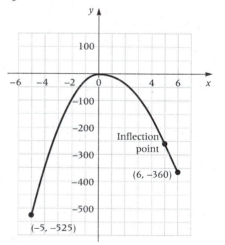

43. relative maximum: $f(1) = 0$;
relative minimum: $f\left(\frac{7}{3}\right) = -\frac{32}{27} \approx -1.18519$;

inflection point at $x = \frac{5}{3}$; no asymptotes.
y-intercept: $(0, -3)$

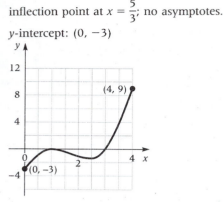

45. (a) $-\infty < x < 0$ **(b)** $0 < x < \infty$ **(c)** $x = 0$; $f''(x)$ is not defined at $x = 0$ **(d)**

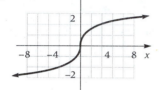

47. (a) relative minimum: $f(2) = 0.75$; inflection point at $x = 2\sqrt{3}$; horizontal asymptote: $y = 1$; y-intercept: $(0, 1)$

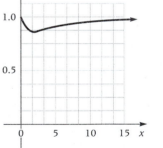

(b) $f(0) = 1$ **(c)** 2 weeks **(d)** After 2 weeks
(e) 0.75; occurring at $x = 2$ **(f)** 1.0; occurring at $x = 0$ and $x = +\infty$ **(g)** The level of oxygen reaches its initial level asymptotically.
49. (a)

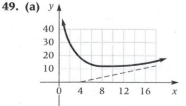

(b) $\overline{C}(8) = 12$ is a relative minimum **(c)** $x = 8$
(d) $\overline{C}(8) = 12$
51. (a)

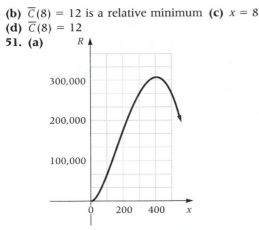

(b) $R(400) = 320,000$ is both a relative and an absolute maximum. $R(0) = 0$ is the absolute minimum.
(c) at $x = 200$ **(d)**

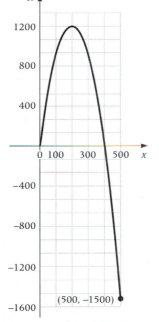

(e) relative and absolute maximum of 1200 at $x = 200$; absolute minimum of -1500 at $x = 500$ **(f)** $x = 200$

SECTION 3-4

1. relative minimum: $f(4) = -7$
3. relative maximum: $f(0) = 7$;
relative minimum: $f(4) = -25$
5. relative maximum: $f(-1) = 7$;
relative minimum: $f(1) = 3$
7. relative maximum: $f(-2) = 21$;
relative minimum: $f(1) = -6$
9. relative maximum: $f(-3) = 90$;
relative minimum: $f(5) = -166$

11. relative maximum: $f(0) = 6$;
relative minimum: $f(-2) = -10$;
relative minimum: $f(2) = -10$
13. relative maximum: $y(-5) = -10$;
relative minimum: $y(5) = 10$
15. relative maximum: $f(-3) = -4$;
relative minimum: $f(3) = 4$
17. absolute minimum: $f(8) = -55$; no absolute maximum
19. absolute maximum: $f(4) = 19$; no absolute minimum
21. absolute maximum: $f(4) = 4$; no absolute minimum
23. absolute maximum: $f(-3) = 58$;
absolute minimum: $f(3) = -50$
25. absolute minimum: $f(5) = 59$; no absolute maximum
27. absolute minimum: $f(3) = 8$; no absolute maximum
29. absolute minimum: $f(0) = -40$;
absolute maximum: $f(4) = 40$
31. absolute maximum: $f(6) = 20$;
absolute minimum: $f(0) = -16$
33. 12 and 12 **35.** 300 and 300 **37.** 60
39. (a) 5 inches **(b)** \$1,093,750
41. $x = 100$ ft, $y = 200$ ft **43.** $x = 100$ ft, $y = 200$ ft
45. $A = xy$; $2x + 2y = P$, a fixed number

$$A(x) = x\left(\frac{P - 2x}{2}\right) = \frac{P}{2}x - x^2$$

$$A'(x) = \frac{P}{2} - 2x$$

$$A'(x) = 0 \Rightarrow x = \frac{P}{4}; \ y = \frac{P}{4}$$

$A''(x) = -2 \Rightarrow$ a concave down. Thus, $A\left(\dfrac{P}{4}\right)$ is the absolute maximum area. Since $x = y$, the rectangle is a square.
47. $x = 500$ ft, $y = 450$ ft; Area = 405,000 sq. ft
49. (a) $P(x) = -4x^2 + 3000x - 10,000$ **(b)** $x = 375$
(c) $P(375) = \$552,500$
51. (a) $P(x) = -0.01x^2 + 19.8x - 40$ **(b)** $x = 990$
(c) $P(990) = \$9761$ **53. (a)** $R(x) = -5x^2 + 3000x$
(b) $P(x) = -5x^2 + 2950x - 6000$ **(c)** $x = 295$ **(d)** \$1525
(e) \$429,125 **55. (a)** $R(x) = -2x^2 + 2000x$
(b) $P(x) = -2x^2 + 1970x - 4000$ **(c)** $x = 492.5$
(d) \$1016 **(e)** \$481,112 **57. (a)** $x = 293$ **(b)** \$1535
(c) increased by \$10 **(d)** 50%
59. (a) $x = 25$ hundred units **(b)** 16 thousand dollars
(c) 15 million dollars **61.** 2 weeks; \$58.80 / tree
63. (a) $R(x) = (40 + 5x)(1000 - 50x)$ **(b)** $x = 6$
(c) \$49,000 **65.** 3 in x 3 in **67.** $x = 8$ ft; $y = 4$ ft
69. $P = 150$; $H(150) = 225$ **71.** $P = 900$; $H(900) = 900$
73. No maximum sustainable harvest

75. $\dfrac{27}{\sqrt{7}} \approx 10.205$ miles

SECTION 3-5

1. (a) $C(Q) = \dfrac{2{,}500{,}000}{Q} + 10Q$ (b) $Q = 500$

3. (a) $C(Q) = \dfrac{18{,}000{,}000}{Q} + 12.5Q$ (b) $Q = 1200$ units

(c) \$30,000/year (d) 250 orders/year 5. (a) \$16/unit

(b) $C(Q) = \dfrac{50{,}000{,}000}{Q} + 8Q$ (c) $Q = 2500$ units

(d) \$40,000/year (e) 200 orders/year

7. $C''(Q) = \dfrac{2KD}{Q^3} > 0 \Rightarrow C$ concave up. Thus, the relative
extremum found in Exercise 6 is a relative minimum. Since
the graph of C vs Q is concave up, the relative minimum is
also the absolute minimum.

• EXTRA DIVIDENDS

1. $C(Q) = \dfrac{1.28 \times 10^8}{Q} + 2Q$ 3. \$32,000 5. \$16,000

7. $C'(Q) = -\dfrac{KD}{Q^2} + \dfrac{H}{2}\left(\dfrac{P-D}{P}\right)$

$C''(Q) = \dfrac{2KD}{Q^3} > 0 \Rightarrow C$ concave up. Thus, the relative
extremum found in Exercise 6 is a relative minimum.
The relative minimum is also the absolute minimum
since C is concave up.

• CHAPTER HIGHLIGHTS

1. Take the derivative of the first derivative. 2. Take the
derivative of the second derivative. 3. (a) Velocity is the
rate of change of distance with respect to time and is given
by the derivative dS/dt. (b) Acceleration is the rate of
change of velocity with respect to time and is given by
d^2S/dt^2.

4. (a)

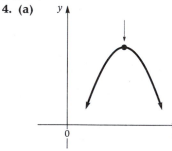

(b)

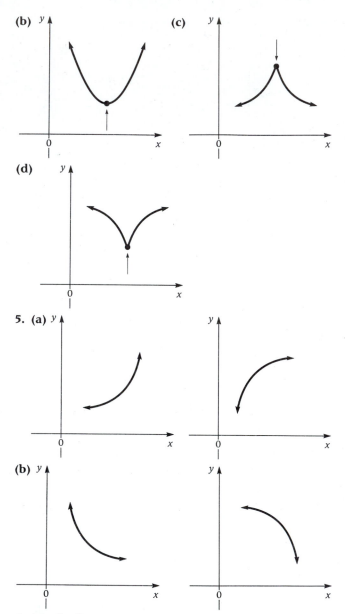

(c)

(d)

5. (a)

(b)

6. (a) The function is increasing over the interval.
(b) The function is decreasing over the interval.
7. (a) Critical values are values of x at which the
derivative of a function is either 0 or undefined. The
function must be defined at a critical value.
(b) Not necessarily (c) We look for a sign change in the
first derivative at the critical value. (d) No.
8. (a) If the sign of the first derivative changes from
positive to negative as we move from left to right across the
critical value, then a relative maximum occurs at the
critical value. (b) If the sign of the first derivative changes
from negative to positive as we move from left to right

across the critical value, then a relative minimum occurs at the critical value.   **9. (a)** A relative maximum is higher than any of its neighboring points on the graph of the function whereas an absolute maximum is the highest or among the highest points on the graph of the function. An analogous statement can be made for minimum points. **(b)** Yes. The figures below show relative maxima that are also absolute maxima. Analogous graphs can be drawn for minima.

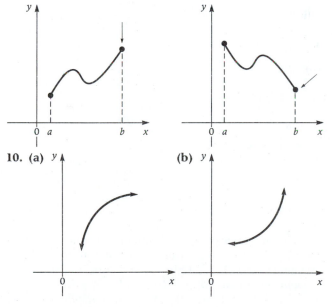

(c) No. The leftmost figure below shows an absolute maximum that is not a relative maximum. The rightmost figure below shows an absolute minimum that is not a relative minimum.

10. (a)   **(b)**

11. (a)   **(b)**

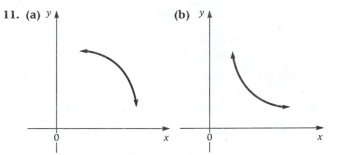

12. (a) The function is concave up over the interval. **(b)** The function is concave down over the interval. **13. (a)** An inflection point is a point where the graph of a function changes in concavity. **(b)** We look for a sign change in the second derivative.   **14.** Vertical asymptotes occur at values of x where the denominator of a rational function equals 0 but the numerator does not equal 0. **15.** No.   **16.** A function $f(x)$ has a horizontal asymptote if and only if either $\lim\limits_{x\to\infty} f(x) = L$ of $\lim\limits_{x\to-\infty} f(x) = M$ where L and M are constants. It might be the case that $L = M$. In any case L would be a horizontal asymptote as x approaches positive infinity and M would be a horizontal asymptote as x approaches negative infinity.   **17. (a)** No, it applies to only those critical values at which the first derivative is 0. **(b)** Yes. **(c)** No.   **18. (a)** A relative minimum occurs at x_0. **(b)** A relative maximum occurs at x_0. **(c)** The test fails and gives no information regarding the existence of a relative extremum at x_0.   **19.** Look for a sign change in the first derivative.   **20.** No   **21.** Yes   **22.** No   **23.** If a function that is continuous over some interval has only one critical value in the interval and the first derivative is 0 at that critical value, then: If the second derivative is negative at the critical value, an absolute maximum occurs at the critical value; if the second derivative is positive at the critical value, an absolute minimum occurs at the critical value; if the second derivative is 0 at the critical value, the test fails.   **24.** *Step 1:* Find all the critical values on the closed interval. *Step 2:* Evaluate the function at the critical values and at the endpoints of the interval. *Step 3.* Write the largest value found in step 2; this is the absolute maximum value of the function over the interval. Step 4: Write the smallest value found in step 2; this is the absolute minimum value of the function over the interval. **25.** The annual ordering cost and annual carrying cost. The total annual inventory cost is given by $C(Q) = K(D/Q) + H(Q/2)$ where D is the annual demand for the product, K is the cost of placing an order, H is the cost of carrying (or holding) one unit in inventory for a year, Q is the order size, D/Q is the number of orders placed in a year, $K(D/Q)$ is the annual ordering cost, $Q/2$ is the average number of units in inventory, and $H(Q/2)$ is the annual carrying cost.

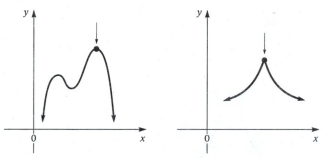

• REVIEW EXERCISES

1. (a) $2x - 6$ **(b)** 2 **(c)** -4 **(d)** 2   **3. (a)** $6x^5 - 32x^3$
(b) $30x^4 - 96x^2$ **(c)** -26 **(d)** -66 **5. (a)** 60 ft/sec;

40 ft/sec **(b)** -4 ft/sec^2 for both   **7. (a)** $x = \dfrac{-1}{2} + \dfrac{\sqrt{41}}{2}$

and $x = \dfrac{-1}{2} - \dfrac{\sqrt{41}}{2}$ **(b)** $-\infty < x < \dfrac{-1}{2} - \dfrac{\sqrt{41}}{2}$ and

$\dfrac{-1}{2} + \dfrac{\sqrt{41}}{2} < x < \infty$ **(c)** $\dfrac{-1}{2} - \dfrac{\sqrt{41}}{2} < x < \dfrac{-1}{2} + \dfrac{\sqrt{41}}{2}$

(d) relative maximum: $f\left(\dfrac{-1}{2} - \dfrac{\sqrt{41}}{2}\right) \approx 169.764$

relative minimum: $f\left(\dfrac{-1}{2} + \dfrac{\sqrt{41}}{2}\right) \approx -92.764$

(e)

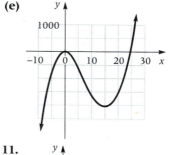

9. (a) $x = 0$ and $x = 16$ **(b)** $-\infty < x < 0$ and $16 < x < \infty$
(c) $0 < x < 16$ **(d)** relative maximum: $f(0) = 6$;
relative minimum: $f(16) = -2042$
(e)

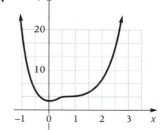

11.

relative and absolute minimum: $f(0) = 2$;

inflection points at $x = \dfrac{1}{3}$ and $x = 1$

13.

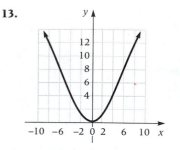

relative and absolute minimum: $f(0) = 0$;
no inflection points

15.

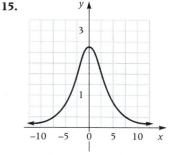

relative and absolute maximum: $f(0) = 2.5$;

inflection points at $x = \dfrac{-2}{\sqrt{3}}$ and $x = \dfrac{2}{\sqrt{3}}$

17. (a) $\overline{C}(x) = x - 8 + \dfrac{100}{x}$

(b)

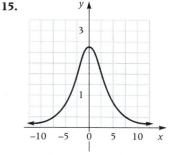

$\overline{C}(10)$ is both a relative and an absolute minimum;
$y = x - 8$ is an oblique asymptote; $x = 0$ is a vertical
asymptote **(c)** $\overline{C}(10) = 12$ is both a relative and an
absolute minimum. **(d)** $x = 10$ **(e)** $\overline{C}(10) = 12$
19. relative maximum: $f(2) = 48$; relative minimum:
$f(8) = -60$ **21.** relative maximum: $f(-10) = -20$;
relative minimum: $f(10) = 20$

23. absolute maximum: $f\left(\dfrac{9}{4}\right) = \dfrac{9}{4}$; no absolute minimum

25. absolute minimum: $f(4) = 31$; no absolute maximum
27. absolute minimum: $f(2\sqrt[4]{12}) \approx 17.9264$;
no absolute maximum   **29.** 200 ft × 200 ft   **31. (a)** $16

(b) $105,600 **(c)** 6600 subscribers **33.** $20\sqrt{3}$ ft $\times \dfrac{40}{\sqrt{3}}$ ft or ≈ 34.64 ft $\times 23.09$ ft

• CHAPTER 4

SECTION 4-1

1. $-\dfrac{4x^3 + y^3}{1 + 3xy^2}$ **3.** $-\dfrac{3x^2 + y^5}{y^3(5xy + 4)}$ **5.** $\dfrac{8y - 3x^2}{6y^5 - 8x}$

7. $\dfrac{3x^2 - 2xy + y^2}{x^2 - 2xy + 3y^2}$ **9.** $\dfrac{x - 2(x + y)^3}{2(x + y)^3 - y}$ **11.** $\dfrac{-7}{36}$ **13.** $\dfrac{7}{16}$

15. $\dfrac{4}{7}$ **17. (a)** $\dfrac{-x}{y}$ **(b)** $\dfrac{-1}{\sqrt{3}}$ **(c)** $y = \dfrac{-1}{\sqrt{3}}x + \dfrac{16}{\sqrt{3}}$

(d)

19. $\dfrac{1}{6}$ **21.** $\dfrac{1}{8x - 3}$; $x \neq \dfrac{3}{8}$

23. (a) $\dfrac{1}{2x - 4}$; $x \neq 2$ **(b)** $\dfrac{1}{2}$ **(c)** $\dfrac{dx}{dy} = \dfrac{1}{2}$ is the rate of change of x with respect to y at $x = 3$

25. (a) $\dfrac{1}{2p - 20}$; $p \neq 10$ **(b)** $\dfrac{-1}{6}$ **(c)** $\dfrac{dp}{dq} = \dfrac{-1}{6}$ is the rate of change of p with respect to q at $p = 7$.

27. $\dfrac{dS}{dt} = \dfrac{2(S - 6t^2 + 1)}{3S^2 - 2t}$ **29.** $\dfrac{dS}{dt} = \dfrac{3t(2S + t)}{4S^3 - 3t^2}$

SECTION 4-2

1. -16 **3.** $\dfrac{1}{4}$ **5.** $\dfrac{-9}{4}$ **7.** 2 **9.** $\dfrac{-1}{7}$ **11.** 1 **13.** -1

15. $-\dfrac{16}{3}$ ft/second **17. (a)** 40,000 **(b)** 4000 **(c)** 36,000

19. 76π or approximately 238.8 cm²/minute

21. $\dfrac{1}{4}$ foot/day **23. (a)** $\dfrac{100\sqrt{6}}{3}$ ft/sec ≈ 81.65 ft/sec

(b) ≈ 55.67 mi/hr **25.** $3200\pi \approx 10,053$ cm³/min

27. $\dfrac{-5}{2\pi} \approx -0.796$ foot/hr **29.** 1.0 ohm/sec

31. $\dfrac{1}{1800\pi} \approx 1.768 \times 10^{-4}$ foot/min

SECTION 4-3

1. $E = \dfrac{-p}{30 - p}$ **3.** $E = \dfrac{-p}{40 - p}$ **5.** $E = \dfrac{2p}{p - 4}$

7. $E = \dfrac{\sqrt{p}}{2\sqrt{p} - 8}$ **9.** $E = \dfrac{-p}{2(200 - p)}$ **11.** $E = \dfrac{-10}{p - 10}$

13. (a) $E = -1.5$ at $p = 10$

Since $E = \dfrac{\% \text{ change in quantity demanded}}{\% \text{ change in price}}$, the value of $E - 1.5$ means that if the price increases by 1% when $p = 10$, the quantity demanded will decrease by approximately 1.5%. If the price decreases by 1% when $p = 10$, the quantity demanded will increase by approximately 1.5% **(b)** elastic

15. (a) $E = -0.80$ at $p = 20$

Since $E = \dfrac{\% \text{ change in quantity demanded}}{\% \text{ change in price}}$, the value of $E = -0.80$ means that if the price increases by 1% when $p = 20$, the quantity demanded will decrease by approximately 0.80%. If the price decreases by 1% when $p = 20$, the quantity demanded will increase by approximately 0.80%. **(b)** inelastic **17. (a)** $E = \dfrac{-p}{65 - p}$

(b) $\dfrac{-10}{3} \approx -3.33$ **(c)** The value of $E = -3.33$ means that if the price increases by 1% when $p = 50$, the quantity demanded will decrease by approximately 3.33%. Also, if the price decreases by 1% when $p = 50$, the quantity demanded will increase by approximately 3.33%.

19. (a) $E = \dfrac{-8}{p - 8}$ **(b)** -4 **(c)** The value of $E = -4$ means that if the price increases by 1% when $p = 10$, the quantity demanded will decrease by approximately 4%. Also, if the price decreases by 1% when $p = 10$, the quantity demanded will increase by approximately 4%.

21. (a) $E = \dfrac{2p}{p - 10}$ **(b)** $\dfrac{-4}{3} \approx -1.33$ **(c)** The value of $E = -1.33$ means that if the price increased by 1% when $p = 4$, the quantity demanded will decrease by approximately 1.33%. Also, if the price decreases by 1% when $p = 4$, the quantity demanded will increase by approximately 1.33%. **23. (a)** $E = -1$ **(b)** $E = -1$ means that an increase of 1% in the price will lead to a decrease of approximately 1% in the quantity demanded; a decrease of 1% in the price will lead to an increase of approximately 1% in the quantity demanded. **(c)** The demand has unit elasticity for all values of p. **(d)** The demand has unit elasticity for all values of p. **25. (a)** $E = \dfrac{-p}{2(100 - p)}$

(b) $\dfrac{200}{3} < p < 100$ **(c)** $0 \leq p < \dfrac{200}{3}$ **(d)** $p = \dfrac{200}{3}$

SECTION 4-4

1. $3x^2\,dx$ **3.** $32x^3\,dx$ **5.** $\dfrac{9}{2}\sqrt{x}\,dx$ **7.** $\dfrac{-32}{x^2}\,dx$

9. $\dfrac{1}{3\sqrt[3]{x^2}}\,dx$ **11.** 6   **13.** ≈ 0.000926 **15.** 16   **17.** 9.03

19. 8.063   **21.** 1.9938   **23.** 0.3975 million dollars
25. $-\$0.024$
27. $dC = 60$ million dollars
    $\Delta C = 60.15$ million dollars
Graphically, the slope of the tangent line at $x = 200$ is 60,
and $60\,dx$ approximates Δy.

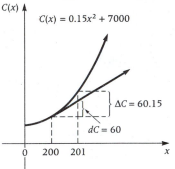

29. (a) $\overline{C}(x) = 100 + \dfrac{50{,}000}{x}$ **(b)** -1.25 **31.** 0.238%

33. (a) 20% **(b)** 10%

SECTION 4-5

1. $x_4 = 1.121531879$ **3.** $x_6 = 2.546818277$
5. $x_4 = 2.236067977$ **7.** $x_3 = 10.00333482$
9. (a) $x_6 = 2.948828358$, $x_7 = x_6$ **(b)** $x_3 = 2.948828358$
(c) The results of (a) and (b) are identical. Starting with
$x_0 = 3$ took fewer steps for convergence.

• EXTRA DIVIDENDS

Using Newton's Method to Find Rates of Return

1. 11.29%   **3.** 12.92%   **5.** 10.30%   **7.** 9.625%
9. (a) 1900 **(b)** 14.37%   **11.** 11.3%   **13.** 9.904%

• CHAPTER HIGHLIGHTS

1. If y is not written completely in terms of x and
constants, then y is defined implicitly in terms of x.
2. time.   **3.** *Step 1:* Identify and list the variables involved.
Draw a sketch if possible. *Step 2:* Find an equation that
relates the variables. *Step 3:* Identify and list the rates of
change that are given and those that must be determined.
Step 4: Differentiate the equation of step 2 implicitly with

respect to time, t. Solve for the derivative that gives the
desired rate of change. *Step 5:* Substitute in all given values.
4. % change in quantity demanded; % change in price.
5. $E = (p/q)(dq/dp)$; negative.   **6.** *Case 1:* If $|E| = 1$, then
the percent change in demand equals the percent change in
price. In this case, demand is said to have **unit elasticity.**
Case 2: If $|E| > 1$, then the percent change in demand is
greater than the percent change in price. In this case,
demand is said to be **elastic.** *Case 3:* If $|E| < 1$, then
percent change in demand is less than the percent change
in price. In this case, demand is said to be **inelastic.**
7. Positive   **8.** Negative   **9.** $dy = f'(x)\,dx$ **10.** dy is an
approximation to y, the change in y, as shown below.

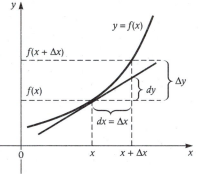

11. $(dy/y)(100)$ **12.** x-intercepts   **13.** $x_{n+1} = x_n - \dfrac{f(x_n)}{f'(x_n)}$
14. If $|x_{n+1} - x_n|$ is less than the desired level of accuracy,
terminate the process.   **15.** Yes. See Figures 4-23 through
4-26 and the accompanying explanations on page 286.

• REVIEW EXERCISES

1. $-\dfrac{3x^2 + y^4}{4xy^3 + 1}$ **3.** $\dfrac{2x - y + y^3}{x - 3xy^2 + 4y^3}$ **5.** $\dfrac{-x}{y}$ **7.** $\dfrac{1}{2(8x + 3)}$
9. -1.8 units/sec   **11.** 1944π cm³/min ≈ 6107 cm³/min

13. $E = \dfrac{2p}{p - 7}$ **15.** $E = \dfrac{-30}{p - 30}$ **17.** $E = -1.4$ at $p = 20$
(a) The value of $E = -1.4$ means that an increase of 1% in
the price when $p = 20$ leads to an approximate decrease of
1.4% in the quantity demanded. Also, a decrease of 1% in
the price when $p = 20$ leads to an approximate increase of
1.4% in the quantity demanded. **(b)** Elastic
19. $(3x^2 - 8x)\,dx$ **21.** $dy = 10x^{3/2}\,dx$
23. $dy = 2(x + 1)\,dx$; 0.5   **25. (a)** 10 million dollars
(b) 3.33%   **27.** 2.347296

• CHAPTER 5

SECTION 5-1

1. $(0,1)$; $y = 0$

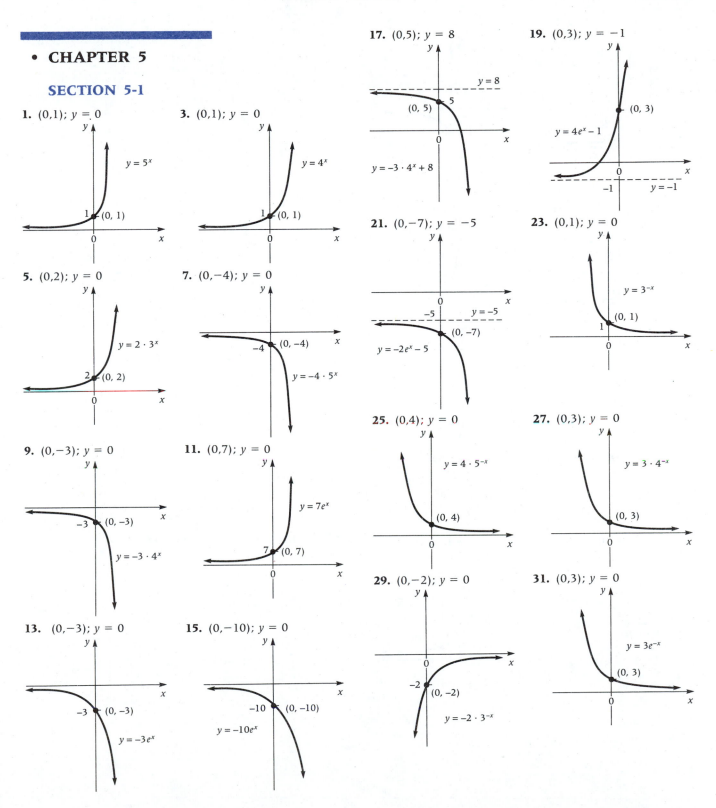

3. $(0,1)$; $y = 0$

5. $(0,2)$; $y = 0$

7. $(0,-4)$; $y = 0$

9. $(0,-3)$; $y = 0$

11. $(0,7)$; $y = 0$

13. $(0,-3)$; $y = 0$

15. $(0,-10)$; $y = 0$

17. $(0,5)$; $y = 8$

19. $(0,3)$; $y = -1$

21. $(0,-7)$; $y = -5$

23. $(0,1)$; $y = 0$

25. $(0,4)$; $y = 0$

27. $(0,3)$; $y = 0$

29. $(0,-2)$; $y = 0$

31. $(0,3)$; $y = 0$

33. $(0,10)$; $y = 0$

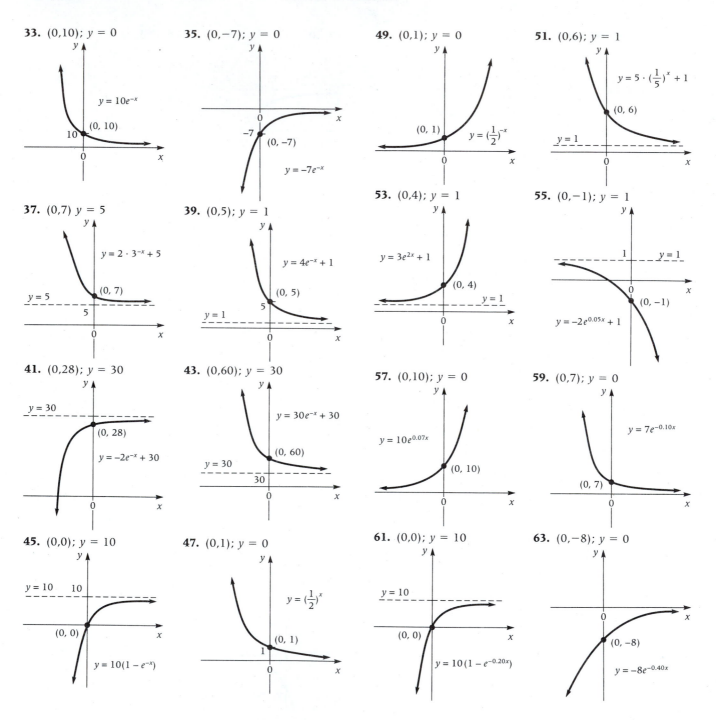

$y = 10e^{-x}$
$(0, 10)$

35. $(0,-7)$; $y = 0$

$(0, -7)$
$y = -7e^{-x}$

49. $(0,1)$; $y = 0$

$(0, 1)$
$y = \left(\frac{1}{2}\right)^{-x}$

51. $(0,6)$; $y = 1$

$y = 5 \cdot \left(\frac{1}{5}\right)^{x} + 1$
$(0, 6)$
$y = 1$

37. $(0,7)$ $y = 5$

$y = 2 \cdot 3^{-x} + 5$
$y = 5$
$(0, 7)$

39. $(0,5)$; $y = 1$

$y = 4e^{-x} + 1$
$(0, 5)$
$y = 1$

53. $(0,4)$; $y = 1$

$y = 3e^{2x} + 1$
$(0, 4)$
$y = 1$

55. $(0,-1)$; $y = 1$

$y = 1$
$(0, -1)$
$y = -2e^{0.05x} + 1$

41. $(0,28)$; $y = 30$

$y = 30$
$(0, 28)$
$y = -2e^{-x} + 30$

43. $(0,60)$; $y = 30$

$y = 30e^{-x} + 30$
$(0, 60)$
$y = 30$

57. $(0,10)$; $y = 0$

$y = 10e^{0.07x}$
$(0, 10)$

59. $(0,7)$; $y = 0$

$y = 7e^{-0.10x}$
$(0, 7)$

45. $(0,0)$; $y = 10$

$y = 10$
$(0, 0)$
$y = 10(1 - e^{-x})$

47. $(0,1)$; $y = 0$

$y = \left(\frac{1}{2}\right)^{x}$
$(0, 1)$

61. $(0,0)$; $y = 10$

$y = 10$
$(0, 0)$
$y = 10(1 - e^{-0.20x})$

63. $(0,-8)$; $y = 0$

$(0, -8)$
$y = -8e^{-0.40x}$

65. (a) $y = 500,000(3^t)$ **(b)**

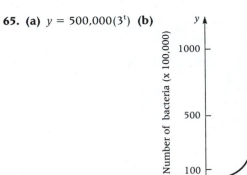

(c) $500,000(3^4) = 40,500,000$ **(d)** $500,000(3^6) = 3.645 \times 10^8$ **67. (a)**

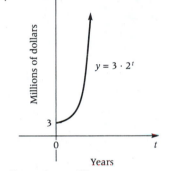

(b) \$3 million; \$6 million; \$12 million
69. (a)

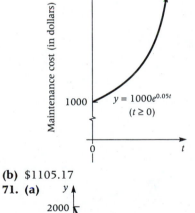

(b) \$1105.17
71. (a)

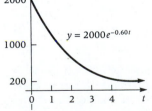

(b) 2000 grams **(c)** 1481.6 grams **(d)** 330.6 grams
73. (a)

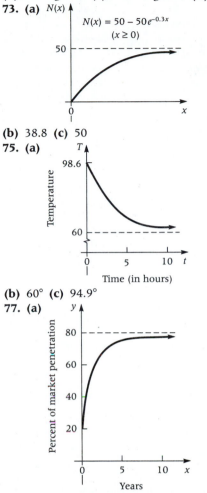

$N(x) = 50 - 50e^{-0.3x}$
$(x \geq 0)$

(b) 38.8 **(c)** 50
75. (a)

(b) 60° **(c)** 94.9°
77. (a)

(b) 65.2% **(c)** 79.9% **(d)** 80%

SECTION 5-2

1. $\log_5 25 = 2$ **3.** $\log_2 64 = 6$ **5.** $\log_{10} 0.01 = -2$
7. $\log_t s = w$ **9.** $\log_b N = x + y$ **11.** 2 **13.** 0 **15.** 1
17. 1 **19.** 3 **21.** 5 **23.** 2 **25.** 5 **27.** 0 **29.** 0 **31.** 1
33. 3 **35.** 5 **37.** (1,0)

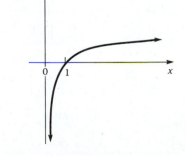

39. 0.5441 **41.** 1.6902 **43.** 1.7481 **45.** 0.1003
47. 0.5731 **49.** 0.9956 **51.** 2.5694 **53.** 4.5694
55. −0.4306 **57.** −2.4306 **59.** 1.791759
61. −0.405465 **63.** 2.079441 **65.** 0.549306
67. −0.287682 **69.** 0.9410 **71.** 3.6776 **73.** −0.0969
75. 2.3026 **77.** −1.8971 **79.** 4.3820 **81.** 8.0297126
83. 8029.7126 **85.** 256,980.4 **87.** 22.9615 **89.** 5.4997
91. $e^{1.22378}$ **93.** $e^{1.7047}$ **95.** $\log x + \log y - \log z$

97. $2 \log x + \log y$ **99.** $\dfrac{1}{2} (\log x + \log y)$

101. (a) \$108,788.9 thousand
\$112,875.5 thousand
\$119,879.3 thousand
\$124,728.3 thousand
(b) \$355.6 thousand; If the company increases its
advertising expenditures from 20 to 21 thousand dollars,
sales increase by \$355.6 thousand. **(c)** \$246.2 thousand
103. (a) \$13.22 thousand; revenue from the sale of 1 unit.
\$16.13 thousand; revenue from the sale of 2
units.
\$20.04 thousand; revenue from the sale of 5
units.
\$23.03 thousand; revenue from the sale of 10
units.
(b) \$0.41 thousand; If the company increases its sales from
10 units to 11 units, revenue will increase by \$0.41
thousand. **(c)** \$0.21 thousand **105. (a)** 2000 **(b)** 5.49
days **(c)** 6.93 days **107. (a)** 13.9 years **(b)** 22.0 years

109. (a) $y = \dfrac{\ln p - 1}{0.3}$ **(b)** 4,341,950

SECTION 5-3

1. $a = 3.19$, $b = 1.37$ **3.** $a = 5.71$, $b = 1.52$ **5.** $a = 9.72$,
$b = 1.54$ **7. (a)** $y = 0.997(1.163)^x$ **(b)** 5.25
9. (a) $y = 2.965(1.157)^x$ **(b)** 9.52

SECTION 5-4

1. $4e^{4x}$ **3.** $-8e^{-2x}$ **5.** $0.2e^{-0.1x}$ **7.** $(5x^4 - 7)e^{x^5 - 7x}$
9. $2e^{2x-5}$ **11.** $(2x - 3)(\ln 4)\, 4^{x^2 - 3x}$
13. $-0.02(\ln 4)4^{-0.02x}$
15. $[x^2(x^3 - 4)(4x^3 - 7) + x(5x^3 - 8)]e^{x^4 - 7x}$
$= (4x^8 - 23x^5 + 5x^4 + 28x^2 - 8x)e^{x^4 - 7x}$
17. $x(x^3 + 8)(3x^2 + 5) + 4x^3 + 8]e^{x^3 + 5x}$
$= (3x^6 + 5x^4 + 28x^3 + 40x + 8)e^{x^3 + 5x}$
19. $\dfrac{x(e^x - e^{-x}) - (e^x + e^{-x})}{x^2} = \dfrac{e^x(x - 1) - e^{-x}(x + 1)}{x^2}$
21. $\dfrac{x(e^x + e^{-x}) - (e^x - e^{-x})}{x^2} = \dfrac{e^x(x-1) + e^{-x}(x + 1)}{x^2}$
23. $\dfrac{[(x^2 - 3x)(3x^2 - 4) - 2x + 3]e^{x^3 - 4x}}{(x^2 - 3x)^2}$
$= \dfrac{(3x^4 - 9x^3 - 4x^2 + 10x + 3)e^{x^3 - 4x}}{(x^2 - 3x)^2}$

25. $\dfrac{-x}{\sqrt{25 - x^2}} e^{\sqrt{25 - x^2}}$ **27.** $\dfrac{1}{2\sqrt{x}}e^{\sqrt{x}}$ **29.** $\dfrac{96,000e^{-3x}}{(1 + 40e^{-3x})^2}$

31. $\dfrac{-160,000e^{-2x}}{(5 - 80e^{-2x})^2}$ **33.** $2(4x + e^{-x})(4 - e^{-x})$

35. $\dfrac{1 - e^{-x}}{2\sqrt{x + e^{-x}}}$ **37.** $\dfrac{x(1 - e^{-x^2})}{\sqrt{x^2 + e^{-x^2}}}$ **39.** $y = x + 1$

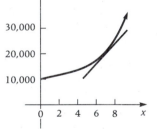

41. (a) $1000e^{0.10x}$ **(b)** 1349.86; $S'(3)$ is the instantaneous
rate of change of S with respect to x at $x = 3$.
(c) 1491.82; $S'(4)$ is the instantaneous rate of change of S
with respect to x at $x = 4$. **(d)** 1648.72 **(e)** \$23,082.09;
\$24,596.03 **(f)**

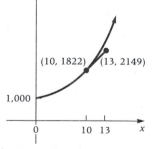

43. (a) 81; increasing **(b)** 109; increasing **(c)** 2149
(d)

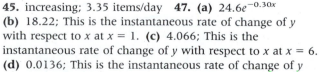

45. increasing; 3.35 items/day **47. (a)** $24.6e^{-0.30x}$
(b) 18.22; This is the instantaneous rate of change of y
with respect to x at $x = 1$. **(c)** 4.066; This is the
instantaneous rate of change of y with respect to x at $x = 6$.
(d) 0.0136; This is the instantaneous rate of change of y

with respect to x at $x = 25$. **(e)** The slope of the tangent line decreases rapidly as x increases. The graph of y vs. x is asymptotic to $y = 90$.

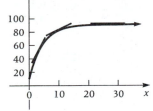

49. (a) 824.36 flies/day **(b)** 1359.1 flies/day

SECTION 5-5

1. $\dfrac{6}{x}$ **3.** $\dfrac{1}{x}$ **5.** $\dfrac{2x - 4}{x^2 - 4x}$ **7.** $\dfrac{2x - 4}{x^2 - 4x + 1}$ **9.** $4x^3 + \dfrac{3}{x}$

11. $\dfrac{-3 + 7x^3}{x^4}$ **13.** $\dfrac{5}{2\sqrt{x}} - \dfrac{3}{x}$

15. $\dfrac{2x^4}{x^2 + 5} + 3x^2 \ln(x^2 + 5)$ **17.** $\dfrac{7(1 - 9 \ln x)}{x^{10}}$

19. $\dfrac{2x(x^2 + 1)}{x^2 + 5} + 2x \ln(x^2 + 5)$

21. $\dfrac{2x(x^2 + 1)\ln(x^2 + 1) - 2x(x^2 + 6)}{[x^2 + 1][\ln(x^2 + 1)]^2}$

23. $60[\ln(x^6 - 8x^3)]^9\left(\dfrac{x^3 - 4}{x^4 - 8x}\right)$

25. $\dfrac{3x^2}{2(x^3 + 7)\sqrt{\ln(x^3 + 7)}}$ **27.** $\dfrac{3x^2}{2(x^3 + 7)}$

29. $\dfrac{e^x(x \ln x - 1)}{x(\ln x)^2}$ **31.** $\dfrac{x^2 e^x(x \ln x + 3 \ln x - 1)}{(\ln x)^2}$

33. $4x^3[\ln(x^3 - 2x)]e^{x^4 - 8} + \left(\dfrac{3x^2 - 2}{x^3 - 2x}\right)e^{x^4 - 8}$

35. 0 **37.** $\dfrac{1}{x \ln 10}$ **39.** $\dfrac{3x^2 + 8}{(x^3 + 8x)\ln 6}$ **41.** $\dfrac{3x^2 - 4}{(x^3 - 4x)\ln 2}$

43. $\dfrac{7(x^3 + 10)}{2x(x^3 + 7)}$ **45.** $\dfrac{15x^2}{x^3 + 7} + \dfrac{5}{2(4 - 5x)}$

47. $\dfrac{8x}{x^2 + 7} + \dfrac{18x^5}{x^6 - 5}$ **49. (a)** $N'(x) = \dfrac{1000}{x}$ items/day

(b) 250; Thus, at $x = 4$, the number of items produced by the worker is increasing at a rate of 250 per day.
(c) 125; Thus, at $x = 8$, the number of items produced by the worker is increasing at a rate of 125 per day.

51. (a) $C'(x) = \dfrac{10}{x + 1}$ **(b)** $\dfrac{10}{11} \approx 0.909$; Thus, at $x = 10$,
total cost is increasing at the rate of 0.909 per unit.

(c) $\dfrac{10}{21} \approx 0.476$; Thus, at $x = 20$, total cost is increasing at
the rate of 0.476 per unit. **53. (a)** $\dfrac{-\ln 3}{r^2}$

(b) -171.66; A small change in r, Δr, when $r = 0.08$,
produces a change in t of approximately $-171.66\ \Delta r$. Thus,

a one percentage point increase in r (i.e., $\Delta r = 0.01$)
reduces the tripling time by approximately $171.66(0.01) \approx$
1.72 years. **(c)** -109.86; A small change in r, Δr, when
$r = 0.10$, produces a change in t of approximately
$-109.86\Delta r$. Thus, a one percentage point increase in r (i.e.,
$\Delta r = 0.01$) reduces the tripling time by approximately
$109.86(0.01) \approx 1.10$ years. **(d)** -27.47; when $r = 0.20$,
a one percentage point increase in r reduces the tripling
time by approximately $27.47(0.01) \approx 0.27$ years.
(e) -12.21; when $r = 0.30$, a one percentage point
increase in r reduces the tripling time by approximately
$12.21(0.01) \approx 0.12$ years.

• CHAPTER HIGHLIGHTS

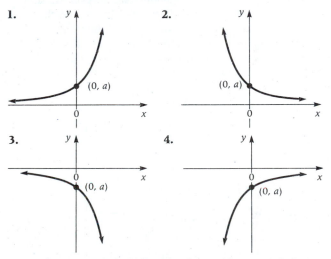

5. *Step 1:* Begin with the graph of $y = ab^x$ or $y = ab^{-x}$.
Step 2: Vertical Shift. If $c > 0$, lift the graph of Step 1
vertically by c units. If $c < 0$, lower the graph of Step 1
vertically by $|c|$ units. **6.** $y = ae^{-kt} + c$ where y denotes the
temperature of the cooling object after t units of time and c
denotes the temperature of the medium surrounding the
cooling object. The letters a and k represent constants
associated with the cooling object.
7. *Modified exponential model:* $y = A - Be^{-mx}$

Logistic growth model: $y = \dfrac{A}{1 + Be^{-mx}}$

where y denotes the percentage of the market penetrated
by the product x years after it has been introduced; A and B
are constants. **8.** Exponent **9.** Natural (or Napierian)
10. Common **11.** $\ln b$ **12.** 1 **13.** Let x, y, and b be
positive real numbers with $b = 1$. Let p be any real
number.
Property 1: $\log_b xy = \log_b x + \log_b y$
The logarithm of a product of two numbers equals the sum
of their logarithms. Example: $\log (5 \cdot 8) = \log 5 + \log 8$

Property 2: $\log_b(x/y) = \log_b x - \log_b y$
The logarithm of a quotient of two numbers equals the difference of their logarithms. *Example:* $\log(7/9) = \log 7 - \log 9$
Property 3: $\log_b x^p = p \cdot \log_b x$
The logarithm of the pth power of a number equals p times the logarithm of the number. *Example:* $\log 5^3 = 3 \log 5$
Property 4: $\log_b b = 1$
The logarithm of its base equals 1. *Example:* $\log_5 5 = 1$
Property 5: $\log_b 1 = 0$.
The logarithm of 1 equals 0. *Example:* $\log_8 1 = 0$
14. $\log y = \log a + x \cdot \log b$ **15.** straight line
16. If $y = e^x$, then $dy/dx = e^x$.   **17.** If $y = e^u$ where u is a differentiable function of x, then $dy/dx = e^u(du/dx)$.
18. If $y = b^u$ where u is a differentiable function of x and $b > 0$, then $dy/dx = b^u(du/dx)\ln b$.   **19.** If $y = \ln x$, then $dy/dx = 1/x$.   **20.** If $y = \ln u$ where u is a differentiable function of x, then $dy/dx = (1/u)(du/dx)$.   **21.** If $y = \log_b u$ where u is a differentiable function of x, $b > 0$, and $b \neq 1$, then $dy/dx = (1/u \ln b)(du/dx)$.

• REVIEW EXERCISES

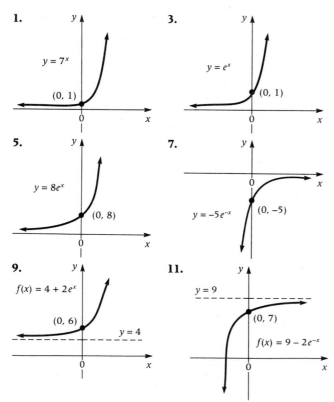

1. $y = 7^x$ (0, 1)
3. $y = e^x$ (0, 1)
5. $y = 8e^x$ (0, 8)
7. $y = -5e^{-x}$ (0, -5)
9. $f(x) = 4 + 2e^x$ (0, 6) $y = 4$
11. $y = 9$ (0, 7) $f(x) = 9 - 2e^{-x}$

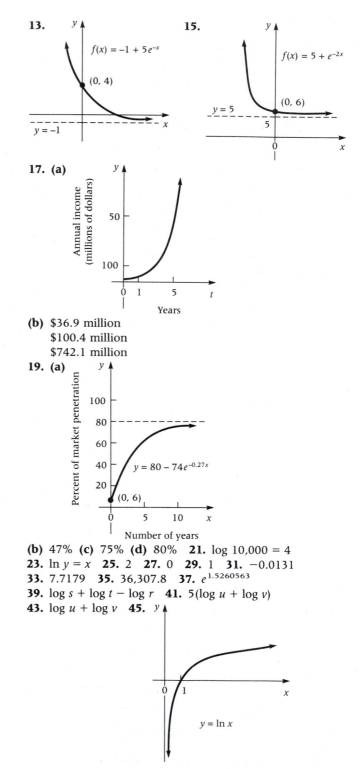

13. $f(x) = -1 + 5e^{-x}$ (0, 4) $y = -1$

15. $f(x) = 5 + e^{-2x}$ (0, 6) $y = 5$

17. (a) Annual income (millions of dollars) vs Years

(b) \$36.9 million
\$100.4 million
\$742.1 million

19. (a) Percent of market penetration vs Number of years, $y = 80 - 74e^{-0.27x}$ (0, 6)

(b) 47% **(c)** 75% **(d)** 80%   **21.** $\log 10{,}000 = 4$
23. $\ln y = x$ **25.** 2   **27.** 0   **29.** 1   **31.** -0.0131
33. 7.7179   **35.** 36,307.8   **37.** $e^{1.5260563}$
39. $\log s + \log t - \log r$ **41.** $5(\log u + \log v)$
43. $\log u + \log v$ **45.** $y = \ln x$

47. $a = 2.10$, $b = 1.95$
$y = 2.10(1.95)^x$
49. $5e^{5x}$ **51.** $8e^{8x+5}$ **53.** $(5x^2 + 42x + 8)e^{5x+9}$
55. $\dfrac{x(4e^x + e^{-x}) - (4e^x - e^{-x})}{x^2} = \dfrac{4e^x(x - 1) + e^{-x}(x + 1)}{x^2}$
57. $(2x + 1)(3x^2e^{6x})$ **59.** $\dfrac{-60,000e^{5x}}{(1 + 20e^{5x})^2}$
61. $2(8x + e^x)(8 + e^x)$ **63.** **(a)** $3200e^{0.08x}$
(b) 4068; A small change in x, Δx, when $x = 3$, results in a change in S of approximately $4068\Delta x$.
(c) 5171.4; A small change in x, Δx, when $x = 6$, results in a change in S of approximately $5171.4\Delta x$.
65. (a) $30e^{-0.60x}$ **(b)** 4.96; A small change in x, Δx, when $x = 3$, results in a change in f of approximately $4.96\Delta x$.
(c) 0.247; A small change in x, Δx, when $x = 8$, results in a change in f of approximately $0.247\Delta x$. **67.** $\dfrac{-7}{x}$
69. $\dfrac{3(x - 4)}{x(x - 6)}$ **71.** $\dfrac{x^2(3x^2 + 7)}{x^3 + 7x} + 2x \ln(x^3 + 7x)$
73. $8[\ln(x^5 + 6x^2)]^7 \left[\dfrac{5x^3 + 12}{x^4 + 6x}\right]$ **75.** $\left(\dfrac{1}{x} + 3\ln x\right)e^{3x+5}$
77. $\left\{8[\ln(x^5 - 6x^2)] + \left(\dfrac{5x^3 - 12}{x^4 - 6x}\right)\right\}e^{8x}$ **79. (a)** $\dfrac{40}{x + 3}$
(b) 2; A small change in x, Δx, when $x = 17$, will result in a change in C of approximately $2\Delta x$. **(c)** 1.6; A small change in x, Δx, when $x = 22$ will result in a change in C of approximately $1.6\Delta x$.

• CHAPTER 6

SECTION 6-1

1. $F'(x) = 7x^6 = f(x)$ **3.** $F'(x) = x^2 - 8x + 5 = f(x)$
5. $F'(x) = e^{2x} = f(x)$ **7.** $F'(x) = \dfrac{1}{x} = f(x)$ **9.** $\dfrac{1}{13}x^{13} + C$
11. $20\sqrt{x} + C$ **13.** $\dfrac{4}{5}x^{5/4} + C$ **15.** $-\dfrac{1}{8x^8} + C$
17. $\dfrac{3}{5}x^{5/3} + C$ **19.** $\dfrac{-28}{5}x^{5/7} + C$ **21.** $-6\sqrt{x} + C$
23. $\dfrac{5}{3}x^{3/5} + C$ **25.** $\dfrac{1}{5}e^{5x} + C$ **27.** $-\dfrac{1}{4}e^{-4x} + C$
29. $4e^{2x} + C$ **31.** $-4\ln|x| + C$ **33.** $300\ln|x| + C$
35. $\dfrac{1}{5}\ln|x| + C$ **37.** $\dfrac{-1}{5x^5} + C$ **39.** $\dfrac{-4}{3x^6} + C$
41. $x^4 - 16x + C$ **43.** $\dfrac{x^6}{6} - \dfrac{7}{2}x^2 + C$
45. $\dfrac{x^4}{4} + \dfrac{4}{x} + 6x + C$ **47.** $\dfrac{t^4}{4} - \dfrac{2}{3}t^3 + C$
49. $\dfrac{y^7}{7} - y^5 + y + C$ **51.** $u^4 - 16\sqrt{u} - \dfrac{5}{u} + C$

53. $7\ln|x| + \dfrac{1}{4}e^{4x} + C$ **55.** $9\ln|x| - e^{-x} + C$
57. $4\ln|x| + \dfrac{1}{5}e^{-5x} + C$ **59.** $\dfrac{-2}{x^2} + 2\ln|x| + C$
61. $\dfrac{-2}{x^3} - \dfrac{1}{4}e^{4x} + C$ **63.** $\dfrac{-1}{x} - e^{-x} + C$
65. $\ln|x| + \dfrac{1}{x} - e^x + C$ **67.** $\dfrac{x^4}{4} + \dfrac{4}{x} + C$
69. $\dfrac{x^3}{3} - x^2 + x + C$ **71.** $\ln|x| + e^{-x} + C$
73. $\dfrac{x^3}{3} - 4x + C$ **75.** $\dfrac{x^3}{3} - \dfrac{x^2}{2} - 6x + C$
77. $\dfrac{x^2}{2} - 2x + C$ **79.** $C(x) = 2x^3 + 2x^2 - 5x + 800$
81. (a) $V(t) = 8000t^3 + 1,000,000$ **(b)** \$2,000,000
83. $S(t) = 2(t^3 + 1)$ **85.** $S(t) = t^3 + 6$
87. $V(t) = 2t^2 + 30$ **89. (a)** $A(t) = \dfrac{20}{t^2} - 0.5$ **(b)** 0.3 cm²

SECTION 6-2

1. 80 **3.** 3 **5.** $\dfrac{15}{8} = 1.875$ **7.** $10\ln 5 \approx 16.09$
9. $e^3 - 1 \approx 19.086$ **11.** $\dfrac{1}{2}(1 - e^{-4}) \approx 0.4908$
13. Lower approximation = 3.53125;
Upper approximation = 3.78125
15. Lower approximation = 4.08;
Upper approximation = 5.28 **17.** $\dfrac{1}{2}$ **19. (a)** 1 **(b)** 1
21. $\dfrac{14}{3} \approx 4.667$ **23.** 64

25. $\dfrac{2}{3}$

27. 15

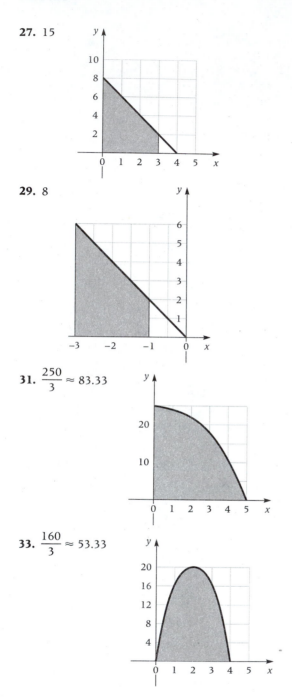

29. 8

31. $\frac{250}{3} \approx 83.33$

33. $\frac{160}{3} \approx 53.33$

35. $\frac{64}{3} \approx 21.33$

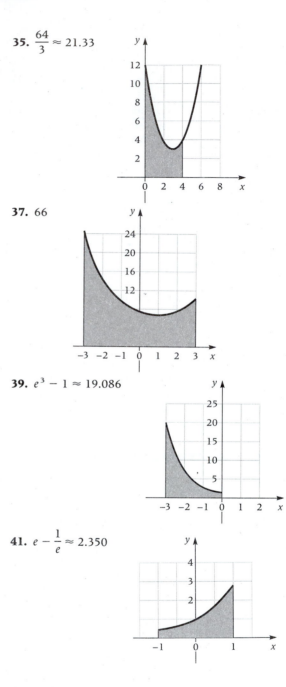

37. 66

39. $e^3 - 1 \approx 19.086$

41. $e - \frac{1}{e} \approx 2.350$

43. $\ln 5 \approx 1.609$

45. $\dfrac{21}{64} \approx 0.3281$

47. $\dfrac{1}{6} \approx 0.1667$

49. $\dfrac{23}{3} = 7\dfrac{2}{3}$

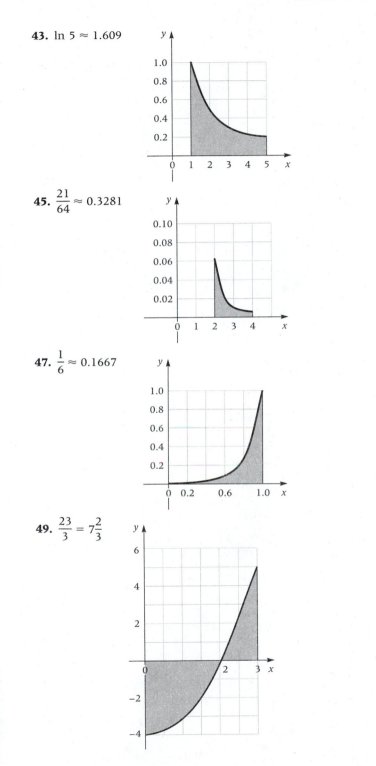

51. 16

53. $\dfrac{23}{3} = 7\dfrac{2}{3}$

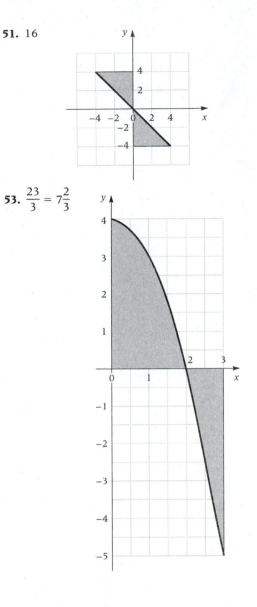

55. 18

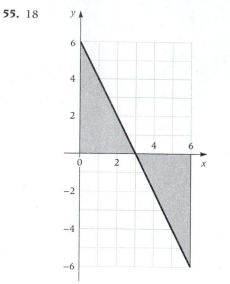

57. 68

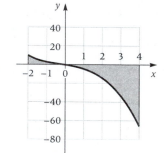

59. $\dfrac{31}{6} = 5\dfrac{1}{6}$

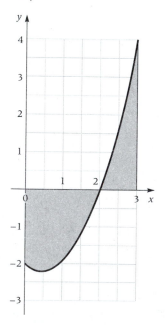

61. $-1 + 4 \ln \dfrac{8}{3} \approx 2.9233$

63. $5\dfrac{1}{2}$

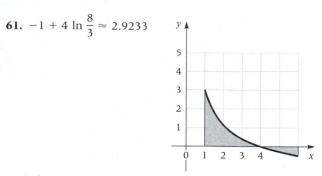

65. 176

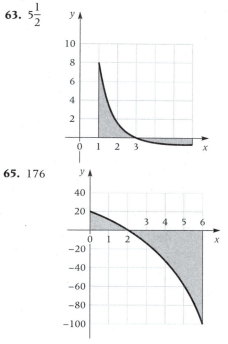

67. 4000   **69.** 1200   **71.** 7700   **73.** 522 ft   **75.** 1 foot
77. (a) 225 cu. ft **(b)** 700 cu. ft **(c)** 65 cu. ft
(d) 75 cu. ft   **79. (a)** $\dfrac{500}{e} \approx 183.94$
(b) $500(1 + e^{-2}) \approx 567.67$ **81. (a)** 190 jobs
(b) 279 jobs **(c)** 442 jobs **(d)** 787 jobs   **83.** $2760
85. $5988.50   **87.** $11,843.50   **89.** $21,743.50

SECTION 6-3

1. $\dfrac{88}{3} = 29\dfrac{1}{3}$

3. $\dfrac{1}{12}$

5. $\dfrac{16}{3} = 5\dfrac{1}{3}$

7. $\dfrac{1}{3}$

9. 21

11. $4 - 3 \ln 3 \approx 0.7042$

13. $\dfrac{5}{2} - 6 \ln \dfrac{3}{2} \approx 0.0672$

15. $e^2 - 3 \approx 4.389$

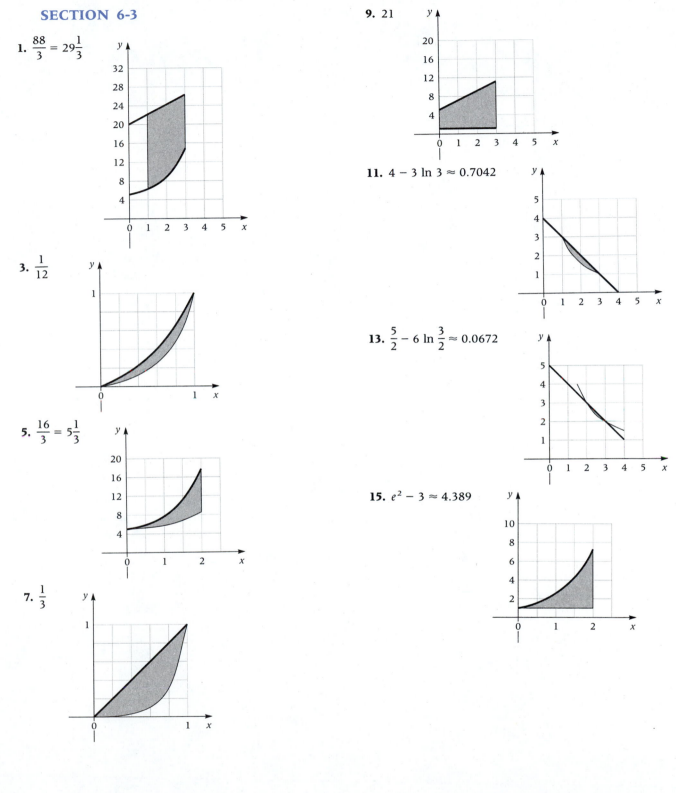

17. 4

19. $\dfrac{1}{20}$

21. $e + e^{-1} - 2 \approx 1.0862$

23. $\dfrac{125}{6} \approx 20.833$

25. 5

27. $\dfrac{29}{6} \approx 4.833$

29. $\dfrac{227}{4} = 56.75$

31. 64

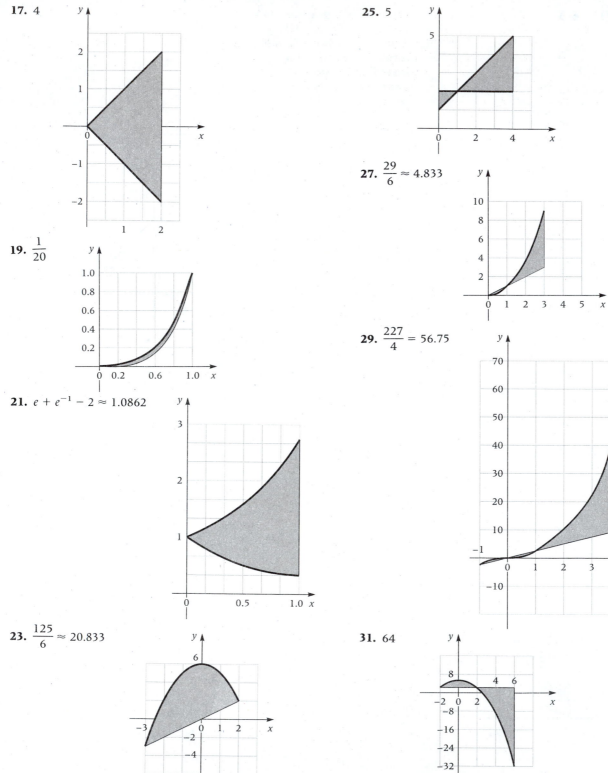

33. $e^3 + e^2 + e^{-2} + e^{-3} - 4 \approx 23.66$

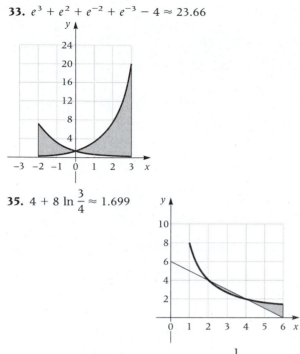

35. $4 + 8 \ln \dfrac{3}{4} \approx 1.699$

37. $CS = \$16$; $PS = \$32$ **39.** $CS = \$2333\dfrac{1}{3}$; $PS = \$666\dfrac{2}{3}$

41. $CS = \$4608$; $PS = \$1152$ **43.** $\$268$ **45.** $\$2,987,862$

SECTION 6-4

1. $\dfrac{1}{11}(x^3 - 7)^{11} + C$ **3.** $\dfrac{1}{6}(x^3 - 4x)^6 + C$

5. $\dfrac{1}{40}(x^4 - 8)^{10} + C$ **7.** $\dfrac{1}{10}(x - 3)^{10} + C$

9. $\dfrac{5}{24}(x^4 + 6)^6 + C$ **11.** $\dfrac{1}{33}(x^6 + 9)^{11} + C$

13. $-\dfrac{1}{27(x^3 - 5)^9} + C$ **15.** $\dfrac{1}{2}\sqrt{x^4 - 6} + C$

17. $-\dfrac{1}{9(3x - 5)^3} + C$ **19.** $\dfrac{1}{3}(125 - 13^{3/2}) \approx 26.043$

21. $\dfrac{1}{10}$

23. 4

25. $\dfrac{5}{6}$

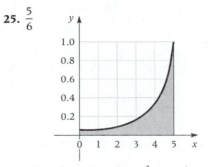

27. The substitution $u = x^3 - 5$, $du = 3x^2 dx$ does not work because we need to multiply $x\ dx$ by $3x$ in order to obtain $du = 3x^2\ dx$. However, we cannot do this because $3x$ is not a constant. **29.** 232,800 barrels
31. $P(x) = 250,000x^2 + 100,000x - 200,000$

SECTION 6-5

1. $e^x + C$ **3.** $\dfrac{1}{4}e^{4x} + C$ **5.** $2e^{x/2} + C$ **7.** $\dfrac{1}{3}e^{x^3-5} + C$

9. $\dfrac{1}{4}e^{x^4+6} + C$ **11.** $\dfrac{1}{2}e^{x^2+2x} + C$ **13.** $5 \ln |x| + C$

15. $\ln\sqrt{x^2 + 1} + C$ **17.** $\ln(x^3 + 4)^2 + C$

19. $\dfrac{-1}{10} \ln |5x^2 - 6| + C$ **21.** $e^4 - 1 \approx 53.598$

23. $\dfrac{1}{2}(1 - e^{-1}) \approx 0.3161$ **25.** $\ln 4 \approx 1.3863$

27. $-6 \ln 6 \approx -10.7506$ **29.** $\dfrac{1}{3}(\ln x)^3 + C$

31. $\dfrac{1}{5}(\ln 3x)^5 + C$ **33.** $\dfrac{1}{2} \ln |x^2 - 4x + 1| + C$

35. $\ln |\ln x| + C$ **37.** $\dfrac{1}{2} \ln |\ln x^2| + C$

39. $\dfrac{1}{2}(1 - e^{-2}) \approx 0.4323$

41. $\left|\ln\dfrac{5}{8}\right| \approx 0.470$

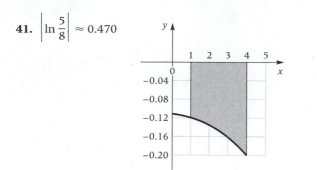

43. $4953.68   **45.** $B(x) = 2000 \ln (5x + 1) + 4204.21$

SECTION 6-6

1. $\dfrac{1}{3}xe^{3x} - \dfrac{1}{9}e^{3x} + C$ **3.** $2x\sqrt{x-3} - \dfrac{4}{3}(x-3)^{3/2} + C$

5. $-e^{-x}(x+1) + C$ **7.** $-\dfrac{x}{2(x-4)^2} - \dfrac{1}{2(x-4)} + C$

9. $-\dfrac{1}{4}e^{-4x}\left(x + \dfrac{1}{4}\right) + C$ **11.** $\dfrac{1}{4}x^4\left(\ln x - \dfrac{1}{4}\right) + C$

13. $\dfrac{x(x-9)^6}{6} - \dfrac{1}{42}(x-9)^7 + C$

15. $-\dfrac{x}{5(6+5x)} + \dfrac{1}{25}\ln |6+5x| + C$

17. $\dfrac{2}{3}x\sqrt{5+3x} - \dfrac{4}{27}(5+3x)^{3/2} + C$

19. $\dfrac{2}{3}x(3x+7)^{3/2} - \dfrac{4}{45}(3x+7)^{5/2} + C$

21. $\dfrac{x^2}{2}\ln 9x - \dfrac{1}{4}x^2 + C$ **23.** $e^x(x^3 - 3x^2 + 6x - 6) + C$

25. Let $u = x^n$ and $dv = e^x\,dx$; $du = nx^{n-1}\,dx$,
$v = e^x$; $\int x^n e^x\,dx = x^n e^x - n\int x^{n-1}e^x\,dx$
27. $x(\ln x)^2 - 2x\ln x + 2x + C$ **29.** Let $u = (\ln x)^n$ and

$dv = dx$, $n = $ integer > 0; $du = n(\ln x)^{n-1}\dfrac{dx}{x}$, $v = x$;

$\int u\,dv = x(\ln x)^n - n\int (\ln x)^{n-1}\,dx$ **31.** $e^2 + 1 \approx 8.3891$

33. $\dfrac{1}{2}$ **35.** $e^x(x^2 - 2x + 2) + C$ **37.** $\ln|x + 6| + C$

39. $\dfrac{1}{2}\left[x - \dfrac{9}{2}\ln |2x+9|\right] + C$ **41.** $83,201.17

43. 5940 decrease in cells

45. $R(x) = \dfrac{x^4}{4}\left(\ln x - \dfrac{1}{4}\right) + \dfrac{1281}{16}$

SECTION 6-7

1. $\ln(x + \sqrt{81+x^2}) + C$ **3.** $\ln 3 \approx 1.0986$

5. $\dfrac{7}{18}\ln\left|\dfrac{9-x}{9+x}\right| + C$ **7.** $3\left(\dfrac{-1}{4x} - \dfrac{7}{16}\ln\left|\dfrac{4-7x}{x}\right|\right) + C$

9. $6 - 2e \approx 0.5634$ **11.** $x\ln |5x| - x + C$

13. $\dfrac{1}{\sqrt{5}}\ln\left|\dfrac{\sqrt{5-2x} - \sqrt{5}}{\sqrt{5-2x} + \sqrt{5}}\right| + C$

15. $\ln |x + \sqrt{x^2 - 100}| + C$

17. $\dfrac{-1}{5}\ln\left|\dfrac{5 + \sqrt{25-x^2}}{x}\right| + C$ **19.** $\dfrac{x}{36(\sqrt{36-x^2})} + C$

21. $x(\ln |x|)^2 - 2x\ln |x| + 2x + C$ **23.** $\dfrac{x^3}{3}\left(\ln |x| - \dfrac{1}{3}\right) + C$

25. $\dfrac{1}{25}\left(\dfrac{x}{\sqrt{x^2 + 25}}\right) + C$

27. $\dfrac{(x+1)^2}{2}\ln |x+1| - \dfrac{(x+1)^2}{4} + C$

29. $\dfrac{4}{3}\ln\left|\dfrac{x}{3+7x}\right| + C$ **31.** $\dfrac{1}{16}\ln 7 \approx 0.1216$ foot

33. 599.64 gallons

• CHAPTER HIGHLIGHTS

1. $f(x)$ **2.** Constant   **3. (a)** *Power Rule:* $\int x^n\,dx =$
$\dfrac{1}{n+1}x^{n+1} + c$ for $n \neq -1$. The power rule states that the
integral of x raised to a power other than -1 is x raised to
the $n + 1$st power divided by $n + 1$ plus an arbitrary
constant. **(b)** *Constant Multiplier Rule:* $\int k \cdot f(x)\,dx =$
$k\int f(x)\,dx$. The constant multiplier rule states that the
integral of a constant times a function is the constant
times the integral of the function. **(c)** *Sum or Difference
Rule:* $\int [f(x) \pm g(x)]\,dx = \int f(x)\,dx \pm \int g(x)\,dx$. The sum or
difference rule states that the integral of a sum or difference
of two functions is the sum or difference of their individual
integrals.   **4.** $kx + c$ **5.** $e^x + c$ **6.** $(1/k)e^{kx} + c$, $k \neq 0$
7. $\ln |x| + c$ **8.** The marginal tax rate is the tax on an
additional dollar of taxable income.   **9.** A definite integral
of a function $f(x)$ is evaluated over an interval of x-values;
the endpoints of such an interval are called limits of
integration. A definite integral of a function $f(x)$ evaluated
over an interval $a \leq x \leq b$ is determined by finding the
antiderivative $F(x)$ of the function $f(x)$ and evaluating
$F(b) - F(a)$. A Riemann sum approximates the area under
a curve over some interval using the sum of areas of
rectangles so that the limit of the sum equals the actual
area as the number of rectangles becomes infinite.
10. The Fundamental Theorem of Calculus states that for a
function $f(x)$ defined and continuous over some interval
$a \leq x \leq b$, if $F(x)$ is an antiderivative of $f(x)$, then the limit
of every possible Riemann sum over this interval equals
$\int_a^b f(x)\,dx = F(b) - F(a)$. The Fundamental Theorem allows
us to compute the area under a curve. If $f(x) \geq 0$ over the
interval $a \leq x \leq b$, the area between the graph of $f(x)$ and
the x-axis over the indicated interval is given by the definite
integral $\int_a^b f(x)\,dx = F(b) - F(a)$. If $f(x) < 0$ over some
interval, then the corresponding definite integral is negative

and, therefore, its absolute value equals the respective area between the curve and the x-axis over the interval.

11. To find areas: *Step 1.* Graph the function. *Step 2.* Find any x-intercepts. *Step 3.* Shade the area to be found. *Step 4.* Note whether the shaded area contains any regions that lie below the x-axis as well as above the x-axis. *Step 5.* Evaluate the appropriate definite integrals.

12. Find each area separately and take the sum. The definite integral corresponding to the area above the x-axis will be positive whereas the definite integral corresponding to the area below the x-axis will be negative and, therefore, its absolute value equals its respective area.

13. The area between the graphs of two continuous functions $f(x)$ and $g(x)$ over an interval $a \leq x \leq b$ where $f(x) \geq g(x)$ (as illustrated below) is given by the definite integral $\int_a^b [f(x) - g(x)]\, dx$

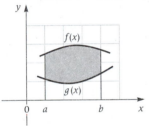

14. Consumers' surplus is the total amount of money saved by consumers as a result of the market being at equilibrium. It is represented by the area between the demand curve and the horizontal line $p = p_E$ over the interval $0 \leq q \leq q_E$ where p_E is the equilibrium price and q_E is the equilibrium quantity. Consumers' surplus is determined by the definite integral $\int_0^{q_E} [D(q) - p_E]\,dq$ where $D(q)$ denotes the demand curve.   **15.** Producers' surplus is the additional revenue gained by producers as a result of the market being at equilibrium. It is represented by the area between the supply curve and the horizontal line $p = p_E$ over the interval $0 \leq q \leq q_E$ where p_E is the equilibrium price and q_E is the equilibrium quantity. Producers' surplus is determined by the definite integral $\int_0^{q_E} [p_E - S(q)]\,dq$ where $S(q)$ denotes the supply curve.

16. $\int u^n\, du = \dfrac{1}{n+1} u^{n+1} + c$ where u is a differentiable function of x and du is the derivative of u times dx.

17. $\int e^u\, du = e^u + c$ where u is a differentiable function of x and du is the derivative of u times dx.

18. $\int du/u = \ln |u| + c$ where u is a differentiable function of x and du is the derivative of u times dx.

19. $\int u\, dv = uv - \int v\, du$ **20.** A table of integrals provides antiderivatives for many integral forms. Such a table allows one to integrate a greater variety of functions.

• **REVIEW EXERCISES**

1. $\dfrac{x^5}{5} + c$ **3.** $20 \ln |x| + c$ **5.** $-e^{-x} + c$ **7.** $7x + c$

9. $x^5 + 2x^3 - 4x^2 + 4x + c$ **11.** $4 \ln |x| + \dfrac{1}{6} e^{6x} + c$

13. $-\dfrac{4}{x} - \dfrac{x^5}{5} + c$ **15.** $\dfrac{x^3}{3} - 25x + c$

17. $C(x) = 3x^3 + 2x^2 - x + 5000$ **19.** 66

21. $20 \ln \dfrac{5}{2} \approx 18.3$ **23.** 80

25. 144

27. $\dfrac{132}{5} = 26.4$

29. 16

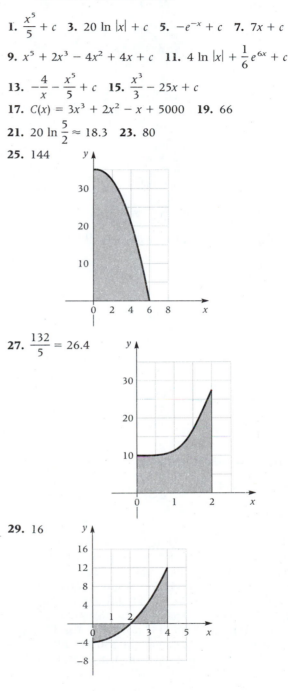

31. $\frac{512}{3} = 170\frac{2}{3}$

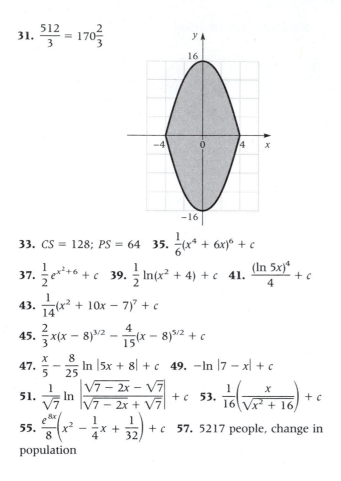

33. $CS = 128$; $PS = 64$ **35.** $\frac{1}{6}(x^4 + 6x)^6 + c$

37. $\frac{1}{2}e^{x^2+6} + c$ **39.** $\frac{1}{2}\ln(x^2 + 4) + c$ **41.** $\frac{(\ln 5x)^4}{4} + c$

43. $\frac{1}{14}(x^2 + 10x - 7)^7 + c$

45. $\frac{2}{3}x(x - 8)^{3/2} - \frac{4}{15}(x - 8)^{5/2} + c$

47. $\frac{x}{5} - \frac{8}{25}\ln|5x + 8| + c$ **49.** $-\ln|7 - x| + c$

51. $\frac{1}{\sqrt{7}}\ln\left|\frac{\sqrt{7 - 2x} - \sqrt{7}}{\sqrt{7 - 2x} + \sqrt{7}}\right| + c$ **53.** $\frac{1}{16}\left(\frac{x}{\sqrt{x^2 + 16}}\right) + c$

55. $\frac{e^{8x}}{8}\left(x^2 - \frac{1}{4}x + \frac{1}{32}\right) + c$ **57.** 5217 people, change in population

• CHAPTER 7

SECTION 7-1

1. (a) $10,000 **(b)** $8052.71 **(c)** $12,629.16
3. (a) $300,000 **(b)** $241,581.23 **(c)** $378,874.79
5. (a) $75,000 **(b)** $55,880.87 **(c)** $87,638.66
7. (a) $10 **(b)** $7.45 **(c)** $11.69 **9. (a)** $17,041.53
(b) $13,595.19 **(c)** $21,321.51 **11. (a)** $181,269.25
(b) $147,062.84 **(c)** $230,640.44 **13. (a)** $5002.50
(b) $4028.22 **(c)** $6317.50 **15. (a)** $9375 **(b)** $7737.51
(c) $12,134.83 **17. (a)** $70,000 **(b)** $50,341.47
(c) $101,375.27 **19. (a)** $80,000,000 **(b)** $58,472,625
(c) $94,496,112

SECTION 7-2

1. 1 **3.** Diverges **5.** Diverges **7.** $\frac{1}{2}$ **9.** 1 **11.** $\frac{1}{2}$

13. Diverges **15.** $\frac{1}{3}$ **17.** $\frac{1}{2}$ **19.** 0 **21.** Diverges

23. Diverges **25.** 1

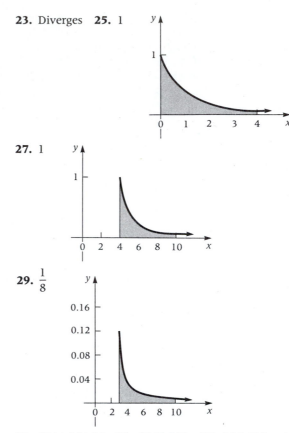

27. 1

29. $\frac{1}{8}$

31. $444,444.44 **33.** $200,000 **35.** 200,000 units
37. 300 gallons

SECTION 7-3

1. (a) 0.40 **(b)** 0.25 **(c)** 0.25
3. (a) $f(x) = \begin{cases} 0.20 & \text{if } 2 \le x \le 7 \\ 0 & \text{otherwise} \end{cases}$ **(b)** 0.20 **(c)** 0.40
5. (a) 0.3935 **(b)** 0.3181 **(c)** 0.1353 **7. (a)** 0.2325
(b) 0.9502 **(c)** 0.00248 **9. (a)** $R(t) = e^{-0.5t}$
(b) 0.6065; $R(1)$ is the probability that the circuitry will
have a lifetime of at least 1 year. **(c)** 0.1353; $R(4)$ is the
probability that the circuitry will have a lifetime of at least
4 years.

SECTION 7-4

1. 7.5 **3.** $\frac{14}{9} \approx 1.556$ **5.** 5

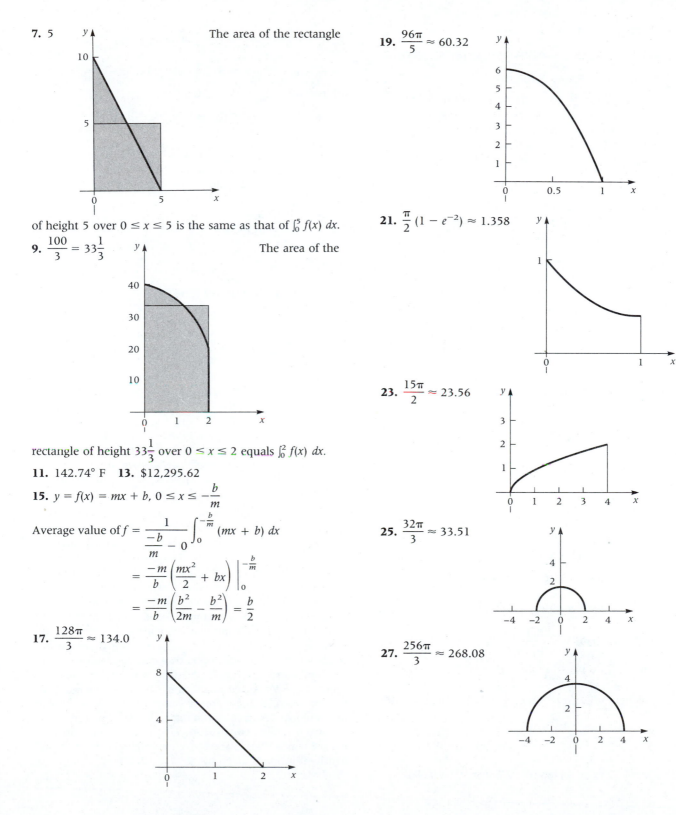

7. 5 The area of the rectangle

of height 5 over $0 \le x \le 5$ is the same as that of $\int_0^5 f(x)\, dx$.

9. $\dfrac{100}{3} = 33\dfrac{1}{3}$ The area of the

rectangle of height $33\dfrac{1}{3}$ over $0 \le x \le 2$ equals $\int_0^2 f(x)\, dx$.

11. 142.74° F **13.** $12,295.62

15. $y = f(x) = mx + b,\ 0 \le x \le -\dfrac{b}{m}$

Average value of $f = \dfrac{1}{\dfrac{-b}{m} - 0} \displaystyle\int_0^{-\frac{b}{m}} (mx + b)\, dx$

$= \dfrac{-m}{b}\left(\dfrac{mx^2}{2} + bx\right)\Bigg|_0^{-\frac{b}{m}}$

$= \dfrac{-m}{b}\left(\dfrac{b^2}{2m} - \dfrac{b^2}{m}\right) = \dfrac{b}{2}$

17. $\dfrac{128\pi}{3} \approx 134.0$

19. $\dfrac{96\pi}{5} \approx 60.32$

21. $\dfrac{\pi}{2}(1 - e^{-2}) \approx 1.358$

23. $\dfrac{15\pi}{2} \approx 23.56$

25. $\dfrac{32\pi}{3} \approx 33.51$

27. $\dfrac{256\pi}{3} \approx 268.08$

SECTION 7-5

1. (a) 0.697024 **(b)** $\ln 2 \approx 0.693147$ **3. (a)** 8.750000

(b) $8\frac{2}{3} \approx 8.666667$ **5. (a)** 1.103210

(b) $\ln 3 \approx 1.098612$ **7. (a)** 8.031250 **(b)** 8.000000
9. (a) 3.396615 **(b)** $2\sqrt{3} \approx 3.464102$ **11.** 0.881704
13. 1.249254 **15.** 0.880555 **17.** 2.962545
19. 1.650543 **21.** 2.157582 **23.** 0.0104 **25.** 0.0208
27. 0.00260 **29.** $n \geq 41$ **31.** $n \geq 116$ **33.** $n \geq 82$

35. $A \approx 1.544910$; Actual area of semicircle $= \dfrac{\pi}{2} \approx 1.570796$

37. 22.83 miles traveled **39.** 0.475010 **41.** 1330 sq ft
43. 21.000450 **45.** 0.231823 **47.** 1.772414
49. 104.023 feet

SECTION 7-6

1. (a) 0.0693254 **(b)** $\ln 2 \approx 0.693147$

3. (a) $8\frac{2}{3} \approx 8.666667$ **(b)** $8\frac{2}{3} \approx 8.666667$

5. (a) 1.098725 **(b)** $\ln 2 \approx 1.098612$ **7. (a)** 8.000000
(b) 8.000000 **9. (a)** 3.435407 **(b)** $2\sqrt{3} \approx 3.464102$
11. 0.882066 **13.** 1.249865 **15.** 0.881375
17. 2.957883 **19.** 1.655748 **21.** 2.158878
23. 0.000521 **25.** 0.00104 **27.** 0.0000163 **29.** $n \geq 7$
31. $n \geq 15$ **33.** $n \geq 11$ **35.** 1.560595; Actual area of

semicircle $= \dfrac{1}{2}\pi r^2 \approx 1.570796$ **37.** 23.28 miles traveled

39. 0.477201 **41.** 1353.3 sq ft **43.** 21.000000
45. 0.231824 **47.** 1.772415 **49.** 104.023 ft

SECTION 7-7

1. $y = Ce^{8t}$, $(C = e^{C_1})$ **3.** $y^2 = \dfrac{-1}{x^2 + C}$, $y = \sqrt{\dfrac{-1}{x^2 + C}}$,

$(C < -x^2)$ **5.** $y = (4x^3 + C)^{\frac{1}{4}}$, $(C = 4C_1)$

7. $y = \ln\left(\dfrac{3}{C - x^3}\right)$, $(C = -3C_1)$ **9.** $y^2 = \dfrac{-3}{2(x^3 + C)}$,

$y = \sqrt{\dfrac{-3}{2(x^3 + C)}}$, $(C < x^3)$ **11.** $y = \dfrac{1}{3}(x^2 + 5)^{\frac{3}{2}} + C$

13. $y = C(4 + x)^5$ **15.** $y = \dfrac{1}{C - e^x}$, $(C = -C_1)$

17. $y = \ln(e^x + C)$ **19.** $\dfrac{dy}{dt} = Ke^{\frac{1}{2}t^2}(t) = ty$

The given equation is a solution of $\dfrac{dy}{dt} = ty$ for all values of

k.

21. $y = \sqrt[3]{3x^3 + 40}$ **23.** $y = e^{\frac{1}{x}}$ **25. (a)** $\dfrac{dS}{dt} = 0.07S$

(b) $S = S_0 e^{0.07t}$ **(c)** $\approx \$9388.05$ **27. (a)** $\dfrac{dS}{dt} = 0.09S$

(b) $S = S_0 e^{0.09t}$ **(c)** $\approx \$11,239.54$ **29. (a)** $\dfrac{dS}{dt} = 0.11S$

(b) $S = S_0 e^{0.11t}$ **(c)** $\approx \$13,456.17$ **31. (a)** $\dfrac{dy}{dt} = -ky$

(b) $y = y_0 e^{-kt}$ **(c)** $y = 40,000 e^{-\left(\frac{\ln 2}{4}\right)t}$

33. (a) $R = k \ln (CS)$ **(b)** $R = 5 + \dfrac{\ln S}{\ln 10}$

35. (a) $\dfrac{dP}{dt} = 4(0.50) - 4\left(\dfrac{P}{10,000}\right)$

$\quad$ = total input rate $\times$ fraction pollutant
$\quad$ $-$ total output rate $\times$ fraction pollutant

$\quad$ Hence, $\dfrac{dP}{dt} = 2 - \dfrac{4P}{10,000}$

(b) $P = 5000 - (5000 - P_0)e^{-\frac{t}{2500}}$
(c) $P = 5000\left(1 - e^{-\frac{t}{2500}}\right)$ **(d)** ≈ 4323.32 gallons
37. $y = 5 + 35e^{\left(\frac{1}{2}\ln\frac{2}{7}\right)t}$

• CHAPTER HIGHLIGHTS

1. If money flows into a fund at a rate $f(x)$ during some time interval $0 \leq x \leq t$, then the total amount of money accumulated is given by $\int_0^t f(x)\, dx$. This formula assumes that the money earns no interest. **2.** If money flows into a fund at a rate of $f(x)$ dollars per year (where x denotes time in years) and is compounded continuously at an annual interest rate r during the tme interval $0 \leq x \leq t$, then the present value of the money flow is given by $\int_0^t f(x)e^{-rx}\, dx$ and the future value is given by either of the following: $e^{rt}\int_0^t f(x)e^{-rx}\, dx$ or e^{rt}(Present value). **3.** If a function $f(x)$ is continuous over the indicated intervals and if the indicated limits exist, then: (1) $\int_a^\infty f(x)\, dx = \lim_{b \to \infty}\int_a^b f(x)\, dx$ (2) $\int_{-\infty}^b f(x)\, dx = \lim_{a \to -\infty}\int_a^b f(x)\, dx$ (3) $\int_{-\infty}^\infty f(x)\, dx = \int_{-\infty}^c f(x)\, dx + \int_c^\infty f(x)\, dx$ where a, b, and c are real numbers. If the right-hand side expressions exist, then the improper integrals are said to be **convergent.** If the right-hand side expressions do not exist, then the improper integrals are said to be **divergent.** **4.** If a continuous stream of money flows perpetually into a fund at a rate of $f(x)$ dollars per year (x = time in years) during the time interval $0 \leq x < \infty$, and if this money flow is compounded continuously at an annual rate r, then its present value at $t = 0$ is given by the improper integral $\int_0^\infty f(x)e^{-rx}\, dx$. **5.** A **random variable** is a letter that represents numerical chance outcomes. If a graph of values of a random variable on a number line results in disconnected points, then the random variable is termed **discrete.** If a graph of values of a random variable on a number line results in a interval, then the random variable is termed **continuous.** **6.** If a random variable x is **uniformly distributed** over the interval $a \leq x \leq b$, its density function is given by

$$f(x) = \begin{cases} 1/(b-a) & \text{for } a \le x \le b \\ 0 & \text{otherwise} \end{cases}$$

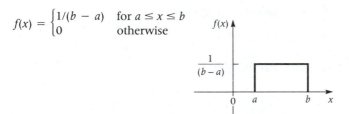

7. Let x be a continuous random variable. A function $f(x)$ is a **probability density function** over some interval $a \le x \le b$ if: (A) $f(x) \ge 0$ for $a \le x \le b$ (B) $\int_a^b f(x)\, dx = 1$. In other words, the area under the graph of the density function over the interval $[a, b]$ equals 1. (C) If $[c, d]$ is a subinterval of $[a, b]$, then $P(c \le x \le d) = \int_c^d f(x)\, dx$.
8. If a random variable x is **exponentially distributed**, then its density function is given by

$$f(x) = \begin{cases} ke^{-kx} & \text{if } x \ge 0 \\ 0 & \text{otherwise} \end{cases}$$

where $k > 0$.

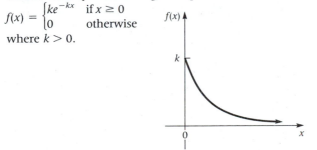

9. The **average value** of a continuous function $f(x)$ over the interval $[a, b]$ is given by $[1/(b-a)]\int_a^b f(x)\, dx$. Graphically, the average value of a continuous function over some interval gives the height H of a rectangle having the same area as that shaded under the continuous function as illustrated in the following graphs.

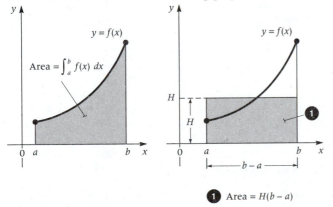

① Area $= H(b - a)$

10. The volume, V, of a solid of revolution formed by rotating about the x-axis the region between the graph of $y = f(x)$ and the x-axis from $x = a$ to $x = b$ (see the accompanying figure) is given by $V = \int_a^b \pi[f(x)]^2\, dx$.

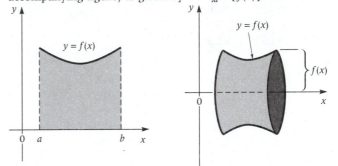

11. If $f(x)$ is a continuous function over the interval $a \le x \le b$, then $\int_a^b f(x)\, dx = \dfrac{b-a}{2n}[f(x_0) + 2f(x_1) + 2f(x_2) + \ldots + 2f(x_{n-1}) + f(x_n)]$ **12.** $K(b-a)^3/12n^2$ where K is the maximum value of $|f''(x)|$ over the interval $[a, b]$. **13.** If $f(x)$ is a continuous function over the interval $a \le x \le b$ and n is even, then $\int_a^b f(x)\, dx = \dfrac{b-a}{3n}[f(x_0) + 4f(x_1) + 2f(x_2) + 4f(x_3) + 2f(x_4) + \ldots + 4f(x_{n-1}) + f(x_n)]$ **14.** $K(b-a)^5/180n^4$ where K is the maximum value of $|f^{(4)}(x)|$ over the interval $[a, b]$.
15. A **differential equation** is an equation that contains one or more derivatives. A differential equation expresses a relationship between a rate of change and other variables.
16. Separation of variables is a method used to solve differential equations. To solve a differential equation by the method of separation of variables, we rewrite it so that one variable occurs only on one side of the equation and the other variable occurs only on the other side so that each side can be integrated. **17.** A **general solution** to a differential equation is an equation that satisfies the differential equation and contains an arbitrary constant. **Initial conditions** (or **boundary conditions**) ensure that the graph of a solution to a differential equation passes through a particular point. Such a solution is called a **particular solution** to a differential equation.
18. Substitute the solution and its derivative into the differential equation and check to determine that the left-hand side equals the right-hand side.
19. If $S = S(t)$ is the value of an investment at time t (in years) where interest is compounded continuously at an annual rate r, then the differential equation $dS/dt = rS$ indicates that the rate of change of S is proportional to S where the annual interest rate is the constant of proportionality. **20.** If $y(t)$ is the temperature of an object at time t and the constant m is the temperature of the surrounding medium, then Newton's law of cooling is

given by the differential equation $dy/dt = k(y - m)$. This differential equation indicates that the rate of change of the temperature of the object is proportional to the difference between the object's temperature and the temperature of the surrounding medium.

• REVIEW EXERCISES

1. (a) $20,000 **(b)** $17,115.69 **(c)** $23,570.49
3. (a) $9836.49 **(b)** $8328.71 **(c)** $11,469.70

5. Diverges **7.** 1 **9.** $\frac{1}{5}$ **11.** $1,250,000 **13. (a)** 0.25

(b) 0.60 **(c)** 0.60 **(d)** 0.45 **15. (a)** 0.3935 **(b)** 0.6988
(c) 0.4493 **(d)** $e^{-1} \approx 0.3679$ **17.** 10 **19.** $1600

21. $\dfrac{36,864\pi}{5} \approx 23,162.33$

23. $\dfrac{256\pi}{15} \approx 53.617$

25. 0.538128 **27.** 0.058128 **29.** 0.911479
31. 0.000028 **33.** $y^3 = \dfrac{1}{C - x^3}$; $y = \sqrt[3]{\dfrac{1}{C - x^3}}$

35. $y^2 = \dfrac{1}{2(C - e^x)}$; $y = \dfrac{1}{\sqrt{2(C - e^x)}}$

37. (a) $\dfrac{dS}{dt} = rS = 0.12S$ **(b)** $S = S_0 e^{0.12t}$ **(c)** $16,435.47

39. (a) $\dfrac{dP}{dt} = kP$ **(b)** $P = P_0 e^{kt}$ **(c)** $P = 4,000,000 e^{\left(\frac{t}{4}\right) \ln 7}$

• CHAPTER 8

SECTION 8-1

1. (a) 2 **(b)** 82 **(c)** 8 **3.** $7\frac{3}{4}$ **5. (a)** 3 **(b)** 34 **(c)** 48
7. (a) 4 **(b)** -104 **(c)** 582 **9.** The domain of g is the set of all ordered pairs (x, y) for which the function is defined, namely, all ordered pairs (x, y) such that $x \neq 2$ and $y \neq 0$.
11. The domain of f is the set of all ordered pairs (x, y) for which the function is defined, namely, all ordered pairs (x, y) such that $x > 3$. **13.** The domain of f is the set of all ordered pairs (x, y) for which the function is defined, namely, all ordered pairs (x, y) such that x and y have the same sign, $x \neq 0$, and $y \neq 0$. **15.**

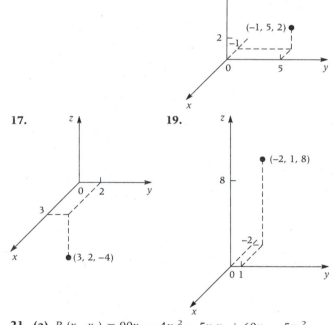

17. **19.**

21. (a) $R(x_1, x_2) = 90x_1 - 4x_1{}^2 - 5x_1 x_2 + 60x_2 - 5x_2{}^2$
(b) 334 **23.** $C(3, 5) = 136$; $136,000. **25. (a)** 5.9033
(b) 5.7217

SECTION 8-2

1. (a) $6x + 6y - 2xy^3$ **(b)** $12y^2 + 6x - 3x^2 y^2$
(c) 2 **(d)** 12 **3. (a)** $3x^2 - 8y + 6x^2 y^2$
(b) $5y^4 - 8x + 4x^3 y$ **5. (a)** $24x^2 - 35x^4 y^8 + 8y^2$
(b) $-4y - 56x^5 y^7 + 16xy + 1$ **(c)** -8904 **(d)** -7143
7. (a) $24x^5 - 24x^2 - 7 + 6y + 3x^2 y^5$ **(b)** $6x + 8 + 5x^3 y^4$
(c) $120x^4 - 48x + 6xy^5$ **(d)** $20x^3 y^3$ **(e)** $6 + 15x^2 y^4$
(f) $6 + 15x^2 y^4$ **9. (a)** $-3x^2 + 12x^2 y^6$
(b) $-2y + 24x^3 y^5 + 8$ **(c)** $-6x + 24xy^6$ **(d)** $-2 + 120x^3 y^4$
(e) $72x^2 y^5$ **(f)** $72x^2 y^5$ **(g)** 36 **(h)** 9718

11. (a) $x^2e^{x^2+y^2}(3 + 2x^2)$ (b) $2x^3ye^{x^3+y^2}$
13. (a) $e^{2x+3y+5}(3x^2+2x^3 + 2y^2)$
(b) $e^{2x+3y+5}(3x^3 + 2y + 3y^2)$ (c) $2e^8$ **15.** (a) $940
(b) $700 **17.** (a) $18,002 ≈ the increase in $P(x, y)$ if x is
increased by 1 (b) $8005 ≈ the increase in $P(x, y)$ if y is
increased by 1

SECTION 8-3

1. $(5, -8)$ **3.** $\left(\dfrac{16}{3}, \dfrac{20}{3}\right)$ **5.** $(-4, 9)$ **7.** $\left(\dfrac{360}{11}, \dfrac{130}{11}\right)$

9. $\left(6, \dfrac{-221}{12}\right), \left(-6, \dfrac{221}{12}\right)$ **11.** $(4, -2), (4, 2)$

13. Relative minimum: $f(4, 5) = -48$

15. Relative minimum: $f\left(-\dfrac{9}{2}, 5\right) = \dfrac{-181}{4}$

17. Relative maximum: $f(20, 50) = 4300$
19. Relative minimum: $f(4, 3) = -58$
21. Relative maximum: $f(10, 4) = 416$
23. $(5, -15.8)$ and $(-5, 15.8)$ are saddle points.
25. Relative maximum: $f(5, -2\sqrt{2}) ≈ 165.25$;
saddle point at $(5, 2\sqrt{2})$

27. $\dfrac{\partial f}{\partial x} = 2x - 18$; $\dfrac{\partial f}{\partial x} = 0, x = 9$

$\dfrac{\partial f}{\partial y} = -4y + 16$; $\dfrac{\partial f}{\partial y} = 0, y = 4$

$A = f_{xx}(9, 4) = 2$; $B = f_{yy}(9, 4) = -4$; $C = f_{xy}(9, 4) = 0$
$AB - C^2 = -8$; Since $AB - C^2 < 0$, $(9, 4)$ is a saddle point.
There are no relative maxima or minima. **29.** (a) $200;
$500 (b) $1,660,000 **31.** (a) 200; 500 (b) 500,000
33. (a) $R(p_1, p_2) = 200p_1 - 20p_1^2 + 3p_1p_2 + 300p_2 - 15p_2^2$

(b) $\dfrac{2300}{397}$; $\dfrac{4200}{397}$ or ≈$5.79; $10.58 (c) $2166.25

(d) $x_1 ≈ 94.71$ cases; $x_2 ≈ 152.90$ cases
35. $h = \sqrt[3]{200}$ in.; $w = \sqrt[3]{200}$ in.; $l = \sqrt[3]{200}$ in.;
     ≈5.85 in.;   ≈5.85 in.;   ≈5.85 in.
37. $h = 25$ ft; $w = 20$ ft; $l = 20$ ft

SECTION 8-4

1. (a) $y = 2.5 + 2.5x$ (b)

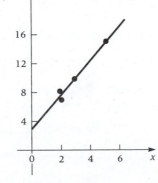

(c) -0.5; 0; 0.5; 0 (d) 0.5 **3.** (a) $y = 2 + 1.4x$
(b)

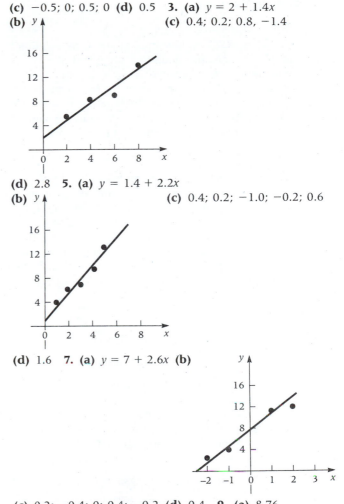

(c) 0.4; 0.2; 0.8, -1.4

(d) 2.8 **5.** (a) $y = 1.4 + 2.2x$

(c) 0.4; 0.2; -1.0; -0.2; 0.6

(d) 1.6 **7.** (a) $y = 7 + 2.6x$ (b)

(c) 0.2; -0.4; 0; 0.4; -0.2 (d) 0.4 **9.** (a) 8.76
(b) 28.5058 **11.** (a) 10.59 (b) 37.6043
13. (a) Quadratic (b) $y = 6.619(1.809)^x$ or
$y = 6.619e^{0.593x}$ (c) 95.43 (d) 107.85 **15.** (a) $2211
(b) $0.841 **17.** 0.655; The change of 1 unit in the S & P
500 results in a change, in the same direction, of
approximately 0.655 unit in the mutual share.
19. 1.29; The change of 1 unit in the S & P 500 is
accompanied by a change, in the same direction, of
approximately 1.29 units in the Neuberger Manhattan
fund. **21.** (a) $y = 320.5(1.082)^x$ or $y = 320.5e^{0.0785x}$
(b) 8.17% (c) 4274; 4623; 5001 **23.** (a) Quadratic
(b) 439.6; 460.4; 481.2 (c) Decreasing (d) 345.9; 319.9;
286.7 **25.** (a) $y = 0.06 + 6.41x$ (b) An increase of 1 unit
in the GPA results in an increase of $6410 in the annual
starting salary. **27.** (a) Decrease by ≈7.8 million bushels
(b) Increase by ≈4.3 million bushels.

SECTION 8-5

1. $f(8, 10) = 44$, relative minimum
3. $f(10, -22) = -252$, relative minimum **5.** No solution (no relative maximum or minimum) **7.** $f(5, 5) = -50$, relative minimum **9.** In Exercise 2, $\lambda_0 = 2x + 6y$ $= 40$ evaluated at $(5, 5)$. λ_0 measures the sensitivity of the optional value of f to a change in c, where $g(x, y) = c = 10$ in this case. An increase of 1 unit in c increases the optimal value of f by approximately 40 units. **11.** In Exercise 4,
$\lambda_0 = 4x + 1 = \dfrac{97}{3} \approx 32.33$, evaluated at $x_0 = \dfrac{47}{6}$.
λ_0 measures the sensitivity of the optimal value of f to a change in c where $g(x, y) = c = 12$ in this case. An increase of 1 unit in c increases the optimal value of f by approximately 32.33 units. **13.** In Exercise 7, $\lambda_0 = -5x + 4y = -5$, evaluated at $(5, 5)$. λ_0 measures the sensitivity of the optimal value of f to a change in c where $g(x, y) = c = 20$ in this case. An increase of 1 unit in c decreases the optimal value of f by approximately 5 units.
15. $x = 26$ units, $y = 14$ units
17. $u = \dfrac{\sqrt{34} - 3\sqrt{2}}{8} \approx 0.1985$, $v = \dfrac{1}{4}\sqrt{7 - \sqrt{17}} \approx 0.4240$
19. $x = 2$ feet, $y = 6$ feet; maximum volume $= 24$ cubic feet.
21. $x = \dfrac{96}{25} = 3.84$ mi, $y = \dfrac{72}{25} = 2.88$ mi; maximum
distance ≈ 4.8 miles **23.** $x = 6000$ units, $y = 3000$ units
25. In Exercise 15, $\lambda_0 = 2x - 5y = -18$, evaluated at $(26, 14)$. λ_0 measures the sensitivity of the optimal value of C to a change in c, where $g(x, y) = c = 40$ in this case. An increase of 1 unit in c decreases the optimal value of c by approximately 18 units. **27.** In Exercise 17,
$\lambda_0 = \dfrac{4u}{v} \approx 1.8726$, evaluated at $(0.1985, 0.4240)$.
λ_0 measures the sensitivity of the optimal value of A to a change in c where $g(u, v) = c = 1$ in this case. An increase of 1 unit in c increases the optimal value of A by approximately 1.8726 unit. (an increase of 1 unit in c is large, relative to c and the approximation is, consequently, not good. It would be more reasonable to increase c by 0.01. Such an increase would increase the optimal value of A by approximately 0.0187 unit.) **29.** In Exercise 19, $\lambda_0 = (2xy - 6x)/(4y) = 1/2$ evaluated at $(2, 6)$. λ_0 measures the sensitivity of the optimal value of f to a change in c where $g(x, y) = c = 60$ in this case. An increase of 1 unit in c increases the optimal value of f by approximately $\dfrac{1}{2}$ unit.
31. In Exercise 21, $\lambda_0 = 0.2$. λ_0 measures the sensitivity of the optimal value of f to a change in c, where $g(x, y) = c = 24$ in this case. An increase of 1 unit in c increases the optimal value of f by approximately 1.92 unit.
33. In Exercise 23, $\lambda_0 = \dfrac{x_0}{4} = 1500$. λ_0 measures the

sensitivity of the optimal value of C to a change in c, where $g(x, y) = c = 9000$ in this case. An increase of 1 unit in c increases the optimal value of C by approximately 1500 units.

SECTION 8-6

1. 67.5 **3.** 45 **5.** $\dfrac{7}{60}$ **7.** -177.3 **9.** $\dfrac{271}{30} \approx 9.0333$
11. $e^6 - e^5 - e^2 + e \approx 250.345$ **13.** 11 **15.** $\ln 2$
17. $6 \ln 6 - 5 \ln 5 - 3 \ln 3 + 2 \ln 2 \approx 0.79382$
19. $\dfrac{15}{2} \ln 2 \approx 5.1986$ **21.** 80; 80 **23.** 69; 69
25. $\dfrac{1}{8}(e^{16} - e^{12} - e^8 + e^4) \approx 1{,}090{,}054$
27. $4 \ln 3 \approx 4.3944$
29. (a) $\displaystyle\int_{0.995}^{1.005} \int_{0.495}^{0.505} 10{,}000 \, dx \, dy$

$= 10{,}000 \displaystyle\int_{0.995}^{1.005} x \Big|_{0.495}^{0.505} dy = 100 \int_{0.995}^{1.005} dy$

$= 100y \Big|_{0.995}^{1.005} = 1$

(b) 0.06

31. (a) $\displaystyle\int_0^1 \int_0^1 \frac{2}{3}(2x + y) \, dx \, dy = \frac{2}{3}\int_0^1 \left[x^2 + yx \, \Big|_0^1 \right] dx$

$= \dfrac{2}{3}\displaystyle\int_0^1 (1 + y) \, dy = \frac{2}{3}\left(y + \frac{y^2}{2}\right) \Big|_0^1 = \frac{2}{3}\left(1 + \frac{1}{2}\right) = 1$

(b) 0.3067

33. $\displaystyle\int_0^\infty \int_0^\infty 2e^{-(2x+y)} \, dy \, dx$

$= 2 \displaystyle\int_0^\infty \left[-e^{-(2x+y)} \, \Big|_0^b \right] dx$
$\quad\quad \underset{b \to \infty}{\lim}$

$= 2 \displaystyle\int_0^\infty (0 + e^{-2x}) \, dx = \frac{-2}{2}e^{-2x} \Big|_0^b = -(0 - 1) = 1$
$\quad\quad\quad\quad\quad\quad\quad\quad \underset{b \to \infty}{\lim}$

• EXTRA DIVIDENDS

Back-Order Inventory Model

1. $C(Q, S) = 5\left(\dfrac{1200}{Q}\right) + 1.15\dfrac{(Q - S)^2}{2Q} + 2.40\left(\dfrac{S^2}{2Q}\right)$
3. $C(124, 40) = \$96.59$ **5.** $Q = 124$ are ordered; $Q - S = 124 - 40 = 84$ are available for sale.

• **EXTRA DIVIDENDS**

Response Surface

1. A relative maximum occurs at the critical point $x_1 = 0.18$, $x_2 = -0.26$ **3.** 111.8° Celsius and 53.7 minutes

• **CHAPTER HIGHLIGHTS**

1. If a function has two independent variables, it is called a **function of two variables.** If a function has three independent variables, it is called a **function of three variables.** Functions of more than one variable are called **multivariate functions.** **2.** The ordered triple $(2, 4, -1)$ is plotted by starting at the origin, then moving 2 units in the positive direction along the x-axis, then moving 4 units in the positive direction parallel to the y-axis, then moving 1 unit in the negative direction parallel to the z-axis.

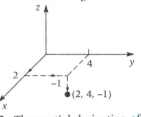

3. The partial derivative of z with respect to x gives the instantaneous rate of change of z with respect to x. It is determined by treating y as a constant and using the derivative rules (i.e., power rule, product rule, quotient rule, etc.). The partial derivative of z with respect to y gives the instantaneous rate of change of z with respect to y. It is determined by treating x as a constant and using the derivative rules (i.e., power rule, product rule, quotient rule, etc.). **4.** The partial derivative of a partial derivative is called a **second partial derivative,** or simply a **second partial.** **5.** Given a function $z = f(x, y)$, there are four types of second partials. They are $f_{xx}, f_{yy}, f_{xy}, f_{yx}$. **6.** A point (x_0, y_0) is called a **critical point** of $z = f(x, y)$ if $f_x(x_0, y_0) = 0$ and $f_y(x_0, y_0) = 0$. **7.** Yes **8.** No. Critical points yield candidates for relative maxima/minima.
9. Let (x_0, y_0) be a critical point of $z = f(x, y)$ such that f_x, f_y, f_{xx}, f_{yy}, and f_{xy} are continuous at (x_0, y_0). Also let $A = f_{xx}(x_0, y_0)$, $B = f_{yy}(x_0, y_0)$, and $C = f_{xy}(x_0, y_0)$. Then:
(a) $f(x_0, y_0)$ is a relative maximum if $AB - C^2 > 0$ and $A < 0$. **(b)** $f(x_0, y_0)$ is a relative minimum if $AB - C^2 > 0$ and $A > 0$. **(c)** $f(x_0, y_0)$ is a saddle point if $AB - C^2 < 0$.
(d) The test fails and no information is given about the point (x_0, y_0) if $AB - C^2 = 0$. **10. Step 1: Search for critical points.** Find f_x and f_y, set them equal to zero and solve for x and y. Determine all possible ordered pairs (x, y) that satisfy both equations $f_x(x, y) = 0$ and $f_y(x, y) = 0$. These are critical points. **Step 2: Apply the second-derivative test for functions of two variables.**

Compute $f_{xx}, f_{yy},$ and f_{xy} and evaluate each at each critical point. Apply the second-derivative test to each critical point. **11.** The method of least squares provides a procedure for determining the best-fitting straight line to a set of data points. Here, the best-fitting straight line is the one that minimizes the sum of squares error. **12.** Given data points $(x_1, y_1), (x_2, y_2), \ldots (x_n, y_n)$, the slope m and y-intercept b of the regression line are given by the formulas

$$m = \frac{\displaystyle\sum_{i=1}^{n} x_i y_i - n\bar{x}\bar{y}}{\displaystyle\sum_{i=1}^{n} x_i^2 - n\bar{x}^2} \qquad b = \bar{y} - m\bar{x}$$

where $\bar{x} = \displaystyle\sum_{i=1}^{n} x_i/n$, the average of the x-values, and

$\bar{y} = \displaystyle\sum_{i=1}^{n} y_i/n$, the average of the y-values. Also,

$$\sum_{i=1}^{n} x_i y_i = x_1 y_1 + x_2 y_2 + \ldots + x_n y_n$$

$$\sum_{i=1}^{n} x_i^2 = x_1^2 + x_2^2 + \ldots + x_n^2.$$

13. Beta denotes the risk of a mutual fund or stock relative to the market. **14.** Fit a linear model to data points $(x, \ln y)$. **15.** a, the coefficient of x^2; b, the coefficient of x; c, the y-intercept. **16.** A multiple linear regression model relates y-values to more than one independent variable. **17.** Maximize (or minimize) $z = f(x, y)$ subject to $g(x, y) = c$ where c is a constant.
18. Step 1: Determine the lagrangian function $F(x, y, \lambda) = f(x, y) + \lambda(c - g(x, y))$ where λ is the lagrangian multiplier. **Step 2: Search for critical values.** Find F_x, F_y and F_λ, set them equal to zero and solve for x, y, and λ. Determine all possible triples (x, y, λ) that satisfy all three equations
$F_x(x, y, \lambda) = 0 \qquad F_y(x, y, \lambda) = 0 \qquad F_\lambda(x, y, \lambda) = 0.$
These are the critical points of F. **Step 3: Apply second-order conditions.** Compute $g_x, g_y, f_{xx}, f_{yy}, f_{xy},$ and f_{yx} and evaluate each at each critical point. Form the bordered Hessian matrix, H, for each critical point. Evaluate the determinant of each bordered Hessian matrix and apply the second-order condition to each such H as follows: If $|H| > 0$, a relative maximum exists. If $|H| < 0$, a relative minimum exists. **19.** The lagrange multiplier, λ, gives the rate of change of z with respect to c or, in other words, dz/dc. **20.** An expression with two integral signs is a double integral. **21.** First evaluate the inner integral, then evaluate the outer integral.

• REVIEW EXERCISES

1. (a) -2 **(b)** 11 **(c)** 25 **(d)** -87 **3.** All ordered pairs (x, y) of real numbers such that $x \neq 4$.

5.

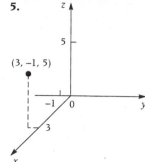

(3, –1, 5)

7. (a) $4x + 6y + 5$

(b) $6x - 32y^3$ **(c)** 9 **(d)** -262 **9. (a)** $x^4e^{x+y}(5 + x)$
(b) x^5e^{x+y} **(c)** $6e$ **(d)** e^3 **11. (a)** 1680 **(b)** 1250
13. (a) $x^3e^{x+y}(4 + x)$ **(b)** $x^2e^{x+y}(12 + 8x + x^2)$ **(c)** x^4e^{x+y}
(d) x^4e^{x+y} **(e)** $x^3e^{x+y}(4 + x)$ **(f)** $x^3e^{x+y}(4 + x)$ **(g)** $5e^2$
(h) e^{-1} **(i)** $5e$ **15. (a)** $12x^2(x^3 + y^5)^3$
(b) $24x(x^3 + y^5)^3 + 108x^4(x^3 + y^5)^2$ **(c)** $20y^4(x^3 + y^5)^3$
(d) $300y^3(x^3 + y^5)^2 + 80y^3(x^3 + y^5)^3$ **(e)** $180x^2y^4(x^3 + y^5)^2$
(f) $180x^2y^4(x^3 + y^5)^2$ **(g)** $-3.338148 \times 10^8 \approx -3.34 \times 10^8$
(h) $92{,}871{,}040$ **(i)** 0 **17.** Saddle point: $(-4, -5)$
19. Relative maximum; $f(6, 9) = 228$ **21.** Relative
maximum: $R(2.4, 1.125) = 77.85$
23. (a) $R(p_1, p_2) = 400p_1 - 12p_1^2 + 20p_1p_2 + 600p_2 - 15p_2^2$
(b) $p_1 = 75, p_2 = 70$ **(c)** $\$36{,}000$ **(d)** $x_1 = 480$ and
$x_2 = 0$. **25. (a)** $y = -0.4615 + 2.5769x$
(b)

(c) $-0.8461, -0.1537,$

$0.7308, 0.2694$ **(d)** 1.346 **(e)** 12.42 **27.** The slope of the
line is the beta value of the xyz Mutual Fund. A change of
1 unit in the $S \& P$ 500 is accompanied by a change, in the
same direction, of approximately 1.90 units in the xyz fund.
29. $\ln y = 6.6993 - 1.7405x$; $y = 811.8e^{1.7405}$; 59.65
31. $x = 42, y = 12$ **33.** In Exercise 30, $\lambda_0 = 2x_0 - 10y_0 = -184$. λ_0 measures the sensitivity of the optimal value of f
to a change in c, where $g(x, y) = c = 52$ in this case. An
increase of 1 unit in c decreases the optimal value of f by
approximately 184 units. **35.** In Exercise 32,
$\lambda_0 = 2x_0 + 6y_0 = 88$. λ_0 measures the sensitivity of the
optimal value of f to a change in c, where $g(x, y) = c = 24$
in this case. An increase of 1 unit in c increases the optimal

value of f by approximately 88 units. **37.** $x = 4$ ft,
$y = 2$ ft. Since $|H| > 0$, $f(4, 2)$ is a relative maximum.
$\lambda_0 = \dfrac{x_0}{40} = 0.10$. λ_0 measures the sensitivity of the optimal
value of V to a change in C, where $g(x, y) = c = 480$, in
this case. An increase of 1 unit in c increases the optimal
value of V by approximately 0.10 units. **39.** 534
41. $-11/12$ **43.** 135

• CHAPTER 9

SECTION 9-1

1. $\dfrac{\pi}{10} \approx 0.314159$ radian **3.** $\dfrac{4\pi}{3} \approx 4.18879$ radians

5. $-\dfrac{2\pi}{15} \approx -0.41888$ radian **7.** $36°$ **9.** $171.887°$

11. 183.346 **13.** $-\dfrac{1}{2} = -0.5$ **15.** $-\dfrac{1}{\sqrt{2}}$ **17.** $\dfrac{\sqrt{3}}{2}$

19. $-\dfrac{\sqrt{3}}{2}$ **21.** $-\dfrac{\sqrt{2}}{2}$ **23.** 0.8 **25.** 0.6 **27.** 0.7660

29. -0.7660 **31.** 0.6428 **33.** -0.6428 **35.** 0.6428
37. 0.8090 **39.** -0.5878 **41.** -0.8090 **43.** 0.8090
45. 0.8090 **47.** 0.3090 **49.** -0.9511 **51.** -0.3090
53. -0.3090 **55.** 0.9511 **57.** 0.3090 **59.** 0 **61.** 0
63. 0 **65.** 0 **67.** 0 **69.** 1 **71.** 1 **73.** 1 **75.** 1 **77.** 1
79. 0.5878 **81.** 0.5878 **83.** $-\sqrt{3}$ **85.** 2 **87.** 1

89. $\sqrt{2}$ **91.** $\dfrac{2\sqrt{3}}{3}$ **93.** $\dfrac{2\sqrt{3}}{3}$ **95.** -1.1917

97. -1.5557 **99.** 1.1917 **101.** -1.5557 **103.** 0.7266
105. 1.2361 **107.** -0.7266 **109.** 1.2361 **111.** 0.7266
113. -1.2361 **115.** 0 **117.** 0 **119.** 0 **121.** 0
123. 0.449319 **125.** 0.999366 **127.** -0.191204
129. 0.995083

SECTION 9-2

1. $y = \cos\left(t - \dfrac{\pi}{2}\right)$

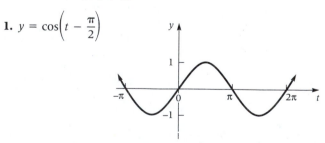

3. $y = \sin\left(t + \dfrac{\pi}{2}\right)$

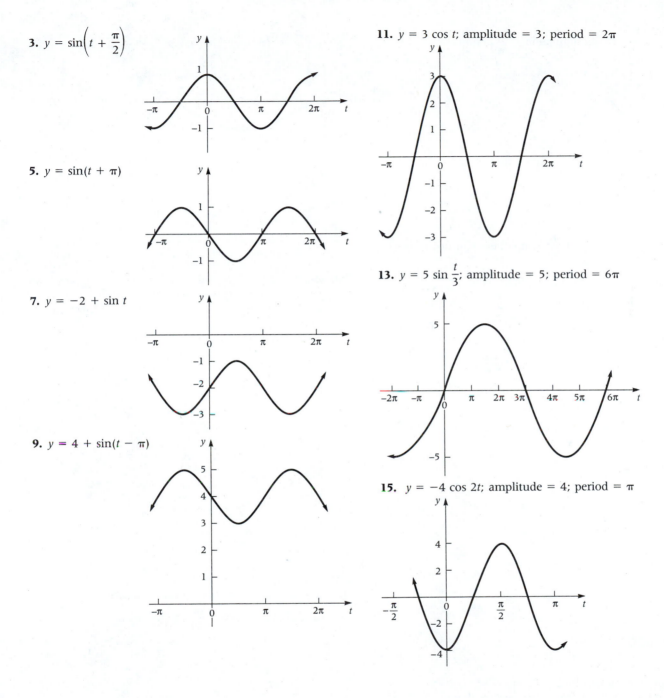

5. $y = \sin(t + \pi)$

7. $y = -2 + \sin t$

9. $y = 4 + \sin(t - \pi)$

11. $y = 3 \cos t$; amplitude $= 3$; period $= 2\pi$

13. $y = 5 \sin \dfrac{t}{3}$; amplitude $= 5$; period $= 6\pi$

15. $y = -4 \cos 2t$; amplitude $= 4$; period $= \pi$

17. $y = 5 + 2 \sin 4t$; amplitude $= 2$; period $= \dfrac{\pi}{2}$

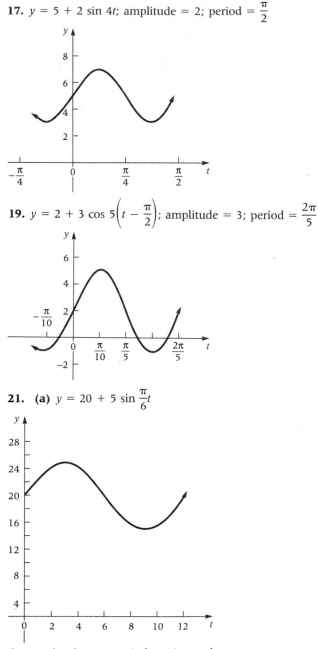

19. $y = 2 + 3 \cos 5\left(t - \dfrac{\pi}{2}\right)$; amplitude $= 3$; period $= \dfrac{2\pi}{5}$

21. **(a)** $y = 20 + 5 \sin \dfrac{\pi}{6}t$

(b) amplitude $= 5$; period $= 12$ months
(c) 20 million gallons **(d)** No upward or downward trend of sales over time

23. **(a)** $y = 100 + e^{0.2t} + 10 \cos \dfrac{\pi}{6}t$

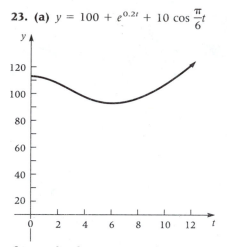

(b) amplitude $= 10$; period $= 12$ quarters
(c) 93.320 thousand gallons **(d)** The water usage exhibits an upward trend over time because of the additive term $e^{0.2t}$. Beyond $t \approx 16$, the periodicity vanishes as y becomes monotonic increasing.

25. **(a)** $y = 500 + 10t + 100 \cos \dfrac{\pi}{2}t$

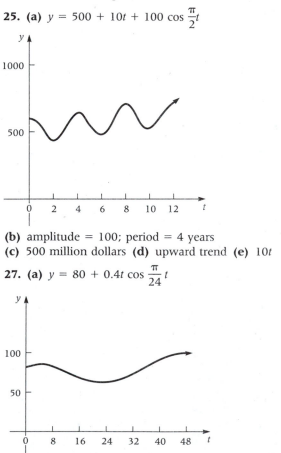

(b) amplitude $= 100$; period $= 4$ years
(c) 500 million dollars **(d)** upward trend **(e)** $10t$

27. **(a)** $y = 80 + 0.4t \cos \dfrac{\pi}{24}t$

(b) 48 months **(c)** 0.4t; $t = 1$, amplitude = 0.4; $t = 5$, amplitude = 2.0; $t = 10$, amplitude = 4.0; $t = 20$, amplitude = 8.0; The amplitude is increasing with time. **(d)** 80 **(e)** no trend over time; The oscillations are increasing in magnitude, however.

29. (a) $V(t) = 120 \sin 100\pi t$

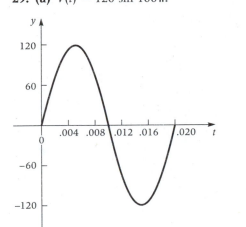

(b) amplitude = 120; period = 0.02 second; frequency = 50 cycles/second **(c)** 120 **(d)** $V(5) = 0$, $V(10) = 0$, $V(20) = 0$

SECTION 9-3

1. $7 \cos 7t$ **3.** $-5t^4 \sin(t^5 - 3)$ **5.** $5 \cos(5t + 4)$
7. $20 \sin^3 t \cos t$ **9.** $5t^4 \cos 4t - 4t^5 \sin 4t$

11. $\dfrac{8t \cos 8t - 5 \sin 8t}{t^6}$ **13.** $\dfrac{1}{\cos^2 t} = \sec^2 t$

15. $-\dfrac{3t^2 \sin \sqrt{t^3 - 6}}{2\sqrt{t^3 - 6}}$ **17.** $\cos^5 t - 4 \cos^3 t \sin^2 t$

19. $-3 \sin(t + \pi)$ **21.** $y'\left(\dfrac{\pi}{3}\right) = -\dfrac{\sqrt{3}}{2}$

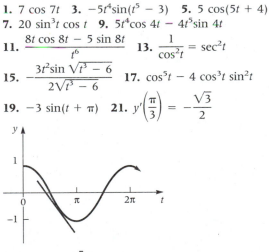

23. $R'(12) = \dfrac{5\pi}{3}$ **25.** $V'(30) = 14{,}400\pi$ volts/second

27. (a) April; 180 thousand dollars
(b) October; 120 thousand dollars
29. (a) 1 P.M. **(b)** 1 A.M.

SECTION 9-4

1. $\dfrac{1}{2} \sin(2t + 1) + C$ **3.** $-\dfrac{5}{4} \cos 4t + C$

5. $4t + \sin t + C$ **7.** $\dfrac{t^5}{5} + 3 \cos 2t + C$ **9.** $\dfrac{1}{3} \sin^3 t + C$

11. $\dfrac{2}{3}(\sin t)^{\frac{3}{2}} + C$ **13.** $-\cos t - \dfrac{\sin^2 t}{2} + C$

15. $-\dfrac{1}{2} \cos t^2 + C$ **17.** $\dfrac{1}{2} \sin(t^2 + 2t) + C$

19. $-\ln |\cos t| + C = \ln |\sec t| + C$ **21.** $\dfrac{1}{2}$

23. $2 \sin \dfrac{\pi}{8} \approx 0.7654$

25. (a) 240 million dollars **(b)** 201.803 million dollars
27. (a) 700.901 thousand dollars
(b) 960 thousand dollars

• CHAPTER HIGHLIGHTS

1. Negative; positive. **2. (a)** Multiply the degree measure by $\pi/180$. **(b)** Multiply the radian measure by $180/\pi$.
3. See the summary box on pages 569-570 and Figures 9-8,

9-9, and 9-10. **4.**

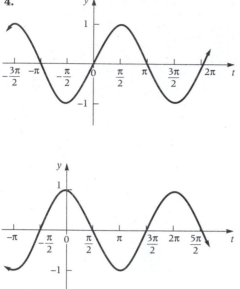

5. If for any value of x and a constant p, a function $f(x)$ has the property $f(x + p) = f(x)$, the function is said to be **periodic**. The smallest value of p for which this property holds is called the **period** of the function. This means that the function repeats itself at regular intervals of length p. The sine and cosine functions each have period 2π.
6. Multiply 2π by $1/B$. **7.** $|A|$. **8.** A wavelike periodic pattern occurring within a 1-year time interval in a time series graph indicates the existence of **seasonal variation**. A time series graph that exhibits long-term upward or downward movement indicates the presence of **trend**. A time series graph that exhibits a wavelike periodic pattern spanning more than 1 year indicates the existence of a **cyclical component** to the time series data. If, in a time series graph, the amplitude changes with time, then the time series data indicates **variable amplitude**.
9. Seasonal variation occurs within a 1-year time interval whereas cyclicality does not occur within a 1-year time interval, but occurs over time intervals of lengths greater than 1 year. **10.** $V(t) = A \sin Bt$ where $V(t)$ is the voltage at time t. **11.** Cosine; negative sine. **12.** The sine function. **13.** The negative cosine function.

• **REVIEW EXERCISES**

1. $\dfrac{\pi}{5} \approx 0.6283$ radian **3.** $\dfrac{13\pi}{15} \approx 2.7227$ radians

5. $\dfrac{720°}{\pi} \approx 229.18°$ **7.** $-504°$ **9.** 0.6428 **11.** -0.7660

13. -0.7660 **15.** 0.7660 **17.** -0.6428 **19.** -0.7660
21. 0.8090 **23.** -0.5878 **25.** -0.5878 **27.** -0.8090
29. -0.8090 **31.** -0.5878 **33.** 1 **35.** 1

37. $y = 4 \sin 2t$; amplitude $= 4$; period $= \pi$

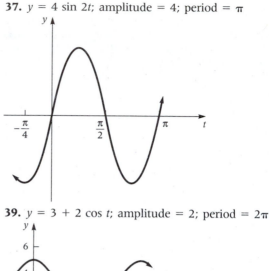

39. $y = 3 + 2 \cos t$; amplitude $= 2$; period $= 2\pi$

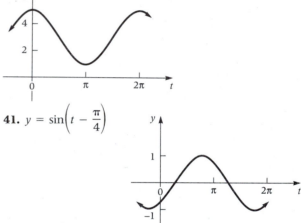

41. $y = \sin\left(t - \dfrac{\pi}{4}\right)$

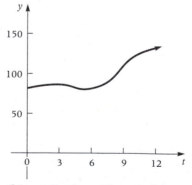

amplitude $= 1$; period $= 2\pi$

43. (a) $y = 80 + 4t + 10 \cos \dfrac{\pi}{6}t$

(b) amplitude $= 10$; period $= 12$ months
(c) 94 thousand gallons **(d)** upward trend over time
(e) $4t$ **45.** $-7 \sin 7t$ **47.** $3t^2\cos(t^3 - 5)$
49. $8 + 6 \sin 6t$ **51.** $6 \cos 6t \cos 5t - 5 \sin 6t \sin 5t$

53. (a) $P'(t) = 0$ **(b)** $t = 24$ gives maximum monthly profit, which is 270 thousand dollars **(c)** $t = 30$ gives the minimum monthly profit, which is 230 thousand dollars

55. $3 \sin(2t + 5) + C$ **57.** $-\dfrac{\cos^5 t}{5} + C$

59. $\dfrac{1}{2} \sin(t^2 + 4t) + C$

• CHAPTER R

SECTION R-1

1. True **3.** False **5.** True **7.** True **9.** True **11.** False
13. True **15.** True **17.** True **19.** False **21.** True
23. True **25.** True **27.** False

29. **31.**
$\quad$ $-5 \quad -1$ $\qquad\qquad$ $-4 \quad -2$

33. **35.**
$\quad$ $-3 \quad 2$ $\qquad\qquad$ 5

37. **39.**
$\quad$ -3 $\qquad\qquad\qquad$ -2

41. **43.**
$\quad$ 2 $\qquad\qquad\qquad$ 2

45. Closed **47.** Open **49.** Closed

51. **53.**
$\quad$ $3 \quad 9$ $\qquad\qquad\qquad$ -4

55. **57.**
$\quad$ 6 $\qquad\qquad\qquad$ $4 \quad 9$

59. 0 **61.** 1 **63.** 2 **65.** 15 **67.** 20 **69.** 4 **71.** 9
73. 6 **75.** 13 **77.** 6
$\qquad\qquad\qquad\qquad\qquad$ $5 \qquad 11$

79. 5
$\qquad$ $-9 \qquad -4$

SECTION R-2

1. $x = 6$ **3.** $x = 9$ **5.** $x = 12$ **7.** $x = 8$ **9.** $y = 10$

11. $\left(-\infty, 5\dfrac{1}{2}\right]$
$\qquad\qquad\qquad\qquad\qquad$ $5\dfrac{1}{2}$

13. $\left(-\infty, 7\dfrac{1}{2}\right)$
$\qquad\qquad\qquad\qquad\qquad$ $7\dfrac{1}{2}$

15. $\left(-\infty, 10\dfrac{1}{3}\right]$
$\qquad\qquad\qquad\qquad\qquad$ $10\dfrac{1}{3}$

17. $(-\infty, 3]$
$\qquad\qquad\qquad\qquad$ 3

19. $[11, \infty)$
$\qquad\qquad\qquad$ 11

SECTION R-3

1. 9 **3.** 25 **5.** $4^6 = 4096$ **7.** $\dfrac{1}{16}$ **9.** 64

11. $5^7 = 78{,}125$ **13.** $\dfrac{9}{25}$ **15.** $\dfrac{1}{64}$ **17.** $\dfrac{1}{8}$ **19.** 4 **21.** 7

23. $8^5 = 32{,}768$ **25.** 343 **27.** 36 **29.** 1
31. $7^5 = 16{,}807$ **33.** 5^{-6} **35.** $(-5)^{-3}$ **37.** x^{-8}
39. $4^{9/2} = 2^9$ **41.** $2^{1/5}$ **43.** $9^{4/7}$ **45.** $5^{7/3}$ **47.** $5^{-3/2}$
49. $x^{-5/2}$ **51.** $x^{-2/3}$ **53.** $9x^2$ **55.** $125x^3 y^3$

57. $2 \cdot 9 = 18$ **59.** $\dfrac{5^3}{6^3} = \dfrac{125}{216}$ **61.** $\dfrac{x^5}{3^5} = \dfrac{x^5}{243}$ **63.** $\dfrac{x^2}{25}$

65. $\dfrac{-8}{x^3}$ **67.** $2^{12} = 4096$ **69.** $\dfrac{1}{3}$ **71.** 4.96×10^2

73. 8×10^9 **75.** 8×10^{-7} **77.** 5.6×10^{-1}
79. 3.57×10^{-3}

SECTION R-4

1. $3x + 12$ **3.** $-2x - 12$ **5.** $9x + 27$
7. $-4x^2 + 12x - 28$ **9.** $5x^4 - 20x^3 + 20x^2 + 25x$
11. $3x^6 y^3 - 15x^2 y^5 + 18x^3 y^4$ **13.** $5(x + 4)$ **15.** $3(x - 9)$
17. $6(x - 5)$ **19.** $3x(x - 9)$ **21.** $-6x(x - 8)$
23. $7x(x + 4)$ **25.** $3xy^2(xy^2 + 2)$ **27.** $-5x^3 y^6(x - 4y)$
29. $3x^2 y^3(y^3 + 3x^3 + 2xy)$ **31.** $P(1 + rt)$ **33.** $P(1 + i)$
35. $x(ax - b)$ **37.** $P(1 + i)^3$ **39.** $3x(2x - 3)$
41. $(x + 3)(2x - y)$ **43.** $x(x - 2)(5y + 8x)$

SECTION R-5

1. $x^2 + x - 6$ **3.** $x^2 + 6x + 5$ **5.** $x^2 - 15x + 56$
7. $3x^2 + 2x - 5$ **9.** $8x^2 - 2x - 21$ **11.** $21x^2 + x - 2$
13. $x^2 - 9$ **15.** $x^2 - 81$ **17.** $9x^2 - 4$ **19.** $x^2 - 4x + 4$
21. $x^2 + 10x + 25$ **23.** $4x^2 - 12x + 9$

SECTION R-6

1. $(x + 9)(x - 2)$ **3.** $(x + 5)(x - 3)$ **5.** $(x - 2)(x - 1)$
7. $(x - 5)(x - 8)$ **9.** $(x - 9)(x + 9)$ **11.** $(x - 7)(x + 7)$
13. $(x + 3)^2$ **15.** $(x - 5)^2$ **17.** $(x + 9)^2$
19. $(x - 9)(x + 3)$ **21.** $(x - 9)(x + 5)$ **23.** $(x + 6)(x + 1)$

SECTION R-7

1. $(2x + 7)(x - 4)$ **3.** $(5x - 2)(x + 4)$
5. $(2x - 5)(3x + 1)$ **7.** $9(x - 2)(x + 2)$ **9.** $(2x + 5)^2$
11. $(5x - 7)^2$

SECTION R-8

1. $2x - 14$ **3.** $-x - 7$ **5.** x **7.** $\dfrac{x - 3}{x - 5}$ **9.** $\dfrac{x + 4}{x + 1}$

11. $\dfrac{x + 3}{x + 2}$ **13.** $\dfrac{1}{x}$ **15.** $\dfrac{x + 3}{x - 2}$ **17.** $\dfrac{x + 3}{x + 2}$

19. $\dfrac{x+6}{2} = \dfrac{x}{2} + 3$ **21.** $\dfrac{9}{x}$ **23.** $\dfrac{-3(x+16)}{x(x+6)}$ or

$\dfrac{-3x-48}{x(x+6)}$ **25.** $\dfrac{9x-49}{x^2-36}$ **27.** $\dfrac{7x-5}{x(x-9)}$ **29.** $x + \dfrac{7}{x}$

31. $3x - 36$ **33.** $4x^2 - 8x + 6$ **35.** $4x^2 + 8x - 12$

37. $5x^3 - 5x^2 + 30x - 10$ **39.** $x^3\left(1 - \dfrac{4}{x} + \dfrac{7}{x^2} + \dfrac{5}{x^3}\right)$

41. $x^2\left(1 + \dfrac{7}{x} + \dfrac{9}{x^2}\right)$ **43.** $\dfrac{1 - (1+i)^{-20}}{i}$

45. $\dfrac{1 + i - (1+i)^{-37}}{i}$

• EXTRA DIVIDENDS

1. 25% **3.** $72 **5.** $428.57 **7.** $14,800 **9.** $16,050
11. 123.3% **13.** 139.3% **15.** -1.6% **17.** $18,148.82
19. $22,321.43

• EXTRA DIVIDENDS

1. 175 **3.** $8,214,286 **5. (a)** 100% **(b)** 17.6% **7.** 1.18
9. 1.35 **11.** 1.1 **13.** 1.32 **15.** $321.44 **17.** $405.19

Index

Continued

assuming that y is held constant. To find f_x, use the derivative rules (i.e., the power rule, product rule, quotient rule, etc.) of Chapters 2 and 5, while treating y as a constant.

2. The partial derivative of z with respect to y is

$$f_y = \frac{\partial z}{\partial y} = \begin{matrix} \text{instantaneous rate of change} \\ \text{of } z \text{ with respect to } y \end{matrix}$$

assuming that x is held constant. To find f_y, use the derivative rules (i.e., the power rule, product rule, quotient rule, etc.) of Chapters 2 and 5, while treating x as a constant.

• SECOND-DERIVATIVE TEST FOR FUNCTIONS OF TWO VARIABLES

Let (x_0, y_0) be a critical point of $z = f(x, y)$ such that f_x, f_y, f_{xx}, f_{yy}, and f_{xy} are continuous at (x_0, y_0). Also, let

$$A = f_{xx}(x_0, y_0)$$
$$B = f_{yy}(x_0, y_0)$$
$$C = f_{xy}(x_0, y_0)$$

Then

1. $f(x_0, y_0)$ is a relative maximum if $AB - C^2 > 0$ and $A < 0$.
2. $f(x_0, y_0)$ is a relative minimum if $AB - C^2 > 0$ and $A > 0$.
3. $f(x_0, y_0)$ is a saddle point if $AB - C^2 < 0$. (A saddle point is illustrated in the graph below.)
4. The test fails and no information is given about the point (x_0, y_0) if $AB - C^2 = 0$.

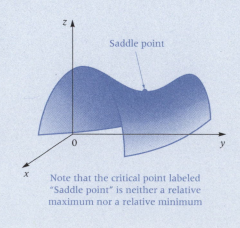

Note that the critical point labeled "Saddle point" is neither a relative maximum nor a relative minimum

• TO FIND RELATIVE EXTREMA FOR FUNCTIONS OF TWO VARIABLES

1. Search for critical points.

   • Find the first order partials f_x and f_y.
   • Set the first-order partials equal to zero, and solve for x and y.
   • Determine all possible ordered pairs (x, y) that satisfy both equations

   $$f_x(x, y) = 0 \quad \text{and} \quad f_y(x, y) = 0$$

   These are the critical points.

2. Apply the second-derivative test for functions of two variables.

   • Compute the second-order partials f_{xx}, f_{yy}, and f_{xy}.
   • Evaluate the second-order partials at each critical point.
   • Apply the second-derivative test to each critical point.

• METHOD OF LEAST SQUARES

Given data points

x	y	(x, y)
x_1	y_1	(x_1, y_1)
x_2	y_2	(x_2, y_2)
$\vdots$	$\vdots$	$\vdots$
x_n	y_n	(x_n, y_n)

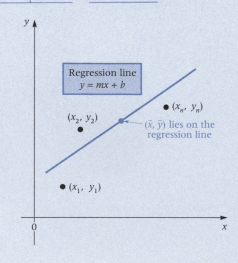

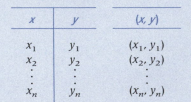

Regression line
$y = mx + b$

(x_2, y_2)

$\bullet (x_n, y_n)$

$(\bar{x}, \bar{y})$ lies on the regression line

$\bullet (x_1, y_1)$